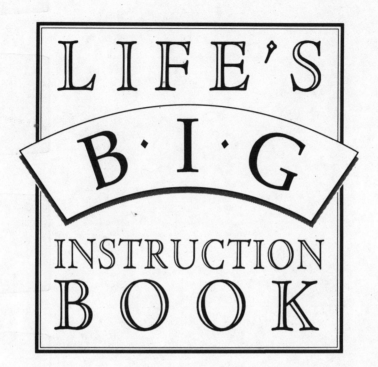

LIFE'S B·I·G INSTRUCTION BOOK

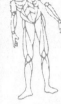

LIFE'S
B·I·G
INSTRUCTION BOOK

THE ALMANAC OF INDISPENSABLE INFORMATION

CAROL ORSAG MADIGAN

Executive Editor of *The People's Almanac*

AND

ANN ELWOOD

Graphics by Ann Elwood

WARNER BOOKS

A Time Warner Company

This book contains information on a broad range of subjects. None of the information is intended as a substitute for the advice of a professional in each of the relevant subject areas. The reader should regularly consult such a professional in connection with all matters that may require professional attention.

Copyright © 1995 by Carol Orsag Madigan and Ann Elwood
All rights reserved.

Warner Books, Inc., 1271 Avenue of the Americas, New York, NY 10020

A Time Warner Company

Printed in the United States of America

First Printing: January 1995

10   9   8   7   6   5   4   3   2   1

Library of Congress Cataloging-in-Publication Data

Madigan, Carol Orsag.
    Life's big instruction book : the almanac of indispensable
information / Carol Orsag Madigan and Ann Elwood.
        p.   cm.
    Includes index.
    ISBN 0-446-51757-7
    1. Handbooks, vade-macums, etc.   2. Conduct of life—Miscellanea-
-Handbooks, manuals, etc.   I. Elwood, Ann.   II. Title.
AG105.M194   1994
031.02—dc20   94-26523
                                                          CIP

To Brook, Betty, Johnny, Linda, and Peg,
with love and gratitude
—C.O.M.

♦

To Casey, Lizzie, Elvira, and Abby,
who kept me company
—A.E.

ACKNOWLEDGMENTS

We are indebted to Lee Clayton, Carol Dunlap, Wendy Hawkins, R. Brook Madigan, and John Zebrowski, who contributed their time and talent to this book. We also want to thank our families, friends, and associates who provided information and inspiration with special mention to: Beth and Doug Beagle, Belinda Borden, Laurie Brannen, John Bronson, Bill Gaupsas, Janet and Bill Goff, Michael Gorman, Larry Hawkins, Aline Hornaday, Micheline Karas, Mary Lou Locke, Arlene Mattioli, Peg Madigan, Betty Orsag, John Raht, Helen Rietz, Simone Taylor, Cynthia Truant, Kristin Webb, Linda Wood.

A book this size requires a publishing team with stamina as well as skill. Thus, we are fortunate to have worked with Joann Davis, Sandra Choron, Moira Duggan, and Grace Sullivan. And our deep appreciation goes to Heide Lange, our literary agent, who guided this project from start to finish with great diligence and enthusiasm.

Finally, we are grateful to the hundreds of organizations that provided us with enormous amounts of research and advice.

TEXT AND ART CREDITS

"Height/Weight Table," reprinted courtesy of Metropolitan Life Insurance Company. "Fitness Benefits of Various Activities," © 1990, *U.S. News & World Report*. "How Healthy Is Your State?" excerpt from *The NWNL State Health Rankings*, © 1993, Northwestern National Life Insurance Company, reprinted with permission. "Are You an Insomniac?" reprinted with permission of National Sleep Foundation. "Contraceptive Failure Rates" reprinted with permission of Alan Guttmacher Institute. Source for "Recovering from Smoking, the Body in Healing," American Lung Association. "Understanding and Helping the Suicidal Person" reprinted with permission of American Association of Suicidology. Source for "Ten Guides to Proper Medicine Use" and "Traveling with Medicines"—Council on Family Health. "Interactions Between Alcohol and Commonly Used Medicines" reprinted courtesy of SRX Regional Program, Medication Education for Seniors, 1095 Market Street #601, San Francisco, CA 94103; © 1993. "Tallying Your Diabetes Risk" reprinted with permission of American Diabetes Association, © 1993. "Clinical Depression" reprinted with permission of National Depressive and Manic Depressive Association. "A Patient's Bill of

INTRODUCTION

"The times they are a-changin'," sang Bob Dylan in the turbulent 1960s. Indeed, they still are but today the roles we play in the changing times are undergoing a radical overhaul. Just a few examples: (1) A two-paycheck family is now the norm rather than the exception: More than 60 percent of all women work outside the home; (2) One in four families is headed by a single parent; (3) Whether by choice or consequence, about 25 percent of adult Americans live alone; (4) Children are not leaving the nest: 54 percent of 18- to 24-year-olds and 12 percent of 25- to 34-year-olds still live with their parents; (5) The average American is likely to devote more years to taking care of an elderly relative than taking care of a child.

The implications? The traditional definitions of typical families and typical roles are relics of the past. Regardless of age, we are all being forced to act more independently, to play a greater number of roles, and to learn basic skills in a variety of arenas. And the basic skills we need cover a lot more areas today than they did 10 or 20 years ago. For instance, we need to know more about safe sex practices, handgun safety, retirement/investment options (gone are the days of the benevolent, secure pension plan), child-care and elder-care alternatives, and a little more about the law (we have become an alarmingly litigious society).

In many ways life has gotten easier because of technology, but the technology itself demands more knowledge. A broom is easier to understand than a vacuum cleaner, a book than a data base, a pen than a computer. While it's wonderful to be living in the "Information Age," there is a downside—too much information and too little time to get our hands on it. If you are like us, you frequently rip articles from newspapers and magazines, stash them somewhere, and promise to one day organize everything into subject areas for easy access. While the stack of information grows, the organization never seems to take place.

The idea for writing *Life's Big Instruction Book* came from our files and boxes overflowing with comprehensive, succinct overviews of subjects we deemed important—whether the subject was reassessing insurance needs, making a compost heap, or how to read a food label. Wouldn't it be nice, we asked ourselves, if all of this nitty-gritty information was made available in one book?

We didn't want to include the kind of information easily found in lots of other reference books—lists of U.S. presidents and world leaders, chronologies of world events, business and economic statistics, professional sports results. Also excluded were lists of famous authors and composers, painters and sculptors, scientists and inventions. We were concerned only with providing practical instruction and advice to help readers cope with everyday life (and some typical once-in-a-lifetime situations).

Life's Big Instruction Book aims to present the core nuggets for living in our highly complex, overly bureaucratic, information-overloaded society. It offers what we consider to be *essential information* that almost everyone will need at some time or other, whether the subject is health, money, etiquette, or crime. Not only does the book include necessary subjects—household matters, family problems, legal concerns—it also focuses on quality-of-life concerns—travel, recreation, personal appearance—things that make life more than just a daily grind.

In some cases, we will provide you with just about all you need to know on a given topic, like how to get a passport, find a lost dog or cat, brew a good cup of coffee, buy quality furniture, or build a campfire. In other cases, such as investments and medical matters, we give you a head start on what you need to know, but you may need to seek additional sources to be truly well-informed. In other words, we don't aim to replace individualized advice from your doctor, your lawyer, your financial advisor.

Life's Big Instruction Book covers the gamut from how to take your temperature to how to survive an IRS audit; from curing insomnia to first aid for pets; from what to do if a child runs away from home to how to look at a work of art; from taking good photographs to buying a home computer. It is a combination of "how-to," problem-solving, insider information, and self-assessment. Because we wanted the book to be enjoyable as well as informative, we snuck in some topics like "What to Do When You Meet the Queen of England," "A Test for Loaded Dice," and "Tooth Fairy Money." Because there are more than 700 articles in the book, we have included a full table of contents, a mini table of contents for each chapter, and an index.

We are greatly indebted to the hundreds of organizations who provided information for this book and to the many people who talked to us on countless subjects ranging from child abuse and neglect to social security benefits. We were genuinely overwhelmed and impressed by the number of groups, many of them nonprofit, that exist solely to provide information and assistance. Regardless of what you need to know, it's likely that there is a group ready to help. We have included names, addresses, and phone numbers of such groups throughout the book and hope that you will contact them.

Final thoughts: Remember Huey, Dewey, and Louie—Donald Duck's adventuresome and indefatigable nephews? Every time they have a problem or need information, they turn to "The Junior Woodchuck Manual," a book that seems to contain all of life's vital survival information. We think of this book as a senior version of the manual. If there's anything we've left out, it wasn't for lack of trying. We had a great time writing the book and we learned a heck of a lot along the way.

CAROL ORSAG MADIGAN
ANN ELWOOD

CONTENTS

1

HEALTH / 1

2
◆

CRIME / *89*

3

♦

MAKING A DIFFERENCE / 127

4

AROUND HOUSE AND YARD / *171*

5

◆

FAMILY / 251

6

◆

PETS / 305

7

MONEY MATTERS / 359

8

TRAVEL / 453

9

TRANSPORTATION / 495

10

◆

RECREATION / 527

11

FOOD AND DRINK / 585

12

ETIQUETTE / 645

13

LOOKING AND FEELING GOOD / 669

14

WORDS/LANGUAGE/ COMMUNICATIONS / 713

15

LEGAL MATTERS / 749

16

FIRST AID AND
DISASTER PREPAREDNESS / 797

17

MEASURES / 823

1

HEALTH

Diet and exercise

Self-care and preventive medicine

DIET AND EXERCISE

Should You Lose Weight?

Your mirror tells you if you look too fat for reasons of attractiveness. But should you lose weight for reasons of health? One or more of these six tests can help you decide.

The Apple-Pear Test.
1. Measure your waist where it is smallest, but don't suck in.
2. Measure your hips at the widest part.
3. Divide your waist by your hips.
If the number is above 0.8 (for women) or 0.95 (for men), you're an apple—that is, you carry your weight around the abdomen rather than the hips. If your waist is smaller in relation to your hips you are a pear, which is good—at least as far as health is concerned. For both sexes, it is best to keep the ratio below 0.76. While you may be able to do nothing about the ratio (it has genetic components), if you are an apple and are overweight by other measures, you probably should lose weight. Even 5 or 10 pounds *at the waist* can be unhealthy—it raises your chance of adult diabetes, high blood pressure, and high cholesterol, according to the Framingham Heart Study of the health of thousands of people. Other studies show it increases cancer risk.

Body-Fat Measurement Test. Ask a fitness counselor or nutritional counselor to perform this test for you. You will find someone qualified at most YMCAs.

Skin-Fold Pinch Test. Pinch your abdominal fat between your thumb and forefinger. Or take a pinch measurement of the flesh at the back of your upper arm or at your waist above the hip bone. If the roll is more than 1 inch thick, you should consider losing weight.

Mirror Test. Look at yourself naked in a full-length mirror. If you see bulges in the wrong places, you are probably overweight enough to need to lose weight.

Health Problems Test. If you have any of the following health problems and you are overweight, you probably should consider losing weight: hypertension, diabetes, high blood pressure, high risk of heart attack.

Tables Test. Look up your ideal weight range on the "U.S. Government Chart of Healthy Weights for Men and Women" or on the "Met-Life® Height and Weight Tables," which follow below. If you are 20 percent or more over the top of your range for your height, you are probably too fat.

WEIGHT PATTERNS IN MEN AND WOMEN

Calculating ratios of fat and muscle in men and women by means of magnetic resonance imaging (MRI), researchers at Yale University School of Medicine discovered that both men and women tend to carry the same proportion of fat—about 23 percent. Men's fat concentrates above the waist, however, while women's fat concentrates

3

below the waist. Earlier studies using other techniques found women's levels of body fat to be higher than men's.

U.S. Government Chart of Healthy Weights

If you are used to height-weight charts that categorize by sex and frame, this Department of Health and Human Services chart of healthy weights may surprise you. Numbers in each height category apply to *both* men and women, though women should pay more attention to the lower end of the range. The chart lists higher weights as healthy for people over 35 because, in general, older heavy people have better life expectancies than was previously thought, according to the National Research Council. In fact the Council claims that people can weigh 30

pounds more at 60 than at 30 (provided they were not overweight at 30) without risk to their health.

MetLife® Height and Weight Tables

Metropolitan Life Insurance has been issuing height-weight tables for decades. This company, too, has raised weights upward. Weight is in pounds according to frame, in indoor clothing weighing 5 pounds for men and 3 pounds for women. Height is taken in shoes with 1-inch heels.

Figuring Your Frame Size

Many estimates of overweight are based on frame size: the bigger the frame, the more generous the weight deemed to be desirable. Most of us fudge by saying we are "big-boned." This test will tell what your frame size actually is.

Bend one forearm upward at a 90-degree angle; keep fingers straight and turn the inside of your wrist toward your body. Place the thumb and index finger of the other hand on the two prominent bones on either side of the elbow of the raised arm. Measure the space between your fingers on a ruler. (A physician would use a caliper.) Compare with tables below listing elbow measurements for medium-framed men and women. Measurements lower than those listed indicate small frame. Higher measurements indicate large frame.

U.S. GOVERNMENT CHART OF HEALTHY WEIGHTS

Height	Weight in pounds	
	19 to 34 years	35 years and over
5'0"	97–128	108–138
5'1"	101–132	111–143
5'2"	104–137	115–148
5'3"	107–141	119–152
5'4"	111–146	122–157
5'5"	114–150	126–162
5'6"	118–155	130–167
5'7"	121–160	134–172
5'8"	125–164	138–178
5'9"	129–169	142–183
5'10"	132–174	146–188
5'11"	136–179	151–194
6'0"	140–184	155–199
6'1"	144–189	159–205
6'2"	148–195	164–210

Source: Department of Agriculture, Department of Health and Human Services

ELBOW MEASUREMENTS FOR MEDIUM FRAME

Men		Women	
Height in 1" heels	Elbow Breadth	Height in 1" heels	Elbow Breadth
5'2"–5'3"	2½"–2⅞"	4'10"–4'11"	2¼"–2½"
5'4"–5'7"	2⅝"–2⅞"	5'0"–5'3"	2¼"–2½"
5'8"–5'11"	2¾"–3"	5'4"–5'7"	2⅜"–2⅝"
6'0"–6'3"	2¾"–3⅛"	5'8"–5'11"	2⅜"–2⅝"
6'4"	2⅞"–3¼"	6'0"	2½"–2¾"

METLIFE® HEIGHT AND WEIGHT TABLES

Men				Women			
Height	Small Frame	Medium Frame	Large Frame	Height	Small Frame	Medium Frame	Large Frame
5'2"	128–134	131–141	138–150	4'10"	102–111	109–121	118–131
5'3"	130–136	133–143	140–153	4'11"	103–113	111–123	120–134
5'4"	132–138	135–145	142–156	5'0"	104–115	113–126	122–137
5'5"	134–140	137–148	144–160	5'1"	106–118	115–129	125–140
5'6"	136–142	139–151	146–164	5'2"	108–121	118–132	128–143
5'7"	138–145	142–154	149–168	5'3"	111–124	121–135	131–147
5'8"	140–148	145–157	152–172	5'4"	114–127	124–138	134–151
5'9"	142–151	148–160	155–176	5'5"	117–130	127–141	137–155
5'10"	144–154	151–163	158–180	5'6"	120–133	130–144	140–159
5'11"	146–157	154–166	161–184	5'7"	123–136	133–147	143–163
6'0"	149–160	157–170	164–188	5'8"	126–139	136–150	146–167
6'1"	152–164	160–174	168–192	5'9"	129–142	139–153	149–170
6'2"	155–168	164–178	172–197	5'10"	132–145	142–156	152–173
6'3"	158–172	167–182	176–202	5'11"	135–148	145–159	155–176
6'4"	162–176	171–187	181–207	6'0"	138–151	148–162	158–179

Source of basic data: 1979 Build Study, Society of Actuaries and Association of Life Insurance Medical Directors of America, 1980. Reprinted courtesy of the Metropolitan Life Insurance Company.

Diet Guide

Boring but true, and, yes, you have probably heard it all before but three phrases are key when it comes to dieting: eat less, exercise more, practice moderation. Quick fixes don't work in the long run. Advertised diet programs tend to work in the short run, but two-thirds or more of their clients regain the weight (and often even add a few pounds) within a year or two. Of those dieters who lose 25 pounds or more, only 10 percent keep their weight down past two years, says the National Center for Health Statistics. Another source says that only 5 percent of dieters succeed in the long run.

Eschewing claims of magical weight loss, the sober experts say that you must change your behavior and attitudes toward food and life permanently in order to achieve permanent weight loss. That said, here is a list of pointers about dieting that most experts agree on:

♦ See your doctor before going on any diet to make sure that dieting is safe for you.

♦ Diet for health, not beauty.

♦ Don't try for impossible goals. A reasonable goal is to lose a pound or less a week. To lose a pound a week, you need to cut 500 calories a day from the amount needed to maintain your weight at its present level. A pound of fat equals 3500 calories.

♦ Don't crash-diet. If you do, you will lose weight but your body will think it is starving. Your metabolism rate will slow down, so that when you eat normally again, you will gain weight.

♦ Avoid the yo-yo syndrome (losing and regaining weight over and over). It is more un-healthy than staying steadily fat at the same weight. Yo-yo dieting greatly increases your risk of dying from heart disease. When weight fluctuates, the body is under stress, and blood pressure and cholesterol levels rise.

♦ Try cutting back on calorie consumption slowly. Don't go cold turkey. For instance, cut back 100 calories a day the first week, 200 calories the second week. That way your body is less likely to produce stress hormones.

♦ Eat low-fat foods. (See "Ten Tips for Lowering the Fat Content of Your Diet," p. 592.) Learn to cook several tasty low-fat dishes. Limit high-fat foods like butter, red meat, cakes.

♦ Increase amounts of foods high in fiber—whole grains, fruits, vegetables, legumes. But do it slowly.

♦ Don't completely deny yourself your favorite foods. Instead, eat them in moderation. Try to eat a variety of foods. Resist feeling guilty.

♦ Eat smaller portions.

♦ Try to avoid eating for emotional reasons. Face your problems. In the long run, excess food will not make you feel better or less tired.

♦ Exercise enough to raise your heart rate to optimum levels three times a week, 20 minutes or more. (See "Exercise for Health," p. 7.)

Fraudulent Diet Aids

The diet business is so lucrative that it attracts phonies in droves. In general, beware of claims that you can magically and easily lose weight without dieting. According to the FDA (Food and Drug Administration), the following weight-loss products and schemes have not been proven effective, or even safe:

♦ Diet patches worn on the skin.

♦ "Fat blockers" that supposedly interfere mechanically with fat you eat, or physically absorb the fat.

♦ "Starch blockers" that claim to impede your digestion of starch. This product can cause nausea, diarrhea, vomiting, stomach pain.

♦ "Magnet" diet pills that purportedly break up into "fat-attracting" particles that grab fat and "flush" it out of the body.

♦ Glucomannan (a plant root), called the "Weight Loss Secret That's Been in the Orient for Over 500 Years."

♦ Bulk-producers or fillers, sometimes fiber-based, that swell in the stomach by absorbing liquid. They quell hunger, but some, like guar gum, can cause obstruction in the gut.

♦ Spirulina, a blue-green alga, that purports to help with weight loss.

♦ Electrical muscle stimulators. These can work in physical therapy, but they are not helpful in weight loss or body toning. They can cause electrical shocks and burns.

♦ Appetite-suppressing eyeglasses with colored lenses that claim to send an image to the retina which kills the desire to eat, usually by making the food look unpalatable.

♦ Magic weight-loss earrings claiming to stimulate acupuncture points that control hunger.

♦ Special belts, pants, or other clothing that will instantly "take off inches." They do take off inches, through dehydration, but the minute you drink water, the inches come back.

DIET FIBBERS—THE EYE-MOUTH GAP

According to a 1992 study published in the *New England Journal of Medicine*, there's no real mystery about people who mysteriously don't lose weight in spite of diet and exercise. The truth is, they don't tell the truth about what they eat or how much they exercise. They underestimate the amount of food consumed in the diet and overestimate the amount of exertion and time spent in exercise. (To catch these fibbers, researchers used an indirect method of metabolic testing.) In fact, most of us (80 percent), fat or thin, underestimate our food intake. The lesson: if you are trying to lose weight, measure or weigh food for a while to get a feeling for what a "serving" is. And keep track of your exercise—honestly.

Exercise for Health

How to Find Your Target Heart Rate for Exercise

At what rate should your heart be beating when you exercise? The answer: not so fast that it is harmful to your health and not so slowly that you gain little or no cardiovascular benefit. You figure out your target (optimal) heart rate by doing arithmetic. First determine your *maximum* heart rate by subtracting your age from 220. Then figure your *target* heart rate for exercise by multiplying the resulting number (your maximum heart rate) by 50 percent (least vigorous) or 75 percent (most vigorous). Of course, the old caveat applies: *see your doctor before starting any exercise program.*

Example:

```
   220
 -  35 (your age)
 = 185 (maximum heart rate)
```

```
   185                    185
 × .50        OR        × .75
 =  93 (least vigorous)  = 139 (most vigorous)
```

Exercise experts suggest that you exercise with your heart beating at 60–75 percent of your maximum heart rate for 20 minutes three times a week. A well-exercised heart pumps blood slowly at greater volume, so that it has to work less.

Stretching Tips

No matter what exercise you engage in, experts recommend that you warm up before it, cool down after it, and incorporate stretching for flexibility. Many people ignore these recommendations, thinking them unimportant. However, that's a mistake—warming up, cooling down, and stretching can prevent injury, improve circulation, enhance performance.

Warm up and cool down by doing a slow version of the workout for 5 to 10 minutes (walking before and after you jog, for instance). Stretch after cooling down.

♦ Stretching should involve the whole body, and it should be slow and gentle, never painful.

♦ Never bounce (ballistic stretching) unless you are very accomplished at stretching and know what you are doing—say, if you are a professional athlete or dancer. Bouncing can injure muscles and it can trigger the stretch reflex that tells the muscle to contract to prevent injury, the exact opposite of what you are trying to accomplish.

♦ Stretch when the body is warm.

♦ Hold each stretch for 20 to 60 seconds. (The American College of Sports Medicine recommends only 20 seconds.)

♦ Match stretching to your workouts. Use a book or ask an exercise consultant for recommendations.

♦ Do not do any stretch that hurts or aggravates a previous injury. If you have knee problems, for instance, some stretches may be harmful.

Walking

Walking is an old and venerable form of exercise—Jefferson, Emerson, and Thoreau were walkers. Walking requires no fancy equipment except a good pair of shoes, and almost all of us know how to do it in some fashion. You can walk almost anywhere and any time, and all your life. You don't need a partner, though a partner is nice. And once you start, you are less likely to drop out than if you take up another form of exercise.

Experts say that walking for a half-hour a day can cut risk of early death in half. The more you have lived as a couch potato, the more immediate the benefit you will get from walking (and other exercise). On the first day your blood pressure and stress level—even your urge to smoke, if you smoke—will drop. Walking will raise your HDL (good cholesterol) level and sharpen your immune system. You will sleep better.

For relaxation and burning of calories, it

doesn't matter how fast you walk, but it does matter that you go a certain distance. Running and walking consume about the same number of calories *per mile*. (The fatter you are, the more calories you will burn.) For cardiovascular benefits, you should walk fast enough to get your heart rate up. (See "Exercise for Health," p. 7.) In fact, studies have shown that walking has close to the same cardiovascular benefits as more strenuous exercise. The Cooper Institute for Aerobics Research studied women who walked three 12-minute miles a day, five days a week.

SOME WARM-UP AND CONDITIONING EXERCISES

The President's Council on Physical Fitness and Sports recommends the following exercises, designed to increase flexibility and strength, as a warmup for walking. (We have eliminated the two most difficult situps.)

Stretcher. Stand facing wall arm's length away. Lean forward and place palms of hands flat against wall, slightly below shoulder height. Keep back straight, heels firmly on floor, and slowly bend elbows until forehead touches wall. Tuck hips toward wall and hold position for 20 seconds. *Repeat exercise with knees slightly flexed.*

Reach and Bend. Stand erect with feet shoulder-width apart and arms extended over head. Reach as high as possible while keeping heels on floor and hold for 10 counts. Flex knees slightly and bend slowly at waist, touching floor between feet with fingers. Hold for 10 counts. (If you can't touch the floor, try to touch the tops of your shoes.) *Repeat entire sequence 2 to 5 times.*

Knee Pull. Lie flat on back with legs extended and arms at sides. Lock arms around legs just below knees and pull knees to chest, raising buttocks slightly off floor. Hold for 10 to 15 counts. (If you have knee problems, you may find it easier to lock arms behind knees.) *Repeat exercise 3 to 5 times.*

Situp. Several versions of the situp are listed in reverse order of difficulty (easiest one listed first, most difficult one last). Start with the situp that you can do three times without undue strain. When you are able to do 10 repetitions of the exercise without great difficulty, move on to a more difficult version.

1. Lie flat on back with arms at sides, palms down, and knees slightly bent. Curl head forward until you can see past feet, hold for three counts, then lower to start position. *Repeat exercise 3 to 10 times.*

2. Lie flat on back with arms at sides, palms down, and knees slightly bent. Roll forward until upper body is at 45-degree angle to floor, then return to starting position. *Repeat exercise 3 to 10 times.*

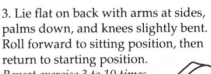

3. Lie flat on back with arms at sides, palms down, and knees slightly bent. Roll forward to sitting position, then return to starting position. *Repeat exercise 3 to 10 times.*

Their cardiovascular fitness increased by 16 percent.

Walking is virtually injury-free, but be sure to check with your doctor before you start this or any other exercise program. To avoid foot problems, wear shoes with good arch and heel support, some cushioning, and flexibility in the front of the foot. The heel of the shoe should raise the heel of your foot one-half to three-quarters of an inch above the sole. (See "Choosing the Right Athletic Shoes," p. 533.)

How to Walk

♦ Rise up and down on your toes 20 times before putting your shoes on. Stretch. Then start walking slowly (3 miles per hour or less) and gradually increase speed over the next five minutes or so.

♦ Maintain proper posture, chin tucked into neck so that ear, shoulder, hip, and ankle are all on the same vertical line. Start by standing this way, then try to hold the posture as you walk. Don't arch your back. Look straight ahead, not at the ground.

♦ Tuck in your rear end and tighten your stomach muscles (pelvic tilt). Walking like this takes weight off your lower back, reducing chances of back pain, and makes your stomach and back muscles stronger.

♦ Swing your arms, elbows bent slightly for regular walking, at a 90-degree angle for aerobic walking. When you take a stride with your right leg, move your left arm for rhythm and balance. Keep your arms close to your body, swinging slightly across. This exercises the upper body, speeds you up, and doubles the exercise value of walking.

♦ Walk with your feet parallel. Don't walk in duck fashion, toes pointed out, or pigeon-toed, toes pointed in. If you do, you put unnecessary stress on your joints.

♦ Walk with a heel-toe roll, landing heel first, then rolling on outside edge of foot to the toe. Drive off the ball of the foot for the next step. This keeps leg bones aligned.

♦ Take long steps, rather than short ones.

WALKING POSTURE

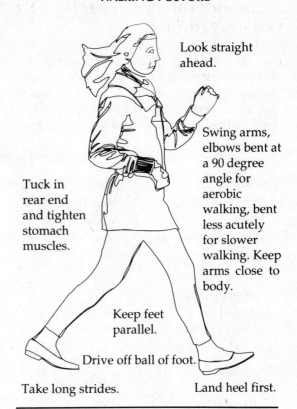

Look straight ahead.

Swing arms, elbows bent at a 90 degree angle for aerobic walking, bent less acutely for slower walking. Keep arms close to body.

Tuck in rear end and tighten stomach muscles.

Keep feet parallel.

Drive off ball of foot.

Take long strides.

Land heel first.

This burns more calories, increases speed, and keeps muscles from tightening too much. However, do not overstride—walk naturally. Lean forward a bit when walking fast or ascending hills.

♦ End with a 10-minute cool-down (a slow walk).

How Far, How Fast?

If you are healthy, start by walking 20 minutes a day four or five times a week at a comfortable pace. Adjust time and speed if this tires you out or seems too easy. Increase time and pace gradually until you can walk three miles in 45 minutes. To find the right pace, use the "talk test": if you can talk and walk without breathlessness, you are not going too fast.

Before you start this exercise program or any other, obtain a doctor's approval.

Calorie Expenditures per Hour for Various Activities

You play tennis with ferocity and energy one day, thus expending a great many calories, and play weakly the next, expending far fewer. Your partner burns more calories than you whatever her level of vigor because she has a higher metabolism rate. Because different people perform an activity with various degrees of enthusiasm and speed at various times, it is impossible to say accurately exactly how many calories each individual burns without individual metabolic testing. The following figures look precise but they are *averages*. If you weigh more or less than 130 pounds, assume you will expend more calories or fewer calories, all else being equal.

CALORIES BURNED PER HOUR

Activity	Calories burned per hour (by a 130-lb. woman)	Activity	Calories burned per hour (by a 130-lb. woman
Aerobics (high/low impact)	600	Rowing (moderate)	273
Badminton	338	Running (10 mph)	600–1,000
Ballroom dancing	176–208	Running (7.5 mph)	750
Baseball (fielding)	240	Sailing	188
Basketball	462	Scrubbing floors	377
Bicycling (12 mph)	545	Shoveling snow	400–507
Bicycling (6 mph)	231	Skating	338
Bowling (nonstop)	158	Skiing (downhill)	462
Calisthenics	231	Skiing (cross country)	600
Canoeing (leisure)	150	Skiing (water)	353
Cleaning	208–222	Soccer	353
Cooking	156–167	Squash	462
Dancing (slow)	176–208	Stationary cycling (10 mph)	375
Dancing (fast)	261	Swimming (backstroke)	273
Dusting	146	Swimming (crawl)	214
Food shopping	169–200	Tennis (doubles)	231
Gardening	169–415	Tennis (singles)	375
Golf	300	Typing	102
Gymnastics	231	Vacuuming	353
Horseback riding	400	Volleyball	176–286
Ice skating	300	Walking upstairs (1 step/sec.)	430–660
Ironing	113	Walking (4 mph)	286–333
Jogging (5 mph)	462	Walking (3 mph)	222
Jumping rope (moderate)	375	Washing floors	222
Making beds	146	Washing windows	231
Mopping	221	Watching television	78
Mowing lawn	206–350	Weeding garden	316
Rollerblading	273	Weight training (light)	300

Fitness Benefits of Various Activities

For all-round fitness, you should engage in several activities—one to make you huff and puff (for cardiovascular health), one to make you grunt (for muscle strength and endurance), one to make you stretch (for flexibility). This list should help you in choosing a variety of activities for overall fitness. Again, check with your doctor before beginning any exercise program.

FITNESS BENEFITS

Activity	Heart	Muscle Tone (strength & endurance)	Flexibility
Aerobics	****	***	***
Basketball (full court)	****	**	***
Bowling	*	*	*
Calisthenics	*	***	****
Cross-country skiing	****	***	**
Cycling (13 mph)	****	***	*
Golf	**	*	**
Hiking	***	***	***
Horseback riding	*	*	*
Racquetball/squash/handball	***	***	**
Roller or ice skating	***	***	**
Rowing	****	***	*
Running (6-min. mile)	****	***	*
Running (9-min. mile)	****	***	*
Stretching	*	*	****
Swimming (slow laps)	****	***	***
Tennis (singles)	**	**	*
Volleyball	**	*	**
Walking (13-min mi.)	***	**	*
Weight training	*	****	*

* *** = Excellent   *** =Good   ** = Fair   * = Poor

Reprinted courtesy of *U.S. News and World Report.*

SELF-CARE AND PREVENTIVE MEDICINE

The Stress Factor

Stress, in itself, can be a positive motivating force that helps you to meet a deadline at work, excel in athletic competition, or complete all the small touches for an elegant dinner party. But at its worst, stress and the inability to cope with it can lead to tension headaches, digestive disorders, insomnia, ulcers, and panic attacks. Stress has also been linked to the six leading causes of death: heart disease, cancer, lung disorders, accidents, cirrhosis of the liver, and suicide. According to one study, 43 percent of adults suffer bad effects on their health due to stress.

While it's long been common knowledge that significant life changes or losses—such as the death of a spouse or changing jobs or residences—are stressful events, more recent medical research shows that constant negative reactions to minor everyday stresses actually pose more of a hazard to our health.

External stress factors are only part of the problem. We all have to deal with conditions such as noise and air pollution, traffic, unemployment, cars or vacuums breaking down, being put on hold by an electronic telephone system, a spouse's irritating habit, or co-workers who are not pulling their weight. The key factor is how we react or cope with the stress. While one person waits happily in line at the supermarket reading a tabloid, the next person impatiently taps a foot and constantly checks the time.

When we have a negative reaction to stress, we feel threatened and the body's physiology assumes the "fight or flight" response. Hormones, including adrenalin, are released that cause blood vessels in the stomach, intestines, and peripheral parts of the body to constrict while more blood goes to the brain and muscle tissue in preparation for physical action. The heart speeds up, breathing becomes shallow and rapid, muscles tense, and perspiration increases. Speech also changes, usually becoming louder, higher in pitch, more rapid, and shaky.

The "fight or flight" syndrome is an emergency response, and when it is maintained too long without relief or repeated too often, the body suffers from exhaustion, the immune system weakens, and the opportunity for stress-related illness increases.

MANAGING STRESS

Although we can't avoid the stresses of modern life, we can learn to manage our responses to stress. The first step is to identify what triggers your reactions—what makes you feel angry, hostile, or frustrated. Learn what your body's stress signals are so that you can then step back from the situation and apply different techniques for managing your response. It's important to take some action, such as calmly expressing your feelings or doing a breathing exercise, so that you reverse or slow down the body's emergency-response mechanism.

Good basic health practices are also important in managing stress. We are much more likely to respond to a tense situation in a volatile fashion when we haven't had enough sleep or have skipped breakfast and lunched on doughnuts. Good nutrition, regular exercise, and plenty of sleep are good anti-stress prescriptions, as is watching your intake of caffeine, alcohol, or any self-prescribed drugs or medications. Some people find smoking "relaxing," but that perception comes from the fact that they are probably shallow breathers and only breathe deeply when inhaling the smoke. It is the breathing, not the cigarette, that brings relaxation.

Talking with a friend, laughing, and physical touching are everyday stress relievers that we sometimes overlook. Studies have shown that petting a dog or cat reduces the heart rate and lowers blood pressure. A joke eases tension during a heated discussion, and laughter as a healing agent for cancer patients has been the subject of recent books. Discussing your problems and concerns with a friend or counselor can provide relief, support, and new perspectives on how to deal with the stresses in your life.

It's important to find a personal source of relaxation—whether it's physical exercise, a hobby, or meditation—and devote at least a half-hour a day to it. Short vacations, such as a day or weekend in the country, also help to lighten the load of daily routines.

Stress Busters

The techniques for reducing tension and relieving stress are many. Some require the services of a paid professional—biofeedback, chiropractic treatments, acupuncture, massage, counseling—but there are numerous things you can do on your own to improve stress-coping skills and develop a more relaxed attitude toward your life and your environment.

Progressive Relaxation. This exercise combines breathing with alternate tensing and releasing of the body's primary muscle groups. Wearing loose clothing, sit in a comfortable chair or lie down in a quiet, dimly lit room. Regulate your breathing. As you inhale, focus first on expanding your abdomen/diaphragm, then your chest. As you exhale, reverse the order. Once you have achieved a slow, relaxed breathing rhythm, tense the lower muscles in your right leg, from the foot to the knee. Tense as you inhale, clenching the muscles as tightly as you can. Hold for 7 seconds, then exhale and release, letting the muscles go limp. Relax for about 45 seconds. Then repeat the tensing/relaxing in the same muscle group on your left side. Move gradually up the body, so you cover these muscle groups: lower legs, upper legs, hands/forearms, biceps, chest/abdomen, upper back/shoulders, neck/jaw, middle portion of the face, forehead.

If after completing the exercise, you still feel tension in an area, repeat the tensing/relaxing for that muscle group. This progressive relaxation can be done on its own or as a preparation for meditation.

Meditation. There are many formal schools of meditation—from Transcendental Meditation to Zen to Sufism to certain Christian prayer practices. Scientific research has shown that individuals in a meditative state have lower blood pressure and a slower heart rate than they do in a normal waking state.

A technique that incorporates all religious and philosophical persuasions has been developed by Dr. Herbert Benson of the Harvard Medical School. Dr. Benson, the author of several books, calls his method "The Relaxation Response" with a "faith factor." His studies show that eliciting The Relaxation Response can help to alleviate the harmful effects of everyday stress.

Here are the steps of his method:
 ♦ Choose a word or a short phrase that reflects your deep personal beliefs, such as "Shalom," the Hebrew word for peace or a phrase from the Lord's Prayer.
 ♦ Sit in a comfortable position, but one that does not induce you to doze off.
 ♦ Let your eyes close slowly.
 ♦ Relax your muscles.
 ♦ Breathe naturally and slowly. Upon each exhalation, silently say your word or phrase.

♦ Passively dismiss other thoughts that enter your mind, by saying to yourself "Oh well," and then return to the silent recitation of your word or phrase.

♦ Practice the technique for 10–20 minutes. Have a clock in plain view so you can easily look at it when you think about the time. Don't set an alarm clock.

♦ At the end of your meditation, open your eyes slowly and sit quietly for at least one full minute before resuming any activity.

♦ Do your meditation once or twice daily. The technique works best on an empty stomach. During relaxation the flow of blood is directed away from the abdominal area. With a full stomach, the digestive process tends to interfere with achieving full relaxation.

Yoga and T'ai Chi. An estimated 3 to 5 million Americans practice yoga. Although there are many different schools of yoga, many of them spiritual meditative practices, Hatha Yoga is the type most widely studied in the West. Hatha Yoga combines focused breathing, proper alignment, and physical exercises or postures. Many of the movements, like those in the Chinese practice of T'ai Chi, were inspired by the movements of birds and animals.

Both Hatha Yoga and T'ai Chi concentrate on calming the mind by directing energy through the body. Through the controlled movements, muscles are alternately stretched and relaxed. The benefits of these ancient alternatives to aerobics can include lower blood pressure, better flexibility and muscle tone, greater lung capacity, improved cardiovascular efficiency, and overall stress reduction.

Guided Imagery. By using the power of your imagination, you can "create" a stress-free retreat from daily cares that will help you to feel rejuvenated in the real world. Soothing music or commercially available relaxation tapes can help you with the technique of guided imagery.

As with other techniques, it's best to do this exercise in a quiet room wearing comfortable clothing. Close your eyes, relax your muscles, and breathe slowly and evenly. Imagine yourself in a place where you felt especially calm and at peace with yourself. Notice all the details of the scene and experience the sensory aspects, such as the sun on your face or the light breeze lifting your hair. When you have completely "explored" this relaxing place, slowly open your eyes and remain at rest for a minute or two to regain your orientation.

Positive Affirmations/Self-Talk. Most of the stress we feel comes from our discomfort over not having control—either control of our own emotions, abilities, and bodies or control of external situations and other people's actions. By keeping a flexible attitude, staying in the present, and limiting negative judgments about ourselves and others, we can learn to cope better with stress.

The first step toward a more positive outlook is recognizing what negative patterns occur in our inner dialogue with ourselves. Negative thinking often is marked by absolute and hyperbolic words such as "never," "always," "horrible," "terrible"; by words that express rigid expectations, like "must" or "should"; and by words that project into the future or the past, tending to magnify the present situation—phrases such as "what if" or "if only." As an example, the following inner dialogue is a sure setup for stress: "I'll never get through this day. I should be better organized. What if my boss has one of his tantrums?"

This type of negative thinking can be replaced with affirming self-talk: "I'll be fine today. I'll do my best and I'm going to focus on achieving one or two important things. My boss's temper is his problem, not mine, and just for today I'm not going to react or take his actions personally."

In developing self-affirming skills, it's important to have compassion for yourself and to praise yourself for your accomplishments. One technique that can be helpful is to write a daily "gratitude list," noting all the things you appreciate about yourself, your life, and those around you.

It is possible to change your outlook if you focus on appreciating yourself and then take action, recognizing that some things are within your control and that things beyond your control simply aren't worth the worry.

DE-STRESS AS YOU GO

Releasing stress throughout the day is a healthful and easy habit to acquire. Whether you're caught in a traffic jam, waiting for an elevator, or chained to a desk, it takes only a few moments to perform a breathing or stretching exercise that will help relieve your tension.

♦ Take 10 deep breaths. Be sure to stand or sit in an erect posture. Breathe slowly. As you inhale, expand the diaphragm first, then the chest. Hold the breath for five counts. As you exhale, deflate the abdomen first, then the chest.

♦ Sing a song loudly. Singing encourages deep breathing and eases tension in the neck and facial muscles.

♦ Yawn deeply three or four times.

♦ Clench a tennis ball for 10 seconds, then release your fist. Repeat until you feel more relaxed.

♦ Take a brief meditation break or visualize yourself lying in the sun on a deserted tropical beach.

♦ Limber up neck muscles by inhaling and slowing moving the head back to look at the ceiling. Exhale, bring the chin to the chest. Then look straight ahead, inhale and turn the head over the right shoulder. Exhale as you look forward again. Repeat, alternating on the left and right sides.

♦ Stretch your upper back by clasping your hands behind your head and pulling your shoulder blades in. Hold the stretch for 10 seconds, then release. Repeat several times.

♦ Release tension in your shoulders by pulling the shoulders up toward the ears as you inhale. Hold your breath as you squeeze the muscles. As you exhale, push your shoulders down and back.

♦ Practice self-affirmations, such as "I can handle this one step at a time."

How Healthy Is Your State?

Northwestern National Life Insurance Company evaluated the state of health in all 50 states. The study compared each state's population in the following categories:

Occupational Safety and Disability (occupational fatalities and work disability status).

Disease (prevalence of heart disease, cancer, AIDS, tuberculosis, and hepatitis).

Mortality (total mortality rate, infant mortality, and years of life lost to death before age 65).

Lifestyle (level of education, prevalence of smoking, motor-vehicle deaths, violent crime, risk for heart disease factors: obesity, hypertension, and lack of exercise).

Access to health care (state unemployment rate, use of prenatal care, and the availability of primary care medical-care providers and state government-funded health care for low-income persons).

All factors were weighted according to their impact on overall health in calculating final rankings. The 1993 list below ranks the 50 states, from the most healthy to the least. *Note:* When rankings are tied, the number or numbers that would have followed have been eliminated. For example, since Hawaii and Connecticut tie for third place, Utah, which ranks next, has been assigned number 5.

State	Rank	State	Rank
Minnesota	1	Ohio	16
New Hampshire	2	North Dakota	18
Connecticut	3	Pennsylvania	18
Hawaii	3	Rhode Island	18
Utah	5	Washington	21
Kansas	6	Indiana	22
Vermont	6	Delaware	23
Massachusetts	8	California	24
Colorado	9	Michigan	25
Iowa	9	Arizona	26
Nebraska	11	Montana	26
Wisconsin	11	Oregon	26
Virginia	13	Missouri	29
Maine	14	Oklahoma	29
New Jersey	15	Idaho	31
Maryland	16	Texas	31

State	Rank	State	Rank
Illinois	33	Nevada	42
South Dakota	33	Alabama	43
Wyoming	35	Alaska	43
New York	36	Arkansas	43
North Carolina	37	New Mexico	46
Georgia	38	South Carolina	46
Kentucky	38	West Virginia	48
Florida	40	Louisiana	49
Tennessee	40	Mississippi	50

Reprinted courtesy of Northwestern National Life Insurance Company.

Home Remedies: What Works, What Doesn't

Some home remedies really work—even doctors and nurses use them. CAUTION: Use these only for temporary relief. If any problem persists, especially with children, see your physician.

Bad Breath. The causes for bad breath are many: throat crypts, where food lodges and rots; periodontal disease; adenoids blocking nasal passages; bacteria on the tongue. Try brushing the top of your tongue, where bacteria collect. Parsley and fennel seeds are natural breath deodorizers. Eat a small amount of sugar but remember that it causes cavities.

Bee stings. Flick out the stinger by putting your fingernail under it and lifting it up and out. Be gentle. Don't use tweezers because pressure will inject more venom. Wash the area with soap and water. Ice packs can reduce swelling. Then apply unflavored meat tenderizer. It works because it contains an enzyme (papain) that can neutralize venom. A paste of baking soda and water can also provide relief. **Warning! One person in 200 suffers an allergic reaction to bee stings that may be life-threatening. Symptoms: itchy rash, dizziness, swelling of the throat and other parts of the body (other than where the sting is), vomiting, nausea, stomach cramps, anxiety, shortness of breath, wheezing, coughing. Get emergency help right away! Epinephrine (adrenalin) can counteract your reaction.**

Black eye. Put an ice pack on it, but don't put pressure on the eye.

Blister. Don't pop it unless it is likely to break on its own. If it looks infected (the liquid is cloudy and red), have a doctor drain it. If you insist on draining it yourself, wash with soap and water and rubbing alcohol, pop by using pressure with cotton swab on one edge, leaving the top alone. Spread with some antibiotic ointment, cover with bandage. Drain every day until healed.

Canker sore: Put a black-tea teabag (previously soaked in lukewarm water and wrung out) on the sore for a minute or two (a recommendation by Ohio dermatologist Jerome Z. Litt, MD). Maalox used topically works too.

Cold. Something in the chemistry of garlic hates cold germs and kills them. Also chicken soup deserves respect: it works. See "America's Favorite Remedy: Chicken Soup," p. 600.

Constipation. The remedy cassia (senna) may work more than you care for, producing watery diarrhea, even serious loss of fluids. And even though it is made of "natural" ingredients, you can become dependent on it. Better to increase your intake of fiber or take a traditional fiber-based laxative.

Cuts. To help healing, 24 hours after bleeding stops (and only then), put a mixture of plain granulated sugar and water (a paste) on the injury, cover with gauze, tape. Change the bandage every day, each time using a new sugar paste. This dehydrates the cut, so that bacteria cannot reproduce.

Earache: Warm a dropper bottle of baby oil with the heat of your hands, then put a few drops in the ear (for temporary relief).

Gas. Drink peppermint tea, which contains carminatives that break up intestinal gas so you can release it.

Hangover. When cymbals seem to clang in your head, you won't think a hangover is funny. Not much will help except time, but drink plenty of water, juice, and bouillon.

Headaches. A herbal remedy, feverfew, actually works, according to a study published in *The Lancet* in 1988. In people prone to migraines who took a capsule a day, attacks were milder. They also vomited less. Those who took a placebo had no such effect. Buy freeze-dried leaves in capsules.

Heartburn: Raise the head of your bed 6 inches or more. This stops the gastroesophageal reflex (backing up of stomach contents with gastric acid into the esophagus). Don't lie down until at least two hours after you have eaten.

Hiccups. According to the Mayo Clinic, massaging the back of the roof of the mouth with a cotton-tipped swab can stop the hiccups. Old remedies known to work, but not in every case: sucking on a piece of ice, breathing into a paper bag 10 times, swallowing a teaspoonful of sugar, drinking water either from the far side of the glass or in many little swallows, lying on your back with your knees against your stomach.

Injuries. Use a package of frozen peas as an ice bag, according to Joseph Burnett, MD, at the University of Maryland, Baltimore. It molds to the shape of the injured part better.

Insomnia. The herb valerian, which smells like dirty socks, depresses the central nervous system and will help you sleep, but don't overdose and don't use every day.

Itching. (1) Make a solution of one-fourth to one-third cup baking soda to a quart of cool water and apply to rashes, insect bites, poison ivy itch, and other itches. It works because it is alkaline and draws residues of itch-causing substances off the skin. One problem: it may dry your skin. (2) Rub the itch with an ice cube.

Nausea. Studies show that pressing the acupressure point in your wrist will reduce nausea. Locate the two tendons on the inside of your wrist from the base of your palm to your elbow. Then find a point about two inches down from the base of your palm (toward the elbow) and apply pressure with your fingers or thumb for a minute or two. Drink room-temperature tea and juices in small amounts; eat crackers or toast.

Pain. Press the muscle in the space between your thumb and forefinger for a few minutes or with an on-off rhythm. This triggers the release of endorphins, the body's natural painkillers.

Premenstrual Syndrome (PMS). Increase your calcium intake. Avoid caffeine. Limit salt

ACUPRESSURE POINT FOR NAUSEA

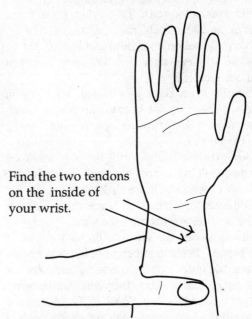

Find the two tendons on the inside of your wrist.

At a spot 2 inches down from the base of your palm, apply pressure to the tendons with thumb or fingers for a minute or two.

ACUPRESSURE POINT FOR PAIN

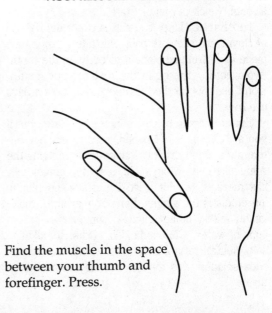

Find the muscle in the space between your thumb and forefinger. Press.

intake. Don't smoke. Exercise. Probably of no use: vitamin B_6 and magnesium supplements.

Sinuses (clogged). Take a hot shower and inhale the steam. Or make a steam tent by putting a towel on your head and leaning over a sink full of steaming water. Eat horseradish (if you can stand it).

Smelly feet. Soak your feet in a solution of cold tea (regular, not herbal), for about a half-hour a week. Use two teabags to a quart and a half of water.

Sore throat: Gargle with hot salt water (½ teaspoon salt in 8 ounces of water). Drink licorice root tea (1 teaspoon licorice root steeped in a cup of hot water for 3 minutes). Glycerrhizin, present in the licorice, is what does the trick.

Stuffy nose: Eat spicy foods with ginger or red pepper. Breathe steam from hot water. Use homemade nose drops (dissolve ¼ teaspoon salt in a cup of boiling water, then cool the mixture); use with nasal atomizer. WARNING: Make nose drops fresh every time—they are easily contaminated.

Sunburn: If you have overdone it in the sun, take two aspirin every two hours (eight total), provided aspirin does not bother your stomach. This will reduce swelling. Use aloe vera juice (from a leaf) on skin. Take a cool bath. Do not use: calamine lotion, witch hazel, or rubbing alcohol, which dry and irritate the skin.

Toothache. Until you can get to a dentist, oil of cloves can alleviate pain. Put a few drops on a piece of cotton and place it directly on the tooth. Avoid getting the oil in the rest of your mouth. Don't use this method for more than seven days in a row.

Upset stomach. Chamomile tea works, but if you are allergic to ragweed, asters, or chrysanthemums, don't drink it—chamomile contains the same allergen. Mom's old remedy, ginger ale, has merit if you let it go flat first—the helpful ingredient is the ginger. For stronger stuff, make ginger tea by boiling slices of ginger root in two cups of water. Club soda also works. Its alkaline salts neutralize stomach acids. *Don't* use baking-soda solutions, as they can cause stomach ruptures.

Warts. Toads don't cause warts, viruses do. Many venerable home cures for warts (milkweed juice, and so on) actually work because they involve covering the wart. Why? Warts probably need air; bandages suffocate them. Put the wart under several layers of adhesive tape, and change it once a week, with one period of 12 hours in the open air. Keep following this pattern until the wart disappears. Incidentally, make sure it is actually a wart that you are treating. Birthmarks and moles are not warts.

Yeast infections. Eat yogurt and use it as a lotion for yeast infections. When women prone to chronic yeast infections ate a cup of yogurt with added acidophilus bacteria a day, they had two-thirds fewer bouts of the condition. Used topically, yogurt soothes itching of vaginal infections.

Sleep

Get your Zzzzs! To live a long and healthy life, you need seven to eight hours of sleep a night, on the average. (Babies require enormous amounts of sleep, and children and young adults need more than adults, up to 10 hours.) If you sleep less than six hours a night, you have a 70 percent chance of dying early of conditions affecting the heart and digestion or from an accident. Much human error results from sleep deprivation: medical mistakes, air disasters, truckers' accidents. And sleep deprivation also leads to irritability, which makes for a testy society.

If you have sleep problems you are not alone. About 40 million Americans have chronic sleep problems, according to the 1992 report of the National Commission on Sleep Disorders Research.

Help exists for people who have sleeping problems. Many medical centers have sleep laboratories, where machines can track breathing and other physiological sleep patterns to help diagnose what is wrong and propose a solution.

What Is a Normal Sleep Pattern?

Sleep cycles include—
♦ light sleep
♦ deep sleep
♦ REM (rapid eye movement) sleep, which happens several times a night. Eyes move, muscles twitch, and heartbeat and blood pressure fluctuate. Most dreaming happens during REM sleep.

All of these stages are necessary, and if any one is disrupted, sleep problems can occur.

Sleeping and waking are controlled by—
♦ a biological clock (a bundle of nerve cells) in the hypothalamus, which responds to variations in sunlight coming into the eye, and
♦ homeostasis, the tendency of the body to seek equilibrium. Scientists think that an as-yet-unidentified chemical that induces sleep accumulates during the day.

Specific Sleep Problems

Insomnia. Insomnia's causes are manifold: stress, hormonal imbalances, allergies, disease, "restless leg syndrome," indigestion. Chronic insomnia can cause short-term memory loss, accidents, misjudgments. If you have long-term insomnia—over six weeks—you should probably see your doctor. Some hints:
♦ Figure out your sleeping pattern by keeping a sleep diary for a week.
♦ Put yourself on a regular schedule of sleeping and waking.
♦ Don't take naps in the daytime.
♦ Exercise regularly, but don't exercise in the three hours before you go to bed.
♦ Start relaxing at least an hour before bedtime. Put your problems and brain-taxing tasks to bed at least an hour before your own bedtime.
♦ Don't ingest caffeine after 12 noon (caffeine is an ingredient of chocolate as well as of coffee).
♦ Abstain from alcohol, which may put you to sleep but later in the night can cause restlessness and sleeplessness.
♦ Sleep in a quiet, cool, dark room.

♦ Go to bed only when you are drowsy. If you are anxious about not sleeping, if you lie awake trying to sleep for more than 15 minutes, get up and do something—read or watch television.
♦ Don't use your bed for anything but sleeping and sex, some experts say. Others disagree. Do what works for you.
♦ Avoid using sleeping pills. You should never take them without a doctor's prescription, and never for more than two or three weeks at a time.
♦ If these suggestions fail, go to a sleep center.

Sleep apnea (apnea means "not breathing" in Greek). There are about 2 million Americans with this condition. While sleeping, they actually stop breathing because the muscles in the upper airway droop and close it down; then, as carbon dioxide increases in the lungs, the brain alarms the person enough to force a big breathy snore. This can happen several hundred times a night, making sleep restless. One cure is a machine that forces air into the nose. Weight loss may help overweight men who are prone to this disorder.

Narcolepsy, falling asleep without warning. About 300,000 Americans suffer from this condition. The pace of narcoleptics' sleep is speedier. They fall asleep fast, in two minutes, and enter REM sleep within 15 minutes. The solution: strong stimulants.

Working at night, particularly the graveyard shift, causing disturbances in biological rhythms. It is possible to turn the clock around with light therapy. That is, exposure to intervals of daylight-bright light and daytime darkness can fool your body into turning night into day, as can capsules of melatonin, a brain chemical from the pineal gland.

Parasomnia, including night terrors, sleepwalking, sleep paralysis. Children who experience these disorders usually outgrow them, but adults may need professional help. Sometimes hynotherapy helps.

For information on a sleep center near you:
National Sleep Foundation, 122 S. Robertson Blvd., 3rd Floor, Los Angeles, CA 90048 (310-288-0466).

American Sleep Disorders Association, 1610 14th Street Northwest, Suite 300, Rochester, MN 55901 (507-287-6006).

Are You an Insomniac?

Check the statements that are true for you.
- ☐ Falling asleep is hard for me.
- ☐ I have too much on my mind to go to sleep.
- ☐ When I wake up in the middle of the night, I can't go back to sleep.
- ☐ I can't relax because I have too many worries.
- ☐ Even when I sleep all night, I'm still tired in the morning.
- ☐ Sometimes I am afraid to close my eyes and go to sleep.
- ☐ I wake up too early.
- ☐ It takes me more than an hour to fall asleep.
- ☐ I am stiff and sore in the morning.
- ☐ I feel depressed when I can't sleep.

If you checked . . .
1–3 statements: You are experiencing occasional—and normal—trouble sleeping.
4–6 statements: You may have a problem. Lifestyle changes—such as in your bedtime rituals or eating and drinking habits—may help improve your sleep habits.
7–10 statements: You may have a sleep problem that requires medical attention.

Reprinted courtesy of National Sleep Foundation.

Chronobiology

Jet lag is well understood. High speed travel over long distances has the effect of either subtracting hours (west-east travel) or adding hours (east-west travel) to our day. This upsets the body's biological rhythms. But many more subtle changes in our bodies occur according to the rhythms of day and night, months, tides, and seasons. We are creatures ruled (at least to some extent) by the movements of the earth and moon. Our brain has its own "clock," the suprachiasmatic nucleus, a clump of neurons, mainly regu-lated by light. Each of us has a pattern, and we acknowledge it when we identify ourselves as "day people" or "night people."

Chronobiologists, who study these rhythms, are finding them important in the diagnosis and treatment of many medical disorders. When is it best to take one's medicine? When is one most at risk from the effects of disease? Some findings:

♦ Asthma and ulcer attacks are more likely to occur late at night. It is better to take medicine before bed.

♦ Some medicines cause more pronounced side effects if taken in the morning, others at night.

♦ For rheumatoid arthritis, anti-inflammatory drugs are best taken in the evening to prevent the morning flare-up that is most common with this disease. For osteoarthritis, on the other hand, medication is more effective if taken in the morning against the peaking of pain later in the day.

♦ Therapy with light seems to help women with lupus, an autoimmune disorder.

♦ Allergic symptoms tend to become worse after awakening, so medication works best if time-released and taken at night.

♦ High blood pressure peaks in the afternoon. Heart attacks and strokes strike most commonly within three hours of waking up.

♦ Daily doses of aspirin or other nonsteroidal anti-inflammatory drugs (like ibuprofen) are best taken in late evening.

Seasonal Affective Disorder (SAD)

A mood disorder that seems to be associated with a deficit of sunlight, SAD is a condition with an easy cure: exposure to bright light (one hundred times brighter than indoor light) for a half-hour a day for two weeks. People afflicted by SAD become lethargic and clinically depressed in the winter months, sometimes manic and energetic with the coming of spring. SAD is associated with the secretion of melatonin, a hormone that acts like a natural tranquilizer. We all experience fluctuations in the production of melatonin, but people with SAD are disabled by them.

Sun Safety

Overexposure to the sun can not only damage your skin, but it can also cause skin cancer. Ultraviolet rays from the sun come in two forms: UVB rays and UVA rays. UVB rays, called burning rays, are the primary cause of sunburn and skin cancer. UVA rays penetrate more deeply into the skin and cause premature aging of the skin; damage from UVA rays can make you more susceptible to damage from UVB rays. It's estimated that as much as 90 percent of skin changes that we attribute to the normal process of aging—wrinkles, brown spots, sagging skin, loss of skin elasticity—are due solely to sun exposure.

While we have long considered a suntan to symbolize youth and vigor and physical fitness, the exact opposite is true. Ninety percent of all skin cancers are due to excessive exposure to sunlight, especially UVB radiation. An equally frightening fact: the most damaging exposure to sunlight occurs in your early years, before you reach age 20. And sunburns that occur in childhood are particularly risky. As few as two or three blistering sunburns sustained in childhood can double the odds of developing malignant melanoma, the most deadly kind of skin cancer. In short, there is no such thing as safe tanning.

To protect yourself from the sun:

♦ Limit *exposure*. Avoid the most intense sun radiation, between the hours of 10:00 AM and 2:00 PM.

♦ Use *sunscreens* liberally when in the sun; don't just use them for sunbathing. Most sunscreens are labeled with a sun protection factor (SPF) and the ratings range from 2 to 50. The SPF indicates the sunscreen's ability to screen out the sun's rays. For example, suppose a fair-haired person, using no sunscreen, turns red in 10 minutes. If that person used a sunscreen rated SPF 2, the skin would need 20 minutes of exposure (two times 10 minutes) to turn red; with a sunscreen rated SPF 15 the skin would turn red in 150 minutes. Likewise, if a darker skinned person burns in 20 minutes, a sunscreen rated SPF 8 would give that person 160 minutes worth of protection before burning. Obviously, fair-skinned people need to be more careful than darker-skinned people. Dermatologists usually recommend an SPF of 15, however, regardless of skin color.

When buying and using a sunscreen, there are other factors to consider. First of all, SPF ratings apply only to the ability to protect against UVB rays; at present there is no federal rating system for UVA protection. Some sunscreen products, however, do contain UVA protection—look for a label that says the product is "broad spectrum" or "full spectrum." Or look for ingredients like benzophenone, oxybenzone, titanium dioxide, zinc oxide, or avobenzone. Also, with a very high SPF number, you don't get very much extra protection. For example, SPF 15 blocks out 93 percent of the sun's rays while SPF 34 blocks out 97 percent. And reapplying sunscreen doesn't increase the SPF; a double dose of SPF 15 doesn't give you SPF 30.

According to the American Academy of Dermatology, sunscreens can be used every day if you are going to be in the sun for more than 20 minutes. They should be applied 15–30 minutes before sun exposure. It takes about 1 ounce of sunscreen to cover the whole body properly. And they need to be reapplied at least every two hours; always reapply after swimming or perspiring heavily. Even sunscreens that are labeled "waterproof" or "sweat proof" can lose some of their effectiveness when you are in the water for extended periods or when you rub yourself dry with a towel.

♦ Be aware that a *cloudy overcast* does not protect you from the sun. Depending on the density of cloud cover, some—but not all—of the sun's rays may be diffused. Also, radiation reflected from water and snow is particularly intense.

♦ Wear *clothing* and accessories like long-sleeved shirts and wide-brimmed hats. In general, the tighter the fabric's weave, the better protection you get.

♦ *Getting a tan* in a tanning booth subjects you to the same risks as getting a tan in the sunshine. Tanning booths emit UVA rays. The artificial light can give you a sunburn, cause premature skin aging, and put you at an increased risk of cancer.

♦ Wear *sunglasses* since ultraviolet rays can permanently damage your eyes. You can't tell whether a pair of sunglasses affords adequate protection by the darkness of the lenses or because the lenses have a mirrored effect. To give protection, lenses must have a UV coating, which is colorless. According to the American National Standards Institute (ANSI), there are three categories of sunglasses: Cosmetic (blocks at least 70 percent of UVB and 20 percent of UVA); General Purpose (blocks at least 95 percent of UVB and 60 percent of UVA); Special Purpose (blocks at least 99 percent of UVB and 60 percent of UVA). The American Optometric Association advises buying glasses labeled, "Meets ANSI Z80.3 General (or Special) Purpose UV Requirements."

Noise and Hearing

More and louder noise assaults us: leaf blowers, jackhammers, loud stereos, target shooting. It does more than anger us—it can destroy our hearing. Of the 11 percent of Americans who suffer from hearing loss, more than a third can point to loud noise as a contributing cause. One proof: people who live under less industrial conditions maintain good hearing into old age.

Sudden loud noise (like an explosion) tears tissue in the inner ear and damages hearing immediately. Sustained noise (like the sound of a jackhammer) flattens hair cells in the inner ear (cochlea) that convey sound to the nerves. Each hair cell is "tuned" to resonate to a different frequency. The wilting of the cells is felt as ear pressure, hissing, roaring, buzzing, or ringing (tinnitus). If noise stops, cells rise up. But too

DECIBEL LEVELS

many assaults over extended periods of time can kill the hair cells.

Too much noise also makes people irritable, gives them headaches, and raises blood pressure and aggression levels. Noise can interfere with concentration and the ability to do work.

How can you protect yourself?

♦ Wear ear protectors (they lessen sound by 35 decibels).

♦ Work to enforce anti-noise ordinances in your community.

♦ Pressure the U.S. Government to establish stronger laws about noise-emission labeling.

How Can You Tell if You Are Hard of Hearing?

Here's an easy test. If you answer yes to any question, you should have your hearing checked.

♦ You shout in conversations.

♦ You have the radio or television on too loud.

♦ You ask people to repeat what they just said.

♦ You favor one ear over the other.

♦ You strain to hear.

Hearing problems can be helped by medical or surgical intervention, hearing aids, and rehabilitation. The latest hearing aids work very well and are inconspicuous.

TYPES OF HEARING LOSS

Nerve deafness involves an abnormality of the inner ear, the auditory nerve, or both. Causes include aging and exposure to loud noise. Some individuals afflicted with nerve deafness respond to medical or surgical treatment. For most, a hearing aid helps.

Conductive hearing loss occurs when an obstruction of the outer or middle ear prevents sound waves from reaching the inner ear properly. Causes: buildup of ear wax, infections, punctured eardrum, rigidity of an inner ear bone. Medical and surgical correction is often successful. Hearing aids work for most.

Tinnitus (hearing a sound that isn't there) can be caused by anything from wax in the ear to

whiplash to a brain tumor to aspirin to hearing loss (most common). Get it diagnosed by your doctor. What helps: a hearing aid; use of white noise—the sound of the ocean, a tone, or other soothing sounds that override tinnitus.

Information:

Better Hearing Institute, Box 1840, Washington, DC 20013 (703-642-0580 or 800-EAR-WELL).

National Institute on Deafness, PO Box 37777, Washington, DC 20013-7777 (800-241-1044; 800-241-1055 TTY).

American Academy of Otolaryngology—Head and Neck Surgery, Inc., 1 Prince Street, Alexandria, VA 22314 (703-836-4444).

American Speech-Language-Hearing Association: 800-638-8255.

American Academy of Audiology, 1735 North Lynn Street, Suite 950, Arlington, VA 22209-2022 (800-222-2732 voice/TTY).

National Association of the Deaf, 814 Thayer Avenue, Silver Spring, MD 20910-4500 (301-587-1788; 301-587-1789 TTY).

Eyes

While your eyes may not reveal the state of your soul, they can be windows on your health. From examining the eyes, physicians find signs of diabetes, hypertension, and other diseases. To preserve your vision, take care of your eyes and have your eyes examined regularly every 2 years, according to the American Optometric Association. If you are over 65, under 20, or at risk, you should be tested every year. Other experts recommend yearly examinations after age 40. These checklists provide tips for taking care of your eyes and spotting vision problems early.

Taking Care of Your Eyes and Your Children's Eyes

♦ Don't save money on low-wattage light bulbs.

♦ Control glare by using translucent lamp shades, window blinds and shades that filter light, matte or flat finishes on walls and other surfaces.

♦ Make sure that light is coming from the right place when you read. If you hold a book to the side, light should come from that side, over the shoulder.

♦ Put the television set in a place free of glare and reflections and separated from you by at least five times the width of the screen.

♦ Make sure you have the right glasses for the right activity (sunglasses, glasses for night driving, reading glasses).

♦ Wear proper eye-safety equipment when handling chemicals, using power tools, or engaging in sports hazardous to eyes.

♦ Take rest breaks from concentrated activities in which you use your eyes.

♦ Don't let children play with firecrackers, peashooters, BB guns, darts, and other missile toys. Don't let them play with others using such toys. Keep them away from power tools, lawn mowers, and chemicals. Teach them not to run with or throw sharp objects.

Signs of Vision Problems

If you notice any of these conditions, see your eye doctor immediately:

♦ Fuzziness or blurring.

♦ Losing one's place when reading or using one's finger to keep place.

♦ Avoidance of close work, especially in children.

♦ Holding reading material too close to eyes.

♦ Rubbing eyes or squinting.

♦ Aching or burning eyes; red eyes; frequent styes and encrusted eyelids.

♦ Headache, eye strain.

♦ Turning or tilting the head to use one eye only.

♦ Reading problems in children, such as making reversals when reading or writing.

♦ Difficulty in concentrating.

♦ Spots or flashes of light in front of the eyes; floaters.

♦ Double vision.

♦ Decrease in side vision.

♦ Haloes around bright lights.

National Eye Institute, National Institutes of Health, Building 31, Room 6A32, Bethesda, MD 20892 (301-496-5248).

If you have very little money, you may be able to get free eye care: call **VISION USA** at 800-766-4466. To qualify, you must have a job (or live in a household where someone has a job); have no health insurance and a low income; have not had an eye examination for a year.

If You Have Vision Problems

♦ Use color contrasts in your house so you can see throw rugs, switches, telephones easily.

♦ If you have lost peripheral vision, compensate when driving by turning your head for better side views and use your sideview and rearview mirrors.

♦ Carry a flashlight when walking in a dark part of the house or outside at night.

Eye-Care Help for Older People

If you are a low-income older person and need eye care, call the National Eye Care Project Helpline: (800)-222-EYES. You will be referred to a physician for an eye examination at no cost to you. You must be a U.S. citizen over 65, you must now be under the care of an ophthalmologist, and you must have had your last eye examination at least three years ago.

If you can only read large print, ask your library what services it offers for the visually impaired, such as large-print books, audiotape, and large-print lenses. Founded in 1986, the project is cosponsored by the Foundation of the American Academy of Ophthalmology and ophthalmology societies throughout the United States.

The Eye Examination

An eye examination should include the following:

♦ Health history and eye history. If you are taking any drugs, tell the eye doctor about them.

♦ Examination of outside and inside of the eye for signs of disease, abnormal conditions, general health problems.

♦ Tests of your ability to see well at various distances. Diagnosis of vision conditions such as nearsightedness or farsightedness.

♦ Refraction—test of your eyes' ability to focus light rays on the retina.

♦ Tests of eye coordination, eye muscle function, peripheral vision, depth perception.

♦ Evaluation of ability to change focus.

♦ Glaucoma test (for intraocular pressure), done by dilating the pupils of the eyes. (See below, under "Vision Problems.")

WARNING: You may be given drops to dilate your pupils and may therefore need someone to drive you home after the examination.

Vision Problems

Astigmatism. An irregularity in the shape of the cornea (front part of the eye) causes you to see objects as blurry or distorted. The treatment: corrective lenses.

Cataracts. If you live long enough, you will get cataracts. Cataracts are usually a result of aging, when the lens of the eye, transparent in younger people, turns opaque. If your cataracts are not treated, you can go blind. The good news: the operation for cataracts—removal of the clouded lens—has been improved enormously in the last twenty or thirty years. Gone are the days when people recovering from cataract operations lay for days with sandbags holding their heads immobile, then wore bottle-bottom glasses. Present-day surgery for cataracts causes no pain, can often be done in an outpatient clinic, and takes less than one hour under local anesthesia. Often an artificial lens is implanted in the eye during the same operation.

Crossed Eyes (strabismus). Usually found in children. One or both eyes consistently turn up, down, out, or in. Strabismus can be treated with corrective lenses, eye patches, prisms, and vision therapy. If not treated, this condition can lead to other problems.

Farsightedness (hyperopia). You can see tele-

phone wires and leaves, but you have difficulty seeing print or anything else close up. The shape of the eye (a short eyeball or flat cornea) is responsible for this condition. It may be hereditary or caused by environmental conditions. The treatment: corrective lenses.

Floaters and spots. In a child, the vitreous body that fills out the eye behind the lens is like jelly. With age, it gradually turns liquid and develops bits of debris (cells and strands of tissue), like specks in Jell-o, that throw shadows on the retina. The bits of debris, usually harmless, are called "floaters."

Glaucoma. Everyone over 60 should be tested every two years for glaucoma, a painless and usually symptomless condition in which the fluid pressure in the eyeball increases. (Blacks should start getting tested when they are 40.) Left untreated, glaucoma can cause blindness. Younger people might also want to be tested every three to four years. (A predisposition toward glaucoma can be inherited.) The recommended test procedure involves dilating the pupils with eye drops. Medication, such as eye drops, can usually control glaucoma.

Lazy eye (amblyopia). One eye (the "lazy eye") stops taking part in seeing, leaving the work up to the other eye. This often comes about because the lazy eye loses clear central vision. Lazy eye can be treated with corrective lenses, eye patches, prisms, and vision therapy.

Nearsightedness (myopia). You may not be able to see telephone wires or leaves on the higher branches of a tree clearly, but you can read print. The curvature of the eye (a too-long eyeball or overly curved cornea) causes nearsightedness, which affects almost one out of three Americans. It usually occurs before age 20 and may be hereditary, though too much close vision work may also be a contributing factor. The treatment: corrective lenses.

Presbyopia. How far from your eyes are you holding this page? The answer is a clue to your age. Some time in their forties, most people discover that print has grown small and blurry. If they put a brighter bulb in the lamp or hold pages farther from their eyes—perhaps 18 inches away—they can see better. This is a normal condition called *presbyopia* ("old man's eye"). The lens of the eye grows less elastic as a person ages. This makes it more difficult for the muscles that control the shape of the lens to adapt for near and far vision. In people in their fifties, the process has usually stabilized. The solution to presbyopia is usually corrective lenses.

Retinal disorders. If you see floaters with bright lights, it is possible that a retina is detaching from the rest of the eye. See an ophthalmologist immediately. A detached retina can be "glued" back with laser surgery under general anesthesia. A dark coloration at the center of the retina (macula) means that the retina is degenerating. In this condition (macular degeneration), peripheral vision remains intact, but the eyes lose fine vision. Those who have it can read with reading glasses and a magnifying glass. Diabetic retinopathy can also be treated.

CORRECTIVE LENSES

To some extent, your eye problem dictates what kind of lenses you should buy. People with certain eye conditions cannot wear contact lenses, for example. Your personality and lifestyle also play a part—you hate the bother of contacts, or the sports you play make contacts desirable, or you like the way you look in eyeglasses. These are the choices:

Eyeglasses. You want eyeglasses to be an asset to your appearance. But the size and shape of frames, first of all, must allow for proper fitting of the lenses. The movie-star look is secondary. Lenses are available in plastic (less likelihood of breakage) or glass (less likelihood of scratching).

Sunglasses. More than a fashion accessory or a lifestyle statement, sunglasses protect against the dangers of sunlight—brightness, glare, and radiation. Ultraviolet radiation can hurt your eyes, and over the long term it may cause cataracts and damage the retina. (See "Sun Safety," p. 21.) To eliminate reflected glare you need polarizing sunglasses. Don't wear sunglasses at night or indoors. They will not help against nighttime glare of approaching headlights.

(You can get a coating for clear lenses that will help with this problem.) Standard tinted sunglasses, in a medium to dark gray (which does not change the way you see colors), suit most people. Some people like light-sensitive (photochromic) lenses that darken and lighten according to the amount of light. Wear mirrored glasses to disconcert other people, if you like, but also for activities under intense glare from water or snow.

Contacts. Contact lenses are classified according to whether they are hard or soft, according to how often they must be replaced, and according to whether or not you can sleep in them (extended wear). If you take care of your lenses according to the instructions (and this is a big *if*), your chance of developing eye infections, even with extended-wear contacts, is very small. You should be scrupulous about cleaning, rinsing, and disinfecting your lenses and lens case. However, if you develop vision changes, eye redness, discomfort or pain, or extreme tearing, take the lenses out and see your eye doctor immediately.

A Warning About Disposable Contacts

A possible link between disposable contacts (those you wear for a week or two, then throw away) and ulcerative keratitis (a rare eye infection) has alarmed the medical community. A study from the Wilmer Eye Institute at Johns Hopkins University Medical School reports that the risk of this infection is 14 times greater among wearers of disposable contacts than those who wear other types of contacts. A Harvard University study found a low risk. What should you do?

Don't buy lenses through the mail or at a chain store.

Follow the advice of your doctor on cleaning.

Don't wear contacts overnight.

Use another kind of lens if you are a teenager, a slob, or a know-it-all (anyone who fails to follow directions).

"Be True to Your Teeth, or They Will Be False to You"

In the old days, most people lost several teeth by the time they were 45 and were toothless by the time they died. No more. Now we keep our teeth into old age. The advice you have heard over and over is true—you can do a great deal to prevent tooth problems by proper brushing and flossing, eating the right foods, and seeing your dentist regularly. The downside: dental care is more expensive nowadays.

Brushing. Your toothbrush should have soft, rounded, polished bristles. You may have to try several kinds to find the one that allows you to reach all tooth surfaces. Replace it every three months or when it is worn out. (You may have to replace children's brushes more often.)

Brush two times a day or every time after you eat. Brush just hard enough so you feel the bristles on your gums.

♦ Outer surfaces. Tilt brush so bristles point toward gums and brush back and forth with short strokes, using a circular motion. Include gums, brushing at a 45-degree angle.

♦ Chewing surfaces of molars. Brush should be flat. Move brush back and forth. Don't forget both sides of the last teeth at the back of your mouth.

♦ Inner surfaces of back teeth. Brush with circular motion at 45-degree angle. Include gums.

♦ Inner surfaces of front teeth. Holding the brush vertically, brush up and down.

♦ Brush your tongue gently.

Flossing. Flossing does what brushing cannot do—it reaches the debris between the teeth and under the gumline. Floss daily, starting with the molars, working toward the other side.

♦ You need about 18 inches of floss. Wind most of it several times around one of your middle fingers, then wind the rest around a middle finger on your other hand.

♦ Holding the floss between thumbs and forefingers, slide between teeth with a sawing motion until it is seated at the gumline. Slide the floss

PROPER FLOSSING TECHNIQUE

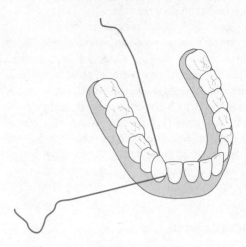

between the teeth, along the side of each tooth, scraping both sides with up-and-down motion. Don't forget to floss all surfaces of your very back teeth.

♦ Unwind floss as you need it.

On the advice of your dentist, you may choose to use interdental cleaning aids (special wooden picks) instead of flossing. Oral irrigators, used in conjunction with brushing and flossing, clean areas that are hard to reach.

Other Ways to Keep Teeth Healthy

♦ Use fluoride. It strengthens tooth enamel, helps prevent cavities. Check to see if your drinking water is fluoridated, and if it isn't, use a fluoride-containing supplement, mouthwash, or toothpaste approved by the American Dental Association.

♦ Eat a balanced diet with enough calcium. (See "Healthy Diets," p. 587.)

♦ Avoid sticky foods that adhere to the teeth. Clean teeth after you snack. Eat carbohydrate-containing foods with meals instead of between meals. Cheese may actually help your teeth to resist decay.

♦ Be careful when you eat hard foods; avoid popcorn kernels and ice. Try not to clench or grind teeth.

♦ Don't smoke, chew tobacco, or use snuff. All are factors in gum disease.

♦ See your dentist every six months.

♦ You may want to use an antimicrobial mouth rinse to reduce plaque. Look for sanguinaria, cetylpyridinium chloride, or domiphen bromide in the list of active ingredients. Mouth rinses work by swishing (which removes debris), and ingredients in the rinse kill germs. When you use a rinse, take in only a couple of tablespoons, and rinse for about 30 seconds two times a day. Swish a lot, and spit it out. If your children use a mouth rinse, supervise them.

Children's Teeth

Don't let infants sleep with bottles in their mouths. Sugary liquid (milk has sugar) may pool around teeth, causing plaque and cavities. Instead, give babies a bottle of water. Clean babies' gums with a clean washcloth or piece of gauze. Brush your child's teeth with a child-sized toothbrush as soon as the first one erupts. When all the primary teeth have erupted, start flossing. On the first birthday, babies should have a trip to the dentist. By age four or five, children should learn how to brush their own teeth, with supervision. Make sure children's teeth are brushed after every meal and before bed.

Dental Glossary

Cavities. Repeated plaque attacks cause a cavity—they are like bombardments that make a breach in a wall. Anyone can get a cavity, not just children. Older adults are prone to cavities in roots, around old fillings and crowns, and along the gum line as gums recede, exposing tooth cementum. For cavity prevention, dentists recommend fluoride and may apply dental sealants on back molars.

Crowns. Crowns are recommended when tooth structure is weak, after some root-canal work, or when the tooth is cracked or broken. The dentist drills out the decay and removes the outer surfaces of the tooth to create a base. He or she then makes an impression of the drilled-down tooth and places a temporary crown over it. On your next visit, the dentist removes the temporary crown and cements on the permanent one, usually made of gold, porcelain, or a metal alloy. Crowns last from 5 to 15 years.

Fillings. The dentist drills out decay, shapes the hole to hold the filling material, and fills cavities with gold, a composite resin (the color of teeth), or an amalgam (a metal alloy). He or she chooses the filling according to the hole's size and position in your mouth. After you have had an amalgam or gold filling put in, you should not eat hard or chewy food for at least 24 hours. A filling can last five years to a lifetime, depending on a number of factors. It takes one visit.

Gingivitis. The early stage of gum disease. Dentists treat it by scaling and root planing to remove plaque and tartar from teeth.

Gum disease. If you are over 35, you have three chances in four of developing gum disease, according to the American Dental Association. The symptoms are bleeding gums, sensitive gums, swollen gums, change in tooth alignment, loose-feeling teeth, bad breath or bad taste in the mouth, pus between teeth and gums. Gum disease is serious—it can lead to tooth loss. It can usually be prevented by keeping the teeth clean and by frequent visits to the dentist for professional cleaning. And it can be reversed. See *Gingivitis* and *Periodontitis*.

Mandibular teeth. Bottom teeth, identified by number.

Maxillary teeth. Top teeth, identified by number.

Plaque. The film you sometimes feel with your tongue on your teeth is bacteria-containing plaque. The bacteria produce acids that attack tooth enamel and irritate gums.

Periodontitis. Later stage of gum disease. From 25 to 50 percent of adults under 65 and nearly 70 percent of adults over 65 suffer from periodontitis, according to the National Institute of Dental Research. Bacterial toxins eat away at gums, causing separation from teeth, formation of pockets, eventual tissue and bone loss. Teeth loosen; eventually they may fall out or need to be removed. Periodontitis can be treated with scaling and planing and other methods, including, in its later stages, surgery. In its early stages, it can be reversed.

Root canals. When deep decay infects or damages tooth pulp, the dentist (or a root canal specialist) may do a root canal by cleaning out the pulp chamber and fixing the damage. A root canal takes one to three visits. If the infection has entered the bone that anchors the tooth, the infection may have to be drained. The dentist fills the pulp chamber with a material, then fills or crowns the tooth to secure the opening. A root canal usually lasts for a lifetime.

Tartar. After 24 hours, plaque calcifies into tartar, a deposit so hard that only your dentist can remove it.

Your Dentist and AIDS

The HIV virus can be destroyed easily through disinfection and sterilization. Dentists take "universal precautions" to protect themselves and you from infectious disease, including AIDS, during all office visits by:
- Wearing gloves, masks, protective eyewear when treating patients.
- Washing hands before and after treatments.
- Changing gloves after every patient.
- Sterilizing or disinfecting instruments after every use in a steam autoclave or with dry heat, or scrubbing followed by chemical solutions that disinfect or sterilize.

WHAT IS THE TOOTH FAIRY UP TO?

Children's teeth can yield vital information about the effects of pollution. The University of Bergen, Norway, wants baby teeth to grind up and analyze for levels of lead, zinc, cadmium, copper, and mercury. Send teeth to: Gisle Fosse, Professor of Anatomy, Bergen University, Asrstadveien, 5009, Bergen, Norway.

- Cleaning and disinfecting treatment room and equipment surfaces after every patient with a chemical hospital disinfectant agent registered with the Environmental Protection Agency.
- Practicing safe disposal methods for needles, scalpel blades, and other sharp items, and for one-use-only materials like gloves, masks, wipes, and paper drapes.

Contraceptive Failure Rates

The chart below shows the estimated percentage of women experiencing an unintended pregnancy in the first year of contraceptive use—by method and type of use. "Perfect use" indicates the failure rate if the method is used exactly as directed. "Average use" indicates typical use of the method by couples and reflects the incorrect and/or inconsistent use of the method.

The data come from the Alan Guttmacher Institute, a nonprofit research group in New York City that studies both birth control and reproductive behavior.

CONTRACEPTIVE FAILURE RATES

Method	Perfect Use (Percent)	Average Use (Percent)
No method	85.0	85.0
Spermicides	3.0	30.0
Sponge	8.0	24.0
Withdrawal	4.0	24.0
Rhythm	9.0	19.0
Cervical cap	6.0	18.0
Diaphragm	6.0	18.0
Condom	2.0	16.0
Pill	0.1	6.0
IUD	0.8	4.0
Tubal sterilization	0.2	0.5
Depo-Provera (injection)	0.3	0.4
Vasectomy	0.1	0.2
Norplant (implant)	0.04	0.05

Reprinted courtesy of the Alan Guttmacher Institute.

Lead Poisoning

Lead poisoning, a sneaky debilitating condition, can damage the brain and nervous system, especially in children. It lowers IQ levels and causes learning disorders and behavior problems. Children are more prone than adults to come in contact with lead, because they play in dust and dirt that may be contaminated; some chew paint chips. Moreover, lead accumulates in the body over a lifetime. The U.S. Public Health Service recommends that all children under the age of six have their blood tested for lead—ideally at the ages of 9–12 months and 24 months, and earlier and more frequently if they live in a high-risk area. The FEP (free erythrocyte protoporphyrin) test for lead in the blood is inaccurate; ask for the "direct-lead" or "blood-lead" test. The U.S. Centers for Disease Control and Prevention state that you should be concerned if blood levels are more than 10 micrograms of lead per deciliter of blood.

Though adults are more resistant to lead poisoning, it can cause neurological damage in them too, and evidence suggests that it may contribute to hypertension and cause stomach pain. Gout may also be exacerbated by lead poisoning, which explains the stereotype of the Englishman drinking his port taken from a crystal decanter (laden with lead) while propping his swollen gouty foot up on a footstool.

To protect yourself and your family from a buildup of lead in the body, eat iron-rich foods (red meat, spinach, iron-fortified foods) and calcium-rich foods (dairy products). Even more important, find ways to eliminate sources of lead poisoning.

Lead in Drinking Water

The Environmental Protection Agency tests water throughout the country for lead levels, concentrating on households known to be at high risk. It tests two samples—first-draw water (water that has been in the pipes for several hours) and purged-line water (drawn after taps have been open for one minute).

However, a 1993 study by *Consumer Reports* found high levels of lead in the water in cities found safe by the EPA (Chicago and Boston), and found "reason for concern" in the lead levels in San Francisco, New York, and Washington. Even in cities with overall low lead levels according to the EPA, *individual* households had high concentrations of lead in the water.

HOW TO PROTECT AGAINST LEAD

♦ Have your water tested for lead. Even if Environmental Protection Agency information lists your city as having water with low lead, you should have the water from your taps tested, particularly if you live in an older house. Lead pipe was used until the late 1970s for service lines carrying water from street mains into houses, and lead pipes for houses and lead-based solder were not outlawed until 1988. If you live in an area where water is "soft" (that is, with low concentrations of dissolved minerals), mineral deposits may not have coated the inside of your lead pipes, making it more likely that the pipes will leach lead into your water. Lead also tends to be more concentrated in water that is (1) acidic, (2) has been sitting in the pipes a long time, (3) is hot. Some cities offer free water testing for lead. Or ask your utility company, local health department, or state department of environmental quality for a list of EPA-certified laboratories. Or you can have it done by mail order. You should test first-draw and purged-line water. If the water has more than 5 ppb on first-draw, and much less on the purged-line sample, the problem comes from within your house. Letting the water run one or two minutes if it has been in the pipes more than a few hours will help. Also, use only cold water for drinking and cooking—that is, start with cold water and heat it up. If the purged-line sample shows more than 5 ppb of lead, it probably is coming from your service line. Get your utility company to inspect the line.

♦ Brass components on new faucets can release lead into your water. Let the water run a little while (a few seconds) before you drink it.

♦ Boiling drinking water kills harmful bacteria, but it may *increase* concentrations of heavy metals and toxic chemicals like lead and asbestos.

♦ If your tap water contains lead, use bottled water for cooking and drinking or buy a good home water-treatment device to remove lead and other contaminants. Make sure it is approved by the National Sanitation Foundation (NSFI), though lack of such certification does not necessarily mean that the device is ineffective. Write for free booklets from **NSF,** PO Box 130140, Ann Arbor, MI 48113–0140, or call 313-769-8010. If you use infant drinking formula, make it with bottled water. And remember that you cannot see the lead in drinking water because it is dissolved.

EPA Safe Drinking Water Hotline: 800-426-4791.

Lead in Cans

Some imported canned food—as much as 10 percent—comes in lead-soldered cans that present a danger, particularly to children.

Lead in Your House

If you live in a house built before the 1970s, painted surfaces may emit lead. According to a 1990 report by the U.S. Department of Housing and Urban Development, 74 percent of private housing built before 1980 has lead paint somewhere. To find out how hazardous your house may be, send dust samples from the windowsills and floor, and chips of the paint itself to a certified lab to be analyzed. The Consumers Union has found two home kits effective for testing surfaces that are highly leaded: LeadCheck Swabs sold by **HybriVet Systems, Inc.** (800-262-LEAD) and Frandon Lead Alert Kit by **Frandon Enterprises, Inc.** (800-359-9000.) You can also have your house tested by X-ray flourescence technicians (XRF). For names of labs and other information, contact your local Environmental Agency

office or the **Lead Institute,** PO Box 591244, San Francisco, CA 94118 (415-885-4645).

Here are some ways to minimize the dangers of lead in the home:

♦ Frequent cleaning of floors and windowsills with a TSP (trisodium phosphate) solution to remove dust will help if lead levels are not too high. For carpets use a shampooer that vacuums up the dirty water, and don't count on vacuum cleaners to sweep up dust—they tend to emit dust (carrying lead) back into the air. Instead, wet down surfaces with the TSP solution two times, wet mop with a high-phosphate soap that has been diluted, then clean with a wet-and-dry shop-type vacuum cleaner. Keep children away from lead-contaminated areas. Wash their toys and keep them away from dirt and sandboxes that can be contaminated by flaking exterior paint.

♦ Don't sand or use a heat gun on lead paint.

♦ Consider using encapsulating paint to cover lead-containing old paint. Or use drywall or wallpaper backed with woven cloth to cover old paint. Replace contaminated woodwork.

♦ Lead abatement by a qualified contractor is the most expensive method. Call your local office of the U.S. Department of Housing and Urban Development to find a qualified contractor. Make sure the people who do the work have attended a lead-paint-abatement program. While work is being done, children and pregnant women should live elsewhere.

♦ Write for information on safe renovation from the **Conservation Law Foundation,** 62 Summer Street, Boston, MA 02110 (617-350-0990).

Lead in Your Wine

♦ If your wine bottle is wrapped with lead foil, wipe the neck of the bottle with a cloth dipped in an acid solution (water and lemon juice or water and vinegar) before pouring from it. Not all lead in wine comes from the foil cap that covers the cork. Grapes can absorb lead from the soil, and lead soldering on the pipes used in the winemaking process can contribute. Screw-on caps contain no lead; the wine won't be great, but it may reduce your exposure to lead.

♦ Generally, imported wines tend to have a higher lead content, according to a 1991 study by the Bureau of Alcohol, Tobacco, and Firearms.

LEAD (IN MICROGRAMS) IN A 3-OUNCE GLASS

	Domestic Wine	Imported Wine
Unpoured	4.2	9.7
Poured	6.0	20.1

Source: Bureau of Alcohol, Tobacco, and Firearms, Environmental Protection Agency

♦ Never store wine in a crystal decanter, because lead can leach out of the crystal into the wine. Researchers at Columbia University performed an experiment on port wine kept in decanters. They chose three decanters with different proportions of lead in the crystal. After one hour, the lead level in wine poured from decanters into crystal glasses was three times higher than the norm given by the EPA for safe drinking water. In four months, it was 108 to 266 times higher.

Lead in Your Soil

If you live near an industry that emits lead (or once did), a military base, dump site, airport, mine, high-traffic route, or farmland, your soil may contain high lead levels.

Lead in Your Dishes

Some ceramic dishes are lead-glazed. Don't buy them, and throw out any that you have. Write for "The Dishowner's Guide to Potential Lead Hazards" from the **Environmental Defense Fund,** 5655 College Avenue, Suite 304, Oakland, CA 94618 (510-658-8008).

For information on lead poisoning:
National Maternal and Child Health Clearinghouse: 703-821-8955.
EPA: 1-800-LEAD-FYI.
Centers for Disease Control, 404-488-7330, for information on childhood lead-poisoning prevention.

Fever

Fever—a symptom, not a disease—means that the body is fighting off infection. The hypothalamus sets a higher body temperature in accordance with immune-system response to infection, immune reaction, tissue inflammation, or death of body tissue (as from a heart attack). A fevered body produces antibodies faster, even shrinks tumors.

When do you have a fever? Body temperatures in normal people rise during the day, varying from about 96° Fahrenheit to about 99° Fahrenheit. The old sacred number of 98.6° degrees Fahrenheit, established in the 19th century, is only an average. Temperatures tend to be higher in children than in adults, in women than in men. Women's body temperatures rise slightly during ovulation. Engaging in rigorous exercise can cause body temperature to rise. Doctors now agree that a temperature of 99° or more in the morning and 100° or more in the evening constitutes a fever.

If you have a fever, drink plenty of fluids to avoid dehydration. In spite of dramatic fiction, sweating is neither a good sign nor a bad one. Fevers naturally rise and fall. For comfort, you can avoid these ups and downs of sweating and chilling with acetaminophens (Tylenol, Panadol, Datril) or anti-inflammatories with ibuprofen (Advil, Nuprin, Motrin). Don't give children aspirin for fever—it is associated with Reye's syndrome.

When to Go to a Doctor

♦ You should report to your doctor immediately when fevers occur in children 18 months old or younger, in people who are old, enfeebled, pregnant, afflicted with AIDS or leukemia, or undergoing radiation treatment or chemotherapy.

♦ See a doctor if you really feel bad or if the fever is accompanied by a preexisting condition (e.g., heart problem).

♦ Fevers of 102°–103° or more may need medical attention, though it is not until temperatures reach 106° that brain function is affected; the brain is damaged at 108°. Very high fevers usually come from a serious condition like encephalitis, heat stroke, or cerebral hemorrhage. Children's temperatures can rise as high as 105° due to chicken pox, childhood viruses, roseola, or strep throat.

♦ See your doctor if high temperature is accompanied by dry skin, even in the armpits (may be heat stroke), or a stiff neck (may be meningitis).

♦ See your doctor if your fever lasts more than two days.

Taking Temperatures

There are three kinds of temperature readings: *oral,* from a thermometer placed under the tongue; *rectal,* from a rectal thermometer inserted in the anus; *axillary,* from an oral thermometer placed under the armpit. Each has advantages and disadvantages. For example, rectal temperatures are more accurate, but must be taken carefully to avoid injury, while axillary temperatures are less accurate (although the procedure is safer). Use ordinary rectal or oral thermometers. Electronic and digital thermometers are not very accurate at temperatures above 102° F. Skin thermometers (plastic strips held on the forehead) are inaccurate at temperatures over 100° F.

Preparing the thermometer: Wash the bulb and lower part of the thermometer with rubbing alcohol or cool soapy water. Hold the thermometer by the upper (non-bulb) end and gently shake the mercury down to 95° or lower, as if trying to shake water off the bulb.

Taking temperatures

♦ Oral temperature. With the thermometer under the tongue, hold lips closed and breathe through the nose. Wait three minutes.

♦ Rectal temperature (about 0.5° to 1° warmer than oral). Insert thermometer no more than 1 inch into the anus and hold it there at the opening for three minutes.

♦ Axillary temperature (less accurate than rectal or oral temperature-taking methods, about 1° cooler than oral). Place oral thermometer under the armpit for five minutes.

Reading the thermometer: Take the ther-

READING A THERMOMETER

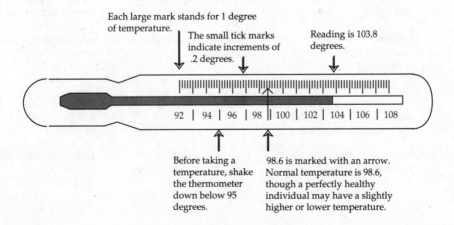

Each large mark stands for 1 degree of temperature.

The small tick marks indicate increments of .2 degrees.

Reading is 103.8 degrees.

92 | 94 | 96 | 98 || 100 | 102 | 104 | 106 | 108

Before taking a temperature, shake the thermometer down below 95 degrees.

98.6 is marked with an arrow. Normal temperature is 98.6, though a perfectly healthy individual may have a slightly higher or lower temperature.

A HEADACHE CHART

TYPE	CAUSES	SYMPTOMS	TREATMENT
Tension headache (about 90% of all headaches)	Stress (physical and emotional), depression that is unrecognized.	Dull pain around head, on both sides and without a center, tension in neck or scalp.	Finding and eliminating the cause, rest, ice packs, aspirin, acetaminophen, ibuprophen, prescription analgesics. Lying in darkened room, hot shower, massaging and relaxing neck muscles. Relaxation techniques, biofeedback, psychotherapy.
Migraine headache	**Common and classic:** heredity, certain foods (chocolate, red wine, cheeses), birth control pills, oversleeping, missing meals, bright or flashing lights, altitude and weather changes, stress. **Menstrual:** changing estrogen levels. More than 23 million people get migraines every year; three times as many women as men get migraines.	**Common migraine:** mild to severe throbbing pain, maybe only on one side of head, perhaps accompanied by nausea, vomiting, tremor, cold hands, dizziness, sensitivity to light and sound. **Classic migraine**: aura– visual disturbances, numbness, smelling strange smells, hallucinations– followed in half an hour by headache. **Menstrual headache:** around period or ovulation.	**Common and classic:** change in lifestyle, ice packs, analgesics or prescription drugs. Lie down in a dark room. Relax, using relaxation techniques. **Classic:** during aura, take ergotamine or practice biofeedback. **Menstrual:** restrict salt, exercise, prescription medications two weeks before menstruation. All migraines usually need a doctor's diagnosis and treatment..
Cluster headache	Smoking, alcohol.	Pain around one eye, tearing, nasal congestion, red face. Headaches attack in groups, for short periods of time, then disappear.	Prescription blood-vessel constrictors. Or oxygen.
Allergy headache	Pollen, molds, other allergens.	Watery eyes, nasal congestion.	Antihistamines or desensitization treatments.
Fever headache	Infection causing inflammation of blood vessels in head.	Generalized, develops with fever.	Aspirin, acetaminophen, antibiotics, if doctor approves.
Hangover headache	Alcohol, which dilates and irritates blood vessels of brain and brain tissues.	Nausea, throbbing.	Liquids, eating foods with fructose to help burn alcohol.
Sinus headache	Infection, nasal polyps, deviated septum.	Pain or pressure over sinuses, often with fever, runny nose, nasal congestion.	Decongestants, prescription antibiotics.

mometer out and read it by turning it slowly until you can see the mercury ribbon (which can be either red or silver).

Headaches

A splitting headache, believe it or not, begins in the physical brain, not necessarily from a state of emotional stress. A headache might come about because you gave up coffee cold turkey, or because you ate Chinese food that contained monosodium glutamate (MSG), or because of some other change or condition in the brain that led the blood vessels to dilate and constrict.

Is your headache a migraine, a cluster, or a tension headache? Or is it a combination? You need to know what it is in order to treat it. Don't assume that if the headache sends you to bed it is necessarily a migraine. Migraines can be minor, and other kinds of headaches can incapacitate you.

Simple advice for preventing headaches: exercise, proper foods, consistent patterns of resting-waking-eating, avoiding excess.

See your doctor if headaches persist. And see your doctor *immediately* if:

♦ The pain came fast without a cause, perhaps in the middle of the night.

♦ You have a high fever and headache and no other symptoms.

♦ You have a stiff neck, fever, and headache (could be meningitis).

♦ Headache is accompanied by confusion or loss of coordination or double vision.

♦ Headaches become progressively frequent and severe.

National Headache Foundation: 800-843-2256.

Infectious Diseases: How to Avoid Them

We all know that infectious diseases are the dirty work of either viruses or bacteria, though we don't always know in what category the culprit belongs. And it's important to know, because antibiotics kill bacteria but not viruses. You should avoid taking antibiotics when they are unnecessary for at least two reasons: (1) because they kill "good" as well as "bad" bacteria, and (2) because bacteria build resistant strains in response to antibiotics, so antibiotic treatment may not work as well later on. Moreover, an individual can develop an allergy to an antibiotic used too often, and antibiotics can cause side effects.

Bacterial infections sometimes follow viral infections—strep throat or an ear infection may follow a cold, for instance. You should not take antibiotics during a viral infection to ward off possible bacterial infections. Antibiotics are effective only *after* the bacterial infection has attacked, and antibiotics are counterindicated for some bacterial infections.

The following should help you to determine whether you have a viral or a bacterial infection:

♦ Viral infections invade several parts of the body—for instance, some give you a runny nose in addition to a headache and muscle ache. The most typical viral infections are flu, the common cold, stomach flu, herpes.

♦ Bacterial infections usually attack one part of the body—the throat or ear, for instance. Typical bacterial infections are strep throat, boils, *turista* (vomiting and diarrhea caused by *E. coli*), and ear infections.

♦ After or during a viral infection, you may develop a secondary bacterial infection, marked by yellow, green or bloody sputum or nasal discharge. If this occurs, call the doctor immediately.

The old advice applies for viral diseases like colds and flu: go to bed, drink plenty of liquids, rest. You should call the doctor if the patient does not improve after four days, or if a cough continues after a cold for more than five days without improving.

Do not self-treat infection with antibiotics prescribed for a previous bout of illness. Specific antibiotics attack specific bacteria, though some are "broad-spectrum." When you take antibiotics prescribed for your particular bacterial infection, be sure to take them for the length of time and in the doses recommended.

Some other advice:

♦ Throw away your toothbrush, which is teeming with microorganisms and may reinfect you.

Avoiding Infections

♦ Don't worry about toilet seats, unless the seats are dirty or you have an open cut or abrasions.

♦ When using a club exercise machine, use a towel to protect yourself from the sweat, saliva, or blister fluid left by the last exerciser.

♦ Don't use poorly maintained public pools, hot tubs, or Jacuzzis, which can harbor pseudomonad and staphylococcus bacteria. In a steam room sit on a fresh towel.

♦ Never share a drinking utensil, towel, washcloth, or a toothbrush.

♦ Wash your hands frequently, for at least thirty seconds each time, particularly after using the toilet and before you eat and while you prepare meals. Studies have shown that colds are spread by surface and body contact more than by transmission through the air.

♦ Clean frequently used surfaces with a disinfectant cleanser registered with the Environmental Protection Agency. ("EPA" followed by a number will appear on the label.) For surfaces like counters and bathroom fixtures, use disinfectant spray with 70–80 percent ethanol and 1 percent phenol once a week and more frequently if someone is sick. Let it stand for 10 minutes or more, wipe with dampened paper towel.

♦ Wash bedding and towels with hot water—at least 130°F. (Remember, though, that a water heater set at temperatures above 120°F. may provide dangerously hot water.)

BEHAVIORAL ILLNESSES

How to Quit Smoking

One of the hardest habits to break, smoking is also the most dangerous habit (in terms of your health) that you can take up in the first place. It is the number one preventable cause of death in the United States, contributing to about 434,000 deaths a year (one in six)—from lung cancer, emphysema, and heart disease. It may help to cause Graves' disease, a thyroid gland disorder, and it increases your risk of getting leukemia. If you quit smoking before age 40, according to a University of Michigan study, you have a much lower risk of contracting lung cancer than if you continue to smoke. Secondhand smoke, the romantic haze of late-night bars, is also a killer—of at least 53,000 Americans a year, according to the Environmental Protection Agency. At least 20 percent of deaths from lung cancer were caused by secondhand smoke. Yet in spite of all this evidence 50 million people were still smoking in 1993. If you smoke, it will pay you to try to quit, both for your own health and the health of those you love. You can do it. More than 3 million Americans quit smoking each year.

A smoker is hooked on nicotine, and people trying to stop smoking often experience withdrawal symptoms during the first week of quitting. Signs of psychological dependency continue for far longer. Situational triggers—morning coffee, a knotty problem—that bring on the desire to smoke can catch you unaware. Giving up smoking can be like giving up a friend—albeit a bad one.

Several programs exist to help smokers quit. You need to find the one that suits you best. A program that works for one person may not work for you.

If you quit and fail, quit again. Sometimes it takes two or three attempts before you achieve permanent success.

Kicking the Habit

According to the U.S. Department of Health and Human Services, most methods of quitting have average success rates of 10 to 30 percent, that is, 10 to 30 percent of smokers using them are still not smoking after a year. The most successful are those methods that combine ways of combating both the physiological and psychological problems of quitting. Beware of any commercial program that promises a success rate of more than 30 percent.

Most important, to succeed you must want to quit smoking for yourself (as well as for others), you must feel that quitting will benefit you, and you must think that you can do it.

Cold turkey. Many smokers quit smoking on their own without tapering off. It is the method of choice for most successful quitters—9 out of 10 of them.

Nicotine patch. The patch, which adheres to the skin, releases nicotine slowly and steadily

SMOKING DEATH TOLL

More lives are lost annually in the United States from smoking than from cocaine, crack, heroin, morphine, fires, homicide, car accidents, suicide, AIDS, and alcohol *combined*. This graph gives the details.

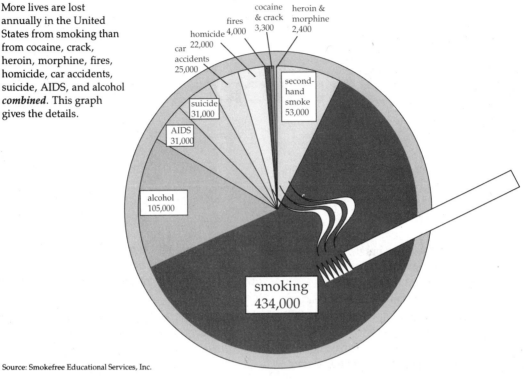

cocaine
& crack
3,300

heroin &
morphine
2,400

fires
4,000

homicide
22,000

car
accidents
25,000

second-
hand
smoke
53,000

suicide
31,000

AIDS
31,000

alcohol
105,000

smoking
434,000

Source: Smokefree Educational Services, Inc.

into the bloodstream. This satisfies the craving for the nicotine drug (and drug it is). This method is costly. You can get the patches by prescription only. You should also join a support group or get counseling to deal with psychological dependence on cigarettes that may be even more difficult to break. WARNING: The patch may irritate skin; it may be harmful to pregnant women and people who are ill with a serious disease, including cardiovascular disease. Several people who smoked while wearing the patch suffered heart attacks.

Nicotine gum and inhalers. Some doctors prescribe one of these rather than patches to put nicotine into the system to ease withdrawal symptoms. Gum can help to cut down on the temporary weight gain experienced by many ex-smokers. (However, within two years of quitting smoking, ex-smokers are no more likely to be overweight than other nonsmokers.) It keeps

your mouth busy. Problems: the gum can be difficult to chew for people with false teeth; nicotine may never reach an effective level.

Hypnosis. Hypnosis, which deals with the subconscious, can plant a suggestion in your mind that will help you stop smoking. It both motivates you and helps you overcome your craving for cigarettes. One in 10 people cannot be hypnotized, however.

Acupuncture. Acupuncture, an ancient Oriental medical system, works on the principle that it can restore the natural energy balance that smoking disrupts.

Clinics. Freedom from Smoking Clinics (American Lung Association) and FreshStart Clinics (American Cancer Society) have been proven successful. Universities and health agencies also offer programs.

Commercial structured programs. Programs like Smokenders provide a structured method for quitting. Smokenders works on changing behavior—smokers cut down, then quit. Ask any group for its success rates one year after quitting, and make sure that it offers help with relapse.

Rapid smoking. A smoker must take a puff every seven seconds—guaranteed to make him or her hate smoking.

Extreme measures. Chain yourself to the sofa for two weeks—this worked for a San Francisco man.

TIPS ON QUITTING

Experts recommend that you prepare to quit before actually quitting, that you give attention to the social as well as physiological components of nicotine addiction, that you obtain follow-up support. Here are just a few tips:

1. Set a time in the future when you will quit smoking. Choose a time that will be relatively free from stress and temptation.

2. Before you quit, taper off:

♦ Buy a brand of cigarettes you don't like instead of your favorite. Or switch to a low-tar, low-nicotine brand before going cold turkey. If you use this trick, do not sabotage yourself by smoking more cigarettes, inhaling more, or covering the holes in the filters.

♦ Cut down by smoking half of each cigarette, postponing smoking in the morning, refraining from smoking during odd or even hours, determining how many cigarettes you will smoke and donating a dollar to charity for every cigarette you smoke over the limit.

♦ Try smoking consciously, only the cigarettes you actually want, not smoking out of habit. Keep ashtrays full so you will see how much you smoke. Look in a mirror each time you light up.

♦ Buy cigarettes by the pack, not the carton.

3. List the reasons for quitting: health and fitness, setting a good example for your children, getting rid of cigarette breath. Be sure to include personal reasons for quitting—not wanting to smell like an ashtray or saving money, for in-

stance. Repeat one of the reasons to yourself 10 times at a specific time of day, like before going to bed.

4. Start getting in shape: exercise, get enough rest, drink more fluids.

5. Before you quit, keep a record of how many cigarettes you smoke and why you smoke them. Do you smoke first thing in the morning? With coffee or alcoholic drinks? After sex? Do you smoke to fill in time between thoughts, to gain time for marshaling an argument, to alleviate boredom? Consider ways of avoiding emotional triggers for smoking.

6. Tell your family and friends you are going to quit. Enlist their help.

7. On the day you quit, get rid of all cigarettes and smoking paraphernalia. Get your teeth cleaned. Keep busy.

8. During the first week you quit (when you may feel withdrawal symptoms as your nicotine level decreases), avoid situations in which other people are smoking, drink lots of liquids, exercise, do something enjoyable. This is the time of greatest danger of relapse.

9. During the first three months after quitting, you are still prone to relapse when something triggers your impulse to light up. When you have an urge to smoke, substitute another activity—walking, eating a carrot, drinking water. If your hand wants a cigarette, give it something else to hold, like a paper clip. If you feel orally deprived, try a fake cigarette, carrots, sugarless gum. Take several deep breaths.

10. Put a jar of smoked butts next to your bed.

11. Never, *never* have "just one." It grows to two, three, and whole packs faster than you can imagine.

12. Be positive! You can do it.

Stop Teen Smoking

As every parent of a teenager knows, adolescence seems to confer a sense of immortality. Teenagers do not respond as well as adults to health warnings about smoking, though they may pay heed to warnings that smoking makes their hair, breath, and clothing smell like an old ash-

RECOVERING FROM SMOKING—THE BODY IN HEALING

The body is a truly remarkable machine. Within minutes of your last cigarette your body is working to correct the damages done by smoking.

20 Minutes from Your Last Cigarette
- Blood pressure drops to normal.
- Pulse rate drops to normal.
- Body temperature of hands and feet increases to normal.

8 Hours from Your Last Cigarette
- Carbon monoxide level in blood drops to normal.
- Oxygen level in blood increases to normal.

24 Hours from Your Last Cigarette
- Chance of heart attack decreases.

48 Hours from Your Last Cigarette
- Nerve endings start regrowing.
- Ability to smell and taste things is enhanced.

72 Hours from Your Last Cigarette
- Bronchial tubes relax, making breathing easier.
- Lung capacity increases.

2 Weeks to 3 Months from Your Last Cigarette
- Circulation improves.
- Walking becomes easier.
- Lung function increases up to 30 percent.

1 to 9 Months from Your Last Cigarette
- Coughing, sinus congestion, fatigue, shortness of breath decrease.
- Cilia regrow in lungs, increasing ability to handle mucus, clean the lungs, reduce infection.
- Body's overall energy level increases.

5 Years from Your Last Cigarette
- Lung cancer rate decreases from 137 per 100,000 people to 72 per 100,000 people.

Reprinted courtesy of American Lung Association.

tray. Several programs exist to help teenagers quit smoking: **DOC** (Doctors Ought to Care), 5510 Greenbriar, Suite 235, Houston, TX 77005 (713-952-4704); **Tobacco-Free Teens** (American Lung Association): 612-227-8014.

Call your local chapter of the American Lung Association (ALA) and the American Cancer Society (ACS) for free pamphlets on how to stop smoking. The ALA offers Freedom From Smoking Clinics; contact: **SmokeFree Educational Services,** 375 South End Avenue, Suite 32F, New York, NY 10280-1085 (212-912-0960).

Understanding and Helping the Suicidal Person

Be Aware of the Facts

- Suicide is preventable. Most suicidal persons desperately want to live. They are just unable to see alternatives to their problems.
- Most suicidal persons give definite warnings of their suicidal intentions, but others are either unaware of the significance of these warnings or do not know how to respond to them.
- Talking about suicide does not cause someone to be suicidal.
- Approximately 30,000 Americans kill themselves every year. The number of suicide attempts is much greater yet and often results in serious injuries.
- Suicide is the third leading cause of death among young people ages 15 to 24, and it is the eighth leading cause of death among all persons.
- Youth (15–24 years of age) suicide rates increased more than 200 percent from the 1950s to the late 1970s. Following the late 1970s the rates for youth have remained stable.
- The suicide rate is higher for the elderly (over 65) than any other age group.
- Four times as many men kill themselves as compared to women, yet three to four times as many women attempt suicide as compared to men.

♦ Suicide cuts across all age, economic, social, and ethnic boundaries.

♦ Firearms are currently the most often utilized method of suicide by essentially all groups (e.g., males, females, young, old, white, non-white), and the rates are increasing.

♦ Surviving family members not only suffer the trauma of losing a loved one to suicide, but are themselves at higher risk for suicide and emotional problems.

Be Aware of Warning Signs

There is no typical suicide victim. It happens to young and old, rich and poor. But fortunately there are some common warning signs which, when acted upon, can save lives. Here are some signs to look for.

A suicidal person may:
♦ talk about committing suicide
♦ have trouble eating or sleeping
♦ experience drastic changes in behavior
♦ withdraw from friends and/or social activities
♦ lose interest in hobbies, work, school
♦ prepare for death by making out a will and final arrangements
♦ give away prized possessions
♦ have attempted suicide before
♦ take unnecessary risks
♦ have had a recent severe loss
♦ be preoccupied with death and dying
♦ lose interest in their personal appearance
♦ increase their use of alcohol or drugs.

Be Aware of Dos and Don'ts

♦ **Be aware.** Learn the warning signs.
♦ **Get involved.** Become available. Show interest and support.
♦ **Ask** if he or she is thinking about suicide.
♦ **Be direct.** Talk openly and freely about suicide.
♦ **Be willing to listen.** Allow expressions of feelings. Accept the feelings.
♦ **Be nonjudgmental.** Don't debate

whether suicide is right or wrong, or feelings are good or bad. Don't lecture on the value of life.

♦ **Don't dare** him or her to do it.
♦ **Don't** give advice by making decisions for someone else to tell him or her to behave differently.
♦ **Don't ask "why."** This encourages defensiveness.
♦ **Offer empathy,** not sympathy.
♦ **Don't act shocked.** This will put distance between you.
♦ Don't be sworn to secrecy. **Seek support.**
♦ **Offer hope** that alternatives are available but do not offer glib reassurance. It only proves you don't understand.
♦ **Take action.** Remove means. Get help from persons or agencies specializing in crisis intervention and suicide prevention.

Be Aware of Feelings

Nearly everyone at some time in his or her life thinks about committing suicide. Most decide to live because they eventually come to the realization that the crisis is temporary and death isn't. On the other hand, people having a crisis often perceive their dilemma as inescapable and feel an utter loss of control. These are some of the feelings and things they experience:
♦ Can't stop the pain
♦ Can't think clearly
♦ Can't make decisions
♦ Can't see any way out
♦ Can't sleep, eat, or work
♦ Can't get out of depression
♦ Can't make the sadness go away
♦ Can't see a future without pain
♦ Can't see themselves as worthwhile
♦ Can't get someone's attention
♦ Can't seem to get control.
If you experience these feelings, get help!
If someone you know exhibits these symptoms, offer help!
Contact a—
♦ community mental health agency
♦ private therapist or counselor

- school counselor or psychologist
- family physician
- suicide and crisis center.

American Association of Suicidology, 2459 S. Ash, Denver, CO 80222 (303-692-0985).

Reprinted courtesy of American Association of Suicidology.

Alcoholism

A person reeking of alcohol and falling down in public gives it away—he or she is very likely to be an alcoholic. Other alcoholics mask their illness by drinking in secret or going on occasional binges. According to the National Clearinghouse for Alcohol and Drug Information, more than 17 million people can be classified as problem drinkers—those who abuse alcohol or are alcoholics. Alcohol abuse is involved in over 100,000 deaths a year. It is a primary factor in many cases of violence and child abuse.

Who becomes an alcoholic? Some people can drink, even drink fairly heavily, and never become alcoholics. Others cannot. To some extent, alcoholism is genetically determined. Drinkers of alcohol can develop psychological and physical dependency on the drug (and it is a drug). Psychologically dependent drinkers use alcohol habitually to handle feelings and problems instead of dealing directly with them. When people physically dependent on alcohol try to give it up, they develop withdrawal symptoms—the shakes, digestive problems, sleep disturbances. Long-term alcoholism increases the risk of developing cirrhosis of the liver, malnutrition, pancreatic disorders, cancer, heart problems, and brain damage. Pregnant women who drink can harm their fetuses.

How do you know if you are addicted to alcohol? If you drink even when you know your abuse of alcohol contributes to work and home problems, you are an addicted drinker. If you drink even when you know that your abuse of alcohol adversely affects your health and safety or that of other people, you are an addicted drinker.

Help exists for alcoholics: Alcoholics Anonymous, detoxification centers, psychotherapy. No one method works for all. Families also need assistance in dealing with the problem.

Where To Find Help

Alcoholics Anonymous. Look in your telephone directory for a local group. If you can't find one, call or write: Alcoholics Anonymous, New York Intergroup, 307 Seventh Avenue, Room 201, New York, NY 10001 (212-647-1680).

Al-Anon Family Groups (support groups for people with alcoholic family members), Al-Anon Family Group Headquarters, Inc., PO Box 182, Madison Square Station, New York, NY 10010 (212-254-7230).

DRUG ABUSE ORGANIZATIONS

Try local sources first. If you cannot find help, call one of the following national organizations for a referral.

- **National Institute on Drug Abuse:** 800-662-HELP (M–F, 9 AM–3 AM, EST; Sa–Su, Noon–3 AM EST); Spanish-speakers: 800-662-9832.
- **National Clearinghouse for Alcohol and Drug Information,** Box 2345, Rockville, MD 20847-2345 (301-468-2600).
- **National Council on Alcoholism and Drug Dependency, Inc.,** 12 West 21st Street, New York, NY 10010 (212-206-6770).

MEDICATIONS

Ten Guides to Proper Medicine

1. When medicine is being prescribed for the first time:

♦ Inform your physician or pharmacist about any other medicines (prescription and nonprescription) you are taking currently. Sometimes, when medicines are taken together, they may interact and produce potentially harmful side effects.

♦ Tell your physician or pharmacist about any allergies or medical conditions you might have such as pregnancy, high blood pressure, glaucoma, or diabetes. Certain conditions may mean you should not take some medicines.

♦ Be sure you fully understand all instructions before leaving the doctor's office or pharmacy. For example, does "four times a day" mean "take one every six hours around the clock," or "take four times during your waking hours only?" Should the medicine be taken before, with, or after meals? Are there any foods, drinks, or activities (such as driving) which should be avoided while taking the medicine?

♦ Write down all instructions for future reference. Doctors and pharmacists need to know the whole story. Help them help you by discussing your health situation fully with them.

2. When buying or taking any medicine, you should always follow these tips to protect yourself against tampering:

♦ Read the label. Tamper-evident packaging identifies the seals and other protective features to note.

♦ Inspect the outer packaging for signs of tampering.

♦ Examine the medicine itself before taking it. Check for capsules or tablets that differ from the others that are enclosed. Do not use medicine from packages that have cuts, tears or other imperfections.

♦ Never take medicine in the dark.

♦ Read the label and examine the medicine at every dose.

♦ If in doubt, tell somebody. Do not buy or use medicine that looks suspicious. Always inform the store manager about questionable products so that they can be removed.

Before buying any medicine, you should STOP and take a LOOK. Before taking it, you should LOOK AGAIN.

3. When buying or taking nonprescription medicine, read the label—including warnings. Medicine labels will tell you:

♦ what symptoms the medicine can relieve
♦ how much to take
♦ when to take it and, just as important, when not to take it
♦ when to stop using the medicine
♦ warnings
♦ if and when to consult a doctor
♦ the medicine's active ingredients.

4. When taking prescription medicines:

♦ Take medicines as prescribed, either until used up, or discontinue as instructed. Symptoms sometimes disappear before the condition has totally cleared up. If you stop taking the medicine too soon, your recovery may take longer. So be certain to follow your doctor's or pharmacist's directions.

♦ Do not take more medicine than prescribed. Taking twice as much never means that you will get better twice as fast. Too high a dose may make the medicine ineffective. It might even be dangerous.

♦ Take medicines at the proper time. In some cases, medicines should be taken either before, after, or during meals. Check with your doctor or pharmacist.

♦ Never take any medicine that has been prescribed for a friend or relative. Only a physician is qualified to determine if a prescription medicine should be used by you at any given time. The same medicine may work differently for different people.

5. When taking all medicines:

♦ Do not consume alcoholic beverages with medicines until you check with your doctor or pharmacist. Mixing alcohol with some medicines may cause drowsiness, hamper the medicine's effectiveness, or create a dangerous situation.

♦ Check for an expiration date on your medicine label to make sure that the medicine is still effective. After the expiration date, the medicine may lose its potency.

♦ Safely dispose of all out-of-date medicines.

♦ Keep all medicines in their original containers. This will eliminate the risk of confusing one medicine with another, not having the proper instructions at hand, or taking outdated medicines.

♦ Always replace child-resistant caps carefully.

♦ Remember that the handicapped, the elderly, and childless families can purchase prescription medicines without a child-resistant cap by asking their pharmacist. Nonprescription medicines are available in non-child-resistant packaging specifically labeled for households without young children.

♦ Be sure to store all medicines as instructed on the label.

6. When medicines don't work . . . Sometimes you may find that a medicine does not appear to be working correctly. Your symptoms may continue or you may experience unexpected side effects. These problems may be due to:

♦ not following the correct dosage schedule— either stopping too soon, taking too much, or taking it at the wrong time

♦ interaction with certain foods or beverages

♦ interaction with other medicines you are taking

♦ trying to treat yourself with a nonprescription remedy when your problem requires professional medical attention

♦ complications that demand further medical attention.

If symptoms continue, or if there are any new symptoms or unusual side effects, always check with your physician or pharmacist.

7. If you are pregnant or nursing a baby, be sure to consult your physician or pharmacist before taking any medicine. If you have children, the following tips will help ensure that they receive the right medicine and the right amount:

♦ Always read the label to determine the proper dose. Never guess the amount of medicine that should be given.

♦ Do not play doctor. Twice the recommended dose is not appropriate, even if your child seems twice as sick as the last time.

♦ Follow the age-limit recommendations. If the label indicates that the medication should not be given to children under the age of two, consult your doctor.

♦ Avoid making conversions. If the label says two teaspoons and you're using a dosing cup with ounces only, get another measuring device.

♦ Always talk to your doctor or pharmacist before giving two medicines at the same time.

8. If you are elderly and a medicine is being prescribed, tell your doctor exactly what medi-

cines you are taking. As you get older, changes in your body may make you more susceptible to drug interactions that could lead to unwanted side effects. There is also the possibility that certain medicines, taken together, could increase or decrease their effectiveness.

9. Ask your pharmacist about patient records. Many pharmacists now keep these records for you so that you'll be able to keep track of all the medicines you are currently taking, as well as allergies and current medical conditions. This service is particularly valuable if you are being prescribed medicines by more than one doctor.

10. Keep a record of the medicines you are taking. If you are taking several different medi-

cines or if you are particularly ill, keeping a record of medication as you take it can help you use medicines properly and safely.

Reprinted courtesy of Council on Family Health.

Medication Mixes

Harmful Effects of Mixing Drugs and Alcohol

We all know that it is dangerous to mix drugs and alcohol, but which drugs in particular, and what are the effects? Here is a chart that gives the details. It is by no means exhaustive, so always check with your doctor or pharmacist.

INTERACTIONS BETWEEN ALCOHOL AND COMMONLY USED MEDICINES

Alcohol combined with. . .	Can cause. . .
☐ Anti-depressants (e.g., amitriptyline, Elavil) ☐ Antihistamines (e.g., diphenhydramine, Benadryl, chlorpheniramine, Chlor-Trimeton) ☐ Motion-sickness pills (e.g., Dramamine) ☐ Pain relievers (e.g., codeine, propoxyphene, Darvon) ☐ Sleeping medications (e.g., Halcion, flurazepam, Dalmane) ☐ Some cough/cold products ☐ Tranquilizers (e.g., lorazepam, Ativan, diazepam, Valium, alprazolam, Xanax) ☐ Ulcer medications (e.g., cimetidine, Tagamet, ranitidine, Zantac)	Excessive drowsiness, impaired coordination, falls, confusion, intoxication, loss of consciousness, impaired breathing.
☐ Anti-anginal medication (e.g., nitrogylcerin, Isordil) ☐ Some high-blood-pressure medications (e.g., prazosin, Minipress, diuretics)	Dizziness, lightheadedness, fainting, loss of consciousness, falls that could result in physical injury.
☐ Aspirin ☐ Anti-arthritic medications (e.g., ibuprofen, Advil, Motrin, naproxen, Naprosyn, Dolobid)	Increase in stomach irritation, possible increase in stomach bleeding.

Alcohol can interact with many medications; check with your pharmacist for further information.

Reprinted with permission of SRx Regional Program, Medication Education for Seniors, 1993.

EFFECTS OF SOME FOODS ON SOME DRUGS

These drugs	with these foods	can cause these problems
ANTIBIOTICS		
Ampicillin, erythromycin, penicillin	Acidic foods like: wine, citrus fruits and drinks, tomatoes, vinegar, caffeine, pickles, cola drinks	Poor absorption of drugs so they are not as effective.
Tetracycline	Foods rich in calcium like: dairy products, calcium and iron supplements	Poor absorption of drugs. Ingest calcium-rich products at least two hours before medication.
ANTICOAGULANTS *Coumadin, Panwarfin, Dicumerol*	Vitamin-K-rich foods like: asparagus, cabbage family (broccoli and kale, for instance), greens, egg yolk, lettuce, liver, potatoes, spinach, vegetable oil	Can work against the effectiveness of the drugs because they produce blood-clotting substances.
MONOAMINE OXIDASE INHIBITORS (MAOIs) Antidepressants Blood pressure drugs The antibiotic *Furoxone*	Tyramine-containing and amine-containing foods and drinks: avocado, raspberries, bananas, canned figs, raisins; nuts; baked potatoes, fava beans; sauerkraut; beer, wine, caffeine; sour cream, yogurt, aged cheese; caviar, pickled herring, liver, cured meat; yeast extract, soy sauce; instant soup mixes; meat tenderizers or extracts	May cause fatal changes in blood pressure. Watch out for headache, red face, sweating, pain in chest and neck, nausea and vomiting, headache. Don't ingest these foods while taking MAIOs and for two weeks *after* taking them.
DECONGESTANTS Any containing phenylpropanolamine and ephedrine	Caffeine-containing foods and drinks (coffee, tea, some soft drinks, chocolate)	Nervousness, insomnia, nausea, tremors.
BLOOD PRESSURE DRUGS Drugs like *Aldomet, Inderal, Lanoxin*	Licorice, the natural kind, which contains glycyrrhiza	Can lead to water retention and send up blood pressure, counteracting the drugs' effect.
TRANQUILIZERS Phenothiazines (*Thorazine, Compazine*, etc.)	Coffee and tea	May counteract effect of drugs.
Benzodiazepines (*Valium, Xanax, Librium*, etc.)	Lots of charcoal-broiled foods	

These drugs	with these foods	can cause these problems
ASTHMA MEDICATION Theophylline	Caffeine-containing foods	Magnifies stimulant effects of drug.
	Low carbohydrate, high-protein diets, charcoal-broiled beef	Lessens effectiveness of drug.
ULCER MEDICATION Cimetidine (*Tagamet*)	Red wine, aged cheese	Headache.
HEART MEDICATION Cardiac glycosides (*Laxolin*, *Crystodigin*, etc.)	High fiber foods taken at the same time prune juice, bran.	Drug does not absorb as well. Swelling, changes in heart rate, shortness of breath.
THYROID MEDICATION *Synthroid*, *Euthroid*, *Proloid*, etc.	Cruciferous vegetables (cabbage, Brussels spouts, cauliflower) and other betacarotene-high foods like carrots, pears, rutabagas; soybeans eaten in large amounts or eaten often.	Lowered heart rate and body temperature; dry skin, drooping eyelids.
PAIN AND FEVER MEDICATION Acetaminophen (*Tylenol, Tempra, Datril*)	Foods high in carbohydrates (pasta, bread, jam, etc.)	Lowers beneficial effects.
OTHER Disulfiram (*Antabuse*) for alcoholism, metronidazole (*Flagyl*) for infections, the anti-fungal griseofulvin	Aspartame	Chest pain, headache, blurred vision, dangerous heart palpitations, low blood pressure.

OVER-THE-COUNTER DRUGS:
Benefits, Warnings, and Side Effects

By no means an exhaustive list, this contains information about those over-the-counter (OTC) drugs that people use most often. General warnings: Be sure to read the labels and inserts, and follow their recommendations. Don't exceed recommended dosage, especially with children. Pay careful attention to warnings about drinking and/or driving when taking OTC drugs. Check ingredients carefully. For example, some products like antacids contain aspirin, which can be dangerous in certain situations (see below), and two drugs may counteract each other or contain the same ingredient. Most important, always consult your doctor for recommendations on using OTC drugs.

Drug	Benefits	Warnings and Side Effects
Aspirin	Relieves pain, reduces fever and inflammation. In daily low doses, can protect against heart attack, stroke, and colon cancer.	Don't give to children (implicated in Reye's syndrome). Avoid during pregnancy unless your doctor advises you otherwise. Can irritate stomach, cause stomach bleeding. Some people are allergic to aspirin. Can cause kidney damage. Do not take aspirin: if you have gout, for a hangover, if you are also taking anticoagulants (blood thinners). Do not use it routinely if you have high blood pressure. Always take aspirin with a full glass of water. Buy buffered or enteric-coated aspirin to avoid stomach irritation. Don't use aspirin that smells like vinegar.
Acetaminophen	Relieves pain and fever.	Can cause upset stomach, liver or kidney damage.
Ibuprofen	Relieves pain and fever.	Similar side effects as aspirin, but less common.
Antihistamines	Allergy and cold symptoms. Itching and motion sickness.	Don't use them with children under 4 months, and ask your doctor before giving them to children 4 months to 1 year old. May prolong colds by drying up mucous membranes, which filter infection. Can cause impaired judgment, dizziness, poor coordination, drowsiness, and hyperactivity. Drink more fluids when taking antihistamines.
Cough medicines	*Expectorants* thin mucus so it can be coughed up. For a productive cough (one that brings up mucus), which you don't want to completely suppress, use expectorants with guaifenesin. *Suppressants* suppress the cough reflex. For a dry, continual, non-productive cough, use cough suppressant with dextromethorphan.	Call the doctor if the cough lasts more than 5 days. Use with caution with children. Home remedy: one part lemon juice, two parts honey (do not give to children under a year old). Don't give cough drops to children under six.

Drug	Benefits	Warnings and Side Effects
Decongestants	Shrink swollen nose membranes, making breathing easier. Relieve runny nose and postnasal drip. Used early in development of a cold, can prevent ear infections.	Check to see if safe for children. Will cause drowsiness or increased activity—this depends on the individual. Don't overuse. Better: homemade saline solution (¾ teaspoon salt, 1 cup distilled water, kept sterile) used as nose drops, dropped in nose from above while patient is lying down on his back, head hanging down over the side of the bed.
Laxatives	Ease passage and cause elimination of feces. Best: those containing psyllium seeds, a natural source of fiber that is nonaddictive.	First try drinking more water, increasing roughage intake (fruits, bran, etc.), and exercise. Do not take laxatives if you have abdominal pain. Do not take regularly—laxatives can be addictive. Drink more water when taking any laxative.
Anti-diarrheal medicines	Thickening mixtures, which contain clay (kaolin or attapulgite) or fruit pectin, absorb toxins and bacteria in the system. Anti-spasmodics stop the intestinal spasm.	Don't take anything for the first six hours of a diarrheal attack—diarrhea often helps to eradicate infection. Don't take regularly, and take a large enough dose. Stop immediately when stool thickens. Drink electrolyte solution (Gatorade, for example) to prevent dehydration.

Drugs and Food

Jane is taking penicillin for a secondary infection from a bad cold, and she is drinking lots of orange juice. The drug doesn't seem to be working—her cold is no better. Max, under a doctor's care for high blood pressure, takes the drug Eutron. He has just been to a party where he abstained from liquor, knowing it was bad for him, but shoveled in gobs of guamacole. Now he feels terrible—his neck is sore, he sweats, he has an awful pain in his chest.

Both Jane and Max mixed drugs with the wrong food, which can lower the drug's potency (by delaying how fast it enters your system or reducing absorption) or—worse—can cause some-times fatal side effects. Most people know not to

YOUR MEDICINE CHEST: PAY ATTENTION TO EXPIRATION DATES

How many of the medicines in your medicine cabinet are past their prime, down to the last few capsules or drops, waiting there just in case you wake up at 2 AM with a bad cold or allergy attack? Or so you can avoid going to the doctor when some condition hits you again? Dump them! They can be ineffective, contaminated, or—worse—toxic. For instance, tetracycline (an antibiotic) becomes toxic after a certain amount of time.

The FDA requires manufacturers of over-the-counter drugs to include expiration dates. Some states require prescription drugs to be dated. If your state doesn't, ask your pharmacist how long a prescription drug will be safe to use.

take drugs and alcohol together. Many do not know about the bad mixtures of food and drugs. Always read the inserts that come with medications and always ask your doctor or pharmacist about side effects you might have.

Don't mix medicines into hot drinks or into food, unless your health professional tells you to. Do take them with a full glass of water, which helps to wash them down and dissolve them.

Generic Drugs

Drug products no longer protected by patent are available as *generic* drugs instead of under brand names. You can save up to 50 percent, sometimes more, by buying generic drugs. They must meet the requirements of the U.S. Food and Drug Administration as therapeutically equivalent to the brand-name drugs, with the same active ingredients in the same strengths, meeting the same test standards. Ask your pharmacist to substitute generic drugs whenever possible.

Drugs are also available through mail order pharmacies at fairly large discounts:

Action Mail Order, PO Box 787, Waterville, ME 04903 (800-452-1976).

Family Pharmaceuticals, PO Box 1288, Mount Pleasant, SC 29465 (800-922-3444).

Medi-Mail, PO Box 98520, Las Vegas, NV 89193-8520 (800-331-1458).

TRAVELING WITH MEDICINES

♦ Keep the medication on your person at all times.

♦ Don't leave medication in checked luggage.

♦ Bring enough medicine to last your entire trip. If traveling to a foreign country, bring copies of your prescriptions in case a Customs officer asks you about the medications and paraphernalia (especially syringes) you are carrying.

♦ Review dosage schedule with your doctor or pharmacist before your trip, especially if changing time zones.

♦ Keep a list of your prescriptions in case you need to refill.

♦ Have health insurance information and card with you.

♦ Carry on your person a list of the names and telephone numbers of your doctor, your pharmacist, and an emergency contact.

Reprinted courtesy of Council on Family Health (except for remarks on traveling in a foreign country, which arose from the experiences of one of the authors while traveling with a diabetic dog in France).

MAJOR DISEASES

Other Health Telephone Numbers and Hotlines

Aging
American Association of Retired Persons, 601 E Street NW, Washington, DC 20049: 202-434-2277; 800-424-3410

American Association of Homes for the Aging, 901 E Street NW, Suite 500, Washington, DC 20004: 202-783-2242; 800-508-9401

Alcohol
Ad Care Hospital (Worchester, MA): 800-AL-COHOL (24 hours a day)

Birth Defects
National Easter Seal Society, 230 West Monroe Street, Suite 1800, Chicago, IL 60606: 800-221-6827

Blind/Vision Impaired
American Council of the Blind: 800-424-8666

American Society of Cataract and Refractive Surgery: 800-451-1339

Guide Dog Foundation for the Blind, 371 East Jericho Turnpike, Smithtown, NY 11787: 800-548-4337

National Association of Parents of Visually Impaired: 800-562-6265

Carpal Tunnel Syndrome
American Physical Therapy Association, 1111 North Fairfax Street, Alexandria, VA 22314: 703-684-2782

Cerebral Palsy
United Cerebral Palsy, 1522 K Street NW, Suite 1112, Washington, DC 20005: 800-USA-1-UCP

Children
American Academy of Pediatrics, PO Box 927, Elk Grove, IL 60009-0927

Childhelp USA, 6463 Independence Avenue, Woodland Hills, CA 91367: 800-422-4453

National Child Safety Council, PO Box 1368, Jackson, MI 49204: 800-222-1464

Colitis/Ileitis
National Foundation for Ileitis and Colitis, 386 Park Avenue South, 17th Floor, New York, NY 10016-8804: 800-343-3637

Cystic Fibrosis
Cystic Fibrosis Foundation, 6931 Arlington Road, Bethesda, MD 20814: 800-344-4823

Digestive Disorders
National Digestive Diseases Information Clearinghouse, Box NDDIC, 9000 Rockville Pike, Bethesda, MD 20892: 301-468-6344

Disabilities
National Head Injuries Foundation: 800-444-6443

National Organization on Disability: 800-248-ABLE

(continued on p. 55)

MAJOR DISEASES: RISKS AND SOURCES OF INFORMATION

By far, the major causes of deaths by disease in the United States are cardiovascular diseases, followed closely by cancer. Together, they cause 2 out of 3 deaths. (See "Heart Disease," pp. 56, and "Cancer: Warning Signs, Risk Factors, and Survival Rates," pp. 59.) This chart presents information about some of the other diseases that afflict us. Three general sources of information are:

1. The National Institutes of Health. This group will provide "Medicine for the Layman" booklets and videotapes. Call 301-496-2563 or write Clinical Center Communications, National Institutes of Health, 900 Rockville Pike, Building 10, Room 1C255, Bethesda, MD 20892.

2. National Health Information Center at 800-336-4797 (9 AM to 5 PM, EST, weekdays), a toll-free line for finding out addresses and telephone numbers of national health groups.

3. Will Rogers Memorial Fund, 785 Mamaroneck Avenue, White Plains, NY 10605 (914-761-5550) for pamphlets on health.

Disease	Risk	Organizations
Allergic diseases, characterized by immune-system reactions (sneezing, itching, hives, migraine headache, and so on) to an allergen, a foreign protein. Include allergic rhinitis (hay fever) and asthma, a disease in which the flow of air into the lungs is blocked as bronchial airways swell with mucus.	50 million Americans suffer from allergic diseases.	American Academy of Allergy and Immunology, 611 East Wells St., Milwaukee, WI 53202 (800-822-2762) American College of Allergy & Immunology: 800-842-7777 The Lung Line: 800-222-LUNG Asthma & Allergy Foundation of America (9 AM–5 PM): 800-7ASTHMA Marion Merrell Dow Pollen Forecast Hotline: 800-POLLENS
Alzheimer's disease, most common of a group of dementias (loss of mental functions) in which brain cells that secrete acetylcholine die off.	Estimated 4 million over-65 Americans, according to National Institute of Aging.	Alzheimer's Association, PO Box 5675-UT, Chicago IL 60680-5675 (800-272-3900) Alzheimer's Disease and Related Disorders Assn.: 800-621-0379 National Institute on Aging, ADEAR Center, PO Box 8250, Silver Spring, MD 20907-8250 (800-438-4380 or 301-495-3311) National Foundation for Medical Research, 1360 Beverly Road, Suite 305, McLean, VA 22101

Disease	Risk	Organizations
Anorexia nervosa, weight loss from dieting, fasting, and exercise, leading to emaciation, even death. Bulemia, a related eating disorder, binge eating followed by vomiting, excessive exercise, or some other behavior to counter weight gain.	Anorexia kills 5–8 percent of affected individuals.	National Anorexic Aid Society Center for the Treatment of Eating Disorders: 614-436-1112 Bulemia Anorexia Self- Help: 800-BASH-STL National Association of Anorexia Nervosa and Associated Disorders: 708-831-3438
Arthritis, joint inflammation. More than 100 different types, among which are osteoarthritis, rheumatoid arthritis.	Estimated 36 million Americans.	American Academy of Orthopaedic Surgeons, 22 S. Propect Ave., Park Ridge, IL 60068 Arthritis Foundation: 800-283-7800
Chronic Fatigue Syndrome (CFS) aka "Yuppie Flu," characterized by low-grade fever, persistent and overwhelming fatigue, and other symptoms; cause unclear.	Affects two times as many women as men.	National C.F.S. Association, 3521 Broadway, Suite 222, Kansas City, MO 64111 (816-931-4777) C.F. and Immune Dysfunction Syndrome Assn., PO Box 220398, Charlotte, NC 28222-0398 (704-362-CFID)
Depression, "the common cold of mental illness," characterized by lingering and incapacitating despair, in the case of manic depression alternating between euphoria and despair.	As many as 30 percent of adults in their lifetimes.	National Mental Health Association: 800-969-6642
Diabetes mellitus: pancreas fails to produce enough (or any) insulin, hormone that helps in the absorption of glucose in the body. Type I: Affected individual is insulin-dependent with insulin-making cells in pancreas destroyed; Type II, late-onset (usually after age 40): Can often be controlled by diet.	14 million people affected, in the top 10 of killer diseases.	American Diabetes Association: 800-232-3472 Juvenile Diabetes Foundation: 800-223-1138 American Diabetes Association: 703-549-1500
Emphysema: breakdown of alveolar walls in lungs, loss of lung elasticity.	Common in heavy smokers.	American Lung Association (local chapters)
Kidney diseases .	11th leading cause of death.	American Kidney Fund: 800-638-8299
Liver disease and cirrhosis	9th leading cause of death..	American Liver Foundation: 800-223-0179

MAJOR DISEASES: RISKS AND SOURCES OF INFORMATION (cont.)

Disease	Risk	Organizations
Osteoporosis (porous bone), a condition in which more bone calcium is being absorbed by the body than is being replaced, thinning of bone mass.	1.5 million Americans have fractures related to osteoporosis every year. One in four women past menopause develops the disease. Other risk factors: having small bones, not being on estrogen replacement therapy, drinking, smoking, low intake of calcium, lack of regular exercise that puts moderate stress on long bones of body and spine.	The National Osteoporosis Foundation, Suite 602, 2100 M St. NW, Washington, DC 20037 American College of Obstetricians and Gynecologists Resource Center, 409 12th St. SW, Washington, DC 20024
Rare diseases.	Not applicable.	National Organization for Rare Disorders in New Fairfield, Conn. (203-746-6518; 800-999-NORD) National Institutes of Health in Bethesda, MD: 301-496-4000
Sickle cell disease, inherited disorder of blood, found primarily in those with African and Mediterranean ancestors.	1500 babies born in the U.S. every year with this disorder.	Sickle Cell Disease Association of America: 800-421-8453
Spinal meningitis: two kinds, bacterial and viral, cause inflammation of the membranes of brain and spinal cord. Symptoms include stiff neck, fever, sensitivity to light, staggering or difficulty walking.	15,000 people a year.	Meningitis and Special Pathogens Branch, Centers for Disease Control: 301-443-2610
Tremor (essential tremor).	Affects 4 million people.	International Tremor Foundation, 360 W. Superior St., Box MM, Chicago, IL 60610
Urinary incontinence (UI), involuntary leakage of urine.	Afflicts 10 million, mostly women.	The Simon Foundation for Continence: 800-23-SIMON US TOO (incontinence after prostate surgery): 800-242-2383 American Foundation for Urologic Disease, 300 W. Pratt St., Suite 401, Baltimore, MD 21201

National Rehabilitation Information Center, 8455 Colesville Road, Suite 935, Silver Spring, MD 20910: 800-34-NARIC

National Spinal Cord Injury Association, 600 West Cummings Park, Suite 2000, Woburn, MA 01801: 800-962-9629

Domestic Violence

National Domestic Violence, 2462 E Street, San Diego, CA 92102: 619-233-3088

Down Syndrome

National Down Syndrome Congress, 1605 Chantilly Drive, Suite 250, Atlanta, GA 30324: 800-232-NDSC

National Down Syndrome Society, 666 Broadway, 8th Floor, New York, NY 10012: 800-221-4602

Dyslexia

Orton Dyslexia Society, 8600 LaSalle Road, Suite 382, Baltimore, MD 21286-2044: 800-ABCD-123; 410-296-0232

Epilepsy

Epilepsy Foundation of America, 4351 Garden City Drive, Landover, MD 20785-2267: 800-332-1000

Genetic Disease

Alliance of Genetic Support Groups: 800-336-GENE

Hearing/Communication Handicaps

American Speech, Language, and Hearing Association, 10801 Rockville Pike, Rockville, MD 20852

Better Hearing Institute, PO Box 1840, Washington, DC 20013: 800-327-9355

Hearing Aid Helpline, 20361 Middle Belt, Livonia, MI 48152: 800-521-5247

National Association for Hearing and Speech: 800-638-8255

Hearing Helpline, PO Box 1840, Washington, DC 20013: 800-327-9355, 800-EAR-WELL, or 703-642-0580 (Virginia)

Infectious Diseases

Centers for Disease Control and Prevention: 404-332-4555

Kidneys

National Kidney Foundation, Inc., 30 E. 33rd Street, New York, NY 10016; 800-622-9010

Lupus

Lupus Foundation of America, #4 Research Place, Suite 180, Rockville, MD 20850-3226: 800-558-0121; 301-670-9292; FAX 301-670-9486

Menopause

National Institute on Aging Information Center, PO Box 8057, Gaithersburg, MD 20898-8057: 800-222-2225

Mental Health

National Mental Health Association: 800-969-6642

For panic disorder: 800-64-PANIC (National Institute of Mental Health)

Multiple Sclerosis

Multiple Sclerosis Association of America, 601 White House Pike, Oaklyn, NJ 08107: 800-833-4672

Myasthenia Gravis

Myasthenia Gravis Foundation, 53 West Jackson Blvd., Suite 660, Chicago, IL 60604: 800-541-5454

Neurological Disorders

National Institute of Neurological Disorders and Stroke, PO Box 5801, Bethesda, MD 20824: 800-352-9424

Nutrition

National Center for Nutrition and Dietetics: 800-366-1655

Organ Transplants

United Network for Organ-Sharing: 800-24-DONOR

Paralysis

American Paralysis Association, 500 Morris Avenue, Springfield, NJ 07081: 800-225-0292

Parkinson's Disease

Parkinson's Educational Program, 3900 Birch Street, #105, Newport Beach, CA 92660: 800-344-7872; 714-250-2975

National Parkinson Foundation, 1501 N.W. 9th Avenue, Miami, FL 33136: 800-327-4545

Phobias

Anxiety Disorders Association of America (Rockville, MD): 900-737-3400

PMS (Premenstrual Syndrome)

PMS Access Hotline: 800-222-4PMS

Reye's Syndrome

National Reye's Syndrome Foundation, PO Box 829, 426 N. Lewis, Bryan, OH 43506: 800-233-7393

Spina Bifida

Spina Bifida Association of America, 4590 Mc-Arthur Blvd. NW, Suite 250, Washington, DC 20007: 800-621-3141

Sudden Infant Death Syndrome

SIDS Alliance, 10500 Little Patuxent Parkway, Suite 420, Columbia, MA 21044: 800-221-SIDS

Thyroid Disorders

Thyroid Foundation of America, Inc., Ruth Sleeper Hall, RSL 350, 40 Parkman Street, Boston, MA 02114-2698: 800-832-8321

For information on doctors' charges for thousands of procedures, call the **Health Care Cost Hotline:** 900-225-2500. A free booklet with instructions and codes for procedures is available by calling 800-383-3434.

A 900 number for medical information is **Medical Information Line:** 900-230-4800.

Heart Disease

If you are an average American, chances are that you will die of heart disease or a stroke. This is why heart disease and stroke dominate health news and why research into their causes and cures is so well funded. If you are at greater-than-average risk for heart disease, changes in lifestyle can greatly reduce your vulnerability.

Risk Factors for Heart Disease and Suggestions for Reducing Risk

Age. The older you are, the greater your risk of having heart disease.

Sex. As a group, men die of heart disease at a younger age than women. Heart attack is the number one killer of women over 40, however.

One in nine women aged 45–64 and one in three women after age 65 has a cardiovascular problem of some kind. After menopause, women can cut their chance of heart attack by 30–50 percent by taking estrogen. *Note:* Women's heart disease symptoms differ from those of men.

Smoking. Give it up. According to the *New England Journal of Medicine* this will lower your risk 50–70 percent. Smoking or exposure to secondhand smoke raises blood pressure, heart rate, and levels of carbon monoxide in the blood. It affects cholesterol, increasing the deleterious effects of low-density lipoprotein (LDL) and decreasing levels of "good" high-density lipoprotein (HDL). A combination of smoking and use of oral contraceptives gives you a risk of heart attack 39 times greater than that of nonsmoking women who don't use birth control pills. If you use oral contraceptives, have your cholesterol levels checked at least once a year.

Height. If you are a short man (5'7" and under), your risk of heart attack is 60 percent higher than men who are 6'1" or taller. This may be because shorter men have narrower coronary arteries or smaller lung capacity.

Blood cholesterol. If your blood cholesterol is over 180, your risk of heart attack increases incrementally. (See "Demystifying Cholesterol," p. 58.) For each 1 percent decline in blood cholesterol higher than the recommended level, you gain a 2-3 percent decline in risk of heart disease.

Iron. A high amount of iron stored in the body may cause oxidation of LDL, which in turn creates plaque that clogs arteries. Experts have not yet suggested curtailing iron intake, especially in infants and pregnant women.

Blood pressure. Danger: any reading over 140/90 may mean hypertension, which is a factor in heart disease. Be on guard if your systolic pressure (the first number) is over 120. For each 1 percent reduction in diastolic pressure (the second and more important number), you lower your risk of heart disease by 2–3 percent. You can reduce high blood pressure by cutting down on salt and monosodium glutamate and by exercising more. Try to minimize those activities that cause you to become angry and raise your blood pressure. If those measures fail, drugs can lower blood pressure.

Aspirin. Taking a quarter of an aspirin tablet a day (40 to 70 milligrams) may lower heart attack risk by 33 percent. However, do not follow this suggestion if you have ulcers or are prone to them. Check with your doctor.

Coffee. If you drink five or more cups of coffee a day you have two times the risk of heart attack than if you drink none at all.

Diet: Fat. A high-fat diet contributes to risk of heart disease. The greatest culprit in the fat family is saturated fat, found in meat, butter, coconut oil, and palm oil. Use liquid oils like canola oil, olive oil, corn oil, safflower oil in cooking. Change your diet: eat more grains, fruits, and vegetables and lower the percent of calories from fat to 30 percent or less. And of that 30 percent or less, get no more than a third in saturated fats. (See "Ten Tips for Lowering the Fat Content of Your Diet," p. 592, "Figuring the Fat in Food," p. 591, and "The Fats in Your Oil and Butter," p. 622.)

Diet: Fiber. Increase your intake of fiber-rich food, particularly soluble fiber like psyllium (which contains eight times more soluble fiber than oat bran does). Other sources: oatmeal, beans, lentils, peas. Add fiber gradually or you may find yourself with a stomachache!

Diet: Vitamins. Be sure you are eating enough foods containing vitamins C and E and beta-carotene, which, experts think, keep LDL from oxidizing and damaging arteries. (See "Vitamins: Should You Stick to the RDA?" p. 594.)

Alcohol. People who drink a moderate amount of alcohol have a 25–45 percent lower risk of heart disease than nondrinkers. Drink a glass of wine or grape juice a day, say some experts. Others claim that the bad effects of alcohol (liver disease, for example), no matter what amount you drink, outweigh the good and advise against drinking to ward off heart disease. Raisins contain resveratrol, the same cholesterol fighter found in wine. Get the artificially dehydrated raisins—sunlight destroys resveratrol, so sun-dried raisins have a much lower concentration.

Exercise. An increase in HDL cholesterol and efficiency of the cardiovascular system result from aerobic exercise. Aim for exercise that raises your heart rate for at least 20 minutes at least three times a week. (See "Exercise for Health," p. 7.) Aerobic exercising can give you a 45 percent lower risk.

Obesity. Because the heart works harder to send blood through fat bodies, heart disease risk is greater if you are very overweight. People with "beer belly" obesity are more prone to strokes. (See "Should You Lose Weight?" p. 3.) Someone at normal weight has a 35–55 percent lower risk of heart disease compared with people 20 percent or more over ideal weight.

Diabetes. If you have diabetes, your risk of heart disease is higher. By lowering your blood sugar (maintaining it at normal levels), you may lower your risk of heart attack.

Signs of a Heart Attack

♦ Heavy pressure, squeezing sensation, fullness, or pain in middle of chest lasting at least two minutes.

♦ Pain in shoulders, neck, jaw, arms, or back that does not go away.

♦ Dizziness, sweating, faintness, nausea, shortness of breath.

♦ One of four heart attacks is without such obvious symptoms, so if you have a vague feeling of discomfort, call your doctor.

Keep emergency numbers near your phone, especially those of facilities that have 24–hour emergency cardiac care. Time is crucial. Two out of three heart attack deaths occur before the person gets to the hospital. *If you suspect you are having a heart attack, don't deny it. Call 911, then call your doctor.* Don't drive. Immediate help can double your chances of staying alive. New treatments for heart attack can reduce heart damage and increase chances of survival. Four of five people who have a heart attack recover completely.

If you already have had a heart attack, be sure a family member or nearby friend knows CPR (cardiopulmonary resuscitation). Training in CPR is available at the Red Cross.

American Heart Association Hot Line, 3640 5th Avenue, San Diego, CA 92103: 800-AHA-USA1

Arizona Heart Institute & Foundation's Hartline, 2632 North 20th Street, Phoenix, AZ 85006: 800-345-HART

Demystifying Cholesterol

There is a correspondence between a high-fat, high-cholesterol diet, blood cholesterol readings, and risk of heart disease. Some people can eat bacon at three meals a day and not have high cholesterol. Others can eat nothing but green vegetables and be plagued with stubborn high cholesterol readings, but such individuals are rare. You usually can lower your blood cholesterol 10–15 mg/dl (milligrams per deciliter) just by changes in diet.

Have your cholesterol checked by a doctor who uses a laboratory affiliated with a teaching hospital or medical school. Laboratory tests should be comparable to the Lipid Research Center (LRC) method sponsored by the Centers for Disease Control. You should fast for 12 hours before the test.

You need to know your arithmetic to understand your blood cholesterol readings. Some cholesterol is good, some bad, and what may matter most is the ratio between kinds of cholesterol. You usually receive results that include numbers for total cholesterol, high-density lipoprotein (HDL), low-density lipoprotein (LDL), and triglycerides.

Total cholesterol. According to the Adult Treatment Panel of the Adult Cholesterol Education Program, a reading of under 200 mg/dl is desirable, 200–239 mg/dl is borderline-high, 240 mg/dl and over is high. High is not good. Anyone with cholesterol over 240 mg/dl should do something about it. For each 1 percent decline in total serum cholesterol, you gain a 2–3 percent decline in risk of heart disease.

High-density lipoprotein (HDL). HDL, "good cholesterol," carries cholesterol away from artery walls and body tissues to the liver, where it is removed. (Recent research has discovered a "bad" protein in HDL—apoA-II; however, beneficial effects of high HDL still stand.) Desirable levels: women, a level of 55 or more; men, 45 or more.

Low-density lipoprotein (LDL). LDL, "bad cholesterol," forms fatty plaques in your arteries that can predispose you to heart attack. The higher your LDL is over acceptable levels, the greater your risk of heart disease. Acceptable level: 160 or less.

Triglycerides. Fatty substances in the blood, triglycerides are "bad" because at high levels they add to your risk of heart disease. Triglyceride levels should be 200 or less.

Ratio of total cholesterol to HDL levels. The ratio between the total cholesterol and HDL, some doctors think, is at least as important as total readings. The lower the ratio, the better. Usually a ratio of 3:5 or less is considered acceptable. To figure out this ratio, divide your total cholesterol by your HDL.

SAMPLE CHOLESTROL CALCULATIONS

TOTAL CHOLESTEROL (in mg/dl)	HDL (in mg/dl)	Ratio*	Result
220	60	3.67	Bad
200	60	3.33	Good
220	65	3.38	Good

*Total cholesterol divided by HDL.

How to Lower Cholesterol Levels:

♦ Keep fat below 30, even 20 percent of calories. (See "Figuring the Fat in Food," p. 591.)

♦ Eat foods rich in soluble fiber. (See "Healthy Diets," p. 587.)

♦ Do aerobic exercise.

♦ Make sure you are getting enough niacin (vitamin B_3).

Children and Cholesterol

Children over two should eat relatively low-fat, low-cholesterol diets, because heart disease begins in childhood.

Cancer: Warning Signs, Risk Factors, and Survival Rates

Cancer strikes fear in the heart of almost everyone. Your chances of contracting it are to some degree genetically determined—there's not much you can do about your relatives. The good news: you can reduce your chances of cancer by simple changes in lifestyle (which also reduce your risk of other disease).

In general, see your doctor if you experience changes in bowel habits, difficulty in swallowing, sores, a thickening or lump, unusual discharge, coughing, hoarseness. Remember, though, that some cancers are symptomless until later stages. Have frequent checkups with recommended tests. (See "What the Doctor Checks For," p. 85, and "What Tests and When?" p. 88.)

The survival rate for cancer has increased—from 20 percent in 1937 to over 40 percent today, according to the National Institutes of Health. Early detection can increase your chance of a cure.

Lung Cancer

If you smoke two packs of cigarettes a day, your risk is 15 to 25 times that of nonsmokers. Pipe and cigar smokers have 5 times the risk of nonsmokers. Symptoms: hard to detect, a "silent" disease until later stages. Survival rate: 13 percent. (See "How to Quit Smoking," p. 37.)

Breast Cancer

You are at greater risk if: (1) you have a "first-degree relative" (like sister or mother) who had breast cancer; (2) you have had other kinds of cancer (ovarian, colon, or uterine); (3) you are older (75 percent of breast cancer cases occur in women over 50). Other risk factors: starting menstruation before age 12; obesity after menopause; having your first child after 30 to 35 (all with moderate risk); menopause after age 55 (low increased risk). Apple-shaped women have three times the cancer risk of pear-shaped women. (See "Should You Lose Weight?" p. 3.) Symptoms include: a lump in the breast, indentation of the skin, retraction of the nipple, blood coming from the nipple. With early detection, survival rate (no sign of disease after 10 years): 85 percent. You should not overemphasize statistics: yes, your chances of developing breast cancer are one in eight, but *only* if you live to age 95. (See "Breast Self-Examination for Women," p. 60.)

RISKS OF DEVELOPING BREAST CANCER

Age	Cancer Risk
30	1 in 2,525
40	1 in 217
50	1 in 50
60	1 in 24
70	1 in 14
80	1 in 10
95	1 in 8

Colorectal Cancer

If you have a close relative who has had polyps or colon cancer, you have three times the risk. Symptoms: sudden changes in bowel habits lasting two or three weeks, discomfort in abdomen, blood in stool. With early detection: 90–95 percent survival rate.

Female Pelvic Cancers

Cervical cancer: Your risk of cervical cancer is greater if you are (and have been) sexually active with multiple partners. Cervical cancer may be caused by the papilloma virus (also responsible for genital warts). Symptom: sudden vaginal discharge, growing worse. Five-year survival rate: 65 percent. *Endometrial cancer* occurs most often in postmenopausal women, women taking estrogen for symptoms of menopause, and women with diabetes. Symptom: vaginal bleeding. Survival rate: 84 percent. *Ovarian cancer:* symptom (swelling of abdomen) occurs late in disease. Survival rate (five-year): 34 percent.

Other Pelvic Cancers

Prostate cancer: Risk increases with age (over 55). Symptom: blood in urine. With early detection: 85 percent (five-year survival rate). *Bladder cancer:* Risk increases if you smoke, if you are male. Symptoms: blood in urine, frequent urination, pain. Survival rate (five-year): 73 percent.

Abdominal Cancers

Pancreatic cancer. Symptoms: jaundice, dark urine, itching, light-colored stools. Survival rate (five-year): 1–3 percent. *Stomach cancer.* Symptoms: stomach upset, gas pains, indigestion, fullness. Survival rate: 15–20 percent.

Blood and Lymph Cancers

Leukemia. Symptoms: weakness, debility. Survival rate: some childhood forms, 75 percent; overall, 33 percent. *Hodgkin's disease.* With early detection: 90 percent survival rate.

Ways to Reduce Your Risk of Cancer

♦ Stop smoking. This habit contributes to one-third of cancer deaths, the major form being lung cancer, together with seven other cancers. (See "How to Quit Smoking," p. 37.)

♦ Avoid the sun, and use a sunscreen with at least a 15 SPF (Sun Protection Factor) when you are in the sun. Overexposure to the sun causes skin cancer. (See "Sun Safety," p. 21.)

♦ Eat a diet that is less than 30 percent fat, better yet, 20 percent fat. (See "Figuring the Fat in Food," p. 591.) High fat consumption increases your risk of developing colorectal cancer, and perhaps other cancers.

♦ Eat fiber, which can lessen your risk of developing colon cancer, perhaps also breast cancer.

♦ Eat vegetables and fruits, especially leafy green and cruciferous vegetables (broccoli, Brussels sprouts, kale, watercress, turnips), as well as yellow and orange vegetables and fruits. These play a role in prevention of several kinds of cancer. (See "Healthy Diets," p. 587.)

♦ Eat less of foods that are smoked or cured with salt or nitrate (hot dogs, bacon, salt cod).

♦ Keep your weight down. (See "Should You Lose Weight?" p. 3.)

♦ Exercise. (See "Exercise for Health," p. 7.)

♦ Take some aspirin every day (if you will not have problems with side effects). Check with your doctor first.

♦ Make sure that you take more than the RDA (but less than toxic doses) of vitamins: A, folic acid, C, and E. (See "Vitamins: Should You Stick with the RDA?" p. 594.)

♦ Avoid unneccesary X-rays.

♦ Cut back on alcohol.

♦ Reduce stress. (See "The Stress Factor," p. 12.)

Cancer Information Service of National Cancer Institute: 800-4-CANCER; 9 AM–7 PM, M–F.

American Cancer Society: 800-ACS-2345.

Breast Self-Examination for Women

Examining your breasts every month can save your life—most breast lumps are discovered by women themselves. Remember, the earlier breast cancer is detected, the better your chances of survival. Discovered early, breast cancer has a 85 percent survival rate. Also remember that not every lump is malignant and that most breast tissue seems a bit lumpy.

Through examining your breasts monthly, you learn what is normal for you, you establish a baseline so that you can more easily spot a lump or changed condition when it occurs.

American Cancer Society Method

♦ Allot a regular time every month for breast examination, perhaps a few days after your period or, if you no longer have periods, on the first of the month.

♦ In the shower or bath with wet soapy hands, using flat straight finger surfaces (not fingertips), move over your entire breast and armpit, feeling for unusual lumps or thickening.

♦ In front of the mirror, look for dimpling, skin retraction, puckering, changes in the shape of your breasts. Don't expect your breasts to look exactly alike. Some asymmetry is normal. Put your arms at your sides, then behind your head and pressed forward. Look again each time.

♦ Still in front of the mirror, put your palms on your hips and press down, bowing toward the mirror, pulling shoulders and elbows forward. This flexes your chest muscles. Look again for dimpling and changes and for significant differences between breasts.

♦ Gently squeeze each nipple between your thumb and forefinger. Look for discharges.

♦ Lie down with a pillow or other support under your left shoulder. Put your left arm under your head. This makes the breast flatter and easier to examine. Examine your left breast with your right hand, fingers relaxed, using the flat surface of your fingers. Move in a circular motion over the breast, looking for lumps or thickening. Work in concentric circles: start at the outside, do a complete circle, move in an inch, do another circle, and so on. Include breastbone, armpit, nipple. Then move the pillow to your right shoulder and repeat for the other breast with your left hand. If you find any lumps, thickenings, or changes, report to your doctor.

The Mammacare Method

With the Mammacare Method, you watch an instructional video and practice on two dummy breasts, one containing a fascimile of normal breast tissue, the other a fascimile of tissue with cancerous lumps. In this way you can learn to tell what is normal. Also, you examine a larger area of the chest and underarm in a vertical pattern and learn to use light, medium, and deep pressure to feel for tumors in tissue. The kit costs about $75.

Cancer Information Service (National Cancer Institute): 800-4-CANCER, M–F, 9 AM–7 PM, EST. Referrals to medical facilities and support groups. Updated by American College of Radiology.

American Cancer Society Cancer Response System: 800-ACS-2345, M–F, 8:30 AM–5 PM. Information and referrals. Sponsors Reach to Recovery, a program pairing breast cancer survivors with women who have recently been diagnosed with breast cancer.

National Alliance of Breast Cancer Organizations: 212-719-0154, M–F, 9 AM–5 PM. Information and referrals to support groups.

Y-ME, National Organization for Breast Cancer Information and Support, 212 W. VanBuren, Chicago, IL 60607: 800-221-2141, M–F, 10 AM–6 PM. Breast cancer survivors answer phones to provide support and referrals.

Tallying Your Diabetes Risk

Write in the points next to each statement that is *true* for you. If a statement is *not true* for you, put a zero. Then add up your total score.

1. I have been experiencing one or more of the following symptoms on a regular basis:
   ♦ excessive thirst   YES 3 ___
   ♦ frequent urination   YES 3 ___
   ♦ extreme fatigue   YES 1 ___

♦ unexplained weight loss   YES 3 ____
♦ blurry vision from time to time. YES 2 ____
2. I am over 30 years old.   YES 1 ____
3. My weight is equal to or above
   that listed in the chart.   YES 2 ____
4. I am a woman who has had a baby
   weighing more than nine lbs. at
   birth.   YES 2 ____
5. I am of Native American descent. YES 1 ____
6. I am of Hispanic or African
   American descent.   YES 1 ____
7. I have a parent with diabetes.   YES 1 ____
8. I have a brother or sister with
   diabetes.   YES 2 ____

Weight Chart

This chart shows weights that are 20 percent heavier than the maximum recommended for both men and women with a medium frame. If your weight is at or above the amount listed for your height, you may be at risk of developing diabetes.

Height (without shoes)		Weight in Pounds (without clothing)	
Feet	Inches	Women	Men
4	9	127	
4	10	131	
4	11	134	
5	0	138	
5	1	142	146
5	2	146	151
5	3	151	155
5	4	157	158
5	5	162	163
5	6	167	168
5	7	172	174
5	8	176	179
5	9	181	184
5	10	186	190
5	11		196
6	0		202
6	1		208
6	2		214
6	3		220

Scoring 3–5 points:

If you scored 3–5 points, you are probably at low risk for diabetes. But don't just forget about it. Especially if you are over 30, overweight, or of African American, Hispanic, or Native American descent.

What to do about it:
Be sure you know the symptoms of diabetes. If you experience any of them, contact your doctor for further testing.

Scoring over 5 points:

If you scored over 5 points, you may be at high risk for diabetes. You may already have diabetes.

What to do about it:
See your doctor promptly. Find out if you have diabetes. Even if you don't have diabetes, know the symptoms. If you experience any of them in the future, see your doctor immediately.

The American Diabetes Association urges all pregnant women to be tested for diabetes between the 24th and 28th weeks of pregnancy.

Check with your local American Diabetes Association chapter or affiliate for more information about diabetes, healthy eating, and exercise. (Numbers are listed in the white pages of the phone book.)

Reprinted with permission from the American Diabetes Association. Copyright 1993.

This test is meant to educate and make you aware of the serious risks of diabetes. Only a medical doctor can determine if you do have diabetes.

Questions and Answers About AIDS

AIDS (acquired immune deficiency syndrome), the result of infection by the HIV (human immunodeficiency) virus, ranks in the top 10 killers in the United States and is moving up the list. AIDS causes the breakdown of the immune system, which renders the body vulnerable to disease. The virus itself does not kill—death follows from the diseases and infections that the immune system can no longer fight. Heterosexuals as well as homosexuals, and women as well as men, can become infected. The World Health Organization predicts that by the year 2000, 40 million people will have been infected with the HIV virus.

How Do You Acquire AIDS?

The HIV virus dies within a few minutes outside the human body. You can contract the virus:

♦ Through a needle contaminated with the blood of someone who is HIV-positive.

♦ Through transfusion of blood or implantation of body tissues or organs from someone who is HIV-positive.

♦ When semen or vaginal discharge from someone who is HIV-positive enters the bloodstream through a sore or cut. Women are more likely to be infected by men than men by women, both because more men are HIV-positive and because the virus is transmitted more easily by men to women than the other way around.

♦ By being born to an infected mother or drinking her breast milk.

You CANNOT Become Infected by:

♦ touching or ordinary kissing—enzymes in saliva destroy the virus.

♦ being sneezed on.

♦ coming in contact with an infected person's sweat.

Are You at Risk?

You are at risk (that is, have a greater chance of becoming infected) if you:

♦ are or have been sexually active, especially with people at risk for contracting HIV, and do not take precautions.

♦ engaged in high-risk behavior such as anal or homosexual sex, even once, since the mid-1970s.

♦ received blood transfusions or body-tissue transplants between 1977 and 1985.

♦ are, or have been, an intravenous drug user.

♦ are, or have been, exposed to infected blood.

♦ are an immigrant from a place where HIV is rife—Haiti and some parts of West Africa or Central Africa.

Are HIV Tests Reliable?

♦ Yes, in the high 90th percentile. The most accurate tests are the Elisa and the Western Blot. They measure HIV antibodies. To be sure to be free of AIDS, a person should be tested for HIV twice in the year, have no sex without a condom, and remain monogamous (as should his or her partner). Sometimes the tests yield false positives.

♦ A woman at risk who is planning to have a baby should be tested twice in the year before getting pregnant to be sure she is negative.

How Can You Avoid Contracting the HIV Virus?

1. Only one way to *completely* avoid sexually contracted AIDS exists:

♦ Practice abstinence.

2. To be *relatively* safe:

♦ Have sex only with a faithful and uninfected partner. This is not as foolproof or as simple as it sounds. The only way to be somewhat sure is if you and your partner are tested negative for HIV twice within a year in which each of you remains completely celibate, then have sex only with each other using condoms and other safe-sex practices for the first six months after. After six months of monogamous protected ("safe") sex, you should be tested again; if both of you test negative, you can stop using protection *if* neither of you engages in any risky behavior. (Even then, you should know that some people infected with HIV don't test positive for as long as 42 months after infection.)

♦ Use a lubricated latex condom every time you have sex. However, you should know that condoms are not 100 percent safe. Use latex condoms—they are less easily penetrated by viruses than lambskin ones. However, any condom can break—and they do, 4 percent of the time, more or less. Use spermicidal products with the condom. Women may use the vaginal pouch, which is not completely foolproof either.

♦ Never share needles with someone else. Nor should you share toothbrushes or razors or other personal devices that could become contaminated with blood.

♦ Avoid engaging in anal intercourse as passive partner. Blood vessels in the anal area rupture easily, giving the virus a highway to the bloodstream.

♦ Take precautions when engaging in oral sex—men should wear a latex condom on the penis, women a dental dam (a nonprescription product available in drugstores) over the vaginal area.

♦ Make sure that medical and dental personnel who treat you

—use a new set of gloves and freshly disinfected instruments for every patient.

—wash their hands after every patient.

—wear gloves, masks, gowns, and protective eyewear when at risk of being sprayed with any body fluid, including blood.

What Is the AIDS Timetable?

♦ Within six to twelve weeks after infection, antibodies for HIV form. However, physicians have documented periods up to 42 months, though this is rare. During this time—the "window" phase—the infected person can infect someone else, even though he or she would test negative for HIV.

♦ The median time between the time a person is infected and full-blown AIDS appears is 10 to 11 years. People carrying the HIV virus can look, feel, and act well.

♦ Once the infected person crosses the line between HIV-positive results and full-blown AIDS (identified by opportunistic diseases), he or she has a 1 in 10 chance of surviving more than

three years. The most common infections are PCP (pneumocystis carinii pneumonia), cytomegalovirus (can cause blindness and infections of brain and colon), cryptococcal meningitis (a fungus invading the brain and lungs), Kaposi's sarcoma (shows up as skin lesions), mycobacterium avium complex (affecting gastrointestinal tract).

Why Hasn't a Cure Been Developed?

The HIV retrovirus mutates faster than scientists can develop weapons against it.

What Are the Signs of HIV Involvement?

♦ Night sweats
♦ Flu-like symptoms
♦ Recurring fever
♦ Diarrhea that lasts more than a month
♦ Weight loss or lack of appetite
♦ Chronic yeast infections
♦ Sores or white spots in the mouth; coating on tongue
♦ Pain or numbness of hands or feet
♦ Mental decline or personality change
♦ Unexplained bleeding from skin growths
♦ Easy bruising
♦ Fatigue or weakness
♦ Shortness of breath
♦ Deep, dry cough, not caused by smoking, that persists
♦ Swellings in throat, armpits, or groin
♦ Rashes
♦ Itching
♦ Herpes (especially genital herpes) that becomes increasingly severe.

Why Be Tested If the Disease Is Fatal?

♦ To avoid infecting others.
♦ Because you can extend your life through treatments that build up the immune system and fight opportunistic diseases.

Centers for Disease Control National AIDS Clearinghouse: 800-458-5231, M–F, 9 AM–7 PM, EST.

National AIDS Hotline: 800-342-2437 (24 hours); TTY 800-243-7889, 10 AM–10 PM, weekdays except holidays.

People with AIDS (PWA) Coalition Hotline: 800-828-3280, M–F, 10 AM–6 PM, EST.

Project Inform: 800-822-7422.

Teen Gay and Lesbian Youth Hotline (manned by teens): 800-347-8336, Th–Sa, 7 PM–11:45 PM, EST.

Teens Tap (manned by teens): 800-234-TEEN, 4 PM–8 PM, CST.

HOW TO USE A CONDOM

♦ Do not use petroleum-based products with condoms.

♦ Use a new condom for each sex act.

♦ Use the condom with a contraceptive product containing the spermicide nonoxynol-9.

♦ Put the condom on *before* genital contact takes place.

♦ Withdraw while still erect.

♦ Hold the rim during withdrawal so there is no spillage.

BEWARE! BEWARE!

♦ If someone shows you a card marketed by Partners for AIDS-Free America (PAFA) "certifying" an HIV-negative test, you can probably believe that what the card says is true. **But** as the Public Health Service warns, the card shows only that the person was HIV-negative on the day of the test. He or she may have become infected afterward. Moreover, since it takes three weeks to six months or more before a blood test can detect HIV once it has entered the body, a negative HIV test does not mean that the individual is "clean."

♦ A survey of 422 sexually active college students by Susan Cochran of California State University at Northridge had some startling results: 20 percent of the men said that, if asked, they would say they had a negative HIV test result even if they hadn't been tested; 47 percent of the men and 42 percent of the women said they would lie about the number of sexual partners they had—downward; 42 percent of the men said they would not admit to a one-night stand.

Sexually Transmitted Disease (STD)

A 1993 study by the Alan Guttmacher Institute reveals that one in five of all Americans is infected with a sexually transmitted disease (STD). Among the 50 sexually transmitted infections and syndromes are syphilis, herpes, and hepatitis B. Though STDs often cannot be cured, they can be controlled. Because women show fewer symptoms, they are more likely to go untreated than men. By definition, STDs are spread by sexual contact. However, babies can contract them from infected women during pregnancy or birth.

To guard yourself from STDs, limit your sex partners, and use a condom with a nonoxynol-9–based spermicide. If you suspect you have contracted a sexually transmitted disease, see your doctor immediately. Left untreated, these diseases can have serious consequences—for example, they can cause women to become infertile.

Chlamydia, the number-one bacterial STD, infects 4 to 5 million people a year. Only half of those affected have symptoms—a discharge from the vagina or penis and burning or itching during urination. Left untreated, chlamydia can cause infertility, but antibiotics cure it.

Gonorrhea ("the clap"), a bacterial infection, is second on the list of STDs in the United States, with 2 million new cases a year. Common symptoms are pain or a burning sensation when urinating and a cloudy discharge, though often there are no symptoms at all. Untreated, it may infect parts of the body other than the genitals. However, like chlamydia, it can be treated successfully with antibiotics.

Genital herpes, caused by the herpes simplex type II virus, is contagious and cannot be cured. (However, medication can relieve symptoms and prevent a secondary bacterial infection.) The symptoms include an itching, burning sensation. Blisters appear within a week of infection (by genital contact). It takes 10–21 days for sores to heal. The disease then becomes dormant, reappearing in a milder form from time to time. About 20 million people in the U.S. suffer from genital herpes; there are 200,000 to 500,000 new cases a year.

AIDS. See "Questions and Answers About AIDS," p. 62.

STD Hotline: 800-227-8922.

Clinical Depression

The zest for life has vanished. It left without giving notice. Hours, days drag on into weeks, months, even years. The simplest tasks loom over us like impossible demands. Energy is gone. Hope and joy are only meaningless words. Truly, darkness rules.

It's natural to feel "blue" at certain times. When these feelings persist for more than two weeks, clinical depression is often the cause. If you, or someone you know, has felt that way for more than two weeks, clinical depression could be the diagnosis. Unfortunately, the majority of us who suffer from clinical depression don't recognize it. And since we don't recognize it we attribute our suffering to all kinds of external events.

Fortunately, help exists. Most of us who are depressed can be helped greatly by a combination of modern treatments. Depression is now one of the most treatable of all brain disorders. Almost all clinically depressed people can be helped substantially.

Don't let the words "mental illness" scare you. You, or your loved ones, aren't crazy. You simply

don't function as well as you did because you are ill. It's not "all in your head." You suffer from a real illness, just as real as the flu or heart disease. You wouldn't think less of yourself or someone you know because of a cold. For the same reason, you need not feel guilty or ashamed if you suffer from clinical depression.

The symptoms of depression aren't exactly the same for everyone. Some of us will experience changes in appetite, sleep patterns, and a loss of interest in activities we used to enjoy. Others will be plagued by fatigue, feelings of worthlessness, guilt, and hopelessness. Many of us will notice an inability to concentrate, persistent thoughts of suicide or death, overwhelming grief and sadness and other disturbed thinking.

Additional problems we might notice concern a change in attitude toward money and sex and problems with drugs or alcohol. In order to soothe our pain some of us spend compulsively, become dependent on mood-altering drugs, alcohol, or both. A distinct loss of interest in sexuality is also a common symptom.

If you, or someone you know, has four or more of these symptoms you should seek medical attention. Your suffering can be alleviated. Many depressed people refuse this type of help because they believe it won't work. That too is a symptom of the disease.

Reprinted courtesy of National Depressive and Manic Depressive Association.

Checklist

Check the following boxes if you notice a friend or friends with any of these symptoms persisting longer than two weeks.
Do they express feelings of—
☐ Sadness or "emptiness"?
☐ Hopelessness, pessimism, or guilt?
☐ Helplessness or worthlessness?
Do they seem—
☐ Unable to make decisions?
☐ Unable to concentrate and remember?
☐ To have lost interest or pleasure in ordinary activities like sports or band or talking on the phone?

☐ To have more problems with school and family?

Do they complain of—

☐ Loss of energy and drive so they seem "slowed down"?

☐ Trouble falling asleep, staying asleep, or getting up?

☐ Appetite problems—are they losing or gaining weight?

☐ Headaches, stomachaches, or backaches?

☐ Chronic aches and pains in joints and muscles?

Has their behavior changed suddenly so that—

☐ They are restless or more irritable?

☐ They want to be alone most of the time?

☐ They've started cutting classes or dropped hobbies and activities?

☐ You think they may be drinking heavily or taking drugs?

Have they talked about—

☐ Death?

☐ Suicide—or have they attempted suicide?

Source: "What to Do When a Friend Is Depressed, Guide for Students," U.S. Department of Health and Human Services.

SURVIVAL RATES FOR TRANSPLANTS
(After One Year)

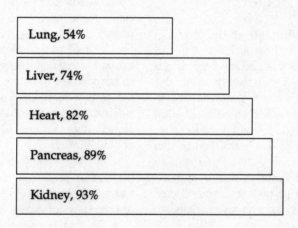

Lung, 54%

Liver, 74%

Heart, 82%

Pancreas, 89%

Kidney, 93%

Source: U. S. Department of Health and Human Resources

Doctors and Hospitals

Choosing Your Doctor

A study at the Health Institute of the New England Medical Center in Boston found that the more patients are assertive and involved during visits to the doctor, the better they do medically. It pays to be a savvy medical consumer—to choose your doctor wisely and to be involved in your own treatment. Your doctor, if a good one, knows the importance of the health information you provide and welcomes your commitment to follow through and cooperate on your own treatment. You should be a partner with your doctor in your own health care, not a passive patient.

How Can You Find Out How Good a Doctor Is?

Be careful when evaluating a doctor's record. Remember that a doctor who deals with patients at great risk will have a poorer "success rate" than one whose practice is devoted to people with minor illnesses.

♦ Call your local medical society or state medical licensing board and ask if your doctor has ever been disciplined. About 40 percent of doctors have been sued for malpractice at least once; however, if your doctor has faced several malpractice suits and lost some, paying large awards, you should investigate further.

♦ Call the **American Board of Medical Specialties** (800-776-2378) to check a physician's credentials. (See the list of specialties and boards in "Who Does What?—A List of Physician Specialties," p. 73.) Don't assume that all certification is meaningful to you as a patient; in order to be certified by some boards a doctor merely has to pay dues. Or write to: **Physician Data Series,** American Medical Association, 515 North State Street, Chicago, IL 60610 (312-464-5000).

♦ If you belong to a health maintenance organization or preferred provider organization, call and ask if there are patient-satisfaction surveys or other physician data you can look at.

♦ To find a pediatrician, write: **American Academy of Pediatrics,** Pediatrician Referral Service, 141 Northwest Point Blvd., PO Box 927, Elk Grove Village, IL 60009-0927 (708-228-5005). State where you live and the kind of pediatrician you are searching for.

♦ Be suspicious of a doctor who continually cancels appointments—he or she could be abusing drugs.

♦ Take a friend along to act as your advocate when you are very sick.

How to Select a Doctor

Ask your friends about their doctors—why they like them, why they don't. If you need a specialist, ask your primary care physician for recommendations. Health Maintenance Organizations often have physician referral services—you pick your doctor from a list, but a representative can give you information about those doctors.

Questions to ask:

1. How close is the doctor's office to your home or work?

2. Is the doctor board-certified?

3. What medical school did he or she attend?

4. Does the doctor accept your insurance?

5. How many years has the doctor been in practice?

6. Does the doctor accept credit cards?

7. How long will you have to wait for an appointment as a new patient?

8. With which hospitals is the doctor affiliated?

9. How old is the doctor?

You may want to consult with the doctor—in a face-to-face visit—before making a decision. This is usually possible, and costs are usually small.

When choosing a surgeon, ask how many times he or she has performed the operation that will be performed on you and what the death rate was. Often there is more than one choice of operation for a certain condition. In that case, your surgeon's experience with a new procedure should weigh in your decision, because statistics show that the more times surgeons perform a procedure, the better their success rate. For instance, laparoscopic operations are relatively new, and your surgeon may be inexperienced at performing them. If so, you may be safer sticking with the old surgical approach, or finding a doctor with more experience performing the new procedure.

Call your county medical board to see if anyone has complained about the anesthesiologist with whom the surgeon plans to work. Before the day of the operation, arrange to talk to the anesthesiologist about the type of anesthetic to be used, and ask if he or she will stay with you throughout the procedure (necessary except for local anesthesia). Mention any medical problems you have and what drugs you take (including illegal and over-the-counter ones).

How Can You Tell How Good a Hospital or Clinic Is?

In many states, agencies collect performance data on hospitals. You may have to twist some arms to get a look at this data, but in some states, pamphlets are available to the public. Generally speaking, municipal, county, and state hospitals injure more patients than other hospitals, probably partly because of under-funding and under-staffing. Best bets: private, nonprofit hospitals; hospitals with high percentage of board-certified doctors; hospitals with medical residency programs. Large hospitals rate better than small ones.

When considering using a hospital, ask someone in the Public Relations office:

♦ Does the hospital keep track of prescriptions by computer? Are computers programmed to warn doctors and nurses when one drug will conflict with another or the dose is wrong?

♦ Does the hospital require double-checking of labels on medications?

♦ What is the hospital's record on frequency of performing the operation, rate of complications, death rate?

People's Medical Society, 462 Walnut Street, Allentown, PA 18102 (215-770-1670). To order books: 800-624-8773, FAX 610-770-0607.

National Association of Health Data Organizations, 254B N. Washington Street, Falls Church, VA 22046 (703-532-3282).

Health Care Financing Administration (information from Government Printing Office): 202-783-3238.

Patient's Bill of Rights: Patient and Community Relations

Introduction

Effective health care requires collaboration between patients and physicians and other health care professionals. Open and honest communication, respect for personal and professional values, and sensitivity to differences are integral to optimal patient care. As the setting for the provision of health services, hospitals must provide a foundation for understanding and respecting the rights and responsibilities of patients, their families, physicians, and other caregivers. Hospitals must ensure a health care ethic that respects the role of patients in decision making about treatment choices and other aspects of their care. Hospitals must be sensitive to cultural, racial, linguistic, religious, age, gender, and other differences as well as the needs of persons with disabilities.

The American Hospital Association presents *A Patient's Bill of Rights* with the expectation that it will contribute to more effective patient care and be supported by the hospital on behalf of the institution, its medical staff, employees, and patients. The American Hospital Association encourages health care institutions to tailor this bill of rights to their patient community by translating and/or simplifying the language of this bill of rights as may be necessary to ensure that patients and their families understand their rights and responsibilities.

Bill of Rights

(These rights can be exercised on the patient's behalf by a designated surrogate or proxy decision maker if the patient lacks decision-making capacity, is legally incompetent, or is a minor.)

♦ The patient has the right to and is encouraged to obtain from physicians and other direct caregivers relevant, current, and understandable information regarding diagnosis, treatment, and prognosis.

Except in emergencies when the patient lacks decision-making capacity and the need for treatment is urgent, the patient is entitled to the opportunity to discuss and request information related to the specific procedures and/or treatments, the risks involved, the possible length of recuperation, and the medically reasonable alternatives and their accompanying risks and benefits.

Patients have the right to know the identity of physicians, nurses, and others involved in their care, as well as when those involved are students, residents, or other trainees. The patient also has the right to know the immediate and long-term financial implications of treatment choices, insofar as they are known.

♦ The patient has the right to make decisions about the plan of care prior to and during the course of treatment and to refuse a recommended treatment or plan of care to the extent permitted by law and hospital policy and to be informed of the medical consequences of this action. In case of such refusal, the patient is entitled to other appropriate care and services that the hospital provides or transfer to another hospital. The hospital should notify patients of any policy that might affect patient choice within the institution.

♦ The patient has the right to have an advance directive (such as a living will, health care proxy, or durable power of attorney for health care) concerning treatment or designating a surrogate decision maker with the expectation that the hospital will honor the intent of that directive to the extent permitted by law and hospital policy.

Health care institutions must advise patients of their rights under state law and hospital policy to make informed medical choices, ask if the patient has an advance directive, and include that information in patient records. The patient has the right to timely information about hospital policy that may limit its ability to implement fully a legally valid advance directive.

♦ The patient has the right to every consideration of privacy. Case discussion, consultation, examination, and treatment should be conducted so as to protect each patient's privacy.

♦ The patient has the right to expect that all communications and records pertaining to his/her care will be treated as confidential by the hospital, except in cases such as suspected abuse and public health hazards when reporting is permitted or required by law. The patient has the right to expect that the hospital will emphasize the confidentiality of this information when it releases it to any other parties entitled to review information in these records.

♦ The patient has the right to review the records pertaining to his/her medical care and to have the information explained or interpreted as necessary, except when restricted by law.

♦ The patient has the right to expect that, within its capacity and policies, a hospital will make reasonable response to the request of a patient for appropriate and medically indicated care and services. The hospital must provide evaluation, service, and/or referral as indicated by the urgency of the case. When medically appropriate and legally permissable, or when a patient has so requested, a patient may be transferred to another facility. The institution to which the patient is to be transferred must first have accepted the patient for transfer. The patient must also have the benefit of complete information and explanation concerning the need for, risks, benefits, and alternatives to such a transfer.

♦ The patient has the right to ask and be informed of the existence of business relationships among the hospital, educational institutions, other health care providers, or payers that may influence the patient's treatment and care.

♦ The patient has the right to consent or decline to participate in proposed research studies or human experimentation affecting care and treatment or requiring direct patient involvement, and to have those studies fully explained prior to consent. A patient who declines to participate in research or experimentation is entitled to the most effective care that the hospital can otherwise provide.

The patient has the right to expect reasonable continuity of care when appropriate and to be informed by physicians and other caregivers of available and realistic patient care options when hospital care is no longer appropriate.

♦ The patient has the right to be informed of hospital policies and practices that relate to patient care, treatment, and responsibilities. The patient has the right to be informed of available resources for resolving disputes, grievances, and conflicts, such as ethics committees, patient representatives, or other mechanisms available in the institution. The patient has the right to be informed of the hospital's charges for services and available payment methods.

The collaborative nature of health care requires that patients, or their families/surrogates, participate in their care. The effectiveness of care and patient satisfaction with the course of treatment depend, in part, on the patient fulfilling certain responsibilities. Patients are responsible for providing information about past illnesses, hospitalizations, medications, and other matters related to health status. To participate effectively in decision making, patients must be encouraged to take responsibility for requesting additional information or clarification about their health status or treatment when they do not fully understand information and instructions. Patients are also responsible for ensuring that the health care institution has a copy of their written advance directive if they have one. Patients are responsible for informing their physicians and other caregivers if they anticipate problems in following prescribed treatment.

Patients should also be aware of the hospital's obligation to be reasonably efficient and equitable in providing care to other patients and the community. The hospital's rules and regulations are designed to help the hospital meet this obligation. Patients and their families are responsible for making reasonable accommodations to the needs of the hospital, other patients, medical staff, and hospital employees. Patients are responsible for providing necessary information for insurance claims and for working with the hospital to make payment arrangements, when necessary.

A person's health depends on much more than health care services. Patients are responsible for recognizing the impact of their lifestyle on their personal health.

Conclusion

Hospitals have many functions to perform, including the enhancement of health status, health promotion, and the prevention and treatment of injury and disease; the immediate and ongoing care and rehabilitation of patients; the education of health professionals, patients, and the community; and research. All these activities must be conducted with an overriding concern for the values and dignity of patients.

Incompetent Physicians

According to statistics, incompetent physicians are disciplined far less often than they should be. The Public Citizen Health Research Group recommends that you file your complaints about doctors with the state medical board and with the Department of Health and Human Resources. Also, if you were in a hospital when the problem occurred, file a complaint with the hospital peer-review committee. Organize groups to improve medical quality in your area, and try to have a representative of your group appointed to the state medical board or the Medicare Review Organization for your state.

Public Citizen: 202-833-3000, x298 (for a list of questionable doctors).

Center for Patients' Rights, Box 4064, Charleston, WV 25364-4064 (304-925-8794).

National Center for Patients' Rights, 666 Broadway, Suite 410, New York, NY 10012 (212-979-6670).

Safe Medicine for Consumers, Box 878, San Andreas, CA 95249 (209-754-4408).

Unnecessary Procedures and Operations

At least 30 percent of all operations done in the United States are unnecessary, according to a recent study by the Rand Corporation. Doctors may spend as much $200 billion a year on unnecessary tests for fear of litigation. In an interview on TV's *Nightline,* obstetrician/gynecologist Herbert Keyser claimed that somewhere around 60,000 people die during the process of an unnecessary procedure each year.

The most common unnecessary operations are on women:

Hysterectomies: By age 65, three quarters of the women in this country will have had their uterus removed, according to John Smith, MD, author of *Women and Doctors.* More than three times as many hysterectomies are performed in the United States as in any other country, according to World Health Organization figures. Complications include blood clots, hemorrhage, and vaginal shortening, making intercourse uncomfortable. The death rate for hysterectomies is about 12 per 10,000 operations. Patients are also responsible for overuse of this procedure. Dr. Richard Soderstrom tells the story of one patient, a golf pro, who wanted a hysterectomy because she believed that premenstrual syndrome and heavy bleeding hurt her golf game. "I have trouble concentrating on my putt and I want that thing out of there," he remembers her saying. After informing the woman of all the possible complications, Soderstrom did the operation. "That woman sends me a Christmas card every year, thanking me," Soderstrom says.

Caesarian Sections. Doing a Caesarian does not always mean better health for mother and infant. Nearly half are unnecessary, according to a recent study by the Public Citizen Health Research Group. Caesarians may be performed for as trivial a reason as convenience, or for fear of a malpractice suit. Many physicians routinely do Caesarians on women who had them before, although the old rule, "once a c-section, always a c-section," no longer holds. More than half of women who have had c-sections can deliver their babies vaginally, according to the American College of Obstetricians and Gynecologists. Caesarians carry risks of injury to the infant (0.4 per cent of cases). The mother can suffer blood loss, infections, injury to other organs, increased death rate (four times more than vaginal birth). However, there are times when c-sections are justified, such as when the fetus is in distress, there is placental bleeding, or the baby's head is too large for the birth canal.

Episiotomies. Episiotomy, a surgical cut widening the vaginal opening to facilitate birth and avoid vaginal tearing, has been fairly routine in childbirth. Doctors once thought that it prevented later problems like relaxation of the pelvic floor and incontinence, and also that it increased sexual pleasure for men because it made the vaginal opening smaller when the cut was sewn up. According to a recent study by doctors at Jewish General Hospital and McGill University in Montreal, the procedure is ineffective and has none of these advantages, except perhaps, the last. To prevent tearing, it is better to allow the mother to lie on her side or squat, using a birthing stool, and most of all, to have patience.

American College of Obstetricians and Gynecologists, Resource Center, 409 12th Street SW, Washington, DC 20024 (202-638-5577).

Taking Charge

How can you tell that you are getting the best and latest treatment for what ails you? The **Agency for Health Care Policy and Research** (part of the U.S. Department of Health and Human Services) may be of help. This agency collects outcome data on thousands of patients to identify the most effective treatments—what works in the majority of cases. The agency uses the findings to prepare "clinical practice guidelines" for doctors and patient guides for some disorders. You can order these free guides by calling 800-358-9295, M–F, 9 AM–5 PM, EST.

To find out the latest treatment for a specific disease, call **Computer Retrieval of Information on Scientific Projects** (CRISP) at the National Institutes of Health: 301-594-7267. You can also call the **National Cancer Institute:** 800-4-CANCER.

Remember, it's your body. If more than one treatment is possible or if you object to a treatment, talk it over with your doctor. If you are anxious about your treatment, seek a second opinion from another doctor. If you decide to change doctors, ask that the former doctor send copies of your medical records to the new one. In the majority of states, you are legally entitled to copies of your records. To find out your state's laws, call **People's Medical Society,** 462 Walnut Street, Allentown, PA 18102 (610-770-1670; 800-624-8773 to order books).

Who Does What? A List of Physician Specialities

Everyone knows what a "medical doctor" is: a physician who has had years of training to understand the diagnosis, treatment, and prevention of disease. The basic training of a physician **specialist** includes four years of premedical education in a college or university, four years of medical school, and after receiving the MD degree, at least three years of specialty training under supervision (called a "residency"). Training in various subspecialties within the general specialties of internal medicine, obstetrics and gynecology, pathology, pediatrics, and surgery can take two to three years longer.

The complexity of the body's structure and the way it functions calls for high levels of skill in understanding body systems and in knowing the effect that each system has on the whole, in health and in disease. That is why, today, most physicians choose to specialize.

Specialists are doctors who concentrate on certain body systems, specific age groups, or on complex scientific techniques developed to diagnose or treat certain types of disorders. Specialties in medicine developed because of the rapidly expanding body of knowledge about health and illness and the constantly evolving new treatment techniques for disease. Today, no one doctor can hope to master the total field of medical knowledge or maintain skills in all diagnostic tests, treatments, and procedures.

A **subspecialist** is a physician who has completed training in a general medical specialty and then takes additional training in a more specific sub-area of that specialty called a subspecialty. This training increases the depth of knowledge of the specialist in that particular field. For example, cardiology is a subspecially of internal medicine; pediatric surgery is a subspecialty of surgery; and child psychiatry is a subspecialty of psychiatry. The training of a subspecialist within a specialty requires an additional one or more years of full-time education in a program called a "fellowship."

Training of a Specialist

The training of a specialist begins after the doctor has received the MD degree from a medical school, in what is called a residency. Resident physicians dedicate themselves for three to seven years to full-time experience in a hospital or ambulatory care setting, caring for patients under the supervision of experienced teaching specialists. Educational conferences and research experience are also part of that training. A doctor in training to be a specialist is called a "resident," although the first year of residency used to be called an "internship."

In each state, the privilege to practice medicine is governed by state law and is not designed to recognize the knowledge and skills of a trained specialist. The physician is licensed to practice general medicine and surgery by a State Board of Medical Examiners after passing a licensure examination. Each state has its own examining procedure to license physicians, and this board sets the general standards for all physicians.

Who Credentials a Specialist and/or Subspecialist?

Specialty boards certify physicians as having met certain published standards. There are 23 specialty boards that are recognized by the American Board of Medical Specialties (ABMS) and the American Medical Association (AMA), 515 N. State Street, Chicago, IL 60610 (312-464-5000). All of the specialties and subspecialties recognized by the ABMS and the AMA are listed in the brief descriptions that follow. Remember, a subspecialist first must be trained and certified as a specialist.

In order to be certified as a medical specialist

by one of these recognized boards, a physician must complete certain requirements.

How To Look up Certified Specialists

Certified specialists are listed in directories published by the American Board of Medical Specialties (ABMS). These include individual directories for each specialty and also the *ABMS Compendium of Certified Medical Specialists,* which can be found in most public libraries, hospital libraries, and medical libraries. Directories are also available in university libraries. Or, you could ask for that information from your county medical society, or from the **American Board of Medical Specialties,** 1007 Church Street, Suite 404, Evanston, IL 60201-5913 (708-491-9091), or from a particular specialty board.

DESCRIPTION OF RECOGNIZED SPECIALITIES

Allergy and Immunology: An allergist-immunologist is a certified internist or pediatrician expert in the evaluation, physical and laboratory diagnosis, and management of disorders potentially involving the immune system. Selected examples of such conditions include asthma, anaphylaxis, rhinitis, eczema, urticaria, and adverse reactions to drugs, foods, and insect bites, as well as immune deficiency diseases (both acquired and congenital), defects in host defense, and problems related to autoimmune disease, organ transplantation, or malignancies of the immune system. *Subspecialty:* Diagnostic Laboratory Immunology.

Anesthesiology: The anesthesiologist is a physician-specialist who, following medical school graduation and at least four years of postgraduate training, has the principal task of providing pain relief and maintenance, or restoration, of a stable condition during an operation or an obstetric or diagnostic procedure. *Subspecialty:* Critical Care Medicine.

Colon and Rectal Surgery: A colon and rectal surgeon is a fully trained general surgeon who has had additional training in the diagnosis and treatment of diseases of the intestinal tract, rectum, and anus. These include such anal conditions as hemorrhoids, fissures, and fistulas, and such colon and rectal diseases as polyps, cancer, colitis, and diverticulitis.

Dermatology: A dermatologist is a physician concerned with the prevention, diagnosis, and treatment of benign and malignant disorders of the skin and related tissues of the mouth, external genitalia, hair, and nails. The dermatologist also diagnoses and treats a number of diseases transmitted through sexual activity. *Subspecialties:* Dermatopathology; Dermatological Immunology/Diagnostic Laboratory Immunology.

Emergency Medicine: Emergency Medicine is the medical specialty that focuses on the immediate decision making and action necessary to prevent death or any further disability. It is primarily hospital-emergency-department based, but with extensive prehospital responsibilities for emergency medical systems.

Family Practice: Family Practice is the primary medical specialty which is concerned with the total health care of the individual and the family. It is the specialty in breadth which integrates the traditional biological and clinical sciences with the behavioral and preventive aspects of the practice of medicine and is not limited by any particular age, sex, organ system, or disease entity. *Subspecialty:* Geriatric Medicine.

Internal Medicine: A general internist is a physician who provides scientifically based, empathic care for the nonsurgical illnesses of adolescents and adults. This care tends to be characterized by a mutual personal commitment between doctor and patient, by stability over time, by substantial breadth, and by an appropriate attention to elements of human support, sensitivity, and concern. *Subspecialties:* Cardiovascular Disease; Critical Care Medicine; Diagnostic Laboratory Immunology; Endocrinology & Metabolism; Gastroenterology; Geriatric Medicine; Hematology; Infectious Disease; Medical Oncology; Nephrology; Pulmonary Disease; Rheumatology.

Neurological Surgery: Neurological Surgery is a discipline of medicine which deals with the diagnosis, evaluation, and treatment of diseases of the brain, spinal cord, and nerves, including the blood supply to these structures. *Subspecialty:* Critical Care Medicine.

Neurology: A neurologist is a physician concerned with the diagnosis and treatment of all categories of disease involving the central, peripheral, and autonomic nervous systems, including their coverings, blood vessels, and all effector tissues, such as muscle.

Nuclear Medicine: Nuclear medicine is the clinical and laboratory medical specialty that employs for diagnosis, therapy, and research the nuclear properties of radioactive and stable nuclides to evaluate metabolic, physiologic, and pathologic conditions of the body. *Subspecialties:* Nuclear Radiology (with ABRadiology); Radioisotopic Pathology (with ABPathology).

Obstetrics and Gynecology: A specialist in Obstetrics and Gynecology has been prepared to provide medical and surgical care for disorders that affect the female reproductive system, the fetus, or the newborn. *Subspecialties:* Critical Care Medicine; Gynecologic Oncology; Maternal and Fetal Medicine; Reproductive Endocrinology.

Ophthalmology: Ophthalmologists are concerned with comprehensive care of the eyes and vision. They are the only practitioners medically trained to diagnose and treat all eye and visual problems including vision services (glasses and contact lenses) and medical disorders of the eye including surgical procedures for treatment.

Orthopaedic Surgery: Orthopaedic Surgery is the medical specialty that includes the preservation, investigation, and restoration of the form and function of the extremities, spine, and associated structures by medical, surgical, and physical means. *Subspecialty:* Hand Surgery.

Otolaryngology: An otolaryngologist—head and neck surgeon—is a physician who provides comprehensive medical and surgical care of patients with diseases and disorders that affect the ears, the respiratory and upper alimentary systems, and related structures: the head and neck in general.

Pathology: Pathology is that specialty of the practice of medicine dealing with the causes and nature of disease. It contributes to diagnosis, prognosis, and treatment through knowledge gained by the laboratory application of the biologic, chemical, and physical sciences to man or to materials obtained from man. *General Certificates:* Anatomic and Clinical Pathology; Anatomic Pathology; Clinical Pathology. *Subspecialities:* Blood Banking; Dermatopathology; Forensic Pathology; Hematology; Immunopathology; Medical Microbiology; Neuropathology; Radioisotopic Pathology.

Pediatrics: Pediatrics is the specialty of medical science concerned with the physical, emotional, and social health of children from birth to young adulthood. *Subspecialities:* Diagnostic Laboratory Immunology; Pediatric Cardiology; Pediatric Critical Care Medicine; Pediatric Endocrinology; Pediatric Hematology-Oncology; Pediatric Nephrology; Pediatric Pulmonology; Neonatal-Perinatal Medicine.

Physical Medicine and Rehabilitation: Physical Medicine and Rehabilitation (also referred to as Rehabilitation Medicine, or Physiatry) is the medical specialty concerned with the evaluation and functional restoration of patients with disabilities regardless of etiology. Some of the more common conditions which produce the disabilities are stroke, multiple sclerosis, Parkinson's disease, amputation, spinal cord injury, cerebral palsy, arthritis, and trauma.

Plastic Surgery: The specialty of Plastic Surgery deals with the repair, replacement, and reconstruction of defects of form and function of the integument and its underlying musculoskeletal system, with emphasis on the craniofacial structures, the oropharynx, the upper and lower limbs, the breast, and the external genitalia. It includes aesthetic surgery of structures with undesirable form. *Subspecialty:* Hand Surgery.

Preventive Medicine: Preventive Medicine is that specialty which focuses on the health of individuals and defined populations in order to protect, promote, and maintain health and well-being, and to prevent disease, disability, and premature death. *General Certificates:* Aerospace Medicine; Occupational Medicine; Public Health and General Preventive Medicine.

Psychiatry: These specialists deal with diagnosis, treatment, and prevention of mental, emotional, and/or behavioral disorders. They also enhance the adaptation of individuals who are coping with stress, crises, and other problems in living. *General Certificates:* Psychiatry; Child Psychiatry; Neurology; Neurology with Special Qualifications in Child Neurology. *Subspecialty:* Child psychiatry.

Radiology: Radiologists are physicians specializing in the use of radiant energy (X-rays and radium) for diagnosis and treatment of disease. *General Certificates:* Radiology; Diagnostic Radiology; Therapeutic Radiology; Radiation Oncology; Radiological Physics. *Subspecialty:* Nuclear Radiology.

General Surgery: A general surgeon is a specialist prepared to manage a broad spectrum of surgical conditions affecting almost any area of the body. The surgeon establishes the diagnosis and provides the preoperative, operative, and postoperative care to patients and is often responsible for the comprehensive management of the trauma victim. *Subspecialties:* Hand Surgery; Pediatric Surgery; Surgical Critical Care; General Vascular Surgery.

Thoracic Surgery: Thoracic surgery encompasses the preoperative evaluation, operative management, and postoperative care of patients with pathologic conditions within the chest.

Urology: A specialist in Urology is competent to manage benign and malignant medical and surgical disorders of the adrenal gland and of the genitourinary system.

Approved Member Boards of American Board of Medical Specialties

ALLERGY & IMMUNOLOGY
American Board of Allergy and Immunology
University City Science Center
3624 Market Street
Philadelphia, PA 19104
215-349-9466

ANESTHESIOLOGY
American Board of Anesthesiology
100 Constitution Plaza
Hartford, CT 06103
203-522-9857

COLON & RECTAL SURGERY
American Board of Colon and Rectal Surgery
20600 Eureka Road, Suite 713
Taylor, MI 48180
313-282-9400

DERMATOLOGY
American Board of Dermatology
Henry Ford Hospital
Detroit, MI 48202
313-874-1088

EMERGENCY MEDICINE
American Board of Emergency Medicine
300 Coolidge Road
East Lansing, MI 48823
517-332-4800

FAMILY PRACTICE
American Board of Family Practice
2228 Young Drive
Lexington, KY 40505
606-269-5626

INTERNAL MEDICINE
American Board of Internal Medicine
University City Science Center
3624 Market Street
Philadelphia, PA 19104
215-243-1500

NEUROLOGICAL SURGERY
American Board of Neurological Surgery
6650 Fannin Street, Suite 2139
Houston, TX 77030
713-790-6015

NUCLEAR MEDICINE
American Board of Nuclear Medicine
900 Veteran Avenue, Room 12–200
Los Angeles, CA 90024
310-825-6787

OBSTETRICS & GYNECOLOGY
American Board of Obstetrics & Gynecology
2915 Vine Street
Dallas, TX 75204
214-871-1619

OPHTHALMOLOGY
American Board of Ophthalmology
111 Presidential Blvd., Suite 241
Bala Cynwyd, PA 19004
610-664-1175

ORTHOPAEDIC SURGERY
American Board of Orthopaedic Surgery
400 Silver Cedar Court
Chapel Hill, NC 27514
919-929-7103

OTOLARYNGOLOGY
American Board of Otolaryngology
5615 Kirby Drive, Suite 936
Houston, TX 77005
713-528-6200

PATHOLOGY
American Board of Pathology
1 Urban Center, Suite 690
4830 W. Kennedy Blvd.
Tampa, FL 33609
813-286-2444

PEDIATRICS
American Board of Pediatrics
111 Silver Cedar Court
Chapel Hill, NC 27514
919-929-0461

PHYSICAL MEDICINE & REHABILITATION
American Board of Physical Medicine and
  Rehabilitation
Norwest Center, Suite 674
21 First Street S.W.
Rochester, MN 55902
507-282-1776

PLASTIC SURGERY
American Board of Plastic Surgery
7 Penn Center, Suite 400
1635 Market Street
Philadelphia, PA 19103
215-587-9322

PREVENTIVE MEDICINE
American Board of Preventive Medicine
Department of Community Medicine
Wright State University School of Medicine
PO Box 927
Dayton, OH 45401
513-873-2300

PSYCHIATRY AND NEUROLOGY
American Board of Psychiatry and Neurology
500 Lake Cook Road, Suite 335
Deerfield, IL 60015
708-945-7900

RADIOLOGY
American Board of Radiology
5255 E. Williams Circle, Suite 6800
Tucson, AZ 85711
602-790-2900
SURGERY
American Board of Surgery
1617 John F. Kennedy Blvd., Suite 860
Philadelphia, PA 19103-1847
215-568-4000
THORACIC SURGERY
American Board of Thoracic Surgery
One Rotary Center
Evanston, IL 60201
708-475-1520
UROLOGY
American Board of Urology
31700 Telegraph Road, Suite 150
Bingham Farms, MI 48025
313-646-9720

Reprinted with permission from The American Board of Medical
Specialties.

Blood Supply

The medical profession takes extreme precautions to assure the safety of the blood supply to be sure it is free of HIV (the AIDS virus) and hepatitis A & B viruses. Since 1985, blood banks have been screening for HIV-1, the virus causing most AIDS cases in the United States. They also test for other viruses: hepatitis, B surface antigen, antibody to HCV, syphilis, HTLV-1 (which causes a form of leukemia), and HIV-2 (a rare AIDS virus). Even so, some tainted blood creeps into the supply. The chance of receiving it is 1 in 225,000 per blood unit for HIV-1 and 1 in 2000 for hepatitis B.

If you face elective surgery, your best bets are:

♦ choose a surgeon who is cautious about giving blood transfusions; *and/or*

♦ before surgery, arrange to have your own blood stored for possible transfusion, called in fancier terms autologous blood donating. In this way, you avoid contaminated blood and the chance of reactions against someone else's blood. Moreover, since you activate bone marrow by donating blood, your body will replace lost blood faster. Most people can donate a little under a pint a week up to three days before the operation. Each pint represents about 10 percent of total blood supply in an adult. You should do this no more than 42 days in advance (if refrigerated), 10 years if frozen. (If frozen, blood contains only red blood cells and it cannot be shipped between states.) Autologous donation is not possible if you have anemia or certain other conditions.

♦ insist that the surgeon collect then retransfuse your own red blood cells from your operation, a procedure called cell salvage. Some hospitals don't have the equipment for this, others do. The equipment, called Cell Saver, collects, cleans, and recycles blood into the patient. This is not possible in bowel or cancer surgery.

♦ speed up red-blood-cell production with presurgery shots of the hormone erythropoietin (EPO), so the body makes its own extra supply.

♦ another possibility is hemodilution, in which blood is expanded with sterile solutions intravenously before surgery. This can strain the heart and aggravate anemia.

Choosing Health Insurance

The rising cost of health care sparks heated debates, and the thought of financial ruin because of a chronic illness haunts most of us. The United States spends more on health care than any of the other industrialized nations, and yet our record on infant mortality, longevity, and other health measures is not encouraging.

The kinds of health insurance break down into two broad categories: fee-for-service (traditional health insurance), and managed care. Which you choose (if you have a choice) depends on your personal philosophy about health care and your general situation in life.

Fee-for-service allows you free choice of doctor and hospital and keeps costs down by limiting the total amount of insurance payments, demanding high premiums, and/or requiring copayments.

The disadvantage to you: unpredictable costs of medical care that is not covered, unnecessary medical care, often lack of coverage for preexisting conditions. With today's medical costs, copayments can cripple you financially. For example, a 20 percent copayment on an operation that costs $50,000 is $10,000. Requirements vary, but some insurers will not provide coverage for a preexisting condition (a condition you have before coverage begins) for six months to a year after coverage begins. The advantage to you: you choose your own doctors; you do not have to run the gauntlet of "utilization review"; you are fairly sure that you will get the treatment you need.

Insurance based on the "managed care" principle seeks to control medical costs by placing restrictions on your choice of doctor and access to specialists and hospitals. It almost always involves a "utilization review" of procedures, in which the insurer will pay only for treatments (nonemergency) approved in advance by an independent expert. The disadvantage to you: lack of choice of doctors, perhaps the chance of being undertreated, and perhaps the risk of delay in getting medical care you need. On the other hand, there can be no forms to fill out, no wait for payment, often no out-of-pocket costs, no dunning by hospital or doctor, no denial of coverage for preexisting conditions.

If you are young and in good health, you might be better off with a fee-for-service policy with high yearly deductibles and copayments. However, be sure there is an upper limit on how much you would have to pay out of pocket for a long-term illness. If you have young children or know you face high medical bills, your choice might be a more comprehensive managed-care plan.

There are myriad variations on each model:

Health Maintenance Organization (HMO): For a flat per-patient fee to employer or private individual, an HMO covers all medical care, provided that the patient receives it from HMO doctors and staff. An HMO either operates its own hospitals and clinics, paying the doctors and staff salaries, or (and this is becoming more popular) it contracts with doctors and hospitals to provide care for patients. Some HMOs do both.

Patients move through the system by first seeing a primary care physician (a "gatekeeper") who determines what kind of treatment they need. If, in his or her opinion, they need the services of a specialist, he or she okays it. More and more, patients see the same "gatekeeper" each time so that they can build a relationship with gatekeepers and so the gatekeepers can become familiar with their medical history. You get to choose your gatekeeper from a list. Gatekeepers get a per capita payment for patients, even if the patients never come to see them.

Preferred-Provider Organization (PPO): A fee-for-service plan by which an employer or group arranges with a group of doctors and hospitals to provide care for a discount. The reimbursement to patients is 80–100 percent vs. 50–70 percent for doctors and hospitals outside the system.

Point-of-Service Plan (POS): A flat-fee system in which patients pay only $5–$15 for a doctor's visit but are reimbursed only 50–80 percent of costs for care outside the system.

The Questions to Ask Yourself

Before you commit yourself to any health plan, make sure that you know the answers to these questions:

♦ Does the plan cover preexisting conditions?

♦ What treatments are excluded from coverage? Mental health? Acupuncture? Bone-marrow transplants? Drugs? Eye care? Experimental treatments?

♦ What out-of-pocket costs will you have to pay? Is there a limit on the yearly amount of out-of-pocket costs?

♦ If it is a managed care plan, does the pool of specialists include all specialties? How many primary care physicians and specialists are on staff? (If equal numbers, that's good—it shows that there is a balance between basic and specialized care.)

♦ What are restrictions on care outside the system? What happens if you become ill away from home?

How to Manage Managed Care Systems

Managed care systems can be manipulated. Demand the care you need. Ask for another doctor or a second opinion if you think you need a procedure or test and the primary care physician is unwilling to approve it. If you disagree with a decision, appeal it. According to a study by the General Accounting Office, only 12 percent of people denied coverage appeal the decision by utilization review. However, one-third of those who do appeal, win. Keep records of conversations with personnel and ask for written explanations. When you ask for a review, request a "specialty-matched physician adviser," a physician who specializes in the procedure under issue. If you need treatment, have it, then fight about it later.

Getting Health Insurance When You Are Unemployed

The Consolidated Omnibus Budget Reconciliation Act of 1985 (COBRA) mandates that businesses employing 20 or more people give their employees the choice of continuing their group health insurance coverage for 18 months after retirement or termination of employment for other reasons. You will have to pay premiums. You may also be able to extend beyond the 18 months.

You may also have the right to convert insurance to an individual policy. (This varies from state to state.)

Why not go straight to a private policy? Because when you are insured under a group policy, premiums tend to be lower and you do not have to wait to cover preexisting conditions.

Medicare

Be careful of Medicare scams. To avoid them, follow these rules:

♦ Guard your Medicare number. Don't give it to strangers, unless you are sure they have a legitimate reason to know it.

♦ If you use mobile labs, make sure that they are sponsored by a reputable organization.

♦ When you are given a listing of Medicare benefits you supposedly received, check it over. Did you really get all services claimed, or was the listing padded?

♦ Tell your doctor or hospital about any coverage by health insurance other than Medicare.

♦ If you suspect Medicare violations or scams, report them to the **Office of the Inspector General:** 800-368-5779, (10 AM–4 PM, EST, weekdays).

Publications explaining Medicare are available at any Social Security office or by writing to:
Medicare Publications, Health Care Financing Administration, 6325 Security Blvd., Baltimore, MD 21207 (410-966-3000).
Consumer Information Center, Department 59, Pueblo, CO 81009 (719-948-3334).

Fringe Medicine

Subtle and powerful connections between mind and body form the basis of most alternative medical systems. Some are ancient Eastern therapies, some date from the 19th century, and some are New Age. By and large, the medical establishment frowns on all but a few of these systems, though traditional doctors do believe in many of the basic tenets of alternative medicine. The notion of body-mind health, the effects of relaxation on the immune system, the importance of lifestyle in determining health, and the effectiveness of folk remedies have recently moved into a position of respectability even among the most skeptical doctors.

Ordinary people have more faith in alternative medicine than the average doctor has. In 1993, the *New England Journal of Medicine* stated that a third of Americans consult practitioners of alternative medicine. Over 30 percent of Americans have gone to a chiropractor and 6 percent to an acupuncturist, according to a telephone poll of 500 adults taken in 1991 for TIME/CNN. Of those interviewed who had not used alternative medicine, 62 percent said they would "consider seeking medical help from an alternative doctor if conventional medicine failed to help" them.

Be aware that the greatest danger of alternative medicine is that you might delay seeing a Western doctor for a dangerous condition that could be fatal. Also be aware that some herbal medicines can poison you, that poorly trained masseuses can injure you, and that some practitioners of alternative medicine are quacks. Your best bet: find a doctor trained in Western medicine who will recommend other therapies.

The following is an eclectic alphabetical list of some of the most popular alternative medicines, with an assessment of their acceptance by practitioners of Western medicine according to their scientific perspective.

Acupuncture. Traditional medicine in China for 2000–3000 years, acupuncture works for asthma, pains (arthritis, rheumatism, back pain), addictions. It has been proven to be an effective anesthetic. Animals respond to acupuncture treatment. Acupuncture *may* alleviate other medical problems: allergies, high blood pressure, gynecological conditions. The procedure: fine needles are inserted into the skin at points on energy pathways that connect to organs and body functions. The needles are left in position for 10 minutes to an hour. The theory: stimulation (with needles or heat) puts physical-mental energy flow (qi or ch'i) in balance. Western explanation: treatments trigger release of endorphins, brain chemicals that impede or override messages of pain. In some states, only physicians are allowed to perform acupuncture, in others acupuncturists without MD degrees are licensed. Acupuncture is sometimes covered by insurance. WARNING: Be sure the acupuncturist uses disposable needles.

The National Commission for the Certification of Acupunturists certifies acupuncturists after they complete acupuncture school or apprentice for three to six years. For information: **American Academy of Medical Acupuncture**, 5820 Wilshire Blvd., Suite 500, Los Angeles, CA 90036 (213-937-5514); **American Association of Acupuncture and Oriental Medicine,**

23632 Rockfield Blvd., Suite 102, Lake Forest, CA 92630.

Aromatherapy. Practitioners of aromatherapy, a Chinese herbal medicine, claim that cure is achieved by aromatic plant oils inhaled, massaged into skin, used as bath oils, and, rarely, eaten. True, smells do affect the body: peppermint arouses, eucalyptus opens sinuses, vanilla soothes. But as for other results, no scientific proof exists.

Biofeedback. When trained in biofeedback techniques, people can alter automatic functions (circulation, heart rate, jaw tension, blood pressure, chronic pain) through concentration while hooked up to a machine with sensors to measure those functions. A display or tone gives patients feedback on their success in bringing the function to the desired level. Biofeedback is considered respectable by the mainstream medical community—the Mayo Clinic uses it. It is considered effective in treating asthma, epilepsy, drug addiction, headache, incontinence, mild hypertension, pain, stress, anxiety disorders, scoliosis, Raynaud's disease (cold and painful fingers in cold weather). Many insurance companies will pay for biofeedback. For information, write or call the **Biofeedback Certification Institute of America,** 10200 W. 44th Avenue, Suite 304, Wheatridge, CO 80033 (303-422-8436).

Chiropractic. Founded in the 19th century, chiropractic requires six years of training in how to manipulate the spine and make other adjustments to the musculoskeletal system. More than 18 million Americans use the services of a chiropractor each year. The medical profession tends to accept that chiropractic works for lower back pain. By freeing the joints, the chiropractor relieves pressure on nearby muscles, joints, and nerves (the as-yet-unproved explanation). Some chiropractors believe in the subluxation theory—that when vertebrae are misaligned they put pressure on nerves arising from the spinal cord, and that this interference increases the body's vulnerability to other diseases. This is less accepted by mainstream medicine—in fact, many chiropractors themselves pooh-pooh this theory. Beware of chiropractors who suggest multiple full-body X-rays, which are costly and submit the body to too much radiation. Don't sign treatment contracts for a certain number of visits. Check a chiropractor's credentials with your state's Chiropractic Board of Examiners. Also contact **American Chiropractic Association,** 1701 Clarendon Blvd., Arlington, VA 22209 (800-986-INFO).

Crystal healing. A New Age fad, crystal healing supposedly cures through the agency of energy passing through quartz crystals and other minerals. Crystal healers claim to alleviate tension and tune up the body. There is no proof that it is effective.

Guided imagery. With the help of their therapists or a recording, patients in a trance-like state envision their immune systems fighting disease (chronic infections and tumors) and chronic pain. Using the senses to calm the mind may help by alleviating stress. Accepted by many doctors, guided imagery is used before minor surgery to aid in faster recovery. It heightens the immune response in cancer patients, but improved odds of survival are uncertain.

Herbalism. This ancient medical system heals with plant parts, eaten or rubbed on the body. However, modern science can duplicate the chemical structure of the substance in the plant that acts medically. Why not just use modern synthetic drugs, so the patient gets a standardized dose? Practitioners claim that natural ingredients in herbal remedies are safer. Assessment by the medical profession: some herbal medicines work, some don't; some are safe, some are dangerous. For instance, chaparral, which comes from the creosote bush, can cause hepatitis.

Homeopathy. The idea behind this 19th-century medical system: symptoms are manifestations of the body fighting disease and should not be suppressed. According to homeopathic doctors, natural substances and treatments that produce illnesses and their symptoms, in very diluted doses, should cause the patient's body to imitate the symptoms and cure the illness. Simply put, they believe that like cures like. The jury is still out on this one in the U.S., though homeopathy is respected in Europe. In European studies, remedies have been found to work in curing influenza, headache, and allergies. Contact **National Center for Homeopathy,** 801 N. Fairfax Street, Suite 306, Alexandria, VA 22314 (703-548-7790).

Hypnosis. Physicians use hypnosis to treat migraines, arthritis, nausea from chemotherapy, burns, and other ills. Patients enter a hypnotic state by focusing on a mental image, a voice, or an object. (One in 10 people is not suggestible.) Hypnosis taps into the body's ability to heal itself, but no one is quite sure how it works. It may provide a way of establishing communication with the limbic system, which controls involuntary activities like digestion and hormone regulation. On the other hand, hypnosis may just make you unaware of pain or other unpleasant body reactions—it changes your perception of your body, but cures nothing. Hypnosis has been labeled legitimate by the American Medical Association since the 1950s. For licensed practitioners: **American Society of Clinical Hypnosis,** 2200 East Devon Avenue, Suite 291, Des Plaines, IL 60018 (708-297-3317); **Society for Clinical and Experimental Hypnosis,** 6728 Old McLean Village Drive, McLean, VA 22101.

Maharishi Ayur-veda. Resuscitated by Maharishi Mahesh Yogi (known as the guru of transcendental meditation), this Indian form of healing works on an imbalance theory that relates respiration, circulation, and metabolism. It supposedly unblocks energy and banishes toxins. Treatment: meditation, massage, herbal medicine. Example: drips of warm oil on forehead for 20 minutes to help those with insomnia, hypertension, digestive problems. Acceptability by medical profession: on the fence, leaning toward the *no* side.

Naturopathy. Naturopathy goes back to 19th-century Germany's big fling with nature. Its medicines are air, sun, water, heat, herbs, massage, fasting, saltwater baths, relaxation exercises, psychotherapy, breathing exercises. It can include acupuncture, herbal medicine, nutrition. How can it lose? Acceptability by medical profession: yes and no. The U.S. has several schools of Naturopathy, among them: National College of Naturopathic Medicine in Portland, Oregon; Bastyr College of Naturopathic Medicine in Seattle, Washington; Southwest College of Naturo-pathic Medicine in Scottsdale, Arizona. Make sure your naturopathic doctor has a degree from one of them. Contact: **American Association of Naturopathic Physicians,** 2366 Eastlake Avenue, East, Suite 322, Seattle, WA 98102 (206-323-7610).

Reflexology. All roads to disease lie in the foot, according to practitioners of reflexology, which originated in ancient China. The big toe is linked to headache, the middle of the right foot to liver function, the left arch to stomachache. Through foot massage, "pathways" allegedly are cleared to other parts of the body. No trials have been done, so no objective proof exists that it works. No matter what else, it feels good.

For general information about alternative medicine, contact: **American Holistic Medical Association,** 4101 Lake Boone Trail, Suite 201, Raleigh, NC 27607 (919-787-5181).

Quackery and Fraud

If you think snake oil salesmen were a thing of the 19th century only, think again. They are alive and well, promoting cures to the desperate and gullible, while their victims often get sicker and sicker. Dr. John Renner of the Consumer Health Information Research Institute (CHIRI), Kansas City, Missouri, says that sales of quack medical devices and pills amount to $30 billion a year. Your best attitude is skepticism. Trust your doctor and major health organizations—the American Cancer Society, American Medical Association, Food and Drug Administration. Don't trust advertisements. No government agency can require prepublication approval; so by the time the government acts on fraudulent advertising, the company who put it out may have shut up shop and taken off for parts unknown. Money-back guarantees are only as good as the integrity of the company that issues them.

Watch out for:

♦ claims of "miracle cures" for life-threatening illnesses.

♦ diagnoses for common ailments like headaches based on fads.

♦ foreign clinics that get most of their business from the United States.

♦ single products advertised as effective for a variety of ailments (often effective with none).

♦ claims of a "breakthrough" ignored or held back by the medical community.

♦ a too-easy fix—"the lazy way" is a clue.

♦ "secret," "foreign," or "ancient" formulas, which are ordinarily just hogwash.

♦ testimonials from "satisfied users" without medical validation.

Some specific medical scams you should look out for:

AIDS cures. Blood-purification procedures, megavitamins, "secret ingredient" pills claiming to change HIV-positive to HIV-negative (this cannot be done).

Vision aids. Pinhole, laser, and "natural" eyeglasses, which are eyeglasses with pinhole lenses, touted as devices that improve vision by forcing eyes to be more industrious, less "lazy." They do not work.

Cancer therapies. Treatment centers set up outside the United States often have chosen the location so as to be out of reach of U.S. authorities. Be wary of claims that one device or remedy can diagnose or treat *all* types of cancer. Currently popular treatments use ozone or electrodes, which are ineffective. Also watch out for

—metabolic therapy, which includes special diets, megadoses of vitamins and minerals, and detoxification by coffee enemas. May cause infection, bowel damage, electrolyte imbalance.

—dietary cures that can lead to nutritional deficiency.

—immune enhancement through injections made of blood from the patient or others—this can cause hepatitis and infection.

Herbal remedies. Herbal remedies are not controlled by the FDA because no claims are made on the packaging. Though some work, others don't or can even be dangerous. For example, an echinacea-goldenseal combination, which tastes vile, is said to ward off colds. There is no real proof that it works.

Uncertified nutritionists. It is possible to order nutrition diplomas by mail from unaccredited "schools." Watch out for words like "certified nutritionist." Qualified nutritionists hold a Bachelor's degree or higher in nutrition or a related field from an accredited institute of higher learning. A registered dietitian (RD) also has completed an internship and has passed a national certification exam. Call the **American Dietetic Association,** 216 W. Jackson Blvd., Suite 800, Chicago, IL 60606-6995 (800-366-1655) for referrals. To verify a nutritionist's credentials, call 312-899-0040.

Medicare fraud. A medical equipment supplier calls people enrolled under Medicare, claiming that their doctor has ordered a piece of equipment for them. During the call, the supplier elicits Medicare and insurance information, which enables the supplier to collect for equipment from Medicare. While the supplier does deliver the equipment, it is unnecessary and never was authorized by a doctor.

Juicers. Turning a fruit or vegetable to juice does not increase its nutritional value, but in fact may lessen it. *Juice made with a juicer is enormously more expensive and no better for you.*

Arthritis cures. Supposed remedies include lemon juice, steroids, cow's milk, DMSO (an industrial solvent), snake venom, and megavitamins. The side effects can be worse than the arthritis. Arthritis cannot be cured. The most any remedy can do is relieve pain and inflammation and increase joint movement. The promoters of arthritis miracle remedies bank on the fact that arthritis symptoms often come and go.

"Fountain of Youth" drugs. Procaine hydrochloride derivatives (sold under various names, including Gerovital H3, GH 3, KH 3, and Zell H3) can cause anaphylactic shock. Zumba Forte, a vegetable-based aphrodisiac, can be dangerous to people with kidney disease. Methyltestosterone can cause liver cancer, jaundice, hepatitis, testicular atrophy, prostate cancer, edema. Cellular therapy—RNA, or ribonucleic acid, from tissues of young sheep or cattle or their fetuses—

supposedly reverses old age and treats various conditions from Graves' disease to Down syndrome. It is dangerous because it can cause allergic complications and can pass on animal bacteria and viruses, including a bovine encephalitis called "mad cow disease."

WD-40. No matter what its valid uses, the silicon spray WD-40 does not oil the joints so that arthritics can go dancing.

Muscle-toners. Electrical stimulators cannot "do the work for you." They can even be dangerous. Rely on exercise.

Chelation therapy. This does help in the treatment of heavy-metal poisoning, but it does nothing for any other condition.

Hair analysis. This is useful only to diagnose heavy-metal poisoning, a relatively rare condition.

"Smart" drugs. These are nootropics (sold under labels like Memory Fuel, Psuper Psonic Psyber Tonic, Powermaster, Mind Mix, Fast Blast) that promise to increase your brain power. The salesmen for these drugs often have impressive scientific vocabularies and talk glibly about amino acids and endorphins and the like. Look for scientific names like pyroglumate, Hydergine, piracetam, vasopressin, DMAE (dimethylaminoethanol). Some of these cause adverse effects like cramping. Vasopressin can trigger heart attacks in people who are prone to them. Even amino acids can be deadly in the wrong doses.

Report your suspicions of Medicare Fraud to the **Inspector General of the U.S. Department of Health and Human Services:** 800-368-5779.

Direct complaints about quackery to:

Council of Better Businesses Bureau, 4200 Wilson Blvd., Suite 800, Arlington, VA 22203 (703-276-0100).

National Council Against Health Fraud, PO Box 1276, Loma Linda, CA 92354 (909-824-4690).

Federal Trade Commission, Public Reference Room #130, 6th Street & Penn Avenue NW, 1st Floor, Washington, DC 20580.

U.S. Food and Drug Administration (local offices); hotline, 800-238-7332; 202-326-2222.

Physicals

The Health History

When you go to the doctor the first time, you will be asked to fill out a family history form, which usually includes information about present complaints and symptoms as well as your health history and that of your family. In addition, you will be asked to answer questions about your occupation, marital status, and so on.

Be ready to answer questions about:

♦ Your symptoms (if any): Where are they? What are they like? How severe are they? When do they occur? What makes them worse? What makes them better? What other symptoms are associated with them?

♦ Your health history: What childhood diseases did you have? What immunizations have you had? (Ask your mother, or look up old records.) Were you ever hospitalized? If so, when and for what reason? What operations have you had? Are you allergic? If so, to what substances? Were you ever injured? What were your injuries?

♦ The health histories of your close relatives: If dead, what did your relatives die of? What medical conditions and diseases did they suffer from? If you don't know, ask Aunt Harriet what Uncle Charley died of before you go in for your exam.

♦ Your medications: What medications are you taking (or have recently taken)?

♦ Your habits: Do you smoke? How many cigarettes a day? Do you drink? How often and how much? Do you use drugs? How often and how much? What is your daily diet? Do you exercise? How often and how long? What are your sleep patterns?

Tell the truth. Don't fudge on the number of cocktails you drink before dinner, or fail to mention the dizzy spell you had a week ago.

Keeping Health Histories

It pays to keep a running record of health information for each member of the family so that you will be able to give acccurate facts to the doctor. Keep records for each individual in one place, a computer file (with backups!) or a three-ring binder with a divider for each. Each person should have a summary sheet containing immunization record, information about birth, and list of medications to which the family member is allergic. On another page, record each significant illness, a drug inventory, a list of doctors.

What the Doctor Checks For

In general, the physician checks the body for infection, growths and swellings, inflammation, sores, abnormal tenderness, signs of healthy condition—for example, skin color. See p. 88.

ROUTINE MEDICAL TESTS

Test	How Often?				
	Age 12–20	Age 21–39	Age 40–49	Age 50–59	Age 60–74
Physical with history, may include blood tests.	Yearly, or up to 4 years between exams.	Every 5 years.	Every 3–5 years.	Every 2–3 years.	Every 1–2 years.
Blood pressure.	Every 3–4 years.	Every 1–2 years.			
Blood cholesterol.	Only if there is a family history of heart disease or a parent has high cholesterol readings.	Every 5 years, more often if high.			At doctor's recommend-ation.
Triglycerides.		Every 5 years.			At doctor's recommend-ation.
Glucose (fasting).	At 20.	Every 5 years.			Every 2½ years.
Dental.	Every 6 months.				
Vision.	Every other year.	Every other year.	Yearly.		
Hearing.	Every other year.	As necessary, every 5–10 years.			
Tuberculin; hemocrit or hemoglobin test.	1 test during adolescence.	As necessary (if exposed or at high risk).			
Urinalysis.	1 test during adolescence.	If pregnant.		Every 10 years.	Every 5 years.
Rubella screening (girls).	If any uncertainty, immunize.	Once (not at all if proof of immunity).	Not routinely necessary.		

Test	How Often?				
	Age 12–20	Age 21–39	Age 40–49	Age 50–59	Age 60–74
Pap smear, pelvic exam.	Yearly (once 18 or sexually active). After 3 normal tests, Pap smear at physician's discretion, sometimes every 3 years.				
Electrocardiogram.	Age 20, baseline.	Every 20 years for nonsmokers, smokers more often.			
Breasts or testicles self-exam.	Monthly for teens, when doctor recommends it .	Monthly.			
Breast examination.		Yearly.			
Mammogram.		Baseline at 35, then every year or two, as physician recommends.		Yearly.	
Skin exam (for signs of skin cancer).	Self-exam, every other month, from age 20.	Self-exam every other month. Yearly by dermatologist if history of heavy sun exposure.			
Chest X ray and lung-function test.		Yearly for smokers. Nonsmokers, baseline chest X ray at age 40.			
Cancer check-up; health counseling.		Every 3 years.	Yearly.		
Digital rectal exam.		Not necessary if asymptomatic.	Yearly.		
Sigmoido-scopy (colon examination).		Not necessary if asymptomatic.		Yearly, starting at age 50. If 2 negative exams a year apart, every 3 to 5 years.	
Fecal occult blood test.		Not necessary if asymptomatic.		Yearly.	

CHECKLIST: PHYSICAL

Body Part	What the Doctor Checks for
Blood pressure	Normal range: 100–140 (top number, systolic) over 60–90 (bottom number, diastolic).
Heart rate	Normal heart rate: 50–90 beats a minute.
Skin	Dark, irregular, bleeding moles or other skin discolorations, sores that don't heal.
Head	Eye movement, facial nerves, ability to swallow.
Eyes	Test of vision with eye chart or machine. Redness, response to light, checks for glaucoma, cataracts, changes in blood vessels, signs of hypertension, diabetes, retinal disease. (See "Eyes," pp. 23.)
Ears	Tests of hearing, inspection for infection, injury to eardrum, fluid, excess wax.
Nose	Check for deviated nasal septum, polyps.
Neck	Check of neck glands (lymph glands, thyroid), ability to move neck, pulse in carotid artery.
Chest	Heart rate and rhythm; abnormal heart sounds, murmurs. Breathing quality and rate.
Breasts	Lumps and discharge, asymmetry.
Back	Curvature (scoliosis), ability to move freely, signs of disc disease.
Abdomen	Organ size, masses, internal sounds, tenderness.
Genitalia	Male: sores and discharge. Female: discharge, pelvic exam to check ovaries and uterus. Pap smear, test for cervical cancer.
Rectum	Rectal tumors and hemorrhoids. Males: prostate gland.
Arms and legs	Circulation, flexibility, muscle strength, reflexes.

What Tests and When?

The experts do not agree on how often medical tests should be performed. In the chart on pp. 86–87, we have leaned toward the recommendations for more frequent exams. However, you should of course do as your doctor advises, and be aware that these recommendations are for those people with no symptoms and a history that does not suggest risk.

2

CRIME

STREET SMARTS

PROTECTING YOUR PROPERTY

ABDUCTED CHILDREN

SEXUAL AND DOMESTIC VIOLENCE

VICTIMS

STREET SMARTS

Avoid Being a Victim of Street Crime

Listed below are some precautions to take so that you will not be a victim:

♦ Always be aware of your surroundings. Criminals target people who are distracted, preoccupied, or in a daze. Be particularly careful if you wear a portable headset when jogging or strolling.

♦ Don't look like a victim. Walk briskly with your head up; stand tall; don't look down at your feet; appear confident.

♦ When walking, stick to the middle of the sidewalk and stay on well-traveled, busy streets. Avoid dark alleys, isolated streets, and wooded areas.

♦ Watch out for your purse; don't ever leave it unattended. When it comes to shoulder bags, safety experts disagree on the best way women should carry them. Some experts say that you should sling the bag strap over your head and carry the bag across your shoulder and chest. Others say that while this method is secure, you might get hurt if a thief is determined to steal the purse. Those opposed to the shoulder/chest method recommend that you carry the shoulder bag on the shoulder, but hold it securely against your body, in front of you. Whenever possible, safety experts suggest that women forgo a purse and carry belongings in a fanny pack around the waist. Further, regardless of what kind of purse you carry, some experts suggest that you carry money, keys, and credit cards in your pockets (not your back pockets); the inside pocket of a coat or jacket is preferred.

♦ Don't display valuables. Diamond earrings and Rolex watches are an invitation to thieves. Also, don't display large wads of money when paying for something.

♦ If you are out late at night, take along a friend. If you are alone and shopping at night at a mall, get a security guard to escort you to your car.

♦ When traveling on a bus, sit as close to the driver as possible; don't sit next to exit doors. Also, if you are the only person waiting for a bus, try waiting in a nearby restaurant or shop.

♦ Beware of pickpockets, especially in crowded areas like bus, train, and airport terminals. Carry belongings in a purse secured against your body or in an inside coat pocket or front pants pocket. Another way to foil a pickpocket if you carry a wallet in your pocket: wrap a rubber band around your wallet. If a pickpocket tries to lift your wallet, the friction caused by the rubber band will alert you to the theft.

♦ Be prudent when riding in elevators. Suppose you are waiting for an elevator, the doors open, and the only person on board is a suspicious-looking character. Don't get on. Or, if you are the only person on an elevator and someone suspicious gets on, you get off. When on an elevator, stand near the button panel in case you need to make a fast exit. If you are attacked, push as many floor buttons as possible—and hit the alarm button. Don't hit the stop button. If an attacker hits the stop button, do your best to pull it back out.

♦ Be as cautious in and around your car as you are walking on the streets (see "Carjacking," p. 101).

♦ If you are attacked, yell "Fire." If you scream "Police" or "Rape" or "Help," people who are safely inside their homes or office buildings may be reluctant to get involved. "Fire" implies that everyone is at risk and some people are likely to venture out to investigate the situation.

Safety at an ATM Machine

What's more likely to attract a robber than someone at a magic money machine? Where 80 percent of transactions are cash withdrawals? No wonder that the "crime of the 90s," muggings at automatic teller machines (ATMs), is something to worry about. Here's how to increase your chances of safety at an ATM.

♦ Look for a well-lighted ATM that is in front of the bank rather than behind it and in a place with plenty of foot traffic. Patronize ATMs with emergency phones, alarms, bright lights, mirrors that enable you to see what is behind you, and cameras that record transactions. If you live in a city, look for an enclosed ATM vestibule with a window so that passersby can see in.

♦ Avoid ATMs near hedges and other hiding places.

♦ Park your car in a well-lighted area. If you must use an ATM after dark, take someone with you. Use machines in open convenience stores or supermarkets rather than those outside banks.

♦ Be wary of strangers, especially those who crowd you or try to view your transaction. Don't accept help from anyone while using the ATM.

♦ Minimize time spent at the ATM. Have your card ready and forms filled out. After com-

pleting your transaction, put everything away and leave quickly.

♦ When using a drive-up machine, make sure all windows but the driver's are closed and the doors are locked. Keep the engine running.

♦ Never keep your code numbers in your wallet. Take the receipt with you.

♦ Be alert and aware of your surroundings at all times.

♦ If anything strikes you as shady or peculiar, postpone or cancel your transaction and go to another location.

♦ Report all ATM-related crimes to financial institutions and police. If someone does hold you up, surrender the money and your card, if the robber demands it.

♦ If your card is stolen or lost, do not give your PIN to anyone who calls about it, even if that person claims to be a banker.

Stalking

In legal terms, stalking is the "willful, malicious, and repeated following and harassing of another person." Every year about 200,000 cases of stalking are reported nationwide. Most victims are women who are stalked by ex-husbands, ex-boyfriends, co-workers, or strangers. It's estimated that one in 20 adults will be stalked sometime during her or his life.

Stalking usually makes the headlines when a celebrity is involved. Rebecca Schaeffer, star of the television show *My Sister Sam*, was stalked for two years and then shot to death when she opened the door of her home and came face to face with her stalker. An obsessive fan has repeatedly broken into the home of talk show host David Letterman. Other celebrities who have been stalked include Johnny Carson, Michael J. Fox, and Jodie Foster. The great majority of victims, however, are ordinary working women.

Stalking can start out with something simple like a gift or compliment. It can escalate into obscene phone calls, assault, kidnapping, rape, and murder. Stalkers can follow a victim's every move, write threatening letters, break into homes and destroy property, badger a victim's family and friends, kill family pets. This threatened violence has forced some women to radically alter their lives, causing them to change jobs and living arrangements. Even when perpetrators are arrested and sent to prison, women live in fear of the day when stalkers will be released and the fear will start all over again.

Who are the stalkers? Many are jilted partners who are angry and hurt and want revenge. Some are obsessively in love with the victim and want to control and dominate that person. Some feel habitually persecuted and need to fixate on an individual as the cause of their failed lives. Some stalkers appear to be quite normal while others suffer severe mental disorders.

Until recently, there was little that the police or the court system could do to protect victims. The only protection a victim could seek was a restraining order against the stalker. This court-issued order prohibits a stalker from coming within a specified distance of the victim. However, police can step in only when the order is violated or harm is actually inflicted upon the victim. Oftentimes, restraining orders turn out to be inadequate since stalkers tend to ignore them.

Today, 48 states have remedied this deplorable protection system by passing "antistalking laws." While the laws differ from state to state, most are written to protect victims *before* any physical harm is done. In order for the law to apply, however, a "credible" threat must have been made against the victim. What constitutes a credible threat is defined by your state law. Those who violate the antistalking laws are subject to arrest, imprisonment, and fines. To find out more about antistalking laws and restraining orders, contact your local district attorney's or prosecutor's office.

Protecting Yourself

♦ If you are a victim of stalking, call your local police department. If there is an antistalking law in your state, it may only take one phone call to generate some law enforcement action. If your state does not have an antistalking law, go to court and get a restraining order.

♦ Report any, and all, crimes committed by the stalker to the police—e.g., breaking into your home, destroying property, physical assault. The perpetrator could be arrested and convicted for any of these crimes. Even if an arrest doesn't happen, your complaints will be documented and that documentation may prove valuable for a future complaint.

♦ Inform family, trusted friends and neighbors, and co-workers about the stalking. If you know the stalker and have a photograph, get copies made and pass them around so that everyone can be on the lookout for the stalker.

♦ Document your case. Save letters and notes from the stalker; keep taped messages left on your answering machine; take pictures of destroyed property. Keep a journal of all incidents that pertain to the stalker.

♦ Take ordinary safety precautions. Make sure your home is secured with dead-bolt locks and outdoor lighting. If you think the stalker may have keys to your home, change all the locks. If you are being harassed by phone calls, change your phone number and be sure the number is unlisted.

♦ Be prepared in case of emergency. Make sure you have written down all phone numbers you might need: police department, local domestic violence shelter, friends, neighbors, family members. Carry those numbers with you and keep them in an easily accessible place in your home.

♦ Whenever possible, keep other people around you. Don't drive alone, shop alone, or go out to dinner alone.

Self-Defense

More and more Americans are choosing to fight back when assaulted. Either they fight back physically or use a self-defense device like a canister of chemical spray or a stun gun. Some escape harm and are hailed as heroes; others end up in the hospital. Nobody can tell you that you should fight back, and it's a very difficult decision to make. However, if you choose to do so, you need skill and confidence. The life you are saving, or endangering, is your own.

Self-Defense Classes

Here you learn how to use your strongest body parts—the heel of your hand, your fingers, feet, elbows, and knees—to strike vulnerable parts of the attacker: eyes, ears, nose, groin, throat, shins. The aim is not to deliver a knockout punch, but to buy time to escape. In other words, these classes teach you how to unbalance an attack, break the attacker's concentration, and inflict incapacitating injury. They don't teach you how to match physical strength with physical strength.

There's a difference between martial arts courses, like karate and judo, and self-defense classes. The martial arts include a wide variety of disciplines, including self-defense, but they take years to master and thus require a long-term commitment. On the other hand, self-defense classes are of short duration and have only one goal—how to fend off an attacker. You can locate self-defense courses in your area by calling YMCAs, women's groups, the police department; also, look in the classified directory under "self-defense."

When choosing a self-defense class, consider the following:

♦ A good class should teach you how to defend yourself verbally as well as physically. It should also teach you how to be alert for danger and how to yell effectively.

♦ A good class should teach you how to fight effectively if you are knocked to the ground. In many assault cases, victims are thrown or knocked to the ground.

♦ It's important that the class conduct fake assaults with fully padded "assailants." If you are going to be prepared, you need some real-life simulation.

♦ The techniques taught should be relatively simple. If they involve too many complicated steps, you're likely to forget them. Before signing up for a class, be an observer.

♦ Evaluate the cost of the classes. Some may be as little as $20 while others cost over $500. Talk to people who have taken the various courses and get their opinions before you fork over a lot of money.

Self-Defense Devices

Sales of nonlethal weapons like chemical sprays, stun guns, and personal alarms have hit record highs in the last decade. While the devices can be effective, police and other safety experts continuously offer an array of cautions:

♦ No device is 100 percent effective.

♦ Incorrect use can further enrage an already violent attacker. Also, incorrect use may cause you to be the victim of the device.

♦ Carrying such a device can give you a false sense of security. You may tend to take greater risks simply because you have the device.

Before buying a device, you should check with your local police department to see if the device is legal. Some states outlaw certain devices; others require that you take a class and get a permit to carry a device. Also, if you buy a nonlethal weapon, it's advised that you do take a course and learn to use it, regardless of whether your state requires instruction. Finally, no device offers any protection if it sits at the bottom of a purse or in a glove compartment.

Chemical sprays. They come in three basic varieties: tear gas (Mace is one brand); pepper spray; a combination of tear gas and pepper spray. Tear gas is directed at the eyes and produces tearing and burning. Pepper spray (made from hot pepper extracts) causes the nose, mouth, throat, and eyes to burn. Pepper spray is believed to be more effective than tear gas against drugged or crazed individuals and vicious dogs. Both, or a combination of the two, are effective for about 20 minutes. *Pro:* If used properly, chemical sprays can be effective against unarmed attackers. *Con:* You must aim the spray accurately and be downwind of the attacker. Otherwise, the spray is not effective or the wind could blow back the spray on you. Also, if you don't use it quickly and correctly, the attacker can grab it and use it on you. *When buying:* Read the labels to be sure you understand what type of spray you are buying. Check the effective range of the spray and be sure it has a safety cap. Canisters of spray should be easy to hold and operate with one hand.

Stun guns. These mechanical devices are about the size of a TV remote control and deliver a high-voltage jolt to an attacker. They also emit a crackling blue arc which is a further deterrent. A stun gun usually incapacitates an attacker for five minutes. *Pro:* A small-sized person can defend against a large-sized person. *Con:* You have to get very close to the assailant and hold the stun gun against the attacker's body. In order to bring down an attacker, not just inflict a little pain, you have to use it for four or five seconds. That can seem an unbearably long time for a victim who wants to get away from, not closer to, the criminal. Also, the stun gun may not be effective if the attacker is drugged or crazed or is wearing thick clothing that can weaken the effect of the jolt. *When buying:* Beware of cheap brands that make sparks and cause a little pain, but cannot immobilize an attacker.

Personal alarms. These screeching hand-held noisemakers are intended to attract attention and scare off an attacker. Legal in all states, they are triggered by a variety of mechanisms—like pulling out a metal pin, using an on/off switch, or squeezing the device. *Pro:* They are pocket-sized; some can be attached to handbags or act as key chains. Also, if an attacker grabs the device, it can't be used to hurt you. *Con:* You are out of luck if there is no one around to hear the noise. Also, people have become so used to the false alarms of car and home security systems, that anyone who hears the noise may not take it seriously. *When buying:* Be sure you are comfortable with the on/off mechanism. And try to purchase one that is not prone to false alarms.

Witnessing a Crime

It's shocking. A crime is committed in full view of a number of witnesses—yet no one steps forward to help, no one even bothers to call the police. Yet it happens often. One of the most prominent cases was the 1964 slaying of Kitty Genovese. She was stabbed to death in a residential neighborhood in the New York City borough of Queens. More than 30 people heard or saw the murder, yet no one helped or called the police.

Psychologists tell us that there are a number of reasons why people fail to get involved. Foremost is the fact that we are afraid to intervene, a very understandable fear when violence is involved. When spousal or child abuse is the issue, many people feel that the matter is none of their business, that it is a family problem that needs to be resolved within the family. And sometimes we just don't know if a crime really is being committed. Overall, doing nothing seems to be the easiest, safest choice.

Psychologists also tell us that when we see an act of violence, our first thought is how to stop the crime—like taking a weapon away from an assailant. When that option is rejected, we tend to forget that there are other, safer ways to help. Should you witness a crime, here are some things you can do:

♦ **Call 911** and report the crime. Tell the operator what is happening, where it is happening, and if an ambulance is needed. Don't assume someone else has called. If you don't want to reveal your name and address, you don't have to. If you are only *fairly* certain, but not 100 percent certain, that a crime is being committed, call 911. You may save someone's life.

♦ If you are at a safe distance from the crime, you can **create a distraction** that might scare off a criminal. Blow your car horn or scream out a window that the police are coming.

♦ **Write down** as much as you can about the criminal. Jot down a physical description including height, color of hair, clothing, any unusual features. If a car is involved, note the color, make and model, and license plate number. All of this information can be given to the police.

Citizen's Arrests

They sound admirable and heroic. Groups like the Guardian Angels, unarmed youths who patrol the streets of New York City, have made citizen's arrests. So have security guards. Of the ordinary citizens who make them, most do so when spotting shoplifters. But citizen's arrests are far more complicated and risky than most people suppose. Not only do you risk physical danger but you also may get sued.

The laws governing citizen's arrests vary from state to state. In general, you have the right to make a citizen's arrest if you witness a felony (a serious crime that oftentimes involves violence). Some states may allow a citizen's arrest for lesser crimes, called misdemeanors. Once you make an arrest, you must call the police. You cannot question the suspect, search the suspect, or obtain evidence against the suspect. Again, laws vary, so if you are interested in your state's law, call the police department or the district attorney's office.

You can put yourself in grave physical danger by making a citizen's arrest. Police departments strongly advise that you not intervene when an armed person is committing a crime, but instead call 911. Neighborhood watch patrols usually are advised to be the "ears and eyes" of the police but are discouraged from making citizen's arrests.

Besides physical harm, what other risk could you face? You could be sued. If the suspect is found not guilty of the crime, that person could sue you for false arrest or false imprisonment. Even if the suspect is found guilty and put in prison, you could still be sued for things like using "excessive force" to arrest the suspect. For example, a cab driver in San Francisco saw a crime in progress, a mugger stealing a woman's purse, and he pursued and captured the thief by

CALLING 911

About 70 percent of the U.S. population are served by an emergency 911 phone number. It is *only* for life-threatening emergencies like fire, a medical emergency, a serious accident, or a crime in progress. A recent survey showed that almost 50 percent of Americans confused 911 with 411 (directory assistance). You should *not* call 911 to report that your car was stolen, to report a broken traffic light, or to inquire about traffic or road conditions.

Once you dial 911, here's how to proceed:

♦ Tell the dispatcher what the problem is. Stay calm and don't ramble on; state the problem in as few words as possible. Say "My house is on fire," "My child isn't breathing," "Someone is breaking into my house."

♦ Give your location with major cross streets, if possible. Give your phone number.

♦ Answer any questions the dispatcher asks and don't hang up until the dispatcher tells you to. Some 911 dispatchers are trained to give medical assistance on the phone, like emergency first-aid measures.

♦ If you get a recording that asks you to hold for a dispatcher, don't hang up and dial again. Calls are answered in the order received.

pinning him against a wall with the cab. In the course of the apprehension, the mugger's leg was broken. The mugger was found guilty of the robbery and sent to prison, but he filed a damage suit against the cab driver for excessive force. The jury ruled in the mugger's favor and awarded him $25,000.

Protecting your property

Burglarproofing Your House

A burglary feels like an invasion—it takes a long time to get over the abhorrent images that haunt your mind when someone has entered your house, gone through your things, taken precious mementoes. Burglaries are difficult to predict. Some happen when you would least expect—in daytime when someone is at home, for example. Even so, there are indicators of risk: some households *are* more vulnerable than others.

Are you in a high-risk category for burglary? You *are* if—

♦ you are middle class. Most upscale neighborhood homes have elaborate security systems, so burglars are more likely to hit middle-class homes.

♦ you have recently moved. Half of burglaries occur in homes that have been lived in less than five years.

♦ you live in a house with easy access—with ground-floor windows, multiple entrances, an attached garage, located on a corner or near a highway for quick getaway.

♦ you have no alarm system. Houses without alarm systems are three times more likely to be burglarized than those with alarms.

Even if you are in a high-risk category, you can do a great deal to prevent burglaries. Police departments will conduct free security surveys of your house. They also sponsor Operation Identi-

fication, lending out engraving tools so that you can etch your name and identifying numbers on possessions, and giving away stickers stating that possessions are marked. Your police department will also help you start or join a Neighborhood Watch program. (See "Neighborhood Watch," p. 104.)

TIPS ON SECURITY

Keys. Don't hide a key outside or have a note on the door.

Doors. Make sure your doors are strong—metal or solid-core hardwood at least 1¾ inches thick. Burglars will kick in a door before they will pick a lock or break a window; it takes a much shorter time and makes less noise than breaking glass. Put hinges on the inside, otherwise a burglar may remove hinge pins and lift out the door. Sliding glass doors should have shatter-resistant glass. Invest in a good lock for your sliding glass door or put a broomstick or thick dowel in the door track (some experts say the lock is better).

Door locks. Make sure the strike plate (metal strip on door jamb) is secured strongly by at least four 3-inch screws. On doors used as exits in case of fire, install single-cylinder dead-bolt locks with 1½-inch bolts that lock on the outside with a key and inside with a·thumb knob. On doors that would not be exit doors in case of fire, install a double-cylinder dead bolt with keys on both sides. Doors from garage or basement should be secured with dead-bolt locks on the inside.

Safety chains can be torn loose by a kicking thief. Get a peephole for your door and consider installing a police lock (a bar that slants from door to floor socket) or horizontal steel bar.

Cover glass on or near doors with Lexan acrylic. That way no one can break the glass to reach the doorknob.

Window locks. Put locks on all windows. On double-hung sash windows, install key locks or pin them closed by drilling a hole at each corner, slanting from top of lower frame into bottom of upper frame, then putting a nail or eye bolt into each hole. If you want to let in air, not burglars, open the window 6–8 inches and make two more holes by inserting the drill through the holes in the bottom sash and drilling two more in the top sash. Use nails to anchor the window. Cover basement windows with iron grates. In high crime areas, consider bars on windows.

SECURING A WINDOW SO THAT IT CAN REMAIN PARTIALLY OPEN

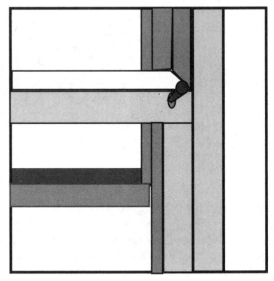

To leave the window open, but burglar-unfriendly, open it 6 to 8 inches and anchor the bottom sash to the top sash with a nail or bolt that penetrates both. Secure both sides of the window.

SECURING A WINDOW FRAME

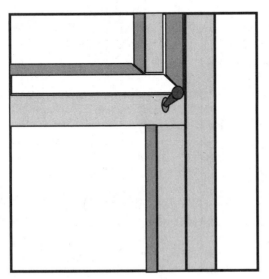

Insert a nail or bolt into a hole that reaches through both upper and lower window frames. Secure both sides of the window.

Landscaping. All windows and doors should be within sight of passing police cars or neighbors. Keep hedges clipped to below the bottom of windows. Use see-through fences. Eliminate hiding places for burglars, like bushes growing too close to windows. (However, *thorny* bushes planted under windows deter burglars.)

Outside lighting. Keep your house and grounds well-illuminated. A test: see if you can read your wristwatch on your grounds at night. If not, they are probably too dark. Put floodlights at each corner of the house. Cover them with wire mesh and put them up high. Electric wires should be high or in a conduit so they can not be easily cut. Leave lights on all night or put in infrared motion detectors that turn on if someone's in the yard.

Habits. Keep the house locked even if you are

working in the yard or going to a neighbor's house for only a few minutes.

When someone knocks on the door, pretend to be talking to someone and ask who's there before you open the door. Be careful whom you let in your house: burglars use various guises to get in: acting as a salesperson, as someone lost needing directions, as someone needing to use the phone, as a utility worker checking the lines. Ask for identification. Offer to make a call for lost souls, but don't let them enter.

Lock up tools and ladders that a thief might use to break in.

Don't leave empty trash cans out.

Be suspicious of hangups on the telephone. Burglars will look at your mail, find out your name, then call to see if you are at home.

Deterrents

Have nosy neighbors.

Keep a noisy dog (third best deterrent after a nosy neighbor and good visibility). If you don't like dogs or can't keep one, connect your doorbell to a barking-dog recording. Put a big dog dish in sight, and nail a sign on your door or gate that says "Fierce dog inside." Or buy a noisy bird.

Belong to a Neighborhood Watch group. Put a sign in your window advertising that fact.

Buy a security system. Post signs and stickers advertising the fact.

Protecting Valuables

♦ Keep lists of valuables with their serial numbers. (See "Taking a Home Inventory," p. 185.)

♦ Don't put the cartons from new appliances out in the trash unless you cut them up and hide them in bags.

♦ Don't put valuables in window view.

♦ Put your keys (car keys, keys to a safe) out of sight.

♦ Don't leave money in the house. Burglars know all about cookie-jar hiding places.

♦ Keep valuables in a bank safe-deposit box. If you must keep valuables in the house, some experts recommend that you spread them around

in various places so you don't lose everything. Safe places:
  a closet with a dead-bolt lock
  a safe bolted to the floor
  a hollow book surrounded by other books
  an old coffee can shelved with other paint cans
  behind books or under insulation.

♦ Engrave your valuables (computer, camera) with your driver's license number. Keep receipts and a record of serial numbers of possessions.

For a brochure on family safety and home security:

Westec Security, Inc., 100 Bayview Circle, Suite 1000, Newport Beach, CA 92660 (800-877-3287).

Where Thieves Look for Valuables

Thieves look first in: dresser and lingerie drawers, under the mattress, in the night table, on the top shelf in the closet, in shoe boxes. They also might look in the freezer, in shoes, under the lid of the toilet tank, in your washing machine or microwave.

When You Are Away

Make your house look as if someone is living there. If you use a lawn service or gardener, keep them coming. Make a deal with a neighbor (one you trust and know) to trade chores while one or the other of you is away: mow lawns, shovel snow, pick up mail and newspapers. Ask your neighbor to park his or her car in your driveway occasionally. Trade house keys so that your neighbor can bring in your mail and other things delivered to your house. Don't hide a spare key.

Ask your neighbor to open and close drapes and turn lights on and off at different times. Or you can use timers for the lights. If you do, make sure you program them to go on and off at random times in different parts of the house.

Let the police know when you will be gone. Some police departments will take special care to observe your house on patrol.

Otherwise tell no one that you will be away.

Make sure all your locks and lights are working.

Unplug the automatic garage-door opener and install slide bolts on the inside.

If you have call forwarding, use it. Someone will answer the phone if a burglar phones to find out if someone is home.

The day before your departure, check and lock every access and set your light timers.

Alarm Systems

Alarm systems deter burglars: they will pass up a house with a decal and will run if the alarm goes off. Ask police for advice on an alarm system for your house. Or call the **National Burglar and Fire Alarm Association**, 301-907-3202. Don't buy an alarm system over the phone (the "salesperson" *could* be a burglar).

You can choose from several different kinds of alarm systems. The least expensive effective setup includes a control panel, hard-wired magnetic contacts on two doors, a motion detector, a sounder, a keypad.

Some alarm systems just set off a siren. Others, for which you are charged a monthly fee, send signals to police or a monitoring station (which then alerts police). No matter what kind of alarm system you decide on, get estimates from at least three companies before you buy. Hire a company that has been in business for a long time.

Equipment should have UL (Underwriters Laboratories) approval, and there should be provision for battery standby during a power failure. If you choose a system that uses a monitoring station, make sure that the station operates on a 24-hour basis.

If you can't afford an alarm system, buy a set of decals and plastic signs to put around the house.

Thwarting a Car Thief

Every 19 seconds a car is stolen. That's about 1.7 million cars a year. The crimes cost Americans over $8 billion a year. It takes an auto thief as little as 7 seconds to break in and about a minute to drive away. And don't think that you are immune from car theft because you drive an older car. It's quite possible that the thief is after car parts, since a car's disassembled parts are worth three times more than the car as a whole.

The prevention tips in this article assume that you are not in your car when a thief tries to steal it. See the following section, "Carjacking," for information on how to prevent your car from being stolen when you are in the car.

BASIC PRECAUTIONARY TIPS

♦ Don't leave keys in the car. Believe it or not, in 20 percent of stolen car cases, the owners left the keys in the ignition.

♦ Park in a well-lighted area; stay away from secluded areas.

♦ Keep packages and valuables out of sight; put them in the trunk.

♦ When parking, turn the front wheels sharply to the left or right and set the hand brake so the car will be hard to tow.

♦ When parking in a driveway, face the car toward the street. A thief will have to tinker with the car in full view of anyone who passes by.

♦ Do not walk away from your car and leave the motor running—even if an errand takes less than a minute.

♦ When you walk away from your parked car, be sure the car is locked, the windows are closed, and you have the key in your pocket.

♦ Don't keep your license, registration card, or car title in your car unless state law requires you to do so. If thieves get these documents, they can use them to sell your car or impersonate you.

♦ If you have a security system, don't display a decal that tells a thief exactly what kind of a system you have installed. A generic sticker that says "This car is equipped with a security system" is okay.

♦ Avoid leaving spare keys in "secret" spots in or on the car; thieves know where to look.

♦ Keep the car locked while in the garage.

♦ Don't leave the garage-door opener in the car. If your car is stolen, you have given the thief access to your home.

♦ When parking in an attended parking lot, give the attendant your ignition key only; make sure the key you leave has no key identification number on it.

ANTI-THEFT DEVICES

Car security devices are not 100 percent effective, but they can stop an amateur thief and frustrate a professional thief. Listed below are brief descriptions of the most commonly used devices. When purchasing a device, always check out what's new on the market—more sophisticated devices are always being designed. In addition, check with your insurance company since many companies offer discounts on premiums if you use an anti-theft device.

Alarms. A noisy alarm is activated by either motion (lifting, shaking, bumping, towing), glass breakage (broken windows), or shock (sharp hits to the car). Usually, you can adjust the sensitivity of these alarms so they won't go off when the wind blows or a cat jumps on the hood. Be aware of how long the alarm will sound so that false alarms won't anger neighbors; some states have laws that limit how long an alarm can sound. Insurance companies favor "passive" alarms, which automatically activate when you leave the car, over "active" alarms, which require an action by the driver to be activated (like using a button, key, or remote control).

Tracking systems. A transmitter is installed in the car and emits signals which the police can track. These systems are expensive to buy and install and usually there is a monthly fee to pay. Insurance discounts, however, are bigger for tracking systems than they are for alarm systems.

Engine disablers. These devices are attached to the ignition system or fuel pump. The thief may successfully break into your car but won't be able to drive it away. Disablers can be activated automatically or manually.

Mechanical devices. These are the least expensive anti-theft devices:

♦ Steering-wheel locks. Some lock the steering wheel; some lock the steering wheel to the brake pedal. The intent is the same: to immobilize the controls. While these devices are very popular, professional thieves slice through the steering wheel and slip the locks off.

♦ Collars. A steel or alloy cover is fitted over the steering column, preventing access to the ignition.

♦ Window etching. The car's vehicle identification number (VIN) is chemically etched, or engraved, on car windows and body parts. Windows must be replaced before a stolen car can be sold. Also, etching makes it more difficult for thieves who strip cars to sell the parts.

Carjacking

Carjacking is the armed theft of an occupied vehicle. While carjacking represents only about 2 percent of all car thefts, it is especially frightening because it can involve violence. Sometimes the thief wants the car to sell (as a whole or in parts); sometimes the thief wants to rob the driver and steal the car. The carjacker may want the car to commit other crimes. Or the thief may simply be out for a joyride.

Carjackings happen in all parts of the country and involve cars of all makes and models. Oddly enough, many experts say that one of the reasons carjacking is on the rise is that more people are installing anti-theft devices in their cars. Since taking a parked, secured car is getting harder, thieves steal cars when people are in them.

Carjacking is a federal crime that carries a 15-year minimum sentence. If someone is injured, another 10 years can be added to the sentence.

If someone is killed, the death penalty can be imposed.

Where do most carjackings occur? While they can happen just about anywhere, they are more likely to happen at red lights and stop signs, at shopping malls and convenience stores, at ATMs (automatic teller machines), at highway exit and entry ramps or anywhere that drivers slow down or stop. They also happen in self-serve gas stations, in parking garages and parking lots. Most carjackings happen at night, between the hours of 10 PM and 2 AM.

Favorite Ploys of Carjackers

Bump and rob. Carjackers stage a minor rear-end accident. When you get out to investigate and exchange information, one thief distracts you (or threatens you with a weapon) and another drives off in your car. You should be suspicious of these minor accidents, especially if there is no apparent reason for it—if you braked suddenly and collided with the car behind you, for example. If you don't feel the accident is real and you do not feel comfortable getting out of your car, don't do it. Motion to the other driver to follow you (don't even roll down the window) and drive to the nearest police station, fire station, hospital, or a well-lighted busy area. Put on your emergency flashers.

Good Samaritan acts. Carjackers stop to "help" drivers whose cars have broken down. Or, a carjacker causes a problem (e.g., lets the air out of your tire while you are in a store), then offers to help you fix the problem. Always be careful when accepting help from strangers.

Impersonating police officers. You stop your car because the car behind you has dash- or roof-mounted flashing lights, but the other driver turns out to be a criminal, not a police officer. It's easy for a thief to buy flashing red lights or spotlights that can be mounted on a car. And it's not that difficult to obtain a uniform that resembles a police uniform. So what do you do? First of all, ask yourself if you have broken any laws. If you don't think that you have, be cautious. When driving during daylight hours, it's reasonably easy

to see if the car behind you is indeed an official police car driven by a uniformed officer. Remember that it's unusual for a plain clothes officer in an unmarked car to pull over a motorist for a traffic violation. And you need to be very careful when driving at night. If you do think that you may be in danger, here's how to proceed: Signal to the officer to follow you, put on your emergency flasher lights, and drive to a well-lighted populated area. Drive at or below the speed limit. Once stopped, if you still don't feel comfortable, stay in the car (doors locked, windows up) and ask to see a badge and identification card (make sure the picture on the ID matches the person).

Protecting Yourself Against Carjacking

♦ Always be aware of your surroundings, especially in isolated or unfamiliar areas.

♦ When driving, roll up the windows and lock the doors. Keep purses, wallets, and other valuables out of sight.

♦ When stopping at a red light or stop sign, leave ample space between you and the car in front of you—in case you need to drive away quickly.

♦ When driving in slow traffic, stay in the center lane, not the curb lane where you are easy prey for carjackers.

♦ Drive on well-lighted, well-traveled streets and park in well-lighted areas. Don't walk across a parking lot alone if someone seems to be loitering around your car. Either wait and walk with other people or ask a nearby store to provide you with an escort. When you approach your car, have your key in hand.

♦ Keep your home driveway well-illuminated. If you have a garage, buy an automatic garage-door opener. And stay inside your locked car until you have closed the garage door.

♦ Plan your route in advance, avoid driving in high crime areas, don't take unfamiliar shortcuts.

♦ Minimize your late-night driving. If you must drive, take a friend along.

♦ If you suspect someone is following you, don't drive home—drive to a police station.

♦ When renting a car, get one without rental

stickers or special rental car license plates. They identify you as a tourist; thieves will assume you are carrying plenty of money.

♦ When confronted with an armed carjacker, don't resist. Give up the car and get yourself to safety. You can get another car; you can't get another life.

Children and Guns in the Home

About half of all American households have at least one firearm (a total of about 200 million firearms); about 25 percent of the firearms are handguns. It's sadly ironic that these guns often hurt or kill the very people they were intended to protect—family members. According to the Center to Prevent Handgun Violence, nearly 90 percent of the accidental shootings of children ages 14 and under happen in the home. In addition, handguns in the home are finding their way into the schools. Schools are being forced to use metal detectors, hire additional security guards, and conduct searches of students' lockers. Here are just a few statistics, taken from prominent national studies, regarding children and guns:

♦ Every day 12 children, aged 19 and under, die in gun-related accidents, suicides, and homicides.

♦ One out of six pediatricians nationwide has treated a young gunshot victim.

♦ Gunshot wounds are the leading cause of death for both black and white teenage boys in America.

♦ Every six hours a youth aged 10–19 commits suicide with a firearm. The odds that potentially suicidal teenagers will kill themselves go up 75-fold when a gun is kept in the home.

♦ About 100,000 students take guns to school every day.

♦ A gun in the home is more likely to be used to kill a family member or friend than a criminal intruder.

♦ A third of all high school students say they can get a gun whenever they want it.

Kids are prone to pick up a gun for any number of reasons. They are curious or want to impress their friends; they are afraid and see a gun as a means of protection. Overall, they have learned that guns and violence are an integral part of our society. Using guns to settle disputes is a model we see frequently in movies, television programs, in news stories of real-life events. Often, children cannot tell the difference between reality and make-believe. After all, TV and movie characters dodge lots of bullets and never get hurt. And a child's favorite actor gets killed in one show but turns up next week on another show.

Children need to be taught that guns are dangerous, that there is a difference between make-believe and real violence, and that arguments and fights should not be settled with guns. While these responsibilities lie primarily with parents, schools increasingly are taking action. Currently, there are a number of gun-awareness programs being implemented in schools. For more information on these programs, contact: **Center to Prevent Handgun Violence,** 1225 Eye Street NW, Suite 1100, Washington, DC 20005 (202-289-7319).

If You Have a Gun in the Home

A survey done by the Harvard School of Public Health revealed that one-third of gun owners store their weapons loaded and more than half fail to keep their guns locked up. This negligence has caused a number of states to pass child safety laws that hold adult gun owners criminally responsible if minor children use a firearm to kill or injure themselves or someone else. Most laws cover any loaded firearm, including handguns, rifles, and shotguns.

The best way to ensure that a child is not harmed by a gun in the home is not to have a gun in the home. Those who choose to have a gun in the home need to take adequate safety measures to prevent minors from gaining access to weapons. There are many kinds of gun-securing devices for sale, and some cost as little as $15. They range from gun cases and padlocks to trigger-locking devices to gun safes. Consult with police or other experts to determine which safety device best serves your needs.

While gun safety begins in your own home, it also needs to take place in the homes where your child visits and plays. Talk to the adults in these homes and make sure that if guns are around, your child is protected. Do this no matter how uncomfortable you may be in discussing the subject. Your child's life could be at stake.

Neighborhood Watch

Make a difference in your neighborhood by joining the Neighborhood Watch program or starting one, if none exists. In Neighborhood Watch, neighbors band together and watch out for each other, working with each other and with local law enforcement agencies to reduce crime and fight apathy.

Neighborhood Watch may also be known as Home Alert, Citizen's Crime Watch, or Block Watch. Whatever the name, it works. Programs like this can reduce crime as much as 50 percent. It's estimated that more than 19 million Americans participate in Neighborhood Watch groups. By cooperating with each other in a common endeavor, people in the neighborhood develop a sense of solidarity and civic pride.

Planning phase. Start by contacting your police department, which probably already has a support program in place. A small group of citizens and a representative from the police department should hold a preliminary meeting to plan the program. This initial group may include members of homeowners' or civic organizations. Use a map of the community to determine the boundaries of the watch's efforts.

Approach a school, police station, or church for a place to hold a larger general meeting, negotiating time and date. Then post notices and send out letters about the meeting. Ask one person from the planning committee and a police representative to speak at the first meeting. A typical and successful agenda: purpose of the meeting, history of the group so far, benefits of a watch group, how to organize and operate a watch group, selection of coordinators and block captains. At the meeting exchange names, home and work phone numbers.

Organization is important. Try to involve everybody: single people, owners of neighborhood businesses, teenagers. Ask for help. Publicize meetings through newspapers, flyers, radio and television stations, announcements in other groups' meetings and bulletins, going door-to-door. Forge strong links with other organizations—other Neighborhood Watch groups and your state's crime prevention association. This will increase your chances of success and will bring in ideas from the outside.

Include socializing as part of the meeting. For instance, bring in refreshments, allow children to attend. Incorporate neighborly activities in your plans: visiting someone who is housebound or checking your immediate neighbor's house when he or she is away. Get to know your neighbors and their routines, without being a busybody.

Forms of Watch Programs

♦ Passive (stationary) watch. Residents keep an eye on the neighborhood in the ordinary course of their lives. Meetings are held quarterly or monthly. Best suited for dense or moderately dense neighborhoods.

♦ Mobile patrols. Law enforcement staff trains citizens to patrol their neighborhood and report suspicious activity with CB or private-channel radio systems. Citizens do not intervene; they only report. Best where homes are far apart.

♦ Walking patrols. Citizens walk in pairs using hand-held radios. Good for inner-city blocks and high-rise buildings.

Crime Prevention Council, 1700 K Street NW, 2nd Floor, Washington, DC 20006-3817 (202-466-6272).

National Sheriffs' Association, 1450 Duke Street, Alexandria, VA 22314-3490 (703-836-7827).

ABDUCTED CHILDREN

National Center For Missing and Exploited Children

A national study by the U.S. Department of Justice showed that in 1988 there were: 354,000 children abducted by family members; 4600 children abducted by nonfamily members; 114,600 attempted child abductions by nonfamily members; 450,700 children who ran away from home.

The National Center for Missing and Exploited Children (NCMEC) is a private, nonprofit organization established by congressional mandate, and it works in cooperation with the U.S. Department of Justice. NCMEC serves as a clearinghouse of information on missing and exploited children, offers advice and assistance to law enforcement agencies and parents in the search for a missing child, makes arrangements to display pictures of missing children nationwide, and offers the use of a toll-free phone number, 800-THE-LOST (800-843-5678), to report information that could lead to the recovery of a missing child.

Through its national hotline number NCMEC has handled more than 700,000 calls, including almost 100,000 calls reporting "sightings" of missing children. It distributes photographs of missing children through its extensive network of 20 federal agencies and more than 1600 private-sector companies. To date, about one in seven children featured in the campaigns has been found.

NCMEC distributes a number of free publications, some for professionals who work on missing children cases, some for parents and children. Among the publications are "Child Protection," "My 8 Rules for Safety" (for children), and "Family Abduction." For a list of NCMEC publications: **National Center for Missing and Exploited Children,** 2101 Wilson Blvd., Suite 500, Arlington, VA 22202-3052.

NCMEC states that there are some actions that parents should take to prepare for the *remote* possibility that a child may someday be missing. These steps are:

1. Keep a complete description of the child. This description must include color of hair, color of eyes, height, weight, and date of birth. In addition, the description should contain their identifiers—eyeglasses or contact lenses, braces on teeth, pierced ears, and other unique physical attributes. The complete description must be written down.

2. Take color photographs of your child every six months. Photographs should be of high quality and in sharp focus so that the child is easily recognizable. Head-and-shoulder portraits from different angles, such as those taken by school photographers, are preferable.

3. Have your dentist prepare dental charts for your child, and be sure that they are updated each time an examination or dental work is performed. Make sure that your dentist maintains accurate,

up-to-date dental charts and X rays on your child as a routine part of his or her normal office procedure. If you move, you should get a copy from your former dentist to keep yourself until a new dentist is found.

4. Know where your child's medical records are located. Medical records, particularly X rays, can be invaluable in helping to identify a recovered child. It is important to have all permanent scars, birthmarks, blemishes, and broken bones recorded. You should find out from your child's doctor where such records are located and how you can obtain them if the need arises.

5. Arrange with your local police department to have your child fingerprinted. In order for fingerprints to be useful in identifying a person, they must be properly taken. Your police department has trained personnel to be sure that they are useful. The police department will give you the fingerprint card and will not keep a record of the child's prints.

What to Do if Your Child Is Abducted

If you believe that your child has been abducted, you need to act immediately. Here are some steps to take:

1. Contact the **police.** Give them as much information as possible concerning the abduction. Provide police with a recent photograph of the child as well as fingerprints and dental records.

2. Make sure the police department enters your child's description into the **National Crime Information Center** (NCIC) computer. If you have difficulty getting this done, contact the FBI and ask that they enter your child's description into NCIC under the Missing Children's Act of 1982. Also, if your state has a clearinghouse for missing children, ask the police to give information on your child to the clearinghouse.

3. Call the **National Center for Missing and Exploited Children** (NCMEC), 800-843-5678. An operator will take down information

concerning your child, and a case manager will follow up and provide you with assistance.

4. Get in touch with nonprofit organizations that help to find missing children. The NCMEC and the police department can provide you with referrals. Some nationally recognized groups: **Vanished Children's Alliance,** 1407 Parkmoor Avenue, Suite 200, San Jose, CA 95126 (408-971-4822); **Operation Lookout/National Center for Missing Youth,** 12128 Cyrus Way, Building B, Suite 400, Mukilteo, WA 98275-5706 (800-782-7335 or 206-771-7335); **Missing Children Help Center,** National Missing Children Division/National Child Safety Council, 410 Ware Blvd., Suite 400, Tampa, FL 33619 (800-USA-KIDS or 813-623-KIDS); **Child Find of America** (parental abductions only), PO Box 277, New Paltz, NY 12561-9277 (914-255-1848).

5. Have **posters** on your missing child printed and distributed (see sample from NCMEC). NCMEC and other missing children's organizations can assist you with this task.

6. There are **actions you can take** even though the police are working on your case. Ask your child's school to notify you if anyone requests your child's records. Likewise, flag any requests for your child's medical records and call the Bureau of Vital Statistics to flag the child's birth certificate.

If you learn the identity of the abductor, there are a great many things you can do. Check with the abductor's bank to find out if an account has been closed and if funds have been transferred to another bank. Also, check with the abductor's last employer, credit card companies, insurance companies, etc. Call the post office to see if any mail is being forwarded. In other words, make a list of any person or group that could know, or may eventually know, the abductor's whereabouts. Be aware, however, that in some instances you will not be able to obtain information without a court order or without the intervention of the police.

7. When the abductor is a parent, there are **legal steps** you need to take. First of all, you need to obtain legal custody of your child if you

Have You Seen This Child?

WANTED
Arrest Warrant
Issued

MISSING CHILD

OPTIONAL

PHOTO
OF ABDUCTOR
(if warrant issued
for arrest)

CHILD'S PHOTO

CHILD'S PHOTO
DIFFERENT ANGLE

(Date of Photo)   (Date of Photo)   (Date of Photo)

NAME OF ABDUCTOR   NAME OF CHILD
Date of Birth: Date of Birth: Age: Race:
Ht.:   Wt.:   Grade in School:
Hair: Eyes: Ht.:   Wt.:   Hair: Eyes:
Complexion: Complexion:
Scars, etc.:   Scars, etc.:
Occupation: Hobbies, sports, etc.:
Race: Details of Abduction— Date, Place:
                                   Indicate violation of court order, warrant on file.
                                   Indicate if abuse has occurred.

IF YOU HAVE ANY INFORMATION, PLEASE CONTACT:

Officer's Name, Police Department:
Phone Number:
Case Number:
Warrant Number (if secured):

National Center for Missing and Exploited Children
1-800-THE-LOST
(1-800-843-5678)

NOTE: A missing child MUST be registered with the National Center for Missing and Exploited Children before adding the organization's name and telephone number to this flier.

have not already done so. You can petition the court for custody even after your child has been abducted. You may consider filing criminal charges against the parental abductor if you intend to press charges after the child has been returned. According to NCMEC: "Under the laws in effect in most states, criminal charges cannot be brought unless the abductor parent has violated a custody order that was in existence at the time the child was taken and there is proof that the abductor parent was aware of the custody order he or she is accused of violating." The NCMEC publishes an excellent and comprehensive free booklet, "Parental Kidnapping: How to Prevent an Abduction and What to Do if Your Child is Abducted." For a free copy, write to: **Center for Missing and Exploited Children,** 2101 Wilson Blvd., Suite 500, Arlington, VA 22202-3052.

8. **Keep a record** of everything that you do as you search for your child. Stay in close contact with the police and any organizations that are helping to find your child. And never give up hope.

Preventing Child Abduction

The odds that your child will be abducted by a stranger are very slim. Nonetheless, there are safety precautions that both you and your child should take.

Children Need to Know

1. Children have a right to say "no" to an adult who is bothering them or making them feel uncomfortable in any way.

2. No adult should ask children to keep a special secret from their parents.

3. A child should not get into a car, go into anyone's home, or go anywhere with anybody unless a parent gives permission.

4. Adults should ask other adults, not children, for help. If a car pulls up and the driver asks for directions, the child should not approach the car.

Another lure used by abductors is to ask a child to help find a missing pet. Children need to know that it is unusual for adults to ask children for help.

5. If a child thinks he or she is being followed, the child needs to quickly get home, to a neighbor's house, to a store—anyplace where there are people—and get help.

6. If a child is grabbed by a stranger or threatened in any way, the child needs to get away fast and make a scene by yelling, "Help. I don't know this person."

7. If a child gets separated from you in a public place, he or she needs to know how to get back to you as quickly as possible. You can either set up a meeting place or instruct the child to go up to the nearest police officer, security guard, or store clerk and get assistance. The child should not go wandering in the parking lot, looking for your car.

8. Children walking or playing alone are easy targets. They need to follow the "buddy system," staying close to other children or adults. They need to know to stay away from isolated places and deserted buildings and to avoid secluded shortcuts.

9. No one has a right to touch a child's "private parts"—the parts covered by a bathing suit.

10. Make sure children know their full names, addresses, and phone numbers (including area code). They also should know how to dial 911 for help. And they should be taught how to use a public telephone and how to call home "collect."

11. A child who is home alone should never open the door to a stranger or tell a stranger that no adult is home. If the child answers the telephone, he or she can say, "My mom (or dad) can't come to the phone right now. Can I take a message?"

12. When strangers offer gifts of money, the child should say "no." Also, if a stranger wants to take a photograph of a child, the answer is "no."

Parents Need to Know

1. Children should not be left alone—in the

car, in a grocery cart, in a rest room, or anywhere in public. Also, they should not be left home alone.

2. Establish strict rules with your school or day-care center concerning who is authorized to pick up your child.

3. Be sure to know where your child is at all times. Keep a written list of your child's friends along with addresses and phone numbers.

4. If an adult is paying too much attention to your child or giving the child gifts, find out why.

5. Don't display a child's name on a visible place on a child's clothing or other belongings. After seeing the child's name, an abductor can easily start up a conversation on a first-name basis.

6. Always have a recent photograph of your child on hand. In addition, have your child's fingerprints taken by a trained person. Know how to get quick access to dental and medical records.

7. If a child expresses an unwillingness to be with a particular adult, be sure you understand the reasons why the child is reluctant.

8. Check out baby-sitters, day-care centers, and any other individuals or groups that will be entrusted with custody of your child.

9. Whatever your child's fears or concerns, always be available to talk about everything that could be upsetting your child. Be alert for any behavior or attitude changes.

10. Practice "what if" games with your child to help the child figure out what to do in various situations. Ask the child, "What would you do if a stranger asked you to help him look for his missing dog?" Or, "What would you do if someone in a car pulled up beside you and asked you for directions?"

Recognizing an Abducted Child

The following information was provided courtesy of the Kevin Collins Foundation for Missing Children, a San Francisco–based nonprofit organization. The foundation was started by David and Ann Collins, parents of Kevin Collins, a 10–year-

old boy who was abducted in 1984. The foundation concentrates all of its energies in one area—abductions by nonfamily members, also called stranger-abducted children. For more information on the foundation and its activities: **Kevin Collins Foundation,** PO Box 590473, San Francisco, CA 94159 (800-272-0012).

How to Know an Abducted Child Next Time You See One

Many abducted children have been found by people who've recognized a face from a poster. So, please, when you see a missing-child poster, milk carton, or postcard, take the time to see if you recognize that child. Unfortunately, abductors take steps to change a child's appearance. Children change over time. And there are so many faces to remember. But don't feel there's nothing you can do.

If you're aware of the problem, and you know what to look for, there are many clues that can help you spot an abducted child. We've compiled a list of signs to look for. Obviously, none of these, in and of itself, is any proof. But they should give you reason to look more carefully.

Most stranger-abducted children who have been returned were exploited or abused. So many of the things to look for are signs of sexual abuse. If you see these signals, and feel a child may be in trouble, please don't talk yourself out of it. But don't try to handle it yourself. Pick up the phone and call the police. There are thousands of abducted children and millions of abused children living at risk out there. What you do could save a child's life.

Who Are Abducted Children?

First, it helps to understand what's going on inside the mind of an abducted child. An abducted child lives totally at the whim of the abductor. Knowing that, he or she doesn't want to anger the abductor at any cost. They become obedient to an extreme. To the point where they'll generally work hard to preserve the "family" masquerade.

Over time, most abductors convince the children that parents don't want them back. Or, wouldn't want them back now because they're "dirty." Some children are actually convinced they've been adopted. They live in shame and fear. But feel they have nowhere else to go.

So don't expect an abducted child to come running up and ask for help. In fact, chances are they're terrified you'll find out the truth and confront the "father" or "mother." Which could put them in real danger.

Even so, abused and abducted children do occasionally slip or give hints of their situation, leaving the door open to help from an adult they trust. This is a cry for help and takes a lot of courage. It's important that you realize this and follow up the lead by asking questions.

What to Look For

♦ You should be sensitive to any "family" situation that doesn't feel right. The most common stranger-abductor relationship is a single child with a single man who's passing as the father or grandfather.

♦ Abductors and their victims generally move around a lot to keep from being found out. As a result, abducted children live a transient life, often living in out-of-the-way cabins and trailer parks. With little sense of permanence, they don't make friends or fit in easily.

♦ They tend not to be enrolled in any one school for very long and don't participate in after-school activities. In fact, often they're not enrolled at all.

♦ They're missing early medical and dental records.

♦ Often, a newly abducted child will have dyed hair to alter his or her appearance.

♦ Because abducted children are living a lie, they must become liars to cover up the truth of their lives—especially as it relates to their parents and family.

♦ Sometimes they're confused about their real name. They trust no one.

♦ They've been brought up to see the police as a threat, a danger.

♦ Abducted children are often overly compliant, since they live in fear.

♦ Children who are being sexually abused will often exhibit pseudomature behavior. They give hints of sexual knowledge or show inappropriate sexual overtones in their play with toys or other children.

SEXUAL AND DOMESTIC VIOLENCE

Child Abuse

Every year an estimated 2.9 million cases of child abuse are reported to child protective service agencies. Every year approximately 2000 children die because of child abuse and/or neglect. And the numbers are growing.

Who are child abusers? According to the National Committee to Prevent Child Abuse (NCPCA): "Child abusers are usually ordinary people caught in situations that are beyond their control. It is a myth that child abuse is confined to minorities, the poor, or those in ghettos. Child abuse cuts across all boundaries of economic level, race, ethnic heritage, and religious faith."

Parents who abuse their children may love their children very much but not very well. The most prominent factors that cause parents to mistreat their children:

♦ Drug and alcohol abuse. It is estimated that nearly 10 million children under age 18 are affected in some way by the substance abuse of their parents.

♦ Parents were abused as children. Parents who have been abused as children are more likely to become abusive parents than those parents raised in a nonviolent environment.

♦ Lack of parenting skills. Parents' lack of knowledge regarding child development may result in unrealistic expectations concerning a child's behavior. When a child fails to live up to expectations, the child may be punished.

♦ Economic stress. Employment and financial difficulties overwhelm parents and leave them unable to cope with children.

♦ Family environment. Specific situations like marital conflict, domestic violence, and physical illness can be factors that lead to child abuse. In addition, social isolation can lead to abuse; parents who are isolated from others may expect children to satisfy their emotional needs.

Definitions of Child Abuse

Child abuse is divided into four categories:

Physical abuse. Defined as "an injury or a pattern of injuries to a child that is nonaccidental." Included in this definition are burns, welts, human bites, strangulation, broken bones, and internal injuries.

Child neglect. Characterized by the failure to provide for a child's basic needs, which include food, clothing, shelter, and health care. It also encompasses abandonment, failure to provide education, and inadequate supervision (like leaving a child alone for extended periods).

Sexual abuse. Includes a wide range of behavior: sexual molestation, intercourse, rape, incest, sodomy, exhibitionism, and exploitation through prostitution or production of pornographic materials. State laws usually distinguish between sexual abuse and sexual assault. An act of sexual abuse is committed by a person responsible for the care of a child (like a parent or baby-sitter). Sexual assault is a sexual act committed by someone who is not responsible for the care of a child.

Emotional abuse. A pattern of behavior that has caused, or could cause, behavioral or emotional or mental disorders. It includes verbal assaults that demean, threaten, shame, reject, and insult a child. It also includes bizarre forms of punishment like confining a child in a locked, dark closet. This kind of abuse can have a very negative effect on a child's self-confidence and self-esteem. It is also an abuse that is very difficult to identify and verify.

When Is Abuse a Crime?

A federal law, the Child Abuse Prevention and Treatment Act of 1974, sets out basic guidelines on what constitutes child abuse and neglect. All states must comply with the guidelines in order to get federal funds. However, each state has its own set of laws that govern child abuse and neglect. Basically, there are three types of laws:

1. State reporting laws. Certain groups of people—like teachers, doctors, and mental health professionals—are mandated by law to report known or suspected cases of child abuse.

2. Juvenile and family court laws. These laws help to resolve family disputes, including those that relate to child abuse. The courts can order specific treatment for parents and children. The courts can also take custody of a child when the child's safety cannot be ensured in the home.

3. Criminal laws. Each state defines what forms of child abuse and neglect are criminally punishable, like sexual abuse, severe physical abuse, or child endangerment.

To find out more about the laws in your state that address child abuse and neglect, contact your local law enforcement agency, the department of social services, or your state attorney general's office.

Reporting Suspected Child Abuse

If you think a child you know is a victim of child abuse, you should call a local child protective service, the child welfare department, or the police department. Be prepared to give: the name, age, sex, and address of the child; the nature and extent of the child's injuries/condition; the name and location of the alleged offender. When reporting a suspected case of child abuse, you can remain anonymous. However, the complaint is more credible if you give your name.

State reporting laws protect those who file reports as long as the report was made in "good faith." In other words, if you have a basis to suspect (an honest belief) that a child is being abused, it's assumed that you acted in good faith. Thus, good-faith reporters are immune from civil or criminal liability.

National Committee to Prevent Child Abuse, 332 S. Michigan Avenue, Suite 1600, Chicago, IL 60604 (312-663-3520).

Clearinghouse on Child Abuse and Neglect Information, PO Box 1182, Washington, DC 20013-1182 (800-FYI-3366).

National Council on Child Abuse and Family Violence, 1155 Connecticut Avenue NW, Suite 400, Washington, DC 20036 (202-429-6695).

Basic Facts About Child Sexual Abuse

What does child sexual abuse mean?

Child sexual abuse should not be confused with physical contacts between an adult and a child that are fond or playful expressions of love. Responsible adults automatically limit their physical exchanges with a child, thereby respecting the child and at the same time maintaining a warm, healthy, affectionate relationship.

Child sexual abuse is quite different. The child is used for the sexual gratification of an adult. Under most state laws a child is defined as anyone under 18 years of age.

Is sexual abuse against the law?

Yes. All 50 states and the District of Columbia identify such abuse as criminal behavior.

Are most sexual offenses against children committed by strangers?

No. The people most likely to sexually abuse children are their own family members, friends of the family, neighbors, and acquaintances.

Does sexual abuse occur more frequently inside or outside the family?

It occurs more frequently inside the family.

What is incest?

Incest is sexual intercourse between family members. The entire spectrum of parent-child sexuality, however, may range from a mother's sleeping with her son but not engaging in sexual relations, to taking pictures of children posed for or engaged in activities to arouse sexual desire and interest, to group sexual activities with children, to torture.

Is it true that incest occurs mostly among rural, isolated, and uneducated poor families?

No. Incest occurs among all groups of the population—both rural and urban and all socioeconomic and educational levels.

Are child molesters sick?

Certainly their behavior is extremely disturbed—and disturbing—but most people who molest appear perfectly normal in other ways. As in other forms of child abuse, less than 10 percent have a specific mental illness, and most do not benefit from the usual types of psychiatric care. Sexual abuse is most often a symptom of severe problems in marriage, family, and life adjustment. Effective treatment requires resocialization, emotional support, changing or controlling sexual interest or behavior, strengthening every member of the family, and at the same time demanding responsibility from the parents and their protection for the children as well as alleviating the psychosocial effects of abuse on the victim.

Are sexual offenders usually prosecuted and convicted?

No. The majority of sexual offenses committed against children are not even reported, let alone prosecuted. And if an individual is brought to trial, conviction is unlikely because these cases are very difficult to prove. Reforms in the legal system and departments of social services are occurring, however.

Are teenagers more frequently the victims of sexual abuse than younger children?

No. Four studies reporting on the age distribution of sexually molested children indicate that the average ages are 8.5, 10.7, 11.0, and 13.0 years.

Are girls sexually abused more often than boys?

Statistics indicate that girls are more frequently the victims of sexual abuse but the number of boy victims appears to be on the increase. Estimates suggest that male abuse is less than 20 to 25 percent of child victims.

If a girl is the victim of incest, is she likely to report it to the authorities?

No. The "courtship" of a child usually begins when she is very young and culminates in intercourse when she nears or reaches adolescence. In many middle-class families the man is "getting even" with his wife for failure to create a happy marriage. Over the child's "courtship years" the entire relationship with the father is shrouded in secrecy, which includes the father's convincing the child that she alone is responsible for maintaining the family as a unit because only her ready availability to him keeps him there. His "line" may also include how special his "fatherly love" is; if she resists, the courtship may include bribes, threats, or violence.

Even if the approach is brutal or humiliating, fear, loyalty to the family, and the nearly total dependency of the child tend to ensure secrecy. If the child discusses it at all, it is when she is older, and then she is most likely to tell a friend or a favorite teacher.

A mother surely must know if her husband or boyfriend is committing incest with her daughter. Isn't she the one most likely to report?

Most mothers do report abuse as soon as they

are aware of it. The problem is that sexual abuse of a child is often a problem difficult to detect. Children often tell their parents in indirect ways or don't tell at all. Mothers often can't imagine that the male they care about would do "such things to a child."

How can I tell whether a child is being sexually abused?

Symptoms of sexual abuse may include physical and behavioral signs as well as indirect comments made by the child. There are several clues to look for when considering the possibility of child sexual abuse. One sign alone may not be a positive indication; if a number are present, it is wise to consider the possibility of abuse.

Physical signs may include:
♦ hematomas (localized swelling filled with blood)
♦ lacerations
♦ irritation, pain, or injury to the genital area
♦ vaginal or penile discharge
♦ difficulty with urination
♦ pregnancy
♦ venereal disease in a young child
♦ nightmares.

Behavioral signs may include:
♦ one child's being treated by a parent in a significantly different way from the other children in the family
♦ arriving early at school and leaving late
♦ nervous, aggressive, hostile, or disruptive behavior toward adults, especially toward the parents
♦ running away
♦ use of alcohol or drugs
♦ sexual self-consciousness, provocativeness, vulnerability to sexual approaches
♦ sexual promiscuity that is "the talk of the town"
♦ withdrawal from social relationships
♦ an appearance of mental retardation
♦ regressive behavior such as acting childishly, crying excessively, sucking the thumb, withdrawing into fantasy worlds
♦ acting out of aggressions, sometimes including petty thefts, giving trinkets to other children to form friendships, stealing merchandise or money
♦ poor peer relationships
♦ inability to make friends.

Comments may include:
♦ "He fooled around with me."
♦ "My mother's boyfriend does things to me when she's not there."
♦ "I don't like to be alone with my father."
♦ "I'm afraid to go home tonight."
♦ "Will you help me go live with my aunt?"

When incest happens, whose fault is it?

The parents bear the entire responsibility. It is not the child. Even if a child is provocative or doesn't object, the law wisely states that incest is the fault of the adult. Where father-daughter incest occurs, the father is the key to the disturbed dynamics and is responsible for *choosing* a sexual relationship with the daughter. Whatever else is said in sympathy with his motivations, and regardless of the wife's and daughter's contributions, the father's responsibility must be emphasized and must be identified in any therapeutic encounter.

What is the greatest obstacle both to preventing and to treating child sexual abuse?

Society. The sexual abuse of children is something most people neither talk about nor believe. A top priority should be a national public awareness and education campaign about sexual abuse. People do not do anything about a problem until they know the problem exists. Also, with more education and treatment programs, more individuals would seek help *for themselves.*

Equally important is society's reluctance to deal with sexuality in a realistic and open way. Certainly one's sexual behavior is a most personal side of one's life, but the attitude that it is dirty or must be whispered about prevents children and many adults from acquiring basic biological knowledge and from experiencing mature and joyful adult relationships.

Reprinted with permission from "Basic Facts About Child Sexual Abuse," the National Committee to Prevent Child Abuse, Chicago, IL.

12 Things to Do So You Won't Hurt a Child

Childhelp USA operates a 24-hour National Child Abuse Hotline that provides crisis counseling, child abuse reporting information, and referrals to self-help groups. The following intervention steps are printed courtesy of this nonprofit organization.

♦ Take a deep breath. Take a few more. Remember *you* are the adult.

♦ Close your eyes and imagine you are hearing what your child is about to hear—or receiving the same punishment.

♦ Press your lips together and count to 20.

♦ Put the child in a "time-out" chair for a number of minutes. The rule is one minute of time out for each year of age.

♦ Put yourself in a "time-out" chair. Are you really angry at the child, or is your anger caused by something else?

♦ Call a friend to talk about it. Or call 1-800-4-A-CHILD.

♦ If someone can watch the children, go out for a walk.

♦ Take a hot bath or splash cold water on your face.

♦ Hug a pillow.

♦ Turn on some music. Sing along if you wish.

♦ Pick up a pencil and write down a list of helpful words, not words that will hurt. Save the list. Use these words.

♦ Write for more information you can keep at home. Send a card or letter to **Childhelp USA,** 6463 Independence Avenue, Woodland Hills, CA 91367.

Battered Women

Domestic violence—also called battering, spouse abuse, wife beating—is the use of physical violence by an abuser to gain control and power over a victim. It happens among couples who are married, who live together, or who have an ongoing or prior intimate relationship. While either partner may be a victim, 95 to 98 percent of the victims are women. According to the American Medical Association, "The American home is more dangerous to women than city streets." The statistics are grim:

♦ Every 15 seconds a woman is battered in the United States.

♦ Every year an estimated 2 to 4 million women are battered by their husbands or partners. The crime is largely unreported.

♦ Domestic violence is the single largest cause of injury to women—outnumbering injuries caused by car accidents, muggings, and rapes combined.

♦ Fifteen to 20 percent of pregnant women are battered.

♦ Weapons are used in 30 percent of domestic violence incidents.

♦ According to the American Medical Association: Every five years, domestic violence kills as many women as the total number of Americans who died in the Vietnam War.

♦ There are almost three times as many animal shelters in the United States as there are shelters for battered women.

Hitting, choking, kicking, pushing, biting, and assaults with weapons are characteristics of physical battering. Battered women are punched with fists, shoved down stairs, slammed against walls, cut with knives. Often, a man will strike a woman in the stomach or other areas where bruises are not readily seen (battering is one of the leading causes of miscarriage). Women who are chronically abused have bruises on various parts of the body—arms, legs, neck, face—and the bruises can be in different stages of healing. Many women have convincing explanations for their injuries since they don't want anyone to suspect that they have been beaten.

Why Do Women Stay?

Here are the reasons why women stay in such abusive relationships:

♦ The batterer threatens to kill the woman if

she leaves. In fact, research has shown that a battered woman faces the most physical danger when she attempts to leave.

♦ The woman is financially dependent on the abuser and feels that she cannot support herself and her children.

♦ Women who have low self-esteem may believe that they somehow deserve the abuse.

♦ The woman feels that she must keep the marriage together at any cost.

♦ She stays for the children's sake; she wants her children to grow up with a father.

♦ She still loves the abuser and holds out hope that he will change.

♦ The battering may cause the victim to become isolated, cut off from relatives and friends; the woman feels she has nowhere to go, no one to turn to.

Who Are the Men Who Beat Up Women?

There is no "typical" profile of an abuser. These men come from all races, religions, economic levels, educational levels, and age groups.

A batterer usually denies the existence of violence. When confronted, he blames the behavior on alcohol or drugs, or blames the woman for provoking the violence. Many of these men have a rigid view of sex roles and believe in male dominance over women; some are very possessive and jealous. A batterer is likely not to be violent at work or in other environments, preferring to vent aggressive behavior at home where there is little chance of punishment or retaliation.

According to the National Council on Child Abuse & Family Violence, here are some reasons why men batter:

♦ Battering is a learned behavior, not a mental disorder. Men who batter choose to do so, and, until recently, there has been no consequence for this behavior.

♦ Acts of violence committed within the family, which would be considered assaults with penalties if perpetrated on a stranger, have gone unnoticed by society and unpunished.

♦ Many batterers were raised in a violent home where they witnessed the abuse of their mother, siblings, or perhaps were themselves a victim of childhood abuse. Witnessing domestic violence in the childhood home is the most common risk factor for becoming a batterer in adulthood.

♦ The batterer has learned to use physical force as a way to maintain power and control in his relationships with women. Battering is the ultimate expression of a belief in male dominance over females.

♦ The batterer has learned to use physical violence as a means to handle anger, frustration, or guilt, and lacks the communication skills necessary to handle these emotions in nonviolent ways.

♦ The batterer generally has low self-esteem and low self-control, often displacing his anger at his boss or himself onto his spouse/partner and children.

♦ A batterer may experience some remorse after the battering and even seek forgiveness from his victim, promising it will never happen again. Such promises rarely are kept. Good intentions will not cure battering. Professional help is needed.

What Can a Battered Woman Do?

The following advice comes from the American Psychological Association:

If you are the victim of violence:

1. Begin to think about how you can plan for your own safety and happiness. Waiting for abusers to change and trying harder to please them will not work.

2. Find out what resources are available in your area for victims of partner abuse. At a safe time, when the abuser is not around, call a local battered women's shelter or domestic violence hotline. Tell them what has happened; ask them what your choices are to protect yourself and to end the violence. Think about the answers to your questions and call again if you need to know more.

3. If you are considering leaving your abuser, make safety plans *before* you talk about separation. Discuss the abuser's pattern of violence with someone at a shelter or crisis line and think

about what risks there might be if you talk about leaving. Try to keep enough money in a protected place to use when you need it to get to safety. Some victims find it best to go to a shelter where they can be safe before they tell the abuser that they are leaving.

4. If you can do this safely, encourage the abuser to go to a group for batterers. There are now many such groups for men who batter their partners. In such a group, batterers can get help from experts specially trained to treat violent people and may learn to change their beliefs and behaviors. You still may need to live apart from the batterer while that person is in the group. Changing patterns of violence can take a long time.

5. If you think you are in *immediate* danger, you probably are. You are expert at sensing when things are getting really bad. Flee at once to a safe location or call the police if you can. When police arrive, ask what legal protections are available to you, and use whatever protections you need to be sure you are safe. Don't let the police leave you alone with the abuser once they've arrived. If you are hurt, ask for medical help. Be sure that the doctor or nurse makes a record of your injuries and notes that those injuries were the result of an assault, not falling down stairs or bumping into a door.

National Council on Child Abuse & Family Violence, 1155 Connecticut Avenue NW, Suite 400, Washington, D.C. 20036 (202-429-6695).

National Coalition Against Domestic Violence, PO Box 18749, Denver, CO 80218-0749 (303-839-1852).

National Clearinghouse for the Defense of Battered Women, 125 S. 9th Street, Suite 302, Philadelphia, PA 19107 (215-351-0010).

Elder Abuse

Mistreatment or neglect of older people by their families or caregivers is called elder abuse. Since most older people live in their own homes or in the homes of family members, rather than in institutions, most cases of elder abuse are called "domestic mistreatment." It's estimated that every year 2 million older citizens in the United States are victims of domestic elder abuse. Domestic mistreatment is grouped into six categories:

Physical abuse: nonaccidental use of physical force that results in bodily injury, pain, or impairment.

Sexual abuse: nonconsensual sexual contact of any kind.

Psychological abuse: infliction of mental anguish by threat, humiliation, intimidation, or other verbal or nonverbal abusive conduct.

Financial abuse: illegal or unauthorized use of an older person's money, property, or other assets.

Neglect: willful or nonwillful failure of a caregiver to fulfill caretaking responsibilities. Willful neglect (also called active neglect) includes things like deliberate abandonment of an older person or denying food or medical services. Nonwillful neglect (also called passive neglect) can also include things like withholding food or health services—but the mistreatment is unintentional.

Self-abuse/neglect: when older people themselves threaten their health or safety due to abusive or neglectful behavior.

Which kind of domestic mistreatment is the most prevalent? Not enough research has been done to answer that question definitively, and even experts in the field disagree when asked to rank the abuses in order of frequency. Some say that about half of all cases are due to self-abuse/neglect; the other half occur because of the actions or neglect of someone else. However, all kinds of abuse can harm or threaten the life of a vulnerable older person. Thus, neglect (even passive neglect) is not necessarily less severe than physical abuse.

Perpetrators and Causes of Elder Abuse

Putting aside the cases of self-abuse/neglect, the people responsible are (in declining order): adult children, other relatives (including grandchildren and siblings); spouses; service providers; friends and neighbors. Some cases of mistreatment are intentional, involve criminal behavior, and are subject to prosecution. Other cases are unintentional and require that the parties involved seek out help from appropriate social service agencies.

Researchers have identified a number of factors that lead to elder abuse. The most common are:

Caregiver stress. Caring for an older person is a great responsibility. It can impose severe financial, physical, and mental strain. Many families take on the responsibility because "it is the right thing to do," but they do not initially recognize the kinds of constraints it places on everyday life.

Lack of knowledge. Home care requires that the caregiver be skilled in a number of areas—everything from cooking nutritious meals to bathing a bed-bound person. Often, caregivers lack these skills, don't know how to get them, and aren't aware of local services that could provide assistance. In addition, many caregivers do not know what to expect as an older person's health deteriorates. For example, some Alzheimer's patients become physically combative. If a caregiver doesn't understand that the older person is striking out because of the disease, not because he or she is defiant and angry, then the caregiver may respond to physical force with physical force.

Cycle of violence within families. Some families are more prone to violence than other families. It is a trait handed down through the generations; violence is a learned behavior that is used to deal with stress and conflict.

Troubled family members. Conditions like alcoholism, drug addiction, or mental or emotional disorders can cause adult children to abuse their parents. Often, the children are financially dependent on the parents.

Sources of Help

Elder abuse is largely unreported because victims are usually afraid and embarrassed. In addition, victims fear losing the only support systems they have, even if the support systems put them in danger.

Most states have instituted Adult Protective Services (APS) agencies that investigate reported cases of elder abuse. Investigation of a case can lead to any number of actions: family counseling can be provided; support services like home health care can be provided; living arrangements can be changed (either the victim or the abuser leaves the home). When criminal conduct is involved, the police and the court system may intervene. Police are often called in cases involving physical assault or sexual abuse.

Reports of suspected elder abuse should be made to an **Adult Protective Service,** an **Area Agency on Aging,** or the county department of social services. In addition, many states sponsor a 24-hour toll-free **Elder Abuse Hotline;** calls are confidential. The numbers for all of the above will be listed in your local phone directory. If you witness an elder abuse situation that requires emergency attention, call 911.

Caregivers who feel overwhelmed and stressed out should seek assistance and take advantage of the many local services available to older persons (see "Area Agencies on Aging," p. 293).

Rape

Rape is *not* a sexual act. A sexual act occurs between two consenting partners. Rape is a violent crime, an act of dominance and control. Rape is *not* a spontaneous act; 70 percent of all rapes are planned. And women are overwhelmingly the victims of rape. Here are some sobering statistics from a 1992 study, "Rape In America: A Report to the Nation":

♦ Every year 683,000 women are raped.

♦ At least 12.1 million American women have been victims of forcible rape.

♦ More than six out of 10 (61 percent) cases of rape occur before the victim reaches age 18.

♦ In 78 percent of rape cases, the victim

knows the rapist: husband or ex-husband; father or stepfather; boyfriend or ex-boyfriend; another relative, a friend, a neighbor.

♦ Only 16 percent of rapes are reported to the police.

♦ An estimated 31 percent of victims develop post-traumatic stress disorder (PTSD).

Reducing the Risk of Rape

1. **Secure your home,** both inside and outside. A large percentage of rapes occur in or around the home. Make sure you have good locks on your doors and windows; make sure the outside areas of your home are adequately lit with floodlights. Consider buying an alarm system or getting a dog. Keep your window shades drawn at night. Don't put your name on the mailbox and never give out your address to a stranger on the phone. Above all, don't let strangers into your home. If a service person comes to your home, ask for identification before opening the door.

2. When outside the home, **use common sense.** Avoid dark, isolated streets. Don't walk close to bushes, alley entrances, or driveways. Don't overload your arms with packages; do carry a whistle or keys in your hand. Wear low-heeled shoes. If you think you are being followed, get help but don't go home or you will be letting a potential attacker know where you live.

3. **Have taxi fare when out on a date,** in case you need to get home on your own. Do not go to secluded places. Don't allow yourself to be pressured into drinking. If your date insists on sex and you are unwilling, be assertive when you say no; don't worry about being polite. Beware of men who show anger and hostility toward women, who act entitled to sex, who show an excessive amount of controlling behavior—those who want to make all of the decisions all of the time.

4. A controversial question concerning rape is, **Should you try to resist an attack?** Conventional wisdom says you should not try to defend yourself physically or do anything that puts you at risk for further injury. However, a recent U.S.

Bureau of Justice report stated that almost 83 percent of female victims of rape, or attempted rape, said they used one or more forms of resistance. How they resisted: 20.8 percent physically resisted the attacker; 19.6 percent screamed or got help; 18.7 percent appeased the offender or persuaded him not to attack; 13 percent ran away or hid; 12.9 percent scared off the offender (doing things like threatening to call the police); 7.9 percent attacked or threatened the offender without a weapon; 0.8 percent attacked the offender with a weapon; the remaining 6.3 percent used other various means of resistance. Of the women surveyed, only 18.9 percent said that resisting made the situation worse or that resisting helped the situation in some ways but worsened it in other ways. Thus, 81.1 percent of the women said that resisting the rape helped them.

Whether or not you choose to resist depends on a number of circumstances. Obviously, resisting could be a fatal mistake if someone is threatening you with a knife or a gun. In addition, halfhearted physical retaliation could worsen a situation; if you are going to fight back, you need to know what you are doing and do it forcefully. Self-defense experts generally recommend that you attack weak spots on the body—eyes, nose, throat, groin, knees, or shins. The best advice of all: take a self-defense class and learn the proper techniques for defending yourself (see "Self-Defense," p. 93). And, if you carry a weapon, like Mace, be sure you know how to use it; the rapist could take it away from you and use it on you.

What to Do if You Are Raped

The following steps assume that you will report the rape to the police. The reasons why women don't report rapes: they don't want their families to know that they were sexually assaulted; they fear that people will think they are somewhat responsible; they don't want their names made public by the media; they feel the police and the court systems are not effective at catching and punishing offenders.

♦ Get yourself to safety.

♦ Do not bathe, douche, shower, or change clothes. Don't even wash your hands until you have been examined medically. You want to preserve as much evidence as possible. If the rape happened in your home, try not to touch anything until the police get a chance to dust for fingerprints.

♦ Call a friend or a rape crisis hotline. You are in need of emotional support and advice. Calls to a rape crisis hotline are confidential; if you want to, you can call anonymously.

♦ Call the police (911) and report the crime.

♦ Seek medical attention. See your own doctor or go to the emergency room of the nearest hospital.

♦ Get counseling. Rape victims experience a number of traumatic issues—everything from fear of pregnancy and AIDS to how family and friends will react to the rape. Even if you consider yourself to be a strong, independent person, get some psychological help.

Helping a Friend Who Has Been Raped

♦ Listen and be supportive. Assure the friend that everything she tells you will be kept confidential.

♦ Do the best you can to convince her that the rape was not her fault; she is a victim. Also let her know that whatever she did was correct because she survived.

♦ Avoid making any comments that are judgmental or insensitive, like "Why didn't you fight back?" or "Lots of women get raped; you'll get over it" or "Why were you out alone that late at night?"

♦ Don't jump right in and take charge. Your friend has just experienced a situation in which her control was taken away. She doesn't need a controlling friend. Help her to make decisions but don't make them for her. Also, it is solely the victim's decision whether or not to report the crime to the police.

Postscript: While rape is most often a crime against women, it is important to point out that males are also the victims of rape. It's estimated that there are approximately 10,000 rapes of males age 12 and over every year in the United States. As is the case with females, males are likely not to report the crime.

Victims

Trauma of Victimization

Dr. Morton Bard, co-author of *The Crime Victim's Book,* has described a victim's reaction to crime as the crisis reaction. Victims will react differently depending upon the level of personal violation they experience and their state of equilibrium at the time of victimization. Victims of nonviolent crimes—such as theft—may experience less of a personal violation than victims of violent crimes. Homicide is the ultimate violation, but it leaves behind the survivors to experience the personal violation. All people have their own "normal" state of equilibrium. This normal state is influenced by everyday stressors such as illness, moving, changes in employment, and family issues. When any one of these changes occurs, equilibrium will be altered, but should eventually return to normal. When people experience common stressors and are then victimized, they are susceptible to more extreme crisis reactions. There are common underlying reactions the victim will undergo either in the immediate hours or days after the crime. Frequent responses to a victimization include: shock and numbness; denial, disbelief and anger; and finally, hopefully, recovery.

Shock and Numbness

Shock and numbness are usually considered a part of the initial stage of the crisis reaction. Victims are faced with a situation beyond their control and may almost immediately go into shock and become disoriented.

Victims may experience what is referred to as the "fight or flight" syndrome. The fight or flight syndrome is a basic physiological response that individuals have no control over. Because many victims do not understand this response, and their lack of control over it, they do not understand why they fled instead of fought, or vice versa. A woman who takes a self-defense course may blame herself when confronted with an attacker because she is unable to put into practice what she has learned. A man may be criticized, or not believed, if he did not fight back when confronted. To question a victim's response is to inflict a "secondary injury."

In many instances, physical and emotional paralyses occur whereby the victim is unable to make rational decisions such as reporting the incident to the police or obtaining medical attention. The individual loses control, feels vulnerable, lonely, and confused; the sense of self becomes invalidated.

Denial, Disbelief, and Anger

In this phase, victims' moods will fluctuate. As psychologist Steven Berglas states in his article, "Why Did This Happen to Me?" [*Psychology Today,* February 1985], victims will think, "This could not have happened to me" or "Why did this happen to me?" Many will replay the disturbing event by dreaming, having nightmares or even fantasies about killing or causing bodily harm to the offender. Survivors of homicide victims may even express anger at their loved one, believing that if the victim had done something differently, he or she would not have been killed. During this period, victims must contend with a variety of stressful emotions such as fear, despair, self-pity, even guilt and shame for their anger and hostility.

Recovery

If victims are to recover from the traumatic event, it is crucial that they be provided with the proper support during the initial impact stage and throughout the criminal justice process. Immediate crisis intervention is needed. Trained crisis intervenors should inquire about victims' welfare by asking if they feel safe, assuring victims that they are if that is true, and determining if they are in need of medical attention. Victims will often blame themselves for the crime. The crisis intervenor needs to assure the victims that they were not at fault. If these initial and crucial steps are missing, the trauma can have a long-term effect on the healing and recovery process. After experiencing the initial traumatic reactions to victimization, victims will most likely undertake the task of rebuilding their equilibrium. Their lives will never be the same, but they begin to regain some form of control and a sense of confidence.

Every victim's experience is different and the recovery process can be extremely different and difficult. It can take a few months or years—or an entire lifetime—depending upon the variables involved. For instance, if an individual has suffered from other traumatic incidents prior to the victimization—such as the death of a close relative or friend—his or her initial emotional reaction, reorganization, and recovery might be different from someone who is experiencing victimization for the first time. The road to recovery is very similar to a roller coaster with unexpected ups and downs. This is why crisis intervention and supportive counseling play a significant role in helping victims recover.

If victims have difficulty rebuilding or finding a new equilibrium, they may suffer from a long-term crisis reaction or post-traumatic stress disorder. Victims never completely forget about the crime. The pain may lessen and even subside, but their lives are changed forever. Victims who suffer from long-term crisis reactions are thrown back into the initial crisis reaction by "triggers." Many victims will have particular triggers that remind them of their victimization, such as sights, smells, noises, birthdays, holidays, or the anniversary of the crime.

Post-Traumatic Stress Disorder

Post-traumatic stress disorder (PTSD) was first applied to military veterans who experienced psychological trauma while serving in combat. Researchers are now applying this syndrome to crime victims. Being a victim of crime does not necessarily mean that an individual will develop PTSD. If victims receive appropriate crisis intervention, the chances of developing PTSD are reduced.

Some recognizable symptoms of PTSD are:
- sleeping disorders; continued nightmares
- constant flashbacks; intrusion of thoughts
- extreme tension and anxiety
- irritability; outbursts of anger
- nonresponsiveness or lack of involvement with the external world
- prolonged feelings of detachment or estrangement of others
- memory trouble.

PTSD is a very complicated diagnosis and the presence of any of the above-mentioned symptoms does not mean that a person is suffering from PTSD.

Secondary Injuries

Victims not only have to struggle with primary injuries in the aftermath of the crime, but they must also battle with the "secondary injuries."

Secondary injuries are injuries that occur when there is a lack of proper support. These injuries can be caused by friends, family, and most often by the professionals victims encounter as a result of the crime. Law enforcement officers, prosecutors, judges, social service workers, the media, coroners, clergy, and even mental health professionals can cause secondary injuries. Those individuals may lack the ability or training to provide the necessary comfort and assistance to the victim. Often, those individuals blame the victim for the crime. Failing to recognize the importance of the crime or show sympathy can be damaging to the victim's self-worth and recovery process.

Perhaps the most agonizing experience for victims involves dealing with the criminal justice system if and when an offender is apprehended. At this level, the crime is considered to have been committed against the state and victims become witnesses to the crimes. This procedure is very difficult for the individual to understand and come to terms with, because, in the victim's mind, he or she is the one who has suffered emotionally, physically, psychologically, and financially. At this stage of the process, a victim can sometimes feel that he or she is losing complete control because he or she is not directly involved in the prosecution or sentencing of the offender.

Participation in the criminal justice system aids victims in rebuilding their lives. If victims are kept well informed about the criminal proceedings, and feel that they have a voice in the process, they will feel that they are a part of a team effort. This added effort enables victims to understand the judicial process and helps to return a sense of control to victims.

In order to have a better understanding of victimization, we must begin to accept the reality that crime is senseless and can happen to anyone regardless of the precautions that are taken to prevent being victimized. We must also understand that a victim's life is turned upside down when he or she is victimized. In order to help victims learn to trust society again and regain a sense of balance and self-worth, we must educate all those who come in contact with victims and survivors. With proper training, all professionals will be better able to assist victims in dealing with the trauma of victimization.

Reprinted courtesy of The National Victim Center.

Crime Victims Have Rights, Too

One of the positive results of politicians' continuing efforts to be "tougher on crime" than their opponents has been increased attention to the individual victims of crime. Most states now have a victim's bill of rights, a victim assistance program, a victim compensation fund, and a witness protection program. Knowing about them could help if you are victimized by crime, as most of us have been or will be.

Victim's Bill of Rights

Since a crime involves breaking a law of government, that government (usually the state) is responsible for finding, trying, and punishing the offender. The offender's victim has a very secondary role. The police, not the victim, are in charge of the investigation. The prosecutor, not the victim, brings criminal charges. The victim can be forced to testify but has no right to do so. A judge or jury, not the victim, sets the punishment. A victim's bill of rights is a way of recognizing that a victim of crime has a special interest in its prosecution and may need special help as well. The bill of rights varies from state to state but generally it gives a victim the right to:

♦ appropriate medical treatment
♦ prompt return of personal property
♦ be kept informed of the progress of the investigation
♦ be notified of hearings and trials, and any postponements
♦ attend the trial
♦ be protected from the defendant and any associates
♦ know when the offender is released from custody.

Victim Assistance Programs

These provide a variety of services on an emergency basis, including medical care, food, shelter, and counseling. Some programs provide help in dealing with the police; others provide an advocate at court hearings. Most programs are closely connected with the police department or prosecutor's office. Details vary. Some programs were started by women's groups and focus on victims of rape and domestic violence. Others are more concerned with the elderly, children, or drugs. Some are connected with witness protection programs.

Victim Compensation Funds

Most states have a fund that helps reimburse crime victims. Only victims of violent crime are usually eligible. Standards vary, but medical expenses, funeral expenses, lost wages, and the cost of counseling usually have priority for reimbursement. Under most programs the offender does not need to be caught or convicted. Victims are sometimes ineligible if the criminal is a household member or relative, or if the victim has a continuing relationship with the offender. Ordering defendants to compensate their victims is becoming increasingly popular. For some crimes restitution is a standard part of the punishment. Restitution often doesn't work, of course, since many criminals, and most prisoners, have no money, property, or job.

Witness Protection Programs

These are meant to offer police protection to witnesses who are in danger because of their expected testimony in a criminal case. Protection through surveillance is the most common. Actual police bodyguards are sometimes used. A witness may also be held in jail or at a secret location to protect him or her. Unfortunately, the emphasis of these programs is on protecting a witness until the witness testifies in court. If the defendant is convicted, remains in jail, and has no

accomplices, that may be enough. Occasionally, however, criminals succeed in retaliating against witnesses later. In rare federal cases, the Department of Justice helps a witness establish a new identity in a new place with a new job, in an effort to prevent retaliation. It's not a perfect answer, but there isn't one.

If you or someone you know becomes a victim of crime, particularly violent crime, be sure to inquire of the police or prosecutor about specific programs that can help.

Reprinted courtesy of the National Resource Center for Consumers of Legal Services.

Civil Legal Remedies for Victims of Violent Crime

Victims of crime are increasingly obtaining monetary damages in civil court actions against those perpetrators who do them harm. Whether damages are ordered against perpetrators; against the perpetrators' insurance, wages, or property; or against third parties who are found to have been negligent, juries are sympathizing with victims of violent crime.

Civil litigation is important for victims of crime, and for society as a whole, for several reasons:

♦ It empowers victims and allows them to be in control of their cases (unlike criminal law, which often relegates victims to the status of witness).

♦ Large verdicts reinforce the idea that victims have suffered important injuries for which perpetrators should pay.

♦ It helps provide victims with unique opportunities to recover monetary damages for the harm inflicted upon them by their assailants.

♦ It acts as a deterrent by holding perpetrators financially accountable for their acts, sending the message that crime doesn't pay.

♦ It promotes enhanced safety policies and practices by holding institutions (third parties) accountable if they acted negligently or failed to protect.

♦ High-profile suits that garner considerable media coverage help heighten national awareness of crime issues.

One of the most common misconceptions about civil litigation is that a perpetrator must have been found guilty in criminal court before a victim may file a civil suit. This is simply not true—no criminal judgment is necessary, nor is it even necessary that a criminal claim be filed. In fact, victory in civil court may be more reachable than in criminal court because there is a lower burden of proof: *beyond a reasonable doubt* in criminal court, versus *a preponderance of the evidence* (more than half) against the perpetrator in civil court.

Although a lower burden of proof is allowed in civil court, victory is not guaranteed. The victim must prove that a crime was committed (called a *tort* in legal terms), that there was a *cause of action* (that the crime committed caused the victim to suffer in the manner she or he claims), and that the perpetrator or third party is liable to pay for that suffering.

Obtaining a civil judgment is only half of the victim's battle. In many cases, the real battle begins when victims attempt to collect the judgments they are awarded. Victims and their advocates recognize that true justice demands that such judgments be fully satisfied—that criminals pay. Many do not. Securing mechanisms to force perpetrators to pay damages is clearly the next civil-law advancement for victim advocates and the criminal justice system.

Reprinted courtesy of The National Victim Center.

ORGANIZATIONS FOR VICTIMS

There are two national organizations that publish a wide variety of materials for crime victims: **The National Victim Center,** PO Box 17150, Fort Worth, TX 76102 (800–FYI-CALL or 817-877-3355); the **National Organization for Victim Assistance** (NOVA), 1757 Park Road NW, Washington, DC 20010 (202-232-6682). NOVA also refers callers to victim services in their areas or provides direct counseling services for victims who live in areas where local programs are not available.

3

MAKING A DIFFERENCE

VOLUNTEERING

The Gift of Time

Once the old and honored activity of volunteering was the province of those who did not work for wages: teenagers, the retired, empty nesters with time on their hands. Today more than half of all adult Americans volunteer their time in some way—to the tune of 21 billion hours' worth, according to a recent survey for the Independent Sector by the Gallup Organization.

Volunteers often say that they are repaid a thousand times over for their efforts—in satisfaction, in camaraderie, in learning. Some see volunteering as a moral or social obligation, a way to repay society for what it has given them. Others find that it looks good on a résumé or that they can network while volunteering.

If you would like to volunteer—no matter what your motive—try to match your talents with the group you want to help. If you are a skilled bookkeeper interested in helping the homeless, you might want to do accounts for a soup kitchen. On the other hand, you may only be satisfied with ladling out meals right on the scene. If you give some thought to what volunteer activities interest you the most, you are likely to "stay on the job." One of the biggest problems faced by organizations staffed by volunteers is turnover. Before volunteering, be committed to work for a reasonable length of time. Of course, some activities by their very nature bring about quick burnout. For instance, those who visit AIDS patients often need time out after several months.

If you are new at volunteering, or need to know about opportunities in your area, contact military installations, family support centers, the United Way, or your Area Agency on Aging. Or write or call one of the following organizations. They will put you in touch with a local agency that can help you:

Points of Light Foundation, 736 Jackson Place, Washington, DC 20503 (800-879-5400, 202-223-9186).

United Way, 701 North Fairfax Street, Alexandria, VA 22314 (703-519-0092).

AARP Volunteer Talent Bank, 601 E Street NW, B3–440, Washington, DC 20049 (202-434-2277).

Community Service Profile

Filling out this questionnaire may give you some insight into the kinds of volunteer activities that would best suit you.

Check any that are appropriate.

The gifts that I have to give are:
- ☐ teaching someone a skill or subject
- ☐ listening to or counseling someone who is troubled
- ☐ mentoring someone who needs a good role model
- ☐ calling on people who are lonely

☐ using my professional skills or hobbies to help others

☐ other (*describe*)

The community problems of greatest concern to me are:

☐ the needs of children and youth
☐ poverty
☐ homelessness
☐ drug and alcohol abuse
☐ education and literacy
☐ the needs of senior citizens
☐ crime
☐ hunger
☐ teen pregnancy
☐ health care
☐ mental illness
☐ other (*describe*)

I would like to work:

☐ on my own or in a situation where I have a lot of freedom
☐ as part of a group that I organize
☐ as part of a group that someone else organizes
☐ in my own neighborhood
☐ outside of my own neighborhood
☐ through my place of work
☐ through my school
☐ through my place of worship
☐ through a club or organization I belong to
☐ with a specific program

I would like to work up to ____ hours a week at the following times:

☐ daytime, Monday through Friday
☐ evenings, Monday through Friday
☐ weekends

Through my involvement, I hope to:

☐ put my ideas to work
☐ develop new skills
☐ make new social connections
☐ use skills I don't use on my job
☐ learn more about problems in my community
☐ feel something real

Reprinted courtesy of Points of Light Foundation.

HELPING THE POOR AND HUNGRY

In addition to preparing and serving food in soup kitchens and homeless shelters, you can pass out leaflets with information about services for the homeless at shelters, soup kitchens, and other places where the homeless go. Or you can conduct a food drive. Or you can experience first-hand the real-life problems of poverty, which will increase your empathy and give you a sense of how to help. **Harvest of Hope** provides an educational weekend or week-long event in living the life of the poor. In classes on hunger, for instance, you see how much food you can buy for a dollar. Call **Society of Saint Andrew: 800-333-4597.**

Gleaning

To feed the millions of hungry people in the United States, philanthropic groups have taken up the ancient practice of gleaning. It goes back at least as far as the Old Testament, which suggested that farmers allow poor widows and vagabonds to glean (pick) the outer edges of their fields.

On modern farms, after the crops have been harvested, at least 5 percent of the produce remains behind. A recent congressional report claimed that *one-fifth* of produce is wasted at harvest. Often the produce is perfectly edible, just unmarketable because it is too ripe, too small, slightly blemished. And whole fields or orchards can remain unpicked when market prices are lower than the costs of harvesting.

The custom of allowing the poor to glean for themselves still lives. The needy, often from the inner city, are allowed to take produce left behind after the harvest, keeping it for themselves and their neighbors. One way for the more affluent to help the poor is to glean in fields and orchards as one of a group of volunteers, with the produce going to churches, soup kitchens, and food banks. (Some volunteers in gleaning groups also donate money for expenses or drive pickers to and from the fields.)

By allowing gleaning, farmers have the satisfaction of seeing produce go to a worthy cause, and they often gain tax advantages. Several states have laws protecting farmers from liability for injury to gleaners.

Organizations that sponsor volunteer gleaning:

The Gleaning Network, Society of St. Andrew, State Rt. 615, PO Box 329, Big Island, VA 24526 (804-299-5956; 800-333-4597; in North Carolina, 919-683-3011). Provides opportunities to glean in Virginia, Maryland, Pennsylvania, North and South Carolina, Louisiana, Florida.

Second Harvest, Chicago, IL: 800-532-FOOD; 312-263-2303. Certifies food banks nationwide. Watch your local paper for opportunities to help with gleaning.

Helping the Disabled

People who have disabilities do a great deal for themselves and other people. However, sometimes they need help—someone to translate a book into Braille, to drive them to an appointment, even to raise a dog that will later help them go about the daily business of life.

The Blind

There are more than 600,000 legally blind people in the United States today. (You are legally blind if you can't see objects more than 20 feet away. Only one person in 10 of the legally blind is totally blind.) About 10 percent of the legally blind can read Braille. However, blind people keep in touch with the world through many other devices: talking books, scales, and thermometers; an identifier that reads and speaks the denomination of a piece of paper money; a gadget that can read LED displays out loud. But sometimes inanimate

gadgets are not enough. Here are some of the things *you* can do to aid the visually impaired:

♦ Write oral descriptions of what goes on during a play. These descriptions are then read onto an audio tape cassette. The vision-impaired can listen to the tape through headphones while attending the play in order to "visualize" the action. You might also volunteer to create tapes for national monuments, museums, and exhibits.

♦ Write Braille transcriptions of menus and other materials.

♦ Read newspapers, magazines, and books over the air for a radio reading service for the visually impaired. Funded by a variety of private and government groups, these stations broadcast on subcarrier channels. Listeners must have a special receiver. To find out if such a station exists near you, call your local library or Chamber of Commerce.

♦ Read textbooks and technical materials for **Recording for the Blind**. There may be a studio near you. The central number is 800-221-4792.

♦ Volunteer for a local agency. In California, for instance, nearly 4000 volunteers for the **Braille Institute** transcribe books, repair talking book machines, act as drivers, teach everything from current events to arts and crafts, and perform many other tasks. Call 800-BRAILLE for referrals.

The Hearing-Impaired

Many public schools and universities offer services through which volunteers take notes for the hearing-impaired. You can communicate with the hearing-impaired by learning American Sign Language (ASL), which indicates words and phrases by hand shape, movement, the way the palm is oriented, and the position of the hand relative to the body. To find out where you can learn American Sign Language, write: **National Association of the Deaf,** 814 Thayer Avenue, Silver Spring, MD 20910 (301-587-1788; TTY 301-587-1789).

RAISING DOGS

If you want to serve humanity and love raising puppies, you may qualify as a puppy raiser for an organization that trains dogs to serve the disabled. In most cases, you give the dog a home, obedience-train it, pay for its care. Part of the job is socializing dogs to deal with a variety of situations. For example, you take them out in public where they can get used to the busy world of streets, cars, and curbs. When in public, dogs often wear special gear (yellow cape and harness, for instance) that identifies them as dogs in training. When the dog is ready for its specialized training, you have to give it up, unless for some reason it is found unsuitable.

Organizations train dogs to serve people with disabilities in many ways:

For the physically or developmentally disabled: dogs help with physical tasks like turning lights on and off, pushing elevator buttons, retrieving things that are dropped, and locking and unlocking as well as pulling a wheelchair. The dogs are trained to take packages from the shelf at stores and carry them to the checkout counter—or bring a beer from the refrigerator.

For the hearing impaired, dogs warn of sounds—the phone, a child's cry, microwave ding, knock, alarm clock.

For the visually impaired, dogs help people negotiate streets, stairs, curbs.

Some dogs, called *social dogs*, provide love and companionship, a bright spot in the day. They may live with an individual or in a group setting, or they may only visit a hospital or nursing home or other institution.

Specific Groups

For a complete list of groups that train dogs, contact: **DELTA Society,** PO Box 1080, Renton, WA 98057–9906 (206-226-7357). Also contact: **Assistance Dogs of America, Inc.,** C/O Mike Roche, Freedom Service Dogs, PO Box 150217, Lakewood, CO 80215–0217 (303-234-9512). This group promoting professionalism of dog-training for the disabled can recommend a nearby member of their group.

Canine Companions for Independence. This organization trains dogs to help people with all disabilities except blindness. The dogs are raised by foster parents from eight weeks until about 18 months of age. Most of the dogs are Labrador and golden retrievers, with some Border collies and Pembroke Welsh corgis.

Bonita Bergin, the director of the program, was inspired by two disparate but related experiences. When she traveled in the Orient, she noticed disabled people using draft animals as crutches to lean on as they sold the wares the animals carried—the animals gave them independence. And she noticed in her special-education classes that more emphasis was put on what professionals could do for disabled persons than on what the disabled could do for themselves. Why not, she thought, train a dog that will give a disabled person more independence?

Requirements are a loving family, a fenced yard, and the willingness of one member to take part in bimonthly obedience training and to make monthly progress reports. The puppy raiser pays for the dog's care, including vet bills. Puppies sleep in the puppy raiser's bedroom. They learn to retrieve and shake hands, to carry paper bags, to sit, and to hold an object.

When the dogs are 18 months old, they go to the center for another 6 months of training. Here they learn dozens of different commands that are eventually strung together in more complex tasks. For the first 3 months, foster families may take the dogs home for the weekend. After training, dog and disabled companion take two weeks of boot camp together. Dogs not accepted into the program may be adopted by those who raised them. Contact: Canine Companions for Independence, National Office, PO Box 446, Santa Rosa, CA 95402-0446 (707-528-0830 voice/TTY).

Okada Hearing/Specialty Guide Dogs. The name of this organization is a Native American word meaning "asking for a place." Most of the dogs once were homeless. Okada has trained dogs since 1986—for the hearing-impaired, for the lonely and physically impaired, for those who need companionship (in group settings like nursing homes). Okada also trains dogs to prevent the wandering of Alzheimer's patients: when the patient starts to wander, the dog goes to and alerts the caretaker. You can provide a foster home for the initial training of an Okada dog if you qualify and live in the Midwest. The task is to housebreak, socialize, and train the dog in basic obedience as well as in responding to a few preliminary task commands. Contact: Okada Ltd., R.R. 1 Box 640F, Fontana, WI 53125 (414-275-5226 voice/TTY).

Dogs for the Deaf, Inc. This organization adopts dogs from Humane Society adoption centers for training. Those under eight months old go to local puppy raisers until old enough for formal training. The puppy raisers socialize the dogs, teach house manners and simple obedience. After that, formal training, which lasts four to six months, begins. Dogs for the Deaf trains dogs as Certified Hearing Dogs, who are allowed legal access to restaurants, stores, public transportation; as Working Companion Dogs, who respond to sounds and are obedience trained but are not allowed in public places; and as Social Dogs. Contact: Dogs for the Deaf, 10175 Wheeler Road, Central Point, OR 97502 (503-826-9220 voice/TTY).

Guide Dogs of America. In their program to train guide dogs for the blind, Guide Dogs of America in Sylmar, California, also uses foster parents to raise puppies, usually Labrador retrievers, golden retrievers, and German shepherds. At about eight weeks, the puppy goes home with its foster parents, who feed and raise it for about a year. They provide a home and teach obedience, manners, how to be social. The school provides veterinary care for free.

Part of the socialization means taking the dog everywhere, which is what the dog will do when it accompanies a blind person. Dogs need to learn to negotiate automatic doors, stairs, elevators, subways.

After their year or more with foster parents, the dogs go back to the institute—the hardest part of the experience, according to many of the foster parents. About 40 percent of the animals have physical or behavioral problems that make them unfit to be guide dogs. In that case, the people who raised them can keep them as pets. Contact: Guide Dogs of America (818-362-5834). Also contact: Guide Dog Foundation for the Blind, 371 E. Jericho Turnpike, Smithtown, NY 11787 (800-548-4337; 516-265-2121).

PET PARTNERS

If your pet (dog, cat, whatever) is in good health and has the right temperament, it might qualify for the Pet Partners Program of the DELTA Society. Pet Partners visit people in institutions. Your dog must successfully pass the Canine Good Citizen Test (see "Canine Good Citizen Title," p. 326). Then your dog or other pet must be checked further for health and temperament by a veterinarian. You yourself will need to go for training in an animal visitation or therapy program through a local group, DELTA chapter, or the SPCA. (If no facility exists, you can learn by using the Pet Partners Volunteer Training Manual.) You also need to pass a written test and visit a facility. At that point you and your pet can register with DELTA Society as an official pet partner. Contact: **DELTA SOCIETY**, PO Box 1080, Renton, WA 98057 (206-226-7357; FAX 206-235-1076).

Helping the Sick

Candy-stripers and pink ladies still brighten hospital corridors. Though you might not have to wear such an official getup, you can still volunteer at a hospital, nursing home, or hospice. For instance, you might entertain sick children by reading to them, playing games with them, or teaching them arts and crafts or music. If you know a foreign language, you might translate for a non-English-speaking patient. Other volunteer jobs include providing transportation, helping with blood pressure monitoring, preparing charts, checking and restocking linens, carrying specimens to the laboratory.

Hugging babies. Some hospitals sponsor hug-a-baby programs for HIV-positive or drug-addicted babies. Crack babies need to be held and rocked by the hour because they are agitated. Often volunteers must undergo training first.

Helping AIDS patients. Programs for AIDS patients are growing all the time. You can assist by acting as chauffeur, preparing and delivering meals, walking or otherwise caring for the patient's pets, just being a friend. Contact the National AIDS Hotline: 800-342-2437; Spanish 800-344-7432; TTY 800-243-7889. Or check your local paper for volunteer activities.

Blood Drives. Of course, you can give blood. But you can also help with the drive itself. Local chapters of the American Association of Retired Persons, Red Cross, and American Association of Blood Banks often need workers.

Hotlines

Sometimes a stranger on the phone can do more to help a frightened, desperate person than a relative or friend can. Since strangers have no personal relationship with the caller, they listen more effectively. Since callers can't read the volunteers' faces they are less likely to hold back. And the anonymity of first names only (both of volunteer and caller) leads to an open exchange. (A few hotlines do not demand confidentiality. For instance, volunteers for a San Francisco program for suicidal elders ask callers for their phone numbers and call them back regularly, even make house calls, to stay in touch until the crisis is over.)

If you are interested in human relationships and their complexity, if you like hanging on the phone, if you are empathetic, this may be the volunteer activity for you. Common sense, of course, helps too. If you want to work for a hotline, look in the paper for opportunities to

volunteer or call a local social service agency. Some hotlines are general and field all sorts of problems—from "my mother doesn't understand me" to serious threats of suicide. Others are more specific: family, gay, ethnic, suicide prevention, rape, drug and alcohol abuse. Some hotlines call older people—many of whom live alone—to check on how they feel and remind them to take medications. Hotlines aimed at teenagers often employ other teenagers as volunteers. Teens counsel teens on problems with parents, siblings, and peers; on alcohol and drug abuse; on sex, pregnancy, and abortion; on self-esteem and puberty. Peer-to-peer influence is more powerful, delivers more impact.

Hotline volunteers provide invaluable service as empathetic listeners and referral agents. Professionals (psychologists and social workers) train volunteers—teaching them, often through role-playing, how to use communication and listening techniques, what the ethical implications of working on a hotline really are, where to find resources for referral.

It is important for volunteers to know that they are not responsible for what callers eventually do. Volunteers must neither diagnose nor treat, just care. They must not give advice but help callers decide. They need to be confident and empathetic yet professional. Part of the training focuses on awareness—awareness of the volunteer's own biases about child abuse, abortion, rape, extramarital sex, bigotry, incest. It is important that volunteers not let their own value systems prevent them from hearing what the caller has to say.

Volunteers are part of the network of social services and act as a kind of clearinghouse. If an agency has food to give away, it will notify a hotline, so that a hungry caller can be fed. Volunteers also refer callers to emergency shelters, food centers, counseling. Volunteers must be up-to-date on the services available. Complete and updated lists of facilities and organizations are an absolute necessity.

Part of the job is to make notes about calls, so that when a new shift comes on they will have information about previous callers (who often call

SUICIDE HOTLINES

Hotline volunteers who handle calls from suicidal persons must immediately separate the caller from the potential means of suicide. While maintaining rapport and keeping the caller on the phone, the volunteer tries to find out if he or she has a specific means planned, if the means are immediately available, how lethal the means are. The immediate goal is to get the caller to take the bullets out of the gun and put it away or flush the pills down the toilet. After that, the volunteer can engage callers in discussion, acknowledging their pain, putting particular attention on getting them to agree to a plan of action like talking to a counselor.

again). One valuable piece of advice is to take a few minutes before starting to answer calls in order to shift gears and clear your head so that you can listen without internal distraction.

One model for handling hotlines—the crisis model—involves four steps:

♦ Reflection. Show empathy, nonjudgmental acceptance, and sensitivity. Empathy (feeling *with* the person) is not the same as sympathy (feeling *for* the person), which can seem condescending. Empathy establishes equality. Listen to everything the callers say—all is significant. Let them vent their emotions. Don't assume you know what their problems are. Don't finish their sentences for them, even if you "know" what they are going to say. Pay attention to emotions as well as words.

♦ Assessment and exploration. Discuss options and decisions, then summarize them. For example, if a caller has a drinking problem, you might discuss (not recommend) the possibility of joining Alcoholics Anonymous.

♦ Agreement. Encourage the caller to agree to take action. This may involve getting in touch with a counselor or social service agency. If the problem is drugs, it may involve getting treatment.

PERSONLESS HOTLINE

The Community Awareness Phone System (CAPS) is an electronic hotline—the machine answers and a recorded voice talks to you, transmitting information. Some people find it easier to listen to a recorded voice than to a real person—it eliminates the fear of being judged and is truly anonymous. And it's available 24 hours a day.

Here's how the system works. After you call the local program's telephone number (using a touch-tone phone), you punch in the number code of the message you want to hear. Lasting from two to four minutes, the messages deal with issues like sexuality, suicide, drug abuse, homework, depression, eating disorders, alcoholism, aging. Examples: How You Don't Get AIDS; Getting Your GED; Date Rape; Fight Osteoporosis: Bone Up On Calcium. Messages encapsulate the wisdom of public health authorities, research centers, universities. They give information in a conversational, unpatronizing way, but do not preach. For example, Are You Tired of Being a Teen-Ager? suggests that the teenager look at problems like a diplomat, and "outguess" adults by doing what they expect before they ask for it. The messages also suggest counseling and emergency treatment.

The system is used by the armed services, communities, colleges, hospitals, and businesses. Luby's cafeteria chain sets up Community Awareness Phone lines in communities it serves. Other groups that have established CAPS lines are Planned Parenthood and United Way.

CAPS was developed by the **Institute for Drug and Alcohol Prevention,** 1655 South Rancho Santa Fe Road, Suite 107, San Marcos, CA 92069 (619-752-7201; FAX 619-752-7210). The Institute charges a one-time fee to initiate the system, then updates it for nothing.

A Pick-and-Shovel Vacation

The best of both worlds: on vacation, a history buff works to restore a European castle, a lover of archaeology unearths artifacts on a Central American dig, a scuba diver examines an underwater site at the Great Barrier Reef, a bug collector gathers insects in the rain forest, a photographer photographs a foreign festival. On such vacations, which are sponsored by a variety of organizations, you often get to work with a professional, to learn about what interests you most—*and* to improve the world. If you are involved in a scholarly enterprise, when the paper is published you receive a copy, maybe even a mention. On other vacation-travel programs, you might help to build a school or a house for an impoverished family in a Third World country.

To become involved in such enterprises, you usually must be over 16, but there is almost always no upper age limit. Most volunteers are screened for physical stamina.

Write or call:

Archaeological Fieldwork Opportunities Bulletin, published by Kendall-Hunt Publishing Company, 4050 West Mark Drive, Dubuque, IA 52002 (800-228-0810). Send for this compendium of information on worldwide digs. It costs about $6.

Archaeological Institute of America, Dept. WT, 505 Park Avenue, 20th Floor, New York, NY 10022 (212-759-4800). A Fieldwork and Opportunities Bulletin costs about $5. This group serves as a clearinghouse for volunteer opportunities in archaeological research.

Council on International Educational Exchange, International Workcamp Dept., 205 East 42nd Street, New York, NY 10017 (212-661-1414, x1139). Young adults over 18 can work for two to four weeks in Canada and Europe on digs and on other projects, including restoring castles and working with handicapped children. The cost includes transportation and a fee.

Earthwatch, Box 403, Watertown, MA 02272 (800-776-0188). This group has sponsored a variety of university and museum programs—from studying animals in the rain forest or on a coral reef, to working with dolphins in Hawaii, to unearthing the prehistory of the Plains Indians on a dig in Nebraska. Cost varies and you pay your own transportation.

Elderhostel, Service Programs, 75 Federal Street, Boston, MA 02110 (617-426-8056). Studying marine mammals, building schools and homes, and other work-travel vacations for people 60 and over (and their spouse or companion if at least 50 years old).

Habitat for Humanity, International, 121 Habitat Street, Americus, GA 31709 (912-924-6935). Founded by Millard Fuller and sponsored by Jimmy and Rosalynn Carter, Habitat for Humanity uses volunteers to help build housing for families in countries all over the world. Depending on the program, you might work for a week or three years, and you might pay your own expenses or receive a small stipend. The work is a joint effort among volunteers and the families, who invest "sweat equity" into their new homes. Volunteers can also give time working in administration, doing word processing, translating, taking pictures, and performing many other useful services. (If you want to contribute money instead of time, $10 buys ten bricks, $75 buys a door, and $2500 buys a roof.)

Kibbutz Aliya Desk, 110 East 59th Street, New York, NY 10022 (212-318-6130). Work on a kibbutz (communal farm) in Israel. Cost is plane fare and registration fees.

Mercy Ships, PO Box 2020, Lindale, TX 75771 (800-772-SHIP). A shipping program that delivers medical and health care, Mercy Ships is part of Youth With a Mission, an international, interdenominational ministry. Mercy Ships puts to work volunteers of all ages—doctors and dentists who fix cleft palates and perform other medical services, accountants, computer specialists, engineers, carpenters, beauticians, secretaries, and more.

The Foundation for Field Research, PO Box 771, St. George's, Grenada (809-440-8854). The Foundation matches you to researchers—

archaeologists, botanists, animal behaviorists. You work hard and pay for the experience—about $300 a week in the United States and about $400 overseas. Transportation is your financial responsibility.

University Research Expeditions Program, University of California, Berkeley, CA 94720 (510-642-6586). Spring and summer expeditions originating from University of California campuses include Mayan archaeology, monkey behavior in Kenya, botany in Alaska. Cost varies and you pay your own air fare.

Note: The Ecotourism Society, 801 Devon Place, Alexandria, VA, 22314 offers a fact sheet on responsible "ecotours" to places of natural beauty and curiosity. You might not do any work on an ecotour, but, if it is properly run, you gain appreciation for nature and do nothing to hurt the environment or its people.

Maintaining the Wilderness

Several groups offer one-day, weekend, one-week, or two-week vacations maintaining trails in the wilderness. The work is backbreaking but satisfying. You hack away undergrowth, construct waterbars to guide water, chop weeds, build bridges, repair shelters, repaint signs. An example: members of the 31 clubs maintaining the 2099–mile Appalachian Trail, which runs from Maine to Georgia, have put in 135,000 hours of volunteer labor; each member may "adopt" a short stretch to keep up. Costs are minimal because you camp out. You pay for your transportation.

♦ Back Country Volunteers, PO Box 86, North Scituate, MA 02060-0086.

♦ American Hiking Society, Volunteer Vacations, PO Box 20160, Washington, DC 20041-2160 (703-255-9364).

♦ National Park Service, Office of Interpretation, Attn. Volunteers in the Parks Program, PO Box 37127, Washington, DC 20013-7127 (202-523-5270).

♦ Appalachian Mountain Club, Trail Program, PO Box 298, Gorham, NH 03581 (603-466-2721).

♦ Appalachian Trail Conference, Trail Crew Coordinator, PO Box 807, Harpers Ferry, WV 25425 (304-535-6331).

♦ Student Conservation Association, PO Box 550, Charleston, NH 03603 (603-543-1700).

♦ Sierra Club, Sierra Club Outing Department, 730 Polk St., San Francisco, CA 94109 (415-776-2211).

Being a Docent

If you like to teach, consider being a docent (from the Latin word meaning "to teach"). Usually all you need is time and a love of the subject. You don't have to be an expert—many institutions train their docents, sometimes in an afternoon or two, sometimes with a long course followed by an apprenticeship. The ability to speak more than one language is often a plus. You may become involved in outreach programs by giving classroom presentations in schools. Or you may lead walking tours to see bird life, old houses, historical artifacts. In addition to tours, docents also devise creative presentations for visitors. Often docents become involved in activities other than teaching, like ushering at the symphony or running a visitor center at a park.

The bonuses, besides your enjoyment of teaching, can include free classes, admission to the institution at all times, making new friends. As an insider, you have access to events the public usually does not attend—the birth of a baby at the zoo, diving with the fish at the aquarium, dress rehearsals.

The following institutions often seek volunteer guides:

♦ museum (art, science, history, natural history)

♦ historical society

♦ architectural foundation

♦ zoo

♦ park

♦ aquarium
♦ symphony
♦ opera
♦ botanic garden

TIME DOLLARS

Law professor Edgar Cahn promotes a notion called "time dollars," in which each hour of time that you spend helping someone else, say by tutoring or baby-sitting, can be "banked" as service credits that you can collect on later. For example, you might bank two hours of baby-sitting you did for a poverty-stricken mother, and later collect by having someone bring you a hot meal when you are sick in bed. You can also give "time dollars" away. His scheme, which assigns the same value to all labor, reinforces the social fabric and a sense of community. Time banks exist in many states, and Congress has given grants to get them going elsewhere.

Working with Youth

Children need adults other than their parents—as friends, mentors, coaches, just someone out of the official loop to talk to. Many children are at risk—because of our violent times, because of the disintegration of family life, because of peer pressure. Volunteers can help. Call your Head Start, local school, YMCA and YWCA, Boys'/Girls' Club, to discover opportunities.

Some possibilities: coaching a team, being a Girl Scout or Boy Scout leader (you don't need to be a parent), tutoring, mentoring, being a foster grandparent, acting as a school aide or crossing guard.

Helping Inner-City Children

To children in the inner city, often (though not always) violence lurks behind everyday activities,

broken homes are the norm, drug dealers sell on the street corner. Hundreds of programs exist to help inner-city youth to stay in school, avoid urban dangers, and acquire hope. Others involve them in volunteer programs that improve the community.

Check this list and your local newspaper for opportunities—if you want to become involved with helping inner-city youth. If, as an inner-city youth, you are interested in community programs and volunteering, go to the next article, "Volunteer Opportunities for Youth," p. 139.

Big Brothers/Big Sisters of America matches disadvantaged young people from single-parent households with adult role models, often creating a kind of extended family. If you want to be a Big Brother or Big Sister, someone from your local chapter will screen, interview, and train you. You can be married or single, with or without children. Usually, program directors ask that you commit to 3–4 hours a week for at least a year. Adults and youths (aged seven through high school graduation) are matched by interests. "Bigs" and "Littles" fish, become involved in sports, watch movies, ride bikes, climb mountains, go to the library, work on community projects together. As a "Big," you become a friend to your "Little" and provide cultural and learning experiences. Many local chapters are in need of Black men to act as Big Brothers in order to expose Black youth to models of success other than professional athletes. Though being a Big Brother or Big Sister takes commitment and energy, the rewards are great—it is possible to change the course of a life. National headquarters: 230 North 13th Street, Philadelphia, PA 19107 (215-567-7000).

Tutoring and Educational Opportunities. Your company may offer an inner-city educational program. For example, volunteers from Grand Met (Pillsbury, Burger King, Häagen-Dazs) teach elementary school classes about work attitudes and habits, kinds of work that are available, the importance of teamwork. The employees of Salomon Brothers, an investment banking firm, serve as one-on-one mentors for juniors and seniors at Paul Robeson High School for Business and

Technology in Brooklyn. Other companies have similar programs—for example, employees of some companies volunteer to tell school children about their work as secretaries, forklift operators, research scientists, marketing experts.

Drug Alliance Program, which is under the umbrella of Corporation for National and Community Service (once called ACTION), strengthens and expands local efforts to prevent illicit drug use and to educate against it. You can volunteer for a local program. See "Corporation for National and Community Service Regional Offices," p. 146.

Concerned Black Men matches black men as surrogate fathers and positive role models to boys in a mentoring program. They teach the boys how to relate to girls, to reconcile conflicts peacefully, to apply for jobs. In Washington, DC, black male professionals teach and mentor in second-grade classes every week at Stanton Elementary School. Call 215-276-2260, Monday, Wednesday, Friday, 9 AM to 4 PM, for information.

Sports. If you are expert in a sport, you might consider volunteering as a coach for an inner-city team. For instance, in St. Paul, Minnesota, volunteers teach children six to eight years old how to play hockey. There are programs like it for older children in other cities. In Los Angeles, volunteers teach inner-city children horsemanship—how to groom, care for, and ride horses.

Tennis player Arthur Ashe was instrumental in bringing the National Junior Tennis League to inner-city kids. Kids get balls and racquets, membership in the U.S. Tennis Association, and instruction from volunteers. Some young players have gone on to compete in college. Contact **U.S. Tennis Association,** PO Box 240015, Los Angeles, CA 90024-9115 (310-208-3838).

Reviving Baseball in Inner-Cities (RBI), established by major league baseball, sponsors inner-city baseball teams, partly to attract more black children to the sport that was first to open its major leagues to black athletes. (Little League has come close to disappearing in black communities.) Each year RBI teams, coached by volunteers, compete in an Inner-City World Series.

Team members are from 13 to 16 years old. Contact: **Reviving Baseball in Inner-Cities** (RBI), PO Box 4387, Diamond Bar, CA 91765 (909-860-9410).

Ballet. Founded by a member of the Sisters of St. Joseph, the St. Joseph Ballet Company of Santa Ana (a city near Los Angeles) has involved 350 children from 9 to 19 in ballet. Much of the work depends on volunteers, parents among them. The young dancers feel safe and challenged. A similar program may exist in your community, or you might consider starting one.

Mentoring. Lawyers in Los Angeles spend time with parolees from the California Youth Authority to help them establish positive goals and work toward them. Mad Dads, a group with its center in Nebraska, runs programs in which men in the community act as role models for youth. Michael D. O'Neal founded Fathers, Inc. in Boston to encourage young black men to shoulder parental and financial responsibility, build self-esteem, train for jobs. Based in Oakland, California, Simba (from the Swahili word for lion) matches inner-city African-American men with African-American boys aged 6 to 18. The men receive personal and business skills training, and in return commit themselves to 12 years of mentoring youths in ways of avoiding violence, among other things. Similar programs may exist in your community.

Volunteer Opportunities for Youth

Young people can volunteer, too. They are a great, underutilized resource, and volunteering helps to build their self-esteem. Kindergarten kids draw pictures for people in nursing homes, teenagers shop for groceries for invalids. Children act as peer tutors or conflict managers. Young adults become involved in youth corps programs.

Environment. Programs to involve youth in saving the environment exist in many cities. "Eco-Teams" in California tell people in parks not to litter. Other young people associated with the project give visitors a plastic bag to use in cleaning up and help in the effort themselves— volunteers have fished out as many as 1000 diapers on a short stretch of the creek running through Big Tujunga Canyon. The project is funded by the Forest Service, Los Angeles Conservation Corps, and California Environmental Project. Similar groups exist in other parts of the country. For instance, Urban Tree House, a community-based program, teaches inner-city youth about environmental ethics and forestry. It is sponsored by the National Park Service, Bureau of Land Management, American Recreation Coalition, and others, including community organizations and leaders. For information, contact Outdoor Recreation and Wilderness Research, Forestry Science Laboratory, Carlton/Green Street, Athens, GA 30602 (404-546-2451), or Robert Stanton, regional director, National Capital Region, National Park Service, 1100 Ohio Drive SW, Washington, DC 20242 (202-690-7005).

Student Community Service Program (SCS), part of Corporation for National and Community Service, gives grants to groups to encourage students to serve in projects that address the needs of poverty. To become involved you must be enrolled in a secondary school or postsecondary school. After receiving training, you may end up working in a hospital, homeless shelter, school, health clinic, senior center, nursing home—even a fire department. Contact: Corporation for National and Community Service, or the regional office nearest you. (See "Corporation for National and Community Service Regional Offices," p. 146.)

Youth Service America (800-394-4972; 202-296-2992) is a network that gives information about youth-corps programs. Participants receive a stipend close to the minimum wage. There may be a postservice benefit, depending on the individual program.

National Association of Service and Conservation Corps will provide a free state-by-state directory of some 80 youth service and conservation corps. Address: 666 11th Street

NW, Suite 500, Washington, DC 20001 (202-737-6272).

Campus Compact. A coalition of colleges and universities offers campus-based public-service programs. For a guide to schools with such programs, send a $20 check to: Campus Compact, Brown University, Box 1975, Providence, RI 02912 (401-863-1119).

Campus Outreach Opportunity League (COOL), started by recent college graduates in 1984, gives encouragement and expert advice to service programs started by young people. Call 202-296-2992.

Hosting a Foreign Student

It is difficult to decide who gains the most when a host family or individual takes in a foreign student. The cultural exchange is rich—host and guest eliminate stereotypes and create country-to-country friendship. Here is a way to learn about another country without leaving home, to do something on a personal level to promote world understanding. For most programs you need not have children or be married. However, you *are* screened. The student may stay in your home for several weeks, a semester, or a year.

Groups

A book of 58 youth exchange programs accepted for listing and operating in the United States can be obtained by sending $8.50 to the accrediting organization: Council on Standards for International Educational Travel (CSIET), 3 Loudoun St. SE., Leesburg, VA 22075 (703-771-2040). Some Future Farmers of America and 4-H Councils also sponsor exchange programs. Call your local branch for information.

American Field Service (AFS) goes back to a World War II dream of peace through intercultural understanding. It is the world's oldest nonprofit student exchange and has sponsored more than 180,000 exchange students. Address:

American Field Service (AFS) Summer International Program, 313 East 43rd Street, New York, NY 10017 (800–AFS-INFO).

Youth for Understanding (YFU) is a private, nonprofit international student exchange organization based in Washington, DC. YFU has arranged for more than 150,000 student exchanges since its inception in the early 1950s. Host families give room and board, provide guidance, help students experience American life. Address: Youth For Understanding International Exchange, 3501 Newark Street NW, Washington, DC 20016 (800-424-3691).

Other youth exchange programs include:

American Intercultural Student Exchange, 7720 Herschel Avenue, La Jolla, CA 92037 (619-459-9761).

Open Door Student Exchange, 839 Steward Avenue, Suite D, Garden City, NY 11538 (800-366-6736).

U.S. Summer Abroad, The Experiment in International Living, World Learning, Inc., Kipling Road, PO Box 676, Brattleboro, VT 05302-0676 (800-345-2929 or 802-257-7751).

Child Advocacy

"As a judge, I had to make tough decisions. I had to decide whether to take a child from the only home he'd ever known, or leave him someplace where he might possibly be abused. I needed someone who could tell me what was best for that child—from the child's viewpoint. That's what CASA does."
—David Soukup, founder of CASA (Court-Appointed Special Advocate Association).

Who will speak in court for children, who often cannot articulate their needs? Children who are victims of violence or abuse, who have been neglected or even abandoned by their parents, can also suffer at the hands of the child welfare system, a complex network of overburdened professionals who are sometimes too busy to give the children the attention they need. Most are

confused and frightened. This problem brought about the Child Abuse Prevention and Treatment Act of 1974, which specified that every abused and neglected child brought before a court should be represented by a guardian *ad litem* (personal advocate). However, the duties of the guardian *ad litem* were not clearly defined by Congress. And funding often isn't available. The remedy—unpaid, well-trained volunteers—comes through **CASA,** 2722 Eastlake Avenue E, Suite 220, Seattle, WA 98102 (206-328-8588; 800-628-3233; FAX 206-323-8137). All fifty states have CASA programs, "a child's voice in court." Endorsed by the American Bar Association, CASA has more than 30,000 volunteers working with more than 100,000 abused or neglected children. Not all children who need an advocate have one. Only about one-fourth do. More volunteers are needed.

Though requirements vary from place to place, CASA volunteers usually must be adults and must submit to law enforcement screening and abuse registry background checks. No special education is required—they do not have to be lawyers or social workers. Some volunteers are students, some have full-time jobs, some are retired. They come from all walks of life and from a variety of racial and ethnic backgrounds. But they have something powerful in common: a concern for children.

Training requirements vary, with the average course lasting about 24 hours. Principals in the system—judges, lawyers, social workers, and others—teach courtroom procedure. Volunteers learn effective advocacy techniques and attend seminars on child sexual abuse, cultural awareness, early childhood development, and adolescent behavior.

Once trained, CASA volunteers are appointed by the court to take on cases of children who have suffered neglect or abuse and who are wards of the court. They get to know the children, to understand the case, and to keep up with the people and agencies that serve the child. They go into the child's home, talk to parents, lawyers, social workers, therapists. They probe. They review records. Most of all, they talk to the child. Once they have explored the case, they report to the judge what they have found. Before the first court appearance, the volunteer may spend 10 hours on research and interviews.

Volunteers keep the court process moving and speak for the children who suffer from that process; and they help the court decide what is in the best interests of the child. Court cases like this tend to stall because they are not made public. Children get lost in the system. For instance, if the court terminates parental rights, the child may be left in a foster home—a kind of limbo. Volunteers provide continuity for children through long court cases, then try to get them into a permanent, stable situation. Sometimes they work to keep the child at home. Volunteers have time for all this, unlike social workers who often have dozens of cases, and judges who have only a few minutes for each case. Most volunteers work 10–15 hours a month. They remain with cases until the cases are permanently resolved.

Each CASA is funded separately, with private or public money. Some are part of the juvenile court. Locally CASA programs are known by several names—Guardian ad Litem, ProKids, Child Advocates, Inc., FOCAS, Voices for Children, and more.

WHY CASA?

> ♦ Children with CASA volunteers have a better chance of living in safe, permanent homes than children who do not have a volunteer.
> ♦ CASA can reduce the number of times a child is moved from foster home to foster home.
> ♦ CASA helps to reduce juvenile delinquency.
> ♦ Children who have a CASA volunteer spend less time in the court system.
> ♦ CASA saves tax dollars.

Reprinted courtesy of National Court-Appointed Special Advocate (CASA) Association.

Volunteer Programs for Older People

Older people are a great social resource, often neglected because of stereotypes of them as helpless and valueless. Many programs—aware of the true value of the old—seek to use their wisdom and talents.

Foster Grandparent Program. The old and the young often have a special tie—grandparents can relax and enjoy their grandchildren in ways they found impossible with their own children. However, often their grandchildren live far away. And poorer senior citizens welcome a chance to make a little extra cash. These two facts play into the success of the Foster Grandparents Program (under the aegis of Corporation for National and Community Service/VISTA), which pays low-income senior citizens over 60 a small hourly wage for working with sick, handicapped, abused, neglected, or troubled children. If you are chosen to be a Foster Grandparent, you will receive training and a small stipend for transportation, a meal here and there while working, accident and liability insurance, and an annual physical exam. You might work with children in a school, hospital, correctional facility, mental retardation center, or day-care center. Some Foster Grandparents help with difficult situations at home. For instance, Foster Grandparents help supervise latchkey children who go to the library after school because the library is safe and it offers something to do. To be a Foster Grandparent, contact the Retired Senior Volunteer Program under Corporation for National and Community Service/VISTA, 202-606-5000. For regional offices, see "Corporation for National and Community Service Regional Offices," p. 146.

AARP Tax Aide. The American Association of Retired Persons (AARP) sponsors a tax aide program that helps people who cannot afford a professional tax preparation service but have difficulty doing their taxes themselves. The aides, senior citizens, have to pass an open-book test before they are allowed to prepare returns for others. People seeking help need not be senior citizens. If their returns are too complicated, the group refers them to a tax professional. Write: AARP Tax-Aide, 601 E Street NW, Washington, DC 20049 (202-434-2277).

RSVP (Retired Senior Volunteer Program), Corporation for National and Community Service Agency, 1100 Vermont Avenue NW, Washington, DC 20525; or contact your regional office (see "Corporation for National and Community Service Regional Offices," p. 146). The talents and interests of people 60 and over are matched with part-time volunteer opportunities under the auspices of local service organizations. You serve without pay but can be reimbursed for some expenses. You might help the chronically ill, handicapped, or other people with special needs; serve teenage parents; work in a literacy or drug abuse program; mentor a young person; care for a baby; tutor educationally disadvantaged children.

AARP Volunteer Talent Bank, 601 E Street NW, B–3–440, Washington, DC 20049 (202-434-2277). Anyone 50 or over can contact the Talent Bank, which matches volunteers with opportunities. Some AARP opportunities:

♦ AARP/Vote—help inform the electorate about issues concerning older persons.

♦ Consumer Housing and Information Service for Seniors (CHISS)—provide one-to-one counseling on housing for older persons.

♦ Health Advocacy Services (HAS)—organize walking events, participate in health fairs, and otherwise help older people comprehend the health care system.

♦ Legal Counsel for the Elderly (LCE)—provide legal and financial help.

♦ Minority Affairs Spokespersons—find ways to promote change in attitudes and actions of minorities and the population at large.

♦ Women's Financial Information Program—offers workshops on money-related topics.

Aging Services Division, Corporation for National and Community Service Agency, 2900 Newton Street NW, Washington, DC 20018 (202-529-8701), or contact your regional office. (See "Corporation for National and Community Service Regional Offices," p. 146.) You may or may not

be paid a small stipend to help someone less able than you to live independently through the Senior Companion Program (SCP). Costs of volunteering are covered by SCP sponsors. To qualify you must be low-income, able to work for 20 hours a week, over 60. You help with shopping and other errands, provide exercise and recreational activities, assist with food preparation, monitor health, care for the terminally ill.

Women's Issues

The battle for justice and equality for women is not over. Women face poverty, violence, employment discrimination, poor health care, lack of reproductive choice. If you want to work directly on women's issues, consider volunteering at your local battered women's center, mentoring girls in the public schools, supporting rape victims, helping single mothers, working to elect women candidates to Congress.

The **National Network of Women's Funds,** Suite 409 North, 1821 University Avenue, St. Paul, MN 55104-2801 (612-641-0742), gives grants and provides training and technical assistance to local groups that help women and girls overcome racial, economic, political, sexual, and social discrimination. This organization includes the following groups:

Astraea, National Lesbian Action Foundation, 666 Broadway #520, New York, NY 10012 (212-529-8021; FAX 212-982-3321). A multiracial, multicultural group of women seeking to eradicate oppression based on sexual orientation, race, age, gender, and other forms of discrimination.

Global Fund for Women, 2480 Sand Hill Road #100, Menlo Park, CA 94025-6941 (415-854-0420; FAX 415-854-8050). Grant-making organization providing funds to seed, strengthen, and link groups committed to work for women's well-being and their full participation in society; has international emphasis.

Harmony Women's Fund, PO Box 300105, Minneapolis, MN 55403 (612-377-8431). Supports organizations and projects run by women dedicated to transforming social systems that oppress women and to eradicating violence against women.

The Kaider Foundation, PO Box 4896, Mountain View, CA 94040 (415-988-8568; FAX 415-493-6367). Gives scholarships to women returning to the health care field.

Ms. Foundation for Women, 141 Fifth Avenue, 6th Floor, Suite 6-S, New York, NY 10010 (212-353-8580, FAX 212-475-4217). A national, multi-issue public women's fund supporting the effort of women and girls to govern their own lives and influence the world around them.

Nokomis Foundation, 48 Fountain Street NW, Grand Rapids, MI 49503 (616-451-0267; FAX 616-451-8481). Named for the Native American word for the passing down of knowledge and wisdom from grandmother to younger women. Works for feminist advocacy, community awareness and education, public policy, and research.

Open Meadows Foundation, PO Box 197, Bronx, NY 10464 (718-768-4015). Offers small grants to programs designed and implemented by women, reflecting the cultural and ethnic diversity of society and promoting the well-being of women.

Shaler Adams Foundation, 2480 Sand Hill Road #100A, Menlo Park, CA 94025 (415-854-9805; FAX 415-233-0816). Promotes national and international efforts to advance the cause of women's rights as human rights. Combats violence against women and supports organizing and advocacy by refugee and immigrant women to raise their voices in affecting public policy.

The Sister Fund, 1255 Fifth Avenue, Suite C–2, New York, NY 10029 (212-722-7606; FAX 212-534-6173). Seeks to empower women economically, socially, politically, and spiritually through grass-roots and national advocacy and media strategies.

The Spring Foundation for Research on Women in Contemporary Society, 316 El Verano Avenue, Palo Alto, CA 94306 (415-856-4121). Funds research on women's strengths, resources, and perseverence in the face of adversity.

Thanks Be to Grandmother Winifred Foundation, PO Box 1449, Wainscott, NY 11975 (516-725-0323). Funds women over 54 years old to encourage them to use their creativity to improve the lives of women.

Also consider:

Planned Parenthood Foundation of America, 810 Seventh Avenue, New York NY 10019 (212-541-7800; 800-829-PPFA). Works on women's issues such as reproductive choice.

Literacy

Few activities bring as much joy as teaching someone to read. The opportunities to do so are great in America—70 other countries have higher literacy rates than the United States. At least one in five Americans is functionally illiterate, which means that he or she lacks the reading skills to live in modern society. Functional illiterates have fourth- to eighth-grade skills but can't fill out a job application, figure out a train schedule, read a newspaper. Many others have basic reading skills but still can't function very well. Most people with this problem are under 50, with at least eight years of school. Why does illiteracy exist? Experts cite immigration and the high school dropout rate (30 percent of high school population). Adult illiterates are not unintelligent—most have learned clever ways to hide their problem. They can't read street signs, menus, recipes— but you'd never know it.

According to the U.S. Department of Health, Education and Welfare, a person learning to read needs 100 hours of instruction in order to advance one grade level. Public libraries have been in the forefront in supporting literacy and in providing direct instruction. The family literacy movement seeks to break the illiteracy cycle and teaches reading and parenting simultaneously, often but not always involving children. A national organization, the Literacy Volunteers of America, might be a way to start finding out how you can become a literacy volunteer.

Laubach Literacy Action, 1320 Jamesville Avenue, PO Box 131, Syracuse, NY 13210 (315-422-9121).

Literacy Volunteers of America, National Capital Area, 1325 W Street NW, Room 312, Washington, DC 20009 (202-387-1772).

National Literacy Hotline: 800-424-7323.

SCALE School of Education, CB # 3500, University of North Carolina, Chapel Hill, NC 27599-3500 (919-962-1524).

Saving Your Library

Civilizations exist on shaky ground when their libraries fail, so they tell us in school. American libraries, bastions of democracy in an age of information, are in big trouble, and it concerns us all. Libraries give us more than books: they also provide adult literacy programs, places to go for latchkey kids, information sources for the jobless, and more. In fact, four out of 10 U.S. citizens visit the library at least once a month.

You can help to keep your library open and flourishing.

♦ Join the "Friends of the Library" in your community. If one does not exist, consider starting one in cooperation with your librarian.

♦ Find out what the library needs and buy it.

♦ Get cooperation from businesses in your area.

♦ Volunteer to shelve books or otherwise help out.

♦ Arrange for guest readers (Guest Reader program) to come to the school or library and read to children, and be one of the readers yourself.

♦ Stage events to raise money for your library—book fairs, used book sales, auctions.

♦ Start a program through which people can donate a book to the library for someone's birthday or in memory of a loved one.

National Full-Time Service Opportunities

Mary Le Baron, mother of nine, became a Peace Corps Volunteer at the age of 61 in Honduras. Working with 69 girls living in a group center, she taught them nutrition, gardening, cooking, English (among other things) and encouraged them to go into business for themselves. Peace Corps Volunteer Oscar Corvison designed and built flood control facilities, silos, floating docks for fishing cooperatives, and a cotton gin for credit cooperatives in Paraguay. Elizabeth Muñoz counseled Denver teenagers during her stint working for VISTA.

If you are committed to helping people and can take a year or more to work full-time, consider one of the more than 33,000 full-time opportunities offered by the government or private organizations.

Volunteers in Service to America, VISTA Recruitment, 1100 Vermont Avenue NW, Washington, DC 20525 (202-606-5000, x230; TTY 202-606-5256; 800-833-3722) or regional Corporation for National and Community Service office. (See "Corporation for National and Community Service Regional Offices," p. 146.) VISTA supports local programs employing full-time people working against poverty in underprivileged urban and rural American communities. You might end up working in a literacy program, teaching substance abuse prevention, helping the mentally ill and developmentally disabled. You might work with Native Americans or migrant workers or refugees. You might fix up houses, provide financial counseling, distribute food. Length of service is one year. You must be 18 or above, and you receive training, a basic living allowance (less than minimum wage), and health insurance. At the end of your service, you receive additional pay for each month served, and you can write off at least part of some college loans.

Peace Corps of the United States, PRU Box 941, Washington, DC 20526 (800-424-8580).

Peace Corps volunteers work overseas in grass-roots development. To qualify, you must be at least 18, in good health, a U.S. citizen, preferably a college graduate or someone with substantive work experience. There is no upper age limit. You might teach, provide technical assistance to small business, work with community development, health, nutrition, or environmental projects. To be more specific, you could:

♦ teach beekeeping, farm mechanics, soil science, forest and wildlife management, fish culture, math or English or library science

♦ practice nursing or health counseling

♦ help people in the community build bridges or houses or irrigation systems.

If accepted, you sign up to serve for two years and spend three more months in training in the country where you will work. The stipends are based on what a local person would make, and you are given free medical and dental care. Most student loan payments are deferred while you are serving in the Peace Corps, and some are forgiven. Service in the Peace Corps does not alter Social Security benefits. On completing service, you receive a readjustment allowance of several thousand dollars. Returning volunteers are eligible for government service and more than 50 college scholarships and assistantships.

Military Service. Joining the military can give you educational opportunities and the satisfaction of serving your country. If you are contemplating joining the military, schedule an interview with your local recruiter. You can find recruiting offices listed in the U.S. Government pages in your phone book under the name of the service branches. Write down any questions you have ahead of time, otherwise you may forget them in the course of your conversation. Bring with you your birth certificate, high school diploma or GED documentation, college transcripts, Social Security card, driver's license or permit, letter from your doctor about any special medical condition you have or have had. In the interview, be honest. Lies can prevent you from being further processed.

The next step is to take the Armed Services Vocational Aptitude Battery (ASVAB), then, hav-ing passed it, to undergo a physical exam. All the services prefer enlistees with high school diplomas. They offer:

♦ housing and meals

♦ free medical and dental care

♦ extra pay for certain types of duty

♦ regular promotions based on ability

♦ thirty days' paid vacation every year

♦ bonuses for enlistment or reenlistment in certain jobs

♦ full pay and allowances during training and while attending school

♦ savings from shopping at exchange stores and commissaries

♦ free and low-cost entertainment facilities

♦ advanced education at little or no cost

♦ excellent retirement programs after 20 years of service.

The Montgomery GI Bill (MGIB) Program gives a considerable sum of money for college education. The military will pay for some or all of your college expenses while you are in the service (after two years of active duty); or up to 10 years after you receive an honorable discharge (provided you put in at least three years of active duty).

Corporation for National and Community Service Regional Offices

Corporation for National and Community Service, the Federal Domestic Volunteer Agency, includes the following programs: Volunteers in Service to America (VISTA), the Foster Grandparents Program (FGP), the Retired Senior Volunteer Program (RSVP), the Senior Companion Program (SCP), the Student Community Service program (SCS), and the Program Demonstration and Development Division (PDDD). Contact a regional office:

Region 1 (Connecticut, Maine, Massachusetts, New Hampshire, Vermont, Rhode Island), Room 473, 10 Causeway Street, Boston, MA 02222-1039 (617-565-7000).

Region II (New Jersey, New York, Puerto Rico, Virgin Islands), Room 758, 6 World Trade Center Bldg., New York, NY 10048-0206 (212-466-3481).

Region III (Kentucky, Maryland, Delaware, Ohio, Pennsylvania, Virginia, West Virginia, Washington, DC), 801 Arch Street, Suite 103, Philadelphia, PA 19107-2416 (215-597-9972).

Region IV (Alabama, Florida, Georgia, Mississippi, North Carolina, South Carolina, Tennessee), Suite 1003, 101 Marietta Street NW, Atlanta, GA 30323-2301 (404-331-2860).

Region V (Illinois, Indiana, Iowa, Michigan, Minnesota, Wisconsin), Room 442. 77 West Jackson Blvd., Chicago, IL 60604-3511 (312-353-5107).

Region VI (Arkansas, Kansas, Louisiana, Missouri, New Mexico, Oklahoma, Texas), Room 6B11, 1100 Commerce Street, Dallas, TX 75242-0696 (214-767-9494).

Region VII (Colorado, Wyoming, Montana, Nebraska, North Dakota, South Dakota, Utah), Suite 2930, Executive Tower Bldg., 1405 Curtis Street, Denver, CO 80202-2349 (303-844-2671).

Region VIII (Arizona, California, Hawaii, Nevada, Guam, American Samoa), Room 530, 211 Main Street, San Francisco, CA 94105-1914 (415-744-3013).

Region IX (Alaska, Idaho, Oregon, Washington), Suite 3190, Jackson Federal Bldg., 915 Second Avenue, Seattle, WA 98174-1103 (206-553-1558).

Note: TTY callers (national number): 202-606-5256.

Donating Time as a Professional

As a professional volunteer—a lawyer, doctor, bookkeeper, teacher—you can provide invaluable help to a poor or isolated community, and in so doing, you can often pay off college loans. Here are some opportunities.

Health Workers. National Health Service Corps, 8201 Greensboro Drive, Suite 600, McLean, VA 22102 (800-221-9393; 703-734-6855 in Virginia). Offers scholarship money and loan repayment to health care workers interested in practicing in underserved areas. Stipend is paid by the clinics where health care workers work.

Lawyers. The National Association for Public Interest Law, 1118 22nd Street NW, Washington, DC 20037 (202-466-3686). Clearinghouse for programs that forgive or repay law school and state loans. For a copy of "Choosing Wisely," a guide to programs around the country, send a $25 check.

Chefs. You can donate expertise to a soup kitchen. Or you might become involved in something more ambitious. For example, some chefs cooked their famous dishes for "Taste of the Nation," a fund-raiser for the hungry and homeless sponsored by American Express Company and "Share Our Strength," (SOS), 1511 K Street NW, Suite 940, Washington, DC 20005 (202-393-2925).

Pilots. AirLifeLine, 6133 Freeport Blvd., Sacramento, CA 95822 (800-446-1231). Pilots volunteer time, planes, and fuel to fly ambulatory medical patients and companions to another city for a visit to a doctor or hospital. They fill in when airlines refuse to carry patients because of their condition or their inability to afford air fare. Patients need a letter from a professional (doctor or social worker) about the diagnosis and reason for the trip, as well as evidence of financial need.

Organ Donation: The Gift of Life

After you die, your body parts can continue to live in the bodies of other people who desperately need them. Every four hours someone needing a transplant dies, often for lack of a donated organ. Of the 31,000 Americans who need a new organ, 75 percent need a kidney. Each year, 12,000–15,000 people become potential donors, able to give multiple organs (the average is 3.5). However, only about a third of those people actually donate organs. Why? Not all hospitals donate. Some potential donors are unsuitable because they are too old or have HIV at death. Families are often too grief-stricken to make the decision, or hospital staff do not approach them. (Yet families who do arrange for donation of their loved ones' organs find it therapeutic.)

In a Gallup poll sponsored by Partnership for Organ Donation, 85 percent of the Americans polled said they support organ donation, 70 percent claimed to be willing to donate their own organs, and 93 percent of families were willing to consent to a donation by a family member if that family member wished it. Yet only one in four Americans (67 million) have *officially* agreed to donate their organs after death. People can officially give permission for organ donation through the Uniform Anatomical Gift Act or another law. Some states allow drivers to sign an organ donor card as part of their licenses, which is, however, only an indication of your wishes, not a legal document. If you want to donate your organs, make sure that you have a donor card signed in the presence of witnesses and that someone in your family knows of your desire. Even if you sign a card, medical personnel are required to ask permission of your family.

For a donor registration card, write to:

CORE (Center for Organ Recovery & Education), 204 Sigma Drive, RIDC Park, Pittsburgh, PA 15238 (800-DONORS7).

Top 10 Misconceptions Regarding Organ Donation

1. *I do not want my body mutilated.*

Organs are surgically removed, similar to gallbladder or appendix removal. Normal funeral arrangements are possible.

2. *Donating my organs probably would cost my family too much money.*

A donor's family is not charged for donation. If a family is billed incorrectly, the family immediately should contact its local organ procurement organization.

3. *I might want to donate one organ, but I do not want to donate everything.*

You may specify what organs may be donated. Your wishes will be followed.

4. *If I am in an accident and the hospital knows that I want to be a donor, the doctors will not try to save my life.*

The medical team treating you is separate from the transplant team. The transplant team is not involved until all lifesaving efforts have failed and death is determined.

5. *I am not the right age for donation.*

Organs may be donated from someone as young as a newborn. Age limits for organ donation no longer exist: however, the general age limit for tissue donation is 60.

6. *If I donate, I would worry that the recipient and/or his family would discover my identity and cause more grief for my family.*

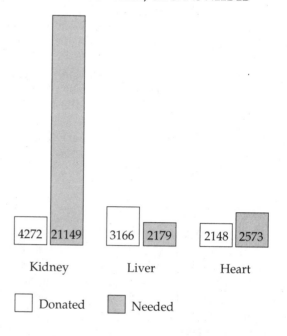

ORGANS DONATED, ORGANS NEEDED

	Donated	Needed
Kidney	4272	21149
Liver	3166	2179
Heart	2148	2573

Source: United Network for Organ Sharing and Health Resources and Services Administration

Information about the donor is released to the recipient if the family that donated requests the information be provided to the recipient.

7. *My religion does not support donation.*

All major religions support donation, typically considered a benevolent act that is the individual's choice.

8. *You can only transplant a heart, liver, and kidney.*

In addition to the heart, liver, and kidneys, lungs and intestine can be transplanted. The islet cells from the pancreas, and in some cases, the pancreas itself, also can be transplanted. Cornea, bone, saphenous veins, tendons, heart valves, and skin are among the tissues that can be used for transplantation.

9. *Wealthy people are the only people who receive transplants.*

Anyone requiring a transplant is eligible for one. Arrangements often are made with the transplant hospital for those requiring financial assistance.

10. *I have a history of medical illness. You would not want my organs or tissues.*

Donors are evaluated on a case-by-case basis. At the time of death, CORE will review medical and social histories to determine donor suitability.

Reprinted courtesy of Center for Organ Recovery & Education (CORE).

Politics

Fulfilling Your Political Responsibilities

If you are like most of us, you read the paper in the morning, become incensed over some issue, decide to write a letter about it to the President or your Congressperson—then never quite get around to doing it. You may believe in voting but forget about it on Election Day. Yet you think the U.S. needs politically active citizens if it is to survive. Feeling guilty? Here are a few tips to galvanize you into action.

Voting

In years past, in order to register to vote, you needed to be enterprising or caught outside a supermarket by someone registering voters. If you refrained from voting for a certain period of time, your name was purged from the voting rolls. The motor-voter law of 1993 has made voting much easier. You can register by mail, when you apply for or renew a driver's license, when you visit some state agencies or military recruiting offices. The only way your name can be purged from the list is if:

♦ you request it
♦ you die
♦ you are convicted of a criminal offense
♦ you become mentally incapacitated
♦ you move to a new jurisdiction.

Making Your Voice Heard

When public hearings on important issues are held in your community, make the effort to go to them and speak up. Before the meeting, call city hall and arrange to be listed as a speaker at the meeting.

Join a citizens' watchdog network for your favorite cause, and respond when called upon to write letters or call government officials.

Communicating with government officials about issues that especially concern you carries great weight, though how much weight varies according to which statistics you read. However, government officials do take letters more seriously than phone calls, which are viewed by some as an annoyance. When you write, be concise, thoughtful, and logical. Tell how the issue affects you personally. Don't threaten.

If you don't know the addresses or phone numbers of officials, including members of Congress, ask at your library or call your local newspaper. For local officials, check the government listings in the white pages of your phone book.

Some computer software makes it easier for you to communicate with Washington:

♦ You can contact the White House through e-mail on Compuserve at 75300,3115; on America Online at "ClintonPz"; on MCI Mail at "White House." Include your postal address if you want an answer. The White House also issues transcripts of speeches, policy statements, and proc-

150

lamations through Compuserve (GO WHITE-HOUSE), America Online ("White House"), and MCI Mail ("View White House").

♦ You can contact members of Congress and other federal officials through Compuserve "Congressgrams." Prodigy performs a similar service, and will even print and deliver your letter—at a price considerably more than that of a stamp, however.

Grass-Roots Politics

Experts agree that grass-roots politics is growing and becoming more powerful. Consider such groups as THRO (Throw the Hypocritical Rascals Out), which works against incumbents. Or, on the political left, We the People and the Independence Party. Opposing them, on the Republican conservative side, are Empower America and Republican Majority Coalition.

Whether you want to become involved in national issues or local issues:

♦ Start at the neighborhood level, asking everyone to talk to friends, so knowledge of the issue and your proposed agenda to resolve it can spread by word of mouth. The other choice is to advertise, which costs money.

♦ Consider affiliating with a larger organization—community or homeowner associations, for instance.

♦ Adopt long-range and short-range goals, but emphasize immediate aims and actions. Make them simple, able to be accomplished immediately. For example, Parent Action has had as objectives: creating baby-sitting co-ops, supporting child care centers, registering parents to vote, fighting drug dealers, working for political candidates.

♦ Get an article about your group published.

♦ Raise money.

Boycotts as Political Weapons

According to the Institute for Consumer Responsibility of Seattle, Washington, a boycott is suc-cessful when it shows that it can cut profits, influence buying decisions through media coverage, and generate unfavorable public relations for the company or the product. It is easiest to boycott products that people often buy, that have an attention-getting brand name, and that are not necessary or can be replaced with other products.

The most important success factor in boycotting is to keep the focus. Before starting the boycott, write to the company and give it a chance to make changes. (Companies fear boycotts, partly because they are usually dominated by well-educated and affluent people—the very people they hate to alienate.) If you have no luck with this tactic, arrange a press conference, letting the company know that you are doing so but not cutting off chances for negotiation. Line up cosponsor support in the community. Decide on what you will claim as victory—a shutdown of the factory, the ending of a practice. Hold the press conference in a place as near the company as possible.

Maintain the boycott, bolstered with letter-writing campaigns, protests, other means. Don't give up.

Does a boycott work? Yes. Consider:

♦ The Rainforest Action Network boycott compelled Burger King to stop buying Costa Rican beef.

♦ Rocky Mountain Humane Society convinced Mary Kay Cosmetics to stop using animals in testing.

♦ An ACT UP (AIDS Coalition to Unleash Power) boycott forced Burroughs-Wellcome to lower the price of AZT.

♦ Tourists boycotted Arizona until it approved a Martin Luther King, Jr. Day.

Jury Duty

Each year 5.6 million Americans face the obligation of jury duty. The reactions of many are negative: They see it as a burden, and assume it's going to be boring. The boss may not be happy at having to pay them while they serve, and they may have to make up work. Their family won't be happy about their absence from home. Overriding all that: it's their civic duty.

Americans try to get out of jury duty for many reasons. Fear is one: they ask, if I find this person guilty, will he or she (or a confederate) follow me home and threaten or kill me? Rarely does this happen, if ever, except on television. When a danger exists, jurors are not named but are given numbers to identify them. A more reasonable fear is that of public reaction to an unpopular verdict. Also, jurors who hear a disturbing, nasty case often require a "psychological debriefing" afterward. Jury duty can be psychologically difficult, too, because of the responsibility.

Another problem is that a jury may be impaneled for 12 weeks, and most people cannot give up working for that long. This has a serious side effect: juries are composed mostly of retired people and individuals on unemployment, so often the group is not representative of society as a whole. In addition, persons from minority groups often are passed over for jury service because they are underrepresented on the lists (voter registration, driver's licenses) from which juries are drawn. And some persons from minority groups slide out of jury duty because they have no belief in the justice system. No matter what your situation, by accepting jury duty, you help to strengthen the American system of justice by making truer the phrase "jury of one's peers."

How the Jury System Works

The court system usually gets your name from voter registration lists or driver's license records. Once you report for jury duty on the designated date, you are interviewed, then are asked to fill out various forms requesting information about your employment status and other pertinent facts. Don't lie on the form—it is against the law. After this, you are given a panel number for selection on a specific jury. In some places you can go home after reporting—once home, you

can telephone a recording every day to find out if your number is being called.

How long will you have to serve? Laws about jury duty vary by jurisdiction—state, city, county. In Phoenix, for instance, grand jurors hear several cases a day two or three days a week for four months and petit jurors hear one case, though it may take several days for the case to close. More than 30 percent of Americans live in jurisdictions with a one-day/one-trial jury system. This means that you spend no more than one day waiting to be selected for a jury. If you are not selected, you are off the hook. If you are selected, you need serve for only one trial, no matter how short it is.

The majority of those called for jury duty do not actually serve. Many are legally exempt—have children and no child care, are police officers or hospital workers, or have some other function that is so important they cannot be spared. You can be excused if you have a physical disability, but if you want to serve, courts offer special assistance to the disabled—someone to translate proceedings into American Sign Language, other forms of printed information, transportation.

According to a study conducted by the Eagleton Institute of Politics at Rutgers University for the Institute for Law and Justice, Inc., 44 percent of people summoned for jury duty did not report, and 19 percent reported but did not serve on a jury. If you are called and do not report, you can be in trouble—a contempt of court charge and eventual arrest.

If You Are Chosen

Many courts give instructions, verbal or videotaped, on how to be a juror. As a juror, you wait until the judge needs you, and if you serve on a jury, you determine only if guilt has been proven, making decisions based on facts and on instructions from the judge. The defendant is presumed innocent until proven guilty. If guilt cannot be proven, he or she should be released, free and innocent.

In most places, you are compensated with a small amount of per diem pay—say, $10–20, and mileage to and from the courthouse. In some places, people who are being paid by employers are not compensated at least for part of their term of jury duty. In some, you receive more pay per day after you have served a certain number of days.

Most people who serve on juries are glad they did. Being on jury duty gives you an inside look into the judicial system. You know you are part of the process. And you might be fortunate enough to serve on a juicy, interesting case. But most of all, you will end up feeling proud that you have fulfilled your most elementary civic duty.

Proposed Jurors' Bill of Rights

This bill of rights, drawn up after a meeting sponsored by the Institute for Court Management, describes what a juror might expect from a system that functions well.

1. The right to be selected fairly: that the process be random, that it cover most of the eligible population and that it remain in place long enough for everyone to have the same opportunity to serve.

2. The right not to be excluded: that the process of exclusion be blind with respect to sex, race, religion, country of origin, physical impairment, or any other categorical criteria, and that there be no challenge of prospective jurors because of these characteristics.

3. The right to avoid hardship: that any reasonable request for postponement ordinarily be granted to allow service at a more convenient time.

4. The right to be properly informed: that the juror be given sufficient notice, that general instructions of the services required be provided, that the juror be advised of length of service, and that proper orientation be provided in all duties.

5. The right to be utilized efficiently: that a prospective juror be summoned only in the strong likelihood that service will be needed in *voir dire* or on a sworn jury, that the juror be treated with respect, that reasonable and comfortable surroundings be provided, that there be little waiting, and that jurors be excused as soon as service is no longer required.

6. The right to be free from employer or other harassment: that a prospective juror's employment not be affected in any way by the call to jury duty, and that the juror not be forced to request excuse from service.

7. The right to reasonable privacy: that citizens' private lives and affairs not be unreasonably investigated, that information made available to counsel be treated confidentially, that jurors be reasonably free from coercion to answer questions of reporters, and that they be protected as necessary from fear of reprisals for their verdicts.

8. The right to participate freely in deliberation: that the court outline the proper rules for deliberation, that the judge's instructions be direct and straightforward, that jurors treat each other with respect, that each be allowed to participate in discussions on issues before voting, that the use of notes be allowed in deliberation, and that deliberation be organized and orderly.

Reprinted with permission of the National Center for State Courts.

Proposed Changes in Treatment of Jurors

A report prepared by the Brookings Institution and the litigation section of the American Bar Association finds problems not with juries but with the judicial system. It suggests that juries have been rendering rational verdicts and are perfectly well equipped to hear complex cases. The judicial system does not respect them enough or involve them enough in the judicial process. It recommends:

♦ Jurors should be allowed to question witnesses and take notes.

♦ Rules of evidence should be simplified.

♦ Lawyers and judges should instruct jurors about the nature and direction of a trial. Judges should speak in plain English, not legal jargon, and they should give printed copies of instructions to the jury.

♦ Jurors should have the right to submit written questions to the judge anonymously, who would then read them to the witness.

♦ Jurors should be better treated and better paid.

MINNEAPOLIS'S 11 COMMANDMENTS OF COURTROOM BEHAVIOR

1. No standing.
2. No talking.
3. No eating, drinking, chewing gum.
4. No tobacco products.
5. No hats.
6. No signs.
7. No garments with trial-related messages or gang symbols on them.
8. No hand signs.
9. No reading in courtroom.
10. No electric/electronic recording devices.
11. No cameras, telephones, or pagers.

Saving the Environment

Ecological Crises and What You Can Do to Stop Them

Human beings and other disasters have laid waste to wetlands, streams and rivers, forests, savannahs. With the destruction of these natural sites goes destruction of the ecosystem—the plants, the trees, the animals.

Simple acts—taken together—can have large and disastrous consequences or a beneficial effect on the planet Earth. We all contribute, for good or ill. Garden runoff can pollute groundwater and rivers. CFCs (chlorofluorocarbons) from the refrigerator contribute to a growing hole in the protective ozone layer. The saving of a butterfly or bird adds to the beauty and complexity of nature. Riding a bicycle to work takes a small bit of the load off the atmosphere.

WATER

Estuaries. Estuaries, nurseries of wildlife where salt and fresh water mix, fringe the coasts of the United States. They are a shrinking fringe. Estuaries often are polluted with toxic wastes and metals. The natural balance of some estuaries is often upset with a nutrient overdose from storm-water runoff that contains lawn fertilizers and waste from defective septic systems, among other things. The runoff causes an excess of algae, which sucks oxygen from the water and drives out sea grasses.

Wetlands. A priceless resource, wetlands are habitats for plants and animals, including aquatic birds, and a place where fish and shellfish spawn. They also act somewhat like sponges to purify water and to store it, which controls the effects of droughts and floods. The National Audubon Society claims that almost 450,000 acres of wetlands are lost each year to development and farming.

Other Water Sources: Rivers, streams, and oceans suffer similar damage. Deforestation can cause erosion that silts streams and kills aquatic life. Pesticides in runoff poison the waters. The average American household uses 243 gallons of water a day. And drinking water supplies are being drained much too fast from natural sources.

AIR

Global Warming. This phenomenon, caused by carbon dioxide and other gases that trap the sun's heat and raise temperatures, may change the world's climate drastically within a hundred years if something is not done. With only 5 percent of the world's population, the United States, the worst culprit, produces 23 percent of carbon dioxide released into the atmosphere. Why worry? Global warming can turn farmlands barren, disrupt the economy. The process is already set in place—it *will* happen, but we may be able to change *how quickly* it will happen. This will give nations time to adjust.

Smog. Automobile emissions and other sources still blanket U.S. cities in smog. Even our national parks are threatened by smog.

Ozone Layer. Chlorofluorocarbons (CFCs), released into the air, break down and combine with oxygen atoms, starting a chemical reaction that destroys ozone in the atmosphere. The ozone layer blocks harmful solar ultraviolet light. When it is depleted, more ultraviolet light reaches the surface of the earth, increasing the incidence of skin cancer and cataracts, perhaps damaging human immune systems, destroying crops, and killing tiny water life. Chlorofluorocarbons, once formed, can last a century or more.

FORESTS

Clear-cutting old forests on steep slopes leads to soil erosion, muddy rivers, and destruction of wildlife habitats. Making products out of trees uses energy. And a tree cut down means more carbon dioxide entering the air. Products made from trees choke landfills. Americans throw out around 75 million tons of paper a year, and for that paper more than a billion trees died.

What You Can Do to Stop Ecological Disaster

♦ Drive less, or carpool. Walk or ride a bicycle instead. Buy an electric car. Keep your tires inflated to the proper pressure, and use radial tires.

♦ Don't dump motor oil or antifreeze down sewers or storm drains.

♦ Take old batteries, used motor oil, antifreeze, and brake fluid to your garage or auto store for recycling. Ask your tire dealer to recycle your tires—they can be retreaded, burned for fuel, made into a material for paving roads, used to produce other rubber products.

♦ Dispose of your toxins (drain cleaner, paint, etc.) at hazardous waste collection days held in your community. Call 800-424-9346, 8:30 AM–7:30 PM, EST, Monday through Friday, for waste collection stations near you.

♦ Buy rechargeable batteries or solar-powered items. Dry cell batteries contain toxic metals that end up in landfills or incinerators and can cause health problems. If you must use them, return them to the manufacturer so that they can be recycled, or work toward curbside pickup of old batteries in your community.

♦ Maintain your septic system.

♦ Clean up after your pets on the street.

♦ To decrease output of CFCs, make sure that if you buy a new car, the air-conditioning system is free of CFCs. Ask your mechanic to check your present air-conditioning system for CFC leaks. When you buy a new refrigerator, ask for a CFC-free model. Make sure that when your old refrigerator is repaired the CFCs are recaptured—encourage your utility company or community to pick up discarded refrigerators and freezers, recapture the CFCs, and recycle the metal.

♦ Don't burn wood in your fireplace or stove. Wood burning causes 15 percent of particulate emissions in the U.S., and it can affect respiratory health, especially of children. Cut back on outdoor grilling.

♦ Use low-flow shower heads and toilets. If we all made this change, the nation would save almost 3 trillion gallons of water a year, enough to supply water for all needs for a week.

♦ Fix dripping faucets. Buy washers for your garden hose where it connects to outdoor faucet. A drip can waste up to 350 gallons of water a month.

♦ Garden with native plants that don't use much water. Use drip systems rather than sprinklers.

♦ Don't overfertilize your lawn or use too many pesticides. Better yet, grow native plants that resist pests and thrive in poor soil.

♦ Save paper, recycle it, reuse it.

♦ Mail unwanted phone directories back to the companies that send them to you.

♦ Buy furniture from "smart wood" companies that harvest tropical wood without helping to destroy a forest. For lists, write to: **Rainforest Alliance,** 65 Blecker Street, New York, NY 10012. (212-677-1900); **Rainforest Action Network,** 450 Sansome Street, Suite 700, San Francisco, CA 94111 (415-398-4404).

Save electricity and other forms of energy:

♦ Replace incandescent bulbs with compact fluorescents, which use less than 25 percent of the electricity that incandescents do. (Make sure they will fit your fixtures.) If everyone replaced just one incandescent bulb with a compact flourescent, the U.S. would use 4 billion watts less electricity a year. This equals the production of four big nuclear power plants.

♦ Air-dry laundry.

♦ When you go on vacation, turn off your electric heater and electric water heater at the circuit breaker. Leave the pilot light burning on a gas water heater, but turn it down to the "pilot" setting. Put gallon jugs of water in the refrigerator to steady the temperature.

♦ If you have a swimming pool, run the pool filter only four or five hours a day.

♦ Turn off lights and other energy-using devices when not using them. Don't heat unused rooms.

♦ Put weatherstripping on doors and windows. (Be careful to allow some outdoor air into the house to provide ventilation and prevent indoor air pollution.)

♦ Use cold instead of hot water whenever possible: laundry, kitchen, bathroom.

♦ Keep the thermostat set at 65 degrees and the air conditioner set 6 degrees lower than usual.

♦ Consider alternative energy sources: solar power, windmills.

♦ Buy local produce when you can—it will taste better and cost less in terms of energy wasted in transportation.

Organizations

Environmental Protection Agency, Public Information Center, 202-260-2080

♦ for Lead and Toxic Substances, 202-554-1404

♦ for Global Climate Change, 202-233-9190; 800-296-1996

♦ for Air Quality, 202-260-7400

♦ for Water Quality, 202-260-7786

♦ for Recycling, 202-260-9327

Department of Energy, Public Information Office, 202-586-5575

FIXING IT

It is possible to restore damaged ecosystems—and scientists and volunteers are engaged in thousands of such projects all over the United States. The EPA's National Estuary Program uses volunteers to monitor water quality and restore damaged habitats. To help, contact the **Environmental Protection Agency,** Coastal Management Branch (WH-4504F), Ocean and Coastal Protection Division, U.S. EPA, Washington, DC 20460 (202-260-2090). Or send $5 to the **Society for Ecological Restoration,** 1207 Seminole Highway, Madison, WI 53711, (608-262-9547) for a list of projects that may take volunteers.

AMAZING POLLUTERS

In the graph below, each little car represents 50 car travel miles to show how much pollution other engines comparatively produce in an hour. An average lawn mower, for example, produces as much smog in an hour as the average car in 50 miles of travel.

Lawn mower

Leaf blower

Chain saw

Farm tractor

Outboard motor

= smog produced in 50 miles of travel by the average car

♦ Energy Efficiency and Renewable Energy Information Service, 800-523-2929
♦ Nuclear Energy, 202-586-6450
♦ Solar Energy, 202-586-1720
♦ Fossil Fuels, 202-586-6503

Department of the Interior, 202-208-3100
♦ Fish and Wildlife Service/Endangered Species, 202-208-5634
♦ Bureau of Land Management, 202-208-5717.

Organizations That Work to Save the Environment

If you wonder how one person can even begin to make a dent in the enormous task of saving the environment, consider joining an organization. Organizations are good for the long haul. They hammer out effective long-range strategies and provide continuity that keeps an endeavor alive. By joining small ad hoc organizations, you can often save a habitat in your community—an estuary, a tree, a river. By joining a larger organization, you can work for more widespread change. There are more than 200 U.S. environmental organizations. Some are political, like the Environmental Defense Fund, others more oriented toward distributing information, like the National Wildlife Federation. Some are focused on one issue, like the Rainforest Action Network; others are more broad-based.

Several environmental organizations are biocentric rather than anthropocentric—radical, if you like—with a belief in the idea that all species have an equal right to exist. They call the movement of which they are a part "deep ecology." This notion has scientific validity, according to some environmentalists who do not necessarily believe in the equality of species. A species that seems to have no human use now may prove to be a vital link in an ecosystem that supports other, more "useful" species, or it may prove later on to provide a medicine that saves human lives.

New Conservation is based on a belief that no compromise is possible, if the Earth is to survive. Radical ecowarriors, like those who belong to Earth First! or Animal Liberation Front, believe in no-compromise, direct action, like blocking bulldozers, sitting in trees so they cannot be cut, freeing animals. They also perform ecotage—putting contaminants in the engine oil of earth-moving equipment, for instance. Edward Abbey, author of *The Monkey Wrench Gang*, lists the rules of being an ecowarrior: honor all life and do not hurt anyone. Don't get caught.

The "compromise environmental movement" includes some of the larger environmental groups, like the Environmental Defense Fund, World Wildlife Fund, and the Wilderness Society.

Environmental Organizations

Ducks Unlimited, One Waterfowl Way, Memphis, TN 38120 (901-758-3825, FAX 901-758-3850). Emphasizes the saving of wetlands, which are decreasing at the rate of about 250,000 acres a year. Wetlands are habitats for ducks, geese, and other wildlife species, which Ducks Unlimited seeks to save. Suggests buying federal duck stamps.

Earth Island Institute, 300 Broadway, Suite 28, San Francisco, CA 94133 (415-788-3666). Fights to protect giant sea turtles, ran successful boycott to protect dolphins against Star-Kist tuna in 1990.

EcoNet, Institute for Global Communications, 18 De Boom Street, San Francisco, CA 94107 (415-442-0220). A worldwide computer network, with public bulletin boards on a huge variety of ecological topics. Subscribers include major environmental organizations. After calling 415-322-0162 (N-8-1) on your modem, at the prompt "LOGIN:" type "NEW"; at the prompt "Password:" hit "Enter." You will then receive further information about EcoNet and its charges.

Environmental Action, 6930 Carroll Avenue, Suite 600, Takoma Park, MD 20912 (301-891-1100; FAX 301-891-2218). Seeks to establish tough standards on environmental cleanup.

Exposed the "Dirty Dozen" (environmentally in-different Members of Congress) and "Filthy Five" (a list of environmentally insensitive corporations). Promotes recycling and energy efficiency.

Environmental Defense Fund, 257 Park Avenue South, New York, NY 10010 (212-505-2100). A research and activist group of scientists, economists, and lawyers that finds practical solutions to environmental problems—for example, EDF was instrumental in the banning of DDT in 1972. Other problems of interest to EDF: pesticides, ozone layer, acid rain, toxic hazards, water pollution.

Friends of the Earth, Global Building, 1025 Vermont Avenue NW, 3rd Floor, Washington, DC 20003 (202-783-7400). A worldwide environmental advocacy group that provides technical help to groups on the subject of acid rain, nuclear weapons, pesticides, the ozone layer, safe groundwater, tropical deforestation, river protection. Mission statement: to create an independent global environmental advocacy program to protect the planet from environmental disaster and to preserve biological, cultural, and ethnic diversity.

Greenpeace, 1436 U Street NW, Washington, DC 20009 (202-462-1177; FAX 202-462-4507). Protests internationally with nonviolent and dramatic methods to protect sea life, oceans, and atmosphere. Works against nuclear testing in the Pacific Ocean, works for nuclear disarmament. EnviroNet, its computer network, offers the chance to communicate with others about environmental issues.

National Audubon Society, 700 Broadway, New York, NY 10003 (212-979-3000). Action line with current information on legislation: 202-547-9009. Main goals: preserve habitats including wetlands, protect habitats from pollution and toxic wastes, promote energy conservation.

National Wildlife Federation, 1400 16th Street NW, Washington, DC 20036 (202-797-6800). Seeks to educate people about conservation and protection of the environment. Focus: energy, pollution, wetlands, other habitats. Publishers of *Ranger Rick* and *Your Big Backyard.*

Sponsors of the backyard habitat program and other practical ways in which ordinary people can help to improve the environment.

Natural Resources Defense Council, 40 West 20th Street, New York, NY 10011 (212-727-2700). Using scientific knowledge and political savvy, seeks to influence policy and to educate the public on the environment, including pollution, global warming, control of toxic substances, energy conservation. Worked with Soviet scientists monitoring worldwide weapons testing.

Sierra Club, 730 Polk Street, San Francisco, CA 94109 (415-776-2211; Washington hotline: 202-547-5550). Public interest organization that works to preserve the environment in North America and worldwide through influencing public policy. Mission statement: to explore, enjoy, and protect the wild places of the Earth; to practice and promote the responsible use of the Earth's ecosystems and resources; to educate and enlist humanity to protect and restore the quality of the natural and human environment; and to use all lawful means to carry out these objectives. You join at the national level, and you can volunteer at the state, chapter, or local level. You might work for a state initiative, a city trail, a recycling effort.

Student Environmental Action Coalition, Box 1168, Chapel Hill, NC 27514 (919-967-4600). A student movement for environmental education with goals of preserving forests, among other issues. Publication: *Campus Ecology*—to assess environmental conditions on campuses.

The Nature Conservancy, 1815 North Lynn Street, Arlington, VA 22209 (703-841-5300). An international private organization devoted to protecting habitats. Establishes sanctuaries for wildlife and advises government on how to acquire public land. Inventories biological resources and species worldwide.

The Wilderness Society, 900 17th Street NW, Washington, DC 20006 (202-833-2300). Lobbies fervently to preserve public wilderness and protect ancient forests. Educates the public. Seeks to improve management of U.S. public lands.

World Wildlife Fund, 1250 24th Street NW,

OTHER ENVIRONMENTAL ORGANIZATIONS

GROUP AND ADDRESS

MISSION AND FOCUS

Animal Liberation Front, address unknown

Underground network of ecoguerrillas who free animals at research labs and fur farms.

Cousteau Society, 870 Greenbriar Circle, Chesapeake,VA 23320; 804-523-9335

Variety of environmental concerns.

Defenders of Wildlife, 1101 14th St. NW, Suite 1400, Washington, DC 20005; 202-682-9400

Protection of habitat.

Earth First!, 1401 Dewey St., PO Box 1133, New Albany, IN 47150; 812-944-5353

A direct-action movement of ecoguerrillas encouraging individuals to act upon their environmental concerns.

League of Conservation Voters, 1707 L St. NW, Suite 550, Washington, DC 20036; 202-785-8683

Election of pro-environment candidates.

National Parks and Conservation Assn., 1776 Massachusetts Avenue NW, Washington, DC 20036; 202-223-6722

Improvement of national parks.

National Recycling Coalition, 1101 30th St. NW, #305, Washington, DC 20007; 202-625-6406

Education, lobbying on recycling.

Rainforest Action Network, 450 Sansome St., Suite 700, San Francisco, CA 94111; 415-398-4404 ; 800-989-RAIN for soaps made from Amazon oil.

Works to preserve tropical rainforests.

Sea Shepherds, address unknown

Radical. Launched by an ex-Greenpeace member in 1977. They have sunk whaling ships, blockaded the Canadian seal fleet.

Seventh Generation Fund, PO Box 2550, McKinleyville, CA 95521; 707-839-1178

A group of Native American elders promoting the notion that we must commit ourselves to protect the earth for at least seven generations.

The Center for Marine Conservation, Pollution Office, 1725 DeSales St. NW, Suite 500, Washington, DC 20036; 202-429-5609

Saving marine habitats.

Trust for Public Land, 666 Pennsylvania Avenue SE, # 401, Washington, DC 20003; 202-543-7552

A national group that seeks to protect open space, especially around cities.

Working Assets Long Distance, 701 Montgomery St., Suite 400, San Francisco, CA 94111; 800-788-8588

One day a month, subscribers can make a number of free phone calls to decision-makers for a social or environmental cause. Gives 1 percent of subscribers' telephone charges to progressive nonprofit groups.

Worldwatch Institute, 1776 Massachusetts Avenue NW, Washington, DC 20036; 202-452-1999

Research on worldwide global environmental trends.

Washington, DC 20037 (202-293-4800). Aims to preserve endangered species all over the planet. Sponsors the newsletter *TRAFFIC*, which reports on illegal trade in endangered species.

The National Wildlife Federation publishes (for a price) a yearly *Conservation Directory* with a complete list of organizations, agencies, and officials concerned with natural resources. For more information, call: **National Wildlife Federation,** 800-432-6564.

Garbage: Going Green

Are righteous parents who buy cloth diapers in order to save the environment really so right? One study says that disposables may be better because washing diapers for one child at home uses up 9620 gallons of water a year. And a diaper service uses trucks, adding to air pollution. Yet disposable diapers help to clog landfills and use up valuable resources in the making. The answer to the question of disposable or cloth? Make your decision based on local conditions. For example, if your community is plagued with water shortages, disposables may be less strain on the environment. If your community is short of landfill space, you might consider cloth diapers.

Once we thought that carrying groceries home in paper (rather than plastic) bags helped the environment, because paper is biodegradable and plastic is not. That would be true, *if* garbage including paper bags was not buried so deep in landfills that it cannot decay—for lack of oxygen. Archaeologist William Rathje has found well-preserved 25-year-old guacamole, 15-year old hot dogs, and a 16-year-old T-bone steak that were buried in landfills. He calls landfill biodegradation "the biggest myth since Santa Claus." On the other hand, paper is made from a renewable resource. Yet . . . paper production generates pollution. Or consider the advantages and disadvantages of plastic—plastic bags and foam cups take less energy and cause less pollution to produce than products made of paper. They take up less space in a landfill and are easier to reuse. Yet they are made of nonrenewable resources and create hazardous waste.

You can bypass making a decision on this problem by recycling your bags, or by using a shopping basket or cloth shopping bag. **This is the main message: don't use or buy unnecessary things.**

These either-or questions are trivialized by the bottom line: the average American produces 4 pounds of garbage a day, more than any other nationality. In 1960, we produced only 2.7 pounds of waste a day. The bright side: recycling and recovery of materials has increased enormously.

You can help by engaging in environmental activism at the community level. Encourage your community to establish curbside pickup for recyclables and to set up recycling facilities and advanced solid waste composting equipment. In addition, recommend community investigation of advanced techniques in "mass burn" of waste. The Environmental Protection Agency recommends burning of waste that cannot be recycled or converted into other useful material.

On an individual level, you can personally reduce the proliferation of garbage.

1. The first and foremost rule is: reduce the amount of garbage you create.

♦ Buy in bulk as much as you can. For instance, buy nails from a bin rather than in a fancy package of cardboard and plastic. Avoid overly packaged convenience food. Much of the material that ends up in landfills is packaging material. And on the average you pay $1 for packaging for every $11 you spend on food.

♦ Buy products in refillable, recycled, reusable containers. *Refillable* is better than *recycled* which is better than *recyclable*. When possible, purchase concentrated products (soaps and detergents, beverages).

♦ Write letters of complaint to companies that use excessive packaging, and suggest they inaugurate source reduction of packaging, a fancy name for packaging more simply with less material. And talk to the manager of your supermarket about carrying "green" and recycled products.

♦ Reuse materials in your home—jars, shopping bags, plastic bags.

♦ Buy containers that can be reused—it's better to buy a plastic container, which can be used over and over again, than to waste aluminum foil.

♦ Pay attention to packaging. Some red and yellow dyes contain cadmium, which can contaminate groundwater.

♦ Use your own bags (string or cloth) for groceries or recycle bags at your market or reuse bags yourself. Don't have anything bagged that does not need to be bagged.

♦ Compost garbage (if your community allows it), along with leaves, grass clippings. (See "Compost," p. 228.)

♦ Don't buy what you don't need. Take good care of the material goods that you own, and replace them when possible with used items. Sell or donate used items to charities rather than throw them away.

♦ When you buy appliances look for the Energy Star seal from the Environmental Protection Agency. Buy good-quality appliances and other items. Maintain them. Cheap appliances fail sooner, causing more junk.

♦ Stop junk mail (catalogs, brochures, and other advertising appeals) you do not want. To do so, write: **Mail Preference Service,** Direct Marketing Association, PO Box 9008, Farmingdale, NY 11735.

♦ Don't use throwaway items when you can use permanent ones—drink from pottery mugs rather than single-use cups, for instance, and bring along regular silverware and reusable plastics for picnics and parties.

♦ Make cleaning rags out of your old clothes to save on paper towels.

2. Recycle. Even though not enough markets exist for recycled products, and even though some recycled material ends up in landfills anyway, *still* recycling is better than not recycling.

♦ If your community recycles metal, be sure to wash out and recycle cans. This lessens strip mining, air pollution, and use of energy in manufacturing new cans.

♦ Recycle glass and plastic. Buy cooking oil in glass. (The plastic used in bottles for cooking oil can produce pollutants when manufactured.) Your recycling company will specify what plastic con-

---

RECYCLING VOCABULARY

The Federal Trade Commission has established voluntary guidelines on terminology used in advertising and labeling products.

Degradable, biodegradable, photodegradable: The product will break down and return to nature within a reasonably short time after it is disposed of in the customary way.

Compostable: All materials in the product or package will break down into, or otherwise become part of, usable compost (e.g., soil-conditioning materials, mulch) in a safe and timely manner if processed correctly.

Recyclable: It can be collected, separated, or otherwise recovered for use as raw materials in the manufacture or assembly of a new product or package.

Recycled content: The product has been made from materials that were recovered from the solid-waste stream (either pre- or post-consumer).

Source: Federal Trade Commission

---

tainers can be recycled—often only beverage containers. Call 800-243-5790, M–F, 9 AM–5:30 PM, EST, for your nearest plastics recycler.

♦ Do not throw glass that cannot be recycled (broken window glass and drinking glasses) in the glass recycling bin. The window glass contains a contaminating chemical, and the drinking glass has a different melting point than a bottle.

♦ Recycle paper. Remove the glossy advertisements from the newspaper you recycle, however. Call 800-878-8878, M–F 8:30 AM–5:30 PM, EST, for your nearest paper recycler.

♦ Encourage your office to recycle white office paper.

♦ Recycle old magazines, if possible, or pass them on to a friend, nursing home, school, library.

♦ Recycle foam "peanuts" at your mailing facility or when you next send a package. Call

Loose-Fill Producers Council at 800-828-2214 or **Association of Foam Packaging Recyclers** at 800-944-8448 for the center nearest you.

♦ Don't forget recyclable items like motor oil, tires, and cars. Each year people dump enough used motor oil down sewers to equal 10 *Exxon Valdez* Alaskan spills.

♦ Recycle your unwanted books by giving them to a library, school, church, thrift store. You can also donate them to developing countries by sending them to the **International Book Bank,** 608-L Folcroft Street, Baltimore, MD 21224 (800-874-7268).

Organizations

National Consumers League, 815 15th Street NW, Suite 928, Washington, DC 20005 (202-639-8140)

U.S. Environmental Protection Agency, Office of Solid Waste and Emergency Response, 401 M Street SW, Washington, DC 20460 (202-260-4610)

Environmental Defense Fund, Recycling, 257 Park Avenue South, New York, NY 10010 (212-505-2100; 800-CALL-EDF). Will tell you where the closest recycling center is.

WASTEFUL AMERICANS

The average middle-class American, born in the 1990s, will in his or her lifetime:

♦ Use more than 28,000 gallons of gasoline, driving 700,000 miles, in a dozen cars.

♦ Read and throw away 27,500 newspapers, at the rate of seven trees a year.

♦ Add 110,250 pounds of trash to the nation's trash heap.

♦ Use enough electricity to burn 16,610 pounds of coal.

♦ Wear and throw away 115 pairs of shoes.

Other facts:

♦ Every three months, we throw away as much aluminum as is in the commercial aircraft fleet.

♦ The office paper we throw away every year could build a 12-foot wall from New York to Los Angeles.

WASTE PAPER WALL

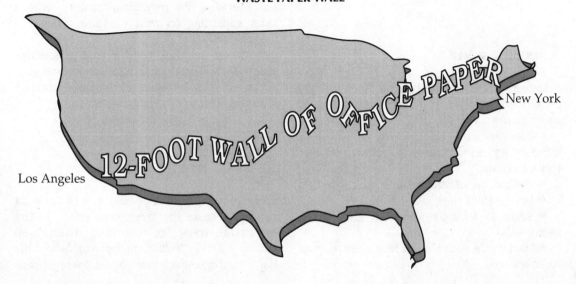

Los Angeles   New York
12-FOOT WALL OF OFFICE PAPER

MISLEADING PLASTIC RECYCLING SYMBOLS

Not all plastic containers labeled with the recycle symbol are actually recyclable. In theory, they *could* be recycled. In actuality they cannot be. The plastics that are most widely accepted for recycling are drink bottles and milk and water jugs. Often items like margarine tubs and yogurt containers, though recyclable, are not accepted by recyclers because facilities for processing them are not easily accessible.

GLASS AND ALUMINUM AND OTHER METALS

Theoretically, glass can be recycled until the end of time. Right now, you can't recycle mirrors, crystal, window glass, drinking glasses, light bulbs, or Pyrex, for reasons having to do with their manufacture.

By recycling aluminum, we save 95 percent of the energy that would be needed to make new cans. Steel and tin recycling saves in landfill costs. To find the nearest aluminum can recycling station, call 800-228-2525.

Become a VIP

Volunteers in Parks (VIPs) for the National Park Service are engaged in a surprising variety of activities. As a VIP, you can:

♦ dress in period costume and participate in living-history demonstrations, conduct oral history interviews.

♦ work at the information desk.

♦ drive a shuttlebus.

♦ serve as a campground host, give guided nature walks.

♦ work in the park library, help preserve museum artifacts.

♦ work with researchers by inventorying underwater resources, making wildlife counts, planting trees.

♦ paint buildings, make cabinets, build fences.

♦ write or design brochures.

♦ take photographs, work in a darkroom, organize photograph and slide files.

♦ design park computer programs.

♦ educate children about the environment.

♦ maintain trails, patrol trails.

♦ participate in preparing and conducting special park events.

♦ pick up litter.

Volunteers need to be in reasonably good health, and disabled individuals are encouraged to volunteer. Work is unpaid, though you may be reimbursed for out-of-pocket expenses. You can volunteer as much or as little time as you want, and hours are flexible. If you are under 18, you can work only at a natural park in your community, with the official consent of your parent or guardian. Or you can work somewhere else if you are part of a family or supervised group. The National Park Service does not want to act *in loco parentis*. If you are over 18, assignments are more flexible. Organized groups can apply.

If interested, write or call the VIP coordinator at the national park where you would like to volunteer. You will be given an application to fill out. Be specific when you describe your skills and interests. You may even want to write a letter expanding on what you have written in the application.

If you are selected, you and your prospective supervisor will first sign an agreement about your duties and responsibilities and outline a tentative schedule, then you can begin work.

Plant a Tree

Trees consume carbon dioxide, one of the eight gases that cause the greenhouse effect. In fact the Earth's trees "fix" into their structure 90 percent of the "solid" carbon dioxide on the Earth's surface. Each year, on the average, each

YEARLY ENVIRONMENTAL VALUE OF A TREE

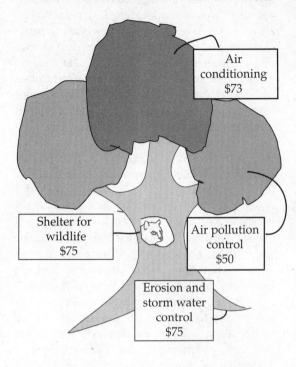

Air
conditioning
$73

Shelter for
wildlife
$75

Air pollution
control
$50

Erosion and
storm water
control
$75

Reprinted courtesy of American Forestry Association.

tree "breathes" in 26 pounds of carbon dioxide and "breathes" out 13 pounds of oxygen. Trees also filter dangerous particulate matter and some toxic pollutants from the air. Trees equalize the temperature, making it cooler in summer and warmer in winter, and they provide an oasis effect in a busy city.

The American Forestry Association program Global ReLeaf seeks to prevent cutting of old-growth forests and to create urban forests throughout the world. Under its aegis, millions of trees have been planted by individuals, businesses, communities, neighborhood associations, and other organizations.

The Famous and Historic Tree Program combines history and the environment. You can plant trees that have descended from famous trees in our history, like trees from George Washington's home at Mount Vernon or from Thoreau's Walden Woods. You can participate as an individual or as part of a group, to plant individual trees, a Historic Grove of 20 or more trees, or trees in America's Historic Forest near Des Moines, Iowa. For more information, call 800-677-0727.

Trees in our cities are not being replaced as fast as they die, and those that are alive are often poorly maintained. Here's how to plant an urban forest as part of the **Global ReLeaf program:**

♦ Get a group of volunteers together.

♦ Take a tree survey. Find a professional forester or arborist through the county extension service agent, local parks, and Recreation or Public Works departments. Convince him or her to help by training volunteers to identify, measure, and rate the condition of trees.

♦ Make estimates of the cost of planting and maintaining trees according to a plan. You may decide to plant a playground or a whole neighborhood.

♦ Publicize results of the survey, make budget estimates, talk with decision-makers. Consider asking for funding from corporations, utility companies, and developers.

♦ Volunteers can help plant, prune, and maintain trees. (See "How to Plant a Tree," p. 240.)

For more information: **American Forestry Association,** PO Box 2000, Washington, DC 20013 (202-667-3300; FAX 202-667-7751). Contributions to AFA support its research, policy, education, and on-the-land conservation action programs, including Global ReLeaf. To learn how to set up a workplace-giving program, call Jim Scott at 800-368-5748.

Endangered Species and Habitats

The U.S. Supreme Court has declared: "Wildlife is a national treasure held in trust for all citizens." In the United States wild animals fight with humans over space—the coyote that sees your cat as prey is competing with humans over territory, as is the least tern that nests in a parking lot. Animals that live in the wilderness, like wolves, are in a perilous position because many people consider them vermin. In other parts of the world, elephants, Bengal tigers, pandas, crocodiles, whales, and other animals are threatened or endangered primarily by loss of habitat, but also by poaching, illegal trade, and pollution. Equally threatened is plant life. Ordinarily we can't save a species without saving a habitat that is home for other plants and animals.

On a more abstract level, the loss of world biological biodiversity is alarming. More than 700 species, subspecies, and populations of animals and plants have been officially listed as threatened or endangered. Worse, unless something is done, by the year 2050 planet Earth will lose 350,000 species of plants and animals. And although the majority will disappear from the complexly rich rain forest, the problem exists elsewhere also. In the U.S., only one-tenth of ancient forests still exists. The tallgrass prairie is one-hundredth of what it once was—and, probably as a result, 7 out of 12 species of Great Plains birds are declining rapidly in population. Only half of U.S. original wetlands, or nurseries for wildlife, still remain.

Why care—except for the loss of the beauty and complexity that animals and plants bring to the world? Except for the fact that they deserve to exist? Loss of plants and animals will impoverish us in ways we cannot predict. Drugs, for example, have their sources in plants: digitalis, which saves heart patients; the yew tree, from which the cancer drug taxol is extracted; the rosy periwinkle, which provides a cure for a type of leukemia that strikes children. Scientists have identified 75,000 edible plants, of which only 5000 have so far been used for food. Moreover, like canaries in a coal mine, endangered and threatened species can act as indicators of the general health of the environment. For instance, when frogs start to die out, something is wrong.

What Can Be Done?

The problem is complicated. Foreign governments do not always cooperate with wildlife groups to save their indigenous animals. The poor see their livelihoods threatened by conservation plans to preserve the wild. For instance, panda skins bring $40,000 each—a fortune. It is difficult for a Chinese peasant to resist that kind of money. The most well-intentioned efforts often do more harm than good. For instance, legal "farming" of endangered or threatened species often provides an illegal outlet for poaching.

Though some gains have been made, even they are cloaked in controversy. Poaching of elephants has fallen dramatically since the 1989 ban on trade in ivory, which brought the price down from $150 a pound to $5 a pound. As a result, in Kenya, though 3000 to 4000 elephants a year were slaughtered for their teeth in the early 1980s, now the annual death toll is fewer than 50. But some experts have criticized the ban. They take a less drastic position that would allow limited culling of elephants for the harvesting of ivory to give African governments money to spend on wildlife reserves. Opponents say that those governments could just as easily raise money by increasing admission prices to game parks. Another argument is that by allowing an increase in elephant herds, other species are made to suffer through destruction of their habitat. One answer is sustainable development, which means harvesting wildlife but not so much that it will be threatened with extinction.

Another answer is for countries to withhold foreign aid unless poaching and smuggling is stopped. Still another is to educate the world to see that poaching and hunting are less profitable than saving wild animals for the enjoyment of money-spending tourists. A lion can deliver $27,000 in tourist dollars. Baby harp seals bring in more money in tourism to Prince Edward Island than the white fur coats made from their skins. One objection to this philosophy is that it promotes "cute" and popular animals over those equally threatened but less appealing. Gray wolves, for instance, have suffered because of the role of the wolf in history (consider "Red Riding Hood"), yet according to some wildlife experts, the wolf, a killing machine with a complex social life, may be a factor in maintaining a healthy ecosystem. In the end, the popular often save the less popular—when the habitat for one animal is saved, those animals that share it are also saved.

Lest you think that the United States is exempt, consider this: the Endangered Species Act of 1973 mandates that the government must restrict use of public land by humans if populations of plants and animals on the endangered list are declining there. Owners of private property also have to guarantee the protection of endangered animals' habitat. And yet . . .

♦ Monarch butterflies, which fly 3000 miles from the Western United States to central Mexico, are losing their habitat.

♦ Manatees of Florida are threatened by powerboats.

♦ Frogs are losing population at alarming rates.

♦ Developers and other business people have opposed plans to put the white ibis on the threatened list because to do so could "thwart development and farming."

♦ Scallops have "all but disappeared" from Tampa Bay.

Success Stories

♦ Of the species listed as threatened or endangered in the United States, the condition of 238 (41 percent) is stable or improving. Five species are recovered (have increased in numbers enough to be taken off the endangered list), including the American alligator and brown pelican.

♦ Decimated by DDT, which thinned shells so that babies could not be born, the peregrine falcon's numbers fell to 30 breeding pairs. Now, through captive-breeding and release programs, the situation is not so dire. Baby peregrines have been introduced into the "wild," which often includes office buildings and other high places that simulate crags.

Many U.S. turtles have died in shrimp fishermen's nets by suffocating; they must be able to breathe air to survive. The Turtle Excluder Device on nets, required by law, has saved many lives.

How You Can Help

♦ Boycott states and nations that do not protect wildlife—and make sure that officials know about your reasons. It works. For example: Alaska's Division of Fish and Game planned in 1992 to kill hundred of wolves from planes and helicopters, in order to increase the size of moose and caribou herds that wolves (and human hunters) prey on and tourists love to see. Their scheme backfired: people planning to tour Alaska canceled reservations in uncommon numbers as part of a boycott against the killing of the wolves. The plan was put on hold.

♦ Boycott companies that maintain practices harmful to animals.

♦ Refrain from overpopulating the Earth. Increase of human population means a decrease in resources for wildlife. (See "Animals and Human World Populations," p. 169.)

♦ Make an effort on your own to alleviate a specific problem. For example, Sherri Tipple of Denver, licensed by Colorado's Division of Wildlife, live-traps beavers that wander into populated areas and transports them to Rocky Mountain National Park.

♦ Plant a tree and maintain it. (See "How to Plant a Tree," p. 240.)

♦ Don't throw away plastic items, which can cause great harm to wildlife. Birds and other animals get caught in six-pack plastic rings; when turtles swallow plastic bags, their intestines can be blocked.

♦ Find ways to save energy. Many fragile habitats are destroyed by oil drilling, the *Exxon Valdez* oil spill being only the most dramatic. (See "Ecological Crises and What You Can Do to Stop Them," p. 155.)

♦ Donate to environmental organizations. (See "Organizations That Work to Save the Environment," p. 158.)

♦ Volunteer at a Fish and Wildlife Refuge. You can do bird counts, build nest structures, and band wildlife.

Adopt an Animal

If your heart goes out to a threatened or endangered animal, you can contribute directly to its welfare. While it is illegal to keep a wild animal in your backyard almost everywhere, you can "adopt" one through an organization committed to the survival of a species. Your money goes to buy food and care for the animal. In return, you may receive its photo and biography.

ANIMALS IN SANCTUARIES AND IN THE WILD

Back to Nature Wildlife Refuge, Inc., 18515 East Colonial Drive, Orlando, FL, 32820; 407-366-1394 (raccoons, cougars, more).

Bats: Bat Conservation International, PO Box 162603, 500 Capital of Texas, Hwy. N, Building 1, Suite 200, Austin, TX 78716; 512-327-9721; FAX 512-327-9724. Adopt a bat. Also ask for plans on how to build a bat house.

Birds: Florida Audubon Society, 460 State Road 436, Suite 200, Casselberry, FL, 32707; 800-874-BIRD.

Dolphins: Oceanic Society Expeditions, Fort Mason Center, Bldg. E., San Francisco, CA 94123; 415-474-3385; 800-326-7491; FAX 415-474-3395.

Manatees: Save the Manatee Club, Inc. 500 North Maitland Avenue, Suite 210, Maitland, FL 32751; 407-539-0990; 800-431-JOIN.

Turtles: Caribbean Conservation Corp., PO Box 2866, Gainesville, FL 32602; 800-678-7853.

Wild Horses or Burros: Adopt-a-Horse. Bureau of Land Management, Room 560, 1849 C Street NW, Washington, DC 20240; 202-208-5717.

Whales: The Whale Adoption Project, International Wildlife Coalition, 70 East Falmouth Hwy., East Falmouth, MA 025536-5957; 508-548-8328.

College of the Atlantic, 105 Eden Street, Bar Harbor, Maine 04609; 207-288-5644 (finbacks).

Pacific Whale Foundation, 101 North Kihei Road, Suite 21, Kihei, Maui, HI 96753; 800-942-5311.

Wolves: Wolf Haven International, 3111 Offut Lake Road, Tenino, WA 98589; 800-448-9653.

Wild Canid Survival and Research Center, PO Box 760, Eureka, MO 63025; 314-938-5900.

Wolf Recovery Foundation, PO Box 793, Boise, ID 83701-0793; and Wolf Foundation and Research Center, PO Box 3832, Ketchum, ID 83340; 800-793-WOLF.

World Society for the Protection of Animals, 55 University Avenue, Suite 902, PO Box 15, Toronto, M5J 2H7, Canada; 800-363-9772; US 800-LIB-BEAR (elephants, rhinos, coral reefs, and more).

ZOO ANIMALS

You can adopt an animal as an individual or part of a group at 75 percent of the nation's zoos. The animal you may adopt depends somewhat on the size of your donation. It could be a lovebird (not so dear), it could be an elephant (expensive). Or it could be an aardvark, prairie dog, monkey, tiger, or bear. If your local zoo is not on this list, call and ask about its adoption programs. For your donation, many zoos allow free admission on certain days.

Buffalo Zoo, 300 Park Side Avenue, Buffalo, NY 14214-1999; 716-837-3900.

Central Florida Zoo, Adopt-an-Animal, PO Box 470-309, Lake Monroe, FL, 32747-0309; 407-323-4450.

Cincinnati Zoo, ADOPT (Animals Depend on People Too), 3400 Vine Street, Cincinnati, OH 45220; 513-281-4700.

Cleveland Metroparks Zoo, 3900 Brookside Park Drive, Cleveland, OH 44109; 216-661-6500, x224.

Como Zoo, Midway Parkway and Kaufman Drive, St. Paul, MN 55103; 612-487-1485; FAX 612-488-5572.

Detroit Zoo. The Adopt an Animal Club, c/o the Detroit Zoo, 8450 West 10 Mile Road, Royal Oak, MI 48068; 313-398-0903.

Houston Zoo, PO Box 66387, Houston, TX 77266; 713-529-2632.

Oakland Zoo, Adopt-an-Animal, 9777 Golf Links Road, Oakland, CA 94605; 510-632-9525; FAX 510-635-5719.

The Brookfield Zoo, 3300 Golf Road, Brookfield, IL 60513; 708-485-0263; FAX 708-485-3532.

The San Francisco Zoo, 40 Fifth Avenue and Sloat Boulevard, San Francisco 94100; 415-753-7083; 415-753-7072.

The Pittsburgh Zoo, Adopt-an-Animal, 1 Hill Road, Pittsburgh, PA 15206-1178; 412-665-3640.

The Philadelphia Zoo, 3400 West Girard Avenue, Philadelphia, PA 19104-1196; 215-243-1100.

Zoological Society of Houston, Adopt-an-Animal, 1513 North MacGregor, Houston, TX 77030; 713-529-2632; FAX 713-522-2823.

Animals and Human World Populations

World human population may double in the next century, to reach 11 billion by 2100. This means starving children, loss of forests and other resources, destruction of the environment. Yet 300 million couples lack access to safe and effective contraception. Family planning programs listed below work in combination with related programs that seek to raise the status of women, improve the health of children, and raise the economic status of the poor.

Population Action International, 1120 19th Street NW, Suite 550, Washington, DC 20036-3605 (202-659-1833). A private, nonprofit, public interest organization concerned with international family planning.

Planned Parenthood Federation of America, Inc. (PPFA), 810 Seventh Avenue, New York, NY 10019 (212-541-7800). Family planning services in the United States and overseas.

Population Reference Bureau (PRB), Suite 520, 1875 Connecticut Avenue, NW, Washington, DC 20009 (202-483-1100). Does research on population issues and disseminates it.

United Nations Population Fund, 42nd Street and First Avenue, New York, NY 10017 (212-963-1234).

U.S. Agency for International Development (USAID), 2201 C Street NW, Washington, DC 20523 (202-647-4000).

Worldwatch Institute, 1776 Massachusetts Avenue NW, Washington, DC 20036 (202-452-1999). A policy research organization, looks to global trends.

Zero Population Growth (ZPG), 3rd Floor, 1400 16th Street NW, Washington, DC 20036 (202-332-2200).

ANIMAL POPULATIONS

Animal	Population in 1993 (in the wild)	Estimated population in 2025
African elephant	600,000	Unknown
Black rhino	2,400	Possibly 0
Bengal tiger	2,300	0
Giant panda	1,000	Estimates vary from 5,000 to 0

4

AROUND HOUSE AND YARD

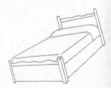

BIG CHANGES

Buying a House

One of us bought a house for its big acacia tree, its view of the ocean, and its multicolored two-by-four ceiling beams. She was lucky. The decision turned out to be a wise one financially even though the carpet smelled and the bathroom floor had a hole in it. Because of the ocean view, the value of the lot has increased enormously. You can't count on such luck, though. Buying a house calls for a fine balance between passion and hard-headedness. Here are some of the other factors (besides the fact that you love it) you might want to consider when buying a house.

Location

1. Location, location, and location—so goes the real estate cliché. Think of location from big to small. Start by picking a region you like, then a town, a neighborhood, a street, and finally a lot (or house). Make sure the whole neighborhood is up to snuff. Look for well-maintained yards. Be suspicious if you see too many "For Sale" signs or commercial businesses spreading into the neighborhood. Visit the area at several times of day, in all seasons. It is all too easy to fall in summer love with a green and lovely region, only to find out later that winters there are fierce.

2. Buy a house that is like other houses in the neighborhood. A very expensive house in a neighborhood with medium-priced houses will lose its value.

3. When moving to a new town or region, check with people who already live there about pitfalls and good neighborhoods—if you can do it gracefully.

4. Take the time to unearth some hard facts about the neighborhood:

♦ Is the house convenient to shopping, public transportation, schools, hospitals, fire stations, and police?

♦ How good are the schools? What are average test scores, how many students go on to college, what is the student-teacher ratio?

♦ Are there other amenities: parks, theaters, stores, restaurants, places of worship?

♦ What is the noise level day and night? Airplane or highway noise? Industrial noise?

♦ Are there any strange smells that waft about?

♦ Has the area ever flooded?

5. Check on city regulations like zoning ordinances at the town hall. What can be built in the neighborhood? What can and can't you do to a house? Who pays for sewers, water, street lights, sidewalks? Is your property up for assessments on any utilities?

How Much House Can You Afford?

1. First ask yourself and your family: What do we need and want in a house?

◆ A view?

◆ House space? Yard space?

◆ Number of rooms? What kind of rooms? How many bathrooms? Bedrooms? A playroom for the kids? A gourmet's kitchen? (Consider using one bedroom for a study.)

2. Consider how much you can spend. Check with mortgage companies to find out how big a mortgage you can carry. If you buy an old house, add the cost of repairs to the purchase price.

3. Match your needs and wants against the amount you can afford. If you come up short on money, start cutting from your list of wants.

Once You Have a House in Mind . . .

1. Determine what the house is worth. Compare its asking price against the average for the neighborhood, which you can determine from a printout of recent home sales (ask a real estate agent for this). You might even pay for a professional appraisal. A bank that makes real estate loans can suggest an appraiser. When considering the price of the house, take extras into account: double-glazed windows, extra insulation, energy-saving appliances, special plumbing so reclaimed water can be used in landscaping and toilets. Is the house well insulated? Do doors and windows fit tightly and open and shut easily? What is under the carpet—concrete or wood?

2. Inquire about tax rates. What is the most recent assessment of the house? Will taxes go up? Look at the owner's real estate tax, school tax, and utility bills for the last year.

3. Consider the house's "mood." Is it well ventilated? Is it light and airy?

4. Inspect the house in the daytime for structural soundness. Also look over electrical wiring, heating and air-conditioning systems, plumbing. Local companies (gas and electric, for instance) often will do this for nothing. If termites could be a problem in the area, have the house inspected by a pest-control firm. Check for asbestos and radon. (See "Indoor Pollution," p. 180).

5. Determine whether the house is built on stable ground. If it is on a slope, is the slope secure? Does the lot have adequate drainage? Is the basement dry when it rains? You might want to request an inspection by a professional engineer or inspector. If you do, ask for a written report.

6. In rural areas, test well water for quality and for flow; have a plumber test the septic system.

7. Find out what goes with the house: appliances, carpets, drapes, screens, storm windows, awnings, light fixtures, bookcases.

PROFITABLE REMODELING INVESTMENTS

If you covet a swimming pool, by all means install one, but don't expect it to pay for itself when you sell the house. *The remodeling that pays off the most:*
◆ Kitchen (minor)
◆ Bathroom (minor)
◆ Painting (neutral colors)
◆ Carpeting (neutral colors)
◆ Skylights
The remodeling that pays off the least:
◆ Swimming pool
◆ Refinished basement

Moving

The consequences of poor planning: trying and failing to jockey that big, old, sagging sofa through a window of your new home while cursing yourself for not having given it away. Or, in the last stages of moving in, wondering in which unlabeled box your opener is, as, hot and thirsty, you stand holding a cold bottle of something wet. Careful planning and knowhow can take some (but not all) of the agony out of moving from one house to another. If nothing else, it will give you some sense of control.

THE SCHEDULE

Several weeks before moving:

♦ Measure rooms and doors in your new home to make sure that they will accommodate your belongings and that you can get them through the doors.

♦ Check regulations on moving plants in and out of your state through State Departments of Agriculture or Natural Resources. Be particularly careful about this if you live in or are moving to California, Arizona, or Florida. If you can move plants, prepare houseplants by repotting them in unbreakable plastic containers. Prune large nonsucculent plants. If you can't take your plants with you, consider cuttings put in a plastic bag with a wet paper towel.

♦ Make a date with a plumber, a utility company, or a service representative from an appliance company to disconnect appliances and take down your television antenna a day or two before the move. Ask your appliance representative about special wedges needed for the washer and other appliances. (You can do all this yourself, but you need to know how.)

♦ Send out change-of-address cards. Change bank and charge accounts. Arrange for disconnecting utilities in old home and connecting them in your new home. Do all this in writing.

♦ Start eating up your food.

♦ Check to see if you need moving permits.

♦ Make arrangements concerning insurance and car licensing and registration.

♦ Obtain records from your doctor, dentist, and veterinarian.

♦ Transfer prescriptions.

♦ Arrange to have deliveries (like newspapers) discontinued.

♦ Go through your items to see what you want to get rid of and hold a garage sale. Give away the rest to local charities. Don't throw out your phone book—you may need telephone numbers from your old community when you move to the new one.

♦ Start collecting cardboard boxes (with lids) from your supermarket. Ask the manager—some supermarkets take boxes apart before putting them in the Dumpster.

♦ Dispose of items that cannot be shipped: pesticides, aerosol cans, caustic cleaners, fertilizers, by taking them to the toxic waste disposal point.

♦ Start packing things that you won't need before the move.

♦ If you are moving to and/or from apartments, arrange for use of elevators.

Several days before moving:

♦ Remove insects and plant parasites from plants, perhaps putting the plants in plastic bags with a pest strip or flea collar.

♦ Drain your water bed.

♦ Continue packing.

Two days before the move:

♦ Empty, defrost, and clean the refrigerator. Leave the doors open. Put charcoal in a clean sock, tie it shut, and put it in the bottom of the refrigerator to prevent mildew and smells.

♦ Keep packing.

A day before the move:

♦ Disconnect all electronic equipment— televisions, VCRs, computers, stereos. Mark cables and cords so you know where they plug in.

♦ Disconnect your washer. Drain the hoses, and put plastic bags secured with rubber bands over their ends. (You may need to have an expert do this.)

♦ Drain gas-powered power tools of fuel. Burn off any propane left in your gas barbecue. Clean the grill; put rocks and other parts in plastic bags and pack them inside the barbecue.

♦ Finish packing.

WARNING: Do not transport dangerous fluids like paint thinner, propane, gasoline in a closed van.

PACKING

Start packing a couple of weeks before the move, beginning with the things you do not need on a daily basis—books, for instance. *Materials you will need:* boxes, twist ties, wrapping paper (unused newsprint bought at packing supply store), bubble wrap, tissue paper, 1- to 3-inch-wide plastic tape, felt-tip marker, utility knife. (You can buy mattress boxes, wardrobe boxes, and other kinds of boxes new from moving company offices or second-hand from individuals.)

General Rules

1. With a marker, write on the side of each box what's in it and what room it belongs to. Keep track of the number of boxes, according to the room they are destined for in the new house.
2. Don't underpack or overpack boxes. If you underpack, the box can be crushed. If you overpack it's hard to shut the lid and have it remain flat. Also, heavy boxes are harder to carry. After the box is packed, rock it. If it rattles, it needs to have the chinks filled up with packing material.
3. When packing fragile items, cushion bottoms of boxes with wadded-up wrapping paper and write "fragile" on all sides. Use linens or paper to protect dishes.
4. Pack the heaviest items in the bottom of the box.
5. Pack contents of drawers separately.
6. Remove all fragile and glass parts (like the glass container of your blender) and pack them separately.
7. Tape down parts that move.
8. Take apart big items like bed frames and tables, and mark the pieces so that they can be put together again easily. Stash nuts, bolts, screws, etc., in a plastic bag, seal it, and tape it to the piece to which they belong.
9. Tape down doors and other parts that can flop open. Tape power cords to back of appliances.
10. Use blankets to sheathe big appliances, tables, and other items from damage.
11. Plan to move important papers, valuables, plants, floppy disks, and items you will need right away in the car.

Kitchen

♦ Wrap each item separately, then bundle several items of a kind in more wrapping paper.

Stack flat dishes (plates, saucers, etc.) on their sides. Nest concave items of a kind together. Cups and glasses should be put upside-down. Pack small appliances together in the same box, wrapped separately, cords coiled. Pack fragile parts separately.

♦ Take as little food as possible. Put liquids in self-closing plastic bags. Tape down lids and opened box tops.

Bedrooms

♦ Remove linens from beds. Cover mattresses and box springs with plastic covers or put them in mattress boxes. Trundle beds should be tied closed.

♦ Leave clothes in dresser drawers.

♦ Pack clothes in closets on hangers in wardrobe cartons, and put shoes on the wardrobe carton floor.

Library, Living Room

♦ Books should be packed upright in small boxes. (Consider shipping them book rate by mail.)

♦ Individually wrap small framed pictures and put them upright in the same box. Individually pack large pictures and mirrors. Crisscross wide tape over the glass of large pictures and mirrors, wrap, and pack individually in mirror cartons.

♦ Lamps should be packed separately from their shades and bulbs. Nest shades in a box.

♦ Tie down sofa beds.

♦ Pack electronic equipment in original cartons, using special packing instructions in owner's manuals. Back up computer files on floppy disks and carry disks with you separately.

Plants: Pack plants in a box with an air hole, placing them so that they cannot fall over. Tape down the lid. Carry plants in the car. If the journey takes less than four days, do not water them.

For more information on moving, write to **American Movers Conference,** 1611 Duke Street, Alexandria, VA 22314 (703-683-7410).

Helpful Tips in Planning Your Interstate Move

This section contains information that may be helpful in planning to use the services of an interstate household goods mover regulated by the Interstate Commerce Commission (ICC). For more complete information, a copy of the pamphlet, "When You Move: Your Rights and Responsibilities," should be provided by any moving company. The "When You Move" pamphlet was prepared by the ICC, and regulated household goods movers are required to furnish a copy to prospective customers.

Things You Should Know Before the Move

Movers are required to prepare an "order for service," a type of work order, for each customer. Be sure to keep a copy of this order for service, as it shows the terms of the initial agreement with the mover for the services requested. Immediately notify the mover about any changes in plans that might affect the order for service. Be sure to have the mover issue a new order for service showing the mover's understanding of any changes that may be needed.

Bill of Lading

The mover must issue a "bill of lading." The bill of lading is the legal contract between the customer and the mover. It is the most important document in the move, so take care not to lose or misplace it.

Do not sign the bill of lading until comparing it with the order for service to be sure that all services ordered are correctly shown. Have the bill of lading on hand at the time of household goods delivery.

Binding Estimates

A "binding estimate" binds the mover to bill only at the price agreed to for the specific ser-

vices needed. Any later increases in the services initially requested or the later addition of any household goods to the shipment will void the binding contract initially agreed to. If changes need to be made, ask the mover for a new binding contract.

A binding estimate must be in writing and a copy of the estimate must be attached to the bill of lading. Under a binding estimate, the mover must be paid by cash, certified check, or money order at the time of delivery, unless the mover has extended credit or otherwise agreed to accept a credit card.

Nonbinding Estimates

The moving company may not charge for a "nonbinding" estimate of what final charges will be. Under a nonbinding estimate, the mover must indicate the amount of the estimate on the order for service and the bill of lading. The final price for the move will not be known until the goods are weighed and the mover calculates the total charges for the transportation and services provided. Movers cannot require the payment of more than the original estimate plus 10 percent at the time of delivery at the new location, though the balance must be paid in 30 days. The mover may require payment in full at the time of delivery for any additional household goods or services that were later added and thus were not shown on the initial nonbinding estimate.

Pickup and Delivery Dates

Agreement should be reached with the mover as to the pickup and delivery dates. Usually, the agreement with the mover will be for delivery within a range of dates and for pickup within another range of dates.

Make sure that these dates are adequate, and do not agree to offers of vague delivery dates, such as "as soon as possible," from the mover. The dates agreed to must be shown on the order for service and on the bill of lading.

The mover is required to pick up and deliver goods within the agreed-upon time periods. The mover may be liable for the consumer's out-of-pocket living expenses for its failure to perform, as promised, unless it can show that any failure was due to a cause over which it had no control.

The mover also is required to make notification by telephone, telegram, or in person if it cannot meet the agreed-upon pickup or delivery dates, and will advise of rescheduled dates for service. Agreement should be reached with the mover to change dates if there is any problem with the dates the mover suggests.

The establishment of a delayed pickup or delivery date does not relieve the mover from liability for damages resulting from its failure to provide service as agreed. However, when a consumer is notified of alternative delivery dates, it is the consumer's responsibility to be available to accept delivery on those dates.

If, after the pickup of a shipment, the mover is requested to change the delivery date, most movers will agree to do so, providing the request will not result in unreasonable delay in the use of their equipment or interfere with another customer's move. However, the mover is not required to consent to changed delivery dates, and it has the right to place a shipment in storage at consumer expense if the consumer is unwilling or unable to accept delivery on the date agreed to in the bill of lading.

The consumer or someone acting on the consumer's behalf should be present to accept delivery of household goods, either at the original agreed-upon time, or at an alternative delivery date. If no one is present at the new location on the designated date, the mover has the right to hold the goods in the truck or to place them in storage and assess additional charges.

Notification of Charges

The mover must be told during initial arrangements if the consumer wants to be notified of the charges for the move. Give the mover the telephone number or address where someone will be available to receive notification of those charges.

The mover must give 24 hours' advance notice of the final charges—excluding Saturdays, Sundays, and legal holidays—so that payment may be arranged. The 24-hour, prior-notice requirement does not apply to a shipment that takes only two or fewer days to deliver, to shipments that are weighed at their destination, or to shipments for which an estimate has been given.

Inconvenience/Delay Claims

If the mover fails to pick up and deliver a shipment on the date entered on the bill of lading and expenses thus are incurred that otherwise might not have been, expenses may be recovered from the mover through an "inconvenience" or "delay" claim. Should a mover refuse to honor such a claim and a consumer believes that he or she is entitled to be paid damages, the consumer may sue the mover in Small Claims Court. Be advised, however, that the ICC has no authority to order movers to pay such claims.

While it is hoped that shipments will not be delayed, consider that possibility and request in writing a copy of the mover's policy on inconvenience or delay claims in advance of the move.

Loss and Damage Claims

As licensed "common carriers" (that is, companies offering their moving services to any and all customers who contact them), movers are responsible for loss or damage to goods caused by the carrier. The consumer and the moving van driver should agree to the number and condition of household goods at the place from which a move is being made. Be sure you are in agreement with the driver's description of the condition of the goods as listed on inventory sheets. A copy of this inventory will be provided.

At the time of delivery, it is essential that any missing or damaged articles be noted on the consumer's and the driver's inventory sheet, because a future claim for loss or damage will be based upon these notations. If there is a failure to note damaged or missing items on the inventory sheet, the mover may decline liability on a subsequent claim.

The consumer should check all boxes and note any loss or damage at the time of delivery.

Added-Value Protection

Consumers should agree with the mover on the amount of liability the mover will assume in case of loss or damage to the goods.

Agreement may be reached for the mover's delivery of goods at a liability value of 60 cents per pound, per article, for any loss or damage claims filed. There is no additional charge for this level of liability. This valuation must be requested specifically in the consumer's own handwriting. The ICC does not recommend this level of protection unless the consumer has other sources of insurance, because the mover's liability is limited to 60 cents per pound, regardless of the true value of the article.

Alternatively, consumers may agree to the mover's delivery of goods at a lump-sum liability value and pay an additional fee to the mover for its assumption of increased liability. There are several programs of this type offered by movers, each of which may require certain declarations of minimum value and may contain various deduct-

ibles. Consumers should carefully consider these liability programs—including any replacement-cost recovery plans that may be available—to ensure understanding of what is being provided, and at what cost.

If no declaration of value is made by the consumer, the mover is required to value them at a lump sum equal to $1.25 times the weight of the shipment. The mover will also charge $5.00 per every 1000 pounds for the additional protection of the shipment. For example, if the goods total 4000 pounds in weight, the mover must value them at $5000 (4000 pounds × $1.25 lump-sum value), and charge $20.00 (4 × $5).

The mover may also arrange for trip-transit insurance. Here, the mover's liability is limited to 60 cents per pound, per article, and the mover's insurance company is liable for additional amounts up to the face value of the trip-transit insurance policy. Evidence of the use of this type of insurance must be provided by the mover.

For additional information:

Office of Compliance and Consumer Assistance, Room 4412, Interstate Commerce Commission, 12th Street & Constitution Avenue NW, Washington, DC 20423 (202-927-7597).

Source: Interstate Commerce Commission

Health and safety in the home

Indoor Pollution

It seems logical that if the air outside is thick with pollution, you can escape it by going inside. But, believe it or not, the air in your house—your refuge—can be more polluted than the air outside, especially when your home is well insulated. Ironically, in attempts to save energy, people have weatherized their houses so that little air escapes and little air enters from outside to dilute pollution. The result is often an indoor air pollution level—of particles, gases, and viruses and bacteria—*higher* than outside. For instance, formaldehyde—a suspected carginogen—can exist inside homes at levels 11 times greater than outdoors. To make it worse, most people spend far more time inside the house than outside—up to 90 percent.

Contaminants in indoor air can adversely affect your health. You can be prey to allergic reactions, infectious diseases, and toxic conditions. Some effects are immediately apparent. Others kill silently over the long term—cancer, heart disease, and damage to liver and kidneys, respiratory system, nervous system.

Health Check List

Watch for the following symptoms. If the symptoms disappear when you are outside, suspect your house. Remember that some people are more susceptible to air pollution than others. Determining factors include age and preexisting medical conditions, as well as individual sensitivity, which may increase with repeated exposure to biological and chemical pollutants.

- Eye, nose, throat irritation
- Headaches
- Dizziness and fatigue
- Cold- or flu-like symptoms
- Attacks of asthma, hypersensitivity, pneumonitis, and humidifier fever.

If you have these symptoms, discuss with your doctor the possibility that they are caused by indoor pollution. If your doctor concurs, do something about it.

If you think your house is polluted, even if you remain asymptomatic, it is important to improve air quality. Some health problems take years to develop.

The chart below lists sources of pollution, health effects, solutions.

Consult with your state or local health department on ways to reduce indoor air pollution if it exists.

Some Other Tips:

- Reduce use of air fresheners, toilet-bowl cleaners, and moth crystals (sources of paradichlorobenzene, a toxic and possibly carcinogenic chemical).

INDOOR POLLUTION CHART

Sources	Pollution	Health Effects	Solutions
Tobacco smoking.	Compounds such as benzopyrene, carbon monoxide, nitrogen oxide, formaldehyde, nitrogen dioxide; respirable particles.	Immediate: eye, nose, throat irritation; respiratory and ear infections in children. Long-term: cancer and possible heart disease.	Don't permit smoking in your house. Send smokers outdoors if they must indulge.
Kerosene and gas heaters; gas stoves; wood stoves .	Carbon monoxide; nitrogen oxide; respirable particles.	Immediate: headaches, fatigue, confusion, impaired vision and coordination, flu-like symptoms. Can be fatal.	Vent stoves, heaters, and fireplaces with fans and other devices. Ventilate your house by keeping a window open a crack. Install exhaust fan to outdoors over gas stoves. Install a CO (carbon monoxide) detector meeting Underwriters Laboratory standard #2034 or place CO gas-testing tablets around the house.
Central heating and cooling systems.	Respirable particles; carbon monoxide.	Immediate: eye, nose, throat irritation; respiratory problems.	Have your heating system inspected annually. Empty humidifier trays often. Change filters on heating and cooling systems and on air cleaners as manufacturer directs. Have heat exchangers, vents, and flue pipes (even on new furnaces) checked for carbon monoxide emissions.
Pressed wood products such as fiber board, particle board, and plywood in walls, floors, furniture.	Formaldehyde.	Immediate: eye, nose, and throat irritation; respiratory problems; fatigue; rash; allergic reactions; nausea. Long-term: Possible cancer; possible coordination problems; possible liver, kidney, nerve damage.	Use air conditioning and dehumidifiers. Ventilate. Use newer pressed wood products with lower emissions of formaldehyde, or coat wood products with polyurethane or lacquer. Leave new cabinets outdoors for a couple of months before installing.
Textiles containing formaldehyde.			Buy 100 percent cotton, wool, or silk products, or wash items before using.
Toilets.	Airborne viruses and bacteria; molds.	Bacterial and viral illnesses; allergic reactions.	Close the toilet lid before flushing.
Moisture-carrying walls, ceilings, carpets, furniture, bedding.			Clean and dry water-damaged carpets or get rid of them. Ventilate. Maintain humidity at 30–50%.
Basements.			If the basement is used as living quarters, leakproof and ventilate.

♦ Put clothes "fresh" from the dry cleaner in a well-ventilated room for several days. They can emit high levels of tetrachloroethylene, a dangerous chemical.

ASBESTOS

If you live in an older house (built between 1900 and the 1970s), it may contain asbestos products like pipe and furnace insulation, shingles, millboard, textured paints, and floor tiles. Asbestos, a mineral fiber, is an excellent insulator and fire-retardant. Unfortunately, it is also dangerous to humans—small fibers, inhaled, accumulate in the lungs: they can cause cancer and scarring and can be fatal. If you find that your house contains asbestos, here is what not to do and what to do:

♦ Do not disturb any items you think contain asbestos. If you do, you may release particles into the air. Instead hire a trained professional to look over your house for asbestos-bearing materials. Some states have asbestos programs; if not, contact your health department.

♦ If you suspect that an area may contain particles of asbestos, don't vacuum or sweep it. Damp mop it.

♦ Consider sealing off rather than removing asbestos-containing material. The only do-it-yourself project approved by the EPA is sealing off very small areas of deterioration (crumbling, flaking, torn, water-damaged) with sealant or wide adhesive tape; while doing this, wear protective clothing, goggles, and a respirator mask approved for asbestos. For larger jobs, call in professionals.

♦ Do not dispose of asbestos in regular trash pickup.

RADON

Radon gas is created when uranium breaks down in rocks and soil—it is a natural phenomenon. Radon seeps into a house, often through dirt floors, cracks in the basement, sumps, or floor drains. It can leak into the water supply, particularly if you have a private well. Radon contamination might be affecting as many as one house in 15 in the U.S. Though radon occurs in greater concentrations in the Northeast, Arizona, and North Carolina, you should not assume that you are safe if you live in another region.

Why worry? According to the U.S. Environmental Agency, radon annually causes from 7000 to 30,000 deaths, mostly from lung cancer. The agency puts the danger level at four picocuries of radiation per liter of air. It claims that radon at this level can cause cancer in 13 to 50 of every 1000 people who live in houses that are affected. It would be as if they smoked 10 cigarettes a day or underwent 200 chest X rays a year. Some experts think this claim is exaggerated because the EPA used as a basis for their conclusions studies of uranium miners, who are exposed to levels thousands of times higher than in homes. But, since controversy exists, why not take the side of caution.

How to prevent radon contamination:

♦ Do not allow cigarette smoking in the house. Radon tends to concentrate on tiny particles in cigarette smoke.

♦ Have your house tested for radon by an Environmental Protection Agency–certified contractor. Be aware that some contractors have been known to manipulate the testing situation—leaving doors and windows open, for instance—so that a false negative results. Others have done a poor job out of ignorance. Check up on the contractor testing your house: Put a piece of tape in an inconspicuous place on windows—if it has moved by the time the contractors leave you can assume that windows have been opened. Insist on a second test if you suspect that the first is inaccurate.

Or,

♦ Test your house yourself with an EPA-approved radon testing kit. Ask your state radiation protection office for advice about kits. There are two types used in homes: charcoal canisters (carbon kits), which should be exposed for a week or more; and alpha track detectors, which should be exposed for one to three months. (The latter are the more reliable, and some states recommend their use only.) Use the kit several times, especially in the lowest-level lived-in part of your house (the basement, for instance). If you consistently find high levels of radon, have your house tested by a professional.

♦ If the level is high, take action.

1. Seal cracks in basement and foundation.

2. Improve ventilation by installing special fans and ducts in crawl spaces, subslab, or basement.

3. Install air-to-air heat exchangers.

4. Open windows evenly on all sides of your house.

5. Have water treated by aerating it or filtering it through granulated-activated charcoal.

6. Forbid smoking in the house.

7. If all else fails, get professional help.

More information on indoor air pollution is available in libraries and elsewhere, including:

Environmental Protection Agency, Public Information Center, 401 M Street SW, Washington, DC 20460 (202-260-2090); Office of Radiation and Indoor Air, 202-233-9340; Radon Hotline, 800-SOS-RADON; TSCA assistance line, 202-554-1404—for information on EPA's asbestos programs and your state's involvement in training and certification program for asbestos-removal contractors.

National Institute of Standards and Technology, Gaithersburg, MD 20899 (301-975-4016), information on reliable asbestos-testing laboratories.

The American Lung Association, GPO Box 3879, 2750 New York, NY 92163-1879 (800-LUNG-USA).

U.S. Consumer Product Safety Commission, CPSC Publications Request, Washington, DC 20207 (800-638-2772); TTY 800-638-8270 (outside Maryland), 800-492-8104 (Maryland only), information on carbon monoxide.

Consumer Federation of America, Suite 604, 1424 16th Street NW, Washington, DC 20036; 202-387-6121, information about formaldehyde.

Ridding Your Home of Allergens

Unfortunately, your house can make you sick with allergies. Experts say that dust mites, tiny little creatures, are the most prevalent of all allergens. They live in places like carpeting, upholstery, mattresses, and pillows. Some ideas to foil them and other allergy-producing things:

♦ Use a double-walled bag in your vacuum cleaner.

♦ Rid the house of old newspapers and houseplants.

♦ Use a dehumidifier in the basement (mites can't live in arid climates).

♦ Watch out for mildew. Throw out mildewed items, and vent damp air.

♦ Buy and use hepafilter air filters.

♦ Ban carpets from your bedroom.

♦ Kill dust mites with acaricides (sold in drugstores).

♦ Put mattress, box springs, and pillows in dust-proof covers.

♦ Use only washable bedding, and wash it in hot water once a week.

♦ Keep dust-attracting toys out of a dust-sensitive child's bedroom.

♦ Replace blinds with window shades.

Also see "Allergies to Pets," p. 309.

EPA Regional Offices

The regional offices of the U.S. Environmental Protection Agency are perhaps the best sources of additional information about environmental hazards in specific state and local areas. Each EPA regional office has information on states and areas within a single geographic area.

EPA REGION 1

John F. Kennedy Federal
  Building Room 2203
Boston, MA 02203
617-565-3420

Areas served: Connecticut, Maine, Massachusetts, New Hampshire, Rhode Island, and Vermont

EPA REGION 2

26 Federal Plaza
New York, NY 10278
212-264-2515
Areas served: New Jersey, New York, Puerto Rico, and Virgin Islands

EPA REGION 3

841 Chestnut Street
Philadelphia, PA 19107
215-597-9800
Areas served: Delaware, Maryland, Pennsylvania, Virginia, Washington, DC, and West Virginia

EPA REGION 4

345 Courtland Street NE
Atlanta, GA 30365
404-347-3004
Areas served: Alabama, Florida, Georgia, Kentucky, Mississippi, North Carolina, South Carolina, and Tennessee

EPA REGION 5

77 West Jackson Boulevard
Chicago, IL 60604
312-353-2000
Areas served: Illinois, Indiana, Michigan, Minnesota, Ohio, and Wisconsin

EPA REGION 6

1445 Ross Avenue
Suite 1200
Dallas, TX 75202
214-655-2200
Areas served: Arkansas, Louisiana, New Mexico, Oklahoma, and Texas

EPA REGION 7

726 Minnesota Avenue
Kansas City, KS 66101
913-551-7000
Areas Served: Iowa, Kansas, Missouri, and Nebraska

EPA REGION 8

999 18th Street
Suite 500
Denver, CO 80202-2466
303-293-1603
Areas served: Colorado, Montana, North Dakota, South Dakota, Utah, and Wyoming

EPA REGION 9

75 Hawthorne Street
San Francisco, CA 94105
415-744-1080
Areas served: Arizona, California, Hawaii, and Nevada

EPA REGION 10

1200 Sixth Avenue
Seattle, WA 98101
206-553-1200
Areas served: Alaska, Idaho, Oregon, and Washington

Taking a Home Inventory

Compiling a detailed inventory of your household possessions for insurance purposes can take many hours—but it's worth the time. In case of a fire, natural disaster, or burglary, an inventory can mean thousands of dollars in insurance claims.

You will need a notebook, an electric engraving device, and a camera or video camera. Collect any available sales receipts. (Insurance companies don't expect receipts for everything, but major purchases should be documented.)

Then tour your house (including attic and basement), garage, and storage sheds, room by room and wall by wall, and:

1. List major items, including purchase date and price.

2. Attach to your list any sales receipts for those items.

3. Record the serial numbers of major appliances.

4. Engrave your driver's license number (or other identifying number) on the back or bottom of items such as televisions, VCRs, and stereos with the electric engraving device, according to manufacturer's instructions.

5. Videotape or take color photographs of your possessions. **First,** take pictures of the room and its contents with closet or cabinet doors open. **Second,** take close-ups of jewelry, antiques, silverware, dishes, and other valuables. If you are using a video camera, describe and value the items as you go. On the back of photographs, write the date, general location, and contents shown.

6. Store your written inventory, photographs, and/or videotapes in a safe place away from home. Make sure others know where records are kept.

7. Keep a copy of your inventory and negatives of the photographs at home so you can update your list and negatives from time to time when you purchase new items, remodel, add a room, or make other changes, even reupholstering. Delete items you no longer own.

8. You may need to have some items appraised: jewelry, art, antiques, furs, collections, and valuables with no bill of sale.

Childproofing Your House

Children investigate everything and tend to ignore danger, part of the reason that accidents are the number-one cause of death for children. You can protect your children by educating them, telling them about things that can be dangerous or can cause pain. It is essential, too, that you childproof your house.

For babies, buy only nursery items approved by the Juvenile Product Manufacturers Association (JPMA). Such items will be identified by a seal that should be stripped off once the item is purchased. (You don't want your baby to choke on it.) Use a safe crib with slats no more than 2⅜ inches apart, sides 22 inches above the mattress, a mattress that fits the frame snugly, no sharp corners. Corner posts should be no more than 1/16 inch higher than end panels. Avoid cribs with cute cutouts on the head and footboards—they can trap a baby's neck.

Once your baby has started getting around on his or her own, childproof your house. Start by pretending you are a child: on hands and knees, crawl around and look for things a child might eat or grab—a lamp cord, dropped pin, tablecloth.

Once you have eliminated those immediate hazards, make other changes that will help to ensure your child's safety:

♦ Install gates at the top and bottom of stairs. Don't use accordion, V-, or diamond-shaped types—they can trap a child's head. Put bars or tight-fitting screens on windows. Install latches on windows that keep them from being opened more than few inches.

♦ Put childproof latches (available at hardware stores) on cabinets and closet doors. Reinstall interior door latches higher up, above the child's reach.

♦ Install childproof covers on electrical outlets. Keep cords out of your child's reach.

◆ Keep matches and cigarette lighters out of reach.

◆ Put chairs in places where a child cannot climb them and lean out the window.

◆ Get rid of poisonous houseplants. (See "Some Plants Dangerous to Children," below.)

◆ Check your house for poisons (cleaning products, etc.) and store them in high cabinets. Keep medicines in childproof containers in locked medicine cabinets.

◆ If you spray your garden with insecticides, don't let children play there for a day or two.

◆ Don't carry aspirin or other medicines in your purse.

◆ Keep the phone number of the poison control center near phones.

◆ Remove breakables from furniture.

◆ Put guards in front of radiators, wall heaters, and fireplaces.

◆ When cooking, turn the pot handles to the back of the stove or make it a habit to use the back burners.

◆ Put antiscald devices on faucets and shower heads.

◆ Lock up power tools. Use extension cords only temporarily.

◆ Keep objects small enough to be swallowed out of children's reach. Don't give little children toys with parts that can come off, or foods like carrot or apple pieces or hard candies.

◆ Store plastic bags out of reach or shred them or tie them in knots. Don't use a plastic cover on your child's mattress.

◆ Lock trunks and unused refrigerators and toilet seats. Disarm interior locks on any container or closet the child can crawl into. Toy chests should have supports that keep the lid from slamming shut and ventilation holes and interior lock releases.

◆ Fill empty lamp sockets with bulbs.

◆ Unplug electrical devices when you are not using them.

◆ Keep fire extinguishers above a child's reach.

◆ Put away cord and string—a child can choke on them.

To Prevent Drowning. See "Swimming: Fear of the Water—Is It Always Bad?" p. 536.

Note: When you travel with children, take an accident prevention kit with you. It should include socket plugs, slide locks, syrup of ipecac, a toilet lock.

U.S. Consumer Product Safety Commission, Office of Information and Public Affairs, Washington, DC 20207 (301-504-0980). Request brochure on child safety; to file a complaint about an unsafe product or obtain information on recalls, call 800-638-2772.

SOME PLANTS DANGEROUS TO CHILDREN

azaleas	lily of the valley
bird of paradise	marigold
bittersweet	mistletoe
black locust	morning glory
bleeding heart	mother-in-law
Boston fern	mountain laurel
boxwood	mushrooms and
buttercup	toadstools
castor bean	narcissus
chrysanthemum	nightshade
crocus	oak
daffodil	oleander
dumbcane	philodendron
(dieffenbachia)	poinsettia
elderberry	poison hemlock
English ivy	poison ivy
English Jew	poison oak
foxglove	potato (sprouts and
geranium	green parts)
holly	rhododendron
horse chestnut	rhubarb leaves
hyacinth	rosary pea
iris	(jequirity bean)
jack-in-the-pulpit	skunk cabbage
jequirity bean	sumac
(rosary pea)	sweet pea
Jerusalem cherry	tomato (green
jimson weed	parts)
jonquil	yew

Juvenile Product Manufacturers Association, Box 955, Marlton, NJ 08053 (609-985-2878). Request brochures on safe cribs and other furniture.

Ageproofing Your House

More than 367,000 people age 65 or older were treated at hospital emergency rooms in 1991 for injuries sustained in bathrooms or on furniture, stairs, carpeting, or rugs. Protect yourself and those you love with simple changes in furniture arrangement, housekeeping, and lighting. Where necessary, install special safety features. Decide today to Live It Safe. Use the following checklist to make your home safer.

Living Areas

♦ Arrange furniture so there are clear pathways between rooms.

♦ Remove low-rise coffee tables, magazine racks, footrests, and plants from pathways in the rooms.

♦ Keep electric appliance and telephone cords out of the pathways.

♦ Remove door sills higher than ½ inch.

♦ Secure loose area rugs with double-faced tape, tacks, or slip-resistant backing.

♦ Do not stand on unsteady stools, chairs, ladders, etc.

♦ Repair loose wooden floorboards immediately.

Stairs and Steps

♦ Do not leave objects on the stairs.

♦ Provide enough light to see each stair and the top and bottom landings.

♦ Do not place loose area rugs at the bottom or top of stairs.

♦ Do not use patterned or dark carpeting on stairs. Repair loose stairway rugs or boards immediately.

♦ Put nonslip treads on each bare-wood step.

♦ Install handrails on both sides of the stairway. Each should be 30 inches above the stairs and extend the full length of the stairs.

Kitchen

♦ Clean up immediately any liquids, grease, or food spilled on the floor.

♦ Store food, dishes, and cooking equipment within easy reach.

♦ Use a step stool with a handrail attached.

♦ Repair loose flooring.

♦ Use nonskid floorwax.

A SAFE CHRISTMAS

A pedestrian but very important Christmas present for your family: a safe holiday. Here are some tips on how to ensure it.

♦ Buy your tree shortly before Christmas. A freshly cut tree, which is much less of a fire hazard than a dried-out one, has pliable needles that spring back into shape when bent.

♦ Choose a place for your tree where it is out of direct sunlight and away from heat sources.

♦ Trim the bottom of the tree trunk, then secure it in a water-filled stand. Refill the stand as needed. Christmas trees are thirsty.

♦ Never use candles on your tree. Lights should be cool enough to hold in your hand when lit. Use only Underwriters Laboratory–approved lights.

♦ Throw away damaged light sets with frayed cords and bad sockets. Make sure that extension cords cannot become entangled with tree stands.

♦ Don't leave your tree lights on when you are not there.

♦ Don't leave pets alone in the room with a tree. They may try to climb it and tip it over.

♦ Take the tree down no later than New Year's Day.

Bathrooms

♦ Place a slip-resistant rug adjacent to the bathtub for safe exit and entry.

♦ Install a night-light in the bathroom.

♦ Place nonskid adhesive textured strips on the floor of the bathtub and shower.

♦ Use a sturdy, plastic seat in the bathtub if you cannot lower yourself to the floor of the tub or if you are unsteady.

♦ Install handrails on the bathroom walls near the toilet and along the bathtub.

♦ Stabilize yourself on the toilet by using either a raised seat or a special toilet seat with armrests.

♦ Mount a liquid soap dispenser on the bathtub/shower wall.

Bedroom

♦ Keep the bedroom floor free of clutter.

♦ Place a lamp and flashlight near your bed.

♦ Install a night-light along the route between the bedroom and the bathroom.

Reproduced with permission from *Live It Safe*, public education brochure, American Academy of Orthopaedic Surgeons.

For a free "Live It Safe" brochure call the American Academy of Orthopaedic Surgeons' public service telephone number, 800-824-BONES, or send a stamped, self-addressed business-size envelope to Live It Safe, American Academy of Orthopaedic Surgeons, PO Box 1998, Des Plaines, IL 60017.

A CLEAN AND WELL-MAINTAINED HOUSE

Doing Laundry

You open the washing machine to see your clothes decorated with shreds of washed tissues from an unemptied pocket. You pluck a shrunken dress from the dryer. Your white socks have gone gray. Then you realize that dumping the laundry from basket into machine and hoping for the best doesn't always work. If that's the case with you, here's a refresher course on doing laundry.

Before Loading

Sort the laundry—by color, by use (towels used for cleaning separate from guest towels), by

fabric (according to need for hot or cold water, vigorous or less vigorous washing action, kind of bleach), by lintiness, by construction (lace-trimmed garments, for instance, need a gentle cycle), by degree of dirtiness. Assign them to specific loads.

Take everything out of pockets and cuffs. Look for clothes that need repair and don't wash them until they are fixed. Close zippers and other fasteners. Take off unwashable attached items (removable shoulder pads, decorations). Wash all pieces of sets of clothing (a matching blouse and skirt, for example) each time.

Pretreat by rubbing dirty spots with concentrated, dissolved detergent. If you pretreat with bleach, do not soak too long. Also treat stains (see "Stains," p. 192).

Some experts on washing say that the water heater should be set to 140°F. Hot will then be 130° (because water will lose some of its heat in the machine); warm will be about 100°F., cold will be less than 60°F. (However, this "hot" temperature can be too hot for safety, according to some safety experts who recommend that the water heater be set at 120° or lower.) Most laundry washes effectively in warm water, and some washes well in cold water. Using cold water saves energy, minimizes shrinkage, keeps colors bright.

Don't overload the washer—clothes should be able to move freely, or dirt removal will be

WHO DOES THE DIRTY WORK?

One woman in three is angry with her husband for not helping more with the housework, according to a poll of about 500 couples by Special Report Network in Knoxville. Other findings: if forced to choose, men would take sex 3 to 1 over a clean house—not women, who rate a clean house on a par with sex, at least when answering polls. And explain *this* strange response: most men—and women—would prefer average sex in a clean house to great sex in a dirty one.

SPECIFIC WASHING METHODS

Washer setting	Washable items	Water temperature	Detergent, bleach, fabric softener
Regular	Nearly everything washable except permanent press, woolens, delicate items. Includes cotton knits if fabric has been treated to resist shrinkage. Washable pillows (do two at a time to balance load).	Whites and very dirty items: hot. Not so dirty colored items: warm. Bright or very dark colors (for color retention) or least dirty items: cold.	Any detergent. Fabric softener optional. Whites and very dirty items (without color problems): chlorine bleach. Don't use chlorine bleach on cotton sweaters. Others: oxygen bleach.
Permanent press with water level at least at *medium.*	Items labeled permanent press or no-iron; washable synthetic knits.	Whites and heavily soiled items: hot. Others: warm. Cold rinse for all.	Any detergent. Use fabric softener. Whites and colorfast items: chlorine bleach. All fabrics: oxygen bleach.
Delicate with water level at least at *medium.*	Washable silk, loose-knit or sheer items, some wool single-knit jersey, washable wool sweaters, lace-trimmed or embroidered items, foundation garments, handwashables, washable down jackets (wash separately), curtains and draperies (except those made of glass fibers). (Put small things and hosiery in mesh bag.	For most items: warm. Items that are not very dirty and bright colors: cold.	Any detergent. Use fabric softener. Whites, except garments of spandex: chlorine bleach. All fabrics: oxygen bleach.
	Wool (only those labeled machine-washable or handwashable).	Cold, though for very dirty items, use warm.	Any detergent. Fabric softener unnecessary. No chlorine bleach. Dry in dryer (at regular setting) only when manufacturer recommends it.

Adapted with permission from *Maytag Encyclopedia of Home Laundry*, 5th ed.

SPECIFIC LAUNDRY PROBLEMS

Problem	Cause	Solution
GRAYING	Not enough detergent	Use extra detergent on very dirty clothes and if your water is hard.
	Washer overload	Reduce load size and make sure you have a mix of large and small things.
	Water not hot enough	See advice above on water heater temperature settings. If your water heater is small, run washer only when hot water is not needed elsewhere.
	Improper soaking	Make sure that you use enough detergent and that it is dissolved for soaking phase.
	Use of soap	Use soap only in soft water.
YELLOWING	Body oils left in fabric (large areas of yellow)	Use hot water and as much as double the recommended amount of detergent. Use a cup of chlorine bleach (diluted in a quart of water) four minutes after first agitation cycle. Agitate four minutes. Let wash soak for 15 minutes. Restart washer at 10-minute wash time, let it go through cycle.
	Iron or manganese in water (many spots, yellow over all)	Use more detergent and a non-precipitating water conditioner in the water, thoroughly dissolved. Don't use chlorine bleach. To remove yellowing, use hot water, detergent, and a rust remover meant for this purpose. Lemon juice removes small spots.
	Tendency of polyester to yellow	Use chlorine bleach; don't overuse fabric softeners.

Adapted with permission from *Maytag Encyclopedia of Home Laundry*, 5th ed.

uneven. Fill a front-loading washer only to the top of the door. Fill a top-loading washer to the top row of holes, if the washer has them. Vary sizes of items in the load. Delicate garments, no matter how small the load, should be washed with water level set to medium; otherwise they may shrink, wrinkle, and develop pulled seams.

Use the correct bleach or none at all, according to clothing labels. In hot or warm water, you can use granular detergent. In cold water, you need a liquid or predissolved detergent.

When clothes are dry, take them out of the dryer and hang them up or fold them immediately.

Special Drying Tips

Dry washable wool on the line or block it. Don't put it in the dryer. Some synthetics can be tumble-dried at low heat, while some (like polypropylene) cannot.

Drip-dry linen.

Handwashing Silk

Silk is probably best handwashed or dry cleaned. Try handwashing a bit of the fabric from an inside seam first. Use warm water to wash, cold water to rinse. If the color runs, dry-clean. Also check interfacings and other fabrics used in the garment. Iron silk damp on the back side of the fabric using a cool setting.

Stains

The universal advice: deal with strains right away. If you don't, time may "set" them so they get worse. Hot water also sets stains, so unless hot water is absolutely required for laundering stained clothes, wash in cold water.

As you work on a stain, blot rather than rub, working from the outside in. Turn your cleaning cloth so you are always using a clean part. Greasy stains generally require solvents; nongreasy stains require detergents or ammonia or vinegar solutions.

WARNING: Use one method with one kind of solution. For instance, don't mix chlorine bleach with ammonia—it creates toxic fumes.

Adhesive tape. Nail polish remover.

Ballpoint ink. Spray with hairspray, then blot with a clean dry cloth and launder. Or soak in milk, wash in warm suds, bleach; rubbing alcohol may work. From suede: use cotton swab dipped in white vinegar.

Beer. On white cotton, use hydrogen peroxide. On colored fabric, use white vinegar.

Berries. Blot, rub with cut lemon, rinse in cold water. Air dry.

Blood. Apply unseasoned meat tenderizer mixed with cool water to make a paste and let it work for 15 minutes. Rinse. Or soak in cold water or ammonia solution. Or use a solution of 1 quart cold water and 2 tablespoons of table salt. Or use hydrogen peroxide (only on fabrics that can be bleached).

Butter. Wash in warm, soapy water.

Candy. Soak in hot water.

Catsup. Put on a mix of half water, half white vinegar, rinse and wash in warm water.

Chewing gum. Soak item in white vinegar or rub with egg white. Or put in a plastic bag in the freezer—frozen gum comes off more easily. Or rub with ice, then scrape. Put waxed paper over the residue and iron lightly. For gum in the hair, work in vegetable oil until the gum loosens up.

Chocolate. Scrape off the excess, then rub cornmeal into the stain. Soak in enzyme prewash for 30 minutes. Or use borax and cold water. Bleach if necessary.

Coffee and tea. Pour boiling water through the stain if the fabric will stand it. Bleach if necessary. Or wipe with a paste of baking soda and water or white vinegar and noniodized salt. Or soak in soda water.

Crayon or candle wax. Put the item between layers of paper towel or brown grocery bags and press with a warm iron.

Egg. Scrape off egg and put on a paste of laundry enzyme cleaner and cold water for 30 minutes. Rinse. Launder warm. Air dry.

Fresh fruit and vegetables. Use hydrogen peroxide or diluted white vinegar—no soap.

Fruit juice. Soak in cold water. Rinse.

Glue. Soak in warm water. Wash in soapy water.

Grass. Rub with isopropyl or denatured alcohol, then soak in a mix of warm water and enzyme detergent; launder.

Grease or oil. Sprinkle with talc or cornstarch, let sit, brush away powder, launder.

Lipstick. Rub with Vaseline and wash in hot soapy water.

Pencil marks. Erase with a pencil eraser. If marks persist, rub in a bit of ammonia, then treat with stain stick and wash.

Mildew. On walls and floors, make a solution of borax and water and apply with a brush. Sprinkle mildewed paper with cornstarch, talcum powder or cornmeal, leave for two days, then brush off.

Mustard. Dampen item, put on prewash stain remover and a bit of white vinegar. Or soak with diluted ammonia. Then rinse and launder as usual.

Nail polish. Use nail polish remover without lanolin for most materials and banana oil for nylon and rayon.

Perspiration. Soak item in warm white vinegar. Or try enzyme presoak. Then launder.

Pet stains. Wet with a solution of half white vinegar, half water, then blot dry. Use baking soda for cat accidents.

Red wine. Pour on club soda, then sponge up. Or sprinkle with table salt, and rinse with cold water. Or soak in a solution of 2 tablespoons of ammonia or ammoniated detergent in a quart of water.

Ring around the collar. Rub shampoo or a paste of baking soda and white vinegar into soiled parts, then launder.

Rust. Put on lemon juice and salt, dry in the sun, rinse. Baking-soda paste works in taking rust off vinyl floor—leave on for several hours, then scrub.

Scorch marks. Soak a cotton ball in 3 percent hydrogen peroxide solution, sponge on, dry in the sun. Or moisten and bleach. Or rub with a lemon, wipe with a damp sponge, repeat until stain is gone.

Scuffs from shoes, on tile, floors. Nail polish remover.

Tar. Rub with kerosene until gone. Launder.

Tarnish on brass and copper. Mix flour and salt in equal parts, then add enough white vinegar to make a paste. Rub the paste on the stain. You may need to do this more than once.

Tarnish from eggs. Use table salt.

Vinegar. Diluted ammonia.

Pest Control

What is our house to what we call a pest? It's a superior habitat, a warm, food-filled refuge. According to urban myth, cockroaches flee from apartments being exterminated, climb down several stories, parade across the no-man's-land of the alley, and invade an apartment next door. They don't even *think* of living out in the open city. Anyone lying sleepless to the tune of a mouse's contented gnawing behind the wall knows the frustration of an infested house. He or she knows that mouse would rather be behind that wall than shivering in an open field. Given that some animal pests have an affinity for human habitation, can we eliminate these unwanted guests?

First, some general advice:

♦ Make food inaccessible to pests. Put it in well-secured containers. Shut lids on trash cans. Clean up spills right away.

♦ Check your house over for entry points—a crack under the door, a hole in the roof. A cockroach can squeeze through a crack only ⅟₆₄th of an inch wide, a mouse through a hole the size of a dime.

♦ If you don't know what a pest is, ask someone at your local museum of natural history.

♦ Trim vegetation, eliminate weeds that grow close to your house.

♦ Follow instructions for pesticides and rodent killers to the letter.

♦ When spreading desiccating dust (boric acid, diatomaceous earth, silica aerogel), wear a mask. Dust only in places inaccessible to children and pets.

Ants. A trillion ants live on earth, and sometimes we think that all trillion are intent on marching into our houses. Ants are not just nuisances, either—they can spread salmonella bacteria when walking on food, for instance. Luckily, there are ways to discourage them.

Spray an ant killer around the outside of your house around the foundation every couple of months. If you see an ant scouting around, kill it, otherwise it will bring word of good living to a horde of its mates. Wash counters or other ant territory with vinegar. When the ants invade, follow the column back to the entry point and shut it off with silicone caulk, plaster, or a line of boric acid. (Boric acid is toxic to children, so be careful how and where you use it.)

For bait, make a mixture of 1 teaspoon boric acid and a cup of sugar water or some tuna fish, depending on the kind of ant. (Ants come in two basic types: those that like sweets, those that like protein.) Put the bait in jars with holes punched into the top and place the jars in spots where children and pets cannot reach. Fairly safe commercial baits contain hydroprene, methoprene, hydramethylnon, sulfuramid.

Cockroaches. Cockroaches, which have a far longer history than humans (300–400 million years), will eat leftovers, clothes in the wash basket, beer, starch, bedbugs, glue in book bindings, almost anything. They can travel at 14 miles an hour or more, and not in a straight line, either. That's why they are difficult to stomp. Roaches carry microorganisms that spread disease, and they can aggravate allergies.

To prevent infestation, put food and water out of their reach, and keep hidden areas clean. Don't leave pet dishes around. Keep sponges and dish towels dry. Fix leaks. Vacuum up roaches and egg cases when you see them.

If cockroaches do appear in spite of all your efforts, spray with insecticide in dark and hidden areas—the back of cabinets, under the sink. (Wait until cabinets are dry. Then line shelves with new shelf paper before putting stuff back.) You need to do this every two to four weeks. Fill a bulb duster with boric acid, diatomaceous earth, or silica aerogel desiccating dust; use it to dust in corners and cracks and under things. You can also make a bait by mixing two parts of boric acid to one part of cornmeal or sugar. Put it in a favorite cockroach hangout. (This may take a couple of weeks to work.) You can also use bait traps. Or try this and see if it works: soak a rag with beer, put it in a corner overnight. Roaches will congregate under it to party all night. Step on the rag in the morning and then clean up the bodies.

Or adopt a gecko—the cockroach is one of their favorite foods.

Fleas. See "Flea Control," p. 355.

Bees and wasps. They are beneficial until they get in your house or under the eaves. If you don't remove bees, they can deposit hundreds of pounds of honey in your walls. The honey can seep through walls and attract ants and cockroaches. Call a professional beekeeper or remover to relocate them. (Yellow jackets, not friendly to forced moves, are usually killed by freezing.)

Mosquitoes. Besides keeping us awake at night with buzzing and bites, mosquitoes carry malaria and encephalitis. To discourage them, screen your house and get rid of standing water. If you cannot eliminate the water source, add *Bacillus thuringiensis israelensis* (Bti), a biological control, to it. Foggers work fairly well. Outside use citronella candles or smoke coils. (See "Wild Beasts and Pests: How to Avoid Them," p. 570, for information on chemical repellents.)

Termites. If, like 600,000 other U.S. householders, you can put an ice pick right through the wood somewhere in your house, termites have made homes there. They munch out chambers in wood, eating out their own house, so to speak. Other signs that you have termites: wood sounds hollow when you knock on it, or you see termite wings or holes in the wood or little piles of pepper-like droppings on a sill.

How can you identify a termite? Beetles make tunnels, carpenter bees make holes, termites make chambers. A termite looks different from an ant—it is shorter and thicker around the waist. All termite wings are the same size.

To prevent termites, eliminate moisture in wood. Keep your house painted, and your gutters clean and watertight. Make sure you have proper drainage around your house and that there are at least 8 inches between wood and ground. (Not all kinds of termites need contact with the ground, however.) Sprinkle the attic with a desiccating dust containing boric acid, diatomaceous earth, or silica aerogel just before swarming season. (Ask your county USDA extension agent when that is.)

Before you resort to calling an exterminator, try tracing the mud tubes of the termites to the nest. Then dig out colonies with a trowel, leaving them out in the open where their enemies (ants, for instance) can get at them. For spot treating, you can use insecticidal soap or borate solution injected into the wood, or pyrethrum/pyrethrin–based insecticides. WARNING: Pyrethrum-based insecticides can kill fish.

In case of massive infestation, you may have to call in an exterminator, most of whom will examine the house and give you a free estimate. Some use trained beagles to sniff out termites. Ask about control by nematodes (tiny organisms), by Electro-Gun (which shoots electricity down the termite galleries), or by Thermal Pest Eradication, which uses heat to treat damaged wood. Other methods use microwaves or cold to kill termites. As a last resort, toxic pesticides may have to be applied. In this case, you may have to leave home for two days while the pesticide is working. *Note:* Carpenter ants can be eliminated by the same methods as those used with termites.

Rodents. Rats and mice have long associated with humans. Rats can get into your house through the roof and might nest inside walls or in your attic. Mice live close to their nests. All kinds of rodents carry disease and spread it through their urine and droppings. (One mouse drops about 18,000 pellets a year.) Ticks carrying Lyme disease may live on rodents.

You can tell if you have mice if you see rub marks along the walls, smell "mouse," find droppings. If you see one, you probably have many more.

To prevent infestation by rodents, seal off entrance points with steel wool, concrete, or metal. Keep lumber and firewood a foot off the ground. Get rid of brush and weeds around the foundation of your house. Once rodents have penetrated all barriers and are infesting your house, how can you eradicate them? If you use poisoned bait to get rid of rodents, they may die inside your house, causing it to smell of death for weeks. Glueboard traps are cruel—the animal can struggle for hours before dying. You can drown a struggling rodent in a pail of soapy water, but it may try to swim. Old fashioned traps are better, and death by trap is kinder. Set traps for rats outdoors, nailed to places along their well-traveled paths. Leave them baitless for a few days so the rats can get used to them. Then use peanut butter or cheese as bait. Or get a cat.

The National Pest Control Association (NPCA), 8100 Oak Street, Dunn Loring, VA 22077 (703-573-8330).

Buying Energy-Efficient Appliances

By law, manufacturers must affix a yellow Energy Guide label to almost all new appliances, even those that are energy hogs. The labels, which are prepared by a national independent testing laboratory, compare energy costs and efficiency of similarly sized appliances. Figure the true

AVERAGE LIFE EXPECTANCE OF APPLIANCES (in years)

gas range (19)
electric range (17)
refrigerator (16)
electric water heater (14)
washer and dryer (13)
microwave oven, room air conditioner, gas water heater (11)
dishwasher, vacuum (10)
VCR, color television (8)

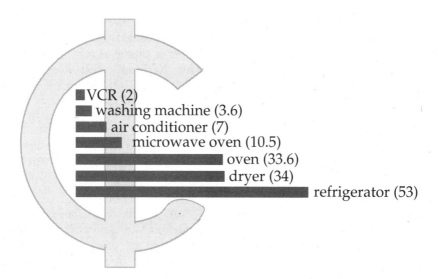

APPLIANCES: HOURLY COST IN CENTS
(based on 7 cents/kw hour cost)

- VCR (2)
- washing machine (3.6)
- air conditioner (7)
- microwave oven (10.5)
- oven (33.6)
- dryer (34)
- refrigerator (53)

prices of appliances by adding their ticket prices to the cost of operating them over their lifetimes, and you may decide to buy the more expensive model. How is this so? Energy costs run high. For example, a refrigerator's energy cost over its 15-to-20-year lifetime can be more than three times its original cost. The appliances that use the most energy are furnaces, air conditioners, water heaters, and refrigerators.

Look in your bookstore or library for *The Consumer Guide to Home Energy Savings,* published every year by The American Council for an Energy-Efficient Economy. The guide lists and ranks top refrigerators, freezers, dishwashers, clothes washers, water heaters, air conditioners, heat pumps, and furnaces.

Auditing Home Utility Bills

To make sure your utility bills are as low as possible, spend more time auditing them. Read your meters, check your bills, analyze your use patterns, and inquire about changes in rates and meters.

Read Your Meters

Read your gas, electric, and water meters at the beginning and end of billing periods to check utility companies' accuracy. Gas and water meters are easy: just read the numerals from left to right, as you read a word. Electric meters are usually read backwards, from right to left.

Some electric meters have a separate demand dial showing maximum use during peak periods. If yours does, take down the reading.

Obtain the Best Rate

Make sure that the rates you have been charged are for the right season. Sometimes utility personnel forget to change from summer rates to winter rates when seasons change.

Most electricity companies offer more than one rate on which you may be billed. Usually, unless you say otherwise, the company charges you at the standard rate—straight billing for kilowatt hours used. If you don't use much electricity during peak hours, you are better off going to "demand rates," which are based on the custom-

HOW TO READ AN ELECTRIC METER

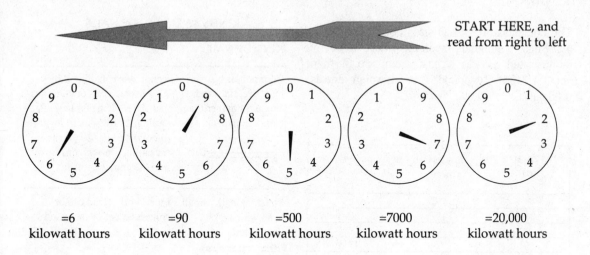

START HERE, and
read from right to left

=6	=90	=500	=7000	=20,000
kilowatt hours	kilowatt hours	kilowatt hours	kilowatt hours	kilowatt hours

Reading=27,596 kilowatt hours

er's highest usage during the day. That is, if you tend to space out usage, you may save. The reading from the demand dial, if you have one, should give you a clue, or call and ask the utility company to analyze a computerized record of your use and then give you the best rate.

Many water companies bill for usage plus a monthly service charge based on the size of your water meter. You may be able to save money by replacing your present meter with a smaller one.

Sewer bills often are based on water-meter readings. That is, you are billed on the amount of water you use whether or not it ends up in the sewer line. If you use lots of water to fill pools, wash cars, water lawns and trees, you might consider installing a meter to measure water that does not end up in the sewer line. Make sure it's worth it, though. The installation is costly.

Many gas companies offer rebates for consumers who switch to gas appliances, which are generally more energy-efficient. And gas is usually cheaper than electricity.

Nails

The nomenclature of nail sizes goes back to the old English monetary system, where a penny (abbreviated *d*) was a basic coin, worth then about 1/240th of a pound. A pennyweight equals 0.05 ounce.

Penny size (d)	Nail length (inches)	Gauge (wire measure)
2	1	15
3	1¼	14
4	1½	12½
5	1¾	12½
6	2	11½
7	2¼	11½
8	2½	10¼
9	2¾	10¼
10	3	9
12	3¼	9
16	3½	8
20	4	6
30	4½	5
40	5	4
50	5½	3
60	6	2

Nails are also made for joining materials other than wood: masonry nails, roofing nails, drywall nails. Shanks of nails may be ringed, spiraled, or barbed for greater holding power.

Nailing tips:

♦ If the wood is hard, drill a hole smaller than the nail in the place where the nail will go.

♦ At the end of a board, blunt the nail with a hammer so it will punch through wood rather than wedge it apart.

Nails come in different shapes for different jobs:

KINDS AND USES OF NAILS

KIND OF NAIL	USE
Common or box nail. Big, flat head. Box nail thinner than common nail. 	Rough work, nailing 2 by 4s. Three basic sizes of common nail: 10 (3-inch) for toe-nailing, 16 (3½- inch) for face-to-edge nailing, 20 (4- inch) for nailing through one board into the end of another.
Finishing nail. Small head with a depression in it. 	Finer work. Head can be concealed below the wood's surface.
Casing nail. Small tapered head with no depression. 	For nailing exterior trim. Can be left flush or set below the surface of the wood.

♦ Put oil or soap or candle wax or beeswax on nails to make for easier nailing into the wood.

♦ Hold the nail between your thumb and forefinger for nailing. Nails too small? Use a paper clip, tweezers, bobby pin, comb (hold between the teeth), fork.

♦ To nail two boards together, nail first through the thin one, then the thick one. Slanting the nails gives more security.

♦ To prevent wood from splitting, try staggering nails rather than placing them in a straight line.

♦ Tap until the nail is planted. Hit the head of the nail with heavier and heavier blows as it becomes more securely implanted in the wood.

♦ To remove a nail: cushion the wood by putting scrap wood under the hammer head and lever out the nail with the claw.

♦ For most nails, use a 14- to 16-ounce hammer. For brads (small thin nails), use a tack hammer.

Screws

Screws come in various lengths (measured from point to widest part of head, ¼ inch to 6 inches) and gauges or body diameter (0–24). You can buy them with flat heads (to be flush with the surface), round heads (to protrude above the surface), or oval heads (to be countersunk, yet protrude). The heads are either cut with one slot all the way across or an x-shaped slot (Phillips head). The heads dictate the kind of screwdriver you use. You can buy screws made of several materials (galvanized steel, aluminum, brass).

Tips for Using Screws

♦ When screwing together two pieces of wood, select a screw that will penetrate two-thirds of the way into the lower layer of material.

♦ Try drilling a hole a bit smaller than the screw before driving it into the wood.

♦ Lubricate the screw with wax or soap for easier insertion; use glue to make it hold better.

A Basic Tool Kit

Every householder needs a tool kit for emergency repairs and a bit of therapeutic weekend work on the house. These tools are recommended by most experts. Keep them all together in a box or empty bucket:

Pliers—to tighten and loosen nuts and bolts and do a bit of plumbing:

♦ regular (small needle-nose and larger blunt-nose) pliers

♦ tongue-in-groove whose jaws open up wide enough to handle any job

Wrench—adjustable so jaws fit any nut, perhaps a set of socket wrenches

Screwdrivers—Phillips-head (cross-shaped head) and slotted-head, one set of five or six.

Hammer—a 14- to 16-oz. claw-head with fiberglass handle (try hammers out to see which feels best in your hand)

Nail sets—one or two to countersink nail heads

Cat's paw nail puller—to pull out small embedded nails

Small pry bar—to pry up heavy nails and trim

Chisels—one or two sizes, for mortising locks and hinges, splitting lumber, shaving it

Cordless drill with drill bits

Handsaw—for cutting lumber

Hacksaw—for cutting pipes or nails

Coping saw—to fit curved molding

Miter box—for making angled cuts

Hand plane—simple block plane to trim, shave, smooth

16-foot tape measure (¾″) and **20–25-foot tape measure** (1″)

Utility knife with spare blades

Roll of electrical tape

Levels—bubble levels, 2-foot and 4-foot, and pocket level

C-clamps—for holding boards together while gluing or nailing or for attaching a level to a 2-by-4

Squares—large, metal carpenter's square and combination square for preset angles

Plumb bob—to tell if something is truly vertical

Chalk line—to mark straight lines on surfaces

Scrapers—small ones for stripping old finishes and large ones for lifting old floor tiles

Wire brushes—to strip fancy surfaces

Safety goggles

Masks

Gloves

Heavy shoes

Rewiring a Lamp

Don't let fear of electricity keep you from rewiring that old lamp that you just can't throw out. It's a simple task—you just need to replace the working insides. Make sure to unplug it before you start, follow some simple directions, and it will light your house a good deal longer.

Tools: wire cutters or strong scissors, utility knife (or old paring knife), slotted screwdriver.

REWIRING A LAMP

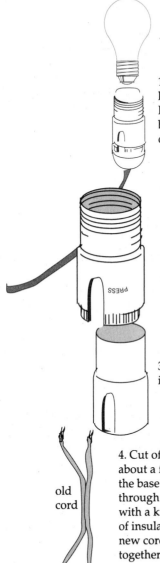

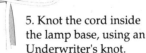

1. Make sure that the lamp is unplugged. Remove lampshade, light bulb, and harp (if there is one).

2. Remove socket shell. Usually there is a spot marked *press*, which yields to thumb pressure.

3. Then remove insulating shell.

4. Cut off the old lamp cord about a foot from the bottom of the base. Cutting very carefully through the insulating material with a knife, strip about an inch of insulation from the old and new cords, then twist them together. Use the old cord to pull the new cord up through the top of the lamp. Split the new cord down the center for about three inches.

old cord

new cord

Twist cords together.

5. Knot the cord inside the lamp base, using an Underwriter's knot.

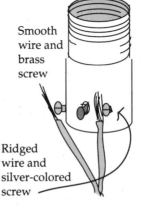

Smooth wire and brass screw

Ridged wire and silver-colored screw

6. Unscrew the screws holding the end wires of the old cord, pull out and discard the old cord, then cut back the bare wire on the new cord to ½ inch. The smooth sheathed wire should be attached to the brass screw, the ridged sheathed wire to the silver-colored screw.

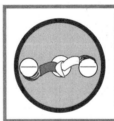

7. Wind wire around screw terminals (in the direction that the screw tightens), then tighten the screws to hold the wires, making sure that no stray wires escape to cause a short.

Reassemble the lamp by putting the socket chell with its insulating sleeve over the socket base. Seat strongly.

When replacing a plug, be sure to use an Underwriter's knot and follow manufacturer's directions on attaching wires to screws.

Materials: New lamp cord. Measure the length of the old cord, then buy what you need by the foot at the hardware store. Be sure to take along a piece of the old cord so you can match its thickness and construction. You may also need to buy a new plug and new replacement socket. Take along the old ones for a correct match. Plugs come in flat-wire and round-wire versions. If the old plug is asymmetrical, buy a polarized replacement plug. If you have to buy a new bulb socket, make sure it has the same amperage and voltage ratings as the old one. Look at the old shell for these numbers.

If necessary, attach a new plug. The flat-wire plug snaps in place according to the manufacturer's instructions. You need not strip wires. The round-wire plug is a bit more complicated. You need to remove about 1¼ inches of outer covering of cord and ¾ inch of the wire insulation. Thread the cord through the plug and tie the part of the wires that are insulated in an Underwriter's knot. Twist the bare wires clockwise and attach to the plug by winding each around its proper screw and tightening the screw. Leave no wires sticking out.

Other Simple Repair Jobs Around the House

Sometimes you can save a bundle by doing a simple repair job by yourself. With a few tools, a bit of patience, and enough sense to know when it is time to call in an expert, you can solve many a household problem.

Repairing a Leaky Faucet

A water-wasting, leaky faucet is caused by a worn washer or O-ring or damaged packing in the stem.

Tools. A box of assorted washers, a screwdriver, an adjustable wrench.

Procedure. Turn off the water below the sink or at the shutoff valve where water enters your house. Let water run until it stops. Take off the decorative cap on the faucet. Loosen the nut that holds the handle to the faucet—it probably turns counterclockwise. Pull out the valve unit. Pad a screwdriver to protect the chrome. Then remove the screw holding the old washer. Be gentle. Replace the washer and screw. You may also have to put in new packing string. Put the unit back in the faucet and turn the handle to the right position. After tightening the nut, turn the water back on.

Comments: Your faucet may demand a slightly different procedure. On some faucets, you have to remove a screw that holds the handle on, or you may need to replace an O-ring or an entire cartridge, a gasket, or water strainers.

Unclogging a Drain

For bathroom or kitchen sink, or tub or shower:

Tools: Plumber's helper (plunger); if you have a double sink, a plastic bag and rags to plug up other sink. Possibly plumber's snake and garden hose.

Procedure: Follow these steps in order.

1. Plug the overflow hole in the bathroom sink (if there is one) with a plastic bag filled with rags. For a double kitchen sink, plug the drain in the unclogged sink in a similar fashion, pushing the plastic bag down into the drain. Then fill the sink with water to same level as clogged sink. For tub and shower, unscrew overflow fitting and plug it. (In some tubs, the overflow fitting is attached to the pop-up stopper and you have to take out the whole thing.) If there are a series of holes, have a helper hold a stopper made of plastic wrap, a sponge, and a piece of wood over them while you work. Fill water to within 2 inches of the top with hot water.

2. Invert the cup on the plunger over the drain hole and push the handle up and down to create suction. Lift off plunger.

3. If that doesn't work, try again.

4. If that doesn't work, use a plumber's snake along with a garden hose. Feed the snake into the pipe, take it out and flush with the hose with the water on full force.

Preventing clogged drains:

1. Once a month pour boiling water and 2 tablespoons of baking soda down them. Or try a mixture of ¼ cup of baking soda and 2 ounces of vinegar in boiling water for lazy drains.

2. Use chemical drain cleaners only on un-clogged drains.

Plugged Toilet

Tools: Funnel cup plunger.

Procedure: Take out water and waste until the toilet is half full, then plunge the funnel-cup plunger up and down 10 times. Try pouring water in the bowl to see if water level goes up. If it does, plunge again. If you have a toilet auger, try it. Then call the plumber.

Sewing Repair

Tools: Needles, thread, straight pins, scissors.
Procedure:

♦ Buttons. Thread a needle and knot it. From the top, put the needle into the cloth where you want the button and pull the thread tight. Put the button over the knot, stitch from underneath through the cloth and a hole in the button. Go down through the hole next to the first one. Put 6 to 10 stitches in each set of holes. Wind the thread around the shank of the button several times, make a loop, and secure thread.

♦ Hems: Run a row of machine stitching about ¼ inch above the bottom of the hem first. Put on

BASTING A HEM

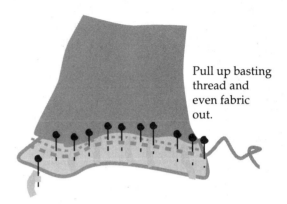

Pull up basting thread and even fabric out.

the garment and shoes, and have someone mark a equal distance on the skirt from the floor all the way around. Press the hem and baste ¼ inch in from the folded edge. Mark the hem at the proper depth (3 inches for a straight shirt, 1½–2 inches for one that is flared) all the way around with pins. Trim. Turn under ¼ inch and stitch. Pin and pull up the basting thread in a wide skirt. To reinforce seam edge, you can use a zigzag stitch on a sewing machine or use seam binding (straight edge) or bias binding (curved edge). To sew, space stitches ¼–½ inch apart. Use blind hemming for a zigzagged or pinked edge; slip-stitch for bias tape or turned and stitched edge; vertical hemming for turned and stitched or seam binding.

BUYING FURNITURE AND DECORATING YOUR HOUSE

Buying Furniture

Decorators offer three simple pieces of advice to furniture buyers. First, buy the highest quality furniture you can afford. If you have little money, pay for basic construction, not details like fancy fabric or curves. Second, buy what you love. Third, sit or lie on it, whatever it is, for a good long time—no matter how visually attractive a piece of furniture is, comfort is more important.

Even if you cannot afford to buy there, go to a store that sells the best furniture to see what determines quality. Check labels and talk to salespeople. If you buy reproductions, make sure that they are well made and true to the period. Not all knockoffs are alike. If you can afford it, buy designer reproductions labeled as "authorized," "licensed," or "limited edition" with seals of approval given by the original designers' estates. Generally speaking, you *do* get what you pay for.

Before actually shopping, measure spaces so that furniture will fit and be in scale. Make sure that furniture will fit through doors and stairwells. In fact it is a good idea to take with you a graph-paper sketch of the room or rooms and all the furniture already in it. At the store, ask about warranties and delivery.

Wooden Furniture

Rock a chest or table to check how sturdy it is. Check doors and drawers to see if they move easily and are flush when shut. Drawers should be made with interlocking dovetail joints. All parts should be smoothly sanded, even those that don't show. Finish should be smooth. Chair legs should be held to each other with horizontal pieces of wood (stringers) for durability.

The more expensive hardwoods are walnut, mahogany, and cherry; less expensive are birch, maple, and oak. The wood under better-grain tops and fronts might be made of furniture board, a quality particle board of compressed sawdust. Experts have differing opinions on the quality of furniture made this way. Check the finish to see that it has the same shine overall. Grain should match from part to part—for example, the grain on the table leaf should continue the grain on the table top. Look underneath the piece of furniture to see if grains match.

Upholstered Furniture

Know what's *under* that fabric you fell in love with—the frame. See how heavy the piece is; the heavier the better, all other things being equal. The best frames are built of kiln-dried hardwoods at least 1¼ inches thick. ("Seasoned" hardwood is not the same; it may have moisture left in it that will cause it to warp or crack.) Hardwoods will not warp or crack like softwoods such as pine.

Check the frame by standing and pushing against the back of it to see if it is stable. Lift a corner. Joints should be solid, there should be no "give." The frame should not jiggle, sag, creak. If the frame squeakily complains when you lift it, it was made of badly dried wood or was nailed rather than screwed together. In the best pieces, legs are part of the frame. If legs do screw in, they should screw right into the frame, not into a metal plate. The best frames are held together with hardwood pegs, and, barring that, screws. (Some manufacturers cover screws with wooden plugs that look like dowel ends, so ask about the joinery of the piece, and if you are suspicious of the answer, request it in writing.) Metal nails, staples, or screws tend to shake loose with the frame's expansion and contraction.

The arms, front panel, sides, and back of an upholstered couch or chair should be well padded. When you sit on the piece, you should not feel the frame or any lumpiness. There should be no extra glue, raveled cloth, rough lumber.

Springs should be double-coil, wired together and attached to the frame, tied by hand in eight directions (anchored springs), and padded. You can tell if they are hand-tied if the space under the material on the bottom is flat and firm. Second best are drop-in pre-tied springs. Third best are S-shaped heavy wires—these are more taut, but still durable. When you pat the underside, you should hear a drumming sound, which means tight coils and webbing. Webbing should be of jute or steel, tacked securely to the frame, without gaps.

The best cushions (and most expensive) are down-and-feather, which need fluffing. If you buy a couch or chair with foam cushions, look for springy polyester or down wrapped around a dense foam or pocketed spring core. Density should be at least 1.8 pounds per cubic foot. Shredded foam will flatten, and the cushion will lose its shape. On zippered cushions, check the interior cushion. It should be enclosed in sewn ticking.

Upholstery fabric should be sewn to fit well. Look for matching and symmetry of pattern. Welts on fabric should be even, without puckering or threads, and cushions should have zipper seams. The skirt should be sewn on, or tacked, not stapled; lined; and without cardboard stuffing.

Choose a fabric you can live with. Take a swatch home and leave it on your present furniture to see if you still like it after you get over your original infatuation with it.

Remember that details—like curves, pleats, braids—cost money. If your budget is limited, it is better to go with a plain piece of furniture that is well made.

Sit on a couch for at least 15 minutes. Your back should be well supported, and you should not sink so low into the couch that you cannot get up easily. Is there a comfortable spot for your arm? Can you take a nap on it? How many people does it seat?

Buying Wall-to-Wall Carpeting

First, sketch and measure your rooms. If a room is not perfectly rectangular, take measurements of the deepest parts. Ask yourself how much you have to spend, and figure out how much you will need in yards, considering that most carpet comes in 12-foot widths. Remember that if you will stay in the house a while, it might be worth it to invest in a better carpet.

The rock-bottom rule on buying carpet is: the denser (not the heavier), the more durable. Ask what the face weight (carpet weight without backing) is. Or check into the stitches per inch or the tufts per inch, the more the better. Try the "thumb test," pressing the carpet to see how easy it is to push through to the backing (the easier, the less durable the carpet). Bend the carpet into a U to see how much backing shows through, the less the better. The yarn should be twisted tight. Cut ends should look neat, well defined.

Take several samples of the carpet home to choose color under various lights. See how you want to place it—in which direction the nap will best go. Small patterns hide soil, as do darker colors or multicolors. However, you are not as limited with color as you used to be, because most carpet is treated to be stain-resistant. Ask what the warranty is—generally speaking, the longer it is, the better the carpet will resist staining and wear. If you cannot afford high-density carpet everywhere, put it in the areas where there is high traffic and buy cheaper carpet for less used spaces.

Before you make any decisions, find out what the price of the carpet you want includes. Is the pad part of the price? What about installation, removing the old carpet, moving furniture, doing stairs? Can you keep remnants? Are seams guaranteed? Insist that installers use power stretchers rather than "knee-kickers." The price should include restretching after a few months. Wait for sales and get several bids. Be suspicious of carpet bargains. Choose a reputable dealer.

FIBERS

Wool is the standard by which all carpet fibers are measured. It is expensive, but it is also naturally resilient, soft, easy to clean, resistant to stains, burns, water. About 70 percent of carpet is made of nylon, which has softness, bulk, and durability. Other choices: acrylic (looks most like wool, but not as durable as other synthetics); polyester (durable, can mat, accumulate dirt); olefin or polypropylene, used mostly for indoor-outdoor carpeting (resists abrasion and dirt, crushes easily). Of course, many carpets are blends of materials.

Tufted carpets (nine out of 10 sold) are made on a machine that stitches yarn loops through a backing fabric made of polypropylene, foam, or jute. The manufacturer applies a latex coating to the carpet, then applies a second backing. The carpet may be left as is or cut to create surface textures.

The fibers come in two forms: staple (bulky, like wool) or filament (continuous strand, very durable).

PILE

Basically, carpet is left in loops or cut to make ends or both looped and cut. The most durable, given equal densities, are in order of most to least durable:
- level loop and frieze
- random sheared and saxony
- multilevel loop, cut-and-loop, plush.

Looped Carpet

Level loop. Smooth, good for areas of high traffic.

Berber. A loose version of level loop with coarse, thick yarn.

Multilevel loop (a.k.a. *sculptured* or *carved loop*). Carpet with pile in which loops are at two or three heights. This carpet tends to wear more than single-level loop pile.

Cut-End Carpet

Plush. A smooth surface cut pile, which can mat and show footsteps.

Textured plush. Ends of yarn show more clearly than in plush.

- *Saxony* is a kind of textured plush, in which yarns are highly twisted so that ends can be more easily seen.

- *Frieze* (pronounced free-*zay*), is a tightly twisted yarn, nubby or pebbly looking, good for high-traffic areas.

- *Shag* is made of long tufts of yarn of various lengths, holds dirt, but also doesn't show it; not much used anymore.

Combination

A cut-and-loop carpet, also known as high-low because the pile is at various heights.

Random sheared

A cut-and-loop pile all the same height, good at hiding footprints, with the effect of plush.

PADS

Buy a high-quality pad to make the carpet feel good under your feet and extend its life. New urethane is best, with a thickness of at least three-eighths inch, but no more than one-half inch. Make sure that it is not too soft and that it is water-resistant.

CARING FOR CARPET

Experts suggest that you vacuum often—light vacuuming every day or twice a week (depending on the expert) with three strokes (forward, back, and forward)—over each area, and heavy vacuuming once a week with seven or more strokes over each area. Deep clean at least every 18 months with a method approved for your kind of carpet.

Cut off snaps and tufts that stick up too far. Never pull out tufts—cut them instead. Raise crushed pile by spraying with a bit of water, using a brush to raise it, then drying it with a hair dryer. Use no hot appliances on synthetics or they may melt into a mess.

Buying Mattresses

If you live an average lifespan, you will spend about 25 years in bed. The average lifespan for a *mattress* is 8–10 years. Don't expect it to live as long as you. To select a new one:

♦ Take your shoes off, lie down, and see how the mattress feels. Have your sleeping partner do the same. Stay there. Do you have enough space? How do your hips and shoulders feel when you lie on your side? Are your lower back, shoulders, and hips comfortable? A mattress should support you, but it doesn't need to be hard as a board.

MATTRESS SIZES	WIDTH	LENGTH
Twin	38 inches	75 inches
Double or full	53–54 inches	75 inches
Queen	60 inches	80 inches
National/ Eastern King	76 inches	80 inches
California King	72 inches	84 inches

♦ Try to get a mattress 6 inches longer than you are tall. Often you can get twin and double sizes extra long, 80 inches.

♦ Mattress and foundation should be solid, at least 6 inches thick, with a heavy, high-thread-count fabric cover. The corners should be well made.

♦ An innerspring mattress should have a sufficient number of coils:

KING SIZE	QUEEN SIZE	FULL
450–576 coils	375–450 coils	300–364 coils

The more coils, the better quality mattress. Look for thick wire coils—the lower the gauge number, the thicker the coil. Extra turns of coil make for a better mattress, as does more padding. Look for several layers of upholstery on an innerspring mattress.

♦ A foam mattress should have a density of at least two pounds per cubic foot. The higher the density number, the better the foam.

♦ Buy mattress pieces together. Twin and full-sized mattresses usually are priced by the piece, queen and king size by the set (two pieces, innerspring and box spring).

♦ The frame of the box spring should have many strong crosspieces.

Waterbeds

Waterbeds have changed since the time they were essentially just bags filled with water that the sleeper(s) sloshed around on. On some of the latest waterbeds, special baffles reduce water movement, and on others separate chambers of air and water produce the same result. The components of a waterbed (flotation sleep system) are:

Water mattress. Usually made of polyvinyl chloride (PVC), the mattress holds the water for the system. A radially constructed mattress is made of two parts and has rounded corners. A mattress constructed like a box has three pieces or more. In either case, make sure the vinyl is at least 20 mils thick.

Liner. The liner—usually made of polyvinyl chloride—keeps the liquid filling from escaping in case the mattress springs a leak. It fits between the mattress and frame. It should be at least 8 mils thick.

Heater. Anyone who has tried to sleep on a waterbed without a heater for the water knows how important the heater is. Without it, you freeze. The heater comes with a thermostat and should be electrically safe in case it comes in contact with water. It usually goes underneath mattress and liner.

Frame. The frame—usually made of wood or plastic—takes much of the pressure from the water.

Base. The base both helps in supporting and distributing the weight of the system and raises the mattress to a comfortable height.

Tips

♦ Never try to use a water mattress without a proper supporting frame and liner.

♦ Water used in the mattress needs to be treated to prevent growth of bacteria and fungi. Use a disinfectant suggested by the manufacturer.

♦ Keep the heater off creases and folds in the liner and water mattress. Don't place the waterbed frame on the heater cord. Don't use an extension cord. Don't attach the heater to the supporting surface with nails, staples, or other metal fasteners unless the manufacturer specially instructs you to do so.

♦ Unplug the heating system before draining the mattress.

♦ Use a mattress pad to help protect against punctures and body oils that can damage vinyl.

♦ Retain heat in the mattress by keeping sheets and blankets over it.

♦ When you change sheets, look for and remove objects that might have fallen between frame and mattress. Also check for moisture in corners that can indicate a leak.

♦ You can fix minor leaks—ask about a repair kit.

Buying Bedding

Quality in bedding is often a matter of numbers, not superficial advertising appeals. For instance, the thread-count of a sheet is more important than the name of its designer. While the puffiness of a comforter seems irresistible, look too at the number that identifies its fill power. Pay attention to the materials bedding is made of: natural materials (down and wool, for instance) have great advantages, while artificial materials (fiberfills) are hypoallergenic and not necessarily inferior.

Sheets. Two things you should look for are: (1) threads per inch—180–220 indicates good quality; (2) fiber content. The higher the thread count, the thinner the thread, the tighter the weave, the softer the sheet. The highest thread count is 330, but 200 to 250 are more common for high-quality sheets. Thread count varies according to fabric, with muslin at 130 threads per inch or less, while by definition percale is woven with 180 or more.

Cotton is the most comfortable fiber, and there are blends of cotton and polyester that come 30/70, 50/50, 60/40, and 65/35. The most luxurious cotton grown in the United States is pima, which has a long staple. Alcala has the second largest staple. Muslin is usually 50 percent uncombed blended cotton. (Uncombed cotton has coarser fibers, because it hasn't been processed to remove them.) Percales can be cotton-polyester blends or all cotton. The top-of-the-line percales are made of 100 percent combed cotton, with a 200–250 thread count. They are wrinkleproof. Cotton-polyester sheets wear better and dry faster than all-cotton. What's more, they cost less. But many people prefer cotton for its softness.

Pillows. You need to look at a pillow from three angles: (1) the degree of softness; (2) the material from which it is made; (3) covering material. Softness is a matter of individual taste and the way you sleep: if you sleep on your stomach, a soft pillow; if you sleep on your side, medium; if you sleep on your back, firm. Go by the way you start out sleeping at night. Incidentally, pediatricians do not advise pillows for babies, and children should have no pillow or only a small one to keep pressure off the spine.

If you want a down or feather pillow, consider the fact that waterfowl feathers (goose and duck) are considered better than those from land birds (chickens and turkeys). They are also more expensive. Pillows labeled "waterfowl feathers" by law can hold only 8 percent landfowl filling. The lowest-grade feather pillows are made with crushed feathers. Polyester fiberfills (Dacron, Kodel, Vycron, Fortrel, and others) are nonallergenic, soft, resilient. In the better ones, the fibers are hollow and trap air. Foam, molded or shredded, provides extra support because of its resilience.

Down-and-feather pillows are best covered with a down or feather-proof ticking with treatment to keep the feathers from sticking out through the fabric. Don't buy a pillow with see-through ticking.

Price varies according to the amount of down (the more down, the higher the price. Synthetics are cheaper than down and feathers). It also varies according to size: A standard size pillow is least expensive, all else being equal. You also pay for the brand name.

Comforter. Comforters come with the same fillings as pillows. Down holds heat and keeps you comfortable all year round, while a fiberfill comforter might not provide enough warmth in winter. If you buy a down comforter, look for the words "white goose down" on the label, which means that it must be at least 90 percent goose down. White down doesn't show through the cover as easily as if it were grey or brown. Comforters labeled "down" simply "all down" are made of duck or goose/duck down. (To label a comforter "down," manufacturers must include 80 percent down. To label it "all down," they must use 100 percent down.) Down is light, made of bits of fuzz that traps air, keeping warmth in, while feathers are stiff and heavy.

Comforter quality has a great deal to do with loft or "fill power"—how many cubic inches down fills when not squeezed. Look for fill power of at least 550. The heavier the down comforter ("loft"), the warmer. Press the center of the comforter between your hands to check for thickness. Try several—you'll feel the difference. One-inch loft will keep you warm in a room of 72°F., a 2-inch loft in a room at 45°F. White goose down comforters weigh from 25 to 50 ounces. The shell covering the comforter should have a high thread count, at least 220, so that the down will not come through and the fabric will be soft.

Quilting also is important. The label lists the type of stitch. More expensive comforters are baffled (which means that the manufacturer has sewn fabric barriers like little walls inside the comforter). With baffles, filling can move and it can fluff up. If the top and bottom pieces are sewn together flat, air can pass through holes made by the needles, and the comforter will be cooler. Overstuffed edges generally mean lower quality.

Comforters can also be filled with silk (very, very expensive), lamb's wool (heavy), or synthetic fill. Polyester filling labeled Hollofil II, Quallofil, and Kodofill has hollow-core fibers that are said to improve warmth. According to Du Pont, lightweight comforters should weigh at least 6.4 ounces a square yard, medium at least 9 ounces, and "continental" at least 12. Generally, for polyester comforters, the thicker the warmer. In a hot house, a synthetic summer-weight comforter may make more sense.

Buy a king-sized comforter no matter what the size of your bed; it will drape nicely over the sides.

Use the comforter with a duvet (pronounced doo-vay) cover, which you can wash to your heart's content. If you do, you can hang the comforter outside to freshen it up and won't have to dry-clean it so often.

When you are not using the comforter, fold it loosely on a shelf, and keep it dry. Don't wash down comforters—when wet, down tends to clump and flatten out. Choose a dry cleaner who specializes in down.

Quilts. Quilts are decorative, with a layer of insulation (polyester) covered with cotton fabric. Patchwork quilts are made of pieces sewn together, while appliqué is sewn on top of one piece of cloth. Quilts are not particularly warm, so you probably need to use them over a blanket or comforter. Dry clean.

Blankets. Cotton blankets can be washed, especially strong cotton blankets made of pima cotton. Wool blankets may be machine washable and permanently mothproofed. Cashmere, soft and warm, is expensive; merino wool is fine and costs less than cashmere.

You can also buy blankets made of synthetics—thermal, nonwoven, flocked. A thermal blanket allows air to circulate in warm weather and traps body heat when covered in cool weather. Nonwoven blankets, made of felt with layers of fiber, are not very durable. Some are foam sandwiched between nylon. Flocked blankets, made of nylon and foam, wash well and feel fleecy.

A blanket should be heavy enough, four to five pounds for queen size, soft with a luxuriant nap. However, if your house is warm you might try two thermal blankets in winter, one in summer.

Buying Tableware

Maybe you covet antiques, like a piece from the five tons of 200-year-old Chinese porcelains salvaged from a ship wrecked in the South China Sea—about $2000 a place setting, over $40,000 for a fish dish (even though when these dishes were made, they were considered quite ordinary). And maybe you'd like to grace your porcelain with a pair of antique Revere sugar tongs priced at over $5000. On the other hand, maybe you don't need a complete set of fancy, expensive porcelain dinnerware, full-lead crystal, fine silver flatware. Maybe you don't even like it. Maybe you like eating take-out Chinese on Chinet plates with a cheap stainless fork. Let your lifestyle and tastes dictate what you buy.

Some experts recommend that you balance: keep two fancy, lavish design elements with one simple, unadorned one. For example, if you have ornate dinnerware and silverware, keep the stemware simple in design. Some people like unmatched pieces—sets of plates different from but complementary to the rest of the dinnerware, or even different glasses that harmonize with each other. Traditional advice is to choose china first, then silver, then crystal.

Where to buy? Many manufacturers now have discount retail outlets with a wide range of designs (the entire line) and lower prices.

Dinnerware

In finer dinnerware, a five-piece place setting usually includes a soup bowl or bread-and-butter plate, a dinner plate, a salad/dessert plate, a cup, and a saucer. Less expensive dinnerware comes in 20-piece sets with place settings for four. Accessories, usually bought separately, include gravy boats and serving platters.

You might buy simple dinner plates and cups and saucers, with salad/dessert plates in a fancier, more colorful design. Coordinate by matching basic colors, picking up a turquoise from a flower design in the fancy piece for the color of the plain one. No matter what you buy, look for patterns that can be bought in open stock.

Remember that some dinnerware is not dishwasher safe and needs to be hand-washed. Dishes with metallic decoration should not go in the microwave.

China, which includes porcelain and bone china, is usually the most expensive, fine dinnerware. Porcelain is glass-like ceramic ware with a fine white grain.

Bone china is porcelain made with some animal bone burned to ash, in order to strengthen it and make it white, translucent, and resonant. In England, bone china must, by law, contain at least 30 percent bone ash; in the U.S., it must contain at least 25 percent.

Stoneware, pottery fired in a kiln, is nonporous, safe in the oven. It is usually opaque, heavier and sturdier than china. However, stoneware can sometimes be elegant—Wedgwood, for example, is stoneware.

Earthenware ranges from a rough clay pot to finer glass-like products. It includes ironstone, delftware, majolica.

Stemware

Crystal. The addition of lead makes crystal glassware clear, heavy, and brilliant. Hand-blown and intricate pieces usually cost more than machine-made and simply designed ones. When you hold the piece against something white, you should see no bubbles or lines.

REGULATIONS ON LABELING OF CRYSTAL

Label	Percent of lead oxide required	
	U.S.	Europe
Full lead crystal	24%	30%
Lead crystal	12–23%	NA
Crystal	under 12%	NA

Flatware

The way you hold your fork has a good deal to do with what kind of fork it is. And holding it is a good way to judge it when you are buying it. Good flatware is balanced in your hand, weighty, and smoothly finished. It is graded—that is, the maker has tapered the tines and made the narrow part of the handle thicker so that it won't bend. Test it for strength. If you can, try spooning out a dishful of ice cream from a hard-frozen carton.

The look of flatware comes from its shape (once called its pattern) and decoration (once called design). European flatware tends to be bigger with plainer fork handles and sharper tines because of the way Europeans use eating utensils. (See "Europe vs. America: Proper Use of Utensils," p. 654.)

Poor-quality flatware is badly finished. Check between the tines of the fork for roughness—a dead giveaway. Make sure that the tips of the tines are smooth and even. Joints between metal and wood or plastic handles should be well finished and almost invisible.

It is not wise to run flatware through the drying cycle of the dishwasher. In the best of all possible worlds, you would handwash and dry it, but you should at least hand-dry it.

Flatware can be made of stainless steel, plated silver, or sterling silver. A brushed (satin) finish shows less wear-and-tear than a mirror (bright) finish.

Stainless. Stainless steel flatware is made from alloys identified by number. The ones used most often are 18/8 (containing 18 percent chromium and 8 percent nickel), 410 (containing 13 percent chromium), and 430 (containing 18 percent chromium). Unless knives are made all in one piece, knife blades are usually made of 410 alloy, which holds a better edge than other alloys. The chromium gives luster, the nickel hardness, making it scratch-resistant and tough.

Plated silver. Silverplate begins with a base metal, usually a brass alloy, that is then electroplated with silver. Better silverplate is doubleplated, first with nickel, which makes the silver adhere better, then silver. Also, the bottom of the bowl of the spoon and the heel of the fork in better silverplate have thicker plating. Some manufacturers guarantee their silverplate against wear-through.

Sterling silver. To meet U.S. government standards, sterling silver must contain at least 92.5 percent silver (925/1000ths); the rest is usually copper. Sterling might not be marked as such. If it is marked, however, it must meet the government standard and include the mark of the manufacturer. American and British sterling is identified as sterling, while other European silver often is marked only with a number indicating the percentage of silver and the country's stamp for a grade of silver (a Minerva head in Austria). European silver is usually 70–80 percent silver to 20–30 percent copper, and heavier than American sterling.

"German silver" and "nickel silver" contain no silver.

You can find discontinued silverware at: **Beverly Bremer Silver Shop,** 3164 Peacetree Road NE, Atlanta, GA 30305 (404-261-4009). **Jean's Silversmiths,** 16 West 45th Street, New York, NY 10036 (212-575-0723). **Past and Present Replacements,** 65-07 Fitchett Street, Rego Park, NY 11374 (718-896-5146).

For information about custom-designed silver, write to the **Society of American Silversmiths,** PO Box 3599, Cranston, RI 02910 (401-461-3156).

Lighting

Artful use of light orchestrates moods, improves health and working conditions, and enhances the looks of your home and possessions. Changes in light can alter your mood—from hyper to serene, for instance. A good desk lamp can improve your work production. A spotlight on a painting can make it suddenly dramatic.

In designing light, consider both "daylighting" (exploitation of natural light) and artificial light in all its forms. By using natural light, you consume less electricity and contribute less to pollution and dependence on fossil fuels. Modern artificial lighting fixtures and bulbs are devised to perform exact tasks, and it pays to know how to use them—for pleasure, energy-saving, money-saving.

DAYLIGHTING

Even after a house has been built, you can change the amount of daylight that enters it, and where that daylight falls. Try to let natural, indirect light into buildings through windows, skylights, transoms, French doors, sliding glass doors, bay windows. Skylights can be stationary, or they can open and close to let in air. In any case, they focus light and project it inside. You might also add a sunroom or atrium. Or you might open floor plans by eliminating walls so light can flow from one room to another.

Consider the quality and duration of light as well as the amount. Light coming in from higher up illuminates, strikes surfaces and bounces off, extending exposure to natural light as long as possible. Other ways to increase natural light:

♦ Use light colors for your walls, floors, furniture.

♦ Trim trees around windows.

♦ Install solar windows and films to eliminate solar heat gain and fading of fabrics.

♦ Install Venetian blinds to control natural light.

ARTIFICIAL LIGHTING

General lighting (ambient lighting). The closest to natural light, general lighting is your main light source; it radiates throughout a room for overall illumination. It should be bright enough so that you can see and get around without falling over things. To provide general lighting, plan on one watt of incandescent light for each square foot in most rooms, twice as much in a kitchen or workshop. If you use fluorescent lights, use one-third of a watt per square foot in living rooms, three-fourths of a watt per square foot in kitchens and workrooms.

Best are overhead lights, with a diffuse spread, like chandeliers, ceiling and wall-mounted fixtures, recessed lights, track lights. Outdoors, use lantern lights.

Task lighting. For specific tasks like reading, sewing, cooking, writing, homework, games, you need focused light. To prevent eyestrain, if you use incandescent lights, you need at least 100 watts; if you use fluorescent lights, you need 22–32 watts. A desk or sewing light should be positioned 15 inches above your work surface. A light over kitchen counters should be placed at least 24 inches above the surface.

For task lighting, use recessed and track lighting, pendant lighting, portable lamps, lamps with movable arms.

Accent lighting. Try accent lighting to show off a painting, plant, or other possession or to bring out the texture of a wall or drapery. To create drama and visual interest, you need to focus at least three times as much light on the focal point as the general lighting around it. Use track, recessed, or wall-mounted lighting. To accent paintings, use a high light with a low-voltage, tungsten-halogen bulb. To create a dramatic plant silhouette, aim a light up at the wall behind the plant. Install it one to two feet from wall and aim it at a 30-degree angle from the wall to prevent blinding people—you don't want it to suggest a police interrogation of the art piece or plant.

Tips

♦ The average-size room needs four to five light sources. A room with dark walls requires more light. Wallcoverings require more light than painted walls, all other things being equal.

♦ Matte finish walls and ceilings diffuse the light, while glossy ones reflect it on to other surfaces.

♦ Keep tops of floor and table lamps at the same level and use shades that are similar in fabric and style.

♦ Set the base of a floor lamp for reading to the left or right of your shoulder (left for right-handed people, right for left-handed people), about 20 inches from the center of book. The bottom of the shade should be at your eye level when you sit.

READING LIGHT

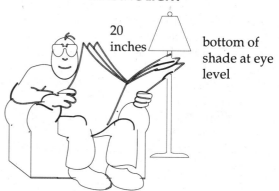

20 inches

bottom of shade at eye level

♦ For television viewing, use a dimmed lamp with 3-way bulb on lowest setting, positioned so there is no reflection on the TV screen. Or put miniature track lighting under shelves on which the TV sits.

♦ The size of a chandelier can be determined in two ways: (1) the diagonal of the chandelier in inches should be equal to the diagonal of the room in feet, (2) the chandelier should be 6 inches narrower than the table on each side. Position the chandelier at least 30 inches above the tabletop.

♦ A pendant lamp over an eating area should be at least 12 inches narrower than the table diameter, 30 inches above the tabletop.

DISTANCE OF LIGHT ABOVE SURFACE OF DESK

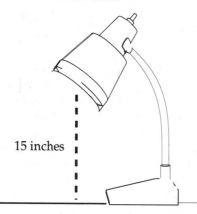

15 inches

KINDS OF ARTIFICIAL LIGHT

LIGHT TYPE	KINDS

Incandescent light. Clear or frosted in 3 shapes: general, globe, decorative. WARNING: pay attention to wattage—don't use more than suggested for a specific lamp.

1. General service (yellow-white light, emitted in all directions).
2. Reflectorized (coated inside to direct light). Floodlights spread light; spotlights concentrate light.
  a. Reflector (R) bulbs, put double the amount of light (footcandles) on the subject as general service bulbs of same wattage.
  b. Parabolic reflector (PAR) bulbs control light more, producing about 4 times the light of general service bulbs.

Tungsten-halogen. Bright white light, longer life and more light per watt than incandescent.

1. High-voltage (120 volts) used in track, recessed, outdoor spotlights and floodlights.
  a. PAR 16, 30, 38 reflectorized bulbs
  b. T-3 Double-Ended bulbs
  c. T-4 Single-Ended bulbs (base types mini-can and bayonet)
2. Low-voltage (12 volts), requiring a transformer to step down voltage, used in spotlights and floodlights, smaller track lights, and recessed lights.
  a. MR-11, MR-16 (Mini-Reflectors)
  b. PAR-36
  c. T-4 Bipin ("peanut" bulbs)

Fluorescent. Lasts up to 20 times longer than incandescent, uses one-fifth to one-third as much electricity.

Shapes: straight tube, U-tube, circle, screw-in, compact "twin," compact "quad."
1. Compact for recessed downlights, wall sconces, track lights, ceiling fixtures.
2. Screw-in types for standard lamp sockets. Use in warm white tones closest to incandescent lights.
A full spectrum bulb duplicates the spectrum of outdoor sunlight, shows colors accurately.

High-intensity discharge. Longer life and more light per watt than any other light source.

Available in mercury vapor, metal halide, high-pressure and low-pressure sodium types. For outdoor security and landscape lighting.

Source: American Lighting Association

♦ Because an opaque shade directs light up and down, a light-diffusing shade is better to read by. Avoid narrow tops that contain bulb heat—they are a fire hazard.
  ♦ Use dimmers for mood. A bright light stimulates, a dim light relaxes.
  ♦ To save energy: Turn off lights when you don't need them. Use dimmers and automatic off-on devices for outdoor lighting. Use **reflector** bulbs for task and accent lights.
  ♦ Light hallways every 8 to 10 feet and stairs top to bottom to prevent accidents. Put switches at either end.

PLANT	WATER, FOOD, AND SPECIAL REQUIREMENTS

Plants needing maximum light: direct sun, open eastern or southern exposure

Aloe	Water only when totally dry once or twice a week in summer, once or twice a month in winter. Use desert-cactus soil mix.
Geranium	Keep fairly dry.
Jade plant	Water when soil goes totally dry. Use desert-cactus soil mix.
Thanksgiving cactus	While dormant, water when soil is totally dry; while flowering, when soil surface dries. Provide diffused light in summer.

Plants needing moderate light: western or obstructed eastern or southern exposure

Amaryllis	Feed and water when soil dries in growth period. Can also tolerate full sun.
Asparagus fern	Moist soil. Spring and summer: foliage plant food monthly.
Boston fern	Keep soil moist in pot resting on wet stones. Use humus soil. Needs diffused light in summer.
Grape ivy	Moist soil. All-purpose plant food every 2 or 3 months. May also thrive in diffused light.
Schefflera	Water when soil almost dry. May also thrive in diffused light.

Plants needing diffused light: northern exposure

African violet	Plant in mix of 3 parts peat moss, 2 parts vermiculite, 1 part perlite, 5 tablespoons crushed eggshell per quart. Keep soil moist. Pot diameter should be three times that of plant.
Fuschia	If it goes dormant, keep dry. Keep cool, also.
Golden pothos	Water when soil is almost dry.
Impatiens	Heavy watering necessary.
Spider plant	Needs moist soil. Every 2–3 months, feed foliage plant food.
Split-leaf philodendron	Does well in moist, humus-rich soil. Spring and summer: feed every month. Mist regularly.
Wandering Jew	Needs moist soil. Spring and summer give plant food once a month.
Wax begonia	Water when soil is slightly dry and feed once a month.

Unfussy plants that will thrive in almost any light

Coleus	Keep moist. Feed foliage plant food spring and summer every 2 weeks.
Rubber plant	Needs moisture. Spray leaves. Give all-purpose plant food every 6 months.
Snake plant	Water when soil is almost dry. Spring and summer: occasional plant food.

Houseplants

Most of us begin decorating with houseplants by choosing a spot. Only then do we choose the plant. The chart opposite lists house plants by light requirements, the most important single factor in their health, so that you can select a plant that will thrive in the spot you want to fill with greenery.

Other Tips for Healthy Houseplants:

♦ Water regularly but never overwater. How can you tell? When the plant is overwatered, its leaves wilt and yellow and drop off. Sometimes bubbles appear on the underside of leaves. Repot the overwatered plant, cutting away rotted and affected parts, then put in good light out of the sun. To keep from overwatering plants, place them in a tray of wet pebbles or crushed egg-shells; use a spritzer (trigger spray bottle) to water.

♦ Put water in an open container for 24 hours so chlorine will dissipate and it will be at room temperature before watering plants.

♦ Plastic pots keep water from evaporating better than clay ones.

♦ If a plant wilts from dryness: water, mist, put out of direct sun.

♦ Fertilize once a month or less in winter; twice a month in summer.

♦ If aphids attack, wash them off your plants under tap water or spray plants with solution of detergent and water.

♦ Get rid of scale, mealy bugs, and some other infestations by swabbing with rubbing alco-hol, then wash with warm water in the sink. Don't use this method on African violets.

Color

Color can fool you. Beware of tiny color chips—a charming pink on the chip can turn shocking pink when painted in the large on the walls of your bedroom. A certain yellow against a nice green can turn that green to a sick avocado. A pleasing off-white can turn "dirty" in shadows. So know that color in a swatch looks different from color in a tiny square, that colors affect each other, and that light affects colors. Invest in a quart of paint and test it on a wall, taking a look at different times of day, in different lights. If you are choosing a fabric, try as large a piece as possible and drape it over your couch or chair to see how it will look. Keep folders of color swatches and chips—you cannot count on your memory.

Some general rules of thumb before you start: Dark colors absorb more light and make a place seem smaller. Using the same color for rooms that are next to each other expands space. Painting rooms next to each other in contrasting colors defines areas and shrinks space. Pick up colors with bright-colored accent pillows, window treatments, artwork.

A color wheel (see next page) can be very useful in choosing colors that go together well. Choose one dominant color for the room from a painting, a piece of pottery, or some other object, then follow one of the three basic color schemes:

♦ Choose opposite colors on the color wheel—this creates contrast. Make sure that one color is dominant. Then choose a color just to the left or right of one of the colors as a third color. Examples: orange-red with blue-green, accented with red; or green with red, accented with red-purple.

♦ Choose colors adjacent to each other on the wheel to create less contrast, for example, purple and purple-blue, yellow and yellow-orange, or blue and blue-green.

♦ For the least contrast, use similar colors of different lightness and brightness—pale pink and red or grey and black.

For help with decorating, call 800-645-8035, a toll-free line sponsored by **Monsanto Corporation** and the **American Society of Interior Designers.** You'll get several decorating hints and the chance to ask questions and receive answers from a decorator.

COLOR WHEEL

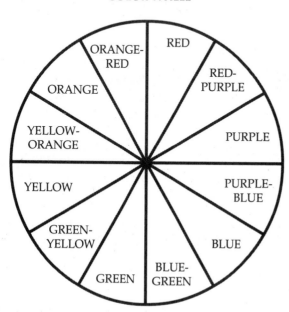

10 Painting Tips

The quickest way to change the looks of your house? Paint it. In your eagerness, though, make sure you do the job right. (*Note:* see "Lead Poisoning," p. 30, for problems that may occur because of lead in old paint.)

1. Prepare the wall or ceiling properly.

♦ Scrape off old flaking paint and smooth the edges with sandpaper. Check for moisture problems—the signal is paint that flakes off in under two years. In this case, you may need a carpenter or roofer to fix the problem.

♦ Wash the surface—with a hose, power washer, or elbow grease. A solution of TSP (trisodium phosphate) and water will remove grease that keeps paint from adhering. (Use rubber gloves.)

♦ Fill nail holes, cracks, and other imperfections. Use the right spackle or putty—exterior for exterior walls, interior for interior walls. Wet the putty knife before putting it in the putty.

♦ After the puttied areas have dried, sand and paint them with a primer coat. Also sand and prime all surfaces covered with slick paint like enamel. Wear a mask while you do it. Dust woodwork with tack cloth.

♦ Caulk window and woodwork joints.

♦ Cover stains, particularly mildew, with a special sealer. If people smoke in your house, prime the ceiling with a stain killer.

2. Move the furniture out of the room, or group it in the center and cover it with a drop cloth.

3. Take off striker plates, doorknobs, and other objects you don't want painted.

Now you can start painting:

4. Prime the surfaces, usually with primer paint. Otherwise you may have to paint the surface an extra time.

5. Use the right-sized brush—you need three for most jobs: 1-inch to 1½-inch trim brush, 2-inch to 2½-inch sash brush, and a 4-inch wall brush. Don't use natural bristle paintbrushes with latex or water-based paint; use one with synthetic bristles instead. If you use a roller, buy a

cover with the right nap for the job—the smoother the surface, the shorter the nap.

6. Paint a room in this order: ceiling, walls, trim, doors, windows. Paint the exterior of a house one side at a time.

7. Don't use too much paint on your brush or roller. Dip brushes only about one-third the length of the bristles into the paint, and don't fill the paint pan for roller painting more than ½ inch deep.

8. Be neat. Take your time. Every spill and drip is more trouble than the time you saved by being sloppy.

9. With a roller, go over the area already painted with up and down strokes.

10. Paint safely. Make sure you have a secure ladder. Don't lean over too far—it's better to move the ladder than break your head.

Note: Trying to get someone to fulfill a promise to paint? Call the Standard Brands Paint Company Nag Line, 800-732-5624. Your procrastinator will be nagged by postcard.

Wallcoverings

Wallcovering your own room is rewarding. Strip-by-strip, a new world emerges, transforming plain surfaces into exciting dimensions of color, pattern, and texture. And, happily, modern technology has made today's wallcoverings a real joy for the do-it-yourself decorator. New manufacturing methods have streamlined the installation process. Many wallcoverings come prepasted; all you do is measure and cut the strips, dip them in water, and smooth them on to the wall.

So, even if you have convinced ourself that you're all thumbs, you really can do a professional-looking job of hanging wallcoverings yourself, simply by following the step-by-step instructions that are yours for the asking from any wallcoverings store. Or send for "The Wallcovering How-To Handbook," an illustrated, 16-page booklet available free from the Wallcovering Information Bureau, Dept. W, PO Box 1708, Grand Central Station, New York, NY 10163.

To help you toward a more professional-looking job, here are seven important pointers:

1. Prepare the walls well. Patch all cracks and holes. The cleaner and smoother the surface, the better your new wallcoverings will look. Apply size or a sealer/primer for better adhesion. If you are doing any painting, such as the ceiling and/or woodwork, do that first to avoid spattering your freshly covered walls.

2. Order all the wallcoverings you need at the same time so they'll all be from the same color run.

PAINT KNOWHOW

Degree of Shininess

Flat Latex. Soft, subdued, not as washable as more glossy paints, good for living rooms and adults' bedrooms.

Satin or eggshell. Low-luster paints that are washable, good for a child's bedroom.

Semigloss. Even more washable and shiny—fine for bathrooms and woodwork.

Gloss. The shiniest, very easily washed, good for woodwork. Shows imperfections more than semigloss.

The Paint Base

Latex. Easy to clean up with soap and water, latex paint is water-based and quick drying. Do not use it over oil-based paints.

Acrylic. Acrylic looks and acts like latex paint, but dries faster.

Alkyd. Alkyd paint (synthetic-based) adheres better than latex paint and is more durable. However, you need chemical solvents to thin paint and clean up. It also dries slowly and creates an odor.

Oil. You will need mineral spirits to clean up after the job because of the oil base. It can be used over water-based paint.

For the outside of the house, you need trim paint for the trim. It comes in all finishes (oil, latex, alkyd, acrylic).

3. Equip yourself with the right tools to make the work go faster and easier. Wallcovering tools may be purchased individually or in a kit.

4. Make sure you have the right adhesive for the wallcovering you've chosen. There are different types of adhesives for different types of wallcoverings. So, consult your dealer.

5. Be meticulous about getting the first strip perfectly straight, with the pattern placed to best advantage. It will govern the alignment of all succeeding strips.

6. Work neatly. Use sharp razor blades. Brush each strip smooth and wrinkle-free as you go. Sponge woodwork and wallcovering clean of paste before it dries.

7. Take your time. Most wallcovering pastes dry slowly, so you can adjust and readjust a strip if need be. You don't even have to do the entire room at one time. A leisurely weekend or a few hours each evening may lead to a better-looking project—one you enjoy doing and showing off afterward.

How Much Will You Need?

To be sure that you purchase the right amount of wallcoverings:

♦ Measure your room carefully and draw a plan of each wall. Note wall height and width—including all nooks and crannies—and the measurement of all windows, doors, fireplaces, and other areas not to be covered.

♦ Take this information to your wallcovering dealer who can determine how many rolls you'll need of the specific wallcovering you have chosen. He or she can also help you determine your requirements for such tricky areas as stairwells.

A Word About Wallcovering Care

Although most wallcoverings can more than stand up to the slings and arrows of everyday home life, accidents do happen. Here's what to do in case of—

♦ Tears and loose edges: Apply paste to both wall and back of loose wallcovering. Press in

place, roll smooth with seam roller, and wipe away excess paste.

♦ Small damages: Paste a new, larger piece of wallcovering over the damaged area, matching pattern exactly. Let the patch set an hour, then cut through both layers with a razor knife. Clean the wall area and repaste the top piece. Wait 15 minutes, then roll fitted edges smooth.

♦ Spots and stains: Clean "washable" wallcoverings with a soapy sponge and water, "scrubbable" wallcoverings with a soft brush, mild soap, and water. For really tough stains, spot removers are available from your wallcoverings dealer. Test a small area first.

Reprinted courtesy of Wallcoverings Association.

Hanging a Picture

It's simple, but there is some art to it. Some people even mat and frame their own pictures, but unless you can buy a precut mat, this is a little tricky. These instructions are for hanging only:

Tools: hammer, awl.

Materials: Choose your hanging method by the weight of your picture:

PICTURE WEIGHTS	MATERIALS
Pictures weighing less than 5 pounds	Picture hook and ring or sawtooth hanger and nail or gum-backed hooks and hangers.
All but very heavy pictures	Hook-and-nail hangers, bought according to the weight of the picture.
Heavy pictures	Picture wire (8 inches longer than frame width) and screw eyes. Hollow-wall toggle bolts or anchors for very heavy pictures hung on plasterboard or fragile paneling. Plastic masonry anchor on brick or concrete.

Nail or screw hooks into studs when possible. To locate studs, which are usually placed 16 or 24 inches apart center to center, wrap a hammer in cloth and tap the wall until you hear a solid sound, which marks a stud. Sometimes you can see nailholes where sheets of drywall or paneling come together, with a stud behind the seam.

Decide whether you want the pictures at standing eye level or sitting eye level. With someone else holding the picture in the proper place, pencil in a mark where the middle of the lower edge of the frame should be. Put the picture hook under the picture wire and pull it into place. Measure the distance from hook to frame bottom. Then take the picture away and measure the same distance on the wall. Mark the spot. Tape an *x* on the plaster, put a hook on the spot with a nail inserted in the holes; hammer in.

Display and Use of the U.S. Flag

There is a lengthy code of etiquette for display and use of the U.S. flag. The rules given below pertain to home use.

1. The flag can be flown on all days, but especially on national and state holidays.

2. The flag is generally displayed from sunrise to sunset. However, it can be flown at night if properly illuminated.

3. The flag can be flown in inclement weather if it is an all-weather flag.

4. The flag should never touch the ground or floor or anything that is beneath it.

5. When flown with other flags, no other flag should fly above the U.S. flag. When a number of flags are displayed, the U.S. flag should be at the center and at the highest point in the group.

6. The flag should not be defaced in any manner. In addition, it should not be used to cover a ceiling, should not be used as a receptacle for holding or carrying anything, should not be used as wearing apparel.

7. The flag should not be drawn back, or up, or in folds, but should always be allowed to fall free.

8. It's all right to wash or dry-clean a soiled flag.

9. When a flag is no longer fit for display, it should be destroyed in a dignified manner, preferably by burning.

10. When hanging a flag horizontally (see A) or vertically (see B), the blue field (called the union) should be uppermost and to the observer's left. When hanging a flag from a staff (see C), the union should be at the peak of the staff.

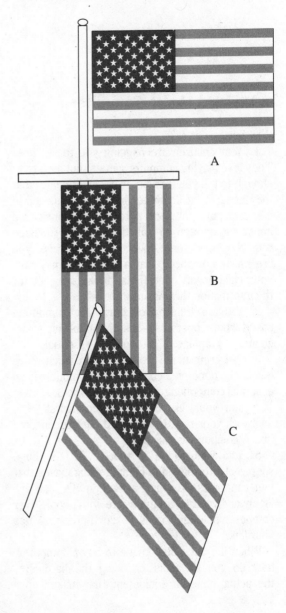

HOME COMPUTERS

Buying a Home Computer

Why buy one at all?

1. Your children are nagging you to get one. They love playing computer games, but are crafty enough to tell you (maybe even sincerely so) that they need to be computer literate to succeed in life. Computer literacy, after all, is considered important enough to substitute for a language requirement in some colleges. In any case, you are finally convinced that a computer may give your children an educational advantage just for the information they assimilate.

2. You are thinking of starting a computer-based home business—desktop publishing, accounting, graphics. A computer is essential.

3. You bring home work that can much more quickly be done on a computer. A computer is an essential component of your home office.

4. You would like to have a personal slave to deal with your monthly bills and file your income tax. A computer is cheaper.

5. You want to be in touch with the huge source of information in computer databases that you can access through a modem. Or you are lonely and want to communicate with people over computer bulletin boards. A computer provides your link.

When the decision is made to buy a computer, how do you go about choosing the hardware, the actual physical equipment that makes up a computer system? The answer is to start with the software, the computer programs that enable you to do specific kinds of tasks. If word processing will be your major task, you probably do not need a computer with a great deal of memory. If you want your children to have an interactive, multimedia electronic encyclopedia and a talking dictionary, you need a multimedia personal computer (MPC). Ask all members of the family what they want to do on the computer, then make up a composite wish list.

Now that you have some preliminary ideas about what you want a computer to do for you, start learning more about computers. Talk to your friends who have computers, talk to the computer wizards you know, read a beginner's book on computers, take a short course at your community college, university extension, or adult school. Some computer stores have computers all set up that you can try out. Many offer computer courses. Remember that a computer is—to put it simply—a set of on-off switches that translate into data. It takes in data and puts forth information based on that data.

Armed with the wish list, go to a reputable software store and start asking questions. Have the clerk show you what software programs will meet your needs. (A software program is comprised of the instructions that tell the computer how to process data. The program and data are stored in the computer's memory.) As you talk, the question of operating systems will probably come up. At the heart of the computer is the operating system: DOS, Macintosh, OS/2, UNIX. The operating system controls the computer hardware and manages the operation of application programs. Software is made to be compatible with specific operating systems, though there may be versions of some software for more than one operating system—for instance, a graphics program made for DOS or Macintosh.

Armed with your expertise, look at prospective computers in these terms:

♦ Compatibility (operating system, application programs, disk size and format).

♦ Expandability (ability to add printer, scanner, modem, and other devices).

♦ Upgradability (ability to keep the original computer and upgrade it with a new chip or other component).

When considering your budget, be sure to factor in the cost of software. Some experts say you should figure it will cost at least as much as the hardware, others that it will cost at least half the price of the hardware.

Make sure that the dealer you buy the computer from offers a money-back guarantee, telephone technical advice, and a free or low-cost service contract.

PERIPHERALS

Printers. Printers come in only a few basic types and can cost from a few hundred dollars to a thousand or more. You should consider the quality of print you need ("letter quality" is best),

BASIC COMPUTER SYSTEM QUESTIONS

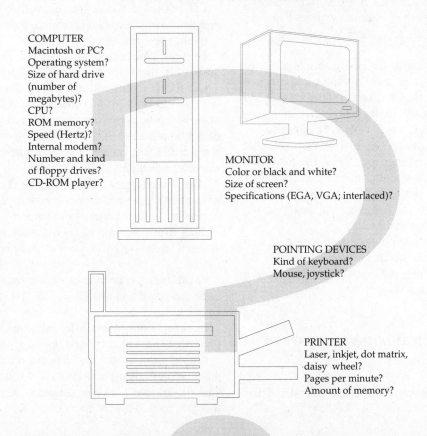

COMPUTER
Macintosh or PC?
Operating system?
Size of hard drive
(number of
megabytes)?
CPU?
ROM memory?
Speed (Hertz)?
Internal modem?
Number and kind
of floppy drives?
CD-ROM player?

MONITOR
Color or black and white?
Size of screen?
Specifications (EGA, VGA; interlaced)?

POINTING DEVICES
Kind of keyboard?
Mouse, joystick?

PRINTER
Laser, inkjet, dot matrix,
daisy wheel?
Pages per minute?
Amount of memory?

whether or not you will be printing graphics, and the speed with which the printer churns out pages. Make sure that the printer will work with your software.

Daisy wheel: The closest approximation to a typewriter, the daisy-wheel printer actually makes impressions with type set in a wheel-like device. It produces letter quality type, but does not print graphics and is fairly slow.

Dot matrix: These printers compose letters and graphics with tiny dots made by ends of

DOT MATRIX LETTERS

wires. The better ones usually can print fast, poorer quality drafts, as well as better-looking final copies that come very close to letter quality.

Inkjet: Inkjet printers produce close to laser quality type and graphics. They work by spraying ink on the paper. For some, you need special paper—otherwise print "bleeds" into the paper fibers.

Laser. The most expensive printers, laser printers are also the most versatile and produce highest quality output. They produce images and type through an electrostatic process that applies toner to a drum in a pattern of very tiny dots.

Modem: A device, internal or external, that connects the computer to a phone line, and from there to other computers, receiving and transmitting data from one to the other. The higher the bps (bits per second) rating, the faster it will transmit and receive data.

Mouse: A pointing device with long cord that looks like a tail (which gives it its name). By moving it and pressing or clicking a button, you send signals to the computer.

Demystification: A Glossary of Computer Terms

accessories: computer clock, calendar, other useful tools.

applications: software programs that contain sets of instructions telling the computer what to do—draw a picture, sort alphabetically, write letters, or process information in some other way. Examples: WordPerfect, Lotus, Paintbrush.

backup: copy of a file, usually made in case the original is lost. Do it!

baud: speed at which *modem* sends and receives information. One baud = one bit a second.

BIOS (Basic Input-Output System), the built-in part (usually) of the operating system.

bit (binary digit): a measure of memory capacity, one on/off setting.

boot: turn on and load the computer (from the phrase "pull up by the bootstraps").

bpi (bits per inch): measure of the density of data on a disk track.

bug: a defect in a program.

bus: circuitry connecting different parts of the computer.

byte: a collection of *bits,* usually eight.

CD-I (Compact Disk Interactive): A compact disk containing data, photos, video, sound.

cache: see *disk caching.*

central processing unit (CPU): microprocessor **chip** that is the brains of the computer.

CD-ROM: a compact disk with read-only memory that can be read by a laser-based disk driver. Material can be *downloaded* to your hard drive but cannot be erased or changed on the disk on which it is resident. Often contains reference materials—for example, a dictionary or encyclopedia.

chip: an integrated circuit; physically a bit of silicon that stores and processes data.

crash: death or coma of computer.

data file: collection of data, usually what you yourself create—a letter or short story or *spreadsheet.*

database: a collection of data arranged to be easily searched and retrieved. Examples: dBase, Dataflex.

desktop computer: a bigger, heavier computer that is not readily portable. See *laptop.*

dialog box: a box that appears on the computer screen giving you choices, establishing a kind of dialogue between you and computer so that you can tell it what to do.

directory: list of *files*.

disk caching: keeping frequently or recently accessed sectors of the disk in memory for fast retrieval.

disk drive: *floppy* disk slot or hard drive slot in the computer.

diskette: a detachable disk, a.k.a. *floppy*.

double density (DD): measure of storage capacity of a *floppy* disk.

DOS: an *operating system*.

download: load information down into the computer from another source: a *floppy* disk or a *database* accessed by a *modem*.

EGA (Enhanced Graphics Adapter): video adapter that works as Monochrome Display Adapter and Color Graphics Adapter and often more.

electronic mail (*E-mail*): messages sent from one computer to another.

expansion board: circuit board to be installed in a computer slot. May add memory, a *port*, *modem*.

file: collection of information with a name and stored on a disk. May be a text file, graphics file, or program file. Can hold numbers, text, or program information.

floppy: disk you put into a slot in the machine, onto which you *download* information or from which you *upload* it. May also contain programs. Works through magnetic storage media.

function keys: special-purpose keys programmed to perform operations, like listing files, indenting, search and replace, sorting.

gigabyte: billion (1,073,741,824) *bytes*.

graphic user interface (GUI): as opposed to command-line or function-key; a way of presenting program operation information, in *icons, pull-down menus, windows, dialog boxes*. Usually needs a *mouse*.

hard disk: permanent disk with much memory. Stores programs and data. Removed only for repair or replacement in case of failure.

hard copy: printed copy as opposed to a computer file.

high density (HD): storage capacity of *floppy* disk. High-density disk can hold much more data than a *double density* disk.

icon: a symbol representing a computer program. Clicking on it with a *mouse* activates the program.

input device: keyboard or *mouse* or your own voice or joystick—anything you use to communicate with the computer.

kilobyte (K): a thousand (actually 1024) *bytes* of memory.

laptop: computer that can fit on your lap, smaller than a briefcase, usually will run on batteries.

logic chip: a microchip that retrieves and manipulates information.

logical drive: a drive recognized by *DOS* as A:, B: (usually *floppy* drives), C: (usually the hard drive), D: (usually the hard drive).

mean time between failure (MTBF): measure of average time a device will run before it fails and needs to be repaired.

megabyte: million (actually 1,048,576) *bytes*.

megahertz: measure of speed—one megahertz is 1 million cycles per second.

memory chip: a microchip that stores information.

modem: a device allowing your computer to talk to other computers by phone line.

motherboard (master board): board into which microchips are plugged.

mouse: a device that helps to input data into the computer.

operating system: The software that runs the computer. Examples: DOS, OS/2, Macintosh.

output device: video display terminal (monitor) or printer.

pixel: a term meaning picture element. The picture on the screen is formed of many of these—they are tiny.

port: a point (plug or socket) where the computer is connected to another device, like a *modem* or *mouse* or printer. There are several kinds, with the main division being between serial ports and parallel ports.

program file: file containing codes that instruct the computer to perform certain functions.

program: a set of instructions that tells the computer what to do in little steps.

pull-down menu: a menu that comes down from the top of the screen, can be dragged by a *mouse.*

microprocessor: the main integrated circuit chip that does the majority of the computer's tasks. The microprocessor's number—e.g., 386 or 586—often identifies the central processor model. See *CPU.*

RAM (random-access memory): memory you can read or change. RAM is where the *microprocessor* puts data while working on it. When the power goes off, RAM forgets.

ROM (read-only memory): the computer or program can read it. You can't change it. It never forgets unless the hard disk crashes.

save: command that keeps all work completed on file.

spreadsheet: display of data in charts, tables, and graphs. Example of spreadsheet program: Lotus 1-2-3.

system software: master program that, with the help of application software, talks to the *input* and *output devices.*

USER GROUPS

Some of the best advice you can get on computer problems comes from other computer users. To tap into this vast resource, consider joining a user group. Each group concentrates on one kind of computer (Macintosh or IBM PC) or software (WordPerfect, Adobe Illustrator).

Most groups have computer bulletin boards that you can call up through your modem. You can ask your questions and get answers through electronic mail, and you can download public domain and "shareware" software. (You first use shareware free or at minimal cost, and if you like it, you register with the creator and pay for it.)

To find a user group close to you, call (with your modem) the **Association of User Groups,** 914-876-6678.

upload: load a file from your computer into another, usually through a *modem.*

utilities: software programs that manage the computer—unerase files or compress data or make *backups* or show the date and time.

window: a part of the screen separated from the rest. Enables working on two files at once.

word processing: software used to create text documents; examples: WordPerfect, WordStar, Ami Professional.

COMPUTERS AND THE ENVIRONMENT

Computers use 5 percent of the nation's electricity. They improve so fast that out-of-date machines end up in landfills. Computer printers annually eat up 9 million trees' worth of paper (200 square miles of forest). Manufacture of computer components adds to the toxic waste problem—Silicon Valley (center of the U.S. semiconductor industry) has more federal Superfund toxic waste sites than any other region. You can lessen the impact on the environment when you use a computer by:

♦ Buying a computer with Energy Star approval from the EPA. These computers "go to sleep," reducing energy usage, when not in use.

♦ Make sure that any computer you buy can be upgraded and that plastic parts are made of recycled plastic.

♦ Shut your computer off if you are not going to use it within the next 10 minutes.

♦ Maintain your computer. Keep it clean. Delete unnecessary files, download little-used files to a floppy disk.

♦ Upgrade rather than buy new whenever possible.

♦ Use computer paper made of recycled fibers, print rough drafts on used paper, recycle your computer paper.

♦ Donate your old computer to a school or nonprofit organization. Or sell it. Or keep it and use it to format disks or to print long documents.

Tips for Healthy Computering

Working at a computer for many hours does not have to cause health problems. First of all, arrange your computer station ergonomically (that is, to avoid strain on all parts of your body).

Other Tips

♦ To circumvent problems stemming from glare, use indirect light or wear tinted glasses. Put a low-wattage bulb in your desk lamp—no more than 60 watts—and make sure it casts no light on the screen or in your eyes. Place your monitor at a 90-degree angle to the windows.

Buy a glass or plastic filter to reduce screen glare. It should have the American Optometric Association seal of approval.

♦ You may want to buy glasses especially ground for computer use.

♦ Look away from the screen for a few seconds every 10 minutes. Focus on something far away.

♦ At least every hour, get up, stretch, and move around.

♦ Change your screen display from a dark background to a light one.

♦ If you can, use a high-resolution VDT (video display terminal).

♦ Use an ergonomically designed keyboard.

HOW TO SIT AT A COMPUTER

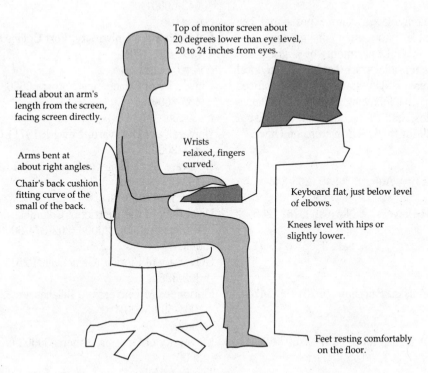

Top of monitor screen about 20 degrees lower than eye level, 20 to 24 inches from eyes.

Head about an arm's length from the screen, facing screen directly.

Arms bent at about right angles.

Chair's back cushion fitting curve of the small of the back.

Wrists relaxed, fingers curved.

Keyboard flat, just below level of elbows.

Knees level with hips or slightly lower.

Feet resting comfortably on the floor.

YARD AND GARDEN

State U.S. Department of Agriculture Extension Offices

U.S. Department of Agriculture personnel can provide valuable information on gardens and yards. The U.S. Department of Agriculture county extension offices are listed in your local phone directory. USDA state extension offices are located in the following land-grant colleges and universities. Call the general number (listed below) and ask for the USDA Extension Office.

ALABAMA
Auburn University, Auburn 36849 (205-844-4000)
Alabama A&M University, Normal 35762 (205-851-5000)
Tuskegee University, Tuskegee 36088 (205-727-8011)

ALASKA
University of Alaska, Fairbanks 99701 (907-474-7211)

ARIZONA
University of Arizona, Tucson 85721 (602-621-2211)

ARKANSAS
University of Arkansas, Little Rock 72203 (501-569-3000)
University of Arkansas, Pine Bluff 71601 (501-543-8000)

CALIFORNIA
University of California, Berkeley 94720 (510-642-6000)

COLORADO
Colorado State University, Fort Collins 80523 (303-491-1101)

CONNECTICUT
University of Connecticut, Storrs 06268 (203-486-2000)

DELAWARE
University of Delaware, Newark 19711 (302-831-2000)
Delaware State College, Dover 19901 (302-739-4924)

DISTRICT OF COLUMBIA
University of the District of Columbia, Washington, DC 20008 (202-274-5000)

FLORIDA
University of Florida, Gainesville 32611 (904-392-3261)
Florida A&M University, Tallahassee 32307 (904-599-3000)

GEORGIA
University of Georgia, Athens 30602 (706-542-3000)
The Fort Valley State College, Fort Valley 31030 (912-825-6211)

HAWAII
University of Hawaii, Honolulu 96822 (808-956-8111)

IDAHO
University of Idaho, Moscow 83843 (208-885-6111)

ILLINOIS
University of Illinois, Urbana 61801 (217-333-1000)

INDIANA
Purdue University, West Lafayette 47907 (317-494-4600)

IOWA
Iowa State University, Ames 50011 (515-294-4111)

KANSAS
Kansas State University, Manhattan 66506 (913-532-6011)

KENTUCKY
University of Kentucky, Lexington 40506 (606-257-9000)

Kentucky State University, Frankfurt 40601 (502-227-6000)

LOUISIANA
Louisiana State University, Baton Rouge 70803 (504-388-3202)

Southern University and A&M College, Baton Rouge 70813 (504-771-2011)

MAINE
University of Maine, Orono 04473 (207-581-1110)

MARYLAND
University of Maryland, College Park 20742 (301-405-1000)

University of Maryland, Eastern Shore, Princess Anne 21853 (410-651-2200)

MASSACHUSETTS
University of Massachusetts, Amherst 01003 (413-545-0111)

MICHIGAN
Michigan State University, East Lansing 48824 (517-355-1855)

MINNESOTA
University of Minnesota, St. Paul 55108 (612-625-5000)

MISSISSIPPI
Mississippi State University, Starkville, 39762 (601-325-2323)

Alcorn State University, Lorman 39096 (601-877-6100)

MISSOURI
University of Missouri, Columbia 65211 (314-882-2121)

Lincoln University, Jefferson City 65101 (314-681-5000)

MONTANA
Montana State University, Bozeman 59715 (406-994-0211)

NEBRASKA
University of Nebraska, Lincoln 68583 (402-472-7211)

NEVADA
University of Nevada, Reno 89557 (702-784-1110)

NEW HAMPSHIRE
University of New Hampshire, Durham 03824 (603-862-1234)

NEW JERSEY
Rutgers State University, New Brunswick 08903 (908-932-1766)

NEW MEXICO
New Mexico State University, Las Cruces 88003 (505-646-0111)

NEW YORK
New York State College of Agriculture, Ithaca 14853 (607-255-2241)

NORTH CAROLINA
North Carolina State University, Raleigh 27650 (919-515-2011)

North Carolina A&T State University, Greensboro 27420 (910-334-7500)

NORTH DAKOTA
North Dakota State University, Fargo 58105 (701-237-8011)

OHIO
The Ohio State University, Columbus 43210 (614-292-6446)

OKLAHOMA
Oklahoma State University, Stillwater 74078 (405-744-5000)

Langston University, Langston 73050 (405-466-2231)

OREGON
Oregon State University, Corvallis 97331 (503-737-0123)

PENNSYLVANIA
The Pennsylvania State University, University Park 16802 (814-865-4700)

RHODE ISLAND
University of Rhode Island, Kingston 02881 (401-792-1000)

SOUTH CAROLINA
Clemson University, Clemson 29631 (803-656-3311)

South Carolina State College, Orangeburg 29115 (803-536-7000)

SOUTH DAKOTA
South Dakota State University, Brookings 57006 (605-688-4151)

TENNESSEE
University of Tennessee, Knoxville 37901 (615-974-1000)

Tennessee State University, Nashville 37203 (615-320-3131)

TEXAS
Texas A&M University, College Station 77843 (409-845-3211)

Prairie View A&M University, Prairie View 77445 (409-857-3311)

UTAH
Utah State University, Logan 84321 (801-797-1000)

VERMONT
University of Vermont, Burlington 05401 (802-656-3131)

VIRGINIA
Virginia Polytechnic Institute and State University, Blacksburg 24061 (703-231-6000)

Virginia State University, Petersburg 23803 (804-524-5085)

WASHINGTON
Washington State University, Pullman 99164 (509-335-3564)

WEST VIRGINIA
West Virginia University, Morgantown 26506 (304-293-0111)

WISCONSIN
University of Wisconsin, Madison 53706 (608-262-1234)

WYOMING
University of Wyoming, Laramie 82070 (307-766-1121)

Source: U.S. Department of Agriculture

OTHER SOURCES OF INFORMATION

The EPA's National Pesticides Telecommunications Network, 800-858-7378 (24 hours a day), FAX, 806-743-3094. Information about health effects of pesticides, help with pesticide emergencies.

Environmental Protection Agency, Office of Pesticide Programs, Field Operations Division (H7506C), 401 M Street SW, Washington, DC 20460 (703-305-5017). Information on integrated pest management.

Bio-Integral Resource Center (BIRC), PO Box 7414, Berkeley, CA 94707 (510-524-2567). Least toxic methods of care of lawns, gardens.

Compost

If you have a compost pile, you spend less time hauling your garbage and other debris to your front gate for trash pickup. You can also feel proud that you have helped the environment. And a bonus—you can enrich the soil in your garden. Called "gardener's gold" for good reason, compost results from a natural process of decomposition. All the instructions about compost have to do with helping the process along. If you left all your garbage, leaves, and lawn clippings in a pile and did nothing, they would still eventually decompose into compost. Microorganisms do the work, ingesting raw organic matter (garbage, leaves, lawn clippings) and turning it into humus, which looks and smells like rich dark crumbly soil. You help by creating the proper environment for the microorganisms.

A few important tips: Don't put cheese, meat, bones, or fat in the garbage you compost. And don't include dog, cat, or bird manure. Keep

COMPOSTING METHODS

1. WIRE MESH
Start with a piece of wire mesh about 5 feet high and 9 feet long.

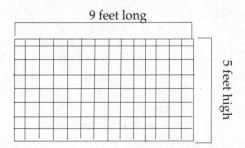

9 feet long

5 feet high

Roll the mesh into a cylinder, and wire the ends together. When the container is full, open it and move it to another location. Then close it up again, and shovel the compost back in to mix it.

2. THREE-SIDED BIN
Stack concrete blocks or hay bales in a three-sided U 4 or 5 feet high.

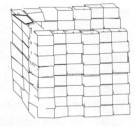

3. GARBAGE CAN
Cut the bottom off a can, punch some holes in the sides, then put it up on a few bricks.

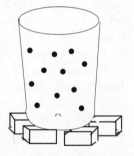

4. PALLET BIN
Make a container of four wooden pallets laced together, with an open top and bottom.

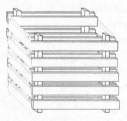

5. WOODEN BIN
Make three compartments, each 3 feet wide by 5 feet long and 3 feet deep. You can space side boards and design the bin so that they slide out. Keep new material in one bin, working compost in another, and finished compost in the third.

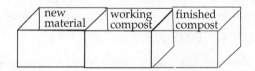

new material / working compost / finished compost

6. INDORE "LAYER CAKE" METHOD

Sprinkling of lime, phospate, or wood ashes

Thin layer of soil

2 inches of green things and manure for nitrogen

6 inches of dry materials for carbon

Repeat in layers until you have a heap 4 to 5 feet high. Mix or poke holes in the side of the pile with a rod to aerate it, adding oxygen for the bacteria. When the pile starts to get dry, add enough water to keep it damp, by sprinkling with the garden hose. Don't soak it. Some piles stay damp from rain or wet organic materials. They don't need sprinkling. The pile should be about as wet as a sponge that has been squeezed out. You can cover it with a tarp to keep the moisture in.

everything in small (but not too small) pieces. Run over leaves with the lawn mower or shred them in a shredder. If a friend has compost, add a shovelful to your pile—it will add microorganisms.

Encourage the pile to heat up by making it at least 3 feet high and 3 feet wide. That way the pile insulates the core so it can reach a temperature of 95–160°F. A temperature of at least 130 degrees for three straight days will kill weed seeds, insect eggs, plant diseases. The pile will not catch on fire. Let the pile "cook" about four to six weeks, then turn it. It will be ready in three months.

The Lazy Man's Way: "Heap Composting"

Pile organic materials on top of each other. The pile will shrink as it decomposes. This method takes much longer, up to a year.

USING COMPOST

Age compost for a month after it has been completely "cooked" before you use it so that the population of bacteria is reduced. Otherwise they may make more compost out of your garden plants.

Use compost as a mulch around beds, or create a potting mix by combining it with soil, sand, and perlite. Your plants will be healthier. Compost suppresses root diseases, nematodes, other soil-borne diseases.

Can you use compost alone as a soil enrichment, a perfect plant food? Some experts say yes, that it contains all that your plants need, particularly if you have used a variety of materials. Others say no—that you should add fertilizer and other nutrients as well.

Good Dirt and Other Plant Requirements

Plants will be grateful (and show their gratitude) for everything you do to make the soil they live in more friable, fertile, and well drained. Stone-picking pays off. And choosing a place that is sunny may make all the difference.

Drainage. Choose a place with well-drained soil, where there are no low places collecting water and there is no runoff from surrounding land or danger of flooding. You can improve drainage by using agricultural tile to draw water off.

Sun. Most vegetable plants like sun all day—lettuces and other leafy greens are the exception.

Soil. Leave wet soil alone. Wait to till it until it is dry enough so that when you pick up a handful and let it go, the soil crumbles. Make sure you check soil a few inches below the surface. After you dig or rototill your soil, mix in compost and other organic material like composted cow manure. Then rake it until it is reasonably fine. Don't rake heavy soil *too* fine, or it may compact.

Mulch keeps the top of the soil from crusting over, retains moisture, and keeps down weeds. As it decays, it releases minerals, nitrogen, and other nutrients into the soil below. You can use almost any plant material as mulch: compost, leaves, lawn clippings, straw.

In order to choose proper fertilizer, you need to know how acid or alkaline your soil is. Generally speaking, soils in dry climates tend toward alkalinity, soils in moist climates toward acidity. Ask your garden center, nursery, university, or county extension office about test kits. Acid soils with pH less than 6 may need lime. Alkaline soils with a pH more than 7 may need organic matter, sulfur, or sulfur-containing materials. Once you know the pH, you can ask at your garden store for proper fertilizer, which also depends on your location and what you want to grow. Some plants require more nitrogen than others, for example. Don't put fertilizer too near the plants—it can burn the roots. And don't overdo fertilizer—it will give your plants herbaceous indigestion.

PRUNING A BRANCH

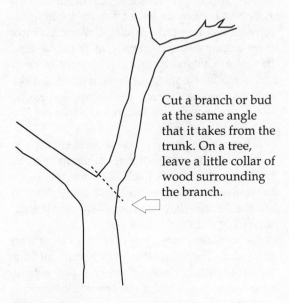

Cut a branch or bud at the same angle that it takes from the trunk. On a tree, leave a little collar of wood surrounding the branch.

CUTTING A BRANCH WITHOUT TEARING THE BARK

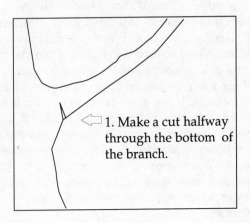

1. Make a cut halfway through the bottom of the branch.

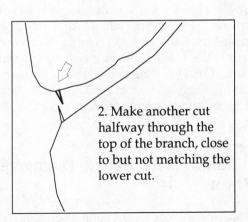

2. Make another cut halfway through the top of the branch, close to but not matching the lower cut.

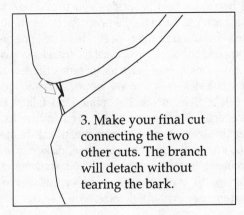

3. Make your final cut connecting the two other cuts. The branch will detach without tearing the bark.

Pruning

General rules:

Shrubs. Prune above a branch or bud, slanting the cut at the same angle that the branch or bud takes from the trunk (or larger branch).

Trees. When cutting off a branch, cut close to but not into the trunk. Leave intact the little collar of wood that surrounds the branch. When you take off a big branch, cut about halfway through the bottom of the branch a little way out from the trunk, then make a top cut that is close to, but does not match, the bottom cut. This enables you to make your final cut without having to worry about tearing bark. If you want to shorten a tree, cut tall branches back to a crotch.

Prune the following:
- Suckers
- Dead wood
- One of two branches that rub or cross each other
- Branches touching the ground
- Wrong-way branches (heading back to the center of the tree or shrub) if terribly wrong-way.

Watering

How much? When? Watering thoroughly but less often is a general rule that saves water and makes for healthy, deep-rooted plants. A good deal depends on your soil and the amount of rain you are getting. Vegetable gardens require about an inch of rain a week—you can put a can in your garden to measure. If you have clayey soil, which holds water well, you can provide that inch in one weekly session. Sandy soils are more porous so it is better to provide a half-inch of water twice a week. Water early in the morning or in late evening, when water will evaporate more slowly. Water vegetables and fruits right after they blossom.

Don't flood your plants or lawn, but water slowly so water has a chance to soak into the ground before running off. Make catch basins around trees and shrubs to create a moat to hold water. Use mulch to retain moisture, and weed often. Consider using drip irrigation for permanent plantings and sweat (soaker) hoses (which ooze water) for strips or winding areas.

Garden Pests: How to Discourage Them

Though the pests munching at your plants put you in the mood to kill, try to control the amount of herbicides and pesticides you use. They are toxic and can harm useful pests, pets, even people. Considering that pesticides are poisons, homeowners are remarkably careless with them—they use as much as six times the amount of pesticides per acre as farmers do. So read the labels, even the fine print, and follow the directions. More is not better. Remember that a healthy lawn or garden may mean sick people. The immediate effects: headaches, dizziness, eye problems, rashes, confusion. The lasting effects: damage to liver, kidneys, and central nervous system; cancer; birth defects; skin disease.

The newest buzz word is IPM (integrated pest management), a new name for some old ideas: the managed use of biological, cultural, and chemical controls of pests for least harm to the environment and long-term results. Biological control means using natural enemies of pests to wipe them out. Cultural control involves use of pest- and weed-discouraging methods of gardening like mowing high so weeds can't grow as easily. Chemical control, the last resort, involves the wise use of pesticides.

Before you spray, assess the pest situation in your garden by going out early in the morning to take a pest census. Look both for the pests themselves (remember to check under leaves) and the damage they have done—holes in leaves, dimpled or distorted leaves.

And consider using kinds of controls other than pesticides. The simplest is to pick pests off your plants by hand. Hose off others, like aphids, with water. Soapy water solution will kill sucking insects like aphids.

You can also try:

Tiny biological controls:
♦ Milky spore bacteria kill Japanese beetle grubs that eat roots and cause them to wilt and die. The bacteria come in pellet or powder form. This method works slowly.

♦ *Bacillus thuringiensis* (BT), a bacterium, comes in a powder used as dust or mixed with water for spraying. BTs can kill caterpillars, potato bugs, and mosquito larvae by paralyzing their digestive systems when eaten.

♦ Nematodes, worm-like tiny organisms, kill insects that live below the surface—potato beetles, weevils, cutworms, grubs.

Good bugs: Good bugs will keep "bad" bugs down. They include ladybugs, green lacewings, syrphid and tachinid flies, and trichogramma wasps. You can attract good bugs by planting the flowers they like—artemisia, asters, chamomile, cosmos, dahlias, daisies, marigolds, yarrow, zinnias. Good bugs also like herbs such as caraway, cilantro, dill, fennel, parsley, tansy. Plant the herbs close to vegetables. You can buy good bugs (lacewings, ladybugs) from: **The Necessary Organics,** 1 Nature's Way, New Castle, VA 24127-0305 (703-864-5103), or **Gardens Alive!** 5100 Schenely Place, Lawrenceburg, IN 47025 (812-537-8650), or **Gardener's Supply Company,** 128 Intervale Road, Burlington, VT 05401 (802-863-1700).

Traps: Traps lure and kill insects. The advantage is that poison is contained within the trap so it is harder for pets and children to get at it. A Japanese beetle trap can eliminate 4000 beetles. Traps are available for gypsy moths and larvae, slugs, yellow jackets, whitefly. Some can be emptied and reused.

Growing Lawns

Time magazine said of a lawn that "it is the decent, respectably dull necktie we knot around our houses." Consider the question: Do we need a lawn at all? If you live in a very hot, dry, or cold place, perhaps not. Some "weeds" can make a lawn—yarrow, for instance. Keep the dandelions: you can eat them and they are pretty. You might decide to grow chaparral or a meadow of wildflowers.

If you do settle on having a lawn, pick your grass carefully. Some seed contains built-in pesticide fungus (endophyte) that cohabits with the grass for generations. It kills insects that eat blades of grass, and it also makes the lawn more resistant to other diseases and drought. Buy cool-climate grasses for the north: Kentucky bluegrass, fescues, perennial rye; seed or use bluegrass sod. Buy warm-climate grasses for the south: Bermuda grass, centipede, carpet grass, *Zoysia japonica.* Of course, new grass varieties are developed all the time—ask your extension service what's best for your area. If you plant sod, do it in spring or early fall. Sod should be thin, no more than ¾ to 1 inch thick, without weeds. No matter where you live and what kind of grass you grow, in early autumn get rid of weeds and apply fertilizer.

The best mowing tool? Sheep, eight to the acre. But if you must use a machine, mow in the evening. Mow when the grass is not more than twice as high as it should be. In shady spots let it grow another half-inch higher. Keep the mower blades sharp, and leave clippings on the lawn or use as mulch in the garden.

Water when you step on the grass and it doesn't come back up, or when it looks blue. Water in the morning, at least a half-hour to each section of grass.

Special Problems

♦ Compacted soil (more a problem in the south): use special tools like spiked roller.

♦ Thatch: a small amount is good, too much is not good. Get rid of it with a power rake.

♦ Weeds: feed the lawn, mow high, and water; dig or pull weeds out when young, trying to get entire root.

♦ Quack grass: put black plastic over patches.

♦ Thistles: cut thistles with a knife below ground.

You might want to substitute ground covers for lawn. (See "Ground Covers," pp. 236–239.) Shallow-rooted kinds are best planted in spring. You can plant those with deeper roots any time if you give them enough water and protection from wind until they are established. Prepare the soil bed, and add balanced fertilizer unless the plant thrives in poor soil. Plant according to variety:

♦ Pachysandra: 6 inches to 1 foot apart.

♦ Periwinkle, ivy, and other plants prostrate in habit; alpine or rock plants: 1 plant per square foot.

♦ Shrubs like cotoneaster and junipers: 3 feet of space per plant.

♦ Vines: 3–5 feet apart.

USDA Plant Hardiness Zone Map

These maps show climate zones for the United States. They range from a cold Zone 1 to a warm Zone 11. Use the maps with "Ground Covers," pp. 236–239 and "Tree Charts," pp. 241–246.

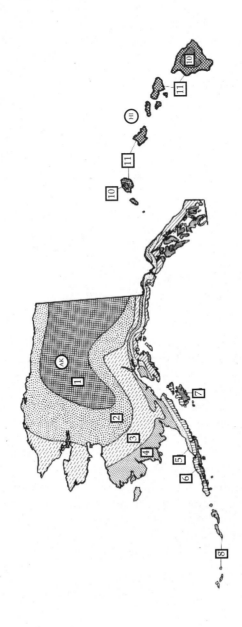

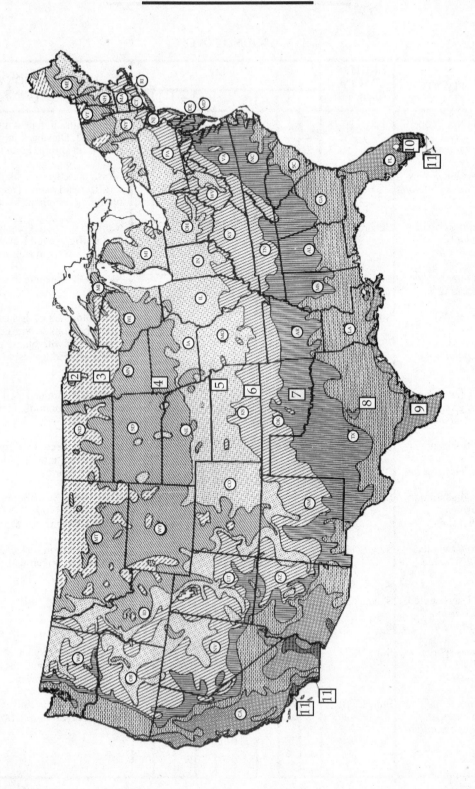

GROUND COVERS

PLANT	LIGHT; SPACING (in inches)	ZONES									DESCRIPTION & CONDITIONS
		2	3	4	5	6	7	8	9	10	
Fern (New York) *Thelypteris noveboracensis*	Shade; 12-18	▓									Moist soil rich in peat moss or leaf mold. Dies back in fall, returns in spring. Long fronds.
Lily-of-the-valley *Convallaria majalis*	Shade; 6-8	▓	▓	▓	▓	▓	▓				Moist, enriched soil. Balanced fertilizer early spring and after blooming. Fragrant flowers.
Creeping charlie *Lysimachia nummularia*	Shade; 12-18	▓	▓	▓	▓	▓	▓	▓	▓	▓	Moist to wet soil. Can stand foot traffic. Round leaves; yellow flowers in summer.
Irish moss *Arenaria verna*	Sun, light shade; 6	▓	▓	▓	▓	▓	▓	▓	▓	▓	Moist soil. Separate in early spring. Looks like moss.
Juniper (Wilton carpet) *Juniperus horizontalis 'wiltoni'*	Sun; 36	▓	▓	▓	▓	▓	▓	▓	▓	▓	Hardy, tolerant of dryness and city conditions. Evergreen 4 inches high with blue-green needle-shaped leaves.
Phlox (creeping, moss, ground) *Phlox subalata*	Sun; 12-18	▓	▓	▓	▓	▓	▓	▓	▓	▓	Needs well-drained soil. Trim back after blooming. Plants 4-6 inches tall.
Pink (maiden, garden) *Dianthus deltoides*	Sun; 6-8	▓	▓	▓	▓	▓	▓	▓	▓	▓	Be sure to weed. Evergreen fine leaves. Fragrant red, pink, white flowers in spring.
Snow-in-summer *Cerastium tomentosum*	Sun; 12-24	▓	▓	▓	▓	▓	▓	▓	▓	▓	Adapts to any well-drained soil. Sows itself. Fuzzy, silvery leaves with summer flowers.
Yarrow (woolly) *Achillea tomentosa*	Sun; 6-12	▓	▓	▓	▓	▓	▓	▓	▓	▓	Hardy, grows in rocks. Can be mowed. Evergreen with yellow blossoms.
Fern (hay-scented) *Dennstaedtia punctilobula*	Shade; 12-18		▓								See Fern (New York).
Cypress spurge *Euphorbia cyparissias*	Sun; 18-24		▓	▓	▓	▓	▓	▓			Grows almost anywhere. 1 foot high. Gray-green leaves and yellow-orange flowers.
Betony, lamb's-ears *Stachys byzantina*	Sun; 12-18		▓	▓	▓	▓	▓	▓			Tolerates dryness. Silvery woolly leaves, purple flowers.

PLANT	LIGHT; SPACING (in inches)	ZONES									DESCRIPTION & CONDITIONS
		2	3	4	5	6	7	8	9	10	
Bird's-foot trefoil *Lotus corniculatus*	Sun, light shade; 6		■	■	■	■	■	■	■	■	Tolerates poor soil. Can be mowed. Clover-like leaves.
Carpet bugle *Ajuga reptans*	Sun, light shade; 6-12		■	■	■	■	■	■	■	■	Good low-growing cover. Shiny leaves and blue flowers.
Chamomile *Chamaemelum nobile*	Sun; 4-12		■	■	■	■	■	■	■	■	Resists drought. Can mow as lawn. Evergreen herb. Fine leaves and daisy-like flowers.
Goutweed *Aegopodium podagraria 'variegatum'*	Shade, part sun; 6-10		■	■	■	■	■	■	■	■	Can take over. Grows almost anywhere. Green and white leaves with white flowers.
Silver mound artemesia *Artemesia schmidtiana*	Sun; 12-15		■	■	■	■	■	■	■	■	Hardy. Silver leaves and tiny yellow flowers.
Stonecrop sedum *Sedum*	Sun, light shade; 9-12		■	■	■	■	■	■	■	■	Thrives almost anywhere. Evergreen or semievergreen.
Strawberry *Fragaria chiloensis*	Sun, light shade; 12-18		■	■	■	■	■	■	■	■	Needs moisture. Dark green leaves and white blossoms, edible red berries.
Thyme (creeping) *Thymus serpyllum*	Sun; 6-12		■	■	■	■	■	■	■	■	Grows best on poor, dry soil. Evergreen herb.
Virginia creeper *Parthenocissus quinquefolia*	Sun, light shade; 36		■	■	■	■	■	■	■	■	Native vine. Needs rich, moist soil. Tree-climber. Turns red in fall. Blue-black berries.
Periwinkle *Vinca minor*	Sun, shade; 12-18			■	■	■	■	■			Thrives almost anywhere. Evergreen, trailing habit.
Violet (sweet) *Viola odorata*	Sun, part shade; 12			■	■	■	■	■			Needs moisture, winter mulch. Spreads. Fragrant flowers.
Pachysandra *Pachysandra terminalis*	Shade; 6-12			■	■	■	■	■	■		Needs rich, moist soil, but little care otherwise. Saw-toothed leaves, white flowers, berries.
Corsican pearlwort, Irish moss *Sagina subulata*	Light shade; 6			■	■	■	■	■	■		Rich, moist, well-drained soil. Evergreen, mat-like plants.
Creeping lilyturf *Liriope spicata*	Sun, shade; 12			■	■	■	■	■	■		Don't walk on it. Grass-like leaves; lavender flowers.
Ginger *Asarum canadense*	Sun, light shade; 12			■	■	■	■	■	■		Needs rich soil. Dried root can be used as flavoring.

GROUND COVERS (cont.)

PLANT	LIGHT; SPACING (in inches)	ZONES 2	3	4	5	6	7	8	9	10	DESCRIPTION & CONDITIONS
Scotch heather *Calluna vulgaris*	Sun, light shade; 12			▓	▓	▓	▓	▓	▓	▓	Plant in spring in zones 4-6, fall elsewhere. Little flowers.
Sweet woodruff *Galium odoratum*	Shade; 10-12			▓	▓	▓	▓	▓	▓	▓	Needs moist, acid soil. Grows well under trees and shrubs.
Yellow-root *Xanthorhiza simplicissima*	Sun, shade; 18-24			▓	▓	▓	▓	▓	▓	▓	Likes moist soil with peat moss. Spreading, about 2 feet tall. Purple flowers in spring.
Paxistima *Paxistima canbyi*	Sun, shade; 12				▓	▓	▓	▓			Good in acid soil. Evergreen foliage, white flowers.
Hall's honeysuckle *Lonicera japonica* 'halliana'	Sun, shade; 24-36				▓	▓	▓	▓	▓		Can take over and even kill trees it climbs on. Oval leaves and fragrant flowers.
Baltic ivy *Hedera helix* 'baltica'	Sun, shade; 12				▓	▓	▓				Requires rich, moist soil. Dark green leaves.
Creeping mahonia *Mahonia repens*	Sun, shade; 12			▓	▓	▓	▓	▓	▓		Needs organic matter. Shrub with yellow flowers, black fruit.
Creeping mazus *Mazus reptans*	Sun, shade; 12			▓	▓	▓	▓	▓	▓		Likes moist, composted soil. Low, with tiny flowers.
Creeping speedwell *Veronia repens*	Sun, light shade; 6-12			▓	▓	▓	▓	▓			Needs moist, enriched soil. 4-inch-tall plant, flowers.
Forget-me-not *Myosotis scorpioides* 'semperflorens'	Shade; 12			▓	▓	▓	▓	▓			Needs moist soil. Self-seeding. Narrow leaves and pale-blue flowers.
Germander *Teucrium chamaedrys*	Sun; 12			▓	▓	▓	▓	▓			Likes well-drained soil. Prune. Saw-toothed hairy leaves and little rose flowers.
Purple winter creeper *Euonymus fortunei* 'colorata'	Sun, shade; 12-24				▓	▓	▓	▓	▓		Hardy. Shiny leaves. Yellow-centered red, pink, or white flowers followed by fruits.
Spreading English yew *Taxus baccata* 'repandens'	Sun, shade; 36-48				▓	▓	▓	▓	▓		Roots well, can use on banks. Evergreen vine with leaves that turn red-purple in fall.

PLANT	LIGHT; SPACING (in inches)	ZONES									DESCRIPTION & CONDITIONS
		2	3	4	5	6	7	8	9	10	
Carmel creeper *Ceonothus griseus 'horizontalis'*	Full sun; 48						▨	▨	▨	▨	Tolerates salt spray. Likes sandy soil. Looks like lilac, grows 18-30 inches tall.
Chaparral broom *Baccharis pilularis*	Sun; 48						▨	▨	▨	▨	Water in first season after planting. Evergreen with holly-shaped leaves, small flowers.
Gazania *Gazania ringens*	Sun; 18-24						▨	▨	▨	▨	Good for banks and poor soil. Daisy-like flowers.
Morning glory *Convolvulus mauritanicus*	Sun, light shade; 24-36						▨	▨	▨	▨	Hardy. Evergreen with large trumpet-shaped blue flowers.
Star jasmine *Trachelospermum jasminoides*	Sun, shade; 24-36						▨	▨	▨	▨	Likes moist, enriched soil. Shiny evergreen leaves with fragrant white flowers.
African daisy (trailing) *Osteospermum fruticosum*	Sun; 24						▨	▨	▨	▨	Withstands drought, but water in extreme conditions. Fleshy leaves and large lavender flowers. Creeping.
Ice plant (trailing) *Mesembryanthemum crystallinum*	Sun; 18						▨	▨	▨	▨	Grows well in sandy soil. Needs water. Thick succulent leaves and red and pink flowers.
Ivy geranium *Pelargonium peltatum*	Sun; 12-18						▨	▨	▨	▨	Grows almost anywhere. Likes well-drained light soil. Trailing. Large flower clusters.
Lantana *Lantana montevidensis*	Sun; 18						▨	▨	▨	▨	Grows almost anywhere with some watering. Fragrant flower clusters. 18-24 inches high.
Parrot's beak (Coral-gem) *Lotus bertheloti*	Sun; 18-24						▨	▨	▨	▨	Likes hot, dry conditions. Trailing. Hairlike leaves and pea-shaped red flowers.
Dichondra, Lawn leaf *Dichondra micrantha*	Sun; 6-12						▨	▨	▨	▨	Grass substitute, but should not be walked on in cold weather. Stains clothing. Water. Keep at lawn height.
Hottentot fig *Carpobrotus edulis*	Sun; 12-18						▨	▨	▨	▨	Grows well in sandy soil. Large flowers, fig-shaped fruit.
Baby's tears *Soleirolia soleiroli*	Shade; 6-12						▨	▨	▨	▨	Needs rich, composted soil. Water until established. Small round green leaves.

HOW TO PLANT A TREE

Three deciduous trees planted to shade the south, southwest, and southeast of your home can reduce your air-conditioning bills by 10 to 50 percent. Windbreak rows of conifer trees to the northwest of your home can considerably reduce heating costs. Shading your outdoor air-conditioning condenser unit will also increase its efficiency.

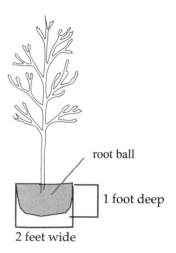

1. Choose a tree at least 5 feet or 6 feet tall grown to nursery standards.
2. Plan to plant in a place with enough room so that branches and roots can reach full size. Avoid overhead and underground utilities.
3. Measure the root ball.

root ball

1 foot deep

2 feet wide

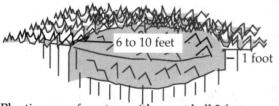

6 to 10 feet

1 foot

Planting area for a tree with a root ball 2 feet wide and 1 foot deep is 6 to 10 feet in diameter and 1 foot deep.

4. Prepare a planting area as deep as the root ball and 3 to 5 times its diameter by loosening the soil.
5. If needed, blend in soil amendments throughout the entire planting area.

6. Dig a hole in the middle of the area and set the root ball even with the ground level.

7. Use water to settle the soil and remove air pockets in the planting area. Do not pack down the soil.
8. Stake the tree to flex with the wind only if tree is unable to stand up to wind.
9. Spread a 2- to 3-inch layer of mulch on the entire area, but not within 6 inches of tree trunk.

NOTE: When planting a seedling, begin with step two. Protect the seedling from damage by lawn mowers, pets, etc., and water as needed to keep it from drying out, especially during its first summer.

Reprinted courtesy of the American Forestry Association.

TREE CHARTS

Unless otherwise specified, trees grow well in moist soil, well drained. Shaded cells indicate zones in which a tree will survive fairly well. (See "USDA Plant Hardiness Zone Map," pp.234–235.) Height varies by climate and soil fertility as well as by type of tree. When a tree has a zone designation ending with *a*, it thrives in the colder section of the zone; a tree with a zone designation of *b* is better suited to the warmer part of the zone.

Size: S=10–25' tall; M=26–50' tall; T=51–80' tall; X=90' tall or more.

CONIFEROUS

Name	Zone 2	3	4	5	6	7	8	9	10	Size	Comments
White cedar (Arborvitae) *Thuja occidentalis*	▓	▓	▓							T	Reddish bark. Dark green to yellow leaves. Many varieties.
Hemlock *Tsuga canadensis*	▓	▓	▓							T-X	Shiny leaves. Shallow roots. Likes moist, slightly acid soil.
White spruce *Picea glauca*	▓	▓	▓							T-X	Bluish-green foliage, drooping tips. Some smaller forms.
Chinese juniper *Juniperus chinensis*	▓	▓	▓							M-T	Pollution-tolerant. Many varieties.
Red pine *Pinus resinosa*	▓	▓	▓							T	Prone to pine bud moth. Shiny, flexible needles. Fast-growing.
Austrian pine *Pinus nigra*	▓	▓	▓							T-X	Fast-growing. Likes alkaline soil. Pyramid shape.
Eastern red cedar *Juniper virginiana*	▓	▓	▓							T-X	Little blue berries. Stripping reddish bark. Likes rocky soil.
White fir *Abies concolor*	▓	▓	▓							T-X	Spicy-smelling needles. Big cones. Hardy. Fast-grower.
Colorado spruce *Picea pungens*	▓	▓	▓							X	Green-blue leaves. Hardy. Susceptible to spruce gall, aphids.
False cypress *Chamaecyparis* sp.			▓	▓	▓					S-X	Size depends on kind. Likes soil a bit acid. Needs pruning.
Oriental arborvitae *Platycladus orientalis*			▓	▓	▓					T-X	Bright green leaves with egg-shaped cones. Many varieties.
Ponderosa pine *Pinus ponderosa*			▓	▓	▓					X	Fast-growing. Dark green needles. Needs space.
Douglas fir *Pseudotsunga menziesi*				▓	▓					X	Fast-growing and hardy. Blue-green needles. Egg-shaped cones.

TREE CHARTS (cont.)
CONIFEROUS (cont.)

Name	Zone									Size	Comments
	2	3	4	5	6	7	8	9	10		
Atlas cedar *Cedrus atlantica*					■	■	■	■		T-X	Fast-growing. Dark green needles. Needs space.
Italian cypress *Cupressus sempervirens*						■	■			T-X	Fast-growing and hardy. Blue-green needles. Egg-shaped cones.
Aleppo pine *Pinus halepensis*						■	■	■	■	T	Pale green. Does well in coastal areas.

EVERGREEN

Name	Zone									Size	Comments
	2	3	4	5	6	7	8	9	10		
Shamel ash *Fraxinus uhdei*			b	■	■	■	■	■		S-T	Semi-evergreen. Shiny bright green leaves. Rounded.
American holly *Ilex opaca*					■	■	■	■		M	Dull leaves. Red fruit. Likes sun or part shade.
Holly *Ilex aquifolium*					■	■	■			M-T	Shiny green leaves, red berries. Plant male and female together.
Privet *Ligustrum*						b	■	■		S-M	Long, glossy, pointed leaves. Late summer flowers.
Strawberry tree *Arbutus unedo*						b	■	■		S	Toothed leaves, red stems. Fall flowers, strawberry-like fruit.
Cork oak *Quercus suber*							■	■		M-T	Tree that cork comes from. Twisted branches. Grows fast.
Live oak *Quercus virginiana*							■	■		T-X	Hardy, fast-growing. Spreads wide. Hairy undersides on leaves.
Camphor tree *Cinnamomum camphora*							b	■		M	Leaves smell of camphor when crushed. Greedy roots.
Olive *Olea europaea*							b	■		S-T	Silvery leaves. Contorted shape. Fruit needs processing.
Red box gum *Eucalyptus polyanthemos*							b	■		T-X	Gray-green leaves. Clustered small flowers. Tolerant of heat.
California pepper tree *Shinus molle*							b	■		M	Gnarled branches, lacy foliage. Yellow flowers. Rosy fruit.
Blue gum eucalyptus *Eucalyptus globulus*							b	■		X	Medicinal smell. Messy. Fast-growing. Easily storm-damaged.
Citrus (various)								■	■	S	Large trees like grapefruit need 25 feet of space, others less.

EVERGREEN (cont.)

Name	Zone 2	3	4	5	6	7	8	9	10	Size	Comments
Carob or St. John's bread *Ceratonia siliqua*								▓	▓	S-M	Shiny green leaves. Source of chocolate-tasting powder.
Cootamundra wattle *Acacia baileyana*								▓	▓	S-M	Bluish-gray leaves, yellow winter flowers. Need water while young.
Jerusalem thorn *Parkinsonia aculeata*							b	▓	▓	S-M	Green bark and lacy foliage. Fragrant spring flowers; pods.
Loquat *Eribotyra japonica*								▓	▓	S-M	Long, stiff leaves. Fragrant fall flowers. Delicious yellow fruit.
Mayten *Maytenus boe[a]ria*								▓	▓	S-M	Toothed leaves. Tiny flowers. Pendulous. Good on terraces.
Mexican blue palm *Erythea armata*								▓	▓	S-M	Fan-shaped tree. White flowers, shiny leaves, yellow fruits.
Mexican fan palm *Washingtonia robusta*								▓	▓	S-M	Fan-shaped. Fibrous matter covers trunk.
Cajeput tree *Melaleica leucadendra*								▓	▓	M	Light green leaves. Cream-colored flower clusters. Bark sheds.
Canary Island date palm *Phoenix canariensis*								▓	▓	M-T	Long feather-like leaves. Fruit hanging in clusters. Thick trunk.
Floss-silk tree *Chorisia speciosa*								▓	▓	M-T	Large yellow, pink, red, or purple lily-shaped flowers. Thorny.
California fan palm *Washingtonia filifera*								▓	▓	T	Spiny stalks, gray-green fan-shaped leaves. Good in dry soil.
Coconut palm *Cocus nucifera*									▓	T	Huge feathery leaves. Coconuts. Thrives at seaside.
Bauhinia or orchid *Bauhinia variegata*									▓	S	White, pink, purplish flowers. Likes soil a bit acid.
Mock-orange *Murraya paniculata*									▓	S	Glossy compound leaves. Flowers smell like jasmine.

DECIDUOUS

Name	Zone 2	3	4	5	6	7	8	9	10	Size	Comments
American linden *Tilia americana*	▓	▓	▓	▓	▓	▓	▓			M-X	White summer flowers attract bees. Blue berries. Yellow fall leaves.
Canoe or paper birch *Betula papyrifera*	▓	▓	▓	▓						T-X	White peeling bark. Likes moist soil. Best grown in groups of two to four.

TREE CHARTS (cont.)

DECIDUOUS (cont.)

Name	2	3	4	5	6	7	8	9	10	Size	Comments
Weeping birch *Betula pendula*	■	■	■	■	■					M-T	White bark. Yellow fall leaves. Short-lived, susceptible to borers.
Mountain ash *Sorbus aucuparia*		■	■	■	■	■				S-M	White spring flower clusters. Red berries in fall. Susceptible to borers.
Ohio buckeye *Aesculus glabra*		■	■	■	■	■	■			S-M	White-green flowers, inedible nuts. Young leaves and seeds poisonous.
Small-leaved Eur. linden *Tilia cordata*		■	■	■	■	■	■			M-X	White fragrant flowers, blue berries. Pyramidal shape. Good city tree.
Sugar maple *Acer saccharum*		■	■	■	■	■	■			M-T	The maple syrup tree. Bright green leaves turn yellow, orange, red in fall.
Yellowwood *Cladrastis lutea*			■	■	■	■	■			M-T	White flower clusters. Gray bark. Bright leaves turn yellow to orange.
Carolina silver-bell *Halesia carolina*			■	■	■	■	■	■		S-M	Bell-shaped white spring flowers. Likes rich soil. Vulnerable to wind.
Common horse chestnut *Aesculus hippocastanum*		■	■	■	■	■	■			M-T	White flowers, inedible nuts. Leaves poisonous in spring.
Scarlet oak *Quercus coccinea*			■	■	■	■	■	■		T	Shiny green leaves turn scarlet in fall. Slightly acid soil. Don't transplant.
Silver maple *Acer saccharinum*		■	■	■	■	■	■	■		X	Yellow orange fall leaves. Moist soil. Prone to iron- deficiency chlorosis.
Apple serviceberry *Amelanchier grandiflora*		■	■	■	■	■	■			S-M	Yellow and orange fall leaves. White spring flowers, then edible berries.
Bradford pear *Pyrus calleryana 'Bradford'*			■	■	■	■	■			S-M	White flower clusters, fruit inedible by humans but attractive to birds.
Norway maple *Acer platanoides*			■	■	■	■	■			M-X	Little yellow spring flowers. Yellow fall leaves. Hardy, with shallow roots.
Red horse chestnut *Aesculus carnea*			■	■	■	■	■	■		M-T	Red and pink flower spikes. Hardy. Reddish leaves, turn yellow in fall.
Red oak *Quercus borealis* or *Q.rubra*		■	■	■	■	■	■			T	Red fall leaves.
Honey locust *Gleditsia triacanthos*			■	■	■	■	■	■		M-X	Ferny leaves. "Moraine" variety lacks thorns. Pods over a foot long.
Blireiana plum *Prunus blireiana*			■	■	■	■	■	■		S-M	Small pink flowers, copper or purple leaves. Needs frequent pruning.
Oriental cherry *Prunus serrulata*				■	■	■	■	■		S	Pink or white fragrant flowers, yellow fall leaves. Varieties differ in size.

DECIDUOUS (cont.)

Name	Zone 2	3	4	5	6	7	8	9	10	Size	Comments
Kentucky coffee tree *Gymnocladus dioica*				▓	▓	▓	▓	▓		M-T	Very large leaves, staying green in fall. Flat pods.
European beech *Fagus sylvatica*				▓	▓	▓	▓	▓		M-X	Dark green, toothed leaves. Copper beech and Fernleaf beech on short side.
Golden chain tree *Laburnum watereri vossi*				▓	▓	▓	▓	▓		S-M	Long, hanging clusters of yellow flowers. Seeds and leaves poisonous.
Saucer magnolia *Magnolia soulangiana*				▓	▓	▓	▓	▓		S	Large, purple-white, cup-shaped flowers. Sometimes multi-trunked.
Franklinia *Franklinia alatamaha*				▓	▓	▓	▓	▓		S-M	Big, shiny, bright green leaves. Large, white, fragrant fall flowers. Pyramidal.
Japanese snowbell *Styrax japonica*				▓	▓	▓	▓	▓		S-M	Slender. Bell-shaped fragrant summer flowers in clusters. Hardy.
Washington hawthorn *Crataegus phaenopyrum*				▓	▓	▓	▓	▓		S-M	Early summer white flowers. Tiny fruit hangs on into winter.
Ginkgo *Gingko biloba*				▓	▓	▓	▓	▓		S-T	Use male trees only. Female fruit smells bad. Fan-shaped leaves.
London plane tree *Platanus acerifolia*				▓	▓	▓	▓	▓		M-T	Fruits in twos. Cream-colored bark peels to reveal yellow inner bark.
Pin oak *Quercus palustris*				▓	▓	▓	▓	▓		M-T	Finely toothed leaves, turn red in fall. Fast-growing.
Sour gum tree *Nyssa sylvatica*				▓	▓	▓	▓	▓		M-T	Dark green leaves, turning orange to red in fall. Will live in wet soil.
Tulip tree *Liridendron tulipfera*				▓	▓	▓	▓	▓		T-X	Yellow and orange tulip-shaped flowers. Needs rich, moist soil.
Chaste tree *Vitex agnus-castus*				▓	▓	▓	▓	▓		S	Summer-fall lavender-blue or white flowers. Pleasant smell when crushed.
Cockspur hawthorn *Crataegus crus-galli*				▓	▓	▓	▓	▓		S-M	White flowers in clusters. Shiny leaves. Hardy and thorny.
Eastern redbud *Cercis canadensis*				▓	▓	▓	▓	▓		S-M	Heart-shaped leaves, yellow in fall. Flowers in red and pink shades.
Flowering dogwood *Cornus florida*				▓	▓	▓	▓	▓		S-M	Pink and white flower-like bracts. Red fruits attract birds. Bright fall leaves.
Japanese pagoda tree *Sophora japonica*				▓	▓	▓	▓	▓		S-T	Sweet-pea-like flowers in long clusters. Pods like bead chains. Good city tree.

TREE CHARTS (cont.)

DECIDUOUS (cont.)

Name	Zone									Size	Comments
	2	3	4	5	6	7	8	9	10		
Zelkova *Zelkova carpinifolia*				▓	▓	▓	▓	▓		M-X	Slow-growing. Vase shape. Hardy, low maintenance. Yellow to red fall leaves.
Goldenrain tree *Koelreuteria paniculata*				b	▓	▓	▓	▓		S-M	Long clusters of yellow flowers. Tan and yellow seed pods. Likes sun.
Yulan magnolia *Magnolia denudata*				▓	▓	▓	▓	▓		M	Needs 30-foot space. Huge white fragrant flowers in late spring.
Chinese redbud *Cercis chinensis*					▓	▓	▓	▓		S-M	Rose-purple spring flowers. Heart-shaped leaves, yellow in fall.
Higan cherry *Prunus subhirtella*					▓	▓	▓	▓		S-M	Pink flowers. Blue-black fruit. Yellow fall leaves. Weeping variety available.
Arizona ash *Fraxinus velutina*					▓	▓	▓	▓		M	Modesto ash (*Fraxinus velunita 'modesto'*) tolerates drought.
Chinese pistachio *Pistacia chinensis*					▓	▓	▓	▓		M-T	Sumac-like leaves. Tolerant of alkaline soil, heat, dryness. Fast-growing.
Sugarberry hackberry *Celtis laevigata*					▓	▓	▓	▓		M-X	Broad tree, resistant of witches' broom. Orange fruit turns purple. Birds like it.
Willow oak *Quercus phellos*					▓	▓	▓	▓		M-X	Thin leaves, turning yellow in fall. Likes soil a bit acid. Grows fast.
Pacific dogwood *Prunus nuttali*					▓	▓	▓	a		T	Slender. White flowers with 4-6 bracts, midspring, perhaps in fall. Red fruit.
American sweet gum *Liquidambar styraciflua*					▓	▓	▓	▓	a	T-X	Star-shaped leaves. Round, thorny seed balls. Fragrant gum in crevices.
Crape myrtle *Lagerstroemia indica*						▓	▓	▓		S	Purple, red, pink, or white flowers. Yellow, orange, and red fall leaves.
Silk tree, Mimosa tree *Albizzia julibrissin*					▓	▓	▓	▓		S-M	Feathery leaves; pink, puffy flowers. Likes dry soil, low fertilization.
Carolina cherry-laurel *Prunus laurocerasus*						b	▓	▓		S	Fragrant white flower clusters. Black fruit. Don't eat leaves or fruit.
European hackberry *Celtis australis*						▓	▓	▓		M-T	Likes moist soil. Resistant to disease, drought, pests. Good substitute for elm.
Coral tree *Erythrina*								▓		M	Red flower clusters, long seed pods. Thorny branches. Poisonous seeds.
Jacaranda *Jacaranda acutifolia*							b	▓		M-T	Violet summer flowers. Feathery leaves. Needs sun. Good street tree.

Backyard Wildlife Habitats

Encroaching humans with their houses and shopping malls have stolen habitats from wildlife. In your backyard you can help to redress the balance by creating a lifesaving ecosystem for many animals—birds, butterflies, bats, squirrels, raccoons, chipmunks, skunks, frogs. The advantage for you—besides the obvious one of your enjoyment from watching the animals—is that you will spend less time and money keeping up your yard.

In the early 1970s, the National Wildlife Federation began the Backyard Wildlife Habitat program through which you can get certification for building a habitat. Since then, the program has grown—more than 12,000 backyards and other properties (a firehouse and miniature golf course among them) have been certified.

What exactly is a Backyard Wildlife Habitat? Simple: landscaping for the needs of wildlife. To be certified, you can have a very small area, as small as a few square feet. But you must show that you have provided:

♦ Food: trees and plants (see next section), feeders for birds, squirrels; birdseed, insects (for lizards and toads).

♦ Water (for drinking and bathing): birdbaths, ponds, water gardens, dripping hose, dish.

♦ Cover: shrubs, crown vetch, a discarded Christmas tree, a dead tree trunk, brush piles, rocks, stone walls.

♦ A place to raise young: heavy cover, birdhouses, squirrel boxes, water (for frogs, salamanders, other reptiles, insects).

You also must send in snapshots and a sketch of the habitat along with a $15 fee. Write to: **National Register of Backyard Wildlife Habitats,** National Wildlife Federation, 1400 16th Street NW, Washington, DC 20036 (202-797-6800).

Trees, Shrubs, and Plants that Provide Food for Wildlife

The National Wildlife Federation suggests utilizing native trees, shrubs, and flowers that usually require less water, fertilizer, and pest control. Ask your state fish and game department to suggest what to plant to attract wildlife. Vary the heights of plants so you have layers of foliage. Consider plants and trees that hold berries into winter: pyracantha, holly, juniper, dogwood, madrone, toyon, bayberry, bittersweet. Include a firebreak, which can be as simple as a mowed path. Once planting is done, try to conserve even more water through mulching and other practices.

To attract hummingbirds: Plant tubular flowers bearing nectar. You can also put out feeders containing a mixture of four parts water to one part sugar. (Don't use honey or red dye.) You should change the sugar water and clean the feeder every three days.

Consider:

acacia	lantana
butterfly weed	lobelia
butterfly bush	morning glory
delphinium	nasturtium
echeveria	nicotiana
eucalyptus	penstemon
fireburst	phlox
fuchsia	red buckeye
hollyhocks	salvia
impatiens	sweet William

To attract other birds: Plant a variety of seed- and fruit-bearing trees, grasses, and plants. Consider:

barberry	holly
bayberry	honeysuckle
black cherry	jewelweed
blackberry, blueberry	juniper
blazing star	mulberry
bluestem grass	oak
buckthorn	phlox
columbine	pine and cedar trees
coralbells	sunflower
cotoneaster	thistle
elderberry	trumpet creeper
flowering crab apple	viburnum
grape holly	Virginia creeper

PLANT PREFERENCES OF SOME BUTTERFLIES

alfalfa	Yellow and Orange Sulphurs
American elm	Mourning Cloak
ash	Tiger Swallowtail
birch	Tiger Swallowtail
black locust	Silver-Spotted Skipper
blueberry	Spring Azure
boneset	Tiger Swallowtail
borage	Silver-Spotted Skipper, Painted Lady
burdock	Silver-Spotted Skipper, Painted Lady, American Painted Lady
butterfly bush (*Buddleia davidii, Buddleia alternifolia*)	Monarch, West Coast Lady, Painted Lady, Tiger Swallowtail
buttonbush	Hairstreak
carrot	Black Swallowtail
cherry	Spring Azure, Viceroy, Tiger Swallowtail
clover	Yellow and Orange Sulphurs, Tiger Swallowtail (red)
clover, red	Black Swallowtail
cosmos	Monarch
dill	Black Swallowtail
dogbane	American Painted Lady
dogwood	Spring Azure
elm	Mourning Cloak
fennel	Black Swallowtail
goldenrod	Monarch, American Painted Lady
heliotrope	Painted Lady
hollyhock	Painted Lady
honeysuckle	Tiger Swallowtail
hops	Red Admiral
knapweed	Painted Lady
kudzu	Silver-Spotted Skipper, Painted Lady
lance-leaved coreopsis	Skippers
lantana	Monarch, West Coast Lady
lilac	Monarch, Tiger Swallowtail
locust	Silver-Spotted Skipper Painted Lady
lovage	Black Swallowtail
milkweed	Monarch, Tiger Swallowtail, Baltimore, Checkerspot

mint	Monarch, American Painted Lady
nettles	Silver-Spotted Skipper, Painted Lady, Red Admiral
parsley	Red Admiral, Black Swallowtail
phlox	Tiger Swallowtail
plantain	Baltimore
plum	Coral Hairstreak
poplar	Mourning Cloak, Viceroy, Tiger Swallowtail
privet	Spring Azure
purple loosestrife	Red Admiral
pussytoes	American Painted Lady
pussywillow	Mourning Cloak
rabbit tobacco	American Painted Lady
rose of Sharon	West Coast Lady
rue	Black Swallowtail
seed grasses	Common Wood Nymph
sumac	Spring Azure
sunflower	Silver-Spotted Skipper, Painted Lady
sweet pepperbush	Hairstreak
thistle	Silver-Spotted Skipper, Painted Lady, Great Spangled Fritillary, Tiger Swallowtail, Red Admiral
tickseed sunflower	Monarch
tick trefoil	Silver-Spotted Skipper, Painted Lady
trefoil	Yellow and Orange Sulphurs
tulip tree	Tiger Swallowtail
turtlehead	Baltimore
vetch	Yellow and Orange Sulphurs
viburnum	Spring Azure
violet	Great Spangled Fritillary
white ash	Tiger Swallowtail
wild anise	Addis Swallowtail
wild cherry	Coral Hairstreak, Tiger Swallowtail
willow	Mourning Cloak, Viceroy, Tiger Swallowtail
wisteria	Silver-Spotted Skipper
wormwood	Silver-Spotted Skipper, Painted Lady, American Painted Lady
zinnia	American Painted Lady

National Wildflower Research Center, Austin, Texas. For $2, the center will supply, for your state, a wildflower list and the addresses of nearby native-plant nurseries and sources for wild seeds.

Department of the Interior, U.S. Fish and Wildlife Service, Washington, DC 20240, has pamphlets on building birdhouses and on feeding birds in your backyard.

National Wildlife Federation, 1400 16th Street NW, Washington, DC 20036 (202-797-6800).

Attracting Butterflies

In a butterfly garden, plants are tattered, but butterflies provide a feast of color for the eyes. For a successful one, locate it in a warm, protected place. Plant flowers in big clumps so butterflies can find them. Some butterflies tend to eat one kind of plant when in the larval stage, another when mature. Monarch larvae, for example, eat only milkweed, while mature monarchs sip nectar from a variety of flowers. Plan your garden so that flowers will be blooming throughout the growing season. Purple is the favorite color of butterflies, so keep that in mind when choosing flowers to plant. (They also like orange, pink, lavender, yellow, and white.)

Provide water and some large, dark-colored stones where butterflies can sunbathe. Don't use pesticide.

Butterfly World, 3600 West Sample Road, Coconut Creek, FL 33073 (305-977-4434).

BUILDING A BAT HOUSE

If you have mosquitoes, why not build a house to attract bats—they will eat the little bloodsuckers. They will also eat moths, corn earworms, and cucumber beetles. You can buy a bat house or plans for a bat house from **Bat Conservation International,** PO Box 162603, Austin, TX 78716 (512-327-9721).

5

FAMILY

PARENTING

COUPLES—MARRIED/NOT MARRIED

PARENTING

Quotes on Parenting

Parenting is a mighty serious job. However, maintaining a good sense of humor is sometimes the only way to preserve your sanity. Thus, here are some entertaining observations and advice from sages of the past, and the present, to keep you afloat when the going gets tough.

I have found the best way to give advice to your children is to find out what they want and then advise them to do it.

—HARRY S TRUMAN

When I was a boy of fourteen, my father was so ignorant I could hardly stand to have the old man around. But when I got to be twenty-one, I was astonished at how much he had learned in seven years.

—MARK TWAIN

There are times when parenthood seems nothing but feeding the mouth that bites you.

—PETER DE VRIES

Parents are people who bear children, bore teenagers, and board newlyweds.

—ANONYMOUS

Oh, what a tangled web do parents weave
When they think that their children are naive.

—OGDEN NASH

Children aren't happy with nothing to ignore,
And that's what parents were created for.

—OGDEN NASH

To be a successful father there's one absolute rule: when you have a kid, don't look at it for the first two years.

—ERNEST HEMINGWAY

It sometimes happens, even in the best of families, that a baby is born. This is not necessarily cause for alarm. The important thing is to keep your wits about you and borrow some money.

—ELINOR GOULDING SMITH

The secret of dealing successfully with a child is not to be its parent.

—MELL LAZARUS

The best way to keep children at home is to make the home atmosphere pleasant, and let the air out of the tires.

—DOROTHY PARKER

My dad once gave me a few words of wisdom which I've always tried to live by. He said, "Son, never throw a punch at a redwood."

—TOM SELLECK in *Magnum, P.I.*

Mothers are fonder than fathers of their children because they are more certain they are their own.

—ARISTOTLE

The reason grandparents and grandchildren get along so well is that they have a common enemy.

—SAM LEVENSON

The first half of our lives is ruined by our parents and the second half by our children.

—CLARENCE DARROW

Literature is mostly about having sex and not much about having children. Life is the other way around.

—DAVID LODGE

Never raise your hand to your children—it leaves your mid-section unprotected.

—ROBERT ORBEN

I could now afford all the things I never had as a kid, if I didn't have kids.

—ROBERT ORBEN

Youth is such a wonderful thing. What a crime to waste it on children.

—GEORGE BERNARD SHAW

If God wanted sex to be fun, He wouldn't have included children as punishment.

—ED BLUESTONE

Happiness is having a large, loving, caring, close-knit family in another city.

—GEORGE BURNS

Babies on television never spit up on the Ultrasuede.

—ERMA BOMBECK

The children despise their parents until the age of forty, when they suddenly become just like them—thus preserving the system.

—QUENTIN CREWE

Before I got married I had six theories about bringing up children, now I have six children, and no theories.

—JOHN WILMONT

Day Care

The growth of two-income families and single-parent families has increased the need for day-care services for young children. Overall, U.S. families are spending upwards of $30 billion a year for child care. In general, this care falls into three basic categories: in-home care, day-care centers, and family day care.

In-Home Care

In-home care providers can be found through want ads or employment agencies. There are even specialized employment agencies that will help you find a nanny or an au pair. However appealing in-home care is—a safe, familiar, convenience—only about 4 percent of all families can afford in-home care since it costs two to four times as much as day-care facilities. In addition, when you hire someone to work in your home, you become an employer and the IRS expects you to pay each year for the caregiver's Social Security and unemployment taxes. For more details about the tax rules for in-home caregivers, call the IRS at 800-829-3676 and ask for IRS Publication 503.

Live-in nannies are becoming increasingly popular, but to date the majority of them have not received any kind of professional education. However, their popularity has spawned more than 60 nanny schools nationwide which teach classes on basic subjects like nutrition, safety, and child development. For help in finding a nanny, contact: **International Nanny Association**, 125 S. 4th Street, Norfolk, NE 68701 (402-691-9628). This group publishes a directory of placement agencies and training programs.

An au pair (which means "on par" in French) is a young (usually between 18 and 25 years old) English-speaking foreigner who is brought to the United States by a host group, like Au Pair in America, for one year. Host families provide room and board and a salary as well as an agency fee which includes transportation costs. For more information on au pairs, contact one of the following two agencies: **Au Pair in America,** The American Institute for Foreign Study, 102 Greenwich Avenue, Greenwich, CT 06830 (800-727-2437); **Au Pair/Homestay USA,** The Experiment in International Living, 1015 15th Street NW, Suite 750, Washington, DC 20005 (202-408-5380).

It's important to note that there are no government laws or regulations for in-home care. While many employment agencies screen applicants and do background checks, you, as a parent, are ultimately responsible for selecting the person who will care for your child.

Day-Care Centers

Approximately 28 percent of preschoolers attend day-care centers. There are about 80,000 of them nationwide. These centers are also called child care centers, learning centers, preschools, and nursery schools. Some are independent businesses and others are sponsored by churches, schools, social service agencies, colleges, and universities. A growing number of American companies are also sponsoring on-site care facilities for their employees.

On average, state and local government agencies inspect day-care centers about once every two years. To find out more about the regulation and licensing of facilities in your area, call your state department of social services. Another source of licensing and accreditation information is the National Association for the Education of Young Children (NAEYC). This group accredits high-quality day-care centers throughout the country. Write or call: **NAEYC,** 1509 16th Street NW, Washington, DC 20036 (202-232-8777; 800-424-2460).

Family Day Care

Child care provided in a private home is called family day care. Oftentimes, the caregivers have children of their own. Estimates of the number of these kinds of caregivers range from 500,000 to more than 1 million. About 19 percent of children

under the age of five participate in family day care. Since the majority are small businesses, many forgo the complicated, time-consuming process necessary for licensing and accreditation. However, more and more are seeking licenses in an effort to present themselves as professional caregivers as opposed to mere baby-sitters.

Family-day-care homes usually are inspected every three to five years. To find out if a family-day-care home is licensed or registered with your state, call your state department of social services. Information on accredited family-day-care providers is also available from the **National Association for Family Child Care,** 800-359-3817.

When you visit a child care setting, there are a number of things you need to know in order to evaluate the provider. The following checklist was compiled by the American Academy of Pediatrics. You might want to make photocopies of the questions and take the list with you when you go to various child care facilities.

What Parents Should Ask About . . .

1. Is the child care center/home licensed or registered with local government? (Ask to see a current document and find out what type of inspection was done.)
2. Can you visit the facility during normal operating hours before registering your child in the program?
3. Will the staff allow you to examine all areas your child will use?
4. Are parents always welcome visitors?
5. Is there a written plan for play and learning activities that includes active play, quiet play, nap/rest time, and snacks and meals? (Ask to see it.)
6. Are there regular opportunities for inside and outside play, and are children supervised at all times?
7. Is television viewing limited to short times and child-appropriate programs?
8. Does the center offer parenting classes or other family support?

9. Is each child assigned to one caregiver who is primarily responsible for his/her care on a regular basis? (Even if other caregivers are involved with the child's group.)

10. Does the caregiver regularly meet with parents? (Ask how often.)

11. Is there a written policy about discipline? (Ask to read it.)

12. Is smoking banned from the child care center or home during the hours children are in care?

13. Are there written policies for the care of ill children that include the responsibilities of parents? (Ask to see the policies.)

14. What is the plan for the care of ill children? Is there a quiet, well-supervised arrangement for the care of ill children until parents pick them up?

15. Will the caregivers give prescribed medications to your children? (If yes, under what conditions?)

16. Is there a health specialist, such as a pediatrician or nurse, that serves as a consultant for the child care program?

17. Have staff members and volunteers had training in child development and providing a learning environment for children? If yes, when was the last time they received training in first aid and the prevention of injury and infection?

18. How long have the caregivers been working at this child care center/home? Do you believe they are experienced, qualified caregivers?

19. Are there arrangements if a caregiver gets sick or has to be away?

20. Can you get recommendations and advice from parents whose children are currently in the program?

21. Are all the costs written out and available for you to read?

What Parents Should Look For . . .

1. Are there enough adult caregivers present at all times? (The desirable range for child care centers is: one adult per three infants less than 24 months old, one adult per four children 25–30 months old, one adult per five children 31–35 months old, one adult per seven children aged 3 years old, one adult per eight children ages 4 and 5 years old.)

2. Does the staff appear to enjoy caring for the children?

3. Is the center/home bright, cheerful, and well ventilated? Is all equipment clean, safe, and well maintained?

4. Do the children in the program appear to be happy?

5. Is the noise level within the child care areas at a comfortable level?

6. Do the adults and the children often talk with each other? Are children encouraged to talk with each other?

7. Does there appear to be enough indoor space for the number of children present? (See if there is a clear area, not including furniture, measuring 35 square feet per child. This is usually equivalent to 50 square feet measured wall-to-wall.)

8. Is there a sleeping (quiet) area large enough for all the children to rest during nap time? (There should be 3 feet of space between cots, cribs, or mats.)

9. Are there individual beds, cots, or mats to sleep on?

10. Are the toilets and sinks clean and easy to reach? Can children reach clean towels, liquid soap, and toilet paper?

11. Is there a clean diaper-changing area for infants? Is a sink well within the caregiver's reach by the diaper-changing surface?

12. Does each child have a place for his/her own belongings?

13. Are infants always fed sitting up, with an adult present during meals and snacks?

14. Is all the food nutritious, well prepared and well served? Are you able to check the menus and meal plans?

15. Are there many toys present that are accessible, safe, and appropriate for your child's age group?

16. Is there an outside play area that is free of

sharp edges, pinch points, sharp rocks, and ditches?

17. Is the outside area free of hazards such as hard surfaces, rocks, high climbers, tall slides, and unsafe swings?

18. Is playground equipment age appropriate, properly installed, and well maintained?

19. Is there impact-absorbing material such as sand, wood chips, or rubber outdoor mats in all areas where children might fall?

20. Do adults closely supervise outside play? Can adults always easily see all the children on the playground?

21. Is your first reaction to the program that it would be a good place for your child?

Child-care checklist reprinted with permission from, "Child Care: What's Best for Your Family," the American Academy of Pediatrics.

Home Alone: Is Your Child Ready?

Project Home Safe, a venture of the Whirlpool Corporation and the American Home Economics Association, has prepared the following checklist which will help you evaluate your child's readiness.

Is your child physically ready to stay alone? Is your child able to:
- [ ] Lock and unlock the doors and windows of your home?
- [ ] Perform everyday tasks such as fixing a sandwich, dialing the telephone, and writing messages?

Is your child mentally ready to stay alone? Does your child:
- [ ] Tell time?
- [ ] Understand what "stranger" and "emergency" mean?
- [ ] Recognize danger and know how to stay safe?

- [ ] Solve small problems on his or her own, but know when to get help?
- [ ] Consider how his or her actions affect others?

Is your child socially ready to stay alone? Does your child:
- [ ] Solve conflicts with brothers and sisters with little help from adults?
- [ ] Talk easily to you about what happens at school, and about his or her feelings?
- [ ] Feel confident enough to contact another adult if a problem arises?

Is your child emotionally ready to stay alone? Does your child:
- [ ] Feel confident and secure when alone?
- [ ] Seem willing to stay alone?
- [ ] Know how to handle fear, loneliness, or boredom?
- [ ] Know how to handle responsibility, such as getting ready for school on time and looking out for younger brothers and sisters?

You may have to do some detective work to answer these questions. Try asking your child to open a window, fix a sandwich, take a message, and answer the door. Play "What if?" games to learn if your child could handle emergency situations safely. Ask, for example, what should be done if the smoke alarm sounds or if he or she gets a bad cut when home alone. Whenever possible, have your child act out his or her response. Sometimes children can give the right answer but can't do what is needed.

If you can answer "yes" to most of the above questions, your child is showing signs of the physical, mental, social, and emotional maturity needed for self-care. Your child needs to be capable in each of these four areas before he or she will be safe and secure staying home alone.

Reprinted with permission from "Assessing Your Child's Readiness for Self Care," American Home Economics Association.

Baby-Sitter Guidelines

The baby-sitter you hire should be capable, mature, experienced, and responsible. Once you have carefully interviewed and selected a sitter, you need to provide the sitter with adequate information and instructions to do a good job.

Hiring a Baby-Sitter

1. The best way to find a baby-sitter is through recommendations from family, friends, and neighbors. Another option is to advertise for a sitter in your local newspaper or check the yellow pages of your phone directory for professional baby-sitting services.

2. When interviewing a baby-sitter, ask about the sitter's previous experience and whether or not the sitter has had any formal child-care training like a first-aid or CPR course. Get the name of several parents the sitter has worked for recently and check out those references.

3. Introduce your child to the baby-sitter and observe how they interact. Does your child respond favorably to the sitter? Does the sitter seem genuinely interested in and comfortable with your child?

4. Discuss the duties and responsibilities of the job with the sitter and make sure you have agreed upon an hourly pay rate.

5. If your child has any special medical or behavioral problems, talk them over with the sitter so that you are comfortable that the sitter can handle them.

6. Invent an emergency situation and ask the sitter how he or she would handle it.

What the Sitter Needs to Know

1. Tell the sitter where you will be, what time you will return, and a telephone number where you can be reached. Write everything down. Also, make a written list of other important phone numbers: fire department, police department, ambulance service, child's doctor, poison control center, neighbors. The phone numbers should be left in an accessible place, preferably next to the telephone. Be sure the sitter knows your exact street address and how to give instructions to get to your house should an emergency situation occur.

2. Give the sitter full instructions on the child's eating, playing, and bedtime routines. Let the sitter know the house rules on watching television, doing homework, snacks, etc.

3. Take a tour of the house so the baby-sitter knows where to find the child's clothing and toys as well as where to find a flashlight, electricity and gas shutoffs, a fire extinguisher, first-aid kit, the house alarm system. If there are any hazardous conditions in your home, point them out. Show the sitter how to lock and unlock doors and windows.

4. Be very specific about instructions that pertain to the safety of your child. How do you want the sitter to answer your telephone (it's not wise to let callers know that children are home alone with a sitter)? If someone comes to the door while you're away, what should the sitter do? Is the child allowed to play outside and if so, under what conditions? Are other children allowed in the house to play with your child? Is the sitter allowed to have any visitors?

5. Don't forget to make the sitter feel welcome by stocking the refrigerator with sodas and munchies. Also, show the sitter how to use the microwave, VCR, and stereo. If anything, like the computer, is off-limits, remember to say so.

Choosing a School for Your Child

Choosing an appropriate school for your child will take time and effort. Before evaluating particular schools, it is important to understand the various kinds of schools in your area. The following list of school options was prepared by the U.S. Department of Education.

Council on Family Health
Babysitter's Checklist

Emergency Telephone Numbers
Police_____
Fire_____
Ambulance/Rescue Squad_____
Hospital Emergency Room_____
Poison Control Center_____
Doctor_____
Pharmacy_____
Parent's Location/Number_____

Other Emergency Contact_____
Neighbor_____
Taxi Service_____

Home of_____
Address_____
Phone number_____

Special Instructions
Medicine_____
_____
Allergies_____
Diet_____
_____

Other Information
Bedtime/Naps_____
Meals/Snacks_____
Household Alarm System_____
Expected Visitors_____
_____
Location of Fire Extinguisher_____

Your Neighborhood Public School

In many public school systems, children attend a school in their neighborhood, according to an assignment system worked out by the school district. Attending a neighborhood public school can make it easy for your child to get to school and to visit friends. If your neighborhood provides a supportive community and the school offers a good program that meets your child's needs, a neighborhood school can be terrific.

Public "Schools of Choice"

In an increasing number of districts, you can choose to send your child to a special public school. These schools of choice are often called "magnet schools" or "alternative schools." Parents from all over the district can ask to have their children attend. If too many children apply, the district may admit children in the order they applied, by drawing names from a hat, or through some other selection mechanism. Racial integration may be one of the factors considered by the school system in such admissions.

Public schools of choice often emphasize a particular subject or have a special philosophy of education. One might emphasize science, art, or language study. Another might offer a firm code of conduct, a dress code, and a rigorous traditional academic program.

Other schools of choice may be designed to serve particular kinds of students. In many areas, students and their parents can decide whether to enroll in a vocational education program or school. There may also be within the public school system an alternative school designed to respond to students insufficiently challenged by the regular school program or likely to drop out.

Other Public Schools

Even if your district does not offer schools of choice, you may still want to investigate public schools around your home. One may be academically stronger than your neighborhood school, or have a special program that would be ideal for your child, or have a philosophy of teaching better suited to your family's values. Getting your child into a school outside your neighborhood may require extra effort. Still, it can often be done.

Church-Affiliated and Other Private Schools

In addition to public schools, there may be a variety of church-affiliated and other private schools available. These schools are all "schools of choice"; they were set up to accommodate parents' differing beliefs about how their children should be educated.

The majority of nonpublic schools are affiliated with a denomination, local church, or other religious organization. Many—but not all—are referred to as "parochial schools." The largest group is the Roman Catholic parochial school system. Lutheran, Calvinist, and other Protestant schools have been expanding in recent years. Jewish, Moslem, and Buddhist groups also have started schools in some communities.

There are also many private schools without a religious affiliation. Some private schools are traditional preparatory schools designed to train students for college; these often have an elite reputation and a long history. Others may be "alternative" schools set up for families and children who may be dissatisfied with various aspects of conventional schools.

If you have questions about public schools in your area, your telephone directory, the school district office, or the State Department of Education can probably help you.

For information on private or church-affiliated schools, you may want to consult your telephone directory or a published guide to nonpublic schools. For example, the Council for American Private Education represents 14 different church-affiliated and private school organizations and has developed *Private Schools of the United States*, a directory of schools in those organizations. If a copy is not available in your local library, you can order one from: **Council for American Private Education,** 1726 M Street NW, Suite 1102, Washington, DC 20036.

Checklist for Choosing a School

In looking at available schools, you may want to use the checklist below as a guide. During your school visit, you can confirm what you heard or read earlier. Once you select a school, you will want to double-check the admissions information you collected to make sure you meet all the requirements.

CURRICULUM

1. Thorough coverage of basic subjects?   ☐ Yes   ☐ No

If no, which subjects are not covered completely?

_____

2. A special focus or theme to the curriculum?   ☐ Yes   ☐ No

What is it?

_____

3. Elective offerings (if appropriate)?

_____

_____

4. Extracurricular programs to enhance learning and character development?

_____

_____

_____

PHILOSOPHY

5. Emphasis on a particular approach to teaching and learning?

_____

6. Belief that every child can learn?   ☐ Yes   ☐ No

7. Encouragement of attributes of good character?   ☐ Yes   ☐ No

IMPORTANT POLICIES

8. Discipline

_____

9. Drugs

_____

10. Homework, how much per subject?

_____

11. Homework hotlines?   ☐ Yes   ☐ No

12. Tutoring?   ☐ Yes   ☐ No

If yes, by whom? _____

13. Grades, feedback, and recognition: How often?

_____

What type? _____

_____

14. Teacher opportunities and incentives?

_____

PROOF OF RESULTS

15. Standardized test scores: Current _____ Past _____

16. Attendance rate: Students _____

Teachers _____

17. Graduation rate _____

18. How many leave school in a year? _____

Why? _____

19. Special achievements or honors for the school?

_____

SCHOOL RESOURCES

20. Staff backgrounds and qualifications? _____

_____

_____

21. Library?   ☐ Yes   ☐ No

22. Classroom books for independent reading?   ☐ Yes   ☐ No

23. Auditorium or other meeting room?   ☐ Yes   ☐ No

24. Physical education facilities?   ☐ Yes   ☐ No

If yes, what type? If no, what alternatives?

_____

PARENT AND COMMUNITY INVOLVEMENT

25. Parent volunteers in school?   ☐ Yes   ☐ No

Doing what?

_____

26. Teachers enlist parent cooperation on home learning?   ☐ Yes   ☐ No

If yes, how?

_____

_____

27. Other community members involved in school?   ☐ Yes   ☐ No

28. Partnerships with local businesses or other institutions?

_____

_____

REPUTATION

29. Views of parents with children in the school

_____

_____

_____

30. Views of friends and neighbors

_____

_____

_____

31. Views of community leaders

_____

_____

_____

SPECIAL QUESTIONS FOR PRIVATE AND CHURCH-AFFILIATED SCHOOLS

Financial obligations, including

32. Tuition? $_____

33. Other fees? $_____

34. Uniforms?   ☐ Yes   ☐ No

35. Book purchases?   ☐ Yes   ☐ No

36. Required participation in fund raising?   ☐ Yes   ☐ No

Financial assistance, including

37. Scholarships up to what percent of tuition? _____

38. Loans? _____

39. Reduced fees if more than one child enrolls? _____

40. State aid available to families? _____

41. Apply how and when? _____

_____

Other

42. School's age and financial status? _____

43. Religious instruction and activities? _____

_____

ADMISSIONS REQUIREMENTS AND PROCEDURES

For a public, church-affiliated, or other private school of choice

44. List of materials to submit (application form, transcript, test scores, references, etc.)

_____

_____

_____

45. Interview required?   ☐ Yes   ☐ No

Date _____ Time _____

46. Date school will decide? _____

47. How will school select students?

_____

_____

For other public schools

48. Borders of the attendance area the school usually serves?

_____

49. Does state law give you a right to transfer your child to another public school?

☐ Yes   ☐ No

50. Tuition or other charges for transferring students? $_____

51. Facts considered important in deciding whether to grant a request for a transfer?

_____

_____

52. When will a decision be made on transfer requests? _____

53. Names of district officials who can permit a child to transfer to a school outside that child's

attendance area

_____

_____

_____

Note: The above checklist was prepared by the U.S. Department of Education. It comes from an excellent 30-page booklet, "Choosing a School for Your Child." For a single free copy of the booklet, send your name and address to: **Choosing a School,** Consumer Information Center, Pueblo, CO 81009.

School Tests

It's estimated that every year students in U.S. schools spend 20 million school days to take 127 million separate tests. In general there are two basic kinds of tests, classroom tests and standardized tests. Classroom tests—quizzes, midterms, final exams—are prepared by the student's teacher and assess how much the student has learned in a particular subject area like reading, science, algebra, etc. Standardized tests are prepared by private test-making firms and their "sameness" enables educators to compare the scores of a student, or a class of students, with the scores of same-grade students, or classes of students in the same school system or in other school systems throughout the state or the entire country.

Test results are used in a number of ways. First of all, they help teachers and school administrators to assess what students have learned and what they still need to learn. In the case of standardized tests, a school district or state education agency can see how its system stacks up against other school systems. Local politicians and legislators use the scores as an accountability yardstick to measure the effectiveness of schools against the amount of taxpayer dollars invested in school systems.

The Basics of Standardized Tests

For the most part, they come in two basic models—one that tests achievement and another that tests ability. The most pervasive is the achievement test, which measures and evaluates what a student has already learned. By the time a student graduates from high school, he or she has probably taken at least one of the following standardized tests: the Comprehensive Test of Basic Skills, the California Achievement Test, the Iowa Test of Basic Skills, the Stanford Achievement Test, the Metropolitan Achievement Test, or the National Assessment of Educational Progress. The various academic skills tested range from reading comprehension, spelling, and listening skills to math, science, and social studies skills. Students who plan to enter college also take a standardized college entrance exam, either the SAT (Scholastic Aptitude Test) or the ACT (American College Testing assessment).

Standardized tests favor multiple-choice questions because they are efficient—can cover a wide range of subjects in a short amount of time—and because they can be inexpensively scored by computer. Critics complain that multiple-choice questions tend to test test-taking abilities rather than a student's thought process and what a student really knows. However, many states are currently experimenting with performance-based tests that ask students to analyze and explain answers as opposed to picking an answer from a list. While these kinds of tests are more expensive to score because they require the time of trained staff professionals, they are expected to become increasingly widespread.

Test results are accompanied by an explanation of how to interpret the scores. These information leaflets contain lots of jargon like national stanine, grade equivalent, scale score, national percentile, and percentile range. Be sure to read the definitions carefully before you attempt to understand test scores.

While the validity of achievement-based standardized tests stirs up minor controversy, the subject of ability-based tests can stir up full-scale verbal warfare. Ability tests supposedly predict what a student is capable of doing in the future, and the most commonly known ability test is the I.Q. or "intelligence quotient" test. An elementary school may administer an I.Q. test as early as the third grade. Advocates of the I.Q. test say it is an accurate measure of a student's fixed or innate capability, but critics say that I.Q. scores are affected by outside factors and thus can change over the course of a lifetime. In addition, critics challenge the validity of I.Q. tests when questions are included that show racial and cultural bias. Because I.Q. tests have become a hot button for many parents as well as educators, many school systems no longer give them.

Lessening Test Stress

The thought of taking a test, any kind of test, can be merely unnerving or can catapult a student into a state of high anxiety. Here are a few tips for parents and students to help reduce the stress.

Parents—

♦ Be supportive and positive. Explain that tests are a routine part of school—and of life. While they are a measurement tool, tests are not a complete assessment of knowledge and capabilities.

♦ If appropriate, help the student study for regular classroom tests. Go over study materials in a low-key manner and don't make studying an all-night session.

♦ Help familiarize students with formats and time limitations of standardized tests. You can get this information from teachers or test administrators. This is particularly important for elementary school children who are taking their first standardized test. Often, young children have more trouble with test-taking procedures than they do with the actual test questions.

Students—

♦ Don't save studying for a last-minute cram session. On the night before an important exam, do something relaxing and enjoyable.

♦ Go to sleep early and get a good night's rest.

♦ Eat a hearty and nutritious breakfast before taking off for school.

Inform Yourself About Testing

Like it or not, students are judged on test results whether the tests are classroom tests or standardized tests. As a parent, you have the right and responsibility to understand, and to question if necessary, the tests and the test procedures of your child's school. The following suggested questions were prepared jointly by the National Parent-Teacher Association and the Educational Testing Service.

1. What tests are being used and why?
2. Will you get to see the test scores and have them explained?
3. What specific areas are being measured in tests? Did your child have an opportunity to learn those things before the test was given?
4. What is the norm group? How is the comparison with the norm group being used? How was the group selected?
5. If your child receives low test scores, what does the school recommend as a positive course of action?
6. How is the school performing as a whole? Are test scores what they were five years ago? Are they declining? Improving?
7. When can I see the test results? How do they relate to my child's classroom work?
8. What procedures does the school have for eliminating bias from classroom tests? Are these tests reviewed by someone other than the test-maker? What are the safeguards followed by the companies or organizations to eliminate bias from their standardized tests?

Being Test-Wise

People make up tests: an important fact to remember, if tests spook you or your children. And good test-makers and test-takers know tricks, some of which we pass on to you:

Preparing for Tests

Find out in advance what form the test will take: multiple-choice, true-false, fill-in, short or long essay. Find out, too, how many points will be allotted to each part.

Obtain any material issued by the test-making company and read it carefully. Some companies include practice questions: do them and analyze them. You can also buy practice books from commercial publishers that contain questions of the same difficulty as those in the test itself.

Learn the Odds

Is it better to guess or leave the answer blank? Consider whether or not points are deducted for wrong answers and the number of choices for each question. If no points are taken away for wrong answers (or they are equated with blanks), it is a good idea to guess. The odds for guessing are better with true-false questions than with multiple-choice.

TAKING TESTS

Pay attention to instructions. Read or listen to instructions carefully. Understand how to mark answers. Ask the proctor if you are uncertain about anything.

Skim. Skim the whole test first (if allowed) and plan your strategy. Be sure you know how much time you have. Plan, in advance, how much time you will spend on each part of the test, and pace yourself. Play the numbers. Figure the weight given to each part—that reveals how much time it is worth.

Strategic Tips

♦ An *an* in front of a blank means that an answer beginning with a vowel is expected.

♦ Do the easy parts first. Skip the questions you are not sure of. Then go back over the test again, picking up what you skipped.

♦ Words like *always* and *never* usually indicate a false answer. True answers often contain words like *sometimes, often,* and *usually.* (However, remember that test-makers know these rules and may fool you—for example, with a true answer

that contains *always:* "Polymaths always are expert in more than one subject.")

♦ If you finish early, go back over your work and look for mistakes. Think again about questions you were not sure of.

Specifics

Essay tests. Make sure that you know what the question is. Look for words like *compare, contrast, describe, analyze, evaluate.* Test-makers try to give clues that confine the field in essay questions. Even the word *the* is a clue: it can indicate that a very complete answer is required. For example, "Give reasons for the killing of Louis XVI" is a different question from "Give *the* [all] reasons for the killing of Louis XVI." In the first case, you might pick three reasons about which you know a great deal and parade your knowledge. In the second case, you should try to be as comprehensive as possible.

Before you start writing answers, jot down ideas and make up an outline. Spend about one-third of your time planning your answers and two-thirds of your time writing.

Multiple-choice. Read *all* the possible answers. Then eliminate those you know are wrong. Watch out for verbal tricks. Avoid wild guesses; if you have eliminated all but two of the answers, follow your hunch.

True-False. Most true statements include qualifiers like *almost* or *except.* On the other hand, one false section makes a whole statement false.

Matching. Count the number of items in each column. If the number is uneven, you know that some items are wrong or that two items in the B column can match with one in the A column. Match those you are sure of first, then use good sense on others.

Verbal analogies. A verbal analogy has four parts that bear a relationship to each other, for example, dog : puppy :: cat : _____.

Your job is to determine the relationship between the first two items, then find the word that will give the second pair the same relationship. Don't read the analogy as mathematics, but as

English: *"Dog* is to *puppy* as *cat* is to what?" Play around with parts of the analogy if you get stuck. For example, go from the second word to the first rather than the other way around.

Number series. Here the task is to find the rule and apply it. Figure the differences between neighboring numbers and see if there is a regular pattern. Look for ratios, exponential relationships (squares, square roots, cubes).

Reading comprehension. Read the questions *before* reading the sample passages. Don't hesitate to read the passages as often as you need to.

Math. Check your work. More people fail math tests because of careless mistakes than for any other reason.

Wear your lucky hat!

Homework Guidelines for Parents

Homework is a classic battleground for parents and children. However, it is a fact that students who do homework on a regular basis get better grades, become better readers, and learn more. According to the National PTA: "In the lowest grades—kindergarten to third grade—very little homework should be given, no more than 20 minutes a day. In grades four through six, a child should be expected to spend 20 to 40 minutes a day. There is no set amount of time for junior high and senior high students."

The following homework tips are geared toward elementary school children.

♦ Set up a regular time period for homework assignments. Assume homework will be done on a daily basis and be sure the schedule adequately provides free, fun time for the child.

♦ Establish a good homework environment, whether the child has a desk in the bedroom or works at the kitchen or dining room table. Lighting should be good, and the child should have all the necessary tools like pencil and paper, dictionary, etc.

♦ Get rid of noisy distractions. Some children work quite well with a low level of music from a stereo or radio, but television is a no-no. Also, other children in the household need to respect the child's homework time.

♦ Try to be at home during homework time. It shows your child that you place a value on homework and education.

♦ Help, but don't do your child's homework. It's okay to be a coach and provide guidance and helpful hints, but resist doing the homework yourself.

♦ Give lots of praise for problems solved and a job well done.

♦ Show genuine interest in your child's work and, when possible, try to relate homework assignments to things that happen in everyday life.

♦ When homework assignments are returned, go over them with your child so that the child understands what has been done correctly and incorrectly.

♦ If your child has difficulty with homework, or if both you and your child don't understand certain assignments, contact the teacher and get the situation resolved.

Twenty Ways to Encourage Reading

Reading Is Fundamental (RIF) is a national nonprofit organization that inspires youngsters to read. Founded in 1966, RIF works through local programs in communities throughout the U.S. Today RIF's nationwide network consists of some 5000 projects that operate programs in more than 16,000 sites. The organization serves more than 3 million kids from preschool through high school, and more than 160,000 volunteers deliver services to these young people each year. A big part of the RIF program is providing books for young people to choose and own at no cost to them or their families. To date RIF has put almost 141 million books into the hands of children.

RIF publishes an excellent series of inexpensive Parent Guide brochures to help parents encourage reading in the home. The series includes "Reading Aloud to Your Children," "Magazines and Family Reading," "Encouraging Soon-To-Be Readers," "Building a Family Library," and "Teenagers and Reading." To get a copy of a brochure or to obtain more information on RIF programs, write to: **Reading Is Fundamental, PO Box 23444, Washington, DC 20026.**

The following is excerpted from RIF's brochure, "Children Who Can Read, But Don't" and is meant to be an aid in leading reluctant readers, aged 9–13, back to books.

1. Scout for things your children might like to read. Use their interests and hobbies as starting points.

2. Leave all sorts of reading materials—including books, magazines, and colorful catalogs—in conspicuous places around your home.

3. Notice what attracts your children's attention, even if they only look at the pictures. Then build on that interest; read a short selection aloud, or simply bring home more information on the same subject.

4. Let your children see you reading for pleasure in your spare time.

5. Take your children to the library regularly. Explore the children's section together. Ask a librarian to suggest books and magazines your children might enjoy.

6. Present reading as an activity with a purpose—a way to gather useful information for, say, making paper airplanes, identifying a doll or stamp in your child's collection, or planning a family trip.

7. Encourage older children to read to their younger brothers and sisters. Older children enjoy showing off their skills to an admiring audience.

8. Play games that are reading-related. Check your closet for spelling games played with letter tiles or dice, or board games that require players to read spaces, cards, and directions.

9. Perhaps over dinner, while you're running errands, or in another informal setting, share your reactions to things you read, and encourage your children to do likewise.

10. Set aside a regular time for reading in your family, independent of schoolwork—the 20 minutes before lights-out, just after dinner, or whatever fits into your household schedule. As little as 10 minutes of free reading a day can help improve your child's skills and habits.

11. Read aloud to your child, especially a child who is discouraged by his or her own poor reading skills. The pleasure of listening to you read, rather than struggling alone, may restore your child's initial enthusiasm for books and reading.

12. Encourage your child to read aloud to you—an exciting passage in a book, or interesting tidbit in the newspaper, or a joke in a joke book. When children read aloud, don't feel they have to get every word right. Even good readers skip or mispronounce words now and then.

13. On gift-giving occasions, give books and magazines based on your child's current interests.

14. Set aside a special place for children to keep their own books.

15. Introduce the bookmark. Remind your youngster that you don't have to finish a book in one sitting; you can stop after a few pages, or a chapter, and pick up where you left off at another time. Don't try to persuade your child to finish a book he or she doesn't like. Recommend putting the book aside and trying another.

16. Treat your children to an evening of laughter and entertainment featuring . . . books! Many children (parents, too) regard reading as a "serious" activity. A joke book, a story told in riddles, or a funny passage read aloud can reveal another side of reading.

17. Extend your child's positive reading experiences. For example, if your youngster enjoyed a book about dinosaurs, follow up with a visit to a natural history museum.

18. Offer other special incentives to encourage your child's reading. Allow your youngster to stay up an extra 15 minutes to finish a chapter; promise to take your child to see a movie after he or she has finished the book on which it was based; relieve your child of a regular chore to free up time for reading.

19. Limit your children's TV viewing in an effort to make time for other activities, such as reading. But never use TV as a reward for reading, or a punishment for not reading.

20. Not all reading takes place between the covers of a book. What about menus, road signs, food labels, and sheet music? Take advantage of countless spur-of-the-moment opportunities for reading during the course of your family's busy day.

Learning Disabilities

Millions of children and adults across this country suffer from a complex problem called learning disability (LD). Believed to be neurological in origin, learning disabilities interfere with someone's ability to store, process, or produce information. Because it is often a "hidden handicap," learning disabilities are not easily recognized, accepted, or considered serious. LD can affect one's ability to read, write, speak, or compute math.

Learning disabilities create a gap between a person's true capacity and his or her day-to-day productivity and performance. These disabilities do not affect intelligence and, in fact, individuals with LD are of average or above average intelligence, and are often gifted.

Early diagnosis and appropriate intervention and support can make all the difference to an LD individual. Without early detection and treatment, LD can lead to a complete loss of self-esteem and self-worth and, consequently, educational failure, illiteracy, school dropout, substance abuse, juvenile delinquency, and other serious social problems. Services and information for individuals with learning disabilities are frequently inadequate. Often people do not even consider that LD may be the reason for an individual's difficulties.

A Few Important Facts

♦ Individuals with LD represent an estimated 10 percent of the total population in the U.S.

♦ LD affects each person differently.

♦ LD appears to run in families and frequently more than one family member has learning disabilities.

♦ LD cannot be outgrown, but can be compensated for.

♦ Federal law (PL 94–142) mandates that all children with learning disabilities have a right to a "free" and "appropriate" education in "the least restrictive environment."

What to Look For

The chart on the next page lists the signs that a child is having trouble keeping up with the flow of expectations. These lists are *guideposts* for parents. They should not be used in isolation, but may lead the parent to seek further assessment. Many children will, from time to time, have difficulty with one or more of these items. They should always be reviewed in a broader context of understanding about a child. For further information and assistance, contact: **The National Center for Learning Disabilities,** 381 Park Avenue South, Suite 1420, New York, NY 10016 (212-545-7510).

Kids and Television

There have been more than 3000 studies on the effects of television on children. While many have provided inconclusive results, TV gets blamed for a lot of social ills, from declining test scores to an increase in street crime. It is accused of promoting drug and alcohol use as well as sexual activity. Television is even blamed for higher cholesterol levels and obesity in children. Whether or not you buy into the theory that TV turns children into "vidiots," the statistics on children and TV viewing are staggering:

♦ Kids watch an average of 27 hours of TV every week.

♦ By high school graduation, the average

LEARNING DISABILITIES: WHAT TO LOOK FOR

Level	Language	Memory	Attention	Fine Motor Skills	Other Functions
Pre-school	Pronunciation problems Slow vocabulary growth Lack of interest in storytelling	Trouble learning numbers, alphabet, days of week, etc. Poor memory for routines	Trouble sitting still Extreme restlessness Impersistence at tasks	Trouble learning self-help skills (e.g., tying shoe laces) Clumsiness Reluctance to draw or trace	Trouble learning left from right (possible visual spatial confusion) Trouble interacting (weak social skills)
Lower Grades	Delayed decoding abilities for reading Trouble following directions Poor spelling	Slow recall of facts Organizational problems Slow acquisition of new skills Poor spelling	Impulsivity, lack of planning Careless errors Insatiability Distractibility	Unstable pencil grip Trouble with letter formation	Trouble learning about time (temporal-sequential disorganization) Poor grasp of math concepts
Middle Grades	Poor reading comprehension Lack of verbal participation in class Trouble with word problems	Poor, illegible writing Slow or poor recall of math facts Failure of automatic recall	Inconsistency Poor self-monitoring Great knowledge of trivia Distaste for fine detail	Fist-like or tight pencil grip Illegible, slow, or inconsistent writing Reluctance to write	Poor learning strategies Disorganization in time or space Peer rejection
Upper Grades	Weak grasp of explanations Foreign language problems Poor written expression Trouble summarizing	Trouble studying for tests Weak cumulative memory Slow work pace	Memory problems due to weak attention Mental fatigue	(Lessening relevance of fine motor skills)	Poor grasp of abstract concepts Failure to elaborate Trouble taking tests, multiple choice (e.g., SATs)

Reprinted courtesy of the National Center for Learning Disabilities.

teenager will have spent more hours watching television than time spent in the classroom.

♦ By the time a child completes elementary school, he or she will have witnessed 8000 murders on TV, as well as more than 100,000 acts of violence.

To curb TV viewing hours and habits, parents might consider some of the following suggestions:

1. Set time limits. Experts generally agree that one to two hours on school nights is acceptable with an increase to three hours per day on weekends.

2. Monitor programs that children watch. Plan in advance what children will view, and participate in the selection process. If you don't want your child to watch a particular program, explain the reasons why. If the child insists on viewing something that you think will be unacceptable, consider watching the program with the child but retain veto power if the program does prove to be unacceptable.

3. Provide alternatives to TV. TV-addicted kids won't give up viewing habits easily. You need to suggest other activities to fill in boredom time. Sports, games, and hobbies are good alternatives. Don't resort to using TV as a baby-sitter.

4. Be aware that you are a role model. It's impossible to convince kids to limit television hours if you spend a lot of time in front of the tube.

5. Turn the TV off during mealtimes and homework time.

6. Consider the consequences of using TV as a reward system. If you allow the child to watch more TV as a reward or less TV as a punishment, the process could backfire. You could elevate the importance of television watching by using it in such a pivotal role.

Discipline

The word conjures up images of a parent spanking or shouting at a child or a teacher scolding a student for misbehaving. To many people *disci-*

pline means verbal or physical punishment. But, actually, to discipline means to teach. Thus, rather than punishment, discipline should be a positive way of helping and guiding children to achieve self-discipline. Parents' beliefs about what is good discipline will have a great effect on how their children live their lives and get along with others.

Studies have shown that physical punishment such as hitting and slapping and verbal abuse are *not* effective discipline. While such punishment may seem to get fast results in specific instances, in the long term it is generally more harmful than helpful. Physical punishment can demoralize and humiliate children and cause them to develop low self-esteem. Some experts argue that it also promotes physical aggression in children by showing them that violence is acceptable.

Discipline Tips for Parents

♦ Set a good example. Children learn more by how parents act than by what they say. If you want, for example, to teach your child that physically aggressive behavior is not the way to resolve conflicts or problems, then don't resort to physical punishment yourself.

♦ Set limits on behavior, but be careful not to impose too many rules. Before making a rule, ask yourself: Is it necessary? Possible criteria would be: Does the rule protect a child's health and safety? Does it protect the rights or property of others? Too many rules overwhelm and hinder creativity and spontaneity and are hard if not impossible to enforce. Generally young children need more rules than older children.

♦ Praise a child for good behavior and accomplishments. Let the child know you appreciate his or her efforts.

♦ Try to ignore unwanted behavior unless it is causing harm to people or is otherwise destructive. But be honest with a child about behavior that is annoying to you or other adults.

♦ Take time to listen to your child, especially if there is a problem or the child wants to discuss a rule.

♦ Involve children as much as possible in making family rules and decisions. Children are less likely to break rules that they have helped establish.

♦ Be consistent. Agree with your spouse on methods of discipline. Consistency reinforces the importance of a rule, and a child can always predict the results if he or she doesn't follow the rule.

♦ Act quickly when a child misbehaves. Don't let a problem or worry build up over a period of time.

♦ Be flexible. Some rules may work when a child is young; but as children get older, they need and want more independence. And remember, not all children respond in the same way.

♦ Don't be afraid of encouraging independence.

♦ Make sure your child understands rules and the penalty for breaking them, and then enforce the rules. If you and four-year-old Timmy agree that he shouldn't cross the street alone, and he breaks this rule, be ready to enforce the penalty. This penalty might be that he can't go out again for one day.

♦ Help your child develop inner control. Young children do not have the self-control needed to follow all the rules all of the time. A five-year-old girl may not be able to exert the self-control necessary not to take a cookie from the cookie jar before dinner. The parent might help by moving the cookie jar out of sight or offering the child something that is allowed.

♦ Give children responsibilities, including household chores. Having something important to do can help children achieve independence and develop high self-esteem. Even toddlers can be responsible for some chores—bringing a diaper or their socks and shoes to you.

♦ Avoid criticism and nagging. Offer positive, constructive suggestions instead. Criticism and nagging can easily become habit-forming, and they can cause your child to become resentful and belligerent and develop low self-esteem.

♦ Avoid power struggles with your children. Discipline is not a game in which there is a winner and a loser. You expect cooperation from your child and your child expects you to be fair. Respect your child enough to allow disagreement at times.

♦ Keep your sense of humor. It can work wonders with children.

♦ Treat your children as you would your friends—with love, respect, and courtesy.

Reprinted with permission from "Discipline: A Parent's Guide," National PTA.

Communicating with Children

Effective communication between parents and children is not always easy to achieve. Children and adults have different communication styles and different ways of responding in a conversation. In addition, timing and atmosphere may determine how successful communication will be. Parents should make time to talk with their children in a quiet, unhurried manner. The following tips are designed to make communication more successful.

Listening

♦ Pay attention.
♦ Don't interrupt.
♦ Don't prepare what you will say while your child is speaking.
♦ Reserve judgment until your child has finished and has asked you for a response.

Looking

♦ Be aware of your child's facial expression and body language. Is your child nervous or uncomfortable—frowning, drumming fingers, tapping a foot, looking at the clock? Or does your child seem relaxed—smiling, looking you in the eyes? Reading these signs will help parents know how the child is feeling.

♦ During the conversation, acknowledge what your child is saying—move your body forward if you are sitting, touch a shoulder if you are walking, or nod your head and make eye contact.

Responding

♦ "I am very concerned about . . ." or "I understand that it is sometimes difficult . . ." are better ways to respond to your child than beginning sentences with "You should," or "If I were you," or "When I was your age we didn't. . . ." Speaking for oneself sounds thoughtful and is less likely to be considered a lecture or an automatic response.

♦ If your child tells you something you don't want to hear, don't ignore the statement.

♦ Don't offer advice in response to every statement your child makes. It is better to listen carefully to what is being said and try to understand the real feelings behind the words.

♦ Make sure you understand what your child means. Repeat things to your child for confirmation.

Source: U.S. Department of Education

Money and Allowances

A recent Gallup poll asked kids, "What things would you like to talk about more often with your parents?" The number one response was "money." It ranked ahead of drugs, drinking, school—even sex. Psychologists say that we don't talk to our children about money because *we* see it as a measure of who we are, a measurement we might not feel comfortable disclosing. In addition, parents are afraid that if children know certain money facts—like how much money the parents earn—the kids will share that information with relatives, neighbors, friends, anyone who will listen.

Since financially responsible adults are a product of financially responsible children, it is essential that children know how to earn, spend, save, and borrow (see "The Five Stages in Raising a Money-Smart Kid," p. 276). And the sooner the child starts to learn about money the better.

Speaking psychologically, there are a few simple guidelines to remember:

♦ Don't manipulate your kids with money; more specifically, don't let them view money as a currency for love or rejection.

♦ Be consistent with your money messages and be sure you and your spouse are sending the same signals.

♦ Give the child real-world experiences with money, not endless explanations.

♦ View your child as an ally—not an adversary—in making family financial decisions.

An allowance is a central ingredient in teaching children how to handle money. Here are some allowance dos and don'ts.

1. *Do* discuss what kind of purchases should be covered by the allowance. Many experts suggest that children be *allowed* to use allowances as they see fit—no strings attached.

2. *Do* encourage wise spending and saving habits but don't dictate them. If you do, you are defeating the purpose of an allowance, which is to teach children how to manage their own money.

3. *Do* agree on the amount of money to be paid. There is no magic formula for deciding how much allowance a child should get. The amount is determined by taking a good look at your child's needs and your particular financial situation. A recent national survey showed that children between the ages of 6 and 8 were getting about $3 a week; children between the ages of 15 and 17 were getting $15 a week. Do renegotiate the allowance as the child gets older; older children need more money.

4. *Do* pay regularly and promptly, preferably on the same day each week.

5. *Don't* link the allowance to a child's chores, behavior, or school grades. If you do, you are using money as a reward or punishment. Children should view routine chores as part of their responsibility to the family unit. If a child fails to do assigned chores, a parent can restrict privileges like watching TV, rather than withholding an allowance. In addition, when you link chores and

THE FIVE STAGES IN RAISING A MONEY-SMART KID

Here is a model program for educating your child about money based on a consensus of experts. The ages are approximate, depending on each child's maturity.

3 to 5.
BEGIN DISCUSSING MONEY. Take your children on shopping trips to buy groceries or gifts. Talk about how you weigh choices and decide. Give them an occasional 50 cents or $1, and ask them to pick among three or four choices.

6 to 7.
INTRODUCE AN ALLOWANCE. Start with 50 cents or $1 a week. Don't link the money to household chores; simply assign chores as part of your child's family responsibility. Discuss what can be done with the money. Give the money every week at a set time, without fail. Don't take it away for punishment.

8 to 10.
GIVE ANNUAL RAISES. Increase the child's allowance and responsibilities each year on an easy-to-remember date like July 4, and provide opportunities to earn extra money by doing additional chores. Help your child to open a savings account and talk about what to save for.

11 to 14.
START TO SET GOALS. Invite your child to join you in family budget conferences. Talk about long-range goals, such as college. As a savings incentive, match any amount that he or she contributes to a savings account.

15 to 18.
PUSH THEM FROM THE NEST. Help your children attain independence by opening a checking account with an ATM card. Consider giving them a family credit card, provided they pay their own bills. Encourage them to get outside jobs. And include them in decisions about paying for college.

Reprinted courtesy of *Money* magazine.

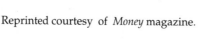

TOOTH FAIRY MONEY

How much money does a child get when he or she puts a tooth under the pillow? According to a survey by *Kids* magazine, the "tooth fairy" usually leaves a quarter, $1, or $5. For some inexplicable reason, girls seem to get a little more, with the average girl getting $1.72 compared with $1.47 for the average boy. The largest per-tooth windfall comes from the very first tooth that falls out. Furthermore, a survey of dentists reports that by the age of eight most kids no longer believe in the tooth fairy, but the young capitalists continue the pillow game until they collect on the very last tooth.

an allowance, you open the door to confrontation: "I'm not doing the dishes tonight and I don't care if you dock my allowance." It's perfectly okay, say the money experts, to pay children for chores above and beyond their normal duties, like babysitting or cleaning out the garage.

6. Don't continually make cash advances to children who run out of money. Children need to budget the money they have, not become deficit spenders. On the other hand, if your child is a prudent spender but keeps falling short, you should review the child's needs and allowance. The allowance may need to be increased.

Zillions (formerly *Penny Power*), a Consumer Reports magazine aimed at children age 8–14, often has articles on money and money management. To order a subscription, write to: ***Zillions,*** 101 Truman Avenue, Yonkers, NY 10703.

Stepparents/Stepfamilies

In days long gone by, stepfamilies usually were created due to the death of a spouse and the remarriage of the surviving spouse. Today, most stepfamilies are created by divorce and remarriage. One out of two marriages fails and approximately 60 percent of all second marriages end up in divorce. That leaves a lot of parents and children in a terribly complex set of relationships. According to The Stepfamily Foundation, Inc., "More than 70 million Americans are currently involved in step relationships, whether remarried, dating, living with a partner or as an absent biological parent." Also, according to the New York–based foundation, "It is predicted that 75 percent of all step relationships will break up. The major causes of these breakups are child- and step-related issues."

Making step relationships work is a daunting task that requires huge amounts of love, understanding, communication, and dedicated effort. Here are a few guidelines that should prove useful:

♦ Instant love is a fantasy. Good relationships are earned, not expected. Psychologists say that even under good circumstances, it can take three to seven years before a new stepfamily functions as a stable unit. Even then, respect and admiration, more than love, may be the family's cornerstone. "Super stepparenting," whether it involves buying loads of gifts for a stepchild or trying to become an immediate confidant and friend to the child, has many drawbacks and usually doesn't work.

♦ Old loyalties present significant roadblocks. Children can feel very guilty responding positively to a new stepparent; it means they are disloyal to the biological parent. Regardless of age, children need to be reassured that caring for more than two adults as parents is acceptable and beneficial. Caring for one parent, or stepparent, doesn't mean that love is being taken away from another person. Also, many children have a difficult time bonding with a new stepparent because they continue to hope that their biological parents will one day reunite. In general, younger children adjust more readily to stepfamilies than older children.

♦ The couple in a new family unit needs to work continually on their relationship in spite of the complexities imposed by stepchildren. Couples need to keep the lines of communication wide open, especially when the issue is money. Who spends what amount of money on a biological child, or stepchild, is a persistent source of friction in many stepfamilies.

♦ Biological parents and stepparents need to work out a clearly defined set of house rules as well as disciplinary policy. Children who live in two distinct households with differing lifestyles can be confused and angry about conflicting standards of expected behavior. The issue of stepparents as disciplinarians is a particularly thorny one.

♦ Ex-spouses need to call a "cease fire" on their past relationship. Divorces are seldom amicable and old emotional baggage dragged into new relationships is pure destruction. Ex-spouses are unlikely ever to be best friends, but they can refrain from bad-mouthing each other, or fighting, in a child's presence.

♦ A new stepparent needs to respect old family ties, even if he or she doesn't particularly like or respect the people involved in those family ties. Family loyalties run deep even in relationships that are far less than ideal.

♦ If the stepfamily unit is not working, seek professional advice. Your family doctor should be able to recommend a family counseling professional.

♦ Never forget that stepfamily situations do have happy endings. Long-term studies have shown that children in successful stepfamily units develop and mature as well as children in first-marriage families. In fact, some stepchildren do particularly well because they have learned to cope and adapt to difficult situations early in their lives.

There are two organizations devoted to providing education and support to stepfamilies. Both are membership organizations, publish a newsletter, and have an array of publications for sale. For more information, write to: **Stepfamily Association of America, Inc.,** 215 Centennial Mall South, Suite 212, Lincoln, NE 68508. Or: **The Stepfamily Foundation, Inc.,** 333 West End Avenue, New York, NY 10023.

Adoption

According to the National Council for Adoption, there are up to 2 million couples or single people who would like to adopt children. Over the last 20 years the number of adoptions has steadily declined due to birth control, more single women keeping their babies, and legal abortion. It's estimated that for every available child there are 20 couples or single parents seeking adoption.

If you want to adopt a child, there are three basic roads to choose from: agency adoption, private or independent adoption, and international adoption. Depending on where you live, your actions will be governed by state law and regulatory agencies. In the case of international adoption, you will also have to comply with U.S. national law. Fortunately, there are numerous nationwide adoption associations that can supply information and guidance for people who want to adopt.

Agency Adoption

Basic operation. There are two kinds, public and private. A public agency is supported by tax dollars and is run by the state or county government. The great majority of children placed by public agencies are older children, children with special needs, or children in foster care. Private agencies can be nonprofit or for-profit; some are sponsored by religious groups. The number and kinds of services provided depend on the particular agency. In addition to handling the screening process and most of the paperwork, some agencies provide counseling to both the adoptive parents and the birth parents. Some counsel the children themselves; some provide assistance after the adoption becomes legal.

Costs. Adoptions through a public agency cost the least, ranging from zero to $500. Private agency fees range from approximately $5000 to $20,000.

Waiting time. First you have to get on an official waiting list. After getting a position on the list, the wait averages two or three years.

Private Adoption

Basic operation. More and more adoptive parents are choosing this option because of long waiting lists at agencies or because they fear rejection by an agency for various reasons like being too old, being a single parent, not being married for very long, or any other number of reasons that might cause rejection. Private, or independent, adoptions are spearheaded by an attorney or other intermediary. Sometimes the attorney is somewhat helpful in finding an adoptive child. In most instances, the adoptive parents are largely responsible for finding the child—through newspaper ads and networking—and then the attorney takes care of all the legal paperwork. Infant adoption resource centers have sprung up across the U.S. to help adoptive parents locate children, do home-study evaluation, and provide parent counseling. However, approximately 20 states in the United States currently ban the use of advertising to locate children.

Costs. Money counts in this type of adoption. Fees vary greatly depending on how much of the work you do, the individual attorney's requirements, and the medical costs of the birth mother. Experts say that the costs range from $5000 to $20,000.

Waiting time. The average is 18 months.

International Adoption

Basic operation. U.S. citizens adopt more foreign-born children than the citizenry of any other country in the world. International adoptions account for more than 10 percent of all adoptions in the United States. The children come from many countries around the world, and the number of adoptees since 1983 has ranged from a yearly total of 7000 to 10,000. The majority of children are from Third World countries. Most Americans arrange adoptions through private agencies that specialize in international adoptions. It's also possible to use an attorney or work directly with orphanages in other countries, but these latter two options are far riskier.

Costs. The cost ranges from $7000 to $20,000. Some agencies operate on a fixed-fee basis.

Waiting time. It usually takes one to two years, depending on the legal procedures in various countries and the age of the child you want to adopt.

Adoptive Families of America, 3333 Highway 100 North, Minneapolis, MN 55422 (612-535-4829).

National Council for Adoption, 1930 17th Street NW, Washington, DC 20009 (202-328-1200).

National Adoption Center, 1500 Walnut Street, Suite 701, Philadelphia, PA 19102 (215-735-9988).

National Adoption Information Clearinghouse, 11426 Rockville Pike, Suite 410, Rockville, MD 20852 (301-231-6512).

International Concerns Committee for Children, 911 Cypress Drive, Boulder, CO 80303 (303-494-8333).

Teenagers and Driving

For teenagers, driving the family car is a symbol of maturity and independence. For parents, teenagers and driving can seem like a toxic combination. It's true that the majority of teenagers are safe, responsible drivers and that vision, hearing, and reflex responses are at their best during the teenage years. However, it's also true that auto accidents are the leading cause of death among the nation's young people.

Parents and teenagers need to come to a complete understanding concerning use of the car and safe driving practices.

♦ Teenagers should take a **driver's education class.** A good high school program will cover the dangers of drinking and driving as well as the rules of the road and how to handle road emergencies.

♦ **Financial guidelines** need to be clear. Adding a teenager to a car insurance policy will oftentimes increase premium rates dramatically. If the teenager gets a ticket for a moving violation, the rates will go up again. Teens should be expected to contribute toward gasoline, maintenance, and insurance. The amounts depend on how often the teen uses the car and if the teen has a part-time job. Teens with no source of outside income can still contribute by washing the car, taking on extra chauffeuring responsibilities, taking the car to a service facility for tune-ups and repairs.

♦ **Ground rules** for use of the car need to be established. Teenagers need to be diligent in abiding by curfews set by parents. Parents should not renege on promises made to teenagers about when they can use the car.

♦ Parents are responsible for **setting good examples** for teenagers. Parents who drink and drive are not believable when preaching about the evils of drunk driving. Also, if you insist that your teenager wear a safety belt, it's best that you buckle up.

♦ Teenagers should be grounded **when they abuse driving privileges.** How long driving privileges are suspended depends on what rules were broken and under what circumstances. However, parents need to be aware that overly harsh punishment only breeds resentment. In addition, parents shouldn't go into orbit when a responsible teen gets a ticket or has a minor accident.

♦ Once you and your teenager have agreed upon the rules concerning use of the car, put those rules into writing and have all parties sign it. Such a **formal agreement** signifies the importance of the rules and helps to resolve disputes that arise later. For example, Students Against Driving Drunk (SADD) recommends that teenagers agree to: "Call for advice and/or transportation at any hour, from any place if I am ever in a situation where I have had too much to drink or a friend or date who is driving me has had too much to drink." Parents agree to: "Come and get (their son or daughter) at any hour, any place, no questions asked and no argument at that time or I will pay for a taxi to bring you home safely."

Teens, Alcohol, and Drugs

The average American youth first tries alcohol or other drugs between the ages of 11 and 14, long before he or she is mature enough to understand the risks involved. As a parent you can help your teens make the right choice. Parents play a key role in how their children look at alcohol and drugs. You can help build your teens' self-esteem, as well as help them learn to make good decisions on their own. Remember, most teens will have to decide about using drugs and alcohol, whether they are well prepared or not. The decision will be theirs. The preparation is up to you.

Why do teens drink or use drugs?

To understand how to help teens avoid alcohol and drugs it helps to understand why they use them in the first place. Teens give these reasons: "To have fun." "Because adults do it, I can, too." "It's exciting to do something illegal." "Everybody else does." Many counselors say that the real reason has to do with teens' insecurities and the pressure they feel to look attractive, "cool," popular and smart.

Teens need your support.

♦ Take time to listen to your teens. This shows you respect their thoughts and feelings and helps them feel important. Don't jump to conclusions or overreact. This causes teens to withdraw. Given the chance, they'll talk things out, using parents as a sounding board.

♦ Respect your teens' need for privacy. It doesn't mean they're hiding anything. If they think you're snooping, they may not be willing to share personal information.

♦ Show your teens you care about them. Look for opportunities to share time with them. Praise talents and qualities they may not have noticed in themselves. Don't set expectations too high or too low. Tell them you love them.

♦ Talk with teens about learning to handle peer pressure. Help them develop some "one-liners" to resist situations they feel pressured about. Having a ready excuse or response can save a teen from getting into trouble in the first place. Tell teens they should respond and then *leave.* Here are some sample conversations:

"What's the matter, are you chicken?" Response: "Yeah, of dying. My parents would kill me, or ground me for the rest of my life."

"If you were my friend, you would." Response: "Come on, you're too smart to want to do something so dumb."

"One drink won't hurt you." Response: "I'm allergic."

♦ Don't be afraid to set firm limits. Explain clearly your standards about alcohol and drugs and the rules you expect your teens to follow. Teens are more likely to respect rules if you explain the reasons behind them. Keep the rules short and simple; having too many rules makes anyone feel harassed.

Be a good role model.

♦ Set a good example. Your actions speak louder than words. Take a hard look at your own drinking and drug use. Don't use illegal drugs and don't give your children the idea that drugs of any sort, such as alcohol, tranquilizers, or cigarettes, can solve problems.

♦ Openly discuss your own use or nonuse of alcohol and drugs. Teens often see drinking and drug use as proof of being mature. Also, be candid about your efforts to change habits such as smoking or drinking too much.

♦ Be alert to signs of trouble. Don't "allow" your children to get into trouble by not looking for signs of trouble or by ignoring the signs you see. Adolescent drug or alcohol abuse can happen in any home.

♦ Take care of yourself. Being a parent can be very stressful. You can set a good example by finding healthy ways of relieving your own stress. These might include regular exercise, eating healthy foods, talking with other parents in similar situations, and spending time doing things you enjoy.

Help your teen make the decision to resist drug use.

Most teens don't intend to start drinking or using drugs. But there is a big difference between knowing the right thing to do and doing it. For teens, following through on a decision is especially difficult because they feel such a strong need to fit in with peers. Parents can help teens make good choices and act on them by teaching them how to make decisions.

♦ Teach your teen the steps that go into making good decisions. Books on the subject agree that good decisions involve: considering a range of choices; examining the consequences of each choice; and being alert to poor reasons for choosing alternatives (such as peer pressure or feeling rebellious).

♦ Give your teens opportunities to practice making decisions. Let them plan a family outing, divide household chores fairly, or choose a way to spend a gift of money. Trust them to make wise decisions. In the end their decisions are theirs to make.

♦ Give teens solid information about alcohol and other drugs. Be prepared to describe how alcohol, marijuana, cocaine, and other drugs affect people. Teens want to know what it feels like to get high, what can go wrong, what it's like to have a hangover. Tell them. Be specific. If you don't give your teens the information they want, they'll find out themselves. Make sure teens know the law: in all states the legal minimum age for purchase and possession of alcoholic beverages is 21. Also, teens should stay informed about other laws regarding drug use.

♦ Look for opportunities to talk about alcohol and drug use in daily life. One conversation is not enough. Discuss movie scenes where alcohol or other drugs are depicted. Suggest books written for teens about alcohol or other drug use. Ask your librarian or school counselor for suggestions.

What if your teen has already started drinking or using drugs?

How can parents tell if their teen has begun to use drugs? Trust your own feelings that something is wrong. Although many of the signs are also common to adolescent behavior, they are usually more severe and last longer. Signs include: a preoccupation with partying, a decrease in extracurricular activities, neglect of personal appearance and hygiene, violent behavior, hostility, secretiveness about friends, and a marked change in sleeping or eating habits.

Drug abuse counselors recommend that parents confront children with their suspicions. You might say, "I'm worried that you're using alcohol or drugs and that it might become a big problem." Be prepared to give the facts about the effects of abuse. Then, set specific limits such as grounding except for school and visits to a counselor, a strict curfew, and no parties or guests when parents are not home.

Recognize that sometimes you can't solve your teen's drug or alcohol problem. If you've tried the above and suspect that your teen still has problems, get help. Call your doctor, religious leader, local mental health center, Al-Anon, or Alcoholics Anonymous. Do it immediately. It's not easy being a teenager's parent in today's world. Although you feel powerless at times, keep in mind that you can make a difference.

Reprinted with permission from "Teens, Alcohol, and Drugs: What Parents Can Do," National PTA.

Runaway Children

Running away can be a frightening experience—for both the child and the parents. Your child becomes vulnerable as soon as he or she leaves home, potentially falling victim to drugs, drinking, crime, sexual exploitation, child pornography, or child prostitution. In the face of this, many parents may feel guilty or depressed . . . or even paralyzed by fear.

It is important for parents to remain calm and rational when they discover that their child has run away. Don't panic or lose sight of the immediate task at hand—to locate the runaway and return him or her safely home.

ACTIONS TO TAKE

The first 48 hours following the runaway are the most important in locating the child. Many runaway children return home during this 48-hour period. To help locate your runaway child, follow these steps immediately:

1. Check with your child's friends, school, neighbors, relatives, or anyone else who may know of your child's whereabouts. Ask them to notify you if they hear from the child.

2. Report the runaway to the local police or sheriff's department. Have an officer visit your home to take the report.

3. Write down the officer's name, badge number, telephone number, and the police report number. Find out from the officer who will follow up the initial investigation. Remember: keep a notebook and record all information on the investigation.

4. Provide the police with a recent photo of your child.

5. Make sure your police department enters your child's name and description into the **National Crime Information Center** (NCIC) computer. This information will *not* give your child a police record, but it may aid in his or her safe return.

6. If your state has a clearinghouse on missing children, make sure that the police pass on the necessary information about your child to the clearinghouse.

7. If your local police won't enter your child into the NCIC computer, the FBI will. The Missing Children Act of 1982 mandates this. Contact your nearest FBI field office for help. Remember: no matter what you have been told, there is no law requiring a waiting period for reporting the child missing to the police or for entry into NCIC. Some police department procedures may still involve a waiting period; therefore, you may have to go to the FBI yourself to get your child entered into NCIC.

8. Call or check several local spots that your child may frequent, and check with area hospitals

MISSING

CHILD'S PHOTO	CHILD'S PHOTO DIFFERENT ANGLE
(Date of Photo)	(Date of Photo)

NAME OF CHILD

Date of Birth: Age: Height: Weight:
Color of hair: Color of eyes: Complexion:
Physical Characteristics: (braces, glasses, pierced ears, scars, marks, tattoos, etc.)

Clothing description:
Circumstances of disappearance: (last seen where, with whom, hitchhiking, etc.)

IF YOU HAVE INFORMATION, PLEASE CONTACT:

Name of Police Department: Police Phone Number:
Officer assigned to case: Police Case Number:
Parents' telephone number:

Personal message to runaway: (We all love you. We want to work this out. Please call. Love, Mom and Dad.)

National Center for Missing and Exploited Children
1-800-THE-LOST
(1-800-843-5678)

Note: A missing child MUST be registered with the National Center for Missing and Exploited Children before adding the organization's name and telephone number to this flier.

and treatment centers. If your child was employed, call the employer or co-workers.

9. If you have not done so, contact the **National Center for Missing and Exploited Children** at 800-843-5678.

10. Call your local runaway hotline (if there is one) as well as the **National Runaway Switchboard** at 800-621-4000. Ask if your child has left a message, and leave a message for him or her. Also contact local runaway shelters and those in adjoining states. There are over 500 runaway shelters throughout the country, and they will be able to give you assistance and advice.

11. Make fingerprints and dental records available to the police. This information may need to be added to the existing NCIC entry.

12. Using the poster format that accompanies this article, have posters or fliers made. Place them in store windows and distribute them to truck stops, youth-oriented businesses, hospitals, treatment centers, and law-enforcement agencies.

When Your Child Returns Home

When your child is recovered or returns home, make sure to show love and concern for his or her safety—not anger or fear. If you react angrily, your child may feel unwanted and unloved and may run away again. Make sure that your child understands that you care about what happens to him or her.

Promptly notify the police, state clearinghouse, the National Center, the National Runaway Switchboard, or anyone else who may have assisted you.

If your child has been away for an extended period of time, a complete medical examination is indicated when he or she returns home, including tests for sexually transmitted diseases.

Most important, when your child returns, try to resolve the problems in your family that prompted your child to leave home in the first place. In general, children run away because of problems or stresses in the family or at home—such as divorce, remarriage, alcoholism, or physical or sexual abuse.

If you are unable to deal with the family problems effectively, seek the assistance of a trained counselor or professional. Parents can contact the local Department of Social Services, Family Services, or other public or private agencies that help families. Members of the clergy, school personnel, or the law-enforcement community can also direct you to available services and resources.

It may be necessary for your child to go to a temporary residence or runaway shelter while the family works toward resolving its problems. A trained counselor can help you make this decision.

Reprinted courtesy of the National Center for Missing and Exploited Children.

COUPLES—MARRIED/ NOT MARRIED

Romance

Romance is good for your health. Researchers on the subject say that romance lessens stress levels and creates a sense of well-being and happiness. A romantic act signifies that you, or your loved one, is special; it stirs up excitement and emotions. Most of us think we are romantic, even if we aren't.

Which sex is more romantic, men or women? The jury is still out on that question, but women are usually given the nod. However, researchers say that after middle age, men generally become more romantic than women.

Raymond Tucker, a professor in interpersonal communication at Bowling Green State University, has done a number of studies on romantic behavior. In one study, working with co-researchers Barbara Vivian and Matthew Marvin, he asked adults between the ages of 18 and 79 to complete an open-ended questionnaire on romantic acts. Participants were asked to list specific acts of romance and space was allotted for up to 12 responses. On average men wrote in 7.8 responses; women offered 11.25 responses. Here are the overall results, in the order of frequency.

Rankings of Romantic Acts

1. The Kiss. (Mostly just "kiss"; several reported "unexpected" kiss; some designated anatomical parts)
2. Flowers. (Roses, wildflowers; both giving and receiving)
3. Dinner. (Dinner out; at home; making dinner for me; with candlelight; with music, wine, no kids)
4. Talking. (Honest conversation; soft and quiet; intimate talking; sharing life goals; being silly; joking; sharing memories)
5. Holding hands.
6. The hug. (In bed after the alarm goes off; unexpected)
7. Sharing outdoor leisure activities. (Picnics; beach; ice skating; skiing at night; moonlight swim or drive; picking apples; fishing; driving to enjoy scenery; walk in the park)
8. Gifts. (Expensive; diamonds; jewelry; candy; homemade, unexpected, or surprise gifts)
9. Walking. (In the evening; at night; in the rain; in the woods; in the moonlight)
10. Touching. (Hand on knee; pat on shoulder or hand; slight caress; petting; caressing; head in lap or sitting on lap; playing with hair)

VALENTINES FROM LOVELAND

If you are a true romantic, you might consider mailing your valentines to Loveland, Colorado, so that they can be remailed from the "sweetheart city" of the United States. Each valentine is individually hand-stamped with a four-line cachet (an endearing, romantic message) and then adorned with a special cancellation mark. The Loveland Valentine Remailing Program, started in 1947, handles 300,000 valentines every year and they go to all 50 U.S. states and 104 foreign countries.

To receive a unique cancellation and a valentine cachet, just enclose your prestamped, preaddressed valentines in a larger first class envelope and mail it to:

Postmaster
Attn: Valentines
Loveland, CO 80537

Your valentines will be removed from the envelope and hand-stamped with the Loveland cachet, then cancelled at the Loveland Post Office. If your valentines are headed to destinations within the United States, make sure they get to Loveland by February 8; if they are to be sent to foreign countries, get the valentines to Loveland by February 3. There is no charge for this special service, but be sure to put correct postage on your valentines.

To offset the costs of the Loveland Valentine Remailing Program, the Chamber of Commerce sells official "Loveland Valentines." If you are interested in purchasing the valentines, and thus supporting the program, write to: **Loveland Chamber of Commerce**, 114 E. 5th Street, Loveland, CO 80537.

Dan Cupid's special arrows fly
From Loveland USA this year
A Rocky Mountain special touch
With messages of love so dear

Fair Fighting

Verbal warfare can be painful and upsetting and can leave long-lasting emotional scars. Often, an argument isn't really about the issue at hand (e.g., overspending, being late, etc.) but is about bigger things like power, control, equality, and respect. Nonetheless, most of us are not fair fighters because we get caught up in the heat of an argument and because we don't know how to argue in a constructive manner.

According to some psychologists, fighting, if handled properly, can actually be beneficial to couples. It can open lines of communication, relieve bottled-up tension, and resolve problems. Most of us would prefer not to fight, but if you must . . .

♦ Stay focused on the subject of the argument. If you are arguing about who does household chores, stick to that issue. Don't bring out a laundry list of everything your partner has done wrong over the course of your relationship. Unrelated past injustices are off-limits.

♦ An argument should have a goal—resolving a problem so that it doesn't happen again. If all you do is vent anger, whether you take an offensive or a defensive stance, you end up with nothing but bad feelings.

♦ Try to remain calm, logical, and positive. Express your feelings and your needs and be direct and brief. And, even though you are having a fight, you don't lose points if you say a few nice things about your partner during the course of the discussion.

♦ If you know you are to blame for some injustice, major or minor, step up and say so and apologize. We all hate to admit that we are wrong. Even if we can get to the point of admitting it, we feel compelled to go further: "Yes, I was wrong, but let me tell you what you did that really bothers me . . ." Don't fall into the trap of escalating the argument into other areas.

♦ Listen to your partner. When the other person is speaking, listen and don't interrupt. Constructive arguing is a two-way dialogue.

♦ Stay away from hot buttons. This includes comments about your partner's family. "You're cheap, just like your father" or "You're a nag, just like your mother" will only add flames to an argument. Also taboo are negative statements in sensitive areas like personal appearance, intelligence, and integrity. Attacking vulnerable areas that are at the root of self-esteem is vicious and unfair.

♦ Beware of statements that your partner will never forget. Grand finale comments like "I want a divorce" or "I never really loved you" linger in your partner's mind long after the argument is over.

♦ Don't fight at all if either you or your partner is beyond anger and into rage. Emotions are on the verge of being out of control and fair fighting is probably impossible. Table the discussion for a more rational time.

♦ Don't argue late at night. It's likely that both parties are tired and fighting will only cost you a good night's sleep.

♦ Argue only when both you and your partner are sober. Fighting while under the influence of alcohol is destructive and nonproductive.

♦ Constant, intense arguments that resolve nothing, or fights that turn from verbal to physical, are a sign that you and your partner need outside help. Consult a psychologist or marriage counselor.

Sex—What Is Normal?

Forget the word *normal* when discussing the sexual habits of Americans. There is no definitive study or consensus of opinion as to what constitutes normal, or average, sexual behavior. What is certain, however, is our collective obsession with defining and categorizing sexual activity. While sex surveys continue to ask numerous questions about frequency of sex, number of sexual partners, turnoffs and turn-ons, sexual fantasies, sexual infidelity, they are asking more questions about a few areas that sex therapists say are common in the 1990s: an increased concern about the quality of sex and an apparent increase in lack of sexual desire.

Our sexual confusion and anxiety seem to stem from a number of basic areas. First of all, say psychologists, is the fact that we get very little honest, helpful information about sex when we are growing up. Frank and open sex talk between parents and children is too often taboo, and sex education in school classrooms is too often nonexistent or inadequate. Without proper knowledge and guidance, it's exceedingly difficult for a child to develop a positive, healthy attitude toward sex and the role it plays in our lives. Adding to the confusion is the constant barrage of sexual images provided by television programs and commercials, movies, and lusty best-selling books. And then there are the ever-present sex surveys, which allow us to compare our sexual selves with what the surveys say is happening in bedrooms throughout the country.

Our enormous attention to matters of sex has even gained a prominent place in our legislative halls. According to author Leslee Welch in *The Complete Book of Sexual Trivia*, "The United States has more laws governing sexual behavior than all of the European nations combined. The only legally sanctioned sexual act in the United States is private heterosexual intercourse between married adults."

Sex therapists seem to agree on the following points, which pertain, of course, to responsible sex between consenting adults.

♦ Frequent sex does not necessarily lead to a happier relationship or marriage.

♦ Lowering sexual expectations can, in the long run, improve a sexual relationship. We ask too much of sex, expecting it to be a cure-all for everything else that goes wrong in our lives.

♦ Trying to perform to an imagined set of sexual expectations can inhibit sex. The more you evaluate yourself and monitor your partner's responses, the less you actually experience.

♦ Talking about sexual expectations is beneficial, even though it can be awkward.

Before you judge yourself according to the results of a sex survey, here are a few more things you should know:

♦ While there are tons of them around, only about six or seven of the national surveys, done since the mid-1980s, are considered scientifically valid.

♦ A study is only as good as the questions asked and the interview techniques used. While both have become increasingly sophisticated, they are not foolproof.

♦ Surveys done by women's and men's magazines get a considerable amount of media attention, but they are usually among the least valid. These surveys are statistically suspect because they are based on voluntary participation of the particular readerships of the magazines.

♦ Honesty is a big issue in sex surveys, particularly in those that use face-to-face interviews. Respondents can have a difficult time answering delicate questions about sex, and sometimes they don't tell the truth.

It's estimated that approximately 50 percent of all relationships at some time experience sexual difficulties. Thus, more and more people are seeking out the advice of sex therapists. Referrals to therapists are made through family physicians, marriage counselors, and family planning clinics. A list of certified sex therapists is available for $2 from: **American Association of Sex Educators, Counselors and Therapists,** 435 North Michigan Avenue, Suite 1717, Chicago, IL 60611.

OLDER PERSONS

Myths About Aging

We are living longer, healthier lives. Every day more than 5000 Americans reach the age of 65. And the older segments of our population are the fastest growing. According to the Census Bureau, the 85-plus age group is growing so fast that by the year 2000 approximately 5.2 million Americans will be 85 or older.

Researchers who study aging adamantly agree that the aging process is taking on a whole new look. In fact, the "new gerontology" has shifted away from a preoccupation with age and disease and is looking at how a combination of factors—physiological, psychological, and environmental—affect the quality of our lives as we age. Some gerontologists predict that in the future people in their 90s will be as active and healthy as those today who are middle-aged. Scientists believe that we are moving toward a new definition of lifespan, one that entails a prolonged healthy life, followed by a relatively short decline into illness and death.

Despite medical breakthroughs that help to prolong life and new research studies that help to identify the process by which we age, we are still a society obsessed with youth. For many of us, growing older means "loss"—loss of our physical attractiveness, our intellectual capabilities, our creative capabilities, our sexual desires. While

the bad news is that we haven't yet figured out how to stop the aging process, the good news is that we have a lot of misconceptions about what happens to us as we age.

Myth: As you grow older, the body turns to flab and the bones deteriorate.

Fact: Muscle loss is a reversible process. Exercise builds muscle in older people the same way it builds muscle in younger people. In addition, exercise along with a proper intake of calcium strengthens the skeletal system and significantly reduces the effects of bone diseases like osteoporosis. Flabby bodies are oftentimes a result of inactivity and lack of exercise as opposed to aging.

Myth: Memory loss is inevitable.

Fact: Not so. Nerve cells in the brain begin to die out when you are two years old and the process continues throughout your life. However, most older people do not suffer significant memory loss, and only 1 percent of those under the age of 75 get Alzheimer's disease. Also, memory loss is often due to causes other than aging like head injuries, depression, side effects of medication, or physical illnesses.

Myth: Aging has a bad effect on intelligence.

Fact: Between the ages of 40 and 60 the ability to solve problems and learn and process new information is about the same as it was in your younger years. Some studies suggest that there may be a decline after the age of 70 but that doesn't mean that you are losing your intelligence. It means that your brain isn't working as fast, and it may take a little longer to solve a problem.

Myth: Sexual activity comes to a standstill.

Fact: There are plenty of studies around that refute this myth. Some studies even suggest that sexy seniors are making love as often as their younger counterparts. Regardless of the discrepancies in the studies regarding the frequency of sex, it is undeniable that older people are doing a lot more than holding hands. In response to the notion that older citizens are lacking in sexual urges, the U.S. Administration on Aging, in its brochure "Healthy Aging," says: "Absurd. Full and healthy sex lives are common over age 70. And so it should be."

AGE AND ACHIEVEMENT

In *The Book of Ages*, author Desmond Morris gives an account of what some famous people were doing at various ages. Here are a few notables who deserve recognition:

♦ Grandma Moses (age 67). An American artist, she started to paint at this age after the death of her husband. By the age of 89, she was famous worldwide and was the recipient of numerous awards. She continued to paint until her death at the age of 101.

♦ William "Buffalo Bill" Cody (age 69). Hero of the American West, he was still an active participant in his Wild West Show.

♦ Charles Blondin (age 72). The French tightrope walker gave his last performance in Belfast in 1896. His legendary stunts over the years included walking the tightrope blindfolded and pushing a wheelbarrow, walking on stilts, and walking with a man on his back.

♦ Antonio Stradivari (age 93). The Italian violin maker was still constructing and modifying violins with the assistance of his two sons.

Gray Power

Interested in joining a group that actively works to promote the interests and rights of older Americans? If so, contact one or both of these groups:

American Association of Retired Persons (AARP). A nonprofit group headquartered in Washington, DC, AARP is "dedicated to helping older Americans achieve lives of independence, dignity and purpose." Membership is open to anyone age 50 or older and annual dues are $8. AARP members receive a bimonthly magazine, *Modern Maturity*, and a newsletter, *AARP Bulletin*, which is published 11 times a year. In addition, the group distributes a large number of publications on subjects that range from retirement and legal issues to personal finance and health care; many of the publications are free.

AARP offers group health insurance, auto insurance, and homeowner's insurance. Nationwide AARP has 33 million members and more than 4000 local chapters. For membership information, write to: American Association of Retired Persons, 601 E Street NW, Washington, DC 20049.

Gray Panthers. According to this nonprofit group: "The Gray Panthers is a national organization of people of all ages who fight to change attitudes and laws which tell the most vulnerable in our society that they must settle for less. . . . The Gray Panthers movement is in the trenches fighting for the values in which we believe— taking the far out positions which lead to real change."

The organization has spearheaded fights against forced retirement at age 65, exposed nursing home abuse, and pushed for every American's right to health care. Currently, there are more than 40,000 members active in over 60 local networks nationwide. The group's agenda includes economic and tax justice, affordable housing, a safe and clean environment, and opposition to ageism, racism, and sexism. Annual dues are $20, which includes a subscription to a newsletter as well as informational bulletins. Membership is open to activists of all ages. For more information, write to: Gray Panthers, 2025 Pennsylvania Avenue NW, Suite 821, Washington, DC 20006.

Being a Grandparent

About 75 percent of all adults over the age of 65 are grandparents. And it's estimated that about half of today's grandparents will eventually become great-grandparents. For grandchildren, grandparents are an endless source of love, guidance, and emotional support. For grandparents, the relationship is a steady stream of giving and sharing, without the responsibilities and headaches of parenting.

The role of a grandparent, however, is somewhat ambiguous, so here are some guidelines to ensure good grandparenting.

♦ Remember that you are the grandparent, not the parent. Grandparents need to respect, and abide by, the child-rearing philosophies of their children. Grandchildren can't be expected to conform to two sets of rules and regulations. Obviously, there is some room for differences and adaptations, but when it comes to the important issues, the parents rule the roost.

♦ Spoiling grandchildren is practically a God-given right, but grandparents need to watch their lavish tendencies, especially when it comes to gift giving. If you simply can't be cured of bestowing presents on your grandchild, at least check with the parents so you can buy some practical, necessary items.

♦ Find time when you can give a grandchild your undivided attention; spending time alone together will make the child feel special and important. Also, the time you spend together need not be centered around a "big event." Being together and sharing an activity is the cornerstone of your relationship, whether you take a trip to the zoo or simply read a book at home.

♦ Don't favor one grandchild over another. Regardless of age, kids seem to have built-in radar when it comes to picking up approval and disapproval signals, however subtle the signals may be. Try to give equal amounts of praise and attention to all grandchildren.

♦ Being a loving, caring grandparent does not mean that you are an on-call baby-sitter. Your children need to understand that you have other interests and responsibilities and that you are entitled to a life of your own. Communicating your needs and desires will prevent uncomfortable situations and bad feelings.

♦ Think of generational differences as an asset instead of a divisive factor. Despite the age gap between you and your grandchild, your perspective on life and your life experiences will add stability and continuity to your grandchild's life. On the other hand, your grandchild is growing up in an environment different from that of your childhood, and you need to be openminded and flexible about changing trends and lifestyles.

♦ Grandparenting from a distance may at times seem frustrating, but there are many things you can do to show your grandchildren that you care. Telephone calls, letters, audiotapes, and videotapes help to make up for a shortage of "in-person" visits. Even if you telephone frequently, don't forget that kids love to get mail. Sending along photographs and other personal items will help to create memories and traditions, even if you live far away from each other.

Elderhostel

Started in 1975, Elderhostel is a nonprofit organization that sponsors inexpensive, short-term study/travel programs for people over 60. According to the group: "Elderhostel is an educational adventure for older adults looking for something different. The later years should be a time of new beginnings, opportunities and challenges. Elderhostel offers you a way to keep on expanding your horizons with people who are interested in the same things you are."

The academic programs sponsored by Elderhostel take place in more than 1900 educational and cultural institutions throughout the United States and Canada as well as 47 countries overseas. Here are just a few of the subjects/programs listed in recent issues of the Elderhostel catalog: volcanoes in Hawaii, Ozark folklore in Arkansas, dolphins in California, Cajun cuisine in Louisiana, the horse industry in Kentucky, the myths and mysteries of wolves in Montana, lighthouses in Maine, marine biology in Alaska, solar energy in Arizona, nature of hurricanes in Florida, biblical archaeology in Israel, opera in Germany, mythology in Greece, calligraphy in China, ecological issues in Brazil. The number and variety of courses offered in the catalog are awesome. Every year more than 250,000 people participate in Elderhostel programs. Some hostelers choose programs close to home and there is very little travel involved. Some participants prefer educational experiences in far-away lands. Still others pick programs based on their proximity to family members so that they can combine an academic adventure with a family vacation.

Basic Academics. The courses offered are equal to college-level liberal arts or science courses and are taught by faculty members at the institution hosting the program. The courses are not for credit, and there are no grades, no exams, and no homework. Also, you need no specific prior educational background. According to Elderhostel staff members, all you really need is an inquiring mind and an adventuresome spirit.

Most Elderhostels in the United States and Canada last five or six nights and start on a Sunday. Each program can involve taking up to three noncredit courses. For example, a participating school in Texas may offer a program with a course on the history and traditions of Texas, a course on the American cowboy, and a course on country-western dancing. Usually, the classes are held in the morning and last for 60–90 minutes. Depending on the program, there may be some extracurricular activities.

Accommodations. The programs take place at colleges, universities, museums, state and national parks, environmental education centers, conference centers, and other educational and cultural facilities. To keep costs down, room accommodations are modest, usually in a dormi-

tory-type facility, and meals are eaten in campus cafeterias and dining halls.

International Programs. Overseas programs are in 47 countries including France, Great Britain, Italy, Greece, Japan, China, Israel, Australia, New Zealand, Brazil, Egypt, Germany, India, and Mexico. While there are some one-week programs, most are two, three, or four weeks long. Unlike most programs in the United States, an international program usually features one major area of study per week. Also, with programs over a week in length, you usually spend each week at a different site. The sites may all be in one country or they could be in different countries. Housing accommodations can be in dormitories, modest hotels, small ships, or barges.

Cost. The average charge for a six-night program in the United States is $315. The price usually includes registration fees, room accommodations, meals, classes, and any extracurricular activities and course-related field trips. The tuition charge does not include your transportation costs to the program site. You are responsible for arranging your own travel to and from the program site, but the sponsoring institution will provide you with information on how to get there.

The cost for an international program covers all major program-related expenses like round-trip international airfare, room and board, academic instruction, as well as travel costs within the host country. Costs vary widely but Elderhostel works hard to keep the prices as low as possible. For example, a two-week program at an environmental center in Costa Rica (with round-trip air from Miami) is $1710. A three-week program in Australia and New Zealand at three different universities (with round-trip air from Los Angeles) is $4580.

Who can participate? Programs are open to anyone aged 60 or older. However, a younger spouse or friend can accompany the 60-plus hosteler as long as the companion is at least 50 years old.

Elderhostel publishes four catalogs a year featuring programs in the United States and Canada and four catalogs a year for the international programs. The catalogs can be found in almost all public libraries in the United States. If you would like to receive a free catalog, write to: **Elderhostel,** 75 Federal Street, Boston, MA 02110-1941.

TRAVELING WITH GRANDCHILDREN

Vacation trips designed for grandparents and grandchildren are becoming increasingly popular. A growing number of tour packagers are offering both domestic and international itineraries that combine fun and adventure with educational experiences. In the forefront is Grandtravel, which provides guides and escorts for every trip. The guide is an expert on the particular destination; the escort is a teacher or counselor who handles the educational aspects of the tour as well as cultural activities and games.

While children of all ages are welcome, Grandtravel says that its trips are particularly enjoyable for grandchildren between the ages of seven and 17. Among Grandtravel destinations are Hawaii, Alaska, New England, the Southwest, England, Kenya, and Australia. Each trip features fun-filled activities "to stimulate curiosity and encourage exploration and discovery." For example, the "Western Parks" tour of Wyoming and South Dakota includes a Mt. Rushmore tram ride, rodeo calf roping and bronco busting, fishing on Lake Yellowstone, a covered-wagon ride, a float trip down the Snake River, and a visit to the Whitney Museum of Western Art. For a free brochure on Grandtravel trips, write to: **Grandtravel,** 6900 Wisconsin Avenue, Suite 706, Chevy Chase, MD 20815 (800-247-7651).

Area Agencies on Aging

When you need information on services available to older people, the first place to contact is your Area Agency on Aging (AAA). There are about 670 AAAs throughout the country. AAAs are government sponsored and their sole mission is to provide free information and assistance for older persons. Your AAA can give you detailed information on a great variety of services including: home-delivered meals, transportation, legal assistance, housing options, recreation and social activities, adult day care, senior center programs, home health services, elder abuse prevention, nursing homes.

There are two ways you can locate your Area Agency on Aging:

♦ Check your local telephone directory under the government listings. However, "Area Agency on Aging" is a generic name and the one closest to you may be called something else, like the Office on Aging, the Department of Elder Affairs, or some similar name.

♦ Call the Eldercare Locator, 800-677-1116. This toll-free service is a collaborative project of the U.S. Administration on Aging, the National Association of Area Agencies on Aging, and the National Association of State Units on Aging. The Eldercare Locator will give you the telephone number of your Area Agency on Aging. The service is available weekdays from 9:00 AM to 8:00 PM EST for callers anywhere in the United States, including the U.S. territories of Puerto Rico and the Virgin Islands.

Staying in Your Own Home

As people reach and pass retirement age, most prefer to remain in their own homes and live as independently as possible. However, if you are living alone or have health problems, there are many community-based services that can provide help and support. Here are just some of the services that may be available in your area.

Home Health Care. The services provided fall into two general categories, skilled care and supportive services. *Skilled care service* is provided at your home by licensed professionals such as registered nurses, occupational and physical therapists, or other medically trained personnel. Typically, skilled care is needed by people who have been discharged from a hospital and are still recovering or those who suffer from chronic medical conditions. Costs for skilled care average up to $70 per visit. Medicare, Medicaid, or Medigap insurance may pay some, or all, of the costs for skilled care but only if you meet strict eligibility requirements, if the skilled care services are prescribed by a doctor, and if the service agency is certified by Medicare. *Supportive services* include everything from assistance with personal hygiene to help with household chores. Since supportive services are not medical services, they are not covered by insurance unless they are approved in conjunction with skilled care services. Home health care is provided through various hospitals, public health departments, and home health care agencies (profit and nonprofit).

Homemaking Services/Chore Services. These help with food preparation, laundry, yard work, grocery shopping, house cleaning, minor home repairs, and other assorted tasks. Costs vary widely and are usually on a per hour basis.

Home-Delivered Meals. Most communities have a "meals-on-wheels" program that will bring nutritionally balanced meals to your home once or twice a day, usually five days a week. Some programs can accommodate special diets. This service can be inexpensive, free, or the cost can be based on your ability to pay.

Transportation. Many volunteer organizations operate a service to get you to important destinations like the doctor, grocery store, drug store, or shopping mall. In some cases, there is a nominal fee.

Telephone Reassurance. If you do not talk regularly with nearby friends and relatives, this service provides daily phone contact and is especially helpful for people who live alone. The call can be initiated by you or the telephone-reassurance volunteer. The service is valuable whether you are concerned about your health and safety or whether you simply want to hear a friendly voice. If the service is available in your area, it is usually free.

To find out about the array of community-based services that are available to you, there are a number of places you can call: city or county social service agencies, senior citizen centers, civic or fraternal organizations. One of the best places to call is your local Area Agency on Aging; look in the listings under Government in your phone book. Or, call the Eldercare Locator (800-677-1116) and you will be referred to the nearest Area Agency on Aging.

Independent Living Arrangements

There are any number of reasons why you may want to change your housing arrangements, even if you are in pretty good health and like being independent. Perhaps you are tired of all the responsibilities that come with being a homeowner. Maybe financial obligations are a concern, or the death of a spouse may cause you to want to make a change. The options listed below are for those who need little, or no, long-term or supportive care.

Home Sharing

Home sharing, or shared housing, means one or more people, usually unrelated, live together in a home or apartment. It used to be referred to as "taking in a boarder." Each person in the living arrangement has his or her own bedroom and, if possible, a bathroom. Shared living areas include the kitchen, living room, and dining room.

Sharing a home requires that you be compatible with your housemate, that each person's need for privacy is respected, and that all parties understand and agree to a division of chores and financial responsibilities. If you are the homeowner, home sharing can provide you with extra income, but you need to consider the financial implications of the extra money. For example, an increase in your income could affect your income tax status as well as any benefits you receive like food stamps or rental and utility assistance. Many homeowners have an arrangement in which their housemates pay no rent, or receive a reduction in rent, in exchange for services like doing housework, shopping, yardwork, and other chores and errands.

Home sharing has become increasingly popular over the last decade, and there are more than 350 organizations nationwide that match up home sharers. It is recommended that home sharers draw up a written agreement so that everyone legally agrees to the rules and responsibilities of shared housing. For more information on home sharing, contact: **The National Shared Housing Resource Center,** 431 Pine Street, Burlington, VT 05401 (802-862-2727).

Accessory Apartments

An accessory apartment is a separate, self-contained unit added to a house. The difficulty of creating this type of housing, as well as the costs, depend on the layout of the original house. The unit usually has a separate bedroom, kitchen, and bathroom, as well as an entrance separate from the main house. Local zoning laws determine whether or not an accessory apartment is permitted in your area.

If you are a homeowner and want to gain additional income by adding an accessory apartment, you need to consider the overall costs of renovation as well as the extra money you will have to pay for property taxes, homeowner's insurance, and utility bills. When renting out the unit, you need to decide if you want your renter to be more of a roommate and companion or if you want a more separate landlord/tenant relationship. And you need to think about the financial implications that will result from additional income, since any money you receive will be considered taxable income.

Accessory apartments can be the answer for families that want close, but separate, housing. Perhaps one of your children, or another relative,

has a home that is adaptable for this type of unit. Obviously, there are many financial and personal issues to be resolved before moving ahead with any plans.

ECHO Housing

ECHO stands for Elder Cottage Housing Opportunity. ECHO housing is a small, portable, totally separate home that is placed in the backyard or sideyard of a single-family dwelling. ECHO units originally were inspired by Australian "granny flats," which allow parents to live close to children and relatives but still maintain privacy and independence.

ECHO is not to be confused with mobile homes. ECHO units are designed especially to meet the needs of older and disabled people and they are energy-efficient. The average cost of an installed one-bedroom unit (approximately 500 square feet) is $25,000. In addition, the units can be modified—with siding, roofing, and window materials—to match and complement the single-family home.

Before you consider ECHO housing, you need to check out local zoning laws in your area, since many communities prohibit ECHO units. Also, you need to be sure that there is ample space for the unit and get estimates for the cost of utility hookups. Finally, how will property taxes be assessed on an ECHO home?

Senior Rental Apartments

These individual units may be in a single building or in a complex of buildings. They usually are designed to accommodate older persons, are in convenient locations, and have good security systems. Many apartments sponsor recreational activities, transportation services, and other special amenities.

Senior rental apartments usually are available for people 60 years and older. Some buildings are allocated only for people of designated income levels. In many cases, government subsidies allow lower rental rates for older persons and disabled persons who qualify according to income.

Retirement Communities

These communities come in varying sizes (up to 5000 units), and the larger ones, called retirement villages, have shopping, medical, and recreational facilities. While most are comprised of apartment units, some are town houses or single-family homes. In most cases, you can buy or rent a unit.

Constructed to meet the needs of older persons, these communities provide a wide variety of social activities, handle property maintenance, and in general provide safe, secure environments. However, they are not intended to provide long-term skilled or supportive care.

For More Information

Contact your local Area Agency on Aging for further details on housing options that are available to you. Also, you might want to consider additional shared living alternatives like professional companionship arrangements (you become a companion for someone who needs assistance in exchange for living accommodations) or caretaker arrangements (you live rent-free, or at a reduced rate, in someone's home in exchange for child care services or household services). There are plenty of choices, but you need to compare them and find the one that fits with your needs and desires, personal style, and financial situation. Also see the following article on supportive housing arrangements.

Supportive Housing Arrangements

When older people are in need of some kind of special care or daily assistance, too many of them, and their families, jump to the conclusion that a nursing home is the only answer. In fact, only 5 percent of the 65-plus population currently reside in nursing homes. There are many housing alternatives that offer varying degrees of help, companionship, and medical assistance.

Congregate Housing

This kind of living arrangement is for older people who need minimal help with day-to-day activities. Each tenant has an individual apartment, including a kitchen for light meals and snacks. Congregate housing is usually an apartment complex in a residential area. While each person lives independently in his or her own unit, you eat one or more meals in a shared dining room. Housekeeping services are provided as well as recreational activities and transportation services.

Many congregate housing facilities have professional staff, like social workers, nutritionists, and counselors, but personal services (e.g., help with dressing and hygiene) and medical services are not provided. In addition, some facilities are not staffed on a 24-hour basis. Congregate housing facilities are operated by government agencies, nonprofit groups, and for-profit companies. They range in size from 30 to 300 units. Monthly costs vary greatly and some facilities have federal subsidies that help to cover some of the rent and service fees.

Assisted Living Facilities

These are also called personal care homes, sheltered care, homes for adults, residential care, domiciliary care, and other various names. They are comprised of private, or semiprivate, rooms with baths and kitchenettes; in some cases, there may be suites or apartments. Like congregate housing, meals are eaten in a common dining room and there are housekeeping, recreation, and transportation services. However, assisted living facilities provide more personal care assistance and medical supervision than are available in congregate housing. There is always a staff member on duty and rooms are equipped with emergency call systems. Assisted living facilities are designed to accommodate ambulatory residents (tenants with wheelchairs and walkers are accepted), but if a resident needs skilled medical care, he or she has to be moved into a nursing home.

Assisted living housing can be quite expensive, with monthly costs ranging from $900 to $4000. Medicare, Medicaid, and private health insurance do not cover these housing arrangements. The majority of costs are paid by residents and their families. However, in some states some facilities are subsidized by the federal government or other sources.

Board-and-Care Homes

These are also known by a variety of names like personal care homes, shelter care homes, foster care homes, group homes, adult care homes, residential care facilities, and domiciliary homes. Most are for-profit privately operated facilities that offer a private bedroom and shared spaces like a living room and a dining room. Three meals a day are provided as well as 24-hour supervision, laundry and housekeeping services, and help with personal care tasks like bathing and dressing.

The cost and quality of board-and-care homes vary enormously. Most have 30 or fewer residents; many are "mom and pop" businesses, and the board-and-care homes are often conversions from private homes, hotels, or apartments. While the manager of the home is responsible for the general well-being of the residents, board-and-care housing is not considered a medical facility and costs are not reimbursed by Medicare, Medicaid, or private insurance. The average monthly rent can be as low as $400 or as high as $3000 a month.

Because of the large diversity of board-and-care homes, it's best to check them out completely before committing to living arrangements. Find out the licensing requirements for the home and how often it is inspected. Even if a home is licensed, evaluate the facility according to your own set of standards and needs.

Continuing-Care Retirement Communities

Also called life care communities, they guarantee that you will receive a vast number of services, including health care services, for the rest of your life. Typically, these communities have three levels of care: independent living, assisted living, and skilled nursing care. In many cases, all three types of facilities are located in one campus-like setting and you move from one to another when your needs change. In most cases, you must be in reasonably good health to get into one of the communities; single people as well as couples move into these communities, most with the intention of remaining there for the rest of their lives.

Independent living accommodations can be an individual apartment, a town house, a cottage, a room, or a small detached house. Services for independent living can include shared meals, recreation and social activities, and transportation services. When you need support, there are housekeeping services and personal assistance services. If you need 24-hour care, you will be moved to an on-site nursing facility or to an affiliated nursing home which is usually close to the community.

While many older people are attracted to these communities because they offer a continuum of care and services for the rest of their lives, many older people can't afford them. Usually you have to pay an up-front entrance fee that ranges from $30,000 to $325,000. In addition, there is a monthly fee to pay and on average it ranges from $600 to $3000.

When you enter a community, you must sign a contract. Basically, there are three types: extensive, modified, and fee-for-service. All three include shelter as well as residential services and amenities. They differ, however, when it comes to covering the costs for long-term nursing care. An *extensive contract* includes unlimited nursing care for little or no substantial increase in monthly payments. A *modified contract* includes a specified amount of nursing care beyond which the resident is responsible for payment. A *fee-for-service contract* sometimes provides for emergency and short-term nursing care. However, if you have a fee-for-service contract and require long-term nursing care, you have to pay an additional per-day rate.

Continuing-care retirement communities are operated largely by nonprofit groups but some are run by commercial developers. Because such substantial amounts of money are involved, you must be sure to understand all aspects of your contract, including the refund policy in case you want to move out of the community. In addition, you need to check on the financial health and integrity of the community, since some have had financial problems.

Nursing Homes

Nursing home care is for those who need extensive and extended care. Some people enter a nursing home after an acute hospital stay and remain there for a relatively short time, until they no longer need full-time supervision. For others, a nursing home becomes a long-term care facility because the resident has a physical or mental condition that requires round-the-clock care.

Nursing homes are very expensive. The cost of a yearly stay ranges from $25,000 to $60,000. Medicare insurance provides only a partial payment for a maximum of 100 days of "skilled nursing care" in a certified facility, following a hospital stay of three or more days. Medicare pays nothing for intermediate nursing care or custodial care. Only when a resident has spent down most of his or her assets, does Medicaid (a federal/state health care financial assistance program for people with low incomes) step in to pay for nursing home costs. Even then, residents must meet eligibility requirements, and those requirements vary from state to state. Medicare supplemental insurance ("Medigap") policies usually pay for very little, or none, of the costs of a nursing home. To protect yourself against the possibility of a long-term nursing home stay, you might consider buying a long-term-care insurance policy available from some private insurance companies. However, while these policies have improved over the years, they are controversial due to policy limitations and high costs.

The quality of life and care varies greatly among nursing homes. However, a federal law that became effective in 1990 holds nursing homes to a new set of standards. Overall, the standards place an emphasis on the rights and dignity of nursing home residents.

For More Information

The world of supportive housing is very confusing, due in large part to the multitude of names given to various facilities. In addition, the range of programs and services offered varies greatly, even within one category of supportive housing. Don't be fooled by labels. When you are checking out a facility, ask numerous questions and take detailed notes. Also, contact your local Area Agency on Aging.

Numerous national groups offer free brochures and booklets on supportive housing arrangements. Among them:

American Association of Retired Persons, 601 E Street NW, Washington, DC 20049.

National Consumers League, 815 15th Street NW, Washington, DC 20005.

American Association of Homes for the Aging, 901 E Street NW, Suite 500, Washington, DC 20004-2037.

American Health Care Association, 1201 L Street NW, Washington, DC 20005-4014.

National Citizens' Coalition for Nursing Home Reform, 1224 M Street NW, Suite 301, Washington, DC 20005-5183.

Living with Your Children

For many people, moving in with their adult children is the best choice when living alone is no longer possible. For other people, it can be a difficult choice (sometimes the poorest of the available options). If you are considering such a move, you need to talk seriously with your family to understand how each one of them feels. You also need to be sure to express all your feelings about the situation. Talk with friends who live with their adult children and try to understand what it's like for them. Think through these questions for both parents and adult children and discuss the issues together before agreeing to join their household.

Questions for the Parent

♦ Does your son or daughter want you to move in? If not, and you move in anyway, will the emotional strain be too much on you?

♦ How will living expenses be shared?

◆ What will you use for transportation? Will you have easy access to shopping, a place of worship, friends, and other interests of your own?

◆ Do you have friends in the area where your children live? Are there people close by with whom you can create friendships?

◆ Will you be able to accommodate your child's lifestyle?

◆ Will you be able to live with your children's children?

◆ Can your children afford to have you live with them?

◆ How will your presence affect family relationships?

◆ How much time will you expect your child to spend with you?

Questions for the Adult Child

◆ Do you want your parent to move in? Have you been honest in expressing your feelings about it?

◆ If you don't want your mother or father to move in but it must happen anyway, will you be able to handle it?

◆ How much time can you spend with your parent? Have you explained what your weeks and weekends are like?

◆ Do you expect your parent to do chores around the house? Is this a reasonable expectation? Have you talked to your parent about what to expect and why?

◆ Can you afford it?

◆ Are you aware of local services that could help you through difficult situations?

Reprinted courtesy of American Association of Retired Persons (AARP).

Adult Day Care

Adult day-care centers can provide a wide variety of support services for older persons including care and supervision, meals, recreation, exercise, personal care, nursing care, group and individual activities, education, counseling, occupational therapy, physical therapy, and speech therapy. Twenty years ago they were virtually nonexistent, but today they are located in all 50 states and are rapidly growing in number. A recent survey of centers showed that the majority of participants live with others—either a spouse, adult children, or other family members or friends. However, 25 percent live alone or in a congregate housing facility.

The National Institute on Adult Day Care, a part of the National Council on Aging, states that day-care activities and services are designed to:

1. Help mentally and/or physically impaired adults to maintain or improve their level of functioning in order to remain in the community.

2. Offer participants the opportunity to socialize, enjoy peer support, and receive health and social services in a stimulating and supportive environment that promotes better physical and mental health.

3. Provide assistance to families and caregivers responsible for an older adult who cannot be left alone during the day and yet does not require 24-hour nursing care in an institution.

4. Help functionally impaired adults who live alone and need supportive services to improve or maintain their level of independence.

The centers may be operated by hospitals, nursing homes, religious or fraternal organizations, neighborhood groups, or local governments, or they may be privately owned. The average cost of care is $30–$65 per day. Transportation services are usually provided for a nominal fee. Most centers are open Monday through Friday, during business hours; a small number of them are open seven days a week. Contact your local Area Agency on Aging. Or, call the National Council on Aging: 202-479-1200.

FAMILY ROOTS

Tracing Your Family Tree

According to the National Genealogical Society, researching family trees has become the third most popular hobby in the United States. Motivated by endless curiosity, thousands of "roots-sleuths" are combing through volumes of documents, on paper and microfilm, and sending out pounds of correspondence in an effort to obtain information about their ancestors. Even though the process is very time-consuming, and oftentimes frustrating, tree tracers say that the search is well worth the effort because it results in a strong sense of family identity and unity.

Because genealogical research has become so popular, there is plenty of help available if you decide to become a family detective. Your first stop should be the local library. The librarian will be able to point out various publications, books and magazines, that are written for beginners in genealogy; some libraries have full-fledged family history departments. In addition, the librarian can tell you if your local college or adult education school has a class in genealogy. And the librarian can help you locate any local, regional, or state genealogical and historical societies.

Another excellent source for all types of genealogical information is the National Genealogical Society. It has extensive library and education services and sells a variety of publications on tracing a family history. For information about the society's services as well as membership information, write to: **National Genealogical Society,** 4527 17th Street North, Arlington, VA 22207–2399.

Documenting your family history requires that you send away for copies of vital records such as birth certificates and marriage licenses. Your search may also lead you to the National Archives in Washington, DC, which has custody of millions of records relating to persons who have had dealings with the federal government. For example, the National Archives has census records, naturalization records, and military service records. Because these documents are useful in genealogical research, the National Archives has published a booklet, "Using Records in the National Archives for Genealogical Research." The booklet includes the following tips for beginners:

Start with Yourself

You are the beginning "twig" on your family tree. Start with the known—yourself—and work toward the unknown. Find the vital information about your parents and write it down. Next, look for information about your grandparents, then earlier generations.

Begin at home. Look for information in family Bibles, newspaper clippings, military certificates, birth and death certificates, marriage licenses, diaries, letters, scrapbooks, the backs of pictures, and babybooks.

Be concerned with extracting four items: names, dates, places, and relationships. These are the keys of the family searcher. People can be identified in records by their names, by the dates of events in their lives (birth, marriage, death), by the places where they lived, and by their relationships to others, either stated or implied.

Relatives

Visit or write to relatives in your family who may have information, particularly older relatives. Often, others before you have already gathered family data. You should write letters, make personal visits, and conduct telephone surveys to locate such persons and to find out what information is already collected. Advertise your family interests in national, regional, and local genealogical magazines.

Non-Federal Records

Vital statistics. Some states began to keep records of birth and death earlier, but, for most of the United States, birth and death registration became a requirement only around the turn of the century (ca. 1890–1915). Before the turn of the century, births and deaths were recorded, generally, only in church records and family Bibles. Marriage records will be found in most counties, often dating from the establishment of the county.

Deeds and wills. Records of property acquisition and disposition can be good genealogical sources. Such records normally are in county courthouses. Often the earlier county records (or copies of them) are also available in state archives.

Visit state, regional, and local institutions in your area. Libraries, historical and genealogical societies, and archival depositories are all good sources for genealogical and family history data.

The National Archives

Records are deposited in National Archives facilities in the Washington, DC, area and in 11 National Archives Regional Archives. These records may contain full information about the person or give little information beyond a name. Searches in the records may be very time-consuming as many records lack name indexes. The National Archives staff is unable to make extensive searches but, given enough identifying information, will try to find a record about a specific person.

Oral History

You are the sum of the family members who came before you. Their lives, values, and beliefs have greatly influenced the person you have become. Each family member has a unique story to tell, full of drama, humor, and surprises. It's likely that you have already heard a number of stories and experiences, whether the storyteller was a parent, grandparent, aunt, or uncle. But unless the stories are recorded, they will fade from memory and large portions of your family history will be lost. Recording interviews with family members is the purpose of oral history. It's a way of preserving your family saga for future generations. It's a way of capturing the thoughts and voices of family members while their stories are still alive and fresh in their minds.

Anyone, child or adult, can easily conduct an oral history interview. A tape recorder, or video camera, and a good set of interview questions are all you need. Most people choose an older relative to interview; the generation gap usually produces a lively and interesting result. Interviewing parents, regardless of your age, is a good place to start; young children often have great success when taping oral biographies of grandparents. However, there need not be a significant age difference between the interviewer and the interviewee.

Preparing for the Interview

Once you have chosen someone to interview, do some advance work. Talk to the subject's friends and relatives so that you can prepare a good set of interview questions.

Test your equipment. Make sure your tape recorder, or camcorder, is working, and have extra batteries on hand.

Choose a comfortable setting for the interview. You want a quiet place, free of noise. Turn off all radios and televisions. Also, it's usually best to conduct the interview in private; involving other relatives or friends can be distracting. If you are using video equipment, create a "set" by filling the room with family photos and other memorabilia.

Remember that you are not the subject of the interview. It's okay to be an active participant in the conversation, but your primary duty is to ask questions and listen.

Interview Questions

Your interview is only as good as your questions, so write them down and have them in front of you. Try to steer clear of too many questions that require a simple yes/no response, and instead ask open-ended, evocative questions. If you ask a sensitive question that makes your subject feel uncomfortable, just drop it and move on. If your subject seems to go off on a tangent, relax and let the person ramble on for a while; you might get some information that you never thought to ask about. Above all, show an interest in the interview. It's essential that your interviewee feel special and at ease.

The following questions are meant as a starting point to help you think about the kinds of questions you want to include in an interview. They are somewhat geared for an interview in which a younger person is interviewing an older person.

1. What do you know about your last name? Its origin or meaning? Did it change when you or your ancestors came to the United States from another country?

2. Who were the first family members to come to the United States? When did they come, where did they come from, and where did they settle?

3. What were your parents like? Where did they grow up? How did they make a living? What kinds of values and traditions did they try to teach you? Do you remember any special stories about them?

4. Where were you born and where did you grow up? What are some of your earliest memories? How many brothers and sisters do you have? Where are they? What are they like? Were you a close family?

5. What were you like in high school? What did you look like? What kind of grades did you get? Did you go to college? Where, and what did you study? Tell me what life was like when you were growing up. Who influenced you the most when you were growing up, and why?

6. What did or do you do to earn a living? What was your first job and how much did you get paid? How many different kinds of jobs have you had? If you had it to do all over again, would you choose another profession? If so, what would it be?

7. Were you ever in the service? Army? Navy? Air Force? Marines? What did you think of military life?

8. When did you first meet your (wife, husband)? How did you meet? What was your first impression? What was your wedding like? How many children do you have and where are they? What was the hardest thing about being a (mother, father)?

9. Can you think of any really unusual relatives in the family or any great family adventures? Like a relative who made and lost a fortune? A relative who became a hero? A relative who created a scandal?

10. What was the best moment in your life? The worst?

11. If you could change one decision in your life, what would it be?

12. What one piece of advice would you give to young people today?

Family Reunions

Planning a family reunion can be fun if you are organized and you start planning months in advance of the event. The basics that you need to consider:

Invitation list. Gather the names, addresses, and phone numbers of all those you plan to invite. Make a master list which you can use during the entire planning stage. Be aware of family sensitivities. For example, if Uncle Jack has three ex-wives, it might not be smart to invite all of them.

Location. Do you want a backyard affair at the family homestead, a picnic at a local park, or an extravagant party at a ski resort? Most families opt for a simple, low-cost location.

Date. If you have a large guest list, this can be a problem. Sometimes a reunion can be planned to coincide with another family event like a wedding or a 100th birthday party, times when many relatives are already likely to gather. Many reunions are planned for the summer months when out-of-towners usually schedule vacation time. If nailing down a date presents difficulty, you might consider sending a preinvitation flyer to all guests and give them a choice of two dates. Ask them to check off the date they would prefer. Tally the results to determine the winning date.

Invitations. Send them out months in advance and ask for an RSVP. Be sure you put a deadline for responses on the invitation.

Food. If most of the guests live near the reunion site, you might have every family bring a potluck meal, but someone will have to coordinate who brings what. Or, you could have the event catered, or buy all the food and prepare it yourself (with the help of others, of course). If you choose one of the latter two options, you will need to collect money in advance from the guests. Figure out the cost per adult and per child and include the information on the reunion invitation. Guests can mail in a check with their RSVPs.

Lodging. Out-of-towners will need a place to stay. If a large number of family members live near the reunion site, some out-of-towners can stay with relatives. However, before you volunteer anyone's home, make sure the relative is willing to put up guests. Call a local hotel or motel and check on the available rates. If you have enough customers, you can usually negotiate a good room rate.

Entertainment. Take a look at the age breakdown of your guest list. Plan age-appropriate games and activities.

Special requests. Perhaps you want to create a large family scrapbook and you need photos from everyone. Or, you want to produce a family recipe book. Maybe you want to have a talent show at the reunion. If you have any special requests, make sure your invitees know what you need and when you need it.

Committee chairpersons. Putting together a family reunion is too much work for one person. You need to delegate responsibility to other family members. Think about the available talent in your family. Who is a logical choice for handling the food? The entertainment? The invitations?

Bottom line. Cost will affect your turnout. The lower the cost, the more family members are likely to attend.

6

PETS

PETS OF MANY KINDS

DOGS

CATS

PETS OF MANY KINDS

Choosing a Pet

Living with an animal of another species can be one of the great joys of life. Poets have written bad verse about it for good reason. The down side to pet owning: an animal takes time and attention and money. The Society for the Prevention of Cruelty to Animals suggests that you consider these questions before you adopt a pet.

♦ Are you willing to care for the animal throughout its lifetime?

♦ Will you give your pet love and attention when it needs you, and not just at your convenience?

♦ Can you afford the cost of food, grooming, and regular veterinary care—including yearly shots and checkups?

♦ Will you see that your pet gets regular, daily exercise?

♦ If your pet is a dog, are you prepared to housebreak your pet and to train it in basic obedience? Will you license it and obey the leash law?

When considering the kind of animal you might adopt as a pet, consult all members of the family, including other pets. If you are thinking about adopting another dog, take the dog that is already

AVERAGE COSTS FOR KEEPING DOGS AND CATS

The lifetime costs of keeping a dog or cat eclipse any money you shell out for a fancy pedigree. One expensive illness can run the total far beyond the average shown here. Dog costs are for a medium-sized dog. You may want to add the cost of boarding, which runs about $10 a day for a cat and $15 for a dog.

Expense	Cat	Dog
First-Year Special Costs		
Getting from shelter*	$25	$55
Vaccines	200	200
Total	$225	$255
Yearly Costs		
Vaccines (after first year)	$27	$65
Toys and grooming supplies	75	160
Feeding	145	250
Other vet care	80	135
Kitty litter	80	
Flea/tick care		80
Training		125
Total Yearly Costs	$407	$815
Total Lifetime Costs**	$6,303	$9,970

*If you buy a purebred animal, add difference between purchase price and cost of obtaining the animal from the shelter.
**15 years for a cat, 12 years for a dog.

COST OF KEEPING PETS

1 horse =

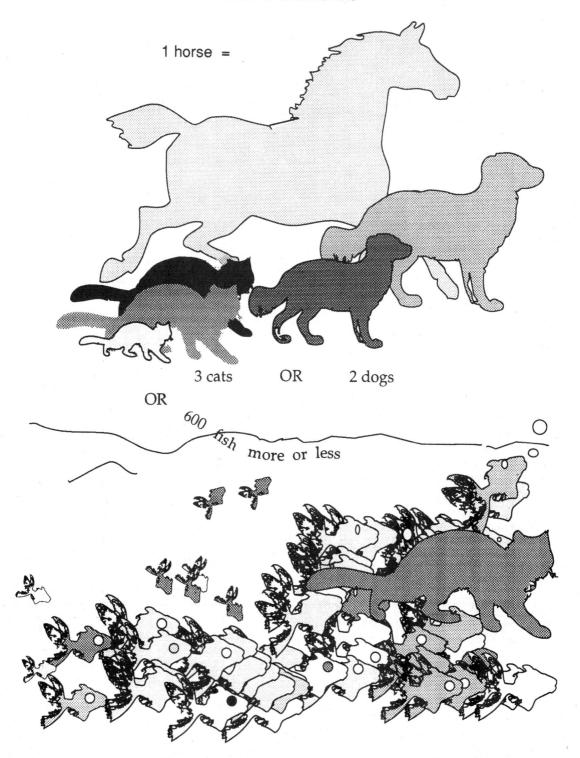

3 cats   OR   2 dogs

OR

600 fish more or less

WHAT THE FAMOUS HAVE TO SAY ABOUT PETS

All animals are equal but some animals are more equal than others.
—George Orwell

Stately, kindly, lordly friend, condescend here to sit by me.
—Algernon Charles Swinburne

A gentle hound should never play the cur.
—John Shelton

Love me, love my dog.
—John Heywood

À bon chat, bon rat. [To a good cat, a good rat.]
—French proverb

Animals are such agreeable friends—they ask no questions, they pay no criticisms.
—George Eliot

The more I see of men, the more I admire dogs.
—Madame Roland

If you pick up a starving dog and make him prosper he will not bite you. That is the principal difference between a dog and a man.
—Mark Twain

Nature teaches beasts to know their friends.
—Shakespeare

Let Hercules himself do what he may, The cat will mew, the dog will have his day.
—Shakespeare

Dogs display reluctance and wrath/If you try to give them a bath.
—Ogden Nash

a member of your family to visit the prospective adoptee to see how the two animals get along. Older cats often will more easily accept a kitten than another grown cat.

Consider adopting an animal from a shelter. (Look in the Yellow Pages under "Animal Shelter," "Humane Society," or "Animal Control.") Some adoptable animals are puppies and kittens, others are older pets who may have been housebroken and trained in obedience. Most shelters try to match people and animals. Almost all require that the animals be spayed or neutered as a condition of adoption.

PETTING YOUR PET EACH DAY CAN KEEP THE DOCTOR AWAY

Having a pet can keep you healthy—both physically and mentally. When your pet is in the same room with you, your heart rate and blood pressure go down. Older pet owners make fewer trips to the doctor than those who are not blessed with pets. Pets have a beneficial effect on abused children, on families in stressful situations, and on people who have neurological disorders, learning problems, and physical disabilities. The survival rate of pet owners who have heart surgery increases after a year above that of those who do not own pets. People with pets may even live longer than people without pets.

Allergies to Pets

At least one American out of 20 suffers from an allergy to furry animals. That allergic American ordinarily is reacting to animal dander (particles from feathers, skin or hair) and saliva. Symptoms include eye irritation, sneezing, and asthma. The allergies are often specific—a person allergic to cats may not be allergic to dogs (or the other way around). About half of sufferers from cat allergies say they will keep their cats in spite of the problem. Even so, a great many pets end up in the pound or are abandoned because their owners are allergic to them. The good news? Allergic children improve with age.

The greater the amount of dander the animal sheds, the greater the allergic person's reaction. The secret to allergy control is to reduce the amount of dander. Some breeds of animals produce less dander: for example, all sizes of poodles, the bichon frise, and the Portuguese water dog are relatively dander-free.

Advice

♦ Talk to an allergist.

♦ Investigate allergy shots (desensitization or immunotherapy). These have been quite successful in solving or alleviating the problem. One-third of allergy sufferers who have had shots improve completely.

♦ Buy an air cleaner, air conditioner, or humidifier for your house.

♦ Dust and vacuum at least once a week; more, if possible. Use a special filter in the vacuum.

♦ Minimize other allergy-causing materials in your house. Cover mattresses and pillows with nonallergenic covers. Avoid down and feathers.

♦ Much as you love sleeping with your animal, keep it out of the bedroom and in places with washable surfaces.

♦ Once a day brush the animal and put the shed hair in a sealed bag. Wipe the animal off with a damp towel. Bathe it at least once or twice a month.

♦ Ask your vet to recommend products that keep down the amount of allergens on the animal.

♦ Feed the animal a pet food with enough fat so that the skin does not dry. Put a teaspoon of oil in its food.

♦ Use unperfumed cat litter, and change it often.

♦ Keep dogs outside in a fenced yard, at least part of the time. Animal experts recommend that cats be kept inside.

♦ If all else fails, buy a snake or turtle.

ANIMAL SUPERIORITY

Any time you start to feel superior to your animal consider these facts:

♦ The dog's olfactory region (the inside of its nose) is 14 times as sensitive as that of a human being. Some dogs can smell sulphuric acid at a concentration of less than one drop in 100 gallons.

♦ Humans can hear sounds up to a pitch of 20,000 cycles per second. Dogs can hear sounds of 60,000 cycles per second.

♦ In a situation in which you would be utterly lost, a cat knows how to find its way home. This may be because of visual memory and sense of smell, perhaps because of changes in Earth's magnetic field.

Finding a Lost Dog or Cat

Pets can't call home when they're lost. They may not be able to find their way back (in spite of stories about pets making crosscontinental trips to find their old homes). Or if they do remember the way, perhaps (temporarily at least), they are having such a good time where they are that they don't want to come home just yet. The dog who takes off in terror at the sound of Fourth of July fireworks can end up happily existing as a member of a feral pack. So it's up to you to find it.

Take heart. Start your search immediately. Time is important because animals travel fast.

Day One

The first thing to do is search your neighborhood. Call your animal and listen for a response. Check garages—animals have been inadvertently locked in garages.

If that search fails, begin a more extensive one.

1. Write up a description of your animal: breed, color, markings, sex, age, weight, size,

tattoos, scars, license number. Remember, your animal might not look the same to other people as it does to you, so be precise.

2. Find a clear photograph of your pet.

3. Then, on a map, with your home as the center, draw a circle with a radius of 25 miles. (Dogs can wander that far very quickly.) Using both the white and yellow pages in the phone book, make a list of phone numbers and addresses of the following within that circle, and start calling:

♦ Animal shelters (both private and public). Give the agency personnel the detailed description of your pet as well as your phone number and the phone numbers of at least two other people. Your pet may have lost his license tag, so be precise. Ask for locations of research labs in your area using animals as test subjects.

♦ Contact research facilities and ask them if they have your pet. If they are uncooperative, enlist the help of the humane society and animal rights activists.

♦ Veterinarians and animal hospitals—to see if your pet has been hurt. Ask vets where unidentified hurt animals are taken.

♦ Dead Animal Pick Up or Highway Maintenance or Sanitation—in case your animal has been killed and hauled away.

♦ Police and sheriffs. Ask if those on patrol will keep an eye open for your dog.

4. Start *visiting* pounds and animal shelters to see if your pet is there. Personnel are busy, and they may not associate your description with a pet in a back cage so it's important to look for yourself.

5. Place an ad in the LOST section in local newspapers.

6. Make up lost-pet posters and put them up at humane societies, veterinarians, and pet supply stores, and on telephone poles and trees around the neighborhood (and beyond). Offer a substantial reward—in cash, no questions asked. Be sure to give *almost complete* information, but withhold something in case someone who calls you claiming to have found your pet is not on the up-and-up. Don't give your dog's name—a dognapper can use your dog's name to control him.

Day Two and Beyond

1. Keep calling and visiting shelters. Most shelters keep dogs for a limited period of time—perhaps a week or two, then euthanize them or pass them off to local research facilities for use as test subjects in experiments.

2. Look in local papers for FOUND ads.

3. Check places where strays hang out: train stations (especially early in the morning), garbage dumps, isolated areas (woods and vacant lots). Ask Animal Control for advice on this. Good times to cruise: early morning and early and late evening. Look for tracks. Every once in a while, get out of your car at a likely spot, turn off the engine, and listen. Call the dog's name, and listen again. If your dog is in trouble—caught in a trap or on a branch by the collar—you may hear it.

After Your Animal Is Found

To make sure this doesn't happen again:

1. Fence your yard (with fencing high enough to contain your animal), and keep the gate shut.

2. Don't leave your pet alone outside.

3. License your animal. You can license a cat as well as a dog. Tell the licensing agency if you change your address.

4. Buy an identification tag of heavy colored plastic. Write your telephone number and pet's license number inside its collar.

5. Have a picture taken of your pet.

6. Tattoo the inner thigh (back leg) of your cat or dog with your Social Security number (or other number). Vets, groomers, and personnel in animal shelters will do the tattooing, which is painless. Don't tattoo the ear! Wicked people can, and often do, slice ears off to remove an ID number.

7. Register the number with a lost-pet registry. Example: **The National Dog Registry** (NDR), in operation since 1966, uses a highly sophisticated computer system to work with vets and various agencies to locate and return dogs. Its success rate is over 95 percent. The hot-line number is open 24 hours a day, seven days a week. For information, call 800-NDR-DOGS.

WHERE TO FIND INFORMATION ABOUT PETS

Your veterinarian, pet store, and book store can be good sources of information about pets—everything from breeds to fleas. For a Dog and Cat Book Catalog, contact: Direct Book Service, 8 Summercreek Place, PO Box 3073, Wenatchee, WA 98807 (800-776-2665; FAX 509-662-7233).

Your Dog and Cat and the New Baby

Because babies cry and flail their arms, some dogs assume they are wounded prey and attack them. For less obvious reasons, cats have been known to claw new babies. That does not mean you have to get rid of your pet when you have a baby. On the other hand, it is important to prepare the animal for the new arrival.

Give your dog obedience training before the new baby comes home. Take it to the vet for a checkup, and if you have not already done so and the dog is old enough, arrange for spaying or neutering.

Train your dog not to be possessive with toys or food, or your dog may snap at the crawling baby who tries to play with the dog's squeak toy.

You may need the help of an animal behaviorist for this. Older children (from the age of three or four) can learn to leave the dog alone when it is eating.

Introduce your dog to the sounds infants make, perhaps by playing a tape. Be reassuring as the dog listens. Accustom the dog to the smells of baby powder and other baby preparations even before the baby arrives. Let it meet babies and toddlers to learn how they smell, move, and sound. Hold the baby and talk calmly to your pet at the same time.

When you first bring the baby home, let someone else hold it while you greet your dog. Pet your dog when the baby is around. Don't let the dog's routine be disrupted (even if yours is). Never leave a baby or toddler alone with any dog.

Do not declaw a cat—it may turn into a biter. (See "Should You Declaw Your Cat?" p. 338.) If the cat hides, don't disturb it, but treat it reassuringly when it comes out. Do not punish a cat for elimination accidents or spraying. The behavior comes from anxiety, so comfort is more appropriate. Don't allow the cat in the crib. And, no, it will not suck away the baby's breath!

Teach children to treat pets with respect and kindness. Toddlers should learn not to grab the cat by the tail or try to ride the dog. Three- and four-year-olds can learn to empathize with a pet's feelings. By age five, a child can help care for a pet by doing chores like filling its water bowl.

Dogs

Adopting a Mixed-Breed Dog

A mixed-breed dog is usually one of a kind. In general, mixed-breeds are less likely to have the physical and emotional problems that result from inbreeding. On the other hand, you are less likely to be able to predict accurately what a mixed-breed puppy will look and act like when it grows up. The size of its feet indicates only *generally* how big it will get, for instance. To get more of an inkling of the puppy's future appearance and behavior, ask to see the puppy's mother and father.

You can adopt a mixed-breed dog from several sources: your veterinarian, an animal welfare group (humane society), animal shelter. Some shelters offer more information about their dogs than others. Try to find out why the dog is up for adoption, if it has had its shots, if it has any health or personality problems. Many shelters will help you find an animal that fits your needs and lifestyle. Be prepared in any case for a period of adjustment when the dog comes to live with you.

Here are some crossbreeds of distinction:

- cock-a-poo: cocker spaniel/poodle.
- chi-poo: Chihuahua/poodle.
- malte-poo: Maltese/poodle.
- peek-a-poo: Pekingese/poodle.

Choosing a Healthy Puppy

Try to observe the puppy with its litter mates for a fair amount of time. An energetic puppy can quickly run out of steam and go to sleep; if you see it half asleep, you may think it is more lethargic than it really is. A healthy puppy has bright, clear eyes, clean, pleasant-smelling ears and skin. It has no excessive overbite or underbite. Male puppies should have two testicles. Look for personality traits that appeal to you. However, it is wise to avoid puppies that are exceptionally intrepid or withdrawn. They can present problems of aggression later.

Dog Breeds

Dog breeds arose through human efforts to produce animals that had certain looks or that were geniuses at skills like fighting, herding, hunting, and guarding. In the recent past, particularly in the United States, some breeders have gone overboard, sacrificing function for form by inbreeding too closely for characteristics like coat color, shape, and markings. As a result, many breeds are plagued with genetic defects.

The American Kennel Club (AKC) registers some, but not all, purebred dogs. It does not guarantee that the dogs it registers are healthy and without genetic flaws. For a regional listing of AKC dog breeds, contact AKC Customer Service, 5580 Centerview Drive, Raleigh, NC 27606 (919-233-9767). Other specialized breed clubs emphasize performance over bloodlines also. Border collie registries, for instance, pay more attention to the dogs' herding skills than to their pedigrees.

Almost all dog breeds arose from crosses of two or more other breeds. For example, many gundog breeds can trace their ancestry to Spanish sporting dogs, like the Spanish pointer, which has existed as a breed for at least 300 years. The English pointer was developed by crossbreeding Spanish pointers with foxhounds.

When choosing a dog, keep in mind what that dog was originally bred to do. That will give you clues to its personality and behavior. However, remember that ancestry is not everything, and that training means a lot. For instance, if a dog breed has a war dog background, that does not mean the dog is untrustworthy or vicious. If you live in a small space, consider small dogs, or more lethargic breeds like the basset hound or English bulldog. On the other hand, remember that some small dogs bark a good deal. If you find grooming a nuisance, consider a short-haired breed.

Categories (By the Job)

In general, breeds fall into certain categories:

Sighthounds (or gaze hounds). Swift dogs that hunt by sight, these breeds probably developed from dogs that aided bow-and-arrow hunters in open country. Sometimes a trained falcon would be released to distract and harry the game while the hounds ran it down. Sight hounds were portrayed often in ancient Persian and Egyptian art. These dogs need exercise, and some, like the borzoi and saluki, need a firm hand.

Scent hounds. Known for "nose" and stamina, scent hounds work in packs, running the prey until it is exhausted. Some breeds bay to let the hunter know about the imminent kill. They are more likely than some other kinds of dogs to run

away, though not intentionally, since once on the trail, they find it difficult to give up. They are affectionate and usually good with children.

Pointers and retrievers. After the invention of guns, dogs' skills became more specialized. A pointer helped the hunter locate the game by pointing to it with its body posture. The dog had to have ultimate self-control. Retrievers—bred for soft mouths—found and brought game back once the hunter shot it. Intelligent and loyal, pointers and retrievers make good pets. They thrive on lots of exercise and working at the jobs they were bred for. Retrievers generally love to swim.

Spaniels. Their name probably comes from "Español," because their ancestors were sporting dogs in ancient Spain. Spaniels have great endurance and a keen sense of smell. Generally they are accomplished at flushing and retrieving game. Like all hunting dogs, spaniels need exercise.

Terriers. Terriers were bred to hunt down animals that live in lairs, like rabbits, foxes, badgers, and rats. They tend to be tough, fiesty, and persistent. Terriers were popular in 18th- and 19th-century Britain, especially among the working classes. They can be excitable and often need obedience training.

Herding dogs. Capitalizing on dogs' talents in separating prey from a herd, humans trained dogs to herd domesticated animals. Herding dogs are usually friendly and intelligent, as well as protective. Some guard dogs evolved from herding dogs. They will help keep track of children, but may be a nuisance if allowed to herd toddlers, because they may accidentally knock them over.

Draft dogs. Dogs whose ancestry included pulling carts or sleds often like to give rides to children. They are gentle, but some, like the husky, will roam.

Fighting dogs. Some dogs bred to fight are affectionate with people, but not trustworthy with other dogs unless socialized. Bulldogs and other breeds were trained to attack tethered bulls in England, but this was outlawed in 1835. Courageous, they make good watchdogs, and are generally reliable with children.

DOG BREED CHART

S=small, M=medium, L=large, VL=very large

Breed	Size	Jobs	Comments
Afghan hound	L	Hunting	Once owned by nobility and used to hunt gazelles, antelope, foxes, wolves. Said to have been on Noah's ark. Perhaps originated in Egypt. Developed long coat living in cold Afghan mountains. Elegant looking. Hard to train. Problems: cataracts, thyroid conditions.
Airedale terrier	M	General (hunting and guarding)	Cross of Black-and-Tan Terrier with Otter Hound, used to hunt badger and otter. Hard, wiry coat. Guard and messenger in World War I. Police dog.
Akita	L-VL	General (hunting and guarding)	Originated in Japan. Hunter of waterfowl, deer, sable, wild boar, bear. Guard dog (an Akita guarded the Emperor) and army dog. Furry, bearlike. Double coat–harsh outer layer, soft undercoat. Problems: aggression. "Owning an Akita is like dating a psychotic model," one dog trainer has said.
Alaskan malamute	L	Draft	Sled-pulling dog, used to carry loads, more powerful than Husky. Bred for pulling freight.
Australian cattle dog	M	Herding (cattle)	Perhaps has some dingo blood. Herds, drives, and pens cattle, darting in and out of herd, dodging hooves. May need obedience training. Also known as Queensland heeler.
Australian shepherd	M	Herding (sheep)	Good watchdogs, easy to train.
Australian terrier	S	General (hunting vermin and guarding)	Brought to Australia by early settlers from England. Cross with other terriers. Good guard dog. Also killer of rats, rabbits, snakes.
Basset hound	M	Hunting (scent hound)	Known in France since the 16th century. Perhaps came from a dwarf strain of bloodhound. Good for hunting through underbrush. Short-haired. Low energy when not at work. Hard to train, but even-tempered and quiet. Problems: prolapsed nictitans, gastric dilatation-volvulus, slipped disc, cervical spondylopathy.
Beagle	S-M	Hunting (hound)	Related to foxhound. Hunter of hares and rabbits. Pocket beagles traveled in coat pockets at start of horseback chase. Strong and good with children. Hard to train. Barking may annoy. Short-haired. Problems: P.R.A., epilepsy, cataracts, kidney disease, spinal disc conditions.
Bearded collie	M	Herding (sheep)	May have originated in Poland, brought to Scotland by medieval traders. Long-haired. Perhaps ancestor of Old English Sheepdog.
Bedlington terrier	S-M	Hunting (terrier)	Rat and rabbit catcher, bred by miners and steelworkers in England for hunting and poaching. Speedy. Looks like a lamb.
Bernese mountain dog	VL	General (draft, herding, guarding)	Bred as cart-puller for weavers and cheesemakers in Berne, Switzerland. Problems: genetic bone cancer.

DOG BREED CHART (cont.)

Breed	Size	Jobs	Comments
Bichon frise	S	Entertaining	In Europe, court dogs and 19th-century circus dogs. Curly, double coat with coarse guard hairs and soft undercoat is nearly hypoallergenic. Sheds very little, but needs much grooming. Affectionate and lively, needs a good deal of human companionship.
Bloodhound	VL	Hunting (scent hound)	At least two millennia old. Known in France, Belgium, and Switzerland as St. Hubert Hound after St. Hubert, patron saint of hunting, who kept a pack of bloodhounds at his abbey. Tends to be low-energy when not working. Even-tempered. Quiet. Problems: prolapsed nictitans, ectropion.
Border collie	M	Herding (sheep)	Bred for skill in sheep herding not for looks. From Scottish border country. Problems: deafness, P.R.A., hip dysplasia.
Border terrier	S	Hunting (terrier)	Chased foxes into their dens and rooted them out. Ran with horses and hounds. Hard, wiry coat.
Borzoi	L	Hunting (sight hound)	Originated in Middle East. Crossed with Russian collie for warm coat. Used by Russian nobles to hunt wolves. Fast runner. Problems: gastric dilatation-volvulus.
Boston terrier	S-M	Pitfighting	Cross of bulldog and White English terrier, never a hunter. Problems: cataracts, keratitis (inflammation of cornea); whelping difficulties.
Boxer	M	Fighting, guarding	Ancestors may have been mastiffs that took part in medieval bull-baiting. Breed developed in 19th century by crossing the bulldog and other breeds to produce a police dog. Good watchdog. Problems: gastric dilatation-volvulus, pyloric stenosis in young dogs, colitis, prolapsed nictitans, cryptorchidism.
Brittany spaniel	M	Hunting (spaniel that points)	Originated in France. Some pointer blood. Known as "poacher's dog." Flushes birds and retrieves them. Works in water and on land.
Bulldog	M	Fighting	Developed from mastiff and used at bull-baiting, until made illegal in 1835. Low energy. Hard to train. Problems: prolapsed nictitans, difficulty in whelping, difficulty breathing (elongated soft palate).
Bull terrier	M	Fighting	Fighting dog of 19th century, refinement of Staffordshire terrier, perhaps crossed with Dalmatian and Pointer. Problems: deafness, aggression.
Cairn terrier	S	Hunting (terrier)	Named after stone piles (cairns) used to mark graves where foxes ran to take cover and terriers chased them. Also used to hunt wildcats. Problems: P.R.A., jaw disorders.
Cavalier King Charles spaniel	S	Companion	Court dogs. Problems: elongated soft palate.

Breed	Size	Jobs	Comments
Chihuahua	S	Companion	May go back to time of Aztecs and Incas, and may have been bred for food. Good city dog. Barks but not excessively. Frisky. Problems: cryptorchidism, hydrocephalus.
Chow chow	M	General (fighting, hauling, hunting)	Brought from China to England in 18th century. Mongolian ancestors used as war dogs, for hauling and hunting, source of food and fur. Possessive and reserved, needs obedience training. Hard to train. May bite. Blue-black mouth and tongue. Problems: entropion, mating and whelping difficulties, territorial.
Cocker spaniel	M	Hunting (spaniel)	Name comes from the word *cock*, which means to flush game, or from the word *woodcock*. English cocker spaniel is larger than American cocker spaniel. Likes to play, but can bite. Needs obedience training. Silky coat, needs frequent grooming. Problems: skin conditions, P.R.A., nervousness, blood-clotting problems, deafness, cataracts, ectropion, ear infections, weakness of spine, elbow dysplasia.
Collie	M	Herding	Came from Scottish herding dogs. Low energy. Even-tempered. Can have rough or smooth coat, with soft undercoat. Problems: Collie eye anomaly, blindness and deafness, epilepsy.
Dachshund	S	General (hunting and guarding)	Name means badgerdog in German. Good watchdogs and hunters of rabbits. A clown, good with children, intelligent. Problems: diabetes, P.R.A.. slipped disc, gastric dilatation-volvulus, juvenile pyoderma, urinary conditions; tiger dachschund—blindness and deafness.
Dalmatian	M	General (coach dog, hunting, guarding, hauling)	The firehouse dog. Not from Dalmatia. Pointer ancestors. In 19th century used as carriage dog, to run along with coach. Affinity with horses. Used in stable to guard and kill vermin. Short-haired, but sheds. Problems: urinary tract infections, deafness, skin conditions, hip dysplasia.
Dandie Dinmont terrier	S	Hunting (terrier)	Named after a character in Walter Scott novel who bred terriers. Was used in hunting fox, badger, and otter.
Doberman pinscher	L	General (hunting, herding, guarding)	Name from the breeder: Louis Dobermann. Bred from Manchester Terrier, Rottweiler, perhaps shepherd dogs. Can track, herd sheep, and retrieve. Good watchdog, easy to train. Short-haired. Problems: cervical spondylopathy, juvenile pyoderma, blood-clotting difficulties, gastric dilatation-volvulus, hip dysplasia, aggression, predisposition to parvo.
English springer spaniel	M	Hunting (spaniel)	Sprung game for falconers, which gave it part of its name. Also follows and retrieves game. Energetic, good family dog. Silky coat. Problems: aggression related to dominance ("rage syndrome"), ear infections, eye conditions, hip dysplasia.

DOG BREED CHART (cont.)

Breed	Size	Job	Comments
German shepherd (Alsatian)	L	Guarding	Produced from several different country dogs at end of 19th century. Used in World War I as army dog. Now a guard dog, police dog, guide dog. Good family watchdog. Devoted, intelligent, easy to train, but may bite. Double coat: rough outer coat, soft undercoat. Problems: gastric dilatation-volvulus, exocrine pancreatic insufficiency, conjunctivitis, cataracts, hip dysplasia, eosinophilic myostitis, osteochondritis dissecans (elbow), eye and heart conditions, epilepsy, bone conditions, diarrhea, hindquarters becoming weak with middle age, diabetes, hydrocephalus; bad temper and nervousness, aggression or over-shyness.
Golden retriever	M	Hunting (retriever)	Cross with setters, spaniels, Newfoundland. Good in water. Often used as guide dog for blind. Excellent family dog, even-tempered, easy to train. Fine watchdog. Problems: P.R.A., cataracts, hip dysplasia, bloat, thyroid disorders, blood disorders, eye and skin disorders.
Great Dane	VL (150 pounds)	Hunting	Royal dog in Middle Ages, used in wild-boar hunts. Was favorite of Bismarck. Problems: gastric dilatation-volvulus, cervical spondylopathy, hip dysplasia, blindness and deafness.
Greyhound	M	Hunting (sight hound)	Bred for track, show, and coursing. Name may mean "gaze hound." Known in time of pharoahs. Can run at 40 mph. Problem: gastric dilatation-volvulus.
Irish red setter	M-L	Hunting	Used for finding game caught in nets. Freezes when it finds game, then drops ("sets"), hence its name. Cross of spaniels, Spanish pointers, other setters. Once red and white. High energy. Problems: entropion, ectropion, P.R.A., gastric dilatation-volvulus.
Irish wolfhound	VL (120 pounds)	General (hunting and fighting)	Lived in noble households, prized for size. Hunter of wolves, wild boar, deer. Also used in battle to pull the enemy from his horse.
Jack Russell	S	Hunting	Named for Reverend John Russell, who bred the dogs from Wire-Haired Fox Terriers to chase foxes into their lairs. Good ratter. Standards for looks are not strict.
Labrador retriever	M-L	General	First bred in Newfoundland to carry rope from ship to shore and to bring in fishing nets; then gundog in England. Named Labrador in 1887 by second Earl of Malmesbury. Retrieves water birds and will flush land birds. Now used often as companion dog for disabled and guide dog for blind. Good with children, even-tempered. Solid build. Short dense coat. Can be taught stunts. Problems: P.R.A., cataracts and other eye problems, osteochondritis dissecans, bloat, hip dysplasia and shoulder dysplasia.
Lhasa apso	S	Guarding	From Tibet, named after its city Lhasa, where it was bred by holy men as a watchdog. Long-haired. Problems: hernias, eye and kidney disorders, hip dysplasia.

Breed	Size	Jobs	Comments
Maltese	S	Lapdog	Favorite of noble households. Long-haired. Good show dog.
Mastiff	VL (150 pounds)	Fighting	War dog in England, was at Agincourt. Used in dog-fighting and bear-baiting in Middle Ages.
Newfoundland	VL (150 pounds)	Hauling and water rescue	Perhaps ancestors were dogs brought to Newfoundland by Vikings or were Pyrenean mountain dogs belonging to Frenchmen who came to the island in 1600s. Even-tempered, good around children, quiet. Problems: hip dysplasia, heart conditions.
Old English sheepdog	L	General (herding and guarding)	Bred as drover and herder for sheep and cattle. Tails once bobbed to show tax-free status as working dogs. Needs frequent grooming. Problems: cataracts.
Papillon	S	Companion	Seen in paintings by Rembrandt and Rubens. Name means butterfly in French: note its large ears. Silky coat.
Pekingese	S	Guarding	Sacred Chinese palace dogs, who were cared for by eunuchs. Good watchdogs. Problems: heart murmur, slipped disc, elongated soft palate.
Pointer	L	Hunting (pointing)	Originally used with greyhounds to hunt hares. Follows, points, retrieves. Problems: cataracts.
Pomeranian	S	Guarding	Toy dog. Good watchdog. Liable to snap. Double-coated with coarse outer coat, soft undercoat. Problems: tracheal collapse, dislocated kneecap.
Poodle	S-M	General (hunting and entertaining)	Bred from German gundogs (*pudels*) that retrieved game from water. Performed in 19th century French circuses. Good family pets, very intelligent, with sense of humor. Easy to train. Curly coat sheds very little, but needs grooming. Problems: standard– diabetes, hip dysplasia, skin conditions, P.R.A., cataracts, heart murmur, hydrocephalus, epilepsy; miniature and toy– skin complications, eye and heart conditions, P.R.A., ear infections, tracheal collapse, neck disc weakness, and kneecap dislocation.
Pug	S	Lapdog	Requires little grooming because of short coat. Short nose. Problems: breathing difficulties, heart and lung conditions.
Puli	M	General (guarding and hunting)	From Hungary. Police dog, watchdog, hunter of small animals. Coat is matted and ropy.
Pumi	M	General (guarding and hunting)	Terrier-like guard dog and vermin hunter. Coat like puli.
Pyrenean mountain dog	VL	General (herding and fighting)	Ancestors came to Europe from Asia over a millennium ago. Used as sheepdogs, to fight bears and wolves in mountain forest, as war dogs. Were at the court of Louis XIV.

DOG BREED CHART (cont.)

Breed	Size	Jobs	Comments
Rhodesian ridgeback	L	Hunting	South African, with ridge along spine of upstanding hair that goes in direction opposite to rest of coat. Used to track and harass lions.
Rottweiler	VL	General (herding and guarding)	German cattle dog, used now as police dog and guard dog. Name from town of Rottweil, but ancestors may have come to Germany with Roman soldiers. In Middle Ages was butcher's dog that herded cattle to market. Needs obedience training, but is a good family watchdog. Problems: diabetes, osteochondritis dissecans, bloat, blood disorders, predisposition to parvo.
Saluki	L	Hunting (hound)	A.k.a. Gazelle Hound. Looks like dogs pictured in pharoah's tomb. Used by Persians and Arabs to hunt gazelles.
Samoyed	M	General (hunting, hauling, guarding)	Named after Samoyed tribesmen of Siberia. Used to hunt, herd, and guard reindeer; pull sleds in pack. Taken on polar expeditions. Double-coated with harsh outer coat, soft undercoat. Problems: hip dysplasia.
Schnauzer	S-M	General (hunting, guarding, herding)	Good ratters and guard dogs. Used to herd cattle. Intrepid but not aggressive. Miniature schnauzer prone to bark. Wiry coat. Problems (miniature): cataracts, clogged hair follicles, kidney disease, swallowing from constriction of esophagus, heart problems, blood disorders, bladder stones.
Scottish terrier	S-M	Hunting	Has history of hunting fox and badger, chasing vermin. Can be snappish. Noisy bark. Problems: esophagus becoming blocked with a bone, diabetes, deafness.
Shar-Pei	M	Guarding and herding	A history as guard dogs for Chinese Emperors; also a hunting dog. Distinguished by loose skin folds, so ugly they're cute though they were bred to look like a Chinese warrior. Problems: entropion, kidney problems, skin diseases from bacteria collecting in skin folds, nervousness and neurosis, hip dysplasia, autoimmune system problems, bad bite, aggression.
Shetland sheepdog	M	Herding	Coat needs grooming. A good, cheerful companion and a fine guard dog. Needs exercise. Easy to train. Problems: Collie eye anomaly, P.R.A., skin sensitive in white parts of face.
Shih tzu	S	Companion	Originated in Tibet, lived in Chinese imperial court. Named after mythological Lion Dog. Long-haired. Problems: slipped disc.
Siberian husky	L	Hauling	Sled-pulling dog. Name comes from Chukchis, Siberian nomads, who used them. Bred more for speed than Malamute. Double-coated with harsh outer coat, soft undercoat. Problems: hip dysplasia, eye conditions.
Skye terrier	M	Hunting (terrier)	Hunter of foxes and badgers. A favorite of Queen Victoria.
St. Bernard	VL (200 pounds)	Guiding	Bred by European monks to help guide people through the mountains and for mountain rescue. Quiet. Problems: ectropion, prolapsed nictitans, osteochondritis dissecans, gastric dilatation-volvulus, nervousness, hip dysplasia.

Breed	Size	Jobs	Comments
Staffordshire bull terrier	M	Hunting and fighting	Cross of bulldog and terrier. Good ratters; used in dog fights. Originally kept by miners. Staffordshire Terrier is American version. Problems: cataracts, problems with aggression.
Weimaraner	L-VL	Hunting	"Gray ghost" German dog, known as far back as the 17th century as a hunter. In the 19th century Weimar noblemen started breeding it for specific hunting tasks, to trail stag, point birds. High-strung and intelligent. Short-haired. Problems: gastric dilatation-volvulus.
Welsh corgi	S-M	Herding (cattle, heelers)	Name comes from Celtic word for dog. Used to herd cattle by nipping heels, for which short legs were an advantage. Double-coated with coarse outer coat and soft undercoat. Two breeds: Cardigan and Pembroke.
West Highland white terrier	S	General (guarding and hunting [terrier])	Fox hunter, good watchdog. Bred to be white so visible in rocks and heather. Frisky, and can be snappish. Noisy bark. Problems: emphysema following bronchitis, esophagus becoming blocked with a bone, liver problems.
Whippet	S-M	General (hunting, racing)	Greyhound was ancestor; crossed with terriers. Name may mean small dog. Used by working class to catch rabbits as sport, then (after anti-cruelty laws put a stop to this) as "rag dogs" trained to run when owners waved a piece of cloth at Sunday races.
Wire-Haired fox terrier	S-M	Hunting (terrier)	Routed foxes from dens. Hard, wiry coat. Frisky. Problems: deafness.
Yorkshire terrier	S	Pet	Companions of English working class. Long, shaggy coat. The nose, eyelids and lips are black or dark. Good city watchdog, but can be snappish. Problems: incomplete tracheal cartilage rings, nervousness and neurosis, low blood glucose level, bone problems (lameness), dislocated kneecaps, diarrhea and vomiting.

Toy dogs and lapdogs. These small breeds were developed mostly as companions, often to royalty. Some lived a pampered life at court. Some make good watchdogs, and most are affectionate and amusing. They need attention.

Inbreeding

Dog breeds are man-made, an artificial construct. Dogs that are inbred, especially for looks, often are plagued with physical deformities, disease, and personality problems. For example, blue merle dogs (blue and gray hair with black marbling) carry a gene linked to blindness and deafness. The old maxim is true: purebreds tend to be less hardy than mutts.

However, with foresight you can own a dog of your favorite breed without encountering problems. Write to the breed association for the type of dog you want to buy. Ask about programs to eliminate inherited problems and request a list of breeders who have bred their dogs away from the breed's problems. When looking at puppies, request documents attesting to the fact that tests on the puppy's parents have shown them free of genetic problems. If the breed has a history of hip dysplasia, consider getting a dog certified free of the condition by the Orthopedic Foundation for Animals. However, to be evaluated by the OFA, the dog must be two years old. Consult your veterinarian. And above all, stay away from puppy mills and pet stores, notorious for stocking puppies from unlicensed breeders.

The chart of dog breeds may help you make a decision when choosing a dog. A breed may have a physical or emotional problem even if none is given. The chart is followed by a list, "Genetic Problems in Dogs," with descriptions of common problems that afflict dogs of certain breeds.

Genetic Problems in Dogs

Cervical spondylopathy: Malformed vertebra (or vertebrae) and the weight of the head cause bruising of the spinal cord. Symptoms: wobbling walk, unsteady hindquarters, trailing forefeet, paralysis. Treatment: surgery.

Collie eye anomaly (C.E.A.): This congenital disorder can lead to blindness from a detached retina or hemorrhage of the retina. The good news is that only one of 20 dogs with C.E.A. goes blind, and then often only in one eye. Solution: breeding away from the disorder.

Cryptorchidism: The puppy lacks one or both testicles or the testis still has not descended as it should by the time he is 10 months old. Treatment: removal of undescended testis.

Diabetes mellitus: The pancreas does not produce enough insulin or regulate glucose levels properly. Symptoms: thirst, tiredness, hunger, weight loss. Treatment: control of the diet in mild cases, home-administered insulin injections in severe cases. Keep glucose syrup (Karo) handy to treat hypoglycemic coma (collapse and convulsions), which occurs when the dog is starved for glucose.

Ectropion: The eyelid turns out, forming a pouch in which tears pool. The cornea then tends to dry out. Treatment: surgery.

Elbow dysplasia: Poorly fitted ball-and-socket joint causes arthritis. See *hip dysplasia*. Treatment: surgery and drugs.

Elongated palate: Short-nosed dogs are prone to this condition. Because the soft palate is too long and floppy, it partially blocks the laryngeal opening, causing chronic inflammation and tonsillitis. Symptom: snorting breath. Treatment: surgery, which does not always provide full recovery.

Emphysema following bronchitis: Carbon dioxide is exchanged for oxygen on walls of lungs' alveoli. Bronchitis can bring on emphysema, in which the alveoli walls break down, so that many small spaces become fewer large ones, reducing the amount of oxygen that is produced. The condition reduces the dog's exercise ability. Treatment: drugs.

Entropion: The edge of eyelid rolls inward under the eye. Treatment: surgery.

Eosinophilic myostitis: The head muscles waste away. Signs: pain, stiffness, weakness, lopsided head. Treatment: painkillers, anti-inflammatory drugs.

Exocrine pancreatic insufficiency (E.P.I.): The pancreas is not fully formed. Symptoms: attempts to eat own feces, bulky feces, dry coat. Treatment: enzymes, oil, and vitamin supplements.

Gastric dilatation-volvulus (GDV): Common name: bloat. The stomach swells and sometimes twists (torsion), trapping gas. Extremely dangerous, fatal in 20 to 40 percent of cases. Symptoms: drooling and panting in distress. Treatment: shock therapy and medications, sometimes surgery (for torsion). Preventives: Raise the bowl for feeding; give several small meals a day rather than one large one; provide water at room temperature and try, if you can, to prevent the dog from gulping it down. Refrain from exercising the dog for at least an hour after it eats.

Hip dysplasia: The flattening of the hip joint socket creates a poor connection between it and the ball. The femur's head rubs on the joint edges, resulting in arthritis. Treatment: restriction of activity in young dogs, surgery.

Hydrocephalus: Commonly called "water on the brain," the condition arises as a result of a deformity in brain's drainage system. Fluid presses against brain tissue. Signs: fits, lack of coordination, blindness. Treatment: surgery.

Juvenile pyoderma: When dermatitis caused by the demodex mite becomes infected, the puppy has juvenile pyoderma. Signs: sores around head and shoulders, mouse-like smell, hair loss, oily skin. Treatment: drugs, antibiotics, shampoos.

Narrow pelvis: Puppies need to be delivered by Caesarian or they and the mother can die during the birthing process.

Osteochondritis dissecans: In large dogs, a "joint mouse" (loose lump) can rub on a joint, leading to arthritis. Symptoms: limping, pain, swelling. Treatment: surgery.

Progressive retinal atrophy (P.R.A.): Lack of blood supply to retina kills off light-sensitive cells. Vision degenerates.

Prolapsed nictitans: A third eyelid shows suddenly or protrudes. Treatment: Call the vet and irrigate the eye.

Pyloric stenosis: The sphincter at base of stomach prevents food from leaving the stomach. Symptom: vomiting of solids. Treatment: surgery.

Slipped disc: Slipped disc is more common in dogs with long backs and short legs. Displacement of the center of the disc damages the spinal cord nerves. Signs: pain, limping, hunching, paralysis. Treatment: drugs or surgery.

Spleen tumor: Symptoms: swelling of abdomen, weakness, pale gums. Treatment: surgical removal.

The Question of Tail Docking and Ear Cropping

Should anyone dock a puppy's tail, crop its ears, and remove its dewclaws? In England and Holland, these practices are forbidden. In the United States, they are standard for some show dogs. If in doubt, ask your dog.

Tail docking is standard for these breeds: poodles, cocker and springer spaniels, bulldogs, Rottweilers, Doberman pinschers, Pembroke corgis, and many terriers. Those in favor of tail docking offer practical reasons: tails can be damaged by banging against things when dogs wag them, tails pick up brambles and burrs, wagging tails make noise giving away dogs' position to game, tails can be grabbed when dogs are fighting or guarding. Those against tail docking say that it works to human, not canine, advantage—to help hunters kill game, homeowners to guard their houses, sportsmen to pit one animal against another.

Docking should be done, if at all, when puppies are young (three to five days old) and bones as yet unformed. If you insist on it for your dog, have a vet do it. Tails are docked in several ways. One way is to put a rubber band around a puppy's tail so tight that it cuts off circulation; eventually the tail atrophies and drops off. Another is to apply a tourniquet and cut the tail off with a scissors, some say a blunt one.

Ear cropping is a more painful procedure than docking. It is traditional for many breeds of dogs to have their ears cropped—Great Danes, Dobermans, boxers and miniature schnauzers. The reasons for the procedure again have to do with the jobs humans have assigned the dogs—guard dogs can be grabbed by the ears and fighting dogs can have their ears bitten off.

Some dog owners arrange to have the vet remove their dogs' dewclaws, the nail that grows up nearer the dog's "wrist." The dewclaw can grow into a kind of canine version of ingrown toenail. Often it is removed just for looks. If you must remove dewclaws, have it done when the dog is three to five days old. For information on how to clip your dog's nails, see "Clipping Your Pet's Nails," page 338.

THE MONKS OF NEW SKETE

W ise in dog rearing, the Eastern Orthodox monks of New Skete, New York, have written two best-sellers on dog training, *How to Be Your Dog's Best Friend* and *The Art of Raising a Puppy.* Their basic premise: to get inside the dog's head. Their fame has also been spread by their mention in the mystery novels of Susan Conant, whose main character, an owner of malamutes, is involved in obedience training.

Training Your Dog

Most trainers agree that your dog must recognize you as top dog (alpha wolf in the pack) for successful training to take place. In recognizing you as leader, your dog also bonds to you as member of the pack. How do you convince your dog that you are above it on the hierarchical ladder? The monks of New Skete, New York, who train German shepherds, say that you should assert dominance by taking the dog by the scruff of the neck and rolling it over on its back, which puts it in a position of extreme submission. Some trainers use a choke chain on the dog to establish dominance. If you do use a choke chain, make sure you put it on correctly. If you don't, you will choke the dog when you don't want to. Jerk on the chain when you want to show who's boss. (Barbara Wodehouse, who was a famous British dog trainer, used to say, "Jerk 'em and love 'em.")

Experts differ on philosophies of training. The two extremes seem to be: (1) make it impossible for your dog to make a mistake and teach it

USING A CHOKE CHAIN

The choke chain should go on the dog's neck so that the chain loosens up when the dog is not straining at the leash. Keep the dog on your left-hand side. Holding the big choke chain ring in your hand, loop the chain around the dog's neck and through the ring, so that it looks like the above illustration. If you put the chain through the ring the other way, it will choke the dog even when it is not straining. Use a choke chain only when walking with the dog or training it.

slowly, in small bits, or (2) trick your dog into making a mistake so that you can correct it.

Whatever your philosophy, you can start training your dog when it is about seven or eight weeks old. At this point the dog can learn the meaning of "no!" To counterbalance this, praise it for everything it does right. When the dog is 13 weeks old, you can begin serious training. If you need to train an older dog, do not despair. In spite of the aged adage, old dogs *can* learn new tricks—it is never too late.

Hounds and terriers are, in general, more difficult to train than herding dogs, retrievers, and guard dogs. This is not because they lack intelligence but because they have been bred toward independence.

Don't give up.

General Rules

1. One person should train the dog. Children can be trainers if they have been taught how.

2. Work with dogs before feeding them, not after.

3. In the beginning, control your dog while training it with a six-foot leash made of leather or cloth. Later, verbal control should be enough. Always kneel so that you are on its level.

4. Before each command, use the dog's name. It will then be alerted to the fact that the command is directed at it, not someone else. For instance, say, "Canina, come," not "Come, Canina."

5. Combine verbal and hand signals. For example, add to the command "Canina, come" a hand motion directing the dog toward you.

6. Use the same tone of voice for commands. Don't yell.

7. Reward the dog immediately for a proper response. Praise is enough—"Good dog!" Praise works better than punishment. And make the praise immediate. If you want, you can use treats—always accompanied by praise—as reinforcers. When using treats, you should reward the dog at first for every correct response, then, as it learns and performs correctly, reward it every third or fourth time, and finally randomly.

8. Capitalize on the dog's pack instinct. When teaching him to come, for instance, walk away first. Dogs tend to follow the leader. And they want to be accepted.

9. Do not punish your dog when he does not understand, only when he disobeys. When the dog seems to disobey, withdraw affection. You might banish it to some room (though not where it sleeps) for a "time-out." Make time-outs at least an hour long. *Never hit your dog.*

10. Don't spend too long a time at one session—puppies have short attention spans. If the puppy wants to play, gently urge it back into the training mode. For puppies, maximum time at one training session is five minutes graduating to 10. For older dogs, the maximum time is 20 minutes.

Housebreaking

Like most animals, dogs do not want to foul their own living and sleeping space. They also want to please you. If you capitalize on those canine motivations, you will find housebreaking your pet much easier. As you would with a child, wait until the puppy is old enough to understand. Don't punish a puppy for mistakes when it is young.

Learn to predict when the puppy needs to go out, usually after eating or when it wakes up. It may signal you by sniffing the floor and circling.

Paper training. In paper training, you teach the puppy to eliminate on newspaper, which you gradually move from inside the house to outside. Some vets advise against paper training because a dog that is old enough to be paper-trained is old enough to go outside. However this is difficult for people who live in apartments or must leave the dog alone for some time each day.

Put the puppy in a small room with the floor covered by newspaper. Watch it to see what part of the room it favors for elimination. Then leave paper in only that section of the room. Once the puppy is accustomed to using the paper, start moving the paper toward the door, then move it outside. Take the paper away entirely the day after you have moved it outside.

Crate training. A crate is a kind of nest for a puppy, and puppies know not to eliminate in the nest—their mothers taught them. Keep the puppy in the crate in the bedroom. Take it out of the crate and outdoors to do its business.

House training. Until the puppy gets to be five months old, make sure you let it out in the morning after it wakes up, after meals, and every two hours. Accompany your puppy outside and give it praise for doing its business outdoors. You can also have a command like "go poop."

Mistakes: Only when your puppy is four or five months old should you chastise it for mistakes. If you find your puppy has messed, put a leash on it and confront it with the mess. Say "no" in a stern voice, look at it with a cold, expressionless face. Add, "You will not do this in the house." (The more your words sound like barks, the better.) Make the puppy look at the mess, but never rub its nose in it, and don't let it see you clean up the mess.

Other Training

Teach commands in the following sequence. (Some experts recommend that you teach heeling first.)

Sit: Push down on dog's hindquarters while saying "sit." When it does sit, say "good dog" until it gets the message. You can use treats also. Hold the treat at the dog's eye level and walk toward it saying, "Sit." The dog will very often sit when you do this. Then give the treat. It will take a while for the dog to associate the word "sit" with the action of sitting. After it learns the command, tell the dog to sit at other times, when it is not in training.

Stay: Start with the puppy sitting. After it has begun to sit for 10 seconds or more, tell it, "Stay." Hold your hand up in front of the dog's eyes, palm forward. Step backward one step. Wait a very short time, then move back to the puppy. Reward it. Repeat this process, increasing distance each time, until you are able to go six or seven feet away without the dog getting up. Then increase time. If the dog gets up, say "No" and tell it to sit. Then temporarily decrease the distance you go away from the dog and the time you require it to sit.

A different method of teaching "stay" is to hold the leash up and to the right and say "stay," while the dog is in a sitting position. Walk around the dog, correcting its attempts to move with jerks of the leash. Use looser control and wider circles as it begins to understand.

Come: You are acting on something the dog already does, which is to approach you when you call its name. Wait until the dog has learned to sit and stay. Then start training it to come. Tell the dog to stay, walk away, turn, and say, "Canina, come." You can open your arms to reinforce this. If the dog is on a leash, tug it as you say come, but not hard. Never call your puppy to you to scold him—this is too confusing for him.

Down: From the sit position, you can maneuver your puppy into the down position. Say, "Rover, down," moving your hand in a sweep toward the floor, palm down. Then ease his front paws forward, which will force him to lie flat. If you use treats, hold the treat at floor level, so that he has to lie down to get it.

Downstay: Once the puppy has learned down and stay, you can put the two commands together. Command it into the down position, then tell it to stay, and back away.

Heel: This means that the dog walks by your side, traditionally on the left, which is still the rule for dog shows. Start off on your left foot, holding a treat in your right hand. Using the leash as gentle reminder, with pulls and releases, keep the dog at your side, rewarding it every 10 or 12 steps with a treat (if you use treats). After the

CANINE GOOD-CITIZEN TITLE

The Canine Good-Citizen Test, created by the American Kennel Club, focuses on good manners for dogs and responsible pet ownership for their human companions. Your dog does not have to be a purebred to be given a title, but licenses, shots, and other required inoculation certificates must be up to date.

During the test the evaluator inspects the dog for health and handles it to see if it is willing to let someone other than the owner touch it. He or she then shakes hands with the owner, paying no attention to the dog, who must not show any shyness (sometimes a sign of masked aggression) or resentment. Other parts of the test are much the same as those for obedience training, except that the dog is tested for its ability to refrain from barking and aggressiveness and to withstand distraction. For example, the dog must react well in two situations in which the evaluator drops a book, jogs by the dog, or does something else distracting. Contact: **The American Kennel Club,** 5580 Centerview Drive, Raleigh, NC 27606 (919-233-3600).

dog has learned a straight-line heel, practice doing turns, starting with right turns. When the puppy has learned to heel on a leash, work with the dog without a leash in a fenced yard or other confined place, then try open spaces. While walking with the dog, practice other commands with it. Condition the dog to traffic, to stopping at the curb, and to refraining from crossing the street until told to do so.

Special Problems

Nipping: Take the dog's muzzle in your hands, shake its head gently, and say "No." Don't hit the dog.

Jumping up: Say, "Off!" then back away and push at dog's shoulders or grab its front feet. Never step on its feet—you can do serious damage.

Car chasing. Get a friend to drive the car, and as the dog runs alongside, spray it with water. Do this on private property.

Hark! Hark! Barking Dogs

Of course you want your dog to bark—when a burglar comes, for instance. Barking is your dog's natural signal for danger. However, if your dog barks too much, you and others will tend to ignore him, even in times of real danger. And, by law, your barking dog may be a public nuisance.

First, ask yourself: Why does Jack bark?

♦ He is complaining about being left alone. Consider leaving the radio on, or get another pet for company. Make sure he has plenty of toys. Or if he is outside, give him more space. Keep him in at night.

♦ He is greeting you at your return home. Don't exaggerate your homecoming's importance to him by making a big fuss about it.

♦ He wants to come in. Let him in.

♦ He is responding to another dog's barking, the sound of children playing, the sound of a siren, neighbors coming home and going out, a passing car. These are intermittent barks and should not be a problem.

♦ He is notifying you that someone is delivering something or the garbage collector is taking what he views as goodies away. Remember he cannot tell the difference between an intruder and the UPS deliverer.

How to stop it? Don't turn the hose on your dog or throw things at him or hit him. Praise him for barking for the *right* reason, as a watchdog, for instance.

You can train your dog not to bark with the water-training method. It will take a day or two.

1. Keep a plant mister filled with water with you.
2. If Jack barks, say "Jack, quiet" and hit him with a couple of squirts of water.
3. If he moves away, say "Quiet," go to him, squirt him again. Do this each time he barks for the wrong reason.
4. Be consistent. Always correct when he barks for the wrong reason.
5. If he barks at night, get up and use the water treatment—it will pay off.
6. After a while, you won't need to use water. The word "Quiet" will be enough.

You can also use a can filled with pennies to startle Jack when he barks.

Note: If Jack has been left alone and has barked for hour upon hour, he may need professional training.

Dogs That Bite

By age 14, one of two U.S. children will be bitten by a dog. In order of number of human *fatalities* caused by dog bites, the breeds with the worst records are: pit bull, German shepherd, chow, malamute, husky, wolf-hybrid, Akita, Rottweiler, and Doberman pinscher. Dogs that bite most (not necessarily fatally), according to a 27-year study, are, in order of most bites to least: German shepherd, poodle, Italian bulldog, and fox terrier. The dogs that bite least: golden retriever, Labrador retriever, Shetland sheepdog, Old English sheepdog, Welsh terrier. If you own a dog of a breed with a bad reputation, do not despair. It can be obedience-trained so that it is not dangerous. On the other hand, dogs of breeds known for gentle temperaments can bite if poorly socialized or provoked. Unneutered males have a greater tendency to bite—one more reason to have your dog neutered.

Signs of aggression in dogs. Dogs show aggression by: excessive barking, overprotectiveness toward food and possessions, fearfulness in strange situations, growling and snapping when given attention, chasing cars and bicycles, getting out and roaming free. If your dog suddenly becomes aggressive, take it to the veterinarian—the dog could be sick. If the vet gives it a clean bill of health, arrange for professional obedience training.

How to act toward an aggressive dog. Remain calm—don't scream or run. Speak to the dog in a calm voice, saying something like "Go home." Don't stare at the dog, but don't turn your back on it either. Let it approach you to sniff you. If and when the dog leaves, back away slowly. If the dog attacks you, give it your hat, purse—anything else besides you—to bite. If the dog knocks you down, curl up and protect your head and neck with your hands. If you are bitten, find out who owns the dog and report the bite to police or animal control. This is important in case the dog has not been given rabies shots. See your doctor.

Your child and aggressive dogs. Train your children not to provoke or abuse dogs and other animals. Also teach them how to act when a dog seems aggressive.

Dog Talk

As a member of the wolf family of pack animals, your dog employs elaborate body language to communicate with you (the leader of the pack), other pack members, and strangers. You know what Canina is telling you when she leaps up, tail wagging, to greet you after a long absence. But did you also know that exposed teeth can be a sign of pleasure as well as aggression? (See opposite page.)

Happiness, Pleasure, Relaxation

- Teeth exposed, showing incisors only.
- Bright eyes. Some happy dogs raise their eyelids to express surprise or a quizzical attitude; sometimes they also tilt their heads.
- A wagging tail usually shows pleasure, invitation. (Be careful, a dog can wag its tail when aggressive.)
- Dogs in an ordinary, relaxed state carry their heads high and tails low. Their jaws are relaxed, and their bodies show no tension.
- Dogs wanting to play crouch down in front with their rear ends high, backs bowed, and jaws relaxed. They wag their tails, yip, bark, and growl playfully.

Aggression

Dogs have two modes of aggression: fearful and dominant. In both modes their lips are drawn back to show their canine teeth.

Fearful aggression.

- Staring eyes: a wild look, skin drawn to show the whites of the eyes, pupils dilated.
- Growling or snarling, perhaps barking.
- Ears laid back or forward and rigid, body tense. The hair in the center of the back often rises on end, tail is down and rigid.

Dominant aggression.

- Pupils constricted with a fixed stare.
- Walking forward, with tail and ears held high, snapping and ready to bite.

Submission

- Tail tucked under, ears folded back.
- Partial submission: crouching, head down. May turn on side presenting flank.
- Complete submission: rolling over and raising one hind leg.

DOG BODY LANGUAGE

Tail low, but not tucked under · Ears up · Relaxed jaws	The happy, relaxed dog looks it. It is alert, but not tense.
Tail high · Ears back · Crouching	The playful dog invites a game with its body posture. Sometimes it yips or emits a high growl.
Ears back · Tail low	The submissive dog crouches a bit.
Hind leg raised · Ears raised a bit · Belly vulnerable	The completely submissive dog presents its flank after rolling over. This is a position of trust.
Tail high · Teeth showing, ready to bite · Ears up	The dog showing dominant aggression moves forward with confidence.
Tail horizontal · Hair on end · Ears back · Teeth bared	The dog showing fearful aggression is tense, in a posture of half-submission, half-aggression.

Dog Work

Some dog experts think that working with a dog at its genetically mandated job makes for a happier dog and a closer tie between human and animal. Most working dogs need—at the very least—exercise and something to keep them interested, even if it is just going on long walks, or chasing and retrieving a ball. You can go further and work with your dog at the specific task its genes give it an affinity for—retrieving game, herding sheep, or pulling a cart, for instance.

Events for dogs may be sponsored by a company (for example, a dog food company), a dog club, or some other organization. Watch listings of special events in your local paper, or ask your veterinarian about training classes and events. Also contact: **The North American Working Dog Association,** Attn. George Theriot, 7318 Brennans Drive, Dallas, Texas 75214 (214-821-3327)

Activities for All Dogs

Obedience Trials: While all dogs need basic obedience training, some dog owners go further and specialize in obedience trials regulated by the American Kennel Club. You can enroll your dog in obedience training classes and belong to a club for dogs and handlers. Dogs are awarded titles in accordance with their competence at certain tasks. The dog begins as a novice. A successful novice is able to:

♦ heel on and off leash, keeping up with the handler.

♦ sit automatically whenever the handler stops.

♦ heel (on the leash) while the handler walks in a figure eight.

♦ allow itself to be touched by the judge, standing still.

♦ come immediately when called, then sit right in front of the handler.

♦ move on command from sitting position to heel position at the handler's left knee, and sit there.

♦ in a line of other dogs, sit and stay for one minute.

♦ lie down with the other dogs for three minutes, handler at the other side of the room.

A *companion dog* (C.D.) must qualify in three separate novice obedience trials, and in each it must score at least 170 points out of a possible 200 *and* receive at least half the points allotted to each of the trial's several exercises. Dogs are judged on speed, enthusiasm, and precision. Points are deducted if the dog shows reluctance to come, lags behind a bit while heeling, even sits with its tail off center. Further titles higher up on the ladder are *companion dog excellent* (CDX) and *utility dog* (UD). Contact: **The American Kennel Club,** 5580 Centerview Drive, Raleigh, NC 27606.

Flyball. Dogs of all breeds can compete in flyball relay races. Organized in teams of four, two to four dogs at a time race to a box over a 55-foot-long course with four hurdles. They paw the box open and a tennis ball pops out. The dogs catch the ball and race back down the track with it. When they return to the finish line, the next set of dogs begins to race. The champions at the sport have been Border collies. Sighthounds (greyhounds, whippets, and salukis) are not very interested in tennis balls. Look for classes and competitions in your local paper or on literature racks at your pet food store.

Agility. The goal is to increase dogs' agility. The method: to teach them to crawl through tunnels, walk a seesaw and swinging bridge, weave their way through poles, and maneuver their way around as many as 20 other obstacles. Usually agility classes are sponsored by obedience clubs, 4-H clubs, and other groups. You can set up your own agility course with big boxes for tunnels, planks (set on the ground to avoid accidents), and poles that the dog can zigzag around (as in slalom skiing).

Frisbee: Consider training your dog to catch a flying disc. Then you and your dog can compete at the FRISKIES CANINE FRISBEE® CHAMPIONSHIPS (address below) at the community, regional, and even national level—if the two of you are good enough. The competitions are free, and you get a free t-shirt and Frisbee flying disc just for entering. Any dog (no matter what its parentage) and any person (no matter what age or sex) can enter. The only exceptions are aggressive dogs and bitches in heat, who are automatically disqualified. The judging is based on showmanship, leaping ability, and the degree of difficulty and elegance of execution for individual catches. You can get a free training manual by writing: Friskies Training Manual, PO Box 2092, Young America, MN 55553-2092. For rules and a schedule of competitions, write to: Friskies, 4060-D Peachtree Road, Suite 326, Atlanta, GA 30319.

The Specialties

Hunting dogs. If you own a hunting dog, you might actually hunt with him. If not, try field trials. An orchestrated exercise, a field trial mimics hunting. In a trial for springer spaniels, two teams of humans and dogs work parallel courses, with judges walking between them. In open trials, both amateurs and professionals compete, while amateur trials do not allow pros. Handlers as well as dogs are judged. A dog who wins two trials becomes a field champion, and national champions are determined at yearly events. Retrievers must become skilled at both blind retrieves (in which the dog retrieves a bird without first seeing it fall) and marked retrieves (in which the dog sees the bird fall before the retrieve). Field trials are sponsored by the **American Kennel Club,** 5580 Centerview Drive, Raleigh, NC 27606.

Herding dogs: Herding-dog associations sponsor about 300 annual competitions where herding dogs like Border collies drive sheep into a pen. A trained Border collie can manage 800 sheep over 3000 acres, responding to commands whistled from as far as a mile away or working alone. In trials, they must perform several tasks consecutively, dealing with obstacles on the course. Contact: **North American Sheep Dog Society,** Route 3, Box 107, McLeansboro, IL 62859 (618-757-2238) registers Border collies

and has publication lists; **American Kennel Club,** 5580 Centerview Drive, Raleigh, NC 27606.

Draft dogs: Draft dogs bred to haul wagons love to be hitched up to a sled or wagon for the kids. You might also consider taking part in dog-sled races. Though you probably won't end up entering the grueling 1000-mile Iditarod race in Alaska, you can race a dog team if you live in snow country. Races are held when snow is a foot deep and temperatures fall to zero or close to it. Dog teams can compete in speed, freight, and long distance races. Traditionally Siberian huskies, Alaskan malamutes, Samoyeds, and Eskimo dogs have been used in dogsled races. However, other purebred dogs and crossbreeds often work out very well. A racing dog usually weighs 45 to 50 pounds, stands a couple of feet tall at the shoulder, has a deep chest and high, sinewy haunches. It has stamina and "heart." Teams range in size from two to 16 dogs, and courses from three miles to 100 miles or more. Children can compete in the Pee Wee Class and Junior Class.

Another event for draft dogs is the Weight Pull, in which the dog pulls a wheeled platform, weighted with increasingly heavy loads. Big dogs can pull as much as 3000 pounds. Contact: **International Sled Dog Racing Association** (ISDRA), PO Box 446, Nordman, ID 83848-0446 (208-443-3153).

Terriers: On walks, your terrier may love to stop and insert himself into holes. You can capitalize on his talent by entering him in terrier trials. The only requirement for entry: that the dog can fit through a 9-inch hole. Dachshunds as well as terriers can compete. On a course 100–150 feet long and 10 feet wide, dogs chase a fox tail or tennis ball on a string pulled by someone on a bicycle. At the finish line dogs must squeeze through 9-inch holes in bales of hay. In another version, called "Go to Ground," dogs race through a 15-foot underground maze, baited with the smell of fox and with a rat in a cage at the end. Look in your local paper or newsletters at your pet food store for classes and events.

Hounds: The American Kennel Club runs trials for dogs in *tracking*—recognizing and following human scent. The dog tracks on a leash between 20 and 40 feet long, with the handler following at least 20 feet behind. Dogs who successfully complete the test receive a Tracking Dog certificate. This qualifies them to enter the more difficult test for the Tracking Dog Excellent (TDX) certificate. Contact: **The American Kennel Club,** 5580 Centerview Drive, Raleigh, NC 27606.

Sighthounds: Sighthounds might enjoy *coursing,* racing after an artificial lure. Scores include evaluation of speed, enthusiasm, agility, endurance, and ability to follow. Events are sponsored by local Sighthound Associations.

CATS

Cat Breeds

The organizing logic of cats? Not much. What makes a Siamese cat a true Siamese? A gene that determines the pattern of its coat. Angoras and Persians are distinguished by long hair. Many "new" breeds are merely varieties of existing breeds. Some cat breeds, recognized because they are old, like the Manx, would not be accepted as breeds if they came into existence today, partly because of genetic handicaps (in the Manx's case, reproductive problems and spinal defects). Understanding it all takes a certain knowledge of genetics and a tolerance for confusion. To compound the confusion, cat associations do not all recognize the same breeds. And there are six cat associations.

No matter what breed you admire, or if you want a mixed breed, when you choose a kitten, look for a glossy coat, clear eyes, and curiosity. The kitten should be 8–10 weeks old before you bring it home.

Training Your Cat

Yes, you *can* train a cat. It is easier to train cats with rewards than punishment. Any negative reinforcement—like a squirt of water from a mister or water pistol—should not seem to come from you. Break down the behavior you want into small tasks, train your cat to do the tasks one at a time, then combine tasks into more complex behavior.

Litterbox training. Most cats learn good bathroom habits from their mothers. If your kitten has not had this training, you have to be its mother and show it what to do. Put it in the litterbox and show it how to scratch by moving its paws. Every time your kitten seems ready to eliminate, put it in the litterbox.

Keep the litterbox clean and put it where your cat has some privacy—otherwise it may seek out someplace else to use as a bathroom. If your cat persists in using an unacceptable place, scrub the place with vinegar to eliminate odor and feed the cat close by it. Put a litterbox within sight of the unacceptable place, then after about a week, gradually move it to where you want it.

If you must give negative reinforcement, spray the cat with water, and say "No." Never rub the cat's nose in its mess. If a cat seems to start urinating inappropriately, take it to the veterinarian—this could be a sign of urinary problems.

Spraying. Cats spray to mark territory. You might want to try draping aluminum foil strips around the place he sprays to discourage him.

Scratching furniture. Cats scratch to sharpen their claws by removing old skin as well as to mark territory. It is important to stop cats from scratching a piece of furniture immediately,

CAT BREED CHART

Name	Characteristics
Abyssinian	Short-haired, brown or red agouti (grizzled) coat, perhaps with tabby markings. Graceful and muscular. Long head. May have ear tufts.
American Wirehair	Like American Shorthair, but with wiry coat.
American Domestic Shorthair	Muscular and strong, round-headed. Short, hard coat.
Balinese/Javanese	Developed in the United States, not Bali. The name comes from the way the animals move, like Balinese dancers. Long silky hair, colored points. Wedge-shaped head and big ears. Thin and long-legged.
Birman	Colored like Himalayan, but paws white. Thinner body and longer head. Long, straight, silky hair.
Bombay	Burmese/American Shorthair cross. Shiny patent-leather-like coat.
British/European Shorthair	Round head and ears. Muscular, heavy body with broad chest and short legs. Rather short tail.
Burmese	Short satiny hair, brown (but some other colors). Muscular, rounded body. Round eyes and head. Can suffer from cleft palate and incomplete formation of skull.
Chartreux	Like British Shorthair but somewhat bigger. Short, gray-blue coat.
Colorpoint Shorthair	Siamese with tabby, tortie, or red point patterns.
Cornish Rex	Short, soft, curly coat. Strong hind legs. Narrow head, oval eyes.
Cymric	Long-haired Manx. Round head and ears. No tail. Long hind legs, compact body.
Devon Rex	Like Cornish Rex, but shorter and with rougher coat. Waif-like face with big ears and eyes.
Egyptian Mau	Short-haired, spotted silver or bronze tabby pattern with elaborate face markings. Medium body.
Exotic Shorthair	Persian-like with short hair. Very round head and ears. Short, thick, soft coat.
Havana Brown	Smooth, brown, short-haired coat.
Himalayan	Resembles Persian in body and coat. Colored like Siamese or in solid colors like chocolate or lilac.
Japanese Bobtail	Short rabbit-like tail. Thin body and legs. Triangular face.
Korat	Silver-blue coat. Big eyes and heart-shaped head. Somewhat rounded body.
Maine Coon	Big, long-haired, muscled cat. Long, bushy tail. Tufts of hair on cheeks and large ruff. Is not half-cat, half-raccoon, and is not from Maine.
Manx	No tail or close to it. Long hind legs (gait like a rabbit) and short, round body. Afflicted by genetic problems, including spina bifida.

Name	Characteristics
Ocicat	Big, short-haired tabby with fairly thin body and long legs. A cross between Abyssinian and Siamese. Resembles a wild cat.
Oriental/Foreign Shorthair	Shaped like Siamese with different coat colors and patterns.
Peke-faced Persian	Persian with face like Pekinese dog. Tabby: red or white. Long hair.
Persian	Short, round head and small round ears. Short body and legs. Long, fluffy hair. May have breathing problems.
Russian Blue	Blue-gray, short-haired "double" coat. Green eyes. Head shape unique.
Scottish Fold	Ears folded forward and down. Similar to American/Domestic Shorthair. If a Scottish fold mates with another Scottish fold, kittens may have excess cartilage, thick tails, swollen feet.
Siamese	Short-haired, pale coat with colored points. Very thin, long legs and tail. Wedge-shaped head. Genetic problem: albinism.
Somali	Long-haired Abyssinian with dense coat. Agouti coloring. Bushy tail, medium-long body.
Sphynx	Hairless cat with big ears and well-fed-looking body. May have immune-system problems.
Tonkinese	Between Siamese and Burmese in body type and coloring.
Turkish (Van)	Long hair. Shorter head and heavier than Angora. Head and tail white and auburn. Likes to swim.
Turkish Angora	Long, fine, silky hair. Thin, sinuous body. Wedged head. Coat colors vary. Gentle and athletic. Sheds in summer.

because the more the furniture is used, the more the cat will use it because it smells of possession. Put a scratching post near the piece of furniture. Take a toy and hang it above the post. When the kitten reaches up to play it encounters the post and becomes used to it. When the kitten starts to scratch furniture, reprimand it and deposit it in front of the scratching post, hold its paws to the post, and make scratching motions to give it the idea. Praise it at the same time. If that fails, try using an animal repellent, available at pet stores, on the furniture.

Teaching the cat to come. When you put out your cat's food bowl, say its name and the word "Come." When it has learned to respond, use this command when you want the cat. Always reward it with a treat and petting. If it just sits and looks at you, tap it with a light object to get its attention, then call again.

Bird hunting. Try this trick to stop cats from hunting birds. Hide. Fool the cat into attacking a toy bird or bird carcass by fluttering it on a string. When the cat attacks, spray it with water. Better yet, keep your cat inside.

Cat Litter

In 1948, Edward Lowe gave some absorbent clay (fuller's earth) in lieu of sand to a friend for a litterbox. The clay worked better than sand, and Lowe—seeing paydirt—started the Kitty Litter company. That was only the beginning. Now there are more than 75 brands of litter available. While some brands of cat litter are made of cedar chips, the majority are based on fuller's earth, which is found by the Georgia seacoast and in the Midwest and central California. The clay is a close relative of kaolin, a diarrhea remedy.

Some people use homemade litter of cut-up newspapers. This is not a good idea—newsprint contains dyes that could be toxic to a cat.

Litter gives the cat a place to hide its urine and feces. The cat is a true carnivore, a protein eater, which makes its waste smell fouler than that of a dog. (Dogs and pigs are omnivores, as anyone who owns a hungry dog and a garbage can knows.) Some cat litters deodorize when activated by pressure or moisture. Others disinfect. All the litters mask odor and slow down the growth of bacteria by absorbing liquids.

The major controversy centers on clumpable litter, which clumps into hard balls when the cat uses it. You can scoop the balls out of the box, leaving clean litter behind. It lasts much longer than other kinds of litter, is odor-free, and may need changing only once a month. The problem: litter sticks to the cat's paws and is tracked through the house. The solution: put a doormat in front of litterbox, so that grains are caught. Clumpable litter is hard to vacuum and clumps when wet-mopped. Clumpable litter can clog the toilet or block sewer lines. You should put it in the garbage, not down the drain, no matter what the package says.

Cat Talk

Your cat doesn't need to know how to speak human language to get its point across. Its sinuous body and expressive face can tell all, if you know the clues.

CAN YOU TOILET-TRAIN YOUR CAT?

Is this a put-on? Paul Kunkel, author of *How to Toilet Train Your Cat: 21 Days to a Litter-Free Home*, would say no. Kunkel was an undergraduate at the University of New Mexico, living with six cats and seven other people, when he first tried to toilet-train a cat. He trained the dominant cat first, then all the others followed suit.

The Kunkel method: Put the litterbox next to the toilet. Raise the level of the litterbox every day, using stacked newspapers, until it is at the same height as the toilet seat. Then take away the litterbox, put plastic wrap between bowl and seat, and place a bit of litter in the center. The cat balances itself on the seat and eliminates on the litter. When the cat has become used to balancing on the toilet, remove the litter and make a hole in the plastic.

While toilet training for cats may seem to spell convenience, we do not recommend it. It seems too dangerous to the cat. What if it falls into the toilet, for instance?

CAT FACE TALK

Happy cat: normal pupils, whiskers relaxed, ears up straight.

Pleased cat: half-closed eyes, whiskers relaxed, ears up straight.

Hunting or playing cat: large pupils but not as large as when frightened, whiskers forward, ears up and forward.

Frightened cat: large pupils, flat whiskers, ears flat to head.

Angry cat: pupils slits, whiskers forward, ears up but furled back.

Other Body Language

Back arched: defensive threat.
Crouch: submissive.
Rubbing: exchange of body odors for recognition in future.

CAT TAIL LANGUAGE

Tail up, a bit bent: greeting.

Tail flailing: threat, cat on offense.

Fat tail up: threat.

Fat tail arched: defensive threat.

Tail wrapped around itself: vulnerability.

INDOORS OR OUTDOORS?

The Humane Society of the United States says without equivocation that all cats should be indoor cats. Here are the reasons:

Roving cats upset the ecological balance by killing wild prey. They defecate in children's sandboxes and rip up flower beds. When allowed to roam, cats pick up and transmit diseases, and if unneutered, they add to cat overpopulation.

Cats live longer if kept inside. An outdoor (or outdoor-indoor) cat lives an average of two or three years. An indoor cat lives 12 to 15 years. The outdoors poses danger for cats—infestation with parasites, poison, traps, attacks by other cats or wild animals. Cruel people have been known to torture cats. However, most outdoor cats are killed by cars.

To keep your cat happy indoors, let in fresh air through screened windows. If your windows do not have wide sills, provide a shelf for the cat to sit on to watch the scene outdoors. Cats like greens—plant some in a pot. Give cats open paper bags and safe toys to play with. Play games with your cat, and consider providing your cat with a companion pet if you are away a good deal. Above all, provide a scratching post.

If your cat is already an outdoor cat, make the transition slowly. Keep your cat inside except for the middle of the day, then slowly shorten the time it is outside until it has become an indoor cat.

Murmurs and Other Talk

Your cat's vocal language differs from that of every other cat. Do you know the sound your cat makes to communicate the following messages?

- Hello.
- Let me in.
- Let me out.
- Please.
- I want.
- I don't understand.
- I am dissatisfied.
- I am in distress.

- ◆ Give me food.
- ◆ No.
- ◆ Look here.
- ◆ I approve.
- ◆ I am angry.
- ◆ I threaten you.
- ◆ I want to mate.

Should You Declaw Your Cat?

Almost all veterinarians agree that only indoor cats, if any, should be declawed. Claws represent safety—an escape up a tree or a set of weapons in a fight. A declawed cat becomes merely prey, a most uncatlike position in life. Moreover, a cat uses its claws to alleviate itches. Many cat organizations will not allow declawed cats to enter shows.

If you insist on having your cat declawed, your veterinarian will put it under a general anesthesia for the operation, which involves a complete removal of the cat's claws, usually front feet only. If declawing is not done properly, with a complete removal of the germinal cells from which claws grow, claws may regrow, but be misshapen.

CLIPPING YOUR PET'S NAILS

Thick edge showing beveling should be at bottom.

The clippers should be held as shown above, with the thick beveled edge showing at bottom. Make sure that the kind you buy has round blades so that you do not injure your animal.

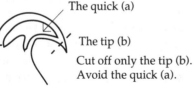

The quick (a)

The tip (b)

Cut off only the tip (b). Avoid the quick (a).

Ideally, the operation should be done between three and four months, but it can be done at any age.

Why is declawing even a question? The answers: shredded furniture or shredded owners. Scratching is a natural activity for the cat. It needs to sharpen its claws and clean them. But not on your good furniture! you exclaim. The solution to shredded furniture: buy a scratching post and teach the cat to use it. (See "Training Your Cat, p. 333.") If the cat shreds you, trim your cat's nails so it will do less damage. Here's how:

1. Buy special nail clippers at your pet store.

2. Find another person to hold the cat, because (at least at first) cats are not fond of this procedure.

3. Take the toe between your thumb and forefinger and squeeze to extend the claw. Then trim off only the tip (b). Avoid the quick, the pink part (a).

FALLING CATS

It all comes from living in trees—a cat can fall 32 stories and survive. Even stranger, cats that fall from a level higher than seven stories are *less* likely to get hurt or die than those who fall shorter distances. Why? Scientists offer this explanation: at five stories, cats reach end velocity of 60 mph as air resistance stops acceleration. (Humans can reach an end velocity of 120 mph. The difference has to do with ratio of body surface area to body mass.) And cats are acrobats. They can turn over in midair to land feet first. It's better to land on four feet than two.

None of these reasons fully explains why cats can fall *farther* and survive. Veterinarians who have studied the problem think it is because, as the cat stops accelerating, it may extend its legs, increasing drag and giving a greater surface for landing so impact is spread.

BUT—close your windows or screen them. Keep cats off high balconies.

Birds and Fish

Birds

Birds delight observers with their intricate behavior. (See the chart on the next page for some examples.) Birds have personalities. And birds are beautiful. If you decide to keep birds, be sure to buy them from reputable dealers. Start with one or two inexpensive, easy-to-raise birds. If you become a bird buff, you might consider financing your hobby by breeding birds to sell or trade for others. Keeping wild birds in captivity is illegal in many countries, and importing endangered birds illegally, a practice notorious for its cruelty to the animals, is not uncommon. In general, it is not a wise idea to place any wild birds in captivity, even those you find in your backyard.

For small pets, birds are surprisingly long-lived. Except for small finches, some of which live only about two years, most birds live from eight to 15 years. Parrots are known for their longevity—from 40 to 70 years. Macaws live 40 to 60 years, and cockatoos from 30 to 40 years.

Check with the dealer about the proper cage for the bird. Cages must give birds enough room to move around and flap their wings. Rectangular cages are better than square or round ones. Make sure the cage comes equipped with a sliding bottom tray for easy cleaning. If you want to keep birds in an aviary, you might consider buying an indoor aviary kit. For building an outdoor aviary, a major undertaking, consult a good bird book.

Make sure, in any case (cage or aviary), that you include the proper accessories—toys, perches, light. Food requirements differ according to species and whether or not birds are breeding. Birds need drinking water; most need a place to bathe. They do not tolerate drafts well and require plenty of light. Keeping birds demands a good deal of work. Cages and aviaries need to be kept clean, and you will have to do some research to learn how to care properly for your birds.

Before introducing new birds to your cage or aviary, quarantine them for at least two weeks in a separate cage. Then before integrating them, put the cage near the other birds for a few days so that they can get used to each other. Allow birds that will be put into outdoor aviaries a chance to acclimate themselves to the weather.

Training a Bird

Though it takes great patience, birds can be trained to obey commands, even to talk if genetically so predisposed. Throughout training, talk to your bird to reassure it. Keep working until even small progress is made. Training should be done by one member of the household.

BIRD CHART

Bird groups	Popular breeds	Cage space per bird, LxWxH (approx.)	Comments
Finches	Gray singing (*Serinus leucopygia*); green singing (*Serinus mozambicus*); society finch (*Lonchura striata*); Zebra finch (*Poephilia guttata*)	Box-type cage or aviary; need perches, some need bath. Cage 20x10x12 inches.	Some good singers, many with fine markings and beautiful color combinations. Popular breeds relatively inexpensive.
Canaries	Roller, gloster, border canary, red-factor canary; smaller varieties	Need perches and bath; cage 20x14x16 inches.	Inexpensive to expensive. Good cage birds or can be kept in aviary with other seed-eating species, even some softbills. Brightly colored, sweet singers (if male, though some hens sing a little).
Soft-billed birds (non-seed-eating)	Pekin robin (*Leiothrix lutea*)	House alone or in pairs; indoor cage 30x18x26 inches.	Strong, lively, fine singers (particularly males). Beautiful plumage. Couples affectionate. Need water daily.
	Shama (*Copsychus malabaricus*)	House alone or in pairs in aviary. Indoors in winter.	Mimics—of everything from rusty gate to nightingale. Exuberant.
	Golden-fronted leafbird (*Chloropsis aurifrons*)	Cage or aviary with other, smaller species. Cage 32x20x24 inches.	Male sings sweetly. Brightly colored. Easily tamed.
Parrots (Psittacidae)	Budgerigar (small species of parrot)	Cage 24x12x16 inches with horizontal wire. May also house in aviary.	Spray cage on warm days with mist sprayer. Many colors, can learn words if taught young. Affectionate, sometimes noisy. Relatively inexpensive.
	Lovebird	Cage 23x12x16 inches with horizontal wire.	Affectionate if hand-reared. Many colors. Relatively inexpensive.
	South American parakeets (conure, Aratinga, etc.); Asiatic parakeets	Cage 47x36 x36 inches.	Curious and beautifully colored, noisy.
	Australian parakeets	Cage 47x36 x 36 inches.	Can be aggressive. Good pet only if hand-reared, can be kept in aviary with other parakeet species and finches.
	Lory, lorikeet		Need nectar mixture, fruits, honey. Beautifully colored. Affectionate.
	African gray parrot (*Psittacus erithacus*)	Cage 59x59x63 inches.	Good talker and mimic, capricious, feather-picker.
	Amazon parrots		Good talkers and mimics. Need space. Hard to breed.

BIRD ON THE HAND

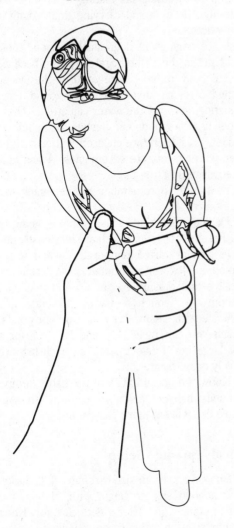

The first step—to accustom the bird to your hand. Put your hand (perhaps leather-gloved) quietly in the cage until the bird gets used to it. Eventually, it will sit on your hand. Move slowly.

Once the bird sits comfortably on your hand, train it to sit on your finger. Put your index finger horizontally against its body in the front above its legs. With big birds you may need to extend three fingers or your entire hand. Keep trying, going back to letting the bird sit on your hand until it has learned to sit on your finger. You can then train it to go from one hand to another, even onto your shoulder.

Teach the bird to go back to the perch by holding it on your finger with its breast against the perch. You may also say something like "up."

You can then let the bird out of the cage to fly free. Be aware that a flying bird may break things in your house. To get the bird back in the cage, use a treat first. You may use a command like "come." If it fails to come, use a stick as a perch, get the bird on it, then walk it back to the cage.

If you decide to use a T-shaped perch for training, remember that the perch can seem to be an aggressive male to your bird. You can leave the T-shaped perch in the cage until the bird becomes accustomed to it. Always approach the bird from the side and very slowly.

Speech Training

This takes patience, and works best if the bird is attached to you. Some researchers think that parrots actually learn to attach meaning to words—they may be more than mere mimics. Do not cut the bird's tongue, a cruel procedure that does nothing for the bird's speaking ability, which is seated mainly in the syrinx below the larynx.

Go to the cage and say words quietly over and over, like "Hi, pretty bird." Open the cage door slowly and put your hand inside. Use a high-pitched voice. Start with one or two words. Birds like the sounds made by *p, t,* and *k.* So include *Pete* or *kiss* or a similar word in the phrase you teach your bird. Birds are not fond of the sounds of *m, n,* and *l.* Forget "I love mommy" or "Nevermore." Put the bird on your finger or hand and say a word or two repeatedly and slowly in a loud, clear voice. Do this several times a day, every day. Mynahs take two to three weeks to learn a couple of words; parrots and parakeets take two or three months.

Once the bird has learned the words, try a short phrase, then after the bird has learned it, another phrase. Only when several phrases are in its vocabulary, should you try to teach a complete sentence.

PARROTS MAY MEAN WHAT THEY SAY

At a University of Arizona laboratory in Mexico, ethologist Irene Pepperberg teaches English to African gray parrots. She has taught parrots to identify shapes, colors, textures. The objects she uses in training have more than one characteristic (shape, color, material): an orange square made of paper, two keys—one of blue plastic and the other of yellow metal, a ball of red fuzz, and others.

Pepperberg's prize pupil is Alex, a parrot she bought in a pet store. She asks Alex, "What is red?" He answers, "Wool." She gives him the fuzzy ball. Alex has a vocabulary of about a hundred words. He can tell items apart, count up to six, tell what object is bigger or smaller. He knows the letters of the alphabet and can sound out words when shown letters together.

In the wild, parrots may shriek to communicate information, using different sounds to convey messages about flight directions or location of ripe fruit. Pepperberg's training method imitates the way parrots probably learn in the wild—she creates a social atmosphere in which parrots learn by watching others learn. Holding an object, she says its name until the model bird says it. The reward is the object.

While no training method has been developed for bird fanciers, perhaps, if you are enterprising, you might try the Pepperberg method to see how smart your parrot really is.

Fish

Fish make excellent pets. They do not need walks and litter boxes, nor do they chew up our shoes. Fur-allergic people can be in their vicinity without sneezing or breaking out in a rash. In their glass house, fish delight and soothe us with their balletic swimming and beautiful colors; they amaze us with their fascinating behavior—like bubble-nest building and carrying their young in their mouths.

Fish are edging out dogs as the second most popular pet in the United States, partly because they are easy to take care of. But they need informed care, as anyone who has found a pet fish floating on top of the water can attest. There is a feeling of failure as one flushes the fish down the toilet, or, if there are children, buries it in the garden with appropriate ceremonies. A fish tank is an ecosystem, after all.

Some things to remember for beginning fish enthusiasts:

♦ Decide what kind of fish you are going to raise. Freshwater tropical fish are less costly and survive well in varied temperatures and water conditions. Saltwater aquariums fascinate but are expensive and difficult to set up and maintain. Try them after you have had at least a year's experience with freshwater fish. Outdoor ponds, in which you can raise carp and koi, call for a rather large initial investment, but such fish are relatively easy to care for.

♦ Know the social habits of the fish you buy. Community fish get along with other fish. Aggressive fish will eat more passive ones.

Tropical Aquarium Setup

♦ Choose aquarium size carefully. A 10-gallon tank is a good size to begin with, though the bigger the tank, the easier it is to care for. Keep the fish population within reasonable limits. Allow at least a gallon of water per inch of fish; one expert says that you should have only one big fish or two or three little fish in a 10-gallon tank.

♦ For the aquarium you need: a hood with a light, a heater, a thermometer, a filter, air pump, a gang valve, airline tubing, gravel, a fishnet, water conditioner, and food.

♦ To set up the tank: (1) rinse it out with tap water; (2) assemble the under-gravel filter and put it in the tank; (3) rinse the gravel (but not with soap or detergent) and add to the tank; (4)

set up the air pump, connect the airline tube to the air stem on the filter and to the gang valve; (5) pour in the water and put in water conditioner (in amount suggested on the package) to dissipate the chlorine; (6) set up the heater, but do not plug it in for 15 minutes.

♦ To introduce the fish: place the plastic bag containing the fish on top of the tank water for several minutes. Then open the bag, but leave the fish in it for a few more minutes before removing it.

♦ About one-fifth of the water should be changed once a month.

Fishbowls for Freshwater Nontropical Fish

♦ Fish in fishbowls are not easier to care for than fish in aquariums for tropical freshwater fish, but the initial investment is less.

♦ You can buy bowls from pint-sized to two gallons.

♦ The water is at room temperature, so you can raise only goldfish or Siamese fighting fish.

♦ Siamese fighting fish must be raised alone. You can put one goldfish in a small bowl, up to three in a large one.

♦ Change the water twice a week. The night before you change it, let the new water sit so that the chlorine dissipates.

General Dos and Don'ts

♦ In the first month, test the water every day; after that, weekly. Water temperature of about 74°F. works for most fish.

♦ Don't put the aquarium in direct sun; use a fluorescent light on the tank.

♦ Do not overfeed fish. Feed them once a day, only the amount of food they will eat in about 30 seconds. Otherwise the food and waste material from the fish begin to break down and create toxic byproducts. You can buy slow-release feeder tablets for times when you are away.

♦ If fish get sick, take them to the pet store. Take little fish in a half-filled mayonnaise jar. Take big fish in trash can liners half-filled with water in a five-gallon bucket; blow some air into the bags. Also take a sample of tank water (3–4 oz.).

Fishes for Freshwater Tanks

The most popular tropical freshwater fishes are zebra danios, tetras, angelfish, scavenger catfish, blue gourmi, platies, mollies, guppies, swordtails, barbs, cichlids, Oscars, pink kissers, neons, cardinals, Caribbean blue angels, lattice butterflies.

When choosing fish you should consider their appearance, interesting habits, and ability to get along with one another. Fish that live together should like the same water properties (softness

CAPTURING OF SALTWATER TROPICAL FISH

Unlike freshwater tropical fish, many saltwater tropical fish are captured in the wild and sent to market. Procedures for capturing them can not only be cruel, they also can ruin the ecological niche in which the fish and other marine animals live. For example, fish collectors capturing fish in the Philippines sometimes shoot sodium cyanide from plastic baby bottles into their faces to slow them down. This deadly poison harms sealife and destroys the coral reefs, according to the International Marinelife Alliance. It also endangers the health of the fish collectors, who often work for only a dollar a day. At least half the fish caught this way die almost immediately. In other areas, like Hawaii and Australia, fish are more humanely caught in nets.

One of five saltwater tropical fish arrives at its destination dead or close to it. By the time they get to your pet store, most fish are under stress. If you want to set up a saltwater aquarium, make sure that the fish you buy have been collected humanely.

FISH CHART

Fish Group	Habits	Requirements
Characins: bright-colored, from South America and Africa. Species include the popular tetras.	Shoaling fishes. Combine with dwarf cichlids, catfishes, other characins.	Need protected areas in the tank. Light not too bright. Slightly soft to medium hard, slightly acid water (pH about 6.5). Keep at least 6 individuals of the same species, with some exceptions.
Barbs and danios, mostly from Asia.	Shoaling fishes. Can combine Schubert's barb, cherry barb, rosy barb, black ruby barb, and fish of the *Brachydanio* species. Some *Puntius* species nibble on other species' fins. *Puntius* barbs stay at bottom, danios at middle and top.	Densely planted tank, with a good deal of open water. Light requirements differ according to species. Neutral to slightly acid water for all but *Sawbwa resplendens*. Keep at least 6 of any one species.
Rainbow fishes, silversides, rice fishes, four different but related families, from the Far East. Many are beautifully colored.	Shoaling fishes. Can be combined with livebearers, small cichlids (from Lake Tanganyika), gobies, catfishes.	Need open water. Keep plants at the back and sides of the tank. Floating plants, java moss for spawning area. Roots at minimum. Medium to hard alkaline water for most. Keep at least 6 of any one species.
Loaches, flying foxes, elephant-trunk fishes, members of order *Cyprinigormes* (carp-like fishes).	Bottom fishes, by and large. Many species need to be kept alone, others live well in groups. Most can be combined with fishes that live at middle and upper levels. Don't combine with other bottom-living fishes.	Need hiding places. No sharp-edged bottom material. Need frequent water changes. Water soft to medium hard, slightly acid to slightly alkaline.
Livebearers, which give birth to live fish, include livebearing tooth carps (the Americas), the *Goodeidae* family (Mexico), the *Hemirhamphidae* family (Southeast Asia). Popular species: swordtails, platies, guppies, mollies, mosquito fish.	Most are shoaling fishes, so you need to keep several individuals of a species, with more females than males. Can be combined with catfishes and smaller cichlids.	Lots of open water, vegetation along the sides. Most like alkaline, medium-hard to hard water, which you should change regularly.
Killifishes. Part of the order *Cyprinodontiformes*. Some species bury themselves in the mud to live through dry seasons. Species include the desert pupfish.	Can be combined with catfishes, small shoaling fishes. Big top-living killies are compatible with dwarf cichlids. Keep small, fragile killies in separate tanks. Males often seek domination.	All except lamp-eyes need densely planted tank, no circulation, dark bottom, shaded water. Cover should be tight -- they can jump out. Soft slightly acid water for all but lamp-eyes from Lake Tanganyika and desert fish, which need hard, alkaline water.
Labyrinth fishes, of suborder *Anabantoidea* (Asia and Africa). Beautiful colors. Includes Siamese fighting fish.	Many species display elaborate courtship behavior, build nests, care for young. Some combine with bottom-dwellers and calm shoaling fishes; others need to be kept alone. Siamese fighting fish: only one male to the tank.	For most species, tanks should be dark, densely planted, and with some floating plants; water slightly acid and soft to medium hard. For bubble-nesting fish, no circulation.

Fish Group	Habits	Requirements
Cichlids, from varied habitats in varied places, classified by areas (Lake Tanganyika, Lake Malawi, Central America, and so on. Central American cichlids include discus and angelfishes. Cichlids are colorful and engage in fascinating brood care.	Territorial fishes, but can be combined: dwarf cichlids with characins and other upper-stratum shoaling fishes; different drawf cichlids with each other if they care for young differently; large cichlids with some large catfishes. When males are aggressive, they may have to be separated from females for a time. Substrate brooders lay eggs on a surface or in cavities and take care of them— and the baby fish when they hatch out. Mouthbrooders keep their eggs in their mouths or deposit them on a substrate, later keeping the young in their mouths. There are many variations on the parent pair and family structure. Start with 6 or 8 fish.	*Tanganyika cichlids*: need rock structures with caves if cavity brooders, with passages if mouthbrooders. Other environment depends on their natural habitat. Need water medium hard to hard, slightly alkaline. *Malawi cichlids*: Many species need rock structures with double-entry caves. Water medium hard to hard, alkaline. *Other African cichlids*: In the wild, many species are doomed to extinction. Smaller species need well-planted tanks with caves and small roots. Larger species need flat rocks and roots. Most can be combined with catfishes and shoaling fishes of upper strata. Most need water medium hard and slightly acid to slightly alkaline. *Central American cichlids*: Most grow to a fairly large size. Need large flat rocks, caves, roots, plants protected by stones. Need medium hard to hard alkaline water. *South American cichlids*: Provide dark tanks with roots, stones, and caves. Some like plants as part of the living space; others eat them. Dwarf cichlids are compatible with characins and other non-aggressive fishes. Most need medium hard, acid to slightly alkaline water, except when breeding (when they need soft, acid water).
Catfishes, one of the most numerous orders of fish.	Can combine with other fishes (except cichlids) because they live mostly on the lower strata. Some are shoaling, others live well in groups, others are meant to live alone. Can be territorial when mating.	Except for those from Lake Tanganyika or Lake Malawi, all like soft to medium hard, slightly acid water. Some need soft bottom material for burrowing. Provide caves and other shelters, shady places.
Gobies (those found in fresh water).	Bottom-dwellers can be combined with fishes that prefer the middle and upper strata. Do not combine with other bottom-dwellers. Gobies are territorial.	Supply them with hiding places. Need medium hard to hard, neutral to alkaline water.

or hardness, acid-alkaline balance), and they should like the same food or be able to tolerate each other's food. In each tank stratum (layer), have only one fish species, unless the tank is over 40 inches long, when you can have two. You can have different fish living in different strata (top, middle, bottom) of the tank. The fewer fish, the easier the tank is to take care of.

PET HEALTH

Your Animal's Shots

The pinpricks of pain aside, shots can save your pet from illness, even extend its life. And, of lesser importance, shots can save you money in vet bills. Vaccinations prevent various diseases by introducing into the animal's body a virus or bacterium that, though it has been made harmless, generates the production of antibodies. Each injection raises the number of antibodies, so booster shots are imperative. Some shots, such as rabies, can provide protection for one to three years. Others need to be administered in a series over a period of weeks.

Usually cats and dogs start receiving shots at 6–8 weeks in a monthly series, until about 16 weeks old. Adult animals should receive vaccination boosters at least once a year. The law requires some vaccinations, like rabies, but others are administered at your discretion.

Dogs: canine hepatitis, canine distemper, tracheobronchitis (bordatella, caused by canine parainfluenza and canine adenovirus), leptospirosis, parvovirus, rabies, coronavirus, Lyme disease. *Note:* Some controversy exists about shots for Lyme disease—consult your veterinarian.

Cats: feline distemper (panleukopenia or feline infectious enteritis), respiratory diseases (rhinotracheitis a.k.a. FVR or herpes virus; calicivirus aka FCV; and pneumonitis aka chlamydia), feline leukemia, feline AIDS, rabies, and sometimes feline infectious peritonitis.

Heartworm, affecting both dogs and cats, is spread by mosquitoes and can prove fatal. Veterinarians sometimes prescribe preventive medication for heartworm.

Neuter Your Pet

When pets are between six and eight months old, it is a good idea to neuter them, unless you are going to use them for breeding purposes. Before neutering, pets should be in good health and have had all their shots. This is the socially responsible thing to do—there is a million-fold surplus of cats and dogs in the United States. For example, for every human child born, seven kittens are born. Many dogs and cats end up in animal shelters, more than half of them to be destroyed because no home can be found for them. Most animal shelters insist that you neuter an animal you adopt so that the animal will not continue contributing to overpopulation.

Female animals are spayed (ovaries and perhaps uterus removed), male animals castrated (testicles removed). The procedures, while not without risk, are not very dangerous. The animal can usually come home the same day. After the operation, you should keep your pet quiet and confined to the house for a day or two. Give water in small amounts. Be careful not to harm the incision through handling. If the incision swells or becomes red or a stitch becomes loose, call your veterinarian. It will be about 10 days before the female animal heals completely, about three days for a male. However, keep male cats indoors for a week to avoid attacks by other cats.

Contrary to pet mythology, altered pets do not become fat and lazy.

The advantages to you of neutering your animal:

♦ Males become less aggressive and lose their wanderlust.

♦ Male cats are less likely to mark territory by spraying with their scent glands, which emit a strong odor unpleasant to humans.

♦ Females will not go into heat. Unspayed bitches go into heat twice a year for up to 21 days, unspayed cats go into heat three or more times a year for three to 15 days. Cats in heat are notorious for their constant nighttime wailing and trilling cries meant to attract a mate. If you value your sleep (and your neighbors' sleep), you will strongly consider having your cat spayed.

♦ You will not have the problem of getting rid of unwanted puppies or kittens.

♦ Your animals will live longer.

♦ Female cats have less risk of uterine infection (pyrometra) and breast cancer; they have no risk of ovarian cancer or uterine cancer (if the uterus has been removed). Female dogs have similar lowered risks.

♦ Male dogs and cats are less likely to contract prostate cancer.

♦ Pets are more affectionate after they are neutered.

AMAZING PET OVERPOPULATION FACTS

One female cat and her young can generate 420,000 cats in just seven years. One female dog and her young can generate 67,000 puppies in just six years.

The Fat Cat and the Fat Dog

Obesity in dogs and cats comes from the same cause as in human beings—the body takes in more energy than it puts out. Life is too easy, food too available. Too much food and too little exercise, along with a low metabolism rate, can make your pet balloon up fast. One cat in every 10 is overweight. Four dogs in every 10 are overweight.

Why worry? You love your pet fat as much as thin. But a fat pet has greater risk of diseases of the skin, heart, stomach, liver, and kidneys. Overweight can contribute to diabetes. It puts a burden on joints and contributes to osteoarthritis. And it increases a tendency to suffer from heat stroke and lengthens recovery time from surgery.

As anyone who has had a fat animal knows, treating obesity is harder than preventing it. If your pet has a tendency to put on pounds, try the following:

♦ Check your dog or cat for extra weight by feeling its sides—you should be able to feel the ribs easily. If there is more than ¼ inch of fat between fur and ribs, the animal is overweight. You should be able see a waistline from above on a dog.

♦ Know what your pet weighs, and keep track of it. Most vets have a scale on which you can weigh your dog. You can also weigh your pet at home if it is light enough to pick up easily in your arms. First weigh yourself. Then hold your pet in your arms and step on the scale. Subtract your weight from the combined weight of you and your pet.

♦ Check with your veterinarian before putting your dog or cat on a diet. In general, reduce caloric intake to 75 percent of what an animal of its weight should normally eat. Buy food that is low in fat—compare labels. For dogs, add fiber, like a bulking agent (Metamusil), bran, or canned vegetables (to 10–15 percent of the animal's food). Commercial diet foods come with instructions on how much food to give to animals of various sizes for safe weight loss. Change the diet in increments (shift foods) rather than all at once, otherwise the animal may get diarrhea. Supplement with multivitamins. Most important, discuss your animal's diet with your veterinarians.

♦ Try feeding an overweight dog or cat more often. Take the daily ration and divide it into three meals, for instance.

♦ Give your dog plenty of exercise, but increase it slowly. Don't exercise the animal within an hour after eating. Small dogs may need only the exercise they get in house and yard. Older dogs may need only to be taken for walks. Other dogs can chase balls or sticks. You can take your cat for a walk on a leash, too, if you use a harness rather than a collar, which might choke it.

♦ Don't feed your animal from the table, and try to stop feeding snacks like kitty treats and dog biscuits, which are high in fats. Animals are very good at begging, and all your efforts to help your pet lose weight may be foiled by one tender-hearted but unenlightened family member who slips the pet treats on the sly. Convince the members of the family that it is a kindness to help the animal lose weight. Be hard-hearted. If you do feed treats, figure in the calories.

Calories in Dog Foods

Dog foods differ in calories per ounce, but, on the average, figure as follows:

FOOD	CALORIES PER OUNCE
Dry food	97
Semi-moist	85
Canned	25
Biscuit	100

Dog food manufacturers change their formulas from time to time so it is a good idea to survey the supermarket shelves and comparison-shop dog food brands. Unless your dog is a working dog, keep the percentage of fat calories low.

Semi-moist dog food and biscuits tend to be higher in fat than other kinds of dog foods. Canned dog foods are lowest in fat per ounce, but they tend to be higher in water.

Dog treats vary in calorie count. Dry dog biscuits range around 100 calories an ounce, while semi-moist treats are about 75 calories an ounce. Jerky treats vary from about 85 calories an ounce to over 150 calories an ounce. If you feed treats, add them in as part of the dog's daily diet. Small and medium biscuits vary in weight from 3 to 10 grams. (A small biscuit from one manufacturer is 9 grams, while a medium biscuit from another manufacturer is 10 grams.) Large biscuits are about 30 grams apiece, and extra large, about 65 grams a piece. Soft-moist treats are about 5 grams a piece, and jerky treats range from 2 to 6 grams a piece. While packages do not list the weight per treat, they do list the total weight. You can determine the weight per treat by counting out the number of treats and dividing into the total net weight per package. You will need to convert grams to ounces to figure the calorie count: an ounce = 28 grams. If a biscuit weighs 9 grams and contains 100 calories an ounce, figure its caloric count as follows:

$$\frac{9}{28} \times 100 = \frac{900}{28} = \text{approximately 32 calories}$$

You can find out *exact* calorie counts for dog foods and treats by writing to the manufacturer. Otherwise, while labels do not list calorie counts, they do list fat, protein, and carbohydrate percentages. Generally speaking, the lower the percentage of fat, the lower the calorie count per ounce.

Serious Signs: When to Rush to the Vet

You should take your animal to the veterinarian *immediately* if you answer yes to any of the following questions. Other signs may also be life-threatening, but these signs are the ones most experts agree on. In any case, better be safe than sorry.

♦ Has your pet lost its appetite for more than two days?

♦ Has your pet vomited more than twice?

♦ Has your pet had diarrhea for more than two days?

♦ Does your pet vomit *and* have diarrhea?

♦ Is your pet behaving with unusual listlessness—brooding, hiding in the bushes, lacking enthusiasm for its favorite activities?

♦ Has your pet collapsed?

♦ Has your pet had a seizure or an uncontrolled muscle spasm?

♦ Does your pet seem confused or disoriented?

♦ Is your pet walking into things or circling without apparent reason?

♦ Is your pet's body temperature more than 103°F.?

♦ Is your pet having problems with breathing?

♦ Does your pet have discharges from mouth and/or nose *and* is it breathing fast?

♦ Is your pet bleeding from mouth, nose, ears, anus, vulva, or penis?

♦ Have you observed blood in your pet's stool or vomit?

♦ Does your pet flinch in pain when touched, when getting up or lying down? Does it display other signs of pain?

♦ Is your pet suffering from a bite, large cut, or cut that bleeds so profusely you cannot stop it?

♦ Do you suspect a broken bone?

♦ Have you any cause to think that your pet has eaten poison?

♦ Does your pet drink abnormal amounts of water? Is it urinating excessively?

♦ Is your cat acting strangely in the litterbox?

♦ Is your pet's ear inflamed or discharging?

♦ Is your pet's eye swollen, glazed, protruding, or discharging purulent material? Is the pupil unusually dilated?

Take your animal to the vet *as soon as you can* if your pet has any of the following signs of illness:

♦ Lack of alertness and interest in the world.

♦ Discharges.

♦ Scratching.

♦ Dull coat, hair loss, or irritated, unhealthy skin.

♦ Lameness.

♦ Overweight or unexplained weight loss.

♦ Coughing or sneezing.

♦ Swellings.

♦ Constipation or incontinence.

♦ Bad breath, abnormal teeth or gums.

♦ Scooting rear end on the ground.

A note about pet birds: See your vet if the bird acts sick, sneezes, or vomits. Observe stools for diarrhea or constipation. Separate the bird from other birds, and keep it warm.

FIRST-AID KIT FOR DOGS AND CATS

♦ Adhesive tape (1–2″)

♦ Gauze bandaging (2–3″ wide, depending on size of pet)

♦ Scissors (blunt-end)

♦ Tweezers

♦ Needle-nosed pliers

♦ Eyedropper

♦ Thick magazine (splint)

♦ Q-tips

♦ Antiseptic products

♦ Commercial eyewash (0.9%–2% boric acid solution)

♦ Commercial ear cleaner

♦ Styptic pencil or commercial product for stopping pet's bleeding

♦ Kaopectate or Pepto-Bismol (for dogs only)

♦ Mineral oil (medicinal)

♦ Karo syrup (for diabetic dogs)

♦ Round-ended rectal thermometer

♦ Chemical ice pack or Ziploc bags for ice

THE FOODS THAT DO NOT COME OUT OF A CAN OR BAG

You can feed your pet "human" food, but keep some facts in mind: feed cooked rather than raw meat and eggs, remove bones from meat and fish, make sure a dog or cat can tolerate milk, give your dog bones only if they are large and do not readily splinter. *Never* feed animals chocolate.

IS YOUR PET FOOD NUTRITIOUS?

The AAFCO (Association of American Feed Control Officials), a nonprofit group of government experts in animal food, establishes legal definitions for ingredients in pet food. They also set nutritional standards that involve testing with live animals for a six-month period. Look for sentences on the label that read:

♦ "nutritionally complete and balanced for **all stages of life** as substantiated through testing in accordance with AAFCO procedures." (Good for all animals—growing, pregnant, nursing, lactating, adult.)

♦ "nutritionally complete and balanced for **growth and maintenance** as substantiated through testing in accordance with AAFCO procedures." (Good for all animals except pregnant or nursing ones.)

♦ "nutritionally complete and balanced for **maintenance** as substantiated through testing in accordance with AAFCO procedures." (Best for older animals.)

If the label reads only that the product "meets or exceeds the nutrient levels set by the National Research Council," it means that the food meets federal nutrition standards and has been subjected successfully to laboratory analysis, but has not necessarily been tested on live animals.

Pet Emergency First Aid

Don't panic. A hurt animal may attack (which does no good to you or the pet). Reassure the animal and gently restrain it. Apply first aid.

What to look for:
♦ Heartbeat
♦ Breathing
♦ Bleeding
♦ Gasping
♦ Pale gums
♦ Fractures
♦ Weakness (animal cannot stand)
♦ Shock
♦ Collapse

Act fast, but without panic. Call the nearest animal hospital. (Keep the number of the hospital by your telephone.) Most veterinarians have referral services. Be ready to describe the condition of the animal.

Be careful when moving the animal. Move it no more than you have to. Remember the Hippocratic Oath: Do no harm.

1. Use an improvised stretcher: a blanket for a large animal, a towel for a smaller one.

2. You may have to muzzle a dog or restrain a cat by wrapping it in a towel (see "Muzzling an Injured Animal," p. 353).

3. Carefully move a cat by holding its rear and the scruff of the neck (if likely to claw) or under the chest; avoid bending its body.

4. With larger animals, if possible, use three people to help move the animal. When moving the pet onto the blanket one person should support the pet's head, another the pet's back, and the third the pet's pelvis. After the animal is on the blanket and you are ready to move it, have two people hold the ends of the blanket taut, with the third person supporting the animal's back.

FIRST-AID EMERGENCIES FOR PETS

Bleeding: Bind a sterile pad tightly over the wound for four or five minutes. If bleeding continues, bandage the pad, changing every hour. Use

ARTERIAL PRESSURE POINTS

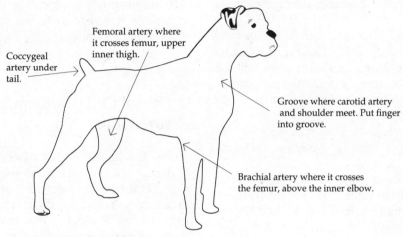

Femoral artery where it crosses femur, upper inner thigh.

Coccygeal artery under tail.

Groove where carotid artery and shoulder meet. Put finger into groove.

Brachial artery where it crosses the femur, above the inner elbow.

Pressure points are the same for a cat.

a tourniquet if blood is spurting or the other methods fail to work. Apply the tourniquet to a pressure point between the wound and the heart, loosening briefly every 15 minutes. Take the animal to the veterinarian.

Burns: Treat for shock by covering the animal with a blanket, putting it in a quiet place, and placing a hot (but not too hot) water bottle beside it. Douse the burnt area with cold water immediately. Take the pet to the veterinarian.

Convulsions: Make the animal comfortable in a dark and quiet room. Clean up the animal and the resting place after the convulsion is over. Give water, but not food until the animal is completely back to normal. Take it to the vet.

Dislocations and broken bones. If you suspect either, immobilize the limb by carefully placing a thick magazine against the affected part and wrapping it loosely with gauze. Do not attempt to put the bone back in place.

Drowning: *Small animals.* Hold the animal upside down by hind legs and swing it carefully for at least 30 seconds. Then have someone else open its mouth and give artificial respiration. *Larger animals.* Pick the animal up, holding it around the abdomen behind the ribs, and put the animal over your shoulder. Then open its mouth and pump its chest. Take your pet to the nearest animal hospital.

Foreign body in the mouth or throat. Open the animal's mouth and find foreign body. If you can, remove it with your fingers or pliers, but only if you can do this without hurting the animal. You can use the Heimlich maneuver on a pet by putting pressure on the lower part of the chest and quickly squeezing up against your own chest to pop the object out. Be careful, though—if you press too hard, you might crack the animal's ribs. Then try methods for *drowning* (holding upside down). If all else fails, rush the animal to the vet.

Foreign body in the eye. Keep the animal from touching its eye, restrain it, and use finger and thumb to open the eye. If the foreign body sits on the eye and is not embedded, try washing it out with eyewash or weak cold tea: squeeze a gauze pad saturated with solution over the eye until the foreign body is dislodged, then put a drop of cod-liver oil or medicinal mineral oil in the eye with an eyedropper. For embedded foreign bodies, take the animal to the veterinarian.

Frostbite or hypothermia. Warm the animal

up slowly in a warm bath or with warm towels (75°F.) for 10–15 minutes, then blow-dry. Keep the animal warm with a hot-water bottle or blanket. If you suspect frostbite, take the animal to the vet.

Heatstroke. Suspect heatstroke if a dog pants heavily, particularly if it collapses. If an animal has heatstroke douse it with cool water, put it in a cool bath, or cover it with cold wet towels. Put an ice pack on its head. Rush it to the animal hospital.

Poisoning: Signs of poisoning: vomiting, seizures, collapse, spasms, weakness, bleeding. *What to do:*

♦ If you can, determine what poison your pet took, then call the veterinarian and the **National Animal Poison Control Center**, 900-680-0000 ($2.95 per minute) or 800-548-2423 ($30 a case, payable by credit card). Follow their instructions.

♦ Wash off any poison left on the pet.

♦ If you know what poison the animal ate, take some to the vet with you, including the container.

♦ If the vet tells you to use an emetic (useful only within 30 minutes after the pet ate the poison), the following are suitable: a small piece (size of pea) of sodium bicarbonate; salted warm water; mustard in cold water.

Shock: Signs of shock—
♦ collapse
♦ fast and shallow breathing
♦ pale gums
♦ fast, weak pulse
♦ cold limbs
♦ dilated pupils.
What to do:
♦ Give nothing by mouth.
♦ Do not prop the animal's head up.
♦ Keep the animal warm.
♦ If breathing has stopped or is irregular, loosen the animal's collar, check inside the mouth and remove anything foreign, then give artificial respiration (below).
♦ If the pulse has stopped, have someone with CPR training carefully give heart massage and artificial respiration (below).

♦ Treat bleeding.
♦ Immobilize broken bones.
♦ Call the veterinarian.
Snakebite: Get the animal to the vet as fast as possible. If the bite is on a leg, put a tourniquet above the wound, and apply ice packs to the bite.

Animal CPR (Cardiopulmonary Resuscitation)

If you find no pulse, you usually will need to perform artificial respiration as you do heart massage. If the heart is beating, but the animal is not breathing, you need only do artificial respiration.

Be extremely careful—it is easy to injure an animal while performing these procedures. Use only in *emergencies.*

Heart Massage: Squeeze the left-hand side of the chest behind the front elbow at one squeeze a second for a dog, two squeezes a second for a cat. With a dog, you may put your other hand underneath the animal, so that you squeeze your hands toward each other. With cats use the finger and thumb, and be very cautious—a cat's rib cage is delicate. Be firm but gentle.

Artificial Respiration:

1. Take off the animal's collar. If it is a small animal, try swinging it to clear the airway. (See the section on drowning, page 351.) Put your pet on its side.

2. Check the mouth to make sure the airway is clear. The mouth should be open, cleaned of debris, tongue forward.

3. Put your hands on the chest over the rib cage behind the elbow (at the sixth rib). Push down gently but firmly to force air from the lungs. Release immediately. Do this every five seconds for a dog, every three seconds for a cat.

OR

If the animal is a cat, put it on its side and cover its mouth so no air can escape. Blow into its

MUZZLING AN INJURED ANIMAL

An injured dog may be so frightened that it will try to bite. You can improvise a muzzle from a piece of cloth (a piece of gauze or a necktie). If a muzzled dog shows signs of troubled breathing, untie the muzzle, open the dog's mouth, and pull its tongue to the front. Keep the muzzle on, but loose, holding the dog's head in your lap.
Warnings: Do not leave a muzzled dog alone. Do not muzzle a short-nosed breed or a dog with chest injuries or troubled breathing.

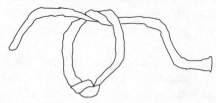

1. Knot the cloth in the middle, then tie another loose knot about 8 inches above the first.

2. Put the loop about halfway between nose and eyes. Pull the loose knot tight.

3. Cross ends under the jaw, then tie them behind the head in an easily loosened knot.

nostrils gently, counting to five (in your mind). The animal's chest should rise. Inhale for a count of eight, then blow again.

4. Continue until the animal breathes on its own or coughs. Then keep pressing on the chest, but without as much pressure.

5. Call your veterinarian.

CPR: For both dogs and cats: 15 heart massages, then two quick breaths. Repeat until normal breathing and heartbeat come back.

Fever? Taking Your Pet's Temperature

When your pet is under the weather, it may be necessary to take its temperature. Use a thermometer with a round bulb, which is less breakable than a thin one. Ask someone to help you.

Normal temperatures: dog, 100.4°–102.2°; cat 101.5°–102.5°F.

1. Shake the mercury down to about 96.8°. Lubricate the thermometer with olive oil or petroleum jelly.

2. With your helper restraining and reassuring the animal, raise the animal's tail and move it aside. If the animal is a cat, hold its tail.

3. Gently insert the thermometer into the rectum about 1 inch. In the case of a cat, you may have to rotate the thermometer gently. *Do not force it.* Hold it still and with the bulb against the wall of the rectum.

4 After one minute, take the thermometer out and read it.

5. Before putting the thermometer away, shake it down, clean it, and disinfect it.

DOG SEAT BELTS

A Love Belt (seat belt) can save your dog's life if you are in a car accident. For a free brochure, call 800-637-LOVE.

Dogs Do Not Belong in Parked Cars!

The Animal Protection Institute (PO Box 22505, Sacramento, CA 95822; 916-731-5521) distributes cards to be put under windshield wipers of dog owners who leave their pets in parked cars on hot days. It reads:

"Your pet may be dying. We understand you meant to be kind by taking your dog with you today, but you could be risking your pet's life.

"On a hot summer day, the inside of a car heats very quickly. On an average 85-degree day, for example, the temperature inside your car—with the window slightly opened—will reach 102 degrees in 10 minutes. In 30 minutes it will go up to 120 degrees. On warmer days, it will go even higher.

"A dog's normal body temperature is 101.5 to 102.2 degrees Fahrenheit. A dog can withstand a body temperature of 107 to 108 degrees Fahrenheit for only a short time before suffering irreparable brain damage—or even death. The closed car interferes with the dog's normal cooling process, that is, evaporation through panting.

"If your dog is overcome by heat exhaustion, you can give immediate first aid by immersing him or her in cold water until body temperature is lowered."

Note: Do not leave cats in parked cars, either.

Other Hot Weather Warnings

Keep in mind that dogs don't wear shoes, and hot pavements can burn their feet.

If you take your dog to the beach, bring along water and an umbrella for shade.

Don't walk your dog in the heat of the day between 10 AM and 2 PM. It's too hot for a dog to run when the temperature is over 85 with 70 percent humidity.

In Cold Weather

Wash your dog's feet free of salt if it has been walking on the snowy street. Trim the fur between its toes so it won't collect ice balls. It's too cold for a dog to run when the temperature is under 40 with a 25-degree windchill factor. And if roads are icy, keep your dog inside—dogs can fall and break their hips, just like people.

Pulse and Breathing Rates

Cats' and dogs' hearts beat at a different rate than humans' hearts; they breathe at different rates, too. Measure pulse rate and breathing when your pet is relaxed, lying down quietly, at rest.

To take your pet's pulse, find the femoral artery, on the inside of the upper hind leg. With small pets you can feel the pulse on the left-hand side of the chest. Place one or two fingers gently on the spot and count heart beats for 30 seconds (using a watch that measures seconds), then multiply by two.

One breath equals one rise and one fall of the chest.

PULSE AND BREATHING RATES FOR DOGS AND CATS

Rates	Cat	Dog
Normal pulse rate (resting)	110-140 beats/min.	Small dogs: 90-120 beats/min. Large dogs: 65-90 beats/min.
Normal breathing rate	30-50 breaths/min.	10-30 breaths/min. (higher in small dogs than large dogs)

Giving Your Pet Medication

Most pet owners have to give their pets medication at some time or other. Because you can't tell your pets it's good for them, administering doses may be a bit difficult. The methods below are easiest on you and your pets.

For Liquid Medication

♦ Fill a syringe or eyedropper with the proper measured amount of medication. *Then* approach your pet, speaking in a reassuring voice.

♦ Put the pet on a table, if you can.

♦ Tip its head, put the syringe into the back corner of its mouth, not between gum and lip. With your other hand, close the animal's mouth gently.

♦ The animal will swallow, and as it does, slowly release the medication through the syringe.

♦ After removing the syringe, hold the animal's mouth closed and massage its throat until you are sure the pet has swallowed all the medication.

For Pills, Tablets, Capsules

♦ Wrap the pill in a piece of the animal's favorite food, and give it to the animal.

OR

♦ Coat the pill with butter. Then grab the animal's mouth in one hand, thumb and forefinger at the angle of the jaw. Tilt the head back. Press on the corners of the mouth to open it. With your other hand, put the pill in the animal's mouth as far back as you can, clamp the mouth closed, and massage the throat until it swallows.

Flea Control

The versatile and tiny flea tortures the animals it bites. It also carries disease and tapeworm. To get rid of fleas, authorities agree that an all-out blitz is most effective—you must treat the animal, the house, and the yard. Though fleas are species-specific (there are cat fleas and dog fleas), any flea can find a home on any warm-blooded animal.

Fleas multiply fast. One flea is capable of laying up to 500 eggs. Pupae can remain dormant until aroused, which explains why an empty house, reinhabited, can seem to spawn fleas by the thousands when they are signaled to arise by vibrations of a potential host's feet or a rise in temperature.

A flea life cycle—egg to mature flea—takes 5 to 14 days. For use on your pet or in your house, you must either use a product that kills eggs and larvae as well as adult fleas and continues to work for a period of time, or you must apply insecticides repeatedly. No matter what pesticide you choose, use it according to the manufacturer's directions. More is not better. Birds can be killed from flea spray, though pyrethrin products often are safe. Check with your veterinarian.

Keep Fleas Out of the House

Before applying the insecticide, vacuum thoroughly, and treat the bag in your cleaner with flea powder or fleas will hatch inside it and cause more trouble. Go under the furniture and in cracks. Wash the pet's bedding in hot water. Put the contents of the filter into the garbage outside or fleas will breed in your washer and dryer.

Other Methods

♦ You can also use nontoxic dehydrators like borax or diatomaceous earth (*without* crystalline silica) in your house. Keep pets away from these products for 24 hours.

♦ *Flea traps:* Put water in a shallow dish and float oil on top of the water. Put a lamp over it. Fleas, attracted to the light, fall into the water; the oil prevents them from escaping.

OR

♦ Put a double-sided flea strip in a dish and put a lamp over it. Fleas again are attracted to the light and come to an end on the flea strip.

Keep Fleas Off Your Pets

♦ Use a flea comb. Make sure you kill the fleas you remove by drowning them in water or some other method.

AND/OR

♦ Apply insecticide (in soap or spray) *if* pets are old enough. Don't use flea products on small puppies or kittens. Bathe pets and treat the house and yard. To treat fleabites, use meat tenderizer paste or cortisone cream.

Allergic Pets

Walking on all fours, pets are closer to the ground than humans. They sniff more than humans. Dust and pollen can stick to their coats more easily than to the slick skin of humans. Consequently, pets tend to suffer from allergies from dust, mites, spores, pollen, and molds. The symptom can be sneezing, but the most common and severe reaction is skin irritation. The difference between human allergies and pet allergies? Humans outgrow them, pets just get worse.

Look for these signs:
♦ pawlicking
♦ chest, abdomen, and armpit scratching
♦ rubbing face and ears
♦ runny eyes
♦ sneezing, coughing, wheezing (mostly in cats).

Before going to the veterinarian, consider the answers to questions he or she is likely to ask: What are the skin problems like? What food does the pet eat? What medicine allergies does it have? Is the problem seasonal? Does it lick the tops of its paws? Does the pet lick the bottoms of its paws or itch all over?

Other Pet Allergies

The most dangerous allergic reaction is *anaphylactic* —to penicillin, incompatible blood transfusions, or insect bites. Anaphylactic reactions can kill by causing cardiovascular breakdown, respiratory failure, and shock. Make sure your vet knows about any reactions to drugs or blood transfusions.

Dogs and cats, like humans, may get *hives* from food or medication. With hives, the tissues around the head swell and other body parts may show round, red places. Signs: the pet itches and

rubs its head on the ground to scratch. Give the pet a bath in mild soap and take it to the vet for treatment.

One of the most common allergic reactions is *flea allergy dermatitis*, which in a sensitive animal can be caused by only one or two fleabites. The most sensitive parts of the body are the base of the tail, the hindquarters, and the lower abdomen. An animal who is severely affected may lose a good deal of hair and be covered with sores. Solutions are control of fleas and allergy treatment. Animals, as well as humans, can suffer from other insect bites. Treat with cold packs and antihistamines. See your veterinarian.

Food allergies can bring about itching, vomiting, diarrhea, and gas. Cats can develop asthma (another allergic reaction) with coughing, wheezing, and sneezing. Solutions: feeding of hypoallergenic foods, bronchodilators and corticosteroids.

Contact allergy, most commonly caused by flea collars, makes the skin red and causes sores, infection, hair loss. Take off the causative agent. Bathe your pet with mild soap. *Feline acne* (pimples under the cat's chin) is contact allergy caused by plastic food and water bowls. Water and feed pets from glass or stainless steel dishes.

Though animals can be desensitized, the treatment is expensive, time-consuming, and often disappointing. The most common treatments are antihistamines, cortisone, and anti-inflammatory drugs. The substance that causes the allergy should be eliminated.

Petproof Your House and Yard

Puppies and kittens, like little children, get into everything. Pet-proof your house by locking up household substances, many of which are toxic to pets, and other objects that might cause harm. For example, cats often play with dangerous objects like marbles and needles and thread. A thread-eating cat can end up undergoing life-threatening operations. Don't assume that animals will instinctively avoid poisonous substances—dogs and cats have been known to drink

SOME PLANTS POISONOUS TO PETS

amaryllis	jimson weed
azalea	large-leaved-ivy
Boston fern	lily of the valley
bulbs	marigold
Christmas rose	marijuana
chrysanthemum	mistletoe
daffodil	morning glory
dumb cane	mushroom
(dieffenbachia)	oleander (deadly)
geranium	philodendron
holly	poinsettia
honeysuckle	rhubarb leaves
iris	sweet pea
Jerusalem cherry	yew

highly poisonous antifreeze. Weedkiller is dangerous to animals. Signs of pet poisoning are: salivating, nausea, vomiting, stomach pain, diarrhea, dilated pupils, depression, difficult breathing. Rush a poisoned pet to the veterinarian. (Also see "Pet Emergency First Aid," p. 350.)
Remember:

♦ It takes less of a poisonous substance to kill a pet than a human. The smaller the pet, the truer this is.

♦ Pennies, because of their zinc content, can kill if swallowed. Tea bags and cigarette butts can be toxic.

♦ Don't give cats acetaminophen, ibuprofen, or aspirin. Ibuprofen and aspirin will harm dogs, as well.

♦ Cats and dogs can chew open containers with child-proof caps.

♦ Pesticides are dangerous to pets. Don't use any flea product on a cat unless it has been made for felines. (Read the label.) Birds are especially sensitive to air pollutants, like roach spray. (Canaries, remember, died to save miners.)

♦ If you treat your lawn or plants with fertilizer or pesticides, keep pets off them. Better yet, use nontoxic products like blood meal, fish emulsion, bone meal, and kelp. Don't use systemic fertilizers.

♦ Be very careful with snail and slug killer, which often comes in pellets that resemble dog food.

Old Animals

The poignancy of taking care of an older animal that you have known since puppyhood is balanced by the companionship and love it brings you. Partly because of the long history you have shared with your pet, you want to give it a happy old age. An old animal needs a good deal more attention and care than a younger one. It often doesn't want to leave your side. Then the time comes when you must agonize over euthanasia to end its pain from a terminal condition or disease.

When Is Your Pet Old?

In nature, small animals tend to live shorter lives than big ones. In the dog world, the reverse is true. In general, a very big dog (over 90 pounds) lives only about eight years and a large dog (51–90 pounds) lives about nine years, while small and medium-sized dogs live to be 10–12 years old or more. Some terriers can live to be 20, but toy breeds are not as long-lived as other small dogs. A dog is aging when it goes gray near its ears and muzzle and loses weight. Cats live to be an average age of 12, and are considered "old" at 18, but have been known to live to be 30.

Signs of Old Age. Like us, animals become stiff and creaky with age, developing joint pain, dental problems, and benign skin lumps. More serious conditions include diabetes mellitus, infections, cancer, and organ failure. Sometimes it is difficult to tell the difference between the normal signs of old age and a treatable, perhaps dangerous condition. Pay more attention to older pets. Take them to the veterinarian at least twice a year and when they display symptoms of illness. Don't ignore symptoms or decide they exist just because the pet is old. For instance, urinary and bowel problems can be treated. Look for change in normal habits and appetite, increased thirst and urination, vomiting, diarrhea, coughing, sneezing, weight loss, blood in urine or anywhere else, lethargy.

How to Treat Old Animals

Be gentle with old dogs and cats. They often don't hear and see as well, and are easily startled. Warn them before starting up the vacuum cleaner, for instance. Even more important, be sure that your pet is out of the way when you back the car out of the garage. If your dog is blind, remember that its senses of smell and hearing compensate for the loss. When you leave the house, turn the radio on to give the pet a sense of company.

Feed your pet well, with easily digested food. Some older dogs need vitamin supplements and fiber or mineral oil to prevent constipation. Keep your pet's weight down—overweight can exacerbate joint problems, put strain on the animal's heart, lower its resistance to disease. A veterinarian can prescribe special diets for overweight and kidney problems. Brush your dog's teeth once or twice a week. Older dogs are susceptible to gum disease.

Protect your pet's bed from cold drafts and keep it cool in summer. Older animals, not as able as younger ones to regulate their body temperature, are more susceptible to heat stroke.

Maintain a regular routine, with regular mealtimes. Try not to leave the pet in strange places, like a kennel, unless it is used to it.

When Its Time to Euthanize

Only you can make this decision, though your veterinarian will offer advice. In advance of the decision, determine what conditions are necessary for your animal to have a decent quality of life. Make up a list of questions: Does your pet have great difficulty in getting up and lying down? Is your pet suffering? Is there no chance of curing your pet? Has your pet lost interest in eating?

When you do decide to put your pet to sleep (the last thing you can do for it), remember that the method most veterinarians use—an injection of a barbiturate in the front leg—is painless. The animal is asleep in a second, dead in 30 seconds. Some owners choose to stay with their pet while it is being put to sleep, others cannot bear to do so. If you think that your emotion will make it more difficult for your pet, you may decide not to be there. Usually, if you want to be with your pet when it is put to sleep, you will have to make an appointment with the veterinarian in advance.

The veterinarian will ask what you want done with the body. You can choose cremation or burial in a pet cemetery. If you want to bury your pet in the garden, check with the city first to make sure it's legal to do so, and be sure to bury it at least three feet deep.

If you are grieving over the loss of a beloved pet, contact: **California Pet Loss Hotline,** 916-752-4200, weeknights 6:00 PM to 9:30 PM; **Florida Pet Loss Hotline,** 904-392-4700, x4080. Also, you may find local support groups and psychological help by asking your veterinarian or humane society.

7

MONEY MATTERS

Sizing up your finances

Buying/selling/giving

Banking basics

SIZING UP YOUR FINANCES

Your Net Worth

The balance sheet on the following page was designed by the Consumer Credit Education Foundation, an affiliate of the American Financial Services Association in Washington, DC. It is designed to help you calculate your assets (how much you own) and your liabilities (how much you owe). Subtracting your liabilities from your assets allows you to figure your net worth. Taking the time to calculate your net worth several times a year will help you to gauge your financial progress and provides a good first step in assuring your future is financially sound.

Tracking Your Spending

The chart on page 363 will help you track your money—what comes in and what goes out. If you think this spending chart is a budget in disguise, you are absolutely correct. Financial people don't use the word "budget" anymore because we Americans hate the very sound of the word. It suggests that we are living beyond our means and need to restrict our spending habits, that we need to live within the constraints of a budget. While *budget* suggests belt tightening, *spending plan* sounds much more positive and upbeat.

Regardless of which word you prefer, it's not all that painful to take a look at your income balanced against your expenses. It can show you where to cut down in order to save for essentials like a child's college education, your retirement fund, or for something you desperately want like a vacation to Europe. It can also point out why you have no money left over at the end of the month or the end of the year. When plugging numbers into the chart, refer to your checkbook register, your paycheck stubs, bills and receipts you have saved, and any other pertinent records.

There are two options below for tracking your spending. If you choose monthly, be sure to divide once-a-year expenses like insurance premiums by 12 (or by 6, if you pay biannually). If your expenses in various categories fluctuate a lot from month to month, you may prefer to track your expenses by using the annual column. The table can be used for a single person or for a couple. And, pencil in any items that aren't listed below but are relevant to your situation.

Improving Spending Techniques

The following list was prepared by the National Center for Financial Education (NCFE), a consumer-oriented, nonprofit organization. NCFE distributes a number of publications on personal finance issues such as spending, saving, credit and debt, investing, insurance, and financial planning. For further information, write to: **National**

NET WORTH BALANCE SHEET

ASSETS

Assets are physical property (such as your home or car) or intangible rights (such as money someone owes you) that have value. Assets are useful to you because you can either spend them, sell them, or use them as security on a loan.

There are two kinds of assets: current and fixed. Current assets can easily be turned into cash. Fixed assets are more difficult to turn into cash.

CURRENT ASSETS

Cash in hand	$_____
Current checking account balance(s) .	$_____
Current savings account balance(s). ..	$_____
Obligations owed you	$_____
Cash value of insurance policies.	$_____
Short-term investments	$_____
Other current assets	$_____

FIXED ASSETS

Real estate.	$_____
Automobile(s).	$_____
Long-term investments.	$_____
Retirement/profit-sharing plan	$_____
Household goods.	$_____
Other fixed assets	$_____
TOTAL ASSETS.	$_____

LIABILITIES

Liabilities are debts, or amounts of money owed by you to someone else. Expressed conversely, liabilities are the claims of your creditors.

Liabilities are expressed as either short-term or long-term or as secured or unsecured. Short-term liabilities are generally paid off within one year. Long-term liabilities usually take longer to pay off. Secured liabilities, such as mortgages or auto loans, require you to pledge a specific asset to ensure payment of the debt. Unsecured liabilities are based on your personal creditworthiness.

SHORT-TERM LIABILITIES

Unpaid bills	$_____
Outstanding credit card balances	$_____
Unpaid taxes	$_____
Other short-term obligations	$_____

LONG-TERM LIABILITIES

Mortgage loan(s) outstanding	$_____
Automobile loan(s) outstanding.	$_____
Installment loan(s) outstanding.	$_____
Margin due (if any) on stocks.	$_____
Other long-term obligations.	$_____
TOTAL LIABILITIES.	$_____

NET WORTH (Total Assets minus Total Liabilities). . . . . .$_____

SPENDING PLAN WORKSHEET

Items	Monthly	Annual
Money coming in		
Salary from job (gross)		
Self-employment income		
Bonuses and commissions		
Interest and dividends		
Capital gains		
Gifts/inheritances		
Alimony and child support		
Tax refund		
Rental income		
Other		
Total income		
Money going out		
Housing		
Rent or mortgage		
Maintenance/repair		
Condo fees		
Utilities		
Telephone		
Electricity		
Gas		
Water		
Fuel		
Insurance		
Life		
Homeowners		
Auto		
Health		
Disability		
Transportation		
Car maintenance/repair		
Gas/parking		
Public transportation		

SPENDING PLAN WORKSHEET (cont.)

Items	Monthly	Annual
Money going out (cont.)		
Installment debt		
Credit-card payments		
Car loan payments		
Home-equity loan payments		
Other		
Child care		
Babysitters		
Day-care center		
Summer camp		
Other		
Child costs		
Clothing		
School lunch money		
School tuition		
Allowances		
Recreation		
Other		
Taxes		
Federal		
State		
Local		
Social Security		
State disability		
Property		
Food		
Dining in		
Dining out		
Savings/investments		
Retirement plan		
Savings plan		
Other		
Miscellaneous		
Clothing/accessories		
Dry cleaning		
Vacation		

Items	Monthly	Annual
Money going out (cont.)		
Miscellaneous (cont.)		
Entertainment		
Hobbies		
Gifts (personal)		
Charities		
Housecleaning help		
Pet care		
Personal grooming		
Membership fees/dues		
Alimony/child support		
Books/magazines		
Furnishings/appliances		
Alcohol/tobacco		
Unreimbursed medical expenses		
Unreimbursed business expenses		
Total expenses		
Cash flow summary		
Total income		
Total expenses		
Total cash flow (income minus expenses)		

Center for Financial Education, PO Box 34070, San Diego, CA 92163.

1. Write down all of the poor spending practices that are to be changed.

2. Write down how you plan to bring about the changes in each area.

3. Construct a cash-flow sheet showing income and outgo.

4. Set up and implement a spending plan.

5. Discontinue all use of credit cards.

6. Begin collecting and making notes on your cash purchase receipts.

7. Review all insurance coverage for duplication, higher deductibles, etc.

8. Begin saving a dollar-a-day (or dollars) and all pocket change, every day.

9. Look for alternatives and substitutes to spending.

10. Start utilizing cents-off coupons and mail in for rebates.

11. Wait for the sales. Comparison shopping can save more than 50 percent.

12. Take advantage of seconds, rebuilt and used items where practical.

13. Start doing things for yourself that others were paid to do previously.

14. Have weekly meetings on improving spending with other family members.

15. Separate shopping trips (when comparing prices, value, repairability, etc.) from spending trips (when actually making the purchase). Avoid carrying credit cards, much cash, or a checkbook on the shopping trips.

BUYING/SELLING/ GIVING

Auctions

You could get the buy of the century; you may overpay; you could get fleeced. The auction industry is booming and consumers are flocking to auction sites in search of good buys. However, "auction fever" is tempered by auction fraud. Some auction houses misrepresent the quality and value of items; some plant "shills" in the audience to create false competition and boost prices. Even if an auction is totally aboveboard (and many are), novice attendees often end up paying too much for secondhand merchandise.

There are a number of things that you can do to make auction-going fun and profitable and to keep yourself from falling victim to a scam.

♦ Be a spectator before becoming a bidder. Get comfortable with the bidding process and other rules of the game before you dive into competition.

♦ Do your homework. If there is an auction catalog, study it carefully and read all the fine print. Understand all "conditions of sale" including payment procedures, removal of property from the auction site, and other specifics (like "merchandise for export only"). Beware of glowing auction-house descriptions that oftentimes exaggerate the value of merchandise. Also, inspect merchandise before buying. Most auction houses have items on display for at least a few hours, often for as long as a week or two, before the sale. And try to find out what the items you want are really worth—wholesale and retail values. If you are interested in a pricey item, like an antique or a valuable painting, consider hiring an independent expert to value its authenticity and reasonable cost.

♦ Decide on your top bidding price before you go. Write it down and don't go beyond that point. It's easy to get caught up in the spirit of competition and become more concerned with winning as opposed to getting a good deal.

♦ Pay attention to who is bidding. Perhaps one person is always in the thick of things—you keep hearing the same bidder number—but the bidder never seems to buy anything. You may be dealing with a phony bidder and an unscrupulous auction house.

♦ Go early and stay late. While the best merchandise may be sold in the middle of the auction, the best buys are at the start and the finish. At the start, bidders can be somewhat scared or tentative. By the end of the auction, a lot of bidders have gone home.

♦ Remember that most of the time you are buying goods sold "as is."

Pawnshops

Pawnshops seem to be cleaning up their image. The old image wasn't too respectable: sleazy shops with iron-bar-covered windows that attracted deadbeats and drug addicts and acted as fences for hot merchandise. But many shops today are spacious, well-lighted, and located in shopping malls, and they cater to a wide variety of clients. It's estimated that there are more than 10,000 pawnshops in the United States. Some call themselves "loan marts" or "collateral lenders." Also, about one in every 10 Americans every year does business at a pawnshop.

How Pawnshops Work

The proprietor of the pawnshop, the pawnbroker, makes loans on personal property left as collateral against the loan. You, the client, pay interest on the loan, and the interest rate is regulated by the state in which you live. Per month, the interest rate can vary from as little as 2 percent to as much as 24 percent—again, depending on the rate set by your state. You get your property back when your repay the loan plus interest plus any special fees that are charged. The average length of time merchandise remains in a pawnshop is three months. If you can't pay off your loan when it is due, your property becomes the property of the pawnshop. However, you can usually renew the loan provided you pay off the interest charges on the original loan. In some states, if you default on the loan, the broker has to sell the pawned item and give you any money that exceeds the cost of the loan.

Customers like pawnshops because they are an easy source of cash. Also, they are the avenue of last resort for people who need a small amount of cash—say three or four hundred dollars—a loan amount most banks don't want to bother with. If the interest rate charged on the loan is small and the length of the loan is short, most customers figure they got a good deal. However,

the industry is still assaulted by critics who say that while the shops may look prettier, they are still operating as legalized usury. If, for example, you get a 3 percent loan and drag out the loan for 12 months, you end up paying 36 percent interest for the year.

In general, you can pawn just about anything: jewelry, cameras, musical instruments, silverware, TVs, guns, etc. You name it and some pawnshop will probably take it. Most loans are made at about 25 to 35 percent of what the pawned item would sell for; loans for jewelry are somewhat lower. Some upper-crust shops even take cars, boats, and Rolex watches.

If you decide to pawn your personal property, be sure you understand the transaction and your legal obligations. What is the interest rate charged per month? How long is the term of the loan? Is there a grace period (some pawnshops give clients five days before taking over the property)? Will the broker notify you that the loan period is about to expire? Can you extend the loan if necessary and, if so, under what conditions? Also, take your merchandise to several shops to get the best loan. If you have any questions about the reputation of a pawnshop, call your local Better Business Bureau.

For many people, pawnshops are more than just loan-givers. Many have lots of property to sell and people of all income levels are hitting the stores in search of a bargain. Some shops offer limited warranties on specific products; many shops take checks and credit cards. And prices are always negotiable. Just remember that pawnshops still vary greatly in reputation, whether you are shopping for a loan or shopping for merchandise. Be a wise shopper and make informed decisions.

Garage Sales

More than 6 million garage sales take place nationwide every year. They are also called rummage sales, tag sales, and yard sales. The best way to make the most profit is to follow the "4Ps" of garage sales: planning, promotion, presentation, and pricing.

Planning

1. Give yourself three or more weeks to prepare for the big event. Stash all the items in one place if you can, like the basement or attic.

2. You may need a license to have a sale; some towns require them. Check with local officials to determine if you need one.

3. Choose a date or weekend that doesn't conflict with a big community event.

4. Ask a few friends for assistance. You will have trouble handling everything yourself. You need help with watching the money, watching over the goods, and watching that no one wanders into your house.

5. Make a plan for handling the money. Where will you keep the profits—a cash box, a carpenter's apron, or where? How much cash will you need in small bills and coins in order to make change? Garage-sale pros suggest $30–$40 in bills and coins should be enough to get started.

Promotion

1. Run an ad in your local newspaper. Keep it short but include all vital information like your address, times and dates of the sale, mention of any specialty or big-ticket items like bicycles, baby furniture, etc. If your home is difficult to find, give a few simple directions. If you advertise your sale to begin at 10 AM, be ready to go at 9 AM. Some customers, wanting to get the best selection of merchandise, always arrive early.

2. Spend some time making up professional-looking signs (block letters, clearly readable, fairly large) which can be tacked up at grocery stores, bus stops, local libraries, community centers. Put them on trees and poles on all major streets in your area if local laws permit such signage.

3. Prepare a flyer that you can hand out to neighbors, friends, and business associates. Include a list of items that you think are likely to draw interest.

Presentation

1. Make your sale items look their very best. Wash glasses and dishes till they shine. Repair and clean clothing, table linens, bedding. Dust off all books and use some steel wool on your tools.

2. Organize your merchandise by category. Clothing in one area, preferably hung on a clothesline or coat rack. Put print materials like old books and magazines on a separate table. Breakable items like glassware and dishes should be together and in a safe spot to prevent breakage. Small, miscellaneous, cheap items can be put in a box or basket, maybe with a $1 sign.

3. Carefully consider where you place small, valuable items like jewelry. Keep such items in a secure area where you can keep your eye on them.

4. Extra touches go a long way. If you have a lot of clothing to sell, you might want to have a full-length mirror on hand. Also, set up an electrical outlet (and have batteries on hand) for items that need testing.

5. Some people like to create a comfortable, friendly buying atmosphere. Toward that end, some sellers set up a refreshment area and charge for beverages and simple snacks. Some put out lawn chairs for customers to relax; some even have low-volume music playing in the background.

Pricing

1. The general rule of thumb is to price an item at 20 percent of retail value if the item is in good condition. The trick is not to price too high—buyers may just walk away. But you also don't want to price too low since buyers notoriously expect to haggle down the price.

2. If you are a real novice at garage sales, visit a few in your area to get a better idea of what various things sell for.

3. Peel-off pricing labels work well for most

items. For clothing you can make small paper labels and use straight pins to attach them.

4. Be prepared to slash your prices on the final day or in the final hours of your sale. When the sale is over, pack up the leftover merchandise and make a donation to a local charity like Goodwill or the Salvation Army. Or, save the remainders for your next sale.

Phone and Mail Scams

Consumers lose an estimated $40 billion a year to con artists using sophisticated sales techniques. The scams use a number of communications methods—cold calls, direct mail notices, broadcast and print advertisements. However, the telephone always plays a vital role, for no matter how initial contact is made, the sale is made over the phone. A recent national poll by Louis Harris and Associates showed that 92 percent of all Americans have received a letter or postcard that stated the recipient had won a "guaranteed" prize of some sort. And the survey stated that more than 53 million Americans responded to the notices.

The list of scams is as long as it is wide and new ones spring up every day to meet consumer needs. For example, when the job market is bad, there is an increase in phony employment services. Other popular scams include:

♦ **Guaranteed prizes.** You have won a prize but when you call to collect, you are informed that you must first buy something—like vitamins, jewelry, a water filter, skin-care products, or any number of items that turn out to be expensive purchases.

♦ **Quick loans.** You are guaranteed a loan regardless of your credit history, but you need to pay a fee in order to qualify.

♦ **Credit cards.** Like the loans mentioned above, you are guaranteed a card but must pay an initiation fee to get it. The cards, of course, have super-low interest rates and are usually "gold" or "platinum" cards.

♦ **Investment cons.** The sales person will offer any number of investment vehicles usually touted as highly profitable and low risk.

♦ **Phony charities.** The names sound very similar to those of legitimate charities, but the only place your money is going is in the con artist's pocket.

♦ **Mortgage payments.** The fraud artist claims to be working with your current mortgage holder in order to work out a new payment schedule (usually a better one than you have) and asks you to start sending your payments to a new address.

♦ **Dirt-cheap products.** They are usually brand-name products at unbelievable prices.

Legally speaking, not all con artists are criminals. If you pay money for something you never receive and the phoney company skips town, that's a pretty clear-cut case of fraud. But many scams operate within one inch of the law. For instance, you do get $1000 worth of travel coupons (after buying $400 worth of vitamins) for hotel accommodations, but you would have to spend thousands more on airfare and "other expenses" in order to use the hotel vouchers. Or, perhaps you bought a $300 camera which you later find out sells elsewhere for $200, or perhaps the camera was just a piece of junk. You figure you are safe because of the guaranteed refund. However, the fine print in the refund clause contains so many stipulations that the camera is virtually impossible to return. Fake charities usually do apply to the government for official charity status but give a mere pittance to those they are supposed to help and keep the lion's share of the money for "other purposes."

How do scam artists find you? It's easy. They buy mailing lists from the same companies that sell lists to legitimate telemarketers. Depending on the list, the swindlers may have a lot of information about you—your age and income, health and hobbies, occupation, education, marital status. Even if the swindler gets your name from a telephone book and makes a cold call, he or she has a good ear for recognizing clients who are receptive to sales pitches.

How Con Artists Work

It doesn't cost much to set up a "boiler room" operation. All you need is a bare-bones room with lots of telephones and salespeople. With the help of computers, mailing lists, and automatic dial phones, a salesperson can talk to dozens of people a day.

According to the Alliance Against Fraud in Telemarketing: "Fraudulent sales callers have one thing in common. They are skilled liars and experts at verbal camouflage." They work from a prepared script and sound believable and understanding. And they are experts at delicately walking around any tough questions or reservations you may have. For instance, you tell the con artist that you want printed information on the company or the product it is offering. The con artist tells you that the company doesn't print brochures anymore because printing costs are high and would add to the cost of the product you are buying. Or, you tell the caller that you want to think about the offer and will call back once you have made a decision. The telemarketer comes back with, "This is a very limited offer that only runs today and we can only accommodate customers on a first-come, first-served basis."

Nine Signs of a Swindle

The following tips are courtesy of the National Futures Association. They were prepared in conjunction with the Alliance Against Fraud in Telemarketing, the Commodity Futures Trading Commission, and the Federal Trade Commission.

1. High-pressure sales tactics. The call may not begin that way, but if the swindler senses you're not going to be an easy sale, he or she may shift to a hard sell. This is in contrast to legitimate businesses, most of which respect an individual's right to be "not interested." High-pressure sales tactics take a variety of forms but the common denominator is usually a stubborn reluctance to accept "no" as an answer.

2. Insistence on an immediate decision. If it's an investment, the caller may say something like, "the market is starting to move even as we talk."

For a product or service, the urgency pitch may be that "there are only a few left" or "the offer is about to expire." The bottom line is that swindlers often insist that you should (or must) make your decision right now. And they always give a reason.

3. The offer sounds too good to be true. The oldest advice around is still the best: "An offer that sounds too good to be true probably is."

4. A request for your credit card number for any purpose other than to make a purchase. A swindler may ask you for your credit card number—or, in the most brash cases, several credit card numbers—for "identification," or "verification" that you have won something, or merely as an "expression of good faith" on your part. Whatever the ploy, once a swindler has your card number it is likely that unauthorized charges will appear on your account.

5. An offer to send someone to your home or office to pick up the money, or some other method such as overnight mail to get your funds more quickly. This is likely to be part of their "urgency" pitch. It could be an effort to avoid mail fraud charges by bypassing postal authorities or simply a way of getting your money before you change your mind.

6. A statement that something is "free," followed by a requirement that you pay for something. While honest firms may promote free phone offers to attract customers, the difference with swindlers is that you generally have to pay in some way to get whatever it is that's "free." The cost may be labeled as a handling or shipping charge, or as payment for an item in addition to the "prize." Whatever you receive for "free"—if anything—most likely will be worth much less than what you've paid.

7. An investment that's "without risk." Except for obligations of the U.S. Government, all investments have some degree of risk.

8. Unwillingness to provide written information or references (such as a bank or names of satisfied customers in your area) that you can contact. Swindlers generally have a long list of reasons: "There isn't time for that," or "It's a brand new offer and printed material isn't avail-

able yet," or "Customer references would violate someone's privacy." Even with references, be cautious, for some swindlers pay off a few customers to serve as references.

9. A suggestion that you should make a purchase or investment on the basis of "trust." Trust is a laudable trait, but it shouldn't be dispensed indiscriminately—certainly not to unknown persons calling on the phone and asking that you send them money. Even so, "trust me" is a pitch that swindlers sometimes employ when all else fails.

What to Do if You Are Defrauded

1. If you paid by credit card, you may have recourse to recoup your loss if you act swiftly. The Fair Credit Billing Act allows you 60 days to contest the billing. In many instances, the credit card company will absorb the loss.

2. The National Consumers League has set up a toll-free hotline for people who think they have been scammed or are afraid of being scammed. The service is called the **National Fraud Information Center** and the number is 800-876-7060. Operators will take down the details of your case, give advice on how to get your money back, and tell you about the newest scams taking place.

3. Call or write your state attorney general and register a complaint. You might also contact your regional office of the Federal Trade Commission. Surprisingly, most victims of scams don't report the incident, either because they are embarrassed that they were scammed or they don't know where to complain. Adding your complaint to the complaints of others who have been conned by the same scam can help to apprehend the crooks.

Using 900 Phone Numbers

While dialing an 800 area code number is free, dialing a 900 area code number costs money—and could cost quite a lot of money. Consumers use 900 numbers to get information in a variety of areas including legal advice, medical advice, personal horoscopes, financial data, sports results, crossword puzzle answers. Some numbers are purely entertainment like dial-a-joke lines or movie review lines; some are used to sell products like books and magazines. Many 900 services are legitimate businesses that provide useful information at reasonable fees. Others are misleading, even fraudulent, and can produce eye-popping numbers on your phone bill.

There are two ways you can be charged for calling a 900 number—by the minute or a flat fee. The cost of the call is determined by the service provider, not by the telephone company. When you are charged by the minute, each minute can cost the same amount or the first minute costs more that any additional minutes. A call based on a flat-fee rate costs the same whether you are on the line for a few minutes or a few seconds.

There are several ploys dishonest services use to keep you on the line. Consumer Action, a nonprofit consumer agency based in San Francisco, states that some 900 services:

♦ Repeat information over and over, or fill time with unnecessary talk.

♦ Put callers on hold, while charging them for every minute.

♦ Hang up in the middle of a program, forcing the caller to call back, paying the higher first-minute fee again. Some 900 services charge first-minute fees of $5 or more.

♦ Refer callers to another 900 number to get the promised information, so that the caller ends up paying for two calls.

Unexpected, large charges on phone bills have caused thousands of complaints to the Federal Trade Commission (FTC) and the Federal Communications Commission (FCC), the two government groups responsible for regulating 900 numbers. Thus, legislation has been passed to protect consumers. What you should be aware of:

♦ Services that charge more than $2 must begin with a statement that reveals the cost of the call, the name of the information provider, and a description of the service offered. A tone is sounded after the disclosure message and you have three seconds to hang up and not be charged for the call.

♦ Print and broadcast advertisements for 900 numbers must display rate charges if the call costs at least $2.

♦ The rules prohibit advertising of 900 services aimed at children under 12 unless the service is educational. The rules are intended to stop children from making expensive holiday calls to Santa Claus and the Easter Bunny.

♦ Local telephone companies must block access to 900 numbers from individual phones, at no charge to customers, if customers request the 900 block.

CHOOSING A LONG-DISTANCE COMPANY

Confused about which long-distance company is right for you? Actually, you should be more concerned with a particular plan as opposed to a particular long-distance carrier. Since the breakup of Ma Bell in the 1980s, the competition for your long-distance business has been fierce. While the average cost of long-distance phone bills has dropped about 40 percent, the dizzying array of plans to choose from is confusing, and always changing. However, a consumer watchdog group, **Telecommunications Research and Action Center** (TRAC), regularly monitors and compares plans for the five biggest long-distance companies. For a copy of TRAC's most recent "Tele-Tips Residential Long-Distance Comparison Chart," send $2 and a self-addressed stamped envelope to: TRAC, PO Box 12038, Washington, DC 20005.

Tip: In general, long-distance charges are the lowest on Sundays through Fridays from 11 PM to 8 AM, all day Saturdays, and Sundays until 5 PM. The most expensive time to make a call is from 8 AM to 5 PM on weekdays.

STOP THE CATALOGS/STOP THE SALES CALLS

Getting too much unsolicited mail or too many telemarketing calls? You need to get your name off of mailing lists and telemarketing lists that are sold to companies that ultimately contact you. The group that can help is the **Direct Marketing Association** (DMA), which distributes such lists to companies that subscribe to its services. To remove your name from national mailing lists, write to: Direct Marketing Association Mail Preference Service, PO Box 9008, Farmingdale, NY 11735. To remove your name from telemarketing lists, write to: Direct Marketing Association Telephone Preference Service, PO Box 9014, Farmingdale, NY 11735. Simply ask that your name be removed from one or both lists. This should cut down on the number of mailings and calls from legitimate companies and telemarketers. It may not, however, affect the mail and telephone solicitations made by con artists and fraudulent companies.

There's another measure you can take to cut down on telephone solicitations. The next time a telemarketer calls, say, "Please put me on your no-call list." According to a recent mandate by the Federal Communications Commission, if you ask to be put on a no-call list, a telemarketer must not call you for five years. The rule, however, does not apply to political groups or nonprofit organizations.

Loans That Turn into Gifts

Loans that go unpaid have been the downfall of many relationships. They start out as a simple transaction—someone who needs money seeks financial assistance from a sympathetic family member or friend. The sum may be small, money needed to pay off a pressing debt, money needed to buy Christmas presents, or any number of immediate money needs. Or, they can involve large sums, like money needed for college tuition or a down payment on a car or home. Whatever the situation or the loan amount, there is usually an implied trust to repay the loan and oftentimes an absence of any written agreement.

In essence, money is just a medium of exchange, but there are countless psychological surveys that show it to be an emotional currency that symbolizes a host of other things like love, security, respect, power, and control. Parents who lend money to a child may consciously, or unconsciously, expect that child to be more attentive or more likely to cater to any special needs and desires of the parents. A friend who lends money to a friend may expect more loyalty or more overt signs that their friendship is special. A loan between those involved in a romantic relationship can set off all kinds of expectations and commitments.

Aside from the emotional side effects that a loan might cause, there is the basic issue of getting the money repaid. You're likely to be pretty unhappy if someone you lent money to goes on an expensive vacation in lieu of repaying the debt. Or what about the friend who keeps promising repayment "as soon as I can scrape it together," but somehow manages to buy new clothes and dine out at expensive restaurants?

Before making a loan:

♦ Consider whom you are lending money to. Is the person reliable or are you dealing with someone who is always in a financial jam?

♦ Consider how you may react if the loan is never repaid. Money can severely alter the dynamics of any relationship. If you think the loan is a bad risk and might cost you a friendship, you can always say no. On the other hand, if you truly want to help out and recognize that the loan may ultimately become a gift, then you are making a deal with yourself that you can live with. Some financial experts go so far as to tell clients that they should not make a loan to family members unless they can afford to consider it a gift.

♦ Think of the loan as a professional business agreement. Communicate clearly with the borrower as to how the money is to be repaid. If the amount of the loan is fairly substantial and can't be paid back in a short period of time, you need to come up with a structured repayment schedule. It's perfectly acceptable to have a written agreement. You can write your own or get a formal promissory note from a stationery store. Whether or not you want to charge interest depends on your needs and desires.

♦ If your loan arrangement starts to go awry, get it back on course before it festers into an ugly confrontation. Give the loan recipient the benefit of the doubt, since unforeseeable circumstances can wreck the best of intentions. However, be clear and direct about your expectations.

The subject of lending has produced some wonderful advice from sages of the past. William Shakespeare said: "Neither a borrower nor a lender be, for loan oft loses both itself and friend." According to Voltaire, "If you lend money, you make a secret enemy; if you refuse, an open one." And British author Sir Philip Gibbs retorts, "It's better to give than to lend, and it costs about the same."

Ten Thoughts on Gift Giving

1. Consider the gift-getter. What kinds of interests and hobbies does the person have? Does he or she have an upcoming important event like taking a trip or changing jobs—something that may suggest an appropriate gift? Is the person likely to appreciate gifts like flowers or dinner at a fancy restaurant, or are you dealing with someone whose great desire is a toolbox, an electric toothbrush, or a flannel nightgown?

2. Be alert for gift hints. People give them all the time whether they are admiring something in a store window, pointing something out in a catalog, mentioning an item that was lost, stolen, or broken. The trick is to write down the brainstorm when it hits you.

3. Don't overspend. This generally happens when you don't know what to buy and you are shopping at the last minute. A little planning can save money. In addition, if you want to—or feel compelled to—buy an expensive gift, the extra

time will allow you to shop the sales and to compare prices.

4. Creativity can save money and endear you to the gift-getter. If you are artistic, make something special. If you are not artistic and you are broke, give a coupon book for a specified number of housecleanings, lawn mowings, baby-sitting services—whatever service you are willing to provide.

5. Forget self-improvement gifts. Much as you want your friend or relative to lose weight, a new diet book is not an appropriate present. Gifts and reminders of shortcomings do not go hand in hand.

6. Don't give a gift that's really meant for you. For example, your husband might salivate over two tickets to a pro football game but not over tickets to the opera. Conversely, your wife might love a new jogging outfit but not a state-of-the-art camping stove.

7. Avoid repeat gifts. Did your father really love the ties you gave him for the last six Christmases? Force yourself to be a bit more original.

GIVING "THE TWELVE DAYS OF CHRISTMAS"

On the first day of Christmas, my true love gave to me. . . . If you used the song, "The Twelve Days of Christmas" as a gift-giving guide during the holidays, you would end up with a hefty bill—$24,728.69 to be exact. Every year a San Francisco investment advisory firm, Hugh Gee & Co., compiles a Christmas index of the various items listed in the song and publishes the prices in its investment newsletter. The annual Christmas-index article describes in humorous detail how the firm arrived at its prices. For example, when the firm called domestic employment companies and asked what the fee would be for "eight maids-a-milking," some of the companies hung up. So the firm had to settle for a cost for eight regular maids and then added to that the cost of the cows. If you want to buy all of the items in the song, get out your gold card.

8. Don't get put off by people who are impossible to please. Do the best you can and hope you get lucky. If buying a gift for a hard-to-please person weighs on your mind, you might ask the person what he or she would like. As a last resort, you can always give a gift certificate to one of the person's favorite stores.

9. Keep all sales receipts. There's no crime in making a wrong choice. Some gift-getters will express delight at your gift even if they dislike it. Others may like the gift but need a different size (if clothing) or prefer a different style or color. Whether the gift-getter asks if the gift can be

CHRISTMAS INDEX

Item	Price (in dollars and cents)
1 partridge	15.00
1 pear tree	39.75
2 turtledoves ($60 a pair)	60.00
3 French hens ($2.98 each)	8.94
4 calling birds ($350 each)	1,400.00
5 gold rings ($375 each)	1,875.00
6 Canada geese ($125 each)	750.00
7 swans ($350 each)	2,450.00
1 portable pool	1,200.00
8 maids (minimum 4 hours: $60 each)	480.00
8 cows ($1,125 each)	9,000.00
9 dancers ($150 each)	1,350.00
10 lords ($150 each)	1,500.00
11 pipers ($200 each)	2,200.00
12 drummers ($200 each)	2,400.00
TOTAL	**$24,728.69**

exchanged or you bring up the possibility of exchange, you will need those receipts.

10. Give gifts on nongift occasions. Sometimes gifts are most appreciated when they are unexpected. For someone you know who has a reason to celebrate or needs cheering up, a small gift signals caring, sharing, and thoughtfulness.

Charitable Contributions

If you are like most people, charitable appeals jam your mailbox, salespeople show up on your doorstep, and voices solicit you over the telephone asking for money for innumerable worthy causes. Therefore, you won't be surprised to learn that in 1992 more than 546,000 U.S. charities were eligible to receive tax-deductible donations. And Americans gave—in 1993, nearly $68 billion in donations, excluding those to religious groups.

How do you sort charities out? How do you know which charities spend too much on fundraising or have bloated administrative staffs? How can you tell if the money you give will be spent on a big salary for an executive or on still more solicitations that end up in your mailbox instead of on the purpose of the charity—to save the starving, clean up the oceans, fund medical research?

Which organizations are unethical? When a child shows up selling candy or trash bags for exorbitant prices, saying that the profits will go to the poor or send the child to summer camp, how do you know whether or not that child is being exploited by a scam organization? What do you do about the charity that sends you unsolicited merchandise (greeting cards or address labels) along with an appeal? How do you resist pressure from a professional fund raiser who catches you at a weak moment?

Watchdogs

Many states require that charities file financial information with a state official. The information is specific—what percent of donations go to ad-

ministration and fund-raising costs as opposed to the charitable program the group was established for? Some states require that charities give such information to prospective donors whether they ask for it or not. (This regulation, however, is being undercut by free-speech considerations.) Cities and counties also have ordinances to protect donors. Again, none of this is foolproof. Often, religious groups, hospitals, and other organizations are exempt. If a door-to-door solicitor does not have a city-supplied card specifying that the charity has met city regulations, the solicitor may still be legitimate. Some businesses, like those employing the handicapped, are not required to have such cards.

The two main consumer groups that provide information about charities are:

National Charities Information Bureau, 19 Union Square West, New York, NY 10003-3395 (212-929-6300).

Philanthropic Advisory Service, Council of Better Business Bureaus, 4200 Wilson Blvd., Arlington, VA 22203-1804 (703-276-0100).

If you want more information about a national charity, contact one, or both, of the above watchdog agencies. Both provide lists and evaluations of numerous national charities (some print materials are free; others are available at a nominal cost).

When evaluating a charity, watchdog agencies consider a number of factors, including:

Public accountability: (1) Soliciting organizations, if asked, should provide annual financial statements that provide information on sources and uses of funds. (2) When an outside fundraising group is used, the terms of the compensation agreement should be disclosed.

Use of funds: At least 60 percent of funds received should be used on programs and activities directly related to the purpose of the charity.

Solicitation material: (1) Solicitations must be accurate and truthful. (2) They must also include a clear description of how the funds will be spent. (3) Solicitors must identify their relationship to the charity, provide another source from which written information is available, and not apply unwarranted pressure.

Governance: (1) The board of the charity should have an independent membership and voting members should have no conflicts of interest. (2) Boards should meet a specific number of times a year, with no fees paid to members for attendance.

Note: **InterAction** (1717 Massachusetts Avenue NW, Suite 801, Washington, DC 20036), an umbrella organization for international relief groups, will send you a list of its member charities, which must also meet rigorous standards.

How to Give Intelligently

1. If you are against door-to-door solicitation, put a "No solicitors" sign on your door.

2. Don't open the door to strangers ostensibly soliciting for charities. Ask who they are first, then keep your door chained until you see a proper ID and have called the charity to verify the ID.

3. Find out the exact name of the charity. Bogus charities often adopt names close to those of legitimate ones. To further check legitimacy, ask for the group's address and phone number and the name of the president.

4. What is the position of the solicitor? Is he or she a volunteer, an employee, or a third-party fund raiser? If an employee, how is he or she paid? Tiers of fund-raising apparatus usually mean less money goes to the charitable purpose of the organization. Some professional fund raisers keep a huge percentage of the money they raise.

5. Ask if the charity is registered with the state. If it is a religious group, ask if it has received the seal of the Evangelical Council for Financial Accountability (PO Box 17456, Washington, DC 20041; 800-323-9473). The ECFA offers a free list of its members, along with financial information.

6. Request financial information about the charity—an annual report or Form 990. The IRS requires charities that accept tax-deductible donations to submit an annual Form 990 on their finances and how money is allocated. (Churches and other religious organizations, which get half

of American charitable contributions, do not have to file IRS returns.) How much goes to administration, how much to fund raising, how much to the philanthropic mission the charity espouses? The charity should spend no more than 30 percent of donations on fund raising and at least 60 percent of donations on programs. Read the fine print. Be suspicious of money spent on education. Some groups put information about a topic like drug abuse in the same envelope as a solicitation so that they can write off the cost of mailing to education rather than to fund raising.

7. Don't give money or checks to solicitors and don't let them force you into a pledge or into giving your credit card number over the phone. Instead, ask for literature and an address. Refuse to let a telephone solicitor send someone over to your home to pick up a check. Mail a check, if (after thoughtful consideration) you decide you want to give.

8. Don't allow intimidation or guilt to rule your decision on whether or not to give. And don't give to an organization you've never heard of.

Other Tips

1. A donation to a tax-exempt group is not necessarily tax-deductible for you. Ask if the group is designated a 501(c)(3) organization by the IRS. If so, your contribution is tax deductible.

2. Be aware that many door-to-door solicitations using young people are under investigation by the Federal Trade Commission for deceptive recruitment practices. Some groups violate child labor laws to operate candy-selling scams in which children are taught to lie. For instance, the children say that they are raising money for inner-city kids when they are not. Such companies may offer students a cut of the money they raise.

3. If you buy something—candy, tickets, magazines—from a charity, you can deduct as a charitable contribution only the part of the contribution that is above fair market value. That is, if you pay $5 for a box of candy worth $2, you can deduct only $3 as a charitable contribution.

4. Be suspicious of a group that presents a

great deal of information concerning a problem but very little concerning what the group is doing about it.

5. All sweepstakes conducted through the mail must be accompanied by a declaration that you need donate nothing in order to win.

6. Be wary of charities that disguise appeals as bills or invoices and do not include a "noticeable disclaimer" that it is an appeal and that you are not obligated to pay.

7. If a charity sends you unordered merchandise, you neither have to pay for nor return the items.

Tipping

How much to tip is a personal decision—there are no rules, only guidelines. If service is good, you'll want to leave a fair tip; if service is exceptionally good, you may want to tip more than the guideline amounts. Below is a list of service providers you are most likely to encounter. People like a headwaiter at a restaurant or a concierge at a hotel are not included; they are tipped only when special services are rendered. Also excluded are cruise ship personnel; normally a cruise line will provide you with a written set of guidelines before you leave the boat. We have, however, included a short list of those people who provide services all year round and are usually tipped once a year, at Christmas.

Christmas Tipping: A gift at Christmas is a nice way to thank the people who provide service to you all year round. The most commonly thought of are: cleaning person/nanny (one week's pay); newspaper delivery ($5–$10); trash collector ($5); mail carrier ($5–$25; even though federal law says no tips are allowed, most people ignore it).

TIPPING CHART

Location	Person	Amount
Restaurant	waiter or waitress	15% of pretax bill
	wine steward	10-15% of wine check
	bartender	10-15% of bar bill
	coat checker	50 cents per coat
	rest room attendant	50 cents
	car park attendant	50 cents-$1
Hotel	bellhop	50 cents-$1 per bag
	chambermaid	$1 per day
	room service waiter	15% of pretax bill
	doorman (to get taxi)	50 cents-$1
Hair salon/ barbershop	hair stylist (cut, color, perm)	10-15% of bill
	manicurist	15% of bill
	shampooer	$1-$2
	pedicurist	15% of bill
Others	taxi cab driver	10-15% of fare
	skycap (airport)	$1 per bag
	shoe shiner at stand	50 cents
	porter (train station)	$1 per bag
	delivery person (take-out food)	$1

BANKING BASICS

Choosing a Bank

When selecting a bank, watch out for:

Customer service. Are there express lanes for rush-hour traffic? Are bank officers usually available to handle questions? Can you make deposits and withdrawals during, and after, operating hours through the use of automatic teller machines (ATMs)? Can you conduct banking by phone, and if so, is the service solely for getting account balances or can you conduct transactions? Does the bank have branches near your home and workplace?

Fees. Banks are making handsome profits on the service fees for your accounts. Ask a bank for a full list of fees that may be levied including those for: maintaining the account, processing checks, using ATMs, bouncing checks, conducting transactions by phone, getting copies of canceled checks, getting cashier's checks or certified checks or money orders, using overdraft protection, and stopping payment on a check. A 1993 federal law, the Truth in Savings Act, requires banks to disclose most, but not all, costs when you open an account. Service fees have risen dramatically over the last few years, and customers are complaining in record numbers. Not only are consumers outraged by steep increases in fees they consider legitimate (bouncing a check can cost as much as $30; a money wire transfer

can cost up to $40), but they are particularly irked by a host of truly offensive bank charges. These offensive charges can include: charging you for depositing another person's bad check; billing customers for a book of deposit slips; imposing fees when you ask for your account balance or most recent transactions; charging you for *not* using some services like an ATM card; making you pay to convert rolls of coins into paper currency.

Freebies. This does not mean a free toaster awarded for opening an account. It means free traveler's checks, free safe deposit boxes, free checks, and other customer perks. However, don't become so enamored of the freebies that you overlook the big factors like what the bank pays on an interest-bearing account.

Types of services. While all banks make loans and handle checking and savings accounts, some provide additional services like selling mutual funds and other investments. Also, some banks provide a single monthly statement that lists balances and transactions for all accounts, including IRAs and CDs.

Safety. Be sure that your deposits are insured by the federal government; look for a Federal Deposit Insurance Corporation (FDIC) logo posted inside a bank. If you are concerned about the financial health of your bank, you can check on its safety by contacting a private rating company. Two companies that provide rating reports: **Veribanc,** PO Box 461, Wakefield, MA 01880 (800-442-2657); **Bauer Financial Reports,** PO Box Drawer 145510, Coral Gables, FL 33114-5510 (800-388-6686). Both companies charge $10 for the first report and less for additional reports.

You don't have to do your banking with a bank. When considering where to stash your cash or where to get a loan, check out savings-and-loan associations and credit unions. Both are competitive alternatives to banks. Credit unions in particular are generally thought to be the best givers of old-fashioned customer service. Also, credit unions are traditionally associated with low-interest loans for consumer purchases like automobiles. To find out if there is a credit union near you that you might be eligible to join, contact: **Credit Union National Association,** Box 431, Madison, WI 53701 (800-358-5710).

Choosing a Checking Account

Some banks offer as many as nine different versions of a checking account. While this array of choices is confusing, there are still only two basic types of checking accounts, non-interest-bearing accounts and interest-bearing accounts. Before choosing an account that's best for you, you need to understand your present banking pattern. To do that, take a look at your last three or four banking statements and analyze the following: number of checks written; number of ATM transactions; monthly checking fees (if any); your average, and lowest, daily balances.

If your checking account hits rock bottom every month, meaning your daily average balance is low, you'll probably opt for an non-interest-bearing account. Even then, what you pay in fees is determined by the minimum balance kept in the account. If no attention is paid to the minimum balance, you'll pay a monthly maintenance fee (from $5–$10) plus a charge for each check written. If you keep a minimum balance (depending on the bank, the minimum can be between $500

and $1000), the fees will be waived. Fall below the minimum balance, however, and fees will be assessed. In addition, many banks offer a "no-frills" checking account for people who write a small number of checks a month; the monthly fee is low and you can write up to 10 checks a month at no extra charge.

Interest-bearing accounts require you to keep a minimum balance—on average between $1000 and $2500—in order to earn interest. As long as you keep enough money in the account to meet the minimum balance, you won't pay a monthly maintenance fee or charges for writing checks. Fall below the balance and some, or all, of the fees will be back in effect. Your bank may have a range of interest-bearing accounts—NOW account, super NOW account, tiered account, etc. Be sure you understand the differences between the accounts offered to you. Also, when figuring your minimum balance, some banks will include the money in other accounts that you hold with the same bank—like savings accounts, CDs, and money-market accounts.

A federal law, the Truth in Savings Act of 1993, included new restrictions on how banks pay interest on interest-bearing accounts. What the law clarifies:

♦ Some banks paid interest only on money above the minimum balance. That's no longer allowed.

♦ Some banks paid no interest at all if an account went below the minimum balance for just one day. That's no longer allowed.

♦ Some banks calculated interest based on a customer's lowest daily balance. That's no longer allowed.

♦ Banks often advertised accounts as "free" even though fees could be assessed for falling below a minimum balance or for things like using ATM machines. Now, an advertised "free" account must really be free. Banks can, however, still charge for certain transactions like bouncing a check or stopping payment on a check.

When choosing an account and a bank, you will, of course, look at interest rates offered and minimum balances required. However, don't forget to ask about all the various fees that might

THREE EASY STEPS TO BALANCE YOUR CHECKBOOK

1. Update your check register.
   ☐ Add any interest. Subtract any service charges.
   ☐ Compare and check off each transaction shown in your check register with those listed on the statement.
2. Determine outstanding items.
   ☐ List below any items shown in your check register but not checked off.

Check No.	Amount		Check No.	Amount			Date	Amount	
	$			$				$	
			TOTAL	$			TOTAL	$	

(Header: Outstanding Checks or Other Withdrawals | Deposits Not Credited)

3. Balance your account.

   ☐ Enter ending balance (from statement front): $_____

   ☐ Add deposits not credited: + _____

   ☐ Subtract outstanding checks/withdrawals: - _____

   ☐ Total (should agree with checkbook balance): $_____

If the balances are different:
   Check the addition and subtraction.
   Make sure all outstanding items have been listed in the appropriate box.
   Compare the amount of each withdrawal and deposit in your checkbook with the amount on this statement.
   Review the figures on last month's statement.

affect your account. For instance, if you are a frequent ATM user, what is the charge for using the bank's machine and what is the charge for getting cash from another bank's automated teller? Some larger banks charge as much as $2 per visit to an ATM that is not their own.

A final word on cutting costs: you don't have to buy your checks from the bank. The average charge is $15 for 200 checks. You can save approximately 50 percent by ordering checks through discounters like **Current Checks** (800-533-3973), **Checks in the Mail** (800-733-4443), or **Custom Direct Check Printers** (800-272-5432). If you choose to go this route, start with a minimal order until you are certain that there will be no problems with the checks. While it's perfectly legal to order checks from a discounter, some banks, disturbed over losing bucks on check orders, seem to find "technical difficulties" when processing the checks.

Balancing a Checkbook

Checking account statements always have instructions printed on the back to help you reconcile your check register with the financial institution's statement. Many customers ignore doing any math and just accept the numbers on the statement—in actuality, the statements are usually correct. Nonetheless, errors are made and balancing a checkbook is easy and painless, especially if you do it every month.

Safe Deposit Boxes

The contents of a safe deposit box are not automatically insured by the bank against theft, fire, or flood. Some banks offer insurance but the coverage is usually low and many items, like cash, are not insurable. In most cases of loss you would need to sue the bank and prove negligence in order to collect; your chances of winning are very slim. However, many homeowner's insurance policies, or tenant's policies, do cover the contents of the box, but the payoff depends on the limits of your policy.

Most people who have safe deposit boxes have them at a bank. Charges for a small box usually carry an annual fee of anywhere from $10 to $60 a year; larger boxes cost more. You get two duplicate keys to your box; it takes your key and the bank's key to open the box. If you lose a key, it can be replaced for a small fee. If you lose both keys, the bank has to drill the box open (it doesn't keep a duplicate of your keys) and the cost can be as high as $100 or more.

What to keep in a safe deposit box is as important as having one. Many of us stuff all kinds of things into a box—valuable jewelry, old love letters, cash, important legal documents. However, aside from the insurability issue, there are other vital matters to consider when deciding what should be kept, and what should not be kept, in a safe deposit box. Foremost is the issue of what happens to the box when you die. Some states "seal" a box when the renter dies. This means that no one can take anything out until the proper legal authorities get in and inventory the contents. After all, you might be hiding some very valuable stuff that will be subject to death taxes. However, in many states a spouse is allowed access to the box if the box was jointly owned. In some states the executor of your will is allowed access.

Ask your bank what happens to your box in the event that you die. Who has legal access? If it's likely that the box will be sealed, you wouldn't want your will, your life insurance policies, your cemetery plot deed—whatever items your heirs need immediately—to be inside. Other legal documents to think about, if you have them, are power-of-attorney papers and a living will (to keep you off of life-support systems).

Below is a list of items that most experts agree are perfectly fine to put into a safe deposit box:
♦ Birth, marriage, adoption, and death certificates
♦ Citizenship papers

♦ Military service records

♦ Divorce and separation agreements

♦ Real-estate deeds and mortgage papers

♦ Car titles

♦ A *copy* of your will

♦ Insurance policies (with the possible exception of life insurance)

♦ Contracts and legal agreements

♦ Social Security cards

♦ Professional licenses and school diplomas

♦ A household inventory (for insurance purposes)

♦ Stock, bond, or savings certificates.

So what do you do with the items you don't want to keep in a bank safe deposit box? You could purchase a fireproof home safe or investigate getting a safe deposit box with a private vault company (rules are a bit different at private vault companies; some people advocate them, but others don't). Also, certain documents can be given to others for safekeeping. Perhaps you want your will in a family member's safe deposit box or home safe; maybe you want your lawyer to keep it for you. Your living will or power of attorney may go to the people who may ultimately be the decision-makers on those matters.

Making a list of all valuable or hard-to-replace items will help you to decide where to keep the various things. As you look at each item, ask yourself who you want to have access to each, while you are alive and in the event you die. And, in the event of death, is the item in a safe, accessible place?

Federal Deposit Insurance Corporation (FDIC)

Your bank, savings-and-loan association, or credit union displays a sign that says that every depositor is federally insured up to $100,000. Thus, if your financial institution goes under, you are protected and will get all of your money back. Well, it's a bit more complex since the whole issue is dependent upon whose name(s) the

money is in, how much money there is, and how many and what kind of accounts you have.

The rules concerning federal insurance come from the Federal Deposit Insurance Corporation (FDIC), which was established in 1933 to insure bank depositors. Some basic guidelines for FDIC coverage:

1. Federal deposit insurance protects $100,000 *per individual, per bank*. All of your accounts—savings, checking, certificates of deposit—need to be added together. For example, suppose you have $50,000 in a savings account and $100,00 worth of CDs in one bank, giving you a total of $150,000; $50,000 of that total is *not* insured. Don't think you are skirting the system if your accounts are in more than one branch of the same bank because the insurance limit is *per bank*. And money in your spouse's name receives its own individual coverage. A joint husband-wife account also has separate coverage. Thus, in the same bank you can have $100,000 in your name, $100,000 in your spouse's name, and $100,000 in a joint wife-husband account. All $300,000 will be covered.

2. Joint accounts do have limitations. While they are covered separately from individual accounts, things get sticky if you have an interest in more than one joint account in the same bank. The basic rule: you have coverage for up to $100,000 on the money that you have in all joint accounts in one bank (or savings-and-loan or credit union). Here's an example from the FDIC people: Harry and Wendy have a joint account totaling $105,000; Harry and Cindy have a joint account totaling $80,000. The bank goes broke. First of all, $5000 of the $105,000 is uninsured since it's over the $100,000 limit. Next, who owns how much of each account? Most of the time the joint owners are considered co-owners with an equal share. Thus, Harry owns half of the $100,000 account (the $105,000 account reduced by the uninsured $5000) and half of the $80,000 account. The total of his money in the two joint accounts is $90,000; Wendy has $50,000; Cindy has $40,000. Since all three people have an insurable share under $100,000, everyone gets paid off. The over-the-limit $5000 is a loss. Suppose,

however, that Harry had a third joint account, this time with Mary, that totaled $40,000. Half of that account, or $20,000, would be added to the $90,000 he already had—giving him a total of $110,000. He's over the limit and stands to lose another $10,000.

3. The rules governing retirement money have changed. Prior to December 19, 1993, the FDIC gave $100,000 of coverage to an individual for each kind of retirement account like IRAs and Keoghs. However, the new regulations now combine the self-directed accounts for insurance purposes, limiting coverage for retirement accounts to $100,000 per person, per bank.

4. In general, FDIC coverage is extended to money that a financial institution receives and keeps. If you buy an annuity or mutual fund through a bank, they are not protected.

There are also special FDIC provisions for testamentary accounts, trust accounts, and other special types of accounts. If this insurance issue gives you a big headache, then follow two simple rules: (1) never put more than $100,000 in one institution, and (2) make sure the institution is federally insured. If the institution is a bank, look for the official FDIC sign. Most savings-and-loans are insured by the Federal Savings and Loan Insurance Corporation (FSLIC), another governmental agency. Insurance for savings in most credit unions is provided by the National Credit Union Association (NCUA). As long as you see one of the acronyms—FDIC, FSLIC, or NCUA—your funds are federally protected.

If you are confused about your coverage, phone the FDIC in Washington, DC: 800-934-3342.

Counterfeit Money

About $20 million of counterfeit U.S. money is circulating throughout the world. Technological advances in both printing and photocopying equipment are making the phony money harder to recognize. In addition to the current methods used to identify counterfeit money (see graphic on next page), the federal government has added two new security features to paper money in order to distinguish genuine bills from counterfeit bills:

Inscribed security thread. A clear, inscribed polyester thread has been incorporated into the paper of genuine currency. The thread is embedded in the paper and runs vertically through the clear field to the left of the Federal Reserve seal on all notes except the $1 denomination. If it is decided to use the thread in the $1 denomination, it will be located between the Federal Reserve seal and the portrait. Printed on the thread is a denomination identifier. On $20 denominations and lower, the security thread has "USA" followed by the written denomination. For example, "USA TWENTY USA TWENTY" is repeated along the entire length of the thread. Higher denominations have "USA" plus the numerical value, such as "USA 50 USA 50" repeated along the entire length of the thread. The inscriptions are printed so that they can be read from either the face or the back of the note. The thread and the printing can only be seen by holding the note up to a light source. Don't panic if your paper money does not have an inscribed security thread. The threads are gradually being phased in as old money is "retired" (is taken out of circulation because it is worn out) and new money is printed to take the place of the old money.

Microprinting. A line of microprinting appears on the rim of the portrait on $50 and $100 denominations, beginning with Series 1990. The words "THE UNITED STATES OF AMERICA" are repeated along the sides of the portrait. As with the new security thread, the microprinting will also be phased in gradually on all denominations, with the possible exception of the $1 denomination. To the naked eye, the microprinting appears as little more than a solid line and can only be read by using magnification.

Neither of the new security features can be reproduced accurately by an office copying machine. Another recent innovation used to detect phony money is a special marking pen used by banks and business owners. When scribbled on a bogus bill, the ink of the marker turns black.

ANATOMY OF PAPER MONEY

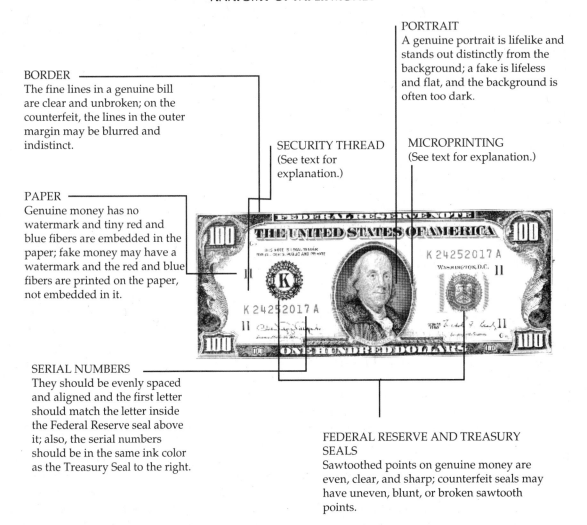

PORTRAIT
A genuine portrait is lifelike and stands out distinctly from the background; a fake is lifeless and flat, and the background is often too dark.

BORDER
The fine lines in a genuine bill are clear and unbroken; on the counterfeit, the lines in the outer margin may be blurred and indistinct.

SECURITY THREAD
(See text for explanation.)

MICROPRINTING
(See text for explanation.)

PAPER
Genuine money has no watermark and tiny red and blue fibers are embedded in the paper; fake money may have a watermark and the red and blue fibers are printed on the paper, not embedded in it.

SERIAL NUMBERS
They should be evenly spaced and aligned and the first letter should match the letter inside the Federal Reserve seal above it; also, the serial numbers should be in the same ink color as the Treasury Seal to the right.

FEDERAL RESERVE AND TREASURY SEALS
Sawtoothed points on genuine money are even, clear, and sharp; counterfeit seals may have uneven, blunt, or broken sawtooth points.

Raised Notes

Some counterfeiters alter genuine paper currency in an attempt to increase its face value. One common method is to glue numerals from high denomination bills to the corners of a note of lower denomination. While this many seem to be a very unsophisticated, even stupid, method and one that's easy to detect, phony money created in this manner is often passed to unsuspecting consumers who hurriedly complete money trans-

actions. To avoid accepting this kind of counterfeit money, you need to compare the denomination numerals on each corner with the denomination written out at the bottom of the note (front and back). Also, you need to know whose portrait appears on which bill; George Washington's face does not appear on a $20 bill. Here are the faces that belong on each denomination:

George Washington—$1

Thomas Jefferson—$2
Abraham Lincoln—$5
Alexander Hamilton—$10
Andrew Jackson—$20
Ulysses S. Grant—$50
Benjamin Franklin—$100
If you are the recipient of a counterfeit bill, you're stuck with the loss. Neither a bank nor the federal government will reimburse you. If you have counterfeit money, it's not very smart to try to pass it on to someone else since you may then become a suspected counterfeiter. Turn the money over to the local police department or the United States Secret Service.

CREDIT AND DEBT

Credit for First-Time Borrowers

According to the Consumer Credit Education Foundation, when a person applies for a loan or credit card, the financial institution makes a judgment based on the "3Cs": character (how a person has handled past debt obligations), capacity (how much debt the person can comfortably handle), and collateral (the person's assets). Obviously, a person without a credit history, who has never had credit, may have problems getting that first loan. In that case, the Foundation recommends the following options:

♦ Ask a close friend or relative to cosign for a loan. In doing this, the cosigner is guaranteeing that payments will be made on time and in full. If the credit user does not repay the loan, the cosigner will be legally responsible for doing so.

♦ Apply for a local retailer's charge card. This can be the first step toward applying for a major credit card, once a person has shown an excellent payment record.

♦ Open checking and savings accounts at a local financial institution. If the customer handles the checking account responsibly and proves to be a valued account holder, the institution may grant the person a small loan or offer a credit card.

♦ People interested in purchasing a new car can apply for an auto loan. Automobile finance companies offer special programs tailored to first-time borrowers.

♦ Buy the appliances or home furnishings you need using the credit plan of a local retailer.

♦ Take advantage of credit cards that are often offered to college students or recent graduates.

♦ Investigate "affinity group" credit cards, which are often made available to members of a particular union or professional or interest group.

Choosing a Bank Credit Card

Approximately 75 percent of all credit card holders owe money on their cards—and the average debt is $2500. The interest rates on bank credit cards (like Visa and MasterCard) range from 12 to 22 percent but extra fees, complex ways of figuring interest, and hidden charges can boost some rates to 30 percent and above. If you are a consumer who regularly pays off credit card debt, you have little to worry about. In fact, you are getting the use of interest-fee money, provided you always pay off the full balance and pay it off on time. Your major concerns are the card's annual fee, its acceptability, and the credit limit it allows you. However, the great majority of credit card holders shell out a lot of money every year in interest payments—payments that are no longer deductible on income taxes.

By law, credit card issuers are required to inform you of all costs and charges on a card. Unfortunately, many of these disclosures appear in a cardholder agreement which you get after you have already applied for, and received, your card. When shopping around for a bank credit card, here are the factors you need to consider, especially if you expect to carry revolving balances.

Interest Rate Calculations: Yes, the card issuer will quote an annual percentage rate (APR). However, there are about six different ways in which a bank can calculate the interest on revolving balances. For example, many banks figure the interest rate on your average daily balance—but some exclude new purchases and some include new purchases in the calculations (excluding is better). To further confuse the issue of interest calculations, some banks have a fixed rate of interest on a card while others have a variable rate. If you don't understand the explanation of interest-rate calculations printed in your disclosure statement, call the bank that issues your card and get someone to explain it to you. Don't hang up until you have a complete understanding.

Annual Fee: Some credit cards have annual fees, some don't. Check your agreement, because some banks offer no annual fee but only for the first year.

Grace Period: A grace period is the number of days (usually 25) between when the billing period ends ("closing date") and when you must pay it *in full* ("payment due date") to avoid interest charges. It does *not* apply, even on new purchases, if you have an unpaid balance. For example, assume that you are carrying forward a balance of $500 and then you make $100 worth of new purchases. When the next statement arrives, you are prepared to pay off the full bill within the grace period. You might expect interest charges on the old balance of $500 but not on the new $100 worth of charges—because you are ready to pay the $100 off within the grace period. Wrong. You get charged interest on the full $600

because the grace period does not apply if there is *any* outstanding debt on your statement. Also, if you have an outstanding balance on your card, make your payment (whatever the amount) as soon as you receive the statement (don't wait for the due date) in order to reduce the average daily balance used to calculate your interest; the longer you wait to pay, the more it will cost you.

Minimum Payment: Banks seem to keep lowering their minimum payment, the amount you have to pay per month. However, the lower the payment, the longer it takes for you to pay off the balance—and the more interest you pay over time to the bank. For example, if you owe $2500 at 18.5 percent interest and make a minimum payment of 2 percent per month, it would take you more than 30 years to pay off the balance and would cost $6500 in interest charges.

FINDING A LOW-INTEREST BANK CREDIT CARD

There are a number of organizations that keep watch over bank credit cards and publish lists of banks around the country that offer the lowest rates. One such group is Bankcard Holders of America (BHA), a nonprofit membership organization. For a small fee you can receive a current list of banks that offer cards at no fee or at low annual fees and/or low interest rates. If you decide to join BHA, you receive a number of membership services in addition to the updated list: a bimonthly newsletter, a toll-free consumer dispute hotline, consumer pamphlets and guidebooks. For more details, contact: **Bankcard Holders of America**, 524 Branch Drive, Salem, VA 24153 (703-389-5445). Another excellent source of information is RAM Research which publishes a monthly newsletter, *Cardtrak*, with names of banks with low-interest credit cards; you can order just one copy of the newsletter at a minimal charge. For further information, contact: **RAM Research**, PO Box 1700, Frederick, MD 21702 (800-344-7714).

Cash Advances: Avoid them. Almost all card issuers charge interest beginning on the day the money is withdrawn (no grace period). In addition, some banks have a different interest rate (a higher one) for cash advances than for credit card purchases.

Additional Fees: There are a number of "nuisance" fees that may show up on your statement: late fee (charges when you fail to make a minimum payment by the due date); over-limit fee (assessed when you exceed your credit limit); cash-advance fee (made when you charge cash to your card). Adding a number of these nuisance fees to your balance can cause your "real" interest rate to skyrocket.

When shopping around for a credit card, there are plenty of issuers to choose from. Generally, the major banks don't offer the lowest interest rates. The better rates usually come from smaller local and regional banks. And the lowest-rate cards are typically issued only to people who qualify as excellent credit risks.

Debit Cards

Debit cards are relatively new but are becoming increasingly popular. They look like a credit card but they work like a check. When you use a debit card, the amount you spend is deducted automatically from your bank checking account. There are two kinds of debit cards, on-line and off-line. The on-line process is similar to what happens when you use an automatic teller machine (ATM). A clerk puts your card through a magnetic reader that is connected to a bank computer. You enter a personal identification number and the computer tells the clerk if there is enough money in your account to cover the transaction. If so, the transaction is processed, and the money deducted from your account. Off-line cards aren't computer linked but are put through the same kind of hand-operated imprinter used with credit cards. The money still gets deducted from your checking account but it can take a few days before the debit is recorded. Debit cards are used mostly in supermarkets, gas stations, and convenience stores—places where cash and check transactions have predominated. Some banks issue ATM cards with debt capability; they can be used at ATMs to get cash and at businesses that accept debt-card transactions.

Banks like the idea of debit cards because they cut down on the costs of processing checks. But there are also advantages for consumers. First, unlike credit cards, there are no interest charges to pay. You don't have to worry about carrying around cash or your checkbook. You don't have to deal with getting check approvals, especially annoying if you are out of town. And using a debit card reduces the number of trips you make to the ATM to withdraw cash.

There are drawbacks to consider. If you don't keep track of the balance in your checking account, it could get very low without you realizing it. Worse yet, you could be overdrawn and be subject to bank penalties. Even if you sign up for overdraft protection at the bank, there can be a high interest penalty for overdrawn accounts. Also, if you are a consumer who pays off all credit card balances every month, you have the advantage of an interest-free grace period (usually 25 days) between the date a purchase is made and the date the payment is due; with a debit card the money comes out of your account right away—no grace period. If your credit card is lost or stolen, federal law limits your liability to $50; debit cards don't have exactly the same protection and if yours is lost or stolen, you could be liable for a lot more, depending on how long it took you to report the loss of the card. So read the debit card agreement to understand liability limits. Finally, there are fees to pay when using debit cards—a monthly or annual charge or a fee for each transaction. Check with your bank to find out exactly how the fees are assessed.

Safeguarding Your Credit Cards

Credit card crime is big business. If your card is stolen and you report the loss before any unauthorized charges are made, you are not liable for anything. If you report the loss after fraudulent use of the card, you are liable for only $50. Nonetheless, the high costs of credit card crime eventually get passed along to consumers (higher annual fees, interest rates, and other charges). Here are some tips to help you avoid fraudulent use of your cards.

♦ Don't give your credit card number, expiration date, or balance to anyone who calls you on the telephone. If you initiated the call and it's to a well-known party (e.g., you are ordering an item from the mail-order catalog of a reputable company), you're usually safe.

♦ Keep your PIN (personal identification number) or PIC (personal identification code) a secret. Don't write the number on your card or on a separate piece of paper that you carry around.

♦ Destroy the carbon paper from credit card receipts.

♦ Review your monthly credit card statement. Keep all receipts from purchases and match them against your statement.

♦ Sign new cards as soon as you receive them. Cut up old cards into small pieces before throwing them in the trash. If your card expires before you receive a replacement card, call your card issuer. The card may have been stolen en route to you.

♦ If you receive a preapproved credit card application in the mail, and you don't want the card, rip up the application before throwing it out. A credit card thief could find it, fill out the application with a change of address, and get a card issued in your name.

♦ Keep a record of all your credit card numbers and the phone numbers of the issuing companies so that you can immediately report the loss or theft of the cards.

Credit Bureaus and Your Credit Report

Whenever you apply for credit, your prospective lender wants to know about your "creditworthiness," your past history of repaying debts. The lender gets this credit report by contacting one or more credit bureaus that collect financial data and generate computer-printed documents. There are three major credit bureaus: TRW, Equifax, and Trans Union. Each one has approximately 170 million files that it constantly updates. Most Americans are tracked by at least two of the bureaus.

What the Files Say About You

Your file is likely to contain many kinds of financial data including: charge accounts and credit cards and other loans (how long you've had them and your payment history); special situations where goods were repossessed or a bill collector was called in; court actions against you like bankruptcy or foreclosure; your employment history; personal data like your marital status and age. The credit bureau itself does not decide whether or not you get the credit you applied for. It simply gives a report to the prospective lender and the lender makes the decision.

You can pretty well guess what lenders don't like to see in a credit report: lots of credit cards with large outstanding balances; accounts closed because you were delinquent in payments; a lien on your property; wage attachments; defaulting on a loan; lawsuits brought against you for money owed; bankruptcy, etc. Generally black marks against your record remain in the file for seven years (except for bankruptcy which stays in your record for 10 years).

You are entitled to get a copy of your file from any bureau that keeps one on you. Sometimes the report is free; sometimes there is a small charge. However, only about one in every 100 credit users requests a credit report—most people aren't aware that they can get them; some people just don't care. However, it is estimated that anywhere from 43 to 50 percent of the files contain mistakes. A great many of the errors are relatively minor and wouldn't affect your credit-worthiness. But there are situations in which you would want your credit record to be completely accurate and as spotless as possible. For instance, you might be applying for a home mortgage. Or you are getting a divorce and you don't want your spouse's financial obligations on your record. Perhaps you've had a bad credit experience which has been resolved and you want to make sure it is deleted from your report. Most people take action only when they have been denied credit and are informed that the denial was based on a credit report.

Credit Repair

If there are mistakes in your credit report, you have the right to get them corrected. Credit bureaus are required to investigate disputed information. If the investigation supports your side of the story, the incorrect information is removed from your file. If the investigation drags on too long (no resolution after about 30 days), you might get lucky, win by default, and get the information obliterated. However, if the credit bureau contacts the creditor who reported the adverse data and the creditor insists there was no error, then you may have to step in and work with the creditor in order to get the situation resolved. If you reach a complete impasse and can't get a negative item removed from your file, you still have one last resort. According to federal law, you can submit a 100-word statement that gives your viewpoint on the disputed information. That statement becomes part of your credit record and will be included in any report sent to a potential creditor.

Every year the Federal Trade Commission is deluged with complaints about the reports generated by credit bureaus. Because of this public outcry, the bureaus have made some improvements in their systems, namely, trying to make the reports more accessible and easier to understand. One of the bureaus, TRW, has offered to send, free of charge, one report per year to any consumer who makes a request. Be aware that if you are denied credit because of a credit report, the bureau in question will send you a report free of charge upon request.

To get a free report from TRW, you need to write to: **TRW Consumer Complimentary Report,** PO Box 2350, Chatsworth, CA 91313-2350 (800-392-1122). You must tell the company your full name (including middle initial), your spouse's first name (if you are married); current address and zip code as well as previous addresses and zip codes for the past five years; Social Security number, date of birth. In addition, TRW requires some kind of identification verification, such as a copy of a driver's license or utility bill.

Equifax and Trans Union charge a fee for a credit report (remember, however, that you get them free upon request if you have been denied credit because of their reports). For information about getting a credit report from **Equifax,** call 800-685-1111; contact **Trans Union** by calling 216-779-2378.

COSIGNING A LOAN

A family member or close friend can't qualify for a loan, so he or she asks you to cosign. If you agree, you may turn out to be a hero, or you may turn out to be a fool. When you become the secondary signer of a loan, you are responsible for paying back every dime if your friend or relative is unable, or unwilling, to meet the financial obligation. In addition, if you apply for your own loan, you must list your cosigned loan as a debt obligation, which may have a bearing on whether or not your loan is approved. Even if your friend or relative declares bankruptcy under Chapter 7 (which cancels out almost all debts), your cosigned loan is not canceled. The creditor will come after you for repayment.

Warning Signs of Debt Problems

Most of us spend more time thinking about credit than we do about debt. That's because the majority of Americans have a relatively easy time getting credit. Preapproved credit card applications frequently arrive in the mail, and most of us carry around a fistful of credit cards. Also, it's more desirable to think about what we can buy as opposed to what we owe. And, besides credit cards, we have a number of other things we can borrow against: our home, our life insurance policies, our investments, our retirement plans.

Financial advisors and credit counselors say that no more than 20 percent of your take-home pay should go toward repaying debt (excluding your housing costs). Unfortunately, a lot of us are overextended and, worse yet, may not fully be aware of it. Listed below are some signs that you may be burying yourself under a mountain of debt.

♦ You don't know the total amount of your debts and other financial obligations.

♦ You can afford to make only minimum payments on credit cards and other revolving loan accounts; you never seem to pay them off completely.

♦ You keep getting new credit cards in order to increase your borrowing power or because your other credit cards are charged up to their limits.

♦ Some of your credit cards have been revoked.

♦ You are taking cash advances on your credit cards to pay other bills or daily living expenses like food.

♦ Every month you have to juggle bill payments; some go unpaid.

♦ You have little, or no, savings.

♦ You put off paying for necessities (like medical checkups) in order to pay off debts.

♦ You get calls from creditors and bill collectors.

♦ You have been denied credit due to a bad credit rating.

♦ You frequently borrow money from friends, family members, and business associates.

♦ You bounce checks.

♦ When buying anything on credit, you choose the longest term for repayment.

♦ You take out new loans before old loans are paid off.

♦ You hate talking about money to anyone, including yourself.

When Your Debts Get Out of Control

Some steps to consider to alleviate debt problems:

1. Face the problem. Until you admit you have a problem, you aren't prepared to fix it.

2. Make a plan. Review the last six months of your spending habits to figure out just where your money goes. How much money comes in each month and what do you need to pay off debts?

3. Curb spending habits. Find ways to reduce spending, and make no new major purchases. Stop using credit cards. If you can't bear to cut them up, tuck them away in a safe deposit box.

4. Consider using your savings, if you have any, to pay off certain debts. If your savings account is paying 5 percent interest and you are paying 20 percent interest on your credit card, you are getting way behind.

5. Can you increase your income? Maybe you can put in extra hours at work or get a part-time job on weekends. Do you have any assets you can sell—extra furniture, a car you really don't need? If you have a lot of personal belongings you can part with, you might hold a garage sale.

6. Consider refinancing your home if interest rates are in your favor and it makes financial sense.

7. Beware of debt-consolidation loans. In theory, the loan sounds appealing: a lender agrees to pay off all of your bills by making you one big loan. The lender handles all the creditors and you

make only one monthly payment to the lender. However, this kind of loan can be very expensive and some of the companies that offer them are not top-quality firms. According to the National Center for Financial Education, a nonprofit organization: "A consolidation loan may be workable ONLY if the loan interest is less than the interest on the debts to be retired AND paid-off charge accounts are closed AND the extra cash-flow is put towards paying off the consolidation loan even faster. Otherwise in a year or two many people who only pay off and not close accounts are often paying off a consolidation loan and also new credit purchases."

8. Don't hide from your creditors. Let them know you are having financial problems and express a sincere desire and commitment to pay your bills. In most cases, a creditor will be flexible and work with you to design a repayment plan that you can meet.

9. If necessary, seek professional advice. There are nonprofit counseling centers across the country that offer assistance to people who are having debt problems. The counselors will work with your creditors to devise debt repayment schedules, help you to create a spending plan, and provide moral support. The fees charged for the services are minimal and are usually based on a client's ability to pay. For low-income clients, the fee is often waived. To locate a counseling center in your area, contact: **The National Foundation for Consumer Credit,** 8611 Second Avenue, Suite 100, Silver Spring, MD 20910 (301-589-5600 or 800-388-2227).

Declaring Bankruptcy

Bankruptcy laws were designed to help consumers in extreme financial distress. People who file for bankruptcy seek to get some or all of their debts eliminated. For people who are faced with truly impossible debt burdens, bankruptcy may be the only way to wipe the slate clean and get a new financial start. However, too many Americans do not view bankruptcy as a vehicle of last resort, but rather as a quick fix, a way to erase bad money habits. The number of personal bankruptcies has risen dramatically over the past 10 years. While declaring bankruptcy doesn't carry quite the social stigma that it used to, it does have a significant downside. Bankruptcy is an admission of financial failure. And it ruins your credit record for up to 10 years. It can make it difficult, or impossible, for you to make major purchases (like a home or car) and to get credit cards and other kinds of loans. Potential landlords may refuse to rent an apartment to bankruptcy filers; potential employers may look adversely on a negative credit record.

There are two types of personal bankruptcy, Chapter 7 and Chapter 13. In Chapter 7, called straight bankruptcy, many of your assets are turned over to a court-approved trustee to be sold in order to pay off debts. Some assets are exempt from liquidation, like personal clothing, a certain amount of equity in your home and car, Social Security benefits and unemployment insurance, a specified amount of jewelry and household belongings, etc. Some states have their own rules regarding bankruptcy exemptions; in some cases, you are allowed to choose between the state and federal exemptions. When all bankruptcy transactions are complete, you are free of debt (with some exceptions that are mentioned below), whether your creditors were paid in full or received only a portion of what you owed.

Under Chapter 13 (called the wage-earner plan) of the Bankruptcy Code, your assets are not sold. Instead, you work with a bankruptcy court to come up with a plan to pay off some or all of your debts, usually over a period of three to five years. The balance of your debt is then forgiven. There are certain requirements for filing under Chapter 13 including your ability to actually pay off debts. In general, a Chapter 13 filing is better on a credit record than a Chapter 7. Future lenders and creditors look more favorably upon someone who has made at least some attempt to honor debts.

Regardless of how you file, some debts are never forgiven. They include alimony, child support, most income taxes, most student loans, court judgments against you for damages. Also, you are liable for any debts that you do not mention on your bankruptcy petition. And you can't run out a few weeks before filing and buy a big-ticket luxury item (like a diamond ring or a Mercedes-Benz) and expect that loan to be partially or totally forgiven.

Federal law dictates that you can file under Chapter 7 rules only once every six years. Under Chapter 13, you can file more often if you have repaid your debts. Before considering bankruptcy, it is advisable to pursue first any and all avenues to *reduce* your debt. If, however, bankruptcy seems to be the only solution, you should seek good legal advice. Do-it-yourself books, workshops, and prepackaged kits may be too simple, or too complex, for your situation.

Saving and Investing

Five Questions to Ask Before Investing

Saving and investing are not synonymous. Money that you save will help to meet immediate needs and emergencies. Money that you invest will be used for longer-term goals. Before you enter the world of investments, ask yourself . . .

1. *Do I really have money to invest?* Take a hard look at your financial status. How much money is coming in, what are your financial obligations, and how much is left over? Financial experts recommend that you set aside a reserve fund of three to six months take-home pay to handle emergencies. That money should be safe and liquid and pay you the highest amount of interest. And, before you start adding up what you can invest, have you adequately met all of your insurance needs?

2. *What are my goals?* Perhaps you want to buy a home or take a long vacation. Or, you need to accumulate money for your child's college education. Maybe retirement income is a major concern. Prioritize your goals, put a price tag on each, and establish time frames for goal attainment.

3. *How comfortable am I with risk?* Surveys have shown that many of us think we can handle more risk than we actually can. In general, higher-return investments require more risk. So,

know thyself before you investigate investment options.

4. *What investments should I choose?* The list of possibilities is long and wide. Fortunately, there are endless books, magazines, newsletters, television programs, and seminars devoted to helping you answer this question. Educating yourself about your money will be the single best investment you can make in your future. Never, ever, put your hard-earned money in an investment vehicle that you don't fully understand.

5. *Who should manage my portfolio?* You can go it alone or seek out, and pay for, the services of a stockbroker, financial planner, tax planner— or a combination of money professionals. Even if you prefer to make all of your own investment decisions, you may still need to go through a brokerage house to buy particular investments. Some investors genuinely love, and need, total control over their money and thus are willing to expend the time and effort to plan out and watch over investments. Others prefer good, expert advice.

Savings and Investment Options

Where you put your money depends on a multitude of circumstances related to your own individual needs and desires as well as the state of the economy. Regardless of your savings and investment choices, you face three kinds of risk: *interest rate risk* (value of your investment changes as interest rates rise and fall); *inflation risk* (inflation diminishes the return on your investment); *price risk* (the actual value of your investment may go down).

Listed below is a brief description of some savings and investment options.

Passbook Accounts

Most of us were introduced to the world of finance with a passbook savings account from our local bank. *Advantages*: No risk; federally insured; convenient. *Disadvantages*: Low interest rates; possible fee for low balances.

Bank Money-Market Accounts

These accounts pay a variable rate of interest and the banks set the rates. There can be a rule on how much you have to withdraw at one time and how many withdrawals you can make by check per month. *Advantages*: In high-interest periods, it usually pays more than passbook accounts; easy to open; convenient access; federally insured; combined bank balances (checking plus passbook plus money market) may get you a free checking account. *Disadvantages*: In low-interest-rate periods, it pays about the same as a passbook account; monthly fees if your account falls below the required minimum balance.

Mutual Fund Money-Market Accounts

In this case money is pooled by a number of investors into a mutual fund that buys short-term securities like Treasury securities, high-quality bank certificates of deposit, etc. They are considered safe (some buy only U.S. Government securities), and you can write a unlimited number of checks on the fund. *Advantages*: Higher short-term returns than with bank money-market accounts; liquid; diverse investments. *Disadvan-*

tages: Don't have federal deposit insurance; management fees.

Certificates of Deposit (CDs)

You deposit money (usually in a bank, savings-and-loan, or credit union) for a specified period at a specified interest rate. Your principal never fluctuates. *Advantages*: Interest rates usually higher than money-market accounts or passbook accounts; federally insured. *Disadvantages*: Penalty for early withdrawal.

U.S. Treasury Bills

You loan money to the U.S. Government when you buy a Treasury bill—or the other two Treasury securities listed below (Treasury notes, Treasury bonds). Treasury bills are short-term obligations that mature in three months, six months, or a year. They do not have a stated interest rate; you buy them at a discounted rate and your profit (or interest) is the difference between what you pay and the face value when the T-bill matures. Minimum investment is $10,000. *Advantages*: Extremely safe; short maturities; exempt from state and local taxes; can buy directly from a Federal Reserve Bank. *Disadvantages*: High minimum investment; no interest payments; interest rates are usually lower than with longer-term investments.

U.S. Treasury Notes

Treasury notes are medium-term obligations with maturities of up to 10 years. They bear a stated interest rate and the owner receives semiannual interest payments. Notes with terms of less than four years require a $5000 minimum; notes with terms four years and over require a $1000 minimum. Interest is paid twice a year to owner. *Advantages*: Extremely safe; exempt from state and local taxes; can buy directly from a Federal Reserve Bank. *Disadvantages*: Longer-term notes not a good hedge in inflationary times; can't sell notes back to government before maturity (if you need to sell before due date, must sell on open market).

U.S. Treasury Bonds

Treasury bonds are long-term obligations, 10 to 30 years. Like Treasury notes, they bear a stated interest rate and the owner receives semiannual interest payments. Bonds are sold at a minimum of $1000. *Advantages*: Extremely safe; exempt from state and local taxes; can buy directly from a Federal Reserve Bank. *Disadvantages*: Can't sell bonds back to government before maturity (if you need to sell before due date, must sell on open market; since value of bonds fluctuates due to changing interest rates, you might get less than you originally paid).

U.S. Savings Bonds

A nonmarketable security of the U.S. Treasury Department, the current Series EE bond has a maturity date of 12 years but can be cashed in six months after the issue date. If you hold the bond for at least five years, you get a guaranteed minimum interest rate or a market-based interest rate—whichever is higher. Bonds cashed in before five years earn interest on a fixed, graduated scale. Bonds come in many denominations starting at $50 and the purchase price is one-half the denomination (a $100 bond costs $50). They can be purchased at most banks, savings-and-loans, and through the payroll savings plan offered by thousands of companies. You can invest as much as $15,000 per year ($30,000 face value). They don't pay cash interest; instead, interest accrues and bonds rise in value until you cash them in. *Advantages*: Extremely safe; exempt from state and local taxes; no fee or commission to buy or sell; federal tax deferred until bond redeemed; totally or partially exempt from federal taxes if used to pay for college tuition and if certain income-eligibility requirements are met (applies to Series EE bonds purchased after 1989). *Disadvantages*: Must be held for five years for guaranteed minimum interest rate; pays less interest than other five-year Treasury securities; no interest payments.

Common Stock

When you buy stock in a company, you become part owner of that company. When the company makes a profit, its management team has three options: pay you dividends; keep the profits and reinvest them in the business; do some of both—pay you some of the profits and invest some back into the company. You can make money in two ways: dividends are steady and rising; the stock increases in value and you can sell it for a profit. The stock market is a very complex world; choosing individual stocks (even with the help of a financial professional) requires diligent research and evaluation. *Advantages*: Potentially high profits. *Disadvantages*: High risk; not insured; value of shares changes daily; brokerage fees.

Preferred Stock

Like owning common stock, owning preferred stock means you are part owner of a company. Unlike common stock, preferred stock stipulates a specific dividend payable before dividends are issued to common-stock holders. Also, in case the company is liquidated, assets go first to preferred-stock holders. However, if a company does exceptionally well, extra profits (or the lion's share of extra profits) go to those who own common stock. *Advantages*: Lower risk than common stock; stable dividends. *Disadvantages*: Still risky; not insured; lower appreciation potential than common stocks.

Corporate Bonds

You make a loan (minimum investment is usually $5000) to a particular corporation and in return it will pay you a certain amount of interest for a fixed period of time (there is a wide range of maturities). When the bond matures, you get your money back. Bonds get a credit rating for safety and quality (AAA is the highest rating). The market value of all types of bonds—corporate bonds, U.S. Treasury bonds (discussed above), and tax-exempt municipal bonds (discussed below)—is tied directly to interest rates.

When interest rates fall, bond prices rise; when interest rates rise, bond prices fall. In addition, corporate bonds have a "call" feature—if a corporation wants to pay off its loan to you early, it can call your bonds and you must surrender them. *Advantages*: Usually pays higher yields than CDs and U.S. Treasuries. *Disadvantages*: Market value of bond tied to interest rates; can be hard to sell at a good price before maturity; bond's current credit rating subject to change; not insured, though some backed by some type of collateral; subject to call; brokerage fees.

Tax-Free Municipal Bonds

Investors buy these primarily because of their tax advantage. These "loans" (usually bought at a $5000 minimum) to government entities are exempt from federal taxes, and if you buy bonds from your own state, they are usually exempt from state and local taxes. Most experts recommend them for individuals in higher income brackets, i.e., 28 percent federal income-tax bracket or above. Issued by government entities—cities, states, counties—they can have short, medium, or long maturities and come in several types, e.g., general obligation bonds, revenue bonds, etc. Like corporate bonds, municipals have a credit rating (AAA is the highest) and have a "call" feature (government entity can redeem them before maturity). Also like corporate bonds, their value on the open market (if you sell before maturity) is dependent on current interest rates. *Advantages*: Steady, tax-free income; some are insured. *Disadvantages*: Market value of bond tied to interest rates; can be hard to sell at a good price before maturity; bond's credit rating subject to change; subject to call; brokerage fees.

Mutual Funds

In a mutual fund your money is pooled with the money of other investors in order to achieve a specific goal (like income, growth, growth and income, aggressive growth). There is an array of funds—stock funds, bond funds, money market funds, real-estate funds, etc. Each is made up of a number of different securities in order to spread investment risk across all the fund's holdings. Funds are handled by full-time money managers who buy and sell the securities in your fund as they see fit. You can buy shares in some funds directly from the company and pay no sales commission (called no-load funds); funds sold through brokerage houses or financial planners or banks (load funds) will require a sales fee. Regardless of how you buy into the fund, you will pay management fees. A fund can make money for you in three ways: (1) dividends or interest on the securities in the fund; (2) selling securities for a profit; (3) owning securities that go up in value, thus increasing the price of the fund's own shares. Most of your profits will come in the form of dividends or capital-gains distributions; payouts can be monthly, quarterly, or annually. *Advantages*: Professional management; diversification of securities; opportunity to reinvest your dividends and capital gains; funds have many different levels of risk; no sales commission on no-load funds; initial minimum investment usually low ($500 or $1000). *Disadvantages*: Low to high risk, depending on choice of fund; profits and value of investments fluctuates; not federally insured; management fees and possible sales commissions (for load funds); filing tax returns can be complicated (you may have dividends, and capital gains and losses).

The above list is a bare-bones look at some savings and investment options. Our intent is not to turn you toward, or away from, any of them. Your financial health—how you manage and save and invest your money—requires maximum study and informed decisions.

Investor's Bill of Rights

In many important ways, an investor is not simply a consumer but a party to a legal contract. Both the offeror and purchaser of an investment have rights and responsibilities. This "Bill of Rights" is designed to assist you the investor in making an informed decision before committing your funds. It is not intended to be exhaustive in its descriptions.

Honesty in Advertising

Many individuals first learn of investment opportunities through advertising—in a newspaper or magazine, on radio or television, or by mail. Phone solicitations are also regarded as a form of advertising. In practically every area of investment activity, false or misleading advertising is against the law and subject to civil, criminal, or regulatory penalties.

Bear in mind that advertising is able to convey only limited information, and the most attractive features are likely to be highlighted. Accordingly, it is never wise to invest solely on the basis of an advertisement. The only bona fide purposes of investment advertising are to call your attention to an offering and encourage you to obtain additional information.

Full and Accurate Information

Before you make any investment, you have the right to seek and obtain information about the investment. This includes information that accurately conveys all of the material facts about the investment, including the major factors likely to affect its performance.

You also have the right to request information about the firm or the individuals with whom you would be doing business and whether they have a "track record." If so, you have the right to know what it has been and whether it is real or "hypothetical." If they have been in trouble with regulatory authorities, you have the right to know this. If a rate of return is advertised, you have the right to know how it is calculated and any assumptions it is based on. You also have the right to ask what financial interest the seller of the investment has in the sale.

Ask for all available literature about the investment. If there is a prospectus, obtain it and read

it. This is where the bad as well as the good about the investment has to be discussed. If an investment involves a company whose stock is publicly traded, get a copy of its latest annual report. It can also be worthwhile to visit your public library to find out what may have been written about the investment in recent business or financial periodicals.

Obtaining information isn't likely to tell you whether or not a given investment will be profitable, but what you are able to find out—or unable to find out—could help you decide if it's an appropriate investment for you at that time. No investment is right for everyone.

Disclosure of Risks

Every investment involves some risk. You have the right to find out what these risks are prior to making an investment. Some, of course, are obvious: Shares of stock may decline in price. A business venture may fail. An oil well may turn out to be a dry hole.

Others may be less obvious. Many people do not fully understand, for example, that even a U.S. Treasury bond may fluctuate in market value prior to maturity. Or that with some investments it is possible to lose more than the amount initially invested. The point is that different investments involve different *kinds* of risk and these risks can differ in *degree*. A general rule of thumb is that the greater the potential reward, the greater the potential risk.

In some areas of investment, there is a legal obligation to disclose the risks in writing. If the investment doesn't require a prospectus or written risk disclosure statement, you might nonetheless want to ask for a written explanation of the risks. The bottom line: unless your understanding of the ways you can lose money is equal to your understanding of the ways you can make money, don't invest!

Explanation of Obligations and Costs

You have the right to know, in advance, what obligations and costs are involved in a given investment. For instance, does the investment involve a requirement that you must take some specific action by a particular time? Or is there a possibility that at some future time or under certain circumstances you may be obligated to come up with additional money?

Similarly, you have the right to a full disclosure of the costs that will be or may be incurred. In addition to commissions, sales charges, or "loads" when you buy and/or sell, this includes any other transaction expenses, maintenance or service charges, profit sharing arrangements, redemption fees or penalties and the like.

Time to Consider

You earned the money and you have the right to decide for yourself how you want to invest it. That right includes sufficient time to make an informed and well-considered decision. High-pressure sales tactics violate the spirit of the law, and most investment professionals will not push you into making uninformed decisions. Thus, any such efforts should be grounds for suspicion. An investment that "absolutely has to be made right now" probably shouldn't be made at all.

Responsible Advice

Investors enjoy a wide range of different investments to choose from. Taking into consideration your financial situation, needs, and investment objectives, some are likely to be suitable for you and others aren't—perhaps because of risks involved and perhaps for other reasons. If you rely on an investment professional for advice, you have the right to *responsible* advice.

In the securities industry, for example, "suitability" rules require that investment advice be appropriate for the particular customer. In the commodity futures industry a "know your customer" rule requires that firms and brokers obtain sufficient information to assure that investors are adequately informed of the risks involved. Beware of someone who insists that a particular investment is "right" for you although they know nothing about you.

Best-Effort Management

Every firm and individual that accepts investment funds from the public has the ethical and legal obligation to manage the money responsibly. As an investor, you have the right to expect nothing less.

Unfortunately, in any area of investment, there are those few less-than-ethical persons who may lose sight of their obligations, and of your rights: by making investments you have not authorized; by making an excessive number of investments for the purpose of creating additional commission income for themselves; or, at the extreme, appropriating your funds for their personal use. If there is even a hint of such activities, insist on an immediate and full explanation. Unless you are completely satisfied with the answer, ask the appropriate regulatory or legal authorities to look into it. It's your right.

Complete and Truthful Accounting

Investing your money shouldn't mean losing touch with your money. It's your right to know where your money is and the current status and value of your account. If there have been profits or losses, you have the right to know the amount and how and when they were realized or incurred. This right includes knowing the amount and nature of any and all charges against your account.

Most firms prepare and mail periodic account statements, generally monthly. And you can usually obtain interim information on request. Whatever the method of accounting, you have both the right to obtain this information and the right to expect that it be timely and accurate.

Access to Your Funds

Some investments include restrictions as to whether, when, or how you can have access to your funds. You have the right to be clearly informed of any such restrictions in advance of making the investment. Similarly, if the investment may be illiquid—difficult to quickly convert to cash—you have the right to know this beforehand. In the absence of restrictions or limitations, it's your money and you should be able to have access to it within a reasonable period of time.

You should also have access to the person or firm that *has* your funds. Investment scam artists are well versed in ways of finding *you*, but, particularly once they have your money in hand, they can make it difficult or impossible for you to find *them*.

Recourse, If Necessary

Your rights as an investor include the right to seek an appropriate remedy if you believe someone has dealt with you—or handled your investment—dishonestly or unfairly. Indeed, even in the case of reasonable misunderstandings, there should be some way to reconcile differences.

It is wise to determine before you invest what avenues of recourse are available to you if they should be needed. One means of exercising your right of recourse may be to file suit in a court of law. Or you may be able to initiate arbitration, mediation, or reparation proceedings through an exchange or a regulatory organization. Additional information about filing complaints can be obtained through various regulatory organizations.

Reprinted courtesy of the National Futures Association.

Financial Planners

In theory, a financial planner is an all-purpose money guru. The planner can assess your overall financial status, map out a plan to help you reach short- and long-term goals, and help you buy and manage your investments on an ongoing basis. With a reasonable amount of knowledge and effort, you can do those tasks yourself and you'll probably do just fine. Some people, however, are hopeless money managers and are willing to pay the price for professional advice.

Some financial planners earn their fees solely from designing a plan for you; some earn their income solely from the commissions on the in-

vestments they sell to you; most receive payments from both a financial plan and sales commissions. There are more than 250,000 men and women who call themselves financial planners. Some are qualified, honest, and financially savvy. But there are also planners who are inexperienced, incompetent, and dishonest. The industry as a whole is largely unregulated. In other words, just about anyone can hang out a shingle stamped "financial planner." It's estimated that planners cause clients to lose at least $600 million every two years.

If you are inclined to work with a financial planner, inform yourself thoroughly in order to ensure that the person you choose is someone who will improve, not sabotage, your financial future. How well does the planner score on all the following points?

Credentials and Experience

What is the planner's background: stockbroker, tax attorney, business analyst, insurance salesperson? Since they come from a variety of backgrounds, planners can have a variety of degrees and licenses. Adding to the credential confusion are the organizations and schools that issue certification designations to persons who have taken courses and passed exams in the field of financial planning, e.g., a CFP (certified financial planner).

Be sure your prospective planner is registered as an investment advisor with the SEC (Securities and Exchange Commission). Ask to see the SEC form ADV Part II, which includes information about education, investment methods, experience, fees, and potential conflicts of interest. In addition, most states require most planners to register with the state's securities department. Finally, advisors who sell securities, as well as recommend them, are required by federal law to pass an exam on basic investment knowledge (or be affiliated with a person who has passed the exam).

If your financial planner is a registered stockbroker, you can find out if the planner has been the subject of any disciplinary actions or if there are any pending disciplinary proceedings by calling the **National Association of Securities Dealers** (NASD). NASD operates a public-disclosure hot line: 800-289-9999.

Scope of Services

Is the planner more of a specialist (e.g., in tax planning) or can he or she give good advice on everything from investments and retirement to insurance, taxes, and money management? Match up your needs with the expertise of the planner.

Costs

Some planners are fee-only: fees typically range from $75–$200 per hour; others ask a flat price for an overall plan, typically from $1500 to $5000. Some planners work solely on a commission basis and their fees are included in the price of the products they sell to you. Most planners have a fee-and-commission arrangement: $200 to $1500 for an overall plan plus commissions on whatever they sell to you. Ask for a written estimate showing the cost of the services you want the planner to provide.

Investment Approach

If you are a conservative investor and the planner boasts of successes in speculative stocks, limited partnerships, junk bonds (all risky investments), then you do not have a match made in heaven. This is particularly important if a financial planner sells securities as well as recommends them. Ask how much of the planner's income comes from various investments—mutual funds, stocks, bonds, etc. If you find out that 70 percent comes from insurance products, then you are dealing with an insurance salesperson, not a financial planner. Also, beware of planners who are affiliated with companies that sell securities (it's likely that they will try to sell you products offered by those companies).

References

Tell the planner that you would like the names and phone numbers of three or four clients. When you call the references, find out how their financial plans are working out, and if they are satisfied with the planner.

For more information on financial planners, as well as referrals, contact one of the following organizations: **Institute of Certified Financial Planners**, 800-282-7526; **National Association of Personal Financial Advisors**, 800-366-2732; **International Association for Financial Planning**, 800-945-4237.

Stockbrokers

More than 15 million Americans use the services of full-service stockbrokers. Some of the well-known brokerage houses give their brokers glitzy names like financial consultants or investment executives. Just remember that stockbrokers are also salespeople. They earn a living from the commissions of products they sell to you.

Most investors are lured to full-service stockbrokers and their brokerage houses because of the great range of services offered: they can buy and sell virtually any kind of security; they have large research departments to analyze investments; and they offer a number of management services and accounts. And, of course, customers are looking for investment advice.

All this service and convenience can be costly. Rarely will a broker volunteer how much commission he or she will get from investments you make. Sometimes, it is fairly easy to figure out: you buy 100 shares of Company ABC at $100 a share and pay $10,250. That's a markup of 2.5 percent which is the sales commission (some of the commission goes to the broker; the rest to the firm that the broker represents). However, often the commission fee is built into the price of the investment (e.g., for many kinds of bonds) and it's not so simple to figure out just what the sales fee amounts to. Besides paying a fee for "buy" and "sell" transactions, there can be processing fees, administrative fees, or maintenance fees on your accounts. These nickel-and-dime charges can add up if you are an active trader.

Obviously, a broker makes more money if you buy high-commission products, which are often riskier and more complicated. In addition, a broker may strongly recommend products (stocks, bonds, mutual funds) that are already owned and/or managed by the broker's firm—but the broker neglects to tell you this. Sometimes these products may be top-notch; however, they may be big-time losers that the broker's firm is eager to dump.

Before searching for a full-service broker, ask yourself if you really need one. If you already know exactly what investments you want, you could save money by dealing with a "discount" brokerage firm, where charges are 20–55 percent less than at a full-service outfit, or with a "deep discount" firm where the charge is about 70 percent less. However, the discount firms are primarily in business to *execute your orders,* not to offer you investment advice or a full range of services.

If you want and need a full-service broker, shop around and ask a lot of questions. Be sure the broker you choose fully understands your financial position, goals, and tolerance for risk. Take notes, in person and on the phone, when you talk to your broker and keep all paperwork (including transaction slips) in a file. Above all, educate yourself about various investments before you entrust your money to someone else.

Unfortunately, there are stockbrokers who put their own financial interests ahead of yours. Listed below are some of the more common abuses committed by brokers.

Churning. Without consideration for your investment goals, a broker engages in heavy trading of your account (lots of buys and sells) in order to generate sales commissions.

Unauthorized Trading. Buying or selling securities not authorized by the customer.

Unauthorized Accounts. A broker may open an account (like a "margin" account) that you never asked for.

Unsuitable Investments. Brokers can be held accountable for putting you into investments that do not fit your stated goals and level of risk tolerance. For example, a retired person concerned with the safety of a small nest egg should not be in high-risk securities. Even if that customer approves a high-risk purchase, the broker can be held liable.

Misrepresentation. Brokers cannot downplay the risk of an investment, conceal pertinent information, or give false information.

Excessive Commissions. The size of commissions and markup is regulated by the stock exchanges and the National Association of Securities Dealers.

If you want to find out if your broker has any history of disciplinary action, you can call the **National Association of Securities Dealers** (800-289-9999). Or, call the **North American Securities Administrators Association** (202-737-0900). This organization will give you a phone number to access the Central Registration Depository (CRD), which is run by the state divisions of securities regulation and the National Association of Securities Dealers. The CRD can tell you about a broker's employment history and any actions taken against the broker.

INSURANCE

Insurance Checkup

Insurance protects you against financial losses, whether you're insuring your health, your car, your home, your life, or your wage-earning capability. What insurance you buy and how much you buy depends on your individual needs and on how much you can afford. Basic information and consumer tips are listed below for the most common types of insurance.

Life

1. Do you need life insurance? Some people don't. If you are young and single (or older and single) with no dependents, you might choose to forgo life insurance. However, the picture changes if your death would cause a financial hardship for your spouse, children, parents—or anyone else you want to protect. Generally, married people with young children have the greatest need for life insurance.

2. How much life insurance do you need? This depends on a great number of factors including your age, how many dependents you have, your assets and debts, if you have a spouse who will continue to work, whether or not you need to figure in the cost of a college education. In short, how much money would it take to get your dependents to a point where they would be financially self-sufficient? In an effort to simplify the calculations, some financial advisors suggest that you multiply your annual income (by a multiple of anywhere from 5 to 8) in order to figure out how much life insurance you need. However, that simplistic approach often goes awry. Getting a more accurate number requires that you diligently look at all your current expenses and future debt and offset them with all expected income (including money from a life insurance policy you have at work, income from savings and investments, Social Security benefits, etc.). That will give you a much clearer idea of just how much insurance you need. Regardless of the numbers, don't commit more money than you can afford.

3. What kind of insurance should I buy? In general, there are two kinds: term insurance and cash-value insurance (which includes whole life, universal life, variable life). The debate over which kind is better is always intense.

Term insurance is the easiest to understand; it's called "plain vanilla" coverage. You buy pure protection against premature death. The policy covers you for a certain amount of time—such as one year, five years, 10 years. If you die within the "term," the policy pays off. At the end of the term, coverage ends, but you can continue it for another term if you have a "renewable" policy. The cost of the policy goes up as you get older. Since term policies are easy to understand, it's not difficult to comparison-shop and find a good buy. They are cheaper than cash-value policies, and for pure protection, you get the greatest immediate coverage per dollar. You cannot cash them in (no cash value) and you cannot borrow against them.

Cash-value insurance gives you protection against death for as long as you live and has a savings or investment feature in the policy. These policies have myriad names—whole life, universal life, variable life, to name just a few. In these policies a portion of your premium goes into a tax-deferred savings account which gives you "cash value." You earn interest on that money and can borrow against it. If you cancel the policy, you get the cash value (after surrender charges). These policies are often very complex, making it difficult to compare them. Premiums are four to nine times higher than initial premiums for comparable term policies (insurance agent commissions are higher, and you are funding a savings account). However, premiums generally don't rise after you purchase the policy (as you get older). If you like the forced savings aspect of cash-value policies, be sure you understand the kinds of returns you are likely to get (what are the returns based on? are they guaranteed?). Do you want to use an insurance policy as a savings/investment vehicle or do you have better investment options?

4. Regardless of what you buy, be sure that you understand all terms of your insurance agreement. If you buy term, it should be renewable automatically, regardless of your health. How often, and by how much, does your premium rise? Does your term policy have a convertible feature—meaning you can change it to a cash-value policy if you so desire—and what are the terms and cost of that conversion? If you buy a cash-value policy, you need to dissect every portion of the policy: fixed or flexible premium, cost, expected dividends, sales commissions, surrender value, etc. Computer-generated proposals for life insurance products are almost always mystifying. Sometimes they are downright deceptive.

5. Constantly reassess your life insurance needs. As you grow older, you may want to make changes in a policy, change policies, cancel policies, change insurance companies. When you reach retirement age, your needs may change dramatically—especially if those you are trying to protect no longer need financial protection.

Disability

1. Between the ages of 35 and 65, your chances of being unable to work for 90 days or more because of illness or injury are about three times greater than your chance of dying. Loss of a steady income can be devastating.

2. Whether you know it or not, you may already be covered by some disability insurance, some of which you may get for free. First of all, your employer may cover you. Second, if you are eligible, the Social Security system provides disability benefits, but the eligibility requirements are strict. Other potential sources of revenue are workers' compensation benefits, veteran's benefits, civil service disability pay, group union disability pay, etc. Among the programs, the amount of money paid, and the length of time benefits are paid, varies widely. Before you buy a disability insurance policy, you need to do some investigative work—and check out any insurance that you already have.

3. Disability insurance is expensive. Experts recommend that before you get an individual policy, you need to add up how much income would be coming into your household (from a spouse's income, investments, from disability insurance you already have, etc.) if you were to become disabled. If you can cover 60 to 70 percent of your income from other sources, you may not need to buy additional coverage.

4. When looking over a disability policy, here are the basic items to look for:

♦ Renewability. A "noncancelable" policy guarantees your right to renew for as long as the policy lasts; the insurance company cannot change the premiums or benefits. "Guaranteed renewable" means the policy will be renewed automatically, but the premium may increase. "Optionally renewable" or "conditionally renewable" means the insurance company can cancel you at each anniversary or premium-due date.

♦ Length of coverage. Policies may extend coverage for one year, two years, five years, to age 65, or for a lifetime. Most people don't need policies that extend beyond their working years.

♦ Size of benefits. Insurers will give you maximum coverage ranging from 40 to 80 percent of your income. Lower-income workers get the higher percentages; higher-paid workers get the lower percentages.

♦ Definition of disability. Some policies pay if you can't return to work in your customary occupation; others pay only if you are unable to engage in any kind of gainful employment. Be sure you understand the definition since policies can differ a great deal.

♦ Residual benefits. This coverage assures that you will receive partial disability payments if you return to work on a part-time basis, at reduced responsibilities and reduced income.

♦ When payments begin. Waiting periods can be anywhere from a month to six months, or longer.

♦ Extent of disability. Are you covered for partial disability or only if you are totally disabled?

♦ Accident and illness coverage. Some policies pay only for accidents; others will cover accidents and illness.

♦ Preexisting conditions. Before getting a policy, you must disclose all past and current medical conditions. Preexisting conditions may be covered at no additional cost. However, because of preexisting conditions, companies can refuse to insure you, insure you but not for a particular ailment, insure you but charge you a higher premium, or restrict the amount of your benefit.

5. People who are self-employed and work at home can have a difficult time getting disability policies. Insurers feel more comfortable dealing with people who show up at an office every day, collect a regular salary, etc. In addition, companies fear that dishonest customers would collect their disability payments and secretly continue to work at home. In order to get policies, the self-employed usually have to produce a lot of income documentation.

Homeowner's

1. Homeowner's policies provide you with two kinds of protection: *property* (covering your house and its contents) and *liability* (protection if someone is injured in your home or on your property). There are several kinds of policies, depending on how many different kinds of risks you want to insure against. For instance, a lower-cost "basic" policy can cover 10 or 11 risks, including fire, vandalism, and theft. A "broad" policy will add more risks like burst pipes and faulty electrical wiring. A "special" policy covers even more. And there are specially designed policies for renters, condominium owners, and owners of unique homes, like Victorian homes. However packaged, homeowner's policies do not provide protection against floods and earthquakes. If you want either, and if you can get it, you will need to buy a separate policy or get a rider to your homeowner's policy.

2. How much insurance you need depends on what you stand to lose. According to insurance experts, the home itself should be insured for at least 80 percent of its replacement value—not what you paid for it or its resale value—but what it would cost to rebuild it. To get this figure, consult a builder, appraiser, or realtor. To get a value on your personal belongings, you'll have to do an inventory of all the contents of your home. Your inventory (plus important receipts, photos of your major items) should be kept in a safe place outside of the home, like a bank safe-deposit box. As for liability coverage: most basic policies include at least $100,000 of coverage; many homeowners pay an additional fee to up the coverage.

3. When making claims for personal property, homeowners are sometimes dismayed to learn that they are paid the depreciated value of an item, not its replacement cost (your damaged five-year-old $800 sofa may get you only $400). You can get replacement-cost coverage but it will

cost extra. You can offset the extra cost, however, by taking a higher deductible.

4. Most policies offer very limited, or no, coverage for costly items like furs, antiques, stamp and coin collections, jewelry, rare books, etc. To insure such valuables, you'll need a special addition to your policy or a special policy called a *floater*.

5. When talking with an insurance agent, ask about special discounts for smoke alarms, security systems, deadbolt locks, fire extinguishers. Also, you might get a discount if you are a nonsmoker, if you are over 65, or if you are retired. And ask for price quotes for different deductible levels.

Health

1. The two basic kinds of health care plans are "fee-for-service" and "managed care." With *fee-for-service* plans, the choice of doctors and other medical providers is up to you. Your plan has a deductible, and after the deductible is paid up, coinsurance provisions of the policy take over (e.g., you pay 20 percent of the bill; the insurer pays 80 percent of the bill). In fee-for-service plans, an insurance company can refuse to pay for part of a bill if the fee does not conform to what the company deems "reasonable and customary." With *managed care* plans, a group of medical providers—doctors, hospitals, lab facilities—join together to provide total health care. You agree to go to the group's doctor and any care you seek outside of the network is at your own expense. An HMO (health maintenance organization) is the most familiar kind of managed health care plan. With HMOs there are no deductibles, no coinsurance conditions, and no need to be concerned with "reasonable and customary" charges. However, some health care plans are hybrids of fee-for-service and managed care—meaning that they contain elements of both. (See "Choosing Health Insurance," page 78.)

2. When evaluating a health care plan, you need to understand exactly what the plan covers (hospitalization, doctors' visits, lab tests, sur-

gery, prescription drugs, etc.) and what your financial obligations are. Also, is it important to you that you choose your own doctors? If so, managed care plans may not be for you. Regardless of the plan, do check out two key money factors: (1) lifetime benefits ceiling (ideally, you want a lifetime cap of $1 million, or unlimited lifetime coverage); (2) cap on your annual out-of-pocket expenses (the plan picks up 100 percent of costs after you pay out so much per year; the lower the cap, the better for you).

3. If you get health insurance as an employee benefit and you leave your job—you quit, get fired, or are laid off—there is a federal law that will temporarily help you keep your old health plan until you are protected by a new one. Called COBRA (Consolidated Omnibus Budget Reconciliation Act of 1985), the law applies to companies with 20 or more employees. Under the law, you can continue coverage for yourself and your dependents for up to 18 months. You must pay the entire premium, up to 102 percent of the cost of the coverage. At the end of 18 months, you can usually convert your group insurance to an individual policy with the same company, but in most cases you will pay considerably more and get less coverage. However, if you or a family member has a chronic medical condition that might cause a new insurance company to reject you, you might consider a conversion policy with your old company—usually medical exams aren't required when you convert from a group policy to an individual policy.

4. If you are having a difficult time getting an individual policy because of a preexisting medical condition, you might be able to get coverage through a state-run insurance pool. Approximately 27 states have these pools for people who have been turned down by insurance companies and are too young to qualify for Medicare. Both premiums and deductibles can be high but at least you would be protected from catastrophic health costs. To find out if your state has a risk pool, ask an insurance agent or broker, or call your state insurance department.

Car

1. An auto insurance policy can have six basic kinds of coverage: liability for bodily injury; liability for property damage; medical payments insurance; uninsured motorists protection; collision insurance; and comprehensive physical damage insurance. These basic definitions alter somewhat if you live in a state that has "no-fault" auto insurance laws. Some kinds of coverage may be required by state law, depending on where you live. Most states require you to carry a minimum amount of liability coverage, while coverage for damage to your car (collision) is optional.

2. How much you pay for car insurance depends on a wide range of factors including your age, sex, marital status, location, and driving record. Also pertinent are the car's age and value, and the frequency of car use. And if you have teenage drivers in your household, be prepared to pay a lot.

3. There are numerous ways to reduce the cost of auto insurance:

♦ Shop around. Prices vary enormously—as much as 50 percent—for the same coverage. Since insurers don't advertise prices, you'll have to make a lot of phone calls. But you stand to save hundreds of dollars.

♦ Choose the highest deductible you can afford. Higher deductibles on collision and comprehensive (fire and theft) can lower your costs substantially.

♦ Consider dropping collision and/or comprehensive coverage on older cars. Your insurer will not pay a repair or loss claim that exceeds the depreciated value of the car. A car dealer or bank can tell you the resale value of your car.

♦ Ask about discounts. An insurer may offer discounts for nonsmokers or nondrinkers, senior citizens, graduates of driver-education programs, students with good grades. There can be discounts for accident-free driving records, cars with low annual mileage, cars with anti-theft devices or automatic seatbelts or airbags or anti-lock brakes. Also, you may be entitled to a cost reduction if you insure more than one car with a company.

♦ Buy a low-profile car. Before purchasing a new or used car, call your insurance agent. Cars that are more likely to be stolen or cost more to repair will cost more to insure.

Help for Consumers

Listed below are two groups that can help you find your way through the complex world of insurance.

The National Insurance Consumer Organization (NICO). NICO is the first national organization established to promote the interests of insurance buyers. A nonprofit public interest group, it offers advice to help consumers buy insurance wisely and works for more equitable insurance laws and policies. If you join NICO (membership is $30 a year), you get a consultation phone call about your personal insurance needs, a bimonthly newsletter, and the book *Taking the Bite Out of Insurance: How to Save Money on Life Insurance.* You also get discounted rates on custom services like having an insurance policy evaluated. Nonmembers can also have policies evaluated for a modest fee and can buy NICO publications. Consumer advocate Ralph Nader serves as an informal advisor to NICO. Contact: National Insurance Consumer Organization, PO Box 15492, Alexandria, VA 22309 (703-549-8050).

National Insurance Consumer Helpline (NICH). NICH is a toll-free consumer information telephone service sponsored by insurance industry trade associations. The associations represent all segments of insurance, including life, health, and home and auto (property-casualty) insurance companies. Trained personnel and licensed agents are available to answer questions about a wide range of insurance matters, are able to refer consumer complaints to appropriate sources, and will send consumer brochures upon request. The helpline (800-942-4242) operates from 8:00 AM to 8:00 PM, EST, Monday through Friday.

UMBRELLA INSURANCE POLICY

If you have a lot of assets to protect, you may not feel totally secure with the protection limits of your homeowner's and automobile insurance policies. For about $200 a year (or more) you can buy a $1 million umbrella liability policy that kicks in after your homeowner's or auto liability insurance runs out. Usually, in order to qualify, you already have to have $300,000 worth of liability on your homeowner's and auto policies. The umbrella coverage typically will protect you against claims of damage or personal injury and may cover such things as invasion of privacy, false arrest, and some forms of libel. For full details on eligibility, cost, and coverage, contact your insurance agent.

How Safe Is Your Insurance Company?

You spend a considerable amount of your money to buy insurance—to be safe. But unlike your bank account which is insured for up to $100,000 by the federal government, there is no federal government protection for insurance companies. So just how safe is the insurance policy you are about to buy or the one you already own?

There are five rating services that routinely issue safety ratings (the ability to pay claims) for insurance companies: A.M. Best (900-555-2378; $2.95 per call plus surcharges); Duff & Phelps (312-629-3833); Moody's (212-553-0377); Standard & Poor's (212-208-1527); Weiss Research (800-289-9222). The toughest "graders" are Moody's and Weiss Research. Each company has a different set of letter grades. For example, the highest rating given at Standard & Poor's is AAA while the highest rating given by Weiss Research is A+ (see chart below). The rating companies will give you an insurance company's grade over

the phone or send you a report; some provide the service for free, some charge a fee. To get a company's rating you can also go to your local library since they have up-to-date reports from all the major rating services. When buying a new policy, don't rely on the rating of just one service. Check out at least two; better yet, check them all.

There's another way to check on an insurance company. Call your state insurance department to learn if the company is licensed and if it contributes to a state guarantee fund that protects consumers if the insurer fails. You might also ask if there have been many complaints against the company.

If you are considering a new insurance company but aren't satisfied after your background check, simply look for another company. But what if you already have a policy and your carrier seems weak, or headed for a fall? Canceling out the policy might seem an obvious decision but it could be quite costly, especially with cash-value life insurance. Surrender fees can be outrageous. Also, before canceling, consider how insurable you are—how easy would it be to replace that policy? Unless your carrier is in severe trouble, switching companies may not be a good idea.

Now comes some surprising news. You've done your homework and have your policies with companies that have the highest safety ratings. What you probably don't know is that even if your insurance company isn't going out of business, or isn't in financial jeopardy, it can transfer your policy to another insurance company—without your permission. If such a transfer happens, you might get an equally good, or even better, company. However, you might land up with a weaker company. Should you get a transfer notice, first check out the rating of the new company. If you don't want the transfer, write to your company and tell them so; also write to your state insurance commission. Consumer advocates insist that policyholders have a right to resist policy transfers but many state laws are fuzzy on the issue. Nonetheless, if you really don't want to switch, kick up a fuss.

Understanding the Grades

In order to understand the safety rating given to an insurance company, you need to know the scoring systems used by the rating companies. The grades listed below are from highest to lowest.

SAFETY RATINGS OF INSURANCE COMPANIES

A.M. Best	Duff & Phelps	Moody's	Standard & Poor's	Weiss
A++	AAA	Aaa	AAA	A+
A+	AA+	Aa1	AA+	A
A	AA	Aa2	AA	A-
A-	AA-	Aa3	AA-	B+
B++	A+	A1	A+	B
B+	A	A2	A	B-
B	A-	A3	A-	C+
B-	BBB+	Baa1	BBB+	C
C++	BBB	Baa2	BBB	C-
C+	BBB-	Baa3	BBB-	D+
C	BB+	Ba1	BB+	D
C-	BB	Ba2	BB	D-
D	BB-	Ba3	BB-	E+
E	B+	B1	B+	E
F	B	B2	B	E-
	B-	B3	B-	F
	CCC	Caa	CCC	
		Ca		

Medicare

Medicare is a federal health insurance program for people 65 or older. It has two separate parts: Part A (hospital insurance) and Part B (medical insurance). You do not have to pay a monthly premium for Part A if you or your spouse are entitled to benefits under the Social Security or Railroad Retirement systems or have worked a sufficient period of time in federal, state, or local government employment to be insured. If you do not meet the qualifications for premium-free Part A benefits, you can purchase the coverage if you are at least 65 and meet certain requirements. Part B is optional (you pay for it) and is offered to all beneficiaries when they become entitled to Part A. It may also be purchased by most persons age 65 or over who do not qualify for premium-free Part A coverage. In addition, certain disabled people under the age of 65 can become part of Medicare as can people of any age with permanent kidney failure.

Part A helps to pay for inpatient hospital care, skilled nursing facility care, home health care, hospice care, psychiatric hospital care. Part B helps to pay for physician services, outpatient hospital services, X rays and laboratory tests, some medical equipment, physical and occupational therapy, and other costs. You are automatically enrolled in Part B when you become entitled to Part A, unless you state that you don't want it. If you receive a Social Security check, you can elect to have your Part B premium deducted from your check.

Some people delay enrollment in Part B if they continue to work and have medical insurance through an employer insurance plan or are covered under a spouse's employment insurance plan. When that coverage stops, you have a special seven-month enrollment period for Part B, beginning with the month you stop work or are no longer covered under an employer plan, whichever comes first. According to Medicare officials, Part B is a good buy since the federal government pays approximately 75 percent of the program's cost.

Even if you have both Parts A and B, there are some things Medicare doesn't pay for at all and there are limits on the services it does cover. First of all, for the services that are covered, there are deductibles and copayments that you must be responsible for. In addition, Medicare has a price list (an approved-amounts schedule) for physician services. If your doctor "accepts assignment," meaning he or she agrees to the fee that Medicare deems acceptable, then you split the bill 80 percent (Medicare pays), 20 percent (you pay)—assuming you have already paid the deductible for your Part B insurance. If your doctor does not accept assignment, you are stuck with the extra part of the bill. However, even if your doctor does *not* accept assignment, there is a limit on how much the doctor can charge—15 percent above the approved Medicare fee. For example: your doctor, who does not accept assignment, charges you $200 for a service that Medicare says should cost $100; the doctor is in error since the most that can legally be charged is $115. Also, Medicare only pays for "appropriate" treatment that is "medically necessary." If a doctor tries to keep you in a hospital for more days than Medicare thinks is appropriate for your illness, then you may be stuck with a bill you didn't count on.

There are a number of things that are totally excluded from Medicare: routine physical examinations, custodial care in nursing homes, most prescription drugs, routine eye exams and eyeglasses, dental care and dentures, routine foot care, treatment while traveling outside the United States, hearing exams and hearing aids, etc.

Because there are so many gaps in Medicare coverage, insurance companies have come up with what are called "Medigap" policies. These plans can cover everything from deductibles and coinsurance payments to prescription drugs, excess doctor charges, preventive screening, foreign travel emergencies, etc. Obviously, the more benefits that are included in a Medigap policy, the higher the premiums.

Until recently, trying to compare Medigap policies was impossible; the insurance companies mixed and matched the components into a dazzling array of options and there was no uniformity among carriers. Thus, consumers were unable to comparison-shop. But the federal government stepped in and forced the insurance industry to come up with standardized packages (there are now 10 of them); not all 10 have to be offered by an insurance company. Now you can put one company's Plan A up against another company's Plan A and compare premiums for the same package of benefits.

Despite the streamlining of Medigap policies, consumers need to understand fully just what benefits they get or don't get under Medicare as well as what benefits they need or don't need in a Medigap policy. Fortunately, there are two good sources for information on Medicare and Medigap policies. First is *The Medicare Handbook*, which is free from your local Social Security Administration office or by writing: **Medicare Publications,** Health Care Financing Administration, 6325 Security Blvd., Baltimore, MD 21207. Also, the United Seniors Health Cooperative puts out a variety of excellent publications (some free; some for a fee). Write to: **United Seniors Health Cooperative,** 1331 H Street NW, Suite 500, Washington, DC 20005.

Living Benefits for the Terminally Ill

It's possible for terminally ill patients to collect a portion of their life insurance benefits before they die. The option, variously called a "living needs benefit" or "accelerated death benefit," allows the insured to get cash benefits in order to cover living expenses, pay medical bills, etc. There are two ways to obtain this option: (1) from your life insurance company if it offers the plan; (2) from a viatical settlement company (a company whose sole purpose is to buy your policy, then give you a discounted cash value once the company is named as beneficiary).

First you need to find out if your insurance company will add a no-cost living-benefits rider to your existing policy or if it adds such riders to new policies only. If a no-cost rider can immediately be added to an existing policy, find out exactly what conditions apply. For instance, most insurance companies will add a rider to cash-value life insurance policies (like whole life) but not to term policies. Most companies require that you submit a doctor's statement that death is likely to occur within six months or a year. And, of course, you need to find out what the payout is—some are as high as 90 percent of the policy's face value.

If you sell your policy to a viatical settlement company, the rules are less stringent, but the money you get is generally 30 to 40 percent less than you would get from an insurance company. In general, these settlement companies, however, will buy term and group policies in addition to cash-value policies. But they also have stipulations that must be met, including: the policy must be A-rated or better; the policy must allow for a change in beneficiary and the beneficiary must sign over the rights; a statement must be produced stating that the insured was of sound mental capacity when selling the policy, etc.

Financial experts generally agree that there is a better way to get cash money from your life insurance policy: get a loan from a family member or friend and designate that person as your life insurance beneficiary. If that is not an option for you or your loved one, then you can investigate the living-benefits option. To find out which life insurance companies provide accelerated options, call the **National Insurance Consumer Helpline** (800-942-4242). For a list of viatical settlement companies, call **Affording Care** (212-371-4140 or 212-371-4741).

Medical Information Bureau

You've probably never heard of the Medical Information Bureau (MIB)—but it may know about you. The MIB is a consortium of 750 life, health, disability, and automobile insurers in the United States and Canada. Acting as a policeman for the insurance companies, it has both medical and nonmedical information on about 12 million people. The MIB's main mission is to catch people who give fraudulent information when applying for insurance policies. For example, if you had a heart attack that was covered by Insurance Company A and you are applying for a policy with Insurance Company B (and neglect to mention the heart attack), Insurance Company B is likely to find out that you conned it when they check your medical records through the MIB.

How does the MIB get all this medical information on you? Every time you walk into the medical system—a doctor's office visit, a stay in the hospital, lab tests, prescriptions filled at a drugstore—you leave behind a paper trail. Also, do you remember signing the section on your insurance company claim form that authorized your insurance company to seek out any information it needs to validate your claim? Then, too, if you have ever applied for an individual policy (health, life, or disability), you gave the company the right to get your medical records from any doctors you ever visited, as well as from other companies that previously insured you.

All in all, the MIB collects information from medical providers as well as insurance companies, puts it on computer, and can generate a report on your medical life. From a medical standpoint, the MIB can know about: specific illnesses, X rays and lab tests and prescribed drugs, alcohol or drug addiction/rehabilitation, family medical history, suicide attempts—anything that may make you a bad insurance risk. And it also has information on nonmedical situations like a bad driving record, counseling for marital problems, participation in hazardous sports.

When you apply for new insurance coverage, there is mention of the MIB on the application form. When you sign the form, you authorize the insurance company to get information from MIB, as well as from other entities that have knowledge of your medical history. If a request is made to MIB by the insurance company, MIB will send out a short, coded report which the insurance

company will compare with the information you have provided. If the two don't match up, the insurance company will conduct a further investigation.

According to a consumer brochure published by the MIB, "MIB is a reasonable balance between an individual's right to privacy and an insurer's need for protection against fraud or omission." The following points are also made in the brochure:

1. MIB does not have a report on most individuals who apply for insurance. Of 10 applicants, MIB will have a record on only one or two. Also, any reports more than seven years old are eliminated automatically by computer edit.

2. If, and only if, an applicant has a condition significant to health or longevity, then authorized personnel at member companies are required to send a brief, coded report to MIB.

3. MIB reports are not used as the basis for an underwriting decision. Underwriting decisions are based on information from applicants and from medical professionals, hospitals, labs, or other facilities.

If there is any incorrect information in the MIB's file on you, you should get it corrected. To obtain a free copy of your report, contact: **Medical Information Bureau,** PO Box 105, Essex Station, Boston, MA 02112 (617-426-3660). You will receive a one-page form to fill out and return. When you get the report, if there are any mistakes, you can ask to have them corrected. Usually, errors are fixed within 30 days.

Insurance Policies You Probably Don't Need

Credit-life insurance. Offered by lenders, this kind of insurance will pay off various loans—car loans, personal loans, credit card loans, installment loans—if you die. The lender is the beneficiary. Sometimes unemployment and disability features are added to entice buyers. But the premiums are costly (sales commissions are high) and often the policy's terms are very restrictive. Usually it's better to buy more life and disability insurance from your insurance agent. However, if you are medically uninsurable, you might consider credit-life insurance.

Mortgage life insurance. It seems downright irresistible. You die and your house is paid off; your beneficiaries don't have to worry about paying off the home loan. However, the cost, and it's not cheap, is usually added to your loan, thus increasing your monthly payment. Also, your survivors must use the proceeds to pay off the loan; perhaps they would rather use insurance money to pay off a more pressing (or costly) loan, but they can't because the insurance can be used only on the mortgage. If you are worried about dying and leaving mortgage payments behind, it's usually better to buy more term life insurance as protection, unless (as mentioned above in the comments on credit-life insurance), you are uninsurable. However, you might be forced to take mortgage life insurance from a lender if you make only a small downpayment on a home, usually less than 20 percent.

Disease-specific health insurance. Rather than insuring against a specific disease, like cancer, it's better to get a good comprehensive health insurance policy.

Life insurance for children. The basic intent of life insurance is to protect against the premature death of wage earners—kids don't fit into that equation.

Accidental-death insurance. Less than 5 percent of all deaths are from accidents. A good life insurance policy is a better buy; it covers death from illness or accidents.

Credit card insurance/hotline registration. With this coverage, you need to call only one hotline phone number if your credit cards are stolen. The insurance issuer will then notify all of your card issuers of the theft. Yes, it may be convenient, but according to federal law, you are liable only for the first $50 of unauthorized purchases on each card (and liable for nothing if you report the theft before a card is used fraudulently).

Contact lens insurance. The cost per year (especially if there is a deductible) may cost more than the cost of a single lens replacement. Unless you frequently lose or abuse lenses, this is probably a bad buy.

INCOME TAXES

Selecting a Tax Preparer

If your tax return is fairly simple, you can probably do it yourself. Or, if you need assistance in only a few areas, you can call the **IRS** toll-free number (800-829-1040) to get your questions answered. Also, every year thousands of tax-trained volunteers, sponsored by the IRS, give free counseling, primarily to the elderly and low-income individuals. It's quite likely that several months before April 15, a tax counseling center will spring up in your local senior citizen center, bank, or library. Call your local IRS office to find out about free counseling services in your area.

When you need help preparing your tax returns, you have a range of professionals to turn to. First are the tax chains like H & R Block and Jackson Hewitt. Depending on the number of forms that need to be filled out, the cost can range from $50 to $100 to prepare uncomplicated federal and state returns. Both of the above-mentioned chains have training courses for their preparers and hire additional employees during tax season. However, there are also lots of mom-and-pop storefront operations that churn out returns every year. The degree of employee training and expertise varies widely among the mom-and-pops.

Filers with more complex financial situations may want to consider using the services of an "enrolled agent." There are about 30,000 of them across the U.S. and about 7500 of them belong to the **National Association of Enrolled Agents** (NAEA). These preparers have passed rigorous tax exams and those belonging to the NAEA are required to take 30 hours of refresher courses every year; many enrolled agents are former employees of the IRS. Costs range from about $75 to $250. If you want the name of a local NAEA member, call the association's toll-free number: 800-424-4339.

Moving up the scale in cost, we come to CPAs (certified public accountants) and tax attorneys. For the most part, they work for high-income individuals or for corporations. To enlist the services of a CPA, you might pay by the hour ($50–$250 an hour) or a flat fee that ranges from $250 to $1500. At the top of the heap are tax attorneys whose fees can top $250 an hour.

When choosing a tax preparer you need to get a few things understood up front. Ask: Are you available only at tax time or all year long? What will you charge to handle my taxes? What is your professional background and training? Beware of preparers who try to sell you anything other than tax services (some sell investments for which they earn commissions). Finally, if you get audited by the IRS, can—and will—the tax preparer represent you? The IRS allows only certain professionals to represent clients in audits (e.g., enrolled agents and CPAs generally are allowed; part-time tax preparers generally are not allowed).

A good tax preparer, whom you can rely on year after year, can amount to more than a seasonal friend. Assuming your pro is a qualified veteran, you should be able to call the preparer whenever you are making major financial decisions that affect your tax standing, like buying a home, getting a divorce, making complicated investments, taking money out of tax-deferred retirement plans, or making cash gifts to your children.

Ten Common Tax Mistakes

1. Failing to sign the tax return.
2. Using the wrong tax tables to figure taxes owed.
3. Making basic math errors, especially in the income section of the tax form and on the bottom line where you find out if you owe money or are due a refund.
4. Believing that getting a tax extension means you have more time to pay taxes (all you are getting is more time to file a return).
5. Incorrectly calculating medical and dental expenses. The deduction allowed is based on your adjusted gross income (AGI).
6. Claiming a deduction for an Individual Retirement Account (IRA) when your circumstances won't allow for the deduction.
7. Not claiming "credits" you are entitled to (carefully read the credit sections in your tax booklet).
8. Miscalculating the interest deductions on refinanced home mortgages.
9. Making calculation errors in figuring out how much tax is owed on unemployment insurance.
10. Not including a Social Security number for children over the age of one whom you claim as dependents.

What Triggers an Audit of Your Tax Return?

When you send your completed tax form to the Internal Revenue Service (IRS), it gets "scored" by a computerized process called DIF (Discriminate Income Function). This program knows what expenses and deductions are usual, and unusual, for the average person in your set of financial circumstances. Unusual expenses and deductions send up a red flag, meaning the program sends out an "audit trigger." The higher your DIF score, the greater likelihood that your return will be audited.

The scoring process for DIF is a highly guarded secret, but the items that most often trigger an audit are common knowledge. Here are some of the triggers to be aware of:

Unusually high itemized deductions. This includes medical and dental expenses; deductions for property taxes and home mortgage interest; state and local income taxes; charitable contributions; job expenses, etc.

Overstated casualty losses. Whatever the calamity that hit you (say your house fell victim to a hurricane), you should file away all the paperwork, like insurance records and appraisals. Also, be sure that what you are claiming as a casualty fits the IRS's definition of a casualty.

Home-office deductions. The IRS has always questioned these deductions, but it got tougher in 1993 when it won a Supreme Court case that further tightened the rules. Now, you can only claim write-offs like home depreciation, utilities, and insurance if your home office is your "most important" place of business or is one where you meet regularly with clients. The court ruling, however, spared the tax breaks allowed for business equipment purchased for home-office use.

Self-employment income. This has always been a hot button for the IRS. To be a legitimate, for-profit entity, your business is supposed to make a profit in three out of five years. Too many taxpayers, says the IRS, claim businesses that they aren't too serious about or businesses that in reality are just hobbies. The reason: to write off lots of wonderful expenses and deductions on Schedule C (Profit or Loss from Business).

Business travel and entertainment deductions. The IRS thinks most of us are making these up or greatly exaggerating them. If you claim them, keep very good records.

Fake dependents. IRS officials will blink more than a few times if your return says you are claiming 10 dependents on a $20,000 income. The current 1040 form asks that you list the age or Social Security number of every dependent you claim.

Nonqualifying IRA deductions. The rules have changed; currently not everyone is entitled to a full or partial deduction for an Individual Retirement Account (see "Retirement Plans," page 442). However, many people aren't aware of the new limitations or don't fully understand them.

Reporting mistakes. Your employer, bank, brokerage house, etc., gives financial information to the IRS. If your numbers don't match their numbers, you could be in for some questioning.

Failure to pay self-employment tax. Self-employed persons oftentimes remember to include all of their deductions but neglect to pay taxes owed for Social Security and Medicare. The taxes are stiff for the self-employed (at least 15.3 percent in 1993), but if you don't pay them, the computer will find the omission.

Early pension withdrawals. If you prematurely take money out of a pension plan, IRA, or other tax-deferred retirement investment, you owe taxes on the money plus a 10 percent penalty. Withdrawals from these kinds of accounts are reported to the IRS. If you fail to report them on your tax return, you are very likely to get caught.

Surviving an Audit

The letter in your mail has the return address of an IRS office. Your heart begins to beat faster and your palms get sweaty. The IRS is after you—what did you do wrong? Maybe nothing, since an audit notice from the IRS means that you are being questioned about a tax return, not that the IRS knows you are guilty of some wrongdoing. There are three kinds of audits: correspondence, office, and field.

A *correspondence audit* means that you can handle the matter by mail. If you receive such a notice, don't automatically assume the IRS is right and reach for your checkbook. Review the notice line by line to make sure you understand the nature of the item in question and how the IRS arrived at its numbers. Once you've figured everything out, if the IRS is correct, you can simply send in a check. However, if there are penalties assessed, you might want to write a letter and try to get the penalties waived, if you have a reasonable excuse for going astray. If the IRS is wrong, write a short letter explaining your side of the story and enclose copies of any documents that support your case. Answer notices promptly and send your letter by certified mail with a return receipt requested.

You're not likely ever to be the subject of a *field audit*. It happens when the audit is so extensive that a field agent comes to your home or place of business in order to pore over your records; it's just simpler for the IRS to come to the records than for the taxpayer to haul boxes and boxes of documents into an IRS office.

The more common "in person" audit is an *office audit*. You get a written notice in the mail that the IRS is questioning something on your return; it wants you to show up, with all the pertinent records, at a local IRS office to discuss the disputed item or items, usually no more than two or three areas (like charitable contributions, business expenses, etc.). Usually you have at least a few weeks to prepare for the audit and if the appointed time is inconvenient, or you need extra time, you can call the IRS and have the appointment rescheduled. Most audits are resolved in one meeting that lasts a few hours at the most.

You can take a tax professional with you to the

audit if your situation is complicated or if you don't trust yourself to handle matters in your own best interests. In actuality, you don't even have to show up if you send a qualified representative with written authorization from you to act on your behalf. Most people, however, do attend the audit and some choose to go it alone. If you attend (with or without a tax expert), here are some tips to help you along:

♦ Be prepared. Gather all important documents and organize them. Review them carefully so you can discuss your records with some degree of familiarity. However, take nothing with you that doesn't specifically address the disputed items. Calling attention to other aspects of your return could prompt an auditor to expand the audit.

♦ Be professional. Answer all questions in a calm, cooperative manner. Avoid taking an argumentative stance. On the other hand, don't get chatty and volunteer all kinds of extra information. Small talk can get you into trouble. Go on and on about your great summer vacation in the year in question and the auditor might decide to look at your travel and entertainment deductions. Also, be aware that you could set traps for yourself. For example, an auditor tells you that a certain deduction is not allowable and you reply that it was allowed on two other previously filed tax returns. That defense could prompt a look at the other two returns and put you in deeper trouble.

♦ Be your own best advocate. Don't give in to pressure just to resolve a situation. IRS agents aren't always right and there is usually room for compromise on any, or all, of the disputed items. If you get a disagreeable or unreasonable agent, you can always ask to see the agent's supervisor.

♦ Be truthful. It's a crime to lie to an IRS official.

Assume the office audit is almost over and the auditor is tallying up the final figures. In the great majority of cases, the taxpayer owes money. If you and the IRS agent are in agreement, you sign a form saying so. You can usually pay the amount owed at that time or wait for a subsequent statement that will tell you what you owe, including any interest or penalty charges.

Suppose you are very unhappy with the outcome of the audit. Then you don't sign the agreement form. You will still receive the final report by mail, and at that time, you can decide if you want to pay up or fight on. If you have a strong case with good documentation, you may want to take your case to the IRS's appeals office; you have 30 days after receiving the audit report to file an appeal. If you lose in the appeals office, you can go on to the U.S. Tax Court. Obviously, if a large amount of money is involved and you believe in your case, you might decide to slug it out to the bitter end. However, before you get involved in any major battles, it's wise to seek out (if you haven't already done so) the advice of a tax expert.

YOUR ODDS OF GETTING AUDITED

Ever wonder what your chances are of getting audited? Here are some numbers from the IRS:

Type of Return	Amount of Income	Odds of Audit
1040A	Under $25,000	1 in 145
1040 (without Schedule C)	Under $25,000	1 in 156
	$25,000–$50,000	1 in 169
	$50,000–$100,000	1 in 99
	Over $100,000	1 in 20
1040 (with Schedule C)	Under $25,000	1 in 67
	$25,000–$100,000	1 in 50
	Over $100,000	1 in 25

Panic Situations

Whether you can't file your taxes on time, can't come up with the money, or haven't filed in the past and fear getting caught, the idea of Big Brother IRS punishing you can be cause for a panic attack.

You Need an Extension

This is one of the most misunderstood aspects of the IRS code. When you file Form 4868, "Application for Automatic Extension of Time to File U.S. Individual Income Tax Return," you are asking for an additional four months to file your completed 1040 tax return. It relates only to paperwork; it has nothing to do with getting an extension on paying any money you owe. Here's how it works: By April 15 you file the extension form. On it you estimate your total tax liability for the tax year, how much tax has already been withheld or paid, and if there is a balance due. If you expect to owe money, you must send in a check, along with the extension form, for the amount you owe the IRS.

When you file Form 4868, your request is granted automatically. The IRS doesn't care if you need extra time because you lost some records, or because you're going on a long vacation. As long as you send them any money owed, you're in fine shape.

However, it is imperative that by April 15 you file either your completed 1040 or file for an extension. If you do neither and just file late, you could be in for some major interest and penalty charges.

What happens if you file for an extension but can't meet the new filing date of August 15? It is possible to get a second extension (Form 2688) but this one is not granted automatically. Your reason for needing even more time has to be a compelling one—like a death in the family or your house burned down and all your tax records were destroyed. If the IRS grants your second extension request, you get two more months before your tax forms are due.

You Can't Pay Your Tax Bill

In an effort to be looked upon as a kinder, gentler tax collector, the IRS has come up with an "installment" plan for Americans who can't pay their tax bill. When you file your tax return, you also send in Form 9465 (Installment Agreement Request), a request to pay part, or all, of your debt in monthly installments. You tell the IRS how much you want to pay per month (average payback time is 14 months). Within 30 days the IRS will tell you if it accepts your request. As good as this sounds, it can be financially painful. Taxpayers on the installment plan must pay interest, currently 7 percent, plus a late-payment penalty of 0.5 percent a month on any unpaid amounts. In other words, it's like having a credit card with the IRS. If you can get a lower-interest loan from another source, you might consider doing so. However, for many taxpayers this may be a very viable option.

You Are a Nonfiler

Perhaps you once paid taxes but dropped out of the system. Perhaps you earn money but never filed a federal tax return. Nonetheless, you live in fear that the heavy hand of the government is one day going to come down on you (maybe it has already found you).

It's estimated that there are about 10 million individuals and businesses that fail to file returns. And that failure costs the government about $7 billion a year. In recent years the IRS has been concentrating on finding nonfilers and that's becoming increasingly easier since so much of our financial lives ends up on some computer.

Most people who drop out of the system do so because of a catastrophic event like the loss of a loved one, loss of a job, or a divorce. They eventually want to get back in but are afraid of what the IRS will do to them. If you are one of those people, you need to know that the IRS usually does not seek criminal penalties (even though it is against the law not to file a return). In addition, the IRS does want your money, so it has to be somewhat flexible.

To get back into the system, you can do one of two things: (1) call the IRS directly (800-829-1040), explain your situation, and work with an agent to reconstruct all the returns you have missed; (2) Work with a good tax preparer to figure out your best tax position before contacting the IRS.

In some cases the IRS will waive some, or all, of the tax penalties you may owe, if you have a legitimate reason for nonpayment. You will, however, have to pay interest charges on money you owe. If you owe money, but can't pay it all back at once, you can usually work out an installment plan. Just remember that the IRS is likely to be more tolerant, reasonable, and flexible with nonfilers who come forth voluntarily as opposed to those whom it catches.

Problems Resolution Office

Solving problems with the IRS—by mail, fax, or phone—can be an endless and frustrating experience. That's where the Problems Resolution Office (PRO) comes in. Every IRS district office and service center has a PRO. These offices will assist you *only* if you have already taken action through "normal channels," namely an IRS district office or service center. PROs generally have a good reputation for resolving problems in a timely manner and for "not passing the buck."

Here is a sampling of the types of problems a PRO can handle:

♦ Your tax refund is long overdue.

♦ You've paid the tax the IRS says you owe, but you keep getting bills.

♦ You have replied to an IRS notice but no one at the IRS seems to have paid attention because you keep getting repeats of the same notice.

♦ You've asked the IRS for help or information but get no reply.

♦ You are notified that the IRS is going to seize your bank account, but you have no idea why.

The Problems Resolution Office primarily attacks administrative problems. It is not set up to be a substitute department for tax audits or tax-audit appeals. To get the phone number of the PRO closest to you, contact your local IRS district office or service center. Or ask a tax preparer, who probably has a listing of PRO offices (the listing is available only to tax professionals).

BURSTING THE REFUND BALLOON

We know of more than just a few people who every year boast that not only did they not have to pay any additional taxes when sending in their tax returns, they also gleefully report that they got a refund—a nice big refund. Well, what these folks really accomplished was giving the federal government an interest-free loan. In other words, the government—rather than the filers—had use of the overpaid money.

If you knowingly overpay year after year because you worry about owing money at tax time, and the overpayment is relatively small, then you've bought peace of mind for a minimal price. But if you continually get large refund checks, you should reconsider your tactics. That extra money you are giving away interest-free could better be placed in an interest-bearing account or be used to pay off high-interest obligations, like revolving credit card balances. If you want to change this situation, you need to lower the amount of money withheld from your paycheck (if you are an employee) and/or lower the amounts you pay in estimated tax payments. The IRS requires that throughout the year you pay 90 percent of your tax bill through the combination of wage withholding and estimated tax payments.

How Long to Save Tax Records

Time frames for holding on to tax records can be three years, six years, or forever. In most cases the IRS has three years to audit your return. The clock starts ticking after the due date of a return (April 15 if you file on deadline; August 15 if you file with an extension). For example, your return for 1994 is filed on April 15, 1995, so the statute of limitations for an audit runs out on April 15 (or August 15), 1998.

However, in some cases the IRS has six years to come after you. This statute applies if the IRS thinks you failed to report income of more than 25 percent of the amount you did report. Unreported income isn't a big worry for most taxpayers because so much income, wage and nonwage earnings, is reported on W-2s and 1099s that find their way to you and to the government.

The last category, the "forever" category, is the one that scares most of us. It can be invoked if the IRS discovers that you didn't file a return or if it believes you filed a "fraudulent" return.

For the most part, fraud is defined as a pretty major offense. Simple math and negligence errors aren't considered fraud. Fraud is something you know is wrong, like claiming dependents who don't exist. Or claiming charitable contributions that are way overvalued or never happened.

What to throw out? What to keep? Three years after a particular return, you are probably safe in tossing out old credit card receipts, old car loan documents, etc. However, when cleaning out your tax files, be somewhat cautious. You might want to keep some summary records like W-2s, 1099s, some check registers, some investment statements.

There are some things you should *never* throw away. Anything that relates to *future* tax filings should be kept, including: paperwork on home buying, selling, refinancing, or home improvements; documentation that relates to your funding of retirement plans; bills of sale for stocks or bonds. As for saving old tax returns, some tax experts say to save them for at least six years; some suggest you keep them all, forever.

BUYING A HOUSE

How Much House (Meaning Mortgage) Can You Afford?

You want to buy a house. What can you afford? The old rule of thumb was easy: multiply your annual family income (before taxes) by 2 and that was your price range. Today, it's not that simple (actually it never was that simple). To figure out what you can afford, there are three basic factors to consider: the down payment (most lenders require between 10 and 20 percent); your ability to qualify for a mortgage; closing costs (they can range between 2 and 7 percent of your mortgage loan).

Whatever kind of lender (mortgage bank, commercial bank, savings-and-loan association, credit union, etc.), the institution is concerned primarily with your willingness and ability to repay the home loan. Basically, here is what the lender wants to see:

♦ that no more than 28 percent of your gross monthly income will be spent on housing (your mortgage principal and interest, taxes, insurance, etc.);

♦ that your total monthly recurring debt (your housing costs plus all your other personal debt—e.g., auto loan, credit cards) does not exceed 36 percent of your gross monthly income.

These numbers, however, are somewhat flexible, depending on your individual financial status.

Also, the limits may vary (go up) for states like California where housing costs are high.

Before granting you a loan, the lender will carefully check out your credit history, your assets, and the property you wish to buy (to be sure the home has adequate value). All lending institutions have their own formulas for determining just how big a mortgage they will give you. Even if you are not quite ready to buy a home, you might want to stop in at a lending institution and "prequalify" for a loan—you'll get some idea of where you stand. Also, if you are in the market for a house, you should delay making any major purchases (like a car, furniture, or appliances); on paper, your debt will be lower and your cash assets higher.

Selecting a Mortgage

Most homeowners choose between two types of mortgages: a fixed-rate mortgage or an adjustable-rate mortgage (ARM). Below is a discussion of both: what they are, pros and cons, what type of homeowner uses each. There are, however, a number of other mortgage options, including two-step mortgages, graduated-payment mortgages, renegotiable-rate mortgages, balloon mortgages. For most people, buying a home is the single

REAL ESTATE BROKERS

If you are buying a home, you need to be aware that 95 percent of real estate brokers, or agents, legally represent the *seller* of the home. That's because the seller pays the sales commission. Called "traditional agents," these brokers are legally required, in most parts of the country, to disclose their loyalty to the seller. However, many home buyers, even if informed of that fact, seem to forget it, because most brokers are very hardworking and go out of their way to help you find a home. It's not unusual for buyers and brokers to enjoy friendly, harmonious relationships.

Sharing too much financial information with the traditional broker could put you at a disadvantage when bargaining with the seller of a home. Remember that the agent's commission is based on the selling price of the home—the higher the price, the higher the commission. Spill the beans to the broker (the top price you are willing to pay for the home) and that crucial fact could find its way to the ear of the seller.

Some buyers enlist the services of a "buyer broker" or "buyer agent" who works solely for the buyer. According to several recent studies, buyer brokers typically negotiate lower selling prices than do traditional brokers. If you work with a buyer broker, you will have to pay a fee out of your own pocket—a flat fee or a certain percentage of the sales price. While that is an option, you shouldn't avoid working with traditional brokers. Just be aware of who is representing whom and reveal only as much financial information as is necessary.

most important purchase/investment they will ever make. So you should leave no stone unturned as you investigate which mortgage plan is best for you. There are numerous books, at bookstores or at your local library, that will give you complete, up-to-date information on all tions. Many will provide step-by-step worksheets to aid in your decision making. Here is the basic lowdown on the two most popular types of mortgages.

Fixed-Rate Mortgage

How it works: It's been around the longest and is the simplest to understand. You pay a fixed interest rate and your monthly payments remain the same for the entire term of the loan. The longest term is usually 30 years; many buyers prefer a 15-year or 20-year fixed loan.

Pros: Most of all, stability and predictability; you know exactly what your payment will be, regardless of what's happening to the economy.

Cons: If interest rates go down significantly from your fixed rate, you may get distraught (but you can always refinance—see article below). Also, since lenders want to protect themselves from increasing interest rates (if that happens, you made a good deal), they often impose tougher qualification standards and charge more up-front points for fixed-rate loans than for adjustable-rate mortgages. (A point is 1 percent of the amount of the mortgage loan. On a $100,000 mortgage, one point is $1000. How many points you pay depends on your lender; the money is paid up front.)

Who gets it: People who need to count on a nonchangeable payment; either they're on a fixed income, are nearing retirement, or can't cope, financially or psychologically, with the possibility that their mortgage payment could change.

Adjustable-Rate Mortgage (ARM)

How it works: Lending institutions invented ARMs to protect themselves against large fluctuations in interest rates. For instance, if you took out a fixed-rate mortgage at 8 percent, and five years later the interest rate was at 13 percent, then the lender is stuck with a bad deal. Thus, lenders developed adjustable-rate mortgages in which interest rates and monthly payments change at specified intervals over the term of the loan. The changing interest rates are linked to any number of established money indexes (like the one-year Treasury securities index or the Cost of Funds for Savings and Loans). To that index the lender will add a "margin" (extra percentage points) in order to calculate a new ARM interest rate. Typically, your payment can change every three months, every year, every three years—sometimes at intervals as long as five or seven years. The fact that your monthly payment will change does not necessarily mean bad news. However, currently there are more than 100 different variations of ARMs offered by lending institutions. They vary in complexity, so be sure you understand the variables before signing up for one.

Pros: If interest rates fall, your payments automatically go down without the hassle of refinancing your loan. The initial interest rate on an ARM is lower than the interest rate for a long-term, fixed-rate loan. Thus, payments on ARMs initially are less. It's easier to qualify for an ARM, and up-front costs and closing costs (points and fees) are lower than for a fixed-rate mortgage. In some cases you get an option to switch from an ARM to a fixed-rate loan (fees vary).

Cons: Interest rates can rise and you could be in for payment shock. However, ARMs normally include a limit (a "cap") on how much the interest rate can increase over a year as well as over the life of the loan.

Who gets it: Those who need lower monthly payments initially but can deal with higher payments when they come; those who have difficulty qualifying for a fixed-rate loan.

About Closing Costs

Remember points? A point is equal to 1 percent of the principal amount being borrowed. Depending on your loan, the lender may charge you one to three points, a one-time charge that you pay for the privilege of getting your loan. And there are other possible closing costs to cover such things as credit checks, appraisal, legal fees, title search and insurance, processing fees, recording fees. Typically, total closing costs range between 2 and 7 percent of your mortgage loan. On a $100,000 loan that would be somewhere between $2000 and $7000. Many first-time homeowners aren't prepared to pay these additional charges. The amounts charged vary from lender to lender so be sure to ask about them—and get a written estimate.

Refinancing a Mortgage

Refinancing your mortgage simply means that you trade in your old mortgage for a new one. When interest rates drop, homeowners, with both

---

ANNUAL PERCENTAGE RATE

The Consumer Credit Protection Act of 1968 requires lenders to disclose the annual percentage rate (APR) on their loans. It's a measure of the cost of credit and provides consumers with a basis for comparing loans, including mortgage loans. The APR for a traditional mortgage takes into account the interest rate charged plus points and other finance charges. Thus, the APR on your mortgage loan will usually be higher than the interest rate quoted to you by a lending institution—giving you a much better idea of the true cost of your loan.

Helpful as the APR is, it has some caveats. First of all, it isn't that much help when applied to adjustable-rate mortgages (ARMs), because the APR is good only until the rate changes on an adjustable-rate mortgage. Second, the APR for a home-equity loan is based on the periodic interest rate alone; it does not include points or other charges. Third, there can always be certain closing costs and hidden fees that don't get included in the APR. Nonetheless, knowing the annual percentage rate at least gets you started when you want to compare loans—so do ask about it.

fixed-rate mortgages and adjustable-rate mortgages (ARMs), rush to refinance. Sometimes they stick with the same kind of mortgage (fixed or ARM); sometimes they switch. For example, if interest rates drop significantly, an ARM holder who is skittish about fluctuating monthly payments might change to a fixed-rate mortgage in order to gain peace of mind by knowing exactly what the payments will be for the life of the new loan.

The traditional rule of thumb says that it makes sense to refinance if the new rate is two percentage points lower than your current rate. But that rule of thumb is subject to a number of other considerations. The most important is, How much can you potentially save? Let's assume you have a $200,000, 30-year fixed mortgage with an interest rate of 10.5 percent (your monthly payment is $1830). You find a new fixed-rate loan at 8.5 percent (your new monthly payment will be $1538). Thus, you will save $292 a month or $3500 a year. However, lending institutions charge refinancing costs for converting a loan (points, appraisal and legal fees—the types of charges you encountered with your original mortgage). Refinancing costs range from 2 to 6 percent.

Back to the example. Let's assume that your lender is on the low end of the percentage range and charges 2.1 percent to convert your $200,000 mortgage. Thus, it will cost you $4200 to switch your loan from an interest rate of 10.5 to 8.5. You are saving $292 a month to convert so if you divide that into the $4200 refinancing cost, it will take you 15 months to recoup your costs. Therein lies a very important factor in your decision to refinance. Will you remain in your home long enough to make your refinancing pay off? The two-percentage-points rule of thumb, however, is tossed aside when interest rates take a nose dive as they did in 1992 and 1993, when record numbers of Americans refinanced their homes. The old rule is based on the assumption that refinancing involves a lot of up-front costs that need to be offset by a new mortgage rate at least two percentage points below the old. The rapid decline of interest rates in 1992 and 1993

caused many lending institutions to compete for homeowner business by offering refinancing deals with low, or no, points and closing costs. Or, when up-front charges were involved, homeowners could add them into the loan amount instead of making an immediate payment—and still save money. Regardless of the status of interest rates when you consider refinancing, your basic goals are to lower your monthly mortgage payment and recoup refinancing costs (if you pay any) within a relatively short period of time.

Tax implications? A lower interest rate gives you less interest to deduct on your income tax, which could increase your tax bill and thus offset the savings you gain from refinancing. Also, the Internal Revenue Service (IRS) stipulates that points paid solely for refinancing your home mortgage must be deducted over the life of the loan—not in the year that you refinance (points paid on an original mortgage, however, can be deducted in a single year).

It's easier to understand the savings benefits of refinancing when dealing entirely with fixed-rate mortgages. Also, potential savings are not too difficult to determine if you are switching from an ARM to a fixed rate. However, the numbers get trickier if you want to switch from one ARM to another ARM. Both the old and the new ARM have interest rates and monthly payments that fluctuate, as well as limits on interest increases.

Home-Equity Loans

Borrowing money against the equity you have built up in your home—that's the basic premise of a home-equity loan. Actually, it's a variation of a second mortgage, but it has extra bells and whistles that make it alluring to homeowners. If used judiciously, it can be a financial asset. However, failure to repay the loan could result in the loss of your home.

A lending institution (savings-and-loan, bank, credit union, etc.) typically will lend you 75 percent of the fair market value of your home, minus your mortgage debt. For example, assume your home's appraisal is $100,000; 75 percent of that is $75,000. However, your mortgage debt is $40,000 which is subtracted from the $75,000. Thus, your potential credit line is $35,000.

Once your line of credit is approved, you can borrow up to your credit limit whenever you want money. Usually, you get special checks; in some cases, you may get a special credit card. There can be limitations on the line, such as a minimum amount for each withdrawal, or a limit on the amount of time over which you can borrow the money. You pay interest only on the money you actually take out of the account.

As with most loans, there are a number of ways of paying back the money. Usually, there is a fixed period of time in which you must repay the loan—say, 10 or 15 years; sometimes the payback time is indefinite. Some plans set minimum monthly payments that cover some of the principal and accrued interest. In other plans you pay interest payments only and nothing toward the principal. Regardless of payment arrangements—whether you pay a small, moderate, or large amount of the principal—when your loan term ends, you might have to pay the entire balance owed, all at once. If you can't come up with this "balloon" payment, you will need to seek out another loan to cover it. If you can't meet your financial obligations, you stand to lose your house.

There are several reasons why homeowners find home-equity loans attractive. First, the interest you pay is deductible on your income tax, unlike the interest you pay on credit cards, car loans, and other personal loans. Usually the interest rates charged are relatively low (compared with other types of credit) and your line of credit is relatively high.

How much will this loan cost you? The interest rate is your first consideration. Home-equity plans typically use variable interest rates rather than fixed rates. The variable rate is based on a public index (like the U.S. Treasury bill rate). Most lenders will add what's called a "margin" (extra percentage points) to the index value in order to calculate the interest rate. When talking to your lender about interest rates, ask what index the lender uses, how often the index changes, what the margin add-on is, and how high the index has risen in the past. Also, find out if the lender has a limit (a cap) on how high your interest rate can rise over the life of the loan. Some lenders may allow you to switch a variable rate to a fixed rate during the life of the plan.

Aside from interest rates, you also need to find out what other costs are involved, many of them similar to those you pay when you buy a home: application fee; property appraisal; closing costs like points (one point equals 1 percent of the credit limit); title search and legal services. In addition, there may be a yearly maintenance fee and/or a transaction charge every time you write a check against your credit line. Some lenders may waive a portion of the closing costs.

Many financial advisors agree that borrowing money against your house for college educations or home improvements (which add value to your home) can be both an intelligent credit choice and a tax advantage. However, Americans are notoriously better at spending than saving, and having a large sum of money available without a specific purpose can be a very dangerous temptation.

If you choose to take out a home-equity loan, most experts advise that you shop around for the best deal, that you borrow only what you need, that you read all the fine print in your loan agreement and understand every financial detail, that you not borrow for luxuries, and that you repay the debt as quickly as you can.

Finally, you might consider the old standard second mortgage as an alternative to the home-equity loan. It's easier to understand because you borrow a fixed amount of money and pay it back over a fixed term (and the interest is deductible on your income taxes). But you need to compare interest rates and all other fees and charges before choosing between the two alternatives.

A federal law, the Truth-in-Lending Act, requires lenders to disclose the important terms and costs of home-equity plans, including payment terms, variable-rate interest features, and all other fees and charges. Usually, you will get a brochure on these legal obligations when you get an application form. The Truth-in-Lending Act gives you three days from the day the account was opened to cancel the credit line. This right allows you to change your mind for any reason.

Hud Homes

The **Department of Housing and Urban Development** (HUD) is a federal government agency that was created to make homeowning easier and affordable for many Americans. HUD takes over properties that have been foreclosed by the FHA (Federal Housing Administration) and then puts them up for sale to the public. These HUD homes can be single-family houses, condominiums, town houses, or two- to four-unit properties, and they are located in many communities throughout the United States. It is important to note that HUD does not make mortgage loans directly to home buyers; home buyers need to secure their own loans through a bank, savings-and-loan, credit union, mortgage company, or one of the various national and government lenders.

According to HUD, there are some very appealing advantages to buying a HUD home. Among them:

♦ Many HUD homes require only a 3 percent down payment instead of the usual 10 or 20 percent down payment.

♦ HUD may pay closing costs charged by your mortgage company for providing your loan.

♦ HUD will pay your real estate broker's commission—up to the standard 6 percent of sales price.

♦ HUD homes are priced at fair market value.

HUD homes are sold through real estate brokers, so you need to find an agent who participates in HUD programs and has a listing of HUD homes in your area. Also, HUD homes are sold through a sealed-bid process, which isn't as complicated as it sounds; a broker will handle all the paperwork for you.

Typically, the largest buyers of HUD homes earn between $15,000 and $50,000 a year; the average price of a HUD home is $40,000. HUD homes are sold "as is," and they often require some fixing-up, which is the responsibility of the buyer. In other words, HUD makes no warranties on the homes it sells; it's up to the buyer to inspect the home fully before making an offer.

To find out about HUD properties in your area, contact a local realtor or contact HUD directly (800–767–4HUD). The department publishes a free booklet, "A Home of Your Own," which you can get by calling the department or by writing to: Consumer Information Center, 614X, Pueblo, CO 81009.

BUYING A CAR

Buying a New Car

Negotiating the price of a new car used to be a consumer nightmare filled with anxiety, confusion, and fast-talking salespeople. Much of the misery was due to the fact that the consumer didn't know what the difference was between the sticker price (or list price) of the car and the invoice price (what the dealer paid for the car). In other words, how much profit is built into the sticker price and how much room is there for negotiation? But now there are a number of sources for that information, and the negotiation process is much more manageable. However, there are still a number of facts you need to know, including some "bewares," before you can be certain that you get the best possible deal.

Do Pre-Deal Homework

Before you start talking price with any car dealer, it's best to narrow down your choice of cars to one or two models. Each model is sold in a choice of trim lines, like *DX* or *LX*, referring to different sets of standard options. You can read up on various cars in any number of auto magazines that rate cars according to driveability, safety, repair record, etc. It's fine to stop by auto dealerships and look at the cars, but steer away from money talk until you are ready to make an offer.

How much money can you afford to spend on a car? If you don't have a number in mind, you are putting yourself at a disadvantage and you can get in over your head. Also, be sure to check with your insurance agent to learn what the various cars will cost to insure.

Find Out the Dealer Invoice Price

You can't begin to bargain until you know what the dealer paid for the car—the dealer's wholesale price, or invoice price. Dealer costs for various cars appear in annual books on car buying or in special car-buying issues of consumer magazines. An excellent source of invoice information is available from *Consumer Reports* Auto Price Service which is affiliated with *Consumer Reports* magazine. For a fee, the service will send you a computer printout for any make, model, and trim line you specify. Each printout notes the list price and dealer cost for the basic car and all standard equipment. It also lists every available factory-installed option and options package along with their list prices and dealer cost.

Finally, the printout has a list of all current cash rebate offers, including the advertised rebates to consumers and those less-publicized ones from the factory to the dealer. Armed with all of these data, you will have a pretty good idea of what the dealer paid for the car you want. To get printouts, write to: ***Consumer Reports* Auto Price Ser-**

vice, Box 8005, Novi, MI 48376 (303-745-1700). The charge is $11 for one car, $20 for two cars, and $27 for three cars.

Figuring Out What to Offer

A dealer's profit margin is usually between 10 and 20 percent. You want to bargain up from the invoice price, not down from the sticker price. You may end up paying as little as $150 to $300 over invoice; you may get a good deal at $500 over invoice. Until you shop around, you won't have a good idea of what qualifies as a reasonable price. In some instances, you may really get lucky and purchase a car *below* invoice price. Selling below cost happens when dealers are offered cash incentives from manufacturers to sell certain models or fill certain sales quotas. When the cash incentives are really appealing, the dealer can sell you a car below cost and still come out ahead. Unfortunately, consumers are not aware of these incentives; if you were, you'd be in a great bargaining position.

Some consumer advocates suggest that buying a car at the end of the month, when dealers are trying to fill monthly sales quotas, might save you some money. It is important to note that some cars will always have less negotiating room, like hot sellers that are in short supply. Also, you'll get a better deal if you buy a car right off the lot as opposed to placing a special factory order. There simply isn't a surefire formula to determine what your first offer should be. It all depends on what car you want, what the supply-and-demand is for that car, and how competitive dealers are when you are shopping. Nonetheless, err first on the side of a lower offer. If you find out that your initial offer was out-of-line low, you can always bump it up. Bumping a price down from your first offer is not going to work.

Beware of Add-Ons

There can be a whole saddlebag of charges that you aren't aware of. First of all, there can be extras like rustproofing, undercoating, fabric finishes, floor mats, and paint sealants. In some

cases, you may find charges for ADM (additional dealer markup), or ADP (added dealer profit), or MVA (market value adjustment). Sometimes, there is a "dealer prep charge" (getting the car ready for delivery) or a "documentation fee" (a charge to process the paperwork). There may even be two price stickers on the car—one that shows the manufacturer's suggested retail price and another dealer-applied sticker that shows accessories and services provided by the dealer. So read all the sticker information carefully. If you don't want the extras like fabric finishes or paint sealants that are already on the car, you can ask to look at a car that doesn't have them. Or you could negotiate the price of any, or all, extras.

After you and the salesperson have agreed on a price, there are still two other supplemental items that a dealer will try to sell you. One is an extended warranty and the other is credit insurance (if you have a car loan, this insurance will pay off the loan if you die or become disabled). Consumer advocates say both are usually a bad buy.

Negotiating the Deal

You know the car you want; you know what the dealer paid for the car; you have carefully read the sticker price information. Here are some negotiating dos and don'ts:

Don't bargain over the telephone. Salespeople will promise you anything to get you in the door.

Do take your paperwork and calculations with you to a dealership, since you'll need to refer to them. There's nothing wrong about letting a salesperson know that you are a serious buyer who has done some homework. However, shoving your documents in a salesperson's face and acting like you know all the dealer's secrets won't sweeten a deal.

Do ask to see the dealer's invoice if the salesperson tells you that your figures are wrong.

Do ask to see the dealer's invoice if the dealer has advertised a special promotion linked to the invoice price (e.g., the car is being sold "at invoice," or "$200 above invoice"). You want to know exactly what items are included, and excluded, from the dealer's invoice price.

Don't agree to shop around and keep coming back to a salesperson so he or she can top other offers. Stand your ground and ask the salesperson for a firm offer.

Don't be pressured into accepting an offer if you are not sure you are getting a fair deal. You can always return another day.

Don't include your trade-in car as part of the negotiation. Doing so can confuse the bargaining process. Most of the time, you will be financially ahead by selling your old car privately. If you want to talk trade-in with the dealer, do it as a separate deal, after you have closed the deal on your new car.

Do read your sales contract before signing it.

Options to New-Car Deals

Say you really don't want to negotiate to buy a new car. In that case you have other options:

No-dicker-sticker dealers. An increasing number of dealers are offering cars at a fixed price—no haggling. This one-price program has been around since 1990 when General Motors started the trend with its Saturn automobile. Currently, about 1000 of the 23,000 U.S. car dealers have switched to the no-dicker-sticker program. However, you're likely to save more money the old-fashioned way at an old-fashioned dealership than you will at a fixed-price dealership. (Some car models are sold only by the fixed-price method.)

Fleet-sale prices. Credit unions and other membership organizations often have agreements with local dealers to sell cars to members at discounted prices—either a fixed price or a specified percentage over invoice.

Brokers. You'll find them listed under "auto brokers" in the yellow pages (they don't operate in every state). Generally, they buy cars through the fleet-sales departments of dealers and then resell the cars to consumers. You do, however, pay for their services—whatever the market will bear. Also, since the car was originally sold to the broker, you will not directly get any recall notices on the car since the manufacturer lists the broker as the original buyer.

Buying services. These services will do the comparison shopping for you. One such service is **CarBargains,** a nonprofit consumer organization in Washington, DC. You tell CarBargains which car you want—make, model, and options. For a $135 fee, the organization will send you a computer printout that gives the invoice price for the car and at least five competitive bids from car dealers in your area. If you end up beating the lowest price, CarBargains will refund your money. For more information, call: 800-475-7283.

Financing a New Car

The best way to buy a car is to pay cash, but almost two-thirds of all new-car buyers need financing for at least part of the car's cost. You can get a loan from a bank, credit union, savings-and-loan, or other loan company. And most dealerships will offer you financing.

Regardless of where you get a loan, if you can, you should put down the largest down payment you can afford and aim for the shortest repayment period. The difference in total interest payments between a three-year loan and a five-year loan can be substantial. It's always a good idea to talk to someone at a bank or credit union before you buy a car in order to get some idea of what your car payments will be.

Special low financing rates offered by a dealer can be a good deal or can be deceptively low. Here are a few things to watch out for if you are considering financing your car through a dealer:

♦ Sometimes the very low advertised rates apply only to specific cars or models and the dealer may not be willing to negotiate on the purchase price for those cars.

♦ Low-cost financing may require a sizable down payment and a short-term loan.

♦ Typically, the finance person at the dealership will try to sell you credit insurance, a policy that pays off your loan if you die or become disabled. Many people already have insurance policies that cover death and disability, or just can't afford the extra cost. When a customer buys credit insurance, the cost is added to the cost of the car so the buyer ends up paying interest on the insurance premiums.

Lemon Laws

If your beautiful new car turns out to be a lemon—a car with a serious defect or malfunction that impairs the car's use, value, or safety—don't despair. Currently, there are lemon laws in all 50 states that protect consumers.

According to Clarence Ditlow, executive director of the Center for Auto Safety: "The theme of state lemon laws is that a manufacturer must provide a refund or replacement for a defective new vehicle that is not repaired within a reasonable number of attempts. Most such laws provide for refund or replacement when a substantial defect cannot be fixed in four tries or the auto is out of service for 30 days, within the first 12,000 miles/12 months. Minor defects such as bad ashtrays would not qualify as substantial but transmission and electrical defects would. A car is out of service while being repaired or waiting for parts."

If you think your new car is a lemon, you should first get information about the lemon law in your state. Write or call your state attorney general's office or local consumer protection office. Be sure to keep meticulous documentation of all repairs and a record that shows all the dates when your car was out of service.

If you need to invoke your state's lemon law, you have to act according to the mandates laid out in the law, and the laws do vary from state to state. In general, you will have to send a certified letter to the authorized dealer and/or manufacturer that lays out your case, supported with copies of all your records; you will ask for either a refund of your money or a replacement vehicle. Sometimes the dealer and/or manufacturer will

cooperate quickly and you will be compensated. Or, you may have to go through an arbitration program—one set forth by the manufacturer in your car's warranty, or a program certified by your state. In some cases, if you are unhappy with the outcome of an arbitration program, you can still go to court. For the names of attorneys who specialize in lemon laws, call your local bar association or send a self-addressed, stamped, business-sized envelope to: **Center for Auto Safety,** 2001 S Street NW, Washington, DC 20009.

Before You Buy a Used Car

Every year more than 17 million used cars are sold. If you are thinking about buying a used car:

♦ Consider all costs of the vehicle you have in mind, including purchase price, insurance costs, loan costs (if you need a loan). Particularly important is the repair record of a car. Every year in its April issue, *Consumer Reports* magazine prints a "frequency-of-repair" survey that points out trouble spots for almost all makes and models of used cars. In addition, the April issue also contains a satisfaction poll of readers ("Would You Buy That Car Again?") as well as a list of reliable used cars in different price ranges.

♦ Is the car covered by any warranty? If you buy a used car from a dealer, there will be a "Buyer's Guide" sticker (required by federal law) in the window of the car. It will tell you whether or not the car has a warranty and, if it does, what the warranty covers (about 50 percent of used cars sold through new-car dealerships have some warranty coverage). If you buy through a private seller, you will have to ask if the car is still covered by a warranty or service contract. Even if a warranty or service contract exists, it may not be transferrable or there may be limitations or costs for a transfer.

♦ Personally give the car a thorough inspection, inside and out. If you don't trust yourself to do a good job, take along a friend who is more knowledgeable. Take the car on a test drive.

And, whether talking with a dealer or a private party, ask to see any available paperwork on the car's history—insurance accident reports, repair bills, and maintenance receipts. Even if you are satisfied with the car, take it to a reputable mechanic to have it checked out. It's money well spent.

♦ Know the fair price for the car. This is easy to find out from the numerous annual used-car books that publish current car values. *Consumer Reports* magazine has a Used Car Price Service that will give you quotes over the phone: 900-446-0500; the charge is $1.75 per minute and the magazine estimates that each call averages at least five minutes.

♦ If you are buying from a private party, be sure the person selling you the car is the registered owner.

♦ To avoid buying a stolen car, make sure the vehicle identification number (VIN) on the car's title is the same as the VIN on the car's dashboard. If you have any doubts, ask your local police department to do a stolen-car check.

♦ Call the U.S. Department of Transportation Auto Safety Hotline (800-424-9393) to find out if the car was ever recalled. If so, ask the dealer or private party for proof that the recall work was completed.

JOBS

Interview Questions

Think of a job interview as a sales presentation. You are sitting down with a prospective employer to discuss why you are the best candidate for the job. Since you've come this far, you have already been effective. Perhaps it was your stellar résumé and/or the screening interview conducted over the telephone. But the real test is the face-to-face encounter.

Before the actual encounter, let's make some assumptions: (1) You have been to the library and done some homework on the company; you understand its basic line of business and how it operates. (2) You are properly dressed, meaning you are conservatively dressed (no flashy ties, no miniskirts); (3) You have had a good night's sleep and are feeling pretty confident and relaxed. (4) You are on time (punctuality is crucial).

Below are some typical interview questions and some tips on how to handle them. This is just a small sampling of questions; there are entire books devoted to job interviews and possible interview questions. If some of the tips do not suit your style or personality, just ignore them or alter them to your comfort level. In general, it's best to give relatively short answers to questions; if the interviewer wants further information, he or she will ask you to elaborate. Don't forget to establish eye contact, be confident but not aggressive, and stay enthusiastic even if the going gets tough or you have a lousy interviewer. Above all, steer clear of negativity. You don't want to complain about, or attack, any previous companies, jobs, or bosses.

♦ *Why do you want to change jobs* (if currently employed)*? Why did you leave your last job* (if currently out of work)*?*

It's easier to answer this if you are still working, because there is a subtle implication (true or not) that you're doing just fine at your current company and the new company has the chance to steal you away. Nonetheless, this can be a tough question because you don't want to say anything derogatory about your current company. Good answers: "I'm looking for greater challenges"; "There's not much more room for advancement in my company"; "I've always been interested in your company and this position sounds like a wonderful opportunity." However you answer this question, be brief and positive.

Being unemployed is nothing to be ashamed of, especially since so many companies have "downsized" in recent years, causing many workers to be laid off. If this happened to you, just say so. If you quit your job voluntarily, you can still honestly give some of the above-mentioned answers—you are looking for greater opportunities, for example.

If you were fired from your last job, you need to know exactly what your former employer will say if contacted by any prospective employers.

Call your former boss or someone in the human resources department of your former company and ask. Ideally, you already asked before you departed. What your former employer will say and what you say in an interview need to be similar. Former employers are usually magnanimous, often saying an employee resigned as opposed to being fired. Obviously, you aren't going to advertise the fact that you were fired, but if it is revealed (some interviewers ask point blank if you were ever fired from a job), do your best to put a positive spin on the situation.

♦ *What do you feel are your greatest strengths?*

Employers usually are looking for qualities like dedication, enthusiasm, reliability, energy, and motivation. Also, they want to be sure that you are a team player, have good communications skills (including listening skills), and will get along with other employees. And, of course, you must have the skills and experience to do the job. This open-ended question about your strengths gives you a great opportunity to put forth the very best case for why you should get the job. Back up your answers with concrete examples from your work history.

♦ *What are your weaknesses?*

This question seems like a catch-22. If you say you have none, you will appear arrogant. If you list weaknesses and start apologizing for them, then you appear to be a bad employment risk. What to do? Give a weakness but frame it as a learning experience. For example, you might say that you are a very decisive person and sometimes people incorrectly assume that you are impatient. What you have done here is really to give a strength (decisiveness) but admit that you sometimes overuse it. Better yet, give a weakness but put it in the past. For example, "When I started out in this business, I fell behind with all the record keeping and paperwork, but I have come to appreciate its value and I've become a master of detail."

♦ *Why have you changed jobs so often?*

No matter how well you have crafted your résumé, if you are a frequent job changer, it's likely to show. Be honest in your answer. Maybe you were having a difficult time finding the kind of job that suits you; maybe you were having personal problems that have since been resolved, etc. However, do point out any jobs in which you had a long tenure and list some job accomplishments, regardless of how long you worked in a particular company. Be convincing when telling the employer that you have always been a hard worker in all of your jobs and are ready to settle down; your job-jumping days are over.

♦ *What kind of experience do you have for this job?*

This seems easy enough. Just give a short discourse on your past jobs, highlighting experience that is relevant to the new position. The key word is "relevant." Remember the company's job description—the specific traits and qualifications that were mentioned. Did the job description focus on managerial skills? Then be sure to mention yours and don't get sidetracked describing your computer wizardry. Before going into a job interview, reread the job description so you can make the connections between your skills and the job's requirements. If the interviewer points out a gap—a requirement that you don't seem to have—don't crumple up and mutter that you are a quick learner. Find a skill in your background that is similar to the one required, point out the similarities, and state confidently that you see no problem in coming up to speed in that area.

♦ *What are your long-term goals?*

This is not the time to talk about your dream of owning your own business. Employers want new hires to stay around a long time. They don't want to spend money training you so that you can go off and find a better job or start a competing company. Talk about goals as goals within the new company.

♦ *Why do you want to work for this company?*

If you have done your homework, it's time to shine. Interviewers are always impressed if you have taken the time to learn about the company. It gives you the opportunity to make complimentary statements about the company, its products or services, the way it is run, whatever deserves applause. Then you can express your desire to be part of a company that you genuinely admire. However, unless asked, don't tell the interviewer what you would do to improve the company. Even if asked, be aware that giving such advice, especially in an initial interview, can be risky. Most bosses don't want high-level advice on how to run their companies from someone who just walked in the door.

Most of us get nervous before a job interview. Advance preparation is the best antidote. Once you are well versed about the company, you can concentrate on giving good, effective answers in a job interview. Anticipate many different questions and interview yourself before you step into the real situation. Practice out loud and judge your answers. Or ask a friend to run through a practice session with you. You can't count on getting a top-notch interviewer who will ask all the right questions and elicit all the pertinent information. Some interviewers just aren't very good, and even the best ones can fall short when they are tired. But if you know what you want to say and how you want to say it, chances are very good that you will be pleased with your performance.

Drug Tests and Psychological Tests

It's becoming increasingly common for companies to ask prospective new hires to take drug tests and psychological tests. Taking such tests seems like an invasion of your privacy, and the tests can be unnerving. But companies are within their legal rights to ask, and if you refuse, you might not get hired.

A recent survey reports that 85 percent of major American companies test workers and job applicants for drug use. Of those tested, 2.5 percent of the workers and 4.3 percent of the job applicants tested positive. It's estimated that more than one-third of all Americans applying for jobs will be asked to take a drug test. The most

common method for drug testing is urinalysis. The problem with the test is that it can result in "false positives" triggered by certain foods, over-the-counter drugs, or prescribed medications. For example, use of the pain reliever ibuprofen may incorrectly signal marijuana use. Similarly, if you eat a poppy-seed bagel for breakfast, you might test positive for heroin use. In addition, laboratories that perform the tests are sometimes to blame for inaccurate readings if lab procedures are faulty or shoddy.

Before giving a specimen for urinalysis, you will usually be given a list of drugs and other ingestible substances that are known to cause false positives. In addition to checking off anything you have taken, be sure to add anything you recently ingested that is not on the list. Also, to ensure the best results, drink a lot of water before the urinalysis. Try to schedule the test as late as possible in the day to give you extra time to flush out your system. The earlier in the day that you give a specimen, the more concentrated your urine will be. If, for whatever reason, you are overly concerned about the test, you might want to have your urine pretested by your physician to see what the likely results will be. If your drug test comes back positive, most companies will retest (sometimes using a test other than urinalysis) in order to be fair.

Psychological tests are a horse of a different color. They test for a lot of intangibles like honesty, loyalty, energy, drive, flexibility, and adaptability. The employer wants to know what kind of a person you are—whether or not you are a good employment risk. The company representative may give the test another name like an "aptitude test," but in essence it is a psychological test. Most are written tests with either multiple-choice or yes-or-no questions. The tests can be relatively short or very long. Most are scored on a total pattern of responses as opposed to single responses. Results are kept confidential; usually you aren't even given the results. And, psychological tests are only one component in an overall evaluation of you as a potential employee.

It's perfectly all right to ask a few questions of

your interviewer or test giver if you are asked to take a psychological test. Ask how the test relates to the job; who in the company is given access to the results; and what, if any, feedback you will receive. When you sit down to take the test, remain calm and "think professional." Some of the answer choices will seem clearer if you think of them in a work context as opposed to a personal context. Also, be aware that identical, or almost identical, questions can pop up as you proceed through the test. This is done to catch you in a lie or inconsistency. In other words, the test preparers want to catch you if you have "psyched out" the test by choosing the answer you think the company wants, not necessarily the answer you would truthfully pick. They figure you might "psych out" question number 6 but by the time you get to question 45 and question 70 (identical, or almost identical, to question 6), you will probably have forgotten how you answered question 6. So be on the lookout for questions that are alike.

Psychological testing, and its role in the workplace, has always been a controversial subject. Psychology is far from an exact science and critics come down hard on tests with questions that tend to screen out people on the basis of race, color, age, or other discriminatory areas. Nevertheless, it looks like these tests are here to stay.

Guidelines for Negotiating a Salary

"You make your deal at the door," says one of our friends who has always been successful at negotiating job salaries. Basically, he means that if you later learn that you could have negotiated a much better salary—tough luck, too late. He also means that you alone are responsible for getting yourself the best deal. Here are some things to know about the art of salary negotiation. Adapt them to your own style and personality.

♦ Know what you are worth in the marketplace. Perhaps you already have a good idea. If not, go to the library and read a few articles on salary ranges for your area of expertise. Professional magazines often publish annual salary survey results. You might also want to contact a few employment agencies or executive headhunters.

♦ Know your salary requirements. Have a minimum figure in mind as well as a top figure, but be realistic in your calculations. These numbers should be kept in your mind until it's time to really talk money.

♦ Avoid putting money figures on a résumé or job application form, unless you absolutely have to. Doing so gives the employer a big advantage. So what do you write on the application form line that says "required salary"? Try putting "open" or "negotiable."

♦ Don't ask about salary in the initial interview(s). Postponing money talk until the company is ready to make you an offer puts you in a much better bargaining position. Once the firm wants you, and you know it, the bargaining chips stack up on your side. In addition, asking up front about money implies that you are more interested in money than you are in the job.

♦ Be prepared to talk money early if the subject is unavoidable. If the interviewer throws you a curve ball and asks about your salary requirements, simply say that you would like to have a complete understanding of the job and its responsibilities before answering the question. However, an interviewer may also ask a more direct question like, "What was your salary on your last job?" That one is hard to sidestep. If you have to name a number, remember that it is fair to add into your base salary items like annual bonuses, profit-sharing money, and money from an anticipated raise. How far you want to go is up to you—for example, do you include the dollar values of your medical plan?

♦ Never lose sight of the fact that you are negotiating for a new job based on new responsibilities. Even if an interviewer has skillfully managed to get some numbers about your salary requirements and salary history (before you were ready to discuss them), you haven't lost the numbers game.

♦ Be money-smart when it's time to cut the deal. Assume the interview process has been ideal: the company is ready to make you a job offer and it's time to resolve the salary issue. The interviewer asks for your salary requirements. Even now, you should turn the table and get the interviewer to say something concrete before you do. Ask, "What salary range did you have in mind?" Or, "What salary range has the company authorized for this position?" Once you hear a number, or range of numbers, you can adjust your answer accordingly. Getting the other party to mention the first number is the single most important element in salary negotiation.

♦ Don't lose enthusiasm or confidence if the offer is too low. Almost always, there is room for negotiation. Remember that the interviewer wants you for the job, and if your number and the interviewer's number aren't too far apart, it's likely that you can arrive at a compromise. As you work the numbers back and forth, be sure to express your sincere interest in the job and the company.

♦ Evaluate the job offer in light of the perks and benefits offered. Perhaps the salary wasn't what you had hoped for but there are generous extras like comprehensive medical insurance, an excellent retirement plan, profit sharing, a lot of vacation time, an expense account, etc. These could add up to a sizable amount.

WHAT A DEGREE IS WORTH

According to a Census Bureau publication, *What's It's Worth*, 25.2 percent of American workers have some type of a post–high school degree. As you will see below, the degrees are worth money in the job market.

Average monthly earnings, by educational level:

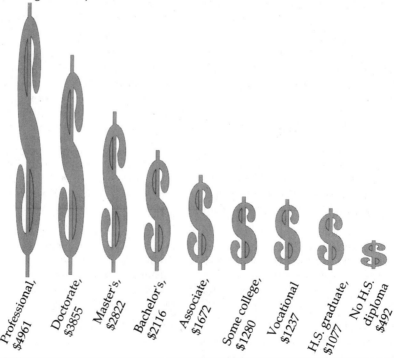

Professional, $4961

Doctorate, $3855

Master's, $2822

Bachelor's, $2116

Associate, $1672

Some college, $1280

Vocational $1237

H.S. graduate, $1077

No H.S. diploma $492

♦ Go out and celebrate after you have accepted a job offer that you earned through your hard work and negotiating skills. Bottoms up!

Turnoffs in a Job Interview

What's likely to create an unfavorable impression in a job interview? That was asked of 320 company recruiters by Victor R. Lindquist, placement director at Northwestern University. Here are the answers from the Northwestern Lindquist-Endicott Report.

1. Arrogance, cockiness.
2. Poor oral communication and presentation skills.
3. Lack of interest.
4. Lack of knowledge about the industry.
5. Early discussion or questions about salary or benefits.
6. Being unprepared for an interview and making excuses.
7. Egotism or overconfidence.
8. Lateness or not showing up for the interview.
9. Poor eye contact.

WOMEN'S WORK

An American woman earns 76 cents for every dollar a man earns for the same job. While women are making progress (the figure was 59 cents back in 1981), they seem overall to be locked into the same kinds of occupations held by their mothers, grandmothers, and great grandmothers. . . . Below are the 10 occupations, according to the U.S. Labor Department, employing the most women in the years 1890, 1940, and 1990.

WOMEN'S OCCUPATIONS

Rank	1890	1940	1990
1	Servant	Servant	Secretary
2	Agricultural laborer	Stenographer, secretary	Cashier
3	Dressmaker	Teacher	Bookkeeper
4	Teacher	Clerical worker	Registered nurse
5	Farmer, planter	Sales worker	Nursing aide, orderly
6	Laundress	Factory worker (apparel)	Elementary school teacher
7	Seamstress	Bookkeeper, accountant, cashier	Waitress
8	Cotton-mill operative	Waitress	Sales worker
9	Housekeeper, steward	Housekeeper	Child care worker
10	Clerk, cashier	Nurse	Cook

10. Being abrasive, rude, or demanding.

11. Dishonesty or fabricating answers in interview or résumé.

12. Poor language usage, slang, or poor grammar.

13. No career direction or not knowing oneself.

14. Shallow or inappropriate questions or answers.

15. Lack of experience, education, activities, or skills.

16. Lack of professional appearance.

17. Know-it-all attitude.

18. Inappropriate attire.

19. Unrealistic goals and career or job expectations.

20. Overly aggressive, hostile, or manipulative behavior.

Losing a Job

Getting laid off or fired can be traumatic and debilitating. Psychologists say that the more our identity is tied to our jobs the harder we take the hit. It's very common to experience an array of feelings and emotions like shock, anxiety, and anger. Even though getting fired or laid off doesn't carry nearly the social stigma that it used to, losing a job usually feels like a large financial and psychological setback. Lousy as it feels, you need to regroup and get your life back on track.

What Benefits Are You Entitled to?

♦ Will you get any severance pay? Unfortunately, severance pay is not mandated by law. In most cases it is considered a gift from a company, unless you have a formal contract that spells out specific severance pay entitlements. The traditional rule of thumb, when a company decides to comply, is one or two weeks' pay for every year of service. If you get severance pay, you might ask that it be paid to you in one lump sum as soon as possible. That way you can file sooner for unemployment insurance.

♦ Besides severance, there may be other issues you need to resolve with your employer. Is any money owed to you for unused vacation time and sick days? What are your options for dealing with your retirement plan? How long will you and your dependents be covered under the company's health insurance plan (usually 18 months) and who will pay the premiums? Will the company do anything to help you find new employment, like paying for retraining programs or outplacement services?

♦ Walk-away benefits are negotiable in many cases. There's no harm in trying to get more severance pay or to negotiate in whatever area you feel you may have some leverage. If you are completely dissatisfied with your package and think that there is anything illegal about your termination (age discrimination, for example), you may want to see an employment attorney. However, be aware that employment attorneys charge about $175 an hour and up.

♦ It is crucial that you and your employer come to a complete understanding about the reasons for your termination. The reason you are leaving can affect your eligibility for unemployment benefits. Also, when you apply for a new job, you are likely to be asked why you left your old job. If your former employer is called as a reference and gives a different reason than what you state, you may be caught in an uncomfortable situation.

Get Your Financial Life in Order

♦ Sign up for unemployment insurance as soon as you can. Eligibility and the size of benefits vary from state to state, but in general you can collect benefits for 26 weeks. During periods of particularly high unemployment, the federal government steps in and extends benefits beyond the initial benefits period.

♦ Reassess your financial picture right away. This is one of those emergency situations that financial experts say you should have been prepared for—that you should have three to six months' salary stashed away for. But many people don't have an emergency fund and need to resort to other tactics like refiguring a budget down to the bare bones, refinancing debts at a lower cost, and selling off some personal property to get cash. If you get into dire straits, you can always consider taking out a home-equity loan or taking some money from your retirement plan, but do so only if you have truly run out of options.

♦ Try hard not to panic. The financial consequences of losing a job can be devastating, but you don't want the anxiety to shake your confidence in your abilities or your chances for getting a new job.

Finding a New Job

♦ Not only should you update your résumé, but you should also create several versions. The one, all-purpose, résumé can work to your disadvantage. It's better to have two or three versions, each one focusing on a different skill.

♦ The obvious sources of new jobs are newspaper ads, employment agencies, and executive recruiters. Try them all if you are so inclined. Also, consider temporary agencies for two reasons: (1) sometimes temporary positions lead to permanent positions; (2) they are a quick source of money. Don't forget about "networking." While it has become an overused yuppie cliché, it works. Call friends and business colleagues and let them know that you are seeking employment; send them a résumé. Join a professional organization in your area of expertise. Cold-call companies that you would like to work for even if they have not advertised job openings. One recent survey of job seekers revealed that 63 percent of those who found work did so through personal contacts and initiatives.

♦ If you know you have difficulty with job interviews, get a book on job-interview techniques. There are plenty of good ones in your local bookstore or library. The key to getting a job is not only the skills and experience you have to offer but also the way in which you present yourself. Advance preparation for a job interview is crucial.

Overseas Job Scams

What about those job agencies that tout big paychecks in faraway countries? Called "employment agencies" or "employment-listing services," they advertise in daily newspapers or on local television stations. For an up-front fee, which ranges from $200 to over $1000, these agencies promise to assist you in finding an excellent job overseas. Convincing telephone salespeople can even offer some pretty outstanding benefits: paying off your credit card debt before you leave; finding jobs for several of your friends so you can all go together; locating great housing accommodations at very affordable costs.

What services do you get for your money? Many of these agencies offer no individualized services but are merely résumé collectors. They pack up stacks of résumés and send them to overseas companies regardless of whether or not there are actual job openings. Some agencies do nothing more than mail you listings of job opportunities abroad, but in many cases the lists are very outdated. By the time you become suspicious that you are dealing with an unscrupulous operator, the agency many have disappeared with no forwarding address or new phone number. Consumer advocates claim that these overseas job scams take in an estimated $100 million a year.

There are legitimate employment agencies that assist clients in finding jobs outside of the United States. Critics say, however, that even the legitimate companies have a low success rate, placing only an estimated 2 percent of clients in overseas jobs. Nonetheless, if you plan to work with an overseas placement agency, here are some tips to help you distinguish the legitimate companies from the con artists.

♦ Up-front fees are a red flag. Most legitimate agencies require fees after a job placement has been made, and often the fee is paid by the employer.

♦ Beware of agencies that deal with you only on the telephone or by mail (usually a post-office box).

♦ When dealing with an agency, check out its reputation by calling the Better Business Bureau or state and local consumer protection agencies.

♦ Get an agreement in writing before you pay a dime for any services offered. Even if you know that all you will be getting is a list of job opportunities, some agencies promise a refund if you don't find a job. But read all the rules about the guaranteed refund, because they can be very restrictive, meaning the refund is almost impossible to collect.

♦ Get specific with the agency. Is it making vague promises about vague companies. Or are there definite job openings? Ask for references; tell the agency representative that you would like to talk to a few satisfied customers.

Retirement

How Much Money Do You Need to Retire?

Only if you have a reliable crystal ball can you get an extremely accurate answer to this question. None of us knows how long we will live or whether we face unexpected financial hardships. And to complicate matters, there are many other unknowns, like how much you will reap from your current investments (if you have them) over the long run or how hard you will be hit by inflation (meaning your current dollars will buy less in future years).

Conventional wisdom says that you will need somewhere between 70 and 80 percent of your preretirement, after-tax, income to live comfortably in retirement. But inflation rates can wreak havoc on this formula.

If you want to get a rough projection of how much money you will need in retirement and how much you need to be saving now, there are numerous worksheets available—from the American Association of Retired Persons (AARP), from financial planners and investment firms. In addition, worksheets usually are included in books on retirement and in personal-finance magazines. The best ones are usually long and somewhat complicated to complete, but they take into account many financial factors and allow you to input more information on your specific situation.

T. Rowe Price, an investment management firm, offers a free "Retirement Planning Kit" and a free "Retirees Financial Guide" which can help you estimate how much you will need to retire as well as plan strategies on how to save and invest. For the free kits, contact: **T. Rowe Price,** 100 East Pratt Street, Baltimore, MD 21202 (800-638-5660).

Whether you are close to retirement or are 30 years away from it, it's wise to start thinking now about your life after work. Here are some interesting facts we thought you might want to know:

♦ Americans are living longer. The over-85 group is the fastest growing portion of the population. In the old days the average person retired at 65 and died at 72 (only seven years of retirement to finance). Today, if you reach age 65, you're likely to live another 20 years.

♦ A Princeton University study, commissioned by Merrill Lynch, states that the average baby boomer is currently saving about 34 percent of the money he or she will need to retire at 65.

♦ Americans are poor savers. In the 1970s the average American saved about 8 percent of earnings. The personal savings rate dropped to 5.3 percent in the 1980s. Currently, it hovers around 4 percent (the Japanese save 15 percent).

♦ Social Security and pension money together account for about 50 percent of preretirement income.

♦ A survey by the New York Life Insurance Company found that aside from the Social Security benefits and company pension plans, four out of 10 Americans do not have a savings program for retirement.

Retirement Plans

Retirement planning used to be thought of as a three-legged stool—Social Security, pension plans, personal savings and investments. More and more, financial experts are saying that a fourth leg needs to be added—part-time employment for some retirees who do not have adequate financial resources for a comfortable retirement.

Since many Americans are behind in planning and saving for retirement, it is especially important to take stock of your retirement plan opportunities, whether you have a pension plan at work, a pension plan of your own as a self-employed person, or a little of both. Listed below are the most common types of retirement plans.

Company Pension Plans

Your employer offers one of two basic kinds of retirement plans: defined-benefit plan or defined-contribution plan. The defined-benefit plan is quickly becoming extinct. It's the kind your father or grandfather probably had. The employer funds the plan, which guarantees a fixed lifetime income usually based on salary and length of service. However, these plans proved to be very costly to employers, and the debt-crazy 1980s caused many companies to replace them with defined-contribution plans.

While there are several different kinds of defined-contribution plans, the most popular by far is known as the 40l(k). Here is how it works: You contribute money from your paycheck into the plan; usually the employer matches part or all of your contribution. All of the money continues to grow, tax-free, until you need to tap it in retirement. However, you must decide how these

funds are to be invested. Typically, a company will offer you different investment options, including mutual funds, fixed-income funds, company stock, etc. Each option carries a different degree of risk. Thus, you are given the responsibility of determining where your money is best placed to meet your retirement goals. How wisely you make these decisions determines the size of the pension you ultimately receive. There is an annual limit on the amount of tax-free money you can put into a 40l(k); and the amount changes every year.

Regardless of the type of plan under which you are covered, there are questions you should ask of someone in the employee benefits department of your company. Most important is how long you must work for the company in order to be "vested"—meaning that you have a legal right to the accumulated benefits. You may be "partially vested" after a certain number of years and "fully vested" after a certain number of years. You never lose any money you put into a plan, but you could lose some, or all, of the company's contributions if you leave before you are fully vested. If you have a paternalistic, defined-benefit plan, your employer would be able to give you a fair idea of what your monthly retirement benefit will be, whether there is a cost-of-living adjustment, what happens to the plan if you leave to work for another company. If you have a defined-contribution plan, namely a 401(k), you need to find out how much you can contribute and what your employer will contribute. There are no problems with the "portability" of 401(k)s; if you change jobs, you can move the money into the new employer's pension plan or keep the lump sum tax-deferred by putting it into an Individual Retirement Account, or IRA (discussed below). Since 401(k) plans require you to make investment decisions, you need to understand fully the potential yields (and risks) of every investment option the company is offering. If you aren't satisfied with the option, or options, you choose, you can switch—within time frames set by the company. Don't forget: the company will not make decisions for you; it will not guarantee an amount of return on your investments; and it will not provide cost-of-living adjustments for your retirement years.

Keogh/SEP Plans

Keoghs were designed for people with self-employment income. Whether you work all by yourself—as writer, consultant, artist—or you own a small, unincorporated business, you qualify for a Keogh plan. Also, if you work for a company (even one that covers you with a retirement plan) but have a job on the side, like teaching night school, you can still get a Keogh. All of your money grows, tax-free, until you retire. And the contributions are deductible on your income taxes. Your money can be placed in any number of investments including mutual funds, CDs, annuities, common stock, bonds, etc. How you decide to invest determines where you go to set up a Keogh (e.g., call a bank or savings-and-loan if you want CDs; call an insurance company if you want an annuity). There is a variety of Keoghs to choose from and each carries different regulations and restrictions.

There is a certain amount (sometimes a lot) of paperwork that needs to be maintained on Keogh plans. If you have few, or no employees, and your contributions are limited and sporadic, you might be better off with a SEP (Simplified Employer Plan). A SEP is handled in basically the same manner as an Individual Retirement Account (discussed below). Thus, there is far less administrative paperwork to deal with. SEPs are usually set up by self-employed persons and small businesses.

There are contribution limits on Keoghs and SEPs—a percentage of self-employment income up to a certain dollar limit; the numbers vary according to the type of plan you choose. For full details on either Keoghs or SEPs, get the IRS publication, "Retirement Plans for the Self-Employed."

Individual Retirement Accounts (IRAs)

When IRAs were fully tax-deductible for everyone, they were enormously popular. But the federal government changed the rules. However, IRAs are still a great tax write-off and investment for millions of people. The individual maximum deduction has remained the same: $2000 ($2250 if you also have an IRA for a nonworking spouse); two-income couples can deduct $4000 if eligibility rules are met. There are two basic guidelines for deductions:

1. You can take the full deduction if neither you nor your spouse is covered by a company retirement plan.

2. If you or your spouse is covered by a retirement plan, you can still take the full deduction if your combined adjusted gross income is $40,000 or less. If you are single and covered by a pension plan, your adjusted gross income has to be $25,000 or less. If your adjusted gross income is larger than the limit, you may still qualify for a partial deduction, depending on how much you are over the limit.

Like all self-directed pensions, you have a wide variety of investment options, from CDs to mutual funds to stocks and bonds. The Internal Revenue Service has a booklet, "Individual Retirement Accounts," which lists all rules and regulations including penalties for early withdrawal and how to transfer, or roll over, IRAs. It's likely that the rules on IRAs will change (even as we write this) because Americans want them restored to their former selves. There always seems to be a bill in Congress that will either restore IRAs to their former identity or make them even better by creating "super IRAs."

Commercial Tax-Deferred Annuities

Because commercial tax-deferred annuities are often marketed as retirement investments, we have included them here. While they are sold by a variety of money professionals—including insurance agents, financial planners, stock brokers, agents at mutual fund companies, and bankers—they are all ultimately backed by an insurance company. While the money you pay into this kind of annuity is not deductible on your income taxes, it does grow tax-deferred until you begin withdrawing it. When you start receiving payments, the amount you receive is determined by how much you have contributed, how long your funds have been in the annuity, and the rate of return earned on your funds. Annuities are not meant to be short-term commitments; many people buy 15- and 20-year annuities. As money guru Jane Bryant Quinn says, "You don't date an annuity, you marry it." You can buy an annuity with one lump sum or a series of payments over time.

Basically there are two types—fixed and variable. With a fixed annuity, your funds grow at a specified interest rate for a specified period of time (like one or three years). After that, the insurance company usually changes the rate once a year or more. Nonetheless, the fixed annuity is a straight interest-rate investment. With a variable annuity, you make the decisions about how you want the money in your fund to be invested, choosing from a portfolio of investment options offered by the insurance company.

Consumers like annuities because of their tax-deferred feature and because, unlike other pension options like IRAs, there is no limit on the amount of money you can invest. Also, if you choose a lifetime stream of income, the insurance company will continue to make payments to you for as long as you live (a nice feature if you happen to live to a very ripe age).

But there are several issues to consider before buying an annuity. First of all, it can be extremely costly to quit the investment altogether or to take out money prematurely. Not only will you pay a bundle to the insurance company, but the IRS will demand a 10 percent penalty for any money withdrawn before age 59½. Also, you will be paying sales commissions on annuities as well as administrative fees. While the contributions you can make to an annuity are unlimited, which is not the case with the money you might put into a 401(k) plan, you buy an annuity with after-tax dollars and contribute to a 401(k) with pretax dollars—a definite advantage for the 401(k) plan.

Annuities are complex agreements and you need to be aware of that when talking to a smooth salesperson who dazzles you with computerized charts of how well off you will be in 20 years. Before buying an annuity, be sure you understand all of its components including surrender fees, administrative costs, walkaway clauses (can you pull out without big penalties?), historic performance of annuity returns (especially if you get a variable annuity), etc. Finally, are you with an insurance company that has a top safety rating?

Social Security Benefits

A great many Americans count on Social Security as a part of their retirement income. The basic foundation of Social Security is simple: you pay taxes into the system during your working years and you and your family receive monthly benefits when you retire or become disabled. In addition, if you die, your survivors are entitled to receive your benefits. Not that long ago, it was virtually impossible to get a good idea of just how much money you were likely to get. However, thanks to the computer age and the improved systems of the Social Security Administration (SSA), it is now possible to get a "Personal Earnings and Benefit Statement" (PEBES) that will give you all the information you need to know (PEBES is discussed below). Here are some frequently asked questions regarding Social Security. Remember that Social Security rules and regulations change every year, so you should always contact your local Social Security office for updated information.

Am I eligible for Social Security?

Most people are. As you work and pay taxes into Social Security, you earn "credits." The maximum number of credits you can earn per year is four. And each credit is based on a specific amount of money earned; in 1994 you earned one credit for each $620 of income earned (the amount of money per credit goes up every year). While the number of credits you need in order to be eligible for Social Security is determined ultimately by your age and the kind of benefit you seek, most people need 40 credits (10 years of work) to qualify. Obviously, you may earn far more than 40 credits, but those extra credits don't necessarily increase your monthly benefit. Also, the credit-system numbers change for those eligible for disability payments or for family members applying for survivor's benefits.

Checking up on how many credits you have earned is a vital issue for some people. Suppose you are a mother who dropped out of the work world to raise your children. You might not have the required number of credits now but maybe you are close. In that case, you may want to reenter the work force, even if it's just to pull you up to the eligibility limit. If you know for sure that you eventually will be able to collect benefits on a spouse's, or former spouse's, account, perhaps you aren't that concerned. But if you have no one else's account to fall back on, be sure that your account is in good shape.

How much will I receive from Social Security?

Your monthly benefit is determined by your age, the type of benefit you are applying for, and your earnings. The Social Security Administration has a specified formula that is used to calculate your benefits. In general, the more earnings you had over the years, the more your benefit will be. However, there is a ceiling on benefits. For example, the maximum benefit for a 65-year-old person who retired in 1994 was $1147 per month. For someone who retired in 1994 at the age of 62, the maximum was $902 a month. Overall, the *average* benefit paid to all retired individuals in 1994 was $674. There are also maximum allowable benefits for couples.

Next you need to decide whether you will take *full* retirement (at age 65), early retirement (between ages 62 and 65), or late retirement (after age 65). The longer you wait to claim retirement benefits, the larger your check will be. Your age at retirement has a significant bearing on your monthly benefit.

Currently, if you were born before 1938, you will be eligible for *full* retirement benefits at age 65. But the rules on full retirement at age 65 are scheduled to change. According to the Social Security Administration: "Beginning in the year 2000, the age at which full benefits are payable will increase in gradual steps from 65 to 67. This affects people born in 1938 and later. For example, if you were born in 1940, your full retirement age is 65 and 6 months. If you were born in 1950, your full retirement age is 66. Anybody born in 1960 or later will be eligible for full retirement benefits at 67."

Regardless of when you qualify for "full" retirement, you can get benefits as early as age 62. However, if you choose to take benefits before your full retirement age, your benefits will be permanently reduced. Again, according to SSA: "If your full retirement age is 65 and you sign up for Social Security when you're 64, you will receive 93⅓ percent of your full benefit. At 62, you would get 80 percent. (Note: The reduction will be greater in future years as the full retirement age increases.)"

What if you delay retirement benefits beyond 65 (or whatever age is your full retirement age)? First of all, if you keep on working, your extra income will boost your "average" earnings— which is part of the formula that determines your benefits. The higher your average earnings, the higher your benefits will be. Also, the SSA gives you extra money, in the form of a special credit, for delaying retirement (the credit applies only until you reach age 70). Currently, the special credit amounts to a 4.5 percent increase a year for people turning 65 in 1994. This rate will increase in future years until it reaches 8 percent for people turning 65 in 2008 or later.

How does any money I earn affect my benefits?

There are limits on how much money you can earn and still collect all of your Social Security benefits. The following 1994 provisions applied to those under the age of 70 who are collecting benefits (after age 70, you get all of your benefits, regardless of earnings):

♦ If you were under age 65 in 1994, you could have earned up to $8040 and still have collected all of your Social Security benefits. However, for every $2 you earned over the limit, $1 was withheld from your benefits.

♦ If you were age 65 through age 69 in 1994, you could have earned up to $11,160 and still have collected all of your Social Security benefits. However, for every $3 you earned over the limit, $1 was withheld from your benefits.

The earnings limits change every year. What constitutes earnings? Money you earn at a job or through self-employment counts. So do bonuses, commissions, and vacation pay. Earnings do *not* include pensions, annuities, investment income, interest, Social Security, veterans or other government benefits.

Are my benefits taxable?

Most people pay no federal income taxes on their Social Security benefits. However, your benefits can be taxed if you are considered a "higher-income" individual or couple. And the rules were changed by the new federal tax bill passed in 1993 that went into effect on January 1, 1994. To figure out whether you will owe taxes on benefits you first need to calculate what's called "combined" income. It is your adjusted gross income as reported on your federal tax return (which will include income like pension money, dividends, interest, etc.) *plus* nontaxable interest (like the interest you get on tax-free municipal bonds) *plus* one-half of your Social Security benefits.

Single retirees with a combined income under $25,000 and couples with a combined income under $32,000 pay no taxes on Social Security benefits. Single retirees with a combined income of $25,000–$33,999 and couples with a combined income of $32,000–$43,999 will pay tax on up to 50 percent of benefits. Single retirees with a combined income of more than $34,000 and couples with a combined income of more than $44,000 will pay tax on up to 85 percent of benefits.

The exact amount of benefits you pay taxes on is determined according to a special tax formula that is included in the annual 1040 federal tax form book and appears on the annual statement that retirees get from SSA. Finally, most states do not levy taxes on Social Security income.

Can I get disability benefits under Social Security?

Yes, if you have worked long enough and accumulated enough "credits" to qualify. However, the SSA has a very strict definition of disability. Also, disability is one of the most complicated of all Social Security programs. If you want more information on the disability program, call or write your local Social Security office and request a free copy of the booklet, "Disability" (publication number 05-10029).

Can my family get benefits when I am eligible?

When you start getting your Social Security checks or disability benefits, members of your family may also qualify for some benefits. According to the SSA, benefits can be paid to:

♦ your husband or wife if he or she is 62 or older (unless he or she collects a higher Social Security benefit on his or her own record);

♦ your husband or wife at any age if he or she is caring for your child (the child must be under 16 or disabled);

♦ your children, if they are unmarried and:
—under 18; or
—under 19 but in elementary or secondary school as a full-time student; or
—18 or older and severely disabled (the disability must have started before age 22).

A family member is eligible for a monthly payment up to 50 percent of your retirement or disability rate—depending on how many family members are eligible. Your spouse can get 50 percent if he or she is 65 or older or is caring for a minor or disabled child. If your spouse is under 65 and not caring for a minor or disabled child, the rate is reduced. Currently, the lowest reduced benefit is 37.5 percent at age 62. There is a limit on how much money can ultimately be paid out to family members. If your family claims are larger than the limit, then benefits to family members will be reduced proportionately. Your benefit will not be affected.

Do I claim benefits on my own account or on my spouse's account?

The issue is getting the most money out of Social Security if both you and your spouse are entitled to benefits. For example, assume you retire and start collecting benefits, but your spouse continues to work. When your spouse finally retires, you may get an increase in your benefits because of a reduced or full "spousal benefit" (because your benefit was less than the amount of a "spousal benefit"). However, if your own benefit turns out to be better than your spouse's, you would not want to switch to a spousal benefit. This whole issue of whose benefit is better and what to do to get the most money is very tricky. Luckily, the SSA has an array of computerized worksheets to help you figure it all out. Just stop by a local office, relate the facts concerning your situation, and SSA personnel will be glad to plug in the numbers and give you an answer. All requests are handled with confidentiality. Also, the SSA is not gender-biased; personnel will figure out the best formula for you regardless of whether a husband's or wife's benefits are greater.

If I die, what happens to my benefits?

If you earned enough Social Security credits, some members of your family can get your benefits. They include:

♦ a widow or widower who is 60 or older;

♦ a widow or widower who is 50 or older and disabled;

♦ a widow or widower at any age if she or he is caring for a child under 16 or a disabled child;

♦ children if they are unmarried and:

—under 18; or

—under 19 but in an elementary or secondary school as a full-time student; or

—18 or older and severely disabled (the disability must have started before age 22);

♦ your parents, if they were dependent on you for at least half of their support.

In addition, if you are divorced (even if you remarried), under certain circumstances, your ex-spouse may be eligible for benefits on your account.

Survivors usually get between 75 and 100 percent of your benefits. However, like payments to family members while you are alive, there are limits to how much money can ultimately be paid out of your account. If your family claims are higher than the limit, the benefits will be reduced proportionately. For full details about survivor's benefits, get the SSA booklet, "Survivors" (publication number 05-10084).

I'm divorced. Can I collect on my ex-spouse's account?

Yes, under certain conditions. Even if your ex-spouse has remarried, you may be entitled to benefits. To qualify, you:

♦ must have been married for at least 10 years;

♦ must be at least 62 years old and unmarried;

♦ must not be eligible for an equal or higher benefit on your own Social Security record, or on someone else's record.

How do I get my Personal Earnings and Benefit Estimate (PEBES)?

You can get a request form at your local Social Security office or by calling 800-772-1213. After providing the SSA with some bare basic information, the department will send you a very detailed estimate of your potential benefits upon retirement. The report will tell you where you stand in terms of the number of credits you have earned, what your monthly benefits would be at various ages, what your spouse and dependent children would receive in monthly payments if you died or became disabled. In addition, it will give you a year-by-year statement of your earnings that were subject to Social Security taxes and the taxes that have been paid into your account.

COLLEGE FINANCING

Saving for a College Education

The chart opposite was prepared by T. Rowe Price Associates, an investment management firm in Baltimore, Maryland. It shows how much you would have to invest a month in order to pay for a four-year education at both public and private colleges—depending on the number of years until a student will enter college. The costs are based on the College Board's Annual Survey of colleges for the 1993–94 school year and include tuition, room and board, transportation, books, and other expenses. In-state residency is assumed for public schools.

The tables assume a 6 percent annual increase in college costs and an 8 percent annual return on investment. No additional investments are assumed once the student starts school, and investments are made at the beginning of each year.

Sources of Financial Aid

More than half of all students attending college are dependent on some form of financial aid. The money is made available through a large variety of grants, scholarships, work-study programs, student loans, and private loans. The best sources for financial-aid information are high school guidance offices and college financial-aid offices. Both will have mammoth amounts of data on specific aid programs including eligibility requirements and forms to fill out.

Grant funds and *scholarship funds* do not have to be repaid; they are gifts. Grants are given predominately on the basis of financial need. Scholarships usually take financial aid into consideration, but they can be awarded solely on the basis of academic achievement, athletic ability, special talents, or other criteria. Most grants come from the U.S. Government, state governments, and colleges. Scholarships are given by state governments and colleges as well as by private foundations, corporations, and civic groups. The federal government gives scholarships in the form of Army, Navy, and Air Force ROTC scholarships with the trade-off that recipients must serve at least eight years of active and reserve duty after graduation.

The College Work-Study program (CWS) is a federally funded program that allows students to earn money to pay for educational costs while attending school. Administered by the colleges, it is usually available to middle-income students as well as low-income students, graduate students as well as undergraduate students. Jobs are secured by the college and can be either on campus or off campus. The amount of money earned can't exceed the total CWS award.

By far the largest percentage of total financial aid money is secured through loans. And the

INVESTING FOR COLLEGE

Years until college	Projected 4-year total cost		Monthly investment	
	Public	Private	Public	Private
1	$39,703	$82,754	$3,168	$6,603
2	$42,085	$87,719	$1,612	$3,360
3	$44,610	$92,982	$1,093	$2,279
4	$47,287	$98,561	$834	$1,738
5	$50,124	$104,474	$678	$1,412
6	$53,131	$110,743	$574	$1,195
7	$56,319	$117,388	$499	$1,040
8	$59,698	$124,431	$443	$923
9	$63,280	$131,897	$399	$832
10	$67,077	$139,810	$364	$759
11	$71,102	$148,199	$335	$699
12	$75,368	$157,091	$311	$649
13	$79,890	$166,516	$291	$606
14	$84,683	$176,507	$273	$569
15	$89,764	$187,098	$258	$537
16	$95,150	$198,324	$244	$509
17	$100,859	$210,223	$232	$484
18	$106,911	$222,837	$221	$461
19	$113,325	$236,207	$211	$441
20	$120,125	$250,379	$203	$422

biggest loan giver is Uncle Sam. For a full roundup of available federal loans (as well as grants), call the *Federal Student Aid Information Center* at 800-433-3243.

A detailed description of all federal loans and grants is beyond the scope of this book, but mention of Stafford loans is warranted because they are the most commonly awarded government-sponsored loans. In addition, Congress recently liberalized the rules and regulations on Staffords, making them available to virtually anyone, regardless of income.

Prior to 1993 there was only one version—a "subsidized" version—of the Stafford loan, which is awarded on the basis of financial need. The loan is considered subsidized because the federal government pays the interest on the loan until the student graduates and begins to pay back the loan. In general, a student whose parents earned a combined income of $45,000 was usually not eligible for the loan; eligibility on the basis of financial need is determined by a complex formula laid out in a federal-aid application form. Also, under the old system for determining financial need, a student also had difficulty showing need if the student's parents had even a modest amount of equity in a home—the amount was factored into the federal application form. However, in 1992 Congress revamped the Higher Education Act and not only made changes to the subsidized Stafford but also created a new "unsubsidized" Stafford.

Major changes in the federal financial-aid formula have had a major impact on Stafford loans as well as on other federal loans and grants. No longer does the formula take into account home equity. Also, the federal aid formula no longer counts the assets of families with adjusted gross incomes of up to $50,000 who don't itemize deductions on their tax returns. These and other changes regarding income and assets make it a lot easier to look poorer, or "needy," on paper. In addition, Congress lowered the interest rates on Stafford loans and increased the amount of money that students could borrow. In 1994 freshmen could qualify for as much as $2625 a year; sophomores could get $3500 a year; juniors and seniors could get a maximum of $5500 a year. Also, the cumulative maximum amounts borrowed also went up: overall, undergraduates can borrow $23,000 while graduate students can get a total of $65,500.

For families who don't qualify for the subsidized Stafford loan, the government has created an unsubsidized Stafford. The only big difference between the two Staffords is the payment of interest charges. As mentioned before, the federal government pays interest charges on the subsidized loan until the student leaves school. With the unsubsidized Stafford, the student is responsible for all interest charges, which must be paid while the student is in school or when the student leaves school.

Regardless of which Stafford loan is in effect, students generally have 10 years after leaving school to repay loans.

NATIONAL SERVICE/COLLEGE LOAN PROGRAM

In 1993 President Bill Clinton signed into law a bill to give financial aid to students in exchange for participation in community service programs. Under the initiative, called AmeriCorps, a student who works 1700 hours per year earns $4725 a year for up to two years; the money is applied to college tuition or to pay off existing college loans. A student also receives an annual living allowance of $7440 plus health and child-care benefits. A total of 100,000 students will be able to participate until 1996 when the law comes up for renewal. For more details, contact: **Corporation for National and Community Service**, 1100 Vermont Avenue, Washington, DC 20525 (800-942-2677 or 202-606-5000).

Financial Aid Forms

Since the federal government is the largest source of college grants and loans, it's likely that you will fill out the Free Application for Federal Aid. This application asks for details about a family's income and assets. The numbers are crunched by a processing firm (according to a federal formula) in order to determine your "expected family contribution" toward college costs. If that amount is larger than the school's annual total costs, then you do not qualify for aid. If there is a gap between expected family contribution and school costs, then you have established "financial need." At that point, colleges and universities can put together an aid package which is usually a mixed bag of grants, loans, and work-study programs.

Since 1993, changes in the federal aid application form have made it a lot easier to qualify for aid. For example, you no longer have to list the value of your home equity as an asset. However, some families are still in "sticker shock" when they learn the amount of the expected family contribution. The government expects a certain amount from you, regardless of whether or not you are pushing the limits of your budget, i.e., living beyond your means.

Strategic planning for getting financial-aid packages has become as popular as financial planning for income tax returns. Entire books have been written on the subject. Regarding the Free Application for Federal Aid, here are some tips for parents from the financial-aid gurus:

♦ Don't keep a lot of money in your child's name. Part of the expected family contribution is calculated on an expected contribution from the student. The federal financial-aid formula assesses 35 percent of a child's assets and up to 50 percent of a child's income as being available to pay for college costs. The rates are far lower on parents' assets and somewhat lower on parents' income.

♦ Defer income if you can. The government scrutinizes your financial status for the calendar year starting in January of the year before the student enters college. For example, if you apply for financial aid for school year 1995–96, much of the information required on the financial aid form comes from your 1994 federal income tax return. If you cashed in a big investment during 1994, you will have to declare any capital gains on the application. And the formula for calculating expected family contributions takes a bigger chunk out of parents' income, including capital gains, than it does out of parents' assets.

♦ Consider putting money into tax-deferred retirement plans like 401(k)s and IRAs. The federal formula doesn't count them as assets on the application form. These "hidden" assets might help to increase federal aid. However, assets are not hit hard by the federal formula, so before shifting money around, make sure the shifting makes sense for more reasons than just financial aid. Also, remember that the application form already excludes consideration of *all* assets if the adjusted gross income line of your federal tax return is $50,000 or less and you don't itemize deductions.

♦ Remember that you need to reapply every year for financial aid so your strategies must continue until you no longer need to apply for aid.

Federal forms are not the end of the line when it comes to qualifying for financial assistance. Many colleges have their own forms and most of those forms delve a lot further into your financial life. And the rules regarding what counts as assets and income are different from what counts on the federal application. Some factor in home equity, tax-deferred retirement plans, life insur-

---

SCHOLARSHIP SEARCH FIRMS

There are thousands of scholarship search firms that provide computerized lists of scholarships for fees that range from $45 to $200. In recent years a number of lawsuits have been brought against these firms by consumers and by the Federal Trade Commission. Usually the firms promise to provide a predetermined number of scholarship opportunities that are selected individually to match up with a student's background and abilities. Oftentimes, the list is a random one and students find themselves ineligible for most of the scholarships that are cited. Sometimes the list never arrives or arrives too late to be of any use. In addition, some firms actually guarantee that students will either get a scholarship from their lists or get their money back. Be aware that no firm can "guarantee" financial aid and very few refunds are ever issued.

The best sources for scholarship information are high school guidance offices and local libraries. Not only do they have all of the data provided by the scholarship search firms, but they are also aware of scholarships offered by local groups and organizations (search firms concentrate primarily on nationwide scholarships). If you are inclined to work with a search firm, do check it out with the Better Business Bureau.

ance policies, etc. You may even have to submit tax returns. However, even if you don't qualify for aid from the college, it won't affect eligibility for federal assistance.

While there are loopholes that can legally make you look needier than you really are, they should be used with caution. First of all, you don't want to make financial decisions that help secure a sizable college loan but have a negative impact on another part of your life. Also, you need to watch how far you push the boundaries of any loopholes that work for you. Financial-aid officers at colleges can be great allies who work hard to make the financial-needs process as painless as possible. But they can be downright unhelpful if they believe that you are lying about your finances or playing manipulative games to take advantage of the colleges they represent.

8

TRAVEL

TRAVEL BASICS

TRAVEL ABROAD

TRAVEL BASICS

Travel Agents/Travel Agencies

Having a good travel agent can mean the difference between a great trip and a rotten trip—whether you are traveling for business or for pleasure. In addition, it will probably make a big difference to your pocketbook. Finding the right airfare, hotel, car rental company can truly be a nightmare in today's largely unregulated travel industry in which prices change daily.

Travel agents act as the go-betweens, or brokers, between you and the companies that provide the services you require. The travel agencies they work for collect commissions (typically 8 percent to 15 percent of costs on airline tickets, hotel bookings, tour packages, etc.) from the service providers—not from you. Thus, you get the assistance of a travel agent/agency for free. However, this no-cost assistance is worthless if you have an agent whose performance is poor. Here's what you need to know when selecting a travel agent/agency:

Knowledge/reputation. Ask your well-traveled friends and business acquaintances for agent recommendations. If money is a major concern, penny-pinching friends may come in handy here—they probably double-check every transaction made by their agents. When you talk to prospective agents, be sure that they are familiar with the particulars of your travel destination.

Also, beware of agents that continually push the same airline or tour packages; they may be getting bonus commissions for doing high-volume business with particular companies. As for the agency—it would be nice if it has been in business for at least five years. Also, is it a member of the International Air Transportation Association (IATA), the Airline Reporting Corporation (ARC), and the American Society of Travel Agents (ASTA)? Remember that agencies come in all shapes and sizes—from mom-and-pop operations to high-volume chains to those that specialize in particular types of travel, like cruises or adventure trips. Try to find one that suits your long-range travel needs.

Equipment/automation. Almost all agencies have a computerized reservation system (CRS). This enables agents to call up quickly a variety of service providers and prices—to get you the best deal. However, not all airlines (especially the no-frills airlines) are on these systems, so if you favor a particular no-frills airline, be sure to let the agent know. In addition, your agent can use the computer to create a data file just for you: your frequent-flyer membership numbers, where you prefer to sit on an airplane, etc.

Good service. Does your agent promptly return your phone calls? Does your agent really try to meet your individual needs, and within your budget? In other words, are you getting personalized, timely, expert advice and attention? If not, it's time to move on and find someone who truly wants your business.

Money matters. Unfortunately, many travel agencies have failed in recent years. And many consumers have gone bust along with them. For instance, if you write out a check to the ABC Agency for a package tour to "anywhere" and the agency goes out of business before it pays the tour company, you may very well be out of a trip and out of your money. This sequence of events is the same for cruise lines and hotels, but airlines usually will honor tickets issued by an agency that is in default or bankruptcy. Very few states in the U.S. have consumer-protection laws requiring travel agencies to maintain accounts solely for the purpose of holding money in escrow until it is passed on to the appropriate tour company, etc. Ideally, your agency, as well as your tour operator, has such an escrow account—you would be wise to ask.

There are, nonetheless, a few things you can do to protect yourself. First of all, get your hands on tickets (and other paperwork) as soon as possible after paying your money. Particularly in the case of a package tour, get written confirmation from the supplier (cruise line, tour operator, etc.). If you start to get nervous, call the supplier yourself to be sure that your reservation has been paid for. Second, pay your travel agent with a credit card. There is a federal law, the Fair Credit Billing Act, that allows you to claim a refund from the card issuer for products or services that weren't delivered. The only stumbling block is that you have to submit a claim within 60 days of payment. If you are booking a package tour well in advance of your trip, pay the deposit upon booking, and, if possible, hold off paying the remainder until 45 days before you depart.

One final thought: If you are dealing with a tour operator, find out if the tour operator is a member of the U.S. Tour Operators Association (USTOA). USTOA has a consumer-protection plan, and its members have to post a bond to cover travelers in case the tour operator goes under. Ask your travel agent to find out if your tour operator is a member of USTOA and if the membership is current. Or, you can call USTOA (212-750-7371).

Finding the Lowest Airfare

Airline ticket prices change daily. The price structures and routing can seem confusing, outrageous, and unfair. Even if you have a travel agent, you might try calling a few airlines yourself to compare prices. Also, continually scan newspapers for advertised specials by the major airlines but be aware that a quoted price usually refers to "one way, based on round-trip purchase." In addition, the seating is usually limited, the fare may not be available on all flights, and there may be some surcharges or add-on costs.

In general, you get the best fares when you book in advance, fly off-peak hours (e.g., the red-eye flights), and fly off-season. Senior citizens usually get a discount, and most major airlines sell special discount coupon books for those 62 or older. If your airfare is included in an air/hotel package or an air/cruise package, you usually get a better price than if you booked the air ticket separately.

Should you buy a ticket from ticket consolidators? These are companies that buy up unsold tickets from the airlines at heavily discounted prices and then offer them to the public. They advertise the bargains in the travel sections of major city newspapers; most of the fares are for international flights. Some consolidators work only through travel agents; others deal only with the public; some deal with both.

There may be substantial savings from dealing with a consolidator, but there are some risks. First of all, you have very limited choice of an airline or departure time and date. If your flight is delayed or canceled, you usually can't use the ticket on another airline. If you need to cancel the ticket, it may be nonchangeable and nonrefundable. During heavily trafficked seasons, consolidators have a difficult time coming up with tickets to match their advertised specials. And you usually can't get frequent-flyer miles when traveling on a consolidator ticket. If you aren't troubled by the drawbacks and want to use a consolidator, find a travel agent who works with one and ask plenty of questions before laying out any money. And pay by credit card so that if something goes wrong (that isn't your fault), you have recourse by refusing payment when the bill arrives.

In the never-ending quest to beat the airlines at their own crazy-quilt fare system, consumers have come up with a number of ingenious ticketing gimmicks. We mention them here, but with a caveat: Airline computer systems are becoming increasingly sophisticated at spotting ticketing gimmicks, and airline representatives are more and more alert to catching travelers who bend, or break, the rules. If you are caught, your ticket may be confiscated and you may have to buy a new ticket before you are allowed to board the plane. Also, if you proudly explain one of the gimmicks to a travel agent and ask the agent to book one for you, the answer may be no.

A few of the most popular fare-saving techniques:

Hidden-city destination. This involves buying a ticket to a city beyond your actual destination. It works because major airlines book many of their flights through "hub cities" (where their operations are based and/or where connecting flights are made). Major hub cities include Dallas, Los Angeles, Miami, New York, Pittsburgh, Chicago, Miami, Atlanta, and St. Louis. Let's assume that Nancy (a passenger) wants to fly from her hometown, Los Angeles, to Pittsburgh. The best super-saver fare she can find costs $600. But after calling around she discovers an airline that is selling a Los Angeles to New York ticket (with a stop in Pittsburgh) for $500. She buys the Los Angeles–New York ticket and when the plane stops in Pittsburgh, Nancy simply gets off and doesn't use the second part of her ticket. She has saved $100. She must carry, not check, her luggage, because if she checked it, the bag would go through to her booked destination, New York.

Fly one way, pay round trip. If logic ruled the airfare pricing systems, the cost of a one-way ticket would cost half of a round-trip ticket. But in actuality, a one-way ticket often costs more than the cost of a round-trip ticket. What to do if you only need a one-way ticket? Buy a round trip and only use the half that you need.

Back-to-back tickets. Business travelers use this method in order to get discounted tickets and avoid the "stay over a Saturday night" requirement. Larry (a Los Angeles–based traveler) is miffed that his short-notice business meeting in New York requires him to pay for a full-fare ticket; he can't get a deal because he must return in a few days and can't stay over a Saturday night. So he buys two discounted tickets (the combined cost is less than a full-fare ticket), making sure that both tickets include a Saturday night stay. One set of tickets originates in Los Angeles and the other set originates in New York. He has carefully mapped out the dates so he can use the first half of ticket number one and the first half of ticket number two to create a ticket to meet his schedule. And he has another "scrambled" ticket to use if he so desires.

♦ Frequent-flyer ploy. Airline frequent-flyer members often sell their free awards via newspaper ads and through consolidators, and the prices are usually discounted. If you buy such a ticket, you will probably be flying under someone else's name. If caught, you will not be allowed to board the flight. Also, you and/or the seller will likely be bounced out of the frequent-flyer program.

Finding the best air fare can be frustrating when you have plenty of time to shop around, but it can be especially harrowing when you need to arrange emergency travel because of the serious illness or death of a family member. Special fares for these situations, called *bereavement fares,* were discontinued in 1992 when the airlines restructured their fare systems but they were subsequently reintroduced. Some airlines now offer these special fares only upon the death of an immediate family member, while other airlines offer them for both death and serious illness. Airlines extend the discounts in one of two ways:

either by offering a discount on a full-fare ticket, or by waiving the advance-purchase requirement on a discounted ticket. If you need to arrange emergency travel, it's best to call at least two or three airlines and ask about the bereavement fares since the rules vary so much among the airlines. For example, the definition of an "immediate" family member varies. Parents, children, siblings, and grandparents usually qualify, but policies differ when it comes to aunts and uncles and other more distant relatives. You can get the discount upon making the reservation or after returning home, but in either case you will have to provide adequate documentation or verification.

A MAGAZINE FOR AIRFARE BARGAIN HUNTERS

Best Fares is a monthly magazine dedicated to helping consumers find the lowest possible airfares. Staff at the magazine research tens of thousands of airfares in order to unearth many unadvertised, nonpromoted bargains that could reduce air travel costs dramatically. Each issue is a hefty 60+ pages and opens with dozens of mini-stories that feature current airfare bargains as well as deals for hotel accommodations and rental cars. In addition, there is news on frequent-flyer programs, senior citizen discounts, discount coupon offers from corporations and credit card issuers, and other travel-related subjects. Each issue of the magazine lists standard economy fares between most major cities in the United States, including super-saver round-trip fares. A 12-month subscription is $58 for the consumer edition; $78 for the corporate edition. For subscriber information, contact: Best Fares, 1111 West Arkansas Lane, Suite C, Arlington, TX 76013 (800-880-1234).

Air Passengers' Rights

Something goes wrong and it's the airline's fault. What compensation are you entitled to? Some situations are regulated by federal law; others are handled at the discretion of the airline; some are resolved in large part by your own negotiating skills. The most common mishaps:

Delayed and Canceled Flights

Airlines are not legally responsible to get you to your destination on time—meaning they don't guarantee their schedules. Regardless of the inconvenience (e.g., you missed a business meeting, family reunion, television appearance), the airline is not required by federal law to compensate you. Most airlines, however, will do their best to get you on another flight if yours is canceled. Also, each carrier has its own set of rules regarding what it will do for delayed passengers—paying for meals and drinks, overnight accommodations, telephone calls. These amenities are usually not offered. When stranded in an airport, you have to ask an airline representative what services the carrier will provide.

Overbooked Flights

When too many passengers have been booked on a flight, the airline will first ask for volunteers to give up their seats. If you volunteer, you will be booked on a later flight and receive one of the following: a free ticket for future travel (usually domestic travel); a certificate with a specified dollar amount that can be used toward the purchase of a ticket; cash. While this can be a good deal, there are considerations to take into account. First of all, when is the next flight out and will you get a confirmed reservation or be put on a waiting list? If the delay is long, will you get a free meal or free hotel room? The deal offered varies, depending on how many passengers volunteer. Obviously, the deal is more negotiable when there are fewer volunteers. In addition, ask about the restrictions on the free ticket:

How long is it good for? Is it transferable? Is it subject to blackout dates (when the tickets can't be used)?

If you are "involuntarily" bumped from an overbooked flight, federal law steps in and stipulates what you are entitled to (called denied-boarding compensation). These rules are based primarily on the length of time you have been inconvenienced.

Situation One. The airline arranges substitute transportation and gets you to your destination within one hour of your original scheduled arrival time. Result: no compensation.

Situation Two. The airline arranges substitute transportation and gets you to your destination between one and two hours after your original arrival time. Result: you get paid an amount equal to the one-way fare to your final destination, with a $200 maximum.

Situation Three. The airline arranges substitute transportation and gets you to your destination more than two hours late (four hours for international flights from the U.S.). Result: you are entitled to twice the amount of your one-way fare, with a $400 maximum.

There are, however, some eligibility requirements that you must fulfill in order to get any compensation for involuntary bumping. You must have had a confirmed reservation, have met the airline's deadline for buying your ticket, and have met the check-in deadline. The compensation rules do not apply if the airline substitutes a smaller plane for the one it originally planned to use, due to operational or safety reasons. Charter flights and planes that hold 60 or fewer passengers are exempt from the compensation rules. And the rules won't help you if you are bumped on a flight to the U.S. from a foreign country, even if you are booked on a U.S. carrier.

Lost Luggage

On domestic flights an airline pays for lost luggage on a per-passenger basis: $1250 maximum per passenger. On international flights, the liability is figured per pound ($9.07 per pound) with a maximum of $635 per bag (a 70-pound bag). In order to receive compensation, you must file a claim with the airline and prove, as best you can, the value of the items lost. Also, even if you have receipts for most of your lost items, the airline will not pay the replacement cost but will pay the depreciated value of items. Airlines will not replace lost cash and most will not pay for valuable items (like jewelry, computers, cameras), so don't put them in checked luggage. If you must pack some valuables in checked bags, then consider buying "excess value" baggage insurance from the airline or get additional travel insurance for luggage from an independent insurance company (some homeowner's insurance covers baggage).

The rules, regulations, and policies of an airline carrier are spelled out in a document called a "contract of carriage." A condensed version of some of the rules is printed on the back of your airline ticket. If you want the long, legal version, you can get it at the airline ticket office or sometimes at the check-in counter.

Flyer's Tips for Health and Comfort

Anyone who has flown in an airplane for a long period of time knows the all-too-familiar symptoms of air-travel fatigue: dry eyes, swollen ankles and feet, stiff back, headache, sore muscles, blocked ears. Add to that a bit of cabin fever from being cooped up in a crowded plane and you get one miserable traveler.

The reasons you feel so wacky are easy to explain. First, you are traveling in a pressurized cabin and are not getting as much oxygen as you would on the ground. Second, you are breathing outside air that has been warmed up for your comfort; in other words, the air has been dried out. Some airplanes have humidifiers; some don't. Also, your body was not meant to sit in one restricted position for long periods of time. Your circulation system and lymphatic systems can't work properly (why your ankles swell up).

Luckily, within a few hours after getting off the

plane, your body returns to normal. There are, however, some preventive measures you can take to reduce the effects of air travel fatigue.

♦ At least once an hour, get up and walk up and down the aisles.

♦ While in your seat, contract and relax your calf muscles every once in a while. Also, you might put pillows in the lumbar region of your back and behind your neck.

♦ Watch what you eat and drink. Avoid excessive eating, especially foods that are hard to digest, like red meat. Stay away from beverages with alcohol and caffeine because they act as diuretics, further dehydrating the body. You need to drink plenty of liquids, but stick to water and fruit juices.

♦ Wear loose-fitting clothes and comfortable shoes. The bloated feeling you get is no illusion; your body can gain as much as four pounds on the plane.

♦ If you get an earache or your ears get blocked, try one of the following: chew gum, suck on hard candy, yawn, swallow.

Jet Lag

Typical symptoms of jet lag include daytime sleepiness, nighttime insomnia, fatigue, disorientation, irritability, digestive disorders, and a general feeling of malaise. Jet lag occurs because high-speed aircraft allow us to cross numerous time zones in a relatively short period of time—and our internal body clocks have a difficult time adjusting to a new time zone. Most people experience little or no jet lag if they cross no more than three time zones. The farther you go and the more time zones you cross (altogether there are 24), the greater the effects of jet lag. You suffer the most when crossing 12 time zones.

Times zones aside, there are other factors that influence your vulnerability to jet lag:

♦ Age (younger people cope better).
♦ Health (poor health increases jet lag).
♦ Personality (extroverts tend to ignore symptoms and push on).

♦ Sleeping habits (in general, if you regularly sleep seven hours or less, you adjust faster).

♦ Direction of travel (east-west or west-east are troublesome, with west-east, against the movement of the sun, causing the most difficulty).

Entire books have been written on how to combat the effects of jet lag—with elaborate preflight dietary and sleep schedules. In addition, there are computer-based programs that allow you to plug in the specifics of your journey in order to get a customized plan for when you should sleep, eat, and exercise. Some travelers swear by these programs; others say they make little or no difference. If you want to expend the time and effort, by all means head to your nearest bookstore/library or software store. If not, here are some basic rules of thumb that should lessen your battle with jet lag. The underlying goal of the recommendations is to get your body clock working in sync with your new time zone.

Booking your departure flight. If you are traveling a short distance eastward or a longer distance westward, try to take a morning flight. If you are traveling a short distance westward or a longer distance eastward, try to book a late-afternoon or evening flight. It's best, if possible, to arrive at your destination in the late afternoon or early evening—in time to eat a light meal and get to bed early.

Sleeping. Be aware of the time at your destination and try to trick your body into believing it is already in the new time zone. If you are flying when it's daytime at your destination, try to stay awake by reading, watching the in-flight movie, talking to other passengers, walking up and down the aisles. If it's nighttime at your destination, try to sleep even if bright sunlight is streaming in your window—close the window blind, turn off your reading light, grab a pillow, put on an eye-mask, and try to sleep, or at least relax. When you arrive at your destination and it's night, you're in luck and can go to sleep, but remember to set your alarm to get up in the morning. Arriving during the day, after a long flight, is much trickier since you will probably be tired and somewhat disoriented. Try not to take a nap since it will only prolong jet lag (if you must take a nap, make it a short one). Freshen up at your hotel and do your best to stay awake until bedtime. One of the best tactics in this situation is to get out into the sunlight. Researchers say that "light therapy" will tell your brain what time it is and help to reset your biological clock.

Food and drink. Eat lightly for the first two or three days of your trip so that you won't overtax your digestive system. On the airplane, drink plenty of liquids but avoid alcoholic beverages and limit your intake of caffeine (avoid drinks with caffeine before you try to fall asleep). Once you get to your destination, try to eat your meals based on local time.

Above all, try not to become obsessed with jet lag. Three out of four long-distance travelers are affected by it. And don't worry if it doesn't disappear right away—every two-hour time difference (or two time zones) usually takes a 24-hour recovery time.

Frequent-Flyer Programs

Frequent-flyer programs, now more than a decade old, have become a national obsession. More than 10 percent of all Americans now belong to one or more of the programs, which are offered by almost all major U.S. airlines. In the early days of the programs the rules of the game were fairly simple: you earned one mile per mile traveled on an airline and when you accumulated enough miles you could trade them in for a free ticket or a free upgrade from coach to business or first class.

While the basic rules still apply, the programs have become much more complex. Now you can earn miles not only by flying on a particular airline, but you can earn them by patronizing companies affiliated with frequent-flyer programs—hotels, car rental agencies, phone companies. In addition, some credit card companies have joined forces with the airlines and offer "affinity cards" whereby you earn one mile for every dollar charged.

Even if you consider yourself an infrequent flyer, you still might benefit from joining a program. Membership is free (usually you get at least a few thousand miles for enrolling), so you might want to join several. Programs are always offering "bonus" miles during slow times of the year or for particular routes, so your miles will add up faster than you think. Before joining, however, you should compare the basic components of several programs. Here are the major points to consider:

♦ Expiration dates. Some airlines stipulate that you lose miles if they are not spent within a certain time period. Avoid those if you are not a very frequent flyer.

♦ Redemption levels. A free domestic ticket may require 20,000 miles on one airline, 25,000 on another. Mileage requirements differ widely among programs for all levels of free tickets as well as for upgrades (both domestic and nondomestic travel).

♦ Minimum credits earned per flight. Even if you are only flying a short distance (i.e., 200 miles), programs will credit you with a guaranteed minimum: some give 500 miles, some 750, some 1000.

♦ Program partners. Is your frequent-flyer program affiliated with your favorite hotels and car rental agencies? Oftentimes, these extra miles earned come in handy when you fall just short of an award level. Also, most U.S. programs have international airline partners like Singapore Airlines, Qantas Airways, Japan Airlines, etc. If you fly on a partner airline, your miles will be credited to your U.S. frequent-flyer account. But before you start celebrating because of all the miles an international flight will bring you, read the fine print in your program's rules-and-restrictions booklet. Many U.S. frequent-flyer programs will not give you credit for the miles on their international partner if you purchase a "restricted" (i.e., discounted) fare.

♦ Transferring awards. Almost all programs will let you transfer your award to someone else but even the fine print gets a little blurred here. Qualifying recipients are variously called "family members" or "relatives" or "family members with the same surname." If this aspect of the program concerns you, do call the program and find our exactly whom you can—and cannot—give an award to.

♦ Blackout dates. These are days when frequent-flyer awards cannot be used. Some programs have a minimal amount of them; some have quite a few.

Don't get carried away and join too many frequent-flyer programs. It's best to concentrate on a few airlines so that your mileage accumulates and pays off with awards. Also, many airlines offer "elite" status to travelers who fly a certain number of miles a year (usually quite a large number of miles). Once you reach elite status, you may be entitled to extra rewards including: free upgrades, mileage bonuses, immunity from blackout dates, preferred baggage check-in. However, once you have spent your miles and collected your awards on an airline program, reevaluate it against other programs. The airlines are constantly changing the programs and you want to belong to those that provide the best benefits.

The U.S. Department of Transportation does not regulate airline frequent-flyer programs. Therefore, complaints regarding programs need to be resolved directly with the airline companies.

Travel Insurance

Travel insurance policies vary widely in coverage, are complex, and are usually misunderstood. In addition, they can be quite costly, as much as 8 to 10 percent of the total cost of a trip. They are sold by travel insurance companies (usually through travel agents) as well as by cruise lines and tour operators. The policies sold by independent insurance companies are called "retail" policies, while the policies sold by cruise lines and tour operators are called "supplier" policies.

Typically, policies from travel insurance companies come in "bundles," meaning you might have to buy several features you don't need or want in order to get the one feature that you do want. And sometimes the features you are forced to take are already covered by your existing health or homeowner's policy. However, some travelers have benefited greatly (sometimes monetarily, sometimes only psychologically) from these policies and would never leave home without them.

When considering whether or not to buy travel insurance, you must read the policy's fine print, all of it, very carefully. Exactly what coverage are you getting? What are the deductibles? What are the exclusions? What is the cost? Are there components in the policy that duplicate coverage you already have?

Following are some of the main divisions of a comprehensive policy that can be bundled together. In some instances, you might be able to get coverage for just one of the items listed below.

Trip cancellation. You've already paid $5000 for a cruise or tour package and you can't go. The very thought of this kind of financial loss is terrifying—and is the reason why trip cancellation insurance is very popular. You can get this coverage directly from the cruise line or tour operator or from a travel insurance company. When comparing policies, be sure to check out a few vital areas. First of all, what are the cutoff dates for cancellation? Can you cancel up to the last minute and get a full refund or does your insurance coverage lapse three or four days before departure? Also, do you need an "acceptable" reason (like a death in the family or an unforeseeable illness) to cancel and collect? And be forewarned that many policies have a "preexisting condition" clause that limits or denies a refund if you cancel because of an illness that occurs due to a preexisting condition. Some companies will cover a preexisting condition if the condition was stable and didn't require medical treatment within a specified period (usually 60 days) before the policy was purchased. Often bundled with cancellation coverage is "trip interruption" coverage.

This covers you if you have to interrupt your trip and return home because of a family emergency or because you have become injured or ill. Again, this coverage usually is limited by preexisting conditions, so ask about the restrictions.

Default. Again, you have prepaid $5000 for a cruise or tour package. Only this time you're all ready to go, but the cruise line or tour operator goes bankrupt. If you bought default insurance from the cruise line or tour operator, you might be out of luck. If you got coverage from a travel insurance company, you will collect. But find out exactly how much you could collect.

Medical. If you already have a major-medical insurance policy, this is duplicate coverage. However, if you are traveling abroad, check your current policy to be sure it covers you for treatment out of the country. Also, Medicare does *not* cover claims made outside of the United States (but some "Medigap" policies—supplements to Medicare—do provide coverage). If you are considering this coverage, do ask about the restrictions for preexisting conditions.

Emergency evacuation. This will cover transportation costs if you need to be transported to a medical facility. It's usually bundled with medical coverage. Consider this coverage if you have a serious health problem or if you are traveling in a Third World country where medical care could be inadequate.

Baggage. If your homeowner's policy has an "off premises" clause, you don't need this. Furthermore, airlines have you automatically covered, both domestically and internationally, if your bags are lost (see "Air Passengers' Rights," p. 458). Finally, if you pay for a trip with a credit card, you may have coverage for lost baggage if your credit card issuer provides traveler's benefits as part of its program.

Accidental death. Almost all travel insurance companies offer this coverage. And one kind of coverage, called flight insurance, is hawked at airports—at counters or in vending machines. Even though it's usually inexpensive insurance, consumer advocates say that you need a good life insurance policy that covers you anywhere and at all times, not just a policy for travel excursions. You may even get this coverage for free if you paid for your trip with a credit card. Like lost baggage coverage mentioned above, accidental death coverage is provided by some credit card issuers as part of their traveler's assistance programs.

If you decide that travel insurance is something you need, shop around to get the best coverage for the least cost and choose a plan from a reputable company.

Filing a Complaint

No matter how well travel plans are constructed, mistakes occur. Whether it's a computer error or a human error, anyone—a hotel, airline, tour company, car rental company, even your travel agent—can blunder and cause you instant aggravation. When something goes wrong on your trip, it's always best to try to resolve the problem immediately. If your hotel room isn't what you expected, or the car rental rate is higher than what you booked, or a tour operator fails to deliver parts of a packaged tour—speak up.

How you complain can determine whether or not you get results. Bursting into an angry tirade, whining, or crying (yes, we weary travelers have these tendencies) may feel good but it is usually nonproductive. First of all, find the appropriate person to speak with—the person who has the authority to fix your dilemma. A growing number of lower-level employees now have the decision-making power to correct mistakes, but you may have to ask to speak to a manager.

Be calm; be firm; be pleasant. Explain your situation and provide any paperwork needed to substantiate your claim. Offer solutions as to how the problem can be rectified and be realistic in what you expect. For instance, if your reserved room with a mountain view simply isn't available, you can suggest a partial refund, an upgrade to an ocean view, complimentary meals in the hotel's dining room. If you are a frequent customer of the company, say so. Most of the time, travel suppliers will do their best to make you happy. However, if the situation is not corrected to your satisfaction, let it be known that you will file a formal complaint with the company.

When you return home, write to the customer service or public relations office of the company. State what happened, as briefly as possible, and what you are seeking in compensation. Enclose copies of all relevant receipts and correspondence and include a synopsis of how you tried to resolve the problem (including the names of the company representatives you talked to). If you think your travel agent may have some clout with the company, ask the travel agent to file the complaint.

When direct contact with the company fails to settle the dispute, there are two groups you can turn to:

1. American Society of Travel Agents. This group represents 20,000 travel agencies, as well as many travel suppliers—tour operators, cruise lines, hotels, airlines, etc. It will act as a mediator if: you submit your complaint in writing; you can prove that you made a effort to resolve the problem; the complaint is not more than six months old. For further information: **American Society of Travel Agents,** Consumer Affairs Department, 1101 King Street, Alexandria, VA 22314 (703-739-2782).

2. U.S. Department of Transportation. Dealing exclusively with complaints against U.S. and foreign airlines, the department helps to resolve disputes on a number of issues, including delayed, canceled, or overbooked flights. It also provides information and assistance for claims involving lost and damaged luggage and ticketing mistakes. For further information contact: **U.S. Department of Transportation,** Consumer Affairs Division, Room 10405, 400 7th Street SW, Washington, DC 20590 (202-366-2220).

Booking a Hotel Room

Calling the toll-free 800 numbers advertised by major hotel chains will not necessarily get you the best room rate. Usually, hotels set aside blocks of rooms for the toll-free numbers and price them at a set rack rate—the highest rate they think they can get. It's better to spend a few dollars on a long-distance call and contact the hotel directly. When you get the reservation desk, ask about a number of rates—weekend rates, senior citizen rates, corporate rates, student rates, auto club rates, etc. At any given time, a hotel (especially those affiliated with major chains) can have in excess of 20 different rates. You're bound to qualify for one or more.

It's always best to make reservations ahead of time and some hotels will give you a discount for early booking. Nonetheless, when you arrive at the hotel, check at the front desk to be sure that you got the best available price. Even if you did, your concern (courteous, of course) may get you bumped up to a better room (at the same price) if space is available. Remember, however, that your best negotiating strategies are subject to supply and demand. You won't get a heavily discounted room in Hawaii at Christmas (peak season) or at your favorite hotel in Las Vegas when a large convention group has been booked.

When you book a reservation, get a confirmation number so that if the hotel is overbooked when you arrive, you won't be left without a room. Using a credit card will guarantee your room even if you arrive later, but you will have to pay for the room if you don't show up. However, there is usually no charge for a guaranteed credit card reservation if you cancel it a few days in advance.

Booking hotel rooms for foreign travel is best done through a travel agent if you plan to stay at a major chain (i.e., more expensive hotel). However, most travel agents have no affiliations with smaller, budget hotels or pensions. After selecting a hotel (dozens are listed in travel books for particular countries), you can phone, fax, or write. Some require deposits for a guaranteed room (usually they will accept an American check). Be aware that the rate you are quoted may be different from that published in your travel book (usually outdated the day it went to press). Also, when you get a written confirmation from the foreign hotel, put it with your travel documents so you won't forget to take it with you.

Hotel Safety

Here are some tips to help protect you from theft and fire:

Theft

Hotel security, even at expensive hotels, is not failsafe. In some hotels and motels, it's practically nonexistent. This does not mean that you should assume the worst or become paranoid, but simply exercise common sense and take some precautions, especially if you are traveling alone.

Ideally, your hotel will have closed-circuit cameras, 24-hour security guards (in the parking garage as well as in the hotel), and peepholes in all room doors. Here are some other safety tips:

♦ If an unexpected delivery or service person knocks on your door, call the desk to make sure the person is legitimate.

♦ Don't leave valuables in your room when you aren't there; even when you are there, don't leave cash and jewelry sitting around on counter tops. Most hotels have safe-deposit boxes in the reception area; some have them in every room.

♦ Try to get maid service to clean your room early, then put out the do-not-disturb sign.

♦ If you don't mind a little noise, book a room close to a heavily trafficked area, like an elevator, lobby, reception desk.

♦ Turn on the lights in the room when you leave. When you return, you will not have to fumble around, looking for the light switch.

♦ When talking with strangers in the hotel—people you meet in the lobby, at the bar or swimming pool—be careful about giving out personal information.

♦ Take along a rubber door jam. When you go to sleep at night, use it to provide absolute security from the inside.

Fire

Knowing what to do, quickly and calmly, in case of a hotel fire could save your life. The following fire safety tips are from "Be Fire Smart: Tips for Travelers," a publication of the Insurance Information Institute.

♦ As soon as you check into a hotel or motel, go into the hallway and locate the nearest exits.

♦ Count the number of doors from your room to the exit and memorize that number. Note which side of the hall the exit is on, or if you must turn left or right.

♦ If a fire should occur, do not panic. Staying calm will increase your chances of survival.

♦ Remember, smoke rises. It also kills. If you should awaken to smoke in your room, roll out of bed, grab your key, and crawl to the door. Even if you can tolerate the smoke while standing, it is safer to crawl.

♦ You should always place your key on your night stand before retiring so you won't have to waste time looking for it in an emergency.

♦ When you reach the door, do not open it until you have checked to be sure there isn't fire on the other side. Brace your shoulder or foot against the door and open with extreme caution. Should you be confronted with a high concentration of superheated air or smoke, close the door immediately.

♦ If the hall is passable, use one of your predesignated escape routes.

♦ Do not waste time gathering personal belongings but shut your door and take your key.

♦ Do not use an elevator. It may stall due to heat or loss of power.

♦ If you must use an inside stairwell, check door for smoke on the other side before entering stairwell.

♦ If the stairwell is safe to enter, walk downward, do not run. Hold onto wall or handrail to prevent falling.

♦ If all of your escape routes are blocked, it may be safer to return to your room.

♦ If you must return to your room or remain in your room because escape routes are blocked, open a window slightly to let smoke escape. If the window will not open, do not break it—a large hole can pull smoke into the room. If the smoke is outside, keep window closed.

♦ Do not jump. You may not survive the fall.

♦ If you must remain in the room, close all vents and air ducts. Wet towels and sheets and stuff them around doors, and into vents and air ducts.

Rental Cars

If you are not a frequent car rental customer, you may not be aware of the complexity of the business or how to go about getting a fair deal. For instance, one of the authors of this book recently arrived at an airport in Hawaii and went to the desk of a major car rental company to get a compact car that she had reserved in advance. The clerk strongly suggested that she consider upgrading to a midsize car—more comfortable, more power, not "that much" more money. She politely refused, preferring to stick with her budget car. A minute later, the clerk informed her that the compact cars were all sold out and she would be given a midsize car, at no additional cost.

Before renting a car you should . . .

Shop Around. The toll-free 800 numbers advertised by major car rental companies do not necessarily produce the best rates. Sometimes, the local franchise in the location where you pick up the car will quote you a lower rate. Watch your newspaper for rental advertisements; ask your travel agent to check the computerized reservation system for the lowest rates. Also, do you belong to an organization or program—auto club, airline frequent-flyer program, etc.—that offers special rates for members? Does the company you work for have a corporate rate with a particular car rental company? And when you call a rental agency, ask if it is running any special promotional deals.

Rent the Least Expensive Car. The least expensive car is usually the smallest. However, sometimes a company has an abundance of a certain-size car, not necessarily the smallest, and they will be offered at a special rate just to get them rented. Whatever the case, the least expensive cars are the ones in greatest demand, so if the company runs out by the time you check in, you might get a free upgrade. When offered a free upgrade, be sure there are no additional charges.

Understand the Rental Agreement. Do you get a specific number of miles free per day and a charge per mile over your allotted miles? Or do you have unlimited mileage? What happens if you book a weekly rate and have to return the car before (or after) the week ends? (You may be charged a higher daily rate.) Ask if there are any extra charges—e.g., for an additional driver, for airport surcharges.

Avoid Buying Unnecessary Insurance. The cost of your rental car can jump up considerably if you need to purchase additional insurance from the rental company. And the car rental companies encourage you to do so. Before you agree, call your insurance agent and see if your personal auto policy extends coverage for a rental car. Also, if you have a major credit card, call the issuer of the card to see if you get free collision-damage coverage if you use the card to pay for the car rental. This credit card insurance is usually secondary coverage, meaning it will pay only after your personal insurance policy has paid up.

Beware of Drop-Off Charges. A drop-off charge is a penalty imposed when you return a car to a location different from the one where you picked it up. The charge can be exorbitant so ask about drop-off restrictions when you reserve a car.

Check the Fuel Charges. Most companies get you on the road with a full tank of gas and ask that you return the car with a full tank of gas. If you don't, the company will fill the tank and charge you at "its price"—considerably higher than what you would pay at the pump.

Packing a Suitcase

For most travelers, packing for a trip is an unwelcome chore. Most of us take too much, end up with bundles of wrinkled clothing, and forget a few essential items. There are, however, some steps you can take to lessen the hassle of packing.

Getting Ready

1. Make a list of what you need to take. Imagine yourself at your destination and think of the activities in which you will participate. Choose clothing that travels well—washable, wrinkle-resistant. Choose a few basic colors and mix and match items to create different outfits. Don't forget to include accessories and toiletries on your list.

PACKING THE INTERFOLDING METHOD

In order to maximize use of suitcase space as well as ensure fewer wrinkles, travel experts recommend a packing method called "interfolding." Here's how it works:

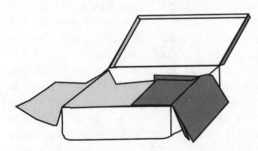

STEP ONE
Begin with your long garments (e.g., trousers, skirts, or dresses). Take one of these long items by the waistband or collar and line it up with a straight edge of your suitcase. Let the rest of the garment hang out over the opposite edge. Continue with the other long garments, using different inside edges of the suitcase, until all long items are packed.

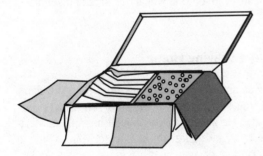

STEP TWO
In the "well" you have created, place folded shirts, sweaters, undergarments, etc.

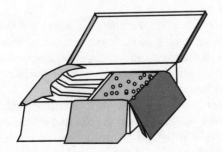

STEP THREE
Then you need to "interfold" all of the clothing that has been hanging out over the edges of your suitcase. Alternate from side to side, folding one garment over another and smoothing out wrinkles as you pack. This method allows garments to cushion each other, causing fewer wrinkles and creases.

2. A week before you leave, start assembling what you will take. Put clothes in a separate section of your closet; put accessories and toiletries in a box.

3. Before putting everything in a suitcase, take a long, hard look at what you have pulled together. Do you absolutely need *all* of it? Usually, the answer is no.

Packing It Up

1. We recommend the interfolding method, which utilizes luggage space ingeniously. It's explained in the accompanying illustration.

2. Shoes and other heavy items should be placed along the hinged side of the suitcase. When the suitcase is closed and standing upright, these heavier items will be on the bottom and won't slip down and wrinkle the clothes.

3. Roll up items like sleepwear, t-shirts, and socks and fit them into available spaces. Smaller items like socks and pantyhose also fit nicely into your shoes. When you are finished, the contents of your suitcase should be comfortably solid (meaning no big, empty spaces). Thus, the contents won't shift too much.

4. If you use a duffel bag, roll all clothing. If you use a hanging garment bag, center all clothing on hangers and bring sleeves up toward the front.

Last-Minute Checks

1. If you check your luggage, there's always a chance it will get lost. Therefore, pack essentials (medications, valuable jewelry, traveler's checks, camera) in a carry-on bag. Important travel documents (passport, hotel and car rental confirmations) should also be placed in the carry-on. Most airlines won't be held accountable for items such as jewelry, cameras, and cash.

2. Be sure you have identification tags on all bags, inside and outside. In order to make your luggage more recognizable, if you will be checking it at airports, you might put a brightly colored

strap around the outside or tie brightly colored yarn around the handle.

3. If traveling on aircraft, be aware that some items cannot go aboard either in checked luggage or carry-on luggage. Some examples: explosives (like fireworks), flammable liquids (like fuel or paint), compressed gases (like butane cylinders for camping). If you plan to take along any knives, even penknives, put them in checked luggage; they can be confiscated from carry-on bags.

Dogs and Cats—On the Road or in the Air

Some pets are eager, happy travelers; other are totally traumatized. Dogs or cats that are ill, very young, old with a medical condition, very nervous or aggressive, are not good candidates for travel. Also, pets that are prone to motion sickness should not be subjected to the rigors of travel. In general, dogs adjust better than cats. If you choose to take along your pet (or if you have to because you are moving to a distant place), there are a number of things you need to know so that your furry loved one will arrive safe and sound.

Before Leaving Home

Your animal's vaccinations must be up to date, and you should take along a current health certificate. Be sure your pet is wearing an identification tag, and take along a color photo and a description of your pet (height, weight, color, distinguishing marks), in case the pet gets lost en route.

Pack a bag for the animal: feeding and water bowls, grooming tools, leash and collar/harness, pet toys, cleanup items (pooper scooper or litter and litter pan, paper towels), food and water, any prescribed medications.

Most important: test your animal for motion sickness. Begin by taking your dog or cat for a short ride in the car and every day increase the length of the trip. Put the animal in a cat or dog carrier and be sure it is large enough for the pet to be comfortable.

Traveling by Car

Pet carriers/kennels are a must, even for dogs who are used to short, frequent car rides. Having your pet in a carrier that is sturdy, well-ventilated, and comfortable (soft mat or cushion inside) will best ensure the safety of the animal as well as the safety of the other passengers. The carrier should be large enough for the animal to stand, turn around, and lie down in. It should not be placed in the sunny side of your vehicle.

Do not feed your cat or dog for at least three hours before setting off in the car. In general, animals should be fed less than usual when traveling. On longer trips, snacks and water or small amounts of food are fine. (Remember that cats need to use a litterbox about every three to four hours.) If possible, the main meal should be given at the end of the day when you are finished driving or have arrived at your destination. Frequent stops are recommended; the dog can stretch and exercise (be sure the leash is on before the dog gets out of the car) and the cat can just get a break from the motion of the car.

Leaving your pet in a closed, parked car can be dangerous, especially in hot weather when car temperatures can rise quickly and cause heat stroke. If you have to leave the animal alone, park in a shaded area, roll down the windows a few inches, and return quickly. Cold weather can be equally threatening, causing hypothermia if your pet is left alone for too long.

Traveling by Air

More than 2 million animals fly in and out of major U.S. airports every year. Each airline has its own company policies for pet travel, so you must contact your airline for its specific rules and regulations. All airlines require health certificates (written no longer than 10 days before departure) to be sure that the pet is in good health.

Your dog or cat must be at least eight weeks old and fully weaned. It must travel in a cage/shipping container that meets the airline's minimum standards for size, ventilation, strength, design, and sanitation (most airlines sell or rent kennels). Depending on the age of your animal, or the length of the trip, food and water may be required (along with written instructions).

If you are traveling on the same airplane as your pet, the animal will be classified as "baggage." If the animal is traveling unaccompanied, it will be called "cargo." The designations are used to determine the cost of transporting the animal (usually the cost is more if the animal is flying solo). Regardless of designation, all pets are shipped in the same pressurized holds of the plane. Some airlines allow a small animal in the passenger cabin as carry-on luggage if the pet is comfortable in the carrier and the carrier fits under the seat.

Pets do die in airplane holds, almost always due to extremely high or low temperatures. Thus, try not to have your animal travel when temperatures are below 40 degrees or above 80 degrees at either end of a flight or at in-between stops. If you are traveling with your animal (the pet is in the airplane hold) and your flight is delayed, be sure that you tell the crew your pet is on board.

The United States Department of Transportation also recommends that all pet owners take the following precautions:

♦ Before traveling, accustom your pet to the kennel in which it will be shipped.

♦ Do not give your pet solid food in the six hours prior to the flight, although a moderate amount of water and a walk before and after the flight are advised.

♦ Do not administer sedation to your pet without the approval of a veterinarian.

♦ Be sure to reserve a space for your pet in advance and inquire about time and location for drop-off and pickup.

♦ Try to schedule a nonstop flight; avoid connections and the heavy traffic of a holiday or weekend flight.

♦ For overseas travel (including Hawaii), inquire about any special health requirements, such as quarantine.

♦ Be sure to put your name and the recipient's name, address, and phone number in large letters on the kennel.

What about taking pets on trains or buses? Amtrak does not permit animals on any of its trains. Most bus lines also prohibit animals, but rules may vary from company to company.

First-Aid Kit

What to put in a medical kit depends on your travel destination, the length of your trip, and your individual needs. While it's advisable to be prepared, you don't want to end up looking like a mobile medical unit. The following suggestions are intended to be a starting point; add and subtract according to your particular situation.

    Aspirin or other minor painkillers
    Band-Aids
    Sunscreen (SPF rating of 15 or higher)
    Insect repellent (with at least a 35-percent solution of deet)
    Antidiarrheal (like Imodium, Kaopectate, Pepto-Bismol)
    Antibiotic ointment (such as Neosporin)
    Antacid tablets
    Gauze bandages (just a few)—and adhesive tape
    Laxatives
    Eyedrops
    Liquid antiseptic (like Betadine)
    Insect sting kit
    Antihistamine (in case of a cold or allergies)
    Thermometer
    Antiseptic "wipes" or alcohol "preps" (for cleansing around minor wounds)
    Moleskin (to put on pressure points on feet where blisters form)
    Tweezers
    Small pair of scissors
    Personal prescription medicines (take an adequate supply; keep medicines in original containers in case you need a refill; know the generic names of your drugs, especially if traveling to foreign countries)

If you are going on a cruise, you might want to take along a motion-sickness remedy. Traveling to malaria-infested regions requires antimalarial drugs. Water-purification gadgets and/or pills are in order when sanitary water supplies are in question. For trips abroad, many tourists like to take antibiotics along—consult your doctor for an appropriate broad-spectrum drug.

Travel Photographs

Disappointed in your vacation photographs? It's discouraging to invest money in equipment and supplies—not to mention lugging the stuff around—only to cringe when you see the developed prints. Assuming you know how to use your camera correctly, there are some basic guidelines that, if followed, will result in travel photos you will be proud of.

Knowing how to use your camera is the cornerstone of good photography. Too many amateurs buy very sophisticated equipment with big instruction manuals and never bother to read them or practice taking photos before leaving on vacation. So be realistic when buying a camera and get one that you are comfortable with. Luckily, modern technology has provided us with a vast array of idiotproof cameras, many of them with sophisticated features that are automatic and easy to use. Once you are at ease with your equipment, you can concentrate on the fun, artistic aspects of photography.

As you get ready to shoot, remember the following:

Get Closer. This is the biggest mistake we all make—trying to get too many elements into one photo. Moving farther and farther away from the subject(s) results in an "overall" photo that shows very little detail of too many things. Ask yourself, "What is the subject of this photo, and what am I trying to capture?" The subject should fill at least one-third to one-half of the picture area.

Beware of Outdoor Lighting Conditions. When taking people pictures, don't pose your subjects squinting into the sunlight. Also, bright, direct sunlight, especially at high noon when the sun is directly overhead, causes harsh shadows on faces and washes out your background. The best time of day for outdoor photos is in the morning or late afternoon (or overcast days).

Choose the Right Film Speed. A film's "speed"—the way it responds to light—is indicated by an ISO (or ASA) number on the roll or box. Use 100- or 200-ISO film on sunny days and when you use a flash. Use 400-ISO film for action shots, in low-light conditions, or when you use a telephoto lens. But, you say, I will probably be using one roll to shoot a number of the above-mentioned conditions. Then, use a 400-ISO, which is the most versatile film. Overall, the higher the number, the "faster" the film—which means that less light will be needed for properly exposed photographs. Special note: if you want to shoot photos in very dim light, with no flash (i.e., in a museum), you want a super-fast, super-low-light film—1600-ISO film.

Experiment with Composition. Do most of your photos have the same look—person or building or pet—smack in the center of the print? To get some variety, try using what photographers call "the rule of thirds." Imagine that the picture area in your viewfinder is divided into thirds—horizontally and vertically. This grid of nine blocks has four intersection points. Put your subject near one of these four imaginary points. Thus, you have moved your subject away from dead center of the photo.

Take More Candid Shots. Your people pictures will be much improved if your subjects are not acutely aware of you and your camera. People are more relaxed, more spontaneous, when they aren't posing before a camera lens. Catch your subjects engaged in an activity and quickly take your picture. Candid shots may take a little more effort, but the results are well worth it.

A final note on travel photos: All of your efforts will be in vain if faulty X-ray equipment degrades your film. If you can, ask the security guard to hand-inspect your film rather then putting it through the X-ray machine. Unfortunately, due to increased security at airports, many inspectors insist that everything, including your film, be X-rayed. In that case, be prepared with a lead-lined bag (available at most photo/camera stores), which should provide adequate protection.

THE RULE OF THIRDS

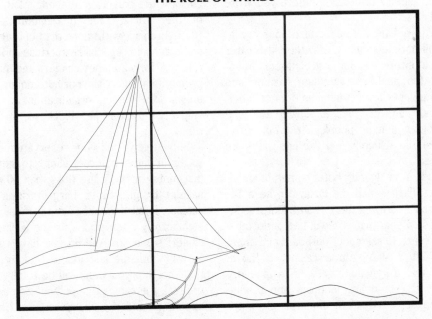

Cruises

A decade ago, cruise vacations were the choice of old people—and their parents. No longer. Today, the ever-booming cruise industry caters to just about everyone—veteran cruisers, honeymooners, singles, families, adventure seekers. There are even special-interest voyages (affinity cruises) for chocolate-lovers, sports fans, wine connoisseurs, opera buffs, murder mystery addicts.

The lure of cruising is undeniably tempting. One price covers most of your major costs: airfare, stateroom, meals, transfers, shipboard activities, and entertainment. Since your room travels with you, you have to unpack and pack only once. In other words, many travel inconveniences are gone, leaving more time for fun and relaxation.

The only downside of cruising is selecting a cruise and shopping around for the best price. Even after deciding where you want to go (the Caribbean is the most popular destination), you need to pick a ship, and the number of choices is staggering. A good travel agent can help you sort out the possibilities, but you should be aware of some major aspects of cruising before you write out a check.

The Cruise Line. While cruise lines try to appeal to all potential customers, they also cater to particular interests. Some are noted for appealing to fun seekers (gambling casinos and discos), some specialize in families (lots of activities for kids), some are ultra-expensive and tend to attract older, affluent people. Ask your travel agent for help in selecting a cruise line that suits your wishes.

The Ship. Your floating hotel comes in small, medium, and large—and the large can be a 14-story megaship carrying more than 2000 passengers. Choose a ship that you will be comfortable with and be sure to ask about on-board activities. Do you want a ship with a casino, a movie theater, a spa, a gym, a library, TVs in every room? Are the on-board lectures about wine tasting, basket weaving, or financial planning?

Also, most cruise brochures do not list the age of the ship; some travelers prefer newer, more modern boats (which usually have more amenities).

The Cabin. All cruise brochures make the rooms look huge; many are not. If space is an issue for you, be sure to ask. While modern cruise ships have stabilizers to lessen the roll and pitch of the boat, some passengers worry about motion sickness. If you are one, then book a room at water level or below, in the center of the ship. Other things to consider: Do you want an outside cabin (with porthole or picture window) or an inside cabin (no windows)? Do you want a full bath (tub and shower) or shower only? In general, the cabins on the top deck are the largest and most expensive; as you progress down the decks, the prices are less. And, as you can guess, outside cabins cost more than inside cabins.

The Price. This part of cruise planning can give you a major headache. The good news: discounts abound on all cruise lines. The bad news: finding and comparing them can seem endless. Once you determine the logistics of your trip (date, itinerary, cruise line and ship, cabin category), then you need to shop around. First, check with a travel agent/agency that is a member of the Cruise Line International Association (CLIA); check with more than one agency, since some agencies specialize in cruises and get better rates. Also, watch newspapers and magazines for promotional ads. Call your automobile club, credit union, or retirement organization; some membership organizations sell blocks of space at good rates.

Should you book your reservation early (three to six months before sailing) to get early-bird discounts, or book late (less than 60 days before sailing) to get super bargain rates on unsold cabins? It all depends. Some cruise lines don't significantly slash prices as the sailing date gets closer; some do. And do you have the flexibility to wait until the last minute, taking the chance that the ship you want will be totally booked? In general, the cabins that sell out first are the most expensive and the cheapest (you'd better book early to get them). Also, you are not likely to get rock-bottom prices during the peak vacation times (Christmas, February, and March in the Caribbean). Before you book, ask the following: If I book a cruise at one price and the cruise line later offers a lower promotional price, and I "qualify" for that promotional price, will I get a refund?

Once on board, there are some costs you will incur. Alcoholic beverages are not included in your ticket price. Neither are massages, beauty shop and barbershop services, on-shore excursions, or tips for the crew.

"Before You Go" Checklist

- ☐ Confirm reservations (airline, hotel, campground, rental car).
- ☐ Gather paperwork/documents (confirmation slips, all tickets, medical and auto insurance cards, travel books and maps, prescriptions for medications and eyeglasses, passport).
- ☐ Get your travel money (cash, traveler's checks, credit cards)—and don't leave it behind.
- ☐ Finish packing (clothing and accessories, toiletries, medical kit, camera and film, etc.).
- ☐ Arrange for pet care.
- ☐ Stop regular deliveries (newspaper, bottled water, food).
- ☐ Hold mail at post office or have friends empty mailbox.
- ☐ Pay bills or arrange to have them paid.
- ☐ Put valuables in safe-deposit box or hide in a secure place.
- ☐ Arrange for plants and lawn to be watered.
- ☐ Clean out refrigerator.
- ☐ Adjust heating or cooling thermostat.
- ☐ Turn down hot-water thermostat.
- ☐ Take out trash.
- ☐ Notify police / security company / neighbors / landlord (whomever you trust) that you will be gone.
- ☐ Leave itinerary (with phone and fax numbers) with family and friends.
- ☐ Give a spare set of house keys to the person in charge of looking after your house.
- ☐ Be sure answering machine is on and tape rewound to beginning.
- ☐ Put car in garage or leave it with a friend (if not traveling in car).
- ☐ Set automatic light timers.
- ☐ Lock all windows and doors and set alarm system.

TOURING THE WHITE HOUSE

If you are in Washington, DC, do stop in for a visit at the White House. There are two types of tours: guided (a tour officer accompanies you and gives historical details), and self-guided (you get a brochure in lieu of an officer but there is an tour officer on hand in every room to answer questions). Some of the rooms you will see: the East Room (largest room in the White House, which is used for receptions); the State Dining Room (for large dinners and luncheons); the Blue Room (considered the most beautiful); the Library. Guided and self-guided tours view the same areas. However, a guided tour (tickets available by writing your Congressperson or Senator) guarantees that you will be admitted on a specific day. Those who choose self-guided tours get same-day tickets at the White House, and if the lines are long, you may not get in. (However, if you arrive early, chances are you won't be turned away.) Public tours are conducted Tuesday through Saturday, unless a White House function interferes. All tickets are free. For further information, call the visitors' information center at the White House: 202-456-7041.

Planning a Family Vacation

According to a recent survey by the American Society of Travel Agents (ASTA), most American families take at least one vacation a year, usually in the summer, and spend between $1000 and $2000. Mothers usually decide where the families will go and make all of the arrangements. The majority of families use the family car as the mode of transportation, and the number one priority for a vacation is the quality and comfort of accommodations, followed by best price and overall value. Here are some tips for making your next family vacation a huge success.

◆ *What destination?* Involve every family member in the planning process. Get each one to jot down three places (in order of preference) that he/she would like to go to and the reasons why. Also, have everybody write down what they liked, and didn't like, about last year's vacation. Once you compare the lists, if you're lucky, a consensus decision will emerge. If not, it's time for negotiation. Obviously, the cost of the vacation is a big determining factor. Once the big decision has been reached, let each family member make at least one decision regarding the vacation.

◆ *Learn about it.* Read up on the place you are traveling to and what activities are available not only at your destination site but also in the surrounding area. Send for free information on your destination by writing to the appropriate state tourist office (see "State Tourist Offices," p. 475). (If you are traveling outside of the country, you can still get free information by calling or writing the government tourist office of the country of your choice; most countries have a tourist office in the United States and a travel agent can give you addresses and phone numbers). Travel books, in bookstores and libraries, are other good sources to pursue. As you gather information, keep it in a central place so all family members can browse through the materials. Remember that if you belong to an automobile club, you can take advantage of membership services, which can include route planning, free tour books, and discounts on hotels rooms and rental cars.

◆ *Costing it out.* Make a budget and comparison-shop. Check out prices on your own and call a travel agent to see if the agent can get you a better deal. Since it's impossible to predict every cost, and since estimated costs usually fall short of actual costs, bump up your budget by about 20 percent.

◆ *Reserving space.* Make all of your reservations well in advance, especially if you are traveling in the summer months.

◆ *Activities.* Plan daily activities but don't overload the schedule. Most people try to cram too many activities into a short period of time, and the vacation ends up being a race against the clock instead of a relaxing, enjoyable trip. Review all of your planned activities to be sure that you've included something for everyone in the family. Also, if some family members need time to be alone, consider how private time can be built into the agenda.

◆ *Ground rules.* Establish travel rules before you leave home. How much spending money does each child get? Is the hotel mini-bar (with its wonderful array of expensive snacks) off-limits? Are your children allowed to be on their own during portions of the trip and will you set curfew hours? Rules spelled out, and agreed upon, at home usually help to avoid bickering and full-blown arguments once you are on the road.

◆ *Attitude.* Preprogram your mind to have a good time even though you know that the best of plans can go awry. You're going on vacation—you earned it, you deserve it—and you will be flexible and deal with anything that goes wrong.

◆ *Coming home.* If you have any energy left, plan a simple family outing to take place shortly after you return from vacation. Having something else to look forward to can soften the blow of having a wonderful vacation come to an end.

Travel for the Disabled

Thanks in large part to the efforts of travel agencies that specialize in travel for the disabled, people with disabilities are heading off on all sorts of travel adventures, both domestic and international. Listed below are just some of these specialized agencies.

♦ **Flying Wheels Travel.** Arranges both group and independent travel for persons in wheelchairs (143 West Bridge Street, PO Box 382, Owatonna, MN 55060; 507-451-5005 or 800-535-6790).

♦ **People and Places.** A nonprofit group that provides escorted vacations for small groups of adults with developmental disabilities (3909 Genesee Street, Cheektowaga, NY 14225; 716-631-8223).

♦ **The Guided Tour.** Specializes in escorted tours for persons with developmental disabilities (7900 Old York Road, Suite 114-B, Elkins Park, PA 19117-2339; 215-782-1370).

♦ **Accessible Journeys.** Handles group, escorted trips and private itineraries for those who are wheelchair-bound or mobility-impaired; specializes in exotic destinations; can arrange for health care professionals to be travel companions (35 West Sellers Avenue, Ridley Park, PA 19078; 800-846-4537 or 610-521-0339).

♦ **Evergreen Travel Service.** Provides escorted tours and individual trip planning for wheelchair-bound and blind travelers (4114 198th Street SW, Lynnwood, WA 98036; 206-776-1184).

♦ **Nautilus Tours.** Specializes in land tours as well as cruises for wheelchair-bound travelers (5435 Donna Avenue, Tarzana, CA 91356; 818-343-6339).

♦ **Wilderness Inquiry.** A nonprofit organization that accommodates people of all ages and abilities, including persons with disabilities; specializes in canoe, kayak, and dogsledding trips in North American destinations (1313 Fifth Street SE, Box 84, Minneapolis, MN 55414–1546; 612-379-3858 or 800-728-0719).

♦ **Dialysis at Sea Cruises.** Arranges cruises for those who need dialysis treatment; handles all aspects of travel and medical requirements; coordinates total setup and operation of a mobile dialysis clinic on board ship (611 Barry Place, Indian Rocks Beach, FL 34635; 800-775-1333 or 800-544-7604).

When talking to disability-travel professionals, you will need to provide them with a clear understanding of your particular needs. Another good source of information for disabled travelers is the **Society for the Advancement of Travel for the Handicapped** (SATH), 347 Fifth Avenue, Suite 610, New York, NY 10016 (212-447-SATH).

State Tourist Offices

Every state in the U.S., as well as the District of Columbia, has an office of tourism and travel to help visitors plan vacations. These offices can provide you with a wealth of free information including maps, brochures on recreational activities, calendars of events, accommodation listings, etc. You can either write or call the tourist offices. Be aware that telephone numbers and addresses are subject to change.

STATES

Alabama Bureau of Tourism and Travel, PO Box 4309, Montgomery, AL 36103-4309; 205-242-4169; 800-ALABAMA

Alaska Division of Tourism, PO Box 110801, Juneau, AK 99811-0801; 907-465-2010

Arizona Office of Tourism, 1100 West Washington, Phoenix, AZ 85007; 602-542-8687

Arkansas Tourism Office, One Capitol Mall, Dept. 7701, Little Rock, AR 72201; 501-682-7777; 800-NATURAL

California Office of Tourism, PO Box 1499, Sacramento, CA 95812; 916-322-2881; 800-462-2543

Colorado Tourism Board, PO Box 38700, Denver, CO 80238; 303-592-5410; 800-COLORADO

Connecticut Department of Economic Development, Tourism Division, 865 Brook Street, Rocky Hill, CT 06067; 203-258-4355; 800-CT-BOUND

Delaware Tourism Office, 99 Kings Highway, Box 1401, Dover, DE 19903; 302-739-4271; 800-441-8846

Florida Division of Tourism, 126 West Van Buren Street, Tallahassee, FL 32399; 904-487-1462

Georgia Department of Industry, Trade & Tourism, PO Box 1776, Atlanta, GA 30301; 404-656-3590; 800-VISIT-GA

State of Hawaii Department of Business, Economic Development & Tourism, PO Box 2359, Honolulu, HI 96804; 808-586-2423

Idaho Division of Tourism Development, PO Box 83720, Boise, ID 83720; 208-334-2470; 800-635-7820

Illinois Bureau of Tourism, 100 W. Randolph, Suite 3-400, Chicago, IL 60601; 312-814-4732; 800-223-0121

Indiana Department of Commerce/Tourism and Film Development Division, One North Capitol, Suite 700, Indianapolis, IN 46204-2288; 317-232-8860; 800-289-6646

Iowa Division of Tourism, 200 East Grand, Des Moines, IA 50309; 515-242-4705; 800-345-IOWA

Kansas Travel and Tourism Division, 700 SW Harrison Street, Suite 1300, Topeka, KS 66603-3712; 913-296-2009; 800-252-6727

Kentucky Department of Travel Development, 2200 Capitol Plaza Tower, 500 Mero Street, Frankfort, KY 40601; 502-564-4930; 800-225-TRIP

Louisiana Office of Tourism, PO Box 94291, Baton Rouge, LA 70804-9291; 504-342-8119; 800-33-GUMBO

Maine Office of Tourism, State House Station 59, Augusta, ME 04333; 207-289-5711; 800-533-9595

Maryland Office of Tourism Development, 217 East Redwood Street, 9th Floor, Baltimore, MD 21202; 410-333-6611; 800-543-1036

Massachusetts Office of Travel and Tourism, 100 Cambridge Street, 13th Floor, Boston, MA 02202; 617-727-3201; 800-447-MASS (for ordering vacation kit only; U.S. only)

Michigan Travel Bureau PO Box 30226, Lansing, MI 48909; 517-373-0670; 800-5432-YES

Minnesota Office of Tourism, 121 Seventh Place East, 100 Metro Square, St. Paul, MN 55101; 612-296-5029; 800-657-3700

Mississippi Division of Tourism, PO Box 1705, Ocean Springs, MS 39566-1705; 601-359-3297; 800-927-6378

Missouri Division of Tourism, Truman State Office Building, PO Box 1055, Jefferson City, MO 65102; 314-751-4133; 800-877-1234

Travel Montana, Room 259, Deer Lodge, MT 59722; 406-444-2654; 800-541-1447

Nebraska Division of Travel and Tourism, 700 South 16th Street, Lincoln, NE 68508; 402-471-3796; 800-228-4307

Nevada Commission of Tourism, Capitol Complex, Carson City, NV 89710; 702-687-4322; 800-NEVADA-8

New Hampshire Office of Travel and Tourism Development, PO Box 1856, Concord, NH 03302; 603-271-2343

New Jersey Division of Travel and Tourism, 20 West State Street, CN 826, Trenton, NJ 08625; 609-292-2470; 800-JERSEY-7

New Mexico Department of Tourism, 491 Old Santa Fe Trail, Santa Fe, NM 87503; 505-827-0291; 800-545-2040

New York State Department of Economic Development, One Commerce Plaza, Albany, NY 12245; 518-474-4116; 800-CALL-NYS

North Carolina Division of Travel and Tourism, 430 N. Salisbury Street, Raleigh, NC 27603; 919-733-4171; 800-VISIT-NC

North Dakota Tourism Promotion, Liberty Memorial Bldg., Capitol Grounds, Bismarck, ND 58505; 701-224-2525; 800-HELLO-ND (U.S. and Canada)

Ohio Division of Travel and Tourism, PO Box 1001, Columbus, OH 43266; 614-466-8844; 800-BUCKEYE (Continental U.S., Ontario, and Quebec)

Oklahoma Tourism & Recreation Department, Travel and Tourism Division, 2401 North Lincoln Blvd., 500 Will Rogers Bldg., Oklahoma City, OK 73105-4492; 405-521-3981; 800-652-6552

Oregon Economic Development Department, Tourism Division, 775 Summer Street NE, Salem, OR 97310; 503-373-1270; 800-547-7842

Pennsylvania Bureau of Travel Marketing, PO Box 61, Warrendale, PA 15086; 717-787-5453; 800-VISIT-PA

Rhode Island Tourism Division, 7 Jackson Walkway, Providence, RI 02903; 401-277-2601; 800-556-2484

South Carolina Division of Tourism, Box 71, Room 902, Columbia, SC 29202; 803-734-0235

South Dakota Department of Tourism, 711 E. Wells Avenue, Pierre, SD 57501–3369; 605-773-3301; 800-SDAKOTA

Tennessee Department of Tourism Development, PO Box 23170, Nashville, TN 37202; 615-741-2158

Texas Department of Commerce, Tourism Division, PO Box 12728, Austin, TX 78711-2728; 512-462-9191; 800-88-88-TEX

Utah Travel Council, Council Hall/Capitol Hill, Salt Lake City, UT 84114; 801-538-1030

Vermont Travel Division, 134 State Street, Montpelier, VT 05602; 802-828-3237; 800-837-6668

Virginia Tourism, 1021 East Cary Street, Richmond, VA 23219; 804-786-4484; 800-VISIT-VA

Washington State Tourism Development Division, PO Box 42513, Olympia, WA 98504-2513; 206-586-2088 or 206-586-2012; 800-544-1800

West Virginia Division of Tourism & Parks, 1900 Kanawha Blvd. East, Building 6, Room B-564, Charleston, WV 25305; 304-558-2766; 800-225-5982

Wisconsin Division of Tourism, PO Box 7606, Madison, WI 53707; 608-266-2161: 800-432-8747

Wyoming Division of Tourism, I-25 at College Drive, Dept. WY, Cheyenne, WY 82002; 307-777-7777; 800-225-5996

DISTRICT OF COLUMBIA

Washington, DC, Convention and Visitors Association, 1212 New York Avenue NW, Suite 600, Washington, DC 20005; 202-789-7000

TRAVEL ABROAD

Passports and Visas

Everyone, including infants, must have an individual, valid passport in order to depart or enter the United States and most foreign countries. If you are applying for your first passport, you must appear *in person* at one of the 13 U.S. passport agencies or at one of the several thousand federal or state courts or U.S. post offices that are authorized to accept applications. Applicants between ages 13 and 18 must appear in person accompanied by a parent or legal guardian. However, for children under age 13, a parent or legal guardian may appear on their behalf.

The 13 U.S. passport agencies are located in Boston, Chicago, Honolulu, Houston, Los Angeles, Miami, New Orleans, New York, Philadelphia, San Francisco, Seattle, Stamford (CT), and Washington, DC. If you do not live near one of the 13 passport agencies, check the government listings in your telephone book for the address of the nearest passport acceptance facility.

To obtain your first passport, you will need to present:

1. *A completed application form (DSP-11).* If you fill it out in advance, don't sign it until instructed to do so.

2. *Proof of U.S. citizenship.* If you were born in the United States, you need a certified copy of your birth certificate, not a photocopy, with a registrar's signature and a raised, impressed, embossed, or multicolored seal. (If you lost yours, you can get one from the Bureau of Vital Statistics in the city, state, county, or territory where you were born.) If you were born abroad, you can present a certificate of naturalization or a certificate of citizenship.

3. *Proof of identity.* A valid driver's license will qualify. (The document you show must contain your signature and a physical description or photograph.)

4. *Photographs.* Two identical, recent (no older than six months), full-face, front-view photographs with a white background (2 × 2 inches in size). They can be black and white or color. Do not wear sunglasses or head covering (i.e., a hat). Snapshots or vending machine photos are not acceptable.

5. *Passport fee.* First-time passports for applicants 18 and over cost $65 and are valid for 10 years. Passports for those under 18 cost $40 and are valid for five years. You can pay with a check, bank draft, or money order (cash is accepted at some, but not all, passport issuance facilities).

If you need to renew a passport, you need not apply in person but can do it by mail—if you have been issued a passport within the past 12 years and after your 18th birthday. Simply get the correct form (DSP-82) which is available at most courthouses, many post offices, or travel agencies. Fill it out and send it, along with your old passport, two new photos, and the required $55 fee (check, money order, or bank draft—no cash) to: **National Passport Center,** PO Box 371971, Pittsburgh, PA 15250. If your name has changed, you will need to submit the original or certified copy of the court order or marriage certificate that shows the change of name.

It is important to be aware of the expiration date of your passport. Some countries will not permit you to enter if the remaining validity of your passport is less than six months. In addition, if you return to the United States with an expired passport, you are subject to a passport waiver fee of $100.

Passports are not technically required for short-term travel between the United States and Mexico, Canada, and some countries in the Caribbean. However, U.S. Immigration requires you to prove your U.S. citizenship and identity when you return to the United States. If you choose to travel to those places without a passport, check with your travel agent or with one of the U.S. passport agencies to learn what documentation you need to take with you.

How much time does it take to get a passport—new or renewed? According to passport officials, you should apply two months in advance of your planned departure (September through December is the best time to apply since demand is down). Generally, it takes less time to get a renewal than a first-time passport. However, if you need visas, allow additional time—approximately two weeks per visa.

Many countries (with the exception of Western European countries) require a visa—a stamp put into your passport by a foreign government that allows you to travel in a particular country for a specified purpose and a limited amount of time. Passport agencies cannot help you to get visas. You have to apply directly—in person, by mail, or through a travel agent—to the embassy or consulate of each country you plan to visit.

In order to find out if you need a visa, call the nearest consulate of the country you are planning to visit, ask your travel agent, or write to the U.S. State Department for a free pamphlet on visa requirements around the world (**Citizens Emergency Center,** 2201 C Street NW, Room 4800, Washington, DC 20520; enclose a self-addressed, stamped envelope).

When a visa is required, you will have to obtain and fill out a form that must be sent to the country's embassy or consulate—*along with your passport.* Most visas require a fee and some require photographs. Since you will have to submit your passport for every visa you need, do start getting all your paperwork together well in advance of your travel departure date.

What do you do if you lose your passport, or if it is stolen? If you are in the United States, report the loss or theft immediately to **Passport Services,** Department of State, 1425 K Street, NW, Washington, DC 20524, or to your nearest passport agency. If you are out of the country, contact the nearest U.S. embassy or consulate as well as the local police. With proper documentation, the U.S. embassy or consulate usually can issue you a new passport within a day or two. Thus, it's a good idea to have a photocopy of the data page of your passport with you, kept in a separate place from your passport. Also, you might want to leave another photocopy with a relative or friend in the United States.

Finally, it is possible to get a passport (new or renewed) in just a few days—either because of your poor planning or in case of emergency. This works only if you live close to one of the 13 passport agencies mentioned earlier. If so, show up with all appropriate legal documents. In addition, take along your airline ticket with a confirmed reservation.

Immunizations

Immunizations may be required, or recommended, for travel to certain foreign countries. Most visitors to Europe, Japan, Australia, and other developed countries will not need any inoculations. However, if an immunization is required for your destination, it must be recorded on a yellow "International Certificate of Vaccination" which you will present upon entering the country.

The most commonly required/recommended immunizations for international travel are for typhoid, yellow fever, and hepatitis. It's relatively easy to find out if you need any inoculations (or pills for malaria) by contacting local and state health departments, travel clinics, your travel agent, or your doctor. In addition, up-to-date information is available by calling the **Centers for Disease Control** 24-hour hotline: 404-332-4559 (listen to recorded messages or get printed material by fax). Other excellent sources of information are the seven United States Public Health Service Quarantine Stations (located in Chicago, Honolulu, Los Angeles, Miami, New York, San Francisco, Seattle).

In many cases your private physician (given the proper amount of time) can administer any necessary immunizations. There are also a growing number of travel clinics (some associated with hospitals and university medical centers) around the country that have a ready supply of travel vaccines. Don't wait until the last minute to get shots, since some of them require two doses with a certain amount of time between doses.

Regardless of where you are traveling, it is always a good idea to make sure that your "routine" immunizations are up to date: measles, mumps, rubella, diphtheria, polio, and tetanus. It is estimated that a high percentage of adults have not received routine immunizations or have not maintained their routine immunization status since their school years.

It's always best to consult with your family doctor about immunizations. For instance, some vaccines are not advisable for pregnant women, very young children, or people with altered immune systems (e.g., people with AIDS). Let your doctor know your exact itinerary and you can work together to determine what inoculations are necessary.

U.S. Customs Service

American tourists who have been out of the country for 48 hours must "clear Customs" when returning to the United States. At that time you will have to declare, usually by filling out a form, the value of all items you have purchased abroad. Currently, each U.S. citizen can bring back $400 worth of merchandise duty-free. If returning from Caribbean and Central American nations, the exemption is $600; the exemption is $1200 if returning from the U.S. Virgin Islands, American Samoa, and Guam. After reaching your exemption level, there is a flat 10 percent tax on the next $1000 worth of goods. If you go over that level, the remaining items will be taxed at various rates of duty that are determined by the kind of article—e.g., the duty rate on a radio is 6 percent while the rate on perfume is 5 percent.

Some of the major points to keep in mind:

1. If you are taking abroad any valuable foreign-made articles—like a camera, watch, fine jewelry, or tape recorder—have proof (like a sales receipt) that this was your possession before you left the country. If there is a serial number on an item, you can register that item with the Customs office nearest you.

2. Designer "knockoffs" or imitation products might be confiscated if they violate trademark laws.

3. Certain articles are prohibited from entering the United States. This illegal merchandise includes products from endangered species (like African elephant ivory), narcotics and dangerous drugs, most firearms, certain food products.

4. Products from some developing countries are totally exempt from duty under the Generalized System of Preferences (GSP). For a list of those countries, obtain the leaflet "GSP and the Traveler" from your nearest Customs office.

5. Beware of "duty-free" shops. Items bought in foreign duty-free shops are subject to U.S. Customs duty but can be included in your personal exemption.

6. If you are traveling with family members,

you can combine your exemptions (a joint declaration), even if the articles bought by one family member cost more than the allowed personal exemption.

For instance, if the allowed exemption is $400 per person and there are two family members, then together you can bring in $800 worth of goods duty-free.

7. Save all your sales receipts and keep them in an accessible place in case the Customs officer asks to see any of them. Also, you might be asked to open your luggage for inspection, so have your purchased items also accessible (perhaps in one suitcase).

8. Don't panic if you are stopped for a search. Calmly answer all questions, don't get defensive or angry, and don't volunteer information.

9. If you get caught undervaluing or failing to declare items, you could face a stiff penalty. Most of the time, however, the penalty is waived but you do have to pay the correct duty.

Tourists who love to shop when traveling are advised to get thoroughly acquainted with U.S. Customs rules and regulations by getting a free copy of the government publication, "Know Before You Go: Hints for Returning Residents." Call your local Customs agency for a copy or write to: **U.S. Customs Service,** National Distribution Center, PO Box 68912, Indianapolis, IN 46268.

Travel Advisories

Every year hundreds of thousands of Americans travel abroad but only a small fraction of them check on travel advisories issued by the U.S. State Department. These advisories target trouble spots around the world and give other vital information on foreign destinations.

The State Department used to have a three-tiered system of advisories—notice, caution, and warning (notice was the least serious advisory; warning was the most serious advisory). However, this system was revamped in 1992 because

it was too confusing and travelers often didn't understand the level of risk associated with each kind of advisory. The new system issues two types of advisories:

♦ *Warnings.* A warning is issued for a country when conditions are so dangerous or unstable that the State Department feels that Americans should avoid travel to the country.

♦ *Consular information sheets.* Issued for all countries, these short reports provide a wealth of information, including: passport and visa requirements, health concerns and medical facilities, unusual currency regulations, areas of unrest or instability, addresses and phone numbers of U.S. embassies and consulates; crime information (what kinds of crime are committed against tourists and where they are likely to happen). These fact sheets are strictly informational and American travelers must decide for themselves whether travel to a particular country is risky.

There are four ways to obtain the travel advisories (both warnings and consular information sheets) issued by the State Department: phone, fax, computer/modem, or secondary sources. The phone numbers listed below are in operation 24 hours a day, seven days a week. There is no charge for the information but you will have to pay for phone charges. However, since the advisory information is available around the clock, you can call at times when your phone rates are low. Be aware that all phone numbers link you into an automated service; there are no live people to talk to.

Phone (202-647-5225). This phone number is for the State Department's Citizens Emergency Center. Using a touch-tone phone, you punch your way through a menu of options until you get to the information you want. The information will be read to you. However, unless you are a fast note-taker, it can be difficult to get everything jotted down; you may have to get the information repeated several times.

Fax (202-647-3000). You call a State Department fax service and a recorded message will lead you through a few simple steps so that the advisories you desire will be faxed to you on the spot. You can order as many as nine documents on a single call.

Computer/modem (202-647-9225). Using this number, you can log on to the Consular Affairs Bulletin Board; there is no access charge.

Secondary sources. You can also get travel advisory information through a travel agent's computerized reservation system or from a U.S. passport agency.

Standard Time Differences—World Cities

The table below lists the Standard Time in selected world cities when it is 12 noon, Eastern Standard Time, in the United States. An asterisk (*) indicates the morning of the following day.

Amsterdam	6 PM	Hong Kong	1 AM*
Athens	7 PM	Istanbul	7 PM
Auckland	5 AM	Jakarta	12 midnight*
Bangkok	12 midnight*	Jerusalem	7 PM
Barcelona	6 PM	Johannesburg	7 PM
Beijing	1 AM*	Lima	12 noon
Belfast	5 PM	Lisbon	5 PM
Belgrade	6 PM	London	5 PM
Berlin	6 PM	Madrid	6 PM
Brussels	6 PM	Manila	1 AM*
Bucharest	7 PM	Mecca	8 PM
Budapest	6 PM	Melbourne	3 AM*
Buenos Aires	2 PM	Mexico City	11 AM
Cairo	7 PM	Montreal	12 noon
Calgary	10 AM	Moscow	8 PM
Cape Town	7 PM	Munich	6 PM
Caracas	1 PM	Nairobi	8 PM
Casablanca	5 PM	Naples	6 PM
Copenhagen	6 PM	Oslo	6 PM
Dublin	5 PM	Panama City	12 noon
Edinburgh	5 PM	Paris	6 PM
Florence	6 PM	Prague	6 PM
Frankfurt	6 PM	Quebec	12 noon
Geneva	6 PM	Rio de Janeiro	2 PM
Glasgow	5 PM	Rome	6 PM
Guatemala City	11 AM	St. Petersburg	8 PM
Halifax	1 PM	San Juan	1 PM
Havana	12 noon	Santiago	1 PM
Helsinki	7 PM	Seoul	2 AM*
Shanghai	1 AM*	Vancouver	9 AM
Stockholm	6 PM	Venice	6 PM
Sydney	3 AM*	Vienna	6 PM
Tel Aviv	7 PM	Warsaw	6 PM
Tokyo	2 AM*	Yokohama	2 AM*
Toronto	12 noon	Zurich	6 PM
Tripoli	7 PM		

Traveler's Checks, Charge Cards, ATMs?

Getting the most value out of your money when traveling overseas usually requires a combination of traveler's checks, charge cards, and automatic teller machines (ATMs). Each has advantages and disadvantages.

Traveler's Checks

They are almost universally accepted and are easily replaced if lost or stolen, but there are commission fees to pay when buying them and cashing them in. If you shop around, however, you can avoid the fee for buying them; many banks, credit unions, and automobile clubs provide them for free.

When cashing in traveler's checks for foreign currency, keep an eye out for the best exchange rate. The worst rates are usually at hotels, shops, and independent exchange agencies. Rates are usually better at airports, banks, or the issuer's local service office.

If the American dollar is on shaky ground and you are concerned about fluctuating exchange rates, you might want to buy some foreign-currency traveler's checks. They can be purchased through American Express, Thomas Cook, and some major banks.

Credit Cards

Credit cards are very convenient, especially if you are short of foreign currency. However, keep in mind that what you will see on your monthly statement is not the rate of exchange at the time

WEATHERGRAPH

REGION/ COUNTRY	Average Daily Temperature (F°)							
	September/ November		December/ February		March/ May		June/ August	
	High	Low	High	Low	High	Low	High	Low
Asia								
Bangkok, Thailand	88	75	89	70	94	77	90	75
Beijing, China	64	43	37	17	67	43	87	68
Bombay, India	87	75	85	68	88	76	86	77
Hong Kong	78	73	65	57	77	65	87	79
Manila, Philippines	88	75	87	70	92	74	89	75
Osaka, Japan	72	55	47	32	65	47	87	73
Seoul, South Korea	65	46	35	18	60	40	84	67
Singapore	88	74	88	74	88	75	88	75
Taipei, Taiwan	81	68	67	55	77	63	89	75
Tokyo, Japan	70	56	48	32	62	46	81	69
Australia/New Zealand/Pacific Islands								
Auckland	63	52	72	59	67	55	57	47
Melbourne	66	48	76	56	68	51	57	45
Perth	71	53	84	63	76	57	64	49
Sydney	70	56	77	64	71	57	61	47
Tahiti	87	71	90	72	90	72	86	69
Canada								
Calgary, Alberta	56	31	24	8	41	18	67	40
Montreal, Quebec	45	33	24	10	54	36	72	54
Toronto, Ontario	56	41	31	17	39	24	76	57
Vancouver, BC	56	44	43	34	57	41	72	53
Caribbean								
Aruba	89	78	86	76	86	77	88	78
Bahamas	85	73	78	65	81	69	88	75
Bermuda	79	68	69	58	72	60	84	72
Jamaica	88	72	86	68	87	70	90	73
Puerto Rico	85	74	80	72	82	72	85	75
Virgin Islands	87	74	85	72	86	74	89	76
Europe								
Amsterdam, Netherlands	57	45	40	32	54	39	69	53
Athens, Greece	76	61	58	44	77	53	90	72
Barcelona, Spain	69	58	56	45	65	52	81	68
Berlin, Germany	54	40	36	27	55	38	72	53
Brussels, Belgium	60	44	43	32	58	42	72	54
Budapest, Hungary	60	45	37	28	61	44	80	59
Dublin, Ireland	57	44	47	36	55	41	67	51
Edinburgh. Scotland	53	44	42	33	50	39	65	52
Frankfurt, Germany	58	45	40	30	60	43	76	58

WEATHERGRAPH (cont.)

REGION/ COUNTRY	Average Daily Temperature (F°)							
	September/ November		December/ February		March/ May		June/ August	
	High	Low	High	Low	High	Low	High	Low
Florence, Italy	63	48	43	31	64	46	82	62
Geneva, Switzerland	59	45	42	31	60	41	75	57
Hamburg, Germany	56	43	38	30	56	38	71	53
Istanbul, Turkey	67	54	48	38	60	46	80	64
Lisbon, Portugal	71	57	58	47	67	53	80	62
London, England	58	47	44	37	56	42	70	55
Madrid, Spain	67	51	51	37	64	45	86	63
Monte Carlo, Monaco	68	61	56	48	61	54	76	69
Munich, Germany	58	40	36	23	56	38	73	53
Oslo, Norway	49	37	31	22	51	34	71	53
Paris, France	62	47	44	36	62	44	76	58
Rome, Italy	72	55	55	42	67	50	85	66
Stockholm, Sweden	49	37	31	22	46	33	67	52
Venice, Italy	64	53	46	36	64	51	81	65
Vienna, Austria	58	44	36	28	56	41	76	59
Zurich, Switzerland	58	43	38	28	59	40	76	56
Mexico								
Acapulco	90	74	88	72	89	74	91	77
Cancun	90	68	85	63	94	67	92	72
Middle East/Africa								
Cairo, Egypt	85	65	67	48	83	57	94	69
Casablanca, Morocco	76	58	64	49	71	52	81	62
Nairobi, Kenya	75	54	76	55	75	57	70	52
Riyadh, Saudi Arabia	93	61	71	48	91	64	107	76
Tel Aviv, Israel	79	58	57	41	74	49	86	65
South America								
Buenos Aires, Argentina	69	50	85	63	72	53	57	42
Caracas, Venezuela	78	61	77	57	80	60	78	62
Rio de Janiero, Brazil	77	66	82	71	81	70	76	64
USA								
Atlanta, GA	72	54	53	37	71	51	87	67
Boston, MA	60	35	40	22	54	38	80	61
Chicago, IL	60	47	34	28	57	39	74	64
Dallas, TX	79	60	58	37	77	56	92	72
Honolulu, HI	82	72	76	68	78	69	84	82
Los Angeles, CA	77	54	66	47	69	50	79	58
Miami, FL	85	73	76	59	81	67	88	75
New York, NY	65	50	41	27	58	42	80	65
Orlando, FL	90	56	75	52	88	55	92	71
San Francisco, CA	68	51	57	45	63	49	65	53
Scottsdale, AZ	87	55	65	41	83	52	102	73
Seattle, WA 60	60	46	47	36	59	42	73	54
Washington, DC	67	48	45	29	64	44	85	64

Reprinted courtesy of Hotel and Travel Index, Reed Travel Group.

of purchase but the rate for the day on which the transaction was processed. You could be charged more, or less, than you expected, depending on whether the value of the dollar rises or falls between the two dates.

Automatic Teller Machines (ATMs)

The most prevalent ATM networks abroad are Cirrus and Plus. Travelers love using them, not only for convenience, but also because ATMs usually give you a "wholesale" commercial exchange rate—one that is usually reserved for transactions of $1 million or more (the rate can be as much as 5 percent better than the rate for cashing in traveler's checks). However, a per-transaction fee may be charged, depending on the bank that issued your card.

Does your credit card work on the Cirrus or Plus system? Even if it does, you need to do a little homework before you leave home. First, find out what the transaction fee is for each withdrawal. If it's too high, then you really aren't gaining any financial advantage by using a cash machine. Also, most ATMs outside North America will not accept a personal identification number (PIN) with more than four digits. Check with your bank; they may need to reprogram your number for use abroad. Also, the keypads on many foreign ATMs have only numbers, not numbers and letters. So you need to be able to translate your password into numbers only. And be sure you find out the limits on your withdrawals and that you have placed sufficient funds in the appropriate account before you leave home.

Final thoughts on money: When you arrive at your destination, it's nice to have about $100 of the local currency so you won't have to wait in a long exchange line just for cab fare and first-day expenses. Most major banks can sell you the more popular foreign currencies, or can tell you where to go. Also, take along a stack of $1 bills (American); they come in handy for tips and small purchases and most countries will gladly accept them.

Value-Added Tax (VAT)

Many Americans traveling in Europe aren't aware that they can get a tax refund on goods that they purchase. The refund is based on what is called a value-added tax (VAT), which is basically the same as retail sales taxes in the United States; most European countries offer a VAT program. Since the tax is a major source of income for European countries, each county refunds it only to foreign tourists, in order to encourage those tourists to spend money.

The rates vary from country to country but some are as high as 30 percent. Also, within one country the tax rates can be different for different categories of merchandise (the rate for jewelry can be different from the rate for clothing). Some purchases may not be subject to the VAT refund, like money spent on restaurant and hotel bills. Also, some European countries allow individual stores and merchants to decide if they want to participate in VAT refund programs. Oftentimes, it's difficult even to be aware of the tax because it's built into, or buried, in the price of the merchandise and does not show up separately on your sales receipt.

Some travelers, aware of VAT, choose not to apply for it either because they haven't bought enough to make it worthwhile (minimum purchase amounts are usually set) or because the process for getting the refund is too cumbersome and time-consuming.

Here is how VAT basically works: You buy merchandise in a store and get a tax-refund form which you or the merchant fills out. You then collect your refund in one of two ways: either at an airport or railroad station before you leave the country or by mail. When you are leaving a country, a Customs official will stamp your form. If the airport, train station, or other exit point has a tax-refund desk (many do), you can get your refund immediately, usually in the local currency. (Allow plenty of time to handle the paperwork). If you must apply for a refund by mail, just be sure the Customs official has stamped your form before you leave the country. In some cases, your refund can be credited to your charge card, if you used a charge card to make the purchase.

Just because the VAT was, say, 15 percent, you won't get a full 15 percent back, since processing charges are deducted before the check is issued to you. Also, if you get your check in the mail, you will have a hard time cashing it because it will be issued in a foreign currency. Most U.S. banks charge a hefty fee for cashing foreign-currency checks; the fee is substantially less if you get the check cashed by an establishment that regularly handles foreign currency like Thomas Cook Currency Services.

Since the rules regarding VAT change so much, you should ask about them before you leave home, or you might be able to get a VAT brochure from a visitor's center when you arrive in a European country. And, of course, before you make a major purchase in any store, ask the proprietor if the store participates in a VAT refund program. You will need to have a passport with you when you make a purchase to prove that you are a foreigner. However annoying the procedures for VAT might be, the sales rebate can turn happy shoppers into very happy shoppers; especially happy are those who make substantial purchases. In addition, a company based in Norway, Europe Tax-free Shopping (ETS), is currently working with thousands of shops and department stores throughout Europe in an attempt to streamline procedures for collecting VAT. If you deal with a merchant who belongs to Europe Tax-free Shopping, you will generally have a much easier time collecting your refund. In some cases, the store will issue you a refund check as soon as you make a purchase. When you leave a country, you get the check stamped by a Customs official and cash your check at a refund counter. Most exit points—airports, ferry terminals, border crossings, railroad stations—have ETS refund counters. For more information on VAT, write for a free brochure: Europe Tax-free Shopping, Box 9012, East Setauket, NY 11733.

BAKSHEESH

In Egypt a street vendor presses a small, colorful bead into the palm of your hand and tells you that the "gift" will bring you good luck, good health. Then he holds out his hand and says, "Baksheesh" (*baksheesh*). In Turkey you politely ask a woman if you can take of picture of her; she agrees and you snap the photo; she demands "Baksheesh." In India a deformed child tugs at your arm and cries, "Baksheesh." All three want money—call it a payment, a tip, or a gift.

Baksheesh is usually regarded as a tip for services rendered. Taxi drivers will ask for it (you expect that) but you are caught off guard when someone voluntarily shows you how to use a public telephone, then asks for payment. And baksheesh is not exclusive to Eastern countries. Called by many different names, a form of baksheesh exists in most poor countries of the world. In some instances, it can amount to a bribe—a local official will expedite processing of paperwork for your visa but only if compensated for the extra effort required.

Baksheesh (or whatever name it goes by) is not directed solely at tourists. Egyptians pay Egyptians; Africans pay Africans; South Americans pay South Americans. Tourists, however, are prime targets. When traveling in a poor country, you need to be aware of what services require payment (including those that appear to be "good Samaritan" services). When gratuities are involved, the sums are usually small; it's a good idea to keep a supply of small change at hand. In the case of beggars, what you do is entirely a personal decision.

Medical Help Abroad

Finding medical assistance in a foreign country can be a bit unnerving, especially if you are in an emergency situation and don't speak the language of the country. You do, however, have a number of good alternatives. First of all, if you are staying at a large hotel or resort, there may be an English-speaking doctor on call. Or, you can call the local U.S. embassy, which maintains lists of doctors and hospitals. In addition, the U.S. State Department **Overseas Citizen's Emergency Center** in Washington, DC, has a 24-hour hot line number (202-647-5225); the Center can help you with a number of emergency problems like finding a doctor or arranging for evacuation home. Finally, many credit card companies offer free travel-assistance services (including emergency medical and referral help) if you are one of their cardholders.

If you anticipate that you may need a doctor, or if you just like to be prepared, then join the **International Association of Medical Assistance to Travellers** (IAMAT), which publishes a booklet listing English-speaking doctors around the world. Cost of membership is minimal (a donation determined by you). As a member, you have access to an English-speaking doctor 24 hours a day—at a preset cost. You will also receive the group's annual, updated publications including "World Immunization Chart" and "24 World Climate Charts." To join, write or call: IAMAT, 417 Center Street, Lewiston, NY 14092 (716-754-4883).

If you have a chronic medical condition, you should consider joining the **Medic Alert Foundation** (800-344-3226 or 800-432-5378), which will maintain an active file on your medical problems. As a member, you will receive a bracelet or necklace engraved with an identification number, a notation of your condition, and the group's phone number. Should you be found unconscious, the person who finds you (or a doctor) can call the organization collect and immediately get your medical history.

In most cases you will have to pay, or arrange to pay, your doctor and hospital bills. Thus, be sure to get itemized bills for services rendered so you can submit them to your insurance company when you return home.

AIDS and Foreign Travel

The spread of the human immunodeficiency virus (HIV) and AIDS throughout the world has become a real concern for travelers. Worldwide about 13 million people are currently infected with the AIDS virus. According to the World Health Organization (WHO), 40 million individuals will be infected by the year 2000; the vast majority of infected people will live in developing countries and will become infected through heterosexual intercourse.

Some international travelers have become so alarmed that they attempt to travel with their own blood supplies, an extreme measure that is not advised by health authorities. Other travelers avoid going to "hot-spot" areas like sub-Saharan Africa. However, the Centers for Disease Control (CDC) states: "Because HIV infection and AIDS are globally distributed, the risk to international travelers is determined less by their geographic destination than by their individual behavior." Thus, travelers need to be cautious and informed and to use common sense.

Travelers abroad can contract the HIV virus the same way they can contract it at home: through sexual intercourse with an infected partner; through contaminated needles and syringes or any other skin-piercing instrument; through contaminated blood or blood products. The World Health Organization says: "AIDS is not spread by daily and routine activities such as sitting next to someone or shaking hands, or working with people. Nor is it spread by insects or insect bites. And AIDS is not spread by swimming pools, public transportation, food, cups, glasses, plates, toilets, water, air, touching or hugging, coughing or sneezing."

Sexual Transmission

Avoid sex with an infected person or anyone whose HIV-infection status is unknown. If you choose to be sexually active, avoid unprotected sex. Use latex condoms and spermicide. Take your own supply of condoms, since the quality of condoms sold in some countries may be questionable; some countries may not even sell them. Repeat: Abstinence is the only safe policy.

Blood Transfusions and Blood Products

Unexpected, emergency blood transfusion is rarely required, according to WHO. The CDC further states: "In the United States, Australia, New Zealand, Canada, Japan and western European countries, the risk of infection of transfusion-associated HIV infection has been virtually eliminated through required testing of all donated blood for antibodies to HIV." While most countries of the world are instituting better blood screening procedures, blood supplies in some countries, especially underdeveloped nations, are suspect. Here are some general guidelines regarding blood supplies and foreign travel:

♦ Unless it's absolutely necessary, try to postpone or avoid any blood transfusions, especially if you are in an underdeveloped country. If the need arises, try to get evacuated out by air—either get home or to a safe location; some travel insurance policies offer air-evacuation coverage. If an immediate transfusion is necessary, do your best to ensure that screened blood is used. In underdeveloped countries, large Western-style hospitals and hospitals in capital cities are usually thought to be less risky. Also, call the nearest American embassy to find out if it has a list of screened blood donors. Also, WHO guidelines suggest that travelers ask about the possibility of using "plasma expanders" rather than blood. According to WHO: "In case of emergency need of blood, use of plasma expanders and urgent evacuation home may be the actions of choice."

♦ Know your own blood type and the blood type of your traveling companions. Someone in your group could be a possible donor. However, this precaution assumes that your companions are HIV-negative.

♦ Take steps to minimize your risk of injury. Wear your seat belt if you drive; don't drink and drive. Don't take unnecessary risks whether you are crossing a street or engaging in a sport.

♦ Prior to leaving on a trip, make a plan to deal with medical emergencies.

Overseas Injections

According to the CDC: "Travelers are at risk if they use or allow the use of contaminated, unsterilized syringes or needles for any injections or other skin-piercing procedures including acupuncture, use of illicit drugs, steroid injections, medical/dental procedures, ear piercing or tattooing."

♦ Whenever possible, avoid injections. If injections are required, the CDC says that "needles used to draw blood or administer injections should be sterile, preferably of the single-use disposable type, and prepackaged in a sealed container." If you question the safety of sterilized equipment that will pierce your skin, ask about sterilization procedures.

♦ Insulin-dependent diabetics or anyone else who needs routine injections should travel with an adequate supply of needles and syringes. Even if you don't need routine injections, you might want to pack some needles and syringes in your first-aid kit, as a precautionary measure. However, be aware that carrying such items can cause problems with Customs inspectors. So, if you pack them, carry along a note or prescription from your doctor.

Eating Abroad

Traveling abroad requires defensive eating habits. While contaminated food and water is most prevalent in Third World countries, you can suffer from stomach and intestinal problems even in European countries. Approximately 40 percent of all international travelers are afflicted with diarrhea.

Some basic food and water precautions to take, especially when visiting underdeveloped countries:

♦ Do not drink tap water and stay away from ice cubes (almost always made from tap water). Don't even brush your teeth with tap water. Fortunately, bottled water is for sale in most parts of the world.

♦ Bottled or canned beverages—soft drinks, fruit juices, beer, wine—are usually okay to drink. Boiled beverages, like coffee and tea, are also generally safe.

♦ If you are traveling to remote locations, pack water-purification tablets, iodine, chlorine, or water-filtration devices to make the water safe. And be sure you know the correct use of whatever sanitary method you choose.

♦ Avoid unpasteurized dairy products.

♦ Stay away from raw or undercooked meat and shellfish, unpeelable fruit (like grapes and berries), raw vegetables and salad greens (usually rinsed in local tap water).

♦ Beware of foods sold by street vendors, especially in underdeveloped countries.

♦ Don't eat sauces, salsas, or anything else that has been sitting on the table for a while.

♦ Avoid food on which flies have settled.

Good common sense should allow you to enjoy all the culinary delights of your trip. Just remember: if you are not absolutely sure the drinking water is safe, consider it contaminated and act accordingly. As for food: boil it, cook it, peel it, or forget it.

In Trouble: What a U.S. Embassy Can/Cannot Do

If you find yourself in a crisis situation, your first instinct will probably be to call a U.S. embassy. There are many things that consular officers at embassies can do; there are also many things they cannot help you with.

U.S. consular officers can: arrange for money to be sent/wired to you; give you the name of a doctor, dentist, or hospital in case of illness; offer assistance in case of a natural disaster or political unrest; help to get you a new passport if yours is lost or stolen; provide information on how to obtain foreign public documents.

U.S. consular officers cannot: act as travel agents, banks, law enforcement officers, or lawyers; get you visas, residence permits, or driving permits; act as interpreters; search for missing luggage; replace stolen or lost traveler's checks; settle disputes with hotel managers.

If you get into legal trouble, or get arrested, there are limits to how much help you can expect from a U.S. embassy. For example, a consular officer cannot get you out of jail. What American officials can do is determined by both U.S. and foreign laws. On average about 3000 Americans every year are arrested in foreign countries; about a third are held on drug charges. It is important to note that few countries provide a jury trial; many countries do not accept bail; foreign prisons often lack minimal comforts.

Following are some legal tips provided in a brochure, "Your Trip Abroad," put out by the United States Department of State:

♦ Learn about local laws and regulations and obey them. Avoid areas of unrest and disturbance. Deal only with authorized outlets when exchanging money or buying airline tickets and travelers checks. Do not deliver a package for anyone unless you know the person well and are certain the package does not contain drugs or other contraband.

♦ Before you sell personal effects, such as clothing, cameras, or jewelry, learn the local regulations regarding such sales. Adhere strictly to local laws because the penalties you risk are severe.

♦ Some countries are particularly sensitive about photographs. In general, refrain from photographing police and military installations and personnel; industrial structures including harbor, rail, and airport facilities; border areas; and scenes of civil disorder or other public disturbance. Taking such photographs may result in your detention, the confiscation of your camera and film, and the imposition of fines.

♦ Do not get involved with illegal drugs overseas. It can spoil more than your vacation. It can ruin your life.

Customs and Manners in Foreign Countries

Like it or not, when you travel abroad, you are viewed as a representative of the United States. Unfortunately, it's not that unusual to overhear an American say such things as: "Don't you have an American cup of coffee?" "You don't speak English?" "This isn't the way we do things at home."

Regardless of where you travel, some things are always in bad taste: taking photographs of people without asking their permission; acting critical or amused by customs that are alien to you; getting too familiar, too fast (e.g., slapping someone on the back, even if the gesture is well intentioned).

To be a good travel ambassador, and save yourself from embarrassment, it's advisable to read a few books about the culture and customs of the country you plan to visit.

Clothing. Wearing shorts in public is generally not acceptable in most parts of the world, including some European countries. In Arab countries low necklines, sleeveless shirts, and short skirts are definitely a bad idea. When in doubt, dress conservatively. Also, while it is tempting to dress in the local style, like wearing a sari in India, be sensitive to the culture—sometimes the local citizenry will appreciate your attempt to fit in; sometimes it will be considered an insult.

Greetings/touching. Handshakes are an almost universally accepted form of greeting, although in some countries, like Japan, a traditional bow from the waist is preferred. Be careful how you address someone; don't use first names unless you are invited to do so. In some countries, you'll see a lot of hugging and kissing going on among the locals (Greece, Italy, Latin countries, Slavic countries); an affectionate hug or peck on the cheek that you share with a new acquaintance is fine, but usually if you are responding to, not initiating, it.

Language/gestures. Taking a crash course in the language of the country you will be visiting rarely results in mastery of the language. Instead, learn some polite expressions (hello–goodbye–thank you) and relax. English is pretty common worldwide, especially in tourist areas, and you can always use body language to get your message across. However, some American gestures have totally different meanings in other countries. For example, in Bulgaria, shaking your head horizontally means "yes"; shaking it vertically means "no." Also, using the American gesture for "OK" (the thumb and forefinger making a circle, with the other fingers pointing up) can be embarrassing. In Brazil that gesture means "screw you"; in Japan it means "money"; in southern France it means "zero" or "worthless."

OK?

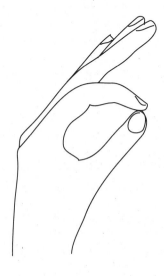

Food/drink. You may find yourself staring down at a local delicacy—snake soup in China, a yak burger in Tibet, sheep's eyes in Saudi Arabia, calves' brains in France—and wonder what to do, particularly if you are a guest in someone's home. Be brave, take small bites, and pretend it tastes like something you like. When presented with a strong alcoholic drink, like ouzo in Greece, take small sips and stop when you must (you can refuse, citing medical reasons as your excuse). Remember that Hindus and some Buddhists don't eat beef (the cow is sacred); Muslims don't eat pork, and strict Muslims abstain from alcohol. And, if you are eating with Muslims, never touch food with your left hand (the left hand is for bathroom use and is considered unsanitary; using it would be very offensive).

Socializing/conversation. If you are ac-

HELLO, GOODBYE, PLEASE, THANK YOU—IN SEVEN LANGUAGES

The pronunciations do not include indications of non-English sounds, like the French *r*, but you will be understood by all but the most arrogant natives in the lands in which you are a foreigner.

The Language	The Words			
	Hello	Goodbye	Please	Thank you
French	bonjour (bohn-ZHOOR)	au revoir (OH ruh-VWAHR)	s'il vous plaît (seel voo PLEH)	merci (merh-SEE)
Spanish	buenos dias (BWEH-nohs DEE-ahs)	adios (ah-dee-OHS)	por favor (POHR fa-VOHR)	gracias (GRAH-see-uhs)
Italian	buon giorno (BWAN JOHR-noh)	arrivederci (ah-ree-vay-DAYR-chee)	per favore (payr fah-VOH-ray)	grazie (GRAH-tsyay)
Russian	zdravstvuite (ZDRAH-st'eh)	do svidanya (duh sv'i DAH-n'uh)	pozhaluista (puh-ZHAHL-stuh)	blagodaryu (bluh-guh-duh-R'OO)
Esperanto	bonan matenon (BOH-nahn mah-TEH-nohn)	adiau (ah-DEE-ow)	bonvole (bohn-VOH-leh)	dankon (DHAN-kohn)
Swahili	salam alekum (SAH-lahm ah-LEH-koom)	kwaheri (kwah-HEH-ree)	tafadhali (tah-fahd-HAH-lee)	asante (ah-SAHN-teh)
Japanese	ohayō (oh-hah-YOH)	sayonara (sah-yoh-nah-ruh)	kudasai (koo-dah-sahee)	arigatō (ah-rih-gah-TOH)

INTERNATIONAL HIGHWAY SIGNS

Curve to right

Double curve

Dangerous curve

Intersection

Danger

Traffic circle

Intersection: main
and secondary roads

Two-way traffic,
one-way road

Steep grade

Steep descent

Pedestrian
crossing

Watch out
for children

Wild animals
crossing road

Loose gravel

Slippery road

Road work

Bumpy road

Falling rocks

Grade crossing
with gates

Road narrows

No entry

Road closed

No entry for
pedestrians

Maximum
width

Maximum
height

Maximum
speed

End of
maximum speed

No passing

No U-turn

No right turn

No parking

No parking
or standing

Main road up
ahead

Main road

End of main road

Mandatory
traffic circle

Mandatory
direction

Mandatory
direction

Superhighway

End of
superhighway

Telephone

Filling station

Mechanical help

HOSPITAL

PARKING

PAID VACATIONS AROUND THE WORLD

In the United States most employees get two weeks of vacation time (10 days) after one year of service. Here's how that average stacks up against vacation days in other countries.

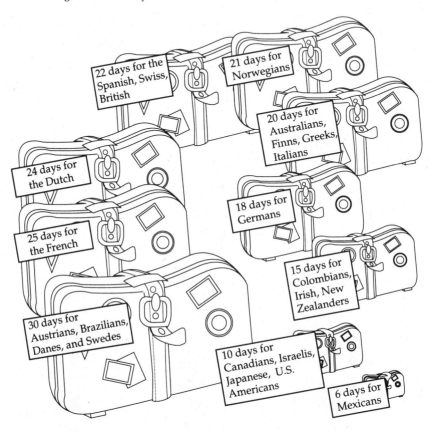

22 days for the Spanish, Swiss, British

21 days for Norwegians

20 days for Australians, Finns, Greeks, Italians

24 days for the Dutch

18 days for Germans

25 days for the French

15 days for Colombians, Irish, New Zealanders

30 days for Austrians, Brazilians, Danes, and Swedes

10 days for Canadians, Israelis, Japanese, U.S. Americans

6 days for Mexicans

quainted with the history and culture of the country, you shouldn't get unnerved. In general, some topics can be touchy or controversial, like money, religion, politics, and sex. But the particular nature of the people is critical: The Japanese do not want to talk about World War II; the French scowl at the classic American question, "What do you do for a living?"; the Chinese call their country "China" or the "People's Republic of China"—not "the Mainland"; people in Scotland are "Scots" or "Scotsmen," not "Scotch" (the drink) or "Scottish" (the language or the terrier).

9

TRANSPORTATION

AUTOMOBILES

AIRPLANES

BICYCLES AND MOTORCYCLES

TRAINS

Automobiles

Car Maintenance

Your owner's manual will give you a specific maintenance schedule for your car. Most manuals give two schedules, one for "normal" driving conditions and another for "severe" driving conditions. If you aren't sure which category you fit into, you might choose to err on the side of safety and follow the more rigorous (severe conditions) schedule. Postponing proper maintenance can not only lead to costly repair bills, but it can also put your life and the lives of your passengers at risk.

It's important to note that the maintenance schedules in the owner's manual, prepared by the car manufacturer, may differ from the schedules recommended by car dealerships that routinely service cars. Many dealers design their own schedules, which look very official and appear to be the services recommended by the manufacturers. However, the dealer-designed schedules are often misleading. A nationwide poll of dealers and their service schedules conducted by *U.S. News & World Report* magazine revealed that many dealers around the country sell far more maintenance services than manufacturers call for or than most cars need. According to the survey, "Two major kinds of questionable maintenance turned up: justifiable services performed prematurely, such as replacing spark plugs and rotating tires; and services of dubious value under any circum-

stances such as supplementing brand-new oil with chemical additives and flushing fuel injectors that work just fine." Thus, before you accept the word of a dealer, or an independent service/repair shop, compare its list of services with the list of services in your owner's manual. While different cars have different service needs, here is a general list of critical areas; you can check many of them yourself.

Oil. Check the oil level whenever you get gas. If you don't know where the dipstick is, check your owner's manual or ask for help at the service station. Most car manuals say that the oil should be changed every 7500 to 10,000 miles under normal driving conditions; every 3000 or 4000 miles under severe driving conditions. Mechanics, however, swear that you should change it every three months or 3000 miles, whichever comes first, and that you should do so regardless of your driving habits. This more frequent schedule is also endorsed by the Automobile Association of America (AAA). Whenever you change the oil, you should also change the oil filter.

Brakes. They should be inspected thoroughly once a year or every 12,000 miles in newer cars, every six months in older cars. Obviously, you need to get to a mechanic quickly if you experience problems, like a slow or fading brake pedal, brake noises like grinding and squeaking, or brake drag (car pulls to one side when you brake).

Tires. Check tire pressure at least once a month to see that your tires are properly inflated. Get your own tire gauge at an auto parts store. The proper tire pressure can be found in any number of places: your car owner's manual, a sticker inside the driver's-side door, a sticker inside the lid of the glove compartment. Also, check tires for cuts and signs of uneven wear.

Fluids. Levels of brake fluid and coolant (anti-freeze mixture) usually show in see-through plastic containers that are easy to find once you get your head under the hood. Check them frequently, every time you check your oil dipstick. Other fluids include transmission fluid (check it when the oil is changed) and power steering fluid (check it at least twice a year or before you take off on a long trip).

Belts and hoses. Give them a quick glance when you are under the hood; have them checked thoroughly when you change the oil. Check for loose belts and signs of fraying on all rubber parts.

Air filter. It's easy to find and easy to replace yourself. Change it when it appears dirty. Most car owners change air filters about once every 15,000 miles or so.

Battery. Check the level of battery fluid a couple of times a year. Look for corrosion (greenish-white deposits) around the battery connections and for any loose connections.

Signs That Your Car Needs a Tune-up

The Car Care Council, a nonprofit educational foundation, states that "symptoms of engine trouble on most vehicles today are subtle. It's not easy to tell if your car needs a tune-up because the symptoms are masked by computerized controls." According to the Council, here are the eight most common signs that your car needs a tune-up:

Hard starting. This is the most common form of car trouble. It's usually due to some unperformed maintenance. If the starter cranks

the engine, the electrical system probably is okay. The culprit could be a starting sensor (on fuel-injected models) or the choke mechanism (on engines with carburetors). Frequently, starting failure can be traced to an electronic component or a computer controlling the ignition system.

Knocking. This noise generally is heard when the engine is under load, such as when accelerating or climbing a hill. While it often may be caused by a tankful of inferior gas, ignition knock frequently is a sign your engine needs attention. It also can be caused by a buildup of carbon inside the engine. Late-model cars are equipped with a knock sensor which "hears" the sound and makes corrective adjustments. But it cannot compensate for a severe malfunction, a condition that can affect engine performance and even damage the engine.

Stalling. This can be caused by incorrect idle-speed adjustments, a malfunctioning sensor or switch, dirty fuel-system parts, worn spark plugs, or other engine deficiencies. Does it stall when hot? Cold? With air conditioning on? To make diagnosis easier, make note of when it happens and advise your technician.

Power loss. How long since the fuel filter was changed? A dirty filter is a common cause of power loss. As noted under "poor gas mileage," there can be many causes of this condition, most of which can be located with a diagnostic procedure.

Poor gas mileage. By keeping a regular check of gas mileage (miles driven divided by gallons used) you can tell if your engine is losing efficiency. Increased gas consumption may be accompanied by other symptoms listed in this section. Note that poor gas mileage also may be due to: underinflated tires, engine running too cold, transmission malfunction, dragging brakes, misaligned wheels.

Dieseling. This also is known as "after-run." The engine keeps chugging and coughing for several seconds after the ignition is shut off. Causes can range from inferior gas to excessive idle speed. Carbon in the combustion chamber also may cause dieseling.

Exhaust odor. The smell of rotten eggs

comes from the catalytic converter, part of your car's emissions-control system. The odor can be due to an engine problem or it can be a sign your car's catalytic converter is malfunctioning.

Rough running. A malfunction in either the fuel or ignition system can cause an engine to run rough. It also can be due to an internal engine condition, such as a bad valve or piston. Does it occur when idling? When accelerating? At all speeds? Your best bet: have a qualified technician perform diagnostic and tune-up services as needed.

Reprinted courtesy of the Car Care Council.

Car Noises

When your car "speaks" to you, it's usually saying that something is wrong, something needs fixing. The Shell Oil Company, in the "answer book" *How to Keep Your Car Healthy*, has selected some of the more common car noises and defined what they mean.

Click (rhythmic, high-pitched metallic tapping)—could indicate a loose hubcap; defective wheel bearing; bent or loose fan blade; low oil level in engine; loose manifold heat-control valve.

Clunk (or dull thump)—possibly a defective universal joint or rear differential; transmission fluid may be low.

Heavy knock (or pounding)—worn crankshaft main bearing, bad connecting rod or loose bolts in torque converter.

Ping (or knock)—car may be in need of tune-up; octane of fuel may be too low for engine.

Screech (or scraping metal sound)—possible brake problem.

Squeak (or high-pitched rubbing)—defective drum brake linings; chassis needs lubrication; worn suspension bushing.

Squeal (high-pitched whine)—underinflated tires, misaligned wheels; loose or worn power-steering fan or air-conditioning compressor belt.

Thud (low, metallic thump)—loose pulley, worn crankshaft bearing; loose exhaust pipe.

DRIVEWAY DRIPS

Drips or puddles under your car could be an early sign of trouble. To make the drips more recognizable, you might want to put a large sheet of paper, preferably paper that won't absorb the liquid, under the car overnight. The most common drips and what they indicate:

Water. Probably just condensed water from your air conditioner.

Green or yellow spots. It's coolant and you could have a bad water pump or a leak in the radiator or heater hoses.

Red drops. Usually transmission fluid. You may need new transmission seals.

Black or dark-colored slippery fluid. Probably oil; you have an engine leak that needs repair.

Thin, watery spots that smell like gasoline. If it smells like gasoline, it probably is. Be very careful since gasoline leaks are the number one cause of car fires.

Oily liquid with little color. Indicates brake fluid; have your braking system checked out.

Checking Tire Wear

When you inspect your tires, look to see if the wear is uneven. You may spot high and low areas or unusually smooth areas (bald spots). Uneven wear patterns may be caused by improper inflation, misalignment, improper balance, or suspension neglect. Also look for foreign objects like stones or nails or pieces of glass that could be stuck in the tire's treads. If you spot a problem early enough and get it corrected by a tire dealer or service facility, you might save the tire.

According to the Tire Industry Safety Council, when the tread on your tire is worn down to one-sixteenth of an inch, the tire must be replaced. Today's tires have built-in tread-wear indicators, or "wear bars," that look like narrow strips of smooth rubber across the tread and show up on the tire when that point of wear is reached. When you see them, you are in the danger zone; replace the tire.

A free guide to tire care and safety, "Consumer Tire Guide," is available by sending a business-size, self-addressed envelope to: **Tire Industry Safety Council,** Box 1801, Washington, DC 20013.

WEAR BARS

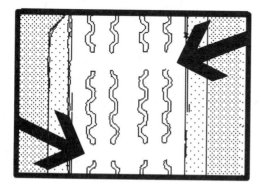

Choosing a Repair Shop

This checklist was prepared by the National Institute for Automotive Service Excellence (ASE), a nonprofit, independent organization dedicated to improving the quality of automotive service and repair through the voluntary testing and certification of automotive technicians. ASE technicians must retest every five years in order to keep up with changing technology and to remain in the ASE program.

ASE certifies technicians, not repair shops, but ASE technicians can be found at every type of repair facility: new-car dealerships, independent garages, service stations, tire dealers, specialty shops, and major franchises. The technicians usually wear a distinctive blue-and-white shoulder insignia and have credentials listing their exact area(s) of expertise. Employers of ASE technicians usually display the ASE sign on the premises and post their technician's credentials in the

customer waiting area. ASE certification does not guarantee trouble-free repair work, and there are good mechanics who simply don't bother with certification testing, but certification does indicate a level of skill and experience.

Checklist: Shopping for Service

☐ Don't just drop your vehicle off at the nearest establishment and hope for the best. That's not choosing a shop, that's merely gambling.

☐ Read your owner's manual to become familiar with your vehicle and follow the manufacturer's suggested service schedule.

☐ Start shopping for a repair facility before you need one; you can make better decisions when you are not rushed or in a panic.

☐ Ask friends and associates for their recommendations. Even in this high-tech era, old-fashioned word-of-mouth reputation is still valuable.

☐ Check with your local consumer organization regarding the reputation of the shop in question.

☐ If possible, arrange for alternative transportation in advance so you will not feel forced to choose a facility solely on the basis of location.

☐ Once you choose a repair shop, start off with a minor job; if you are pleased, trust them with more complicated repairs later.

☐ Look for a neat, well-organized facility, with vehicles in the parking lot equal in value to your own and modern equipment in the service bays.

☐ Professionally run establishments will have a courteous, helpful staff. The service writer should be willing to answer all of your questions.

☐ Feel free to ask for the names of a few customers. Call them.

☐ All policies (labor rates, guarantees, methods of payment, etc.) should be posted and/or explained to your satisfaction.

☐ Ask if the shop customarily handles your

vehicle make and model. Some facilities specialize.

☐ Ask if the shop usually does your type of repair, especially if you need major work.

☐ Look for signs of professionalism in the customer service area: civic and community service awards, membership in the Better Business Bureau, AAA-Approved Auto Repair status, customer service awards.

☐ Look for evidence of qualified technicians, such as trade school diplomas, certificates of advanced course work, and ASE certifications—a national standard of technician competence.

☐ Keep good records; keep all paperwork.

☐ Reward good service with repeat business. It is mutually beneficial to you and the shop owner to establish a relationship.

☐ If the service was not all you expected, don't rush to another shop. Discuss the problem with the service manager or owner. Give the business a chance to resolve the problem. Reputable shops value customer feedback and will make a sincere effort to keep your business.

Talking to a Mechanic

If you can, talk directly to the mechanic/technician who will work on your car. However, in many instances, especially in high-volume repair shops, you will have to talk to a service writer/advisor or a clerk in the front office. Regardless of whom you tell your story to, you need to be prepared to give accurate information about what is wrong with your car.

♦ Make a written list of the car's symptoms and hand it to the mechanic or service writer. Keep a copy for yourself.

♦ Describe the problem in as much detail as possible. When did the problem first occur? Does it happen when the engine is hot or cold? Does it happen at all speeds, or only upon acceleration, braking, or shifting? Does the problem happen constantly or only every once in a while? If the problem is a noise, what does the noise sound like: rattling, thumping, clanking, squeaking, knocking, a scraping metallic sound? If you are at a complete loss to describe the problem, have someone at the shop go with you for a short test drive.

♦ Don't be shy or embarrassed about asking questions. If the answers are technically over your head, ask for an explanation in lay person's terms.

♦ If the problem has been handled previously by another shop, mention it and indicate what repairs were done.

♦ Don't insist on diagnosing the problem yourself and asking for specific repairs. That's what you are paying the shop to do. And you could end up paying for a repair that wasn't necessary.

♦ Don't demand an on-the-spot answer. Get a written estimate of repairs based on your initial conversation and leave a phone number where you can be reached. Have the shop call you when the diagnosis is complete and tell you what needs to be done and what the repair will cost.

♦ If you are unhappy with the repair work, take the car back to the shop. Stay calm and reasonable, but stand your ground until the car is fixed to your satisfaction. Most repair shops will be accommodating since they want your continued business.

Seat Belts and Air Bags

Consumers, as well as the federal government, are demanding safer cars. As a result, auto manufacturers are continually adding new safety features to new cars. An *anti-lock braking system* (ABS) prevents wheel lock-up and keeps you from skidding or losing control of the car when you slam on the brakes in an emergency. *Traction control* adjusts power to the wheels and keeps you from spinning out or fishtailing. More and more cars are including rear-window wipers and defrosters as well as built-in child safety seats.

While the two primary safety features, seat belts and air bags, receive considerable attention in the media, there is still some consumer confusion as to their reliability and effectiveness. Listed below are some of the misconceptions about both. First, here are a few statistics.

♦ Approximately 40,000 people die every year in car accidents. Another 4.5 million are injured.

♦ Although safety-belt laws exist in most states, only 66 percent of Americans regularly buckle up.

♦ At some time in their lives, two out of three motorists will be in an accident in which someone in the car is killed or hurt.

Seat Belts

Myth: I only drive short distances and I drive slowly. I don't need a safety belt.

Fact: Three out of four accidents happen within 25 miles of home. Approximately 80 percent of deaths and injuries happen at speeds under 40 mph. Unbelted drivers and passengers have been killed at speeds as low as 12 mph.

Myth: A safety belt could trap me in the car. It's better to be thrown free, especially in the case of fire or water submersion.

Fact: The odds of you being killed are 25 times greater if you are thrown from a car. Death by fire or drowning accounts for less than one-tenth of one percent of car accident fatalities. Regardless of the conditions of an accident, a safety belt is likely to keep you conscious so that you can help yourself and your passengers.

Myth: My car has an air bag. I don't need to buckle up.

Fact: Air bags protect against frontal collisions. Seat belts will protect you in frontal collisions and in other kinds of potentially deadly accidents like rollovers, rear-end collisions, and side collisions. Also, in a multiple-crash accident you need your seat belt since air bags won't reinflate.

Myth: Pregnant women shouldn't wear seat belts.

Fact: Both mother and baby are safer with a seat belt. According to the National Highway

Traffic Safety Administration, here is how the belt should be worn: "Lap belts, as well as the lap portion of a lap-shoulder belt combination, should be placed low, across the hips and over the upper thighs. To be most effective, they should lie snugly over the pelvis, one of the stronger bones of the body. Never place the belt over the abdomen. Adjust the shoulder belt for a snug fit. If it cuts across your neck, reposition your car seat for a better fit."

Air Bags

Myth: I almost always wear my seat belt, so an air bag is an unnecessary expense. Besides, they only protect you against frontal collisions.

Fact: Frontal and front-angle crashes account for more than half of all accident deaths. According to the National Highway Traffic Safety Administration, "To argue that air bags are a poor idea because they do not provide protection from all types of crash injuries is like arguing that polio vaccine shouldn't be used because it doesn't cure cancer." Also, in serious frontal collisions, if you neglect, or forget, to wear your seat belt, the air bag will still provide significant protection.

Myth: Air bags themselves are a real health hazard and cause serious injuries.

Fact: They do inflate instantly upon impact and at a great speed. According to a recent study, about one in three air-bag inflations left a driver or passenger with burns, bruises, and neck sprains. But with few exceptions, the injuries were minor. The odds of sustaining an injury do, however, go up if you sit too close to the steering wheel (3 inches or less). Nonetheless, numerous federal and auto industry studies attest to the fact that air bags save lives and prevent serious injuries. The federal government, convinced of the safety benefits of air bags, has mandated that by 1998, all new cars and most new trucks will have dual front air bags.

Myth: Air bags won't work unless they are properly maintained and that's expensive.

Fact: Air bags last throughout the life of the car and require no maintenance. A few car manufacturers, however, suggest that you have them inspected at intervals ranging from three to 10 years.

Myth: Air bags don't work all of the time, and they also go off accidently, causing a driver to lose control of the car.

Fact: According to some studies, air bags work 99 percent of the time. Some consumers, however, have complained to federal agencies that air bags failed to deploy when they were in an accident. What is important to remember is that air bags are designed to inflate when a car hits an object head-on and at speeds of 12 mph or more; customers who complained usually weren't aware of those facts. Air bags rarely inflate accidently. They won't be activated when you hit a bump or pothole or when you stop suddenly. And air bags are designed so that you will not lose control of your car.

Child Safety Seats

Car accidents are the leading cause of death and serious injury for infants and children. It's estimated that 75 percent of the fatalities could have been prevented by the proper use and installation of child safety seats. There are laws in all 50 states and the District of Columbia that require children to ride in safety seats, yet one out of every three infants and children rides in a car without one. In addition, a number of studies have shown that up to 90 percent of child safety seats are misused in some way.

Holding a child in your lap, even if you wear a seat belt, is extremely dangerous. In a car crash at 30 mph, a 10-pound child would be thrown from your arms with a force of almost 300 pounds. A safety seat would keep the child from being hurled through the car until he or she hits something.

Take the following into account when you buy and use a child safety seat:

Safety standards. Buy and use only child safety seats that meet Department of Transportation standards. There should be a label on the seat that reads: "This child restraint system conforms to all applicable federal motor vehicle safety standards." The stamp of manufacturing should be after January 1, 1981.

Throw out any car seats made before 1981, when federal safety standards went into effect. Throw out a car seat that has been used in a crash. Buy a new child safety seat if you buy a new car and the old safety seat doesn't fit properly.

Call the **Auto Safety Hotline** (800-424-9393) to make sure the seat you have hasn't been recalled. Since 1981, the federal government has recalled more than 20 million faulty car seats. Seats are recalled for any number of reasons including defective buckles and harnesses, cracks in the body seat, and failure to meet flammability standards. Personnel at the hotline number, operated by the National Highway Traffic Safety Administration (NHTSA), can provide you with a list of recalled seats and tell you what action to take if your car seat is on a recall list.

Fit/car. Make sure your car seat fits your car. Not all child safety seats are compatible with all cars or all car seats. If the seat you have doesn't fit your car, don't use makeshift measures to make it work.

Fit/child. Use a car seat that fits your child's size and weight. In general, there are three basic types of seats: infant seats (birth to about 20 pounds; seat faces the rear of the car, meaning the child rides backward); convertible seats (birth to about 40 pounds; rear-facing for infants up to 20 pounds but can be converted to forward-facing for toddlers from 20 to 40 pounds); booster seats (40 to 60 pounds; forward-facing). As your child ages and grows, reassess his or her safety seat. Using a seat that is too small for an older child can be just as dangerous as using a seat that is too big for a baby.

Installation. Read carefully the installation instructions that come with the child safety seat. Also, read your car owner's manual for installation instructions. Many problems of "failure" occur because the seat isn't properly installed, the child isn't properly secured in the seat, and the seat isn't correctly fastened with the car's safety belt. Be especially diligent if your car has automatic crash protection, like air bags. For example, a rear-facing infant seat should *not* be installed in the front seat of a car that has an air bag on the passenger side. The bag hitting the back of the infant seat could injure a child.

Position. Regardless of the type of seat you have, most safety experts agree that the best place for your child safety seat is in the center position of the back seat. Also, a baby under age one and/or 20 pounds should be in a rear-facing infant seat. This allows the baby's strong back to absorb the forces of a crash.

Choosing the right seat for your child can be confusing because there are a multitude of makes and models available. For details on how to select a car seat, write for the free brochure, "Family Shopping Guide to Car Seats," from the **American Academy of Pediatrics,** 141 Northwest Point Blvd., Elk Grove Village, IL 60009. Or, write for a free tip sheet, "Size and Weight Guide for Child Safety Seats," from the **National Highway Traffic Safety Administration,** 400

HOW SAFE IS YOUR CAR?

Every year the National Highway Traffic Safety Administration (NHTSA) crash-tests 30 or more new cars. Two excellent sources for the safety results are the April issue of *Consumer Reports* magazine and an annual book by Jack Gillis, *The Car Care Book.*

The NHTSA also operates a toll-free Auto Safety Hotline so consumers can report suspected safety problems and get information on automobile recalls and safety defect investigations. NHTSA encourages consumers to call the hotline because, "Consumers provide the first information we use to identify safety problems." If you live in the Washington, DC metropolitan area, call 202-366-0123; otherwise call 800-424-9393.

7th Street SW, Washington, DC 20590. Another excellent source for publications on child safety seats is **SafetyBeltSafe USA,** PO Box 553, Altadena, CA 91003.

Better Gas Mileage

If you want to increase your fuel efficiency, here are some items to take into consideration.

Tires. If your tires are underinflated, you could be losing up to one mile per gallon of gasoline. Tires should be inflated according to the pressure specified by your car manufacturer and should be checked often, when the tires are cold. If the wear on your tires is irregular, have the wheel alignment checked. Radial tires are preferable to bias-ply tires because they improve mileage by 3 to 6 percent.

Tune-up. Poorly running engines consume gas. A tune-up can increase your mileage by as much as 20 percent.

Speed. Most cars get the best mileage at a cruising speed between 35 and 45 mph. Also, driving at 55 mph instead of 65 mph can increase mileage by three to five miles per gallon.

Extra weight. Unnecessary items carried around in your trunk and back seat, or on top of your car (e.g., a luggage rack), are costing you miles. Get rid of heavy items; a weight loss of 100 pounds can result in a mileage gain of up to one mile per gallon.

Air conditioning. When you don't need it, don't use it. Your gas consumption increases 5 to 20 percent with the air conditioner on.

Driving techniques. Frequent starts and stops waste gas. Gentle acceleration is better than rapid acceleration. Excessive engine idling is also a gas guzzler.

New car. If gas mileage is a major concern, remember that smaller engines are more fuel efficient. Manual transmissions usually get better mileage than automatic transmissions; an overdrive gear on either type of transmission will save gas. Power options like power steering and brakes as well as trim options like undercoating add weight to the car and will decrease your gas mileage.

Octane ratings. Using gasoline with a higher octane rating will not improve your gas mileage. Use the octane level recommended in your car owner's manual.

Gas-saving products. There are many types of products on the market that claim to improve fuel economy. They come in many forms including air-bleed devices, vapor-bleed devices, ignition devices, fuel line devices, mixture enhancers, and fuels and fuel additives. After testing and evaluating more than 100 alleged gas-saving devices, the Environmental Protection Agency (EPA) has found only a few that improve mileage and none that do so significantly. In fact, says the EPA, some "gas-saving" products may damage a car's engine or cause substantial increases in exhaust emissions. So beware of such products, especially those that claim to be approved by the federal government. No government agency endorses gas-saving products for cars.

Road Emergencies

Unexpected breakdowns can be annoying, upsetting, and downright dangerous. Here are some tips to help you deal with car trouble.

♦ Join an auto club. For an annual membership fee, you should get emergency road service, lock and key service, and towing service.

♦ Get familiar with your owner's manual. A typical manual will have a section on emergencies, with specific information on how to jump-start a car, how to change a tire, what to do if your car overheats, what to do if your engine stalls, what to do if your brakes fail, and the proper procedures for having your car towed. Keep the owner's manual in your car. If you don't have one, get one from a local car dealership or buy a book on your specific car at a bookstore. Even if you have no intention of ever handling a car repair, the information in the manual will be of use to the person who comes to your aid.

♦ Be sure you have a car emergency kit on board (see article in this section for the items to include).

♦ In the glove compartment keep some spare change in case you need to use a pay telephone. Also keep important phone numbers on hand like the auto club number, numbers of 24-hour towing services, the number of the local police department, and the numbers of close relatives or friends.

♦ Pay attention to your car's warning lights. If the *oil pressure light* goes on, pull off the road as quickly and safely as possible, turn off the engine, and check the oil dipstick. Running the engine on insufficient oil will cause serious damage. If the *temperature light* or *gauge* comes on, your car is overheating. Pull off the road and check for a broken fan belt or a leak in the heater or radiator hoses. If the *alternator light* or *gauge*

FIGURING OUT YOUR MPG

From time to time, it's a good idea to check on how much gas your car uses, or how many miles you get per gallon. A sudden increase in gas consumption could signal car trouble. The calculations are easy.

1. Write down the mileage on your odometer when you fill up your tank.

2. The next time you fill up your tank, write down the odometer reading again and note the number of gallons you put in.

3. Subtract the first odometer reading from the second and divide that answer by the number of gallons put in.

Example: In step 1, your odometer reading was 20,000 miles. In step 2, the reading was 20,250 miles and you put in 10 gallons of gas. The difference in odometer readings is 250 miles. Divide that 250 miles by the 10 gallons you put in and you get 25 miles per gallon.

comes on, you are draining your battery, meaning your battery is not being recharged properly. Turn off the air conditioner and radio and get to the nearest service station (if you turn off the engine, it may not restart). If the *brake light* comes on, you may be low on brake fluid or you may have a problem in your braking system. Pull off the road, check your brake fluid, and test your brakes. If you are uncertain about the safety of your car, regardless of which light comes on, get help.

♦ If you need to pull off the road, turn on your emergency flashers and move your car to a safe spot, out of the line of traffic. If you need to signal for help, raise your hood or trunk lid. You can also tie a white cloth or a scarf on the antenna or door handle. Many drivers carry a "help" or "call police" sign (available in auto parts stores) written in large block lettering that can be read easily from a distance; put the sign in the high-way-side window of your car.

♦ When help arrives, whom do you trust? If you are stranded on a major highway regularly patrolled by the police or highway patrol, a uni-formed officer will likely come to the rescue. Stay in your car with the doors locked, windows closed. If you are in doubt about the authenticity of a uniformed officer, ask to see his or her identification. If a good-Samaritan stranger stops, crack the window and ask the person to call for help; give the person some change and ask that the person stop at the nearest pay phone. Do not let a stranger into your car and do not get into a stranger's car. For the most part, it's best not to leave your car when you break down; both you and your car are left in a vulnerable state. Obvi-ously, this rule can be bent if you break down during the day in a safe area and there is a pay phone within short walking distance.

♦ Remain calm and be patient. You need a clear head to get through any car emergency, especially if it occurs at night and in a remote area. If you have a real fear of coping with car troubles, consider getting a car phone or a CB radio.

Car Emergency Kit

Auto experts suggest that the following be stored in your car:

♦ Spare tire (properly inflated)
♦ Jumper cables
♦ Jack and lug wrench
♦ Tire-pressure gauge
♦ Aerosol tire inflator/sealant
♦ Small fire extinguisher
♦ Basic tool set—pliers, screwdrivers (slot-head and Phillips-head), small wrench, pocket-knife
♦ Duct tape or electrical tape
♦ Flares or reflective warning triangles
♦ Flashlight with new batteries
♦ Spare parts (fuses, fan belt, wiper blades)
♦ All-purpose wire, like baling wire
♦ Funnel
♦ Unopened containers of oil, brake fluid, an-tifreeze
♦ Work gloves
♦ Clean-up supplies (rags or paper towels)
♦ First-aid kit

For winter driving you will want to add some extras: can of de-icer, ice scraper, bag of sand or road salt, small shovel, tire chains and traction mats, blanket, and nonperishable snacks.

If You Have a Car Accident

Whether you have a fender bender or a major accident, it's likely that emotions will run high and you will be upset and confused. If you have a car accident:

1. Stop and survey the scene. Is it safe for you to get out of your car? Do you need to get clear of the car right away, e.g., is the car on fire or do you smell gas?

2. Check for injuries. If anyone in the accident is hurt, call 911 for assistance.

3. Call the police. Many local jurisdictions do send officers to the scene of an accident, regard-

less of the circumstances. However, if the accident is minor (no injuries, no severe damage to automobiles), the police may not show up, or they may respond but not file an accident report. If police officers are on the scene, do get their names, badge numbers, and telephone numbers. If an accident report is filed, you will want to get a copy of it.

4. Move your car out of traffic if it is safe to do so. If you have an injured person inside, you might have to leave the car where it is. Flip on emergency flasher lights and/or put out warning devices.

5. Exchange information. Ask the other driver for his or her name, address, and phone number. Get the other party's driver's license number as well as insurance information (name and address of insurance company and the driver's policy number). Also jot down the make, model, and color of the car along with the car's license plate number and registration number. Get the names, addresses, and phone numbers of any passengers in the other car.

6. Look around the scene for any witnesses to the accident. If there are any, get their names, addresses, and phone numbers.

7. Do not admit fault to anyone. Fault will be determined later and anything you say may come back to haunt you.

8. Before you leave the scene, write down your recollection of the accident (if you can). Make note of the location, time, road conditions, weather conditions, traffic conditions. Draw a simple diagram of the scene and where the vehicles were positioned. If you happen to have a camera in your car, or someone at the scene has a camera, take photos of the positions of the cars as well as close-ups of damage that occurred. If you can't write down your recollections immediately, do it as soon as you get home and have calmed down.

9. Call your insurance company as soon as possible. Your agent will handle most of the details on any claims made as a result of the accident. If you have to do anything, like filling out an accident report or getting an estimate for damage

done to your car, the agent will tell you how to proceed.

10. If you feel even slightly hurt, get yourself checked out immediately at an emergency room or schedule an appointment with your family doctor as soon as possible.

Safe-Driving Tips

Everything mentioned below is pure common sense. However, cars can be weapons, so even common sense bears repeating.

♦ Don't drive under the influence of drugs or alcohol. Both dull your mind and reflexes. Alcohol is involved in at least half of all fatal crashes.

♦ Keep your mind, as well as your eyes, exclusively on your driving. While driving, don't put on makeup, write letters, or eat a meal.

♦ Chill out when you encounter a hostile driver. No doubt you'll see red when an obnoxious driver cuts you off, plows through a red light, or is tailgating. But dangerous situations are not the time to be competitive or combative.

♦ Beware of falling asleep at the wheel. It results in at least 200,000 traffic accidents per year. Driving between midnight and seven in the morning is particularly bad. If you are heading off on a long trip, get plenty of rest the night before, wear comfortable clothing, listen to the radio, and make frequent stops. If you are experiencing drowsiness, stop at a hotel or motel and get some sleep.

♦ Don't be a "yellow-light accelerator" or a "green-light anticipator." These names were designed by driving school instructors for drivers who play driving games with traffic lights. Yellow-light accelerators speed through an intersection to beat the red light. Green-light anticipators speed up when they think the light is about to change from red to green. A large number of traffic accidents happen at intersections, and many are due to drivers who second-guess signal changes.

♦ Steer clear of large vehicles like trucks and trailers. Too often your view is blocked. Carefully work your way around them and stay far away.

♦ Avoid the far left lane except when you need to pass another car. Drivers who like to drive fast usually remain in this lane; insurance company representatives call it the "death lane."

♦ Observe all basic driving rules and regulations. Adjust your speed to coincide with weather and traffic conditions.

♦ Wear your seat belts. Wear your seat belts. Wear your seat belts.

How Many Drinks Does It Take to Be Legally Drunk?

The blood-alcohol level at which a driver is considered "driving under the influence" (DUI) varies from state to state. In most states, it is .10 percent. In a growing number of states, like California, Oregon, and Maine, it is lower—.08 percent. Most experts estimate that the ability to drive begins to become impaired when the driver's blood alcohol level is at .05 percent.

0.08% DUI (DRIVING UNDER THE INFLUENCE) CHARTS

BAC Zones: 90 to 109 lbs.								110 to 129 lbs.								130 to 149 lbs.								150 to 169 lbs.							
TIME FROM 1ST DRINK	TOTAL DRINKS								TOTAL DRINKS								TOTAL DRINKS								TOTAL DRINKS							
	1	2	3	4	5	6	7	8	1	2	3	4	5	6	7	8	1	2	3	4	5	6	7	8	1	2	3	4	5	6	7	8
1 hr	░	■	■	■	■	■	■	■	░	■	■	■	■	■	■	■	░	■	■	■	■	■	■	■	□	░	■	■	■	■	■	■
2 hrs	□	░	■	■	■	■	■	■	□	░	■	■	■	■	■	■	□	░	■	■	■	■	■	■	□	░	■	■	■	■	■	■
3 hrs	□	░	■	■	■	■	■	■	□	░	■	■	■	■	■	■	□	□	░	■	■	■	■	■	□	□	░	■	■	■	■	■
4 hrs	□	░	■	■	■	■	■	■	□	░	■	■	■	■	■	■	□	□	░	■	■	■	■	■	□	□	░	■	■	■	■	■

BAC Zones: 170 to 189 lbs.								190 to 209 lbs.								210 lbs. and up							
TIME FROM 1ST DRINK	TOTAL DRINKS								TOTAL DRINKS								TOTAL DRINKS							
	1	2	3	4	5	6	7	8	1	2	3	4	5	6	7	8	1	2	3	4	5	6	7	8
1 hr	□	░	■	■	■	■	■	■	□	░	■	■	■	■	■	■	□	░	■	■	■	■	■	■
2 hrs	□	□	░	■	■	■	■	■	□	□	░	■	■	■	■	■	□	□	░	■	■	■	■	■
3 hrs	□	□	░	■	■	■	■	■	□	□	░	■	■	■	■	■	□	□	░	■	■	■	■	■
4 hrs	□	□	□	░	■	■	■	■	□	□	□	░	■	■	■	■	□	□	□	░	■	■	■	■

□ (.01%–.04% BAC)

░ (.05%–.07% BAC)

■ (.08% BAC and up)

The chart from the California Department of Motor Vehicles shows Blood Alcohol Concentration zones for various body-weight levels after one hour to four hours from the time the first drink was consumed. For the purposes of the chart, one drink = 12 ounces of beer, 4 ounces of wine, 1¼ ounces of 80-proof liquor. For example, if you weigh 120 pounds, you would probably be *legally* under the influence in California and other states with a DUI level of .08 after two drinks in one hour, certainly after three drinks in one hour. Remember, though, people react differently, and these are *averages*. To drive safely, you probably should not get behind the wheel if you have been drinking at all.

AIRPLANES

Personal Air Safety

It's quite a long shot—about one in 1 million—that you will be in an airplane accident in which at least one person is killed. Nonetheless, many passengers get somewhat nervous before or during a flight. There are some simple guidelines that you can follow to help ensure your safety in case of an accident.

Choice of Aircraft. In general, wide-body, or twin-aisle, airplanes like the 747, L-1011, and DC-10 can better withstand a crash than narrow-body, or single-aisle, airplanes (see "Survival Rates," opposite).

Seat Selection. If possible, book an aisle seat near an exit door. While there is no substantial evidence that one section of the plane is safer than another, some experts claim that the rear third of an airplane is safer.

Knowledge of Aircraft. About 50 percent of airline passengers do not listen to the flight attendant's initial safety briefing and do not read the plastic emergency-instruction card inserted in the seat pocket. It's a good idea to pay attention to both.

Preplan Escape. In case of an accident, how would you get out of the plane and are there any obstacles in your way? Make a mental map of your escape route. Memorize the number of rows between you and the nearest emergency exit. If the lights go out or the cabin fills with smoke,

you may have to feel your way to safety by counting the seat backs to reach your exit. Experts say that you have 90 seconds to get out of a plane after it has crashed. After 90 seconds, you are likely to succumb to smoke and toxic fumes.

Appropriate Clothing. Avoid nylon and polyester clothing because they can melt in extreme heat. Also, you might consider wearing a bright red or white shirt/blouse since those colors are easily spotted by rescue teams if you are thrown from the aircraft. Finally, wear flat, sturdy shoes that have traction.

Child Considerations. While a child under the age of two is not required to have his/her own airline seat, it is advisable to purchase one. In case of a crash, a child could fly out of your arms or lap and suffer serious injuries. In addition, take along your automobile child-restraint seat to place in the airline seat. The child-restraint seat must be on the Federal Aviation Administration's (FAA) approved list; most seats manufactured after 1985 are approved. To find out if your child-restraint seat is on the approved list, call your airline or the FAA (800-322-7873).

Fear of Flying

Fear of flying has a technical name, *aviaphobia*, and it affects about one out of every six Ameri-

SURVIVAL RATES

The figures below show survival rates for various kinds of aircraft. The percentages are from a 1992 study commissioned by *Condé Nast Traveler* magazine that looked at accidents in which at least one person survived and the aircraft sustained a considerable amount of damage. According to the study, "The figures reflect the survivors aboard aircraft that have had an accident—not the likelihood that a particular kind of aircraft will be in an accident."

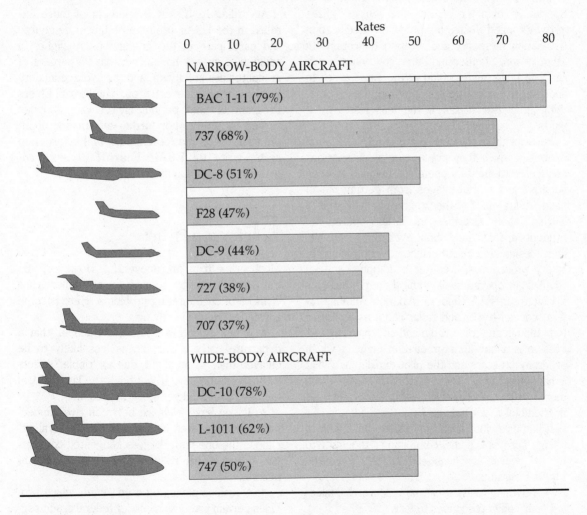

Rates

0 10 20 30 40 50 60 70 80	

NARROW-BODY AIRCRAFT

BAC 1-11 (79%)

737 (68%)

DC-8 (51%)

F28 (47%)

DC-9 (44%)

727 (38%)

707 (37%)

WIDE-BODY AIRCRAFT

DC-10 (78%)

L-1011 (62%)

747 (50%)

cans. Some "aviaphobes" have never flown on an airplane; some won't even enter an airport terminal. However, many do fly but experience white-knuckle anxiety from takeoff through landing; some perpetually turn to alcohol or tranquilizers to get them through a flight. Aviaphobes encompass a wide cross section of people. They can be found in every age group and every professional field. Of particular interest is the fact that the great majority of them have never been in an airplane accident nor had a bad flying experience.

To help passengers overcome their fear of

flying, several major airlines have instituted fear-of-flying programs. Foremost among the airline programs is USAir's Fearful Flyers Program. Started in 1975, the seven-week course was created and is directed by Carol Stauffer, a clinical social worker and psychotherapist, and Captain Frank Petee who has more than 45 years of commercial flying experience and is Director of Special Projects for USAir. The course utilizes a two-pronged focus on behavior modification (relaxation methods) and aviation education. In other words, Stauffer and Petee contend that you can't be tense and relaxed at the same time. In addition, the more you understand about something (i.e., the airplane), the less fearsome it will be.

Participants in the course are taught relaxation exercises which they practice between sessions and learn "thought-stopping" techniques to keep negative and fearful images from getting out of hand. A large part of the program is dedicated to learning about airplanes and airline operations. Students are informed about everything from airliner design and maintenance to pilot training, safety procedures, weather conditions, and en route flight operations. A typical course includes a visit to an FAA (Federal Aviation Administration) control tower and radar room as well as a tour though an airline cabin and cockpit. The last session is a one-hour graduation flight in which program directors and the pilot explain just what is happening during each stage of the flight. Class members can, if they wish, bring along a spouse or friend for moral support.

If you or a close friend or relative has a fear of flying, here are some comforting "thoughts to fly by" which are included in USAir's Fearful Flyers Program:

♦ Anything learned can be unlearned, including your bodily responses to fear.

♦ Ninety-nine and ninety-nine one-hundredths percent (99$\frac{99}{100}$%) of all airline flights are routine and normal.

♦ You don't have to like turbulence. You don't even have to feel comfortable with it. But it won't hurt you, and it won't hurt the airplane. This assumes that you are in your seat with your seat belt fastened.

♦ Airline accidents that are attributed to "weather" still occur, but they're few and far between.

♦ When there are more flights than airspace, it means delay, not danger.

According to USAir, 97 percent of those enrolled in the USAir program do finish the course and participate in the graduation-day flight. In addition, a survey has shown that 95 percent of graduates are still flying, and the average anxiety level has taken a severe drop. The Fearful Flyers Program is held periodically in various cities served by USAir. For further information about program dates and locations as well as program costs, write to: **USAir Fearful Flyers Program,** Box 100, Glenshaw, PA 15116.

Defensive Flying

Most airline trips are uneventful. However, you can take steps to reduce even further your chances of encountering problems. Here is some advice for "defensive flying."

♦ When selecting a flight, remember that a departure early in the day is less likely to be delayed than a later flight, due to "ripple" effects throughout the day. If you book the last flight of the day, you could get stuck overnight.

♦ If you have a choice between two connections and the fares and service are equivalent, choose the one with the less congested connecting airport. This reduces the risk of misconnecting.

♦ Consider paying by credit card, which provides certain protections under federal credit regulations. For example, in all recent airline bankruptcies, passengers who had charged their fare and were not provided service were able to have their credit card company credit their account for the amount of the fare.

♦ If possible, pick up your ticket from a travel

agency or from one of the airline's airport or city ticket offices. Airline procedures for replacing a ticket that you claim was lost in the mail can be inconvenient. Safeguard your ticket after you receive it; it is an accountable document and has value, much like cash. Keep a separate record of the ticket number.

♦ As soon as you receive your ticket, check to make sure all of the information on it is correct, including your name. Have any necessary corrections made immediately.

♦ Bring a photo I.D. when you fly. Many carriers are requesting such identification at check-in, both for security purposes and in an attempt to cut down on the reselling of discount tickets. (This is why it is important for your name on your ticket to be correct.)

♦ Keep checking your fare after you buy a ticket. Fares change all the time and if that same fare goes down before you fly, the airline will often refund the difference. But you have to ask.

♦ Call a day or two before your flight to reconfirm your reservation. Flight schedules sometimes change, and while airlines usually call to notify you if this happens, it's wise to double-check.

♦ Check in early. Airlines rescind specific advance seat assignments 30 minutes before scheduled departure, even if you already have your boarding pass. You can lose your entire reservation if you haven't checked in 10 minutes before scheduled departure time on a domestic flight (longer on international flights). Allow time for traffic and parking problems. If a flight is oversold, the last passengers to check in are the first to be bumped, even if they have met the 10-minute deadline.

♦ Check your ticket immediately after checking in for each leg on your trip. Airline agents sometimes accidently lift two coupons instead of one.

♦ If you are "bumped" because your flight is overbooked, read the Overbooking Notice in your ticket, then ask for a copy of the rules mentioned in that notice. This information applies to oversales, where your flight operates and leaves you

behind; it does not apply to canceled or delayed flights.

♦ Before agreeing to accept a travel voucher as compensation for being bumped, ask about restrictions. For example, with some vouchers you can't make a reservation until a few days before you want to fly.

♦ Put a tag on the outside of your baggage with your name, home address, and home and work phone numbers. The airlines provide free stick-on tags. Most carriers also have "privacy tags" which conceal this information from passersby.

♦ Put the same information *inside* each bag, and add an address and telephone number where you can be reached at your destination city.

♦ Verify that the agent checking your bags attaches a destination tag to each one. Check to see that these tags show the three-letter code for your destination airport. Remove tags from previous trips to avoid confusion.

♦ If your bag arrives open or unlocked, check immediately to see if any of the contents are missing or damaged.

♦ Report any baggage problems to your airline *before leaving the airport*. Insist that the airline fill out a form and give you a copy, even if they say the bag will be in on the next flight. Before leaving the airport, ask the airline if they will deliver the bag without charge when it is found.

♦ Open your suitcase immediately when you get to your destination. Report any damage to contents or pilferage by telephone right away. Make a note of the date and time of the call, and the name and telephone number of the person you spoke with.

Source: U.S. Department of Transportation

Selecting a Good Airline Seat

If safety is the main concern in your selection of an airline seat, your choice should be an aisle seat near an exit door. Here are some additional tips for seat selection:

♦ Don't rely on seat configuration charts that appear in old travel books and other publications. They are likely to be outdated. When reserving a seat yourself, ask the airline representative to explain the seating arrangements on your aircraft or make sure your travel agent is aware of your particular needs.

♦ The roomiest aircraft are generally considered to be Boeing 767s (wide-body jets) and McDonnell-Douglas MD-80s (narrow-body jets). However, even if you book a seat on a roomier aircraft, there's no guarantee that the airline won't switch planes on you at the last minute.

♦ While coach seating is never as comfortable as first class or business class, some airlines like TWA have increased "seat pitch" (the front-to-rear spacing of seat rows, measured from any point on a seat to the same point on a seat in the row in front or behind) by pulling out a number of coach seats. This distance between seats determines your legroom as well as your eating/working/sleeping space. Most coach sections have a seat pitch of 31 or 32 inches; TWA increased seat pitches in coach class on some planes to as much as 36 inches. If extra legroom is important to you, ask about it when you book your flight. Also, the most legroom can be found in bulkhead seats (those directly behind a cabin divider) or seats next to exit doors. Be aware that passengers in the exit-row seats are asked to be prepared to lend assistance in case of an emergency evacuation. Also, children under the age of 15 are not permitted in exit rows.

♦ While bulkhead seats have ample legroom, there is no underseat storage so all of your carryon items will have to be stored in overhead bins. In addition, your armrests might not lift up and your seating position will make it hard to watch an in-flight movie.

♦ Last-row seats on an aircraft do not recline. Seats in front of emergency exits usually do not recline. Also, some emergency-row seats do not recline.

♦ If you are traveling with a companion and face a choice of seats with a three-seat configuration (aisle-middle-window): book an aisle and a

WHY THE PLANE WOULDN'T FALL IF THE ENGINES STOPPED

From Takeoff to Landing: Everything You Wanted to Know About Airplanes But Had No One to Ask, a book by veteran commercial pilot Ed Sternstein and co-author Todd Gold, takes you through all aspects of a commercial flight, from preflight planning and flight-crew training to aircraft safety and maintenance, how and why a plane flies, and just what happens during takeoffs and landings. It answers all kinds of questions like, Could someone accidently, or intentionally, open a door in mid-flight? The answer is no because when the plane is pressurized, the interior pressure locks the doors in place.

Foremost on some passengers' minds is what would happen if all the engines shut down? First off, as Sternstein says, the odds of a malfunction in a turbo-fan "jet" engine are less than one per 50,000 hours of flight. Obviously, the odds of all engines failing at once are statistically way out in left field. Nonetheless, here is what Sternstein has to say on the subject: "A car that loses its engine might try to coast downhill. A plane only has to lower its nose. If all the engines were to fail at once, the pilots would point the airplane downhill. Enough lift will be generated to keep the plane safely airborne until an engine is restarted. At 35,000 feet even a jumbo jet can glide for about 70 miles, simply by coasting. . . . In fact, on almost every flight there comes a point on descent when the pilots will pull the power back to idle and let the plane glide. Gliding is a normal part of almost every flight."

window. The middle seats are the least desirable and chances are no one will book that seat. Thus, you and your companion will have more space. If someone does end up in the middle seat, and you and your companion really want to sit next to each other, you can always ask the middle-seat passenger to switch places with one of you.

♦ Seats over a wing block your view and subject you to more noise.

♦ Seats near the food service areas, flight attendants' stations, and bathrooms are in heavily trafficked areas and are noisier.

♦ Seats toward the front of the plane are quieter than seats in the back. However, rear-row seats usually fill up last so those areas are more likely to have empty seats, even empty rows.

♦ If you are unhappy with your seat assignment, go back to the desk shortly before boarding. Seats for passengers who didn't show up will be available and you might get a better seat.

♦ Board the aircraft when your seat is called; don't lag behind. Errors do happen and sometimes two people are assigned the same seat. Generally, the first person seated is given priority.

ABOARD AIR FORCE ONE

The odds are slim to none that you'll ever get invited to fly in Air Force One, but if you are, here's what to expect: The $181 million Boeing 747 has 85 telephones, 18 televisions, and a computer center and conference room. The Presidential suite has a bedroom, shower, dressing area, and a mini Oval Office. There is an operating room in case of medical emergency and a lounge with fully reclinable sleeping chairs. The plane has two food galleys; each can handle meals for 100 people. And you can cruise along for 7140 miles without stopping to refuel.

BICYCLES AND MOTORCYCLES

Bicycle Safety

More than 52 million adults and 44 million children ride bicycles. Every year bicycle accidents kill 950 Americans and cause injuries to another 580,000. Most of these injuries do not involve motor vehicles, but 90 percent of bicycle fatalities do involve a collision with a motor vehicle.

The National Safety Council offers the following tips for safe and enjoyable bicycling:

♦ Obey traffic rules. Get acquainted with ordinances. Cyclists must follow the same rules as motorists.

♦ Know your bike's capabilities. Remember that bicycles differ from motor vehicles; they're smaller and can't move as fast. But they can change direction more easily, stop faster, and move through smaller spaces.

♦ Ride in single file with traffic, but not against it. Bicycling two abreast can be dangerous. Bicyclists should stay as far right on the pavement as possible, watching for opening car doors, sewer gratings, soft shoulders, broken glass and other debris. Remember to keep a safe distance from the vehicle ahead.

♦ Make safe turns and cross intersections with care. Signal turns half a block before the intersection, using the correct hand signals (left arm straight out for left turn; forearm up for right turn). When traffic is heavy and the cyclist has to turn left, it is best to dismount and walk the bicycle across both streets at the crosswalks.

FIVE COMMON BICYCLE ACCIDENTS
1. Bicycle Left Turn or Sudden Swerve

The bicyclist swerves to the left without checking traffic, without signaling, and moves into the path of an overtaking motor vehicle. The motorist does not have enough time to avoid the collision.

Advice to the bicyclist: Always ride in a straight line. When changing lanes, look behind you and yield to overtaking traffic. When turning left, give hand signal and move to left lane when it is safe. Signal again and make the turn.

2. Motorist Overtaking Cyclist

This accident occurs because the motorist fails to see and react to the bicyclist until it's too late. This accident type is more frequent at night, on narrow rural roads, involves driver inattention, and also involves drunk driving.

Advice to the bicyclist: Avoid riding at night, on narrow roads, and where highway speeds are over 35 mph. Always use lights and reflectors if you must ride at night.

3. Stop-Sign Rideout

This accident occurs when the bicyclist enters an intersection that is controlled by a sign and collides with a motor vehicle approaching from an uncontrolled lane. The bicyclist fails to stop/slow and look for traffic before entering the intersection. This improper action leaves the motorist too little time to avoid a collision.

Advice to the bicyclist: When riding your bicycle, obey all traffic signs and signals. At busy intersections, get off your bike and walk across the road as you do when you are a pedestrian.

4. Midblock Rideout

This is the most frequent accident type for young riders and occurs soon after the bicyclist enters the road from a driveway, alley, or curb without slowing, stopping, or looking for traffic. The bicyclist's sudden entry leaves the motorist too little time to avoid the collision.

Advice to the bicyclist: Stop and look left-right-left for traffic before entering the road.

5. Wrong-Way Riding

Motorists do not expect traffic to be approaching from the wrong way. It is the exception to the rule that creates the condition for an accident, which is the main reason why it is unlawful to ride facing traffic.

Advice to the bicyclist: Go with the flow. Ride with traffic just as cars do.

Source: National Highway Traffic Safety Administration, U.S. Department of Transportation

♦ Never hitch on cars. A sudden stop or turn could send the cyclist flying into the path of another vehicle.

♦ Before riding into traffic: stop, look left, right, left again, and over your shoulder.

♦ Always be seen. During the day, cyclists should wear bright clothing. Nighttime cycling is not advised, but if riding at night is necessary, retroreflective clothing, designed to bounce back motorists' headlight beams, will make cyclists more visible.

♦ Make sure the bicycle has the right safety equipment: a red rear reflector; a white front reflector; a red or colorless spoke reflector on the rear wheel; an amber or colorless reflector on the front wheel; pedal reflectors; a horn or bell; and a rear-view mirror. A bright headlight is recommended for night riding.

♦ Wear a helmet. Head injuries cause about 75 percent of all bicycling fatalities. The Council strongly urges all cyclists to wear helmets. The first body part to fly forward in a collision is usually the head, and with nothing but skin and bone to protect the brain from injury, the results can be disastrous. Look for helmets with approval stickers (Snell Memorial Foundation, or American National Standards Institute).

A helmet is well designed if it has these features:
1. a stiff outer shell designed to distribute impact forces and protect against sharp objects;
2. an energy-absorbing liner at least one-half inch thick;
3. a chin strap and fastener to keep the helmet in place;
4. is lightweight;
5. is cool in hot weather; and
6. fits comfortably.

Bicycle Helmets

About 85 percent of head injuries and 88 percent of brain injuries sustained by cyclists could have been prevented if the riders had been wearing helmets. Less than 10 percent of Americans regularly wear them, however. To date some states have laws requiring the use of bicycle helmets for children, but there is a growing movement toward compulsory helmet laws for both children and adults.

Bicycle helmets come in three basic models: no shell, thin shell, and hard shell. Each contains a dense inner cushion of expanded polystyrene (EPS) foam; the thicker the cushion, the more protection you get. No-shell helmets have a Lycra cover and are the lightest of the three models. Thin-shell helmets are covered with a thin layer of semirigid plastic and weigh a little more than no-shell helmets. Hard-shell helmets have a plastic or fiberglass shell and are the heaviest type of helmet.

All helmets come with chin straps, and it's important that the straps be adjusted for a perfect fit. When the helmet is on your head, it should sit level and fit snugly. The top half of your forehead should be covered and the helmet should touch the head all the way around at the brim. According to the Bicycle Institute of America, "When the strap is properly adjusted, you should not be able to push the front edge of the helmet upward more than 30 degrees from level."

When shopping for a helmet, you should first look for an ANSI or Snell sticker which will be inside the helmet. ANSI stands for American National Standards Institute, a group that sets safety standards for helmets; the sticker will say "This helmet meets ANSI Z90.4 standard." An ANSI sticker means that the helmet manufacturer has followed voluntary industry standards for helmet construction; in this case, the manufacturers themselves test the helmets. The strictest test standards around are those used by the Snell Memorial Foundation, an independent, nonprofit organization that tests helmets not only for bicycle use but also for use with motorcycles, automotive sports, and equestrian sports. The Snell decal for bicycles is green or blue and has the name "Snell" prominently displayed. If the helmet you are considering does not have an ANSI or Snell sticker (preferably, it has both), then don't buy the helmet.

It's generally agreed that the life span of a helmet is five years. However, if you are in a crash in which your head and the helmet are hit, replace the helmet. The foam part of the helmet is designed for a one-time impact; after it has been crushed, it no longer gives you adequate protection.

Bicycle helmets have come a long way over the years in terms of style and comfort, as well as safety. Most have large air vents to "air condition" your head and they come in a number of appealing colors and designs. But safety should always be the number-one consumer consideration. If you think of a helmet as an air bag for your head, you will have an easier time adapting to wearing it on a regular basis.

Motorcycles and Cars: Sharing the Road

The following questions and answers were developed by the Motorcycle Safety Foundation (MSF), a nonprofit organization whose purpose is to improve the safety of motorcyclists on our nation's streets and highways. The information below is written for the motorist and is intended to increase a motorist's awareness of motorcyclists on the road.

Why is it so important to give motorcyclists room on the road?

A rider is exposed to all the elements. There is no steel compartment surrounding the rider to protect him or her in the event of a collision.

Motorcyclists will also use more of the road in responding to changing traffic and/or highway conditions. Motorcycles are generally more maneuverable than cars, and riders use this maneuverability to avoid potential danger. In order to make such maneuvers, a rider needs room.

Don't crowd a rider in a lane. The motorcyclist is entitled to the entire lane, regardless of where he or she may be riding.

Why should you look more carefully for motorcyclists?

A study conducted at the University of Southern California showed that motorists' failure to detect and recognize motorcycles in traffic is the predominant cause of accidents involving motorcycles and other vehicles. Many motorists fail to detect motorcyclists because they don't expect to see them or aren't looking for a motorcycle. They expect to see other cars and don't realize there are many motorcycles on the road as well.

If motorcyclists are hard to see, why don't they make themselves more visible?

Experienced riders will do all they can to be conspicuous. That's why you almost always see the motorcyclist's headlight on, day or night. It's the best way to attract attention.

You may also notice that some riders wear brightly colored helmets and clothing. This helps them to be more visible to other motorists.

However, you still see many riders wearing black riding gear. Black was made fashionable by Hollywood movies, but many riders still prefer to wear darker clothes because they don't show the dirt and grime picked up from being out in the open.

And motorcyclists don't wear leather jackets, jeans, boots, and studded gloves to look tough, like the characters immortalized in the movies. Leather provides some of the best protection from the elements and from potential injury should the rider fall.

Motorcyclists wear jackets on warm days not only for protection, but also because riding can make the weather seem much cooler than it actually is. A rider must contend with a wind-chill factor that corresponds to the speed he or she is traveling.

Why do motorcyclists ride in different parts of the lane?

That's another way riders make themselves more visible to motorists. Usually you'll see motorcyclists ride in the left portion of the lane. That makes them more visible to oncoming traffic and gives them the best view of traffic as well.

Riders may switch lane position so they're not in your blind spot. Having a motorcyclist appear out of nowhere may come as a sudden surprise to some drivers, but the rider is merely trying to get your attention so that you realize he or she is there.

Visibility isn't the only reason riders switch lane position. Safe motorcyclists try to maintain a "space cushion" between themselves and traffic. This space cushion gives them time to react to changing traffic conditions, unexpected moves by cars, or to debris in the road. While a car is relatively unaffected by road debris, it can be a real hazard to the motorcyclist and he or she will most likely take evasive action to avoid it. The same holds true for potholes or oil.

Sometimes a rider will get blown across a lane by strong gusts of wind. Even the wind created by a passing truck in the other lane can be enough to move a motorcycle around. If you see an oncoming truck, expect the motorcyclist to move to the right side of the lane.

A rider will also move about within a lane in order to prepare for a turn. Watch for the motorcyclist's turn signal, but don't assume that means he or she will actually turn. Most motorcycle turn signals are not self-canceling like those on a car. It's not uncommon for even the most experienced rider to inadvertently let a turn signal continue to flash.

Where is a motorcyclist most likely to be involved in an accident with another vehicle?

At an intersection. According to a study conducted at the University of California, intersections are the most likely place for motorcycle accidents. And two-thirds of those accidents occurred when another vehicle violated the motorcyclists' right-of-way.

A motorcycle's small size makes it more difficult to spot in traffic, so motorists must aggressively and consciously look for motorcycles in changing traffic conditions. Because of the small silhouette, it's not easy to determine the speed of an oncoming motorcycle; it's common to misjudge the actual distance between the car and motorcycle. So before proceeding at an intersection, check the scene no less than three times and make it a point to look for motorcyclists.

Tips for Safe Motorcycling

Motorcycling is a fun, exciting, and practical way to get around. But, like any other activity, it has risks. The reality is that you are exposed and vulnerable; it is up to you to avoid accidents and injury. Risk, and how you treat it, is what safe cycling is all about. To help you reduce and manage risks:

Know your skills. Take a beginning or experienced RiderCourse from a **Motorcycle Safety Foundation** recognized training center. Call 800-447-4700 for the RiderCourse nearest you. The more you know, the better rider you become.

Know the rules of the road and respect other road users. Don't forget, riding is a privilege. Get yourself and your motorcycle properly licensed; get insurance if required. Know the limits of your skills, your motorcycle, and the road conditions so you don't ride over your head.

Ride with the right gear. A helmet, eye protection, sturdy jacket, pants, boots, and gloves are your best defense against accident injury. It can happen to you.

Ride aware. A car turning left across your path causes the most frequent accident. Three-fourths of motorcycle accidents involve collisions with other vehicles, the majority caused by the other driver. Intersections can be bad spots, so slow down and be prepared to react.

Ride to survive. Be seen and not hit. You aren't as big as a Mack truck, but you can attract attention. Wear bright clothing, use your headlight and bright-colored fairings, select a lane and a position within a lane to be seen, avoid rapid lane changes, and keep looking around; you don't need surprises.

Ride straight. Alcohol and other drugs do not let you think clearly or make sound judgments. Up to 45 percent of all fatal motorcycle accidents involve alcohol.

Keep a safe bike. Know your owner's manual, follow recommended service schedules, and have repairs made by an authorized dealer. Always check your bike's tires, suspension, and controls before riding.

Reprinted courtesy of the Motorcycle Safety Foundation.

Motorcycle Helmets

Helmets are the most effective piece of safety equipment available to the motorcyclist. Here are some facts taken from recent studies on motorcycle accidents:

♦ Per mile driven, a motorcyclist is about 20 times more likely to die in a crash than is an automobile passenger. But wearing a helmet reduces the motorcyclist's risk of death by almost one-third (29 percent).

♦ Head injury is the leading cause of death in motorcycle crashes, and helmets go a long way toward preventing these injuries. Among riders involved in crashes, those who don't wear helmets are 40 percent more likely to sustain a fatal head injury than those who wear helmets, and they are also 15 times more likely to incur nonfatal head injuries.

♦ From 1984 through 1989, helmets saved the lives of more than 4100 motorcyclists. But another 4000 deaths could have been prevented if all riders had been wearing helmets.

Mandatory helmet laws have been the subject of much controversy, especially among some motorcyclists who believe that helmet laws are a violation of their basic rights as Americans. Currently, there are 24 states that require all motorcycle riders and passengers to wear helmets. Another 23 states have laws requiring helmet use, but only some people, usually minors, must wear them. Only three states have no helmet laws. Numerous studies have shown that when a state helmet law goes into effect, more people use helmets and more lives are saved. When helmet laws are repealed, fatalities are estimated to increase by 20 percent.

Buying a Helmet

Guidelines for buying and wearing a helmet:

1. There are two basic kinds of helmets: a full-face helmet and an open-face helmet. A *full-face* helmet gives more protection simply because it covers more of your face; a full-face helmet usually has movable faceshields for eye protection as well as a chin bar. An *open-face* helmet does not have the same face and chin protection afforded by a full-face helmet. According to the Motorcycle Safety Foundation: "If you use an open-face helmet, you should have a snap-on faceshield in place when you ride, or buy a pair of goggles that can withstand the impact of a stone. Ordinary glasses or sunglasses are not sufficient protection for a motorcyclist, and they might move or fly off."

2. All helmets have three layers: an outer shell, made of fiberglass or plastic; an impact-absorbing liner of expanded polystyrene (Styrofoam) that is designed to absorb shock upon impact; and comfort padding that cushions your head and enables the helmet to fit snugly on your head.

3. By law, all adult-sized motorcycle helmets sold in the United States must meet certain safety standards set by the Department of Transportation (DOT). When buying a helmet, be sure it has a sticker that signifies DOT approval. In addition, the Snell Memorial Foundation, an independent, nonprofit organization, certifies helmets that meet its high-quality, rigorous safety standards. Look for a DOT sticker and/or a Snell sticker on the inside or outside of the helmet. If you do not find one, or both, of these stickers, do not buy the helmet.

4. Always use the helmet strap. When the helmet is securely in place, it should sit squarely on your head and fit snugly. The fit should not be too loose or too tight.

5. Most helmets need to be replaced every two to four years even if they haven't been in an accident. If a helmet has been in an accident, it needs to be replaced immediately. If the helmet suffers damage because you drop it, it may also

need to be replaced. Helmets are not designed to sustain repeated blows. When in doubt about the safety of a helmet, get a new one or at least have it checked out. Some manufacturers will repair helmets if the damage is minimal.

Helmet Myths

In its brochure, "Motorcycle Helmets: The Facts of Life," the National Highway Traffic Safety Administration addresses three common myths about motorcycle helmets:

Myth #1: Helmets Cause Injuries

In its report, "Head Protection for Cyclists," the American Medical Association found no valid evidence that helmets caused head, neck, or shoulder injuries. In addition, after investigating 900 motorcycle crashes, the University of California concluded that:

♦ Helmeted riders and passengers experienced significantly fewer and less severe head and neck injuries than unhelmeted riders and passengers.

♦ There is a critical need for the use of protective equipment by every motorcycle rider. The contemporary motorcycle helmet provides spectacular reduction of head and neck injury, without any adverse effect on vision or hearing, or vulnerability for other injury. The research shows no reason for any motorcyclist to be without a safety helmet.

♦ Only four of the 861 head and neck injuries were attributed to safety helmets and all were minor injuries. . . . In each case, the helmet prevented possible fatal or critical head injury.

Myth #2: Helmets Impair Vision

Helmets don't obscure vision. According to a study done to investigate helmets and vision, helmets limit peripheral vision by less than 3 percent. Not only that, all helmets provide a field of vision of more than 210 degrees—well above the 140-degree standard that state driver-licensing agencies use to identify vision problems.

Myth #3: Helmets Impair Hearing

In practical terms, a motorcyclist out on the

THE TYPICAL MOTORCYCLE RIDER

According to the Motorcycle Industry Council, the typical motorcycle rider is male, 33 years old, married, has attended college, and earns a mean household income of about $39,200 a year. Some other interesting facts from the Council:

♦ Women riders are likely to be married and tend to be slightly younger than males riders (32 versus 33 years old).

♦ The largest percentage of riders (30 percent) live in the Midwest.

♦ Motorcyclists love outdoor activities. When asked to pick their favorite "other recreational activity," the most popular activity was fishing.

♦ About 25 percent of riders are white-collar workers; blue-collar workers total 29 percent. Twenty-two percent are "gray-collar" including service workers, clerical/sales personnel, and students. The remaining 24 percent is comprised of farmers/farm laborers, retired military, housewives, and other groups.

road will hear just as well or better with a helmet as without one, according to the Department of Transportation. Why? Because for someone without a helmet, the wind and the sound of the engine are very loud. Any other important sounds have to be even louder to be heard over all that noise. With a helmet on, everything quiets down somewhat, but in equal proportions. This means that if something can be heard over wind and engine noise without a helmet, it can be heard in the same way with one—because wind and engine noise also will be less. Technically speaking, the signal-to-noise ratio stays the same.

For More Information:

The Motorcycle Safety Foundation (MSF) offers a vast array of materials for motorcyclists, including, "What You Should Know about Motorcycle Helmets," "Riding Gear for the Motorcyclist," and "Riding Tips." Also, MSF has a brochure on its RiderCourse instruction programs which are taught at over 800 sites throughout the United States; to date more than 780,000 motorcyclists have graduated from RiderCourse programs. Write to: **Motorcycle Safety Foundation,** 2 Jenner Street, Suite 150, Irvine, California 92718-3812.

TRAINS

Tips for Traveling on Amtrak

Amtrak, the only nationwide passenger train system in the United States, operates about 250 trains that go to more than 500 destinations. Listed below are some of the basic rules, regulations, and services that pertain to travel on the Amtrak system.

Baggage. Most trains allow two carryon bags per passenger. If you have reserved overnight sleeping accommodations, you can take on board as much luggage as will fit safely and comfortably in your room. On trains that offer checked baggage service, each ticketed passenger can check up to three bags without charge; weight limitations are 75 pounds per bag or 150 pounds per passenger. Amtrak assumes no liability for carry-on baggage and has a liability limit of $500 per ticketed passenger for checked baggage; you can buy additional coverage up to $2500 if you wish, when you check in.

Overnight travel. There are sleeper cars on Amtrak's overnight routes but they are fully booked months in advance. The charge for sleeping accommodations is separate from the charge for your rail fare. Sleeping accommodations vary according to the train and destination; they include an economy bedroom, a roomette, a family

bedroom, a deluxe bedroom, or a slumbercoach room. If you book a sleeping compartment, all necessary bedding is provided. Most sleeper accommodations are designated as first-class service. Passengers traveling in coach class will sleep in their reclining seats and pillows are provided. If you want a blanket, you can bring your own or buy an Amtrak souvenir blanket, on sale on most long-distance trains.

Pets. Animals are not permitted unless they are certified guide or service animals accompanying passengers with disabilities.

Food. On long-distance overnight trains, there are dining rooms that serve complete meals, either served at your table or cafeteria style. Some dining rooms on long-distance trains are deluxe with table linens, glassware, and china dinnerware; most are more informal. Trains that travel shorter distances will have a café, or lounge car that serves sandwiches, snacks, soft drinks, and beverages.

Unaccompanied children. Children cannot travel unaccompanied if they are under eight years old. Children ages eight through 12 years may travel alone but only under certain circumstances; they pay the full adult fare.

Entertainment. Long-distance trains provide the most entertainment as well as other amenities. For example, the Superliner trains that travel through the western United States have lounge cars that feature full-length movies, cartoons for kids, games like bingo, hospitality hours, and other activities and services. Some long-distance trains have interpretive guides on board who provide narration about the history and geography of places or regions that you pass through on the trip. Whatever the length of the train trip, many passengers take along their own games, books, and playing cards to keep themselves occupied. It's all right to take along a radio or tape player, but only if you use earphones and keep the volume low.

Passengers with disabilities. Amtrak can provide special services for disabled persons, including special seating, sleeping, and dining arrangements. If you or a traveling companion needs extra assistance, it's best to make reservations in advance and let Amtrak know exactly what kind of help you need.

Reservations. In general, you need to make reservations for first-class travel, all long-distance coach seating, and for sleeping-car accommodations. Also, a small number of trains/routes always require advance reservations. When talking to your travel agent or an Amtrak agent, remember to ask if you need a reservation. Reservations can be booked 11 months in advance. Amtrak reservations lines are open 365 days a year, 24 hours a day. Call 800-USA-RAIL (800-872-7245).

Ticketing. You can get a ticket through a travel agent. Or, you can buy tickets directly from Amtrak. If you call Amtrak and make a reservation, you can pay with an approved credit card and get your tickets in the mail, as long as you make a reservation 10 days in advance. If you make a reservation by phone, you need not pay immediately with a credit card. The Amtrak agent will give you a reservation number and a deadline date for payment. If you don't pay for and pick up the tickets by the deadline date, the reservation will be canceled.

Cancellation policy. Amtrak's cancellation policy requires 48 hours notice to avoid penalties on first-class accommodations.

Tipping. Tipping is not required for any services, but it's a nice gesture, especially for the employees who check your bags (Red Cap Service) and for the attendants who take care of you in sleeping cars and dining cars.

Fares. Like airline fares, they change, depending on whether you are traveling during peak or off-peak times of the year. Also, Amtrak frequently offers special promotional fares. Amtrak agents are trained to give you the lowest possible fare when you call for price information. Children under the age of two travel free as long as they ride on a parent's lap. Reduced rates are available for children ages two through 15 if they are traveling with adults.

Making Reservations on Amtrak

Amtrak suggests that you do the following before you call an Amtrak agent or your travel agent:

1. Have a pen and paper ready to jot down information you receive from your travel agent or Amtrak reservationist.

2. Have an idea where you want to go, and where you'd like to stop along the way.

3. Know when you want to travel. Amtrak offers many discount fares, but some fares have restrictions and "blackout periods." Your best fare depends on the time and the date you travel.

4. Consider alternative dates. Discount fares depend on the availability of seats, so they may not always be available for your first choice.

5. Know the number of people you'll be traveling with and the accommodations you prefer.

6. You're eligible for discounts if you are: over 62; military personnel on active duty; an individual with disabilities. Don't hesitate to ask for them.

7. If your plans change and you are unable to travel, cancel your travel and tour bookings immediately so that if your tickets are refundable, you can get the maximum refund possible.

8. Do not hesitate to ask questions. Amtrak needs to know your concerns in order to help you as much as possible.

10

RECREATION

SPORTS AND GAMES

528 RECREATION

Sports and Games

What Sport Is for You?

Sports can bring well-being—from competition, from playing in the outdoors, from feeling centered in an agile, energetic body. People who play sports find that they have lower levels of stress, sleep better, think better. Nobody except a dyed-in-the-wool couch potato challenges the fact that sports are fun and good for you. The real question is: What sport suits you best?

Here are some tips, gleaned from sports and fitness experts, that should help you chose a sport that is compatible with your fitness level and lifestyle:

♦ Always have a physical examination before you start.

♦ Focus on one sport, not several, because you are more likely to stick to it. Once committed, in a routine, you can add other sports if you feel the need.

♦ Pick a sport that will demand a variety of physical and mental skills, and one that you can do for life. You can play singles tennis fiercely when young, and cut back to slower games of doubles when you are older, if you like. (Plenty of seniors continue to play fierce singles, but you may not be one of them.)

♦ Ask yourself what benefits you want from the sport: A cardiovascular workout or an increase in flexibility or strength? A mental challenge or pure pleasure? Competition or solitary enjoyment?

♦ Does the sport provide exercise that is age-appropriate? Fitness-appropriate? (If you have a trick knee, it's probably not a good idea to take up surfing or squash, for instance.)

♦ Make sure that you can afford the sport—some sports, like downhill skiing, are more expensive than others. Find out what equipment you need to rent or buy, if you need to join a club in order to play, and if you need lessons.

♦ Does the sport demand that you travel someplace to do it? If so, are you willing to put in travel time?

♦ If you play with a partner, choose a partner at your level or slightly better.

♦ Enjoy yourself. Pay attention to your bodily feelings and your physical surroundings. If you ski, revel in the snow. If you swim in the ocean, notice the patterns of the waves.

♦ Have goals and focus on them.

♦ Always warm up and cool down.

♦ Don't overdo.

For more information:

Amateur Athletic Union (AAU), AAU House, PO Box 68207, Indianapolis, IN 46268 (317-872-8680) (or a local office), offers programs and competition in Olympic and non-Olympic sports at the local, state, and national levels.

Women's Sports Foundation, 800-227-3988;

in New York, 516-542-4700, for information about women's sports teams or organizations in your area.

Locally, check the phone book for: YWCA and YMCA; recreation and parks departments; fitness clubs or country clubs.

Most Popular Sports

According to a 1990 survey by Lieberman Research for *Sports Illustrated*, Americans enjoy an eclectic assortment of sports—everything from tennis to hunting. The survey asked respondents to check all sports they participated in at least once in the previous 12-month period. Surprisingly, one person out of five did nothing at all; 69 percent of women and 74 percent of men participated at least once. This list includes all sports chosen by at least 10 percent of the respondents.

Participation Sports (In Order of Popularity)

Swimming	Hiking/backpacking
Bicycling	Boating (except
Fishing	sailing)
Using exercise	Weight lifting
machines	Basketball
Bowling	Volleyball
Calisthenics/	Hunting
aerobics	Golf
Baseball/softball	Football
Pool/billiards	Tennis
Jogging	

Spectator Sports

In spite of tradition, which claims baseball as the national pastime, the top American spectator sport is now football, with baseball second and basketball third. (In 1937, the number one spectator sport *was* baseball.) Whether male or female, young or old, white Americans ranked football as their favorite sport to watch. Black

Americans placed basketball at the top, with football a close second. The majority of all respondents felt that players in these three top sports were overpaid, and that student athletes should not play for pay.

Special Olympics

"Let me win, but if I cannot win, let me be brave in the attempt." (Special Olympics Oath)

Children and adults who are mentally retarded can train for one or more of 23 sports, then compete in those sports in Special Olympics, athletic training, and competitions in a variety of sports. Participants in Special Olympics work their way up through Chapter and National games to International Games, which occur every two years. (The First International Special Olympics Games, organized by Eunice Kennedy Shriver, took place in 1968 in Chicago.) Special Olympics athletes have set records in track, won boxing titles, and played in the National Basketball Association and National Football League. Special Olympics provides a way for athletes to develop physical fitness, show courage, experience the joy of achievement, be included in the community, and make friends. Families of Special Olympics athletes are encouraged to become involved. The Unified Sports Program sponsored by Special Olympics brings together people with and without mental retardation on the same teams, matched for athletic ability.

Volunteers organize and run local Special Olympics programs. They serve as coaches, officials, drivers, and in other capacities. People who want to compete in Special Olympics may do so through school programs, community recreation programs, and other organizations. They must be at least eight years old.

The official summer sports are:

aquatics	cycling
athletics	equestrian sports
basketball	football (soccer)
bowling	gymnastics

roller skating	tennis
softball	volleyball

The official winter sports are:

alpine skiing	floor hockey
cross-country skiing	poly hockey
figure skating	speed skating

Demonstration sports are:

badminton	table tennis
golf	team handball
powerlifting	

Special Olympics also provides a comprehensive motor activity training program (MATP) for individuals with severe and profound limitations. In this program, emphasis is on training and participation, not competition.

To participate as an athlete or volunteer contact your local Special Olympics chapter. Or contact **Special Olympics International Headquarters,** 1350 New York Avenue NW, Suite 500, Washington, DC 20005 (202-628-3630; FAX 202-737-1937).

How to Play Mental Games: The Psychology of Winning

Winners' mental strategies have probably existed since the first sports contest. However, it is only recently that sports psychologists have codified the techniques that athletes have always intuitively known. The New Age of sports psychology began with the application of Zen principles in the book *The Inner Game of Tennis,* by W. Timothy Gallwey. Since the book's publication in 1974 sports psychology has turned increasingly scientific.

Mental practice (armchair rehearsal): Though close to daydream, mental practice is a more ordered system than idle fantasy. First, relax. Sit in a comfortable chair, breathe deeply several times. Then imagine yourself going through the steps of a *successful, perfect* move. For instance, if you want to improve your tennis serve, imagine your initial stance, the toss of the ball as you raise your racquet and let it drop behind your back, then the up-and-over move of the racquet and the forward explosive lunge as you hit the ball. You are programming your brain to send the right signals to your body—visual, auditory, and kinesthetic.

This practice, according to psychologists, can have the same effect as actual physical practice. They suggest that you build an "image bank" of various scenarios for various situations.

Concentration: When actually playing, you must reach the proper arousal level (neither too "psyched" nor too relaxed) in order to play at peak levels. Shut off your analytical self, focus on positive results, tune out distractions. Easy to say, but hard to accomplish. Techniques do exist:

♦ Scientists have found that changes in the brain take place during peak performance and intense concentration. Using electrodes, they have tracked bursts of alpha waves (which come with a relaxed, trance-like state) just before skilled archers let an arrow go, basketball players shoot a free throw, or marksmen shoot at a target. Biofeedback training may help you learn to control your brain waves, so that you can go into an alpha state just before crucial moves.

♦ Before actually making a move, mentally rehearse it, if the sport allows. The basketball player can do this for a free throw, but it is more difficult during the rough-and-tumble of regular play.

♦ Different sports demand different levels of arousal: the golfer must intermittently reach a low level of arousal, the weight lifter must gear up for a short burst of intense energy. Keep this in mind.

The "spaces between": What you do between moves can improve your performance. During those times, think positively, concentrating on what you have done well, not what you have done poorly. Relax.

Garner your energies for the next move. Focus only on the things you can control.

Trusting your "muscle memory": Let

yourself go into "automatic"—trust your brain to know the skill. In a 1992 study, neurologist Scott Grafton of the University of Southern California tracked brain patterns in skill learning and found that the brain fine-tunes neural circuits so that it becomes more focused as the athlete becomes more proficient.

Creating short-term goals: Divide long-term goals into several short-term goals, so that you are rewarded more often and can use the positive feedback to catapult yourself to a yet higher level. Think about improving your score rather than winning the game.

Relying on superstition: Those crazy little rituals actually work. They help you to focus your attention, provided that they are not out of control. Know that your little routine is a coping strategy; the gods of sport are not watching—you will not necessarily lose if you misplace your lucky hat.

Children and Sports

Why so much emotion in the screaming Mom or Dad as they exhort a young athlete to greater accomplishment? What is the coach really doing when he or she plays the role of acerbic critic after the Little League team has lost a game? How can you determine what sport is best for your child? Perspective—in parents, audiences, and young players—matters when it comes to the question of whether sports are beneficial or damaging for children.

Adults should be careful not to invest too much of their own ambition into their children's sports programs. Just because you loved volleyball does not mean your child will. A father yelling at his child at a Little League game says more about his own disappointments than his interest in his child. Children's sports programs should not degenerate into spectator sports for adults.

Most sports psychologists and pediatricians agree on the following:

♦ When participating in a sport, a child should concentrate on mastery of skills, not just winning.

♦ Pushing children to enter a sport too early may cause them to drop out because they become discouraged. Glyn Roberts, a University of Illinois professor of sports psychology, estimates that 80 percent of children who try competitive sports drop them forever by age 17, many because they feel that it is too psychologically painful to continue.

♦ Make sure that your child has proper safety equipment and that the leaders of the program are safety-conscious. Tumbling and gymnastics demand protective mats, hockey demands helmets.

♦ Insist on a proper ratio of instructors to children. For children under five, at least one instructor for every four or five children; two coaches for a baseball team of nine-year-olds.

♦ Instructors should be good and patient teachers, fond and respectful of children. Watch a couple of practices to assess the instructor's attitude and skill.

♦ All children should be allowed to participate. Canadian researchers found that 90 percent of children would rather play on a team that loses than not play at all. Children should have a say in what goes on in the program, to present and develop creative ideas.

♦ Don't worry if you cannot attend every game, but show an interest.

Competition

Is competition good for children? This is an important question because 30 million children are involved in competitive sports. The answer? Yes, say most sports psychologists, provided that playing gives pleasure, not undue stress. More emphasis should be put on fun than on winning. Through playing competitive sports, children can master skills, learn to cooperate, break down class and racial prejudices. Experts say that it is best to get satisfaction from the competition itself. To quote the old adage, "It's not whether you win or lose but how you play the game." Still, winning itself has great power for many people—it says that the gods are smiling upon you. Children feel that power, too.

What Physical Activities When?

The consensus among physical fitness experts is that children under three do not need fitness classes. They get all the exercise they need on their own. For older children:

Choosing the Right Athletic Shoes

When most of you were kids, a pair of canvas shoes (any kind) would do for all our activities, from running to playing dodgeball. Not anymore. Now we require a separate athletic shoe for

CHILDREN'S BEST PHYSICAL PROGRAM, BY AGE

Ages	Psychological	Best physical program
3 4	Children of 3 to 4 are more concerned with how well they do in a physical skill than with how they compare with others. They are more likely to say, "I threw the ball very high!" than "I threw the ball higher than Alex!"	Children of these ages need to develop strength and flexibility, to learn skills like skipping, hopping, kicking, balancing, catching a ball, and throwing a ball overhand and underhand. Begin participation in noncontact sports at age 6.
5 6	Children begin to compare themselves with others, trying to better others' efforts. Finally they learn to keep score and care about it.	
7 8 9 10	Children under 11 enjoy sports for a sense of accomplishment. If they can swim a lap or ride a two-wheeler, that's what charges them up.	Participation in noncontact sports —baseball, tennis, track, swimming. Participation in contact sports like basketball, soccer, wrestling.
11 12 13	Children on the verge of adolescence enjoy competition, but are sensitive to social comparisons.	With proper safety precautions, participation in collision sports like hockey and football may be appropriate for children of these ages.

almost every sport. Why? Isn't this just another consumer scam? No, say the experts, because different sports place different demands on your feet and legs, and proper shoes can prevent injuries and increase performance. For example, the three-mile run of a 150-pound jogger has a cumulative impact on each foot of 150 tons. Between them, your two feet, intricate structures of exquisite balance, have 26 bones (one-fourth of all those in the body), 33 joints, and a network of more than 100 tendons and ligaments.

In general, follow these suggestions:

♦ Buy new shoes when the foam in the midsole of your old shoes has gotten hard.

♦ Before you go to the shoe store, find out if you walk more on the outside or inside of your feet (you can tell by looking at the wear on an old pair of athletic shoes), and if you have high arches or low arches. (Wet your feet and walk on a piece of paper to see the outline of your feet. If the part of the foot between the heel and ball appears thick, you may have low arches.) Tell the clerk about these peculiarities of your feet.

FOOT OUTLINE

♦ Show uneven wear on your old shoes (if any) to the clerk. Some shoes may be designed to minimize such wear and to compensate for the poor habits such wear may disclose.

♦ Buy shoes when your feet are biggest—in the afternoon.

♦ Pick a reputable shoe store with an informed staff.

♦ Put on socks and other foot gear before trying on shoes.

♦ The heel on the shoes should fit tightly, but your toes should have plenty of room, at least a half an inch between the end of your big toe and the shoe when you are standing. The shoe should be just wide enough—so the foot fits but does not hang over.

♦ Test out both shoes in a pair. Lace them up. Move your feet around in the shoes. Flex your foot, extend it, rock from side to side in both shoes. Curl your toes. Make sure the shoes do not wobble when you walk in them. Check tops to see if they are symmetrical. The shoes should be flexible yet supply support.

♦ Try several movements, running and jumping, for instance. Make sure your feet do not slide in the shoes.

♦ Inside seams should be smooth. Stitching should be complete.

When buying shoes for specific sports, keep several factors in mind: cushioning, support and stability, flexibility, and durability. You are playing with variables: you can have light weight *or* strong support—but not both.

Walking Shoes: Look for a good tread pattern, strong support for forward movement, and spring in front cushioning for a strong push-off. Your heel can be lower to the ground than in a running shoe. Heel counter should be strong, and the shoe should be designed to keep your foot from moving side to side. Look for an upward sweep of the toe, which augments heel-toe motion.

Breathable uppers keep your feet from becoming too hot.

Running shoes: Running shoes should be lightweight and designed for forward motion. The sole of a running shoe should provide enough friction with the ground so that you don't slip, and there should be precise beveled edges on side and back soles. The shoe should arch up front and back, have elevated heels with strong heel

ANATOMY OF AN ATHLETIC SHOE

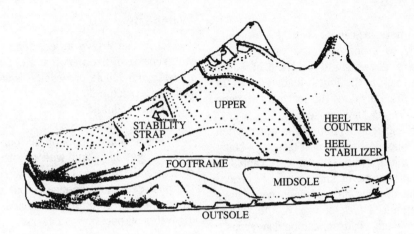

counters, strong arch supports that work against lateral movement. It should also provide spring through air pockets and foam wedges. When you land on the heel of your front foot, enormous force is created and stored as the Achilles tendon compresses into a "spring." As you move onto the ball of your foot, the tendon pushes you ahead by expanding. Good running shoes multiply this energy storage. The heel of the shoe should be well cushioned and elevated a bit (¾-inch higher than the sole) and the base of the heel should be wide to provide stability, at least as wide as the shoe's top. The front area should be flexible so that the shoe bends as your foot does.

Aerobic Dance Shoes: Because of side-to-side movements in aerobic dance, shoes should be constructed with a stiff heel, a strong and well-designed arch, a sturdy midsole and insole, and a wrapped outsole to keep your feet stable. Shoes should support your feet while you leap, twist, turn, slide. The toebox should be high enough so that you don't irritate your toes, and the midsole and the front of the sole (for the ball of your foot) should be well cushioned. The heel should be lower than in a running shoe. Don't wear tennis or running shoes for aerobic dance.

Tennis Shoes: If you play on a clay-type surface or on a wooden court, you need a special tread for increased traction. On nonporous surfaces, the shoes should provide a minimum of traction. The soles should have a hard, square, flat edge, midsoles should be cushioned, and heel cups and counters should be firm and cushioned. The shoes should provide good arch support. You can wear aerobic shoes, if you like.

Basketball: Soles and heel counters should provide good support during side-to-side moves. The midsole should have extra cushioning and the heel and forefoot should absorb shock. You also need good traction, preferably with rubber or rubber-based material dotted with pivot-point inserts. High-top or three-quarter cut provides support.

Soccer: For grass, you need molded cleats; for hard ground, shorter cleats and midsole cushioning; for indoors, a tennis-type outsole and well-cushioned midsole.

Organizations:
Call the **American Podiatric Medical Association** at 800–FOOTCARE (800-366-8227) for literature about feet. Also, the **American Academy of Podiatric Sports Medicine**, 800-438-3355.

Swimming: Fear of the Water—Is It Always Bad?

One of two Americans cannot swim, even though knowing how to swim can save one's life or someone else's. According to the National Safety Council, drowning is the fourth leading cause of accidental death. Why does this alarming statistic exist? The obvious answer: fear of the water. Some aquaphobes learned to fear the water when given a childhood swimming "lesson"—being tossed in to sink or swim. Others were caught in a wave. Still others never knew a pool or beach. However, the obvious answer does not always apply. Sometimes a *lack* of fear of the water, particularly in young children, can be dangerous.

Swimming Lessons for Babies?

According to the American Academy of Pediatrics, children under three should not be given swimming lessons. They may pick up bacterial infections or hepatitis, and they may risk becoming "intoxicated" or develop seizures by swallowing too much water. While experts do not agree about the value of infant *swimming* classes, they do agree that children should have experience in the water at a young age. Some say it should be fun. Others stress that it should promote a healthy respect for the water and emphasize safety. Young children can be taught ways to stay alive if they fall in the pool. They can learn to roll over on their backs, rest, and breathe (the survival float). And they can learn to reach for the wall and hold on to it.

The YMCA offers classes that expose children under three to water and teach safety to parents, but it does not teach toddlers to swim. While the Red Cross does offer swimming lessons to children under four, the instructors are not allowed to submerge the children. Many instructors agree that swimming is best learned between the ages of four and five. And they unanimously agree that no matter what competence children have in the water they need constant supervision.

Parents should never relax their vigilance while children are near or in the water.

Water Safety

A child can drown in less than two inches of water inside of five minutes. Keep anything with more than a couple of inches of water away from children's reach.

♦ Close toilet lids.

♦ Empty inflatable pools.

♦ Fence home pools on all four sides with a fence 4 feet high and with a gate that is self-closing and latching. Don't allow riding toys on the pool deck, and keep toys out of the water. Keep pool cover completely closed. Drain standing water off pool or spa covers.

♦ Keep rescue equipment near the pool—a buoy, a long pole, a plastic jug attached to a line.

♦ Keep doors and windows near the pool locked, with locks above the child's reach.

♦ Don't allow your child (or anyone else) to dive into the shallow end of the pool or into water that is less than 9 feet deep.

♦ Adults should know CPR and first aid (see "Guide to First-Aid Emergencies," page 799), and all family members should know how to dial emergency telephone numbers.

Adults and Fear of the Water

Adults who never learned to swim may have had no opportunities to visit pools or bodies of water when children. Others have childhood fears to overcome. Once made afraid of water, people tend to continue to fear it and avoid it, and fear complicates the learning process.

Experts in teaching adults to swim stress the importance of eliminating fear, partly by learning in warm, relaxing water. The first step is often just going under water, perhaps wearing goggles and a nose clip, and learning to breathe in the water—exhaling under water, inhaling above it. Pierre Gruneberg, who teaches swimming on the French Riviera, says that breathing problems cause people to panic in the pool. To allay their fears, he has them practice breathing in a water-filled glass salad bowl, blowing bubbles and singing while exhaling. The secret is to inhale with face out of the water, and to exhale with face in the water.

The second step is to learn to float. Anyone can float—prone and spread-eagled on his or her back. Once having learned to float, beginning swimmers may need help in learning how to regain their feet.

For more information, **United States Masters Swimming,** 2 Peter Avenue, Rutland, MA 01543 (508-886-6631).

SWIMMING IN A RIP CURRENT

Swim parallel to the beach until you are out of the rip current. Don't try to swim against it (*toward* the beach). Generally the ocean will bring you back in once you are past the rip current.

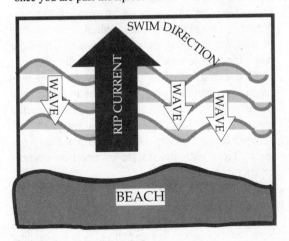

Buying a Bicycle

In the old days, all you needed to know when buying a bike was the proper bike size. Now with more than 82 million Americans riding bicycles—and for many different reasons—the options

when you buy a bicycle are dizzying. The job becomes easier if you analyze your bike usage and match it against what is available.

All-terrain bikes (a.k.a. ATBs or mountain bikes) can go almost anywhere—into the woods, through streams, over tree roots and rocks. However, they are not limited to rough terrain and many people ride them on city streets. ATBs have small-diameter wheels with thick, deeply treaded tires for lots of traction. You can inflate them with a car tire nozzle at a gas station. ATBs have 21 to 24 gears, with options for all terrains. They weigh from 22 to 30 pounds.

On an entry-level ATB you ride upright, which gives a better view of the terrain. But it also creates drag, so you have to work harder. The saddle is big and wide, and you have a better grip for rough riding. The bike is easy to turn but not particularly precise. The less expensive mountain bikes can be used as street bikes. On a more expensive mountain bike that you plan to use for off-road riding, look for a shock fork at the front wheel. The sport ATB has lower handlebars and a narrower saddle, and racing ATBs put you in a racing position.

Road bikes or racing bikes have more delicate frames, and are good for long-distance riding; they should be ridden only on the road. The handlebars are designed to give you more positions for placing your hands. Leaning over streamlines the ride, and your weight is distributed between arms, feet, and buttocks. However, it is more difficult to see traffic in this riding position. Tires are thin, with not much tread, and require high air pressure. You need a special adapter to fill them at a gas station. Road bikes have 16 gears, more or less.

Hybrid, cross, city, or fitness bikes (mix of mountain and racing bike) have a robust but light frame, medium tires, up to 21 gears, handlebars that allow you to sit up straight. You can't ride these off the road as easily as you can mountain bikes.

Cruisers are also good for casual riders. They have no gears, their handlebars let you sit upright, and their tires are wide.

EVALUATING A BIKE

How to decide? Ask yourself these questions:

1. Where and why do I intend to ride the bike? If off-road, an ATB is really a necessity, but many people who ride bikes in the city chose ATBs rather than racing bikes. For pleasure riding, the ATB is more comfortable. If you intend to do road racing, a racing bike is a necessity. You can get exercise from all kinds of bikes.

2. How often will you ride a bike? The more you will ride, the more durable a bike you will need. (And durable often translates into expensive.)

3. Which means more to you: performance or comfort? The higher the performance, the lower the comfort.

When you buy a bike, don a helmet and take a test ride. Check the brakes by accelerating quickly and braking hard. Work the shifters. How smoothly does the chain shift gears? Also consider the following:

Top tube: The horizontal bar running between seat and handlebars is what defines a boy's bike. It makes the frame more rigid. You can more easily step off a bike with a sloping bar (a girl's bike).

Size: Straddle the top tube with feet flat on the ground, and measure the gap between your crotch and the top tube of the bike. It should be

BIKE SIZE

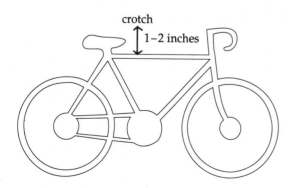

1 to 2 inches (3 to 4 inches for off-road riding). (On a bike without a top tube, use a yardstick or something like it to simulate the horizontal bar.) While sitting in the seat, you should be able to touch the ground with the balls of your feet. Children should have a 1-inch gap between crotch and top tube. Don't buy a bike that is too big with the notion that your child will "grow into it"—it will be hard to control and therefore unsafe. You can adjust a bike as the child grows by adjusting the handlebar stem and seat post.

Frame: Materials, from heaviest to lightest: steel alloy, aluminum, titanium. Aluminum is rigid, some steel alloys corrode, titanium is very expensive.

Seats: A gel seat, which costs $20–30 more than a foam seat, is also more comfortable and will wear longer.

Gears: You can overdo it on the number of gears—most riders use only 40 percent of their gears. If you are not going to ride up and down steep hills, you don't need so many gears. Indexed gear systems click when you change gears. You can buy automatic gears. The best place for gear levers is under the handle bar.

Tires: Narrow tires (about 1 inch) have less traction so you don't need to use as much energy pedaling them. Wide tires (to 2½ inches) provide control. Some foam tubeless tires never go flat, survive broken glass, nails, and other sharp objects. Tires with Presta valves need an adapter or special pump.

Brakes: Cantilever brakes are better than side-pull brakes.

Pedals: The ordinary pedal has no binding. Some pedals have clips and toe straps for holding the foot to the pedal. Serious riders may want clipless pedals with spaces for cleats to snap into. For these you need cycling shoes.

Lights: Rechargeable dual headlights have high and low beams. Some rear lights have many flashing red and white lights. Note: Children should not ride bikes at night—it is about 20 times more dangerous than riding in the daytime.

Biking Organization: **National Off-Road Bicycle Assn.** (NORBA), One Olympic Plaza, Colorado Springs, CO 80909-5775 (719-578-4717). Has a trail riding program for clubs.

Fly-Fishing Schools

According to fly fishers, their elegant sport is as far from worm fishing as Cordon Bleu is from fast food, as a symphony from rap, as archery from bazooka-blasting. And—like most true contests—fly fishing isn't easy. Anyone who has tried it knows: hook and line snarled in the underbrush, the wily fish that got away. Because the fly is weightless, you must be a convincing puppeteer to manipulate it so that it mimics true insect and arthropod movements. It takes time and patience to learn to tie the clinch knot and the blood knot, to choose a fly, to know when fish are rising, to cast, and to place the fly.

To become an expert, you might start with a short course sponsored by a fishing supply store like Orvis. Or you can go to fly-fishing school:

♦ L. L. Bean Inc. Fly Fishing Schools, Casco Street, Freeport, ME 04033 (800-341-4341). Basic three-day course or four-day intermediate course, spring–summer.

♦ The Wulff School of Fly Fishing, Beaverkill Road, Lew Beach, NY 12753 (914-439-4060). Instructor-student ratio is four to one. Weekend classes in trout fishing and fly casting, end of April through end of June.

♦ Fishing Creek Outfitters, RD 1, Box 3101, Benton, PA 17814 (800-548-0093 or 717-925-2225). One-day beginner class (teacher-student ratio is three to one), early May, June, October; one-day intermediate fly-fishing class (limited to two students), scheduled individually.

♦ Fish Hawk/Orvis Fly-Fishing School, 279 Buckhead, Atlanta, GA 30305 (404-237-3473). Two-and-a-half-day classes for up to five students, April through the end of October.

♦ Gates AuSable Lodge, 471 Stephen Bridge Road, Grayling, MI 49738 (517-348-8462). Individual casting lessons and in-stream instruction, minimum half-day.

♦ P.J.'s Resort Lodge Schools, PO Box 61, Norfolk, AR 72658 (501-499-7500). Instructional guide trips for one person or two people, fly-tying demonstrations, casting instruction.

♦ The Flyfisher Ltd. (an Orvis Shop), 252 Clayton Street, Denver, CO 80206 (303-322-5014). Specializes in walk-and-wade fly fishing, encourages catch-and-release. One-day trips from Denver with instructor-guide, six-evening fly-tying class (March–November), two-day evening class (April into September), one-day stream-side class for graduates of evening classes (April into September), some weekend schools, private lessons.

♦ Kaufmann's Fly Fishing Expeditions, Inc., PO Box 23032, Portland, OR 97223 (800-442-4359; 503-639-6400; FAX 503-684-7025). Stream-side classes for groups of up to eight anglers, weekends and some midweek May to early October; three three-day fly-tying classes (with fishing) in March, May, and June; four-day steelhead schools for up to six anglers, instructor-guide ratio is three to one, one in August and one in November.

♦ Mel Kreiger's School of Fly Fishing, 790 27th Avenue, San Francisco, CA 94121 (415-752-0192). Weekend seminars, and three-day, five-day, and week-long schools featuring on-stream instruction. Classes offered in California, Kansas-Missouri, Colorado, Idaho-Montana, Texas. April through September, depending on the location. Also offers two videos, "The Essence of Fly Casting I" and "The Essence of Fly Casting II."

♦ Mike Lawson's Henry's Fork Anglers, PO Box 487, St. Anthony, ID 83445 (800-788-4479). Two-day seminars, held throughout the West. One-day Sage Fly Fishing school in June.

Catch-and-Release Fishing

Do not release a tired fish until it has *completely* recovered. Firmly hold a played-out fish by the tail with one hand and *gently support* the fish from underneath just behind the head with your other hand. Face the fish upstream in an upright position in fairly calm water, but where there is enough oxygen to allow the fish to breathe easily. By moving the fish back and forth in this position the gills will begin pumping life-giving oxygen into its system, while at the same time allowing the fish to rest and regain strength lost during the battle. Fish being revived in this manner will often attempt to escape *before* they are completely recovered. A good rule of thumb is not to let the fish swim away the first time it attempts to. When fish are released prematurely they will often swim out of sight, lose their equilibrium, turn onto their side and die. It doesn't hurt to revive fish a bit longer than you feel is necessary. This will ensure a complete recovery without complications. This process usually takes a minute or two, but fish that are extremely tired can require several minutes. This is especially true preceding, during, and after spawning periods. When you do release a fish, do so in calm water, allowing the fish to swim into the current at its leisure.

After releasing a fish, move slowly, for sudden movement may spook them prematurely. *Never toss* a fish back into the water. If you wish to take a photo, set up everything before you remove the fish from the water. Cradle the fish and lift it just a little way above the water so if it should happen to fall, it will not crash onto the hard shoreline. Fish can also be laid on wet grass for a couple of seconds. Do not put undue strain on fish by lifting them high or in an unnatural position. *Never put your fingers in their gills* for this is like puncturing a lung. *Never squeeze* fish, since vital organs are easily damaged. Fish will seldom struggle when handled gently. A quick, harmless way to measure fish is to tape off measurements on your rod or buy a "fish tape" that adheres to your rod. Simply slide the rod alongside the fish in the water and you get an accurate measurement. Spring scales are deadly on fish and should be used only for hoisting a net with the fish inside. It is easy to estimate the weight by the length and condition of the fish. The important consideration is to release fish quickly and unharmed. A fish that is bleeding slightly will probably survive just

fine. Even a fish that is bleeding profusely can usually be revived if you are patient enough.

Try to land fish in a reasonable amount of time. The longer some fish are played the more lactic acid builds up in the blood stream and the more difficult it becomes to revive such fish. Most fatal damage occurs to fish through improper handling, not during the actual hooking and playing of fish. It is best not to handle or remove fish from the water. When a fish is removed from the water it begins to suffocate immediately and the risk is great that fish will slip from your grasp and flop about on the bank, or that you may unknowingly squeeze the fish to death. If you *must* handle fish, be certain your hands are wet, for wet hands will not destroy the protective mucous film on fish, especially trout.

To remove the hook, gently grip the fish by the tail or jaw with one hand, removing the hook with the other. If you are wading, both hands can be freed by slipping the rod into your waders. If a fish is hooked really deep, the hook can often be removed with the aid of a long-nose pliers or forceps. If not, it is best to cut the leader, leaving the fly in the fish. Nature supplies a built-in mechanism that will dissolve the hook in a matter of days. Oftentimes a friend can lend a hand in unhooking and reviving tired fish.

A barbless hook will help ensure safe handling and facilitate a quick release. (To debarb a hook, smash it flat using a flat-nose pliers; be careful not to damage the hook point.) You seldom have to touch the fish since barbless hooks can usually be backed out very quickly using only one hand. Under specific conditions, a net, if used properly, can be a tremendous advantage, allowing you to land and release fish quickly. A net can alleviate fish flopping and thrashing over rocks in shallow water and can greatly aid you in landing a fish when you are waist deep in water. Be careful that fish do not become entangled in the net.

More fish are landed with barbless hooks than with barbs! Sometimes fish will escape but such instances have nothing to do with the absence of a barb.

Reprinted (abridged): courtesy of *Kaufmann's Streamborn* (1993).

Choosing a Health Club

Don't let glossy ads or high-pressure salespeople fool you into signing up at a health club. Remember that your choices are many: school facilities; community centers; YMCA or YWCA; body-building clubs like Gold's Gym; national spa facilities like Jack LaLanne; storefront establishments. Look in the Yellow Pages, badger friends for recommendations. Ask yourself some questions before you begin to make a decision.

What do you want in a health club?

What do you want from the club: fitness, weight training, aerobic dance, swimming, martial-arts training, sports facilities? Do you want to lose weight, gain strength, practice aerobics for fitness? Don't pay for what you don't want.

—Should the club include both men and women?

—How close should it be to home or work?

—Is a spa, Jacuzzi, sauna, or massage room necessary?

—What are you prepared to spend?

Does the health club meet standards?

Choose a few facilities and visit each at the time you plan to use it to make sure it is not too crowded then. Talk to members about the club. Then ask the staff some questions:

♦ Does the club have the right number of members for its space? According to the International Association for Fitness Professionals, each person should have at least 34 square feet of workout space per person, or, put another way, there should be about a body's length between exercisers.

♦ What is the professional training of the staff? A staff member's well-muscled body is not enough evidence of competence to teach physical skills. (The best is a Master's degree in exercise physiology, but a Bachelor's in physical education is good, too.) Instructors should be certified through one of the following organizations: the American College of Sports Medicine (ACSM), the American Council on Exercise (ACE), the Aerobic and Fitness Association of America (AFAA), the Association for Fitness in Business (AFB), the Cooper Institute of Aerobic Research (CIAR), International Dance Exercise Association (IDEA), the National Intramural Recreational Sports Association (NIRSA), the National Strength and Conditioning Association (NSCA), the Young Men's Christian Association (YMCA).

♦ What is the ratio of staff and members?

♦ Does the facility offer orientation and provide instruction in using the equipment?

♦ Is the facility clean? How many showers does it have? Is the exercise equipment in good condition?

♦ What are the hours and schedule of classes?

♦ Does the facility provide for safety and a health screening? Is there a completely stocked first-aid kit? Does the staff know CPR?

♦ Is there well-lighted parking at the facility?

♦ Is the facility a member of a trade organization that is nationally recognized?

How well equipped is the club?

Does the club have an array of modern, well-maintained facilities?

♦ Weight training: Look for 10–12 stationary machines. About half should concentrate on lower-body development, half on upper-body development. Free weights should also be available.

♦ Exercise bikes, cross-country ski simulators, and rowing machines: These go from the simple to the fancy, but make sure that they are in good condition.

♦ Track: A running track is best, but a treadmill or jogging track can substitute.

♦ Aerobic exercise room: The best room is big, with carpeting or springy wooden floor. The class format should include warm-up and stretching, strength and firming exercises, aerobic exercise, and cool-down.

♦ Swimming pool: Most pools are too small for lap swimming, but can be used for aerobic exercising.

♦ Courts: Racquet courts include tennis, squash, handball, racquetball.

Signing up:

When you decide to join, you might want to sign up for just three months to test your commitment and the club's facilities. Take advantage of complimentary offers. However, consider a year's membership only if you are committed and sure that the club is right for you. Be aware that rates for years after the first year may be lower, so you might want to back away from multiple-year offers. Some clubs demand an initiation fee up front, usually about three times the monthly dues. They are counting on you not showing up later on. Laws in some places require that a cooling-off clause be included in the contract, which gives you a couple of days or more to change your mind without financial penalty. Be careful of financing plans—often the interest will cost more than the membership. Find out if your membership is good at all the club's facilities, including those in other cities. Ask what the membership includes: court fees, locker rental, pool privileges, baby-sitting. You can often get a membership at a lower price if you use the club only during off-peak hours or forgo some services.

SPORTS DIMENSIONS: FIELDS AND COURTS

Softball Field

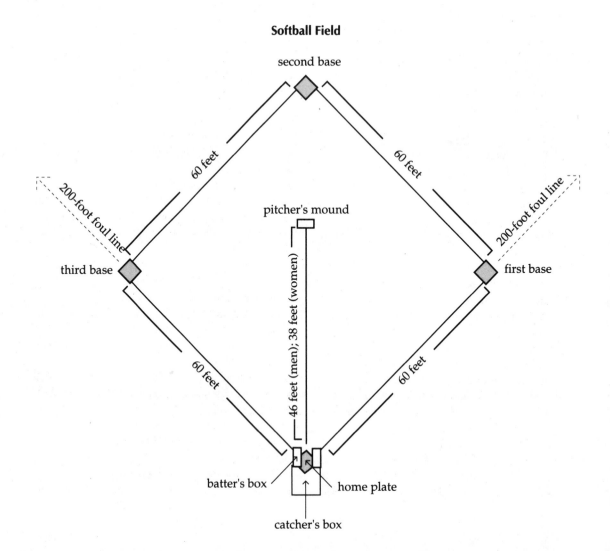

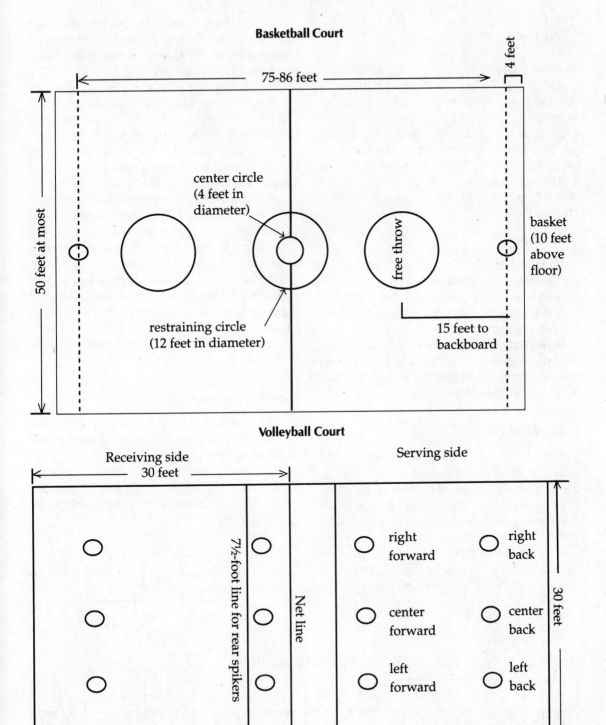

Basketball Court

75-86 feet

4 feet

50 feet at most

center circle
(4 feet in
diameter)

free throw

basket
(10 feet
above
floor)

restraining circle
(12 feet in diameter)

15 feet to
backboard

Volleyball Court

Receiving side
30 feet

Serving side

7½-foot line for rear spikers

Net line

right
forward

right
back

center
forward

center
back

left
forward

left
back

30 feet

7½
feet

Bowling

Bowling ranks high as a participant sport—a study by the Billiard and Bowling Institute of America found that nearly 50 million Americans went bowling at least once in 1992. The following pointers on scoring are excerpted from "Bowling for Everyone, Fundamentals of the Game," a pamphlet issued by **Billiard and Bowling Institute of America,** 200 Castlewood Drive, North Palm Beach, FL 33408 (407-840-1120).

How to Score

Many bowling centers have automatic scorers that display your scores on a video screen. All you have to do is punch in a few commands (fellow bowlers or the center staff can assist) and the rest is automatic.

If your center does not have automatic score, you will be given a scoresheet and a pen to keep your own score. You'll find that keeping your own score can be enjoyable.

Frames and Games

A game is made up of 10 frames. At the beginning of each frame, the bowler tries to knock down all 10 pins. If successful, the result is a strike and the frame is over. If any pins are still standing after the first shot, a second ball is rolled. If these pins are knocked down it is a spare. If a pin or more are standing after the second shot the result is an "open" frame. The bowler is credited with just the number of pins that fell.

When a spare is made the bowler gets credit for 10 plus the number of pins knocked down on the next throw. No score is marked in that frame until the next shot is made.

For instance, a player who follows a spare by rolling a 6 count on the next ball will get credit for those six pins added to the 10 for the spare. It is now known that the spare was worth 16.

A strike is worth 10 plus the number of pins knocked over on the next two tosses. Say a strike is followed by a frame in which the bowler knocks down five on the first ball and three more on the second throw. The strike would then be worth 10 + 5 + 3 for a total of 18. The score of each frame is added to the score of the previous frame until reaching a final total after 10 frames. In the final frame, if a spare is recorded, another ball must be rolled to determine how much that spare will be worth. For the same reason, when a strike is made in the tenth frame, two more shots are needed to find out how much the strike will be worth.

Scoring Premiums

The scoring system is not just a simple count of pins knocked down. Spares and strikes provide a bonus opportunity to get extra credit.

The scoring system greatly rewards consecutive strikes. In fact, real high-scoring games—over 200—are possible only by bunching together strikes.

STRIKE   SPARE

BOWLING SCORESHEET

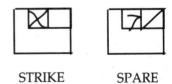

Reprinted Courtesy of Billiard and Bowling Institute of America.

Pool: A Changing Image

Perdition used to await low-life denizens of seedy pool halls, according to moralizers. (Remember the crafty Robert Preston warning against River City's pool halls in *The Music Man*? "Trouble with a capital T, and that rhymes with P and that stands for pool!") And once drug dealers, bookies, and hustlers did indeed hang out in pool halls—they were dangerous places, where fights broke out. Today most pool halls are not so smoky and decadent. In fact, pool has gone upscale and popular—it is a family sport, played by almost 38 million Americans, one-third of them women. You don't need to be tall to play pool, or male, or young. It is a more popular sport than golf or tennis. A billiard center is the modern, cleaned-up version of the old-time pool hall. No gambling is allowed, so you won't run into the modern-day counterpart of Minnesota Fats.

Nine out of 10 players shoot pocket billiards (pool) while the rest play snooker (bigger table, more balls, smaller pockets) or carom (fewer balls, no pockets). (The European game of billiards is played on a table without pockets.)

Here are some tips if you are playing for the first time:

♦ Hold the cue in the four fingers and thumb of your right hand (left, if you are left-handed). Cradle it, don't grip it.

CUE GRIP

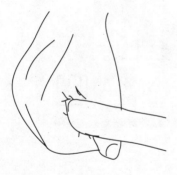

♦ Plant both feet firmly on each shot. Don't stretch for a shot.

♦ The bridge, which you make with your other hand, steadies and aims the cue. Your hand (left if right-handed, right if left-handed) should be 7 to 10 inches away from the cue ball. Beginning or sometime players usually use the open-thumb bridge. Your fingers should be together and you should cup your hand enough to raise your palm off the surface of the table. The only parts of your hand that should touch the table are the heel, the base of the thumb, and three fingertips. The cue slides between the ridge between your thumb and forefinger.

OPEN-THUMB BRIDGE

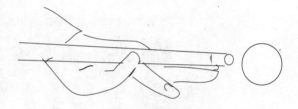

♦ Aim by imagining a line between the pocket and the center of the ball you are aiming at. Visualize the cue ball hitting the object ball at the correct point to sink it.

♦ Keep your movements easy and relaxed and your shooting arm close to your body. Try three or four practice shots before hitting the ball. Try for good follow-through, with the cue passing 4 to 6 inches through the place formerly occupied by the cue ball.

♦ Reminders (reprinted from *How to Play Pool Right* by George Fels with Alvin Blick, published by Billiard Congress of America):

1. Remember to chalk your cue properly after each and every shot. The correct way to do this is to chalk the cue instead of cueing the chalk.

2. Concentrate on every shot. Don't become absentminded, careless, or indifferent. The importance of this reminder cannot be overestimated.

3. Strive to do whatever's easiest, as long as that's possible.

4. Decide on how a shot should be made and stick with your decision.

5. Observe how you miss certain shots and correct for those aiming flaws. Admit your faults to yourself and correct them, one at a time.

6. Before and during your stroking of the cue ball, forget about everything in the universe except the shot.

7. Practice the shots that give you trouble, not just the ones you like. Take the time to study, analyze, and replay any misplayed shot or shots which puzzle you.

8. Practice makes perfect. It might be a cliché, but it's totally true in pool.

For information about competitions and rules for billiards write to: **Billiard Congress of America,** 1700 South First Avenue, Iowa City, IA 52240 (319-351-2112).

Chess

THE CHESS BOARD

CHESS MOVES

The pawn moves forward. For the first move, it may advance one or two squares. After that, it advances only one square at a time. It may move diagonally only to capture pieces adjacent to it, but it may not capture a piece in front of it. Once a pawn reaches your opponent's back row, you may raise its rank as high as queen, but not to king.

The knight may move three squares, but the move must be L-shaped. That is, the piece can move one or two squares forward, backward, or sideways, then one or two squares at right angles to the first move. The knight may jump over pieces in its path, but captures only the piece occupying the square on which it finally lands.

The bishop moves diagonally forward or backward, any number of empty squares.

The queen may move in any direction and any number of empty squares. She is the most powerful of all the pieces.

A rook (or castle) moves any number of squares forward, backward, or sideways. The only other move it makes is castling.

The king ordinarily moves only one square at a time, but in any direction.

Castling

You may castle if your king and rook (either one) have not yet moved and the spaces between them are empty. This example shows the two ways in which white may perform the move. Black may castle using the same principles.

Move the king two spaces toward the rook.

Then move the rook to the square that the king jumped.

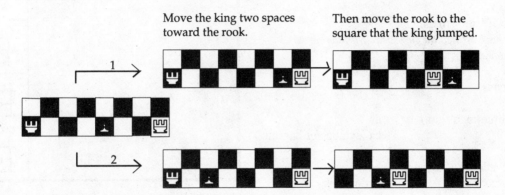

Scrabble™

The game of Scrabble was invented in 1933 by unemployed architect Alfred Butts, who incidentally was not a good speller. He originally called it Criss-Cross. Now more than one in four U.S. households has a Scrabble set. Over the years, more than 100 million games have been sold. You can even buy Scrabble as a computer program.

♦ Consider buying *The Official Scrabble Players Dictionary*, published by G. & C. Merriam Company, as a source for accepted and unusual Scrabble words.

♦ Learn all the two-letter words and as many three-letter words and four-letter words as you can. These account for 75 percent of words in an ordinary game and more than 50 percent of points scored.

♦ Learn four-letter words that can be made from legitimate three-letter words (for example, *mark* from *mar*), five-letter words that can be made from four-letter words (for example, *bathe* from *bath*).

♦ The best combination for a seven-letter word is three vowels and four consonants.

♦ Don't waste your *s*—it is invaluable for hooking one word on another if your rules allow it. For example, you can hook *severe* to *lamp* by turning *lamp* plural.

♦ Save one *u* in case you get the *q*.

♦ Learn the *q* words that do not use a *u*: *faqir, qaid, qanat, qat, qindar, qindarka, qintar, qoph, tranq*.

Two-letter words:
(We have defined the not-so-well-known words.)
aa (cindery lava)

ad	at
ae (one)	aw
ah	ax
ai (three-toed sloth)	ay
am	ba (symbol for barium; sheep's bleat)
an	
ar (the letter *r*, symbol for argon)	be
	bi (bisexual)
as	bo

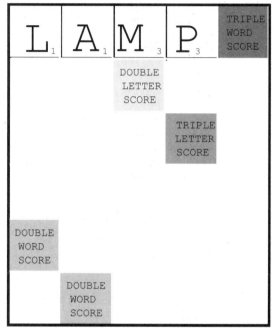

SCORE: 8

SCORE: 54

by

da

de

do

ef (the letter *f*)

eh

el (the letter *l*; elevated train)

em (the letter *m*; unit of measure)

en (the letter *n*; unit of measure)

er (symbol for erbium)

es (the letter *s*; symbol for einsteinium)

et (symbol for ethyl)

ex

fa (musical note)

go

ha

he

hi

ho

id (a division of the psyche, skin rash)

if

in

is

it

jo (sweetheart)

ka (cathode)

la (musical note)

li (Chinese measurement—about 1/3 mile)

lo (behold)

ma

me

mi (musical note)

mu (Greek letter)

my

na (symbol for sodium)

no

nu (Greek letter)

od (expletive)

oh

om (mantra)

on

op (optical art)

or

os (bone)

ow

ox

oy

pa

pe (Hebrew letter)

pi

re (musical note)

sh

si (symbol for silicon; musical note variant of *ti*)

so

ta (thank you)

ti (musical note)

to

um

up

us

ut (musical note variant of *do*)

we

wo (interjection; variant of "woe")

xi (Greek letter)

xu (South Vietnamese coin)

ya

ye (you or the)

Unusual Words:

euoi (cry at a bacchanal)

eupnoeas (regular breathing)

gid (sheep disease)

hox (partly drugged and totally disabled)

iynx (bird that twists its neck)

jin (genie)

kef (Australian fool)

logy (groggy)

oxy (oxygenic)

quidnunc (busybody)

quondam (former)

revehent (carrying back)

swink (work hard)

teapoy (a tea table)

tzarevna (a tzar's daughter)

ywis (certainly)

zyzzyva (a tropical weevil)

Vowel-Heavy Words (to help you balance your rack):

aecia (bodies of a fungus)

aureolae (lights around something)

epopoeia (epic poems)

eulogiae (funeral orations)

zoeae (larval forms)

Consonant-Heavy Words:

nth (greatest)

cwm (basin on a mountain)

crwth (crowd)

Organization: **National Scrabble Association,** PO Box 700, Greenport, NY 11944; 516-477-0033.

Crossword Puzzles

According to those on the inside in the crossword puzzle world, crosswords are undergoing a revolution. It is becoming rarer to encounter those old short crossword puzzle words that live only in crossword puzzle land, like the nearly extinct Hawaiian goose called the *nene*. And some constructors (a.k.a. cruciverbalists) tend to break new ground by doing what was once verboten—for example, using brand names as answers to clues. If you are one of the close to 40 million Americans who do crossword puzzles, here are some tips from the experts on how to outwit the constructors.

♦ Know that *The New York Times* (and other newspaper) puzzles grow progressively harder from Monday through Saturday.

♦ *In Across and Down,* the late Eugene T. Maleska suggests that you start by doing the easy Down clues, then the easy Across clues, put an *s* at the end of plurals and *ed* at the end of past tense words (even if you don't know the word). You might also fill in *est* for clues demanding the superlative.

♦ Work from the edges. It is easier to find an answer when you know the first letter rather than one in the middle of the word. For instance, in the following example, it is easier to figure out the answer to the clue "current occupation" (1 Across) if you know that 1 Down is "clue," than if you know that 4 Down is "sense."

```
C R O S S W O R D
L       E
U       N
E       S
        E
```

♦ Watch out for the "two letters in one square" trick:

```
M A I D E N
    S
    L
    E
```

♦ When all else fails, constructors often use Roman numerals as an answer:

```
    M
    O
I X     (nine)
    I
    E
```

♦ Even trickier, more up-to-the-minute constructors will sometimes use Arabic numerals as part of an answer.

```
3 M I L E L I M I T
R
I
N
G
C
I
R
C
U
S
```

♦ Once you have discovered the theme of a thematic puzzle, which is usually hinted at in its title, the rest is easy.

♦ Learn to interpret puns and jokes. Some examples: The clue "two pints make one cavort" leads to the answer "Champagne" (constructor Jack Luzzatto); the "Trapp family dog" leads to "Hound of Music" (constructors Sylvia Bursztyn and Barry Tunick).

♦ Know your crosswordese: *ai* (three-toed sloth), *unai* (two-toed sloth), *obi* (Japanese sash), *emir* or *emeer* (Arab chieftan), *esne* (feudal slave), *alate* (winged), *orts* (table scraps), *nene* (Hawaiian goose), *stoa* (Greek porch), *brae* (Scottish river), *Ra* (sun god, Egypt), *ted* (spread), *anoa* (ox of the Celebes), and thousands more that you can find in a crossword puzzle dictionary. Constructors try to avoid these (the easy way out), but sometimes it is impossible.

♦ If you see a long blank stretching all (or almost all) the way across or down the puzzle, it is probably a thematic answer and probably contains more than one word.

MONOPOLY—FACTS THAT CAN HELP YOU WIN

♦ The most frequently landed-on spaces are Illinois Avenue, Go, and B & O Railroad.

♦ The worst investments are the Utilities: Water Works and Electric Company.

♦ The most profitable square in any color group is the one on the left as you are facing the group.

♦ The most commonly thrown dice total is seven.

Casino Games: How to Win

Luck rides on a toss of the dice, a card dealt. You can't trick random chance and the gods of fortune. Or can you? If you play gambling games at casinos, some strategies can improve your chances of winning.

Over the long run, in games in which you bet against the house, the house will win, because the house has a built-in mathematical edge over the bettor every play. In games you play against other players, you have a better chance, particularly if you play well; in these games, strategy counts.

TESTS FOR LOADED DICE

Hold the die at diagonally opposite corners, and loosely. If dice are loaded, the die will pivot when the weighted side is up. Or:

Drop each die in a tall glass of water several times, with a different number on top each time. Watch to see if the die turns so that the same couple of numbers keep showing up. If so, it's loaded.

General Advice

♦ Bring enough money and divide it into equal parts according to the number of sessions you will participate in. (A good rule of thumb is to bring at least 20 times your minimum bet per session. That is, if you play at a $5 table, bring $100.)

♦ If you start to lose, take a break, and never play more than two hours at a stretch. Bring your own watch—casinos don't have clocks.

♦ If you win, play with the house's money, saving your original stake.

♦ Leave when you are still ahead.

♦ Don't spend any more than you originally brought. If you lose all your stake, quit. Never forget that you are playing with real money. And that you are playing for fun.

♦ Stick with one game. But if the table is not to your liking, move on.

♦ Don't take too many long-shot bets ("proposition bets")—the odds are terrible.

♦ Avoid drinking and playing when tired.

♦ Tip the dealer by giving him or her a stake in your game.

♦ If you win big, don't advertise it.

♦ If you are a good player, your best bets are poker and blackjack. If you are not, you may do better at craps or baccarat.

DICE: THE ODDS

For one toss. . .

Total	Odds against
2	35 to 1
3	17 to 1
4	11 to 1
5	8 to 1
6	31 to 5
7	5 to 1
8	31 to 5
9	8 to 1
10	11 to 1
11	17 to 1
12	35 to 1

Slot Machines

Some things to remember: there is no such thing as a hot machine, a machine that is due, a machine that is better because of where it is placed, a machine that pays better because it returns warm coins. All these fictions are contradicted by a basic probability law: every play is a completely independent event and the chances of winning are exactly the same each time. (Some expert gamblers would dispute all the above claims, so you choose.) The million-dollar jackpot has terrible odds. If it paid fairly (according to odds), you would get $29.

Sports Events

The odds on these are often not bad. The sports books make their money on the "vigorish" (fee, usually of close to 5 percent) that they charge gamblers. To give yourself an advantage:

♦ Bet early on a popular favorite, because later, the line tilts to the underdog. Bet late on the underdog.

♦ The best sport to bet on (in terms of your odds advantage) is baseball. One of the worst is boxing. Sports like jai alai and horse racing, where the public creates the odds, are good only if you know what you are doing. The house gets a big cut (up to 20 percent).

Lottery

The odds depend on the state. But the "house" gets a huge percent (in California 50 percent), so if you play, consider it a game.

Gambling

Compulsive and problem gambling is a health disorder, according to the American Psychiatric Association. More than 8 million Americans are compulsive gamblers, most of them male. What distinguishes the male compulsive gambler from everyone else, says an article in *Psychology Today*, is a damaged psyche, often from a poor childhood, with a perfectionistic or abusive or addicted father and a doormat mother. Female compulsive gamblers often have guilt problems. Money rules gamblers' lives—they have been taught that personal worth and happiness come from the possession of money. Robert M. Politzer, director of research of the Washington Center for Pathological Gambling, claims that all gamblers seek a sense of power and control and try to fill a void emanating from feelings of rejection and isolation.

When is gambling a problem? As with most addictions, when it takes over your life. The progress from gambling for fun to compulsive gambling can be slow. A compulsive gambler rarely quits while he is ahead *or* while he is behind. A chronic gambling problem can lead to broken marriages, financial ruin, and even suicide.

Signs:

Missing money. Compulsive gamblers explain it away by citing paycheck payment prob-

POKER HANDS

Poker hands are ranked as follows, top to bottom. Odds of your drawing each on a first draw are in parentheses after the hand:

Royal flush: five highest cards of the same suit and in sequence (649,739 to 1).

Straight flush: five cards of the same suit and in sequence (72,192 to 1).

Four of a kind: any four cards of the same rank (4,164 to 1).

Full house: three of a kind and a pair (693 to 1).

Flush: any five cards of the same suit (508 to 1).

Straight: five cards in sequence (the suit doesn't matter) (243 to 1).

Three of a kind: any three cards of the same rank (46 to 1).

Two pair: two cards of the same rank along with two other cards of the same rank (20 to 1).

One pair: two cards of the same rank (4 to 3).

lems, an emergency, a robbery. They steal valuables and cash from their own homes.

Behavioral changes. Switches in mood, withdrawing from the family or starting arguments, nervousness, anxiety, abusiveness.

Health changes. Stress shows up as stomach problems, eating problems, headache, insomnia, breathing problems, backaches, dizziness and more.

Work problems. Compulsive gamblers don't show up for work, or are late for work or leave early. Their performance is poor.

Teen Gamblers: More than 1 million children in the United States have gambling-related problems, and the problem is increasing. A high school student is two and a half times more likely to have gambling problems than an adult; a college student eight times as likely. Teenaged gamblers come from all social and economic groups. How do they get away with gambling when they are underage? One answer: though minors are prohibited from playing the lottery and from entering gambling casinos in most states, the rules are difficult to enforce. The signs that a teenager may be gambling: money missing in the house, lottery stubs in large numbers, changes in behavior. Not many groups exist for teen gamblers. The best bet is to find a mental-health professional specializing in treating addictions.

Organizations:

Gamblers Anonymous, PO Box 17173, Los Angeles, CA 90017 (213-386-8789). Support group, self-help.

Gam-Anon, PO Box 257, Whitestone, NY 11357 (718-352-1671). Support group for spouses.

The National Council on Problem Gambling, Inc., 445 West 59th Street, New York, NY 10019 (212-765-3833 or 800-522-4700). Will refer individuals with gambling problems to local groups of Gamblers Anonymous and members of the family to Gam-Anon.

National Center for Pathological Gambling, 924 East Baltimore Street, Baltimore, MD 21202 (800-332–0402). Treatment, referrals, information.

Compulsive Gambling Center, Inc., 24-hour hotline: 800-332-0402; 410-332-1111.

Minnesota Council on Compulsive Gambling, an information clearinghouse, over-the-phone counseling: 218-722-1503.

Are You a Compulsive Gambler?

Only you can decide. Compulsive gamblers are those whose gambling has caused continuing problems in any facet of their lives. The following questions may be of help to you:

1. Do you ever lose time from work because of gambling?

2. Has gambling ever made your home life unhappy?

3. Has gambling ever affected your reputation?

4. Have you ever felt remorse after gambling?

5. Do you ever gamble to get money to pay debts or otherwise solve financial difficulties?

6. Does gambling cause a decrease in your ambition or efficiency?

7. After losing, do you feel you must return as soon as possible and win back your losses?

8. After winning, do you have a strong urge to return as soon as possible and win more?

9. Do you often gamble until your last dollar is gone?

10. Do you ever borrow to finance your gambling?

11. Have you ever sold anything to finance gambling?

12. Are you reluctant to use "gambling money" for normal expenditures?

13. Does gambling make you careless of the welfare of your family?

14. Have you ever gambled longer than you had planned?

15. Have you ever gambled to escape worry or trouble?

16. Have you ever committed, or considered committing, an illegal act to finance gambling?

17. Does gambling cause you to have difficulty sleeping?

18. Do arguments, disappointments, or frustrations create within you an urge to gamble?

19. Do you ever have an urge to celebrate any good fortune by a few hours of gambling?

20. Have you ever considered self-destruction as a result of gambling?

Most compulsive gamblers will answer yes to at least seven of these questions.

Reprinted courtesy of Gamblers Anonymous.

Winning Contests and Sweepstakes

The skepticism with which most of us open the letter saying, "You are already a million dollar winner" is balanced by the fact that people *do* win sweepstakes. In fact, in the United States, more than $100 million ends up in the pockets of sweepstake winners every year. Are the odds worth the stamp you use to send in your entry? Jeffrey and Robin Sklar say that it often is. They have won eleven 19-inch televisions, three months of free hotel stays, dozens of free airline flights, thousands of dollars in cash, and more. They tell their secrets in their book *Winning Sweepstakes* and in their *Winning Sweepstakes Newsletter*. In the newsletter, they give tips for winning and rate specific sweepstakes. They will send a free issue, and entry details for the best currently open sweepstakes, if you send a standard legal size envelope with two first-class postage stamps to: *Winning Sweepstakes Newsletter*, PO Box 1468-0107, Framingham, MA 01701. Or call 1-800-WINNING.

Here are the Sklars' 23 secrets and strategies for winning sweepstakes:

Random-Draw Sweepstakes

♦ The more difficult it is to enter a random-draw sweepstakes, *the easier it is to win*. This applies to sweepstakes that require a store visit, a research qualifier, an understanding of complex or confusing rules, a two-step entry procedure (request entry form by mail and then submit), and hard-to-learn-about (limited advertising) sweeps.

♦ The more restricted a random-draw sweepstakes is, the easier it is to win. This applies to sweepstakes that are advertised or limited to a local or regional area, open for a short period of time, and sponsored by alcohol or tobacco companies.

♦ Sweepstakes are easier to win during the summer months when your competition is on vacation.

♦ Sweepstakes that permit automatic cents-off coupon entries double the odds *against* winning.

♦ Sweepstakes with great middle and lower prizes have fewer entrants than similar sweepstakes with a gigantic grand prize because many players enter for the grand prize.

♦ Sweepstakes with a prize structure geared toward a special interest are easier to win.

Game and Second-Chance Sweepstakes

♦ Most game sweepstakes have poor odds. It is seldom worth writing for game pieces by mail.

♦ The best (four-star) game sweepstakes have sensational odds and are the closest thing to a sure thing.

♦ Game sweepstakes are worth entering (that is, writing away for game pieces by mail) when the total value of all prizes divided by the number of game pieces printed is greater than your cost of round-trip postage (to obtain your game piece).

♦ When playing scratch-off game cards, be sure to use a penny or nickel. Sometimes the opaque gray covering adheres too closely to game cards. If you use a coin with ridges on its edge (such as a dime or quarter), it can mutilate a game card and disqualify a potential winner.

♦ Second-chance sweepstakes of collect, match, and decode games are among the most lucrative and most worth entering. It is not uncommon for over 90 percent of the prizes (from the game portion of the sweepstakes) to be unclaimed and awarded in these types of second-chance sweepstakes.

Multiple-Draw Sweepstakes

♦ A multiple-draw sweepstakes is a random-draw sweepstakes with several drawings spread out over a period of time in which nonwinning entries are retained and remain eligible for subsequent drawings. Submit multiple-draw entries as early as possible so that: (1) you are entered in the early drawings where there are fewer entries, and (2) you are entered in more drawings thus giving you more chances to win.

Entry Tips

♦ Make sure that your entries are legible. Illegible printing is one of the prime reasons for disqualification from a sweepstakes.

♦ Always include any required qualifying phrase exactly (with the same capitalization and quotation marks) as it appears in the official rules. "Block letters" are all capital letters.

◆ Watch out for tricky rules. Some sweepstakes restrict the size of the envelopes permitted for entry, the number of entries you can submit, and the number of prizes per person.

◆ Although it is unlikely you would ever be disqualified for using a 3″ x 5″ card when a 3″ x 5″ piece of paper is requested, it's always best to play it SAFE by interpreting rules in the most stringent manner. So . . . when the rules ask for paper, use a regular paper stock and when a card is asked for, use a blank index card.

◆ There are sometimes separate sets of rules for the same sweepstakes with different details or entry addresses. This enables sponsors to test the strength of their advertising sources. Consider all sets of official rules to be correct.

Winning Sweepstakes

◆ Sweepstakes sponsored by service industries frequently offer the best combination of great prizes and excellent odds. Rather than offering expensive tangibles (such as cars, boats, and computers), service businesses can offer prizes that cost them considerably less. For example, when an airline gives away a flight, in many cases it is really just giving away an empty seat.

◆ Most promotions are not judged by the sponsor, but rather by an independent judging organization. The presence of such an organization assures that the promotion will be honestly run.

◆ Winners often are required to sign an affidavit of eligibility. Prizewinners should allow 6–8 weeks after date of notification for receipt of their prizes. Winners of major (and sometimes even minor prizes) may be required to sign an affidavit swearing that they are eligible to win a prize.

◆ You never lose in taxes by winning. The cost of taxes is only a fraction of the value of your winnings. You need only pay tax on the fair market value of the item. The fair market value is the price that a willing seller who is not forced to sell, or a willing buyer who is not forced to buy, would pay. The fair market price need not be the retail price. For example, airline flights with blackout periods or restrictions are not as valuable as regularly priced airline tickets. You should consult an accountant after a major win.

◆ Always save dated photocopies of your winner's affidavits and prize notification correspondences.

◆ When you win a game sweepstakes, photocopy your winning game piece and send it via certified mail, return receipt requested. This will provide documentation that it was received.

Reprinted from "Special Report: The Guide to Winning Sweepstakes," Jeffrey and Robin Sklar.

CAMPING

Camping Tips for the Inexperienced

For some families, camping means living in a luxurious motor home at a campground with tennis courts and swimming pools, perhaps movies at night. For most backpackers, it means truly roughing it in the wilderness, away from the amenities of civilization, in tune with nature in the raw. No matter what your bent, here are some tips on camping for the first (and even the second and third) time.

Consider borrowing or renting equipment. You could decide that camping is not for you—you hate those little rocks that turn into boulders under your sleeping bag, you don't like roughing it.

Try car camping rather than trekking into the wilderness. It allows you to carry more supplies, and you are safer. Go to a place within an hour of your home and plan to stay two or three days. Find out if you need to make advance reservations. Buy a topographical map of the area.

Watch the weather forecast for the place you are going for at least a week ahead. Plan your clothing and equipment accordingly.

Check on the need for a forest permit (free at ranger stations); ask about fire restrictions. Fishing usually demands a fishing license, and you should know about regulations.

If you are tent camping, make sure you have proper equipment. (See "Packing for an Overnight Camping Trip," p. 560, and "Sleeping Bags: How to Buy and Care for Them," p. 562).

When you pitch your tent, find a flat, smooth place. Clean away rocks and twigs. Then put down your ground cover. If you think it might rain, dig a little trench around the tent to divert water.

Keep meals simple, but bring plenty of food. Keep your food in containers so that animals cannot get at it. (See "Wild Beasts and Pests: How to Avoid Them," p. 570, for how to deal with food in bear country.)

Don't drink water or even brush your teeth with it unless you purify it first. (See "Purifying Drinking Water," p. 570.)

Dogs should be leashed, and children should understand how to behave at camp.

Be careful of fire. Build fires in fire rings. Make sure they are out before you leave.

Pack out your garbage or leave it in garbage cans at the campsite.

Divide up chores so that no one gets stuck with all the unpleasant jobs.

Make sure you have a ground cloth—it can be a cheap tarpaulin.

Use plastic, but not disposable, plates and containers for food.

When you come home, turn the tent inside out and hose it, then hang it up to dry. Store it in a dry place, but not in its bag—keep it loose.

Organizations and Sources for Hikers and Campers

Adirondack Mountain Club, R.R. 3, Box 3055, Luzerne Road, Lake George, NY 12845 (518-668-4447).

Appalachian Mountain Club (AMC), 5 Joy Street (Headquarters), Boston, MA 02108 (617-523-0636).

American Hiking Society (AHS), PO Box 20160, 1015 31st Street NW, Washington, DC 20041-2160 (703-255-9304).

Sierra Club, 730 Polk Street, San Francisco, CA 94109 (415-776-2211).

National Campers and Hikers Association, c/o Fran Opela, 4808 Transit Road, Depew, NY 14043 (716-668-6242).

KOA Directory, Road Atlas and Camping Guide. Available for $3 from Kampgrounds of America, Dept. PS, PO Box 30162, 550 North 31st Street, Billings, MT 59114 (406-248-7444).

Woodall's Campground Directory: 800-323-9076.

Best Holiday Trav-L Park Association, 1310 Jarvis Avenue, Elk Grove Village, IL 60007 (708-981-0100).

Leisure Systems, Inc., Yogi Bear's Jellystone Park, Camp-Resorts, 6201 Kellogg Avenue, Cincinnati, OH 45230 (800-558-2954).

American Automobile Association, 8111 Gatehouse Road, Falls Church, VA 22047 (703-222-6000). Has a variety of benefits and services for its members, including campground guides and directories.

State tourist bureaus also have information about camping-related clubs.

Camping on Public Land

Camping under the stars (or a tent roof) appeals to Americans enormously, as proven by crowded campgrounds on our public land. To do it, you need more than transportation and a tent. You need some basic information—about reserva-tions, visiting hours, and seasonal openings and closings, which vary from park to park.

You must make reservations at most public campgrounds and for cave tours at popular parks like Yosemite, Mammoth Cave, Yellowstone. (For specific information, see the list below.) Consider going in spring and fall when the parks are less crowded, and consider visiting the less-well-known places.

The Department of the Interior advises you to stop first at the visitor's center (if there is one) for free literature and presentations that help you understand the area and use it safely.

National Park Service, U.S. Department of the Interior, Public Affairs, PO Box 37127, Washington, DC 20013-7127 (202-208-4747). National Parks have 29,000 campsites available. The Service offers a national park information kit. Write: Superintendent of Documents, U.S. Government Printing Office, Washington, DC 20402-9325 for a National Park Camping Guide, $4, stock #024-005-01080-7, or for "The National Parks: Lesser-Known Areas," $1.50, stock #024-005-00911-6. *Reservations*: Reserve space through MISTIX at 800-365-2267 or Ticketron. Hearing-impaired persons may call TTY 800-274-7275. Pay with credit cards over the phone, or send personal checks or money orders within 14 days. You can ask which parks are heavily used, and ask for alternative locations. You can reserve a family campsite at a national park campground no more than eight weeks in advance. Group (eight or more people) site reservations are accepted no more than 12 weeks in advance with one exception—reservations at Ozark National Scenic Riverways, Missouri, must be made 25 weeks in advance. If you don't reserve space, the policy is first-come, first served.

Golden Eagle Passport. For $25 a calendar year, you can buy a Golden Eagle Passport, which covers entrance fees for people in a single, private, noncommercial vehicle or the holder, spouse, children, and parents. It does not cover use fees. You can buy it at park entrances.

Golden Age Passport. If you are 62 or older, you are eligible for a free lifetime Golden Age Passport that covers admissions and a 50 percent

TYING A MOUNTAIN KNOT

The mountain knot, used for tying shoes, does not come accidentally undone as easily as the more common double knot. And yet you can quickly untie it by pulling one of the laces. It is as useful for city shoes with slick laces as it is for hiking boots. The first time you tie a mountain knot, you may find it hard. Once you master it, though, you won't use another knot.

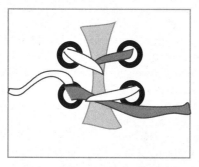

1. Start with a simple knot. (For clarity, one lace is shown dark-colored, the other light-colored.)

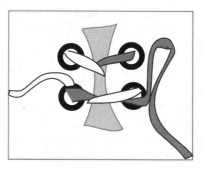

2. Create a full-sized loop with the right-hand (dark-colored) lace.

Hold loop with right hand.

Make twists with left hand.

3. Twist the left-hand (light-colored) lace around the right-hand loop twice, front to back.

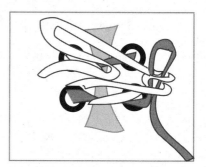

4. Make a loop with the same (light-colored) lace.

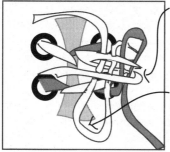

Hold double twist open with right thumb.

Push new loop into double twist with right forefinger.

5. Pull the loop through the double twist top to bottom.

6. Pull the loops out to tighten the knot. To release the knot, pull the left-hand (light-colored) lace.

KNOTS FOR CAMPING

SQUARE KNOT. Easily tied and untied, the square knot joins two ropes of the same size.

1. Start with two ropes or rope ends and a simple couple of twists. Loop one rope over and under and over the other rope, then loop it back to the right.

2. Take the right-hand end of the other rope and loop it under and over and under the first rope to make a knot.

2. The finished knot should look symmetrical, something like this.

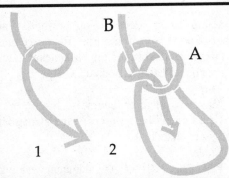

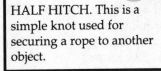

HALF HITCH. This is a simple knot used for securing a rope to another object.

CLOVE HITCH. Use this knot to tie the end of a rope to a tree or other object.

BOWLINE. This knot forms a secure loop. After making a twist in the rope, take the working end (marked with an arrow) and pull it up through loop A, then behind the part of the rope marked B, and down through the first loop. Pull the rope end (arrow) tight to make the knot.

SHEET BEND. Try this knot for joining two pieces of rope of different thickness. Start by looping the thicker rope. Then pass the thinner rope through the loop and around the straight part of the thicker rope as shown.

discount on campground and other user fees. These are available at park entrances.

National Forest Service has developed 4000 campgrounds in its 155 forests. For a list write: Forest Service, U.S. Department of Agriculture, Office of Information, PO Box 96090, Washington, DC 20090-6090 (202-205-8333). Campground reservations: 800-283-CAMP.

Bureau of Land Management (BLM) manages over 270 million acres of land, some of it with facilities for camping, fishing, and boating. Contact: BLM, Department of Interior-MIB, 1849 C Street NW, Room 5600, Washington, DC 20240 (202-208-5717).

U.S. Army Corps of Engineers has created 53,000 campsites at recreation areas, often on the water. Contact: Bureau of Land Management, Department of the Army, U.S.A.C.E. Regional Brochures, IM-MV-N, 2909 Halls Ferry Road, Vicksburg, MS 39180-6199 (601-631-5000).

Packing for an Overnight Camping Trip

Packing for camping demands careful planning. To be dramatic, it can make the difference between life and death. To be practical, it can make the difference between basic comfort and the misery of being damp, cold, itching, and hungry. For backpacking, go lightweight, but do not forget safety and first-aid items, which can save your life. For car camping, you can bring more of everything, but don't forget items for day trips.

Cooking

♦ Camp stove (depends on portability and number of persons: three-burner for car camping with family; single-burner for backpackers, foldable and no more than 2 pounds)
♦ Fuel
♦ Matches or lighter (butane)
♦ Grill (should be tip-proof, have strong legs and stay-cool handles)
♦ Cooler
♦ Fry pan (or set of aluminum camping cookware; wrap outside of pots with aluminum foil)
♦ Can opener and/or bottle opener
♦ Water jug (large size)
♦ Bowl, cup, eating utensils for each person
♦ Food (buy dehydrated food for longer trips and backpacking)
♦ Water (five-gallon container); purification tablets (see "Purifying Drinking Water," p. 570)
♦ Fishing line and hooks (for emergencies)

SEEING AUTUMN LEAVES

Nature puts on one of her most spectacular displays when leaves turn in the fall. She's fickle enough that the peak times vary from year to year. You can find out when those peak times are by calling one of the following fall foliage hot lines.
National Forest Service Fall Color Hot Line: 202-205-1780
Alabama: 800-252-2262
Arkansas: 800-628-8725
Connecticut: 203-566-5348
Delaware: 800-441-8846
Georgia: 800-847-4842
Indiana: 800-289-6646
Iowa: 800-345-4692
Kentucky: 800-225-8747
Maine: 800-533-9595
Massachusetts: 617-727-3201
Minnesota: 800-657-3700
New Hampshire: 800-262-6660
New York: 800-225-5697
North Carolina: 800-847-4862
    Asheville: 800-257-1300
    Blue Ridge Parkway: 704-271-4779
Pennsylvania: 800-847-4872
Tennessee: 615-741-2158
Vermont: 802-828-3239
Virginia: 804-786-4484
    Shenandoah National Park: 703-999-2266

Sleeping

♦ Tent. Manufacturers describe tent sizes in terms of the persons they will theoretically hold. It's often a tight squeeze, and you might consider getting a slightly bigger tent than manufacturers suggest. Figure about 25 square feet for each person—a 10 x 12 tent sleeps five. If you have kids, consider getting two tents, one for them and one for you. Make sure you can stand up at the highest point in the tent.

Basically there are three shapes of tent: wall tent (more comfortable), umbrella tent (free-standing with tubes replacing center pole), A-frame (more portable but not much space). All tents should have an inner lining made of material that "breathes," and a rain shell for the outside that can be rolled back. Ventilation should come from two opposing ends. All openings should have flaps that can close in bad weather, and mosquito netting with very fine mesh. Look for well-sewn seams like those on good jeans. The tent material should be flame-retardant. Check door and window zippers for sturdiness and precision (they should close tightly). Get the salesperson to demonstrate how the tent is set up.

♦ Sleeping bag (see "Sleeping Bags: How to Buy and Care for Them," p. 562).

♦ Mylar space blanket

♦ Ground cover. A cheap tarpaulin will do, but it should be big enough so that the tent can stand on it.

♦ Shade. A tarp with grommets to shade your dining area.

Setting Up and Cleaning Up

♦ small shovel
♦ nylon rope
♦ safety pins
♦ string
♦ plastic bags
♦ towels
♦ knife (Swiss Army type)

Light and Safety

♦ lantern (propane type is more expensive, safer, easier to use; liquid fuel is less expensive)
♦ compass
♦ flashlight (and extra batteries)
♦ package of small emergency flares
♦ police whistle
♦ sunscreen
♦ map
♦ flares
♦ mirror

Clothing

Think layering. Choose large outer garments that will fit over other clothing. Think pockets.

♦ shorts
♦ t-shirt
♦ thermal underwear (of synthetic fibers that pull moisture away from the body)
♦ long pants
♦ long-sleeved wool shirt
♦ sweater or wool shirt
♦ heavy jacket
♦ rain gear (poncho or large garbage bag)
♦ socks (for hiking wear two pairs, thin liners—perhaps of polypropylene for dryness, wool or synthetic socks for warmth)
♦ hiking boots (good ankle support, good traction, thick soles, broken in)
♦ sun hat
♦ bandanna
♦ warm hat
♦ gloves (for warmth)
♦ work gloves
♦ comfortable shoes
♦ sleeping gear (underwear or polypropylene material for cool weather)

Personal Items

♦ toothbrush and toothpaste
♦ soap (in a tube)
♦ sunglasses
♦ toilet paper

Packs

♦ day pack (carry enough gear and food and water for a day hike—look for foam-padded shoulder straps and leather bottoms)

♦ backpack (with external metal frames to provide air between pack and body; internal frames so rough terrain won't throw you off balance)

Other Suggestions

♦ detachable inner pouch with belt loops for day trips
  ♦ camera
  ♦ books
  ♦ binoculars
  ♦ trash bags

First Aid

  ♦ insect repellent
  ♦ thermometer (reading below 75 degrees, in case of hypothermia)
  ♦ iodine tablets
  ♦ tincture of benzoine
  ♦ prescription medicines
  ♦ bandages
  ♦ adhesive tape
  ♦ antiseptic
  ♦ hydrocortisone
  ♦ lip balm
  ♦ aspirin
  ♦ survival manual

Think about: ephinephrine (treats anaphylactic shock, produced by allergic reaction to sting by insect like a bee); Sawyer Extractor (snakebite kit that extracts up to 30 percent of venom); Sam Splint (can be used on any part of the body); irrigating syringe and 18-gauge catheter (for wound cleaning).

Sleeping Bags: How to Buy and Care for Them

Take time to choose a sleeping bag, keeping in mind how you will use it. Don't buy more or less sleeping bag than you need. If you car camp in summer, you need one kind of bag, if you camp in the cold snow, you need another.

Temperature ratings: The rating tells you the coldest temperature at which you will sleep comfortably. The colder the rating, the more expensive the bag, all else being equal.

Recreational: rated to about 30°, can be roomy, rectangular, weighty (4–6 pounds).

Three-season backpacker: rated to 20° or lower, lighter, more compact.

Expedition/winter: rated to 0°, up to 6 pounds.

Ask yourself if you are a warm sleeper or cold sleeper. If you are a cold sleeper, buy a bag rated at least 5 degrees colder than the temperature conditions you expect to use it in. Smaller people may not be as warm as someone who fills up the bag. Other factors to consider: difference between air and ground temperatures; if you sleep in a tent; the thickness and warmth of the pad you use underneath.

Lengths: How tall are you? Bags come in different lengths: short (to 5' 4"; regular, to 6'; and long, 6'6". Inner length of the bag should be about 4 inches longer than you are.

Shape: Bags come in shapes from mummy to rectangular, with modifications in between (modified mummies, modified rectangles, barrels). The mummy bag, wider at the shoulders than the feet, conserves heat.

System bags: System bags come with layers, liners, and shells, so you can add or subtract warmth. Radiant-heat barrier liners raise warmth. Vapor barrier liners can reduce heat loss through evaporation (but the bag can become a sweat box). Shells and liners should be of dense nylon (high thread count); liners should be slippery so they don't "follow" you as you turn in your sleep.

Interior insulation: Interior insulation

should be long-fibered synthetic or baffled to keep it from wandering. Synthetics are light, durable, and quick-drying. Goose down is even lighter, and it costs more.

Workmanship: Look for even stitching on the seams. Check seams and workmanship on the inside. The zipper should be nylon and should move smoothly without catching. Big zipper pulls are a plus. There should be material between the sleeper and the zipper to keep out air currents. If you want to zip bags together, make sure one is a left-hand model and the other is a right-hand model.

Storage: Store the bag loosely, folded or hung in the closet. It needs air. Some experts say you can wash sleeping bags made of synthetics in the machine; others say you should not. If you do, use a front-loading tumble machine, mild soap, low temperatures, and gentle cycle. Air-dry indoors for 24 hours, or use a commercial dryer set at low heat. Do not dry-clean sleeping bags made of synthetics. Some experts say that you can dry-clean down bags, though others recom-

mend against it. If you opt for dry cleaning, choose a cleaner that specializes in down. Air-dry for a week afterward.

Pads Under Sleeping Bags

Every camping princess feels the pea, that little pebble she missed when she cleaned off the camping site, unless she has a good pad underneath her sleeping bag.

No matter what kind of pad you buy, make sure it is big enough—measure your sleeping bag where it is widest. It can be full length (72 inches) or about 42 inches (shoulder to hip), which means it is less to carry but you have no lower leg insulation, or full length (72 inches). Some foam pads roll up compactly, and self-inflate through a valve when opened. Others are plain (and less expensive). Look for "cold crack temperature," the temperature at which the material breaks down. (The more ultraviolet light the pad is exposed to, the higher its cold crack temperature, as time goes on.)

Here are the choices, with pros and cons.

SLEEPING BAG PADS

Kind of padding	Characteristics	Comments
Closed cell foam	Won't let in moisture; better insulation for thickness. Made of: Ensolite (trademark for a polyvinyl chloride), durable, mar-resistant, but may break down; EVA (ethyl vinyl acetate), durable, good insulation, mars easily, not as comfortable as others; polyethylene, not expensive, good insulation, inflexible, can tear.	Should be at least ⅜" thick.
Open cell foam	Heavier. Made of polyurethane, soft, compressible, durable. Cons: bulky and absorbs water. Store unrolled.	Should be at least 1½" thick. You may want to invest in a foot pump to blow it up.
Air mattress	Choose vinyl laminate of cotton, rayon, nylon.	

Finding Your Way With and Without a Map and Compass

The wilderness talks to you—tells you directions, gives hints of danger—if you can read it. Sharp observation of your surroundings is essential to keep your bearings when you are in the wild. As you walk, remember landmarks—like unusual rocks and trees. Notice the direction of running water. Such observational skills can help you decide the direction in which you want to go. But what about the obstacles that lie *between* you and your destination? If you were a crow, you could fly over them. But human beings rarely can go "as the crow flies." A sheer 200-foot unclimbable cliff or a mosquito-laden, treacherous swamp may prevent you. A topographical map and compass can keep you oriented and help you plan a route around such natural obstacles. WARNING: If you are lost, your best bet is to stay where you are. (See "How to Survive in the Wilderness," p. 572.)

Topographical Maps

Before venturing into the woods, buy a topographical map of the area. All of the United States has been mapped, and you can buy the maps in 7½- and 15-minute series. (They come in other series, but these two are best for hikers.) A 7½-minute map covers about seven miles (7½ minutes or ⅛ degree of longitude, at a scale of about 3⅝ mile to the inch). Most experts consider it better than the 15-minute map because it shows more detail.

Contouring on the map mimics three dimensions. Each contour line on a topographical map delineates an elevation above sea level, at an arbitrary height, say, 20 feet, 40 feet, and so on. Thicker lines are labeled with elevations, as are high points. The closer the lines are together, the steeper the slope. Usually contour lines are colored brown, and man-made features (buildings, roads) are colored green. The maps show cliffs, waterfalls, valleys. You can find them at sporting goods stores and from the **U.S. Geological Survey,** Earth Science Information Center, Building 3, MS532, 345 Middlefield Road, Menlo Park, CA 94025.

WITH A COMPASS

Compasses can cost from $2 to $100. Look for:
♦ a rotating housing with points of the compass (N, S, E, W) and degrees marked on the rim, intermediate marks every 5 degrees

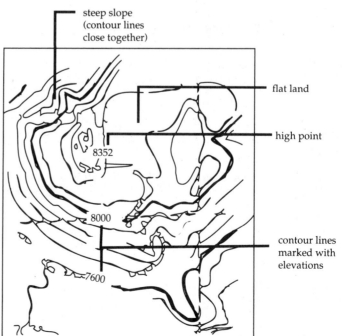

TOPOGRAPHIC MAP OF LOOKOUT MOUNTAIN (California)

steep slope (contour lines close together)

flat land

high point

contour lines marked with elevations

8352

8000

7600

♦ an orienting arrow on the bottom of the housing

♦ transparent baseplate that enables you to see the map

♦ a liquid-dampened needle

♦ a good instruction book.

All compasses contain a needle that points toward magnetic north, not the North Pole. The difference between true north and magnetic north, the angle of declination, is indicated on all topographical maps. Some compasses have a movable collar which allows you to set the compass in accordance with the angle of declination. (The needle should point to N on the collar.) In any case, use the instructions on dealing with the angle of declination on the instruction sheet that comes with the compass.

THE ACTUALITY OF TRAVEL

In the best of all possible worlds, you can walk straight to your destination right along the line of travel. In actuality, you may find obstacles in your path. If you do, here are two ways to get around them.

New technology: Portable (1–4 pounds), easy to use, infallible, and expensive (the cheapest unit is about $900), the **Global Positioning System** was developed by the Department of Defense. It uses satellites orbiting 12,000 miles above the earth as sources of information and operates on batteries or with an electrical adapter. It can tell you where you are, where you have been, how fast you are walking, how far back to a starting point. Positions are given in latitude and longitude on a tiny screen. The unit stores your starting position in its memory if you want, and when you want to know how to get back, it displays a compass direction. For information, call Challenge, 800-LAT-LONG.

FINDING OUT WHERE YOU ARE

If you cannot find your location on the map (in short, if you don't know where you are), sight on two landmarks and determine their bearings with your compass. In this case, they are Mt. Baldwin at 320 degrees and Mt. Morgan at 85 degrees. Make sure you take the angle of declination into account. On the map, draw lines at the same angles from the landmarks until they intersect. The point of intersection is your location.

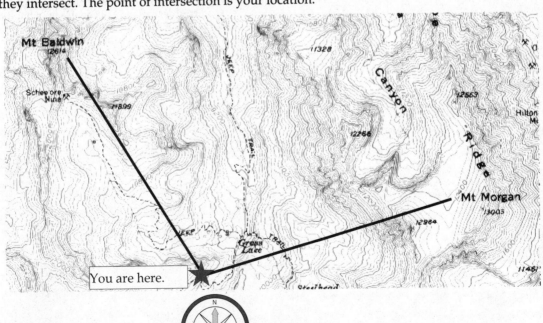

CLEARING AN OBSTACLE

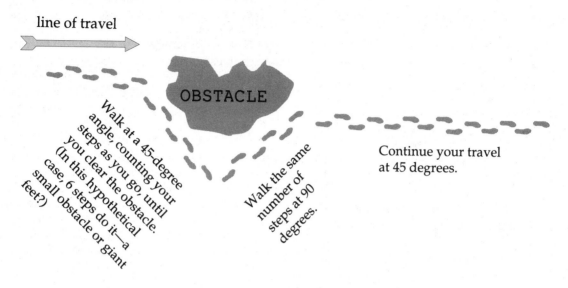

line of travel

OBSTACLE

Walk at a 45-degree angle, counting your steps as you go, until you clear the obstacle. (In this hypothetical case, 6 steps do it—a small obstacle or giant feet?)

Walk the same number of steps at 90 degrees.

Continue your travel at 45 degrees.

FINDING YOUR DESTINATION

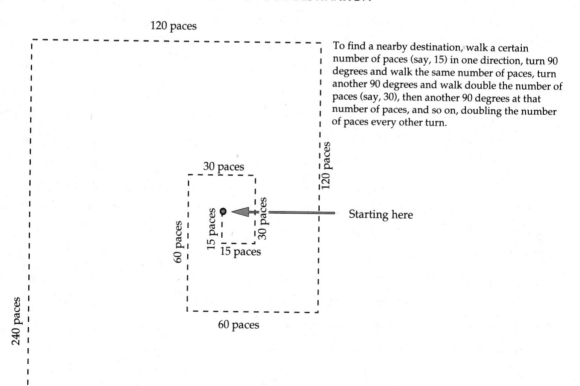

120 paces

To find a nearby destination, walk a certain number of paces (say, 15) in one direction, turn 90 degrees and walk the same number of paces, turn another 90 degrees and walk double the number of paces (say, 30), then another 90 degrees at that number of paces, and so on, doubling the number of paces every other turn.

120 paces

30 paces

30 paces

15 paces

60 paces

15 paces

30 paces

Starting here

15 paces

240 paces

60 paces

WITHOUT A COMPASS

If you are without map or compass, use landmarks to stay on course. Walk from one to another, always looking ahead to find the next. If you stop, lie or sit facing your direction of travel, and if you want to go to sleep, scratch an arrow on the ground to show you the direction in which you were going when you awaken.

To find directions to help you plot your course (and stay on course), here are three methods:

THE STICK METHOD

Put a stick in the ground and mark the tip of its shadow. At the end of an hour, mark the tip again. The line between the two shadow tips will be east-west, with the stick south of the line.

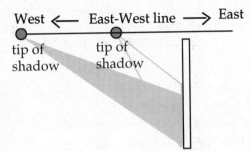

Stick is south of the east-west line.

THE WATCH METHOD

This method is not very accurate, but will do in a pinch. Holding your watch flat (horizontal to the ground), point the hour hand toward the sun. South is halfway between the hour hand and 12 o'clock.

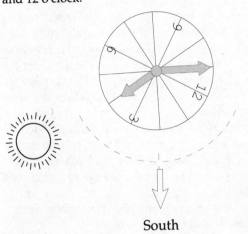

South

THE STAR METHOD

1. Find the two stars that delineate the front lip of the Big Dipper. Imagine the line between them.

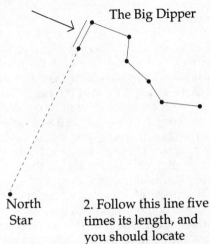

The Big Dipper

North Star

2. Follow this line five times its length, and you should locate Polaris (the North Star), which is within one degree of true north.

ORIENTEERING ("Cunning Running")

Invented by Scandanavian military to train messengers, orienteering is popular in 30 countries, including the United States. Though fitness helps, it is a "thinking sport," which has been compared to treasure hunting and to a car rally on foot. Basically, it is cross-country racing in which participants navigate an unfamiliar course using compasses and maps. Orienteering aficionados range from serious competitors dressed in nylon track suits and shin guards to families in ordinary clothes out for a day's recreation in the woods.

Races range in length from 2 kilometers to 11 kilometers. (There is even an event for toddlers, called Stringo.) Participants work with a topographical map and sheet of clues, given to them at the beginning of the event, to follow a course marked by control points. They may use a compass, if they wish—compasses are often available for rent at the site of the event. The individual who completes the course in the shortest amount of time wins.

The orienteering map includes details like cave openings, ponds, ditches, knolls, anthills, and changes in vegetation. Circles mark checkpoints. At each checkpoint is a flagged cardboard box, sometimes tacked to a tree. Boxes contain hole punches, each with a different shaped hole, with which contestants punch their cards. Between one control point and another are obstacles, and contestants who win generally are not the fastest runners but those clever at maneuvering their way around them.

No one gets lost because of two principles: (1) the course is usually in an area bounded by roads; (2) participants only become "temporarily misoriented," never "lost."

Wild Plants That You Can Eat

Edible wild plants live in open spaces (backyards or vacant lots). Many of them are not natives, but imports brought in as seeds on the coats of domestic animals or in food. The imports often overwhelm native plants, and harvesting them may help restore the natural landscape. If you are camping near towns or cities, you may find it adventurous and fun to find and eat them. Two warnings: Don't pick within 100 yards of a road because of automobile pollution (cadmium and lead from exhaust); avoid areas where you suspect pesticides might have been used. And look up any plant you plan to eat in three separate field guides to determine whether it is safe.

EXAMPLES

cattail	nasturtium
clover	oxalis
dandelion	pine nut
lamb's-quarters	seaweed
miner's lettuce	thistle root
mint	wild onion
mushroom (if not poisonous)	wild radish

Dangerous and Annoying Wild Plants

"Leaves of three, let them be" and "berries white, poisonous sight"—the rhymed rules warn against poison ivy and poison oak, which cause so much summertime itching. But these are not the only plants that can plague you. Plants' wiles are many—some attack your skin, others are toxic when eaten.

Other rules besides "leaves of three" to follow: Avoid wild plants with milky or colored juices; avoid fruits, seeds, roots, and tubers of wild plants (which can be toxic storage organs); avoid bulbs unless they smell like onions or garlic. Don't eat or touch anything you cannot identify as harmless in three plant books.

Children react badly to dangerous plants, partly because they are smaller—it takes less poison to lay waste to a small body than to a large one. Teach children not to eat anything except what is on their plates.

Urushiol-Containing Plants

The substance that causes itching in several plants, like poison ivy and poison sumac, is a colorless oil called urushiol, an allergy-producing oleoresin. (Oleoresins also occur in mango rind, Florida poisonwood leaves and branches, ginkgo nut pulp, and cashew shells.) Don't assume that if you have been immune to urushiol in the past, you will not become sensitive to it in the future. About 85 percent of Americans are sensitive to poison ivy or will become sensitive to it. The good news: sensitivity declines with age.

The oleoresin is inside the plant. Leaves that are injured, allowing the oleoresin to ooze out, will cause grief when you touch them. However, the poison can travel on animal fur, on clothing, on any object. If you suspect you have had contact with urushiol, wash it off as soon as you can with water and detergent. If no detergent is available, use water. Take off your clothing, keeping it separate for washing. Never burn the offending plants—the smoke can cause lung irritation.

Avoiding contact: Wear protective clothing—long-sleeved shirts, long pants, gloves, and socks. According to Duke University researchers, barrier creams, rubbed on like suntan lotion before exposure, can block urushiol. Researchers are working on desensitization methods. Be warned, though, that the old Indian remedy of eating a few leaves a day to build a resistance sounds good, but it doesn't work. In fact, it may produce an itchy bottom. A reaction to urushiol (itching and redness) occurs anywhere from six hours to three days after exposure. Blisters form and ooze, then crust over. A bout with urushiol can last for two or three weeks.

Don't scratch—it can start an infection. However, the rashes are not contagious.

Treatment: Try cold compresses, oatmeal baths, a paste of baking soda, painkillers (aspirin, for example). Herbal experts recommend rubbing the skin with crushed plantain leaves to relieve itching. Go to a dermatologist quickly if you have had problems with urushiol in the past. Steroids can help severe reactions and rashes in sensitive places.

Poison ivy: The noxious weed grows in every state and in many different habitats, including the beach. It does not look the same everywhere—it can appear as a bush or a tree-like shrub, though its most common guise is as a climbing vine. Three leaflets cluster together, though sometimes more than three are found. The leaves are most often shiny, but can also be dull, and they turn red in the fall. Birds eat the berries.

Poison oak: Poison oak, which grows on the West Coast and elsewhere, also contains urushiol. It grows as a small tree or shrub, with hairy leaflets clustered in threes. Berries are yellow.

Poison sumac: Poison sumac, which grows in the wetlands of the Northeast, Southeast, and West, is a third usushiol-containing plant. This tall shrub bears leaflets in clusters of seven to 13. Its berries are cream-colored.

Other Dangerous Plants

Baneberry (*Actaea*): The plant, which grows up to 2 feet high, with notched leaves, bears beautiful, shiny, and deadly berries of pink or white. They can be fatal very quickly.

Deadly nightshade (*Atropa belladonna*): A big plant with bell-shaped purplish flowers and shiny black berries that are fatally poisonous. This is the plant from which atropine (used to dilate the pupils of the eyes) comes.

Hemlock (*Conium maculatum*): It looks like a wild carrot, with lacy foliage and a taproot, but it is poisonous. The leaf stalks are spotted purple, flowers white.

Jack-in-the-pulpit (*Arisaema triphyllum*): The name comes from the hood over the flower spike, resembling a little person under a canopy. An irritant, it can cause swelling on contact.

Jimsonweed (*Datura stramonium*): Also called thorn apple, a poisonous and bad-smelling weed, all of whose parts are highly toxic. Eating it can cause death. Leaves are toothed; flowers, white or purplish and trumpet-shaped.

Mandrake (*Mandraga officinarum*): Mandrake plant has been considered sexually magical because its root resembles the forked bottom of the human body. (No, it is not an aphrodisiac.) Some teenagers think that mandrake can get them high (also not true). According to folklore, mandrake shrieks when uprooted, and those who hear the shriek go mad or die. People *can* die from mandrake, but from eating it, not hearing it. Mandrake contains scopolamine. An emetic, it can also cause dizziness, increased heart rate, upward moving paralysis, even death. A member of the nightshade family (like tomatoes), it grows up to 6 feet tall, with large clusters of leaves that look like horseradish. The bell-shaped flowers are small and greenish.

Pokeweed (*Phytolacca americana*): The flowers are white, the berries reddish, and the root, which looks like horseradish, is poisonous.

Stinging nettle (*Urtica dioica*): The stinging nettle, which grows in wet places, attacks with its formic-acid-containing hairs. Come in contact with one and you will feel as if you had been stung by ants. Luckily, the stinging itch doesn't last very long, at the most a few hours. It can be treated with an alcohol rub or the juice from the nettle. The fuzzy-looking plant grows up to 8 feet tall; it has serrated, spiny leaves. In Europe, nettles, high in vitamin A and plant protein, are used to make soup.

Note: Many other dangerous plants exist.

Purifying Drinking Water

Water that bubbles crystal clear down rocks in the streambed may teem with bacteria, viruses, and parasites that can ruin your camping trip. You don't know where that water had been before it arrived in a woodsy paradise. It may have been contaminated by outhouses, seepage, agricultural pesticides.

If you are going on a short trip, carry water with you. Otherwise, purify all water you find by one of these methods:

♦ Boil the water for at least five to 10 minutes.

♦ Use water purification tablets, either iodine or chlorine. WARNING: Iodine tablets may lose potency once the bottle is opened. Use one iodine tablet for a quart of lukewarm water, and give it 30 minutes to work. If the water is cold, warm it and allow it to sit longer. Don't add ascorbic acid (in fruit-flavored powders) for at least 30 minutes after you add the iodine. If water is cloudy, use two tablets. Chlorine tablets are less reliable. Their ability to purify varies according to the form of chlorine and the water itself—its pH, temperature, and organic content. Halazone (chlorine tablets) purifies a quart of water in about an hour.

♦ Use portable water purifiers that filter the water and kill organisms. There are two basic kinds. With one, the more convenient, a hand-held pump forces the water through a filter with microscopic holes. With the other, which processes more water, the water drips by gravity through a filter. Don't be fooled by the words "EPA Est." plus a number. This only means that the filter was made in a factory handling pesticides or water-treatment devices. Look instead for "EPA Registration" followed by a number. This means that the EPA reviewed data the manufacturer submitted showing that the filter can kill all microorganisms. Popular filters include First Need (made by General Ecology Inc., Lionville, Pennsylvania), M.S.R. Waterworks (made by Mountain Safety Research of Seattle), and Pocket Filter (made by Katadyn Products Inc., Switzerland).

Wild Beasts and Pests: How to Avoid Them

Only in Disney movies do critters sing songs to human beings. In real life wild animals are not particularly friendly to human beings. It is best to give them a wide berth—to avoid them if they are dangerous and, even if they are not, to keep from disturbing their habitat. After all, the woods are their home, not ours.

Bears: No matter how appealing they look, bears are wild animals that can be dangerous. Avoid them. Never hike alone or after dark, and be cautious on blind corners. Keep away from places where bears feed, like berry bushes. Wear no cosmetics (bears may be attracted by their scent), and don't go near bear country when you have your menstrual period. Human sexual activity has been known to attract bears, so save it for when you are home. Don't bring your pets, and leave dead animals alone.

If you do see a bear or a cub, do not approach it. Leave the area instead. Make noise by singing or wearing bells, so that the bear will know you are there and can avoid you. Detour if you can, walking upwind so the bear will smell you and know you are there. Do not make eye contact, which looks like a threat to many bears. If the bear is a grizzly or black bear, try to climb a tall tree. Drop something big, like your pack, to distract the bear.

If you come face to face with a bear, do not run—it can outrun you. Drop slowly to a fetal position, locking your hands behind your neck. Keep your backpack on to protect your back. Don't move until you are sure the bear is gone.

Carry only dried or freeze-dried foods with you—fresh foods will attract bears. Bears can get at food stored in your tent or car. Public campgrounds in bear country have storage cupboards where you can keep your food. If storage cupboards are not available, put all food and garbage in plastic bags, seal them, and hang them at least 12 feet above the ground and 10 feet away from the tree trunk. Tie off the rope on another tree. Pitch your tent upwind from the cooking-eating area, near a tree you can climb. Don't sleep in the clothes you wore when you cooked a meal. Pack out all garbage.

Snakes: Snakes are shy, and usually bite only when startled. In the United States, there are only about 20 species of venomous snakes, but they bite people 8000 times a year, and of those

people nine to 50 die. Most bites (98 percent) are from pit vipers (the Crotalidae family), which include rattlesnakes, copperheads, and cottonmouths. The other venomous snake family is the Elapidae—the most familiar member of this family is the coral snake. Not all bites from venomous snakes contain venom—one-fourth of rattlesnake bites, for example, are without venom. You are most likely to be bitten in North Carolina, Arkansas, Texas, Georgia, West Virginia, Mississippi, and Louisiana.

Plan to know where ranger stations are so that you can get help quickly. Wear hiking boots and heavy pants. Sleep in a closed structure, so that snakes, attracted by body heat, cannot crawl in to sleep with you. Always know where you are stepping or reaching.

Bring a snake bite kit, with instructions, on all your excursions into undeveloped land.

Scorpions: There are 1600 known species of scorpions in the world. Of those species only 25 can kill humans, and only one U.S. species is fatal (*centruroides exilicauda*). Most stings are about as toxic as that of a honeybee. All scorpions have pinchers, eight legs, and a tail with a stinger. They are from one-half inch to 8 inches long. What to do about scorpions? Avoid them. For example, look inside your boots before you put them on.

Bees, ticks, and other small creatures: Wear long pants, long-sleeved shirt, cap. Tuck your pants legs into your boots or sock cuffs. Don't walk barefoot—you might step into a yellow jacket nest.

When camping, check yourself over often for ticks, arthropods that can spread Rocky Mountain spotted fever. To keep ticks from attaching themselves to you, apply a product containing 0.5 percent permethrin to your clothes, sleeping bags, and other equipment. You should let it dry at least two hours before wearing or using them. If a tick does get on you, put paraffin or rubbing alcohol or a drop of nail polish on the tick, then pull it straight out with a tweezers.

Ranger stations usually stock epinephrine to treat bee sting allergies.

For mosquitoes and other flying insects, use a

good insect repellent, either citronella-based or with no more than 30 percent "deet" (N,N-diethyl-meta-toluamide). WARNING: Do not use a deet-based repellent on children under two, and consider protecting adults by putting it on clothing, not on skin (though it can damage spandex, rayon, and acetate); or, if you must put it on the body, apply over sunscreen and only on the hands. Don't use it near eyes or lips, or on broken skin. Don't breathe it, don't use it near food. Wash it off after you don't need it anymore. As you may have guessed, deet can have side effects. Call the EPA at 800-858-7378 with questions about it. (Why consider it at all? Because it is the most effective against most crawling and flying pests.)

If bitten, put on ice, soap and water, mud, jewelweed sap, alcohol, hydrocortisone cream. If allergic, ask your doctor what to carry with you and how to use it.

Stingrays and jellyfish: About 750 Americans are bitten every year by stingrays, which hide in sand in shallow water. Wash wounds with seawater, remove the stinger, and put the affected part in hot water (as hot as the person can stand it) for an hour or more. *Get medical help.* The wound may need to be stitched and the patient may need painkillers.

Jellyfish stings are painful. Take off tentacles, bathe area with seawater, followed by alcohol. Then cover the area with flour or baking soda and scrape this off (after it dries) with a sharp knife (not a razor). Wash again with seawater. You can also use ammonia, vinegar, unflavored meat tenderizer (papain), boric acid, lemon juice, or cortisone cream.

How to Survive in the Wilderness

The biggest danger to people stranded in the wilderness is not hunger or thirst, but cold. Hypothermia, which occurs when body temperature drops below 95°F., kills more travelers outdoors than anything else. A human being can live six to eight weeks without food, but cold kills fast.

The best advice about survival is to make contingency plans in advance in case you do lose your way. Take these precautions:

♦ Give your itinerary to someone. Call in at designated times, so that if you fail to call, your contact will suspect a problem.

♦ Dress for warmth in breathable, water-repellent fabrics—polypropylene (which dries quickly and provides warmth) or wool (which does not dry so fast). Protect your head, neck, and hands by wearing gloves, scarf, hat.

♦ Always carry a fire starter—bits of candle or fire-starter paste. Bring matches that light under all conditions, along with the striker panel.

♦ In a thunderstorm, seek shelter away from trees or hide under a boulder.

♦ Carry a garbage bag, preferably of yellow or orange for visibility. You can cut holes in it to make a poncho, and it will provide emergency shelter.

♦ If you plan to take children into the woods, footprint them by having them step on a piece of padded tinfoil; identify each footprint with the child's name. Do this for each pair of shoes the children will be wearing. This will help searchers distinguish your child's tracks from those of others.

♦ Put a whistle around your child's neck and teach him or her that three blasts is a signal for help.

If you are stranded:

♦ Unless you know how to walk out, stay where you are. Before you go camping, tell your children what to do if they are lost—to hug a tree. This will keep them in one place and prevent them from panicking. (Hug a Tree is a national program to teach children how to survive in the wilderness. It was developed by Ab Taylor, a retired tracker for the U.S. Border Patrol.)

♦ If you do decide to move on, leave a trail as Hansel and Gretel did. You might drag a stick, for instance. Do not move at night—you can't see where you are stepping.

♦ Find shelter in a high place out of the wind—in a cave, a hollow tree, rocks. Remember that windchill, brought on by wind, can reduce air temperature. Know how the wind blows—up valleys by day, down them at night.

♦ An International Distress signal is three of anything—a yell, a whistle blast, a column of smoke. Make three piles of firewood, ready to light if you hear rescuers. Flash signals at planes with a mirror or any surface that is reflective (a metal pot, for instance).

♦ In a clearing, make a big cross or "SOS" from rocks or another material visible from the air as a clue to searchers.

♦ After you have started a fire for warmth, make a heat reflector of a rock or stack of wood. (See "Building a Campfire," below.) Build a foot-high platform of dirt or branches for sleeping. Find some material to put between you and the ground—dry pine needles, for instance.

♦ Drink plenty of water, which will help you maintain body heat. If snow is the only water, melt it first. Eating snow can lower your body temperature, which can be dangerous.

♦ Lie on the ground to wave if a search plane comes over. You will be easier to see.

♦ Yell at frightening noises. Animals may be frightened away, and searchers may more easily find you.

♦ If you accidentally step into quicksand, lie flat, which provides more surface so that you won't sink. Use the back stroke to swim out.

♦ Don't try to conserve water. Drink what you need.

Avalanches

Associated with an unstable layer of snow, avalanches, once begun, travel very fast—up to 70 mph (in the Cascades). Storms, sonic booms, and warm rain can trigger them. Your chances of surviving are slim—the fast-moving snow can hit you like a truck, and if you are buried, the weight of the snow is enormous. For instance, if an avalanche buries you 3 feet deep, you are under pressure of 200 pounds per square foot, so weighty that your lungs can not expand to enable you to breathe. The best bet is to avoid avalanches.

Here are safety tips from the U.S. Forest Service:

♦ If you want to avoid avalanche risk completely, stay in developed ski areas.

♦ Outside developed areas, pick your route carefully. Avoid old avalanche paths, such as treeless gullies, where snow might slide again. If you must cross dangerous slopes, stay as high as possible. Trees and brush usually help anchor the snow. Use areas of dense timber or rocky outcrops for rest stops.

♦ Eighty percent of avalanches are storm-related. Rapidly falling snow can destabilize a slope. So can rain or a sudden warming. A storm that starts cold and then warms is more likely to cause avalanches because cold, dry snow makes a slippery boundary between old snow below and heavier snow above.

♦ If the snow sounds hollow under skis or snowshoes, or if cracks spread in the snow, conditions are probably dangerous.

♦ All members of a party should carry a collapsible shovel and a radio transmitter-receiver to speed location and rescue of avalanche victims. Experts say survival chances drop 50 percent after the first 20 minutes.

Building a Campfire

Make sure you are allowed to start fires where you are going. The Forest Service discourages campfires because they cause a hazard and leave an ugly scar in the forest. So if possible use a stove for low-impact ("no trace") camping. If you have to start a fire—if you are lost it may make the difference for survival—here's how.

Pack your own firewood if you can. If you gather wood in the forest to burn, use only wood from the ground that you can break with your hands. Keep your fire small.

Choose a place away from tree roots and branches, a place where a fire was lit in the past if you can find one. Clear a circle about 10 feet in diameter and build the fire in the center. Taking away all debris decreases the chance that the fire will spread.

Gather tinder (easily burning small fuel like fire starters, dead evergreen twigs, dry dead bark); kindling (dry sticks); firewood (larger wood). Start by placing the kindling crisscross over the tinder. The general rule is to go from small to large. You can fuzz sticks to make them burn better—just whittle the outside into scales.

If you are stuck without matches, you can start a fire using a long, thin stick and twirling it fast between your palms into a board with some tinder next to the point of friction. Or use a magnifying glass to focus the rays of the sun on a piece of paper to start a fire.

Cone fire: Make a tepee of tinder and sticks, with the tinder inside. Cone fires burn fast.

Hunter's fire: This is also a quick fire. Start a small fire, then as coals start forming, put two logs straddling the fire, so the wind blows between them. Let them support the pots as they burn.

Keyhole fire: This is a good long-lasting fire. With stones, mark out the shape of a keyhole. The long section should be 3–6 feet long, wide enough to support pots. Start a fire in the circular section and push burning wood down into the corridor as needed to heat pots.

Pyramid fire: Put down tinder, then build a log cabin of wood around it. On top lay wood to make the whole thing into a box.

KEYHOLE FIRE

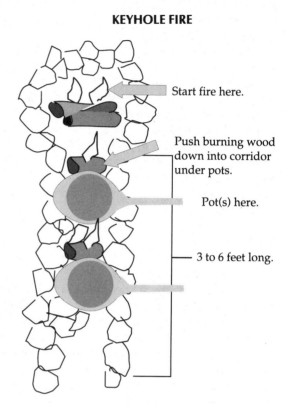

Start fire here.

Push burning wood down into corridor under pots.

Pot(s) here.

3 to 6 feet long.

Never leave a fire alone. Pour water and dirt over it twice before you leave. Stir the embers, make sure the fire is cold. If you see steam, it is not out. Bury the ashes and put forest debris over the spot.

THE ARTS

DAVE BRUBECK ON MUSIC

"Music is the most profound form of communication. Its influence, sometimes subliminal, often supersedes language as a means of human expression. We celebrate the significant events of our lives—private and public—with appropriate music. We are lulled as infants by our mother's song. Our social life is brightened by it. Our prayers are lifted with it. Our most profound emotions and our most frivolous ones are expressed through music. Have you ever noticed that when an event of great magnitude is projected on the screen, or on the theatrical stage, when words, action, and pictures have failed to express the immensity of the moment, it is always music that is called upon to express the inexpressible? Ask yourself why this is so, and in your answer you will understand how truly important music is to our humanness."

Reprinted from *Testimony to Music* (p. 19), Music Educators National Conference (MENC), 1986, 1806 Robert Fulton Drive, Reston, VA 22091.

The Orchestra

If you don't know a piccolo from an oboe, a map of the orchestra may keep you from making an idiot of yourself when talking about the music. It might even help you understand better how those thrilling cascades of sound are produced.

You should realize, however, that conductors may remove some instruments or add some, depending on the piece to be played. For instance, the orchestra may include an English horn, or it may not. The placement of some groups of instruments may change—clarinets might be to the right in some orchestras, to the left in others. You can count on the following broad plan: strings in the front, woodwinds behind the strings toward the center, piano and harp behind the violins to your left, brass in the back or in the row in front of the back row, percussion in the back. The strings usually play the most continually, the woodwinds sometimes carry the melody, the brass amplifies, the percussion supplies the beat.

The Instruments

Strings: Violins (divided according to the parts they play into first and second violins), violas, violoncellos (or cellos), double basses (or contrabasses), harp.

Piano

Woodwinds: Piccolo, flutes, clarinets, bass clarinet, saxophones, oboes, English horn (or cor anglais), bassoons, contrabassoon.

Brass: French horns, cornets, trumpets, trombones, tuba.

Percussion: Timpani, bass drum, snare drum, cymbals, triangle, xylophone, Chinese woodblocks, castanets, gongs, glockenspiel, chimes.

THE BEST SEAT

A high-priced ticket does not guarantee the best sound in a concert hall—except for chamber music. To hear an orchestra best, you should be a distance above it and away from it—in the boxes on the sides of the hall or the rows of the balcony from the first through the center. If you sit in the first rows, you can see the orchestra better; if you sit toward the center rows, you hear richer sound.

Why? If you are too close, the sound of one part of the orchestra may be exaggerated, and the instruments do not blend as well to your ear into a total sound. Think of the stage as a shell, in which the sound gathers and blends—you need to be far enough away to get the full effect.

Avoid seats under an overhang, which dulls and traps the sound.

Opera for Beginners

Opera is definitely an acquired taste. But more and more people are acquiring it, so why not give it a whirl?

By definition, opera is musical theater or sung drama, with an orchestral accompaniment, in one to five acts usually preceded by an overture. In practice, just think of opera as a sort of musical Halloween, a carnival of emotions.

However archaic or up-to-the-minute the subject of an opera (from ancient history to a modern terrorist attack), the common basis of all opera is intense human emotion expressed in music, and the transformation of sound into spectacle. Themes tend to cluster around courtship, seduction, betrayal, love, and death, with a whole spectrum of obsessive pathology: jealousy, hatred, insanity. Opera has even been described as *the* primal scream—of pain, ecstasy, triumph, love, despair.

But it's all foreign, you say—you can't even understand opera if it's sung in English. The answer to that one, developed in the last decade, is called supertitles, similar to the subtitles under

THE ORCHESTRA

PERCUSSION (timpani, bass drum, snare drum, cymbals, triangle, xylophone, Chinese woodblocks, castanets, gongs, glockenspiel, chimes)

BRASS (French horns, cornets, trumpets, trombones, tuba; can also be in last row)

WOODWINDS (piccolos, flutes, clarinets, bass clarinets, saxophones, oboes, English horns, bassoons, contrabassoons)

PIANO

HARP

STRINGS (violins, violas, violoncellos, double basses)

CONDUCTOR

foreign films but projected above the opera stage. Supertitles are becoming ever more sophisticated. When actual librettos were simply projected, audiences tended to snicker at a lot of the text. (At the musical peak of one Puccini opera, the caption above the stage read, "Go get me a pair of shoes.") Special titles are now being written and edited for sophisticated contemporary consumption. And because sung language is so much more difficult to understand than spoken, even operas written in English are now being supertitled for American audiences.

The next objection to opera is that it is somehow the province of foreigners (and hyphenated-Americans). Not so any longer. Never before have there been so many American opera companies—besides the great Metropolitan in New York City, there are functioning operas in Cleveland, Houston, Hartford, Boston, Baltimore, San Diego, Miami, Seattle, St. Louis, Philadelphia; even Long Beach, a Los Angeles suburb, has an excellent little opera company performing ambitious and innovative projects. And in the last generations, the U.S. has produced numbers of world-class stars. Some great American singers, now retired or past their prime, include Robert Merrill, Leonard Warren, Leontyne Price, Grace Bumbry, Shirley Verrett; now at the peak of their careers are the Americans Jessye Norman, Kathleen Battle, June Anderson, Marilyn Horne, Sherrill Milnes, Samuel Ramey.

You may be more familiar with opera than you think. If you go to the movies, even if you are a TV couch potato, you have already been exposed to a lot of operatic music. A famous aria from *I Pagliacci* was once used as a TV breakfast food commercial, while another aria from the French opera *Lakmé*, its soaring notes suggesting celestial activity, is now televised as an airline ad. Most film composers up to the 1960s were classically trained musicians who borrowed heavily from their great predecessors. In his 1954 Academy Award acceptance speech, film composer Dmitri Tiomkin acknowledged his professional debts to Beethoven, Brahms, and Wagner. Al Pacino's *Serpico* (1973) borrowed an aria from Puccini's *Tosca*, while another famous Puccini aria

was heard in *The Killing Fields* (1984). And if you saw *Apocalypse Now* (1979), you will never forget Wagner's "Ride of the Valkyries"—which also played, along with an entire Wagnerian medley, in *Excalibur* (1981).

Places to Experience Opera

The world's great opera houses include:
♦ La Scala in Milan, famous since 1778 for its demanding and demonstrative audiences
♦ Covent Garden, London's operatic center since 1858
♦ The Metropolitan Opera, New York (est. 1883)
♦ The Vienna Opera (est. 1869), a center of European opera
♦ The Semperoper, Dresden, and the Munich Opera, Germany's operatic capitals.

For summer opera, with picnicking between the acts:
♦ Glyndebourne, England
♦ Bayreuth, Germany
♦ Spoleto, Italy
♦ Santa Fe, New Mexico
♦ Verona, Italy
♦ The Baths of Caracalla, Rome, Italy.

The Vocabulary of Opera

aria: vocal solo
bel canto: "beautiful singing"; classic Italian style of beautifully sustained vocal lines
bravura: characterized by great dash, skill, brilliance
castrato: male singer castrated before puberty; common in 16th-century Italy
coloratura: specializing in elaborate vocal ornamentation
diva: Greek for "goddess"
duet: composition for two voices
intermezzo: a short work, usually comic, performed between acts
legato: smooth connection of successive notes
leitmotif: a musical motive or theme used to signal a character, idea or event

libretto: the text or "little book" of an opera

operetta: light opera

overture: orchestral piece played before the curtain rises, possibly incorporating musical material from the opera

prelude: introductory orchestral piece, similar to an overture, leading directly into the opera

prima donna: "first lady" or leading female voice; typically synonymous with imperious, demanding, impossible, capricious, willful

recitative: recitation, or spoken dialogue

tremolo: "trembling" or excessive vibrato, sometimes called a "wobble"

verismo: Italian for realism, a style of opera derived from naturalism, with contemporary, everyday settings and characters

vibrato: a vibration or fluctuation of pitch or volume

Recommended Starter Operas

Commonly performed operas ranked by degree of difficulty (from *, easiest, to ****, most difficult)

*La Bohème**

*La Traviata**

*Aida**

*Carmen**

*Rigoletto**

*Tosca**

*Madama Butterfly**

*Turandot**

I Pagliacci and *Cavalleria Rusticana** (one-act operas typically performed together)

*Otello***

*Nabucco***

*Lucia di Lammermoor***

*La Cenerentola*** (Cinderella)*

*Samson and Dalila***

*Tales of Hoffmann***

*Der Rosenkavalier***

*La Forza del Destino***

*The Barber of Seville***

*Don Carlo***

*The Marriage of Figaro***

*Don Giovanni***

*The Magic Flute***

*The Flying Dutchman***

*Die Meistersinger***

*Electra****

*Semiramide****

*Norma****

*Tannhauser****

*Lohengrin****

*Così fan Tutte****

*Orpheo ed Euridice****

*Salome****

*Fidelio****

TEENAGERS' CHOICES OF INSTRUMENTS

According to a survey by the American Music Conference, teenagers are more likely to play the synthesizer or keyboards more than any other instrument. This is how instruments stack up. (Some chose more than one instrument.)

Synthesizers and keyboards	34 percent
Woodwinds	32 percent
Acoustic piano	31 percent
Brass	21 percent
Guitar	13 percent

SIX TIPS TO MAKE YOU A BETTER DANCER

1. Steps should be no bigger than the width of your hips.

2. Shift weight easily from one foot to the other.

3. Know your center—feel a cord pulling on your sternum.

4. Keep your eyes forward and off your feet. With your head up, your balance is better and you look better.

5. Don't stop. It's time wasted and it's obvious you made a mistake. Move smoothly through the mistake.

6. Don't try to teach your partner to dance. It may make her or him self-conscious. Concentrate on your own performance instead.

Julius Caesar***
Wagner's *Ring* cycle****
Parsifal****
The Coronation of Poppea****
Wozzeck****
Lulu****
all Russian opera****

How to Look at a Work of Art

Like most of us, you have probably found yourself
in an art burnout—moving unthinkingly from
painting to painting in a museum, seeing nothing

and thinking about lunch. It's all too much. Maybe
it's a good idea to slow down and look at only a
few paintings, you say. But how? Much of the
time the inability to look, really look, at a painting
comes from lack of knowledge. Here are some
tips compiled from brochures from the Los
Angeles County Museum of Art and the New
Britain (Conn.) Museum of American Art.

When confronted with a piece of art, first look
long and hard, and allow yourself to respond
emotionally. Are you puzzled? Why do you react
as you do?

You may then begin the task of looking intellec-
tually. At this point, you analyze the parts of
the painting, then put the whole back together.

Reproduced by courtesy of the Trustees, The National Gallery, London

Behind analysis are some larger questions: Why is this art? Who made it? What is the artist trying to communicate? Is the artist trying to express an idea or tell a story, show what someone looked like, enhance a useful object like a bowl, express a mood or emotion, make a beautiful pattern of colors and shapes, lead the viewer to think in a different way about the world?

Description

Look at all the parts of the painting, including the details. In Jan van Eyck's *Giovanni Arnolfini and His Bride*, it is all too easy to focus exclusively on the couple, without noticing the convex mirror in the background that reflects two people we cannot see in "reality." Above the mirror is written "Johannes de Eyck fuit hic 1434" (Jan van Eyck was here 1434). Is van Eyck one of the men reflected in the mirror? What does the dog mean? The shoes? The chandelier? The more you know about van Eyck and Flemish painting of the Renaissance, the more meaning you will prize from this particular painting. Even if you are not well versed, noticing the details and pondering their meaning adds to your enjoyment of the painting.

Formal Analysis

Art historians contend over the best way to analyze works of art—psychological, sociological, existential, Marxist, deconstructivist, post-modernist, you name it. The most common method is formal analysis, which separates the work of art into parts in order to examine their function.

Composition

♦ What are the shapes in the work and how are they arranged? Does the arrangement seem random, in planes, overlapping, side by side? In van Eyck's painting, the shapes of the two figures are boxed by the three walls and their objects.

♦ Do you see vertical, horizontal, or diagonal shapes? Curves or zigzags? In this painting the shapes are vertical, with several curves—for in-

stance, the drape of the bride's dress that ends in the shape of the dog.

♦ What does this analysis suggest about the artist's intentions? In *Arnolfini and His Bride*, you might think that the arrangement of the figures—apart but with joined hands—suggests formality as well as connection. Yet the other objects—the shoes, the fruit, the dog—convey informality.

Point of view. Where is the artist in relation to what he or she has wrought? In this painting, van Eyck looks up, but he is also in the mirror. The room is open to us.

Balance. Are the elements in the painting arranged in such a way that the painting is symmetrical or asymmetrical? Symmetry may express calmness and order, asymmetry may express tension or excitement. Mentally draw lines down the middle and across the middle of the work. How does the image fit in the canvas? This painting has a rough symmetry: the two figures are on either side of a line formed by the chandelier, mirror, and dog. But little details keep it from being so symmetrical that it is boring—the sandals, the placing of the figures so that the groom is a bit higher than the bride. The window and the bed balance each other but are in different planes and sizes.

Space. Does the painting have depth? How is our eye drawn through the space: in a circle, in a zigzag, erratically? Is there more than one perspective? Here, the painter has given us a three-dimensional view, with some distortion of the perspective—in the floor, for instance.

Geometry. Look for geometrical forms as clues to the underlying structure of the painting. The more geometric, the more order suggested by the painting. In van Eyck's painting, the two figures form a parallelogram.

Color and light. Color adds emphasis. Primary colors (red, yellow, blue) are usually viewed as strong. Colors change when placed next to other colors. Artists may seek to imitate the colors of nature or not. With light and shadow, the artist spotlights parts of a painting, suggests mood.

Technique. Notice the brushwork, paint

thickness. When we see paintings with strong brushwork, we are aware that the painting was made by a human being. What does the texture of the work evoke?

Interpretation

After your analysis, which of course need not be as detailed as the foregoing, speculate about what the painting means. You might add to the analysis what you know about the period in which the art was created—in the case of the van Eyck painting, the Renaissance. What does this painting tell you about marriage, how people lived? Also consider biographical information—who was van Eyck? How did he fit into the art movements of his time? Think back to your first reaction to the painting. Is it confirmed?

Reprint courtesy of Los Angeles County Museum of Art.

How to Visit a Museum

Many of us are intimidated by museums. We pussyfoot from one object to another, afraid to pass anything by, talking in whispers. Relax, say the experts. A museum is to be enjoyed. Here are some tips on how to get the most from your museum visit:

♦ Before you visit the museum, try to find out something about its collections or exhibits. Try to get a brochure from the museum before you go. Even if the museums you are going to visit are in foreign countries, you often can get guides beforehand by asking your travel agent for them. Libraries often have books on hand that can help you decide what you want to see, like the *Official Museum Directory* or the *International Dictionary of Arts*.

♦ Find out about parking.

♦ Wear comfortable clothes and shoes.

♦ If you want to videotape or take pictures, make sure the museum allows such practices before you lug everything to the museum.

♦ If you have no advance information, ask the

SHOULD ART BE REALISTIC?

Works of art may be executed in three different styles—realistic: close to the way things actually look; abstract: related to the way things look but altered in some significant way; nonrepresentational: unconcerned with the presentation of figures or objects, focused instead on shapes, lines, and colors.

The term *realistic* is very subjective and has different meanings in different cultures. Even within the same culture, the conception of what is realistic can change over time. There is a tendency among museum visitors to think that realistic art is in some way better than other kinds of art, but this is not necessarily true. The basis for understanding and appreciating why something looks the way it does is knowing who made it and why.

people at the desk what the museum is famous for. You might say, "If I were to look at only five things, what should they be?"

♦ Many museums offer self-guided tours, with cassettes or booklets stressing certain themes. You might want to take advantage of them.

♦ Once in the museum, follow your bent. Some people go quickly through the whole museum (if possible), then return to contemplate those objects or rooms that most appealed to them. Others go immediately to what interests them. Still others start at the beginning and try to go through to the end. Do the museum at your own pace, in your own way. *Idea*: If you have visited the museum before, try going through it backward.

♦ Look at details through opera glasses so that you can appreciate them better. Or draw them—drawing will help you focus your attention.

♦ Pay attention to the museum building itself—it, too, is often a work of art.

♦ Supervise your children so they will learn something and not disturb others.

♦ Don't overdo. Plan to have lunch to break up museum visits.

♦ Relax, enjoy yourself. Respond honestly to what you see. Don't let a phantom expert keep you from connecting with the things that are right before your eyes.

The Movie Rating System

The movie ratings that some filmmakers bitterly dispute are determined by a film rating board of the Classification and Rating Administration (CARA), a voluntary system of the Motion Picture Association of America and the National Association of Theatre Owners. The board, made up of parents, views each film and discusses it as a group. It then votes on its rating, making an educated estimate of which rating most American parents would consider the most appropriate.

In the decision-making process, the board considers theme, language, violence, nudity, sex, and drug use—without putting undue emphasis on any one element. Then it assesses how each of these elements is used in the context of the film.

Filmmakers do not have to submit their films for ratings, but the great majority do. All five of the rating symbols are trademarked—they cannot be self-applied. Movie producers can reedit their films and resubmit them in the hope of having ratings changed. They may also appeal a rating decision to the Ratings Appeals Board, composed of people from the industry organizations that govern the rating system. A two-thirds secret ballot vote of those present on the appeals board may overturn a rating board decision.

Enforcing the ratings is voluntary, but the overwhelming majority of theaters follow CARA's guidelines and enforce its provisions.

The following descriptions are taken verbatim from a pamphlet distributed by AMC Theatres. (To supplement the ratings, you may want to look at other movie rating guides.)

The Rating Symbols

G *General Audiences—All ages admitted.* Signifies that the film rated contains nothing most parents will consider offensive for even their youngest children to see or hear. Nudity, sex scenes, and scenes of drug use are absent; violence is minimal; snippets of dialogue may go beyond polite conversation but do not go beyond common everyday expressions.

PG *Parental Guidance Suggested—Some material may not be suitable for children.* Signifies that the film rated may contain some material parents might not like to expose their young children to—material that will clearly need to be examined or inquired about before children are allowed to attend the film. Explicit sex scenes and scenes of drug use are absent; nudity, if present, is seen only briefly; horror and violence do not exceed moderate levels.

PG-13 *Parents Strongly Cautioned—Some material may be inappropriate for children under 13.* Signifies that the film rated may be inappropriate for preteens. Parents should be especially careful about letting their younger children attend. Rough or persistent violence is absent; sexually oriented nudity is generally absent; some scenes of drug use may be seen; some use of one of the harsher sexually derived words may be heard.

R *Restricted—Under 17 requires accompanying parent or adult guardian* (age varies in some jurisdictions). Signifies that the rating board has concluded that the film rated may contain some adult material. Parents are urged to learn more about the film before taking their children to see it. An R may be assigned due to, among other things, a film's use of language, theme, violence, sensuality, or its portrayal of drug use.

NC-17 *No Children Under 17 Admitted* (age varies in some jurisdictions). Signifies that the rating board believes that most

American parents would feel that the film rated is patently adult and that children under the age of 17 should not be admitted to it. The film may contain explicit sex scenes, an accumulation of sexually oriented language, and/or scenes of excessive violence. The NC-17 designation does *not*, however, signify that the rated film is obscene or pornographic in terms of sex, language, or violence. NC-17 is CARA's new name for the old X rating—but unlike the X, NC-17 is a registered trademark and cannot be self-applied.

For more information, write: **The National Association of Theatre Owners,** 4605 Lankershim Blvd., Suite 340, North Hollywood, CA 91602, or **The Classification and Rating Administration,** 14144 Ventura Blvd., Suite 210, Sherman Oaks, CA 91423.

Reprinted courtesy of Motion Picture Association of America.

Great Old (and Relatively Obscure) 1930s and 1940s Movies to Rent

When the latest Hollywood concoction seems thin, resort to those old movies from the great period of moviemaking, the 1930s and 1940s. This list may lead you to some you have never seen.

Thrillers and Horror

♦ *La Bête Humaine* (1938), also called *The Human Beast* and *Judas Was a Woman*. Jean Renoir's *film noir* adaptation of an Emile Zola novel, starring Jean Gabin and Simone Simon, focuses on a love triangle that ends in murder.

♦ *Criss Cross* (1949). In a tale of robbery, Burt Lancaster stars as an armoured-car guard, Yvonne de Carlo as his wife. Anthony (Tony) Curtis makes his first film appearance here.

♦ *49th Parallel* (1941). A Nazi U-boat is sunk off the coast of Canada, and its crew tries to sneak into the United States. The cast includes Laurence Olivier, Leslie Howard, Raymond Massey, Glynis Johns.

♦ *Gun Crazy* (1949). If you relish getaway crime scenes, see this thriller about a young couple (gun-crazy John Dall and *femme fatale* Peggy Cummins) on the lam. You are there during the car chase because the camera was—right in the car.

♦ *I Walked with a Zombie* (1943). Jane Eyre (Frances Dee) on a creepy Haitian plantation, if you can imagine it, with skeletons in the closet and voodoo rituals. Directed by Jacques Tourneur.

♦ *Marked Woman* (1937). Crime drama, based on the hooker-caused downfall of Lucky Luciano, stars Bette Davis as a woman gone bad and Humphrey Bogart as a somewhat gutless D.A. Directed by Lloyd Bacon.

♦ *They Live by Night* (1949)—Directed by Nicolas Ray; Farley Granger and Cathy O'Donnell star as fugitive lovers in the 1930s.

Comedy

♦ *His Girl Friday* (1940). Directed by Howard Hawks, recently restored. Stars Cary Grant, Rosalind Russell, and Ralph Bellamy in a newspaper romance, complete with murder, with a terrific script by Ben Hecht and Charles Lederer.

♦ *Ninotchka* (1939). Greta Garbo, Bela Lugosi, Melvyn Douglas in a romantic comedy in which Garbo, as a Russian agent, falls in love in Paris with the dashing Douglas.

♦ *Swing Time* (1936). Fred Astaire and Ginger Rogers dance away, even though Astaire is engaged to a girl back home (Betty Furness). Songs include "A Fine Romance," "The Way You Look Tonight," and "Pick Yourself Up."

Drama, Romance, and Melodrama

♦ *Becky Sharp* (1935). Miriam Hopkins stars in the title role of this film version of William Thackeray's novel, *Vanity Fair*. First full-Technicolor movie ever made. As director Rouben Mamoulian said, "Now it [the screen] is given a palette with paints." One critic compared it to a "fresh fruit sundae."

♦ *Black Narcissus* (1947). Michael Powell directed this beautiful (color), sharply written psychological drama, starring Deborah Kerr, about a steamy group of British nuns establishing a mission at a Himalayan outpost.

♦ *Caught* (1949). Max Ophuls directed this chilling romance about a young woman (Barbara Bel Geddes) who marries a dashing but nasty millionaire (Robert Ryan) and lives to regret it.

♦ *Cleopatra* (1934). Director: Cecil B. DeMille. Well-acted and beautifully filmed version of the story of the temptress of the Nile, starring Claudette Colbert and featuring lavish sets and costumes, passion, battle scenes, party animals of ancient times.

♦ *Deception* (1946). Bette Davis plays a classical pianist, Claude Rains a composer, and Paul Henreid a cellist in this well-acted drama about jealousy in a romantic trio.

♦ *Dodsworth* (1936). Walter Huston and Ruth Chatterton in a William Wyler–directed adaption of the Sinclair Lewis novel, a drama about a middle-aged retired industrialist who faces life changes during a trip abroad.

♦ *Home of the Brave* (1949). Produced by Stanley Kramer, a pace-setting drama about racism and war (WWII), with James Edwards and Lloyd Bridges.

Musicals

♦ *Show Boat* (1936). Paul Robeson, Irene Dunne, Helen Morgan, Hattie McDaniel, and others in the fine cast dance and sing the Jerome Kern–Oscar Hammerstein musical. It's worth it to hear Robeson singing "Old Man River" and Morgan singing "Bill."

♦ *Good News* (1947). Football star Peter Lawford meets a beautiful tutor, June Allyson, and everyone starts dancing—to, among other things, "Varsity Drag."

Impossible to Classify

♦ *Dancing Lady* (1933). Joan Crawford, Fred Astaire, Franchot Tone, and the Three Stooges mix it up in a musical romance.

If it's difficult to find old treasures and other not-so-popular movies at your video store, try renting them through a mail-order club.

Discount Video Tapes, Inc., 833-A North Hollywood Way, PO Box 7122, Burbank CA 91510 (818-843-3366; FAX 800-253-9612 or 818-843-3821).

Eddie Brandt's Saturday Matinee, 6310 Colfax Avenue, North Hollywood, CA 91606 (818-506-4242; 818-506-7722).

Evergreen Video Society, 228 W. Houston Street, New York, NY 10014 (800-225-7783; 212-691-7362).

Facets Video, 1517 W. Fullerton Avenue, Chicago, IL 60614 (800-331-6197; 312-281-9075; FAX 312-929-5437).

Home Film Festival, 305 Linden Street, Scranton, PA 18503 (800-258-3456).

Video By Mail, PO Box 1515, Whitney, TX 76692 (800-245-4996).

Video Library, 7175 Germantown Avenue, Philadelphia, PA 19119 (800-669-7157).

11

FOOD AND DRINK

FOOD: HEALTH AND SAFETY

Healthy Diets

The recommendations of the U.S. Department of Agriculture (USDA) for the daily American diet are easy to understand. You can readily identify foods in the six basic food groups, and you can't avoid seeing that foods in five of those groups are essential for health while those in the sixth group (fats, oils, and sweets) are largely expendable. But identification is one thing, following the recommendations is another. It's easy to load up on those unnecessary fats and sugars, not so easy to eat five to nine servings of vegetables and fruits a day. Be honest now—have you eaten all your vegetables?

Food Groups

- Bread, cereal, rice, pasta: 6–11 servings a day
- Fruits: 2–4 servings a day
- Vegetables: 3–5 servings a day
- Meat, poultry, fish, dry beans, eggs, and nuts: 2–3 servings a day
- Milk, yogurt, and cheese: 2–3 servings a day
- Fats, oils, and sweets: Use sparingly.

What Is a Serving?

Another problem: it's difficult, particularly if you live alone, to arrange to eat five servings of vegetables a day without having some of them molder into compost in your refrigerator. However, servings are small, as this chart shows, and you can occasionally eat a double portion of a vegetable you like to fulfill the daily recommendation. Remember, too, that juice counts as fruit, banana on cereal counts as fruit, vegetable sticks as snacks count as vegetables. (See the chart on the following page.)

Recommended Daily Calorie Levels

The trick to healthy eating? The sleight of hand it sometimes takes to eat the right foods *and* the

RECOMMENDED DAILY CALORIE LEVELS (U.S.D.A. Suggestions)

If you are...	You probably can consume
A sedentary woman An older adult	1600 calories
A child (most children) A teenage girl An active woman A sedentary man (most)	2200 calories
A teenage boy An active man (most) A very active woman	2800 calories

FORTY-FIVE FOOD SERVINGS

Foods	Serving Amount	Foods	Serving Amount
Bread, Cereal, Rice, Pasta		**Fruits**	
Cereal, shredded wheat, grits, rice, barley, bran, bulgur, pasta or noodles (cooked)	½ cup	Banana, grapefruit	½
Bagel, English muffin, hamburger roll	½	Apple, nectarine, orange, peach, pear	1
Bread	1 slice	Cantaloupe, raspberries	1 cup
Croutons	1 cup	Blueberries	¾ cup
Stuffing*	¼ cup	Strawberries, watermelon	1¼ cup
6-inch taco shell*	2	Cherries	12
6-inch tortilla*	1	Grapes	15
4-inch pancakes*	2	Unsweetened fruit juice; frozen and canned fruit in own juice or light syrup	½ cup
4½-inch waffle*	1	**Milk, Yogurt, Cheese**	
Air-popped popcorn	3 cups	Low-fat buttermilk, 1% milk, skim milk, low-fat yogurt	1 cup
Animal crackers	8	Evaporated skim milk	½ cup
Pretzels	¾ oz.	Low-fat cheese (Mozzarella, farmer's, Jarlsberg Swiss, Ricotta, Romano)	1 oz.
French fries*	10		
Starchy vegetable (peas, corn, lima beans)	½ cup	Low-fat cottage cheese	¼ cup
Sweet potato	⅓	**Meat, Poultry, Fish, Dry Beans, Eggs, Nuts**	
Vegetables		Chicken or Cornish hen or turkey (without skin); fish; wild game; veal chop or roast; Canadian bacon, ham, pork tenderloin; lean beef	1 oz.
Asparagus, beets, Brussels sprouts, cabbage, mushrooms, spinach, zucchini	½ cup		
Broccoli, carrots, cauliflower, green beans, peppers, tomatoes	1 cup	Clams, crab, lobster, scallops, shrimp	1 oz.

Foods	Serving Amount	Foods	Serving Amount
Meat, Poultry, Fish, Dry Beans, Eggs, Nuts (cont.)		**Fats, Oils, Sweets**	
Canned tuna (light, in water)	¼ cup	Butter, margarine, mayonnaise, oil	1 tsp.
Egg whites	3	Olives	5
Dry beans, cooked (garbanzos, navy beans, peas, red beans, lentils, soy beans, pinto beans); tofu	1 cup	Salad dressing	1 tbs.
		Bacon	1 slice
Nuts and seeds, unsalted, without oil; peanut butter***	2 tbs.	Sour cream	2 tbs.
		Heavy cream	1 tbs.
		Cream cheese	1 tbs.
Ground beef, meat loaf, rib roast, chuck roast, rump roast, Porterhouse steak, T-bone steak, pork chops or cutlets, lamp chops or roast, veal cutlet, chicken or turkey (with skin)***	1 oz.		
Canned salmon, tuna (in oil)**	¼ cup		
Corned beef, ground lamb, ground pork, luncheon meat, ribs, sausage***	1 oz.		

> * counts as one fat serving
>
> ** medium high in fat
>
> ***counts as two fat servings; high in fat

right amount of calories. You can start with this chart. Of course calorie levels also depend on metabolism and other factors.
Contact: **Consumer Nutrition Hotline** at 800-366-1655.

Food Labels

The Food and Drug Administration requires that all processed food be labeled according to a set of guidelines. A label must list values for a 2000-calorie diet as well as limits for both a 2000- and a 2500-calorie diet. Serving sizes have been standardized based on how much of a food people really eat. If manufacturers list an ingredient, they must also list the amount of that ingredient and what proportion of the recommended intake it represents.

Food manufacturers cannot:
♦ use the term "no cholesterol" for food that never had any cholesterol—for example, pure peanut butter, a plant food, never contains cholesterol;
♦ list nutrients like thiamine and riboflavin that are not missing from our diets;
♦ make a claim based on only one part of a food (like saying a chocolate-covered cherry is low-fat because the cherry is);

ANALYZING A FOOD LABEL:
ANOTHER LOOK AT MACARONI AND CHEESE

The Food and Drug Administration requires that all processed foods be labeled according to a set of guidelines that include the format below. Labels are both more informative and (a bonus) easier to read than before.

Serving sizes are standardized.

Saturated fat, considered to be the most harmful, is included as a category of fat content.

The label lists the amount of each nutrient in each serving. Dietary fiber may help to prevent disease. Diabetics and hypoglycemics need to know the sugar content of foods.

Micronutrients considered most important in American diets—vitamins A and C and minerals calcium and iron—are shown for every product. Micronutrients almost never deficient in diets —like riboflavin and thiamine—are not listed.

The label also reminds us that fat has more than twice the amount of calories per gram than carbohydrates or protein.

Nutrition Facts

Serving Size ½ cup (114g)
Servings Per Container 4

Amount Per Serving

Calories 260 Calories from Fat 120

	% Daily Value*
Total Fat 13g	**20%**
Saturated Fat 5g	**25%**
Cholesterol 30mg	**10%**
Sodium 660 mg	**28%**
Total Carbohydrate 31g	**11%**
Dietary Fiber 0g	**0%**
Sugars 5g	—
Protein 5g	—

Vitamin A 4%	●	Vitamin C 2%
Calcium 15%	●	Iron 4%

*Percent Daily Values are based on a 2,000 calorie diet. Your daily values may be higher or lower depending on your calorie needs:

	Calories:	2,000	2,500
Total Fat	Less than	65g	80g
Sat Fat	Less than	20g	25g
Cholesterol	Less than	00mg	300mg
Sodium	Less than	2,400mg	2,400mg
Total Carbohydrate		300g	375g
Fiber		25g	30g

Calories per gram:
Fat 9 ● Carbohydrates 4 ● Protein 4

Serving size must be what an average person would normally eat.

Label lists total calories.

Fat and cholesterol content is shown in both grams and percent of daily value for a 2000-calorie diet. Sodium, restricted in many diets, must be listed in percentages and in milligrams.

Every label lists dietary recommendations for both a 2000-calorie diet and a 2500-calorie diet. These recommendations make it easier to evaluate food from a nutritional standpoint. This macaroni and cheese has enough saturated fat and sodium that you might consider cutting back on other fat and sodium sources on the day that you eat it. It has no fiber—another minus. Its percentages of vitamins A and C are negligible though it is a fairly good source of calcium.

♦ list information for ingredients that are in a package without including those one must add to make the food (for instance, a cake mix must include in its calorie count the eggs the purchaser must add to make the cake).

Manufacturers' claims must follow certain rules:

♦ "Low in calories" means that the food can be eaten frequently without going beyond guidelines for a good diet.

♦ "Low in sodium" means less than 140 mg. a serving.

♦ "Reduced" means the product has at least 25 percent fewer calories of an ingredient than the regular product.

♦ "Good source" (say, of fiber) means one serving has 10 to 19 percent of Daily Value for that nutrient.

♦ "Low-fat" means the product contains no more than 3 grams of fat a serving.

♦ "Lite" means that a food contains at least 50 percent less fat than the food it's being compared with.

♦ "Fresh" means that the food cannot have been frozen, processed, heated, or chemically preserved.

Figuring the Fat in Food

Most experts say that less than 30 percent of the calories in your diet should come from fat. Some think that we should get no more than 10 percent of our calories from fat. No matter how sincere we are about lowering the percentage of fat in our diets, we can make mistakes in our calculations. One of the problems: fat contains 9 calories per gram, while protein and carbohydrate contain 4 calories per gram.

The formula for determining fat calorie limit at 30%:

1. Multiply the recommended day's calories by 0.3.

2. Divide that number by 9 (because each gram of fat has 9 calories).

Example: You eat 2000 calories a day. Multiply 2000 by 0.3 = 600, then divide 600 by 9 = 67 grams of fat. That is your daily fat allowance.

The formula for determining the percentage of fat calories in a food:

1. Multiply the number of grams of fat by 9.

2. Divide that number by the number of calories per serving.

3. Multiply the result by 100.

Example: A serving of three cookies contains 5 grams of fat and 150 calories. Multiply 5 by 9 = 45. Divide 45 by 150 = 0.3. Multiply 0.3 x 100 = 30% of calories from fat.

Choose Fats Carefully: According to their chemical structure, fats are classified as saturated, polyunsaturated, and monounsaturated. Food products may contain varying amounts of these kinds of fats. Saturated fat is the one to avoid most—experts think that only 10 percent of the fat you eat should be saturated. This does not mean that you can never eat another potato dripping with butter (largely saturated fat), but that you include the butter in your fat budget and cut back somewhere else. You find saturated fat in animal foods, chocolate, coconuts, coconut oil, palm and palm-kernel oils. (For more information on kinds of fat, see "The Fats in Your Oil and Butter," p. 622. Also see "Ten Tips for Lowering the Fat Content of Your Diet," p. 592.)

To get more information:

Order the "American Heart Association Fat and Cholesterol Counter" (102-page booklet) containing AHA recommendations, how to calculate fat, and information for 450 foods. Call: **American Heart Association:** 800-733-3000.

Order "The Eating Smart Fat Guide" slide-chart, listing recommended fat intakes by age and sex; includes fat, saturated fat, and calories in 300 foods. Write: **Center for Science in the Public Interest,** 1875 Connecticut Avenue NW, Suite 300, Washington, DC 20009.

Jack Sprat's Choice: Meat— Fat or Lean?

Just "giving up red meat" may be too simple a solution for the health of your arteries. It's the cut that counts, as much as the kind of meat. This United States Department of Agriculture chart shows how various cuts of meat (in 3-ounce servings) compare in terms of fat and calorie

CALORIES AND FAT IN VARIOUS CUTS OF MEAT
(in 3-ounce servings)

Meat	Cut	Calories	Fat Grams
Beef	eye of round	143	4.2
	top roast	153	4.2
	tip round	157	5.9
	top sirloin	165	6.1
	chuck roast	189	7.6
	top loin	176	8.0
	flank	176	8.6
	tenderloin	177	8.6
	T-bone steak	182	8.8
	Porterhouse steak	185	9.2
Veal	cutlet	140	3.5
	chop	177	6.6
Chicken (skinless)	breast	140	3.0
	leg	162	7.2
	thigh	178	9.2
Pork	tenderloin	139	4.1
	loin roast	165	6.1
	rib chop	186	8.3
Lamb	leg roast	117	4.4
	loin chop	116	4.6
Turkey	breast	132	1.8

Source: U.S. Department of Agriculture

content. Beef is somewhat redeemed from its reputation as a red-meat villain when you compare the fat contents of eye-of-round and a chicken leg. Cattle and pig farmers have trimmed the fat from their animals by breeding and feeding programs—for example, a University of Wisconsin study showed that pork had 31 percent less fat in 1990 than in 1983.

Meat has B vitamins, easily absorbed iron, and zinc. However, though farmers have reduced the fat in the meat they sell, fat is still high and at least 20 percent saturated. (See "Figuring the Fat in Food," p. 591.) So limit how much meat you eat in one day, and balance it with other less fat-heavy foods.

Note: Children over the age of two need two to three servings of protein foods a day.

TEN TIPS FOR LOWERING THE FAT CONTENT OF YOUR DIET

1. Measure oil in cooking; use less.
2. Poach, broil, or roast foods.
3. Remove skin from meat.
4. Eat no more than 6 ounces of meat a day. And make it lean fish, meat, and poultry. Turkey has less fat than chicken, and white meat has less fat than dark meat.
5. Buy low-fat or nonfat dairy products.
6. Limit egg yolks to four per week.
7. When choosing a butter-like spread, your best bet is diet margarine in a tub, the softer the better.
8. Feature fat-free foods in your diet. You will find them among plant foods, including grains, fruits, vegetables, beans.
9. Be aware that "fat-free" foods can by law contain some fat (less than 1 gram per serving).
10. Look for low-fat items in food categories. For instance, some cookies low in fat are graham crackers, fruit cookies (Fig Newtons), and vanilla wafers.

RULES FOR VEGETARIANS

Vegetarians are not all alike. Their vegetarian motives differ—from love of animals to environmentalism to a desire for better health. And they range from semi-vegetarians, who merely refrain from eating red meat (at least some of the time) to vegans who eat no animal products, including eggs and dairy products. ("Ethical vegans" also use no leather, soap made of animal fat, or other animal products.)

A vegetarian diet is not a sure ticket to health. After all, potato chips contain no meat, nor do candy bars. Vegetarians, like everyone else, should limit the fat and sugar in their diets.

	Semi-vegetarians	Ovo-lacto vegetarians	Vegans
Diet	Avoid red meat, but may eat a little.	Eat no meat, poultry, or fish, but do eat dairy products and eggs.	Eat no animal products at all, including no eggs, and no dairy products.
Advantages	May lessen risk of heart disease and some cancers.	May lessen risk of heart disease and some cancers.	Less risk for some cancers, heart disease, adult-onset diabetes, obesity. NOTE: This is a naturally low-fat diet, and a greater proportion of vegans do not smoke or drink.
Risks	Iron deficiency, perhaps low intake of zinc.	Iron deficiency, perhaps low intake of zinc. Too much fat from dairy products.	Iron deficiency, low intake of zinc. Possible deficiencies of calcium and vitamins B^{12}, B^6, riboflavin, and D. Short on good-quality proteins. Tendency for babies to be born with low birth weight. Children can be vitamin-deficient. Not enough calories for pregnant women.
What to add	To increase iron intake, eat foods like fish, poultry, tofu, beans, and iron-fortified cereal. Use cast-iron pots, especially for cooking acidic foods. Eat food rich in C to increase iron absorption. Pregnant women: ask physician about an iron supplement. For zinc: shellfish, seeds and nuts, legumes, tofu, fortified cereal. Watch intake of fat.	To increase iron intake, eat foods like tofu, beans, and iron-fortified cereal. Use cast-iron pots, especially for cooking acidic foods. Eat food rich in C to increase iron absorption. Pregnant women: ask physician about an iron supplement. For zinc: nuts and seeds, legumes, tofu, fortified cereal. Watch intake of fat. Eat low-fat rather than high-fat dairy products. Consume no more than 3 or 4 egg yolks a week.	Ask a nutritionist about your diet. You may need more protein, iron, and other nutrients. Perhaps you should eat fortified foods and take supplements. Be especially careful if you are pregnant, breast-feeding, convalescent. Child vegetarians have special needs. For calcium: beans, dried figs, broccoli, dark leafy greens, tofu, and fortified cereals. For iron: dark green vegetables, dried fruit, seeds, dried beans, fortified foods—and eat these with food rich in vitamin C.

How to Read a Meat Label

The Food and Drug Administration regulates labeling of meat, but there's a catch—such labeling is voluntary. If you are concerned about fat content, buy meat labeled "select" (by grade) and "extra lean." When you want a specific cut, look for meat labeled "light" and "lower fat," which, believe it or not, actually must mean something.

Grade. The degree to which the meat is marbled with fat determines its grade. The fattiest meat is *prime*, the next fattiest is *choice*, and the leanest is *select*.

Other Terms: Meat must have at least 25 percent less fat than regular cuts to be labeled *light, lite, leaner,* and *lower fat.*

If no more than 10 percent of the meat is fat, it can be labeled *lean* and *low fat.*

If no more than 5 percent of the meat is fat, it can be labeled *extra lean.*

However, ground beef can be labeled either *lean* or *extra lean* when it has no more than 22.5 percent of fat, by weight.

Vitamins: Should You Stick with the RDA?

Tricky business, vitamins. One of us once tried to cross-reference the vitamins recommended by a famous 1960s diet guru only to find that using optimum levels of two vitamins canceled out the benefits of a third. Our suspicions about the intricacy of vitamin relations were confirmed by several scientific studies—for instance a study showing that consuming more than 15 milligrams of zinc a day can cause a deficiency in copper.

Should you take vitamin and mineral pills? To avoid deficiencies you may not have to—if you eat right, are healthy, not dieting, not pregnant. Conservative medical specialists advise against taking extra vitamins and suggest the following. If you feel compelled to take a vitamin:

♦ Make it a multivitamin and/or mineral pill.

Don't take separate specific vitamins (like B-complex) unless your doctor recommends them.

♦ Don't take a vitamin preparation that includes more than 100 to 150 percent of RDA (Recommended Daily Allowance). Vitamins in doses over the RDA can be toxic, especially those that are fat-soluble (A, D, E, and K).

♦ Look for equal proportions of vitamins and minerals according to RDA. That is, if a vitamin capsule contains 100 percent of the RDA for vitamin A, it should contain 100 percent of the RDA for B_{12}—not 500 percent.

On the other side of the vitamin-mineral debate are medical experts who recommend large *therapeutic* doses of vitamins—not to prevent deficiency, but to ward off disease. For example, they say that antioxidants in vitamins may thwart free radicals, reactive oxygen molecules implicated in diseases like cancer, rheumatoid arthritis, and cardiovascular disease. Beta-carotene, which converts to vitamin A in the body but tends not to be toxic, is a hot new contender for the role of free-radical battler.

Some recommendations that neither side would argue with are:

♦ Vitamins in foods: After foods are harvested, they start to lose their nutrient values, so buy fresh, locally grown vegetables and fruits. Barring that, buy them frozen or canned. Produce that has traveled long distances or spent too much time in the supermarket tends to have *fewer* nutrients than canned or frozen fruits and vegetables, which ordinarily are processed right after they are picked.

♦ Don't overcook your food.

♦ Don't duplicate vitamins you are getting in fortified cereals or other food sources.

♦ Avoid taking antacids with calcium in combination with calcium supplements.

♦ Tetracycline (an antibiotic) and iron supplements will cancel each other out unless you take the iron three hours before or two hours after the tetracycline.

♦ Take the average for your recommended intake of a vitamin or mineral over a three-day period. You don't have to ingest each vitamin up to the maximum every day.

♦ Remember that it is far easier to overdose on fat-soluble vitamins (A and D). If you want to increase your intake of A, eat vegetables and fruits high in beta-carotene, which converts to A in the body if needed.

RDAs (Recommended Daily Allowances) of Vitamins and Minerals

A panel of scientists and nutritionists at the National Academy of Sciences meets about every five years to decide amounts of 26 vitamins and minerals Americans need. Needs vary, of course, according to gender and age. Pregnant and nursing women's needs are higher than average. The panel usually chooses to publicize the amount needed by teenaged boys.

To make it more difficult to understand, recommendations about vitamin intake, sometimes doses are given in milligrams (mg., 1/1000th of a gram), sometimes in micrograms (mcg., 1/1,000,000th of a gram), and sometimes in International Units (IU). And to *further* compound the problem, there is no standard equivalency between milligrams and International Units. For example, for beta-carotene, 1 mg. equals 1667 IU. However, with some forms of vitamin E, 1 mg. equals 1 IU. Go figure!

YOU MIGHT NEED TO TAKE EXTRA VITAMINS AND OR MINERALS IF YOU ARE . . .

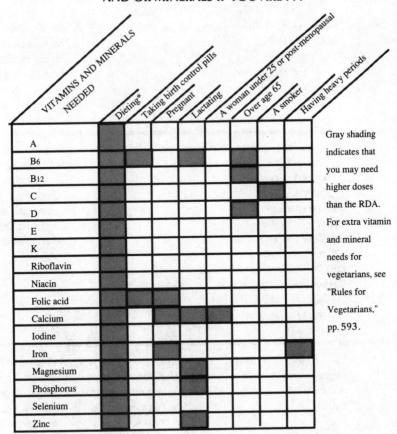

VITAMINS AND MINERALS NEEDED	Dieting*	Taking birth control pills	Pregnant	Lactating	A woman under 25 or post-menopausal	Over age 65	A smoker	Having heavy periods
A	■							
B6	■	■		■	■			
B12	■					■		
C							■	
D					■			
E								
K	■							
Riboflavin	■							
Niacin	■							
Folic acid	■	■	■					
Calcium		■	■	■	■			
Iodine	■							
Iron	■							■
Magnesium				■				
Phosphorus								
Selenium				■				
Zinc	■							

Gray shading indicates that you may need higher doses than the RDA. For extra vitamin and mineral needs for vegetarians, see "Rules for Vegetarians," pp. 593.

*Taking in less than 1500 calories a day

VITAMINS AND MINERALS

Vitamin or mineral	RDA	"Optimum levels"	Health benefits	Effects of overdose
A	1000 mcg. RE (retinol equivalents) or 4000 IU	No more than 10,000 IU.	Help keep hair, skin, eyes, nails, and immune system in good condition; prevent night blindness; may reduce risk of various cancers, heart disease, stroke, cataracts, macular degeneration.	Nausea, headache, lethargy, blurry vision, hair loss, skin peeling, vomiting. Spleen enlargement and damage to liver and bones over long term. Harm to fetal development.
Beta-carotene	None	15–30 mg. or 6000-20,000 IU (Jeffrey Blumberg, Tufts University antioxidant researcher).		Skin might turn orange, but this effect is harmless. Heavy drinkers who take beta-carotene supplements may develop liver damage. Perhaps lowers effects of vitamin E.
B^3 niacin	20 mg.	To lower cholesterol, niacinamide is prescribed in doses of 1–3 grams. (Don't take without medical advice.) Symptoms of overdose can appear at 100 mg. According to the Council for Responsible Nutrition, 500 mg. should be maximum daily dose in supplements.	Prevents pellagra; possibly works against cancer.	Jaundice and liver damage. Flushing, headache, nausea, cramps, diarrhea. High blood sugar. Can make asthma and ulcers worse. Can cause deficiency of other vitamins.
B^6 pyridoxine	2 mg.	50–150 mg. (to relieve carpal tunnel syndrome and PMS). Overdose: 500 mg.	Aids in prevention of anemia, skin conditions, damage to nervous system; may protect against neural-tube defects (in fetuses).	Problems walking; pain or numbness in extremities; depression; headaches; tiredness; nerve damage. Can cause deficiency of other vitamins.

Vitamin or mineral	RDA	"Optimum levels"	Health benefits	Effects of overdose
B^{12} cobalamin	2 mcg.	Be careful not to take over the RDA because it is stored in the body.	Aids in prevention of pernicious anemia, helps build and maintain cells; may be effective in prevention of heart disease, nerve damage, fetal neural-tube defects.	None known (at doses up to 100 mcg.)
C	60 mg.	250–1000 mg. (Jeffrey Blumberg, Tufts University antioxidant researcher). Other researchers say that any dose over 500 mg. can cause problems.	Prevents scurvy and promotes tooth and gum health, lessens hemorrhage, helps the body to absorb iron and to heal wounds; may lessen risk of heart disease, cancer, cataracts, macular degeneration, birth defects, colds, lung problems caused by pollution.	Megadose of over 500 mg. daily with estrogen may cause breakthrough bleeding. 1000 mg. may cause diarrhea and distort medical test results. Acetaminophen (Tylenol) with over-RDA amounts of C can damage liver and kidneys. Digestive problems possible. "Rebound scurvy" from overdosing and suddenly stopping.
D	400 IU	1000 IU and over may be dangerous.	Needed for bones and teeth, function of nerves and muscles, blood clotting; prevents rickets; may prevent osteoporosis, kidney disease, and cancer.	Weight loss, anorexia, constipation, nausea, irritability and weakness, kidney stones, elevated calcium levels causing calcium deposits in heart and arteries, high blood pressure, kidney damage, cardiovascular problems.
E	20 mg.	400 IU with d alpha tocopherol on label (Jeffrey Blumberg, Tufts University antioxidant researcher); 400 IU (Mohsen Meydani, USDA researcher). 100 IU okay according to University of California at Berkeley Wellness Letter.	Aids in prevention of retrolental fibroplasia, anemia; may lessen risk of heart problems, cancer, lung damage, cataracts, spinal cord damage in cystic fibrosis patients; helps prevent muscle aches; may slow macular degeneration and effects of Parkinson's disease; reduces hot flashes, strengthens immunity in elderly.	No known effect except may change effectiveness of anti-clotting medications. Don't take with anti-coagulants.

VITAMINS AND MINERALS (cont.)

Vitamin or mineral	RDA	"Optimum levels"	Health benefits	Effects of overdose
Folic acid	400 mcg.	400 mcg. for women of childbearing age.	Important in formation of blood cells, metabolism of proteins, division of cells; aids in preventing cervical dysplasia; may reduce risk of cancer and heart disease, nerve damage, neural-tube defects and anencephaly; helps conception.	Overdose: kidney damage, enlargement of organs. Can mask symptoms of pernicious anemia.
Iron	18 mg.	Most people excrete excess iron, but some are genetically predisposed to store it.	Helps form red blood cells, carries oxygen, prevents anemia; may help insomniacs to sleep, improve mental function.	Diarrhea, constipation, diabetes. Liver damage, impaired immunity. Can interfere with absorption of zinc. Too much iron in blood may contribute to heart disease. An intake of 300 mg. can be toxic for children weighing 20–30 pounds.
Zinc	15 mg.	None	Helps in digestion, metabolism, protein formation; important in fetal development; has effect on immune system, sense of taste, healing of wounds; deficiency may affect memory and mental performance.	Digestive problems like nausea, vomiting, diarrhea. Too much zinc can interfere with copper absorption.
Calcium	1000 mg.	Up to 2500 mg. is considered safe.	Bone development, prevention of osteoporosis, perhaps hypertension.	Lethargy, muscle pain and weakness, excessive thirst and dehydration, nausea, constipation, confusion, abdominal pain, kidney stones.

Sources for Vitamins and Minerals

Vitamin A: Fish oil and fish liver, dairy products, egg yolks, dark green leafy vegetables, yellow and orange vegetables and fruits (yellow winter squash, carrots, sweet potatoes, cantaloupe, apricots, mangoes).

Vitamin B_1: Whole grains, pork, beans, liver, enriched flour.

Vitamin B_2 (Riboflavin): Dairy products, whole grains, liver, meat, poultry, fish, dark green vegetables.

Niacin (Vitamin B_3): Meat, poultry, seafood, whole grains, legumes.

Vitamin B_6: Liver, fish, chicken, eggs, nuts and seeds, whole grains, bananas, watermelon, potatoes with skins on, soybeans.

Vitamin B_{12}: Meats, poultry, dairy products, eggs, liver, fish and shellfish, nutritional yeast.

Vitamin C: Citrus fruits, bell peppers, green leafy vegetables, broccoli, sweet potatoes, snow peas, tomatoes, potatoes, kiwi fruit, strawberries, papaya.

Vitamin D: Sunlight, fatty fish, egg yolks, liver, fortified milk.

Vitamin E: Vegetable oils and fish liver oil, wheat germ, seeds, nuts, olives, egg yolks, asparagus, green leafy vegetables.

Folic acid: Asparagus, green leafy vegetables, liver, black-eyed peas, pinto beans, brewer's yeast, lima beans, broccoli.

Vitamin K: Leafy vegetables, corn and soybean oils, liver, whole grains, dairy products, meats, fruits.

Iron: Liver, beef, clams, oysters, beans, parsley, spinach.

Zinc: Meats, especially liver; turkey; beans; wheat germ.

Calcium: Dairy products, tofu, broccoli.

Contaminants in Food

You won't find it in the headlines, but unsafe handling of food at *home* is responsible for 30 percent of food-borne illness. Opportunistic bugs with fancy names team up with unsafe food handling to lay us low with diarrhea, stomach cramps, vomiting. Food-borne diarrhea costs the U.S. economy somewhere between $1 and $10 billion a year. Salmonella sickens 2.5 million of us every year. Most food-borne illnesses won't kill us and don't last very long, except if we are very young, very old, already ill, or have a damaged immune system. But fun they are not.

The main organisms that cause food-borne illness include seven bacteria (*Campylobacter jejuni, Salmonella, Staphylococcus aureus, Clostridium perfringens, Vibrio vulnificus, Listeria monocytogenes,* and *Shigella*), two protozoa (*Giardia lamblia* and *Entamoeba histolytica*), and a virus (hepatitis A). They live in meat, poultry, raw seafood, dairy products, coconut, fresh pasta, spices, chocolate products, seafood, salads, desserts made with milk products, and vegetables grown in soil fertilized with contaminated manure.

Of all the foods, poultry has the greatest incidence of contamination—60 percent or more of raw poultry carries some bad bacteria.

How to foil the little monsters?

♦ At the supermarket, pick up packaged and canned foods before fresh and frozen foods.

♦ Examine containers and reject cans that are bulging or dented, jars that are cracked or have loose or bulging lids.

♦ Never buy outdated food. Check expiration and "sell by" (or "use by") dates.

♦ Don't eat raw milk, cheese, or shellfish if you have a health problem, especially one that may have impaired your immune system. You might want to avoid these products in any case.

♦ Buy only refrigerated eggs marked Grade A or better. Check to make sure no eggs in the carton are cracked or leaking.

♦ Buy meat, poultry, fish, frozen foods, and other perishables last. Put in separate plastic bags.

♦ Look for cleanliness at the salad bar and fish counter. Beware if you see cooked shrimp in the same bed of ice as raw fish—they could become contaminated.

AMERICA'S FAVORITE REMEDY—CHICKEN SOUP

Mom was right—chicken soup actually works in alleviating the symptoms of a cold, specifically by helping to release virus-laden fluids from nasal passages. It's not just the heat that causes this beneficial runny nose. A recent study showed that chicken soup was more effective than plain hot water, even when sipped through a straw. The cold-fighting hero may be arginine, an amino acid found in chicken. Here's one recipe:

Chicken Soup

1 frying chicken (all except giblets)

For broth:
2 stalks of celery
1 brown onion, cut up, skin still on
1 carrot, cut into chunks
5 parsley stalks
1 bay leaf
½ teaspoon dried thyme
5–6 peppercorns
salt to taste

For soup:
½ cup white rice
1 onion or leek, sliced or chopped
1 celery stalk, chopped
1 carrot, chopped
2 tablespoons chopped parsley
½ teaspoon dried thyme
salt to taste
juice of ½ lemon or splash of white wine
½ cup frozen peas

1. Wash a frying chicken (whole or cut up), and put it in a large pot with water to cover. Add ingredients for broth. Simmer until chicken is done.

2. Take chicken from pot, let cool, then remove skin, bones, and fat. Set chicken meat aside. Put skin, bones, and fat back into the pot of broth and cook for another hour, then strain, discarding cooked vegetables and herbs. Cool, put in refrigerator, and remove fat after it congeals.

3. Add rice and onion (or leek) and cook for 5 minutes, then add celery, carrots, parsley, thyme, and any other vegetables and seasonings you like and cook about 10 minutes. Add lemon juice or wine, and cook 5 more minutes. At the last minute, add frozen peas and cut-up chicken meat.

♦ Buy shellfish only from markets that buy from state-approved sources.

♦ If it will be more than an hour before you get home, put frozen and perishable foods in an ice chest.

♦ Refrigerate or freeze perishable foods right away—fresh meat, vegetables, dairy products, mayonnaise, catsup. Check labels for storage advice. Throw out items that you neglect to refrigerate. Keep your refrigerator at 40° Fahrenheit, freezer at 0° Fahrenheit. Check them often to see that proper temperatures are maintained.

♦ Make sure juices from meat and poultry don't contaminate other foods in your refrigerator.

♦ Store eggs in their carton in the refrigerator, not in the door.

♦ Don't crowd the refrigerator or freezer, and throw out spoiled food often, especially food that has molded.

♦ Don't store foods under the sink or near household cleaning products and chemicals.

♦ Put older cans to the front when storing canned goods so you will use them first. Don't use canned food that is sticky on the outside.

♦ Don't leave hot or cold foods standing at room temperature for too long. Keep foods meant to be hot, hot, and foods meant to be cold, cold.

♦ Cook eggs until yolk begins to harden and white is firm.

♦ Cook seafood thoroughly. (See "Cooking Meat, Poultry, and Fish," p. 616.) Eat cooked seafood right away.

♦ Cook hot dogs to 160°F. for several minutes. Never eat them raw.

♦ Don't leave cooked foods standing out for more than two hours. Store in refrigerator in small packages. Store stuffing separately.

♦ Use leftovers within three days.

♦ Don't thaw frozen foods at room temperature. Thaw in the refrigerator or microwave, defrost in cold water, or cook frozen.

♦ Never taste food that you suspect is spoiled or is from damaged, bulging, or leaky cans.

♦ Reheat foods until they reach a temperature of at least 165° Fahrenheit.

♦ Thoroughly clean cooking utensils and cutting boards every time you use them to prepare a food that may be contaminated, especially poultry. Don't cut up vegetables on a cutting board that has been used for preparing meat unless you wash it first. Bacteria contaminate wooden cutting boards less than plastic ones, but no matter what kind you use, you should always wash it with soap and water afterward.

♦ Wash your hands before starting to cook and after you handle raw meat or poultry. Don't cook if you have an infected cut.

♦ Keep the blade of the can opener clean. Take apart and clean food processors and meat grinders right after you use them.

♦ Don't put cooked meat on an unwashed plate that held raw meat.

♦ Wash fruits and vegetables in water.

USDA Hotline: 800-535-4555; 202-690-1622 in Washington, DC.

Buying Fish and Meat

Sushi Lover? Be Careful

According to the FDA, the newsworthy notion that seafood is unsafe is untrue. It is much riskier to eat chicken. Proof? The incidence of illness from eating chicken is one for every 25,000 servings, but for seafood, it is one in 250,000 servings. If raw shellfish is eliminated, seafood causes only one illness per 1 million servings. Still, the

FDA urges extreme care when eating *raw* fish. Sushi may be contaminated with larvae of parasites like tapeworms, flukes, and roundworms, which, however, can be killed by freezing. One of every 1000–2000 servings of raw mollusks (oysters, clams, mussels) makes somebody sick. If you must eat raw shellfish, do it in the cold months. The old rule about eating shellfish only in months with the letter *r* has merit, though some *r* months may still be unsafe. Shellfish also can pick up pathogens from polluted water, including hepatitis A. And two diseases caused by toxins—paralytic shellfish poisoning (PSP) and neurotoxic shellfish poisoning (NSP)—are caused by eating shellfish that have fed in "bloomed" ("red tide") water. The illness in humans comes from eating the plankton (dinoflagellates) in the shellfish. Some fin fish can be the cause of ciguatera poisoning, also caused by plankton.

How to eat seafood, which not only tastes good but is nutritious and low in fat and calories? First of all, always buy any kind of fish from a reputable dealer; beware of roadside stands. If you fish for sport, don't eat fish caught in contaminated waters. In tropical climates, avoid reef fish (barracuda and grouper, for example).

No matter what kind of fish you buy, choose smaller, younger fish. Always trim off skin, dark meat, belly flap. Avoid eating fatty parts, the green "tomalley" in lobsters, and the "mustard" in crabs. Pregnant women should avoid swordfish, which is known for accumulating methylmercury.

Cook fish until it flakes with a fork and has gone opaque. Cook oysters and clams by putting them in boiling water and then, after water boils again, cooking for four to six minutes. If you steam them, steam for six to eight minutes. Never eat shellfish if their shells remain closed after cooking.

Meat, Poultry, Fish: How to Tell If It is Fresh

If it smells bad, meat is obviously not good to eat. But what of more subtle ways to tell if meat and fish are fresh? Is green-tinged aged beef "off"? What about that open clam—is it just taking a breather? Here are some guidelines to help you choose the freshest meat and fish.

Fish. As with lovers, eyes tell all, some say. When fish eyes are fresh and bulging (except for naturally cloudy-eyed walleye pike), the fish is fresh. Flesh should be firm, skin and flesh should shine, reflecting light. Brown marks may indicate age, red marks indicate bruising. Only whole fish should be covered in ice. Smell fish after it has been rinsed. If you notice an ammonia smell or a fishy smell, reject it.

Shellfish. Shells should be closed or should shut when you tap them. Otherwise look for movement: steamer clam necks should twitch when you tap the shell, crabs should quiver if you touch them, and lobsters should curve their tails under their bodies when you pick them up. Scallops should be translucent. All live mollusks should be refrigerated, not kept in water. Shrimp should be headless.

Storing fish. Don't keep unfrozen fish for more than two days before eating it. And it is better to eat tuna, bluefish, mahi-mahi, and other fish prone to scromboid poisoning within one day of buying it. Rinse fish under cold water and dry before refrigerating. Refrigerate fish at 32–37°F. This includes live shellfish. Keep moist but do not store in water or in airtight packages. Thaw frozen fish in the refrigerator.

Meat. Rely on the "sell by" dates on the packages at the market. Ground beef sometimes looks brownish on the inside, but is perfectly good. Oxygen reacting with myglobin (a meat protein) and iron gives the meat the red color.

Wrapping the meat in plastic film reduces the amount of oxygen. The meat on the inside has the least amount of oxygen and therefore turns brown. Aged meat is more tender. Montana State University recommends that packers age carcasses in a cooler for eight to 10 days to improve flavor and make the meat more tender. But rely on your nose—if meat *smells* bad, it *is* bad.

HONEY IN INFANT FOOD—NO!

Spores of *Clostridium botulinum* present in honey can cause infant botulism, which often leads to paralysis. The intestines of older children and adults have bacteria that kill the organism, but infants' intestines do not. Don't feed honey to a child less than one year old.

CHINESE RESTAURANT SYNDROME

MSG (monosodium glutamate), found in Accent, Ve-Tsin, Ajinomoto, and Mejing, is the suspected culprit in Chinese Restaurant Syndrome (CRS), also known as Kwok's disease. People with Chinese Restaurant Syndrome suffer from heart palpitations, dizziness, nausea, numbness, muscle pains, headache, sweating. MSG's scientific name is sodium hydrogen L-glutamate, a kind of glutamic acid extracted from proteins. Though glutamates occur naturally in foods, commercial manufacturers make it by fermenting a carbohydrate such as sugar with ammonia or slow-fermenting soybeans.

Worcestershire sauce has MSG, so do fish sauces. You find it in canned foods, bouillon cubes, and Chinese food products. If the phrase *monosodium glutamate* does not appear on a food label, you can still not be sure that it is MSG-free. The following phrases may signal the presence of MSG: hydrolyzed vegetable protein (HVP), hydrolyzed plant protein, sodium caseinate, autolyzed yeast, Kombu extract, natural flavor, flavoring, seasoning. It has been deemed safe by the Food and Drug Administration. Why then CRS? Critics say it is from *overuse* of MSG in Chinese restaurant kitchens. If you ask, kitchens in restaurants will forgo its use. However, the FDA is reexamining its use. If you have had a reaction to MSG, tell the FDA about your symptoms (in detail). Mail a letter to the FDA, 5600 Fishers Lane, Rockville, MD 20857, or call Kenneth D. Fisher, Life Sciences Research Office, 301-530-7030.

FOOD ORGANISMS THAT CAN LAY YOU LOW

Disease and Organism	Source of Illness	Symptoms
Botulism: Botulinum toxin (produced by *Clostridium botulinum* bacteria)	Spores of these bacteria are widespread. But these bacteria produce toxin only in an anerobic (oxygenless) environment of little acidity. Found in a considerable variety of canned foods, such as corn, green beans, soups, beets, asparagus, mushrooms, tuna, and liver paté. Also in luncheon meats, ham, sausage, sttuffed eggplant, lobster, and smoked and salted fish.	Onset: Generally 4–36 hours after eating. Neurotoxic symptoms, including double vision, inability to swallow, speech difficulty, and progressive paralysis of the respiratory system. **Get medical help immediately. Botulism can be fatal.**
Campylo-bacteriosis: *Campylobacter jejuni*	Bacteria on poultry, cattle, and sheep can contaminate meat and milk. Chief food sources: raw poultry, meat, and unpasteurized milk.	Onset: Generally 2–5 days after eating. Diarrhea, abdominal cramping, fever, and sometimes bloody stools. Lasts 7–10 days.
Listeriosis: *Listeria monocytogenes*	Found in soft cheese, hot dogs, unpasteurized milk, imported seafood products, frozen cooked crab meat, cooked shrimp, and cooked surimi (imitation shellfish). The Listeria bacteria resist heat, salt, nitrate, and acidity better than many other microorganisms. They survive and grow at low temperatures.	Onset: From 7–30 days after eating, but most symptoms have been reported 48–72 hours after consumption of contaminated food. Fever, headache, nausea, and vomiting. Primarily affects pregnant women and their fetuses, newborns, the elderly, people with cancer, and those with impaired immune systems. Can cause fetal and infant death.
Perfringens food poisoning: *Clostridium perfringens*	In most instances, caused by failure to keep food hot. A few organisms are present after cooking and multiply to toxic levels during cooling and storage of prepared foods. Meats and meat products are the foods most frequently implicated. These organisms grow better than other bacteria between 120–130°F. So gravies and stuffing must be kept above 140°F.	Onset: Generally 8–12 hours after eating. Abdominal pain and diarrhea, and sometimes nausea and vomiting. Symptoms last a day or less and are usually mild. Can be more serious in older or debilitated people.
Salmonellosis: *Salmonella* bacteria	Raw meats, poultry, milk and other dairy products, shrimp, frog legs, yeast, coconut, pasta, and chocolate are most frequently involved. Wash utensils used in preparing raw poultry in very hot water and soap.	Onset: Generally 6–48 hours after eating. Nausea, abdominal cramps, diarrhea, fever, and headache. All age groups are susceptible, but symptoms are most severe for elderly, infants, and infirm.
Shigellosis (bacillary dysentery): *Shigella* bacteria	Found in milk and dairy products, poultry, and potato salad. Food becomes contaminated when a human carrier does not wash hands and then handles liquid or moist food that is not cooked thoroughly afterwards, Organisms multiply in food left at room temperature.	Onset: 1–7 days after eating. Abdominal cramps, diarrhea, fever, sometimes vomiting, and blood, pus, or mucus in stools.

Source: Food and Drug Administration

COMMON USES OF FOOD ADDITIVES

American food contains more than 2000 additives—preservatives, flavorings, colorants, conditioners, sweeteners, and more. Without them, canned green beans would turn gray, ice cream would suffer from "curdy meltdown," salt would turn to rock. In the modern world, food additives are necessary to preserve food and prolong its shelf life. Some additives may be harmful, particularly to people who suffer from certain conditions. Asthmatics, for instance, may suffer from allergic reactions to sulfites.

Additive Function	Examples*	Foods Where Likely Used
Impart/Maintain Desired Consistency	Alginates, Lecithin, Mono- & Diglycerides, Methyl Cellulose. Carrageenan, Glycerine, Pectin, Guar Gum, Sodium Aluminosilicate	Baked Goods, Cake Mixes, Salad Dressings, Ice Cream, Process Cheese, Coconut, Table Salt, Chocolate
Improve/Maintain Nutritive Value	Vitamins A and D, Thiamine, Niacin, Riboflavin, Pyridoxine, Folic Acid, Ascorbic Acid, Calcium Carbonate, Zinc Oxide, Iron	Flour, Bread, Biscuits, Breakfast Cereals, Pasta, Margarine, Milk, Iodized Salt, Gelatin Desserts
Maintain Palatability and Wholesomeness	Propionic Acid and its Salts, Ascorbic Acid, Butylated Hydroxyanisole (BHA), Butylated Hydroxytoluene (BHT), Benzoates, Sodium Nitrate, Citric Acid	Bread, Cheese, Crackers, Frozen and Dried Fruit, Margarine, Lard, Potato Chips, Cake Mixes, Meat
Produce Light Texture; Control Acidity/Alkalinity	Yeast, Sodium Bicarbonate, Citric Acid, Fumaric Acid, Phosphoric Acid, Lactic Acid, Tartrates	Cakes, Cookies, Quick Breads, Crackers, Butter, Soft Drinks
Enhance Flavor and Impart Desired Color	Cloves, Ginger, Fructose, Aspartame, Saccharin, FD&C Red No. 40, Monosodium Glutamate, Caramel, Annatto, Limonene, Turmeric	Spice Cake, Gingerbread, Soft Drinks, Yogurt, Soup, Confections, Baked Goods, Cheeses, Jams, Gum

* Includes GRAS (generally recognized as safe) and prior sanctioned substances as well as food additives.

Source: Food and Drug Administration

How Long Can You Keep Food?

It's obvious that that unidentifiable moss-covered object in the back of the refrigerator should be thrown out, but what about the other food? Just because a food does not smell foul or look as if it had seen better days does not mean that it is safe to eat.

The chart on the next page offers some general guidelines on food storage. Be more careful in hot weather, when you cannot rely on expiration dates on dairy products and when some foods can spoil in an hour at room temperature. *When in doubt, throw it out!*

Cook food well to kill bacteria, and don't use the same plates for cooked food as raw food. Bring marinades to a boil. Wash vegetables under running water, and scrub melon rind with a mild detergent and rinse well before you cut it. Never refreeze meat thawed on the counter or in the microwave. *Note:* Canned food can be kept for two years or more.

Call: **USDA Meat and Poultry Food Hotline,** 800-535-4555, or **Cornell University Cooperative Extension Food Hotline,** 516-454-0900 (weekdays, 1PM–3PM, EST).

Is Your Drinking Water Safe?

By law, the Environmental Protection Agency has set National Primary Drinking Water Standards for contaminants like lead, sodium, insecticide and herbicide residues, other chemical toxins, minerals, bacteria, and viruses. Within a large safety margin, limits were based on what you can consume over a lifetime without ill effects on your health, given that you consume two liters (a little more than two quarts) of water a day. By law, your water supplier must sample and test your water. If your water does not meet national standards, your supplier must tell you and do something to correct the problem.

The EPA notes that only two substances on the list pose an *immediate* threat to health when found to exceed limits: bacteria and nitrate (a threat to children under a year old). Follow instructions in notices from your water company in cases where these substances exceed limits. Do not boil water with nitrates—this only concentrates them.

If you are worried about your drinking water (and some experts would say that in spite of regulations, you should be worried), have it tested. Call your state or local health department or your state department of environmental quality to get a list of state-certified laboratories in your area. Or call **Clean Water Lead Testing,** 704-251-0518, or **National Testing Laboratories,** 800-458-3330. (See also "Lead Poisoning," p. 30.)

If your water is not safe, consider buying a filtration system. Reverse-osmosis and distilling systems remove lead and nitrates, while carbon filters remove chlorine and odors. Water softeners remove calcium and magnesium, which leave scaly deposits and affect taste. Before buying a water purifying system, write to the **National Sanitation Foundation,** a nonprofit group that certifies filters, for free booklets: NSF, PO Box 130140, Ann Arbor, MI 48113-0140 (313-769-8010).

Bottled water is also regulated by the Food and Drug Administration. Bottles must be labeled truthfully according to type, as defined by the FDA: mineral water, municipal water, distilled water, purified water, spring water, artesian water. Water labeled "flavored" contains mineral, spring, or public-supply water; it can be carbonated and have flavoring additives (natural or artificial). Water labeled "full-flavored" may have sugar and artificial additives. Ceilings set on levels of lead and other substances are even more stringent than those set by the EPA on public water systems. Incidentally, 25 percent of "designer" waters come from municipal water systems.

For information about all drinking water, including bottled water, call the EPA's **Safe Drinking Water Hotline** 800-426-4791, M–F, 9AM–5:30 PM, EST.

FOOD STORAGE CHART

Food	Storage Period	
	In Refrigerator	**In Freezer**
Ground beef	1–2 days	3–4 months
Beef steaks and roasts	2 days	6–12 months
Pork chops	2 days	3–4 months
Ground pork	1 day	1–2 months
Pork roasts	2 days	4–8 months
Lamb chops	2 days	6–9 months
Lunch meat	3–5 days opened, 2 weeks unopened	1–2 months
Sausage	1 day	1 month
Gravy	1 day	3 months
Lean fish		up to 6 months
Fatty fish	1–2 days (at 37°F.)	2–3 months
Shellfish		4 months
Whole chicken, whole turkey	1–2 days	10–12 months
Chicken parts, giblets	1–2 days	3–4 months
Soft cheese	1 week	Can be frozen
Hard cheese	6 months	
Milk	1 week after "sell by" date	1 month
Butter and margarine	1 month after "sell by" date	Can be frozen
Yogurt	7–10 days	
Fresh eggs in shell	3–4 weeks	Don't freeze
Hard-boiled eggs	1 week	

Food	Storage Period	
	In Refrigerator	**In Freezer**
Berries, cherries	1–2 days	12 months
Apples	1–3 weeks	NA
Corn (in husk)	1–2 days	NA
Spinach	3–5 days	8–12 months
Peas (unshelled)	3–5 days	NA
Celery	1–2 weeks	NA
Citrus fruit	1 week	12 months (juice)
Peaches, pears	1 week	12 months
Tomatoes	1–2 days	8–12 months
Lettuce	5 days	NA
Beans	1–5 days	8–12 months
Carrots	1–2 weeks	8–12 months
Onions	3–4 weeks	NA
Mayonnaise (commercial) and vinegar-based salad dressings; catsup	No more than 6 months—throw out when they smell "off" and the color darkens	NA
Applesauce	2 weeks	NA
Spaghetti sauce	1 week to 10 days, capped	NA

Flatulence

"Beans, beans, the musical fruit"—intestinal gas is a folklore joke, but not to people who are afflicted with it. And beans are not the only culprit. Others include high-fiber cereals, bran, and whole grains. Surprisingly some intestinal tracts react gassily to white-wheat-flour products such as bagels, pasta, pretzels, and pastries as well as to oats, potatoes, and corn. Only rice seems safe from gas-producing problems. Most animal-derived foods—meat, fish, poultry, and eggs—aren't problems, or they're associated with "normal" levels of flatulence. The one exception to this rule is milk. The carbohydrate (sugar) in milk is lactose. Some people's bodies don't have the enzyme lactase, which is needed to break apart and absorb lactose.

Gas results when carbohydrates (sugar and starches) and fiber get as far as the large intestine without being digested or absorbed. The source of gas in beans (and in other vegetables and grains) is the family of raffinose sugars. No one has the enzyme (alpha-galactosidase) to break them down. When those raffinose sugars reach the large intestine, bacteria have a feast. As the bacteria eat the sugars, they give off as by-products hydrogen, carbon dioxide, and, in some people, methane.

Gas-producers in the plant kingdom:

Vegetables: cabbage, brussels sprouts, onions, turnips, radishes, eggplant, celery, avocados, beans, broccoli, cauliflower, corn, cucumbers, peas, peppers, and radishes.

Fruits: apples and apple juice, melons, raisins, and prune juice.

"Remedies"

Ineffective: simethicone, prokinetic agents (to move things through the innards faster), activated charcoal, antibiotics, and carminatives like peppermint oil.

Effective:

1. An elimination diet. Experiment by cutting out suspect foods for a while, then reintroducing them one by one.

2. Beano (on anecdotal, not laboratory, evidence). An enzyme product (alpha-galactosidase), which reduces excessive gas in the large intestine by breaking down gas-producing sugars

FLATULENCE LEVELS OF 10 POPULAR BEANS

Nutritionists recommend beans as a low-fat source of proteins, carbohydrates, vitamins, and fiber. The problem? Because they are high in nonabsorbable carbohydrates, they can cause flatulence about 4 hours after eating. This means pain to you, offense to those around you. If you have this problem, the following list, by Dr. Louis B. Rockland of the Western Regional Research Laboratory of the U.S. Department of Agriculture in Berkeley, California, might help you to make choices. It is arranged in order of most to least (soybeans cause the most flatulence).

Note: Garbanzos and blackeyes are not really beans but are included because most people think they *are* beans, and they do cause gas.

1. Soybeans
2. Pink beans
3. Black beans
4. Pinto beans
5. California small white beans
6. Great northern beans
7. Lima beans (baby)
8. Garbanzos
9. Lima beans (large)
10. Blackeyes

Not tested by Rockland but a wise choice are small, red-brown Abasazi beans. Joseph Maga, Ph.D., director of the food research and development center at Colorado State University, recently analyzed the beans. He found that they contain less than 25 percent of the gas-causing sugars of pinto beans but about the same nutritional value as pinto beans. Fat content? 1 percent.

in the colon. Available at health food stores. Take a few drops with first bite of food. For a free sample call 800-257-8650 weekdays, 8:30 AM–9:30 PM, EST.

3. For lactose intolerance: over-the-counter lactase, which you add to milk or eat before consuming dairy products.

Tips on Avoiding Flatulence

♦ If you have trouble digesting milk, try a lactose-reduced brand.

♦ If beans are a new diet addition, start by choosing small amounts of more easily digestible types (lentils, limas, split peas) and then gradually increase intake. Soybeans are among the worst gas offenders.

♦ To break down starch troublemakers, rinse beans and discard the water, then cover them with boiling water and let them soak for at least four hours. Discard the soaking water and add fresh water for cooking. Cook beans until soft. (Red beans are toxic unless cooked on the boil for several minutes.) Tofu (soybean curd) is less likely to be a problem than plain soybeans. And soybeans cooked with an equal amount of rice have only two-thirds the flatulence potential of solo soybeans. Tempeh and fermented black beans are easily digested.

♦ Try canned beans instead of dried, but drain and rinse them before using them in a dish.

♦ Cooking makes the starches and proteins in beans more digestible. Try soaking them, discarding the water, then cooking them to a boil for five minutes in 2 inches of water, discarding the water, rinsing them, then covering them with more water for final cooking. Why does this work? The liquid in which the beans are soaked, cooked, or canned becomes loaded with raffinose sugars. Eliminating those sugars helps to solve the problem. Try cooking beans with garlic and the Mexican herb epazote.

♦ Some people have excess gas because they swallow too much air. Gum-chewers take note. It may help to eat slowly, chew with your mouth closed, and avoid gulping food. Limit intake of carbonated beverages and don't drink out of a bottle (it promotes air swallowing.)

♦ Eat only small amounts of beans and gas-causing vegetables at any one sitting. Don't mix the two in the same meal or recipe.

♦ Increase fiber intake slowly.

♦ Avoid stress.

♦ Read labels and steer clear of products that list fructose and sorbitol as major ingredients.

♦ You should not stop eating gassy foods entirely, because you would become nutrient-starved. Besides, it is not practical.

Cooking

Cooking Schools

There are many good reasons to go to cooking school—to learn an art, to pick up tricks that will make cooking easier, to save money by making your favorite complicated dishes at home. You should have no trouble finding a good cooking school. Supermarkets run excellent ones, as do community colleges. Television stations often offer cooking series by famous cooks.

No matter what your choice, make sure that the school will give you what you want—techniques, specialty cooking, demonstrations by master chefs, hands-on experience. If you want to get your hands into the cooking, you will be disappointed by a class that features a demonstration by a famous cook and a no-touch policy toward student participation. Here is a short list of schools:

Foreign

La Varenne, Château du Fey, Villecien, Joigny 89300, France (800-537-6485). One-week summer series and one-week *grand luxe* gastronomic course in fall.

L'école de Gastronomie Française Ritz-Escoffier, Hotel Ritz, 15 Place Vendôme, 75001 Paris, France (800-966-5758). Short-term courses in French and English.

Le Cordon Bleu, Paris, France (800-457-

CHEF in the United States; 011-48-56-0606, calling U.S. to Paris). Courses include one-day workshop, three-day Gourmet Sessions, 55-week Classic Cycle.

Marcella Hazan, Venice, Italy; Hazan Classics, PO Box 285, Circleville, NY 10919 (914-692-7104). Five-day classes, spring and fall, master classes in Northern Italian cuisine, long waiting list.

United States

Peter Kump's New York Cooking School, 307 East 92nd Street, New York NY 10128 (800-522-4610; in New York, 212-410-4610).

Taste of the Mountains Cooking School, Box 240, Glen, NH 03838 (800-548-8007). Weekend and five-day courses specializing in healthful cuisine.

Captiva Cooking School, Plantation Resort & Yacht Harbour, Box 194, Captiva, FL 33924 (800-237-3102). Four-day courses in seafood cooking.

Great Chefs at the Mondavi Winery, Box 106, Oakville, CA 94562 (707-944-2866). Two- and three-day cooking demonstrations, specializing in international cuisine.

The Natural Gourmet Cookery School, Institute for Food and Health, 48 West 21st Street, 2nd Floor, New York, NY 10010 (212-645-5170). Classes in low-fat, flavorful, healthful national and international cuisine.

Cooking with Steven Raichlen, Snowvillage Inn, Snowville, NH 03849 (603-447-2818). Hands-on and demonstration classes in country cooking and low-fat international cuisine.

Channel Bass Inn, Chincoteague Island, VA 23336 (804-336-6148). Three-day classes in cooking sauces, soufflés, seafood, vegetables, desserts.

Jane Butel's Southwestern Cooking School, 800 Rio Grande NW, Suite 14, Albuquerque NM 87104 (800-473-8226). Weekend and five-day classes in New Mexican and Southwestern cooking.

Buy the *Guide to Cooking Schools*, which lists the nearly 200 institutions in the U.S., or write to the **International Association of Cooking Schools,** 1001 Connecticut Avenue NW, Washington, DC 20036, for a listing of schools in your area.

Fruits and Vegetables: How to Choose Them

Generally speaking, look for fruits and vegetables that are beautiful—bright-colored and unwithered—and yield slightly when pressed. However, don't be fooled by bright colors—highly colored fruit can still be "green." Some fruits, especially peaches and nectarines, are picked so underripe that they never will ripen, but will slowly rot from within. You can tell these fruits by their rock-hardness.

Refrigerate vegetables—except for garlic, tomatoes, potatoes, sweet potatoes, and winter squash. Most fruit should be kept at room temperature for maximum flavor and aroma.

Apples: Don't buy apples that are bruised or shriveled. For eating out of the hand: Delicious, McIntosh, Granny Smith, Jonathan, Winesap. For cooking: Gravenstein, Jonathan, Delicious, Granny Smith, and other tart, dense apples. Store in the refrigerator in a plastic bag.

Apricots: Never buy green ones. Look for velvety skin.

SINKIES, FAST FOOD AS HIGH ART

❝Sinkies swallow everything but their pride,❞ is one slogan for the Sinkies, members of the International Association of People Who Dine Over the Sink. Another is "I am at your disposal." The club was founded by Norm Hankoff in 1991, as he stood over the kitchen sink wolfing tuna salad with ruffled potato chip spoons. "The Official Sinkies Don't Cook Book" contains "recipes" like meat loaf in your fist, cakeless frosting, curry in a hurry, and hash in a flash. You can join or send your recipes to the group. Part of the profits go to organizations devoted to eliminating world hunger. Contact: **Sinkie World Headquarters/N.H. Associates,** 1579 Farmers Lane, No. 252, Santa Rosa, CA 95405.

Artichokes: Choose a good artichoke at the market. It should squeak when squeezed, feel heavy in your hand, have fleshy leaves, and look fresh. Brown or purple coloration near the base of the leaves, which indicates that the artichoke has been touched by frost, marks a prize—such artichokes are sweeter and tastier. Trim the stem and thorns from outer leaves.

Asparagus: Choose fresh asparagus, without woody pores at the end of the stalk and with tight scales at the bud end. Break each stalk where it "wants" to break to eliminate tough ends.

Avocados: Press lightly with your thumb at the stem end. If the rind gives a little, the fruit is ripe. If the rind is hard and has sunken spots, it's over the hill. Avocados will ripen at room temperature in a closed paper bag.

Beans (green or snap): Buy crisp beans—you should be able to hear them break if you bend them. Don't buy bumpy beans—they will be tough.

Bananas: Partially green fruit will ripen at room temperature. After it is ripe you can store it in the refrigerator, in spite of what Chiquita Banana used to say.

Blueberries: Look for a white bloom on the skin.

Broccoli: Choose broccoli that is dark green, with tight buds, and firm, blemish-free stems.

Cabbage: Heads should be firm, solid, and heavy.

Carrots: Medium-sized are best. Don't buy hairy carrots or carrots with shriveled ends.

Cherries: Look for glossy, brightly colored fruit with stems that are bright green and attached. Don't buy cherries that have brown spots or are shriveled.

Citrus fruit: Pick up citrus and feel its heaviness in your hand—the heavier, the juicier. Choose fruit with thin, smooth, flexible peels. Pointed fruit tends to have thick peels.

Corn: Freshness counts with corn, so buy it from a vendor who guarantees that it is picked the day it is sold. Ears should have fresh-looking green husks with young but plump and developed kernels. Silk should be shiny and yellow. If you can't use corn right away (what a pity!), husk it, wrap each ear in plastic and store in the refrigerator.

Cucumbers: Yellow on the skin indicates overripeness, except in Kirby's cucumbers. Look for firmness and a svelte look—fat cucumbers are not as good as medium or skinny ones.

Eggplant: A shiny skin and green cap means eggplant is fresh. The lighter in weight, the fewer seeds.

Melons: Sniff the melon for ripeness. It should smell rich and fruity. Press the stem end—it should give a little. If the melon feels heavy in your hand for its size, it is probably ripe. For watermelons: Thump to see if it sounds hollow, a sign—not infallible—of ripeness; look for a yellowish patch (not dead white) on the bottom. For canteloupes: choose those with an underlying creamy color. Honeydews should give slightly when pressed on the blossom end.

Peaches and nectarines: Don't buy green-tinged fruit. To ripen peaches, store them in a paper bag that is closed loosely.

MUSHROOMS AND OTHER EXOTIC FUNGI

Used to be you bought white or brown mushrooms, and that was all there was. But now, in almost any supermarket, a gallery of mushrooms delights your eye and perhaps later your palate.

Oyster. Almost no calories and subtle flavor. Delicious with cream or in puff pastries, or in light sauces, or raw in salads.

Morel. Appears after forest fires. Wonderful with veal.

Shiitake. Strong and delicious, with woodsy, meaty flavor, somewhat spongy in texture. Contains a compound called lentinan that fights viruses. May be effective against cancers and may lower cholesterol. Cook in soups, sauces, stir-fries.

Crimini. The "poor man's shiitake," but not really so cheap. Meaty flavor and firm texture. Use in any mushroom recipe calling for white buttons.

Chanterelle. Grows in the Northwest. Woodsy and fruity with firm texture. Sauté and serve with meats or cook in pasta sauces.

Enoki. Wonderful raw, in salads.

Wood ear. High in protein and tastes like meat.

Peppers: Look for bright, waxy skins. Wrinkles mean old age, as does softness.

Pineapples: Smell them at the stem end for ripeness. Heft them in your hand—they should feel heavy. The rind should be tinged with orange. Also pull one of the leaves away from the fruit—it should come off easily. The leaves should be green and fresh-looking. Don't buy bruised fruit or fruit that has soft, moist spots.

Raspberries: Look carefully for mold, and do not buy berries in boxes that have stains (an indication that the berries may be overripe).

Strawberries: They should be red all over, with no green or white parts. Check the carton to make sure that berries packed on the bottom are not green. Look for mold.

Summer squash: Buy shiny-skinned squash less than 7 inches long. Press on the ends—if ends are soft, they are probably too old.

Tomatoes: Tomatoes should be bright red and yield to slight pressure, but should not be too soft. Buy vine-ripened ones. To ripen tomatoes, cover them with a cloth and keep at room temperature.

Note: To ripen unripe fruits and vegetables, put in a paper bag, close up and keep in warm place for a couple of days. This will not work with strawberries, which do not ripen once picked.

Glossary of Cooking Terms and a Few Tips

Al dente ("to the tooth"): Cooked until tender but not mushy—used for pasta, vegetables.

Baste: Spoon juices, fat, or marinade over food as it cooks.

Baton: A cut for a vegetable—3 × ⅜ × ⅜ inches.

Blanch: Precook for a short time in boiling water.

Bouquet garni: Seasoning (parsley, thyme, celery leaves, bay leaf, etc.) tied in a bundle and tossed into various dishes like soups and stews.

Braise: Brown food in a little fat, then add liquid and cook slowly, usually covered. Best for tougher cuts of meat that need moist cooking—brisket, chuck or round steak, lamb and veal shanks.

Broiling, grilling: Direct intense heat used to quick-cook food. In broiling, the heat comes from above, in grilling, from below. Preheat: wait 15 minutes for gas or electric heat or until coals are covered with white ash for charcoal. Never add extra lighter fluid after the fire has started. Good for steaks, chops, poultry pieces; flattened birds or butterflied lamb, fish steaks and fillets; vegetables.

Broth: Liquid in which meat or vegetables were cooked.

Chiffonade: Green leaves cut into thin strips. Tip: roll them up and slice.

Coulis: Purée (e.g., tomato or red pepper or raspberry) used as a sauce.

Dash: Small amount, determined by taste. Start with a pinch (what you can hold between thumb and forefinger).

Deglaze: Use a bit of water, wine, or other liquid and stir to loosen bits of food and other residues left in the pan after cooking. Basis for a sauce after degreasing.

Degrease: Take fat off pan or cooking liquid. More easily done if food is cold, when fat congeals and can easily be lifted off the liquid. To hasten the process throw ice cubes into a small amount of hot sauce or put it into refrigerator. Several gadgets capitalizing on the fact that fat rises to the top can be used for hot liquids.

Dredge: Lightly coat food by dipping it into flour or crumbs. Can be done by putting food and dredging material into a paper bag and shaking it.

Duxelles: Minced mushrooms and shallots (shallots are optional) cooked down to make mushroom essence for flavoring dishes.

Emulsify: Combine ingredients that usually don't mix well by adding one to the other gradually, constantly mixing. For vinaigrette, first mix acid (vinegar or lemon) with mustard, then slowly pour oil into it while beating constantly.

Fold: Gently mix ingredients, usually with a spatula, by bringing the mixture up from bottom and turning it over.

Fricassee: Cook meat, cut up into pieces, with vegetables in liquid.

Fry: Quick-cook in hot fat—½ to 1 inch deep for shallow frying, several inches deep for deep-frying. Food should keep sizzling. Coatings (bread crumbs, batter, flour and egg) keep food crunchy, prevent overcooking, and seal in moisture. Don't crowd the pan. Temperature: 360°–365°. Thermometer is helpful. Good for all foods recommended for stir-frying, and also for fritters and croquettes.

Gratin: Crust formed when foods are topped with grated cheese or bread crumbs and baked.

Julienne: A cut for a vegetable—about 1¼ × ⅛ × ⅛ inches (matchstick).

Jus (juice): Natural juices of meat, made by deglazing the pan.

Marinate: Combine foods with other ingredients to add flavor and tenderize before cooking or serving. Example of a marinade: olive oil, wine, dry herbs, garlic.

Mince: Chop fine.

Mirepoix: Onion, carrots, and celery, diced, cooked, and used as flavoring. Can also include other ingredients like salt meats and herbs.

Parboil: Precook food by boiling.

Purée: Mash until smooth. Can be done in food mill, blender, food processor.

Reduce: Boil liquid ingredients until concentrated.

Roast: Use dry heat to cook uncovered food on a spit or in the oven. Preheat oven for 15–20 minutes. Best for large and tender cuts of meat—rib roast, pork loin, leg of lamb, whole poultry, whole fish.

Roux: Equal amounts of flour and fat cooked together and used to thicken sauces and other liquids.

Sauté (or panfry): Quick-cook in small amount of fat over high heat. Good for small or flat food pieces. Use a heavy pan. Make sure fat is hot before putting food in, and don't overcrowd the pan. After food is cooked, deglaze the pan to make sauce. Good for cut-up food—

vegetables, tender cuts of meat like chicken, steaks, chops, scallops, small fish, fish fillets, scallops and shrimp.

Scald: Heat a liquid just to the edge of boiling.

Sear: Brown the outside of a food.

Simmer: Cook in liquid just under the boil (tiny bubbles, very little movement of the water).

Steam: Cook with steam from boiling liquid trapped in a closed container. The food should not touch the water. Good for low-calorie cooking of chicken breasts (boneless), filleted fish, shellfish, most vegetables.

Steep: Keep food sitting in hot liquids.

Stir-fry: Quick-cook food with high heat in small amount of fat by tossing it. Use a wok or heavy skillet. Add foods that need longest cooking first, and make sure all pieces are the same size. Good for same foods as sautéing, except food should be cut small.

Stock: Liquid made from bones, vegetables, flavorings cooked in water.

Truss: Tie up a chicken or turkey so that it is more compact. Look at the bird from breast side. Put wing tips under the bird, tie legs together with kitchen string. Some turkeys

TRUSSED BIRD

From the top: Put legs under band of skin or tie together. Sew up body cavity with a large-eyed needle and string.

From underneath: Tuck wings under bird and sew up neck cavity.

come with a band of skin under which you can tuck the legs.

Velouté: A sauce or soup made with broth thickened with egg yolks, cream, and butter.

Zest: Colored part (not the bitter white pith) of citrus rind.

Cooking Tips

Bacon slices won't separate: Refrigerate rolled into a tube secured with rubber bands.

Baking powder too old: To tell if it is still active, mix 1 teaspoon in 1 cup of hot water. Watch for lots of bubbles, which are clues that it is still good.

Beets, peeling: Cook for 15 minutes, cool under running water, cut off ends. Peel will slip off. Or cook until done, then peel.

Browning food: Use hot pan and do not crowd it.

Brussels sprouts, onions. Cut a cross in the bottom end before cooking.

Celery, limp: Put in ice water; or stand, bottom down like a bunch of flowers, in a pitcher partly filled with water.

Cheese, cooking: Use a low temperature for short time—otherwise you have a stringy, rubbery mess. Melt cheese over simmering water in double boiler.

Cooking smells: Simmer several whole cloves in vinegared water. Or put ground coffee into a frying pan and heat it up. For cruciferous vegetables (broccoli, cauliflower, brussels sprouts), throw a piece of rye bread into the pot.

Crystallized honey or syrup: Heat it up in pan of hot water or put in microwave (without metal cap) for a few minutes.

Dough stuck to rolling pin: Put it in the freezer.

Eggs—are they fresh? Put eggs in a pan of water. Those that float are not fresh.

Fish, smelly: If poaching, add celery. If baking, turn the heat down.

Fruit and vegetable discoloration: To prevent discoloration of cut apples, avocados, bananas, peaches, and other fruits, sprinkle on some lemon juice. Red cabbage: 1 tablespoon of vinegar in cooking water.

Garlic, peeling: Bang with the flat edge of a large heavy knife. The skin should come off easily, and the garlic will be not so difficult to chop or mince.

Meringue: Before putting in egg whites, wipe the bowl with a small amount of white vinegar. Make sure the egg whites have begun to foam before adding sugar.

Olives, pitting: Roll with rolling pin on paper towel, then hit with the heel of your hand.

Onions, cooking: Sprinkle with a little sugar for better flavoring and browning.

Pasta: Put a bit of oil in the cooking water to keep pasta from sticking together. Drain well. Toss with a little oil or sauce immediately.

Peppers (bell), roasting: Roast over a gas flame on end of fork or broil on foil-lined baking sheet or grill. Make sure the pepper is blackened everywhere. Wrap in foil or plastic bag until cool and peel.

Prunes, raisins, and currants: Plump them before adding to your recipe by covering them with boiling water and letting them stand for 5 minutes. Drain. Or, put in microwavable dish, add an equal amount of water, and microwave on HIGH until boiling, 1–3 minutes for ½ cup or 3–5 minutes for 1 cup. Drain. To keep fruit from settling at the bottom of cakes or breads, coat it with flour first (put fruit and some flour in a paper bag, close the bag, and shake).

String beans, stringing: Plunge them in boiling water for a few minutes before stringing.

Tomatoes, peeling: Immerse them for 30 to 60 seconds in boiling water, remove, rinse under cold water. Skin should slip off. Other fruits that peel more easily if dipped in hot water: grapefruit, oranges, lemons, peaches.

Winter squash, cutting: Cook for 2 minutes on HIGH in a microwave oven, let stand for 2 minutes. Cutting up the hard squash will be much easier.

Correcting Cooking Mistakes

If you didn't learn how to correct cooking mistakes from your mother, you may be at a loss. Cookbooks rarely help—they assume you follow directions and get it right. Here are some tips from the experts.

Bread too soft to slice: Freeze it and slice it frozen.

Bread stale: Sprinkle it with a small amount of water, put it in foil, and bake in an oven at moderate heat for about 10 minutes.

Cake stuck to pan: Let it sit until it is a little cooler, then try again. If it is already cold, reheat it for a minute or two.

Cheese tough or rubbery after cooking: Blend in a blender or food processor at low speed for a minute or two, then cook slowly.

Coffee or broth cloudy: Add eggshells.

Coffee overcooked: Add a pinch of salt.

Custard or pudding curdled: Put 1 tablespoon of the pudding or custard and 1 tablespoon milk in a bowl. Beat the mixture until it is creamy. Add another tablespoon of pudding or custard and beat until creamy. Keep doing this until you have used up all the pudding or custard.

Dough is lumpy: Add more liquid and pound the dough into submission.

Dough won't rise: Put the bowl of dough in a warmer place—for instance, an oven with a pilot light (don't turn the oven on). Or mix a bit more yeast in ¼ cup warm water and knead into the dough.

Dough won't shape: Let it rest for 15 minutes.

Eggs crack when cooking: Put in 1 teaspoon of salt or a bit of lemon or vinegar into the water to keep whites from oozing out of the shell.

Egg whites won't whip: Add a bit of baking soda or salt.

Fudge hard: Add a tablespoon of milk and 2–3 tablespoons of corn syrup and beat, then pour. Put in an airtight container for 24 hours.

Gelatin stuck in mold: Dip the mold in hot water, but not so the gelatin is touched by the water—just for a few seconds. Put the mold on a plate, turn it upside down and shake.

Gravy gray: Add red currant jelly, soy sauce, a bit of sherry, meat extract, or 1 teaspoon instant coffee.

Gravy lumpy: Beat it with eggbeater or wire whisk. Strain it.

Gravy salty: Make more. Sometimes adding a bit of brown sugar helps. Cook small pieces of potato in the gravy.

Gravy or sauce fatty: Skim fat off top. If the fat is not readily accessible, chill, skim the fat, and reheat.

Ham salty: Soak slices in milk for 15 minutes to a half-hour. Wash off.

Icing sugared: Add a bit of vinegar and keep cooking.

Lemon hard: Heat it for 5 minutes in boiling water or for 15 seconds in a microwave on HIGH, then try juicing it.

Main course burned: Take it off the heat, then fill the sink partially with cold water so you can set the pan in it without flooding it. Put the pan of burned food in the water to cool. Lift out whatever is loose and put in another pan. If the saved food tastes burned, cover it with a damp cloth and set aside for a half-hour. Meanwhile make a highly spiced sauce and use it to disguise the food.

Meat burned: Cut off burned parts, cube and sauce the rest. Serve over pasta.

Pasta stuck together: Put back in boiling water with a tablespoon or so of oil in it.

Pie dough burning on edge: Cover edge with aluminum foil.

Popcorn won't pop: Soak corn in water for 5 minutes, dry off and try again. For very recalcitrant corn, freeze overnight and pop while frozen.

Rice burned: Get it off the flame, then put a piece of bread on top of it, cover for 5 minutes.

Sauce curdled: When sauces like hollandaise or mayonnaise separate into an ugly mess, keep them warm, then beat them a spoonful at a time into a bit of warm water or a beaten egg yolk. Reheat gently. For curdled hollandaise drop an ice cube or tablespoon of cold water into it and stir. To save a curdled mayonnaise, beat an egg yolk and a little mustard, then dribble in the mayonnaise.

Scummy stock: Add leek tops and tomato peels, which absorb the scum.

Soup too salty: Slice in a potato, simmer until potato turns translucent, then lift potato out. Or add a pinch or two of brown sugar, a splash of fortified wine, or a can of tomatoes and simmer 10 minutes.

Stew meat tough: If you haven't time to let the stew continue cooking under gentle heat, add a few tomatoes or a teaspoon of sugar to tenderize it.

Vegetables old: To pep them up, add a pinch or two of sugar and a little salt to the cooking water.

Vegetables overcooked: Purée them. Or make a cream soup of them. Or put them in an oven-safe dish, cover them with bread crumbs and grated Parmesan cheese, and broil for a couple of minutes.

Vegetables too salty: Pour the water out, rinse them off, return them to the stove in new water. If they are already done, wash in hot water.

Whipping cream won't whip: Chill everything (cream, bowl, beaters) and try again. If that fails, add an unbeaten egg white or 3–4 drops of lemon juice and whip like mad.

THE TOP 10 CAMPBELL'S SOUPS

Chances are you have fond childhood memories of Campbell's chicken noodle or tomato soup. Campbell's was the soup your mother brought you when you were sick in bed and put in front of you when you came home from school for lunch. And we're willing to bet that you have in your back pocket a fall-back recipe using a Campbell's cream soup for a dip or casserole. The top 10 Campbell's soups, in terms of numbers of cans eaten, are: chicken noodle, cream of mushroom, tomato, cream of chicken, vegetable beef, chicken with rice, cream of broccoli, vegetable, cream of celery, vegetarian vegetable.

Cooking Meat, Poultry, and Fish

Timing counts when cooking meat, poultry, and fish. And the timing differs according to the cut of the meat as well as its size.

Fish: The "10-minute rule": Measure the fish's thickness where it is thickest, and tuck thin ends under. Cook 10 minutes for each inch of thickness. Fish a half-inch thick, for instance, should cook 5 minutes. If fish is frozen, double the cooking time; if you wrap it in foil or cover it with sauce, add 5 more minutes. Turn the fish over halfway through cooking time. If it is less than a half-inch thick, don't turn it. For baking, set the oven temperature at 400°–450° and broil the fish 5 inches from the heat source. How to tell if it is done? Flake it with a fork—if it is not opaque inside or fails to flake, it needs more cooking. If you use a thermometer, internal temperature should be 145°.

For shellfish, simmer shrimp 3 to 5 minutes or steam 10–15 minutes or sauté 5 to 10 minutes—until flesh turns white-pink and is opaque. Cook shellfish until shells open (5 to 10 minutes).

Microwave: Put in dish with thicker parts to outside edge, cut skin of whole fish. Cover with microwavable plastic wrap vented by turning a corner back. Cook on HIGH for 3–6 minutes a pound. Rotate halfway through cooking. Take fish out when it *almost* flakes, then let it sit, covered, for a minute more.

Beef roasts: Braise tougher cuts; roast or grill more tender cuts. Place roasts in a 325-degree oven. Roasting time will depend on the size of the roast and whether you prefer it rare or medium (see chart).

On a meat thermometer, meat is rare at 140°F. and medium at 160°F. Temperature is measured by inserting the meat thermometer in the thickest part of the roast, not touching bone or fat. Roast in the oven until the meat registers 5–10 degrees below desired final temperature, then remove from oven. Cooking times are based on meat taken directly from the refrigerator.

Pork: Parasites are killed at 137°F. For medium doneness, 160°F., for well done, 170°F.

Weight (in pounds)	Degree of doneness	Minutes per pound
4 to 6	Rare	26 to 30
	Medium	34 to 38
6 to 8	Rare	23 to 25
	Medium	27 to 30
8 to 10	Rare	19 to 21
	Medium	23 to 25

Source: National Live Stock Board

Turkey: If the turkey is frozen, thaw it in the refrigerator in its wrapper 5 hours for each pound; or cover it with cold water, changing the water every half-hour, for one half-hour per pound. Wash the turkey inside and out and dry. Never leave it at room temperature. Thermometer-test for doneness: thrust thermometer into

USDA ROASTING TIMETABLE FOR TURKEY AT 325°F

Weight (in pounds)	Hours (unstuffed)	Hours (stuffed)
6 to 8	2¼ to 3¼	3 to 3½
8 to 12	3 to 4	3½ to 4½
12 to 16	3½ to 4½	4½ to 5½
16 to 20	4 to 5	5½ to 6½
20 to 24	4½ to 5½	6½ to 7
24 to 28	5 to 6½	7 to 8½

Source: U.S. Department of Agriculture

the thickest part of the thigh—it's done if the temperature is 180° to 185°F. Other tests: Pinch the thigh at the fleshy part to see if it is soft; wiggle the leg to see if it moves easily at the hip; pierce inner thigh to see if the juices run clear.

Turkey Hotlines: Weekday, office-hour hotlines except weekend before Thanksgiving and Thanksgiving Day.

USDA Meat and Poultry Hotlines: 800-535-4555.

Butterball Turkey Talk-Line: 800-323-4848; TTY 800-TDD-3848. Weekdays, early November through December 23.

CARVING MEAT

Traditionally assigned to "the man of the house," who may not have been endowed with much talent for the job, meat carving demands a sharp knife, skill in using it, and knowledge of the anatomy of the piece of meat.

To carve, cut a slice off one end, stand the roast on that end, and slice across the top with a sharp knife, holding the roast in place with a meat fork. Hold the knife as an extension of your arm, and let it work for you, sliding through the grain of the meat. Use your fork to lay the slice across the knife.

CARCINOGENS

Contrary to what you might think, most cancer-causing agents in food are natural ingredients—nitrosamines in dairy products and mushrooms, benzopyrenes in vegetables and grains. You can't avoid them.

You can, however, avoid other carcinogens, like those that form when you grill meats. Some experts recommend that you microwave meats for a couple of minutes before you grill them—this releases the chemical that makes the carcinogens.

CARVING A BIRD

Give the turkey 20–30 minutes of rest after it comes out of the oven, then begin carving. Use a sharp carving knife and a fork with long tines. Work first on one side of the bird, then the other. Cut the leg off at the thigh joint first, pulling the leg away from the body and slicing down through skin. Cut the bone off at the joint.

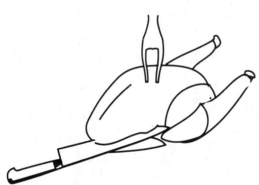

Holding the bird steady with the fork, make a cut parallel to the wing all the way to the ribs. This is the stopping point for each breast slice you will now cut.

Make thin, even slices of the breast down to the parallel cut. Carve leg and thigh separately, cutting with the grain of the meat.

Reynolds Turkey Information Line: 800-745-4000. Operates 24 hours, seven days a week in November. How to defrost turkey and roast in cooking bag or foil.

Chicken: Follow the chart for cooking times. If the chicken is stuffed, add 15–20 minutes to the roasting time. Let chicken rest for 15–20 minutes after taking it out of the oven.

ROASTING TIMETABLE FOR CHICKEN

Weight (in pounds)	Sear at 400°F. (in minutes)	Then roast at 325 °F.
2 to 2½	20	30 to 40 minutes
3 to 3½	25	40 to 50 minutes
4	30	50 to 60 minutes
5	30	1 to 1¼ hours
6	30	1¼ to 1½ hours
7	30	1½ to 2 hours
8	30	2 to 2½ hours

Cooking Rice

For best results, follow package directions. Otherwise, use this easy method. Combine 1 cup rice, liquid (see chart), 1 teaspoon salt (optional), and 1 tablespoon butter or margarine (optional) in 2- to 3-quart saucepan. Heat to boiling; stir once or twice. Lower heat to simmer; cover with tight-fitting lid. Cook according to time specified on chart. If rice is not quite tender or liquid is not absorbed, replace lid and cook 2 to 4 minutes longer. Fluff with fork.

Microwave Oven Instructions: Combine 1 cup rice, liquid (see chart), 1 teaspoon salt (optional), and 1 tablespoon butter or margarine (optional) in

2- to 3-quart deep microwavable baking dish. Cover and cook on HIGH (maximum power) 5 minutes or until boiling. Reduce setting to medium (50% power) and cook 15 minutes (20 minutes for parboiled rice and 30 minutes for brown rice). Fluff with fork.

COOKING RICE

1 Cup uncooked rice	Liquid	Cooking time
Regular-milled long grain	1¾ to 2 cups	15 minutes
Regular-milled medium or short grain	1½ to 1¾ cups	15 minutes
Brown	2 to 2½ cups	45 to 50 minutes
Parboiled	2 to 2½ cups	20 to 25 minutes
Precooked, flavored, or seasoned mixes	Follow package directions	

Source: USA Rice Council

POP! POP!

The average American eats about 48 quarts of popcorn a year. A high-fiber food, it is also nonfattening (27 calories a popped cup), if you don't add too much fat to it. Popcorn packaged for the microwave, though, often contains enough oil to take popcorn out of the healthful category.

To make popcorn, use an air popper, or pop in a heavy pan with a very small amount of oil. Keep the lid on but open it a crack occasionally during the popping to let out moist air. Dress it with a bit of grated Parmesan cheese or eat it plain. Don't oversalt it.

STRANGE GRAINS?

Rice, wheat, and potatoes are not the only starches to serve at dinner. According to the Center for Science in the Public Interest, nutritionally speaking, the 10 top grains are: quinoa, amaranth, buckwheat groats, bulgur, barley, wild rice, millet, brown rice, triticale, and wheat berries.

Cooking the Perfect Egg

Artists praise the egg's perfect shape. Nutritionists praise the egg as a perfect food (except for its cholesterol). It deserves perfect cooking, doesn't it?

Hard Boiled Eggs

The trick? Don't boil eggs too hard or they turn out to be tough. Prick a little hole in the large end of each shell, going through the shell and membrane into the egg a fraction of an inch. Otherwise the air bubble at the large end will expand with heat and possibly crack the shell.

Two cooking methods:

♦ Simmering. Lower the eggs (no more than a dozen) gently into boiling water, then wait until the water returns to a simmer, lowering the heat to keep the water at a simmer. Cook eggs 12–13 minutes if they were chilled, a minute or two less if they were at room temperature.

♦ Coddling. Put chilled eggs in cold water, 6 cups for one to four eggs and another cup for each additional egg. Bring the water to a boil, then turn off the heat and cover the pan. In 17–18 minutes, the eggs will be done.

To prevent a dark ring between yolk and white (a harmless chemical reaction), chill the cooked eggs in a pan of ice cubes and water.

Peeling the eggs: Crack the shell all over with gentle tapping. Peel from the large end under running cold water. If the egg won't peel well, drop the eggs three at a time into boiling water for 10 seconds, then put them back in the ice water.

Always refrigerate hard-boiled eggs in cold water in an uncovered container.

Poached Eggs

If the egg is very fresh, you can drop it into simmering water. If not, boil the egg in the shell for 10 seconds, then break it into simmering water or use a perforated egg poacher. In any case, water should be an inch deep. Poaching time: 4 minutes.

Scrambled Eggs

Break the eggs (four to six) into a bowl and add a tablespoon of cold water, salt, and pepper. Whip with a fork only until yolks and whites blend. Put a tablespoon of butter in a pan over moderately low heat. When the butter has melted, put most of the egg (all but 2 tablespoons) into the pan and scrape with a spatula over the bottom of the pan, slowly at first, then more quickly, moving the pan on and off the heat to slow cooking. When eggs are done to your liking, fold in the reserved egg.

Frying

Preheat the oven broiler. Put $1/16$ inch of fat (butter, olive oil, bacon grease) in a pan over moderate heat on the stove top until hot, then break the eggs (up to eight) into the pan. Cook until the white has set on the bottom. Baste the eggs with fat, then put the pan under and close to the broiler, moving it in and out, basting all the while, until done.

A Glossary of Greens

The art of mixing a good salad lies in combining textures (the crispness of romaine with the soft-ness of butter lettuce), colors (the red of radicchio and the dark green of watercress), shapes (the round leaves of mache, the tangled leaves of curly endive), flavors (bitterness of endive, pepperiness of arugula, blandness of iceberg, tartness of sorrel). Generally it is wise to start with milder greens (butter lettuce, romaine) and accent them with spicy, bitter, and tart greens. However, it is also possible to make a salad of just one green—endive, iceberg, romaine, spinach—with appropriate accents.

Arugula (rocket, roquette, rugula): Thin leaves with peppery flavor, use sparingly.

Belgian endive (witloof chicory): White, multileaved heads, mild but bitter.

Butter lettuce (and Bibb, Boston, limestone, buttercrunch): Loose-leaved heads, tender texture, and sweet, buttery flavor.

Curly endive (chicory): Curly leaves ranging from dark green to pale green, prickly and bitter taste, to spice up blander greens.

Escarole (broad-leaved endive): Paler and straighter than curly endive, and less bitter, but bitter nonetheless. Use sparingly.

Iceberg lettuce (crisphead): Tight heads, mild flavor, crisp texture.

Mache (lamb's lettuce, corn salad): Dark green, oval leaves with sweet flavor.

Radicchio (red chicory, Italian red lettuce): Red leaves with white veins, good to add color, bitter in flavor.

Red-leaf lettuce or oak-leaf lettuce: Loose-leaf lettuce with ruffled leaves, soft-textured, sweet flavor.

Romaine (Cos): Long, medium to dark green leaves in loose head, crunchy, mild but distinctive flavor.

Salad Bowl: Loose-leaf, curly pale-green leaves, soft and delicate in flavor.

Sorrel (dock): Long, dark green leaves with lemony, tart flavor. Good as accent.

Spinach: Dark green leaves, coarse texture, distinctive flavor.

Watercress: Round, very dark green leaves, with sharp flavor, good to spice up a salad.

Drying and Preparing Greens

Dry leaves after washing them and roll them in paper towels, then put in plastic bags, or roll them in terry cloth towels. You can also dry them in a plastic salad spinner. (Metal baskets bruise lettuce.) Tear into bite-sized pieces.

Dressing

Choose dressings to suit greens. Iceberg holds up under rich, creamy dressings like Thousand Island. Romaine goes well with a citrus vinaigrette. Boston lettuce (and others like it) need mild vinaigrettes. Bitter lettuces mix well with sweetish dressings such as sherry vinaigrette. Peppery lettuces like arugula and watercress are piqued by vinaigrettes of lemon or balsamic vinegar.

Vinaigrette: For strong red and white vinegars, use 1 part vinegar to 4 parts of oil (to begin); for aged balsamic and sherry wine vinegars, 1 part vinegar to 3 parts oil. Add more vinegar if needed. *Tip:* Mix the salt and vinegar, then beat in the oil bit by bit. (Oil won't dissolve salt, vinegar will.)

All About Olive Oil

Choosing olive oil can seem almost as complicated as choosing wine. It varies in flavor, color, and quality. The type of olive used makes a difference, as does the method of extracting the oil. To be sure that olive oil is not too old, buy it in a store that has a good turnover of olive oil. Put it

OLIVE OIL VOCABULARY

Oil	Acidity	Flavor	Use
Extra-virgin, unrefined, cold-pressed, drawn from first pressings. High quality.	Low: no more than 1 gram of oleic-free fatty acid for each 100 grams of oil.	Flavorful; greenish colors tend to be peppery; yellow colors tend to be nutty.	As condiment, flavoring; flavor breaks down when heated. Try sautéing with half olive oil, half butter. Or cook food in another oil and add a splash of olive oil at the last minute.
Virgin, unrefined. Usually combined with refined olive oil.	Amount of oleic-free fatty acid ranges from more than 1 gram to less than 3.3 grams for each 100 grams of oil.	May have some flavor imperfections. Otherwise tastes like extra-virgin olive oil.	Rarely sold alone.
"Pure" or plain refined. A combination of virgin olive oil and less high quality refined olive oil. Low cost.	Contains less than 1.5 grams of oleic acid for each 100 grams of oil.	Mild flavor.	Good for salads and dishes with other strong flavors. Can be used in high-heat cooking.
Light or extra-light.	Lighter in color, neutral in flavor, not lighter in calories.	Mild flavor.	Use in place of vegetable oil or melted butter for baking.

in a glass or pottery jar and keep it in a cool, dark place, and it will last for one to two years. Throw away old and rancid olive oil.

According to Michele Anna Jordan, author of *The Good Cook's Book of Oil and Vinegar,* you can test for virginity in olive oil by putting a drop of the oil in a glass container and putting it in the refrigerator for a few days. If it crystallizes, it's really virgin; if it clumps, it probably contains some oil that was chemically refined.

Microwaves

By microwaving rather than using a conventional stove, you often save cooking time and the mess of dirty pots. Microwaves cook by causing food molecules to vibrate so that friction creates heat. Food cooks from outside in.

Some general rules: Always remove store wraps from food before putting it in the microwave. Never put anything metallic in the oven, including foil. Use only microwave-safe cooking utensils. Plastic containers may be unsafe because chemicals from them can leach into food.

Allow the food to stand for one-third of the original cooking time once it is out of the microwave—it will keep on cooking. This equalizes temperature in the food and raises internal temperatures, which kill bacteria. Contrary to modern folklore, letting the food stand does not let

THE FATS IN YOUR OIL AND BUTTER

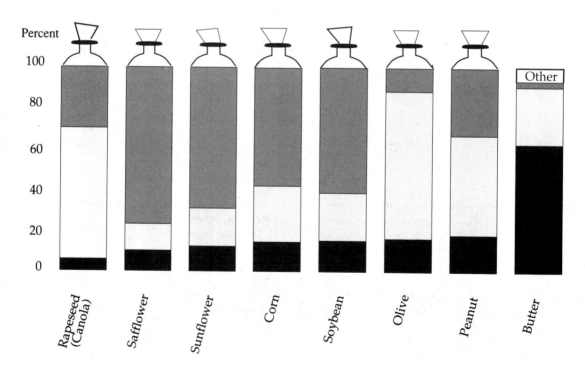

Saturated
Monounsaturated
Polyunsaturated

out the microwaves—there were none in the food to begin with. The food should be slightly underdone as it leaves the microwave because it will keep on cooking. A baked potato, for instance, should give a bit on the outside but still be firm on the inside as it leaves the microwave. Tent or cover food during standing time and make sure the containers rest on a flat, solid surface. Some examples of cooking and standing times:

MICROWAVE COOKING AND STANDING TIMES

Food	Cooking time in microwave	Standing time
Fish (1 pound)	2½ to 5 minutes	2 minutes
Two potatoes	8 minutes	5 minutes
Two ears of corn on the cob (husk and wrap with microwavable plastic wrap)	5 to 6 minutes	2 to 3 minutes
Carrots (thin sliced)	4 to 5 minutes	1 minute

Defrosting in a microwave: Put the food in microwave-safe dish, and follow the oven manual for times and power levels. Turn and rearrange food during defrosting, taking foods out as they defrost. Cook food right away after defrosting.

Cooking: Cut food into uniform sizes, and if you can't, arrange food in the dish so that thick parts are toward the outside. Cover the dish with lid or plastic wrap, turned back at one corner. Wrap should not touch the food. Rotate the dish halfway through cooking, stir the food, rearrange it, turn big items over.

Danger! Don't cook in the microwave:
♦ Large pieces of meat or thick pieces of meat with bones—they won't cook evenly.

CHECKING MICROWAVE SAFETY

To check the output efficiency and for possible radiation leakage in a microwave oven more than 15 years old, put an 8-ounce cup of water in the microwave, turn on HIGH for three minutes. If the water has not reached a rolling boil by then, get your oven checked out. (If your oven has less than 600–1000 watts, you may need to give it more time to reach a rolling boil.)

Other signs of problems: a flashing LED sign, strange noises, poor heating, electrical arcing, lights dimming when microwave is in use.

Do not try to repair the oven by yourself.

MICROWAVE DISH TEST

Put a glass measuring cup holding 4 ounces of water in the oven; put the dish you want to test near the cup but not touching it. Set microwave on HIGH for one minute. At that point, the water in the cup should be at least warm. If the dish being tested is cool to lukewarm, it is safe to use for microwave cooking. If it is hot, it has absorbed microwaves and is not safe. Generally, you can microwave in ovenproof glass, Pyroceram, porcelain (not trimmed with metal), paper (except for foods that have high sugar or fat content), glazed pottery and stoneware.

♦ Fried foods—the fat may catch on fire.
♦ Anything on recycled paper towels or plates—flecks of metal in the paper may cause a fire.
♦ Popcorn in a bag unless it's a commercially packaged brand—again, a possibility of fire, so use a microwavable plastic popper.
♦ Eggs in the shell—they'll explode.

Failures in the microwave: Homemade pies will end up with raw crust. Breaded and batter-dipped food will be soggy unless specifically packaged for microwaving. Steak will steam. Yeast bread will cook unevenly, and the crust will be pale and sodden.

Herbs and Spices

Herb aficionados like to describe their favorites in the way that wine-lovers describe fine wines. To some experts, chervil, for instance, has a "hint of pear." Perhaps taste is the most difficult of all senses to describe in words. Could we be so bold as to say that chervil tastes of chervil, as a wine-taster we once knew described a fine wine as tasting of grapes?

To learn the tastes of herbs and spices, try a tiny leaf or seed, crush and smell it, chew it, and imagine it in various foods. And if your culinary imagination comes up with nothing interesting, fall back on our handy chart—a list of herbs and spices with the foods that they are compatible with.

Many people kill culinary sensibility by their cruel treatment of herbs and spices. The jars are made to sit in the light close to the stove. Some are so old that they've turned gray. The right way? Spices should be stored away from the stove, even in the refrigerator, with containers tightly sealed. Red spices should be refrigerated in air-tight containers to keep them from going brown.

Fresh herbs and spices will keep for two weeks stored in self-sealing plastic bags in the refrigerator. They can also be frozen. More delicate herbs survive better with their stems in water, in the refrigerator. Don't wash herbs until you want to use them. If you buy spices whole, you can grind them as you need them—they will taste fresher.

Throw away old spices from time to time. Don't keep them for more than a year or two. The older the spice, the more you will need, and even then, the only flavor you are likely to get is of dried hay.

When cooking food on top of the stove, use one-quarter teaspoon of herbs and spices for each pound of food to begin with, then add more if needed. Double the amount of fresh herbs in recipes that call for dry ones—except rosemary: use the same amount.

A BASIC LIST OF HERBS AND SPICES

Herb or Spice	Description	Use
Allspice	The dried fruit of a pimento tree, available in whole berries or powdered. Tastes like a combination of cinnamon, clove, nutmeg, and pepper.	Beets, yellow squash, rutabaga, baked goods, oat bran.
Arugula (rocket)	Peppery leaves.	Use in salad, pasta, frittata.
Anise	A strong fruity, licorice taste. You can use both seeds and leaves.	Leaves: salads, fish, poultry. Seeds: baked goods, for example biscotti, Christmas cookies.
Basil	A kind of mint with a sweet but strong and spicy flavor of anise and clove.	Add at the last minute. Used in Mediterranean and Oriental dishes. Try fresh tomatoes dressed with an olive oil and basil dressing. The principal ingredient in pesto, a pasta sauce, and in other tomato-based spaghetti sauces. Try with cucumbers, eggplant, zucchini, summer squash. Garnish for fish.
Bay leaves	The leaves of the sweet bay tree. Needs long simmering except when used for marinades and barbecue.	Simmer in food for a long time. Stews, split-pea soup, spaghetti sauce. Use as flavoring with lemon slices threaded with seafood on kabobs for barbecuing.
Burnet	Delicate plant with compound leaves. Leaves taste of cucumber.	Soups, sauces, egg salad, French dressing.
Borage	Tastes like cucumber.	Eat young leaves in salads. Use blossoms to garnish salads, fruit, summer drinks.
Caraway	Parsley family. Seeds have a pungent flavor.	Seeds in rye bread, leaves in vegetables, meats, fish.
Cardamom	A spicy, sweet taste and aroma. Comes in seeds and pods.	Pickles, winter squash, sweet potatoes, rice, meatballs, Danish pastries, gingerbread.
Chervil	A delicate herb, tastes of parsley and anise, perhaps pear, if you have a discriminating sense of taste.	A gourmet herb that goes well with parsley, chives, and tarragon. Good with chicken, fish, eggs, carrots, mushrooms, avocados, asparagus.
Chili pepper	Any one of a number of hot peppers, some of which are thousands of times hotter than others. Generally, the smaller the pepper, the hotter it is. On the Scoville Heat Unit scale, sweet peppers rank zero, jalapeños rank 2500–5000, habañeros and Bahamian peppers rank 300,000.	Use in chili and salsa, other Mexican food, Oriental dishes.
Chives	A member of the onion family, stronger tasting, slightly bitter.	Add at last minute. Cucumber, baked pototoes, potato salad, eggs, seafood, pasta, omelets, any cheese dish, fish sauces.

A BASIC LIST OF HERBS AND SPICES (cont.)

Herb or Spice	Description	Use
Cilantro	Leaves are used in Oriental and Mexican cooking. Cilantro tastes of sage, citrus, and, some people say, mintiness or mustiness. For seeds, see Coriander.	Add at last minute. Leaves for flavoring corn, tacos, guacamole, chili, salsa, lentil soup, chicken soup, tabouli, Asian noodles and salads. Use with red onion and sliced oranges for salad.
Cinnamon	Comes from the bark of tree, with warm, spicy aroma and taste. You can buy it in sticks or ground.	Breads and other sweet baked goods, Middle Eastern and North African foods, South American foods, barley, oatmeal, chicken.
Cloves	The flower buds of the clove tree, dried and sold ground or whole. Warm, spicy flavor that numbs your tongue.	Beets, poached pears, baked goods.
Coriander	See Cilantro.	Ground seeds in gingerbread, puddings, baked apples; whole seeds in pickles, soup, grog, poached pears.
Cumin	A warm flavor, smells a bit like caraway.	Chilis and curries, North African and Middle Eastern food, Mexican cooking, meat dishes, carrots, eggplant, cabbage, chickpeas, lentils.
Dill	You can flavor with both leaves and seeds. The leaves taste like caraway or anise; the seeds are stronger tasting, slightly bitter.	Add leaves at last minute. Leaves used to flavor cucumbers (in sour cream or low-fat yogurt), poached salmon (dill sauce), chicken, fish salad, salads, pickles, vegetables like summer squash and green beans. Use seeds in breads, potatoes, eggs, chicken, apple pie, pickles.
Fennel	Tastes a bit like anise and licorice. You can eat the seeds or the bulb.	Fresh bulb can be cooked as a vegetable, used raw in salads. Seeds used in breads, sauerkraut.
Ginger	A rhizome, ginger varies according to where it is grown. You can buy it whole, powdered, dried, candied. The taste: hot and spicy.	Broccoli, carrots, Oriental dishes, chicken and duck, beef, oat bran and oatmeal, baked goods.
Mace	The outer covering of the nutmeg fruit, which tastes sharper and stronger than nutmeg itself.	Oatmeal, spinach, rutabaga, sweet potatoes, yams, some baked goods.
Marjoram	Like oregano, but more delicate and sweet.	Add at last minute. Eggplant, tomatoes, zucchini, beans, meats, poultry, eggs. Try in salads, with raw tomatoes. cornbread and risotto, meat loaf, pork chops. Add to vinaigrette.
Mint	Many kinds of mint, with different flavors, but all possessing a sharp flavor and cool aftertaste. Spearmint is more delicate than peppermint. Other flavors: pineapple, lemon, orange, chocolate, apple.	Garnish melon balls. Tabouli, falafel, Indian dishes, curry. In jelly to accompany lamb. Mint juleps, teas.

Herb or Spice	Description	Use
Nutmeg	The seed of an evergreen myrtle tree. Warm and pungent taste.	Asparagus, spinach, winter squash, chicken, baked goods.
Oregano	A kind of mint. Strong smell; warm, sharp flavor, hinting of clove and balsam. Good dried.	Use in Mediterranean and Mexican dishes. Tomatoes, beans, meats, poultry, shellfish, olive spread, vinaigrette salad dressing.
Paprika	A pungent red powder. Two versions: Hungarian (bright red, hot) and Spanish (less red, milder).	Chicken, turkey, game birds, scallops, cauliflower, potatoes.
Parsley	Italian: flat-leafed, good in cooking. Curly-leafed: best fresh chopped for salads and garnish.	Good in almost all main dishes, from soups to stews to steamed vegetables. Add to salads and biscuits. Good breath freshener, eaten raw.
Peppercorns	Pungent seeds of the pepper vine, *Piper nigrum.*	Add to poultry, meats, and stews and cook for a long time. Grind on meats, poultry, seafood, vegetables.
Red pepper	The pungent, hot flavor that hurts so much it is good.	Beef and fish, crab and mussels, turnips, broccoli, okra, pasta.
Saffron	Stigmas of a crocus flower. Aromatic, mineral flavor. Turns food yellow.	Bouillabaisse, paella, buns, biryani, stews with tomatoes, rice.
Rosemary	Tastes like pine.	Tomatoes, zucchini, tuna, lamb, pork, veal. In marinades and added to barbecue coals. Good in stuffing; with potatoes and carrots; Italian dishes.
Sage	Leaf used dried or fresh. A good salt substitute. Warm, spicy flavor.	Eggplant, tomatoes. Turkey stuffing, sausage, pork, veal. French onion soup (a leaf added to broth).
Savory	Dried or fresh leaves. Hints of clove and pepper.	Beans, meatloaf, pork stuffing, cabbage, brussels sprouts, corn.
Sorrel	Tart green, used fresh. A marriage between lemon and spinach.	Raw in salads (with less vinegar or lemon in dressing). In sorrel soup or sorrel sauce for fish. Eggs, vegetables, mayonnaise. Add to spinach.
Spearmint	A sweet, mild mint.	Spicy dishes of Middle East and Asia: dipping sauce, lamb, eggplant. Iced tea, fruit salads.
Tarragon	A leaf that can be used dried or fresh. Spicy, with a taste of licorice and pepper.	With cucumber, in French sauces, eggs, potatoes, sautéed mushrooms, tomato soup, fish, chicken. In mustard, wine vinegar. With beans, carrots, tomato.
Thyme	A leaf that can be used dried or fresh. Spicy, tasting of clove.	Flavor tomatoes, clam chowder, rice, mushrooms. Fresh leaves in cottage cheese. Sauces, soup, stews.
Vanilla	The fruit of a Mexican orchid, sold as an extract or in the pod. Warm, rich, sweet taste, at times with a hint of chocolate.	Put pods in sugar or brandy for flavor. Indispensable in many baked goods.

Basic Pasta Shapes

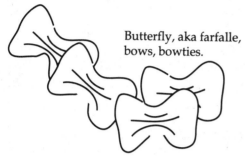

Butterfly, aka farfalle, bows, bowties.

Flat pasta, like linguine, fettuccine, and lasagna.

Medium-sized tubes, which come as elbow macaroni, ziti, penne, and others.

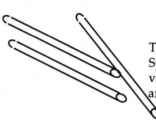

Thin tubular pasta. Spaghetti, spaghettini, vermicelli (little worms), angel hair.

Large tubes, like rigatoni (grooved and slightly curved), manicotti and mostaccioli (diagonal ends), and cannelloni, many of which are used for stuffing.

Wheels, like ruote and wagon wheels.

Spirals, including fusilli, rotini, and rotelle.

Shell shapes, large and small. For instance, conchiglie.

Tiny pasta for soup. Comes in various shapes, tiny tubes, stars, rings (anelli), tiny shells. And stars, little hats (cappelletti), ears (orecchioni), radiators (radiatori) and a variety of eyes, such as occhi di trota (trout's eyes) and occhi di lupo (wolf's eyes). Alphabets, of course.

Chocolate

The average American eats 11 pounds of chocolate candy a year. Those who dare, break tradition and have chocolate cakes at their weddings—as one of us did. Remember those winter afternoons after school drinking cocoa with marshmallows in it? Making fudge on a winter evening? When life turns ugly, what do we turn to? Chocolate! Chocolate is our comfort food of choice—warm, rich, smooth, consoling. In that spirit, we offer a few tips on how to use it in cooking.

Quality chocolate. All chocolate begins with the cacao bean, which grows in pods on trees cultivated in the cacao belt hugging the equator in Brazil and other South American countries, Central America, the Caribbean, West Africa, and

CHOCOLATE: BAD GUY OR GOOD GUY?

Chocolate-eaters tend to be mildly depressed, according to a study at Richard Stockton State College in Pomona, New Jersey. But they should cheer up, because more than one study has also shown that chocolate does not, repeat, *does not* trigger acne outbreaks. Chocolate is also cholesterol-free (unless it contains milk), though it does contain saturated fat (which, interestingly enough, does not elevate blood cholesterol as much as animal fats do).

Indonesia. Some beans are better than others. Once harvested, the beans are husked, fermented, and sun-dried. Chocolate makers, who guard their formulas ferociously, then blend the

DECORATING WITH CHOCOLATE

Some of those fancy chocolate decorations you see at the bakery or on the dessert tray are actually easy to make.

Leaves

Select clean, small leaves (rose or lemon, for instance).

Brush a thin coat of melted chocolate on the underside of the leaves. Don't coat the stems. Let set on parchment paper.

Peel the leaves off the chocolate starting with the stem end.

Zigzag

On a sauce or glazed cake, pipe stripes or concentric rings of chocolate.

Then pull a knife tip (the dull side) across the stripes or rings, first in one direction, then the other.

The final product should look something like this.

beans and roast them for varying lengths of time. After the outer shells are removed, the beans are broken into pieces, heated, and ground to a fine paste until they become a fine chocolate liquor or cocoa paste, from which various kinds of chocolate are made. (See the following list). The chocolate maker then kneads the chocolate (usually by machine), pours it into molds, and cools it.

Chocolate blends:

Unsweetened chocolate a.k.a. *baking chocolate* and *bitter chocolate*. Pure chocolate liquor, hardened and molded. It has from 50 to 58 percent cocoa butter.

Unsweetened cocoa powder. Chocolate liquor from which about 75 percent of the cocoa butter has been pressed. It is low in fat.

Natural (nonalkalized) cocoa powder tastes strongly chocolate.

Alkalized (Dutch process) cocoa powder is less acid (mellower) and tastes not so strongly of chocolate. If a recipe uses baking soda, you should use nonalkalized cocoa powder (above) unless the recipe specifically calls for alkalized cocoa powder. If a recipe uses baking powder, you should usually use alkalized cocoa powder.

Dark sweet chocolate. Blend of chocolate liquor, cocoa butter, sugar, lecithin, and vanilla or vanillin.

Semisweet and *bittersweet chocolate*: Dark chocolate with at least 35 percent chocolate liquor.

Milk chocolate. Dark sweet chocolate with milk added. It contains at least 10 percent chocolate liquor and at least 12 percent milk solids.

White chocolate. Not officially a chocolate because it contains no chocolate liquor. Made from cocoa butter (or another vegetable fat), sugar, milk, lecithin, and vanilla or vanillin.

Storing chocolate. Wrap chocolate in foil and plastic wrap in an airtight container. Keep the container in a cool, dry place at 60°–70°. Store it in the refrigerator only for a short time. If you see whitish streaks (fat bloom) or graininess (sugar bloom) on chocolate, do not throw it out. Blooms, which come from improper storage, are harmless. Dark chocolate keeps its quality up to five years, milk chocolate for about one year, white chocolate for six to eight months.

Melting chocolate. First chop the chocolate into small pieces. Melt in a double boiler over hot (not boiling) water or in the microwave on HIGH for 1 to 3 minutes, stirring every minute. If you have the nerve, you can try melting it over very low direct heat. The chocolate will often "seize" if any water is present when you melt it. If this happens stir in 1 tablespoon vegetable shortening (not butter) for every 3 ounces of chocolate.

Substitutions. You can use these equivalents:

1 oz. unsweetened baking chocolate = 3 tbsp. of cocoa + 1 tbsp. shortening.

1 oz. square semisweet baking chocolate = 1 oz. (2 tbsp.) semisweet chocolate morsels.

1 6-oz. (1 cup) package of semisweet chocolate chips, or 6 1-oz. blocks of semisweet chocolate = 6 tbsp. cocoa + 7 tbsp. sugar + ¼ cup vegetable shortening.

Hillary Rodham Clinton's Chocolate-Chip Cookie Recipe

In a taste comparison test of several recipes for fresh-baked cookies and 25 packaged cookies, *Consumer Reports* (September, 1993) gave Hillary Clinton's recipe for chocolate chip cookies a high rating ("delicate crispness, chewy; smooth, chocolatey chips"). Here's her recipe:

Hillary Clinton's Chocolate-Chip Cookie Recipe

1½ cups unsifted all-purpose flour
1 teaspoon salt
1 teaspoon baking soda
1 cup solid vegetable shortening
½ cup granulated sugar
1 cup firmly packed light brown sugar
1 teaspoon vanilla extract
2 eggs
2 cups rolled oats
12-oz. package semisweet chocolate chips

Heat oven to 350 degrees. Combine flour, salt, baking soda. Beat together shortening, sugars, and vanilla until creamy. Add eggs, beating until fluffy. Gradually beat in flour mixture and rolled oats. Stir in chips. Drop teaspoonfuls of batter onto cookie sheets. Bake 8 to 10 minutes. Cool cookies on sheets for 2 minutes before placing them on wire rack for further cooling. Yield: 7½ dozen cookies.

Measuring

When measuring dry ingredients, first stir, then put into cup or spoon and level off with a knife. For both wet and dry ingredients, look at the cup at eye level to assure accuracy. Press down solid cooking fats and brown sugar in the measuring cup.

Abbreviations:

t. or tsp. = teaspoon
T. or tbsp. = tablespoon
c. = cup
oz. = ounce
lb. = pound

Equivalents:

1 tablespoon = 3 teaspoons
1 cup = 16 tablespoons = 8 oz.
1 pint = 2 cups (liquid)
1 quart = 4 cups or 2 pints (liquid)
1 gallon = 4 quarts
1 jigger = 3 tablespoons (liquid)

Can sizes:

8-oz. can = 1 cup
No. 1 can = 11 oz. = 1⅓ cups
No. 303 can = 16 oz. = 2 cups
No. 2 can = 20 oz. = 2½ cups
No. 2½ can = 28 oz. = 3½ cups

Substitutes and Equivalents

Acids: 1 t. lemon juice = ½ t. vinegar.
Baking powder:
♦ 1 t. double-acting = 1½ t. phosphate baking powder or 2 t. tartrate baking powder.

♦ substitute—for each cup of flour in the recipe, 1 t. baking soda, 2 t. cream of tartar, ½ t. salt instead of baking powder. Use immediately.
Butter: 1 stick = ½ cup or 8 T.
Cocoa-chocolate: See "Chocolate," p. 629.
Eggs: 2 egg yolks = 1 whole egg.
Garlic: 1 t. minced = 1 clove = ½ t. garlic powder.
Ginger: 1 t. fresh minced = ¼ t. ground ginger.
Herbs: 1 t. fresh herbs = ½ t. to ⅓ t. dried.
Lemon juice: 1 t. lemon juice = ¼ t. vinegar.
Milk:
♦ Cream: 1 c. = ¾ c. milk + ⅓ c. melted butter.
♦ Buttermilk: ¼ c. milk and ¾ c. yogurt, or sour milk with enough lemon juice or vinegar to sour it.
♦ 1 c. whole milk = 1 c. buttermilk + ½ t. baking soda, or 1 cup skim milk + 2 T. fat or oil.
Mustard: 1 T. prepared mustard = 1 t. dry mustard + 1 T. water, vinegar, or wine.
Onion: 1 T. dry chopped = 2 T. fresh chopped = 1 small onion = ½ T. onion powder.
Starches:
♦ Flour, all-purpose: 1 c. = 1⅛ c. cake flour or whole wheat flour or 1⅓ c. rye flour.
♦ 1 t. cornstarch = 2 t. flour.
♦ 1 c. flour = 1⅓ c. oats.
♦ Arrowroot: 1 t. = 1 T. flour; 2 t. = 1 T. cornstarch.
♦ Cake flour = 1 c.–2 T. all-purpose flour + 2 T. cornstarch.
Cornstarch: 1 T. = 2 T. white flour, 1 T. arrowroot, 1 T. tapioca.
Sweeteners: 1 c. sugar = ¾ c. honey or 1½ c. molasses or 2 c. corn syrup or 1½ c. maple syrup; 1 c. honey = 1¼ c. sugar and ¼ c. any liquid.
Tomatoes: 1 c. canned tomatoes = 1½ c. fresh tomatoes (chop and simmer 10 minutes).
Vanilla: 1-inch piece vanilla bean = 1 t. vanilla extract.
Yeast: 1 6-oz. compressed yeast cake = 1 envelope active dry or quick-rise yeast (but be careful, mixing directions may need to be changed).

Drinks

Coffee

For many of us coffee starts the day—and ends it. It provides the excuse for a break from work, a chat with a friend, a look at the scenery. Some of us haunt specialty stores for the latest in trendy gourmet beans, while others of us just pick up a handy name brand at the supermarket. In either case, knowing a few things about beans and brewing methods can make all the difference in the quality of your coffee.

To Brew Coffee

1. If you can, buy good quality beans and grind them yourself each time you make coffee. Fresh-roasted beans retain good flavor for three weeks, ground coffee only for one week. Arabica beans (mainly from Central America) may be preferred to robusta beans, since they are lower in caffeine. Beans range in color from almost black to light tan. The darker the beans, the longer they have been roasted and the fuller the flavor.

2. Store the beans in a sealed container in the freezer.

3. Choose the grind according to your coffee-maker. Grind the coffee fine for drip coffeemakers, coarser for percolator and plunge coffeemakers. If the grind is too fine, it may clog up your coffeemaker, and it may make bitter coffee. If the grind is too coarse, the coffee will be watery.

4. Measure your coffee—one level scoop (2 tablespoons) for each 6 ounces of water. Make only as much coffee as you will use right away. Reheated coffee usually tastes like the water at the bottom of a drainage ditch.

5. Use good-tasting water, and use it cold. Tap water should be freshly drawn. If your coffee tastes funny, try bottled water or invest in a water filter.

6. Don't use grounds a second time.

Coffeemaking Methods

Percolators make a strong, hot cup of coffee that has less caffeine than coffee made in a drip pot. Use a coarse grind.

Drip method coffee can be made with a filter cone or in an electric drip machine. Because it brews at a lower temperature, it keeps the flavor. Use a fine grind.

Plunger method coffee is usually strong coffee. The method, which comes from Europe, works on the same principle as used in making "cowboy coffee" (put the ground coffee in a pot of boiling water). The trick with the plunger pot (or French press) lies in the plunger, which filters out grounds. Use a coarse grind.

Expresso method coffee is usually made through pressure in a special pot.

WHAT'S IN THE CUP?

Coffee now comes in several guises, brewed extra strong, laced with foamy steamed milk, embellished with chocolate. If you are bewildered by the choices, this list of definitions should help.

Espresso: Rich, black coffee, served in a small cup, often with a sliver of lemon peel and sugar.

Caffé latte: Coffee, covered with hot steamed milk, topped with foam.

Café au lait: Coffee served with hot milk.

Cappuccino: Coffee with about a half cup of steamed milk and a large amount of foamed milk.

Expresso con Panna: Expresso with whipped cream on top.

Caffé Mocha: Chocolate syrup, then expresso coffee, steamed milk, whipped cream, chocolate sprinkles.

Tea

Tea drinking—which eases the mind, relaxes the body, and encourages social life—is a simple pleasure with a long, rich tradition. More tea is consumed on this planet than any other beverage except water. Rituals focusing on tea are common in both East and West. The Japanese tea ceremony (*chanoyu*) has existed for 500 years. Afternoon tea, formal or informal, is a fixture of English life. And nothing stops us from developing our own tea ceremonies.

How to Brew Tea

1. Use a good brand of loose tea. (Tea bags do not yield as aromatic a cup of tea and often are made of inferior leaves.) The leaves from a package of loose tea should be rolled; they should crumble if you rub them between your fingers, but should not turn to powder right away. Keep tea in a tin caddy. You can keep black tea for about two years, green and brown about six months *if* the caddy is airtight.

2. Water should be fresh and cold. If you use tap water, run it for a couple of minutes.

CAFFEINE—SHOULD YOU GIVE IT UP?

No study has yet proved any *serious* bad effects on health from caffeine. However, coffee does raise blood pressure and heart rate. Some people experience insomnia, nervousness, heartburn, diarrhea, and more severe premenstrual syndrome symptoms. Women who consume less than recommended amounts of calcium may have a greater incidence of osteoporosis.

How to give it up. Do it slowly, or you may have withdrawal symptoms (headache, depression), according to researchers at Johns Hopkins University School of Medicine (Baltimore).

How much caffeine? Generally speaking, arabica beans (such as Colombian) contain less caffeine than robusta beans. Drip coffee tends to be stronger than percolated. Instant coffees and teas tend to be relatively low in caffeine, compared to their regular counterparts. Chocolate contains caffeine—if you eat a piece of chocolate cake, you are consuming the equal of about a half cup of tea. Dark chocolate has more caffeine per ounce than milk chocolate. Some soft drinks also contain caffeine—check the labels before you buy. And beware of over-the-counter remedies for premenstrual syndrome and pain, some of which pack a real caffeine wallop.

Drinks	Caffeine (in milligrams)
Strong coffee (5-oz. cup)	180
Strong tea or weak coffee (5-oz. cup)	80
Weak tea (5-oz. cup)	50
Cola drinks (5-oz. glass)	15–23
Cocoa (5-oz. cup)	15

Source: *FDA Consumer*

3. Bring the water to a rolling boil.

4. Pour a little water in the teapot to warm it, then pour the water out.

5. Put the tea in the teapot: a teaspoon for every person, and one for the pot. Immediately pour in boiling water. Let the tea steep for around three minutes. If tea leaves are large, the tea may need to brew a little longer.

6. Serve with milk or lemon.

Kinds of Tea

Except for herbal teas, all teas come from the plant *Camellia sinensis*. Most are grown in India, Sri Lanka, China, Japan, Taiwan, Indonesia, and Africa. Teas fall into categories according to their degree of fermentation. *Green tea* is unfermented and mild, pale in color; it is ceremonial in Japan and often served in Oriental restaurants. Drinking green tea may cut the risk of cancer and heart disease. *Oolong tea* is semifermented; it brews light brown and has a distinctive flavor. *Black tea* is completely fermented and requires a good deal of attention during the process.

Distinctive blends and flavors include:

Assam—from India, a strong, wake-up tea.

Black Currant—Oriental teas with black currant.

Darjeeling—fruity taste, the "Champagne of teas," from India.

Earl Grey—blend of black China and Darjeeling, with oil of bergamot.

English Breakfast—blend of teas from Ceylon and India.

Flowery Orange Pekoe—a black Ceylon (Sri Lanka) tea with subtle flavor.

Formosa Oolong—brown tea with a peachy taste.

Gunpowder—very delicate Chinese tea.

Jasmine—green or black-green blend, with jasmine flowers.

Keemun—a delicate tea from China.

Lady Londonderry—black blend.

Lapsang Souchong—from China, smoky and rich.

Rose Pouchong—Chinese tea with rose petals.

Russian Caravan—China and Taiwan oolong blend.

Yunnan—strong but subtle Chinese tea.

TEA AS MEDICINE

Tea has always been used as a folk remedy, and now scientists have found that tea (especially green tea) contains less caffeine, may reduce tooth decay (because of its fluoride and tannin content), may act as an antibacterial and antiviral agent (because of its tannins), perhaps reduces risks of heart disease and cancer. Compounds called polyphenols, components of green tea, may affect cholesterol production in the body and reduce platelet clumping. In parts of Japan where large amounts of green tea are consumed, death rates from cancer are lower, and again scientists credit polyphenols, which may help to block cell changes and act as antioxidants to inhibit the growth of tumors that have already started. Most research has been done with green teas, though oolong and black teas may have similar effects. Herbal teas contain few or no polyphenols.

Wine: What's Pretentious, What's Important

At a wine-tasting party in France, one of the American guests asked the wine expert about cork smelling as part of the wine ritual. He smiled and said that in France corks were not for smelling, however, labels were. He got almost as many laughs as the woman who, when asked to identify the fruit aroma of a burgundy (raspberry, etc.), replied, "Grape." Wine is a serious drink that does not need always to be taken so seriously.

About aging: Past a certain point, wine does not necessarily improve with age. Most wines are better drunk young, within 10 years of when they were made.

What's in the Name

With some exceptions, French wine makers name their wines according to region, American wine makers according to kinds of grape (variety). There is some reason for this. Wine is produced almost everywhere in France. The French believe strongly in the importance of soil, climate, and growing conditions. American wine tends to be grown only in a few regions. Americans tend to focus on grape varieties. Other countries follow a mix of classification schemes. This chart identifies grape varieties and their use in wines named for regions.

Wine Labels

How to read a wine label in a foreign language—or even in English? Meanings of terms often vary according to country—for example, "estate-bottled" does not mean the same thing in the United States as it does in France. But spending a little time deciphering a label pays off. Hidden in it is valuable information about the kind and quality of the wine.

United States:
♦ Brand or winery name.
♦ Vineyard name. At least 85 percent of the grapes must come from that vineyard.
♦ Varietal name (e.g., Chardonnay, Cabernet Sauvignon). Wine is labeled according to the variety of grape. By law, it must contain at least 75 percent of that variety (e.g., Chenin Blanc must contain 75 percent Chenin Blanc grapes).
♦ Estate-bottled. The grapes were grown in one county by the same producer. The term "made and bottled by" means that a winery has made at least 10 percent of the wine—the rest can come from anywhere.
♦ Vintage (a year). At least 95 percent of the grapes used in making the wine were harvested in that year.

♦ Other statements (size of bottle, alcoholic content, etc.). If you see the words "table wine," percentage of alcohol need not be mentioned.
France:
♦ Brand name or name of estate. The producer of the wine.
♦ Regional name. In France, wine is labeled by region. Burgundy wine comes from the Burgundy region, but it might be made of a blend of several kinds of grapes.
♦ Estate-bottled. Grapes were grown and produced on the estate.
♦ AC or VDQS: Guarantee by French government that wine is authentic.
♦ Perhaps *Cru* or *Premier Cru.* Better than ordinary quality of grapes.
♦ Vintage.
♦ Other statements (size of bottle, shipper, etc.).
♦ Appellation. Place of origin.
Germany:
♦ Name of village where wine was made, ending in *er.* For example, wine from Wehlen is called Wehlener.
♦ Vineyard (*Weinberg* in German).
♦ Grape variety.
♦ Indication of dryness. *Trocken,* meaning dry; *Halbtrocken,* half-dry.
♦ Perhaps *Erzeugerabfüllung,* meaning "put in bottles at the Château."
♦ *Weingut:* winery.
Contact: **Wine Institute,** 425 Market Street, Suite 1000, San Francisco, CA 94105 (415-512-0151) for a brochure on buying and serving California wine and a chart showing what wine goes with what food.

Entertaining with Wine

How Much Wine?

Count on one bottle per person, and buy wines that you can afford. Don't worry about being an expert. Share the wines you like with your guests without apology.

WINE CHART

Grape Variety	Description	Wines
Cabernet Sauvignon (red)	Herbal, often minty. Can taste of cedar, black currant, violets. Full-bodied, somewhat mouth-puckering when young.	Some Tuscan wines (e.g. , Sammarco, Sassicaia); American, Australian, Italian Cabernet Sauvignon; ingredient in red Bordeaux.
Chardonnay (white)	Fruity, medium- to full-bodied, rich. Tastes of vanilla, butter, apple, melon, tropical fruit. Can be high in alcohol.	French white Burgundy; French Chablis; American, Australian, Italian Chardonnay.
Chenin Blanc (white)	Honey and floral tastes, citrus, earth, perhaps damp hay. Tart, off-dry or sweetish.	French whites (Vouvray, Anjou, Touraine); American Chenin Blanc.
Gamay (red)	Grapey, light, fresh. Flavors: berry, spice, bacon fat, tar.	French Beaujolais; American "gamay beaujolais" grape may be Pinot Noir.
Gewürztraminer (white)	Distinctive taste. Varies in dryness by region.	California and Germany, semisweet; Alsace, dry.
Merlot (red)	Fruity, lush. Flavors: cherry, red fruit, plum. Tannins.	Blended with Cabernet in French Bordeaux; California Merlots.
Nebbiolo (red)	Sturdy.	Italy: Barolo, Barbaresco, Gattinara, and others.
Pinot Noir (red)	Fruity, silky, but rich. Flavors: strawberry, raspberry, black and red fruits. Softer than cabernet.	French Burgundy; German Spätburgunder; California and Australian Pinot Noir.
Riesling (white)	Intense, floral and fruity, rich. Flavors: floral, apple, honey, mineral. Medium-dry to sweet but tart. Good aperitif.	German Riesling (kabinetts, spätlese, auslese); Alsace Riesling; California Johannesburg Riesling, white Riesling, Rhine Riesling. German and California, medium-dry to sweet; Alsace, dry.
Sangiovese (red)	Less thick than Cabernet.	Italy: in many wines including Chianti Riserva. Also California.
Sauvignon Blanc (white)	Grassy, herbal, mineral, citrus flavors, usually dry and acidic, though some are finished sweet.	Some French whites (Pouilly Fumé, Sancerre); South American Sauvignon Blanc; California Sauvignon Blanc, Fumé Blanc.
Scheuerbe (white)	Cross of Riesling and Sylvaner.	German.
Syrah (red)	Berry or vegetal taste, full-bodied.	Ingredient in French Rhône wines; Australian Shiraz; California Syrah.
Zinfandel (red)	Fruity, tannic. Flavors: red fruit, spice, licorice, maybe tar. Used to make "white" (rose) zinfandel.	California Zinfandel, ingredient in generic reds (Gallo Hearty Burgundy).

A U.S. WINE LABEL

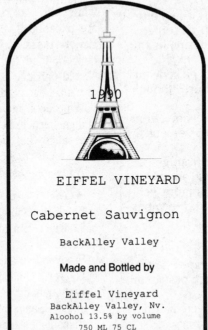

The vintage year was 1990. At least 95% of the grapes were harvested in 1990.

The wine was made with at least 75% Cabernet Sauvignon grapes.

The bottle contains 75 centiliters (750 milliliters) of wine.

At least 85% of the grapes come from Eiffel Vineyard.

Eiffel Vineyard made at least 10% of the wine but perhaps no more than that.

EIFFEL VINEYARD

Cabernet Sauvignon

BackAlley Valley

Made and Bottled by

Eiffel Vineyard
BackAlley Valley, Nv.
Aloohol 13.5% by volume
750 ML 75 CL

A FRENCH WINE LABEL

Produit de France
Anne Vigneron

1985
Domaine Chanson du Lit

CÔTES DE RHÔNE
APPELLATION COTES DU RHONE CONTROLLEE

MIS EN BOUTEILLE AU DOMAINE
75cl
Anne Vigneron et Jon Skinner Proprietaires-
Recoltants, 30760 St. Grigoire

Anne Vigneron is responsible for this wine.

The vintage year was 1985.

The estate where it was made is called Chanson du Lit.

The wine was bottled at the estate.

The appellation, place of origin, is the Côtes du Rhône. This is the name of the wine.

The bottle contains 75 centiliters of wine.

GERMAN WINE TERMINOLOGY

Auslese: Grapes picked in selected bunches, according to natural alcohol content. Can be sweet dessert wines or dry, in any case powerful. Age well.

Beerenauslese: Grapes are picked one at a time. Usually sweet and lush, though some are dry.

Deutscher Tafelwein: Table wine, from Germany, with minimum of 8.5 percent alcohol.

Eiswein: "Ice-wine," made from grapes frozen on the vine, bringing about reduced water content and thus more richness and intensity. Highly acid, the wines need aging. Can be expensive.

Halbtrocken: Not so dry.

Kabinett: Wine that has fermented only on natural sugar from the grapes. Light. Can age well, though not much past 10 or 15 years.

QbA Hochgewächs: High-weight wine, with some added sugar.

Qualitätswein: High-quality wines meeting government standards. However, most German wine meets the qualifications.

♦ *Qualitätswein eines bestimmer Anbaugebiete* (QbA) comes from a specified region and may have had sugar added. Wine of this category from the Moselle-Saar-Ruwer comes in a green bottle, that from the Rheingau in a brown bottle.

♦ *Qualitätswein mit Prädikat* (QmP) must ferment only from natural grape sugar, has special attributes. The category includes Spätlese, Auslese, and other wines made special ways.

Sekt: Sparkling wine, usually made from Riesling grapes.

Spätlese: Wine made from late-picked grapes, tending to be—but not always—sweet. Very intense. Ages well.

Trocken: Dry.

Trockenbeerenauslese: Rare, made from individually picked grapes, dried on the vine by *Botrytis* mold ("noble rot"). Very sweet and highly acid. Ages very well. Very expensive.

What Wine to Serve with Dinner?

The old general rules—red with red meat, white with poultry and fish—still apply, but there are exceptions, qualifications, nuances of intensity, tartness, dryness. Wine can alter the taste of food, food the taste of wine. Food and wine should enhance each other, not fight each other or cancel each other out.

Wine does not go well with chocolate, citrus, vinegar, artichokes, peppers, sweet corn, barbecue sauce, ketchup. If you do serve wine with these foods, make it a rosé, Gamay, or Zinfandel.

A few suggestions:

♦ *Fish:*
Shellfish: Sauvignon Blanc, Chablis, Chardonnay, white Burgundy, Muscadet, Soave, sparkling wines.

Smoked fish and fish soup: Sauvignon Blanc.

Oysters: Chablis, Muscadet.

Light fish: dry Riesling, Chenin Blanc, Gewürztraminer, Sancerre, white Burgundy.

Fish dishes made with red wine: young Bordeaux.

Salmon and other meaty fish: Chardonnay, Pinot Noir, Gamay, Sauvignon Blanc, white Burgundy, white Zinfandel.

♦ *Meat:*
Veal and pork: Beaujolais, Chardonnay, Dolcetto, white Rhône wine, Riesling.

Veal, beef, meat loaf: Merlot.

Grilled steak: Zinfandel.

Lamb: Cabernet Sauvignon.

Roasted meat: Barolo, Cabernet Sauvignon, Merlot, Bordeaux reds, Zinfandel.

Meat stew: Zinfandel, Côtes-du-Rhône, Châteauneuf-du-Pape, Gigondas.

♦ *Poultry:*
Chicken: Beaujolais, Chardonnay, Dolcetto, white Rhône wine, Riesling.

Duck: Cabernet Sauvignon, Merlot.

Poultry stew: Côtes-du-Rhône.

♦ *General:*
Spicy Southwestern, Mexican, Oriental food: Côtes-du-Rhône.

Shrimp or chicken salad: Soave, Sauvignon Blanc, Fumé Blanc.

Fruit salad or fruit soup: dry Riesling.

Salty and highly seasoned foods: sparkling or sweet wines.

Thanksgiving dinner: any color, young, matched to the stuffing—Rhône wine for chestnut dressing, Riesling or Gewürtztraminer with apple stuffing, for instance.

Pasta with tomato sauce: Barbera, Zinfandel.

Pasta with vegetables: Riesling, Sauvignon Blanc, Soave, sparkling wines.

Cold salmon and oriental food: dry Riesling.

Wineglasses

Invest in some good wineglasses—they do not have to be very expensive. Wineglasses should be plain, tulip-shaped, with stems, and large enough to hold 6 ounces of wine when half full. The rim should be thin. If you buy separate glasses for red and white wine, the larger glasses are for red, the smaller for white. Flutes and long tulip-shaped glasses are good for Champagne and sparkling wines. For aperitifs or dessert wines, smaller glasses are appropriate.

Temperature of Wine

Serve light white, rosé, and sparkling wines at a cool temperature, but not too cold. An hour in the refrigerator or a half-hour in an ice bucket is enough. Heavy white wines and light reds should be lightly chilled, just below room temperature.

Uncorking Wine

In processing, cork bark is boiled for 90 minutes, sorted, and punched out in the shape of corks. The problem with the traditional cork: it sometimes goes bad so that the wine is "corky" (the only reason for smelling the cork).

Cork won't come out? Try holding the neck of the bottle under warm water so that the glass expands. Don't wet the cork. Insert a screwpull corkscrew at an angle for more leverage. When the cork breaks off and half stays in the bottle or

the cork crumbles, push the cork down into the wine. Then strain the wine through a coffee filter into a carafe or decanter.

Kinds of corkscrews:

♦ Waiter's Friend: Small, with three hinged tools (a knife blade, a screw, a hinged brace) that swing out. Look for one with a sharp point on the screw. The knife blade cuts the foil off the bottle. You next twist the screw into the center of the cork until you can clip the brace over the rim of the bottle neck. Then pull the handle up to draw the cork. Problem: It can eat up the cork's center.

♦ Winged corkscrew: You set the plastic-lined cup on the cork, then turn the handle to drive the screw into the cork. As you do this, the wings rise. Press down on the wings and the cork comes out. Problem: It also sometimes takes out the center of the cork.

♦ Screwpull: Long spiral bore connected to a handle. You turn the handle to insert the screw, then pull the cork out. The kind with a plastic guide frame makes pulling unnecessary.

♦ Cork Pops: A device that injects gas so that air pressure pushes the cork out of the bottle.

♦ Ah So: Two steel blades attached to a handle. You put the blades between cork and bottle, rock them to insert them farther, then twist and pull until the cork—left whole—comes out.

Problem: The Ah So can crack bottle lip or push the cork down into the bottle.

Note: If you are keeping old red wines, drink one now and then to check the corks. Replace corks if they are failing. (You can get supplies at a wine-supply store.) When you open the one bottle, you should drink the whole thing because the bottle is now "ullaged"—i.e., less than full, with air space between the wine level and the cork.

How to Uncork Champagne and Sparkling Wines:

Don't stir the Champagne up. Hold the bottle at a 45-degree angle pointing away from you, any other human, and priceless objects. Take off the foil hood and the wire cage. You can open the bottle by brute human force or with a key or a star, two gadgets that fit over the cork. If you use brute force, turn the bottle, holding it by the base, while you hold the cork firmly with the other hand. Use your thumbs to prod a stubborn cork on its way. Let the foam settle a bit before filling glasses, and hold a towel under the neck of the bottle to catch falling foam.

CORKSCREWS

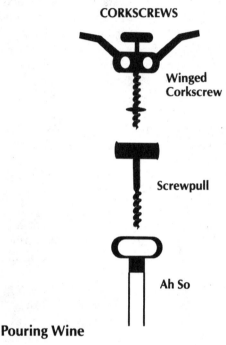

Winged Corkscrew

Screwpull

Ah So

Pouring Wine

After you have removed the cork, pour a small amount of wine in your own glass. Swirl and sniff the wine (without ostentation) and taste it. If you approve of the wine, pour for the rest of the group, serving yourself last. Don't overfill wine glasses—they should be no more than two-thirds full.

Wine Talk—Glossary of Basic and Frivolous Wine Terms

Acidity: Amount of acid; necessary for proper aging in reds, for balancing sweetness in whites.

Appellation. Place of origin.

Appellation Contrôllée (AC): In France, wines from a region where wine making is controlled by certain standards.

Austere: Tannic, acidic, or without much fruit. May be undeveloped.

Backward: Behind schedule in aging.

Body: Term indicating the weight of a wine, important mostly with reds meant for aging and just a few whites.

Bottle-sick: Wine that is unstable due to bottling or rough handling, usually temporary.

Bouquet: All of a wine's smells, a.k.a. *nose.* This is the sum of the odors that come from a wine.

Breathing: Allowing wine to stand, cork removed, for a certain amount of time.

Cépage: Grape variety, in French.

Color: In white wines, gold, greenish, straw hues; in reds, purple to crimson hues. Look at a wine's color at the edge where wine's surface meets the glass, with glass tilted away from you, against a white background. Old wine may appear to be dull and brown.

Corky: A bad smell from a bad cork, which has caused the wine to spoil.

Cru: Means "growth" in French. Better-than-ordinary quality of grapes, usually from a certain village or geographic area. *Premier cru* means "first growth"; *Grand cru* means "great growth."

Decant: To pour wine from the bottle into another container, usually to separate it from sediment.

DOC: In Italy, wines from a region where wine making is controlled by certain standards.

Dry: Not sweet.

Finish: Aftertaste. If long, that's good.

Forward: Ahead of schedule in aging.

Flinty: The taste that is like the smell of struck flint, usually in very dry white wine.

Grapy: Tasting of grapes, not good.

Grassy: Tasting of grass, not necessarily bad.

Legs: Swirl wine in your glass and watch the streaks running down the side—the streaks are "legs."

Nose: See *Bouquet.*

Oaky: Taste of the oak barrels in which some wine is aged. Flavors associated with oak are vanilla, butter, coffee, toast, and coconut.

Oechslé: German measure of grape ripeness, expressed in numbers and degrees, e.g., 110 degrees.

Ordinaire: French for undistinguished.

Spumante: Italian term for sparkling wine.

Tannic: Tasting of tannin from wine skins, bitter and perhaps astringent. Not necessarily bad, since the presence of tannin indicates the wine may be fit for aging.

Vin délimité de qualité supérieure (VDQS): French term meaning wine of superior quality.

Vin de pays: In French, "wine of the country." A better *vin de table,* it can be quite good.

Vin de table: Table wine. Like jug wine.

WINE TASTING

Reams have been written about wine tasting, some silly, some portentous but wise. Much has to do with the smell of the wine, which may be because human taste buds differentiate among four basic sensations while the human nose can detect 2000–4000 aromas.

A fast fix:

♦ In general, first look at the wine's color and clarity. If white wine has a greenish tint, it is probably at least slightly acid. If yellow, it has low acidity or was aged in a barrel. In red wines, blue hues indicate youth, brown or brown-red, age.

♦ Watch the legs after swirling—if thick and slow in a dry wine, the wine has more body.

♦ Smell the wine's aroma without sniffing pretentiously (be subtle), holding your nose a bit away from the rim, perhaps swirling the wine a little. Notice hints of fruit, vanilla, grass, spices, garlic. Is the smell complex or simple?

♦ Taste, moving the wine around to all parts of your mouth. Does the wine have body? Does it taste the way it smells? Is it acid, sweet, tannic?

♦ After you swallow, is there a pleasant, long aftertaste?

CHAMPAGNE TERMS

Method: The better sparkling wines and Champagne are made by the *méthode Champenoise.*

Levels of Sweetness (from driest to sweetest): brut, extra dry, dry (sec), demi-sec, doux, riche. *Note:* The tinier the bubbles, the better the Champagne.

Big Champagne Bottles

You need a cork wrench to open these. Give the empty bottle to the guest of honor.

Magnum: 2 quarts

Jeroboam: 0.8 gallon (1.6 magnums, as much as four or five bottles)

Rehoboam: 3 magnums

Methuselah: 4 magnums

Salmanazar: 6 magnums

Balthazar: 8 magnums

Nebuchadnezzar: 10 magnums.

BEAUJOLAIS PRIMER

Beaujolais is a wine meant to be drunk young. How young? When it's only a few weeks old to seven years from its making, say the experts.

Beaujolais Nouveau: The first of the harvest, sold starting the third Thursday of November, to be drunk within a few weeks.

Beaujolais or *Beaujolais Superieur:* Should be drunk within a year.

Beaujolais-Villages: Beaujolais wines made from any of 37 villages, to be drunk within a year.

Beaujolais Grand Cru: These wines come from the places they are named for: St.-Amour, Juliénas, Chénas, Moulin-à-Vent, Fleurie, Chiroubles, Morgon, Régnié, Brouilly, and Côte de Brouilly. Most can be kept for two to four years. Moulin-à-Vent and Morgon can be kept even longer, for six to seven years.

Beer

You drink a widely advertised brand with potato chips and hot dogs while you watch a game—that's the traditional picture of a beer drinker. Or you search out a microbrewery that serves its own beer with a fine meal. Whether you like it or not, beer is changing its image. Yet hasn't it always been versatile? Hasn't it always come in a surprising variety of brews?

How Is It Made?

The basic ingredient in beer is grain—barley is best, though rice and corn may be added. The brewer may or may not toast the grain before soaking it in water. Hops, which vary in taste, go into the vat, then the mixture is boiled and cooled. At this point yeast is added, and the mixture ferments for several weeks until it becomes what we know as beer. *Ales* are top-fermented—yeast rises to the top—at warmer temperatures, usually 60°–70°F. *Lager* beers are made with bottom-fermented lager yeast, which works at lower temperatures—50°–55°F. Lager beer is smoother, clearer, and less sweet.

Pilsener refers to the lighter beer that the brewers of Pilsen, Czechoslovakia, invented in a long-gone time of thick, dark beer. The word has become generic. *Malt liquor* is a term created to label higher-alcohol beer in states where the amount of alcohol in anything called "beer" must be below a certain limit—usually 3.2 percent.

Serving Beer

The tricks to serving beer? Keep beer at between 36°–46°F., and pour it down the side of the glass to control the volume of the head. Too much foam is worse than too little.

Beer Gazetteer

Many styles of beer exist in the world. Here are a few.

Ale: Ale is top-fermented at a warm temperature. It tastes fruity, comes in colors from dark gold to deep black, and can be delicate to very forceful. Some U.S. states define ale as any malt beverage with alcohol content above 5 percent by volume. Ale does not need aging.

Altbier (German): Top-fermented beer made of an all-barley mash, later cold-conditioned (which makes it more like a lager). Sometimes brewers add malted wheat. The beer is copper in color, medium-bodied.

Barley Wine (English): A strong, top-fermented ale. It is not unusual for it to have from 6 to 10 percent alcohol by volume. Flavor: malty, bitter, alcohol. Comes in light and dark.

Bitter (English): Served on draft, tasting of hops, colored yellow to copper. Alcohol content is 3.5 to 4 percent by volume or lower. "Special bitter" has a slightly higher alcohol content, and "extra special bitter" is even higher—up to 5 to 5.5 percent alcohol.

Bock (German): Made with a barley mash, tasting of hops and malt, with alcohol content over 5 percent. Pale or dark. *Maibock* (on sale March through May) tends to be pale. *Double bock,* or *doppelbock,* is stronger, can have more than 7 percent alcohol, amber to brown in color. *Eisbok* ("ice bock") has been frozen, making it more potent because water is removed.

Brown Ale (English): A darker ale with lower alcohol content, similar to a porter, but sweeter and lighter. Can range from sweet and very brown to drier and red-brown.

Canadian Lager: A pilsener, with more hops and body than American pilseners.

Cream Ale (American): A light ale in body and taste, sometimes called "sparkling lager-ale." It can be made by either the top-fermented or bottom-fermented style when warm, then cold-fermented like a lager. May be a blend of ale and lager beers.

Dortmunder (German): Pale, bottom-fermented. Sweeter than a pilsener with more body and alcohol content.

Dry (Japanese): Dry, like its name, without much aftertaste. Made, like most dry beers, from a strain of yeast that ferments more ingredients into fermentable sugars. Pale and clean, good with fine food.

Lager: Any bottom-fermented beer. Can be light in color to very dark, and alcohol content from close to zero (nonalcoholic beer) to over 12 percent. Needs to be aged.

Marzen (German): Very malty, medium-bodied, gold to amber in color, 5.5 to 6 percent by volume. Drunk at Oktoberfest.

Münchener or *Munich* (German): Spicy and dark brown, 5 to 5.5 percent alcohol.

Old Ale or *Strong Ale* (English): A medium to strong ale, dark in color, containing quite a bit of hops and malt. Can be aged to the point where it should be sipped from a brandy snifter.

Pale Ale (English): Bronzy or coppery, bitters with more body, more hops, more alcohol. The name is confusing—but once in the old days this ale was lighter than other ales.

Pils or *Pilsener* (Czechoslovakian): Original dates to 1842 in Bohemia. The name once indicated high quality. Golden, clear, bottom-fermented, with flavors of hops and flowers, dry finish. Medium alcohol content. European pilseners are all malt, with varied amounts of hops and degrees of bitterness, with more body than American pilseners. American pilsener is light, often with rice or corn added to mash, and fewer hops. Golden color, alcohol between 3.5 and 4 percent.

Porter (English): An old kind of beer, now made mostly by microbrewers. Lighter than a stout, with 5 percent alcohol content by weight.

Scotch Ale (Scottish): Malty, high in alcohol content.

Stout (Irish): Black, top-fermented, containing roasted barley, giving it a roasty flavor. *Sweet,* or *milk, stouts* are lower in alcohol (3.5 to 4 percent) and slightly sweet. *Dry stout,* made from unmalted roasted barley, is dry. *Imperial stout,* which originated in Russia, has up to 10 percent alcohol.

Trappist Ale (Belgian): Made by Trappist monks, top-fermented, made with candy sugar, alcohol between 6 and 9 percent, conditioned in the bottle. Double and Triple ales have more alcohol, usually drunk during holidays.

Vienna (Austrian): Like marzen, with malt flavor and dry finish.

Weisse or *Weizenbier* (German): Pale beer, made with up to 75 percent malted wheat, top-fermented with a special kind of slightly sour yeast. Bavarian weizen can taste of cloves and fruit. Colors from pale gold to bronze, alcohol between 5 and 6 percent. Dunkelweizen is darker, more malty. Hefeweizen is unfiltered and should be decanted.

Beer and Food

A powerful beer can overshadow delicate food. A too-light beer seems weak when drunk with heavy food. Choosing the proper beer is as much an art as choosing wine.

Fish: Bohemian or German pilsener-style beer, Dortmunder lager, Munich pale, lighter Canadian ale.

Oysters: Dry stout.

Chicken or pork: Vienna or marzen beer.

Game: Belgian ale.

Pasta: Munich dark lager.

Rich food: German pilseners, English ales and beers.

Aperitif: Light beers, pilseners from Czechoslovakia or Germany.

After dinner: Sweet stout or bittersweet ale.

12

ETIQUETTE

EATING AND DINNER PARTIES

WEDDINGS AND FUNERALS

NICETIES

EATING AND DINNER PARTIES

Where We Stand

Etiquette, it seems to us, operates from two principles: the Golden Rule and social hierarchy. We are assuming you are all kind people and don't need to be reminded of the Golden Rule. And, as much as possible, we are downplaying the sticky little etiquette dictates that remind people of where they stand in society. This chapter emphasizes common occasions and traditional manners, with the understanding that many people may ignore tradition.

How to Eat Difficult Foods

The plate of food looks delicious, but you haven't a clue about how to eat it. You watch the people around you, but they seem to have a variety of styles, and you can't decide which one is correct. Don't pass the food up—be it lobster or asparagus. This list describes how to eat difficult foods, according to etiquette mavens. Notice that the preferred way of eating a food is often dependent on the formality of the occasion.

Artichokes: Pull the leaves off a couple at a time. Dip the base of the leaf into the sauce, then put it in your mouth and pull it through your teeth to extract the tender part. Put the chewed leaves in a pile on your plate. After you have consumed the leaves, lift the spiny leaves off the heart, then use a spoon to scrape off the fuzz (choke) still clinging to the heart. Cut the heart into bite-sized pieces with your fork and eat.

Asparagus: You can eat it with your fingers, tip down, dipping it in the sauce. But if a stalk is long, use a fork to cut it up.

Bacon: If it's crisp, eat with your fingers. If it's limp, use a fork and knife.

Bouillon and other thin soups: You can drink them from the cup. But use a spoon to eat any bits of meat and vegetable first.

Bread: Break the bread into pieces as you eat it. Use the bread plate if there is one. You can use a piece of bread as a pusher. Etiquette experts differ on how to eat bread used as a pusher.

Cherry tomatoes: Eat all in one bite.

Chicken: Don't eat chicken with your fingers at a formal or even informal dinner party. It's okay at a barbeque.

Corn on the cob: Pick your expert. You can eat down the rows (the typewriter method, according to Miss Manners) or around them. You can butter the whole ear at once or a couple of rows at a time. However, most etiquette arbiters think that corn on the cob should be served only in informal situations.

Fish, whole: The head of the fish should be to the left. Remove the head if you want, then slit the flat of the fish in the middle, head to tail with the fish knife or a fork. Open the fish out, and eat the top flesh, first one segment, then the next. Then put the knife under the backbone at one end and lift it out with the fork or the fish knife. You can use your fingers to extract any bones that are left. When you use lemon, shield other guests from the spray with your hand.

Fortune cookies: You can eat the cookie if you like, according to Elizabeth L. Post.

Frog's legs: Eat with your fingers.

Kabobs: Slide the food off the skewer onto your plate before eating it.

Lobster: Start with the little claws, removing them and sucking out the meat from the end. Take the meat out of the body and cut it into small pieces. Dip into the sauce with your cocktail fork. Crack the big claws with a nutcracker, open them with your fingers, and pry the meat out with your fork.

Parsley or watercress garnish: You can eat it, but only with a fork in a formal situation.

Peas: Crush them a bit before eating them—that way they won't roll off your fork.

Potato, baked: Break the top with your fingers, and put the butter on with your fork. You may eat the skin with knife and fork.

Salad: Don't cut lettuce with a knife. Use your fork instead.

Snails (escargots): Use the metal holder to grip the shell. If there is no metal holder, use a napkin, pry out the snail with a little fork and eat. Experts disagree on what to do with the juice left in the shells. Some say you may drink the juice from the shells, others that you may up-end them so the juice runs out on your plate, then use bread speared on a fork to sop the juice up. Still other experts frown on both techniques.

Soup: You should eat the soup from the side of the spoon, and you may tip the bowl away from you to extract the last drops.

Spaghetti: Twirl the spaghetti around the fork, then put in your mouth.

Sushi: Elizabeth L. Post says that if you are in an informal restaurant you can eat sushi with your fingers, but a fork or chopsticks are better.

HOW TO EAT A WHOLE FISH

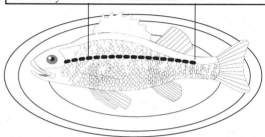

Cut along the dotted line down to the bone. You may remove the head first.

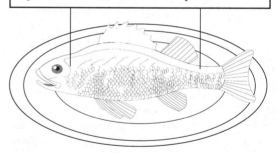

Open the fish out, and eat the top flesh first.

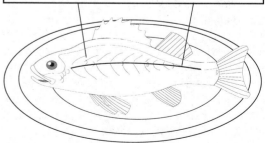

Then eat the bottom part of the exposed flesh. Finish by lifting off the backbone, preferably in one piece, with your fish knife, and eating the meat under it. You may also flip the fish over to eat the meat.

PECULIAR EATING UTENSILS

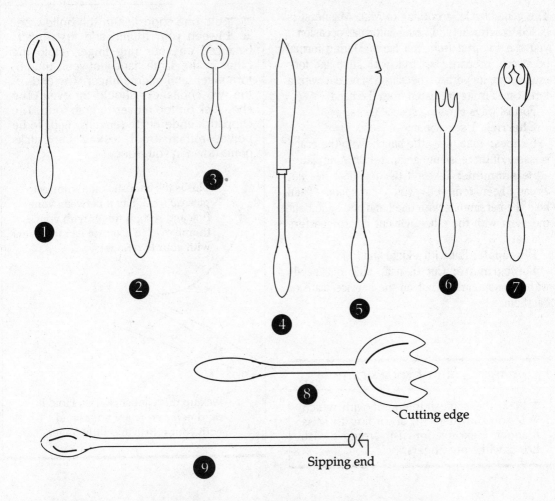

Cutting edge

Sipping end

1. Ice cream spoon (or sherbet spoon). Spoon with a flat bowl for eating ice cream.
2. Nut shovel. Used for moving nuts from serving dish to plate.
3. Salt spoon. This goes along with a salt dish. It replaces the salt shaker.
4. Fruit knife. Knife made with a silver blade, because the metallic taste of baser metals could be brought out by the acid in the fruit.
5. Fish knife. Used to debone and divide fish.
6. Shellfish fork (or shrimp, cocktail, or seafood fork). A tiny fork used for eating shrimp cocktail and other appetizer fish dishes.
7. Ice cream fork. Fork with short prongs, good for eating Baked Alaska. Originally invented because in the 19th century one ate dessert with a fork, which is pretty tricky when ice cream is served. Ergo, a utensil that is both fork and spoon.
8. Runcible spoon. Used to eat mince and slices of quince, a big slotted spoon with three thick prongs at bowl's end and a cutting edge on the side.
9. Iced tea spoon. A long spoon with a hollow handle that serves as a straw.

Eating Fruits

The general rule, according to Miss Manners, is based on formality. During informal occasions, you can eat fruit from the hand. During formal occasions, prepare your fruit with knife and fork (quartering it, perhaps peeling it) and eat with a fork. Small fruits are eaten from the hand.

Formal ways of eating special fruits:

Cherries: Use a spoon.

Grapes: Take off a little bunch (with the grape scissors, if there is one) and put it on your plate.

Persimmons: Take off the top (if it has not already been removed) with your spoon. Then hold the persimmon with one hand and spoon out the meat with the other. Or cut it into quarters and eat it.

Pineapple: Eat with a knife and fork.

Pomegranate: Cut in half, pick out seeds with your spoon and put on the service plate or eat them.

TAKING THINGS OUT OF YOUR MOUTH

Use the same implement with which you put them in, according to Miss Manners, except for fish—remove fish bones with your fingers.

Dinner Etiquette

Planning a dinner party can cause a certain amount of anxiety, in spite of the eager anticipation with which you look forward to the occasion. Who sits where? Will so-and-so get along with the dinner partner you have assigned him or her? What about the food? We can't do much to allay your quite proper trepidation, but we can tell you the rules—for you to embrace or break.

USING CHOPSTICKS

Hold one chopstick in the hollow between your thumb and first finger, balanced on your ring finger. Hold the other in the same hand between thumb, forefinger, and middle finger. The ends of the two chopsticks should be even. The chopstick on top moves to grab food. The chopstick underneath remains rigid. To be polite, refrain from resting chopsticks point-down in your food.

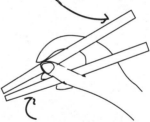

This is the chopstick that moves to pick up food. Lay it between your first and second finger with your thumb over it. Control its movement with your two fingers.

Pick up this chopstick first. Hold it rigid in the crotch of your hand with your fourth and little finger.

Seating Arrangements

At formal dinner parties, the host and hostess sit at the two heads of the table, with the male guest of honor on the right of the hostess and the female guest of honor on the right of the host. Other guests are assigned places, often with men and women alternating, though not always. Husbands and wives may be seated together or separately.

If you have two tables, the host should sit at one, the hostess at the other. At informal parties, you don't need specific seating arrangements.

Place Settings

Behind the placing of tableware lies one simple concept: ease of eating. Forks and bread plate are on the left, knives, spoons, and glasses on the right. Sometimes the soup spoon can be placed horizontally, bowl to the left, above the plate. Two exceptions: the oyster fork (if there is one) is on the right, resting in the bowl of the teaspoon, and the butter knife lies across the bread plate. Knife blades face toward the plate. The napkin is on the left or on the plate; if folded decoratively, it may even end up in the wineglass. Salad plates are placed on the bottom left (if not a separate course), tea (or coffee) cups and saucers to the right.

Formal Place Setting. While most of us will never have to worry about laying a formal place setting, we probably will have to contend with one as a guest at a formal dinner. The simple rule is to work from outside in while using tableware. However, it's easy to freeze when you see the arsenal awaiting you. To allay your anxieties, while doing research for this book we found at least three different "official" formal place settings, all with formidable sets of eating equipment. In one the bread knife was placed diagonally across the bread-and-butter plate, in another, horizontally. On the other hand, Miss Manners says that bread-and-butter plates are not in good taste at formal dinners. (You put your roll on the tablecloth.) She also says that formal settings should not include soup bowls and coffee cups. In all cases, however, the general rule (outside in) applied to all.

Make a mistake and use the wrong utensil? Miss Manners has a fine solution—"Lick clean the wrong fork you have just used and slip it back on the tablecloth while no one is looking."

For the illustration we have chosen the most complicated plate setting.

Note: Dessert is a separate occasion, in terms of tableware—sometimes. The plate arrives with dessert spoon and fork, perhaps a fingerbowl, on it. You move the spoon (a tablespoon or dessert spoon) to the right and fork (a salad fork or dessert fork) and fingerbowl to the left. Letitia

Baldrige shows a table setting with the dessert spoon and fork placed horizontally above the dinner plate, the bowl of the spoon facing to the left, the tines of the fork facing to the right.

Informal Place Setting. For informal occasions, this place setting is considered correct. Notice that it is a simplification of the formal place setting.

Serving Food

Food is served from the left and plates removed from the right. The oldest woman at the dinner (or the guest of honor) should be served first. All the women should be served before the men, or a woman is served first, then the other guests in the order in which they are seated, the hostess last. If eight or fewer people are at the table, wait until all are served before starting to eat.

Table Manners

Question: How fashionable is it to arrive late at a dinner party?

Answer: Not fashionable at all. In fact, if you are more than fifteen minutes late, the hostess is quite correct in starting dinner without you. Incidentally, it is not polite to be early, either—it puts your hosts at a disadvantage because they have to get ready for the party and entertain you.

Question: Where do I put the olive pits?

Answer: On the butter plate (if there is one).

Question: Where does the spoon go when I'm not using it?

Answer: On the underplate or saucer. However, if, when you are finished eating, there is no room on the underplate, it can be placed in the bowl or cup.

Question: I don't drink alcohol. How do I indicate that I don't want any?

Answer: Just put your hand over your glass and say, "No, thank you."

FORMAL PLACE SETTING

INFORMAL PLACE SETTING

water goblet

dinner fork

dinner knife

teaspoon

Question: In what direction is food passed?

Answer: From left to right, in the same direction that it is served, according to some experts, from right to left according to others. Just make sure it all goes in the same direction or someone will end up trying to juggle two big plates of food at once.

Question: How do you indicate you have finished eating?

Answer: By placing your knife and fork in the middle of the plate, knife (blade in) to the right of the fork. Or by placing them across the top of the plate, knife blade facing you. Or by placing them diagonally across the plate. If you are not finished, and wish to put your knife and fork down, cross them, fork handle to the left, knife handle to the right. If you pass your plate for more food, put the knife and fork on the right side of the plate, at right angles to the table edge.

Question: What about napkin etiquette? Can I tuck it under my collar?

Answer: No. Large napkins go half-folded on

your lap, smaller ones completely unfolded on your lap. Keep it on your lap until the meal is over, then fold it in the shape of a triangle or drape it loosely and put it on the table. Or in its napkin ring at a family dinner. (You may have been issued a napkin ring if you are a guest.) And put your napkin in place when you sit down at the table.

Question: Is it proper to soak up gravy and sauce with a piece of bread, then eat it?

Answer: Yes and no. Etiquette experts reluctantly agree that it is acceptable if you use a small piece of bread, impale it on your fork, and sop up the sauce. Miss Manners really disapproves of sopping except at family dinners. We like it and do it in France (and when home alone).

Question: Can I blow my nose at the table?

Answer: No, go to the bathroom and do it.

Question: What do I do when someone asks me a direct question when I have my mouth full?

Answer: Wait to answer the question until you have chewed and swallowed the food.

Question: I get food stuck in my teeth. May I use a toothpick at the table?

Answer: No, and you should not use your finger either. Wait until the meal is over, then go to the bathroom to dislodge the food.

Question: What can I do if I burp at table?

Answer: Say "Excuse me."

Question: What if I find a bug in my food?

Answer: Quietly pick it up and put it in your napkin. Don't mention it, or you will embarrass your hosts.

Question: Why can't I put my elbows on the table?

Answer: You can—in between courses. While eating, you look sloppy and tired with your elbows on the table.

Question: Is it correct to pick up a chicken leg or lamb bone to eat the last meat off it?

Answer: Only at a family dinner or a picnic.

Question: In what order are people served at a family dinner?

Answer: In this order: (1) unrelated women, oldest to youngest; (2) women in the family, oldest to youngest; (3) unrelated men, oldest to youngest; (4) men in the family, oldest to youngest. Children are served according to the same principles.

Question: Is it proper to share food?

Answer: Yes, if you ask for separate plates and utensils.

Question: How do I dispose of a tea bag?

Answer: Put it on a spoon, wrap the string around bag and spoon to squeeze out the moisture. Put it on your saucer.

EUROPE VS. AMERICA—PROPER USE OF UTENSILS

An etiquette debate rages about the "best" way to use a knife and fork. Proper Americans cut their food (one bite at a time) by holding the fork in the left hand, knife in the right. Then they put the knife down and put the fork (tines up) in the right hand to pick up and carry the food to their mouth. Proper Europeans hold the fork in the left hand and the knife in the right hand. They use the knife to ensure that the food stays on the fork. They transport the food in the fork, tines down, to their mouth. Letitia Baldrige approves of the European system as "best." Miss Manners believes that Americans should eat like Americans, Europeans like Europeans.

Weddings and Funerals

Weddings

Wedding etiquette has loosened up considerably. According to most etiquette arbiters, any bride may wear a white dress. If a map will help the wedding guests to find their way to the wedding, you may include it even in the most formal invitation. Weddings may be held at any time of year. The bride need not promise to obey and need not have her father give her away. If you like, both parents may accompany their marrying children, as is the Jewish custom. Common sense and the desires of the wedding couple and their families (if involved) should rule decisions. Even Miss Manners, who leans toward the traditional, gives bridal couples much more slack than Emily Post originally did. A few general principles apply:

♦ All the components of the event should be in harmony. That is, if the wedding is an informal affair held on a mountaintop, formal engraved invitations are out of place.

♦ All grudges should be set aside.

That said, we here outline the rules of the battered traditional wedding and a few controversies as battled out by the etiquette experts. For help planning a wedding, call the **Association of Bridal Consultants** at 203-355-0464 or **National Bridal Service** at 804-355-6945.

Wedding list: The bride and her family are in charge of compiling the list of those to be invited to the wedding, a task that should be done at least 10 weeks before the event. Half of the invitations should go to family and friends of the groom. About 10 percent of the people you invite will not be able to accept. Include those you know cannot come. More people may be invited to the reception than to the religious ceremony (or the other way around).

Invitations: The formality of the invitation should match the formality of the wedding itself. For a formal wedding, printed (less expensive) or engraved (more elegant) invitations are appropriate. Handwritten notes on white paper suit less formal weddings. Order invitations 8–10 weeks before the wedding; send them 6–8 weeks before the wedding. Those cut from the wedding list should receive wedding announcements. Envelopes should be addressed by hand. Even if other people are paying for the wedding, the bride's parents traditionally "request the honor" on the invitations.

Wording of the invitation: Perhaps no other invitation has inspired as much advice, turmoil, and controversy as the wedding invitation. Who should issue it? What wording should be used— the usual, or something interesting that expresses the feelings of the bridal couple? Should it be handwritten, printed, engraved? Handwritten invitations are the most informal. And while engraved invitations are elegant, printed ones are quite proper. As for other questions, debate rages. It is up to you, after all. However, if you

WEDDING INVITATIONS

If the bride and groom are giving their own
wedding, they may use their own names:

Felice Penny Parent
and
Norman Chance Fortune

If the wedding is not
held in a house of
worship, you may say
instead:
*the pleasure of your
company*

If you are inviting
everyone to both the
ceremony and the
reception, you may
include:
*and afterward
at Mill Lodge*

In this case, add
"R.s.v.p." at the bottom
left-hand corner.

Mr. and Mrs. John Parent

request the honor of your presence

at the marriage of their daughter

Felice Penny

to

Mr. Norman Chance Fortune

Saturday, the seventh of November

at twelve o'clock noon

First Presbyterian Church

Prosperity, Idaho

If the bride's parents
are divorced, their
names appear on
separate lines:
Mrs. Alicia Fedora
and
Mr. John Parent

You may add the year,
spelled out on a
separate line:
one thousand and one

It is not necessary to
add the name of the
city and state.

stray from traditional wording, make sure that
your invitation is clear about what people are
being invited to (church, reception, both), who is
marrying whom, where the event or events will
take place, and when the events will take place.
Proofread your invitation before you have it dupli-
cated and sent out. And you might think about
what future generations will say about it before
you become too creative.

To guests: Those invited should respond to
the invitation with acceptance or regrets. The
formality of the wording should match the formality of the invitation. Don't bring uninvited dates
or children to a wedding.

Wedding announcements: Wedding announcements are sent on the day of the wedding
or shortly thereafter to people who would want
to know about the wedding but would not expect
to attend. They are similar to invitations except
for some changes in wording.

At-Home cards: At-Home cards may accompany the invitation or announcement. They give

AT-HOME CARD

> *Ms. Felice Penny Parent*
> *Mr. Norman Chance Fortune*
>
>
> *After the 25th of November*   *12 Golden Lane*

The bride and groom announce how they wish to be addressed.

The card lets friends and family know where the couple will be living and when they will be back from their honeymoon.

---

the bridal couple's new address and state when they will be in residence. This information is useful to friends of the couple, especially those who send late presents.

Gifts: Listing choices in bridal registries in stores is still considered suitable. Once you receive gifts, you may display them on a large table with donors' cards attached (except for checks and money). You may type a list of people who sent checks (but without amounts). Thank-you notes should be written within three months of the wedding. If the wedding is called off, you must return the gifts with a note.

To guests: Though you are obligated to give presents only to people getting married for the first time, a gift is never wrong. It is not crass to ask the bridal couple what they need or to buy an expensive gift with someone else. Send the gift right after you receive the invitation. Don't bring the present to the reception—send it to the couple's home or the home of the bride's parents. (Some etiquette experts reluctantly allow you to bring presents to the reception.)

Who pays: Traditionally, the bride's family pays for most of the wedding costs. The groom's family pays for the clergyman's fee, tips for altar-boys, bride's rings, expenses for ushers, bachelor dinner and rehearsal dinner, honeymoon, corsages for family members, and the bride's going-away corsage. Bridesmaids and ushers pay for clothing, transportation to and from the town in which the wedding was held, a gift to the couple, and a group gift to person they were attending. Often ushers give the bachelor dinner. At the wedding site, all other attendants' expenses are paid by whoever is paying for the wedding. Out-of-town guests pay for their own accommodations and a gift to the couple. Today, the people who can best afford it (including the groom's parents or even the bridal couple themselves) may pay for the wedding. The bride and her mother make the wedding plans, however.

Responsibility for wedding events:

Bride: Her side of the family is in charge of compiling the wedding list. She chooses her attendants (maid and/or matron of honor, bridesmaids), making sure that one of her sisters and a sister of the groom are included. She selects their dresses. Before the wedding, she gives some sort of party for them. She also gives each one a gift.

Bride's parents: Traditionally, the wedding arrangements have been the province of the bride's mother. No matter who pays for the wedding, she is its official hostess. The father of the bride hosts the wedding. He escorts his daughter down the aisle.

Bride's attendants: The maid and/or matron of honor help the bride dress and perform other services when asked. During the wedding the attendants may hold the bride's bouquet, arrange her train, hand her the groom's ring.

Groom: He chooses his attendants (best man and ushers), making sure to include a brother of his own and a brother of the bride. He takes charge of the bachelor dinner, though he may leave the arrangements to someone else. He gives each attendant a gift.

Groom's parents: The bridegroom's parents invite the bride's parents over. Then the bride's parents reciprocate. The bridegroom gives the bachelor dinner, and the bridegroom's family gives the rehearsal dinner.

Best man: The best man may be the busiest individual of all at a wedding. He

♦ supervises the activities of the ushers, including their apparel;

♦ makes sure the ushers' presents are wrapped in time;

♦ sees to it that the men's boutonnieres and bride's bouquet have been ordered;

♦ helps arranage for transportation for all wedding events;

♦ leads off toasts and assigns toasts at the bridal dinner and wedding reception (toasting the bride first), and takes charge of seeing that everyone who should be is toasted;

♦ makes sure that the groom is dressed (wedding license in pocket) and on time for the wedding;

♦ carries the ring and payments for clergyman and church;

♦ witnesses the signing of the wedding certificate;

♦ acts as general problem solver.

Ushers: Ushers seat wedding guests, giving an arm to all women and escorting them down the aisle. The bride's friends and relatives are seated on the left, the groom's on the right except when there is a lopsided guest list—in which case, it is more important to even out the numbers of people sitting on each side of the church. Five minutes before the wedding ceremony is to begin an usher escorts the mother of the groom to her place (first row on the right), then an usher escorts the bride's mother to her place (first row on the left).

Wedding Events

Bridal shower: A close friend should give the shower, *not* a member of the family. The bride makes up the guest list (unless the shower is a surprise), and the person hosting the shower determines the number of guests. Unless the wedding is to be very small, all people invited to the shower should also be invited to the wedding. Traditionally, only the women friends of the bride attend. However, showers for the couple, with both men and women attending, are perfectly acceptable. Only the wedding party should be invited to more than one shower. The rule of thumb is that no more than two showers per bride should be given, though in reality if the bride moves in several circles of friends, several may be more practical. At the shower, someone should keep track of the gifts and who gave what. The bride should write thank-you notes for the gifts she receives.

Bachelor dinner: Takes place one to three days before the wedding, may be Dutch treat. Groom and ushers may exchange gifts at this affair. Though it was once customary to break glasses after the toast, this is no longer appropriate.

Bride's tea or luncheon: Also takes place one to three days before the wedding.

Rehearsal and rehearsal dinner: The rehearsal of the ceremony often takes place the day before, about 4 o'clock, after which the wedding party, their spouses, and close friends and family eat dinner together. The best man toasts the bride, then the bride toasts the groom; the groom, the mother of the bride; the father of the bride, the parents of the groom, and on until all members of the bridal couple's families have been toasted.

Wedding ceremony: The order of the processional varies according to religion. Guests stand for the processional and remain standing until told to sit. The ceremony itself is dictated

WEDDING PROCESSIONAL

Christian	**Jewish**

ALTAR   CHUPPAH

Christian	Jewish
best man and bridegroom (enter from side, wait at altar)	rabbi (walks down aisle if wedding is not held in temple or synagogue)
ushers	ushers
flower girl	best man
bridesmaids	bridegroom in between parents
maid and matron of honor	bridesmaids
bride with father	maid or matron of honor
pages carrying bride's train	flower girl
	bride in between parents
	pages carrying bride's train

NOTE: Miss Manners puts the bridesmaids before the flower girl.

WEDDING RECESSIONAL

Christian	**Jewish**

ALTAR   CHUPPAH

Christian	Jewish
ushers and bridesmaids (paired off)	rabbi
flower girl	ushers and bridesmaids (paired off)
maid or matron of honor and best man	flower girl
bride and groom	maid or matron of honor and best man
	groom's parents
	bride's parents
	bride and groom

NOTE: The flower girls and pages may walk immediately after the bride and groom.

by religious custom or civil law, with variations often allowed. The wedding party should meet with the person who will perform the ceremony to determine its form and content.

♦ The bride switches her engagement ring (if she has one) to her right hand before the wedding. After the wedding it goes on top of her wedding ring.

Reception:

The reception may occur right after the wedding, later in the day, or even a week or month or two after.

♦ The photographer might want to take group pictures as the guests arrive at the reception.

♦ The receiving line should be formed right away, in this order: bride's mother, groom's father, groom's mother, bride's father (optional), bride, groom, matron of honor or maid of honor, bridesmaids. As guests go down the receiving line (and they should be quick about it), they identify themselves, say something complimentary about the beauty of the bride and the wedding, congratulate the couple, and wish them happiness. A more informal alternative: the guests seat themselves and the bridal couple makes the rounds of the room.

♦ As the receiving line breaks up, the bridal couple dance. The father of the bride cuts in, as does the father of the groom and other members of the wedding party.

♦ The bride and groom sit at the bride's table—bride on groom's right, best man on her right, maid or matron of honor on groom's left—along with members of the wedding party. The parents of the couple may sit at a special table, too. The bride's mother, acting as hostess, is flanked on her right with the groom's father, her own husband across the table from her, with the groom's mother on his right. Others at the table may include the clergyman, grandparents, distinguished guests.

♦ Sometime during the reception, usually when everyone is seated, the best man toasts the couple, followed by the groom's toast to the bride, and other toasts.

♦ The cake cutting is ceremonial. The couple, as one person, cuts the first slice from the bottom of the cake and shares eating it. Someone else slices the rest of the cake and passes it around to the other guests. The top of the cake is saved for the bridal couple. Many couples freeze it and eat it at their first wedding anniversary.

♦ The order of dancing: bridal couple, bride with groom's father, groom with bride's mother, bride with best man, and groom with maid of honor, then with other members of wedding party.

ETHNIC WEDDINGS

Planning an African-American wedding demands some research and imagination. It's different from the sterotypical American wedding, not just in its ceremonial customs like the tasting of honey and kola nuts (to emphasize the sweet and the bitter). The African-American wedding (a mélange of African custom and American adaptation) celebrates the joining of two families, including the dead ancestors, more than the joining of two individuals. Brides often wear African dress. Drums and dancers take part in the ceremony.

Some Afro-American couples incorporate the jumping of the broom, an old tradition from the times of American slavery that symbolizes the joining of two households.

Chinese weddings may feature very long ceremonial dinners and "ang pows" (money in a red envelope as a wedding gift). The Kirgiz people of China tie the bride and groom together on the wedding day and release them only when relatives and friends give gifts.

At Puerto Rican weddings, a young girl, also dressed as a bride, takes part.

You can buy books on wedding planning—ethnic and otherwise. There are even tapes on how to dance at a wedding.

♦ The bride throws her bouquet, she and the groom retire to change into their honeymoon clothes, then they say goodbye and leave, showered by rice, flower petals, or confetti. Then it is time for everyone else to leave.

Second weddings: The ceremony should be small, simple, and quiet, though the reception can be as big a bash as you want. (Remember, these are the rules—you can break them.)

VIDEOTAPING A WEDDING

Yes, you can. However, it is most polite to limit the videotaping to the ceremony and ritual events like the cake cutting. It is voyeuristic to tape guests' casual conversations. Though those who do not attend will enjoy seeing the videotape, don't bore people with it.

CREATIVE (ODD) WEDDINGS

You might have the ceremony performed in a balloon, on the beach, in a cave, on a bus. And who dictates the white wedding dress? One bride did wear one—with a white motorcycle jacket over it. Another carried a bouquet made of healing crystals. "I'll Love You Always" is nice, but some couples choose reggae music. The wedding cake can be topped with almost anything—a lighted dome, the Sydney Opera House, cupids.

ANNIVERSARY GIFTS

Traditionally, wedding anniversary names have dictated gifts for the anniversary couple—a paper gift for the first anniversary, a silver gift for the twenty-fifth. Here is a list including both traditional and modern takes on the subject.

Year	Traditional	Modern
1	paper	plastics, clocks
2	cotton	calico, china
3	leather	crystal, glass
4	linen, silk	synthetics, electrical appliances
5	wood	silverware
6	iron	wood
7	copper, wool, brass	desk sets
8	bronze	electrical appliances, linens, lace
9	pottery	leather
10	tin	aluminum, diamonds
11	steel	accessories, fashion jewelry
12	silk	pearls, gems
13	lace	textiles, furs
14	ivory	gold jewelry
15	crystal	glass, watches
20	china	platinum
25	silver	sterling silver
30	pearl	diamond
35	coral, jade	jade
40	ruby	rubies, garnets
45	sapphire	sapphires, tourmalines
50	gold	gold
55	emerald	emeralds, turquoise
60	diamonds	gold, diamonds

Funerals

Death calls for more than sympathy. Though death seems to dwarf practical matters, in truth there is much to do. If you are a good friend of the family, you may be able to help.

Things a friend can do:
- Call the funeral home and lawyer.
- Call the cemetery (if the person is to be buried).
- Call friends and relatives to tell them of the death and of funeral arrangements.
- Put a death notice in the classified section of the newspaper.
- Answer the phone.
- Take care of the food.
- Be a pallbearer.
- Speak at the funeral or memorial service.

Funeral Protocol

It is no longer obligatory to wear black to a funeral. For instance, a widow may wear a dress that her husband especially liked at his funeral. At Roman Catholic funerals and Orthodox Jewish services, women may wear hats. Men at most Jewish services wear yarmulkes.

Anyone may go to a public funeral; otherwise wait to be invited.

Flowers: Do not send flowers to an orthodox Jewish funeral, perhaps not to a conservative or a reform funeral. In Catholic funerals, only flowers from the family are allowed in the church. Often it is better to send flowers to the funeral home.

Mass cards: You can arrange with the priest to have a mass or several masses said "for the soul of" the dead person. Nuns and monks may also pray for the dead. Mass cards tell about these prayers and are mailed to the dead person's family by someone from the church or are brought to the funeral home by friends and left on a special tray. You can buy mass cards for someone even if you are not Catholic.

Contributions to a charity: Often the family of the deceased requests contributions to a charity in place of flowers. Be sure that you contribute to an appropriate charity—one that the dead person was active in, for instance.

Condolence Letters

Etiquette dictates that you write a personal condolence letter—it is the one occasion when it is absolutely not proper to send a card. The condolence letter should be handwritten on white paper. All that is easy enough—the hard part is deciding what to say. Condolence letters need not be long, however—just a sentence or two saying that you are sorry, with some short comments (complimentary, of course) about the dead person and what he or she meant to you, along with an offer of help.

The family of the deceased should send handwritten thank-you notes to those people who sent flowers or made contributions in the person's name or (according to some etiquette experts) sent condolence letters.

Note: In the procession of cars to the cemetery, you traditionally put your headlights on. You must obey traffic laws unless a uniformed police officer or motorcycles from a professional escort service accompany the procession.

NICETIES

White Tie, Black Tie—What Else?

Most Americans need consider the question of white vs. black tie only a few times in their lives. It is ordinarily required only for formal occasions like weddings.

White tie: The most formal evening dress for men, white tie includes tails ("white tie and tails," *à la* Fred Astaire). You should not wear white tie before 6 PM. Specifically, "white tie" means:

♦ a tailcoat with tails reaching to behind your knee;

♦ matching pants without cuffs, and satin or grosgrain faille stripe down the outside seam of the leg;

♦ a white waistcoat;

♦ a white, wing-collared shirt with studs rather than buttons;

♦ a white bowtie;

♦ plain black oxfords or evening shoes with bows;

♦ thin black socks;

♦ optional: top hat, white scarf, white gloves.

Women at a white-tie affair wear long evening dresses.

Black tie: According to Miss Manners, this has meant "informal" dress. Other etiquette experts say that it is "semiformal," though semiformal can, in some parts of the country, mean that you should wear a dark business suit. If an invitation for a semiformal late afternoon or evening occasion does not specify dress, you are safe with black tie. Black tie implies the wearing of:

♦ a dinner jacket, black in winter, white in summer;

♦ matching black pants without cuffs, and satin or grosgrain faille stripe down the outside seam of the leg;

♦ a wool vest *or* cummerbund in winter; cummerbund in summer;

♦ white shirt, pleated or not (but no button-downs);

♦ a dressy bowtie, usually black;

♦ plain black oxfords or evening shoes with bows;

♦ thin black socks;

♦ optional: homburg, white scarf, gray gloves.

Women at a black-tie affair wear short dressy dresses.

Gifts

No etiquette advice can completely alleviate the anxiety that goes into selecting a proper gift. Experts agree that a little gift is almost always appropriate. You can't go wrong with flowers. Incidentally, you don't need to play tit-for-tat with gift giving. That is, if a wealthy friend gives you an expensive gift, you are not obligated to spend the same amount of money on him or her. On the other hand, the person to whom you give a gift is not obligated to reciprocate.

Question: I received a birthday party invitation with the annotation "no gifts." However, I would like to give a gift. What is the correct protocol?

Answer: You may give a present—just don't bring it to the party because it may embarrass the guest of honor and the other guests who obeyed the directive on the invitation.

Question: When is it considered proper to give money?

Answer: It depends on custom. Some people welcome money at a confirmation, a bar or bat mitzvah, or a wedding. If it bothers you to give money, consider giving a gift certificate or a stock or bond.

Question: I sent a gift months ago to a favorite niece, and I have received no thank-you note. May I ask her if she received the gift? I am worried that it was lost in the mail.

Answer: Yes.

Question: As our family has grown, gift giving at holidays has become expensive and time consuming. How might I call a halt to it?

Answer: In cases like this, it is best well ahead of the holidays to write to or meet with members of the family to suggest a name drawing so that each family member gives to only one other family member. Or you might suggest giving less expensive gifts.

Question: In a new relationship, what gifts are appropriate?

Answer: Impersonal ones.

Question: When it is all right to exchange a gift?

Answer: When it is not one of a kind.

Question: I was embarrassed to receive a gift from someone who came calling during the holidays. How can I avoid future embarrassment?

Answer: Keep a store of small gifts (of food, say) just for such occasions.

Question: What is appropriate for a fiftieth wedding anniversary?

Answer: The family may pool resources to buy a special expensive present, like a trip to Europe. It is not proper to ask other guests to chip in on such a gift. Some enterprising families request that guests write up an experience shared with the guests of honor, then bind them in a book. Some experts approve of a money tree (provided that children of the anniverary couple suggest it); others don't.

Question: What are proper ceremonial gifts?

Answer: For a christening, a bar or bat mitzvah, a graduation, and other ceremonial occasion, try to give something of permanent value, such as a book, a pen, stocks or bonds.

Question: An acquaintance sent me an announcement of his graduation. Is it necessary for me to send a gift?

Answer: Only if you want to. You should bring a gift if you are invited to the ceremony.

Question: What gift should I bring when invited to dinner?

Answer: Flowers or wine, perhaps candy.

When Are Thank-You Notes Necessary?

The overriding rule: write a thank-you note when you are grateful for some kindness or gift. Be specific—for instance, mention the gift and why you were pleased to receive it. However, don't mention money amounts when thanking people for gifts of money. But do tell how you are planning to use the money.

Thank-you notes should be sent within two or three days. However for gifts you received at a big occasion, like a wedding, you have up to three months before anyone will consider you an ungrateful boor.

If you and the gift giver are in the same room when you open the gift, and you thank the giver personally, thank-you notes are not always necessary, say the experts. However, you should always write thank-you notes in the following situations:

♦ When someone has had you over for dinner as guest of honor. (Some experts say you should thank your host or hostess with a letter or phone call after any sit-down dinner.)

♦ When you are a house guest (stay overnight or longer).

♦ In response to a note congratulating you for some achievement.

♦ For a gift for which you did not thank the giver personally.

♦ For any wedding gift.

Godparents

Who? Ordinarily godparents are not members of the family, but close friends. Traditionally they were of the same religion as the baby, but now the real requirement is that they have the same attitude toward life as the parents. According to Miss Manners, the baby should have two

godparents of its own sex and one of the opposite sex.

Job? It is an honor, with the only real obligation to be a friend to the child, to provide moral advice, perhaps religious advice, if wanted. Traditionally godparents oversaw the spiritual education of the child, but that no longer holds. It is not the godparents' responsibility to bring up the child if the parents should die. (A legal guardian is responsible for such upbringing.) At the christening, a godparent holds the child.

Present: When the child is baptized or at the bris (Jewish circumcision) ceremony, you give a gift. The gift has traditionally been of silver—a mug or matching fork and spoon, engraved with the baby's initials and birthdate. You can also give a baby book, photograph album, savings account.

Invitations

Most of the invitations we issue are informal—with a note or phone call. When you use formal engraved or printed invitations (proper only for formal occasions), follow the same general guidelines as for wedding invitations ("Weddings," p. 655). Mail at least three weeks before the event, state the reason for it, and if you include "r.s.v.p." or "please respond," give an address for responses.

FORMAL INVITATIONS

You might add a line specifying the kind of event it is, for example:
at dinner

If the replies should be sent to an address other than where the event is being held, include that address under the *R.s.v.p.*

Mr. and Mrs. William Bucks
request the pleasure of your company
on Saturday, April 1
at eight o'clock
449 Penny Lane
Goldmine, Idaho

R.s.v.p.   *Black tie*

You may also want to state the reason for the event, for example:
in honor of our daughter's graduation
However, if you are throwing the party for yourself, don't mention the reason.

Mention dress only if it is black tie or white tie,

Always respond to an invitation with an acceptance or regrets. Match the formality of the response to the formality of the invitation.

CHILDREN'S NAMES

Catholic children must be given a saint's name, either as a first name or middle name. Jewish children may be given a name that is close to that of a dead relative (beginning with the same initial, for instance). If a boy is named for his father, his father becomes Senior (Sr.) and the boy is Junior (Jr.) If a boy is named for another relative (grandfather, for instance), he is "the second" (II).

Smoking

No matter what your stand on smoking, etiquette rules apply. (For health implications of smoking and secondhand smoke, see "How to Quit Smoking," p. 37.)

Smokers should:

♦ Put out their cigarettes when food arrives at their table or a neighboring one. Make sure the butt is not smouldering.

♦ When smokers visit someone's home, ask permission to smoke.

♦ Position their cigarettes so that smoke does not blow in someone else's direction.

♦ Ask if their smoking is bothersome, and put out the cigarette if it is.

♦ Refrain from insisting on sitting in the smoking section of a restaurant when the friends accompanying them are nonsmokers.

♦ Pay attention to the missing ashtray. One does not have to be a detective to figure out why it is missing.

Nonsmokers should:

♦ Refrain from making a crusade out of their abstinence. While it is perfectly proper to ask someone to put out a cigarette when it is bother-

some, it is priggish to ask people to put out cigarettes just on principle.

♦ Warn smokers in advance that they do not allow smoking in their house. Suggest that smokers smoke outside.

♦ Put a sign saying "Thank you for not smoking" in their office, not their house.

Note: It is not only proper but preferable that you say something to smokers who smoke in places where it is against the law. But be polite about it.

Telephone Manners

As telephones have become technological marvels, telephone etiquette problems have gone from not listening in on a party line to questions much more complicated.

Answering machines: Long, funny messages amuse the first time, but soon become tiresome. Unless you can change messages often, confine yourself to the simple: "Hello. This is Fritz Outalot. I am unable to come to the phone right now, but please leave your name and telephone number, and I will call you back as soon as I can."

If you screen calls by letting your machine answer, be careful about what you say if you pick up the phone after someone has started to leave a message. You don't want to give the impression that you are screening calls—otherwise the person you are speaking to will be suspicious when he or she calls again and your machine answers. Say that you were busy and could not come to the phone right away.

Telephone solicitation: It is perfectly polite to say, "I'm sorry, but I am not interested." If the solicitor asks, "When would be a convenient time to call?" feel free to answer, "Never, I don't like telephone solicitation." You can also say that you don't like to discuss unsolicited appeals over the phone, but you would appreciate materials sent you through the mail.

Two lines or call waiting: If you have call waiting, do not put the original caller on hold while you talk at length to the one whose call interrupted you. If the second call is an emergency or a very important long-distance call, switch back to the original caller to explain and say you will call back.

If you are put on hold by a friend, it is perfectly proper to hang up. When the person calls you back, you can say, according to Miss Manners, "We seem to have been cut off."

Beepers and cellular phones: Unless you are a doctor, or a member of the police or fire department, use beepers and cellular phones with discretion. They don't belong at social occasions or in a restaurant.

General telephone manners:

♦ Always give your name when you call— "Hello, this is Fritz Chatter. May I please speak with Marjorie Prattle?"

♦ When you get a wrong number, don't just hang up—apologize. Don't ask what number you have reached. Instead, tell what number you

are calling. If you are on the other side of this contretemps and don't want to give out your number to a complete stranger, say, "Sorry, I don't like to give my number. What number are you calling?"

♦ Keep three-way conversations to a minimum.

♦ Teach your children to answer the phone correctly.

♦ Only servants should answer the phone with "This is the Chatter residence."

♦ Don't call too early in the morning or too late at night.

♦ Give people at least six rings to get to the phone. (One expert says 10.)

♦ If you have a speaker phone, say so. The caller has the right to know.

♦ If you call long distance from someone else's phone, ask the operator to charge it to your home phone.

♦ If you have a visitor, do not indulge yourself in a long phone conversation. Say you will call back later.

WHAT TO DO WHEN YOU MEET THE QUEEN OF ENGLAND

First of all, don't even think about hugging and kissing her. While some areas of royal protocol are up for debate, exuberant physical contact isn't one of them.

Next, the big controversy: do you curtsy if you are a woman, or bow if you are a man? Depends on where you are. If the introduction takes place in the United States, it is acceptable for both women and men to make a slight bow, while shaking hands with the queen. However, if you are on British soil (especially "at court"), royal protocol dictates that women execute a deep, formal curtsy and men a full-fledged bow.

In addition, if you are presented to the Queen of England, you do not speak first. After she speaks to you, you can reply, but be sure to keep it short—one or two sentences is appropriate. And be sure that you address her as "Your Majesty."

Miscellaneous Manners

Abbreviations: On a formal invitation, you may abbreviate only "Mr.," "Mrs.," and "Ms."

Adoption: Adoption announcements might read:

Mr. and Mrs. George Parent
take pleasure in announcing
the adoption of
Jeanne Marie
born December 3, 1996

You may give a shower for an adoption, but wait until the child has been adopted. For an older child, an adoption party is appropriate.

Birth announcement: Traditional wording is as follows:

Mr. and Mrs. George Parent
are proud to announce
the birth of their daughter
Jeanne Marie
born December 3, 1996

Divorce announcement: It is in poor taste to send out a divorce announcement or to have a divorce party.

Gloves: You are expected to wear gloves (long ones) at formal White House dinners and when meeting the Pope.

Kissing: Don't kiss someone if you have a cold, and even if you are in perfect health, it is better to stick to kissing a cheek. When meeting a woman, the man should follow her lead. If she sticks out her hand, he should shake it. In general, social rank directs who initiates handshaking—the most important, the older.

Meeting the Pope: Yes, you must kneel and kiss his ring if he comes up to you.

Putting on makeup: You may put on lipstick, nothing more, at the table in restaurants. Don't interrupt a conversation to do it. And no mascara, lip pencil, or hair combing—which should take place in the ladies' room.

Videotaping: If you want to take close-ups, you should ask permission.

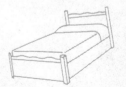

13

LOOKING AND FEELING GOOD

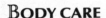

BODY CARE

ADDITIONS AND ACCENTS

Sᴘᴇᴄɪᴀʟ PROBLEMS

BODY CARE

Skin Care

Male or female, the basics of good skin care are the same: frequent exercise, a good diet, plenty of sleep, regular cleansing, moderate moisturizing, no smoking or excessive drinking, and staying out of the sun. If you follow this prescription, have the advantage of some good genes, and live in a temperate climate with clean air, you're bound to have flawless skin.

A Cleansing Routine for the Face

Most dermatologists recommend washing the face twice a day with a mild soap. For people with dry skin or allergies, the detergent ingredients and alkaline properties of fatty soaps can cause irritation or chapping. If that occurs, you should buy a cleansing bar that is less alkaline. People with oily skin should avoid soaps with a high content of lanolin or mineral oil, which can clog the pores and cause pimples. Products labeled "noncomedogenic" eliminate pore-clogging ingredients.

Applying toner or an astringent to the skin after cleansing helps remove any residue of oil and dirt and makes the pores appear smaller. For men, the alcohol content of aftershave accomplishes this purpose. Women have a variety of products to choose from, but a homemade alternative of witch hazel (for oily skin) or lemon juice and water (for dry skin) can be just as effective. People with dry skin should avoid witch hazel and other products with high alcohol content—look for ingredients on the product label that end in "ol."

Moisturizers

While people with very oily skin do not need a moisturizer, people with normal or dry skin can benefit from a moisturizer that smoothes and plumps up the facial skin. A decade ago, moisturizers contained mostly water, oil, and waxes. Today, there are many products that contain humectants—substances that promote the shedding of dead skin and encourage the skin to absorb and retain water. These substances include urea, lactic acid (a substance found in fermented milk products), and glycolic acid (found in sugarcane).

Most of these new "anti-aging" moisturizers are quite expensive. Before you spend $35–$40 an ounce, consider that moisturizing is a temporary effect—it does not change the texture of the skin and it does not prevent wrinkles. Sunscreen is the only effective anti-wrinkle ingredient.

Aging of the Skin

Twenty percent of the sags and wrinkles that occur in the face as we grow older are caused by the biological process of aging. An estimated 80 percent are caused by exposure to the sun. Whether the agent is Father Time or the sun, the effect is the same. The sun destroys the fibrous proteins in the dermis, the skin's supporting structure. These fibers—collagen and elastin—also lose their firmness and elasticity as we age. Once this substructure is weakened, the upper layer of the skin, the epidermis, loses its tone, and wrinkles and sags develop.

Various factors can define where on the face wrinkles will develop:

♦ Habitual facial expressions, such as squinting, frowning, scowling, or smiling. These repetitive movements can stretch the facial muscles and make them more vulnerable to wrinkles.

♦ Sleep postures. Putting habitual pressure on your face during sleep encourages wrinkles. Sleeping on the back is a good remedy.

♦ Smoking. The mechanics of smoking cause constant restriction of the lips. Smoking also promotes squinting and reduces oxygen in the capillaries of the dermis.

♦ A cycle of weight gain and loss. As we age, the elastic qualities of the skin are diminished and the skin can't "bounce back" as it once did.

Acne

Acne affects 80 percent of teenagers, as well as many adults. It is caused primarily by overactive oil glands—a condition that can be influenced by hormones, diet, weather, and hereditary factors. As mentioned above, people with oily skin should avoid fatty cosmetic products. Avoiding fatty and heavily-sugared foods is also in order.

While consulting a dermatologist is often necessary, some people with acne will see results from self-treatment with benzoyl peroxide, the strongest nonprescription medication available for the condition. Start with a low concentrate of 2.5 percent and gradually increase the strength if you see no improvement. Whether you have a serious case of acne or an occasional pimple, never squeeze blemishes, either whiteheads or blackheads. It can lead to infection and scarring.

Common Myths About Skin Care

There are many misunderstandings about what is good for the skin. Our preoccupation with the signs of skin aging can lead to some odd notions. Here are some of the common myths about skin:

MYTH: Dry skin causes wrinkles.
FACT: Whether skin is dry or oily has no influence on wrinkles. Wrinkles are caused by the breakdown of protein fibers in the substructure of the skin, as a result of aging or sun exposure.

MYTH: Sunscreen is only for days at the beach.
FACT: A *daily* application of SPF 15 sunscreen is the second best antiwrinkle treatment available. The best is staying out of the sun, particularly between 10:00 AM and 2:00 PM. Using one sunscreen product is sufficient. Women who apply an SPF 15 moisturizer and a foundation with sunscreen are getting no additional benefit and may be inviting skin irritation.

MYTH: Steaming the face opens the pores and allows for a better shave.
FACT: Steaming the face actually closes the pores by plumping up the skin around the pores. It's best to shave after washing the face in warm water and after shaving cream has further softened the skin on the face or legs.

MYTH: A rigorous daily scrub is good for the face.
FACT: As part of its biological cycle, the skin is continually sloughing off dead cells to make way for new cells in the epidermis. Exfoliating products or "cell-renewal agents" are good in moderation to enhance this natural process, but once a week is normally sufficient. Scrub products should never be used on blemished or irritated skin.

MYTH: Flaking is always a sign of dry skin.

FACT: Too much moisturizing can actually inflame the oil glands and create irritation and flaking.

MYTH: Facial exercises and facial massages can prevent wrinkles by toning the muscles.

FACT: Sagging skin and wrinkles are due to a loss of support in the substratum of the skin—not because facial muscles are relaxed or have a lack of tone.

Basic Hair Care

Like other parts of the body, hair looks its best when it is cleaned regularly and its proper moisture balance is maintained. The outer layer of the hair shaft is composed of cells that overlap to form a protective cuticle. When the cuticle is burned or broken by the sun, heat drying, or harsh chemicals, the hair looks dull. In healthy hair, the cells of the cuticle lie flat and the resulting appearance is shiny hair.

Haircuts

In order to minimize bad hair days, start with a good cut in a style that fits your face and lifestyle. Be sure your stylist knows your limitations in terms of available time and styling ability. Remember, you're on your own once you leave the salon.

One way to find a good stylist is to ask someone whose hair you admire where they have their hair cut. When you encounter a new stylist or are braving the scissors for a new cut, it's helpful to take along pictures from magazines that approximate the look you want to achieve. Be realistic about what your hair can and cannot do. One expert on women's hair recommends, "Never layer thin, fine hair—a blunt cut is best."

Brushing and Combing

Brushing your hair 100 strokes a day, contrary to folk wisdom, is not a good idea, as it can damage the hair cuticle, cause split ends, and make the hair excessively oily. A light brushing or combing once or twice a day is all that's needed. Brushing hair before shampooing helps to distribute scalp oils and prevent tangles, but never take a brush to wet hair—hair stretches more when it's wet and more readily snaps and breaks in this elasticized condition. Use a wide-tooth comb to detangle wet hair.

Choose a hairbrush that has rounded tips and smooth shafts. The bristles can be nylon, plastic, or natural. A comb should also have smooth teeth and no sharp edges that can rip the hair shaft. Don't forget to wash combs and brushes frequently. Try soaking them in a sink full of water with a tablespoon of baking soda and just a drop of household bleach, then rinse.

Shampooing/Conditioning

Some hair problems are caused by not shampooing frequently enough, by using too much shampoo, or by not rinsing adequately. The following techniques are recommended for the best possible at-home shampoo:

♦ Shampoo in warm or tepid water, not hot.
♦ Rinse hair first to dislodge oils and dirt.
♦ Apply a small quantity of shampoo, not more than a quarter-size amount.
♦ Spread the shampoo on both palms for even distribution on the hair.
♦ Shampoo with the pads of your fingers, not your fingernails.
♦ Begin massaging at the hairline and move backward and down to reduce tangling.
♦ Lather only once if you shampoo daily. Lather and rinse twice if you wash your hair less frequently.
♦ Rinse thoroughly, until pulling on a strand of hair produces a "squeak."
♦ Apply conditioner only on the ends of the hair, not on or near the scalp, and rinse again.
♦ Blot hair dry with a towel, don't rub.

Many hair stylists recommend changing hair products frequently to avoid "build-up," or using a special clarifying shampoo weekly to remove shampoo residues or hard water deposits. A homemade rinse of half lemon juice, half water accomplishes the same effect.

There are also many homemade recipes for conditioning dry hair, including an overnight application of olive oil (be sure to cover your pillow with a towel). When buying commercial conditioners, read labels and experiment to determine which ingredients work best for you. If you have oily hair, try a balsam conditioner alternated with a body-building product. If you have permed hair, avoid products with sodium hydroxide, which can straighten the hair.

When you don't have time to shampoo, you can refresh oily or dirty hair by using a commercial "dry shampoo," or dusting the hair with dry oatmeal, cornstarch, corn meal, or talcum powder and then brushing thoroughly.

Heat Styling

To most women and many men, the blow dryer has become as indispensable as the microwave. Just remember that too much heat can hurt the hair. If you shampoo daily, give your hair a once-a-week break from the dryer by letting it dry naturally. Here are some tips for effective heat styling:

♦ Allow hair to air-dry for 10 minutes or so after shampooing.

♦ After blow-drying hair nearly dry, switch to a cool setting for a better set to the style and less damage to the hair.

♦ Dry straight hair or straighten curly hair by blow-drying hair until no dampness remains. Using a brush, lift the hair near the roots and move the dryer from the roots to the tips of the hair, using the brush as a guide.

♦ Blow-dry curly hair in a circular motion. Leave it slightly damp so the curls will set.

Dandruff

According to a recent study, 85 percent of the population experiences flaky scalp, but only 33 percent of the causes merit medicated treatment.

If you have fine, dry flakes in the scalp, you can usually remedy it by using a conditioner or conditioning shampoo that has moisturizing properties, by avoiding the hot setting on your hair dryer, and by not using hair sprays or other hair products with propyl or isopropyl alcohol.

If the flakes on your scalp are oily and stick together, a medicated dandruff shampoo is in order. Dandruff shampoos slow the growth of excessive bacteria in the scalp and usually stop the flaking within two or three weeks. The shampoos have ingredients of varying strength. Some common ingredients are salicylic acid (relatively mild, can be used every other day), pyrithione zinc (can be used every third day), selenium sulfide (strong-acting, use only once a week—not for pregnant or nursing women). Tar shampoo is also very strong-acting and can potentially cause inflammation of the scalp.

Once the flaking has stopped, taper off on the dandruff shampoo and alternate it with your regular shampoo until you find a regimen that keeps you flake-free.

Beards and Moustaches

A beard, moustache, or both may save a man time while shaving, but they still require committed care for a neat appearance. They should be washed daily to remove dirt and bacteria and to keep the hair conditioned and soft. A trim is in order weekly and at haircut time. The whiskers should be trimmed only when dry, since wet whiskers lie differently on the face.

When growing a beard or moustache, allow approximately three weeks for full growth. Some itching and discomfort can be expected. Wash the growing hair daily, using a mild dandruff shampoo if there is excessive flaking of the skin.

Beards and moustaches can help to balance facial features. A full beard and moustache can minimize a long, thin face; a weak or pointy chin; and a less-than-perfect nose. They can also draw attention away from a receding hairline. A moustache on its own diminishes the impact of a big nose, low hairline, jutting chin, or an especially wide face.

Hair Options—Color and Perms

Curling and coloring the hair are age-old options for changing one's appearance. Permanent waves, which are not really permanent, cut down on the time it takes to create daily curls or a fuller style. Color treatments can be dramatic, like changing you from a brunette to a blonde, or they can simply be a way to hide gray hair. One in every four persons has some gray hair by the age of 25, and nearly 65 percent are partially gray by age 35.

Hair Coloring

Applied properly, a hair-color product can add body and manageability to the hair, as well as change the color. On the negative side, hair-coloring products can trigger allergies and, if improperly applied, can damage the hair and result in a color that horrifies you and everyone you know. In addition, while there has been concern that hair color can be linked to cancer, a 1994 study by the American Cancer Society showed that for more than 99 percent of women who use hair color, the products do not increase the risk of cancer even with long-term use. However, there is a small risk for permanent-dye users who have been using black hair dye for 20 years or more.

Cautionary tales aside, it's a foregone conclusion that hair coloring will increase among both men and women as the population grows older and grayer. While the graying process is not thoroughly understood by the scientific community, we do know that a pigment called melanin colors the hair and that the production of melanin is affected by genetic, environmental, and nutritional conditions.

According to Clairol, the hair-color products company, 8 percent of the 40 million gray-haired men in America color their hair and most women today consider that acceptable, or even desirable, for men to do so. Hair coloring appears to be most prevalent among men in their early forties,

when gray hair is not quite a hallmark of being "older and wiser."

Whether you color your hair at home or go to a salon, the type of color product you choose will determine your level of commitment:

Temporary color. Temporary hair-color products come in foams, rinses, and shampoos. They coat the hair shaft with color rather than penetrate it and gradually wash out after one to three shampoos. Because of the coating affect, they reflect less light and are less natural-looking than the other types of hair color.

Semipermanent color. These solutions partially open the hair cuticle to deposit color. Typically, they last from three to six washings, but some are advertised to last up to 24. With repetitive use, some semipermanent products tend to deposit permanent color.

Permanent color. Permanent color products penetrate the hair cuticle, take out the natural pigment, and lock in the dye. The color stays in the hair until new hair growth at the roots shows your natural color.

When choosing a color, it's advisable to pick a color that's just a shade or two lighter or darker than your natural hair. That way you're more likely to select a color that's flattering to your complexion and eye color. If you're coloring at home, do a color test before jumping in. Snip off a strand of your hair and test the solution on it, paying close attention to the timing. You should also do a patch test on your skin a day before coloring to see if you develop any redness, itching, or other signs of allergic reactions. If you do, don't use the product.

Once you have made the commitment, your color-treated hair will need some special care. Apply a conditioner at least once a month and be sure to wear a bathing cap in chlorinated pools to protect the color.

Permanents

The chemical magic that makes straight hair curl is a process that rearranges the protein molecules of the hair. The waving solution of a perm breaks the bonds that hold these proteins together. The neutralizing solution stops the chemical action of the waving lotion and encourages the reconnection of the bonds in a new shape—the shape dictated by the perm rods.

There are three basic types of permanent waves. The choice you or you and your stylist make will depend on the texture, elasticity, and porosity of your hair—and the desired hair style.

Conventional/alkaline perms. The active "bond-breaking" chemical in these perms is ammonium thioglycolate. This is the strongest type of perm available and creates the firmest curls and the most volume. It's especially good for long hair or any hair that is reluctant to take a perm.

Acid perms. In acid perms, the active agent (glycol monothioglycolate) breaks down the bonds of the hair more slowly than in conventional perms, and thus is less damaging to the hair shaft. These perms create softer curls and are better for damaged hair or fine, fragile hair. Heat is applied generally during the waving-lotion phase of these perms; the heat speeds up the bond-breaking process.

Soft waves. The active ingredients in these perms are bisulfites. Like the acid perms, they give a gentler effect and are less likely to frizz or break the hair. This is the mildest form of perm and it is usually found in retail products, not at professional salons. These at-home products may last only two to three months, as opposed to a conventional/alkaline perm that can last up to six months.

Wrapping Techniques

The newest perms give a natural, softly curled effect partly because of new wrapping techniques and new shapes in perm rods:

Root perms—only the first inch of the hair from the root outward is wrapped on the rods. This gives a lift to the roots and works especially well on short hair.

Weave perms—only sections of the hair are wrapped. This technique adds body to medium-length hair.

Spiral perms—the hair is wrapped around rods with spiral grooves which are placed hanging down from the head, instead of resting horizontally on the scalp. The spiral wrap works well to give long, medium-textured hair volume and springy curls.

Words of Caution

Processing the hair with a permanent wave and color at the same time can cause serious damage. It may be best to rely on a professional if you're undertaking this double treatment. In any case, do not do both processes on the same day.

It's best to perm first and wait 7 to 10 days before coloring. The chemicals in the perm can strip color from the hair. If you have already colored your hair at home (even with a rinse or spray-in color), be sure to tell the stylist when you arrive at the salon for a perm. Color-treated hair tends to be more porous and requires a gentle perm with special conditioners, or it may be best to wait on the perm until your hair is in better condition.

For heavily processed hair, regular at-home conditioning is important. Try the "leave-in" conditioning products that are not rinsed off the hair when you shampoo. Also, avoid styling products with alcohol and always protect your hair from the sun.

Nail Care

During 1992, Americans spent $3.4 billion on nail care. While many of the products and processes used were superfluous to basic nail care, the amount of money spent does demonstrate that we consider our nails to be an important part of our personal appearance.

Dos and Don'ts of Nail and Hand Care

♦ Don't subject your hands and nails to extremely hot water, harsh chemicals, and strong household cleaners. Do wear gloves.

♦ Do apply hand lotion regularly to keep the

hands moisturized and aid nails that crack or chip. If nails are soft and tend to tear, avoid putting lotion on the nails themselves.

♦ Do use a cuticle cream daily or massage a dab of olive oil into the cuticles.

♦ Don't file or buff the nails excessively. This can thin and weaken nails.

♦ Do be alert to allergic reactions from form-aldehyde in nail polish or acrylics in sculptured nails, tips, and nail glues. The reaction may show up as a rash or itchiness on places touched by the nails, like the eyelids, cheeks, or neck—rather than on the less sensitive skin of the hands.

Manicure Basics

A home manicure, once you learn the basics, can be an easy weekly routine to improve the appearance of your nails and hands.

♦ File each nail with an emery board from the sides in toward the center. File in one direction only, don't "saw" back and forth.

♦ Soak fingertips in warm soapy water to soften cuticles.

♦ Apply cuticle remover and gently push back the cuticle with the blunt end of an orangewood stick.

♦ Trim any hangnails with a small nail scissors. Do not otherwise cut the cuticle, as it is the protective barrier for the growth center of the nail.

♦ Scrub nails in soapy water and clean under the nails with an orangewood stick wrapped in cotton.

♦ Dry hands and apply hand lotion.

Polish Tips

Polishing the nails creates a finished look, but your nails will be healthier if you let them go at least one day a week without polish. Here are some tips for a professional-looking polish job:

♦ Wipe nails with polish remover after the manicure to remove any residue of soap or lotion.

♦ Don't polish the underside of the nail. When it's time to remove the polish, chemicals in the polish remover can lift the nail away from the nail bed, providing a chance for infection to develop.

♦ Apply a base coat and two to three thin coats of polish, rather than one thick one, for better coverage. An additional clear top coat protects against chipping.

♦ Tidy up polish that's strayed onto the fingers with the following tool: a moistened tooth-pick wrapped in a bit of cotton puff and saturated in nail polish remover.

♦ If you have to dry polish quickly, try dipping fingers carefully in a bowl of ice water.

♦ Polish nails away from direct sunlight, which may cause bubbles in the finish.

Nail Salon Safety

If your idea of doing your nails is a weekly visit to the salon, you need to find a nail salon that is hygienic and safe. Although most states require manicure/pedicure salons to be licensed, safety and health practices vary widely in the industry and government controls are not strict. The nail-salon environment can provide an opportunity for the transmission of bacterial diseases and fungal infections—even hepatitis, warts, and other viruses (although there has been no documented case of AIDS being transmitted in this fashion). Here are some guidelines and suggestions for monitoring nail-salon standards:

♦ Metal implements should be cleaned between client visits. Implements should be washed and then soaked for a minimum of 10 minutes in a hospital-grade disinfectant.

♦ You may choose to bring your own manicure implements, properly sterilized.

♦ Both you and the technician should wash your hands before beginning the manicure.

♦ Fresh nonmetal products (emery boards, cuticle sticks, towels) should be used for each client.

♦ Ask your manicurist not to cut your cuticles, since cutting increases the risk of infection and overcutting the cuticles can affect nail growth.

Special Effects

Women who like sculptured or acrylic nails should be aware that they can cause allergic reactions. Also, covering the nails for extended periods of time can create an environment for bacterial and fungal infections. Silk wraps rarely produce allergic reaction or fungi, but the silk material can invite bacterial growth. Protect yourself by taking an occasional break from these types of treatments and always work with a manicurist who has high professional standards.

Happy Feet

Although the feet are complex structures—with 26 bones, 33 joints, and more than 100 tendons and ligaments—it is not normal to have sore or aching feet. Other than wearing the proper shoes (see "Buying Shoes That Fit," page 684), the best way to keep your feet happy is proper and consistent care:

♦ Bathe the feet daily and dry them thoroughly, especially between the toes.

♦ Apply a light moisturizer over all the foot, except between the toes.

♦ Dust or spray feet with foot powder.

♦ Don't wear the same shoes every day. Switching shoes allows the foot muscles to relax and helps to prevent foot odor.

♦ Strengthen the feet and increase circulation through walking or special foot exercises.

♦ Treat your feet to an occasional massage and pedicure.

♦ Consult a podiatrist if you experience persistent pain, redness, swelling, or irritation.

Common Foot Ailments

The American Podiatric Medical Association provides the following definitions of the leading foot complaints and what can be done about them.

Athlete's foot is a skin disease, usually start-ing between the toes, which can spread to other parts of the foot and the body. It is caused by a fungus which most commonly attacks the feet because the warm, dark humidity of shoes fosters fungus growth. The signs of athlete's foot are drying skin, itching, scaling, inflammation, and blisters. You can prevent infection by washing your feet daily in soap and warm water; drying carefully, especially between the toes; and changing shoes and hose regularly to decrease moisture.

Blisters are caused by skin friction and moisture. Don't pop them. Apply moleskin or a Band-Aid over a blister, and leave it on until it falls off naturally in the bath or shower. Keep your feet dry and wear a layer of socks as a cushion between your feet and shoes. If a blister breaks on its own, wash the area, apply an antiseptic, and cover with a sterile bandage.

Bunions are misaligned big-toe joints which become swollen and tender. The deformity causes the first joint of the big toe to slant outward, and the second joint to angle toward the other toes. Bunions tend to be inherited, but the tendency can be aggravated by shoes that are too narrow in the forefoot and toe. There are conservative and preventative steps which can minimize the discomfort of a bunion, but surgery is frequently recommended to correct the problem.

Corns and calluses are protective layers of compacted, dead cells. They are caused by repeated friction and pressure from skin rubbing against bony areas or against an irregularity in a shoe. Corns ordinarily form on the toes and calluses on the soles of the feet, but both can occur on either surface. The friction and pressure can burn or otherwise be painful and may be relieved by applying moleskin on the affected areas. Never cut corns or calluses with any instrument, and never apply home remedies, except under a podiatrist's instructions.

Ingrown nails are nails whose corners or sides dig painfully into the skin. They are frequently caused by improper nail trimming, but also by shoe pressure, injury, fungus infection, poor foot structure, and heredity. Toenails should be trimmed straight across, slightly longer than the end of the toe, with toenail clippers.

For more information on foot-health conditions and concerns, contact: **American Podiatric Medical Association,** 9312 Old Georgetown Road, Bethesda, MD 20814 (800-FOOTCARE).

Body Odors—Causes and Prevention

The sense of smell acts as a warning device. Our noses screen out our normal body odors in order to detect other smells in the environment. While we react quickly to the malodorous scents of others, and we can detect sudden changes in our own systems (such as body odor after exercise), we are basically immune to our own odors, whether they be pleasant or strongly offensive.

Since we can't rely on ourselves and perhaps not even on our best friends to alert us, it's best to prevent body odors through a consistent regimen of good personal care.

Body Odor

The ancient Egyptians, and not the heavily perfumed courts of Europe, knew the best way to control body odor—bathing daily. Body odor is caused by bacteria acting upon perspiration and body oils, primarily in the glandular areas under the arms and near the genitals. Washing away the bacteria gives you a fresh start, whereas perfumes and lotions merely create a more complex body bouquet.

If you have a persistent body-odor problem, try changing brands of soap, as some may have ingredients that react negatively with your body chemistry and can actually cause odor. Deodorants, which have antibacterial agents, and antiperspirants can be helpful. Antiperspirants contain an aluminum compound, usually aluminum chloride or aluminum chlorohydrate. Aluminum chloride is more effective at inhibiting perspira-

tion, but it can cause skin irritation and damage clothing. Test different products carefully, or try a mild homemade deodorant of baking soda—just dab a little under your arms after you've dried off from the shower.

Be sure to wear clean underwear and clothes every day, preferably garments of natural materials (silk, wool, cotton) that allow air to circulate.

Foot Odor

As with body odor, the culprit that causes smelly feet is bacterial growth in a medium of perspiration. Each foot has more than 250,000 sweat glands, so it is imperative to keep the feet dry, clean, and well ventilated.

If your daily shower does not prevent foot odor, try bathing your feet in warm water with a little baking soda or vinegar. Foot powders and antiperspirants can also help the problem. Most shoe inserts advertised to stop odor don't stop feet from perspiring, but they contain an ingredient, activated charcoal, that can absorb odor.

Don't wear the same pair of shoes two days in a row. Give them a chance to air out. Likewise wear fresh socks every day, or even change your socks at midday. Wear wool or cotton socks and leather shoes, avoiding synthetic materials that keep air out and moisture in.

Bad Breath

The constant moisture in the mouth provides an ideal growing ground for bacteria and the odor-causing toxins they produce. To avoid bad breath, clean the mouth thoroughly by brushing the teeth and massaging the gums with a soft toothbrush and by brushing the tongue. One dental study showed that brushing the teeth and the tongue reduced mouth odor by 85 percent, while brushing teeth alone reduced it by only 25 percent. It is also important to floss daily to ensure that all food particles are removed. For extreme bad breath, you may have to floss after every meal.

A homemade toothpaste of baking soda and water can help neutralize the acids in the mouth that encourage bacterial growth. A mouthwash of hydrogen peroxide and water has the same affect. Most commercial mouthwashes, however, merely cover up mouth odor for a short time.

While it's difficult to detect bad breath in yourself, taste can serve as a clue. When you experience a strong aftertaste from eating garlic, onions, pungent cheese, or other foods, it's likely there's an associated odor. Should you be caught without toothbrush and floss, chewing fresh parsley or mint after meals provides a natural neutralizing action.

As with other persistent body odors, continual bad breath can be the symptom of a health problem. If you've done everything you can and you're still not smelling sweet, consult your dentist or physician.

ADDITIONS AND ACCENTS

Dress Tactics for Men and Women

Feeling good about what you wear begins with feeling good about yourself. Next, you must dress for the occasion, whether it's the office, the golf course, or a wedding. Then you need a clear idea of what looks good on you—the colors, lines, and textures that flatter and how to combine them. Once you understand these principles, you can slowly build a functional wardrobe and you'll be able to open the closet without anxiety.

To begin, make a list of your daily, weekly, and occasional activities and the clothes that are required for each. Also note the percentage of time you spend on the activity and rate how important it is to you to look your absolute best. This evaluation will help you decide where to spend your fashion budget. You may discover you're spending 80 percent of your budget on sportswear, when what you really need are more impressive office outfits that indicate you're ready for a big promotion.

Dressing for Business

In a work environment, the primary dress tactic is to be accepted as part of the team. While men have long had a well-defined business uniform, women have more latitude at the office (and more opportunities to make mistakes).

Each industry and each company within that industry has a corporate culture that defines "appropriate dress." If you work for a postal service, you wear the uniform. If you're a banker, you wear a three-piece suit. However, if you're a banker with a Wall Street firm, you'll dress differently than if you are a banker in a one-branch Midwest bank that deals in farm loans.

To determine your company's dress standards, evaluate the appearance of the company's top people and try to emulate them within your budget and according to your own style. If you're starting out in a new career or with a new company, dress conservatively and within the corporate guidelines until you've established yourself and your credentials. Once you're accepted as part of the team, you can demonstrate some fashion flair that reveals your individuality.

Color

A good way to simplify your wardrobe is to limit the colors you wear. During the 1980s, color analysis—"having your colors done"—was a cottage industry built on two basic principles. One, most people can wear most colors—it's the *shade* or *intensity* of the color that determines whether it's flattering or unbecoming. Secondly, colors come in *warm* and *cool* shades, and each of us looks better in one type or the other.

To determine whether you're in the warm or cool category, look at the skin on the inside of your forearms. If you see yellow, golden, or red undertones, you're warm. If you see pink, blue, even green undertones, you're cool. All skin, no matter how dark or light, usually falls into one of these categories. This self-examination is not always easy, because sallowness or ruddiness of the skin can be confused with the skin's undertones.

Another color test is to stand in good light (women should not wear makeup) and hold fabrics of different colors up to your face. The successful colors will bring out a vibrant, healthy look in your skin and eyes; the wrong colors will wash out your features.

If this test is still beyond your color aptitude, take a cue from compliments. When two or more people in a single day comment that they've never seen you looking better and you happen to be wearing a rose-pink sweater, you probably belong to the cool color group.

Remember, it's not the color but the shade that counts. Even blacks and navies can have a warm or cool cast to them. The lists below show cool versus warm tones.

Cool Colors	Warm Colors
Winter white	Ivory
Pure red	Brick red
Gray	Brown
Pink	Peach
Emerald green	Olive green
Taupe	Beige

Style—Accentuating the Positive

To determine what styles work for you, start with a careful inventory of your body—height, weight, body type, and features—the positive and negative. When choosing the best styles, your goal is to accentuate the positives and balance out the negatives.

Style is a matter of appealing to, or tricking, the eye. When we see vertical lines, the field of vision lengthens, whereas horizontal lines widen the field. If we look at a smooth, dark surface, it recedes. A light color moves forward and a field of bright color and patterns "pops."

In general, heavy-set people will look thinner if they wear darker clothes or solid light colors, smooth textures, and small prints or pinstripes in straight, unconstructed styles. A thin person can wear brighter colors, bigger prints and florals, and more heavily textured, nubby fabrics in close-fitting styles. Excessive pleats and pockets (horizontal details) also add weight.

A short person wishing to appear taller will avoid cuffs on trousers and a sharp contrast of colors between the top and the bottom half of the body. Uniform color and vertical style lines will add height.

The Mark of Quality

Once you've narrowed your fashion field by determining the colors and styles that look best, you should pay more for fewer clothes. Well-cut, well-made clothes in quality fabrics are a good investment, and they can be updated each fashion season with accessories.

Buying quality does not mean buying a designer suit just for the label. Look for good tailoring (finished seams, ample hems) and clothes with linings (they wear more comfortably and last longer).

While the fashion industry is inventing, promoting, and improving synthetic fabrics such as polyester and rayon, the classic fabrics—cotton, linen, silk, and wool—still can't be beat. Natural-fiber fabrics generally hold their shape better, are more comfortable because they allow ventilation, and provide more flexibility season to season.

Men's Suits—The Fit and the Finished Look

A good suit is a major investment. The quality you choose is often limited by your budget, but a good fit can make even a less expensive suit look custom-made. When trying on a suit, you should walk, sit, bend, reach, even crouch, to make sure the fit will take you through a typical day and not just out of the store's dressing room.

SUIT AND ACCESSORY COLOR GUIDE

Suit tones	Gray	Dark gray	Blue	Brown	Tan
SHIRT Solid, stripe, or check	1. Blue 2. Yellow 3. Pink	1. Red/pink 2. Gray 3. Blue	1. Blue 2. Yellow 3. Light green	1. Red/pink 2. Blue 3. Yellow	1. Tan 2. Green 3. Blue
TIE	1. Blue 2. Black/gold 3. Red	1. Red/blue 2. Blue/green 3. Blue/red	1. Black/blue 2. Navy/gold 3. Green/blue	1. Red/brown 2. Blue/ brown 3.Yellow/brown	1. Green/gold 2. Blue/green 3. Yellow/blue
SOCKS	1. Navy 2. Black 3. Dark gray	1. Black 2. Navy 3. Black/navy	1. Black 2. Black 3. Navy	1. Brown 2. Brown 3. Brown	1. Brown 2. Green 3. Brown
SHOES and BELT	1. Black 2. Black 3. Black	1. Black 2. Cordovan 3. Black	1. Black 2. Black 3. Black	1. Brown 2. Brown 3. Brown	1. Brown 2. Brown 3. Brown
SILK SQUARE or SCARF	1. Blue/white 2. Black/ gold 3. Red/pink	1. Red/blue 2. Blue/green 3. Blue/red	1. Black/blue 2. Navy/gold 3. Green/blue	1. Red/brown 2. Blue/ brown 3.Yellow/brown	1. Green/gold 2. Blue/green 3. Yellow/blue
HAT	1. Medium gray 2. Black 3. Gray	1. Gray 2. Brown 3. Gray	1. Gray 2. Gray 3. Black/navy	1. Brown 2. Medium brown 3. Brown	1. Brown 2. Brown 3. Brown
OUTER COAT	1. Black 2. Gray 3. Navy	1. Gray 2. Tan 3. Navy	1. Navy 2. Black 3. Navy	1. Brown 2. Camel 3. Brown	1. Natural 2. Brown 3. Brown
GLOVES	1. Gray 2. Black 3. Gray	1. Gray 2. Brown 3. Gray	1. Navy 2. Gray 3. Navy	1. Natural 2. Brown 3. Brown	1. Brown 2. Camel 3. Brown
JEWELRY (Finish)	1. Gold 2. Gold 3. Silver	1. Silver 2. Silver 3. Gold	1. Gold 2. Gold 3. Gold	1. Gold 2. Gold 3. Gold	1, Gold 2. Gold 3. Gold

Reprinted courtesy of The Fashion Association of America, Inc.

The following fitting tips are provided by the Wool Bureau, a nonprofit fashion industry group:

1. The suit should have ample room in armhole, across back, and through the body for comfort.

2. When jacket is buttoned:
  ♦ Collar lies flat across the back
  ♦ Vent(s) show no sign of pulling
  ♦ Sleeves hang straight
  ♦ Hem of sleeve extends to break of wrist
  ♦ Shirt cuff extends ½–¾" beyond jacket
  ♦ No signs of "twisting" fabric in front or back.

3. Trousers:
  ♦ Fitted on the waist, not the hips
  ♦ Enough room in waistband to fit one finger
  ♦ Seat of pants should lie smooth
  ♦ Hem of pant touches top of shoe with slight break in leg.

Once you have a few basic suits, use the color guide on the previous page to help you build a well-coordinated, fashion-right wardrobe.

Ties & What Knot

A man's tie seems the simplest (and certainly the least utilitarian) of fashion components, but it does raise some knotty issues. First, there's the question of width, which varies with the fashion season. The guiding principle: the width of the tie should be in direct proportion to the width of the suit lapels. A narrow tie works with narrow lapels; a wide tie should be worn with wide lapels.

Next is the question of whether or not to match the tie to the pocket square (the decorative handkerchief) in the suit jacket. Fashion experts have an uncharacteristically uniform response on this issue. The answer is, "Don't." Accessories should complement the basic outfit and each other. Exact matching shows a lack of imagination and, as the fashion columnist G. Bruce Boyer points out, creates a "uniform" look that might invite people to mistake you for an airline employee.

On the subject of pattern, the safest approach is to wear a patterned tie with a plain jacket and shirt. If you're a little more daring, two of the garments can be in patterns. Wearing jacket, tie, and shirt in patterns, however, is an invitation for fashion disaster.

Finally, there is the question of knots—how to tie them and what knot to wear with what collar. The basic rule here is that the wider knot works with the wider collar; you don't wear a full Windsor knot with your wing-collared tuxedo shirt. Whichever knot you choose, tie it just firmly enough to keep it in position. A man dressed for success never wears a tie tied in a tiny tight knot.

The diagrams on pages 686–687 on knot tying are compliments of The Fashion Association of America, Inc. If you are a novice, try tying the necktie around your thigh until your technique improves.

Buying Shoes That Fit

According to a recent national poll by the American Podiatric Medical Association, 44 percent of American women and 20 percent of American men wear uncomfortable shoes. Most people buy shoes that are too narrow and too short. Another study by the American Orthopedic Foot and Ankle Society found that 9 out of 10 women were wearing shoes one size smaller than their actual foot measurement. Considering that the average person walks 70,000 to 100,000 miles in a lifetime, and that many foot problems are caused or aggravated by ill-fitting footwear, perhaps it's time America reconsidered its shoe-buying habits.

Here's a checklist to help you on your next shoe-shopping trip:
  ♦ Have your feet measured by a salesperson. Foot size typically increases with age.
  ♦ Have both feet measured. Often one foot is larger than the other. If that's so, buy to fit the larger foot.
  ♦ Always try on both shoes.

◆ Shop after work or in the late afternoon. Since feet swell during the day, you want a fit that will be comfortable until you kick off your shoes at home.

◆ When you go shopping, take with you the socks or stockings you intend to wear with your new pair of shoes.

◆ When going for a test walk, step onto a hard surface, such as tile or concrete, before you make a selection. Walking on carpet does not give a true indication of comfort.

◆ Buy shoes that hug the heel and allow one-half inch of room at the end of the toe.

◆ Don't plan on "breaking in" stiff shoes. In time your feet may stretch the shoes, but it could be a long, painful process. Shoes should feel comfortable immediately.

◆ Check the thickness of the sole. If it's too thin, it won't protect your foot from the pavement, and the ball of your foot will do more than its share of shock absorbing.

◆ Be sure the widest part of your foot fits comfortably in the widest part of the shoe. Don't squeeze a "C" foot into an "A"-width shoe.

◆ Steer clear of shoes made of synthetic materials, such as plastic. Natural materials like leather and canvas have more give and allow ventilation to the feet.

◆ If you're a woman and you must buy heels, try to settle for a heel under 2 inches high, so the ball of the foot is not overstressed.

◆ Last, but not least, try to shop in a store where you can return the shoes if they're just not comfortable.

SLEIGHT OF FOOT—ELEVATOR SHOES FOR MEN

Women can adjust their height for any occasion by stepping into a pair of high heels. While many men would probably like to add 2 or 3 inches to their height, most don't consider elevator shoes unless they're much shorter than the national average of 5'10".

Today, elevator shoes come in a surprising variety of styles. The Richlee Shoe Company (800-343-3810) in Frederick, MD, which holds the trademark "Elevators," markets more than 50 different shoes—everything from boat shoes to wing tips, oxfords to cowboy boots, even high-top sport shoes (although running full court for 48 minutes is not advisable).

A few other words of caution: It takes some adjustment to learn to walk with ease in elevator shoes, just as it does for women in heels. Also, your podiatrist may not approve of daily wear. But for an occasional golf game with a tall business associate or a date with a statuesque beauty, elevator shoes may just give you the boost you need.

Fine Jewelry

Although "fine jewelry" is not a phrase regulated by the government or the jewelry industry, it usually refers to karat gold and sterling silver jewelry, gemstones, and higher-priced watches. As a fashion statement, fine jewelry calls attention to the wearer and is an indicator of his or her financial status.

Today more men are wearing jewelry, going beyond the wedding ring and the wristwatch. In the 1970s, gay men wore an earring in the right earlobe to signify their sexual preference, but now earrings are so mainstream that even the Ken doll (of Barbie and Ken fame) sports a small silver hoop in his left ear. Chain-link gold I.D. bracelets are also popular with men, and the jewelry industry reports a 78 percent increase in sales of diamond jewelry to men during the past decade.

Whether you are a jewelry fanatic or a once-in-a-while shopper, having some basic knowledge of fine jewelry can protect you from purchasing a bargain that is no bargain.

HOW TO TIE A TIE

The illustrations below represent what you see when you look in the mirror.

THE WINDSOR KNOT

Wide and triangular— for wide-spread shirt collars.

1. Start with wide end of tie on your right and extending a foot below narrow end.

2. Cross wide end over narrow and bring up through loop.

3. Bring wide end down, around behind narrow, and up on your right.

4. Then put down through loop and around across narrow as shown.

5. Turn and pass up through loop and . . .

6. Complete by slipping down through the knot in front. Tighten and draw up snug to collar.

THE HALF-WINDSOR KNOT

Medium Symmetrical triangle— for standard shirt collars.

1. Start with wide end of tie on your right and extending a foot below narrow end.

2. Cross wide end over narrow and turn back underneath.

3. Bring up and turn down through loop.

4. Pass wide end around front from left to right.

5. Then, up through loop . . .

6. And down through knot in front. Tighten carefully and draw up to collar.

THE FOUR-IN-HAND KNOT

Long and straight—to complement a standard shirt collar.

1. Start with wide end of tie on your right and extending a foot below narrow end.

2. Cross wide end over narrow and back underneath.

3. Continue around, passing wide end across front of narrow once more.

4. Pass wide end up through loop.

5. Holding front of knot loose with index finger, pass wide end down through loop in front.

6. Remove finger and tighten knot carefully. Draw up tight to collar by holding narrow end and sliding knot up snug.

THE BOW TIE

For the man who dresses with a certain flair.

1. Start with end in left hand extending 1½" below that in right hand.

2. Cross longer end over shorter end and pass up through loop.

3. Form front loop of bow by doubling up shorter end (hanging) and placing across collar points.

4. Hold this front loop with thumb and forefinger of left hand. Drop long end down over front.

5. Place right forefinger, pointing up, on bottom half of hanging part. Pass up behind front loop and . . .

6. Poke resulting loop through knot behind front loop (see illustration). Even ends and tighten.

Gold and Sterling Silver

Gold. According to the Federal Trade Commission (FTC), the word "gold" means "all gold" or 24-karat (24K) gold. It's rare to find jewelry that is 24K because gold, a soft mineral, is usually mixed with baser metals to make it more durable. The "karat" designation tells you how much gold is in the piece of jewelry. From a possible total of 24 karats, a ring that is 14K will have 14 parts of gold mixed with 10 parts of other base metals.

In the United States, any jewelry marked less than 10 karats cannot be sold legally as gold jewelry. No regulation states that jewelry must be marked, but if there is a karat mark on the piece, it must be accompanied with a U.S. registered trademark that identifies the person or company that stands behind the gold content.

Karat marks can be assigned to jewelry that is merely gold plated, gold filled, gold overlay, or rolled gold plate, but the karat designation has to be followed by a qualifying term, such as "14K Gold Overlay." These kinds of jewelry are 10 karat gold that is mechanically bonded over a base metal. While you may buy it because you like a particular piece of jewelry, be aware that the gold coating can eventually wear off.

Sterling Silver. According to the Jewelers of America, Inc., the United States government has the highest standards in the world for classifying sterling silver. Silver is not a strong metal as compared to gold; it is hardened by the addition of copper. The proportion of silver to copper determines the quality of the silver product. Sterling silver, the highest quality, is 92.5 percent silver and 7.5 percent copper. Sterling silver carries the mark .925. Lesser qualities of silver (marked .875 or .750) are sold outside the United States.

Gemstones

All but a few gemstones are minerals formed in the earth's crust as a result of changing temperatures and pressures. Those gemstones that are not minerals are organic animal substances (pearls and coral) or are of vegetable origin (jet and amber). The traditional "precious" stones are diamonds, emeralds, rubies, and sapphires, but many kinds of gemstones are set in today's fine jewelry—including jasper, jet, carnelian, citrine, spinel, and zircon.

Synthetic or imitation stones are often used in jewelry in place of gemstones. *Synthetic stones* are fabricated in a laboratory and mimic the properties of natural stones, including hardness and color. *Imitation stones* (glass, plastic, or cheaper stones) only resemble the surface appearance of the true stones. The FTC guidelines state that if a stone is not natural, the seller of the stone must disclose that it is "synthetic," "created," "laboratory grown," "man-made," or "imitation."

Even when a stone is natural, it does not mean that it has gone untreated or unprocessed. There are many "enhancement" techniques used in the gemstone industry to improve the appearance and durability of stones. Some of these techniques may affect the value of the stone, some may affect the appearance of the stone only temporarily, and some may require that you give special care to the stone once it's in your possession. You should always deal with a jeweler you trust and question him or her about enhancements before you make a purchase.

There are seven common gemstone enhancements:

♦ Heating some natural gems—including aquamarines, rubies, and tanzanite—can improve their color and sometimes their clarity.

♦ Irradiating gems can add more color to colored diamonds and some other stones. All blue topaz, for example, is irradiated. The Nuclear Regulatory Commission has established standards for this procedure, and your merchant should be able to document that the standards have been met.

♦ Oiling or waxing some gems masks imperfections, hides cracks, and improves color. It is a common enhancement for emeralds.

♦ Stabilizing certain gems with plastic bonding improves durability and color, especially for low-grade turquoise.

♦ Dyeing some gems increases and evens the color of the stones. Saltwater cultured pearls are treated with a very light pink dye, primarily to make it easier to match the colors within a necklace strand. Onyx, lapis lazuli, and low grades of coral, opal, ruby, and emerald are also regular candidates for a dye job.

♦ Bleaching is done on organic substances such as ivory and pearl to even out nature's discolorations.

♦ Lasering is a technique used to whiten internal black spots in diamonds. A recently developed process enables diamond cutters to use lasering to conceal less-than-perfect clarity of the diamond—a definite concern to diamond shoppers.

Watches

Today's watches are fashion and sports accessories, as well as timekeepers. When buying a watch with gold, silver, or gemstones, use the same caution you would in buying any piece of fine jewelry. Other than the aesthetic aspects, there are two basic categories of watches—mechanical and electronic.

Traditional mechanical watches are operated by a mainspring wound by hand; as the mainspring unwinds, it turns the interlocking wheels that make the watch hands revolve. Automatic or self-winding watches work on the same principle, but the mainspring is wound from the natural movement of the wearer's arms and wrists.

Electronic watches are powered by batteries that send electronic impulses through a small synthetic quartz crystal, setting up vibrations. These vibrations are channeled within the parts of the watch to equal one impulse per second, thus moving the display on the face of the watch—either the "hands" on an analog display or the numerical "digits" in a digital watch. Analog quartz watches have some moving or mechanical parts, whereas digital watches have none.

As a general rule, quartz watches are more accurate timekeepers than mechanical watches, simply because they have fewer moving parts that can wear or break. Mechanical watches that have jewel movements employ gemstones—usually synthetic sapphires or rubies—as bearings. Highly polished jewels reduce friction, increasing the accuracy and wear of the timepiece. Most experts agree that 17 jewels are a mark of good quality in a mechanical watch.

Other durability features to look for include "water-resistant" and "shock-resistant." Watches must meet FTC standards to earn these labels. If a watch can be submerged 80 feet in salt water without leaking or losing accuracy, it can be labeled water-resistant. Shock resistant watches have to be able to withstand a 3-foot fall onto a hardwood surface.

Whether you choose to spend $15 or $1500, you are legally entitled to a warranty on any watch over $15. Look carefully at the warranty—the length of the warranty, the parts covered, and what happens if the watch can't be repaired; all are aspects to be considered when you make a purchase. In making your selection, also consider the cost of repairs once your warranty has expired. Keep in mind that while mechanical watches can almost always be repaired at a local jewelry store, quartz watches usually have to be shipped to the manufacturer.

What to Do About Problems

Although the Federal Trade Commission (FTC) cannot intervene in individual disputes over jewelry transactions, the FTC is interested in hearing about problems that involve gold jewelry, gemstones, watches, or warranties. When sending complaints to the company from which you purchased your jewelry, send copies of the correspondence to the **Federal Trade Commission,** Public Reference, Washington, DC 20580.

If you would like additional information on fine jewelry or related subjects, write to the **Jewelers Vigilance Committee,** 1185 Avenue of the Americas, New York, NY 10036.

What Determines the Value of a Diamond?

When purchasing a diamond, your guidelines are the "Four C's"—carat weight, color, clarity, and cut.

Carat. This is the unit of weight used for diamonds, a word derived from carob seeds used to balance scales in ancient times. A carat is equal to 200 milligrams, and there are 142 carats to an ounce. Carats are further subdivided into points. There are 100 points to a carat. For example, a 45-point diamond weighs a little less than half a carat. Because larger diamonds are quite rare, they have a greater value per carat.

Color. Although a diamond may be any color of the spectrum, grading a cut stone for color means deciding the amount by which it deviates from the whitest possible (truly colorless). Completely colorless, icy-white diamonds are rare and, therefore, more valuable. White diamonds with a tinge of blue—known as "blue white"—are rarer still. The best way to see the true color of a diamond is to look at it against a white surface. Although most diamonds are a shade of white, they do come in all colors—pale yellow, canary, pink, red, green, blue, and brown. These are called "fancies," and they are valued for their depth of color, just as white diamonds are valued for their lack of color. The famous Hope Diamond is blue, and the well-known Tiffany Diamond is canary.

Clarity. A diamond's clarity is determined by taking into account the number, size, placement, color, and the nature of any internal "inclusions" or external surface irregularities. Inclusions are nature's birthmarks—imperfections such as spots, bubbles, or lines—included in the stone when it was crystallized from carbon millions of years ago. These marks make each stone unique, for no two diamonds have the same inclusions in the same places. When inclusions do not interfere materially with the passage of light through the stone, they do not affect its beauty. However, the fewer the inclusions, the more valuable the diamond. Under Federal Trade Commission

rules, a diamond can be called "flawless" only when no imperfections are visible to a trained eye under 10-power magnification and in good light. The Gemological Institute of America (GIA) quality-analysis system is the most widely used for grading gemstones in the United States. Clarity

GEM CUTS

Round

Emerald cut

Heart shape

Pear

Oval

Marquise

Reprinted courtesy of Jewelers of America, Inc.

is graded according to the relative position of the diamond on the Flawless-to-Imperfect scale.

Cut. Diamonds are cut according to an exact mathematical formula. A finished diamond has 58 "facets," which are the small, flat, polished planes cut into a diamond so that the maximum amount of light is reflected back to the viewer's eye. This reflection is called "brilliance," and is extremely important in evaluating the quality of a diamond. The widest circumference of a diamond is the "girdle." Above the girdle are 32 facets plus the "table," the largest and topmost facet. Below the girdle there are 24 facets plus the "culet," or point. Cut also deals with the shape of the diamond. Traditional shapes are round, emerald, marquise, pear, oval, and heart.

Baubles, Bangles, and Beads

Jewelry should be chosen not only to complement your wardrobe, but also to complement the shape of your face. The four basic shapes are oval, round, heart-shaped, and rectangular.

Oval

Considered the ideal shape, an oval face has near-perfect proportions with a forehead that is not too wide and a slightly rounded chin.

♦ Triangular-shaped earrings are especially attractive. Button and hoop earrings are also good choices. Dangling earrings are fine, but if they are too long they will not complement the slightly long jaw of the oval face.

♦ Any kind of necklace looks wonderful with an oval face.

Round

The length and width of a round face are equal; the jawline is round and the chin is short. The most flattering jewelry will add length to the face.

♦ Earrings in geometric shapes (square, rectangle, diamond) are good choices. Dangle earrings in angular shapes also help to make the face

look more slender. Avoid hoop earrings as they only draw attention to the roundness of the face and make it look wider.

♦ Choose long necklaces (26 to 32 inches) or those that end in a "V" shape.

Heart-shaped

The distinguishing characteristics of a heart-shaped face are a wide forehead, wide cheeks, and narrow (pointed) chin. Since the face looks like a triangle, you want to use jewelry to add width to the chin area.

♦ Wear earrings that are wider at the bottom than at the top. Wide hoops or triangle-shaped dangles also work well since they tend to fill out the lower half of the face.

♦ Choker necklaces will soften the pointy chin; avoid necklaces that end in a "V" shape.

Rectangular

This face has more length than width. The forehead and chin are the same width and the jawline is somewhat narrow. Carefully selected jewelry will add width to the face and draw attention away from the length of the face.

♦ Circular or horizontally shaped earrings will camouflage the length of the face; stay away from dangles, which only make the face seem longer.

♦ Chokers or short necklaces (16 to 18 inches) that end in a "U" shape are good choices.

Applying Cosmetics

Applying makeup can be quick and easy once you know what products to use and how to use them. Remember that less is better and that a soft, natural look is the end goal. Once you figure out what works for you, don't trade in your natural colors for chartreuse eyeshadow and fuschia lips, just because you're dressing up for a special occasion. To glamorize your look, simply go a shade darker, using your basic colors.

There are two keys to a quality makeup job: selecting the proper colors and blending the makeup. Selecting colors is easier once you know what your underlying skin tone is. There are two basic groups of skin undertones—either yellow/gold/red or pink/blue. All skin, no matter how dark or light, usually falls into one of these categories.

Women in the yellow-undertone group will find their skin is complemented by warmer colors such as peach, ginger, brown, or cinnamon. Women who have blue undertones will find that cooler shades of color—pink, plum, and burgundy—work best for them. Shades of makeup should never be chosen because they match your hair, eyes, or the outfit you happen to be wearing. Foundation makeup should match your face color as closely as possible.

The true color of your skin is found on the underside of your forearm. Do not confuse sallowness or ruddiness with the underlying skin tone. If you can't determine the tone from your forearm, hold a white sheet of paper against the forearm and next to the palm of your hand.

To achieve an even blending of your makeup, don't rely on the small brushes that come in compacts. Invest in two large, soft makeup brushes—one for face powder and blush and one for the eyes. Other blending tools include cotton balls and a small sponge. Translucent powder, which contains little or no color, is a useful product not only for blending, but for setting makeup to give you longer-lasting effects. If you use powder-type blush and eye shadow (preferred by most women), apply translucent powder before application. If you use cream-based products (some women with dry skin prefer these), apply the powder afterward. Translucent powder can also be used as a fixative between coats of lipstick or mascara.

There are nine steps to a complete makeup application, but depending on your skin, your features, your schedule, and your mood, you may choose to skip a few. Before applying any makeup, your face should be cleaned and moisturized.

1. Concealer. To lighten dark circles under the eyes and hide blemishes and pronounced wrinkles, use a liquid concealer or a foundation that is one shade lighter than the foundation you use on your face. Don't go any lighter, or you'll achieve an owl effect around the eyes.

2. Foundation. Select a foundation that matches as closely as possible the color of your face. Try the color on your face at the jawbone—in bright sunlight it should blend evenly with your face color. You may also need to buy some foundation that is a shade or two darker to wear if you get a tan. Apply foundation by dotting it on your face. Then blend with a clean, damp makeup sponge, using downward strokes to keep the downy facial hair smoothed. Blend just to the hairline and slightly over the jaw. If you have chosen the right color of foundation and blended thoroughly, you will not see a noticeable line at the jaw. Never apply foundation to the neck—it only leads to dirty collars.

3. Powder. After letting your foundation set a moment or two, fluff on loose, translucent powder with your large brush. If you use pressed powder from a compact, apply it with a powder puff or cotton ball. *Note:* If you're in a hurry, or you have a naturally even complexion, you can forego concealer and foundation and just use the powder to even out the skin color in your face.

4. Blush. Select a warm or cool blush color depending on the undertone of your skin. Apply blush to the outside "apples" of the cheeks (you'll find them by smiling) and the hollows of your cheeks, which are the areas just below where the cheekbone and jawbone meet. Using your large brush or a cotton ball dipped in loose powder, blend upward toward the temple. Blush color should not extend below the bottom of the nose or reach any closer to the side of the nose than the width of two fingers.

5. Eyeshadow. Limit your use of eyeshadow to a maximum of three colors at a time; one or two colors are certainly sufficient. Eyeshadow should contrast with your eyes, *not* match it. If your eyes are baby blue, try mauve or gray shadow. Plum or olive-green shadows provide a good contrast to brown eyes. A standard application for oval eyes is to apply a light shade over the entire eye area. Then put a medium shade of shadow between the lashes and the crease and a slightly darker shade just above the crease. Blend all colors upward and outward, using a little translucent powder on your brush. Another option is to apply shadow in a horizontal "V." Use your darker color across the bone above the crease. Take the color just past the outer edge of the eye, and then bring it back into the lash line.

The guiding principle in experimenting with shadow is that light colors emphasize an eye area, while a dark shadow will minimize it. For example, to draw forward deep-set eyes, highlight the brow bone with a light shadow; to widen close-set eyes, apply light shadow near the nose from the lash line to the brow and darker shadow on the outer third of the lid and brow bone.

6. Eyeliner. Eyelining today is done typically with a soft pencil for a "smudged" look, as opposed to a severe painted line. Outline the eyes close to the lashes. Never line on the inside of the lashes next to the eye itself, as this could invite eye infection. Put eyeliner on only the top of the eye or the top and the bottom, but don't line only the bottom as you'll have an unfinished look. Retracing the line with eyeshadow will further soften the look and make it last longer.

7. Eyebrow pencil. Tweezing eyebrows is the first step, although the best time to tweeze is after a shower or bath. Thick, bushy brows may also need a trim with small manicure scissors. As part of your daily makeup routine, brush the eyebrows up, then fill in sparse areas using a brown powder eyeshadow and a brow brush to create a fuller look. Brush the inner corners of the brow straight up for a squared-off look and dust the brows with translucent powder.

8. Mascara. According to a study done by L'Oréal, the beauty products company, if women in the United States could have only *one* cosmetic, they would choose mascara. Black mascara is most commonly used, but navy or dark brown mascara can offer a softer look. An eyelash curler used before the mascara application makes the lashes look fuller. Don't overcurl the lashes, and be sure to clean the rubber part occasionally with an oily mascara remover. Makeup experts apply several light coats of mascara to both the upper and lower lashes and comb the lashes, using an eyebrow or metal-pronged comb, between each layer to prevent the mascara from clumping or flaking. Most smudging can be prevented if the area around the lashes is well powdered.

9. Lipstick. As part of your daily makeup, lipstick color should be warm, muted, and within the same color range as your blush. Lipstick with beige or brown tones looks good on everyone. On special occasions, when only a red lipstick will do, select a brick red or tomato red if your skin has yellow or red undertones; choose a red more toward plum if you have blue undertones to your skin.

A lip pencil, which should match the color of your lipstick, prevents lipstick from bleeding outside the lipline or feathering into the little lines around the mouth. You can use lip pencil to draw a more pleasing lip shape, but for a convincing effect, draw it close to the natural lip line. For easy application of lip pencil, soften the point first by rubbing it on tissue. Once you've drawn your lip outline, use the pencil to fill in the entire lip area—this provides a good base for your lipstick. Putting foundation on your lips before you apply liner and lipstick will help keep your lips moist during the day. Another way to protect your lips from drying is to choose one of the lipsticks on the market that contains a sun-blocking agent.

Cosmetic Safety

Any cosmetic product—including nail and hair products, fragrances, soaps, lotions, deodorants, and skin and eye makeup—can potentially irritate and inflame the skin of susceptible individuals. Sometimes this condition, known as contact dermatitis, may occur immediately upon using a new product. In other cases, a person may use a product for months or years before his or her skin has a negative reaction to it.

In a recent study, half of the patients with contact dermatitis and their doctors did not initially suspect that this unfortunate condition—which can include itching, swelling, reddened skin, and hive-like welts—was caused by a cosmetic.

Such adverse reactions to cosmetics affect about 5 percent of the population. Research done by the North American Contact Dermatitis Group, a council of dermatologists, showed that 713 out of 13,216 patients developed skin reactions to cosmetic products. The allergic reactions of these patients were traced (in order of the number of occurrences) to:

♦ Fragrances or fragrance additives found in bath powders, facial cosmetics, and even household paper products

♦ Preservatives, which are found in almost all cosmetics

♦ Emulsifiers, which keep oil and water from separating in a cosmetic formula

♦ Lanolin, a purified, natural wax that softens the skin and is a key ingredient in many products.

According to the American Academy of Dermatology, some of the other ingredients that have been documented as allergens are:

♦ PABA (para-aminobenzoic acid) in sunscreen products (the irritation and itchiness it causes can be mistakenly attributed to sunburn)

♦ Aluminum salts in antiperspirants

♦ Detergent in bubble baths (some acute reactions have occurred with children who developed genital or urinary conditions)

♦ Ammonium persulfate, added as a booster to hydrogen peroxide in some hair dyes.

If you have sensitive skin or allergies, you can try products labeled "fragrance-free" or "hypo-allergenic," but don't expect any guarantees. Cosmetics, unlike drugs, do not have to pass approval of the Food and Drug Administration (FDA) before they are marketed, and the FDA does not regulate or define such terms as "natural" or "hypo-allergenic." The prefix "hypo" simply means "less than" and a "hypo-allergenic"

product is one that a cosmetic manufacturer believes to be less likely to cause an allergic reaction. Some manufacturers just omit perfumes or other potentially allergenic ingredients from their standard product formulas. Other manufacturers do extensive clinical testing on their products. Also, beware of the term "fragrance-free." Often these cosmetics still contain traces of fragrance to cover unpleasant odors of other ingredients in the product, such as fatty soaps.

Contamination

All of us, whether or not we have allergic tendencies, can be exposed to health risks when we come in contact with contaminated cosmetics. Cosmetic products—through exposure to air, sunlight, dirt, and heat—can become the breeding ground for bacterial organisms, molds, and other fungi. Most products have adequate preservatives to prevent the growth of these organisms during normal use and expected shelf life, although, as noted above, the preservatives themselves can be a problem to sensitive persons.

Normal use of a cosmetic does not extend to sharing lipstick with a friend or testing every product at the department store. In a recent study by the FDA, researchers collected cosmetic samples from department store makeup counters and found that more than 5 percent of the samples were seriously contaminated. The conclusion of the study was that common cosmetic preservatives are adequate for solo use in the home, but some cosmetic products cannot handle the constant use and sharing that goes on at the makeup counter.

Safety Guidelines

Common sense and good personal hygiene are the guiding principles for protecting yourself against potential health risks when using cosmetics.

♦ Wash your hands before applying makeup.

♦ Close makeup containers tightly after use and store away from heat and sunlight.

♦ Clean brushes and makeup applicators regularly.

♦ Never share makeup.

♦ Insist on a fresh, unused applicator when testing makeup at the store, or look for individual samples.

♦ Don't use eye cosmetics when you have an eye infection, such as conjunctivitis, and discard all products used from the time you first noticed the infection.

♦ Never apply makeup in a moving car, especially mascara. The mascara wand could scratch the eye and cause serious, even sight-threatening, infections.

♦ Throw away makeup and other beauty products if the color changes or an odor develops, or if there is a noticeable change in the texture of the product.

Products that have lost their preservative power and turned rancid are not always apparent to the user. The following guidelines on when to toss out commonly used products are provided by the Society of Cosmetic Chemists:

MAKE-UP SHELF LIFE

Type of makeup	Shelf life	Replacement signals
Liquid foundation	2 years	Oil separation
Lipstick	2–3 years	Beads of oil on sides
Liquid mascara, eye pencil	3 months	Contamination by bacteria and fungi, though not detectable, occurs with use and presents risk to delicate eye tissue
Eye shadow, pressed face powder	2–3 years	Flaking
Suntan lotion	5 years or more	No visible signs

Fragrance—An Age-Old Mystique

The use of fragrant ointments by men and women extends from the earliest civilizations when our ancestors applied oils and rendered animal fats to soothe skin cracked and dried by hot weather and wind. Early religious ceremonies included the burning of aromatic gums and woods as offerings to the gods, and the Bible makes many references to perfume, oils, and incense. The word *perfume* is derived from the Latin—*per* meaning "through" and *fumum* meaning "smoke."

Ancient cultures also prized perfume for its sensual and health-enhancing aspects. In the Far East, perfume was thought to help prolong life. In Greece, Hippocrates, the "father" of modern medicine, prescribed perfume for nervous disorders. At Greek and Roman banquets, the revelers refreshed themselves between courses with water perfumed with flowers. Famous fragrance lovers included Cleopatra and Hammurabi, the Babylonian king who decreed in 200 BC that all men and women in his kingdom must wash in perfume.

The first modern perfume, made of essential oils blended with an alcohol solution, was created in Hungary in the 14th century. During the Renaissance, the Italians, through their far-flung trade routes, introduced exotic new fragrances and raised perfume popularity in Europe to new heights. The marriage of Catherine de Medici to Henry II of France and her love for perfume may have been the beginning of the French passion for fragrance.

Today the flower fields in the south of France, which first flourished in the 18th century, are an important source of raw materials for the perfume industry. However, nearly every quarter of the modern world contributes natural ingredients used in concocting perfumes: flowers, grasses, spices, herbs, citrus products, woods, and leaves.

Today's Fragrances

With advances in chemistry, today's perfume manufacturers have thousands of ingredients from which to choose. A fine perfume may contain up to 300 elements, including essential oils derived from natural materials, aroma chemicals (such as synthetic musk or synthetic gardenia, a flower which does not yield oil), and fixatives derived from mosses, resins, or chemicals that mimic animal ingredients. These elements are then diluted in a specially prepared, aged alcohol, usually a wood alcohol, that "carries" the fragrance. The amount of alcohol added determines the strength of the fragrance, whether it will be perfume (the least amount of alcohol), eau de parfum, toilet water, or cologne.

Although there are no government controls to regulate the alcohol content in fragrance products, the classifications generally are as follows:

FRAGRANCE CLASSIFICATIONS

Product	Fragrance Concentration	Alcohol Content
Perfume	20–30%	70–80%
Eau de Parfum	18–25%	75–82%
Toilet water	15–18%	82–85%
Cologne	5–7%	93–95%

The higher the fragrance concentration, the longer the fragrance will last on your body. Aftershave products for men have even more alcohol than cologne, therefore aftershave fragrance dissipates quickly.

Cologne, a light form of fragrance, was first created in the city of Cologne, Germany, in the 17th century as a fragrant citrus "water." Toilet water is a somewhat unfortunate translation of the French phrase *eau de toilette*, meaning water (*eau*) used in the act of dressing oneself (*toilette*).

How to Apply Fragrance

Even the most expensive perfume is not formulated to last all day. Perfume may last up to five hours, while cologne lasts only one to two hours, so any form of fragrance requires refreshing for a day-long effect. Since fragrance rises, a quick dab behind the ears is not enough to get the most mileage from your perfume or cologne.

Perfume should be applied, preferably with an atomizer, at all the body's pulse points, where the body's heat will help to release the fragrance—behind the ears, inside the wrists and elbows, at the temples, the base of the throat, the bosom, behind the knees, and inside the ankles.

Eau de parfum and toilet water may be sprayed lightly on the entire body, from the feet up, before dressing to create an aura of fragrance around the body. Then apply it to the body's pulse points, or use perfume of the same scent. If you're worried that you may be overdoing it, use the rule of thumb that your fragrance should not extend more than an arm's length from the body. Eau de parfum and toilet water can also be sprayed on clean hair, but no fragrance should be applied to clothes, since the fibers can change the smell of the fragrance and the fragrance product may stain the clothing.

Cologne, as typically the lightest form of fragrance, may be applied like eau de parfum and toilet water and may also be used as an after-bath refresher, as a rubdown for sore muscles or aching feet, or to keep your hands cool and dry (an astringent effect of the high alcohol content).

Colognes and toilet water can be kept in the refrigerator for a cool pick-me-up, but extreme temperatures and dampness can change the delicate balance of perfume. However you choose to apply the various types of fragrance, don't hoard them for the Christmas party or your fiftieth wedding anniversary. Once opened, fragrance products deteriorate with time and exposure to air, heat, and sunlight.

Tips for Fragrance Shoppers

A "note" is the term perfumers use to describe a single, unblended scent. Each essential oil or aroma chemical in a fragrance blend has its own note. Top notes, such as citrus, are the odors that first strike our sense of smell. They evaporate quickly to reveal the middle notes, usually floral or spicy scents. The longest-lasting odors are the bottom or base notes, rich essences like sandalwood, musk, or vanilla.

When selecting a new fragrance, test only two or three at a time so your sense of smell will not become overwhelmed and fatigued. Apply the fragrance at the inside of the wrists or elbows or the palms of your hands. Your first impression, as you're smelling the top notes, will change in about 10 minutes when the middle notes surface. It can take up to 45 minutes to smell the base notes of the fragrance, so you may want to do some other shopping before making your decision. If you still can't decide, try the fragrance another time. Various internal and external factors can alter the way a perfume or cologne smells on the body—including external temperature, humidity, the ingestion of spicy foods or garlic, smoking, some medications, and hormonal changes in women.

Fragrance Questions and Answers

The following questions and answers are courtesy of The Fragrance Foundation, the nonprofit, educational arm of the international fragrance industry. Founded in 1949, the foundation publishes a variety of materials, conducts surveys, and sponsors seminars on fragrance.

Is it true that a person has his or her own individual "smell fingerprint"?

Yes. Each of us has our own unique odor identity which is the sum total of our heredity (genes), skin chemistry, skin type (dry/oily/light/dark), hair color, diet, whether or not we take medications, are under stress, and the environment in which we live.

Do women have a keener sense of smell than men?

Yes, but much of it is learned. On a day-to-day basis women in our society are encouraged to use their noses more often than men through their interest in cooking, flower arrangements, creating interior environments, and the early use of fragrance products.

In addition, according to scientific research, the fluctuation in a woman's sense of smell, during a 24-hour period, is systematically greater than a man's. These changes appear to be influenced by the secretion of female hormones—scientists are testing to determine if estrogen increases smell acuity in the first half of the month and progesterone decreases acuity in the last half. It also appears that odor awareness changes when a woman is pregnant and often her perception of scents changes. She may be more conscious of some odors and unable to experience others.

Is it true that the sense of smell is keener in the morning than it is later in the day?

No, our sense of smell is *not* as sharp in the morning as it is later in the day. More upbeat "bright" scents can be appreciated at the beginning of the day to sharpen the senses. Once you've awakened your sense of smell, choose fragrances that correspond with your mood, fashion, or the occasion.

As we get older, can our sense of smell begin to diminish as it does with our eyesight and hearing?

Many men and women over 50 begin to lose their ability to fully appreciate smell sensations. Though current research reveals that women are less apt to lose their sense of smell as quickly as men at the same age, older people often prefer stronger scents. They must be careful not to overdo their fragrance applications, particularly in warm weather or if they know they are going to be in stressful situations.

Can one improve one's sense of smell after 50?

Constant, creative use of all our senses can help to keep them at peak performance well into old age. It may be the time in a person's life to

CUE CARD FOR WOMEN'S FRAGRANCES

**Exhilarating/
Energetic**
GREEN
Usually the top
note of a fragrance
composition which
denotes the zest
and energy of
freshly cut grass
and dewy-green
leaves. Green notes
add lift and create
a young, vigorous
mood in a
fragrance.

SPICY
Connotes
fragrances which
obtain their notes
from several
sources: actual
spices such as
cinnamon, cloves,
ginger, and
cardamom; and
flowers that
possess traces of
spicy notes such
as carnation and
lavender.

WOODSY
MOSSY
Fragrances with
unmistakably
clean, clear
crispness.
Sandalwood,
rosewood, cedar
and other aromatic
woods are
combined with
earthy oakmoss
and fern to create
scents refreshingly
"foresty."

**Relaxing/
Understated**
SINGLE
FLORALS
A single floral,
which captures the
scent of a single
flower such as a
rose, carnation,
violet, or lilac.

FRUITY
Fruity blends are
recognized by a
clean, fresh citrus
quality of oranges
and lemons, and a
smooth, mellow
peachlike warmth.

**Romantic/
Poetic**
FLORAL
BOUQUET
An intricately
blended bouquet of
individual flower
notes which are
given balance and
body by a
combination of
bass notes
including woods,
greens, ambers,
etc.

**Erotic/
Mysterious**
ORIENTAL
BLEND
Sophisticated,
mysterious, and
sultry, this
uninhibited
fragrance type is
achieved through a
blending of
brilliant exotic
flowers, herbs, and
fixatives. It is
designed to have a
strong, erotic
appeal.

**Sophisticated/
Confident**
MODERN
BLEND
A type of
fragrance noted
for a brilliant
sparkle that
intensifies as it
warms on the
skin. Personified
by an extremely
individualistic
fragrance
personality that
defies specific
description, it
expresses the
imagination of the
perfumer. Also
known as
aldehydes.

Reprinted courtesy of The Fragrance Foundation.

CUE CARD FOR MEN'S FRAGRANCES

Exhilarating/ Energetic
CITRUS
A popular scent made from oils derived from the lemon, lime, orange, and bergamot trees. It is noted for its fresh, brisk quality.

SPICE
Another highly popular male scent. Nutmeg from the West Indies, cinnamon from Asia, clove bud oil from Zanzibar, bay oil from the West Indies, and basil from the Mediterranean are most often used to create fresh, masculine spicy scents.

Relaxing/ Understated
LEATHER
Cade oil from the juniper trees of Morocco and birch tar, a resin from Finnish birch trees, are used to create this scent.

Romantic/ Poetic
LAVENDER
One of the oldest scents favored by men, it is made from the oils of lavender and lavandin plants which are grown in France and spike lavender from Spain.

Erotic/ Mysterious
ORIENTAL BLEND
Sophisticated, mysterious, and sultry, this uninhibited fragrance type is achieved through a blending of brilliant exotic flowers, herbs, and fixatives. It is designed to have a strong, erotic appeal.

Sophisticated/ Confident
FOUGERES (Ferns)
Forest notes from Yugoslavian oak moss, labdanum resin from Spain, geranium oil from the island of Reunion.

WOODY
A most popular note based on vetiver from Bourbon, Haiti, and Java; sandalwood from India, and cedar from Virginia.

Reprinted courtesy of The Fragrance Foundation.

change fragrance type, i.e., one that gives a fast and stronger odor impression.

Can one lose one's sense of smell?
Yes, particularly if you have a cold or the flu or if you have suffered a head injury. If the condition persists, see a physician.

Does dry skin require a more generous fragrance application?
Yes, dry skin does not hold fragrance as long as oily skin, and fragrance should be reapplied more often throughout the day.

Is it true the sense of smell is not as keen in the winter as it is in the summer?
Yes, heat increases the impact of odor. In the summer, there are so many fascinating "smell" signals around us, and we are more conscious of our sense of smell. In hot weather, each fragrance application goes a long way—so lighter fragrances should be worn.

Is it true that fragrance reacts differently on blondes, brunettes, and redheads?
Yes. Blondes—with fair skin—will be happiest with long-lasting multifloral creations. Their skin

is often dry, causing fragrances that are too subtle to evaporate rapidly.

Brunettes usually have medium-to-dark skin which contains natural oils, allowing scents to last longer. Dramatic oriental scents are often favorites.

Redheads usually have fair and delicate skin which may be incompatible with fragrances which have predominant green notes.

If a person is inclined to perspire, does this affect the impact of fragrance?

Yes, as body heat builds up, fragrance intensifies.

When traveling to a high altitude, will fragrance be affected?

Yes, high altitudes decrease the long-lasting effects of fragrance so it should be applied more often. High altitudes also weaken the strength of a fragrance message. Choose stronger fragrances.

SPECIAL PROBLEMS

Is Plastic Surgery for You?

In a recent Gallup poll, more than half of the respondents considered cosmetic surgery acceptable for older adults and just under half felt it was acceptable for young adults. Only about 2 percent of those polled, however, had themselves been under the beautifying knife.

The growing acceptance of cosmetic surgery reflects the changing demographics of patients who undergo the procedures. Today, the patient profile is no longer famous and wealthy—it's young and middle-income. Seventy percent of patients have annual incomes less than $50,000 and almost 50 percent earn less than $35,000. Nearly 40 percent are between the ages of 35 and 50, 32 percent are between 19 and 34, and only 26 percent are over the age of 50.

If you have toyed with the idea of cosmetic surgery for yourself and find these statistics encouraging, don't reach for the yellow pages. First, it's not the best way to choose a doctor (see "How to Choose the Right Doctor," page 703) and second, cosmetic surgery requires long and serious consideration. It is a significant financial and emotional investment. And it *is* surgery, with associated risks of infection, blood clots, and adverse reactions to anesthesia, to name just a few possible complications.

Before embarking on your face lift or tummy tuck, here are some questions to ask yourself:

Do I generally take good care of my health and my appearance?

A patient who dresses slovenly, overdoes makeup, and is excessively overweight with no diet or exercise plan is not a good candidate for cosmetic surgery. Neither are patients with body-image disorders, such as anorexia and bulimia, and drug or alcohol addictions. Cosmetic surgery can improve appearance and give self-confidence a boost, but it is not a cure-all for psychological problems or low self-esteem.

Before resorting to surgery, even healthy individuals may want to explore new cosmetic options or health regimes in order to improve their looks—from using foundation makeup to diminish the contours of a prominent nose to giving up cigarettes. Smoking causes fine lines to develop around the lips and eyes and long-term smokers develop a grayish cast to their skin. Also, many plastic surgeons will not operate on smokers because of increased vascular problems.

Just as a chemical peel is not a solution for "smoker's face," liposuction is not a remedy for obesity. Liposuction, now the most widely performed plastic surgery in the U.S., was developed as a way to remove small, concentrated areas of fat that can't seem to be exercised away. The ideal candidate for liposuction is not more than 10 pounds overweight and has good skin elasticity. This treatment should be used as an incentive to maintain your figure, not as a way to avoid aerobics and bran cereal.

What exactly do I want to change about myself?

Patients who walk into the plastic surgeon's office and ask for a "whole new look" or express the desire to change their ethnic appearance are not being realistic about what plastic surgery can accomplish. Actually, the trend in facial plastic surgery today is to accomplish small changes that keep the patient's features in balance. The better cosmetic surgery candidate will want to remedy *one* feature that has been a source of unhappiness for years. For example, he or she may say, "My receding chin has bothered me since I was 16. I just feel a chin implant would improve my profile and make me feel better about the way I look."

Am I doing this just for myself?

If you're undertaking cosmetic surgery in order to look more like Christie Brinkley or Mel Gibson or because you're hoping to please a husband, family members, or friends—put your surgery date on hold. Cosmetic surgery should be an inner-directed decision. It's not going to save a marriage, or get you a date every Saturday night if you're single. People with unrealistic expectations of cosmetic surgery are bound to be disappointed. Often the results are very subtle. After you've undergone a face lift, your best friend may only remark that you look well rested.

Do I really understand the procedure and what the risks are?

According to a publication of the American Society of Plastic and Reconstructive Surgeons, cosmetic surgery has a 2 percent risk of serious complications, the same as most major surgical procedures. Most of the complications are infections and cardiac problems related to undergoing anesthesia. Patients with diabetes, heart or lung disease, or poor circulation face even higher risks, and some plastic surgeons may refuse to work with them.

In addition to facing the fact that you could potentially die as a result of cosmetic surgery, you should be willing to face the almost certain fact of scarring, although with a successful sur-gery the scars will most likely be visible only to you and your intimates.

There are other medical worries to consider, including the uncertainties of introducing foreign substances, such as silicone and collagen, into your body. Silicone breast implants were outlawed by the Food and Drug Administration in 1992 because of potential hazards. Saline implants are still allowed; however, the pockets that hold the saline solution are made of silicone.

The risks of plastic surgery also encompass botched jobs. A tummy tuck could potentially set your navel 2 inches off center. A chemical peel by a poorly trained physician or cosmetologist could leave you with paper-thin skin disfigured by scars.

Your best protection is to know your physician's qualifications, know *exactly* what the procedure entails, what can go wrong, and what will be done, at whose cost, to correct any problems. If your physician makes you feel that you're asking too many questions, you have the wrong doctor. Last, but not least, know yourself and what risks you're willing to chance.

Can I afford this operation, in terms of money and time?

Since most cosmetic surgery is elective, it is not covered by health insurance. The average cost of a tuck to the upper eyelids is $1514, while a facelift runs about $4156. There may be additional charges for an anesthesiologist and other hospital personnel and for follow-up visits with your surgeon. Be sure you understand up front all the costs involved. Time is another factor to consider. Most surgeries require at the very minimum a one- or two-week recovery period. Are you willing to trade your annual vacation for a forehead lift?

Once you've evaluated yourself, your motivations, and your pocketbook, there's one more consideration. While nose surgery, the most popular cosmetic surgery, is permanent, other procedures need to be repeated to keep the aging process at bay. A face lift typically lasts five to seven years. Will you be willing to do it all again?

How to Choose the Right Doctor

It's not generally known that anyone with a medical degree can advertise as a plastic surgeon and legally perform outpatient surgeries, even if that doctor has no specialized training and no experience in the field of cosmetic surgery. Since there are no laws to protect you, protect yourself by choosing a *qualified* plastic surgeon.

Many plastic surgeons advertise themselves as "board certified." This can be a very misleading claim. Some doctors are "certified" by a professional group whose only requirement is membership dues and they may have no specialized training in plastic surgery.

You want to find a plastic surgeon whose "board certification" is from the American Board of Plastic Surgery (ABPS), one of the 24 examining boards governed by the American Board of Medical Specialties (ABMS). The ABMS is recognized by the American Medical Association and is the authoritative agency on medical competency. To obtain a certification in plastic surgery from ABPS/ABMS, doctors undergo five to seven years of specialized training beyond the completion of their MD degree. They also have to pass examinations to prove their skill and knowledge.

While a physician may have ABMS certification in dermatology or otolaryngology (head and neck surgery), he or she may still lack the certification in plastic surgery. You may, nevertheless, choose to select the doctor to perform your procedure, but you should be fully aware of what the credentials mean.

The **American Board of Medical Specialties** has a toll-free number for patient inquiries: 800-776-2378.

If you have not yet selected a doctor and are looking for qualified recommendations, or you need additional information on a specific cosmetic surgery procedure, you can call the American Society of Plastic and Reconstructive Surgeons. All of their members are certified by the American Board of Plastic Surgery. They also offer free pamphlets on the various procedures: **American Society of Plastic and Reconstructive Surgeons, Inc.,** 444 East Algonquin Road, Arlington Heights, IL 60005 (800-635-0635).

Once you have narrowed down your choice of surgeons, you need to sit down with each one for a consultation visit (usually you must pay for the visits). Here are some important questions to ask:

1. What is your area of specialty and what training do you have in the specific cosmetic surgery procedure I want? Are you certified by the American Board of Plastic Surgery?

2. How many operations like mine have you done in the last year? During your career?

3. What happens if I don't get the results you expect? Will I need additional surgery? If so, will you do the additional/corrective procedures at no extra cost?

4. How safe is this procedure? What are the risks? What are the side effects and how long will they last?

5. Do you have a book of "before and after photos" of patients who have had the same kind of surgery?

6. Do you have hospital privileges? Where will the surgery be done? Will you perform the operation yourself? Who will administer the anesthesia?

7. What will the surgery cost? What are your fees, and what other charges can I expect? What kind of follow-up care is involved and what will it cost?

8. How much time will the operation take? How long will I be out of work?

9. Can I contact a few of your former patients who have had the same surgery?

If the physician you choose suggests that your surgery will be performed in his or her office, check with one of the following organizations to see if the facility has passed an inspection: **Accreditation Association for Ambulatory Health Care, Inc.,** 708-676-9610; **American Association for Accreditation of Ambulatory Plastic Surgery Facilities,** (708-949-6058); **Joint Commission for the Accredita-**

tion of **Healthcare Organizations,** (708-916-5600).

The **Food and Drug Administration** is a good information source for the hazardous effects of certain procedures, such as silicone breast implants, which were banned by the FDA in 1992. The federal agency will send you detailed information about breast implants, collagen injections, and liquid silicone injections. To obtain this information, send a postcard to "Breast Implants" or "Collagen and Liquid Silicone Injections": FDA, HFE–88, 5600 Fishers Lane, Rockville, MD 20857.

The FDA also has a toll-free hotline on breast implants: 800-532-4440. For the hearing impaired, the number is 800-688-6167.

Common Cosmetic Surgery Procedures and Their Potential Risks

Before having any operation, it is important to have realistic expectations about the benefits that can be achieved, and understand the possible risks and side effects. Those issues should be discussed thoroughly with your surgeon. Below is a brief, simplified overview of some of the potential complications and side effects of common cosmetic surgery procedures. It cannot substitute for a consultation with a properly trained physician.

Any of these operations can result in infection or blood collecting beneath the skin, conditions requiring additional treatment and, in a few cases, further hospitalization. In rare instances, permanent and conspicuous scarring can result. Further, although many of these operations are not done under general anesthesia, those that are carry additional risks.

Face-lift (rhytidectomy): Although a face-lift can improve some signs of aging, surgery will not stop the aging process. Following the operation, there may be significant puffiness and bruising for several weeks, and some individuals may feel a temporary numbness or tightness in the face or neck. Nerve damage that causes permanent loss of sensation or movement in the facial muscles can occur in rare instances.

The scars resulting from a face-lift are normally in the hairline and folds of the ear, and usually lighten with time until they are barely visible. The kind of scars cannot be predicted with total accuracy, because everyone heals differently.

Nose surgery (rhinoplasty): Changing the shape of the nose is one of the most complex procedures, even for a skilled surgeon. If too much cartilage or bone is removed, the nose can look misshapen. Additionally, if care is not taken with the internal structure of the nose, you can end up with a nose that does not function correctly. Before the operation, make sure you and your doctor thoroughly discuss what kinds of changes you would like and how the changes will "fit in" with your other facial features.

It can take several weeks for bruising around the eyes to go away and several months for any swelling that occurs to completely disappear. You may experience some difficulty breathing for some weeks following the procedure.

Eyelid surgery (blepharoplasty): Performed to remove excess skin and fat above and below the eyes, this procedure usually causes bruising that fades within a week to 10 days. However, discoloration can last for several weeks. The physician must be very careful not to remove too much skin, which could cause too much "white of the eye" to show. In addition, though rare, risks include dry-eye syndrome (the eyes stop making tears) and drooping of the lower lid.

Hair transplants: The most common of these procedures, called punch grafting, is performed by transplanting small pieces of skin with healthy hair follicles to bald spots. This process may be repeated several times over a period of 8 to 18 months. Common temporary aftereffects include pain, swelling, bruising, and the formation of crusts on the scalp. In another technique, called scalp reduction, part of the bald scalp's skin is removed, and the skin with hair is stretched and sutured together over this area. Some discomfort, including headaches and scalp tightening, may follow for a short time. Less frequently, flap surgery is performed by rotating wide strips of skin with hair to cover areas where bald skin has been removed. In another procedure, the hair-bearing scalp tissue may be expanded so that the enlarged tissue can replace the bald area. The latter two procedures require general anesthesia, and more serious complications, such as damage to tissue, can result.

Breast augmentation (enlargement): In this procedure, silicone envelopes filled with salt water (saline solution), silicone gel, or a combination of both can be implanted to enlarge the breasts. In April 1992, the FDA announced that because it continues to be concerned about the safety of silicone gel–filled breast implants, all patients to receive these implants must be enrolled in clinical studies. Silicone implants for the purpose of breast augmentation will be available only to a very limited number of women. (Women who need the implants for breast reconstruction will be assured access to the studies.) The FDA made this decision because it determined that manufacturers of silicone implants have not proven that these devices are safe.

As of May 1992, saline-filled implants continue to be freely available. In the future, manufacturers of saline implants will be required to submit data to the FDA to prove that these devices are safe and effective in order to continue marketing these devices. Known risks of saline-filled implants include the possibility of infection, hardening of the scar tissue surrounding the implant, formation of calcium deposits in the surrounding tissues, implant rupture, and interference with the detection of early breast cancer. Evaluating the risks and benefits of breast implants can be a difficult issue. Discuss this issue thoroughly with your doctor.

Breast reduction: With breast reduction or lift surgery (mastoplexy), there will be some degree of scarring, and there may be unevenness in breast size. You will want to ask your physician about this and other possible effects, such as a temporary or permanent change in nipple sensation or a decreased ability to breast-feed.

Tummy tuck (abdominoplasty): The common nickname for this procedure—which removes excess, sagging skin and underlying fat from the abdomen—belies the fact that it is a major surgery normally done under general anesthesia. An incision is made from hip bone to hip bone and, although it is located low along the "bikini line," a significant scar results. Full recovery, as with other major surgery, may take a couple of months or longer.

Injections: Facial wrinkles may be treated by injecting them with collagen or fat. Neither substance produces permanent results, and the longevity of the results depends on the patient's skin and reaction to the substance. People may be allergic to collagen and not know it. Also, the FDA is investigating whether there is a cause-and-effect relationship between having collagen treatments and later developing "PM/DM" (chronic, progressive, sometimes fatal inflammatory disorders) or similar diseases.

The injection of liquid silicone has not been approved by the FDA for any purpose, and the FDA prohibits manufacturers and doctors from marketing or promoting this product.

Chemical Peels and Dermabrasion: These two techniques may be used to treat scarring (such as those from acne or skin injury), skin wrinkles, or splotchy pigmentation. To perform chemical peels, an acid or other agent is applied to destroy the top layers of the skin. Temporary pain, swelling, and redness may result. Dermabrasion is performed by using machines that remove the top layers of skin. This helps smooth skin irregularities. Treated skin may be sensitive to sunlight. Risks include scarring and uneven pigmentation which, in rare cases, may be long-term or permanent.

Liposuction (suction-assisted lipectomy): To perform this very popular procedure, a doctor inserts a thin tube into a fatty part of the body and, using a special vacuum pump, suctions out unwanted fat, leaving a flattened area with little scarring. The growing popularity of the procedure has attracted many physicians with widely varying training and experience. There have been reports of blood clots, fluid loss, infection, and even death following liposuction. Make certain the doctor you choose is well trained and experienced in performing this procedure. Contrary to popular belief, liposuction is:

1. Not a substitute for good routines of diet and exercise. Ideal candidates are close to their ideal weight, but have pockets of resistant fat on their hips, thighs, abdomen, or chin.

2. Not a cure for "cellulite," the popular term for the dimpled skin often found on the thighs.

3. Not a solution for people with stretched-out, inelastic skin that cannot redrape around body contours.

If you are a good candidate and proceed with the surgery, you will need to wear a girdle or other compression garment until any bruising and swelling disappear.

Source: "Facts for Consumers . . . Cosmetic Surgery," a brochure from the Federal Trade Commission (FTC).

Cosmetic Dentistry

Practicing good oral hygiene at home plus regular visits to the dentist for dental care and professional cleaning are vital to keep teeth strong and healthy. In addition, there are a number of cosmetic dental procedures that can improve the appearance of your teeth, and thus improve your smile.

Bleaching. The dentist will use a peroxide-based solution to lighten surface stains caused by coffee, tea, and tobacco or discoloration caused by aging. Bleaching, however, may not work on discolorations that are caused by injuries or by the use of certain antibiotics. The bleaching solution is applied to the teeth and activated by heat or a combination of heat and light. The number of office visits required depends on how many teeth you want bleached and how many the dentist will do at one time. Also, some teeth may have to be bleached more than once in order to achieve the desired effect. Some dentists have patients use

an at-home method in which a mold is made of the patient's mouth; the mold is then taken home, filled with solution, and worn for a prescribed number of hours.

Over-the-counter tooth-bleaching kits are not recommended since unsupervised application can prove hazardous for consumers who don't follow instructions properly or who have teeth and gum problems that could be aggravated by the treatments. Before buying any over-the-counter tooth-whitening treatment, including toothpaste, consult with your dentist. Also, you can always fall back on the old-fashioned method of whitening teeth: brush them with a paste of baking soda and water.

Bonding. Bonding can be used to treat teeth that are fractured or chipped, or to fill in gaps between teeth (especially between front teeth), or to mask discoloration and stains caused by the use of certain antibiotics, like tetracycline. Here's what happens: The tooth surface is etched with a weak acidic solution to create a rough surface; a tooth-colored composite resin (like putty) is applied to the tooth and shaped to fix the problem; the resin hardens and the bonded tooth is smoothed and polished. Bonded teeth chip more easily than regular teeth, and like regular teeth, they are prone to stain if you smoke, drink coffee or tea, or eat certain foods. A bonded tooth usually lasts for three to five years and then has to be replaced. Bonding is not recommended in some instances, e.g., for teeth that are poorly aligned (and need orthodontic treatment); for badly damaged back teeth (which usually require crowns).

Veneers. An offshoot of tooth bonding, veneers are custom-made shells, usually made of porcelain or acrylic materials, that are affixed directly to the teeth. They can be used to fix the same kinds of problems that bonding fixes: teeth that are damaged, discolored, have small gaps between them, or are poorly shaped or slightly out of alignment. In the veneering process, a small amount of enamel is usually removed from the tooth, and an impression of the tooth is taken and used to make the custom-fitted shell. The surface of the tooth is etched with a mild acidic solution and the veneer is set in place using a composite resin cement. A veneer, rather than bonding, is usually chosen for more severe teeth problems. Veneered teeth are usually more resistant to chipping and staining than bonded teeth, but they are also more expensive. Once teeth are veneered, they must be periodically reveneered; usually a veneered tooth lasts for four years or longer.

Cosmetic dentistry is only as good as the dentist who performs the procedure. Before you wade in, be sure you select a skilled dentist and understand what you are getting, what follow-up is required, what the cost will be. Remember, cosmetic procedures are not covered by health insurance.

Hair Loss

Losing hair—it happens to all of us. The average scalp has 100,000 hairs on it and a person typically loses 50 to 100 hairs a day. With normal hair growth, the hairs that are shed, having finished their two- to six-year growth cycle, are replaced by new hair from the same follicles. While 90 percent of the hair is in a continual growth cycle, no new hair follicles are formed during a person's lifetime.

Abnormal hair loss can occur for a variety of reasons. It may be the result of illness, high fever, drug or radiation therapy, nutritional deficiency (usually a lack of protein), a hormonal readjustment (as occurs after pregnancy), or due to harsh chemical treatments or styling techniques. Hair loss from these causes is usually temporary because the hair follicles themselves have not been damaged.

One cause of potentially permanent hair loss is alopecia areata, a condition that affects 2.5 million Americans. It usually starts as one or more small, round patches on the scalp. In some cases, all the scalp hair is eventually lost (alopecia totalis) and in others, all the hair on the entire body is lost (alopecia universalis). Recent research indicates that this condition is probably an autoimmune disorder, a type of "self-allergy" that diminishes the growth capacity of the hair follicles. Because the hair follicles remain alive beneath the skin surface, it is a treatable condition, most commonly treated with cortisone injections and topically applied drugs.

The Major Cause of Hair Loss

The major cause of permanent hair loss is a condition called androgenetic alopecia. The result of inherited genes that can be passed through the maternal or paternal side, it accounts for an estimated 95 percent of all permanent hair loss, what's called male-pattern baldness and female-pattern baldness.

In the United States, 20 million women and 35 million men have this genetic predisposition. The condition often has an early onset. By age 39, 40 percent of American males have some degree of permanent hair loss. At the same age, 29 percent of women have experienced hair loss.

Women usually experience hair loss as a general thinning, spread evenly across the scalp. The syndrome of male-pattern baldness manifests in hair loss on the forehead and the top of the skull, leaving a fringe of hair on the sides and back of the scalp. This effect is sometimes called the "Hippocratic wreath," after Hippocrates, the father of modern medicine, who tried to "cure" his own hair loss with an ointment of opium, rose oil, and unripened olives. His concoction is only one of many folk remedies through the ages that have raised hope, but not hair.

Today, Americans spend close to $100 million a year on non-prescription cosmetics that profess to promote hair growth or retard hair loss. And this is several years after the Food and Drug Administration outlawed the advertisement of such claims. Unfortunately, the FDA does not have adequate staff to police the industry.

The bare truth is that no superficial treatment can stop the process of hair loss, which is governed by genes and hormones. In those persons who have androgenetic alopecia, the hair follicles have a negative reaction to androgens, the male hormones, and over time lose the ability to generate new hair growth.

The notion that losing hair is a loss of "manliness" is simply a myth. As a matter of fact, balding men generally have much higher levels of testosterone, the male hormone responsible for the development of male genitalia in the fetus and during puberty and for the growth of facial, chest, and pubic hair.

In women, the female hormone estrogen acts as a protection to the hair follicles, but when the level of estrogen drops, as it does during menopause, the follicles become more susceptible to the damaging effects of androgens.

Until a true miracle drug is found through gene therapy—a possibility some experts predict—there are only three options available to the legions of those who suffer hereditary hair loss—and none of them is a cure.

Hair Transplants

Surgical rearrangements of hair follicles and scalp are expensive, lengthy undertakings. Some procedures can cost as much as $10,000, take up to two years to complete, and still not yield the desired results.

There are 30,000 to 40,000 hair transplants performed annually in the United States. Less than 5 percent of the patients are women. Candidates for the surgery must have adequate healthy hair to transplant. (For more information on the operation and how to choose a plastic surgeon, see "Common Cosmetic Surgery Procedures and Their Potential Risks," page 704.)

Minoxidil

The drug minoxidil, which was approved for hair loss treatment by the FDA in 1988, has not panned out to be a miracle drug, but it has been shown to produce limited hair growth. The drug acts to extend the growth phase of the hair, the desired result being more hairs growing longer and thicker at the same time for better scalp coverage.

Men who seem to benefit the most from minoxidil are under 30 and have been balding for less than five years. A study of women using the drug found that 23 percent had moderate regrowth, 34 percent had minimal growth, and 43 percent had no change at all. Minoxidil costs upwards of $600 for a year's supply. It takes at least four months to tell whether you're getting any results, and the topical solution must be applied twice daily *indefinitely*—until you're too old to care.

Some doctors will not prescribe the drug, which originally was used to treat high blood pressure, for people over 50 because of potential side effects and especially for patients with cardiovascular disease.

Hairpieces

During the past decade, the manufacturers of synthetic fibers used in wigs and toupees have significantly improved their products. Hair additions made from human hair have always been popular. The quality of human hair varies widely.

In addition to the quality of the hair or fibers, the cost of a hairpiece (which can fetch $39 or

$3900) is determined by whether the hair is hand-tied to the base of the wig or machine made. Hand-tying results in a finer, more natural-looking product. Fitting is also an aspect of cost and quality. There are ready-made, semi-custom, and custom-made hairpieces, with the price and delivery time going up in that order.

Of American men who wear hairpieces, 80 percent choose synthetic and 20 percent wear human hairpieces. Almost all men opt for the hand-tied product. Since the wefts in machine-made pieces allow a "see-through" effect to the scalp, machine-made wigs are commonly worn by women with an overall thinning of hair, rather than men trying to cover bald areas.

Posture

People with good posture project self-confidence and generally wear their clothes well. Good posture can also have a slimming effect—a sloucher with paunch or double chin is much more noticeable than someone who stands with his or her stomach slightly lifted and head held high.

Other than simple inattention, poor posture can be caused or aggravated by a number of conditions, including poor self-image, depression or other psychological problems, being overweight, lack of physical exercise, wearing high-heeled or platform shoes, one leg being shorter than the other, injury to the back, or medical conditions such as osteoporosis (bone deterioration).

The back is a complex structure of muscles, ligaments, and vertebrae that protect the spinal column and the 31 pairs of spinal nerves. The cartilage discs between the vertebrae serve to absorb the pressure and shock of the body's movements. When the alignment, flexibility, and muscle tone of the back are maintained, the individual has a good sense of balance and ease of movement.

Correct posture follows the natural curves of the back at the neck and the lower back—a ramrod straight, military stance is *not* good posture. You can check your posture by looking straight on at yourself in a mirror. Your shoulders should be even on a parallel plane, as should your hips. Your head should be in the middle of your shoulders, not inclining toward either side. From a side view (you may need a friend to make the inspection), your shoulder, hip, knee, and ankle should be aligned. If a part of your body juts out, your posture needs improvement.

Some visualization techniques that can help you get the "feel" of relaxed, natural posture include: imagining a straight plumb line that travels from the top of your head to the balls of your feet; imagining your head as a helium balloon that rises above your shoulders; or pretending that you are a marionette dangling from a string attached to the top of your head.

If your mind can't make these leaps of imagination, here are some more concrete tips to help you achieve good posture:

♦ Stand with the feet apart, about the width of the shoulders
♦ Distribute your weight evenly on both feet
♦ Point the toes straight forward
♦ Relax the knees
♦ Don't flatten or arch the lower back
♦ Tuck the pelvis slightly forward
♦ Slightly lift the diaphragm (the area above the stomach), but don't suck in the stomach
♦ Hold the head level and straight
♦ Pull the chin in just a bit toward the neck
♦ Relax the shoulders.

Sitting posture is also important, especially since many of us spend hours a day at a desk or in front of the television.

♦ Sit with the buttocks against the back of the chair
♦ Sit with your weight evenly distributed and the lower back mildly arched
♦ Rest both feet on the ground (after you assume the correct posture, you can cross your legs)
♦ Relax the shoulders and neck.

Ideally, your chair should allow you to sit with your knees resting at a level slightly higher than your hips. An extra support for the lumbar re-

POSTURE: CORRECT AND INCORRECT

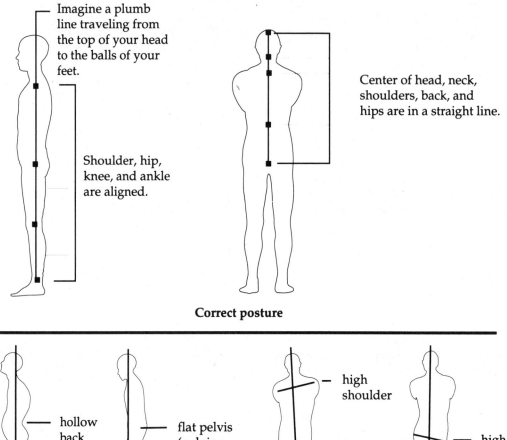

Imagine a plumb line traveling from the top of your head to the balls of your feet.

Shoulder, hip, knee, and ankle are aligned.

Center of head, neck, shoulders, back, and hips are in a straight line.

Correct posture

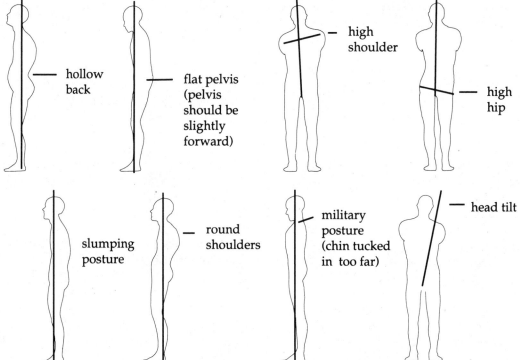

hollow back

flat pelvis (pelvis should be slightly forward)

high shoulder

high hip

slumping posture

round shoulders

military posture (chin tucked in too far)

head tilt

Incorrect posture

gion, or lower back, is also a good idea, since this is the back area where the majority of strains or injuries occur. You can make a lumbar pillow by rolling a towel to the width of 4–6 inches; it can also be used to make driving more comfortable.

Remember, the key to good posture is keeping the back strong and flexible. Stretching exercises, walking, swimming, and other moderate physical workouts are good for the back and your posture.

Snoring

British novelist Anthony Burgess said, "Laugh and the whole world laughs with you; snore and you sleep alone." The observation may be funny, but snoring is not a laughing matter for snorers and "snorees," the people kept awake because of snoring. Snoring can reach a noise level of 90 decibels (louder than a power lawn mower) and can put a big strain on any relationship.

Snoring occurs when the soft tissues at the back of the throat vibrate; the vibrations occur from turbulence caused by the narrowing of breathing passages. What causes snoring? It happens if you have poor muscle tone in the throat tissue, if there is a mass that obstructs the airway (like tonsils), if your nasal breathing is obstructed, or if the airway is blocked due to a deformity like a broken nose.

It's estimated that more than 20 million Americans are chronic snorers. Men snorers far outnumber women snorers. And, the older you get, the more likely you are to snore; the largest percentage of snorers are in the 50-plus age category.

Some snoring can be corrected by relatively simple adjustments to sleeping habits and lifestyle. Some snoring needs to be corrected by surgical procedures. Of particular concern are those snorers who suffer from sleep apnea—when snoring is interrupted by repetitive pauses in breathing. In sleep apnea, the snorer stops breathing for 10 seconds or longer, then snorts or gasps for air. If you suspect that you are a victim of sleep apnea, you should talk with a doctor. Sleep apnea can cause heart problems.

Following are some things you can do, or should not do, to help eliminate the causes of snoring:

♦ Discuss your snoring with your doctors. If a medical condition is the culprit, perhaps it can be corrected. Ask your dentist if a dental appliance will help. These orthodontic anti-snoring devices pull the jaw forward, thus creating more air space; they also help to keep the tongue in place so it doesn't fall back and block the air passage. Also, your doctor may be able to teach you a few exercises that will strengthen the muscles under the palate.

♦ Don't sleep on your back, a position that invites the tongue to fall back and obstruct the airway. If you tend to sleep in this position, sew a tennis ball or golf ball into a pocket sewn on the back of your pajama top.

♦ Sleep on a firm mattress in a well-ventilated room. Use a single, flattish pillow to keep your neck straight and your air passage open. If your nasal passages are always congested, you might try putting bricks under the legs at the head of your bed; the tilted position of your bed, and you, might help to drain the nasal passages.

♦ Avoid alcohol, tranquilizers, and antihistamines late in the day. And don't take sleeping pills. All depress the central nervous system and over-relax the tissues and muscles in your airway passage.

♦ If you are overweight, go on a diet. Obese people are far more likely to snore than thin people, even though doctors aren't exactly sure why.

♦ If you smoke, quit. Smoking irritates the throat and causes the mucous membranes to swell, which in turn narrows your airway.

14

♦

WORDS/ LANGUAGE/ COMMUNICA-TIONS

Writing

Speaking

WRITING

How to Write Clearly

Ask any group of writers and editors how to improve writing skills, and you usually get the same answers.

1. Make an outline. An outline acts as a road map; without it, your writing is going nowhere. Using paper or note cards, jot down all the main points you want to make. Then sort the points into various subject areas. For example, if you are writing an article on how to buy a new car, your points might fall into categories like narrowing down your choices, shopping for a car loan, negotiating with a car dealer, etc. Once you have figured out your main topic areas, then put them into a logical order.

2. Write in a natural style. Don't try to imitate your favorite author or English professor.

3. Keep your writing simple and straightforward. When constructing sentences, concentrate on nouns and verbs, not adjectives and adverbs. Don't get carried away with figures of speech, like similes and metaphors. Don't use foreign words or expressions unless you know they fit. And, avoid jargon and clichés.

4. Use the active voice instead of the passive voice. "Jack drove the car" is better than "The car was driven by Jack."

5. Keep your audience in mind while you write. How much do the readers know about the subject—a lot or very little? The answer to that question determines how detailed you need to be on particular points or whether you have to explain any special terms or technical words.

6. Use specific, concrete language. Write, "He laughed as he watched the child imitate the monkey," not "He gained great satisfaction upon perceiving that the child was able to move around in a manner similar to that of a monkey."

7. Review and revise. This can be harder than writing a first draft. First of all, is every sentence necessary, and if so, is every sentence in the right place? Are some sentences too vague? Are you guilty of overexplaining a point? Overall, you need to be ruthless when editing. Make your writing as tight and as easy to read as possible. Here are a few examples of how to get rid of superfluous wording: "if" instead of "in the event of"; "clearly" instead of "it is obvious that"; "soon" instead of "in the near future."

8. Review your revision, but first take a breather. Writing and editing are exhausting, and when you are finished, nothing may seem clear. A short rest will restore your sanity and enable you to tackle the piece one last time.

Parts of Speech

Grammarians divide the words we use into eight categories, called the "parts of speech"—even though they are just as important in writing as in speaking. Anyone who has survived an English composition class has learned them. Here is a brief refresher course:

1. A **noun** is a word that names people, places, or things. Specific people and places (*Irving; Indianapolis*) are called proper nouns and are usually capitalized, as distinct from common nouns (*man; city*). Other categories of nouns include collective nouns (*team, orchestra*), which usually take a singular verb; concrete nouns (*moon, spoon, balloon*); and abstract nouns (*time, trouble, kindness*).

2. The **pronoun** substitutes for a noun that has already been mentioned or is known. Some of the most important types of pronouns are as follows:

♦ personal: *I, you, he, she, it, we, they*
♦ interrogative, posing questions: *who, what, which*
♦ indefinite: *one, all, both, few, some*
♦ relative, linking clauses: *that, which, who*
♦ demonstrative: *this, that, these, those*

3. An **adjective** modifies, describes, or limits a noun. It is usually placed before the noun (the *red* barn), or it may be in the predicate, meaning everything in the sentence but the subject (the barn was *red*). Adjectives also come in the form of phrases, which may include all parts of speech, as in: the barn *that stood by the road*. An important property of adjectives is their ability to take comparative and superlative forms. One-syllable adjectives add *-er* and *-est* (*high, higher, highest*), while longer adjectives use the auxiliaries *more* and *most* (*more beautiful, most beautiful*).

4. **Verbs** are words expressing action and condition. Very versatile, they change form according to subject, tense (the basic tenses are past, present, and future), voice (active or passive), and mood (indicative, imperative, and the little-used subjunctive). Grammarians also find it useful to distinguish between transitive and intransitive verbs, or those which take an object (she drove the car) and those which do not (the sun set).

5. **Adverbs** are words that modify, describe, or limit verbs and also adjectives and other adverbs. Adverbs often end in *-ly*: He walked *slowly*. (However, some words ending in *-ly* are not adverbs—*ugly* and *lovely* are two such exceptions.) Like adjectives, adverbs have comparative and superlative forms, and are formed similarly. Adverbs of one syllable (thus excluding all those of the *-ly* type) add *-er* and *-est* (*far, farther, farthest*), while longer adverbs use the auxiliaries *more* and *most*. Some of the most commonly used adverbs are irregular in the comparative and superlative: *well, better, best; badly, worse, worst*. An example of an adverb modifying an adjective: a *very* pretty dress.

6. A **preposition** indicates a relation or link between words, phrases, or clauses. It can describe position, direction, scope, or timing. Some of the most common prepositions: *above, after, around, behind, below, down, during, from, outside, through, to, under, upon*, and *with*. In addition to being single words, prepositions also come in phrase form: *toward evening* is a prepositional phrase.

7. **Conjunctions** connect words, groups of words, and parts of sentences. The most common are *and* and *but*. Grammarians distinguish among coordinating conjunctions, which directly link relatively equal parts of a sentence (*and, but*); correlative conjunctions, which come in pairs (*either/or; not only/but also*); and subordinating conjunctions (*because, after, unless, until, when, where*).

8. An **interjection** is a word interjected into a sentence without introduction or link: *Indeed*, the barn is red. Interjections often express feeling and may culminate in an exclamation point: *Oh my*, we don't want that!

When in doubt, remember that dictionaries identify words by parts of speech, usually abbreviated: n., pron., adj., v.i. and v.t. (verb transitive and verb intransitive), adv., prep., conj., interj.

How to Punctuate

(*Authors' note:* Plodding through the endless pages of punctuation rules in a grammar book can be frustrating and tedious. Below is a concise punctuation primer written by Pulitzer-Prize–winning author Russell Baker. The article was part of a series on communications topics that was sponsored by the International Paper Company.)

When you write, you make a sound in the reader's head. It can be a dull mumble—that's why so much government prose makes you sleepy—or it can be a joyful noise, a sly whisper, a throb of passion.

Listen to a voice trembling in a haunted room:

"And the silken, sad, uncertain rustling of each purple curtain thrilled me—filled me with fantastic terrors never felt before . . ."

That's Edgar Allan Poe, a master. Few of us can make paper speak as vividly as Poe could, but even beginners will write better once they start listening to the sound their writing makes.

One of the most important tools for making paper speak in your own voice is punctuation.

When speaking aloud, you punctuate constantly—with body language. Your listener hears commas, dashes, question marks, exclamation points, quotation marks as you shout, whisper, pause, wave your arms, roll your eyes, wrinkle your brow.

In writing, punctuation plays the role of body language. It helps readers hear you the way you want to be heard.

"Gee, Dad, have I got to learn all them rules?"

Don't let the rules scare you. For they aren't hard and fast. Think of them as guidelines.

Am I saying, "Go ahead and punctuate as you please"? Absolutely not. Use your own common sense, remembering that you can't expect readers to work to decipher what you're trying to say.

There are two basic systems of punctuation:

1. The loose or open system, which tries to capture the way body language punctuates talk.

2. The tight, closed structural system, which hews closely to the sentence's grammatical structure.

Most writers use a little of both. In any case, we use much less punctuation than they used 200 or even 50 years ago. (Glance into Edward

Gibbon's *Decline and Fall of the Roman Empire,* first published in 1776, for an example of the tight structural system at its most elegant.) No matter which system you prefer, be warned: punctuation marks cannot save a sentence that is badly put together. If you have to struggle over commas, semicolons, and dashes, you've probably built a sentence that's never going to fly, no matter how you tinker with it. Throw it away and build a new one to a simpler design. The better your sentence, the easier it is to punctuate.

Choosing the right tool

There are 30 main punctuation marks, but you'll need fewer than a dozen for most writing.

I can't show you how they all work, so I'll stick to the 10 most important—and even then can only hit highlights. For more details, check your dictionary or a good grammar book.

Comma [,]

This is the most widely used mark of all. It's also the toughest and most controversial. I've seen aging editors almost come to blows over the comma. If you can handle it without sweating, the others will be easy. Here's my policy:

1. Use a comma after a long introductory phrase or clause: After stealing the crown jewels from the Tower of London, I went home for tea.

2. If the introductory material is short, forget the comma: After the theft I went home for tea.

3. But use it if the sentence would be confusing without it, like this: The day before I'd robbed the Bank of England.

4. Use a comma to separate elements in a series: I robbed the Denver Mint, the Bank of England, the Tower of London and my piggy bank.

Notice that there is no comma before *and* in the series. This is common style nowadays, but some publishers use a comma there, too.

5. Use a comma to separate independent clauses that are joined by a conjunction like and, but, for, or, nor, because or so: I shall return the crown jewels, for they are too heavy to wear.

6. Use a comma to set off a mildly parentheti-

cal word grouping that isn't essential to the sentence: Girls, who have always interested me, usually differ from boys.

Do not use commas if the word grouping *is* essential to the sentence's meaning: Girls who interest me know how to tango.

7. Use a comma in direct address: Your majesty, please hand over the crown.

8. And between proper names and titles: Montague Sneed, Director of Scotland Yard, was assigned the case.

9. And to separate elements of geographical address: Director Sneed comes from Chicago, Illinois, and now lives in London, England.

Generally speaking, use a comma where you'd pause briefly in speech. For a long pause or completion of thought, use a period.

If you confuse the comma with the period, you'll get a run-on sentence: The Bank of England is located in London, I rushed right over to rob it.

Semicolon [;]

A more sophisticated mark than the comma, the semicolon separates two main clauses, but it keeps those two thoughts more tightly linked than a period can: I steal crown jewels; she steals hearts.

Dash [—] and Parentheses [( )]

Warning! Use sparingly. The dash SHOUTS. Parentheses whisper. Shout too often, people stop listening; whisper too much, people become suspicious of you.

The dash creates a dramatic pause to prepare for an expression needing strong emphasis: I'll marry you—if you'll rob Topkapi with me.

Parentheses help you pause quietly to drop in some chatty information not vital to your story: Despite Betty's daring spirit ("I love robbing your piggy bank," she often said), she was a terrible dancer.

Quotation marks [" "]

These tell the reader you're reciting the exact words someone said or wrote: Betty said, "I can't tango." Or: "I can't tango," Betty said.

Notice the comma comes before the quote marks in the first example, but comes inside them in the second. Not logical? Never mind. Do it that way anyhow.

Colon [:]

A colon is a tip-off to get ready for what's next: a list, a long quotation or an explanation. This article is riddled with colons. Too many, maybe, but the message is: "Stay on your toes; it's coming at you."

Apostrophe [']

The big headache is with possessive nouns. If the noun is singular, add *'s*: I hated Betty's tango.

If the noun is plural, simply add an apostrophe after the *s*: Those are the girls' coats.

The same applies for singular nouns ending in *s*, like Dickens: This is Dickens's best book.

And in plural: this is the Dickenses' cottage.

The possessive pronouns *hers* and *its* have no apostrophe. If you write *it's*, you are saying *it is*.

Keep cool

You know about ending a sentence with a period (.) or a question mark (?). Do it. Sure, you can also end with an exclamation mark (!), but must you? Usually it just makes you sound breathless and silly. Make your writing generate its own excitement. Filling the paper with !!!! won't make up for what your writing has failed to do.

Too many exclamation points make me think the writer is talking about the panic in his or her own head. Don't sound panicky. End with a period. I am serious. A period. Understand?

Well . . . sometimes a question mark is okay.

Reprinted courtesy of the International Paper Company.

Ten Tricks of the Trade

Our language provides us with a number of devices to add color, originality, intensity—even humor—to our writing. Collectively, these devices are called "figures of speech" (or figurative language), and they are used to compare dissimilar things as well as to create sounds and images. In other words, they allow us to walk outside the realm of "literal" language. Most of us use these devices daily, in speaking as well as writing, even though we may not know the technical name for them. Used properly, they can turn mundane writing into a work of art. Used improperly, they can make you sound absurd.

Simile. Compares two essentially different things by using *like* or *as* or *as if:* a heart as big as all outdoors; tears flowing like wine. Similes can tend to become clichés: filthy as a pig; stubborn as a mule; blind as a bat; fit as a fiddle; ugly as sin.

Metaphor. Like a simile, a metaphor makes a comparison between two unlike things but does not use the words *like* or *as* or *as if*. The comparison can be in the form of a substitution: Sam Smith is a dead duck. Or, the unlike things can be identified with one another: Mary really went to bat for me at the stockholder's meeting. Metaphors create wonderful images but too many dissimilar images can lead to what is called a "mixed metaphor": Bob is a sharpshooter who always has his eye on the ball, and he never lets his antennae down. Mixed metaphors bombard the reader with mixed messages; avoid them.

Alliteration. Appeals to the ear by repeating initial sounds in two or more neighboring words in a phrase, line of poetry, or a sentence. "Peter Piper picked a peck of pickled peppers" is an extreme use of alliteration. More moderate examples: wild and woolly; slipped silently; bravely approach the bloody beast. Be careful not to overuse this figure of speech. It works best when the reader is not quite conscious of it.

Onomatopoeia. Using words whose sounds imitate what they mean: Over the cobbles he clattered and clashed in the dark inn yard. Some onomatopoeic words: babble, bank, bowwow, buzz, cackle, croak, cuckoo, hiss, moo, sizzle, twitter, and zoom.

Hyperbole. An extravagant overstatement that is not intended to be taken literally; it is used only to heighten the effect of your writing. Some hyperboles: This book weighs a ton; I'm eternally grateful; they're stuffed in that car like sardines; my stack of work is a mile high. Used ironically, the hyperbole can be potent: A boss says to an employee who has just made a costly mistake, "You're an absolute genius, aren't you?"

Meiosis. Understating something to get a desired effect; the opposite of hyperbole. Mary just won a $100-million lottery and her husband says, "I guess we can get by on that." A stunningly beautiful woman walks by and a male observer says, "She's acceptable." This device is usually employed to get a humorous or satiric effect.

Euphemism. Substituting an inoffensive expression for one that is considered offensive. The funeral industry is full of euphemisms: casket has replaced coffin; internment has replaced burial; memorial garden has replaced graveyard. Sometimes there are good reasons for using this device. Perhaps you'd rather say that a couple "spent the night together" rather than talk about "sexual intercourse." However, we tend to get carried away with euphemisms: a used car can be called a pre-owned car; a dog catcher can be called a canine control officer; a prostitute can be called an available, casual, indigenous female companion.

Oxymoron. Combining two contradictory or incongruous words in order to express a startling paradox. Some oxymorons: pretty ugly, small fortune, random order, awfully good, jumbo shrimp, deafening silence, open secret, minor miracle, old news.

Anticlimax. Something trivial or commonplace that concludes a series of significant things; often used for humorous effect. Example: He was a scholar, a humanitarian, and one heck of a poker player.

Paronomasia (the technical and outdated word for "pun"). A play on words. Puns can involve words that sound alike but have different meanings. "Trees a crowd" is a pun. Common phrases with words reversed are also puns: the greatest earth on show; the hand that cradles the rock. And puns have taken on the full-fledged flavor of a joke: An actress was hired for the lead in *Joan of Arc* but she ended up getting fired; the dessert most popular with carpenters and boxers is a pound cake; how can you tell that the dog is young? because of his short pants.

Commonly Misused Words

Don't know which of two words to choose? Either they sound exactly alike or pretty much alike. Here are some pairs of words that send just about everybody to the dictionary:

accept: to receive; to make a favorable response to
except: to leave out; with the exclusion of

affect: to influence
effect: a result or impression; to bring about or to accomplish

allude: to make an indirect reference to
elude: to avoid or evade

antagonist: an adversary or opponent
protagonist: the principal or leading character

anybody (one word): any person
any body (two words): any corpse; any human form; any group

canvas: a heavy woven fabric
canvass: to solicit something (like votes or orders)

capital: a city that is the seat of government; the top part of a column
capitol: a building in which a legislative body meets

climactic: refers to a climax
climatic: refers to the weather

complement: to make complete; something that completes
compliment: to praise; an admiring remark

discreet: prudent
discrete: separate or distinct

disinterested: unbiased or impartial
uninterested: not interested or not concerned

dyeing: to color with dye
dying: to stop living

emigrate: to leave a country to live elsewhere
immigrate: to come into another place of residence

eminent: conspicuous or prominent
imminent: ready to take place

elicit: to call forth or bring about
illicit: illegal

faze: to disturb or bother
phase: a stage or distinguishable part

ingenious: clever or resourceful
ingenuous: innocent

personal: relating to a person; private
personnel: the employees of a company or organization

principal: the chief person or thing
principle: a fundamental truth or law

prostate: relating to the prostate gland
prostrate: lying flat with face on the ground

qualitative: relating to quality
quantitative: relating to number

stationary: immobile
stationery: writing material

tortuous: winding or crooked
torturous: unpleasant or painful

viral: relating to a virus
virile: manly

Capitalization

When speaking, you obviously do not have to worry about whether to uppercase or lowercase a word, but as soon as you put pen to paper you encounter numerous questions relating to capitalization. Here are some answers:

1. The first word of a sentence or a direct quotation is capitalized.

2. In the titles of books, movies, paintings, and musical compositions, all words are capitalized except conjunctions, prepositions, and articles (a, an, the). Example: *How to Win Friends and Influence People.*

3. Capitalize days of the week, months, and holidays, but not seasons.

4. Names of persons are capitalized, as is the pronoun "I." When a common noun is used as a name, it is capitalized: "Father just left"—but, "My father has not left." Even fictitious people and abstractions are capitalized: Jane Doe, Uncle Sam, Mother Nature. The names of corporations (Coca-Cola, Levi Strauss, Kimberly-Clark) are capitalized, and so are their trademarks (Coke, Levi's, Kleenex). But according to a recent court ruling, the trademark Formica has become generic, hence deserving only a lowercase letter (formica).

5. Racial and ethnic groups are usually capitalized (Aryan, Afro-American, Hispanic), but there are some exceptions—white, black, redneck. (The U.S. Census Bureau, however, capitalizes White and Black.)

6. Geographical place names are capitalized: cities and states (Washington State, but the state of Washington); areas (the Panhandle, the Pacific Rim); mountains, rivers, and lakes (even Walden Pond). Regions are capitalized—the West, back East—but not directions (going east, heading south). Buildings and monuments are often capitalized (the White House, the Statue of Liberty) but not always (city hall). Street names, parks, and bridges begin with capital letters.

In the world of outer space, we write Mars and Venus, but the earth, sun, and moon.

7. For political and administrative institutions and bodies, we write Congress, Parliament, the Supreme Court, and the Census Bureau—but cabinet, both houses of Congress, the federal government. We write Democratic party and Nazi party—but democracy and nazism.

8. Historical, cultural, and socioeconomic periods, events, and styles are particularly tricky. According to the *Chicago Manual of Style*, you should capitalize Prohibition but not the gold rush; the War on Poverty but not the cold war; the Great Depression but not just the depression. We refer to the Dark Ages, the Renaissance, and the Roaring Twenties, but baroque, romanticism, and cubism. The Bronze Age requires two capitals but the Jurassic period only one.

9. Titles are full of potential capitalization problems. We write President Lincoln and Pres. Abraham Lincoln when the title comes before the name, but Abe Lincoln, president of the United States. (Lincoln's epithet, the Great Emancipator, is capitalized.) When a title is used in direct address in place of a name, it begins with an uppercase letter ("Excuse me, Senator").

10. Concerning the military, you write lowercase army, navy, etc. when used in their plural forms (the armies) or when they are not part of an official title (the British army). However, full titles are capitalized (the United States Marine Corps) as are specific names for corps, regiments, fleets, and battalions (the Seventh Fleet, the First Battalion).

11. Religious names, terms, and events incline heavily to capitalization. We write God, the Supreme Being, the Messiah, and the Prophet; the Gospels, the Talmud, the Koran; the Creation, the Crucifixion, Original Sin. The word *church* is capitalized when it is part of a proper name: the Church of England or Westfield Memorial Church (but the Roman Catholic church).

12. The names of ships, aircraft, satellites, and space vehicles are capitalized (U.S.S. *Arizona*, the *Spirit of St. Louis*, Voyager II).

Spelling Tips

Most poor spellers consider themselves beyond help. Yes, of course, there are rules ("*i* before *e* except after *c*") but there are exceptions (when sounded like *a*, as in neighbor and weigh). And what about either and neither, seize and sheik? And have you ever been shopping at Neiman Marcus?

According to one school of thought, the ability to spell is an innate neuromuscular skill, not a measure of intelligence. In any case, poor spellers either resign themselves to constant, humiliating error, or steel themselves to use the dictionary (or telephone book, encyclopedia, or anything handy that is in alphabetical order). Even then, you have to know approximately how a word is spelled before you can find it.

If you really want to feel like a spelling ignoramus, take a look at some of the winning words at the annual Scripps Howard National Spelling Bees:

eczema
chihuahua
macerate
narcolepsy
elucubrate
sarcophagus
psoriasis
milieu
staphylococci

There are some things you can do to improve your spelling:

1. Use mnemonic aids to help you remember words that always give you trouble. For example: there's a *rat* in separate; the word *science* is in conscience.

2. Confused about whether a words ends in -*efy* or -*ify*? There are only four words that end in -*efy*: liquefy, putrefy, rarefy, and stupefy. Use -*ify* for all other words.

3. Other than technical words, only two words in our language end in -*yze*: analyze and paralyze.

4. Only one word ends in -*sede*—supersede.

5. The endings -*ery* and -*ary* are particularly troublesome. If a word has a primary accent on the first syllable and a secondary accent on the next-to-last syllable (sec-re-tar-y), the word almost always ends in -*ary*. The only exceptions to the rule: cemetery, confectionery, distillery, millinery, monastery, and stationery (writing paper).

6. There are only three words in our language that end with -*ceed*: exceed, proceed, and succeed.

7. Saying words out loud will improve your spelling—provided you are pronouncing them correctly. For example, if you correctly say "Feb-*ru*ary," not "Fe*bu*ary," then you won't forget the letter "r."

8. Always have a dictionary on hand when you are writing. And be sure it isn't too outdated.

Affirmative-Action Grammar

The goal of affirmative-action grammar is to avoid offending or excluding any sector of the population. The sector that has been most active in

50 COMMONLY MISSPELLED WORDS

accommodate	diarrhea	independent	necessary
acquainted	dilemma	inoculate	occurrence
advantageous	embarrass	irresistible	parallel
amateur	exhilarate	laboratory	permanent
anonymous	foreign	liaison	privilege
bureau	fulfill	lightning	receipt
commitment	grammar	maintenance	rhythm
conscience	guerrilla	maneuver	separate
counterfeit	harass	miniature	sergeant
deceive	heighten	minuscule	similar
desirable	hemorrhage	misspell	subtle
desperate	humorous	mysterious	transferred
	incidentally		yield

seeking language reform is women, but they are not alone. New words such as *weightism* and *heightism* have been suggested by respective pressure groups to designate discrimination against the fat and the short. A professional association of Asian-Americans has requested that they no longer be described in such stereotypical terms as *industrious* or *smiling.* You should no longer use expressions like "Indian giver" or "beat the drums," to avoid provoking native Americans, and *niggardly* should be dropped from the dictionary as a racial slur against Black Americans.

Wordsmith Willard Espy points out that many words in the dictionary are offensive to one group or another: gypsies might object to *gyp,* the Welsh to *welshing,* the *Slavs* to slavery. But it is American women who have spoken up the loudest and most effectively, launching a growing movement for reform and elimination of sex discrimination in English usage.

Ms. was coined as a new title for women. *Ms.* is equivalent to *Mr.* in that it reveals nothing about the woman's age or marital status (which *Miss* and *Mrs.* do). Although controversial (grammarians call it etymologically nonsensical, as well as basically unpronounceable), *Ms.* has achieved surprising acceptance, probably for sheer convenience when one does not know a woman's marital status.

Even more basic than forms of address is the matter of what to call that sector of the population that is not male. In a more innocent era, *female* was considered a biological term, *lady* a social designation, and *woman* all-inclusive of mature females; under the age of puberty, females were called *girls* (although this designation, and its slang spin-off, *gals,* is used by some men for females of any age).

Girls can still be called girls, up to the age of about 14, but to call any older female a girl (or gal) is now considered demeaning. *Lady* has come under fire as presumptuous and patronizing, and occupational titles incorporating it—*saleslady, lady doctor*—are now taboo (see following table). According to some revisionists, *female* should be scrapped because it suggests that the female sex is a subspecies of the male. Even *woman,* say some critics, is tainted by its obvious relationship to *man;* an alternative spelling proposed by feminists is "womyn." (A recent cartoon satirizing the dilemma showed a young boy telephoning from the maternity floor of a hospital: "It's a woman," he announced, "an infant woman!")

Instead of *man* or *mankind,* you should now use *humans, humanity* or *humankind, men and women,* or just plain *people.* (For example, man did not discover fire; people did.) As a general rule for gender-neutral nouns, you should no longer use any word ending in *-man* or *-lady* and avoid the suffixes *-ess* and *-ette.* If a sexual bias is conveyed in some other fashion, then you have to use some ingenuity in finding an acceptable substitute. Herewith, some nonsexist alternatives to tainted words:

No	Yes
saleslady	salesperson
seamstress	sewer
poetess	poet
waitress	waiter
lady doctor	doctor
heiress	heir
cleaning woman	housecleaner
workmen's compensation	workers' compensation
chairman	chair, chairperson
craftsman	artisan
fireman	firefighter
tomboy	active child
maneater	cannibal
mastermind	leader
old wives' tale	superstitious folklore
manhole	conduit
brotherhood	community
bachelor's degree	undergraduate degree
grandfather clause	existing-condition clause
man of the world	cosmopolite

All derogatory or less than respectful terms for women—including *chick, bitch, battle-ax, the weaker sex, witch, nymphomaniac, pinup, nag, whore,* even *coed*—should be eliminated from your vocabulary. Likewise, references to sexist men—*womanizers, wolves*—should not be used.

A *male chauvinist* is now simply a *chauvinist,* a *playboy* a *pleasure seeker.* And what about that old fallback, the unknown "Dear Sir" or "Sirs" to whom you address letters? You might start with a reference line ("Re: Job Application"), or substitute a department name ("To: The Personnel Department").

Moving from nouns to pronouns, the problem becomes a little thornier. In English, fortunately for equal opportunity linguistics, the first- and second-person pronouns, *I* and *you,* are gender-neutral; the difficulty begins with the third person, *he* and *she* and their objective and possessive forms, *him* and *her, his* and *hers.* (In the third-person plural, *they, them,* and *their* are again gender-neutral.)

One humorous suggestion for combining *he, she,* or *it* was "h'orsh'it." (Long ago, sardonic writer Ambrose Bierce anticipated this whole brouhaha when he suggested combining *Miss, Mrs.* and *Mr.* into "Mush.") As things stand now, you should use a gender-neutral noun (as listed above, or "one" instead of he or she) with a similarly appropriate pronoun when the sex of the person is not known.

There are several ways to walk around all this linguistic confusion. Omit the possessive altogether ("everyone must carry I.D.") or cover all bases with *"his or her* I.D." You can also use plural nouns and pronouns (instead of "a child should learn to tie *his* own shoelaces," use "children should learn to tie *their* shoelaces"). You can always repeat the subject to avoid sexism: "when the doctor arrived, the doctor was behind schedule," rather than ". . . *he* was behind schedule." Another possibility is to rewrite your sentence in the passive voice: instead of "a secretary should know how to repair *her* typewriter," say "typewriter repair should be part of secretarial training." Finally, grammarians are becoming more receptive to the idea of using the gender-neutral plural with a singular antecedent. As W. H. Auden once wrote, "anyone in *their* senses . . ." The problem is that when you hear someone say this, you don't know whether they are illiterate or gender-conscious.

If you think this is unnecessarily difficult, be grateful that English nouns (with rare exceptions like cars and boats, which are traditionally assumed to be female) generally have no gender. The problem of sexism increases enormously in languages in which all nouns have gender, and that includes most of the world's languages.

Letter Writing— the Difficult Ones

Job Application Letter

You are unemployed. You desperately need a job. But thousands of others who share your predicament are knocking on the same doors. How then do you rise above the herd, calling attention to yourself and your skills without appearing to be a grandstander? Besides a résumé, you must compose an accompanying letter that will compel the recipient's attention, impressing the recipient with your drive and self-confidence (even when they may be at their lowest) as well as your qualifications—all this without sounding like a braggart.

Whether you are replying to an ad or just mass-mailing letters at random, you want to find out as much as possible about your target companies. Look them up in the *Dun & Bradstreet Directory* or *Standard and Poor's Register.* Try to find and read the company's annual report. If a company is too small or local to be listed in the above sources, check with the relevant trade association or even the Better Business Bureau, so you can custom-design your pitch to the employer's activities and needs.

Next, you want to compose an impeccable letter with correct grammar, punctuation, and spelling. It must be typed. Appearances are especially important, so use good-quality paper. Some people favor brightly colored stationery so their letters will stand out from the heap, but this strategy can backfire.

The opening and closing sentences of your letter are key; they should be exciting, provocative, to the point. Instead of beginning, "I am responding to your advertisement in today's paper," you might write, "I have carefully studied your operations for the last year and . . ." Be different and original: you might want to start with a question, anecdote, famous saying, or expert opinion. However, be careful that your originality doesn't end up sounding eccentric or bizarre.

The body of the letter should enumerate your capabilities (paraphrased from your résumé) and relate them to the employer's needs. In other words, concentrate on what you can give to the employer instead of what you want from the employer. Do not criticize anyone (for example, your former employer); be diplomatic and positive. Keep the letter as short as possible. When you have finished, read the letter out loud to see if it sounds natural and appealing.

The Bantam Book of Correct Letter Writing includes many samples of job application letters, including one that we find particularly inspired:

Dear _____:
　　I am a typist, but not an ordinary one! I like typing. I thoroughly enjoy it. I take pride in turning out clean, attractive, well-spaced copy.
　　Your advertisement . . . appeals to me because I know I'd especially enjoy typing radio scripts. . . . It would be fascinating to type scripts again after a year of nothing but dull legal documents. . . .

Consider this letter written in 1482 by an unemployed man named Leonardo da Vinci. Although best known as an artist, Leonardo was also an inventor. The letter, seeking employment, was sent to the Duke of Milan:

Having, most illustrious lord, seen and considered the experiments of all those who pose as masters in the art of inventing instruments of war, and finding that their inventions differ in no way from those in common use, I am emboldened, without prejudice to anyone, to solicit an appointment of acquainting your Excellency with certain of my secrets.
　　1. I can construct bridges which are very light and strong and very portable. . . .
　　2. In case of a siege I can cut off water from the trenches and make pontoons and scaling ladders. . . .
　　3. . . . I can demolish every fortress if its foundations have not been set on stone.
　　4. I can also make a kind of cannon which is light and easy of transport . . . of which the smoke causes great terror to the enemy. . . .
　　5. I can noiselessly construct to any prescribed point subterranean passages either straight or winding. . . .

And so on. Needless to say, Leonardo got a job and it lasted for 16 years.

Complaint Letter

Defective merchandise and poor service are the most common reasons for writing a complaint letter. Since your goal is to get speedy and just compensation, it's important that your letter be as effective as possible. Here are some rules of thumb:

♦ Make your letter as professional-looking as possible. Type it, if you can, and use good-quality, white paper. Be sure that your address and phone number are included.

♦ Keep your letter brief and to the point. State the problem up front and list all the important facts like date and place of purchase, model and serial numbers, and *exactly* what is wrong with the product. If you are complaining about service, describe the service and who performed it as well as why the service was not satisfactory.

♦ Include copies of all relevant documentation. Keep the original paperwork in a file with a copy of your letter.

♦ State what you want done to resolve the problem—repair, replacement, or refund. The more specific you are, the more likely you are to get a prompt response.

♦ Carefully review the tone of your letter. You want it to be courteous and businesslike. Anger, sarcasm, and threats will get you nowhere. The person reading your letter may not be directly responsible for the problem and won't look kindly upon an insulting letter. Assume that the recipient of the letter will be helpful; that assumption will help you to write in a polite manner.

♦ Be sure your letter is addressed to the right person. You do not have to write to the president of a large food products company to complain about a box of stale cookies. Someone at a lower level, like a customer-service representative, will usually have the power to resolve the problem. If you're not sure whom to complain to, call the company and ask (many large corporations have toll-free phone numbers).

♦ Sit back and wait. Smaller companies usually respond faster than large corporations. If you haven't received a reply in four to six weeks, send off another copy of your letter and attach a note expressing your concern and disappointment at not hearing from the company. In addition, you may consider sending a copy of your letter and a copy of your note to someone higher up in the organization's chain of command; perhaps it's time to go "straight to the top."

♦ Recognize when you need help. You've been a polite, reasonable, patient complainer and no one is paying any attention to you. Then it's time to seek assistance from a group like the Better Business Bureau or your local consumer protection agency. If a significant amount of money is involved, you can ask your lawyer to write a letter on your behalf.

Condolence Letter

It's a lot easier to buy a sympathy card than to sit down and write a condolence letter. However, a condolence letter is a more heartfelt way to express your thoughts to a bereaved family or friend. Most people avoid writing these letters because they are afraid of saying something wrong and because they are uncomfortable talking about death. Here are some suggestions to help you pen an appropriate letter:

♦ It must be handwritten. White or cream-colored stationery is preferred.

♦ The letter should be written as soon as possible after hearing of someone's death.

♦ The letter can be short—as short as two

sentences or two paragraphs. However, if you want to write a one-page letter, feel free to do so.

♦ It's permissible to express shock and dismay and to use the word *death*.

♦ Don't be concerned that your letter be eloquent; simply say what you feel. The thoughts behind the words you use are more important than the actual words.

♦ Talk about the things you liked or admired about the deceased. If you want to share a personal memory, do so. Humorous anecdotes are also okay.

♦ There are some definite "don'ts" to be aware of when writing the letter. Don't focus on specific details of the deceased's illness or death. Don't say things like: "I don't know how you will go on without her"; "You're lucky to have had him for so long"; "It's time to get on with the rest of your life."

The Love Letter

Few missives are as eagerly awaited, long-remembered, and tenderly cherished as the love letter. Nearly everyone has written some kind of a love letter. The main concern is to translate the rapture in your mind into rapture on paper, using your own customary expressions.

The best thing about love letters: there are no rules to follow. You can be clever, foolish, funny, intimate. You can whisper sweet nothings, exaggerate as much as you want, even tell little white lies. If you want to write poetry, this is your chance; or, if you have no talent, crib a few lines from someone else. And there are no laws governing the length of a love letter; make it as long as you want.

Creating an intimate nickname for your loved one can be great fun. Remember, however, that it can come back to haunt you (Charles Dickens to his wife Kate: "Dearest darling Pig"; Zelda Fitzgerald to F. Scott Fitzgerald: "Dear Goofo"). Most love-letter writers aren't overly concerned that their passionate verse may fall into the hands of someone other than their loved ones. However, if the possibility frightens you, write your letter, or parts of your letter, in secret code. Just be sure your loved one knows how to decipher the code.

Some of the world's greatest love letters were written by a man whose fame was for military, not amatory, conquest. Early in their relationship, Napoleon Bonaparte sent Josephine Beauharnais a thousand kisses by letter—"but give me none in return, for they set my blood on fire." In 1796, after their marriage, he wrote of his obsession with his wife:

> I have not spent a day without loving you; I have not spent a night without embracing you; I have not so much as drunk a cup of tea. . . . In the midst of my duties . . . my beloved Josephine stands alone in my heart, occupies my mind, fills my thoughts. . . .

Separated from Josephine while campaigning in Italy in 1797, the jealous general wrote his wife, who had neglected to maintain her end of the correspondence: "Beware, Josephine; one fine night the doors will be broken down and there I shall be." Napoleon closed this letter, however, with his usual ardor: "I hope to hold you in my arms before long, when I shall lavish upon you a million kisses, burning as the equatorial sun."

Perhaps you need a few more sample love letters to inspire you and get you started. If so, there are a number of love-letter collections available at your library or bookstore. Two of the best are Cathy Davidson's *The Book of Love: Writers and Their Love Letters* and Antonia Fraser's *Love Letters: An Illustrated Anthology*.

How to Write a Résumé

There are certain standard ingredients that any résumé should contain, but you can mix and match, and customize them to maximize your strengths, minimize your weaknesses, and zero in on your objectives.

A résumé should be one-page long, two pages maximum; more, and nobody will read it. Remember, the function of a résumé is to get you in the door for an interview, not to tell the story of your life and overwhelm readers with your accomplishments. Margins should be 1½ to 2 inches on each side: do not overload the page, for the eye can take in only so much. Write clearly, correctly, and avoid jargon. The résumé should be printed on good white stock, and each copy should look like an original, a simple matter in the age of computers.

The basic ingredients of any résumé are seven-fold:

1. Your name, address, and telephone number (both day and evening, if necessary), at the top. There is no need to type "Résumé" as a heading; it's obviously a résumé.

2. A "job objective" statement is optional and works best when a résumé is customized for a particular employer. If you use it, focus on what you can do and want to do.

3. A summary of your qualifications is also optional; generally and briefly, describe your skills.

4. Your employment experience is the meat of your résumé. List positions in reverse chronological order, with dates, names and addresses of employers. Include your job titles (sometimes you have to use a little imagination, like "computer specialist," but do not lie), responsibilities and accomplishments, goals and results, any awards received. Use action verbs like "created," "directed," "achieved," and "organized." Give this section your very best effort.

5. Your education should also be outlined in reverse chronological order, listing schools, degrees, dates, major/minor fields of study, extracurricular activities when relevant, scholarships and work-study programs. If you did not get a degree but attended college, indicate the number of credits earned. Do not list high school unless you did not attend college. Show vocational (such as computer) training courses.

6. Supporting data, also optional, may include professional affiliations or names and addresses of references.

7. Personal data are optional. State your mari-

tal status if you like, and your age, but provide height, weight, and a photo only if relevant (as for an acting or modeling position). This is where to mention personal projects, activities, volunteer work, special skills, bilingual capabilities. You might want to inject some personal flavor here, like "semiprofessional folk singer," but don't get too clever. Fund-raising activities, roles in school plays, hobbies such as chess, and travel might also be mentioned here.

There is no need to date your résumé; this may give away the fact that you have been job-hunting for a long period. And do not state the reasons why you left previous employers; that is a subject for the interview (if at all).

The résumé described above, a chronological résumé, is the one most people use. However, it may not work well for people who have changed jobs frequently or have big gaps of time between jobs; these special problems may stand out in a chronological format. If this format doesn't work for you, then create a more functional one that stresses skills and responsibilities and has a minimum of dates and company names. Whatever format you design, be sure it is logical and presents you in a favorable manner.

If you have difficulty writing a résumé, or just hate writing one, you might consider hiring someone to do it for you. There are many résumé services (listed in your yellow pages), and they will write up the résumé, choose an appropriate format, and print it on quality paper. When calling around, be sure to ask about price; one page can cost as much as $100.

Once you have written the résumé, what do you do with it? The sad fact is that most résumés never get read because they land on the wrong desk, usually that of the secretary in the personnel department. Unless you have specific instructions to the contrary, you should send your résumé to the person in charge of the department where you would like to work, the highest authority that you can reach. It may take some research to get the name of that person. Use friends, neighbors, the library, your alumni association, and trade publications to help you identify your target.

Forms of Address

You want to write a letter to the president, or to a member of the clergy, a military officer, or the mayor. Since all of them have some sort of official title, you aren't sure how to write the name on the envelope or how to pen the name for the inside address. To make matters worse, after you write the word "Dear" (the salutation), you are again stumped.

This difficult subject is called "forms of address," and the proper forms are a matter of convention and etiquette rather than grammatical usage. You need two different forms of address to write to a person of title, rank, or public office: one form for a written address and another for a written salutation. Listed below are some common forms of address. If the one you need is not included, you should consult an etiquette book. But if you consult two different sources, you may find two different versions, for we are dealing here with propriety, not right or wrong.

In the following list you will notice a few appellations common to different VIPs, such as the address "The Honorable," followed by the full name. This designation (written, and also used for public introductions) is shared by cabinet members, U.S. senators and representatives, ambassadors, governors, mayors, state legislators, and judges. (Some sources say that former U.S. presidents should also be addressed as "The Honorable," but more often they are treated honorifically, as if they were still president.) One step up from honorable, "The Right Honorable" is accorded to members of the British nobility lower than marquis, while "His" or "Her Excellency" is reserved for foreign ambassadors (American ambassadors are just plain "The Honorable") and "His" or "Her Majesty" for royalty.

The forms of address given below are in the following sequence: letter address, then letter greeting (salutation).

Elected and Appointed U.S. Officials

President: The President; Dear Mr. President, or Mr. President

Vice-President: The Vice-President; Dear Mr. Vice-President, or Mr. Vice-President

Cabinet Member (other than Attorney General): The Honorable (full name), Secretary of _____; Dear Mr./Madam Secretary

Attorney General: The Honorable (full name), Attorney General; Dear Mr./Madam Attorney General

Senator: The Honorable (full name); Dear Senator (surname)

Representative: The Honorable (full name); Dear Mr./Madam (surname)

Governor: The Honorable (full name); Dear Governor (surname)

Mayor: The Honorable (full name); Dear Mayor (surname)

The Judiciary

Chief Justice of the Supreme Court: The Chief Justice of the United States, or simply The Chief Justice; Dear Mr. Chief Justice

Associate Justice: Mr./Madam Justice (surname); Dear Mr./Madam Justice, or Dear Mr./Madam Justice (surname)

Judges: The Honorable (full name); Dear Judge (surname)

Diplomatic Corps

U.S. ambassador: The Honorable (full name), Ambassador of the United States; Dear Mr./Madam Ambassador

Foreign ambassadors: His/Her Excellency (full name), The Ambassador of _____; Excellency, or Dear Mr./Madam Ambassador

Secretary-General of the United Nations: His/Her Excellency (full name), Secretary-General of the United Nations; Dear Mr./Madam Secretary-General

Consul-General: The Honorable (full name); Dear Mr./Mrs./Ms. (surname)

Clerical Orders

The Pope: His Holiness, the Pope, or His Holiness, Pope (name); Your Holiness, or Most Holy Father

Cardinals: His Eminence (first name) Cardinal (surname); Your Eminence, or Dear Cardinal (surname)

Bishops: The Most Reverend (full name), Bishop or Archbishop of (diocese); Your Excellency, or Dear Bishop/Archbishop (surname)

Priest: The Reverend (full name); Reverend Father, or Dear Father (surname)

Protestant clergy: The Reverend (full name); Dear Dr./Mr./Ms. (surname)

Rabbi: Rabbi (full name); Dear Rabbi (surname), or Dear Dr. (surname)

Military and Naval Officers

The appropriate way to address a letter is the same for any member of the armed forces: full or abbreviated rank + full name + comma + abbreviation for branch of the service (USA, USN, USAF, USMC, USCG). Example: First Lieutenant James L. Moore, USAF.

When it comes to the greeting of the letter (the salutation), it is generally acceptable to shorten the rank. Thus, you can write "Dear General Smith" whether Smith is a general, a lieutenant general, a major general, or a brigadier general. Just be sure to get your rankings straight: a lieutenant colonel is addressed as a colonel, not a lieutenant.

Miscellaneous Professional Ranks and Titles

You will notice in some instances below that when a professional title or degree is written after a name, the designations Mr., Mrs., Ms., and Dr. are not used.

Attorney: Mr./Mrs./Ms. (full name), Attorney-at-Law; Dear Mr./Mrs./Ms. (surname)

Certified public accountant: (full name), C.P.A.; Dear Mr./Mrs./Ms. (surname)

Dentist: (full name), D.D.S.; Dear Dr. (surname)

Physician: (full name), M.D.; Dear Dr. (surname)

Veterinarian: (full name), D.V.M.; Dear Dr. (surname)

Abbreviations

To abbreviate means to make shorter; an abbreviation is therefore a shortened form of a word or words. Sometimes a period ends an abbreviation; sometimes the period is omitted. In fact, there is considerable variation in the use of periods and in capitalization; for example, miles per hour could be abbreviated as mph or m.p.h. or MPH. Some abbreviations are always used instead of a word, like Mr. and Mrs. Here are some common abbreviations:

a	acre
A.A.	Alcoholics Anonymous
AAA	American Automobile Association
ABM	antiballistic missile
AC	alternating current
ACLU	American Civil Liberties Union
A.D.	*anno domini* (Latin: in the year of our Lord)
ADP	automatic data processing (computers)
AFDC	Aid to Families with Dependent Children
AFL	American Federation of Labor
AIDS	acquired immune deficiency syndrome
A.M.	*ante meridiem* (Latin: before noon)
AMA	American Medical Association
anon.	anonymous
APB	all points bulletin
APO	Army post office
ASAP	as soon as possible
assn.	association
attn.	attention
B.A.	bachelor of arts
BBB	Better Business Bureau
bbl.	barrel(s)
B.C.	before Christ

blvd.	boulevard
B.P.O.E.	Benevolent and Protective Order of Elks
B.S.	bachelor of science
B.S.A.	Boy Scouts of America
B.T.U.	British thermal unit
bu.	bushel
BYO	bring your own
C	centigrade, Celsius
c., ca.	*circa* (Latin: about)
cc	carbon copy
CDC	Centers for Disease Control
CEO	chief executive officer
CIA	Central Intelligence Agency
cm	centimeter
c/o	in care of
COD	cash (or collect) on delivery
corp.	corporation
C.P.A.	certified public accountant
CPR	cardiopulmonary resuscitation
CPU	central processing unit (computers)
CST	central standard time
cu.	cubic
D.A.	district attorney
D.A.R.	Daughters of the American Revolution
DC	direct current
D.D.	doctor of divinity
D.D.S.	doctor of dental surgery
DOA	dead on arrival
DOS	disk operating system (computers)
doz.	dozen
DNA	deoxyribonucleic acid
DST	daylight saving time
D.V.M.	doctor of veterinary medicine
EEO	equal employment opportunity
e.g.	*exempli gratia* (Latin: for example)
EPA	Environmental Protection Agency
Esq.	Esquire
ESP	extrasensory perception
esp.	especially
EST	eastern standard time
et. al.	*et alii* (Latin: and others)
etc.	*et cetera* (Latin: and so forth)
F.	Fahrenheit
FAA	Federal Aviation Administration
FBI	Federal Bureau of Investigation

fc	foot candle
FCC	Federal Communications Commission
FDA	Food and Drug Administration
FDIC	Federal Deposit Insurance Corporation
FHA	Federal Housing Administration
fn.	footnote
f.o.b.	freight on board
ft.	foot
FTC	Federal Trade Commission
FY	fiscal year
FYI	for your information
gal.	gallon
GAO	General Accounting Office
GMT	Greenwich mean time
GOP	Grand Old Party (Republican party)
GPO	Government Printing Office; general post office
G.S.A.	Girl Scouts of America
HMO	health maintenance organization
H.M.S.	his/her majesty's ship
Hon.	the honorable
hp	horsepower
H.R.H.	his/her royal highness
HUD	(Department of) Housing and Urban Development
ibid.	*ibidem* (Latin: in the same place)
i.e.	*id est* (Latin: that is)
in.	inch
INS	Immigration and Naturalization Service
I.O.U.	I owe you
I.R.A.	Irish Republican Army/individual retirement account
I.Q.	intelligence quotient
IRS	Internal Revenue Service
J.D.	*jurum doctor* (Latin: doctor of laws)
J.P.	justice of the peace
k.	karat
kg	kilogram
km	kilometer
kw.	kilowatt
l	liter
lat.	latitude
lb.	pound
LL.B.	*legum baccalaureus* (Latin: bachelor of laws)

LL.D.	*legum doctor* (Latin: doctor of laws)
long.	longitude
L.P.N.	licensed practical nurse
m	meter
M.A.	master of arts
M.B.A.	master of business administration
MC	master of ceremonies
M.D.	*medicinae doctor* (Latin: doctor of medicine)
mfg.	manufacturing
mi.	mile
ml	milliliter
mm	millimeter
Mme.	madame
mos.	months
M.P.	member of Parliament; military police
mph	miles per hour
M.S.	master of science
MSG	monosodium glutamate
Msgr.	Monsignor
N/A	not applicable
NAACP	National Association for the Advancement of Colored People
NASA	National Aeronautics and Space Administration
NATO	North Atlantic Treaty Organization
No.	number
NOW	National Organization for Women
NP	notary public
NSC	National Security Council
op. cit.	*opere citato* (Latin: in the work cited)
OSHA	Occupational Safety and Health Administration
oz.	ounce
PC	personal computer
Ph.D.	doctor of philosophy
P.M.	*post meridiem* (Latin: after noon); prime minister
POW	prisoner of war
pro tem.	*pro tempore* (Latin: for the time being)
P.S.	postscript
pt.	pint
PTA	Parent-Teacher Association
PX	post exchange (commissary)
qt.	quart
rbi	runs batted in (baseball)
R & D	research and development

REM	rapid eye movement
Rev.	Reverend
RFD	rural free delivery
RIP	*requiescat in pace* (Latin: rest in peace)
RN	registered nurse
ROTC	Reserve Officers' Training Corps
rpm	revolutions per minute
R & R	rest and relaxation (military)
R.S.V.P.	*repondez s'il vous plaît* (French: please answer)
Rx	prescription
s	seconds
S.A.S.E.	self-addressed stamped envelope
SEC	Securities and Exchange Commission
SPCA	Society for the Prevention of Cruelty to Animals
sq.	square
St.	saint; street
syn.	synonymous
T	ton
TD	touchdown (football)
TM	trademark
T.N.T.	trinitrotoluene (dynamite)
UFO	unidentified flying object
U.K.	United Kingdom
U.N.	United Nations
UNICEF	United Nations International Children's Emergency Fund
U.S.S.	United States ship
UV	ultraviolet
v. (or vs.)	versus (against)
VA	Veterans Administration
V.F.W.	Veterans of Foreign Wars
VHF	very high frequency
V.I.P.	very important person
V.P.	vice-president
w	watt
w/o	without
yd.	yard
Y.M.C.A.	Young Men's Christian Association
yr.	year
Y.W.C.A.	Young Women's Christian Association

U.S. Postal Regulations

The United States Postal Service has a number of free consumer publications covering everything from express mail services to mail-order problems and stamp collecting. If you would like to receive a publications list, write to: **Consumer Affairs Department, United States Postal Service,** 475 L'Enfant Plaza WSW, Room 5821, Washington, DC 20260-2207.

Listed below are some of the basic services and regulations of the U.S. Post Office.

Mail Services

Express Mail Service. This is the fastest service. It offers guaranteed delivery service, or your money will be returned upon filing a refund application at your local post office. Express Mail Next Day Service provides several options for both private and business customers who require overnight delivery of letters and packages. To use Express Mail Next Day Service, take your shipment to any designated Express Mail post office, generally by 5 PM, or deposit it in an Express Mail collection box, call for on-demand pickup, or hand it to your letter carrier. Your local post office can provide specific Express Mail acceptance times for your area. Your mailing will be delivered to the addressee by noon the next day if you are mailing between major markets, or by 3 PM the next day (weekends and holidays included). Express Mail can also be picked up at the destination post office as early as 10 AM the next day. The U.S. Postal Service also offers International Express Mail to over 120 countries.

First-Class Mail. Use First-Class Mail for letters, postcards, postal cards, greeting cards, personal notes, and for sending checks and money orders. Use Priority Mail for first-class items weighing 11 ounces or more. Insurance is available only for *merchandise* sent as First-Class Mail. However, additional services, such as certificate of mailing, certified, return receipt, and restricted delivery, can be purchased at the option of the mailer. If your First-Class Mail is not letter-size, make sure it is marked "First Class" or use a large green diamond-bordered envelope. First-Class Mail is generally delivered overnight to locally designated cities and in two days to locally designated states. Delivery by the third day can be anticipated for remaining outlying areas.

Priority Mail. Priority Mail is First-Class Mail weighing 11 ounces or more. When the speed of Express Mail is not needed, but preferential handling is desired, use Priority Mail. Priority Mail offers a two-day expedited delivery. The maximum weight for Priority Mail is 70 pounds, and the maximum size is 108 inches in length and circumference combined. Priority Mail should be well identified. Your local post office has Priority Mail stickers, labels, envelopes, and boxes available at no extra charge. Priority Mail can be insured, registered, certified, or sent COD for an additional charge.

Fourth-class mail (parcel post). Use this service for packages weighing one pound or more. If First-Class Mail is enclosed or attached, first-class postage must usually be paid for the enclosure or attachment. You can purchase insurance to cover the value of articles mailed at the fourth-class rate. Packages mailed within the continental United States can weigh up to 70 pounds and measure up to 108 inches in length and girth combined. Your post office also has information about lower local mailing rates and special mailing rates for books, catalogs, and international mailings. The delivery goal for parcel post is seven days or less to most areas, depending on distance.

Second-class mail. Only publishers and registered news agents who have been approved for second-class mailing privileges may mail at the second-class rates of postage. The applicable single-piece third- or fourth-class rate must be paid for magazines and newspapers mailed by the general public.

Third-class mail. Third-class mail, also referred to as bulk business mail, or advertising mail, may be sent by anyone, but is used most often by large mailers. This class includes printed material and merchandise weighing less than 16 ounces. There are two rate structures for this class: single-piece and bulk rate. Many community organizations and businesses find it economically attractive to use the bulk rates. Also, individuals may use third-class mail for mailing lightweight parcels. Insurance can be purchased, at the option of the mailer, to cover loss or damage of articles mailed at the single-piece third-class rate.

Special Services

◆ Cash receipts. Customers needing proof of payment of postage and other services are entitled to cash receipts.

◆ Certificate of mailing. A certificate of mailing proves that an item was mailed. It does not provide insurance coverage for loss or damage or provide proof of delivery. Your post office will provide a certificate of mailing for a fee, but no record is maintained at the post office.

◆ Certified mail. Certified mail provides a mailing receipt, and a record of delivery is maintained at the recipient's post office. A return receipt to provide the sender with proof of delivery can also be purchased for an additional fee. For valuables and irreplaceable items, use insured or registered mail. Certified mail service is available only for First-Class Mail. Certified mail service is not available for international mail.

◆ Insurance. Insurance coverage up to $600 can be purchased for third- and fourth-class mail, as well as for third- and fourth-class matter that is mailed at the Priority Mail or First-Class Mail rate. Insurance coverage up to $25,000 can be purchased on the Postal Service's most secure service—registered mail. For articles insured for more than $50, a receipt of delivery is signed by the recipient and filed at the delivery post office. Do not overinsure your packages. The amount of insurance coverage for loss will be the actual value, less depreciation, and no payments are made for sentimental losses or for any expenses incurred as a result of the loss.

◆ Recorded delivery (international mail). Recorded delivery service is similar to certified mail service in that it is intended for letters, documents, and items of little or no value. It is for the customer who wants a record of mailing on international mail, and who wants to know that a record of delivery exists, if an inquiry is necessary. For an added fee, the customer can purchase a return receipt at the time of mailing.

◆ Registered mail. Registered mail is the most secure option offered by the Postal Service. It is designed to provided added protection for valuable and important mail. Insurance may be purchased on domestic registered mail up to $25,000 at the option of the mailer. Return receipt and restricted delivery services are available for additional fees. Registered mail to Canada is subject to a $1,000 indemnity limit. For all other foreign countries, the indemnity limit is currently $32.35. Registered articles are placed under tight security from the point of mailing to the delivery office. First-Class or Priority Mail postage is required on domestic registered mail.

◆ Restricted delivery. Restricted delivery means that the sender's mail is delivered only to the addressee or to someone authorized in writing to receive mail for the addressee. Restricted delivery is offered in connection with return-receipt service and is available only for registered mail, certified mail, COD mail, and mail insured for more than $50. Restricted delivery mail addressed to officials of government agencies, members of the legislative and judicial branches of federal and state governments, members of the diplomatic corps, minors, and individuals under guardianship can be delivered to an agent without written authorization from the addressee.

◆ Return receipts. This is the sender's proof of delivery. A return receipt can be purchased for mail that is sent COD or Express Mail, is insured for more than $50, or is registered or certified. The return receipt shows who signed for the item and the date it was delivered. For an additional fee, the sender can get the addressee's correct address of delivery or request restricted delivery service. Return receipt for merchandise service, another form of return-receipt service that provides a mailing receipt, return receipt, and record of delivery, is available for merchandise sent at

the First-Class, Priority, third-class, and fourth-class rates of postage.

◆ Special delivery. You can obtain special-delivery service on all classes of mail except bulk third-class. It provides for delivery even on Sundays and holidays, and beyond normal delivery hours. This delivery service is available to all customers served by city carriers and to other customers within a one-mile radius of the delivery post office. The purchase of special delivery does not always mean the article will be delivered by special messenger. Special delivery may be delivered by your regular carrier if the mail piece is available before the carrier departs for morning deliveries.

◆ Special handling. Special-handling service is available for third-and fourth-class mail only, including insured and COD mail. It provides for preferential handling to the extent practical in dispatch and transportation, but does not provide special delivery. The special-handling fee must be paid on parcels that require special care, such as baby poultry or bees, except those sent at the First-Class Mail rate. Special handling does *not* mean special care of fragile items. Anything breakable should be packed with adequate cushioning and marked "fragile."

International Mail

Airmail and surface mail can be sent to virtually all foreign countries in a variety of ways:

1. Letters/postcards and letter packages—includes items of mail containing personal handwritten or typewritten communications.

2. Aerogrammes—air letter sheets which can be folded into the form of an envelope and sealed.

3. Printed matter—includes regular printed matter, books, and sheet music, publishers' periodicals, catalogues, directories.

4. Small packets—items of merchandise, commercial samples, or documents which do not have the character of current and personal correspondence.

5. Parcel post—packages of merchandise or

U.S. POSTAL SERVICE ABBREVIATIONS

Place	Abbreviation	Place	Abbreviation
Alabama	AL	Montana	MT
Alaska	AK	Nebraska	NE
American Samoa	AS	Nevada	NV
Arizona	AZ	New Hampshire	NH
Arkansas	AR	New Jersey	NJ
California	CA	New Mexico	NM
Colorado	CO	New York	NY
Connecticut	CT	North Carolina	NC
Delaware	DE	North Dakota	ND
District of Columbia	DC	Northern Mariana Islands	MP
Federated States of Micronesia	FM	Ohio	OH
Florida	FL	Oklahoma	OK
Georgia	GA	Oregon	OR
Guam	GU	Palau	PW
Hawaii	HI	Pennsylvania	PA
Idaho	ID	Puerto Rico	PR
Illinois	IL	Rhode Island	RI
Indiana	IN	South Carolina	SC
Iowa	IA	South Dakota	SD
Kansas	KS	Tennessee	TN
Kentucky	KY	Texas	TX
Louisiana	LA	Utah	UT
Maine	ME	Vermont	VT
Marshall Islands	MH	Virginia	VA
Maryland	MD	Virgin Islands	VI
Massachusetts	MA	Washington	WA
Michigan	MI	West Virginia	WV
Minnesota	MN	Wisconsin	WI
Mississippi	MS	Wyoming	WY
Missouri	MO		

any other articles that are not required to be mailed at letter postage rates.

6. Express Mail International Service—high priority or other urgently needed items, including merchandise in many instances, can be sent to more than 120 countries around the world. Registry service, with a very limited level of indemnity protection, is available for letter-class mail, small packets, and all printed matter. Insured parcel service is also available to many countries. All categories of international mail, other than Express Mail, may be sent either airmail or surface mail. However, all U.S. originating letters and postcards intended for delivery in either Canada or Mexico receive First-Class Mail treatment in the U.S. and airmail treatment in those two countries. Check with your local post office for specific information about the country to which you are mailing.

Source: United States Postal Service

SPEAKING

The Good Conversationalist

Ralph Waldo Emerson said, "The best of life is conversation." True, if you are a good conversationalist. Not so true if you feel tongue-tied and awkward in social situations. Or, perhaps you consider yourself a good conversationalist (you're never at a loss for words), but others disagree. Below are some guidelines on how to shine in social situations:

1. Be a good listener. Give your full attention to the speaker and maintain eye contact. Don't allow outside noises to distract you, and don't interrupt the speaker. Sometimes it's very difficult not to interrupt because your mind has raced ahead and you know how you want to respond. Resist the temptation; it's rude to interrupt.

2. When it's your turn to speak, get to your point in as few sentences as possible. If someone asks you a question, don't ramble on for five minutes before you get to the answer. Answer first, then elaborate. Avoid giving too much detail. If people want further details, they will ask for them.

3. Assume that everyone you meet has something interesting to say. Don't assume someone is boring because of physical appearance, age, or occupation. Give everyone a fair chance.

4. Try not to ask too many questions that require a yes/no answer. Ask open-ended questions.

5. Know when a topic has run its course. When you and your conversation partner have run the topic into the ground, give it up and move on to something else.

6. Don't panic when silence occurs. You don't need to rush in and fill the void. Silence doesn't mean someone is bored and is going to walk away.

7. Watch out for controversial subjects. Topics like politics and religion can spark lively, interesting discussions but can also lead to heated arguments. If a conversation is headed for trouble, change topics. When you need a noncontroversial subject, try family, work, or travel.

8. In the course of conversation, mention the person's name: "Yes, Bob, I agree that . . ." It's a nice gesture and also helps you to remember the person's name.

9. Don't hesitate to ask what you may think is a "dumb" question. You can't be an expert on every subject, and it's unlikely that anyone will think you are stupid for asking a basic question.

10. Don't be a passive guest. If you don't know a single person at a party, introduce yourself to someone and start up a conversation. If you are very shy, join a group of people and join in the conversation when you feel comfortable.

11. Be careful how you disagree with someone. Don't say, "How can you possibly believe that?" Say, "I understand what you mean, but I have a different point of view. . . ."

12. Don't disagree over minor details. For instance, suppose you are having a wonderful discussion about an old movie and there is a difference of opinion about who played one of the lead roles. Even if you are sure that you are right, don't ruin the flow of conversation just to make sure that everyone knows you are right.

13. Don't talk over, or under, the knowledge level of your audience. No one likes to be talked "down to"; nor is anyone impressed by technical jargon and 12-letter words.

14. Never forget the number-one rule of good conversation: equal time for all.

Remembering Names

You're at a party and someone is approaching you from across the room. The face is familiar, but you can't quite place the name. . . . Forgetting someone's name is quite embarrassing, especially if you have met the person on more than one occasion. You forget a name, not because you have a bad memory, but because you didn't learn how to remember the name in the first place. Some steps to help you remember names:

♦ When you are first introduced to a person, make sure you hear the person's name and hear it pronounced correctly. Pay attention during the introduction instead of concentrating on what you plan to say. If you aren't sure you heard the name correctly, ask to have it repeated. Most people won't mind that you asked; they will be flattered.

♦ Repeat the name a few times. Say it when you are introduced: "It's nice to meet you, Mary"; "It's a pleasure to meet you, Mr. Simmons." Also repeat the name during the course of the conversation, "Well, Mary, I do see your point." And say it at the end of the conversation, "I enjoyed talking to you, Mr. Simmons."

♦ Create a ridiculous cartoon in your mind that links the person's name with an outstanding physical characteristic. For example, you meet Fern Fadness and she has a prominent nose; imagine ferns growing out of her nose. You meet Ben Armstrong who is very tall and skinny; imag-

ine him as a strongman in a circus, in a silly costume and flexing his arms. The trick here is to create a mental image (the more ridiculous, the stronger the image) that will help you remember a name. If physical characteristics don't seem to work, try other associations. Maybe Mrs. Noyes is a very quiet woman. Or, Mr. Pierce looks fierce.

♦ If you are going to a small social event and will be meeting a number of new people, find out ahead of time who will be in attendance. If you hear the names before you arrive, then repeat the names during introductions, you're likely to remember them.

Swearing

Swearing. Everybody's doing it—even two-year-olds. There's no evidence to suggest that we swear more today than people did hundreds of years ago. But we no longer do it behind closed doors. In part, swearing seems more acceptable because we hear so much of it every day in movies, television programs, radio talk shows, popular music.

Why do we seem to have a growing addiction to cuss words? They allow us to relieve frustration and stress and express rage without becoming physically violent, says an expert on swearing, Timothy Jay, who is a psychology professor at North Adams State College in Massachusetts. Jay has been studying how and why we swear for more than 20 years. His book *Cursing in America* is a serious and exhaustive study on profanity. In the book Jay points out that there was one bad word (Clark Gable's "damn") in the 1939 movie *Gone With the Wind* (and producer David O. Selznick was fined $5000 for using it). In contrast, the 1983 movie Scarface had 299 bad words (about 1.8 bad words per minute).

Professor Jay estimates that about 1 percent of all words spoken are dirty words. While that may not seem excessive, Jay points out that if a conversation takes place at one word per second and the conversation lasts five minutes, then it is likely to be peppered with three swear words.

College students are quite proficient at swearing. According to Thomas Murray, associate professor of English at Kansas State University, college years seem to be the time for all kinds of experimentation—everything from sex to alcohol to cuss words. Swearing seems to be one way of closing the gap between childhood and adulthood. Murray conducted a survey of Midwestern college students and here's what he found:

♦ Ninety-four percent of the college students said they regularly used dirty words.

♦ Women use the same kinds of dirty words as men and swear almost as frequently as men.

♦ Women tend to increase their dirty-word usage when they are around other women; men tend to swear indiscriminately.

If you want to curb your use of profanity, here are some suggestions:

1. Come up with another expression to take the place of cuss words. Since "darn" and "Oh, poo" aren't adequate substitutes, you'll have to be a bit more creative.

2. When you swear, choose *one* good word or phrase and stop. A long string of cuss words or repeating the same word or phrase only diminishes the effect of your outburst.

3. Washing your child's mouth out with soap is not the way to stop a child from swearing. Kids pick up swear words from parents as well as from other people. The best way to keep your child from swearing is to stop swearing yourself. When very young children swear, psychologists say parents should not overreact and not try to explain the meaning of whatever dirty word was said. Instead, explain to the child that the word is not acceptable because it might hurt someone. Give the child another word or phrase to use instead of the swear word.

Gossip

Defined as idle talk and rumor, gossip is a universal phenomenon. "The power of remaining silent is always highly valued," said the Nobel Prize–winning writer Elias Canetti. But who among us has that power? Besides being a source of information and entertainment, gossip evokes the thrill of risk and complicity, power, and—above all—malicious pleasure. It is the latter quality, the appeal to our lower instincts, that gives gossip a bad name.

While gossip about celebrities is always in the headlines, it seems that what we most like to gossip about is ourselves. A recent survey by the women's magazine *Self* revealed that 74 percent of the respondents said they liked to gossip. The top four subjects of choice were (in declining order): work, friends' personal lives, people we dislike, and celebrities. When asked for a personal opinion of gossip, 38 percent of the respondents considered gossip a harmless diversion, 28 percent said it was a lot of fun, and 26 percent claimed gossip is destructive and malicious. Other, less popular opinions were: it's petty and a waste of time; it's a practical way to get the office scuttlebutt.

Jack Levin, sociologist at Northeastern University and author of *Gossip: The Inside Scoop*, says that there are five secrets that even your best friends won't keep:

♦ Paycheck information
♦ Dangerous liaisons
♦ Personal details about a mutual friend
♦ Private dreams
♦ Anything prefaced by, "Please don't repeat this."

Remember, the juicier the gossip, the more likely it is to get passed on.

One of the most insightful observations about gossip comes from Mark Twain; remember it the next time you are about to divulge one of your most carefully guarded secrets. According to Twain: "It takes your enemy and your friend, working together, to hurt you to the heart. The one to slander you and the other to get the news to you."

The Art and Medicine of Humor

We use humor to break the ice, relieve tension, create rapport. Most speeches incorporate humor, and it is usually vital to the success of every social situation. And now, it turns out, humor is also good for your health.

According to Dr. William Fry of Stanford University, laughing can be considered a cardiovascular workout. Laughing a hundred times a day equals about 10 minutes of rowing, and provides health benefits to your heart and your lungs. What's more, tickling the funny bone seems to trigger the release of a natural painkiller and to mobilize antibodies that help to fight infection.

Perhaps you need to become a better joke-teller? Comedian Steve Allen points out that the line between comedy and tragedy is not finely drawn. Many jokes concern the seven deadly sins (pride, lust, anger, envy, etc.) and innumerable lesser peccadillos like stupidity, drunkenness, and laziness. The trick is to make these subjects funny by word play, exaggeration, and implication—by providing the unexpected. Allen advises that the most effective anecdotes involve something that happened to you or a friend. He also suggests improving the quality of your jokes by immersing yourself in the works of the world's great humorists, like Mark Twain and James Thurber.

If you need to polish your joke-telling skills, here are a few bits of advice:

♦ Tell jokes you really like and practice them until you've got them down. Keep them short and simple.

♦ Timing is very important but what works for one person may not work for another. Experiment so you can determine the best way to time the delivery of each part of the joke.

♦ Puns may evoke groans rather than laughter; use them selectively.

♦ Avoid long and off-color jokes.

Besides jokes, there are many other ways to inject humor into everyday life. Make it a habit to tell amusing stories at the dinner table. Collect cartoons and put them up in conspicuous places. When you are in a bad mood, turn on the television set and watch a comedy. Above all, try to find some humor in all stressful situations; it's good for your health.

Making a Speech

Everyone suffers stage fright when making a speech, whether the speech is before a handful of colleagues or an auditorium full of strangers. You are the center of attention and the only voice in the room is yours. The anxiety can be overwhelming, but on the other hand, the extra adrenalin flow can work to your advantage. The key to an effective speech is preparation.

Writing the Speech

1. After choosing the topic for your speech, think about your audience. How much do your listeners know about the subject? Also consider the intent of your speech. Is it to instruct, to persuade, to inspire, or to entertain? Perhaps you have more than one goal.

2. Gather together all the research necessary to write your speech and organize the main points in a logical order. Your speech will break out into three parts: the introduction, the main body, and the conclusion. As you write the speech, keep this in mind: What one main idea do I want the audience to remember? That should help you to tighten up your copy and keep you focused. While it's important that all of your main points be backed up with facts and supporting data, remember that people like personal stories, funny anecdotes, interesting examples—anything that adds a little "life" to a speech.

3. Devote a lot of time to your introduction. You need to grab your audience's attention right away or they may be tuned out by the time you get to your best material. You can open with a provocative thought or question, a startling statement, a human interest story, a relevant quote. Be careful about opening up with a joke

since you could be very embarrassed if the joke is a big failure.

4. Fine tune your conclusion. Briefly review the major points of the speech and end with a personal touch—a dramatic story, an inspiring message, a call to action (if you want the audience to do something). A joke at the conclusion is usually fine; if it bombs, it doesn't really matter since it comes at the end of a terrific speech.

5. How long should a speech be? Most experts say 20 to 30 minutes is ideal. An hour is the maximum length.

6. What kind of written materials should you take to the lectern? Some people insist upon taking the entire typed manuscript with them. If you do, however, you'll be tempted to read the whole speech, and it could sound stilted and formal. A better idea is to write down your main points on 3 × 5 notecards and use them to guide you.

Rehearsing the Speech

1. At home, rehearse your speech in front of a mirror and use a tape recorder. A video recorder is very helpful if you happen to have one. Play back your recording and judge your performance. Do you appear natural? Are you using your hands effectively? Do you sound breathless and nervous? Is your speech riddled with "um" or "now" or "you see"? Are you pausing in the right places? Seek feedback from family and friends.

2. If you are using any special equipment, like a slide projector, be sure to use it in a rehearsal.

3. If possible, visit the place where you will be speaking and get comfortable with the size of the room, the acoustics, and any equipment that is available for your use.

Delivering the Speech

1. Many speakers talk too fast. If you have this tendency, write "slow down" on the top of your notecards.

2. Assume a relaxed stance with your feet slightly apart. Check your posture.

3. Be sure that you can be heard at the back of the room. This is especially important if you aren't using a microphone.

4. Establish eye contact with one person at a time. Talk to someone in the left section of the audience, then the center, then the right.

5. Before you begin speaking, take a few deep breaths and try to relax. To loosen up your body and mind, comedian Art Buchwald suggests that you imagine that the entire audience is naked—a thought that should at least put a smile on your face.

HOW TO SAY NO

It's more difficult to say "no" than "yes." Here are some ways to utter an effective no:

♦ Simply say no; do it without a long-winded explanation. "I'd rather not" or "I prefer not to" or "Thanks, but I can't" will work if you respond assertively, yet nicely. If you sound matter-of-fact, most people won't push for an explanation.

♦ Say no with an explanation: "I can't go because I'm having dinner with my mother."

♦ If someone is really making it hard for you to say no, stall for more time. Just say, "I need a little time to think about it." Then come up with a reasonable excuse for saying no.

♦ Use humor: "I'd really like to go on vacation with you but I'd have to rob a bank to get the money."

♦ When all else fails, tell a little white lie.

FOREIGN LANGUAGES

Learning Foreign Languages

According to a 1992 report by the U.S. Department of Education: "The United States is virtually alone in the world in delaying foreign-language study until high school and concentrating its energies in two-year programs. . . . Fluency in foreign languages is no longer a luxury for Americans; it is a necessity if our nation is to compete successfully in the global marketplace and to function effectively in international affairs."

Senator Paul Simon states the case even stronger in his book *The Tongue-Tied American:* "We are linguistically malnourished. Yet never in history has there been one nation with such a variety of ethnic and language backgrounds." In fact, a recent U.S. Census report showed that there are 329 languages spoken in the United States. About 14 percent of U.S. residents speak a foreign language at home, a result of the large influx of immigrants from Asia and Latin America. The census report further stated that the great majority of those who speak a foreign language at home also speak English "well" or "very well."

Some language experts say that when it comes to language, Americans tend to be ethnocentric—that is, we believe English to be the superior language and the only one we need to know. After all, in almost 30 nations English is the only official language; it is one of the official languages in another 16 countries. But while English is still considered "the language of commerce," we are living in an increasingly interdependent world, in a global economy that requires some shifts in thinking.

Our attitude toward foreign-language instruction is changing. Today about 30 percent of U.S. students study a foreign language. At least five states—Louisiana, Arkansas, Oklahoma, Arizona, and North Carolina—require foreign language instruction in elementary school. Most four-year colleges and universities in the U.S. require language instruction as an entrance requirement; many require a demonstrated proficiency in a foreign language for graduation. And surveys show that parents want their children to learn a foreign language because they want them to have a competitive edge in the job market.

Economic reasons aside, there are other good reasons for learning another language. Studying foreign languages gives us an understanding and appreciation of peoples and cultures other than our own. It also helps to enhance reading comprehension and oral and written skills. According to the American Council on the Teaching of Foreign Languages (ACTFL), students who study a foreign language do better than those who have not on standardized tests like the Scholastic Aptitude Test (SAT).

We have a long way to go to catch up with other nations. Students in all countries of the European Community (EC) learn two languages in addition to their native tongues. In Japan, two foreign languages are required for university graduation. Egypt mandates six years of English and three years of French. Iran requires seven years of foreign language, starting in the sixth grade. In Afghanistan, English, French, and German are taught, starting in elementary school. And so on.

Learning a foreign language takes a lot of hard work. According to the ACTFL, studying for a year or two results in limited basic communication and reading skills; you must study longer in order to become fluent in a language. If you want to learn a new language, you can learn it in a classroom environment or you may want to purchase a self-study kit. For classroom opportunities, check with local colleges and universities as well as adult education programs at high schools. Also, check your yellow pages under "language schools" for private organizations, like Berlitz, that offer classroom and individualized instruction.

There is a multitude of self-study kits on the market. Before you choose one, ask friends, relatives, or language instructors for recommendations. Be sure that you purchase a program with cassettes that feature authentic, native-like speakers. If a manual is included, look through it to be sure you like the approach and that the manual is user-friendly. Some of the more popular self-study cassettes:

Berlitz Cassette Pack. Available in 321 languages; mostly for travelers who want "survival" language skills; includes a phrase book.

Living Language Basic Course. Available in nine languages; for beginners; method developed by U.S. government to teach foreign languages to diplomats; includes manual and dictionary.

Teach Me Tapes. Includes the basics of seven different languages; geared for children ages four to 12; uses songs and stories to instruct; includes study manuals.

Foreign Words and Phrases

Foreign words and expressions enrich our writing as well as our conversation. Many foreign words have slipped comfortably into our language and we handle them with ease. From the French language, we use sauté, quiche, connoisseur, and gourmet. From Italian, we borrow soprano, prima donna, and dilettante. From Spanish, we take rodeo, guerrilla, pronto, and chile con carne. Some foreign words and phrases, however, can be difficult to decipher if you haven't studied the particular language. Sometimes you can figure out the meaning of a word or phrase by studying how it is used within the context of a sentence; sometimes you have to pick up a dictionary. Listed below are some commonly used foreign words and phrases. The abbreviation following the expression indicates the language from which the word or phrase is derived: Arabic (A), French (F), German (G), Italian (I), Latin (L), Russian (R), Spanish (S), Turkish (T), Yiddish (Y).

ad hoc (L)	for a particular purpose or end
ad infinitum (L)	forever; endless
ad nauseam (L)	to a sickening degree
aficionado (S)	enthusiast; devotee
alfresco (I)	in the open air
apparatchik (R)	Communist party functionary
arriviste (F)	social climber
au contraire (F)	on the contrary
au courant (F)	up-to-date
avant-garde (F)	in the forefront
beau geste (F)	a noble gesture
bête noire (F)	pet peeve; annoyance
billet doux (F)	love letter
blitzkrieg (G)	lightning war
bon marché (F)	inexpensive
bon mot (F)	witty comment
bon vivant (F)	person who enjoys the good things in life
carpe diem (L)	seize the day
carte blanche (F)	complete freedom; no restrictions
cause célèbre (F)	a celebrated case; scandal
caveat emptor (L)	let the buyer beware
c'est la vie (F)	that's life

chutzpah (Y)	arrogance; audacity; nerve
corpus delicti (L)	evidence of a crime
coup de grâce (F)	the final blow
coup d'état (F)	forceful overthrow of a government
crème de la crème (F)	the very best; the top level
cri de coeur (F)	heartfelt plea
déclassé (F)	fallen in social standing
de facto (L)	in fact
de rigueur (F)	necessary; compulsory

CONCORDIA LANGUAGE VILLAGES

Concordia College, a private Lutheran liberal arts institution in Minnesota, operates an innovative and highly successful series of 10 summer language villages for students seven to 18 years of age. These camps in Minnesota's lake country are set up as complete foreign environments. For example, the German village (called Waldsee, lake of the forest) has an authentic Bavarian train station, restaurant, and German mailboxes; students pass through customs on arrival and exchange their dollars for German marks.

Besides German, the other villages are Chinese, Danish, Finnish, French, Japanese, Norwegian, Russian, Spanish, and Swedish. Students master vocabulary in the same way they acquired their native language as children: by hearing it, repeating it, and using it in daily life. In other words, they become immersed in the lifestyle and traditions of another culture. The villages feature lots of singing and dancing, games and costume parties, as well as an incredible array of international foods.

Every year more than 5000 students from all 50 states and several foreign countries participate in the language programs. Concordia College offers one-week sessions, two-week sessions, and four-week sessions (ninth- through twelfth-graders can earn language credits for four-week sessions). For more information, write to: **Concordia Language Villages,** 901 South Eighth Street, Moorhead, MN 56562.

SANTA CLAUS IN OTHER LANGUAGES

Austria	St. Nikkolo
Brazil	Papa Noël
China	Shen Tan Lao Jen (Christmas Old Man)
Denmark	Jul emanden
Finland	Ukko (Father Christmas)
France	Le Père Noël
Germany	St. Nicholas
Holland	Sinter Klaas
Hungary	Kriss Kringle
Italy	Babbo Natale
Sweden	Jultomten

double entendre (F)	word or phrase with two meanings
enfant terrible (F)	terrible child; one whose behavior causes embarrassment
ennui (F)	boredom
e pluribus unum (L)	from many, one
ersatz (G)	substitute; imitation
esprit de corps (F)	group spirit; team spirit
ex post facto (L)	after the fact
fait accompli (F)	accomplished fact
faux pas (F)	a social blunder
femme fatale (F)	attractive, dangerous woman
flagrante delicto (L)	caught in the act
glasnost (R)	openness; candor
haute couture (F)	high-fashion dress-designing
ipso facto (L)	by the fact itself
jihad (A)	holy war waged on behalf of Islam
joie de vivre (F)	joy of living; high spirits
kitsch (G)	trash
kismet (T)	fate or destiny
kvetsch (Y)	to complain or gripe
laissez-faire (F)	allow to do; nonaction
machismo (S)	maleness
magnum opus (L)	major work
mea culpa (L)	my fault
ménage à trois (F)	three-sided relationship
modus operandi (L)	method of operation
mot juste (F)	the right word
noblesse oblige (F)	responsibility of nobility or rank

nolo contendere (L)	no contest
nom de plume (F)	pen name; pseudonym
non sequitur (L)	something that does not follow
nouveau riche (F)	a newly rich person
paparazzi (I)	photographers of celebrities
perestroika (R)	restructuring
persona non grata (L)	unacceptable or unwelcome person
pièce de résistance (F)	most outstanding item; showpiece
prima facie (L)	on the fact of it; self-evident

quid pro quo (L)	something for something; a fair exchange
raconteur (F)	skilled storyteller
raison d'être (F)	reason for being
savoir faire (F)	social tact or know-how
schlemiel (Y)	unlucky or clumsy person
semper fidelis (L)	always faithful
tabula rasa (L)	a clean slate
tour de force (F)	a very skillful act
verboten (G)	prohibited; forbidden
vis-à-vis (F)	with regard to; relating to
wunderkind (G)	child prodigy
zeitgeist (G)	spirit of the times

NONVERBAL COMMUNICATIONS

Body Language

There are innumerable ways in which you can express yourself without saying a word. According to social anthropologist Edward T. Hall, more than half of all communication is nonverbal. Lift your eyebrows, and you are sending the classic signal of doubt, disbelief, or surprise. A frown typically suggests annoyance or that you are making an effort to concentrate. Shrugging your shoulders expresses indifference; tapping your fingers, impatience; swinging your legs, tension. And so on. These signals are called body language, or the science of kinesics.

The face is by far our most important means of expression. Researchers estimate that there are some 250,000 different facial expressions, from joy and sorrow to anger and frustration. We even have a special descriptive vocabulary for facial expressions: pout, grimace, wince, blanch, gape, smirk. The face can express an enormous and sometimes quite subtle range of emotions and conditions, including recognition, rejection, insult, chagrin. Our facial expressions may reinforce, contradict, or even conceal what we really feel. And we acquire a series of all-purpose facial masks: one for parties, another for funerals, one for business matters.

The most universally understood facial expression is probably the smile; one researcher claims to have identified 1.8 million variations. Certainly one of the most famous is the Mona Lisa's enigmatic smile, which has intrigued generations of art lovers. Sigmund Freud even wrote an entire book on the smile's meaning. While it may evoke mystery, the smile is usually a universal expression of happiness, pleasure, pride, confidence.

While the head and face are the most expressive parts of the body, we use all parts of the body to communicate. Listed below are some common nonverbal messages and how we send them.

Nervousness: excessive blinking of the eyes; tapping foot; fidgeting; wringing hands; tugging ears; clearing the throat.

Frustration: clenching hands into fists; rubbing hand through the hair.

Confidence: hands held behind the body while standing; hands held in "steeple" position (tips of fingers touching, palms apart); leaning backward.

Defensiveness: arms crossed in front of body; touching and rubbing the nose.

Arrogance: looking sideways; clasping hands behind the head.

Aggressiveness: hands on hips.

Friendliness: tilting head slightly; open palms; leaning slightly forward when seated in chair.

Even something as routine as a handshake can convey your mood and personality. When engaging in a handshake, you want to appear friendly, confident, and cooperative. To ensure a good handshake, use only one hand and shake vertically. Shakes should come from the elbow; four or five shakes are sufficient; palms should touch. Grip the hand firmly but don't crush it. When you shake, make eye contact, lean forward slightly, and smile.

Another matter to consider is "personal space," or the private territory we need to feel comfortable. Moving your body into someone else's space can be awkward and embarrassing. In social situations, the rule of thumb is as follows: Everyone is entitled to a personal space of about 5 feet; it's best to keep at least 3 feet between you and the other person when you begin a conversation. If the conversation is going well and you're "invited in," it's okay to move a little closer.

THE STEEPLE

Walking Styles

Did it ever occur to you that your gait, or the way you walk, reveals clues about your mood and personality? Sara Snodgrass, a psychologist at Florida Atlantic University, has identified six basic gaits through a series of studies conducted when she was at Skidmore College in New York. Here are the gaits and the message that each one sends:

The stride. Long steps with a bounce; arms swinging. Message: self-confident, independent, successful.

The shuffle. Small steps; pigeon-toed; drooping shoulders. Message: meek and disorganized.

The duckwalk. Toes point out and body swings from side to side. Message: impulsive, independent, charming.

The chopped-up walk. Short, heavy steps. Message: unfriendly and frustrated.

The mince. Short, prim steps. Message: submissive, not self-assured.

The swagger. Shoulders back and hips swaying. Message: not self-confident, unsympathetic.

The gait that won the most positive rating is the stride. People like, and are attracted to, those who walk with strong, long steps, those who swing their arms and have a bounce to their step. These "striders" are considered to be friendly, high achievers who are in control of their lives.

Once Dr. Snodgrass determined that you can decode someone's mood and personality by

THE STRIDE

watching walking behavior, she turned the equation around. Can you influence your mood by changing your walking style? In another study, some participants were instructed to be striders: take long, brisk steps, swing the arms, look straight ahead with head held erect. The other participants were asked to be shufflers: take short steps, shuffle the feet, keep the head down. Mood questionnaires, filled out before and after the experiment, showed that the striders felt energetic, happy, and self-confident. Shufflers felt tired and depressed. The moral to the study: Assume the stride style, even if you are in a bad mood; it could lift your spirits.

15

LEGAL MATTERS

LAWYERS AND COURTS

FAMILY LAW

CONSUMER LAW

WORKPLACE LAW

ESTATE PLANNING

LAWYERS AND COURTS

Hiring a Lawyer

Before you decide to hire an attorney, ask yourself if you really need one. Many problems, even those that involve an area of the law with which you are not familiar, can be resolved without the high-priced services of a lawyer. If your problem is not too complex, you may be able to resolve it on your own, through skillful negotiation and letter writing. Also, there are many good legal guidebooks for sale, specifically written for consumers, that will help you to understand the legal technicalities of whatever area of the law your problem involves.

Your local, county, or state government is likely to have a consumer-protection agency that can provide advice and counseling; the Better Business Bureau in your area can put you in contact with the appropriate consumer-protection agency. In addition, the Better Business Bureau can refer you to an arbitration or mediation service, an impartial third-party organization that is designed to resolve disputes. Another alternative is to take your problem to small-claims court. Finally, many local television and radio stations have "watchdog" reporters whose sole job is to investigate and solve consumer complaints.

There are, however, times when you will need the services of a lawyer. According to a study by the American Bar Association, the three most common matters taken to lawyers involve real estate, estate planning, and marital problems. You may also need an attorney if you are in an accident involving personal injury or property damage, if you are establishing a new business, if you have severe tax problems, if you are sued in a civil lawsuit, or if you are arrested for a crime.

Hiring a private attorney is an unaffordable option for many people. There are a few lower-cost alternatives when you are in need of legal services:

Legal clinics. They are best for handling routine, uncomplicated matters like a simple will, an uncontested divorce, traffic offenses, personal bankruptcy, name changes, or landlord-tenant disputes. Widely advertised on television, clinics can vary widely in their scope of services. Clinics usually use standard legal forms and have standard fee schedules.

Prepaid legal services plans. These plans are typically sponsored by employers, credit unions, labor unions, associations, churches, and consumer groups. The way they work is similar to the way a medical insurance plan is run. In other words, a group is banded together in order to allow members easy access to affordable legal services. Sometimes the sponsoring organization pays all of the costs; sometimes members pay monthly fees. While most plans allow you to get free legal advice, there are many plan variations, each offering a specific kind of structure and coverage. The simplest, and lowest-cost, plans offer free advice on the phone or in an office, follow-up services, and document reviews, as well as discounts on services if the legal problem is complex and requires extensive work. More comprehensive plans will provide extra services like representation in a divorce, civil or criminal trial, and other more complicated legal matters. There are legal services plans that accept individuals who are not affiliated with a sponsoring group. For a free list of plans in your area, send a self-addressed, stamped envelope to: **The National Resource Center for Consumers of Legal Services,** PO Box 340, Gloucester, VA 23061.

Legal Aid. For civil cases, free or low-cost help may be available through Legal Aid societies. Located in many cities in the United States, these offices will usually be listed in the yellow pages of your phone book under "Legal Aid" or "Legal Services." You can also call your local bar association to find out if there is a Legal Aid Society in your area. Not everyone is entitled to help from these groups; eligibility is based primarily on financial need.

Finding a Lawyer

When you have a legal situation that requires the help of a private attorney, you need to be a wise and prudent shopper.

1. Begin by getting recommendations from family members, friends and co-workers. Be aware, however, that many lawyers specialize in a particular area of law. The attorney who successfully helped your sister resolve a child custody case may not be the best lawyer to help you with complicated estate planning. Also, recommendations from a friend of a friend of a friend usually don't turn out to be very reliable. Good referrals come from someone whose judgment you trust and who has had a legal situation similar to yours.

2. Local bar associations sponsor referral services, but there is no guarantee that this is the best avenue for finding an attorney who's right for you. There is very little quality control over these services, and any attorney can become part

of the service simply by paying a fee to be listed. Private referral services also exist but often have the same downsides as those operated by bar associations. That's not to say that you won't find a good attorney from a referral service. However, don't automatically assume that the names you get from services have been anointed with some kind of seal of approval.

3. Lawyers advertise in the yellow pages of phone books as well as on radio and television. Oftentimes, the ads will list specialty areas but will not indicate costs.

4. If you live or work near a law school, you could try calling the dean's office for a referral.

Interviewing a Lawyer

Once you have a short list of possible lawyers to hire, it is advisable to meet personally with each candidate. Lawyers usually will not charge you for an initial get-acquainted meeting. The meeting is to decide if the two of you want to work together; you will not be getting free legal advice.

If you do not use the services of a lawyer on a regular basis (most people don't), the meeting can seem intimidating. You need to be prepared to ask the right questions and never lose sight of the fact that you are in the driver's seat because you are doing the hiring. Since you could be looking at a considerable amount of money, you need to understand, and be comfortable with, a number of important issues:

Expertise. Does the attorney have the experience to properly handle your case? And how long has the attorney and/or law firm been practicing law? Is the attorney a specialist in an area of law (like domestic relations or personal-injury law), or is the attorney a general practitioner? As best you can, you need to understand the complexity of your case before choosing a lawyer. On the one hand, you don't want to hire someone who is underqualified and inexperienced. On the other hand, your case many not require a $200-an-hour lawyer, regardless of the person's outstanding credentials or impressive office.

Communications. Legal jargon, commonly

called "legalese," can make you feel like you have been transported to a foreign country. If you cannot communicate with a lawyer in plain, simple language, then that lawyer is probably not a good choice for you. Also, you need to be clear about what kind of ongoing communications you need to have with an attorney. Some people don't care if they are regularly informed about the progress of their case. Most, however, want frequent updates, especially if something happens that results in an unexpected delay of the case or increased costs.

Handling of the case. You will be relieved to find an attorney that suits your needs and budget, but you may be irked to find out that the attorney you hired isn't personally doing all the work on your case. It's not unusual for lawyers to turn over some, or much, of the work to junior associates or paralegal assistants. Ask who will actually do the work on your case, and if much of the work will end up being delegated to others; ask how closely the work will be supervised by the lawyer. Also, you need to inquire if the services of assistants are billed at a rate that is different (lower) from the lawyer's rate.

ELDER LAW

A new breed of lawyer, the elder-law attorney, has evolved in recent years to handle legal issues that affect older persons. These lawyers deal with a wide range of issues including estate planning, age discrimination, long-term health care financing, Medicare and Medicaid claims and appeals, retirement and pension benefits, and elder abuse. Most elder-law attorneys specialize in one or more of these areas but most do not practice in all areas. For a free brochure on how to find and select an elder-law attorney, write to: **National Academy of Elder Law Attorneys,** 655 North Alvernon Way, Suite 108, Tucson, AZ 85711.

Fees. When it comes to fear of the unknown, lawyer bills rank at the top of the heap. Before hiring an attorney, you want to know exactly what the costs will be and you need to have all agreements put in writing (see article below).

Lawyer Fees

There are three ways to pay a lawyer:

Hourly fee. This is the most common arrangement. You are billed by the hour for work done on your case, and fees can range from $50 to $300 an hour. Since the unknown amount of hours required to resolve your case may unnerve you, ask for a written estimate of probable costs.

Flat fee. Flat fees, or fixed fees, are used for routine matters like writing a will, when an attorney can pretty accurately predict how much time and effort is required.

Contingency fee. In this case, the lawyer is paid only if your case is successfully resolved. This type of fee is most common in personal-injury cases and workers' compensation cases. If you win your case, the lawyer gets a percentage of the money you recover (usually 33 percent). If you lose, the lawyer gets nothing. You do, however, have to pay for certain things like court costs and other case-related expenses. Whether the lawyer calculates his or her percentage *before* or *after* the expenses are subtracted from the award will affect how much money you ultimately receive. Suppose that you get an award of $100,000 and the "costs" of conducting the case are $15,000. If the attorney calculates the fee *before* expenses, the fee amounts to $33,000; you get the remainder of the money after the $15,000 worth of expenses are deducted (giving you $52,000). If the attorney calculates the fee *after* expenses, the fee amounts to about $28,000, which is 33 percent of $85,000 ($100,000 minus the $15,000 of expenses); you get $57,000. Obviously, lawyers prefer that their fees be calculated before expenses are deducted, but the issue is negotiable.

Points to Remember

1. Fees are negotiable, even though lawyers certainly don't advertise that fact. It's possible to negotiate a lower hourly rate which you propose, or to ask an attorney to match a fee quoted to you by another lawyer you've interviewed. You can also negotiate on contingency fees. For example, some lawyers will agree to a sliding scale whereby the money they get depends on how long the case takes to resolve or the amount of the award. For instance, when the sliding scale is based on how long the case takes to resolve, the attorney may get 25 percent of the award if the case is resolved before trial, 30 percent if you actually go to trial, and 40 percent if there is an appeal. If the sliding scale is based on the amount of the award, it might be calculated as follows: 25 percent on the first $100,000, 15 percent on the next $100,000, and 10 percent on any money over $200,000.

2. Regardless of the attorney's billing method, you will likely incur case-related costs and expenses. These costs can be for any number of items including filing and court fees, postage, phone and fax charges, copying documents, and the advice or testimony of expert witnesses.

3. Some lawyers require a retainer, which is an advance payment, or downpayment, for legal services. Once the work actually begins, the lawyer will bill the fees against the retainer at the agreed-upon hourly rate. Retainers, if required, are often negotiable.

4. Depending on your particular case, you may be able to lower your costs by doing some of the work yourself. For instance, you might be able to make some information-gathering phone calls or pick up and deliver documents.

5. Be sure that you understand your attorney's billing methods and how often you are expected to pay. Ask that the bills be itemized so you understand exactly what you are being billed for.

6. Once you have completed fee negotiations, get everything in writing. Many lawyers have a simple, short contract. If it excludes items that are of concern to you, ask to have those items included. Be sure that all fee arrangements and extra costs are spelled out. Also, get a written estimate of what your total payout is likely to be.

7. Don't pay your lawyer to be your buddy. If you are paying at an hourly rate, every time you talk on the phone to your lawyer, you get billed. Most lawyers charge per minimum billing units. If the attorney's interval is 15 minutes, and you talk on the phone for 5 minutes, you will still be billed for 15 minutes of the lawyer's time based on the hourly rate. So keep your visits and phone calls short, and don't waste time talking about sports or the weather or anything else that doesn't relate to the business at hand.

Dissatisfied with Your Lawyer?

If you are not pleased with the manner in which your lawyer is conducting your case, your first step is to try to resolve the problem yourself. Be specific and let the lawyer know what is bothering you, whether it's unreturned phone calls, excessively high bills, long delays in getting your case resolved, or whatever else is causing your blood pressure to rise. In many cases of unhappy lawyer-client relationships, problems can be ironed out once both parties have been honest and frank in expressing their points of view.

If the dispute is over the lawyer's fees, there is usually room for compromise. However, if you are unable to reach a compromise and the amount of money is sizable, you can choose to go before an arbitration committee. Most state, county, or local bar associations have such committees. While procedures vary in different states, the general process is similar. Both you and your attorney present your case to a panel that renders a decision that can be binding, not binding, or binding only on the attorney. The panel may be comprised partly or entirely of lawyers, but there is a growing trend to include non-lawyers on the panels. When you contact the appropriate bar association, you will be sent written materials that explain what you have to do. Some arbitration committees allow you to bring an attorney to represent you if you so desire, but the hearing is informal and most people represent themselves.

When the attorney-client relationship is broken down and there is no hope of repairing it, you do have some options. However, be advised that each alternative carries with it a degree of risk, the possibility of additional legal fees, and no assurance that your version of truth and justice will prevail.

Changing Lawyers

1. When you fire a lawyer, you still have to pay for the work that has been performed. In some states the lawyer has a right to hold on to your files until your bills have been paid.

2. If your case has been on a contingency-fee basis (a lawyer's fee is paid only if the case is won; the fee is a percentage of the money awarded), resolving money issues gets more complex. If you hire a second attorney and that attorney wins your case, it's likely that the fee for the money recovered will have to be shared between the first and second lawyers. How they split up the contingency fee is based on how much work, and the value of the work, each has performed.

3. You might have a tough time finding a second lawyer once you've dismissed the first one. This is more likely to happen in small communities where lawyers are more likely to stick together. Also, as mentioned above, if your case is based on a contingency fee, a prospective second lawyer may balk at the idea of sharing a damage award. Thus, it's best to find a second lawyer before you fire the first.

4. It's hard to tell how changing lawyers will affect the total cost of your legal fees. If you dismiss your first lawyer before much work has been done on your case, and the second lawyer is more capable (and perhaps charges a lower fee), you could end up with a reasonable legal bill. However, if the second lawyer has to duplicate a lot of the work done by the first lawyer, and/or if the second lawyer turns out to be a clone of the first lawyer, you could be faced with legal bills far beyond what you had originally anticipated.

5. Switching lawyers is a decision that requires careful consideration. However, if you feel convinced that it is the right move, do it as quickly as you can. The real lesson here is to choose the right lawyer in the first place.

Filing a Complaint

1. If your lawyer has handled your case improperly, you can file a complaint with the disciplinary board of your state supreme court. Usually, your state bar association will investigate the misconduct complaint and a grievance committee will recommend punishment, if punishment is warranted. Punishment can range from a reprimand to disbarment.

2. According to the National Resource Center for Consumers of Legal Services: "Bar association grievance procedures are the most misunderstood of the remedies available to dissatisfied clients. . . . The system is concerned with violations of the lawyers' 'code of professional responsibility' (different names are used), not with routine fee or other disputes. . . . Most grievance proceedings involve fraud or willful misconduct. . . . You should regard filing a grievance as a civic duty like reporting a crime. It should be done to further justice, but not with any expectation of compensation." In other words, you may be able to punish the lawyer, but the odds are very slim that you will be awarded any monetary damages.

3. If you file a grievance and it is resolved in your favor, the decision may be beneficial to you if you sue your lawyer for malpractice.

Suing for Malpractice

1. If you have a strong case that shows you suffered damage due to a lawyer's mistake, you might choose to sue your lawyer. The National Resource Center for Consumers of Legal Services says, "The most common claims are for failing to act in time, for taking actions without the client's consent, and for careless investigations."

2. Lawyers don't like to sue other lawyers, so you'll probably have a hard time finding a lawyer to take your case. When you do find one, he or

she is likely to be a personal-injury attorney, usually one who handles medical malpractice cases.

3. Malpractice cases are very hard to win. According to a study by the American Bar Association, two out of every three clients who file them lose their cases. Only a small percentage of those who win get more than $1000, and only 4.3 percent of the winners get $100,000 or more.

Small-Claims Court

Small-claims courts can also be called magistrate's courts or justice of the peace courts. Their purpose is to resolve minor civil lawsuits (not criminal lawsuits). The monetary awards are limited by your state law and the amount ranges from hundreds of dollars to thousands of dollars. Typical of the many different kinds of cases that find their way to small-claims court are tenant-landlord disputes, claims against companies or individuals for defective products or services improperly performed, claims against people who fail to repay loans.

The average consumer will find a lot to like about small-claims court. Court procedures are simplified, hearings are informal, costs are minimal, and you don't need an attorney. Your grievance is heard, and decided upon, by a judge or arbitrator; thus, there is no jury. In addition, small-claims courts process cases a lot faster than regular courts. Some small-claims courts even hold hearings at night so that you won't have to take time off from work in order to attend the hearing.

If you want to file a grievance in small-claims court, here is how you should proceed:

1. Do your best to resolve the dispute before taking it to court. Settling out of court is almost always preferable to filing a lawsuit. If you do end up in small-claims court, the judge will look favorably upon you if you have made an honest effort to compromise and settle the claim.

2. Call your local small-claims court and ask what the limit is on monetary damages that the court can award. For example, if you have a $2500 claim and the most the court can award is $2000, then you are out $500 even if you win your case. However, the advantage of a speedy, inexpensive hearing may outweigh the disadvantage of not being able to collect the full amount of your claim. Also, when you call your nearest small-claims court, be sure to ask in which jurisdiction your claim needs to be filed. Depending on the circumstances of your case, the hearing may be held in a court where you live, where the defendant lives, or where the problem or damage occurred.

3. File your claim. The forms are fairly simple and a court clerk is on hand to help you out. Basically, you will need to state the name and address of the person you are suing and a short explanation of your complaint. If your claim is against a business, you will need to know the name of the owner. If a business license, with the owner's name, isn't on display in the store or place of business, you will have to call your local licensing agency or the county clerk's office in order to get the name of the owner. Once your complaint is filed, the court will set a hearing date and will notify the defendant of your action, either by registered or certified mail or in person (a summons delivered by a sheriff or marshall). The fee for filing your complaint is minimal, usually around $20. There can be an additional fee for mailing or hand-delivering your complaint to the defendant.

4. Prepare your case. Gather all documentation that is relevant to your case. This can include any number of items like itemized bills, receipts, copies of canceled checks, correspondence, contracts, warranties, other legal documents. If the complaint is over a damaged item, be prepared to take the item to court, if possible, or take a photograph of it along. If you have witnesses to support your case, be sure they will show up at the hearing to testify. If your witnesses, or other independent experts, cannot attend the hearing, ask the court if written statements are admissible.

5. Present your case. Once in court, you don't need to act like Perry Mason to be effective, but you do need to be logical and organized. Keep your answers simple and stick to the facts. Be honest and direct, but don't volunteer information that isn't asked for. Remain calm and listen carefully to all testimony. Don't interrupt anyone, especially the judge. It's a good idea to attend a small-claims session prior to your own case in order to familiarize yourself with the way things work. Once you see the actual proceedings, you're likely to be more comfortable with the process on the day you actually go to court.

6. Wait for the judge's decision. The judge may render a decision on the spot, or you and the defendant may get the decision in the mail. If you win, the court will direct the defendant to pay you damages. If the defendant does not comply with the court's orders, you will need to ask the court for advice on how to collect the money owed to you. In most cases, you can attach the defendant's bank account or wages or put a lien against the defendant's property.

Mediation and Arbitration

When involved in a legal dispute, most people would prefer to avoid a lengthy and costly trial. Two alternatives to a full-blown trial are mediation and arbitration; both are forms of "alternative dispute resolution." These kinds of legal mechanisms can be used in almost all kinds of civil cases including employment, family, neighbors, landlord-tenant, consumer, personal injury, and contracts. In addition to saving time and money, these legal alternatives are less stressful than a traditional courtroom trial. They are also a good alternative for someone who might want to take a case to small-claims court but can't because the case is too complicated or the monetary damages sought exceed the limit that a small-claims court can award.

Mediation involves a neutral third party called a mediator. The mediator, who is trained in dispute resolution, sits down with both parties and tries to get them to reach a mutually acceptable agreement. Acting as an advisor and negotiator, the mediator may suggest solutions but the final agreement is made by the disputants. Mediation proceedings are informal and the parties usually do not need to hire an attorney. Either party, unhappy with the proceedings, can refuse a proposed settlement and still take the matter to court.

In *arbitration,* the disputing parties agree to let a neutral party, or an arbitrator, make the decision. Many kinds of arbitration ask the parties to agree in advance that the decision is a final, binding decision. In that case, the decision is a legally enforceable contract and if you don't like the decision, you can't take the matter to court. While arbitration proceedings are informal, they are a step up from mediation proceedings. Witnesses and evidence are presented and both sides may need to be represented by lawyers. The arbitrators are oftentimes retired judges, lawyers, or business persons with expertise in a particular field. In short, arbitration is a more adversarial process than mediation. Like mediation, arbitration proceedings are confidential and private.

Despite the many advantages of mediation and arbitration, the proceedings are not advisable for all people and all cases. For example, you may not want to give up your right to appeal a decision, which is what happens with binding arbitration. Or, you may want a trial by jury. When a case involves complicated legal issues and interpretations, you may prefer to take your case through the regular judicial system.

Alternative dispute resolution centers are set up all across the country. To find one that is close to you, check the yellow pages of your phone directory under "mediation services." For more information on mediation and arbitration, write or call one or more of the following organizations: **National Institute for Dispute Resolution,** 1726 M Street NW, Suite 500, Washington, DC 20036 (202-466-4764); **American Arbitration Association,** 140 West 51 Street, New York,

NY 10020 (212-484-4000); **American Bar Association/Standing Committee on Dispute Resolution,** 1800 M Street NW, Washington, DC 20036 (202-331-2258).

Another organization to contact is your local **Better Business Bureau** (BBB). BBBs across the country assist in the resolution of disputes between a business and its customers; they even provide binding arbitration and nonbinding mediation services. The Better Business Bureau is also noted for its BBB Auto Line program which settles problems between consumers and automobile manufacturers. If you have a problem with your car that has not been corrected to your satisfaction, call the BBB Auto Line phone number: 800-955-5100.

FAMILY LAW

Getting Married

The laws governing marriage vary from state to state. To get a marriage license in most states, you and your partner need to have a blood test for venereal disease. A few states require a complete physical examination, which can be done by your doctor. All states have a minimum age at which you can be married without parental consent and a minimum age with parental consent. Each state also has its own set of rules regarding marriage between blood relatives; for example, marrying a first cousin is usually illegal. And, of course, all states forbid you to marry if you are still legally married to another person.

To find out what laws apply to you, call your local marriage license bureau. You will be told what papers you need to bring when you apply for a marriage license (medical documents, proof of age, proof that a former marriage is legally ended, etc.). Most marriage license bureaus will accept only original documents; photocopies, unsigned papers, or altered or incomplete documents are usually not accepted. Most states require a waiting period, anywhere from one to five days, between issuance of the marriage license and the marriage ceremony. Once you have a marriage license, it must be signed by an official sanctioned by your state government. Most couples have either a civil or religious ceremony, and the license is subsequently signed by a public official or a member of the clergy.

"Common-law marriages" are recognized in a minority of the states in the U.S. By definition, a common-law marriage is cohabitation, living together as husband and wife without the benefit of a marriage ceremony. If a common-law marriage is recognized by your state, it may confer some of the same legal rights as other marriages. However, simply living with a person for a certain number of years does not constitute a common-law marriage. Strict definitions of these marriages exist in the states that recognize them. Also, even if you and your partner have orally agreed that you have a common-law marriage, it's easy for one of you to later deny that agreement since you have no signed legal documents. If you want the legal rights and obligations that go with a marriage, you can only be assured of them if you get married the old-fashioned way.

Prenuptial Contracts

Formerly the exclusive domain of wealthy individuals, prenuptial contracts, also called premarital contracts or antenuptial contracts, have hit mainstream America. About 5 percent of first marriages and 20 percent of remarriages include a prenuptial agreement. Basically, the contract is signed prior to a marriage and sets out how assets are to be divided in the event of death or divorce.

The contract makes the most sense for a person who has children from a previous marriage and who wants to ensure the financial security of those children and other dependents. Also, anyone with substantial assets (e.g., an inheritance, a family business) may want to protect his or her property. Prenuptial agreements are oftentimes considered when one person in the impending marriage is worth considerably more than the other person.

How airtight are prenuptial contracts? Actor Sylvester Stallone and his ex-wife, actress Brigitte Nielsen, had one; it held up in court. So did the agreement between actress Joan Collins and her former husband, Swedish pop singer Peter Helm. Not so lucky was business tycoon Donald Trump when he divorced his wife Ivana; she contested the prenuptial and won an additional settlement. Just how well a prenuptial holds up in court depends on the laws in your state as well as o. the quality and fairness of the document. In the old days, the courts generally frowned upon prenuptials and upheld few of them. Today, however, the documents are more common and more widely enforced, even though the judicial system puts them through a rigorous scrutiny.

Think carefully before you ask your intended to sign a prenuptial contract. It may indeed be a wise and necessary move on your part. But critics of prenuptials say that they often are not needed, particularly in first marriages when both parties are financial equals. The critics charge that a prenuptial agreement can signal distrust and ruin romance as well as appear like a ready-made blueprint for divorce.

If a prenuptial contract is right for you, here are some issues to consider:

1. Oral agreements are hard to enforce. Do-it-yourself kits are rarely worth the paper they are printed on. If your aim is to protect your financial assets, get a good attorney to draw up the contract. Each party should have an attorney—and not the same attorney. The contract is much more likely to be upheld if each person was represented by his or her own lawyer, which tends to indicate that the contract was fair and nobody was coerced.

2. The court always looks at how fair and reasonable the conditions of the contract are. If the contract is totally lopsided in one person's favor and seems to go against the general financial obligations of marriage, the court will refuse to enforce it. Also, some states look at the contract not only in terms of fairness at the time the contract was signed but also at the time when the contract needs to be enforced. For example, suppose your financial situation changes dramatically between the time of your marriage and your divorce 20 years later. What may have seemed fair on your wedding day may not seem fair to the court on your divorce day.

3. When reviewing a prenuptial contract, the court assumes that you and your spouse were entirely honest about your respective financial positions when you signed the contract. If you told your spouse that you were worth $100,000, and later it is discovered that you were worth $1 million, your contract is in trouble.

4. The last-minute signing of prenuptials considerably weakens the agreement. Many lawyers will refuse to execute an agreement a day or two before the wedding. It's best to have the contract signed weeks, or months, in advance of the wedding. Last-minute signings can lead to charges later that one party was forced to sign "under duress."

5. Courts will not enforce provisions in a contract that relate to child custody if the conditions are not in the best interests of the child. Also, child support issues will be questioned if the agreement takes away a child's legal right to parental support.

6. Some couples include a "sunset clause" in a prenuptial. It stipulates that the contract is terminated after a certain number of years, after the birth of a child, or after some other set of circumstances occurs.

Getting Divorced

Judicial attitudes about divorce have changed considerably over the years. In the "old" days, divorces were granted primarily when one spouse was deemed "at fault," whether the fault that ruined the marriage was adultery, desertion, or mental or physical cruelty. Today, all states permit "no-fault" divorce, which means that the divorce can be granted for any number of reasons, with "irreconcilable differences" being the most common no-fault grounds. Thus, it's virtually impossible to stop one spouse from getting a divorce from the other spouse. It should be noted, however, that in some states the "fault" of one spouse can affect the financial settlement of the divorce.

What are your options when you need to dissolve your marriage legally? Do-it-yourself divorces have become increasingly popular. You can get standard forms from your state courthouses, in office supply stores, or in divorce law books written for consumers. Legal clinics also provide low-cost divorce services, usually at a preset standard fee. Another alternative is a divorce mediator, an independent third party who helps couples work out equitable agreements (see full explanation below). Or, you and your spouse can each hire a divorce attorney. Hiring divorce lawyers is the most expensive option. However, when financial and family circumstances are complex and you and your spouse cannot reach an agreement, divorce attorneys may be the best alternative. Whichever way you go, once you have arrived at an agreement, it must be submitted to the court for approval. Only about 10 percent of all divorce cases ever go to trial.

Division of Property

A divorce settlement will lay out the rules for division of property and debt, spousal support, child support, and child custody. Assets of the couple include bank accounts, investments like stocks and bonds, real estate and personal property, pension funds—even a professional degree earned while the couple was married. How the property is divided depends on the state in which you live.

♦ *Community-property states* (Arizona, California, Idaho, Louisiana, New Mexico, Nevada, Texas, Washington, and Wisconsin). The courts in these states view anything (job earnings, real estate, investments, etc.) that was acquired during the marriage as community property. The spouses are considered equal partners and community property is split 50/50 in a divorce. The 50/50 split applies even if only one spouse was responsible for all money earned during the marriage. Also, it applies regardless of who purchased an item, whose name is on the title to a car, whose name is on a bank account or stock certificate. Provisions do exist in community-property states that protect "separate property," or property that one spouse had before a marriage like a house that you owned when you were single. Also protected are gifts or inheritances given solely to one spouse during the marriage. However, the definition of separate property gets dicey when separate property gets mixed in with community property. Suppose you and your spouse have a joint savings account and you get a $10,000 inheritance which you deposit into that account. If you never take any money out of the account and you keep all the paperwork regarding your inheritance, you will easily be able to prove in a divorce that the $10,000 was your separate property. But if you continually withdraw and deposit money into the account, your separate property will look more and more like community property and is likely to end up in a 50/50 split. Couples in community-property states often "commingle" separate property assets with community-property assets. In a divorce, figuring out which is which can be an awesome and aggravating task.

♦ *Equitable-distribution states* (all other states). The husband and wife are viewed as economic partners and anything earned, saved, or acquired during the marriage is subject to an "equitable" distribution, but the distribution may not be a 50/50 split. An equal division of marital assets is more likely after a "long" marriage (generally viewed as 10 or more years). The court looks at a great number of things when deciding who gets what, including: the length of the marriage; the health, age, occupation, and earning potential of each spouse; how much each spouse has contributed to the marriage (including homemaker contributions); the particular needs of the spouse with custody of the children; whether one spouse will receive alimony or spousal maintenance support. Equitable-distribution states have different rules when it comes to handling separate property (property that one spouse owned prior to the marriage, or property inherited or given as a gift during marriage). Some states only divide up marital property (the assets acquired during marriage), and separate property remains untouched. In other states, the courts have the right to divide up separate property and can give part of a spouse's separate property to the other spouse.

Special Concerns for Women

Divorce is a miserable process for both husbands and wives, but numerous studies have shown that women ultimately suffer more when it comes to the financial repercussions of a divorce. This is due to a number of factors including the fact that women, even if they are gainfully employed, generally earn less than men. Also, women are usually the primary caretakers of the children, which adds to the financial burden. And, if fathers are delinquent in child support payments (many are), money problems can become severe. Women contemplating, or involved in, a divorce should keep the following in mind:

♦ Alimony is rapidly becoming a thing of the past. At present only 15 percent of divorces result in an alimony payment. Sometimes a court will award what is called "spousal maintenance" or "rehabilitative support" to help a wife make a transition from being financially dependent to self-supporting. The money awarded, however, is usually for a limited amount of time.

♦ It is important to have a full picture of the financial history of your marriage. Collect all pertinent documents including old income tax records, real estate transactions, pension fund and insurance information, debt information, and all other relevant financial data. Before you agree to any divorce settlement, you need to have a full inventory of all assets and debts.

♦ If you have children, assess the costs of raising and supporting those children. The list of expenses should include everything from day-care costs and medical costs to clothing, food, and other necessities.

♦ Don't minimize your contributions to the marriage because you do not work outside of the home or because you are the lower-income earner. The court puts a value on homemaker responsibilities whether they relate to child care or are deemed helpful to furthering the career of the husband.

♦ If you are completely baffled by the divorce process, seek legal help. If you hire an attorney, be sure he or she is an expert in divorce matters (this area of the law is usually called family law or domestic relations).

Obviously, the above issues could apply to a husband in a divorce proceeding. While women typically have a tougher time with the money side of a divorce—especially those who will become single parents—there are many men who could find themselves in the same financial circumstances.

Divorce Mediators

For many people, divorce mediators are a practical alternative to long, oftentimes expensive and hostile divorce litigation. A mediator is an independent counselor who helps couples resolve their disputes. The mediator may be a lawyer, a psychologist, a social worker, or another trained professional. According to the Academy of Family Mediators: "Mediators help families resolve conflicts involving custody, parenting arrangements, child and spousal support, and property and debt division. . . . Settlement options are developed and discussed to be sure they fairly meet everyone's goals." In some states, mediation is mandatory for couples involved in child custody disputes.

In many cases, couples use a mediator to help them work out tentative agreements that are then reviewed by each spouse's lawyer. The mediator acts as a facilitator to help the couple talk through their divorce issues in a nonthreatening environment (no lawyers are present). The respective lawyers watch out for the best interests of their clients, coach the mediation process along, and hammer out the final agreement.

Proponents of divorce mediation say that the use of mediator services cuts down on the total cost of divorce, since mediators charge substantially less by the hour than do lawyers. In some states the agreement you reach can be filed directly with the court, but it's usually advised that you have an attorney review it.

Critics of divorce mediation say that it shouldn't be used, especially in lieu of a lawyer, if you doubt the financial honesty of your spouse. Also, some women's groups say that financially unsophisticated women may not fully understand the legal and financial implications of the agreement reached. Also, critics charge that women are usually more open to compromise than men and may have a tendency to give up too much just to smooth things over and reach an agreement. Also, if a spouse is subject to physical or mental abuse, direct negotiation with the abuser, even with the help of a mediator, may not be a good idea.

If you think that a divorce mediator is an alternative for you, the best way to find one is through references from friends or co-workers. To locate a mediator who is also an attorney, call your local bar association. You can also check the yellow pages of your phone directory under "divorce mediators." Or, call the **Academy of Family Mediators** in Eugene, Oregon (503-345-1205). You may want to interview several mediators before making a decision so that you can find one whose style and qualifications suit your personality and situation. Also, remember that not all states require mediators to be licensed to practice, so choose carefully.

Child Custody

Who gets custody of a child after a divorce is determined by a court. When sole custody is awarded, it has traditionally been given to the mother; the father is given visitation rights and must provide financial support for the child. However, fathers who file for sole custody have increasingly been awarded custody. In addition, there is a trend in many states to award couples joint custody of children. The court's guiding principle for awarding custody is that the decision must be made "in the best interests of the child."

When a court makes a decision based on sole custody, it takes a number of issues into consideration. The judge will look at each parent in terms of mental, physical, and financial health and stability. The relationship and emotional ties of the child with each parent will be considered as well as each parent's willingness to provide and care for the child. While no state will allow the child to make a custody decision, the preference of the child is sometimes a factor. When parents cannot agree on custody arrangements, some states require them to enter a mediation process. Also, a court can seek out the professional advice of an independent social worker or psychologist to help resolve child custody battles.

There are two kinds of joint custody arrangements. One is joint legal custody and the other is joint physical custody; you might have one or both. When you and your ex-spouse have joint legal custody, you are responsible for making decisions that will affect your child's health, education, and general well-being. Joint physical custody means that the child will live in the homes of both parents, but not necessarily for equal amounts of time. For example, one parent may care for the child on school days and the other parent may care for the child on weekends. If the parents live far apart, the child may spend the school year with one parent and summer vacations with the other parent.

Custody arrangements can be changed without too much difficulty if you and your former spouse are in agreement. If you aren't, you must present a compelling case to the judge to show just cause for your requested changes, and the changes must still be in the best interests of the child. Snatching or kidnapping a child away from the other parent is a serious offense. Federal and state laws dictate that all states must uphold custody decrees and that children who are unlawfully taken by a parent must be returned to their home states.

Child custody arrangements and child support arrangements are two different things. If your ex-spouse is delinquent in child support payments, you cannot violate joint custody rights or visitation rights. On the flip side, if you are the one making the child support payments and your ex-spouse is the one violating custody or visitation rights, you should not withhold child support money. When such problems arise, it's time to get advice from a lawyer and/or the court, not to take matters into your own hands.

Child Support

Children are legally entitled to financial support from parents. When parents divorce, the court determines the financial obligation of each parent, and most states have a preset formula that is used to figure out that financial obligation. For example, a noncustodial parent (usually the father) will have to make monthly child support payments to the custodial parent (usually the mother). One parent usually makes a payment to the other parent regardless of the custody arrangement—sole custody, joint legal custody, and/or joint physical custody. If financial circumstances change, one parent can ask for a reduction in payments, or the other parent can ask for an increase, but the court must approve the change.

Federal and state governments have plenty of laws that guarantee financial support to children, but many parents are reneging on child support payments. The offenders are called "deadbeat dads" (and some moms), and collectively they owe some $20 billion in support to 16 million U.S.

children. The delinquent parents include divorced parents who ignore court orders as well as unwed parents. (Children of unwed parents are entitled to the same support as children of formerly married parents.)

Because the problem has become a national disgrace, government enforcement programs across the country have beefed up their collection efforts, and new laws have gone into effect to force deadbeat parents to pay up. Those who fail to pay can have money withheld from their paychecks; a lien can be placed against their property, or their property can be seized and sold; their state and federal income tax refunds can be withheld.

In order to collect child support you must have a court order. It may be issued as a result of a divorce or legal separation. When parents are not married, paternity must be established to get a court order. How the legal relationship of paternity is established is a matter of state law. The alleged father can usually sign a consent agreement admitting paternity, which can then be filed with the court. In cases of contested paternity, a genetic test (usually a blood test) will be given to the alleged father and to the mother and the child.

If you do not have a court order for child support, you can get one by representing yourself in court, by hiring a private attorney, or by working with the **Child Support Enforcement** (CSE) office in your area. The CSE program is a federal/state/local effort to collect child support from parents who are legally obligated to pay. Your state's CSE program will help you:

♦ *Locate an absent parent.* Your CSE office has a "state parent locator service" and a "federal parent locator service." The state service checks records like motor vehicle registration, unemployment insurance, income tax, correctional facilities. The federal service can search the records of the Internal Revenue Service, the Department of Defense, the Social Security Administration, and the Veterans Administration.

♦ *Establish legal fatherhood (paternity).* Your CSE will guide you through the steps necessary to establish paternity. All information given to the CSE is confidential. While CSE offices will try to establish paternity for any child up to the child's eighteenth birthday, it's best to establish paternity soon after the child's birth.

♦ *Establish the legal support order.* Most of the time this can be done without going before a judge in a courtroom. The CSE will obtain information on the delinquent parent's income and assets and verify all data before the support order (court order) is legal.

♦ *Collect child support payments.* The CSE will encourage voluntary payment. If that fails, other enforcement techniques (mentioned above) will be used.

To find your local CSE office, check the county/state government listings in your telephone directory. A free 40-page government booklet, "Handbook on Child Support Enforcement," answers dozens of questions about child support issues. To receive a copy, write to: Consumer Information Center, Pueblo, CO 81002.

Because state child support agencies are often overloaded with a backlog of cases and because collecting delinquent child support money can be a lucrative business, many private child support collection agencies have sprung up across the country. These businesses usually charge an up-front fee (around $25) and work on a contingency basis. Typically, their fee is 25 percent of any money collected; if they collect no money, they get no fee. In order to use a private collection agency, you must have a valid court order awarding you child support and you must not be receiving Aid to Families with Dependent Children (AFDC). To get more information about private agencies, call the **American Child Support Collection Association**: 800-PAY-CHILD.

Trouble with the Neighbors

Like it or not, your neighbors tend to become part of your extended family. Whether you own your own home or live in an apartment or condo, the mere proximity of neighbors forces some sort of a relationship upon you. Regardless of how friendly you are with your neighbors, any number of conflicts can arise. State and local laws oftentimes determine who's right and who's wrong in a dispute, but the manner in which you resolve a dispute can have long-lasting effects on personal relationships as well as on goodwill in the neighborhood.

In general, the best way to settle a dispute is one-on-one negotiation, either in person or through letter writing. If that fails, you can try mediation, which is a process whereby a neutral third party sits down with both sides and assists in reaching a solution; the mediator simply acts as a facilitator and does not make the decision. In recent years neighborhood mediation centers have proliferated across the country (some services are free; some charge a small fee). If you want to use a mediator, look in the yellow pages of your phone directory under "mediation services" or "conflict resolution." If you have an apartment manager or a co-op/condo board, a complaint letter to either may also be an avenue to consider. Depending on the nature of your

ADOPTION SEARCH LAWS

Adoption records are sealed in all states and only a few states permit adopted children to see the records, and only when the children reach a certain age. However, 35 states permit mutual-consent registries where birth parents and adopted children (who are "of age") can independently express a desire to find and meet one another. If both the biological parent and the adopted child register, a state social service agency or an adoption agency will assist in setting up a meeting. In addition, approximately 15 states have a search-and-consent provision. In these states the adopted child states that he or she wants to find a biological parent and the parent is subsequently informed of the request; the biological parent can approve or reject the release of information to the adopted child. Laws exist in all states that help adopted children to obtain critical medical information.

conflict, calling the police might be an option. Finally, you can take the matter to court if you want to collect monetary damages. You can file a lawsuit in either a small-claims court or a local court.

Noise. High on the list of neighbor complaints is excessive noise—barking dogs, loud parties, lawn mowers that rev up at 6:00 AM. Most state and local laws protect your right to the "peaceable enjoyment" or "reasonable comfort" of your home. Loud noise that might be permissible in the afternoon may not be permissible early in the morning or late at night. If excessive noise is a problem, you need to get a copy of your local noise ordinance from city hall or your public library; the ordinance will explain what constitutes a violation and tell you what hours of the day are protected from excessive noise. In addition to the rights afforded you by civil law, you may also be protected by criminal law. For example, loud parties late at night can be considered "disorderly conduct."

Property. Branches from a neighbor's tree block your view, dump unwanted fruit on your property, or keep sunlight from reaching your vegetable garden. The fence built by a neighbor is on your property. A neighbor's home and land are a blight on the neighborhood; the lawn is never mowed, trash is strewn everywhere, the place is simply a mess.

Regarding tree issues: in general, you own not only your house and land but the air space above both, so you are within your rights to ask that branches be removed or trimmed when they interfere with your property rights. In the case of the "illegal" fence, you need to check the deed to your property to be sure the fence falls within your property lines. If the fence is on your land, you may be able to get it removed or grant your neighbor an "easement" that will allow the fence to remain on your land. When it comes to the overall "look" of a neighbor's property, the law usually comes down on the side of the property owner. If a neighbor refuses to mow the lawn or chooses to paint pink polka dots on the exterior of his or her house, the neighbor is oftentimes acting legally. However, if conditions of a neighbor's property present a safety or health hazard to you and your family, then you do have a justified complaint.

Illegal activities. Suspect that illegal activities, like drug sales or prostitution, are going on in your neighbor's home? If so, you should contact the police department; you can choose to give your name when calling or register an anonymous complaint. Results, however, will not happen overnight, since the police will need time to investigate your charge before taking any legal action.

To sum up, a property owner has a great many legal rights as long as the owner's actions comply with local laws and building ordinances, and provided the actions do not infringe upon the legal rights of others. But even if the law is on your side, neighborhood disputes are more easily resolved, and tend to stay resolved, if both parties are open to compromise and exercise common courtesy.

Consumer Law

Contract Basics

A contract is a legal agreement between two or more persons or parties. You enter into a contract when you get married, buy or rent a car, take out an insurance policy, sell your bicycle to a friend, hire someone to fix your leaking roof, make a credit card purchase. Most contracts involve the exchange of something for money: you give or take money in exchange for certain goods or services. Of the countless contracts you make during your lifetime, most are everyday occurrences that require little time or effort. However, there's no denying that we live in a very litigious society and any mistakes we make when executing an important legal contract can cost us plenty. Here are some basic tenets of contract law:

1. Not everyone can enter into a contract. Both parties must be of sound mind and be a certain age. Evaluating mental health is a complex area and state laws vary greatly on their definitions. Age requirements are determined by the "age of majority" and in most states the age of majority is 18.

2. Oral contracts are enforceable. Proving the existence of an oral agreement may be difficult, but if there is sufficient evidence, the court may consider the oral contract valid. When dealing with matters that are truly important to you, don't rely on an oral contract; get everything down in writing.

3. Certain contracts must be in writing. For example, most state laws require written contracts for land sales and sales of goods over $500. In addition, promises to bequeath property (wills) and promises to be responsible for another person's debts (when someone cosigns a loan) must also be in writing.

4. Persons entering into a contract must do so voluntarily, not "under duress" or because of "undue influence." For example, if you signed a contract because of physical threats, you did so under duress (not of your own free will), and the contract would not be considered legal. Undue influence usually occurs when someone who is at a disadvantage (e.g., someone who is very young, very old, or in poor physical or mental health) is pressured into signing a contract by someone whom he or she trusts. In other words, the person in the position of trust used the trust unfairly and exerted undue influence to get the disadvantaged person to sign the contract. Again, the court will look at whether or not the person who signed the contract would have done so of his or her own volition, if undue influence had not been used.

5. In addition to the reasons mentioned above, there are other factors that can void a contract. For instance, illegal terms in a contract may void a contract. Also, if someone outright lies, or commits fraud, the contract may not be legal. If you have signed a contract that you want to get out of and think you have just cause, you should get expert legal advice before taking action.

6. The number-one rule to follow before signing a contract: *read it, then read it again.* It's not as formidable as it looks. Many states have "plain English" laws that require consumer contracts to be written in language that consumers understand. When you come across something that puzzles you, make a note of it or place a checkmark next to it and get an explanation from someone knowledgeable and trustworthy. And don't forget to scrutinize the small print, painful as it may be. Oftentimes, the small print includes important items that you need to be aware of—and things you might not like. For instance, hidden in the small print may be the fact that you waive your right to sue the other party if a problem occurs.

7. No contract is really a "standard" contract. All parts of a contract are up for negotiation. You are within your legal rights to delete parts of a contract, add provisions, change the language to your liking. Obviously, you need to be realistic and reasonable in your demands. The other party does not have to agree to your contract changes and you may end up with no contract at all. Be sure that any oral agreements not in the contract are written in before you sign.

8. You can write your own contract without using the services of a lawyer. Whether or not you pay a lawyer to draw up a contract for you depends on the substance and importance of the contract. If you lend a friend $500, you shouldn't find it too difficult to write your own agreement that stipulates the repayment terms. If your friend doesn't live up to the conditions of the contract, you can try to resolve the dispute yourself or take the matter to small-claims court. However, when sizable amounts of money are involved, when you are negotiating business deals, or when you are resolving complicated family issues, you need an attorney. To put it simply, don't get in over your head. If the contract is important to your health, wealth, and overall well-being, play it smart and call a lawyer.

Warranties

Before you make a major purchase, there is an important promise you should read. It is called the *warranty*—the manufacturer's or seller's promise to stand behind a product. Warranties vary in the amount of coverage they provide. So, just as you compare the style, price, and other characteristics of products before you buy, you can also compare their warranties. The Magnuson-Moss Act of 1975 requires that warranties be available for you to read before you make a purchase.

Written Warranties

Written warranties come with most major purchases, although this is not legally required. The protection offered by written warranties varies greatly, so it is important to compare warranties before making a purchase. Here are some questions to keep in mind when comparing warranties.

♦ What parts and repair problems are covered by the warranty? Check to see if any parts of the product or types of repair problems are excluded from coverage.

♦ Are any expenses excluded from coverage? Some warranties require you to pay for labor charges.

♦ How long does the warranty last? Check the warranty to see when it expires.

♦ Does the warranty cover "consequential damages"? Many warranties do not cover consequential damages. This means that the company will not pay for any damage the product caused, or for your time and expense in getting the damage repaired. For example, if your freezer breaks and the food spoils, the company will not pay for the food you lost.

♦ Are there any conditions or limitations on the warranty? Some warranties only provide coverage if you maintain or use the product as directed. For example, a warranty may cover only personal uses—as opposed to business uses—of the product. Make sure the warranty will meet your needs.

♦ Whom do you contact to obtain warranty service? It may be the seller or the manufacturer who provides you with service.

♦ What will you have to do to get repairs? Look for conditions that could prove expensive, such as a requirement that you ship a heavy object to a factory for service.

♦ What will the company do if the product fails? Find out if the company will repair it, replace it, or return your money.

Spoken Warranties

Sometimes a salesperson will make an oral promise, for example, that the seller will provide free repairs. However, if this claim is not in writing, you may not be able to get the promised service. Have the salesperson put the promise in writing, or do not count on the service.

Service Contracts

When you buy a car, home, or major appliance, you may be offered a service contract. Although often called "extended warranties," service contracts are not warranties. Warranties are included in the price of the product. Service contracts come separately from the product, at an extra cost. To decide whether you need a service contract, you should consider several factors: whether the warranty already covers the repairs that you would get under the service contract; whether the product is likely to need repairs and their potential costs; how long the service contract is in effect; and the reputation of the company offering the service contract. To learn more about buying a service contract, write: "Service Contracts," Public Reference, **Federal Trade Commission,** Washington, DC 20580.

Implied Warranties

Although warranties are not required by law, there is another type of warranty that is. It is called an "implied" warranty. Implied warranties are created by state law, and all states have them.

Almost every purchase you make is covered by an implied warranty. The most common type of implied warranty is called a "warranty of merchantability." This means that the seller promises the product will do what it is supposed to do. For example, a car will run, a toaster will toast.

Another type of implied warranty is the "warranty of fitness for a particular purpose." This applies when you buy a product on the seller's advice that it is suitable for a particular use. For example, a seller who suggests that you buy a certain sleeping bag for zero-degree weather warrants that the sleeping bag will be suitable for zero degrees.

If your purchase does not come with a written warranty, it is still covered by implied warranties unless the product is marked "as is," or the seller otherwise indicates in writing that no warranty is given. Some states do not permit "as is" sales.

If problems arise that are not covered by the written warranty, you should investigate the protection given by your implied warranty.

Implied warranty coverage can last as long as four years, although the length of the coverage varies from state to state. A lawyer or a state consumer protection office can provide more information about implied warranty coverage in your state.

Preventing Problems

To minimize the chance of a problem with your warranty, take these precautions:

♦ Consider the reputation of the company offering the warranty. If you are not familiar with the company, ask your local or state consumer protection office or Better Business Bureau if they have any complaints against the company. A warranty is only as good as the company that offers it.

♦ Before you buy, read the warranty. See exactly what protection the warranty gives you.

♦ Save the sales slip and file it with your warranty. You may need it later to document the date of your purchase or, in the case of a warranty limited to the first purchaser, that you were the original buyer.

◆ Perform any maintenance or inspections required by the warranty.

◆ Use the product according to the manufacturer's instructions. Abuse or misuse of the product may cancel your warranty coverage.

Resolving Disputes

If you are faced with any problems with a product or with obtaining the promised warranty service, here are some steps you can take:

◆ Read your product instructions and warranty carefully. Do not expect features or performance that your product was not designed to give, or assume warranty coverage that was never promised. Having a warranty does not mean that you automatically get a refund if the product is defective. The company may be entitled to try to fix it first. In addition, if you reported a defect to the company during the warranty period and the product was not fixed properly, the company must correct the problem, even if your warranty has expired.

◆ Discuss your complaint with the seller. Disputes usually can be resolved at this level. But if you cannot reach an agreement, write the manufacturer. Your warranty should list the company's mailing address. Send all letters by certified mail and keep copies.

◆ If you cannot get satisfaction from either the seller or manufacturer, contact your local consumer protection agencies. They may be able to help.

◆ Inquire about dispute resolution organizations. They arbitrate disagreements when both you and the company are willing to participate. The company or local consumer protection office can suggest organizations to contact. Consult your warranty; dispute resolution may be a required first step before going to court.

Source: Federal Trade Commission

Mail-Order Sales

Catalog and magazine sales have grown dramatically over the past 10 years because shopping by mail is both quick and easy. Federal laws enforced by the Federal Trade Commission and the U.S. Postal Service give consumers certain rights when shopping by mail, and the rights also protect consumers against fraudulent sales practices.

Timely delivery. Your merchandise has to be in the mail within 30 days of your order, unless the company's advertising designates another time frame. If there is a delay in shipping your order, the company should inform you of the delay and give you the option of canceling the order and receiving a refund (the refund should be mailed within seven business days). Not responding to a delay notice means you have agreed to a later shipping date. There are some exceptions to the delivery rules including: flower seeds or growing plants; the first issue of a magazine subscription; film development; C.O.D. orders.

Returns. When you get something that isn't what you ordered (the company made a mistake), or the item isn't what the catalog promised, you can return it for a full refund. When a mail-order company knowingly sends you a substitute item, you are under no obligation to keep it; however, you must pay for anything that you do not return. Most companies have very liberal return policies and you can get a refund if you aren't completely satisfied with the merchandise.

Unordered merchandise. Legally, there are two kinds of unordered merchandise that you can get in the mail: a free sample (it should be clearly marked "free sample") and items sent by charities (e.g., greeting cards, key chains, return-address stickers) that are seeking donations. These unordered items are gifts and are yours to keep, give away, or throw away. A company or organization that bills you for such items can be charged with mail fraud.

Some helpful hints for mail-order shopping:

1. Place orders with reliable companies. If you are not familiar with the company or it's the first

time you have dealt with the company, place a small, inexpensive order.

2. "Too good to be true" prices and products usually are. Beware of slick advertising photos and catalog descriptions.

3. Pay by credit card, check, or money order so that you have proof of purchase. Sending cash is a bad idea.

4. Keep track of when you ordered and received merchandise. Make sure you make a note of the company's name, address, and telephone number.

5. If you can't resolve a problem with a company, call or write your local or state consumer protection agency. If you suspect intentional fraud, you should also write to the **U.S. Postal Service,** Washington, DC 20260 and the **Federal Trade Commission** (FTC), Washington, DC 20580. While the FTC will not intervene in individual cases, it may investigate to see if the company has a pattern of similar complaints.

Door-to-Door Sales

A Federal Trade Commission rule, called the "Cooling-Off Rule" or the "3-Days-to-Cancel Rule," allows you to change your mind about any purchase you make from a door-to-door salesperson. The salesperson is required to inform you about the cancellation rights and to provide you with a cancellation form or receipt. Listed below are the important aspects of the rule as well as the exceptions to the rule.

1. The law is not confined solely to sales made by a person who appears uninvited on your doorstep. It applies to sales made anywhere other than the seller's normal place of business. Thus, it covers sales made at other people's homes (like consumer product parties), sales made on street corners or in rented hotel rooms. It even applies if you have invited the person into your home or you met the salesperson at a restaurant.

2. You can cancel your sale by signing and mailing the cancellation form before midnight of the third business day after the date on the contract. When you count up the days allotted to you, don't count Sundays or federal holidays since you are only counting business days.

3. You do not have to state a reason for canceling the sale. The Cooling-Off Rule is intended to give you time to reflect on your purchase and change your mind, whatever the reason.

4. Once you cancel the transaction, the salesperson must refund your money, return any trade-in goods you turned over, cancel and return your contract. The salesperson has 10 days to do these things. In addition, the salesperson must pick up the merchandise within 20 days or give you money to return the product by mail.

5. There are some exceptions to the 3-Days-to-Cancel Rule. It does not cover the following sales categories:
♦ purchases under $25
♦ real estate, insurance, or securities
♦ emergency home repairs
♦ purchases made entirely by mail or telephone.

6. If you want to cancel your contract and the salesperson refuses to comply with the law, you should contact your local or state consumer protection agency. Also, you might want to notify the **Federal Trade Commission,** Washington, DC 20580.

Lost or Stolen Credit Cards and Debit Cards

When your credit cards are lost or stolen, federal laws impose limits on your liability when the cards are fraudulently used.

Credit cards. If you report the loss or theft before any unauthorized charges are made, you are not liable for anything. If you report the loss after fraudulent use of the card, the most you will have to pay is $50 on each card.

ATM (automatic teller machine) cards and **debit cards.** Your liability for an ATM card or debit card is different than the liability for a credit card:

♦ Your loss is limited to $50 if you notify the financial institution within two business days after learning of loss or theft of your card or code.

♦ You could lose as much as $500 if you do not tell the card issuer within two business days after learning of loss or theft.

♦ If you do not report an unauthorized transfer that appears on your statement within 60 days after the statement is mailed to you, you risk losing all the money in your account plus your maximum overdraft line of credit.

Telephone credit cards. You are not responsible for paying for the unauthorized use of your phone credit card, provided the calls are determined to be unauthorized calls.

Correcting Billing Errors

Month after month, John Jones was billed for a lawn mower he never ordered and never got. Finally, he tore up his bill and mailed back the pieces—just to try to explain things to a person instead of a computer. There's a more effective, easier way to straighten out these errors. The Fair Credit Billing Act requires creditors to correct errors promptly and without damage to your credit rating.

A case of error? The law defines a billing error as any charge—

♦ for something you didn't buy or for a purchase made by someone not authorized to use your account;

♦ that is not properly identified on your bill or is for an amount different from the actual purchase price or was entered on a date different from the purchase date; or

♦ for something that you did not accept on delivery or that was not delivered according to agreement.

Billing errors also include:

♦ errors in arithmetic;

♦ failure to show a payment or other credit to your account;

♦ failure to mail the bill to your current address, if you told the creditor about an address change at least 20 days before the end of the billing period; or

♦ a questionable item, or an item for which you need more information.

In Case of Error

If you think your bill is wrong, or want more information about it, follow these steps:

1. Notify the creditor *in writing* within 60 days after the first bill was mailed that showed the error. Be sure to write to the address the creditor lists for billing inquiries and to tell the creditor:

♦ your name and account number;

♦ that you believe the bill contains an error and *why* you believe it is wrong; and

♦ the date and suspected amount of the error or the item you want explained.

2. Pay all parts of the bill that are not in dispute. But, while waiting for an answer, you do not have to pay the amount in question (the "disputed" amount) or any minimum payments or finance charges that apply to it.

The creditor must acknowledge your letter within 30 days, unless the problem can be resolved within that time. Within two billing periods—but in no case longer than 90 days—either your account must be corrected or you must be told why the creditor believes the bill is correct.

If the creditor made a mistake, you do not pay any finance charges on the disputed amount. Your account must be corrected, and you must be sent an explanation of any amount you still owe.

If no error is found, the creditor must send you an explanation of the reasons for that finding and promptly send a statement of what you owe, which may include any finance charges that have accumulated and any minimum payments you missed while you were questioning the bill. You then have the time usually given on your type of account to pay any balance, but not less than 10 days.

3. If you still are not satisfied, you should notify the creditor in writing within the time allowed to pay your bill.

Maintaining Your Credit Rating

A creditor may not threaten your credit rating while you're resolving a billing dispute. Once you have written about a possible error, a creditor must not give out information to other creditors or credit bureaus that would hurt your credit reputation. And, until your complaint is answered, the creditor also may not take any action to collect the disputed amount.

After the creditor has explained the bill, if you do not pay in the time allowed, you may be reported as delinquent on the amount in dispute and the creditor may take action to collect. Even so, you can still disagree in writing. Then the creditor must report that you have challenged your bill and give you the name and address of each person who has received information about your account. When the matter is settled, the creditor must report the outcome to each person who has received information. Remember that you may also place your own side of the story in your credit record.

Source: "Consumer Handbook to Credit Protection Laws," Board of Governors of the Federal Reserve System, Washington, DC.

Landlord-Tenant Disputes

Can a landlord refuse to return your security deposit? Doesn't a landlord have to paint your apartment as well as make necessary repairs? Can your landlord evict you just because you invited a friend to share your apartment? These issues and dozens of other landlord-tenant questions flood consumer hotline numbers and oftentimes find their way into the nation's court systems.

In general, landlords provide renters with a "warranty of habitability," which guarantees that your rental apartment or house will be safe and livable. And the landlord must apply "reasonable" standards in making your rental unit safe and livable. However, a reasonable repair standard for a gas leak or burst water pipe is different than the standard for a broken dishwasher; the first

instances require *immediate* attention while the latter does not.

Many disputes between tenants and landlords could be prevented if tenants would carefully read, and negotiate, their lease agreements, which spell out the rights and responsibilities of both landlord and tenant. These agreements do tilt in favor of the landlord, but tenants can try to add and delete conditions as well as modify them. Remember that you are legally obligated to follow the stipulations of your lease; oral promises made by a landlord may not be enforceable unless they are written into your contract.

Here are some of the basic items to watch out for before you sign a lease:

1. What are the conditions under which you get the security deposit back?

2. What does the lease say about repairs and maintenance?

3. Are there any restrictions on who can occupy your residence? Can you, at a later date, share the rental unit with another person? Are children and pets permitted?

4. Are there limitations to the alterations you can make to your home and do all alterations require landlord approval? Also, if you make alterations that might be considered a permanent fixture, like a built-in bar, be sure that the lease allows you to walk away with your property.

5. What does the lease say about rent increases as well as your right to renew the lease?

6. Do you have a right to cancel the lease? Do you have the right to sublet the unit?

7. If you anticipate operating a full-time or part-time business from your home, does the lease prohibit you from doing so?

8. What kind of insurance is provided for your rental unit?

9. What are the conditions under which you can be evicted?

10. If the building is sold, will your lease automatically be canceled?

11. Are there any conditions that you don't fully understand? If so, ask for an explanation in plain English and/or get a legal opinion before signing. Hidden somewhere in fine-print "legalese" may be a clause that imposes extra charges

and penalties for particular situations or a clause that says you do not have a right to withhold rent, no matter what the landlord does wrong.

Asking for a change in a standardized lease will give you a preview of how you and your landlord are likely to get along, whether you want to make a minor addition or radically alter an unfair condition. If a landlord is not open to compromise or cannot adequately explain the reasons for certain contract stipulations, you might be in the wrong building.

When you and your landlord do not see eye to eye, it's best to try to resolve your differences on your own. If that doesn't work, contact your local tenant's rights association for advice and assistance. If you have to go to court, many municipalities across the country have special housing courts that deal solely with tenant-landlord problems; most of these courts allow you to file a lawsuit without hiring a lawyer. In addition, you can always file a complaint in small-claims court. Finally, think twice before you withhold your rent, even if you feel totally justified in doing so; failure to pay rent is likely to get you evicted. Before you consider withholding rent, get expert legal advice.

Bites, Barks & Messes: Pets and the Law

Is every dog really entitled to "one free bite"? Can you sue the owner of a barking dog or a cat that scares away the birds? Can you leave money to your pet through a trust? These are just a few of the most common questions people have about animals and the law. Here's a look at the basic rules and how they can be applied to common situations.

♦ *Pets are property.* The law doesn't prescribe what animals may not do, only what people may not do. You can't sue an animal, only its owner. You can't give money to an animal either (see below).

♦ *A pet's owner is responsible for it.* The traditional rule is that an owner is responsible only for "known dangerous propensities" of his/her animal. The trend is toward making an owner liable for any harm done by his/her animal, regardless of whether he/she should have anticipated the harm. This is called strict liability. An owner is also responsible for obeying all laws relating to owning an animal, such as leash and scoop laws.

Bites. The "one bite rule" for dogs is based on the fact that, unlike some animals, dogs don't normally bite people. Under the traditional rule an owner of a lion or a snapping turtle would be responsible if it bit anyone, but a dog owner would not be as long as the dog had never bitten anyone before. An owner of a cow was liable if it trampled crops, but not if it bit someone. And so on. Today, some courts have abandoned the rule and some states have passed a law to change it. Some of the new laws apply just to dog bites; others are broader.

Damage to Property. Traditionally, a dog owner was unlikely to be held responsible for his or her dog's digging up a neighbor's garden or chewing up furniture, or for causing an accident by chasing cars or running into the street unless the owner knew the dog tended to do such things. Today, an owner may well be liable in all these situations. Homeowner's insurance would probably cover amounts over the policy deductible.

Injury to Pets. In theory, you can sue someone who kills or injures your pet, but in practice it's seldom worthwhile. You can only recover the amount of the vet's bill for injuries or the market value of the pet at its death. Since the real value of the pet is sentimental and you can't recover for that, suing seldom makes financial sense. In addition, you have to show that the person doing the harm was negligent. That is difficult in the typical case of a driver hitting a dog or cat. The driver who says the animal "darted out in front of the car" or that traffic precluded any avoidance maneuver is hard to refute.

Barks. An incessantly barking dog is considered a nuisance. In most places "maintaining" a nuisance either violates a local ordinance or is a misdemeanor. This means you can file criminal charges against a dog owner who lets a dog bark for long periods. Barking dogs, and complaints about them to the police, can really arouse a neighborhood, so be sure to complain to the owner yourself first, if you can. Sometimes a dog only barks when its owner is gone, so the owner might be unaware of the problem. However valuable a good night's sleep might be, it is hard to sue successfully for being kept awake.

Leaving Money. Everyone's heard of the recluse who left millions to her cats or his old dog. It is always a problem, because pets are property and can't own property themselves. You can leave your pet to someone in your will, and you can leave money to a person to care for your pet, but you can't leave money to the pet. What about a trust? People have left money in trust for the care of a pet, but it's not the solution you might think. The beneficiary of a trust is considered the owner of rights in the trust. A beneficiary must be able to sue to enforce trust provisions. Pets, as property, can neither own interests in a trust nor sue to enforce those interests. The trust will only work if your survivors, recognizing your intentions, do as you wish. You are dependent, with or without the trust, on their goodwill.

Reprinted courtesy of the National Resource Center for Consumers of Legal Services.

WORKPLACE LAW

Federal Discrimination Laws and the Equal Employment Opportunity Commission (EEOC)

The U.S. Equal Employment Opportunity Commission was created by Congress and enforces Title VII of the Civil Rights Act of 1964, which prohibits employment discrimination based on race, color, religion, sex, or national origin.

The EEOC also enforces the Americans with Disabilities Act of 1990, the Equal Pay Act of 1963, and the Age Discrimination in Employment Act of 1967. EEOC is also responsible for enforcing any subsequent changes to the above statutes.

Title VII of the Civil Rights Act

Employment discrimination based on race, color, religion, sex, or national origin is prohibited by Title VII of the Civil Rights Act of 1964.

Title VII covers private employers, state and local governments, and educational institutions that have 15 or more employees. The federal government, private and public employment agencies, labor organizations, and joint labor-management committees for apprenticeship and training also must abide by the law.

It is illegal under Title VII to discriminate in:

♦ Hiring and firing;

♦ Compensation, assignment, or classification of employees;

♦ Transfer, promotion, layoff, or recall;

♦ Job advertisements;

♦ Recruitment;

♦ Testing;

♦ Use of company facilities;

♦ Training and apprenticeship programs;

♦ Fringe benefits;

♦ Pay, retirement plans, and disability leave; or

♦ Other terms and conditions of employment.

Under the law, pregnancy, childbirth, and related medical conditions must be treated the same as any other non-pregnancy-related illness or disability.

Title VII prohibits retaliation against a person who files a charge of discrimination, participates in an investigation, or opposes an unlawful employment practice.

Employment agencies may not discriminate in receiving, classifying, or referring applications for employment or in their job advertisements.

Labor unions may not discriminate in: accepting applications for membership; classifying members; referrals; training and apprenticeship programs; and in advertising for jobs. It is illegal for a labor union to cause or try to cause an employer to discriminate. It is also illegal for an employer to cause or try to cause a union to discriminate.

The Immigration Reform and Control Act of 1986 requires employers to be able to prove that all employees hired after November 6, 1986, are legally authorized to work in the United States. However, an employer who requests employment verification only from individuals of a particular national origin, or individuals who appear to be or sound foreign, may have violated both the Immigration Act and Title VII.

Citizenship requirements, preferences, or rules requiring employees to be fluent in English or speak only English at work may be unlawful if they disproportionately exclude individuals of a particular national origin and are not justified by business necessity.

The Americans with Disabilities Act (ADA)

Title I of the Americans with Disabilities Act of 1990 prohibits private employers and state and local governments with 25 or more employees (15 or more after July 26, 1994), employment agencies, and labor unions from discriminating against qualified individuals with disabilities in job application procedures, hiring, firing, advancement, compensation, fringe benefits, job training, and other terms, conditions, and privileges of employment. The ADA does not cover the executive branch of the federal government. The executive branch continues to be covered by Title V of the Rehabilitation Act of 1973, which prohibits discrimination in services and employment on the basis of handicap and which is a model for the requirements of the ADA. The ADA, however, does cover Congress and other entities in the legislative branch of the federal government.

An individual with a disability is a person who:
♦ Has a physical or mental impairment that substantially limits one or more major life activities;
♦ Has a record of such an impairment; or
♦ Is regarded as having such an impairment.

A qualified employee or applicant with a disability is an individual who satisfies skill, experience, education, and other job-related requirements of the position held or desired, and who, with or without reasonable accommodation, can perform the essential functions of that position.

Reasonable accommodation may include, but is not limited to:
♦ Making existing facilities used by employees readily accessible to and usable by persons with disabilities;
♦ Job restructuring, modification of work schedules, reassignment to a vacant position; or
♦ Acquiring or modifying equipment or devices; adjusting or modifying examinations, training materials, or policies; and providing qualified readers or interpreters.

An employer is required to make a reasonable accommodation in order to provide an equal employment opportunity to a qualified applicant or employee with a disability, unless this would impose "undue hardship" on the operation of the employer's business. Undue hardship is defined as an action requiring significant difficulty or expense when considered in light of factors such as a business's size, financial resources, and the nature and structure of its operation.

An employer is not required to lower quality or production standards to make an accommodation. Nor is an employer generally obligated to provide personal use items such as eyeglasses or hearing aids.

Before a job offer is made, employers may not ask job applicants about the existence, nature, or severity of a disability. Applicants may be asked about their ability to perform specific job functions. A job offer may be conditioned on the results of a medical examination, but only if the examination is required for all entering employees in the same job category. Medical examinations of current employees must be job-related and consistent with the employer's business needs.

Employees and applicants currently engaged in the illegal use of drugs are not covered by the ADA, and an employer may act on the basis of such use. Tests for illegal use of drugs are not subject to the ADA's restrictions on medical examinations. Employers may hold individuals who are illegally using drugs, and alcoholics, to the same performance standards as other employees.

Equal Pay Act (EPA)

The Equal Pay Act prohibits employers from discriminating between men and women on the basis of sex in the payment of wages where they perform substantially equal work under similar working conditions in the same establishment. The law also prohibits employers from reducing the wages of either sex to comply with the law.

A violation may exist where a different wage is paid to a predecessor or successor employee of the opposite sex. Labor organizations may not cause employers to violate the law.

Retaliation against a person who files a charge of equal pay discrimination, participates in an investigation, or opposes an unlawful employment practice also is illegal.

The law protects virtually all private employees, including executive, administrative, professional, and outside sales employees who are exempt from minimum wage and overtime laws. Most federal, state, and local government workers also are covered.

The law does not apply to pay differences based on factors other than sex, such as seniority, merit, or systems that determine wages based upon the quantity or quality of items produced or processed.

Many EPA violations may be violations of Title VII of the Civil Rights Act of 1964, which also prohibits sex-based wage discrimination. Such charges may be filed under both statutes.

Age Discrimination in Employment Act (ADEA)

Persons 40 years of age or older are protected by the Age Discrimination in Employment Act of 1967. The law prohibits age discrimination in hiring, discharge, pay, promotions, and other terms and conditions of employment.

Retaliation against a person who files a charge of age discrimination, participates in an investigation, or opposes an unlawful practice also is illegal.

The law applies to private employers of 20 or more workers, federal, state, and local governments, employment agencies and labor organizations with 25 or more members. Labor organizations that operate a hiring hall or office that recruits potential employees or obtains job opportunities also must abide by the law.

It shall be unlawful to cease or reduce the rate of pension benefit accruals or allocations because of age for employees who have at least one hour of service in pension plan years beginning on or after January 1, 1988. Limitations on the amount of benefits, years of service, or years of participation may be permissible, if the limits are imposed without regard to age.

The Older Workers Benefit Protection Act (OWBPA) was enacted on October 16, 1990, effective generally on April 15, 1991. There are delayed effective dates for certain collectively bargained plans and certain state and local government employers. OWBPA makes clear that employee benefits and benefit plans are subject to the ADEA. The Act codifies EEOC regulations addressing employee benefits and states that the employer has the burden of proving the lawfulness of certain benefits-related actions. New provisions were enacted affecting early retirement incentive plans and permitting certain offsets against severance payment and long-term disability. Title II of OWBPA sets out minimum criteria that must be satisfied before a waiver of any ADEA right or claim will be considered a "knowing and voluntary" waiver.

State and local governments may make age-based hiring and retirement decisions for firefighters and law enforcement officers if the particular age limitation was in effect on March 3, 1983, and the action taken is pursuant to a bona fide hiring or retirement plan that is not a subterfuge to evade the purposes of the Act. The section in question was scheduled to expire on December 31, 1993.

Institutions of higher education may involuntarily retire an employee at age 70 who is serving under a contract of unlimited tenure or a similar arrangement. The section in question is scheduled to expire on December 31, 1993.

The ADEA does not prohibit the compulsory retirement of certain bona fide executives or high policymaking personnel as discussed in section 12(c)(1) of the Act.

How to File a Charge

If you believe that you have been discriminated against by an employer, labor union, or employment agency when applying for a job or while on the job because of race, color, sex, religion, national origin, age, or disability, you may file a charge of discrimination with the U.S. Equal Employment Opportunity Commission. Charges may be filed in person, by mail, or by telephone by contacting the nearest EEOC office. If there is not an EEOC office in the immediate area, call toll-free 800-669-4000 or 800-800-3302 (TTY) for more information. To avoid delay, call or write beforehand if you need special assistance, such as an interpreter, to file a charge.

There are strict time frames in which charges of employment discrimination must be filed. To preserve the ability of EEOC to act on your behalf and to protect your right to file a private lawsuit, adhere to the following guidelines when filing a charge.

Title VII charges must be filed with EEOC within 180 days of the alleged discriminatory act. In states or localities where there is an antidiscrimination law and an agency authorized to grant or seek relief, a charge must be presented to that state or local agency. In such jurisdictions, you may file charges with EEOC within 300 days of the discriminatory act, or 30 days after receiving notice that the state or local agency has terminated its processing of the charge, whichever is earlier. It is best to contact EEOC promptly when discrimination is suspected. When charges or complaints are filed beyond these time frames, the private right of action may be unavailable.

EEOC may file a lawsuit if it finds reasonable cause to believe that discrimination occurred and conciliation efforts fail. An individual may file a private suit within 90 days of receiving a notice of right-to-sue from EEOC.

Americans with Disabilities Act (ADA) enforcement procedures and time line requirements are the same as those for Title VII charges.

Age Discrimination in Employment Act (ADEA) charges may be filed by or on behalf of an aggrieved person. If a charge is filed on behalf of another, the aggrieved individual's identity may be kept confidential. Individuals who are aware of practices that may involve age discrimination, but who do not wish to file a charge, may bring the matter to the EEOC's attention by filing a complaint. If a complaint is filed, the identity of the complainant ordinarily will not be disclosed without prior written consent. A complaint does not preserve the right to file a private suit. However, if a charge is filed, the charging party's name will be given to the employer.

ADEA charges must be filed with EEOC within 180 days of the alleged discriminatory act. In states where there is a law prohibiting age discrimination in employment or authorizing a state agency to grant or seek relief, a proceeding must be commenced with the state agency as a prerequisite to private suit. In such jurisdictions, a charge may be filed with EEOC within 300 days of the discriminatory act, or 30 days after receiving notice that the state terminated its processing of the charge, whichever is earlier. When charges or complaints are filed beyond these time frames, the private right of action may be unavailable.

Persons who file timely charges of age discrimination, or who are the beneficiaries of timely filed charges, may file suit against the respondent named in the charge within 90 days of receipt of notice that the Commission has dismissed or otherwise terminated proceedings. EEOC is also empowered to file suit to remedy violations of the Act.

Equal Pay Act (EPA). Individuals are not required to file an EPA charge with EEOC before filing a private lawsuit. However, some cases of wage discrimination also may be violations of Title VII. Charges may be filed concurrently under both laws. If an EPA charge is filed with EEOC, the procedure for filing is the same as for charges brought under Title VII.

An EPA lawsuit must be filed within two years (or three years for willful violations) of the discriminatory act, which in most cases will be a payment of a discriminatorily lower wage. Filing a charge with the EEOC will not stop the running of the two-year (or three-year) period for filing a lawsuit.

If a complaint is filed under EPA, the identity of the complainant will not be disclosed. However, if a charge is filed under both Title VII and EPA, the charging party's name will be given to the employer.

If EEOC finds reasonable cause to believe that discrimination occurred and conciliation efforts fail, EEOC may file a lawsuit on behalf of the victim in federal district court. Should EEOC take action first, a private lawsuit may not be filed.

General Procedures

1. EEOC interviews the potential charging party to obtain as much information as possible about the alleged discrimination. If all legal jurisdictional requirements are met, a charge is properly drafted and the investigative procedure is explained to the charging party.

2. EEOC notifies the employer about the charge. In investigating the charge to determine if discrimination occurred, EEOC requests information from the employer that addresses the issues directly affecting the charging party as well as other potentially aggrieved persons. Any witnesses who have direct knowledge of the alleged discriminatory act will be interviewed. If the evidence shows there is no reasonable cause to believe discrimination occurred, the charging party and the employer will be notified. The charging party may exercise the right to bring private court action.

3. If the evidence shows there is reasonable cause to believe discrimination occurred, EEOC conciliates or attempts to persuade the employer

to voluntarily eliminate and remedy the discrimination, following the standards of EEOC's Policy on Remedies and Relief for Individual Cases of Unlawful Discrimination. Remedies may include reinstatement of an aggrieved person to the job he or she would have had but for the discrimination, back pay, restoration of lost benefits, and damages to compensate for actual monetary loss. Limited monetary damages may also be available to compensate for future monetary loss, mental anguish, or pain and suffering, and to penalize a respondent who acted with malice or reckless indifference. The employer may also be required to post a notice in the workplace advising employees that it has complied with orders to remedy the discrimination.

4. EEOC considers the case for litigation if conciliation fails. If litigation is approved by the Commission, EEOC will file a lawsuit in federal district court on behalf of the charging party(ies). Charging parties may initiate private civil action on their own in lieu of EEOC litigation.

State and Local Fair Employment Practice Agencies (FEPAs)

Under Title VII and ADA, EEOC must defer charges of discrimination to state or local Fair Employment Practice Agencies. The charge may be processed initially by either EEOC or the state or local agency, where a work-sharing agreement so specifies.

Litigation

Most charges are conciliated or settled, making a court trial unnecessary. EEOC's Statement of Enforcement Policy commits the agency to consider for litigation each case in which reasonable cause has been found and conciliation has failed. If EEOC decides not to litigate a case, a notice of right to sue is issued, permitting the charging party to take the case to court if he or she chooses.

Relief

The Commission's policy is to seek full and effective relief for each and every victim of employment discrimination, whether it is sought in court or in conciliation agreements reached before litigation.

In general, relief that may be sought includes:

♦ Back pay (all);

♦ Hiring, promotion, reinstatement, benefit restoration, front pay, and other affirmative relief (Title VII, ADA, ADEA);

♦ Actual pecuniary loss other than back pay (Title VII; ADA);

♦ Liquidated damages (ADEA, EPA);

♦ Compensatory damages for future monetary losses and mental anguish (Title VII, ADA);

♦ Punitive damages when employer acts with malice or reckless disregard for federally protected rights (Title VII, ADA);

♦ Posting a notice to all employees advising them of their rights under the laws EEOC en-

forces and their right to be free from retaliation (all);

♦ Corrective or preventive actions taken to cure the source of the identified discrimination and minimize the chance of its recurrence (all);

♦ Reasonable accommodation (ADA); or

♦ Stopping the specific discriminatory practices involved in the case (all).

The above information is intended as a general overview and does not carry the force of legal opinion.

Source: Equal Employment Opportunity Commission (EEOC)

Questions and Answers About Sexual Harassment

1. What is sexual harassment?

Sexual harassment is a form of sex discrimination which is a violation of Title VII of the Civil Rights Act of 1964. The U.S. Equal Employment Opportunity Commission's (EEOC's) guidelines define two types of sexual harassment: "quid pro quo" (Latin for "something given or received for something else") and "hostile environment."

2. What is "quid pro quo" sexual harassment?

Unwelcome sexual advances, requests for sexual favors, and other verbal or physical conduct of a sexual nature constitute "quid pro quo" sexual harassment when (1) submission to such conduct is made either explicitly or implicitly a term or condition of an individual's employment, or (2) submission to or rejection of such conduct by an individual is used as the basis for employment decisions affecting such individual.

3. What is "hostile-environment" sexual harassment?

Unwelcome sexual advances, requests for sexual favors, and other verbal or physical conduct of a sexual nature constitute "hostile-environment" sexual harassment when such conduct has the purpose or effect of unreasonably interfering with

GAY RIGHTS IN THE WORKPLACE

Contrary to popular belief, there is no federal law that expressly protects gays against discrimination in the workplace. Title VII of the federal Civil Rights Act of 1964, the most substantial antidiscrimination law that governs the workplace, protects workers against discrimination based on race, color, religion, sex, or national origin. It says nothing about sexual orientation. However, a number of states (including Wisconsin, Massachusetts, Hawaii, and Connecticut) have enacted laws that specifically prohibit employment discrimination due to sexual orientation, and more than a hundred municipalities in the U.S. have passed gay-rights laws. In addition, some major American corporations have rewritten their policy manuals to protect gay workers. Nonetheless, gay activists continue to press for passage of a federal gay-civil-rights bill.

an individual's work performance or creating an intimidating, hostile, or offensive working environment.

4. What factors determine whether an environment is "hostile"?

The central inquiry is whether the conduct "unreasonably interfered with an individual's work performance" or created "an intimidating, hostile, or offensive working environment." The EEOC will look at the following factors to determine whether an environment is hostile: (1) whether the conduct was verbal or physical or both; (2) how frequently it was repeated; (3) whether the conduct was hostile or patently offensive; (4) whether the alleged harasser was a co-worker or supervisor; (5) whether others joined in perpetrating the harassment; and (6) whether the harassment was directed at more than one individual. No one factor controls. An assessment is made based upon the totality of the circumstances.

5. What is unwelcome sexual conduct?

Sexual conduct becomes unlawful only when it is unwelcome. The challenged conduct must be unwelcome in the sense that the employee did not solicit or incite it, and in the sense that the employee regarded the conduct as undesirable or offensive.

6. How will the EEOC determine whether conduct is unwelcome?

When confronted with conflicting evidence as to whether conduct was welcome, the EEOC will look at the record as a whole and at the totality of the circumstances, evaluating each situation on a case-by-case basis. The investigation should determine whether the victim's conduct was consistent, or inconsistent, with his/her assertion that the sexual conduct was unwelcome.

7. Who can be a victim of sexual harassment?

The victim may be a woman or a man. The victim does not have to be of the opposite sex. The victim does not have to be the person harassed but could be anyone affected by the offensive conduct.

8. Who can be a sexual harasser?

The harasser may be a woman or a man. He or she can be the victim's supervisor, an agent of the employer, a supervisor in another area, a co-worker, or a non-employee.

9. Can one incident constitute sexual harassment?

It depends. In "quid pro quo" cases, a single sexual advance may constitute harassment if it is linked to the granting or denial of employment or employment benefits. In contrast, unless the conduct is quite severe, a single incident or isolated incidents of offensive sexual conduct or remarks generally do not create a "hostile environment." A hostile-environment claim usually requires a showing of a pattern of offensive conduct. However, a single, unusually severe incident of harassment may be sufficient to constitute a Title VII violation; the more severe the harassment, the less need to show a repetitive series of incidents. This is particularly true when the harassment is physical. For example, the EEOC will presume that the unwelcome, intentional touching of a charging party's intimate body areas is sufficiently offensive to alter the condition of his/her working environment and constitute a violation of Title VII.

10. Can verbal remarks constitute sexual harassment?

Yes. The EEOC will evaluate the totality of the circumstances to ascertain the nature, frequency, context, and intended target of the remarks. Relevant factors may include: (1) whether the remarks were hostile and derogatory; (2) whether the alleged harasser singled out the charging party; (3) whether the charging party participated in the exchange; and (4) the relationship between the charging party and the alleged harasser.

11. What should a sexual harassment victim do?

The victim should directly inform the harasser

that the conduct is unwelcome and must stop. It is important for the victim to communicate that the conduct is unwelcome, particularly when the alleged harasser may have some reason to believe that the advance may be welcomed. However, a victim of harassment need not always confront his/her harasser directly, so long as his/her conduct demonstrates that the harasser's behavior is unwelcome. The victim should also use any employer complaint mechanism or grievance system available. If these methods are ineffective, the victim should contact the EEOC as soon as possible.

12. How do I file a charge of discrimination?

Charges of sex discrimination may be filed at any field office of the U.S. Equal Employment Opportunity Commission. Field Offices are located in 50 cities throughout the United States and are listed in most local telephone directories under U.S. Government. To reach the nearest EEOC field office, dial toll free: 800-669-4000. More information on sexual harassment and information on all EEOC laws may be obtained by calling toll free: 800-669-3362.

13. What are the limits for filing a charge of discrimination?

A charge of discrimination on the basis of sex must be filed with EEOC within 180 days of the alleged discriminatory act, or within 300 days, if there is a state or local fair employment practices agency that enforces a law prohibiting the same alleged discriminatory practice. However, to protect legal rights, it is recommended that EEOC be contacted promptly when discrimination is believed to have occurred.

14. What types of evidence will the EEOC look at to determine whether sexual harassment has occurred?

When investigating allegations of sexual harassment, EEOC will look at the whole record: the circumstances, such as the nature of the sexual advances, and the context in which the alleged incidents occurred. The EEOC recog-

nizes that sexual conduct may be private and unacknowledged, with no eyewitnesses. Corroborative evidence of any nature will be explored.

EEOC also will investigate whether any complaints or protests occurred. However, while a complaint or protest is helpful to a charging party's case, it is not a necessary element of the claim. Victims may fear repercussions from complaining about the harassment and such fear may explain a delay in opposing the conduct. If the victim failed to complain or delayed in complaining, the investigation must ascertain why.

15. If I file a discrimination charge, what types of relief are available?

If you have been discriminated against on the basis of sex, you are entitled to a remedy that will place you in the position you would have been in if the discrimination had never occurred. You may also be entitled to hiring, promotion, reinstatement, back pay, and other remuneration. You may also be entitled to damages to compensate you for future pecuniary losses, mental anguish, and inconvenience. Punitive damages may be available, as well, if an employer acted with malice or reckless indifference. You may also be entitled to attorney's fees.

16. Can my employer retaliate against me for filing a charge with EEOC?

It is unlawful for an employer or other covered entity to retaliate against someone who files a charge of discrimination, participates in an investigation, or opposes discriminatory practices. Individuals who believe that they have been retaliated against should contact EEOC immediately. Even if an individual has already filed a charge of discrimination, he or she can file a new charge based on retaliation.

The above information is intended as a general overview of sexual harassment and does not carry the force of legal opinion.

Source: U.S. Equal Employment Opportunity Commission

Facts about Pregnancy Discrimination

The Pregnancy Discrimination Act is an amendment to Title VII of the Civil Rights Act of 1964. Discrimination on the basis of pregnancy, childbirth, or related medical conditions constitutes unlawful sex discrimination under Title VII. Women affected by pregnancy or related conditions must be treated in the same manner as other applicants or employees with similar abilities or limitations.

Hiring

An employer cannot refuse to hire a woman because of her pregnancy-related condition as long as she is able to perform the major functions of the job. An employer cannot refuse to hire her because of its prejudices against pregnant workers or the prejudices of co-workers, clients, or customers.

Pregnancy and Maternity Leave

An employer may not single out pregnancy-related conditions for special procedures to determine an employee's ability to work. However, an employer may use any procedure used to screen other employees' ability to work. For example, if an employer requires its employees to submit a doctor's statement concerning their inability to work before granting leave or paying sick benefits, the employer may require employees affected by pregnancy-related conditions to submit such statements.

If an employee is temporarily unable to perform her job due to pregnancy, the employer must treat her the same as any other temporarily disabled employee; for example, by providing modified tasks, alternative assignments, disability leave, or leave without pay.

Pregnant employees must be permitted to work as long as they are able to perform their jobs. If an employee has been absent from work

as a result of a pregnancy-related condition and recovers, her employer may not require her to remain on leave until the baby's birth. An employer may not have a rule which prohibits an employee from returning to work for a predetermined length of time after childbirth.

Employers must hold open a job for a pregnancy-related absence the same length of time jobs are held open for employees on sick or disability leave.

Health Insurance

Any health insurance provided by an employer must cover expenses for pregnancy-related conditions on the same basis as costs for other medical conditions. Health insurance for expenses arising from abortion is not required, except where the life of the mother is endangered.

Pregnancy-related expenses should be reimbursed exactly as those incurred for other medical conditions, whether payment is on a fixed basis or a percentage of reasonable and customary charge basis. The amounts payable by the insurance provider can be limited only to the same extent as costs for other conditions. No additional, increased, or larger deductible can be imposed.

If a health insurance plan excludes benefit payments for preexisting conditions when the insured's coverage becomes effective, benefits can be denied for medical costs arising from an existing pregnancy. Employers must provide the same level of health benefits for spouses of male employees as they do for spouses of female employees.

Fringe Benefits

Pregnancy-related benefits cannot be limited to married employees. In an all-female work force or job classification, benefits must be provided for pregnancy-related conditions if benefits are provided for other medical conditions. If an employer provides any benefits to workers on leave, the employer must provide the same benefits for those on leave for pregnancy-related conditions. Employees with pregnancy-related disabilities must be treated the same as other temporarily disabled employees for accrual and crediting of seniority, vacation calculation, pay increases, and temporary disability benefits.

Filing a Charge

Charges of sexual discrimination may be filed at any field office of the U.S. Equal Employment Opportunity Commission. Field offices are located in 50 cities throughout the United States and are listed in most local telephone directories under U.S. Government. Information on all EEOC-enforced laws may be obtained by calling toll free 800-669-3362. EEOC's toll free TTY number is 800-800-3302.

If you have been discriminated against on the basis of sex, you are entitled to a remedy that will place you in the position you would have been in if the discrimination had never occurred. You may be entitled to hiring, promotion, reinstatement, back pay, or other remuneration. You may also be entitled to damages to compensate you for future pecuniary losses, mental anguish, and inconvenience. Punitive damages may be available, as well, if an employer acted with malice or reckless indifference. You may also be entitled to attorney's fees.

The above information is intended as a general overview and does not carry the force of legal opinion.

Source: Equal Employment Opportunity Commission (EEOC)

Family Leave Bill

The Family Medical and Leave Act (FMLA) went into effect in 1993. It gives workers the right to take up to 12 weeks of unpaid leave from their jobs for the birth or adoption of a child or to care for a seriously ill child, spouse, or parent. In addition, workers can take the time to recover from their own serious illnesses. While the employee is on leave, he or she is entitled to full health coverage and when the employee returns to work, he or she is guaranteed the same job or an equivalent job. To be eligible for the unpaid leave, an employee must have spent at least 1250 hours on the job during a 12-month period.

While the federal law is a breakthrough step for families, it does have limitations. First of all, it only covers people who work for companies with 50 or more employees; 61 percent of American workers are employed by companies with fewer than 50 employees. Because the leave is unpaid, low-income workers, who would like to take advantage of the law, simply might not be able to afford the luxury. Here are a few other essential provisions of the law:

♦ Companies can require workers to use up vacation time, or other leave, before taking advantage of FMLA.

♦ Spouses who work for the same company can be limited to 12 weeks' total leave a year.

♦ Workers must provide employers with 30 days' notice in foreseeable cases like birth, adoption, or planned medical treatment.

Most European countries have family leave laws that put FMLA to shame. For example, parents in Sweden get 15 months of government-paid leave that can be split between them during the first eight years of their child's life; the pay is based on a percentage of salary with most of the days paid at 90 percent. In Finland, women get 35 weeks of leave at full pay; German women get 14 to 18 weeks at full pay; French women get 16 weeks at 90 percent pay. An Italian woman gets five months of leave at 80 percent of salary and another six months at 30 percent of salary.

If you are not eligible for FMLA, don't despair. At least 34 states have some kind of family-leave legislation on the books and some states do not exempt small businesses. So be sure to make inquiries about the rights afforded you by state law. Also, if your state law is more generous that FMLA, you get the more generous benefits.

Frequently Asked Questions About Workers' Rights in the Workplace

Your rights in the workplace are not determined by one uniform law. Instead, workplace law is defined by a combination of laws including federal and state laws, collective bargaining agreements, and policies written by independent employers. Thus, if you question a policy or action instituted by your employer, it is important to understand what law, or combination of laws, governs that policy or action. Then you can begin to figure out if your rights have been violated.

Below are some common questions that employees have regarding their rights on the job. Obviously, the answers to the questions are not ironclad since how the law applies to your situation depends on a number of circumstances including your job status or classification, whether you work in private industry or for a government entity, and the state in which you live. In addition, workplace law is constantly evolving—new laws are written, old laws are struck down, and the court systems add new interpretations to existing laws.

1. Do I have a right to see my personnel file?

Most workers employed by the federal government have this right, given to them by the 1974 Privacy Act. Also, if you are working under a union contract, chances are you have access to your personnel file. Most workers in the private sector are governed by the laws of their state. At least 17 states have passed laws that allow workers access to their files but there can be restrictions on what you are permitted to see. In some states the only way you can obtain your file is in the event that you file a lawsuit against an employer or former employer. Usually a request to see your file must be made in writing. For specific details on the law as it pertains to your personnel file, call or write your State Department of Labor.

2. What kind of tests can my employer make me take?

♦ *Polygraph tests (lie detector tests).* A 1988 federal law virtually wiped out the use of these tests. They can, however, be required in some instances—e.g., jobs that relate to company security or national security. Also, the test may be allowed if you are a suspect in an employment-related crime. In addition, the federal law does not cover government workers—federal, state, or local government.

♦ *Drug tests/medical tests.* More and more companies are testing new job applicants for the use of illegal drugs. Asking you to take such a test (usually urinalysis) is legal, and if you refuse, the employer may not consider you for the job. When it comes to drug testing for existing employees, there are more legal constraints. In general, companies in the private sector cannot randomly subject all employees to drug testing without having a very good reason for doing so. However, companies may ask an employee to take a test if there is evidence that drug abuse is affecting job performance, especially if that job performance could cause bodily harm or property damage. Periodic random testing does legally take place in some companies that are linked to the federal government. For example, airline pilots can be asked to take drug tests that are mandated by the U.S. Department of Transportation.

Mandatory medical exams and company medical questionnaires have taken on a whole new look since passage of the Americans with Disabilities Act (ADA), a federal law that gives new rights to both disabled and nondisabled workers who are hired by companies that employ 15 or more people. ADA makes it illegal to ask questions about the disability or medical history of any job applicant. Thus, medical questionnaires and checklists are no longer permitted in the workplace. In addition, an employer may not ask or require a job applicant to take a medical examination before making a job offer. An employer may, however, ask questions about an applicant's ability to perform specific job functions, and may, with certain limitations, ask an individual with a disability to describe or demonstrate how he/she would perform these functions.

According to the Equal Employment Opportunity Commission: "An employer may condition a job offer on the satisfactory result of a post-offer medical examination or medical inquiry *if* this is required of all entering employees in the same job category. A post-offer examination or inquiry does not have to be job-related and consistent with business necessity. However, if an individual is not hired because a post-offer medical examination or inquiry reveals a disability, the reason(s) for not hiring must be job-related and consistent with business necessity. The employer also must show that no reasonable accommodation was available that would enable the individual to perform the essential job functions, or that accommodation would impose an undue hardship."

♦ *Psychological tests.* Since lie detector tests have, for the most part, been banned from the workplace, many employers use a variety of other tests to learn about an applicant's honesty, flexibility, adaptability, and a number of other intangible factors. These psychological tests can be called by a variety of names including "aptitude tests" and "integrity tests." Employers are within their legal rights to ask prospective new hires to take these tests, and if you refuse, you may not be considered for employment. Most of the tests are written tests and all results are kept confidential.

3. Can an employer run a credit check on me?

Yes. A current or prospective employer can get complete financial information on you by contacting one or more national credit bureaus that compile this information. What the employer learns may influence a decision to hire or promote you. However, a federal law, the Fair Credit Reporting Act, does give you certain rights. If you lose a job or promotion because of a credit check, the employer must tell you so and give you the name of the credit bureau that issued the report. Once you obtain the report, you have the right to correct any mistakes that are in it. If

there is a dispute over correcting certain information and the credit bureau will not change that information, you still have the right to write up your own version of the dispute and have it placed in your credit file. Obviously, it's in your best interests that your credit report be accurate (see "Credit Bureaus and Your Credit Report," p. 389). Pending legislation in Congress would require employers to get your written consent before obtaining your credit record.

4. Can my employer force me to abide by a dress code?

Yes, but within certain limits. In general, employers can have a dress code, provided it doesn't discriminate against a particular group of employees or potential employees. For instance, if men in a company are allowed to wear casual clothing but women are not, the dress code may be illegal.

5. What can I do about unsafe conditions at my job?

First of all, you should point out any dangerous conditions to your employer and give the employer a fair chance to correct them. If a hazardous situation is not corrected, you can file a complaint with a federal agency, the Occupational Safety and Health Administration (OSHA). OSHA enforces the Occupational Safety and Health Act which covers almost all private employers in the United States; the federal law requires employers to maintain a safe and healthful workplace.

You can get a complaint form by contacting the nearest OSHA office. You can request that your identity be kept confidential. It is illegal for an employer to fire you or take any discriminatory action against you because you have filed a complaint or have cooperated with OSHA in investigating a complaint. In addition to the federal law, there are many state and local laws that also guarantee employees a safe place to work.

6. Can an employer stop me from serving on a jury?

Most states have a law that specifically prohibits an employer from firing you for serving on a jury. In addition, most state laws add that an employee cannot be "otherwise punished" for jury duty. That usually means that an employer can't dock your vacation time or reduce your sick days. Several states even require employers to pay employees for the time missed at work, but jury-duty pay may be deducted from an employee's paycheck. In the great majority of states, it's up to the employer to decide whether or not you get paid while serving on a jury. If you are unclear about your rights, ask your employer, or when you get a summons, call the clerk at the court in which you are to serve.

7. Does my boss have to pay me for overtime hours?

A federal law, the Fair Labor Standards Act (FLSA), sets out the rules for overtime pay: An employee who works more than 40 hours a week must receive overtime pay for all time over 40 hours; the overtime rate must be at least one and a half times the regular pay rate. However, there are quite a few jobs that are not covered by FLSA. Most prominent among them are "executive, administrative, and professional employees." Considered "white-collar" employees, these exempted people are thought to earn ample salaries and thus don't need to be covered by federal overtime laws. For more information about whether you qualify for overtime pay, contact your local office of the Wage and Hour Division of the United States Department of Labor; look in the phone book under the federal government listings.

The FLSA also covers areas such as federal minimum wage and child labor laws. The law, however, is very complex, full of exceptions, and is constantly changing. In addition, you may have additional rights under state laws. For example, your state may have a higher hourly minimum wage than the minimum wage established by the federal government. In that case, you will be paid according to the higher state standard. If you want a detailed explanation of FLSA, you can get a free pamphlet, "Handy Reference Guide to the Fair Labor Standards Act" by calling the nearest office of the Wage and Hour Division of the United States Department of Labor.

8. If I quit my job, can I collect unemployment insurance?

Yes, but only if you quit with "good cause." The reasons that qualify for "good cause" vary from state to state. In general, most acceptable good-cause reasons relate to actions of the employer. Perhaps you quit because working conditions were so unsafe that your health, or your life, were in danger. Or, you were forced to do work very different from the job you were originally hired to do. Maybe you were a victim of sexual harassment and your employer would not take action to correct the problem. In some cases, your own personal reasons can constitute "good cause." For example, if your spouse gets a new job in another state and you have to move, you might be able to quit your job and get unemployment insurance. Be aware, however, that "good cause" means different things to different people, and your employer may disagree with you and challenge your claim. And, even if your claim is likely to hold up, you still must meet other federal/state eligibility requirements to collect benefits. Call your local unemployment insurance office for further details on eligibility; the phone number will be in the state government listings of your telephone directory. The office probably will not be called an "unemployment" office. In an effort to be more positive and user-friendly, most claims offices go by another name like "Employment Development Department" or "State Employment Service."

ESTATE PLANNING

Wills

Approximately 70 percent of us don't have a will. The reasons why are pretty basic. First of all, we don't want to confront the reality that we will die one day. In addition, making a will seems like we are putting price tags on our relationships, since wills specifically spell out who gets our assets when we pass on. However, if you die intestate (that is, without a will), your state government will decide how to divide up your property. The government will appoint an administrator for your estate and that person will, according to your state laws, determine who gets what. In general, spouses and children are the primary beneficiaries, and if there is no spouse and/or children, the estate passes to other blood relatives—again, according to a formula of succession designed by your state government.

Regardless of the size of your estate, if you care about how your hard-earned money and other assets will eventually get distributed, you need a will. Also, another very important reason for having a will is to stipulate who will get guardianship of your minor children in the event of your death. The court doesn't have to follow your guardianship mandate (children aren't property), but it usually does. When families are intact and one parent dies, the surviving parent almost always gets custody of the child. The guardianship issue gets much more complex when di-

vorces and remarriages are involved. Also, while it is improbable that you and your spouse will die in a common accident, you need to consider the possibility and name a guardian in your will.

Making a Will

1. In general, you have to be of "sound mind" and at least 18 years of age to make a will. Husbands and wives should have separate wills.

2. Who should draw up your will? It's best to have legal advice. You can draft your own will, but a single technical mistake could invalidate the entire document. In addition, verbal wills are hardly ever recognized; holographic wills, those done in your own handwriting, are acceptable in some states but are usually not as ironclad as a formally executed will. A simple will done by an attorney or legal clinic (using standardized formats) can cost as little as $100. If your situation is complex and your estate is sizable, you need an attorney who specializes in estate planning and who understands all of the federal and state tax laws that will apply to your estate.

3. When you are ready to make your will, there are three major issues to be addressed. *First*, how do you want your property to be distributed? *Second*, who are you going to name as the executor of your will? The executor is the person who, upon your death, will take charge of the estate and carry out your wishes. It's a big

job so you need someone you trust and that person need not be a financial genius; most people name a spouse or other major beneficiary as executor. *Third,* if you have minor children, you need to name a guardian. Obviously, you should ask your chosen executor and chosen guardian if they agree to the roles you have assigned to them.

4. Before your will is ready for your signature, be sure you have compiled an exhaustive inventory of your assets. Gather together bank statements, investment papers, real estate papers, tax records, and any other relevant financial records that your lawyer will need to see.

5. While you do have considerable control over the distribution of your estate and can disinherit just about anyone (including your children), you cannot leave your spouse penniless. Surviving spouses almost always are entitled to a portion of the estate, regardless of what you say in your will.

6. Depending on how you hold title to your assets, some of them will pass on to your survivors outside the realm of your will. For example, if you and your spouse own your home in joint tenancy (with a right of survivorship), your share of the house automatically goes to your spouse. If you leave your share of the house to your brother in your will, he will not get it. In other words, your prior contractual arrangement wins out over your will. Another example of an asset that is not affected by your will is a life insurance policy. The designated beneficiary of your policy gets the money. If you want to change the beneficiary, call your insurance company; a change of heart made in your will has no legal bearing.

Signing/Storing/Changing a Will

1. Your will must be witnessed, usually by two or three people, when you sign it. These witnesses must also sign your will. It's advised that the witnesses not be beneficiaries; they should be impartial (they have no financial interest in your estate). Self-written and self-executed wills run the risk of being improperly witnessed

and therefore can later be declared invalid. If you are a do-it-yourself will maker, be sure you are following correct witnessing procedures.

2. Your safe-deposit box may be the worst place to store your will, depending on the laws in your state. In some states a safe-deposit box is sealed when a person dies and it takes a court order to get it opened. Call the institution where you have a safe-deposit box and ask what your state laws are before you deposit the will in the box.

3. You can change your will at any time either by drawing up an entirely new will or by adding a codicil (a supplement to the will that alters its original provisions). In order for codicils to be legal, they must be executed and witnessed in an appropriate manner. Don't try crossing out things in your will or writing in corrections; those kind of changes could make the entire will invalid.

4. It's a good idea to review your will periodically, at least every three years or so. However, you should always review it when there is a major change in your life: when you get married or divorced; when you become a parent; when your spouse dies; when one of your beneficiaries dies; when you inherit or purchase new property; when your assets substantially increase or decrease; when you move to another state; when your named executor is unable or unwilling to serve; when a change in federal or state tax laws affects the provisions of your will.

Revocable Living Trusts

A trust is a legal instrument that manages and disposes of property. You can set up a living trust (one that is in effect while you are alive) or a testamentary trust (one that is created by your will and takes effect when you die). In addition, trusts can be revocable (you can cancel it) or irrevocable (you can't cancel it). While a trust is not a substitute for a will, in actuality, it does perform many of the same functions, especially in terms of bequeathing your property when you die. There are a wide variety of trusts including charitable trusts, tax-saving trusts, trusts for the management of property. A discussion of the complexities of the various types of trusts is beyond the scope of this book. However, there is one trust that deserves special attention because it has taken center stage in the arena of estate planning—revocable living trusts.

Like a will, a revocable living trust is a legal document that allows you to determine how you want your estate to be disposed of when you die. You as the "grantor" (or settlor) establish the trust and transfer ownership of your property into the trust. The person who controls the management and disposition of assets of the trust is called the "trustee." Most grantors name themselves as trustees so they can control all the assets of the estate while still alive; a back-up trustee or successor trustee is named to take over when you die. Like the "executor" named in a will, your successor trustee will follow the trust's instructions for distribution of the estate when you die. A trust is not a trust until you put property into it. Thus, you have to change the title on your home and alter other ownership documents so that your property is no longer owned by Jane Doe but by "Jane Doe, the trustee of the Jane Doe Trust" (assuming, of course, that you are both the grantor and the trustee). While your property is in the trust, you can do whatever you want with it—sell it, spend it, or give it away. You conduct business as usual, including filing your income tax returns. Because the trust is revocable, you can change it or cancel it at any time.

Why would you consider setting up a revocable living trust? The first word uttered by any proponent of these trusts is "probate." A will must go through a probate court; a revocable living trust does not. Probate is the legal process by which your estate is settled; wills and probate go hand in hand. When you die, your will is submitted to a probate court. Once the will is declared valid, your executor carries out the provisions of the will. Your assets would be inventoried and assessed; debts and taxes are paid; your estate is

then distributed to the beneficiaries in your will. While probate is a relatively easy process to understand, it can be costly both in terms of time and money. Probating a will can be accomplished in months or in years. The time, as well as the cost, depends on the complexity of the will and the administrative duties that are involved. Even if you die intestate (without a will), your property (or at least some of it) is likely to be subject to the probate process.

Is the fear of probate a good enough reason to consider a revocable living trust? Not necessarily. Probate laws in most states have improved considerably; procedures have been simplified and most probate judges and clerks are used to dealing with inexperienced executors whose duty it is to settle the estate. In addition, some states don't even probate relatively small estates (the amount depends on where you live) or have designed alternative legal procedures to replace the probate process.

Proponents of revocable living trusts also point out that the trusts ensure a far greater degree of privacy than wills. A will becomes a matter of public record once it is probated. The trust agreement is usually not filed with a probate court and thus it does not become a public document. Thus, a revocable living trust can avoid probate and protect privacy. It can also provide that your successor trustee take over management of your affairs should you become physically or mentally incapacitated, without the need for guardianship or conservatorship proceedings. Finally, a living trust can continue long after you die. For example, you might be concerned that your children or other beneficiaries will squander lump-sum payouts from your estate. You can direct your successor trustee to limit the payments according to your wishes until the beneficiaries reach a certain age.

Despite the advantages of a revocable living trust, they are overused and misused by people who really may not need them. Here are some items to consider:

1. A revocable living trust does not save money on income taxes or estate taxes. Your

successor trustee will have to file federal and state income taxes. Regarding federal estate taxes (called death taxes), federal law currently allows for a $600,000 exemption for every U.S. citizen; federal estate taxes are owed only if the estate is worth more than $600,000. Whether or not the estate is subject to estate taxes in your state depends on where you live.

2. There are other ways to avoid probate. For instance, jointly owned property (with a right of survivorship) passes to the surviving joint owner(s) outside of probate. Other contractual agreements, like a life insurance policy or pension proceeds (cases in which you have already legally designated a beneficiary), are probate-proof. These kinds of assets are considered nonprobate property even if you have a will. In addition, if you know that your estate is sizable enough to warrant a hit by estate taxes, you can always give some of your assets away while you are alive. At the present time, you can give away, free of gift taxes, up to $10,000 per year to whomever you wish; a married couple can give twice that amount.

3. Probate can't be avoided, even with a revocable living trust, if there is a lawsuit against you at the time you die or if you were subject to an income tax audit.

4. Setting up a trust can be costly (from $500 to $2000 or more) and may not be cost-effective for someone with a small estate, or someone who simply cannot afford the up-front costs. Those with smaller estates may be better off with a finely tuned will and a lawyer who understands the various ways of protecting property from the probate process. In general, it costs less to write a will than to write a living trust. However, the difference in the up-front costs can be offset later on when you die. The costs of probating a will can be far greater than the costs of administering a living trust.

5. Just as there are costs involved with probating a will, there are costs involved with administering a trust. You will be charged when you

alter, or completely redo, a trust. Also, when you die, the nonprobate assets of your trust still need to be managed and distributed. This may require the services of an attorney or appraiser in addition to the work performed by your successor trustee.

6. A living trust can be a good idea if you own real estate in more than one state. With a will, property in another state may have to go through a probate court in that state, a procedure called ancillary probate. A living trust, valid in all states, allows the beneficiaries quicker access to property without going through the multiple probate proceedings that a will might require.

7. If you have established a revocable living trust, you still need a will. First off, some property is simply difficult to put into a trust, like jewelry or furniture. Also, the will covers things you did not put into the trust, whether you did so deliberately or unintentionally. Finally, if you have minor children, you need to have a will in order to name a guardian.

8. Sometimes the transfer of property titles into a trust can cause problems. An insurance company may not want to insure a car that is owned by a trust, not an individual. Likewise, a lending institution may not want to refinance your home unless it's in your name, not the trust's name.

A revocable living trust may be an excellent estate-planning tool for you and it may resolve a lot of worries that you have about your estate. On the other hand, it's not a panacea for everyone. You need to understand exactly how the benefits of a revocable living trust fit into your personal financial picture. Since these trusts have become quite popular, there are plenty of books and lengthy magazine articles on them. In addition to reading up on trusts, you should also inquire about the probate process in your state. Once you have a layperson's understanding of the issues, get your questions ready and see an attorney. And talk to one who is experienced in estate planning.

Advance Medical Directives (Living Will and Health Care Proxy)

Medical technology has enabled physicians and hospitals to keep patients alive for extended periods of time even when patients are terminally ill. Many people abhor the thought of being institutionalized, hooked up to life-sustaining systems, and robbed of their dignity, when there is little or no hope of recovery. On the other hand, some people may want doctors and hospitals to try everything possible to prolong life even in very adverse circumstances.

A *living will* and a *health care proxy* (also called a *durable power of attorney for health care*) are two types of advance directives that allow you to specify the kind of medical care you want, or don't want, if you become incapacitated and unable to make decisions. Both are signed, legal documents that must be made while you are competent. Advance directives only go into effect when an individual is rendered incapable of communicating medical treatment preferences, and that decision is made by one or more attending physicians.

All states in the United States recognize advance medical directives but the laws vary. In the great majority of states there is a combination of laws that recognize living wills and health care proxies. In several states only health care proxies are recognized, while in several other states only living wills are recognized. State laws also differ when it comes to the restrictions placed on advance directives, such as whether or not a state will allow life support to be withdrawn from a pregnant patient. While no advance directive is an ironclad legal document, it usually goes a long way in providing "clear and convincing evidence" of your wishes.

Living Wills

Also called a "directive to physicians" or a "treatment directive," a living will specifies what kind of medical treatment you want to accept, or reject, if you become terminally ill and unable to communicate your desires. Treatments can include feeding tubes, artificial respiration, CPR (cardiopulmonary resuscitation), kidney dialysis, chemotherapy, drugs (including pain medication or antibiotics), and other medical procedures. It bears repeating that a living will is not only a device for choosing what treatments you do not want, but is also a device for choosing the treatments that you do want. Before you enact a living will, it's advised that you discuss the benefits and risks of specific treatments with your doctor. You can always change or cancel your living will.

A living will does have some limitations. In some states it is binding only if it is signed after you have been informed that you have a terminal condition. In some states, it applies only to the use of life support, not other health care conditions. In some states, the living will must be extremely specific, and if an error exists or an omission is made, the patient's wishes may not be carried out.

Health Care Proxy (or Durable Power of Attorney for Health Care)

A health care proxy, also called a "durable power of attorney for health care" or a "proxy designation," allows someone else to make health care decisions for you when you become incapacitated. In other words, you choose an individual (your "proxy") to act on your behalf to make medical and life-sustaining decisions. No one, however, can be forced to act as a proxy. Therefore, you must thoroughly discuss your concerns and wishes with the person you want to act as your proxy and be sure that the person is willing to accept the responsibility.

According to the nonprofit group, Choice in Dying, "A health care proxy is flexible and avoids the need to anticipate every medical crisis that may arise. In some states, if an individual fails to accurately predict potential medical crises in the living will, medical treatment wishes may not be carried out." In addition, the society notes, "The scope of the proxy's authority is generally broader than with a living will." Like a living will, you have the right to change or cancel your health care proxy.

Where to Get Help

Simply sitting down and writing out your wishes for medical care is not advisable. State laws concerning advance directives can be very specific and your document may not carry much legal weight. To get advice and information about your rights, talk to your family doctor or lawyer. Also, a federal law, the Patient Self-Determination Act of 1991, requires that medical institutions that receive Medicare or Medicaid funds (about 95 percent do) inform patients about advance directives. Thus, your local hospital should also be able to provide you with any information that you need.

Whether you want to have, or need to have, both a living will and a health care proxy depends on the state in which you live as well as your particular circumstances. Free, state-specific living-will and health-care proxy forms are available from Choice in Dying (CID), a nonprofit organization that is dedicated to protecting the rights and serving the needs of dying patients and their families. Every year CID sends out more than 250,000 copies of advance directives. The group also provides free legal counseling and assistance. Contact the group by writing or calling: **Choice in Dying,** 200 Varick Street, New York, NY 10014 (212-366-5540).

Once you have the proper documents, be sure to have them properly signed, witnessed and notarized—per the requirements of your state. In most cases you will not need the services of an attorney. When the documents are complete, give a copy to your proxy (if you have a proxy), your doctor, your lawyer, and any other relatives or friends who may one day need them. You might want to keep a card in your wallet that states that you have advance medical directives. Most important, keep the signed original documents in an easily accessible place and be sure that someone you trust knows where they are. Do *not* keep the original documents in a safe-deposit box. Periodically, you should review your advance directives, make changes if you wish and inform all appropriate parties of any changes.

Durable Power of Attorney

If you are concerned about what would happen to your financial and business affairs if you become incapacitated, you might consider a *durable power of attorney.* Like a regular power of attorney, this document gives another person legal permission to make decisions on your behalf. You, the "principal," give authority to another person, your "attorney in fact." What is the difference between a regular power of attorney and a durable power of attorney? The powers granted in a regular power of attorney end if you become incapacitated. With a durable power of attorney the powers granted remain in effect if you become incapacitated; that's why it's called "durable." If you die, the durable power of attorney is no longer effective.

If you have a durable power of attorney and become disabled or incompetent, your attorney in fact can sign checks, enter into contracts, file tax returns, buy and sell property, and conduct other financial transactions. On the other hand, if you become unable to handle your own affairs and have not provided for the orderly transfer of your financial decision making, your family may have to go to court, and the court will appoint someone to take over (perhaps not the person you would choose).

You should only have a durable power of attorney if you have complete trust in the person to whom you are granting power. Most people choose a spouse, a parent, or an adult child. Even then, you can put limits on the powers you turn over to an attorney in fact. Remember that you are usually granting sweeping financial authority, or as one estate lawyer says, you are "giving away signed blank checks." Theoretically, an attorney in fact could try to use his or her power before you become incapacitated, but usually there are safeguards to prevent that from happening. However, if you want to be sure that no one takes over for you until you are truly unable to fend for yourself, you can prepare a "springing" durable power of attorney. In this case, the legal power springs into effect *only* if you become incapacitated. You can stipulate in the document the conditions under which your incapacity or mental status will be determined.

If you are considering a durable power of attorney, see a lawyer. Laws that permit durable powers of attorney differ among states. When talking with a lawyer, you need to fully understand your options, the limitations (if any) that you want to place on your attorney in fact, and the legal consequences of your actions. Also, you can't force anyone to become an attorney in fact, so discuss the responsibilities with the person you choose. Even if you draw up a durable power of attorney, some institutions may not recognize it as legally binding. For example, some institutions may not abide by a document that's too old. Also, some institutions, especially banks, have their own legal forms and won't recognize any others. Before you do anything, call your bank, your broker, your insurance company and get the specifics on what they will accept. Finally, as long as you are mentally competent, you can revoke a durable power of attorney—at any time and for any reason.

16

FIRST AID
AND
DISASTER
PREPAREDNESS

FIRST AID

DISASTER PREPAREDNESS

FIRST AID

Guide to First-Aid Emergencies

The following first-aid information is excerpted from the *First Aid Book,* published by the U.S. Department of Labor. It is intended to give you an overview of first-aid practices and is not intended to replace the instruction you will get if you take a first-aid course in which you will learn first-aid procedures under the supervision of trained instructors. To find out about first-aid courses offered in your area, contact your local chapter of the American Red Cross. The authors are not responsible and assume no responsibility for any action undertaken by anyone utilizing the first-aid procedures that follow.

General Principles

No two situations requiring first aid are the same, and first aiders must be able to select and apply appropriate first-aid measures in different circumstances. However, the following procedures are generally applicable:

1. Take charge. Instruct someone to obtain medical help and others to assist as directed.
2. Secure the scene. Make area safe, if necessary.
3. Make a primary survey of the victim.
4. Care for life-threatening conditions.
5. Use a tourniquet only under extreme conditions as a last resort.
6. If several people have been injured, decide upon priorities in caring for each victim.
7. Make a secondary survey of victim.
8. Care for all injuries in order of need.
9. Keep the injured person lying down.
10. Loosen restrictive clothing when necessary.
11. Cover victim to keep him or her warm and dry.
12. Keep onlookers away from the victim.
13. When necessary, improvise first-aid materials using the most appropriate materials available.
14. Cover all wounds completely.
15. Prevent air from reaching burned surfaces as quickly as possible by using a suitable dressing.
16. Remove small, loose foreign objects from a wound by brushing away from the wound with a piece of sterile gauze.
17. Do not attempt to remove embedded objects.
18. Place a bandage compress and a cover bandage over an open fracture without undue pressure before applying splints.
19. Support and immobilize fractures and dislocations.
20. Except for lower jaw dislocations, leave the reduction of fractures or dislocations to a doctor.
21. Unless absolutely necessary, never move

a victim unless fractures have been immobilized.

22. Test a stretcher before use, and carefully place an injured person on the stretcher.

23. Carry the victim on a stretcher without any unnecessary rough movements.

Patient Assessment

Primary Survey

Several conditions are considered life-threatening, but three in particular require immediate action:

♦ respiratory arrest
♦ circulatory failure
♦ severe bleeding

Respiratory arrest and/or circulatory failure can set off a chain of events that will lead to death. Severe and uncontrolled bleeding can lead to an irreversible state of shock in which death is inevitable. Death may occur in a very few minutes if an attempt is not made to help the victim in these situations. Before caring for lesser injuries, the first aider should perform the primary survey and then perform the following procedures to correct any life-threatening conditions:

♦ A—Open the airway.
♦ B—Check breathing (restore if necessary)
♦ C—Check circulation (pulse) (CPR if necessary)
♦ Control bleeding

Establish unresponsiveness, position the victim, and to ensure adequate breathing, establish and maintain an open airway. If there are no signs of breathing, artificial ventilation must be given immediately.

If a victim experiences circulatory failure, a person *trained* in cardiopulmonary resuscitation (CPR) should check for a pulse, and if none is detected, start CPR at once.

Make a careful and thorough check for any severe bleeding. Control serious bleeding by using proper methods.

In making the primary survey, do not move the victim any more than is necessary to support life. Rough handling or any unnecessary movement might cause additional pain and aggravate serious injuries that have not yet been detected.

Secondary Survey

When the life-threatening conditions have been controlled, the secondary survey should begin. The secondary survey is a head-to-toe examination to check *carefully* for any additional unseen injuries that can cause serious complications. This is conducted by examining for the following:

1. *Neck:* Examine for neck injury—tenderness, deformity, medical identification necklace, etc. Spine fractures, especially in the neck area, may accompany head injuries. Gently feel and look for any abnormalities. If a spinal injury is suspected, stop the secondary survey until the head can be stabilized. Follow these same precautions for any suspected spinal injury.

2. *Head:* Without moving the head, check for blood in the hair, scalp lacerations, and contusions. Gently feel for possible bone fragments or depressions in the skull. Loss of fluid or bleeding from the ears and nose is an indication of possible skull fracture.

3. *Chest:* Check the chest for cuts, impaled objects, fractures, and penetrating (sucking) wounds by observing chest movement. When the sides are not rising together or one side is not moving at all, there may be lung and rib damage.

4. *Abdomen.* Gently feel the abdominal area for cuts, penetrations, and impaled objects, observing for spasms and tenderness.

5. *Lower back.* Feel for deformity and tenderness.

6. *Pelvis.* Check for grating, tenderness, bony protrusions, and depressions in the pelvic area.

7. *Genital region.* Check for any obvious injury.

8. *Lower extremities.* Check for discoloration, swelling, tenderness, and deformities which are sometimes present with fractures and dislocations. Paralysis in the legs indicates a fractured back.

9. *Upper extremities.* Check for discoloration, swelling, tenderness, and deformities which are sometimes present with fractures and dislocations. Paralysis in the arms and legs indicates a fractured neck. Check for a medical identification bracelet.

10. *Back surfaces.* Injuries underneath the vic-

tim are often overlooked. Examine for bony protrusions, bleeding, and obvious injuries.

Artificial Ventilation

Principles

Artificial ventilation is the process for causing air flow into and from the lungs when natural breathing has ceased or when it is very irregular or inadequate.

When breathing has ceased, the body's oxygen supply is cut off and the brain cells start to die within four to six minutes. This process may result in irreversible brain damage, and if breathing is not restored, death will occur. In some cases the heart may continue to beat and circulate blood for a short period after a person stops breathing. If artificial ventilation is started within a short time after respiratory arrest, the victim has a good chance for survival.

Certain general principles must always be kept in mind when administering artificial ventilation by any method:

♦ Time is of prime importance; every second counts.

♦ Do not take time to move the victim unless the accident site is hazardous.

♦ Do not delay ventilation to loosen the victim's clothing or warm the victim. These are secondary in importance to getting air into the victim's lungs.

♦ Perform head-tilt/chin-lift method for opening airway, which will bring the tongue forward.

♦ Remove any visible foreign objects from the mouth.

♦ An assistant should loosen any tight-fitting clothing in order to promote circulation and go or send for help.

♦ Use a blanket, clothing, or other material to keep the victim warm and dry.

♦ Maintain a steady, constant rhythm while giving artificial ventilation. Be sure to look for rise and fall of the chest; and look, listen, and feel for return air. If there is none, look for upper airway obstruction.

♦ Continue artificial ventilation until one of the following occurs: 1) Spontaneous breathing resumes; 2) You are relieved by a qualified person; 3) A doctor pronounces the victim dead; 4) You are exhausted and physically unable to continue.

♦ Do not fight the victim's attempts to breathe.

♦ Once the victim recovers, constantly monitor the victim's condition, because breathing may stop again.

♦ Keep the victim lying down.

♦ Treat the victim for physical shock.

Performing Artificial Ventilation (Mouth-to-Mouth)

The first thing to do when finding an unconscious person is to establish unresponsiveness by tapping on the shoulder and asking, "Are you OK?" Place the victim on his or her back. Open the airway by using the head-tilt/chin-lift method. Remove any visible foreign objects from the mouth. To assess the presence or absence of spontaneous breathing in a victim, the rescuer should place his or her ear near the victim's mouth and nose while maintaining the open airway position. Look toward the victim's body and while observing the victim's chest:

♦ LOOK for the chest to rise and fall,

♦ LISTEN for air escaping during exhalation, and

♦ FEEL for the flow of air.

If the chest does not rise and fall and no air is heard or felt, the victim is not breathing. This assessment should take only three to five seconds. If it is determined that the victim is not breathing, begin artificial ventilation.

The method of artificial ventilation being taught for use on a victim of respiratory arrest is mouth-to-mouth ventilation. Mouth-to-mouth ventilation is by far the most effective means of artificial ventilation.

1. Open the airway. The most common cause of airway obstruction in an unconscious victim is the tongue. The tongue is attached to the lower jaw; moving the jaw forward lifts the tongue away from the back of the throat and opens the airway.

♦ Kneel at the victim's side with knee nearest the head opposite the victim's shoulders.

♦ Use the head-tilt/chin-lift maneuver (if no spinal injury exists) to open airway. Place one of your hands on the forehead and apply gentle, firm, backward pressure using the palm of your hand. Place the fingertips of your other hand under the chin. The fingertips are used to bring the chin forward and to support the jaw.

2. Pinch the nose closed. Inhale deeply and place your mouth over the victim's mouth (over mouth and nose with children), making sure of a tight seal. Give two full breaths into the air passage, watching for the chest to rise after each breath.

3. Keep the victim's head extended at all times.

4. Remove your mouth between breaths and let the victim exhale.

5. Feel and listen for the return flow of air, and look for fall of the victim's chest.

If neck injury is suspected, used modified jaw-thrust:

♦ Place victim on his or her back.

♦ Kneel at the top of the victim's head, resting on your elbows.

♦ Reach forward and gently place one hand on each side of victim's chin, at the angles of the lower jaw.

♦ Push the victim's jaw forward, applying most of the pressure with your index fingers.

♦ Do not tilt or rotate the victim's head.

6. Repeat this procedure giving one breath 12 times per minute for an adult, 15 times per minute for a small child, and 20 times per minute for an infant (giving gentle puffs of air from the mouth).

Note: After giving the initial two full breaths, you must check the victim's carotid pulse at the side of the neck to see if the heart is beating. If the victim has a pulse but is not breathing, continue rescue breathing and recheck the pulse every minute. If there is no pulse or the pulse stops, begin CPR, which is discussed below.

HEAD-TILT/CHIN-LIFT METHOD FOR OPENING AIRWAY

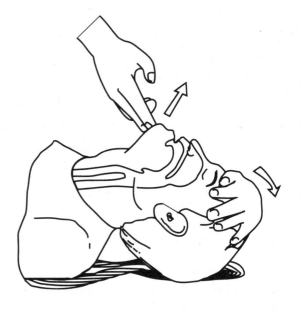

MOUTH-TO-MOUTH VENTILATION

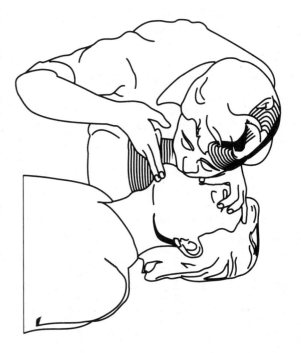

One-Person CPR (Cardiopulmonary Resuscitation)

Cardiopulmonary resuscitation (CPR) involves the use of artificial ventilation (mouth-to-mouth breathing) and external heart compression (rhythmic pressure on the breastbone). These techniques must be learned through training and supervised practice. Courses are available through the American Heart Association and American Red Cross. Incorrect application of external heart compressions may result in complications such as damage to internal organs, fracture of ribs or sternum, or separation of cartilage from ribs. (Rib fractures may occur when compressions are being correctly performed but this is not an indication to stop compression.) Application of cardiopulmonary resuscitation when not required could result in cardiac arrest, so never practice these skills on another person. When CPR is properly applied, the likelihood of complications is minimal and acceptable in comparison with the alternative—death.

Recognizing the Problem

The person who initiates emergency heart-lung resuscitation has two responsibilities:

♦ To apply emergency measures to keep the clinically dead victim biologically alive;

♦ To be sure the victim receives proper medical care.

When sudden death occurs, the rescuer must act immediately upon recognition of heart failure. In order to prevent biological death, the rescuer must be able to do the following:

♦ Recognize rapidly the apparent stoppage of heart action and respiration.

♦ Provide artificial ventilation to the lungs.

♦ Provide artificial circulation of the blood.

In addition to performing CPR, the rescuer must summon help in order that an ambulance and/or a physician may be called to the scene.

CPR Procedure for Single Rescuer

The CPR procedures should be learned and practiced on a training mannequin under the guidance of a qualified instructor. The step-by-step procedure for cardiopulmonary resuscitation is as follows:

1. Establish unresponsiveness. Gently shake the victim's shoulder and shout, "Are you OK?" The individual's response or lack of response will indicate to the rescuer if the victim is just sleeping or unconscious.

2. Call for help. Help will be needed either to assist in performing CPR or to call for medical help.

3. Position the victim. If the victim is found in a crumpled-up position and/or face down, the rescuer must roll the victim over; this is done while calling for help.

♦ When rolling the victim over, take care that broken bones are not further complicated by improper handling. Roll the victim as a unit so that the head, shoulders, and torso move simultaneously with no twisting.

♦ Kneel beside the victim, a few inches to the side.

♦ The arm nearest the rescuer should be raised above the victim's head.

♦ The rescuer's hand closest to the victim's head should be placed on the victim's head and neck to prevent them from twisting.

♦ The rescuer should use the other hand to grasp under the victim's arm furthest from rescuer. This will be the point at which the rescuer exerts the pull in rolling the body over.

♦ Pull carefully under the arm, and the hips and torso will follow the shoulders with minimal twisting.

♦ Be sure to watch the neck and keep it in line with the rest of the body.

♦ The victim should now be flat on his or her back.

4. Open the airway. The most common cause of airway obstruction in an unconscious victim is the tongue.

♦ Use the head-tilt/chin-lift maneuver to open airway. (This maneuver is not recommended for a victim with possible neck or spinal injuries.)

5. Establish breathlessness. After opening the airway, establish breathlessness:

♦ Turn your head toward the victim's feet

with your cheek close over the victim's mouth (three to five seconds).

♦ Look for a rise and fall in the victim's chest.

♦ Listen for air exchange at the mouth and nose.

♦ Feel for the flow of air. Sometimes opening and maintaining an open airway is all that is necessary to restore breathing.

6. Provide artificial ventilation. If the victim is not breathing, give two full breaths by mouth-to-mouth ventilation. Allow for lung deflation between each of the two ventilations.

7. Check for pulse. Check the victim's pulse to determine whether external cardiac compressions are necessary.

♦ Maintain an open airway by holding the forehead of the victim.

♦ Place your fingertips on the victim's windpipe and then slide them toward you until you reach the groove of the neck. Press gently on this area (carotid artery).

♦ Check the victim's carotid pulse for at least 5 seconds but no more than 10 seconds.

♦ If a pulse is present, continue administering artificial ventilation once every 5 seconds or 12 times a minute. If not, make arrangements to send for trained medical assistance and begin CPR.

8. Perform cardiac compressions:

♦ Place the victim in a horizontal position on a hard, flat surface.

♦ Locate the bottom of the rib cage with the index and middle fingers of your hand closest to the patient's feet.

♦ Run your index finger up to or in the notch where the ribs meet the sternum (breastbone).

♦ Place your middle finger in notch and index finger on sternum.

♦ Place the heel of the other hand on the sternum next to the index finger in the notch in the rib cage.

♦ Place the hand used to locate the notch at the rib cage on top and parallel to the hand which is on the sternum.

♦ Keep the fingers off the chest, by either extending or interlocking them.

♦ Keep the elbows in a straight and locked position.

♦ Position your shoulders directly over the hands so that pressure is exerted straight downward.

♦ Exert enough downward pressure to depress the sternum of an adult 1½ to 2 inches.

♦ Each compression should squeeze the heart between the sternum and spine to pump blood through the body.

♦ Totally release pressure in order to allow the heart to refill completely with blood.

♦ Keep the heel of your hand in contact with the victim's chest at all times.

♦ Make compressions down and up in a smooth manner.

Perform 15 cardiac compressions at a rate of 80–100 per minute, counting "one and, two and, three and . . . fifteen."

9. Use the head-tilt/chin-lift maneuver and give two full breaths (artificial ventilation).

ONE-PERSON CPR

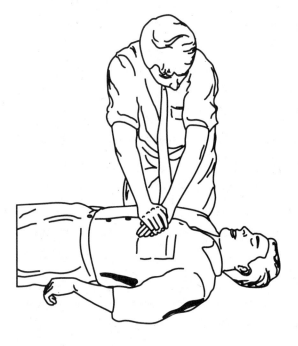

10. Repeat cycle four times (15 compressions and 2 ventilations).

11. After the fourth cycle, recheck the carotid pulse in the neck for a heartbeat (5 to 10 seconds).

12. If breathing and heartbeat are absent, resume CPR (15 compressions and 2 ventilations).

13. Stop and check for heartbeat every few minutes thereafter.

14. Never interrupt CPR for more than 5 seconds, except to check the carotid pulse or to move the victim.

Child Resuscitation

Some procedures and rates differ when the victim is a child. Between one and eight years of age, the victim is considered a child. The size of the victim can also be an important factor. A very small nine-year-old victim may have to be treated as a child. Use the following procedures when giving CPR to a child:

1. Establish unresponsiveness by the shake and shout method.

2. Open the airway using the head-tilt/chin-lift method.

3. Establish breathlessness (three to five seconds).

4. If the victim is not breathing, give two breaths.

5. Check the carotid pulse for at least five seconds.

6. Perform cardiac compressions:

♦ Place the victim in a horizontal position on a hard, flat surface.

♦ Use the index and middle fingers of your hand closest to the patient's feet to locate the bottom of the rib cage.

♦ Place your middle finger in notch and index finger on sternum.

♦ The heel of the other hand is placed on the sternum next to the index finger in the notch in the rib cage.

♦ The fingers must be kept off the chest by extending them.

♦ Elbow is kept straight by locking it.

♦ The shoulders of the rescuer are brought directly over the hand so that pressure is exerted straight downward.

♦ Exert enough pressure downward with one hand to depress the sternum of the child 1 to 1½ inches.

♦ Compress at a rate of 80 to 100 times per minute.

♦ Ventilate after every five compressions.

Infant Resuscitation

If the victim is younger than one year, it is considered an infant and the following procedures apply:

1. Establish unresponsiveness by the shake and shout method.

2. Open the airway; take care not to overextend the neck.

3. Establish breathlessness (three to five seconds).

4. Cover the infant's mouth and nose to get an airtight seal.

5. Puff cheeks, using the air in the mouth to give two quick ventilations.

6. Check the brachial pulse for five seconds.

7. To locate the brachial pulse: Place the tips of your index and middle fingers on the inner side of the upper arm. Press slightly on the arm at the groove in the muscle.

8. If heartbeat is absent, begin CPR at once.

♦ Place the index finger just under an imaginary line between the nipples on the infant's chest. Using the middle and ring fingers, compress chest ½ to 1 inch.

♦ Compress at the rate of at least 100 times per minute.

♦ Ventilate after every five compressions.

Obstructed Airway

An obstruction in the airway can result in unconsciousness and respiratory arrest. There are many factors which can cause the airway to become partially or fully obstructed such as gum, tobacco, or loose dentures. Foreign-body obstruction sometimes occurs during eating. A variety of foods cause choking, but meat is the most common.

When the airway is completely obstructed, the victim is unable to speak, breathe, or cough and will clutch the neck. Most people will use the universal distress signal. If the person is choking, movement of air will be absent. Unconsciousness will result due to lack of oxygen and death will follow quickly if prompt action is not taken.

Obstructed Airway: Conscious Victim Sitting or Standing

1. Determine if airway obstruction is partial or complete.
2. If partial obstruction (air exchange), encourage victim to cough.
3. If there is no air exchange, stand behind the victim and place your arms around the victim's waist.
4. Grasp one fist in your other hand and position the thumb side of your fist against the middle of the victim's abdomen just above the navel and well below rib cage.
5. Do not squeeze victim.
6. Press your fist into the victim's abdominal area with a quick upward thrust.
7. Repeat the procedure if necessary.

Note: The above abdominal-thrust method is commonly called the Heimlich maneuver.

Obstructed Airway: Unconscious Victim

When you attempt to give artificial ventilation and you feel resistance (the air not getting in), the victim's airway is probably obstructed. The most common cause of airway obstruction in an unconscious person is the tongue falling back into the airway, which can be corrected by using the head-tilt/chin-lift maneuver. When the airway is obstructed by a foreign body, the obstruction must be cleared or ventilation will be ineffective.

Here's how to do the abdominal thrust with the victim lying down:

1. Position victim on his or her back, face up.
2. Straddle victim's hips, if possible.
3. Place the heel of one hand against the middle of the victim's abdomen between the rib cage and the navel with fingers pointing toward the victim's chest.

UNIVERSAL DISTRESS SIGNAL FOR CHOKING

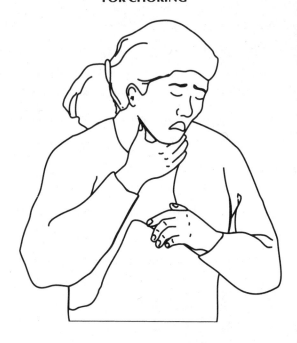

ABDOMINAL THRUST (HEIMLICH MANEUVER) WITH VICTIM STANDING

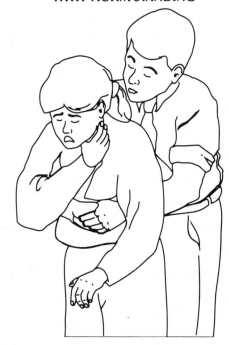

4. Place your other hand on top of the first.

5. Move your shoulders directly over the victim's abdomen.

6. Press into the victim's abdominal area with a quick, upward thrust.

7. Do 6 to 10 thrusts.

8. Follow with opening mouth and finger sweep to dislodge a foreign object.

9. Attempt artificial ventilation.

10. Repeat the procedures until obstruction is cleared.

Bleeding

Controlling bleeding is almost always very simple. Most external bleeding can be controlled by applying direct pressure to the open wound. Direct pressure permits normal blood clotting to occur.

In cases of severe bleeding, the first aider may be upset by the appearance of the wound and the emotional state of the victim. Remember that a small amount of blood appears as a lot of blood. It is important for the first aider to keep calm and do what is necessary for the victim.

When it is necessary to control bleeding, use the following methods:

♦ Direct pressure with sterile bandage, if available.

♦ Elevation.

♦ Pressure points.

♦ Tourniquet, if necessary (use as a last resort).

Direct Pressure

The best all-around method of controlling bleeding is applying pressure directly to the wound. This is best done by placing gauze or the cleanest material available against the bleeding point and applying firm pressure with the hand until a cover bandage is applied. The cover bandage knot should be tied over the wound unless otherwise indicated. The bandage supplies direct pressure and should not be removed until the victim is examined by a physician. When air splints or pressure bandages are available, they

may be used over the heavy layer of gauze to supply direct pressure.

If bleeding continues after the bandage has been put on, not enough pressure has been applied. Use the hand to put more pressure on the wound over the bandage, or apply a second bandage. Do not remove the original dressing. Either method should control the bleeding. In severe bleeding, if gauze or other suitable material is not available, the bare hand should be used to apply direct pressure immediately. This will control most bleeding.

Elevation

Elevating the bleeding part of the body above the level of the heart will slow the flow of blood and speed clotting. Use elevation with direct pressure when there are no fractures or fractures have been splinted, and it will cause no pain or aggravation to the injury.

Pressure Points

Arterial bleeding can be controlled by digital pressure applied at pressure points. Pressure points are places over a bone where arteries are close to the skin. Pressing the artery against the underlying bone can control the flow of blood to the injury. There are 26 pressure points on the body, 13 on each side, situated along main arteries.

Shock

The state of shock may develop rapidly or it may be delayed until hours after the event that causes it. Shock occurs to some degree after every injury. It may be so slight as to not be noticed; or so serious that it results in death where the injuries received ordinarily would not prove fatal.

Some of the major causes of shock are as follows: severe or extensive injuries; severe pain; loss of blood; severe burns; electrical shock; certain illnesses; allergic reactions; poisoning inhaled, ingested, or injected; exposures to extremes of heat and cold; emotional stress; substance abuse.

The signs and symptoms of shock are both physical and emotional. Shock may be determined by any or all of the following conditions: dazed look; paleness in light-skinned individuals and ashen (grayish) in dark-skinned individuals; nausea and vomiting; thirst; weak, rapid pulse; cold, clammy skin; shallow, irregular, labored breathing; pupils dilated; eyes dull and lackluster.

Treatment

While life-threatening, shock is a serious condition that is reversible if recognized quickly and treated effectively. Always maintain an open airway and ensure adequate breathing. Control bleeding.

First aid for the victim of physical shock is as follows:

1. Keep the victim lying down, if possible. Make sure that the head is at least level with the body. Elevate the lower extremities if the injury will not be aggravated and there are no abdominal or head injuries. It may be necessary to raise the head and shoulders if a person is suffering from a head injury, sunstroke, heart attack, stroke, or shortness of breath due to a chest or throat injury. However, it should be noted that if an accident was severe enough to produce a head injury, there may also be spinal damage. If in doubt, keep the victim flat.

2. Provide the victim with plenty of fresh air.

3. Loosen any tight clothing (neck, chest, and waist) in order to make breathing and circulation easier.

4. Handle the victim as gently as possible and minimize movement.

5. Keep the victim warm and dry by wrapping in blankets, clothing, brattice cloth, or other available material. These coverings should be placed under as well as over the victim to reduce the loss of body heat. Keep the victim warm enough to be comfortable. The objective is to maintain as near normal body temperature as possible, not to add heat.

6. Do not give the victim anything by mouth.

7. The victim's emotional well-being is just as important as his or her physical well-being. Keep calm and reassure the victim. Never talk to the victim about the injuries. Keep onlookers away from the victim, as their conversation regarding the victim's injuries may be upsetting.

Burns and Scalds

Classification of Burns

Burns may be classified according to the extent and depth of damage as follows:

♦ First degree (minor). The burned area is painful. The outer skin is reddened. Slight swelling is present.

♦ Second degree (moderate). The burned area is painful. The underskin is affected. Blisters may form. The area may have a wet, shiny appearance because of exposed tissue.

♦ Third degree (critical). Insensitive due to the destruction of nerve endings. Skin is destroyed. Muscle tissues and bone underneath may be damaged. The area may be charred, white, or grayish in color.

First Aid for Burns

The first aid given to a burn victim largely depends on the cause of the burn and the degree of severity.

Emergency first aid for burns or scalds should primarily be exclusion of air from the burned area, relief of the pain that immediately follows burns, minimizing the onset of shock, and the prevention of infection.

Remove all clothing from the injured area, but cut around any clothing that adheres to the skin and leave it in place. Keep the patient covered, except for the injured part, since there is a tendency to chill.

First-aid dressings for burns and scalds should be free of grease or oil. The use of greases or oils in the treatment of burns makes it necessary to cleanse the burned or scalded areas with a solvent before medical treatment can begin. This delays the medical treatment and is very painful.

Be careful when dressing burns and scalds. Burned and scalded surfaces are subject to infection the same as open wounds and require the same care to prevent infection. Do not break blisters intentionally.

Never permit burned surfaces to be in contact with each other, such as areas between the fingers or toes; the ears and the side of the head; the undersurface of the arm and the chest wall; the folds of the groin; and similar places.

Cover bandages should be loose enough to prevent pressure on burned surfaces. As swelling often takes place after burn dressings have been applied, check them frequently to see that they are not too tight. Watch for evidence of shock and treat if it is present.

In cases of severe burns, remove the victim to the hospital as quickly as possible. The victim will probably require an anesthetic, so ordinarily, nothing should be given by mouth.

In addition to the general principles listed, certain other principles must be followed when giving first aid for specific types of burns.

A. Thermal Burns (minor)

♦ Use cool, moist applications of gauze or bandage material to minimize blistering.

♦ Treat for physical shock.

B. Thermal Burns (moderate and critical)

♦ Do not use cold applications on extensive burns; cold could result in chilling.

♦ Cover the burn with a clean, dry dressing.

♦ Treat for shock.

♦ Transport to a medical facility.

C. Chemical Burns

♦ Remove clothing containing chemical agent.

♦ Do not use any neutralizing solution, unless recommended by a physician.

♦ Irrigate with water for at least 15 minutes; use potable water if possible.

♦ Treat for shock.

♦ Transport to a medical facility.

First aid for dry chemical (alkali) burns is an exception to the general first aid for chemical burns because mixing water with dry alkali creates a corrosive substance. The dry alkali should be brushed from the skin and water should then be used in very large amounts.

D. Electrical burns

♦ Conduct a primary survey, as cardiac and respiratory arrest can occur in cases of electrical burns.

♦ Check for points of entry and exit of current.

♦ Cover burned surface with a clean dressing.

♦ Splint all fractures. (Violent muscle contractions caused by the electricity may result in fractures.)

♦ Treat for physical shock.

♦ Transport to a medical facility.

Respiratory failure and cardiac arrest are the major problems caused by electrical shock and *not* the burn. Monitor pulse and breathing while preparing victim for transportation.

Poisoning by Ingestion (Eating or Drinking)

The chief causes of poisoning by ingestion are as follows:

♦ Overdose of medication (intentional or accidental). This includes the combining of drugs and alcohol.

♦ Household cleaners, chemicals, and medications left within the reach of children.

♦ Original labels being left on containers which are now used to store poisons.

♦ Improperly stored food.

The signs and symptoms of poisoning by ingestion are as follows:

♦ nausea, vomiting, and diarrhea

♦ severe abdominal pains and/or cramps

♦ altered respiration and pulse rates

♦ corroded, burned, or destroyed tissues of the mouth

♦ unusual odors on the breath

♦ stains around the mouth

The following is first aid for poisoning by ingestion:

1. Call your local Poison Control Center.

2. The Poison Control Center may instruct you to dilute the substance by giving the victim milk or water or induce vomiting so that the substance is removed from the stomach. Vomiting will prevent absorption into the circulation system.

3. Vomiting should *not* be induced in the following cases:

♦ If the victim has swallowed a strong acid or

alkali which would cause further damage when vomited.

♦ If a petroleum product has been swallowed, because it can be easily inhaled into the lungs and cause pneumonia.

♦ If the victim is unconscious or semiconscious because the victim may inhale the vomit into the lungs.

♦ If the victim is convulsing.

♦ If the victim has a serious heart problem.

Check with the Poison Control Center to determine the best method to induce vomiting. The victim should be sitting and leaning forward to prevent vomit from going into the lungs. Collect the vomit and take it to the hospital with the victim, along with the poison's container.

Insect Bites and Stings

Many insects bite or sting, but few can cause serious symptoms by themselves, unless, of course, the person is allergic to them. However, some insects transmit diseases. For example, certain types of mosquitoes transmit malaria, yellow fever, and other diseases; certain types of ticks transmit spotted or Rocky Mountain fever; and certain types of biting flies transmit tularemia or rabbit fever.

Occasionally, stinging or biting insects that have been feeding on or have been in contact with poisonous substances can transmit this poison at the time of the sting or bite.

Persons who have experienced serious reactions from previous insect bites should be urged to secure any possible immunization or have an antidote readily available to prevent more serious reactions from future insect bites and stings.

The signs and symptoms of insect bites and stings are as follows:

♦ The stings of bees and the bites of mosquitoes, ticks, fleas, and bedbugs usually cause only local irritation and pain in the region stung or bitten.

♦ Moderate swelling and redness may occur; and some itching, burning, and pain may be present.

The first aid for insect bites and stings is as follows:

1. The sting area should be inspected to determine whether the stinger is still left in the body. If it is, remove it in order to prevent further injection of toxin. The stinger should be carefully scraped off the skin, rather than grasped with tweezers, so as not to squeeze toxin into the body.

2. Application of ice or ice water to the bite helps to slow absorption of toxin into the bloodstream. A paste of baking soda and water can also be applied to the bite.

3. The victim should be observed for signs of an allergic reaction. For people who are allergic, maintain an open airway and get the victim to medical help as quickly as possible.

Bites of Animals

Any warm-blooded animal may suffer from rabies. If a person is bitten by an animal, always suspect the animal to be rabid until it is proven otherwise. The saliva from a rabid animal enters the wound caused by the bite, transmitting the disease to the victim. If possible, the animal should be captured or identified and held for medical observation. First aid for animal bites is as follows:

1. Control bleeding.

2. Wash the wound with soap and water and rinse with alcohol.

3. Dress and bandage the wound.

4. Splint if dealing with an extremity.

5. Take the victim to a medical facility as quickly as possible.

Heatstroke

Heatstroke is a sudden onset of illness from exposure to the direct rays of the sun or too high temperature without exposure to the sun. Physical exertion and high humidity definitely contribute to the incidence of heat stroke.

The most important characteristic of heatstroke is the high body temperature, which is caused by a disturbance in the heat-regulating mechanism. The person can no longer sweat, and this causes a rise in body temperature.

This illness is more common in the elderly. Alcoholics, obese persons, and those on medication are also very susceptible to heatstroke.

The signs and symptoms of heatstroke are as follows:

♦ The skin is flushed, very hot, and very dry. (Perspiration is usually absent.)

♦ The pulse is usually strong and rapid, but may become weak and rapid as the victim's condition worsens.

♦ The respirations are rapid and deep, followed by shallow breathing.

♦ The body temperature can reach 108 degrees.

♦ The victim rapidly becomes unconscious and may experience convulsions.

Care should be centered around lowering the body temperature as quickly as possible. Failure to do this will result in permanent brain damage or death. The care for heatstroke is as follows:

1. Maintain an open airway.

2. Move the victim to a cool environment.

3. Remove all clothing.

4. Wrap the victim in a cool, moist sheet and use a fan to cool the victim.

5. Immerse the victim in cool water if the above treatment is not feasible.

6. Use cool applications if neither of above treatments is feasible.

7. Transport the victim to the hospital as rapidly as possible, continuing cooling en route.

Heat Exhaustion

Heat exhaustion occurs in individuals working in hot environments. It is brought about by the loss of water and salt through sweating. This loss of fluid will cause mild shock.

This illness occurs most commonly to persons not accustomed to hot weather, those who are overweight, and those who perspire excessively. The signs and symptoms of heat exhaustion are as follows:

♦ The skin is pale and clammy.

♦ The skin shows evidence of profuse perspiration.

♦ Breathing is rapid and shallow.

♦ The pulse is rapid and weak.

♦ The victim may complain of nausea, weakness, dizziness, and/or headache.

The first aid for heat exhaustion is as follows:

1. Move the victim to a cool and comfortable place, but do not allow chilling.

2. Try to cool the victim by fanning and/or wiping the face with a cool, wet cloth.

3. Loosen the victim's clothing.

4. If fainting seems likely, have the victim lie down with feet elevated 8 to 12 inches.

5. Treat the victim for shock.

Hypothermia

Hypothermia is a general cooling of the entire body. The inner core of the body is chilled so the body cannot generate heat to stay warm. This condition can be produced by exposure to low termperatures or to temperatures between 30°F. and 50°F. with wind and rain. Also contributing to hypothermia are fatigue, hunger, and poor physical condition.

As the body tissues are cooled, the victim begins to shiver as a result of an involuntary adjustment by the body to preserve normal temperature in the vital organs.

Cold reaches the brain and deprives the victim of judgment and reasoning powers. The victim experiences feelings of apathy, listlessness, indifference, and sleepiness. The victim loses muscle coordination. The victim of hypothermia may not recognize the symptoms and deny that medical attention is needed.

First aid for a victim of hypothermia is as follows:

1. Get the victim out of the elements (wind, rain, snow, cold, etc.).

2. Remove all wet clothing.

3. Wrap the victim in blankets. Be certain the blankets are under as well as over the victim. Maintain the victim's body heat by building a fire

or placing heat packs, electric heating pads, hot water bottles, or even another rescuer in the blankets with the victim. (Do not warm the victim too quickly.)

4. If the victim is conscious, give warm liquids to drink.

5. If the victim is conscious, try to keep him or her awake.

6. CPR is indicated if the victim stops breathing and the heart stops beating.

7. Get the victim to a medical facility as soon as possible.

8. Remember to handle the victim gently. In extreme cases rough handling may result in death.

Frostbite

Frostbite results from exposure to severe cold. It is more likely to occur when the wind is blowing, rapidly taking heat from the body. The nose, cheeks, ears, toes, and fingers are the body parts most frequently frostbitten. As a result of exposure to cold, the blood vessels constrict. Thus, the blood supply to the chilled parts decreases and the tissues do not get the warmth they need.

The signs and symptoms of frostbite are not always apparent to the victim. Since frostbite has a numbing effect, the victim may not be aware of it. Frostbite goes through the following stages:

A. *Frostnip.* The affected area will feel numb to the victim. The skin becomes red, then white during frostnip. Treatment for frostnip is as follows:

1. Place hand over frostnipped part.
2. Place frostnipped fingers in armpit.

B. *Superficial Frostbite.* As exposure continues, the skin becomes white and waxy. The skin is firm to the touch, but underlying tissues are soft. The exposed surface becomes numb. The treatment for superficial frostbite is as follows:

1. Remove the victim from the environment.
2. Apply a steady source of external warmth.
3. Do not rub the area.
4. Cover the area with a dry, sterile dressing (when dressing foot or hand, pad between toes and fingers).

5. Splint if dealing with an extremity.

6. Transport to the hospital. As area thaws, it may become a mottled blue, and blisters will develop.

C. *Deep Frostbite.* If freezing is allowed to continue, all sensation is lost, and the skin becomes a "dead" white, yellow-white, or mottled blue-white. The skin is firm to the touch, as are the underlying tissues. Treatment for deep frostbite is as follows:

1. Leave it frozen until victim reaches hospital.
2. Dress, pad, and splint frostbitten extremities. (When dressing injury, pad between fingers and toes.)
3. Transport the victim to a hospital.

4. If there is a delay in transport, rewarming may be done at the site. Place the affected part in a water bath of 100–105 degrees F. Apply warm cloths to areas that cannot be submerged. An extreme amount of pain is associated with rewarming.

5. Rewarming is complete when the area is warm and red or blue in color and remains so after removal from the bath. Do not rewarm if there is a possibility of refreezing.

General Rules for Treating Frostbite

1. Apply loose, soft, sterile dressings to affected area.
2. Splint and elevate the extremity.
3. Give the victim warm fluids containing sugar to drink if he or she does not have an altered level of consciousness.
4. Do not rub, chafe, or manipulate frostbitten parts.
5. Do not use hot water bottles or heat lamps.
6. Do not place the victim near a stove or fire, because excessive heat can cause further tissue damage.
7. Do not allow the victim to smoke, because nicotine constricts the blood vessels.
8. Do not allow the victim to drink coffee, tea, or hot chocolate, because these substances will cause the blood vessels to constrict.
9. Do not allow the victim to walk if the feet are frostbitten.

Source: U.S. Department of Labor

Pediatric Emergencies

Almost 16 million children are treated each year in emergency departments of hospitals, many of them incorrectly. Emergency teams and hospitals sometimes fail to take children to the right hospital, diagnose them improperly, use the wrong equipment, or administer the wrong dosages of medicine. Hospital personnel commit similar errors. Why? They have not been trained to treat children and tend to treat them as tiny adults. But children's bodies are not just smaller than adults, they are also different. For example, children's blood pressure does not drop as quickly as adults when they are in shock; they can be near death before it begins to fall. They need to receive emergency treatment more quickly than adults, partly because they do not tolerate blood loss as well. Traumatized adults need treatment within an hour, children within 30 minutes or less. Children need smaller oxygen masks, smaller blood pressure cuffs, smaller plastic airway tubes, smaller cervical collars. They require drug doses carefully calibrated according to their age and weight.

What you can do:

♦ Before any emergency occurs, ask your pediatrician whom to call in case one does. Also ask what hospital is best equipped to deal with injured or critically ill children.

♦ Keep a list of medical emergency numbers by all phones.

♦ Personnel at your child-care facility or school should have a medical-release form, dated, with the child's name, stating that you authorize necessary emergency medical services requested by the bearer.

♦ Know how to perform CPR (cardiopulmonary resuscitation), Heimlich maneuver, and first aid. See "Guide to First-Aid Emergencies," page 799.

♦ Keep medical documents for your child all together in an easily accessible place. These should include your pediatrician's name and phone number, list of your child's allergies, your child's medical history, your health insurance card.

♦ In advance of emergency, if emergency technicians in your area do not have advanced pediatric life support, insist that they get it.

♦ Don't rush to the pediatrician's office in an emergency. Instead get your child to a hospital that has a Pediatric Intensive Care Unit.

♦ Make sure before and during the ambulance ride that emergency medical teams can take your child to the nearest *appropriate* hospital (one with a Pediatric Intensive Care Unit) with links to pediatricians. If not, make sure your child can be transferred to one. Know where the nearest regional pediatric critical care center is and if there is a mobile intensive care unit to take your child to it. Make sure in advance that these facilities are available for your child.

♦ Encourage your school to send for urgent care guidelines for schools from **American Academy of Pediatrics:** 800-433-9016. And arrange to be on the mailing list of the **EMSC** (Emergency Medical Services for Children) National Resource Center: 202-939-4927.

DISASTER PREPAREDNESS

General Preparedness for Disasters

Acts of God, they're called, and you can feel helpless in the face of the awesome rages of nature—floods, hurricanes, tornadoes, earthquakes. A flood can make matchsticks of your house, a tornado can travel at 200 miles an hour to carry you off to some other Oz. On the oceans, hurricanes create huge domed storm surges that rise as much as 20 feet above normal tides. An earthquake turns the ground beneath you into a terrifying, massively vibrating trampoline. Fire can suddenly roar out of control, moving 80 miles an hour down a canyon or eating your house alive. However, you are not entirely helpless—you can prepare for disasters ahead of time, increasing your chances for survival. Here are some tips gleaned from the American Red Cross and the Federal Emergency Management Agency.

♦ Make sure your insurance covers you for disasters that are likely to take place in your area. Most homeowners' policies cover tornadoes and hurricanes, but you may need extra coverage for earthquakes or floods. If you rent, get a replacement-cost renters' insurance policy.

♦ Know emergency preparedness plans of your workplace, children's school, or other place you and your family spend a good deal of time.

♦ Develop a plan for escape from your house. Know escape routes and practice using them.

Have regular practice drills for fire, earthquake, and other disasters.

♦ Decide how and where you will get back together after a disaster—choose two places, one in your neighborhood and another outside it. (Your neighborhood may become inaccessible in flood or other disaster.)

♦ Plan for evacuation—where can you go? A friend's house in another area, a shelter, a motel? If authorities advise evacuation, do it immediately or you may be trapped where you are.

♦ Choose a friend or relative from out of state as a liaison person for everyone to call. Teach your children to make a long-distance call.

♦ Talk to your neighbors about how you can help each other in an emergency.

♦ Learn first aid and CPR. (See "Guide to First-Aid Emergencies," p. 799.)

♦ Prepare a list of emergency telephone numbers. Teach children how to dial 911 and report an emergency.

♦ Know the location of main valves and switches for electricity, gas, and water. Learn how to shut them off. Put a wrench near the gas and water shut-off valves with written instructions on how to turn the utilities off.

♦ If you or someone in your family is disabled or has special medical needs—medication, diet, equipment—provide for them.

♦ Leave a disaster kit near the door you are mostly likely to leave from.

814

♦ Keep your pet vaccinations up to date—you may have to leave your pet at a boarding kennel, veterinary clinic, or animal shelter. They may require proof of vaccination. Dogs should be vaccinated against distemper, parvovirus, infectious canine hepatitis, leptospirosis, parainfluenza, bordatella, coronavirus, and rabies. Cats should be vaccinated against panleukopenia, rhinotracheitis, pneumonitis, calicivirus, feline leukemia, and rabies. Make sure your pet has a collar with I.D. and license tags, a leash, and a carrier in which it can stand, turn around, and lie down. Have available a three-day supply of food and water and medications for your pet, along with written instructions about its care.

♦ Put family records in a container that is waterproof and fireproof.

♦ Cut down dead trees and trim branches from live ones. In case of a severe storm, trees and branches can fall and block driveways or doors.

Shortly Before a Disaster

♦ Listen for instructions that come over emergency channels on radio or television.

♦ Put on protective and comfortable clothing and shoes.

♦ Fill the gas tank on your car.

♦ Store drinking water in clean receptacles: bathtub, jugs, pots and pans.

♦ Protect windows with a large *X* of wide masking tape or fiber tape, first diagonally, also in a checkerboard, or cover windows with plywork, or use storm windows.

If You Must Evacuate . . .

♦ Put a note on a previously designated place telling when you left and where you are going. Take your disaster kit with you. Lock up.

♦ Take a map with you. Take routes suggested by authorities.

♦ If you have time, turn off gas, water, and electricity if so instructed.

♦ Take pets somewhere where they will be safe. Many public shelters will not accept them.

Disaster Preparedness Kits

For the Car. Store the following in a nylon backpack or metal or plastic container in the trunk of your car:

♦ First-aid kit with bandages, gauze, tape, and handbook

♦ Water (change every three months)

♦ Nonperishable food like granola bars, raisins, peanut butter (change every six months)

♦ Personal items: toothbrush, toothpaste, comb, soap, towel, razor, antiseptic cream, aspirins, bandages, gauze, and any needed prescriptions

♦ Pocketknife

♦ Leather gloves

♦ Bottle opener

♦ Flashlight, with extra batteries and bulb (replace batteries before expiration date)

♦ Pocket radio with extra batteries (replace batteries before expiration date)

♦ Blanket

♦ Canned food and snacks

♦ Jumper (booster) cables

♦ Traction mats or chains

♦ Rope

♦ Pry bar

♦ Fire extinguisher (5-pound A-B-C type)

♦ Screwdriver and crowbar

♦ Plastic trash bags

♦ Pencil and paper

♦ Sterno canned heat

♦ Maps

♦ Shovel

♦ Tools for tire repair

♦ Flares

♦ Important legal documents, identification for all family members

♦ Bright-colored cloth to tie to antenna

For the Home. The following can be stored in an old barrel or trash can:

♦ Flashlight with extra batteries and bulb (replace batteries before expiration date)

♦ Portable radio with extra batteries (replace batteries before expiration date)

♦ Water, one gallon per person per day for three days (replace every three months)

♦ Foods: store only canned, powdered, and freeze-dried foods, enough to last one week, and a nonelectric can opener (replace every six months)

♦ First-aid kit (including tampons, toilet paper, and first-aid handbook); prescription medications

♦ Personal items: toothbrush, toothpaste, comb, soap, towel, razor, antiseptic cream, adhesive tape, alcohol, aspirins, bandages, gauze, and any needed prescriptions; an extra pair of glasses

♦ Gloves
♦ Plastic trash bags
♦ Aluminum foil
♦ Household bleach
♦ Tissues
♦ Pocketknife
♦ Mini barbecue grill or hibachi
♦ Screwdriver, wrench, and crowbar
♦ Sleeping bag or blankets
♦ Change of clothes, underwear, and shoes; rain gear
♦ Pencil and paper

♦ Keep copies of important papers, documents, medical history, list of family physicians, style and serial number of devices like pacemakers.

After the Disaster

1. In a power failure, shut off large appliances like air conditioners, washers and dryers, and electric stoves.

2. Look everyone over for injuries. Give first aid.

3. Put on sturdy shoes, to protect you from broken glass injuries.

4. Using a flashlight if it is dark, look the house over for:

♦ gas leaks (by smell only—do *not* try to find them by lighting matches)—shut off main valve, open windows and doors;

♦ electricity and water-line damage—turn everything off if you find any damage;

♦ cracks and damage, especially roof, chimneys, foundation.

5. Don't turn utilities back on until the utility company representatives have checked your home over. You can obtain emergency water from water heaters, ice cubes, toilet tanks (not bowls), canned vegetables.

6. Turn on a radio (portable or car) to listen for instructions from public safety agencies.

7. Do not use the telephone unless you have an emergency—fire, medical, public safety. Dial 911 in case of emergency.

8. Unless there is an emergency, stay put. If you must drive, be aware that traffic signals may not be working, and watch out for fallen objects. For further information, write for the free brochure, "Disaster Driving," from **Aetna,** 151 Farmington Avenue, RWAC, Hartford, CT 06156–3220.

9. Don't touch any loose or dangling wires or metal objects that might be in contact with electrical wires. Stay out of water that such wires and objects are touching.

10. Don't smoke. Don't use fire or flames.

Earthquakes

In our nightmares about earthquakes, the earth opens up beneath us into a widening, bottomless chasm and we fall into it, screaming. In reality, an earthquake usually shakes us up, may break a few dishes, leave us with the lasting realization that solid earth is not as solid as we thought. We are more likely to be hurt by flying glass and falling objects than the actual movement of the earth.

And we are not helpless in the face of an earthquake. There is much that can be done to prepare for one, and there are ways to lessen the danger when it occurs.

Before the Quake

1. Discuss safety rules in the section "General Preparedness for Disasters" with your family and other people you see frequently—in the neighborhood, at work.

2. Conduct earthquake practice drills, where you search out and stay in safe places.

3. Take any big, heavy objects and breakable objects that are on higher shelves and put them on lower shelves.

4. Secure water heaters, gas appliances, refrigerators, heavy furniture, bookcases, shelves.

5. Secure mirrors, pictures, and hanging plants, especially those hanging over beds.

6. Keep hazardous and flammable liquids in cabinets or on low shelves.

7. Check your house for structural flaws that could cause problems in an earthquake.

8. Prepare emergency kits as listed above.

During the Quake

1. Stay calm.

2. Find a secure place. Stay there until the shaking stops.

♦ Inside a house, go under a bed, desk, table, or bench and cover your head with cushions or some other soft objects. Otherwise, stand in a doorway or against a wall away from windows and glass dividers.

♦ Inside a public building, get under a desk or something similar, or crouch against an interior wall, head protected with your arms or an object like a briefcase. Do not rush to an exit— stairways may be overcrowded with people and they may be unsafe. Stay away from elevators— power may fail. If you happen to be inside an elevator, stomp on the floor after the quake to get help. If you are in immediate danger, you might try to escape through the trapdoor on top of the elevator—there may be danger from fire.

♦ Outside, keep away from anything that can fall on you—buildings, trees, telephone and electrical lines. Watch out for falling debris, especially window glass. It is better to duck into a doorway

than expose yourself to falling debris. If you are on the beach, get off—to escape a tsunami (wall of water) that may be generated by the quake.

♦ On the road, stop in a safe place, away from underpasses, overpasses, trees, telephone and electrical lines. Stay in the car.

3. Be prepared for aftershocks. Decide where to take cover if they occur.

4. Don't use matches, candles, any flame because of possible gas leaks. Put out fires.

Weather Disasters

Floods

A massive flood can dislodge your house from its underpinnings, collapse walls, ruin insulation and wiring. Of all weather-related disasters, flash floods kill more people every year. Don't think you can survive trying to get through flood waters over 6 inches deep—they can sweep you away and drown you. If you are driving when a flash flood appears, get out of your car and walk to higher ground.

Keep plywood and nails available to board up windows.

Get to high ground, but don't drive, walk, or swim through spots that are flooded. Have ready an evacuation route that bypasses roads near rivers, creeks, lakes, or the ocean. When a flood hits, protect your valuables and furniture by moving them to a higher floor.

If you stay in your house, stay in a windowless interior space.

Tornadoes and Hurricanes

Before the storm hits, if you have time, bring in lawn furniture, planters, garden tools, trash cans, and anything else that can blow away and bang into someone or something. Cover windows with plywood to protect against shattering glass. Remember some tornadoes ("frog-stranglers") can travel up to 200 miles per hour. If you live in

Tornado Alley, a piece of the Great Plains stretching 900 miles from Texas to Iowa, watch out.

When a tornado or hurricane hits, head for an inside bathroom or basement or central hall on the first floor with no clutter (otherwise you can be hit by flying objects). The best place in a tornado is in a basement under a table or workbench. Don't stay inside a mobile home. Don't take time to open windows. If you are outside, go inside a building to the basement, avoiding buildings with wide freespan roofs like some gymnasiums. Go to the corner closest to the tornado. Stay indoors until authorities tell you it is safe to go out. The storm may not be over—the eye is the calm center, but there may be more storm after it passes over.

Don't drive.

Keep away from chimneys. Or lie in a ditch or other depression in the ground with your hands over your head. If you are in a car, get out and find a safe place away from the car so it can't roll over and hurt you.

If you see a tornado, move at right angles to it.

Blizzards

Put a battery-powered National Oceanic and Atmospheric Administration weather radio in your disaster kit.

Put on warm clothing in layers, and a hat. If you are caught in your car, stay in it, engine off. Every hour turn it back on and run the heater for 10 minutes with one window a bit open and after making sure the exhaust pipe is clear of ice and snow. Move your arms and legs to keep your blood circulating. Tie a brightly colored cloth to the antenna as a signal to rescuers.

Fire!

Fires and burns kill 4500 Americans a year, most of them at home in the middle of the night, and they are the number-one cause of childhood death

from accidents in the home. You can help prevent this from happening in your family with prevention measures and a plan in case of fire.

Smoke Detectors

Smoke detectors will give you two extra minutes of escape time from a fire. They come in two basic kinds: ionization and photoelectric. You should have both kinds in your house, in all bedrooms and hallways, at all levels. Use heat detectors in rooms where smoke detectors are not practical—kitchens, for example.

The **ionization smoke detector** responds more quickly to the fumes of a hot, blazing, fast-burning fire. Keep it on the ceiling.

A **photoelectric detector** responds to smoke from a slow-burning fire—for instance, from a cigarette smouldering away in an overstuffed chair or mattress. It is less likely to be activated by harmless kitchen fumes. Keep a spare battery and bulbs handy. The bulb emitting the beam must be replaced every three years.

Choose smoke detectors that have been certified by a known testing organization. Check the instructions: are they clear and complete? They should tell you how and where to install the detector, how to test and maintain it. Look for a step-by-step explanation with diagrams. Make sure that the detector will emit a signal to tell you when bulbs or batteries need to be replaced. Place smoke detectors in halls leading to bedrooms and at the head of stairs leading to living areas. Avoid places where there are air currents (vents and radiators), dead-air corners, and ends of halls. A ceiling detector should be 20 inches or more from any wall. A wall detector should be 15 to 30 inches below the ceiling. Clean smoke detectors once a year. Test them monthly. Test a ionization smoke detector by holding a burning candle flame 6 inches below it. Test a photoelectric detector by putting out a candle and letting the smoke drift into the detector. You can also blow a large quantity of tobacco smoke into it. The smoke detector should go off within 20 seconds and stop after you move the flame or wave away the smoke.

Power for both types of smoke detectors comes from batteries or house current. If a detector is battery-operated, it should produce a signal when batteries are running down—a chirping or beeping sound. (Don't think you have crickets when you hear the sound.) It is wise to change batteries yearly (or according to directions from manufacturer). If the detector runs on house current, plug it into a receptacle that cannot be switched off or directly into a circuit. Choose a detector with a backup battery in case of power failure. To remove the battery, take off the cover. If you can't figure it out, ask your fire department to help. After putting in the battery, replace the cover and test the detector according to manufacturer's directions. If it doesn't pass or if it continues to beep, look for a burned-out bulb, replace it, and test again. If it still fails the test, replace the detector.

Sprinklers

Though expensive (1 to 2 percent of the purchase price of a new house, 3 to 4 percent of an existing home), sprinklers can save the lives of the handicapped, the very young, and the very old. They respond to a fire within 35 seconds and do far less damage than fire and smoke.

Fire Extinguishers

Fire extinguishers should weigh at least 5 pounds. They come in four types:
- Type A—for paper, wood, and fabric fires
- Type B—for flammable liquid fires (grease, oil, gasoline)
- Type C—for electrical fires
- Type ABC—for all three types of fire.

All are for extinguishing small fires before they get out of control. If you must choose between trying to put out a large fire and escaping, escape! In 1992, some 500 people died with fire extinguisher in hand, trying to put out a fire.

To Prevent Fires

Screen fireplaces and keep chimneys cleaned. Use only dried woods and never use flammable liquids to start fireplace or stove fires. Keep the damper open and screen closed when the fire is burning. Keep flammable materials away from fireplaces and stoves. Never leave a fireplace fire unattended. Let ashes cool and put in lidded containers to dispose of them.

Don't smoke in bed. Of all multiple-death home fires, one-third are caused by people smoking in bed. Keep matches in places safe from children. Empty ashtrays into toilets rather than the trash.

Use only UL-tested electrical appliances. Repair frayed cords and plugs—not just by wrapping broken places with electrical tape. Don't fold or crimp cords of electrical appliances—this can disturb insulation, exposing wires, which might short out and spark. Unplug and store electric blankets when not in use. Keep hair dryers, electric razors, and curling irons away from combustible materials when you are using them. Be careful when using heating pads. Leave them on only for 30 minutes or less and never fall asleep with a heating pad on. (You can set an alarm clock to wake you up in 30 minutes.) Don't put too many plugs in one outlet.

Don't let grease build up in the oven or try to broil very fatty meats. Don't leave cooking oil heating unattended. Keep combustible materials away from the stove, and don't hang dish towels or pot holders above the stove where they can fall down and catch fire in the flames.

Follow manufacturer's instructions on how long to leave synthetics, plastics, rubber, or foam in the dryer. Keep the lint screen cleaned and keep combustibles away from the dryer. Vent the dryer to the outside and give it its own electrical outlet.

Some materials can generate heat and ignite spontaneously—newspapers, barbecue charcoal, oily rags. Dry oily rags by spreading them out in a well-ventilated place, then wash them. Keep all these materials and all flammable liquids in a cool, dry place, stored in metal containers with a tight lid, at least 3 feet away from heat sources like pilot lights.

BRUSH FIRES

Fast-moving brush fires can roar into your neighborhood. If you are threatened by a brush fire, here are some safety tips. Have your car gassed up and ready, backed into the garage, with a way to open the garage door if electricity fails. Close the doors and windows of your house, remove gauzy curtains, close heavy curtains. Seal vents to attic and basement. Have a 100-foot hose attached to a spigot. Put combustible things in the garage. Put trash cans full of water around the house, with sponges, little rugs, or sacks available to dip into them to extinguish small fires. Turn off propane tanks. Leave your lights on because smoke makes the house dark. Put on clothing with long sleeves and pants; use a damp cloth to cover your face, goggles if you have them.

If the fire comes to within 600 feet of the roof, you might want to wet it down with the hose. If you do, be very careful not to fall, and once you are done quickly (but prudently) get down from the roof.

If the fire is moving very fast, you might be better off staying in the house. Sometimes fires move so fast they roar by the house. If the roof is on fire, get in your car, pull into the driveway, and turn on the air conditioner.

After the fire has passed, put out small spot fires on roof and around the house. Keep windows and doors closed. If you can, wait around for at least four hours, checking to see that embers have not gotten into attic or eaves.

Clean up all dry, combustible brush at least 30 feet around your house. Keep woodpiles safely away from the house. Make sure that your house numbers are clearly visible from the street so that the fire department can easily find you.

Check your roofing material. If you have untreated wood shakes, consider replacing them with a material that is more fire-resistant. Cover your chimney with half-inch steel mesh so that sparks cannot escape to set the roof or brush on fire. Clean rain gutters and roofs. Trim tree limbs near the house.

When a Fire Breaks Out

Turn off the source that has ignited the fire—the stove, appliance, gas supply. Pull out plugs.

TYPES OF FIRES AND HOW TO EXTINGUISH THEM

Type of fire	Smother or cool	Comments
Cooking	Smother with pan lid or baking soda; by shutting oven door.	Don't move pans, use water, or turn on the exhaust fan. Let fat cool in the oven.
Electrical appliance	Smother with blanket.	Never use water—it conducts electricity.
Gas	Smother with rug or blanket. Cool with water.	Ventilate to let gas out. Call fire department to check gas pipes for immediate danger. Then call gas company.
Heating	Electrical: smother with blanket. Gas: use water. Fireplace: smother with baking soda.	Call fire department when stovepipe is red or there is a fire in the chimney.
Storage	Smother with blanket or rug.	Be careful storing rags, charcoal, solvents, hairspray, glue, newspapers.

RISKIEST PLACES TO LIVE

The riskiest places to live in terms of major disasters are Texas and California (20 major natural disasters each since 1982), followed by Illinois, Louisiana, and Oregon (11 each); then come Washington and Mississippi (10 each), New York and Oklahoma (9 each), Iowa and Florida (7 each). Last are Wyoming and Delaware (1 each).

What disasters are the most lethal?

The number-one killer is flash floods, which kill 165 people a year, because more of us live in places that are prone to floods. Your chance of being killed by a hurricane is about 1 in 20 million. It was much greater before the days of modern weather forecasting. Now we can evacuate. Lightning strikes and kills about 70 people a year, the vast majority male. Tornadoes kill 100 people a year.

In 1900, the Galveston hurricane roared through Texas, carrying death in its wake. It killed more than 6000 people, 10 times that of the San Francisco earthquake of 1906, making it the worst U.S. disaster of all time.

If you think you are safe from earthquakes because you don't live in California, think again. In the early 1800s, the Midwest suffered earthquakes of 8.0 or greater on the Richter scale. They changed the course of the Mississippi River.

The hurricane belt hugs the Atlantic and Gulf coasts, Texas to Maine. Tornado Alley cuts a swath through large parts of the Southwest and Midwest. If you live near a coast, you face tidal waves (tsunamis), floods, and hurricanes. There are volcanoes in Washington and Montana.

On National Public Radio's "All Things Considered," September 2, 1993, Richard Krimm, acting associate director for state and local programs for FEMA (Federal Emergency Management Agency), found it difficult to identify a place safe from natural disasters in the U.S.: "I would have a hard time doing it . . . perhaps you could live in a state like Wyoming, where the hazards are more minimal than many other places, but you still would have to watch the flood plain; you have to watch the severe cold and snow; and perhaps you would want to live there during the summer and spring and fall months and then move to New Mexico or Arizona for the winter, but you have to be careful where you go in Arizona because they get terrible floods."

If a Fire Is Out of Control

Planning: Have a plan set up in advance. All rooms in your house should have two means of escape. Draw a picture showing the escape routes for every room and explain it to everyone. Upper floor windows should have hook-on fire escape ladders or rope ladders. If you live in a high-rise, make sure all members of the family know a safe exit and warn them not to use the elevators if there is a fire. Assign one older person to be responsible for each child. Establish a method of communication (knock, yell, whistle). Plan on a meeting place outside. Have practice fire drills every three months, some of them at night. All members of the family should know how to call 911—to give the address and tell the dispatcher that there is a fire.

During the fire: Stay calm. If one escape plan set up in advance doesn't work, try the other. Before opening a door, feel it for intense heat and check to see if smoke is coming in around its edge. If it is hot or you see smoke, stuff wet towels or clothing in the cracks. Don't open it. Try another escape route or wait for help. If you are more than two stories above ground and no ladder is available, open the window slightly at the top or bottom (after checking for nearby flames). Crouch near the open window for fresh air and to let the firefighters know you are there. If the door seems safe, open it slowly; be ready to close it if heat and smoke invade. Close doors behind you.

Crawling on the floor, mouth and nose covered with a damp cloth (to keep down smoke inhalation), may be the best mode of travel. If your clothes catch fire, stop, drop, and roll.

Once outside the house, do not go back in.

Organizations:

American Red Cross (your local chapter).

Burn Institute, 3702 Ruffin Road, Suite 101, San Diego, CA 92123; 619-541-2277.

National Fire Protection Association, Batterymarch Park, Quincy, MA 02269; 617-770-4543.

17

MEASURES

International Alphabet, Morse Code, Flags and Pennants

Letter Morse code	Flag or Pennant	Letter Morse code	Flag or Pennant	Letter Morse code	Flag or Pennant	Letter Morse code	Flag or Pennant
A Alpha • —		B Bravo — • • •		C Charlie — • — •		D Delta — • •	
E Echo •		F Foxtrot • • — •		G Golf — — •		H Hotel • • • •	
I India • •		J Juliet • — — —		K Kilo — • —		L Lima • — • •	
M Mike — —		N November — •		O Oscar — — —		P Papa • — — •	
Q Quebec — — • —		R Romeo • — •		S Sierra • • •		T Tango —	
U Uniform • • —		V Victor • • • —		W Whiskey • — —		X Xray — • • —	
Y Yankee — • — —		Z Zulu — — • •					

NUMERAL PENNANTS; MORSE CODE

1 • — — — —		2 • • — — —	
3 • • • — —		4 • • • • —		5 • • • • •		6 — • • • •	
7 — — • • •		8 — — — • •		9 — — — — •		0 — — — — —	

PENNANTS FOR ANSWERING OR REPEATING AND SIGNALING CODE

1st repeat		2nd repeat		3rd repeat		Code and answering pennant	

Semaphore Code

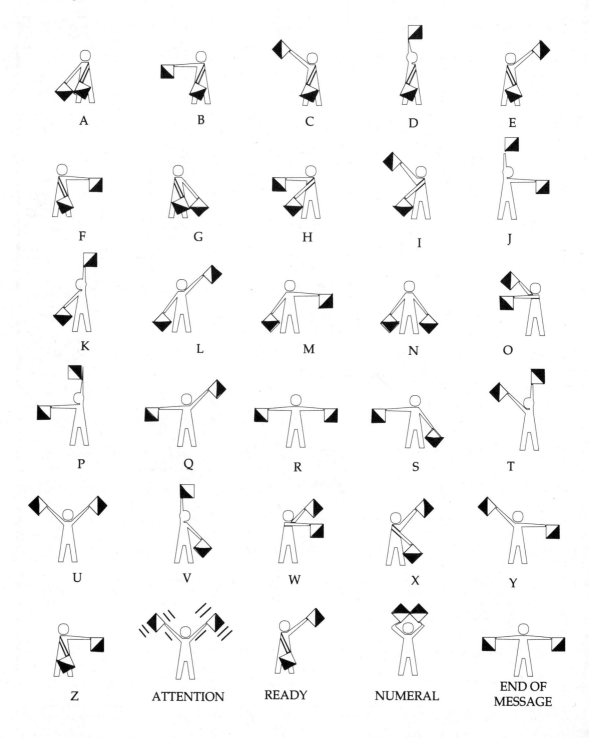

Distress Signals

Three of any sound or visual signal (smoke or flashes from a mirror) indicates distress. If you are lost in the woods, spell out SOS or HELP in large letters by using pieces of clothing or by trampling the snow. Other distress signals used at sea and elsewhere include: red flares, orange smoke signals, many foghorn blasts, an upside-down flag, "Mayday" (on radiotelephone channel 16—156.8 MHz.

I   Send doctor

II   Send medicine

X   Can't go on

F   Send food and water

K   What direction?

↑   Going in this direction

△   You can land safely

LL   All is well

⌐L   I don't get it

☐   Send map and compass

O   No

N   Yes

Y   Send signal light

Braille Alphabet

A language of raised dots, spoken and read by the fingers: in 1824, Louis Braille, a young blind teacher in Paris, perfected writing words with a sequence of dots, using a sharp stylus to punch indentations onto paper fitted over a metal slate. Today slate and stylus are lightweight, portable tools, with Braille typewriters and electronic adaptions available as well.

The six dots of the Braille cell are arranged and numbered thus:

```
1  ●  ●  4
2  ●  ●  5
3  ●  ●  6
```

The capital sign, dot 6, placed before a letter, makes it a capital. The numeral sign, dots 3, 4, 5, 6, placed before a character makes it a figure and not a letter. The apostrophe, dot 3, like the other punctuation marks, is formed in the lower part of the cell. The symbol for beginning quotation marks and the question mark is the same.

BRAILLE ALPHABET AND NUMBERS

Capital sign		A / 1		J / 0		S	
Comma		B / 2		K		T	
Semi-colon		C / 3		L		U	
Period		D / 4		M		V	
Single quotation mark		E / 5		N		W	
Dash		F / 6		O		X	
Exclamation point		G / 7		P		Y	
Question mark		H / 8		Q		Z	
		I / 9		R		Number sign	

Source: American Foundation for the Blind

FINGER SPELLING

Finger spelling is sometimes used by the deaf to spell names and other words not in the vocabulary of American Sign Language.

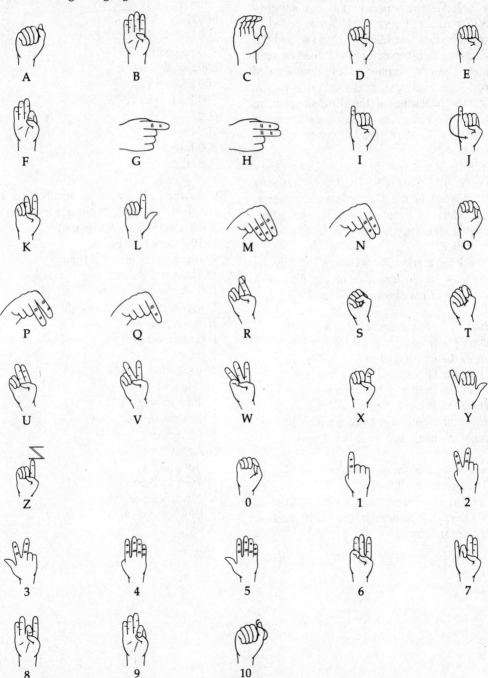

ISBN (International Standard Book Number)

Every book, like every person, has its number—the ISBN number. Every ISBN is composed of 10 digits. The first nine identify the book, and the tenth is a check digit to determine if the first nine are right. The first number tells in what part of the world the book was published. A *0* means that it was published in the English-speaking world. The second group of numbers identifies the publisher. The third group of numbers identifies the book itself.

The ISBN of the *New York Public Library Desk Reference* is 0-13-620444-9. The 0 identifies it as being published in the English-speaking world. The 13 refers to Prentice-Hall, the publisher. The 620444 identifies the book itself. The last is the check digit.

To check the number for accuracy, multiply the first digit by 10. In the case of the *New York Public Library Desk Reference*—10 x 0 = 0 . . . then

  multiply the second digit by 9: 1 x 9 = 9
  multiply the third digit by 8: 3 x 8 = 24
  multiply the fourth digit by 7: 6 x 7 = 42
  multiply the fifth digit by 6: 2 x 6 = 12
  multiply the sixth digit by 5: 0 x 5 = 0
  multiply the seventh digit by 4: 4 x 4 = 16
  multiply the eighth digit by 3: 4 x 3 = 12
  multiply the ninth digit by 2: 4 x 2 = 8
Total = 123

Now ask what is the next multiple of 11 after 123. The answer is 132 (11 x 12). The difference between the two numbers (132 and 123) is 9. And 9 is the tenth numeral in the ISBN number. The number is accurate.

Library Classification Systems

The Dewey Decimal System (widely used in public libraries):
  000 General Works
  100 Philosophy
  200 Religion
  300 Social Science
  400 Philology
  500 Pure Science
  600 Useful Arts
  700 Fine Arts
  800 Literature
  900 History

The Library of Congress classification system (used mostly in research and academic libraries):
  A General Works, Polygraphy
  B Philosophy, Religion
  C Auxiliary Sciences of History
  D Universal History
  E-F American History
  G Geography, Anthropology
  H Social Sciences
  J Political Science
  K Law
  L Education
  M Music
  N Fine Arts
  P Language, Literature
  R Medicine
  S Agriculture
  T Technology
  U Military Science
  V Naval Science
  Z Bibliography, Library Science

Metric Conversions

To convert from	To	Multiply by
Linear measure		
centimeters	inches	.3937
inches	centimeters	2.54
meters	feet	3.281
feet	meters	.3048
meters	yards	1.094
yards	meters	.9144
kilometers	miles	.621
miles	kilometers	1.609
Area measure		
square centimeters	square inches	0.155
square inches	square centimeters	6.4516
square meters	square feet	10.764
square feet	square meters	0.09290341
square meters	square yards	1.196
square yards	square meters	0.836
square kilometers	square miles	0.386
square miles	square kilometers	2.58998811
Cubic measure		
cubic centimeters	cubic inches	0.06102374
cubic inches	cubic centimeters	16.387064
cubic meters	cubic feet	35.31467
cubic feet	cubic meters	0.0028316847
cubic meters	cubic yards	1.307951
cubic yards	cubic meters	0.764554858
Fluid volume		
milliliters	ounces	0.0338
ounces	milliliters	29.573528
liters	ounces	33.814
ounces	liters	0.02957
liters	cups	4.2268
cups	liters	0.236588
liters	quarts	1.0567
quarts	liters	0.9463529
Dry volume		
grams	ounces	0.03527
ounces	grams	28.3495
kilograms	pounds	2.2046
pounds	kilograms	0.45359
metric tons	short tons	1.1023
short tons	metric tons	0.907

Area and Volume

Measure	Equivalents	
Linear measure		
1 foot	12 inches	
1 yard	3 feet	36 inches
1 rod	5½ yards	16½ feet
1 mile	1760 yards	5280 feet
Area measure		
1 square foot	144 square inches	
1 square yard	9 square feet	
1 square rod	30¼ square yards	272½ square feet
1 acre	160 square rods	4840 square yards
1 square mile	640 acres	
Cubic measure		
1 cubic foot	1728 cubic inches	
1 cubic yard	27 cubic feet	
Fluid volume		
1 tablespoon	3 teaspoons	0.5 fluid ounce
1 cup	8 fluid ounces	
1 pint	2 cups	16 fluid ounces
1 quart	2 pints or 4 cups	32 fluid ounces
1 gallon	4 quarts or 8 pints or 16 cups	
Dry volume		
1 pound	16 ounces	
1 short ton	2000 pounds	
1 long ton	2240 pounds	

Temperatures

In the Fahrenheit system, water freezes at 32° and boils at 212°. In the Celsius (Centigrade) system, water freezes at 0° and boils at 100°.

The conversion formulas are:

Fahrenheit to Celsius: Subtract 32 from the Fahrenheit temperature, multiply the result by 5; divide by 9. Example: To find out the Celsius equivalent of 90°F.:

$$90 - 32 = 58$$
$$58 \times 5 = 290$$
$$290 \div 9 = 32.2°C.$$

Celsius to Fahrenheit: Multiply the Celsius temperature by 9, divide the result by 5, and add 32.

Example: To find the Fahrenheit equivalent of 25°C.:

$$9 \times 25 = 225$$
$$225 \div 5 = 45$$
$$45 + 32 = 77°F.$$

Decimal Equivalents of Common Fractions

For any fraction not on the list, divide the numerator by the demoninator (top number by the bottom number). Example: for ¾, 3 divided by 4 = 0.75.

DECIMAL EQUIVALENTS OF COMMON FRACTIONS

Fraction	Decimal	Fraction	Decimal
1/2	.5000	3/11	.2727
1/3	.3333	4/5	.8000
1/4	.2500	4/7	.5714
1/5	.2000	4/9	.4444
1/6	.1667	4/11	.3636
1/7	.1429	5/6	.8333
1/8	.1250	5/7	.7143
1/9	.1111	5/8	.6250
1/10	.1000	5/9	.5556
1/11	.0909	5/11	.4545
1/12	.0833	5/12	.4167
1/16	.0625	6/7	.8571
1/32	.0313	6/11	.5455
1/64	.0156	7/8	.8750
2/3	.6667	7/9	.7778
2/5	.4000	7/10	.7000
2/7	.2857	7/11	.6364
2/9	.2222	7/12	.5833
2/11	.1818	8/9	.8889
3/4	.7500	8/11	.7273
3/5	.6000	9/10	.9000
3/7	.4286	9/11	.8182
3/8	.3750	10/11	.9091
3/10	.3000	11/12	.9167

Roman Numerals

The Roman numeral system follows the same general logic all the way through. For example, 16 is XVI, just as 6 is VI; 19 is XIX, just as 9 is IX. The rules are these:

1. When a letter repeats, add its value to the previous value. For example, X = 10, XXX = 30.

2. When a letter is followed by letters of lesser value, add the value of the subsequent letters to that of the letter of greater value. Example: L = 50, LX = 60, MCCC = 1300.

3. When a letter of lesser value is followed by a letter of greater value, subtract the value of the letter of lesser value from that of the letter of greater value. Example: X = 10, IX = 9, CM = 900.

4. A dash placed over a letter increases its value by a thousand times, V = 5, $\overline{V}$ = 5000.

ROMAN AND ARABIC NUMERAL EQUIVALENTS

1	I	600	DC
2	II	700	DCC
3	III	800	DCCC
4	IV	900	CM
5	V	1000	M
6	VI	1500	MD
7	VII	1900	MCM or
8	VIII		MDCCCC
9	IX	1910	MCMX
10	X	1920	MCMXX
15	XV	1930	MCMXXX
20	XX	1940	MCMXL
25	XXV	1950	MCML
30	XXX	1960	MCMLX
40	XL	1970	MCMLXX
50	L	1980	MCMLXXX
60	LX	1990	MCMXC
70	LXX	2000	MM
80	LXXX	2010	MMX
90	XC	2020	MMXX
100	C	2030	MMXXX
150	CL	3000	MMM
200	CC	4000	MMMM or $\overline{IV}$
300	CCC	5000	$\overline{V}$
400	CD	10,000	$\overline{X}$
500	D	100,000	$\overline{C}$
		1,000,000	$\overline{M}$

Time

Twenty-four hour time (used by scientists, in the U.S. Military, and in European transportation systems):

Standard Time	24-hour time
1 AM	0100 (one hundred hours)
2 AM	0200
3 AM	0300
4 AM	0400
5 AM	0500
6 AM	0600
7 AM	0700
8 AM	0800
9 AM	0900
10 AM	1000
11 AM	1100
12 noon	1200 (twelve hundred hours)
1 PM	1300
2 PM	1400
3 PM	1500
4 PM	1600
5 PM	1700
6 PM	1800
7 PM	1900
8 PM	2000
9 PM	2100
10 PM	2200
11 PM	2300
12 midnight	2400

PERPETUAL CALENDAR

In the key below, look up the year. The number next to it indicates which calendar from the following pages to use for that year. For instance, for 1800 it is calendar 4.

Year	Cal	Year	Cal	Year	Cal	Year	Cal	Year	Cal	Year	Cal	Year	Cal
1800	4	1838	2	1876	14	1914	5	1952	10	1990	2	2028	14
1801	5	1839	3	1877	2	1915	6	1953	5	1991	3	2029	2
1802	6	1840	11	1878	3	1916	14	1954	6	1992	11	2030	3
1803	7	1841	6	1879	4	1917	2	1955	7	1993	6	2031	4
1804	8	1842	7	1880	12	1918	3	1956	8	1994	7	2032	12
1805	3	1843	1	1881	7	1919	4	1957	3	1995	1	2033	7
1806	4	1844	9	1882	1	1920	12	1958	4	1996	9	2034	1
1807	5	1845	4	1883	2	1921	7	1959	5	1997	4	2035	2
1808	13	1846	5	1884	10	1922	1	1960	13	1998	5	2036	10
1809	1	1847	6	1885	5	1923	2	1961	1	1999	6	2037	5
1810	2	1848	14	1886	6	1924	10	1962	2	2000	14	2038	6
1811	3	1849	2	1887	7	1925	5	1963	3	2001	2	2039	7
1812	11	1850	3	1888	8	1926	6	1964	11	2002	3	2040	8
1813	6	1851	4	1889	3	1927	7	1965	6	2003	4	2041	3
1814	7	1852	12	1890	4	1928	8	1966	7	2004	12	2042	4
1815	1	1853	7	1891	5	1929	3	1967	1	2005	7	2043	5
1816	9	1854	1	1892	13	1930	4	1968	9	2006	1	2044	13
1817	4	1855	2	1893	1	1931	5	1969	4	2007	2	2045	1
1818	5	1856	10	1894	2	1932	13	1970	5	2008	10	2046	2
1819	6	1857	5	1895	3	1933	1	1971	6	2009	5	2047	3
1820	14	1858	6	1896	11	1934	2	1972	14	2010	6	2048	11
1821	2	1859	7	1897	6	1935	3	1973	2	2011	7	2049	6
1822	3	1860	8	1898	7	1936	11	1974	3	2012	8	2050	7
1823	4	1861	3	1899	1	1937	6	1975	4	2013	3	2051	1
1824	12	1862	4	1900	2	1938	7	1976	12	2014	4	2052	9
1825	7	1863	5	1901	3	1939	1	1977	7	2015	5	2053	4
1826	1	1864	13	1902	4	1940	9	1978	1	2016	13	2054	5
1827	2	1865	1	1903	5	1941	4	1979	2	2017	1	2055	6
1828	10	1866	2	1904	13	1942	5	1980	10	2018	2	2056	14
1829	5	1867	3	1905	1	1943	6	1981	5	2019	3	2057	2
1830	6	1868	11	1906	2	1944	14	1982	6	2020	11	2058	3
1831	7	1869	6	1907	3	1945	2	1983	7	2021	6	2059	4
1832	8	1870	7	1908	11	1946	3	1984	8	2022	7	2060	12
1833	3	1871	1	1909	6	1947	4	1985	3	2023	1	2061	7
1834	4	1872	9	1910	7	1948	12	1986	4	2024	9	2062	1
1835	5	1873	4	1911	1	1949	7	1987	5	2025	4	2063	2
1836	13	1874	5	1912	9	1950	1	1988	13	2026	5	2064	10
1837	1	1875	6	1913	4	9851	2	1989	1	2027	6	2065	5

1   **PERPETUAL CALENDAR (cont.)**

JANUARY

Su	M	Tu	W	Th	F	Sa
1	2	3	4	5	6	7
8	9	10	11	12	13	14
15	16	17	18	19	20	21
22	23	24	25	26	27	28
29	30	31				

FEBRUARY

Su	M	Tu	W	Th	F	Sa
			1	2	3	4
5	6	7	8	9	10	11
12	13	14	15	16	17	18
19	20	21	22	23	24	25
26	27	28				

MARCH

Su	M	Tu	W	Th	F	Sa
			1	2	3	4
5	6	7	8	9	10	11
12	13	14	15	16	17	18
19	20	21	22	23	24	25
26	27	28	29	30	31	

APRIL

Su	M	Tu	W	Th	F	Sa
						1
2	3	4	5	6	7	8
9	10	11	12	13	14	15
16	17	18	19	20	21	22
23	24	25	26	27	28	29
30						

MAY

Su	M	Tu	W	Th	F	Sa
	1	2	3	4	5	6
7	8	9	10	11	12	13
14	15	16	17	18	19	20
21	22	23	24	25	26	27
28	29	30	31			

JUNE

Su	M	Tu	W	Th	F	Sa
				1	2	3
4	5	6	7	8	9	10
11	12	13	14	15	16	17
18	19	20	21	22	23	24
25	26	27	28	29	30	

JULY

Su	M	Tu	W	Th	F	Sa
						1
2	3	4	5	6	7	8
9	10	11	12	13	14	15
16	17	18	19	20	21	22
23	24	25	26	27	28	29
30	31					

AUGUST

Su	M	Tu	W	Th	F	Sa
		1	2	3	4	5
6	7	8	9	10	11	12
13	14	15	16	17	18	19
20	21	22	23	24	25	26
27	28	29	30	31		

SEPTEMBER

Su	M	Tu	W	Th	F	Sa
					1	2
3	4	5	6	7	8	9
10	11	12	13	14	15	16
17	18	19	20	21	22	23
24	25	26	27	28	29	30

OCTOBER

Su	M	Tu	W	Th	F	Sa
1	2	3	4	5	6	7
8	9	10	11	12	13	14
15	16	17	18	19	20	21
22	23	24	25	26	27	28
29	30	31				

NOVEMBER

Su	M	Tu	W	Th	F	Sa
		1	2	3	4	
5	6	7	8	9	10	11
12	13	14	15	16	17	18
19	20	21	22	23	24	25
26	27	28	29	30		

DECEMBER

Su	M	Tu	W	Th	F	Sa
					1	2
3	4	5	6	7	8	9
10	11	12	13	14	15	16
17	18	19	20	21	22	23
24	25	26	27	28	29	30
31						

2

JANUARY

Su	M	Tu	W	Th	F	Sa
	1	2	3	4	5	6
7	8	9	10	11	12	13
14	15	16	17	18	19	20
21	22	23	24	25	26	27
28	29	30	31			

FEBRUARY

Su	M	Tu	W	Th	F	Sa
				1	2	3
4	5	6	7	8	9	10
11	12	13	14	15	16	17
18	19	20	21	22	23	24
25	26	27	28			

MARCH

Su	M	Tu	W	Th	F	Sa
				1	2	3
4	5	6	7	8	9	10
11	12	13	14	15	16	17
18	19	20	21	22	23	24
25	26	27	28	29	30	31

APRIL

Su	M	Tu	W	Th	F	Sa
1	2	3	4	5	6	7
8	9	10	11	12	13	14
15	16	17	18	19	20	21
22	23	24	25	26	27	28
29	30					

MAY

Su	M	Tu	W	Th	F	Sa
		1	2	3	4	5
6	7	8	9	10	11	12
13	14	15	16	17	18	19
20	21	22	23	24	25	26
27	28	29	30	31		

JUNE

Su	M	Tu	W	Th	F	Sa
					1	2
3	4	5	6	7	8	9
10	11	12	13	14	15	16
17	18	19	20	21	22	23
24	25	26	27	28	29	30

JULY

Su	M	Tu	W	Th	F	Sa
1	2	3	4	5	6	7
8	9	10	11	12	13	14
15	16	17	18	19	20	21
22	23	24	25	26	27	28
29	30	31				

AUGUST

Su	M	Tu	W	Th	F	Su
		1	2	3	4	
5	6	7	8	9	10	11
12	13	14	15	16	17	18
19	20	21	22	23	24	25
26	27	28	29	30	31	

SEPTEMBER

Su	M	Tu	W	Th	F	Sa
						1
2	3	4	5	6	7	8
9	10	11	12	13	14	15
16	17	18	19	20	21	22
23	24	25	26	27	28	29
30						

OCTOBER

Su	M	Tu	W	Th	F	Sa
	1	2	3	4	5	6
7	8	9	10	11	12	13
14	15	16	17	18	19	20
21	22	23	24	25	26	27
28	29	30	31			

NOVEMBER

Su	M	Tu	W	Th	F	Sa
				1	2	3
4	5	6	7	8	9	10
11	12	13	14	15	16	17
18	19	20	21	22	23	24
25	26	27	28	29	30	

DECEMBER

Su	M	Tu	W	Th	F	Sa
						1
2	3	4	5	6	7	8
9	10	11	12	13	14	15
16	17	18	19	20	21	22
23	24	25	26	27	28	29
30	31					

3 PERPETUAL CALENDAR (cont.)

JANUARY

Su	M	Tu	W	Th	F	Sa
		1	2	3	4	5
6	7	8	9	10	11	12
13	14	15	16	17	18	19
20	21	22	23	24	25	26
27	28	29	30	31		

FEBRUARY

Su	M	Tu	W	Th	F	Sa
					1	2
3	4	5	6	7	8	9
10	11	12	13	14	15	16
17	18	19	20	21	22	23
24	25	26	27	28		

MARCH

Su	M	Tu	W	Th	F	Sa
					1	2
3	4	5	6	7	8	9
10	11	12	13	14	15	16
17	18	19	20	21	22	23
24	25	26	27	28	29	30
31						

APRIL

Su	M	Tu	W	Th	F	Sa
	1	2	3	4	5	6
7	8	9	10	11	12	13
14	15	16	17	18	19	20
21	22	23	24	25	26	27
28	29	30				

MAY

Su	M	Tu	W	Th	F	Sa
			1	2	3	4
5	6	7	8	9	10	11
12	13	14	15	16	17	18
19	20	21	22	23	24	25
26	27	28	29	30	31	

JUNE

Su	M	Tu	W	Th	F	Sa
						1
2	3	4	5	6	7	8
9	10	11	12	13	14	15
16	17	18	19	20	21	22
23	24	25	26	27	28	29
30						

JULY

Su	M	Tu	W	Th	F	Sa
	1	2	3	4	5	6
7	8	9	10	11	12	13
14	15	16	17	18	19	20
21	22	23	24	25	26	27
28	29	30	31			

AUGUST

Su	M	Tu	W	Th	F	Sa
				1	2	3
4	5	6	7	8	9	10
11	12	13	14	15	16	17
18	19	20	21	22	23	24
25	26	27	28	29	30	31

SEPTEMBER

Su	M	Tu	W	Th	F	Sa
1	2	3	4	5	6	7
8	9	10	11	12	13	14
15	16	17	18	19	20	21
22	23	24	25	26	27	28
29	30					

OCTOBER

Su	M	Tu	W	Th	F	Sa
		1	2	3	4	5
6	7	8	9	10	11	12
13	14	15	16	17	18	19
20	21	22	23	24	25	26
27	28	29	30	31		

NOVEMBER

Su	M	Tu	W	Th	F	Sa
					1	2
3	4	5	6	7	8	9
10	11	12	13	14	15	16
17	18	19	20	21	22	23
24	25	26	27	28	29	30

DECEMBER

Su	M	Tu	W	Th	F	Sa
1	2	3	4	5	6	7
8	9	10	11	12	13	14
15	16	17	18	19	20	21
22	23	24	25	26	27	28
29	30	31				

4

JANUARY

Su	M	Tu	W	Th	F	Sa
			1	2	3	4
5	6	7	8	9	10	11
12	13	14	15	16	17	18
19	20	21	22	23	24	25
26	27	28	29	30	31	

FEBRUARY

Su	M	Tu	W	Th	F	Sa
						1
2	3	4	5	6	7	8
9	10	11	12	13	14	15
16	17	18	19	20	21	22
23	24	25	26	27	28	

MARCH

Su	M	Tu	W	Th	F	Sa
						1
2	3	4	5	6	7	8
9	10	11	12	13	14	15
16	17	18	19	20	21	22
23	24	25	26	27	28	29
30	31					

APRIL

Su	M	Tu	W	Th	F	Sa
		1	2	3	4	5
6	7	8	9	10	11	12
13	14	15	16	17	18	19
20	21	22	23	24	25	26
27	28	29	30			

MAY

Su	M	Tu	W	Th	F	Sa
				1	2	3
4	5	6	7	8	9	10
11	12	13	14	15	16	17
18	19	20	21	22	23	24
25	26	27	28	29	30	31

JUNE

Su	M	Tu	W	Th	F	Sa
1	2	3	4	5	6	7
8	9	10	11	12	13	14
15	16	17	18	19	20	21
22	23	24	25	26	27	28
29	30					

JULY

Su	M	Tu	W	Th	F	Sa
		1	2	3	4	5
6	7	8	9	10	11	12
13	14	15	16	17	18	19
20	21	22	23	24	25	26
27	28	29	30	31		

AUGUST

Su	M	Tu	W	Th	F	Sa
					1	2
3	4	5	6	7	8	9
10	11	12	13	14	15	16
17	18	19	20	21	22	23
24	25	26	27	28	29	30
31						

SEPTEMBER

Su	M	Tu	W	Th	F	Sa
	1	2	3	4	5	6
7	8	9	10	11	12	13
14	15	16	17	18	19	20
21	22	23	24	25	26	27
28	29	30				

OCTOBER

Su	M	Tu	W	Th	F	Sa
		1	2	3	4	
5	6	7	8	9	10	11
12	13	14	15	16	17	18
19	20	21	22	23	24	25
26	27	28	29	30	31	

NOVEMBER

Su	M	Tu	W	Th	F	Sa
						1
2	3	4	5	6	7	8
9	10	11	12	13	14	15
16	17	18	19	20	21	22
23	24	25	26	27	28	29
30						

DECEMBER

Su	M	Tu	W	Th	F	Sa
	1	2	3	4	5	6
7	8	9	10	11	12	13
14	15	16	17	18	19	20
21	22	23	24	25	26	27
28	29	30	31			

5   **PERPETUAL CALENDAR (cont.)**

JANUARY

Su	M	Tu	W	Th	F	Sa
				1	2	3
4	5	6	7	8	9	10
11	12	13	14	15	16	17
18	19	20	21	22	23	24
25	26	27	28	29	30	31

FEBRUARY

Su	M	Tu	W	Th	F	Sa
1	2	3	4	5	6	7
8	9	10	11	12	13	14
15	16	17	18	19	20	21
22	23	24	25	26	27	28

MARCH

Su	M	Tu	W	Th	F	Sa
1	2	3	4	5	6	7
8	9	10	11	12	13	14
15	16	17	18	19	20	21
22	23	24	25	26	27	28
29	30	31				

APRIL

Su	M	Tu	W	Th	F	Sa
			1	2	3	4
5	6	7	8	9	10	11
12	13	14	15	16	17	18
19	20	21	22	23	24	25
26	27	28	29	30		

MAY

Su	M	Tu	W	Th	F	Sa
					1	2
3	4	5	6	7	8	9
10	11	12	13	14	15	16
17	18	19	20	21	22	23
24	25	26	27	28	29	30
31						

JUNE

Su	M	Tu	W	Th	F	Sa
	1	2	3	4	5	6
7	8	9	10	11	12	13
14	15	16	17	18	19	20
21	22	23	24	25	26	27
28	29	30				

JULY

Su	M	Tu	W	Th	F	Sa
			1	2	3	4
5	6	7	8	9	10	11
12	13	14	15	16	17	18
19	20	21	22	23	24	25
26	27	28	29	30	31	

AUGUST

Su	M	Tu	W	Th	F	Sa
						1
2	3	4	5	6	7	8
9	10	11	12	13	14	15
16	17	18	19	20	21	22
23	24	25	26	27	28	29
30	31					

SEPTEMBER

Su	M	Tu	W	Th	F	Sa
		1	2	3	4	5
6	7	8	9	10	11	12
13	14	15	16	17	18	19
20	21	22	23	24	25	26
27	28	29	30			

OCTOBER

Su	M	Tu	W	Th	F	Sa
				1	2	3
4	5	6	7	8	9	10
11	12	13	14	15	16	17
18	19	20	21	22	23	24
25	26	27	28	29	30	31

NOVEMBER

Su	M	Tu	W	Th	F	Sa
1	2	3	4	5	6	7
8	9	10	11	12	13	14
15	16	17	18	19	20	21
22	23	24	25	26	27	28
29	30					

DECEMBER

Su	M	Tu	W	Th	F	Sa
		1	2	3	4	5
6	7	8	9	10	11	12
13	14	15	16	17	18	19
20	21	22	23	24	25	26
27	28	29	30	31		

6

JANUARY

Su	M	Tu	W	Th	F	Sa
					1	2
3	4	5	6	7	8	9
10	11	12	13	14	15	16
17	18	19	20	21	22	23
24	25	26	27	28	29	30
31						

FEBRUARY

Su	M	Tu	W	Th	F	Sa
	1	2	3	4	5	6
7	8	9	10	11	12	13
14	15	16	17	18	19	20
21	22	23	24	25	26	27
28						

MARCH

Su	M	Tu	W	Th	F	Sa
	1	2	3	4	5	6
7	8	9	10	11	12	13
14	15	16	17	18	19	20
21	22	23	24	25	26	27
28	29	30	31			

APRIL

Su	M	Tu	W	Th	F	Sa
				1	2	3
4	5	6	7	8	9	10
11	12	13	14	15	16	17
18	19	20	21	22	23	24
25	26	27	28	29	30	

MAY

Su	M	Tu	W	Th	F	Sa
						1
2	3	4	5	6	7	8
9	10	11	12	13	14	15
16	17	18	19	20	21	22
23	24	25	26	27	28	29
30	31					

JUNE

Su	M	Tu	W	Th	F	Sa
		1	2	3	4	5
6	7	8	9	10	11	12
13	14	15	16	17	18	19
20	21	22	23	24	25	26
27	28	29	30			

JULY

Su	M	Tu	W	Th	F	Sa
				1	2	3
4	5	6	7	8	9	10
11	12	13	14	15	16	17
18	19	20	21	22	23	24
25	26	27	28	29	30	31

AUGUST

Su	M	Tu	W	Th	F	Sa
1	2	3	4	5	6	7
8	9	10	11	12	13	14
15	16	17	18	19	20	21
22	23	24	25	26	27	28
29	30	31				

SEPTEMBER

Su	M	Tu	W	Th	F	Sa
			1	2	3	4
5	6	7	8	9	10	11
12	13	14	15	16	17	18
19	20	21	22	23	24	25
26	27	28	29	30		

OCTOBER

Su	M	Tu	W	Th	F	Sa
					1	2
3	4	5	6	7	8	9
10	11	12	13	14	15	16
17	18	19	20	21	22	23
24	25	26	27	28	29	30
31						

NOVEMBER

Su	M	Tu	W	Th	F	Sa
	1	2	3	4	5	6
7	8	9	10	11	12	13
14	15	16	17	18	19	20
21	22	23	24	25	26	27
28	29	30				

DECEMBER

Su	M	Tu	W	Th	F	Sa
			1	2	3	4
5	6	7	8	9	10	11
12	13	14	15	16	17	18
19	20	21	22	23	24	25
26	27	28	29	30	31	

7 **PERPETUAL CALENDAR (cont.)**

JANUARY

Su	M	Tu	W	Th	F	Sa
						1
2	3	4	5	6	7	8
9	10	11	12	13	14	15
16	17	18	19	20	21	22
23	24	25	26	27	28	29
30	31					

FEBRUARY

Su	M	Tu	W	Th	F	Sa
		1	2	3	4	5
6	7	8	9	10	11	12
13	14	15	16	17	18	19
20	21	22	23	24	25	26
27	28					

MARCH

Su	M	Tu	W	Th	F	Sa
		1	2	3	4	5
6	7	8	9	10	11	12
13	14	15	16	17	18	19
20	21	22	23	24	25	26
27	28	29	30	31		

APRIL

Su	M	Tu	W	Th	F	Sa
					1	2
3	4	5	6	7	8	9
10	11	12	13	14	15	16
17	18	19	20	21	22	23
24	25	26	27	28	29	30

MAY

Su	M	Tu	W	Th	F	Sa
1	2	3	4	5	6	7
8	9	10	11	12	13	14
15	16	17	18	19	20	21
22	23	24	25	26	27	28
29	30	31				

JUNE

Su	M	Tu	W	Th	F	Sa
			1	2	3	4
5	6	7	8	9	10	11
12	13	14	15	16	17	18
19	20	21	22	23	24	25
26	27	28	29	30		

JULY

Su	M	Tu	W	Th	F	Sa
					1	2
3	4	5	6	7	8	9
10	11	12	13	14	15	16
17	18	19	20	21	22	23
24	25	26	27	28	29	30
31						

AUGUST

Su	M	Tu	W	Th	F	Sa
	1	2	3	4	5	6
7	8	9	10	11	12	13
14	15	16	17	18	19	20
21	22	23	24	25	26	27
28	29	30	31			

SEPTEMBER

Su	M	Tu	W	Th	F	Sa
				1	2	3
4	5	6	7	8	9	10
11	12	13	14	15	16	17
18	19	20	21	22	23	24
25	26	27	28	29	30	

OCTOBER

Su	M	Tu	W	Th	F	Sa
						1
2	3	4	5	6	7	8
9	10	11	12	13	14	15
16	17	18	19	20	21	22
23	24	25	26	27	28	29
30	31					

NOVEMBER

Su	M	Tu	W	Th	F	Sa
		1	2	3	4	5
6	7	8	9	10	11	12
13	14	15	16	17	18	19
20	21	22	23	24	25	26
27	28	29	30			

DECEMBER

Su	M	Tu	W	Th	F	Sa
				1	2	3
4	5	6	7	8	9	10
11	12	13	14	15	16	17
18	19	20	21	22	23	24
25	26	27	28	29	30	31

8

JANUARY

Su	M	Tu	W	Th	F	Sa
1	2	3	4	5	6	7
8	9	10	11	12	13	14
15	16	17	18	19	20	21
22	23	24	25	26	27	28
29	30	31				

FEBRUARY

Su	M	Tu	W	Th	F	Sa
			1	2	3	4
5	6	7	8	9	10	11
12	13	14	15	16	17	18
19	20	21	22	23	24	25
26	27	28	29			

MARCH

Su	M	Tu	W	Th	F	Sa
				1	2	3
4	5	6	7	8	9	10
11	12	13	14	15	16	17
18	19	20	21	22	23	24
25	26	27	28	29	30	31

APRIL

Su	M	Tu	W	Th	F	Sa
1	2	3	4	5	6	7
8	9	10	11	12	13	14
15	16	17	18	19	20	21
22	23	24	25	26	27	28
29	30					

MAY

Su	M	Tu	W	Th	F	Sa
		1	2	3	4	5
6	7	8	9	10	11	12
13	14	15	16	17	18	19
20	21	22	23	24	25	26
27	28	29	30	31		

JUNE

Su	M	Tu	W	Th	F	Sa
					1	2
3	4	5	6	7	8	9
10	11	12	13	14	15	16
17	18	19	20	21	22	23
24	25	26	27	28	29	30

JULY

Su	M	Tu	W	Th	F	Sa
1	2	3	4	5	6	7
8	9	10	11	12	13	14
15	16	17	18	19	20	21
22	23	24	25	26	27	28
29	30	31				

AUGUST

Su	M	Tu	W	Th	F	Sa
			1	2	3	4
5	6	7	8	9	10	11
12	13	14	15	16	17	18
19	20	21	22	23	24	25
26	27	28	29	30	31	

SEPTEMBER

Su	M	Tu	W	Th	F	Sa
						1
2	3	4	5	6	7	8
9	10	11	12	13	14	15
16	17	18	19	20	21	22
23	24	25	26	27	28	29
30						

OCTOBER

Su	M	Tu	W	Th	F	Sa
	1	2	3	4	5	6
7	8	9	10	11	12	13
14	15	16	17	18	19	20
21	22	23	24	25	26	27
28	29	30	31			

NOVEMBER

Su	M	Tu	W	Th	F	Sa
				1	2	3
4	5	6	7	8	9	10
11	12	13	14	15	16	17
18	19	20	21	22	23	24
25	26	27	28	29	30	

DECEMBER

Su	M	Tu	W	Th	F	Sa
						1
2	3	4	5	6	7	8
9	10	11	12	13	14	15
16	17	18	19	20	21	22
23	24	25	26	27	28	29
30	31					

9   **PERPETUAL CALENDAR (cont.)**

JANUARY

Su	M	Tu	W	Th	F	Sa
	1	2	3	4	5	6
7	8	9	10	11	12	13
14	15	16	17	18	19	20
21	22	23	24	25	26	27
28	29	30	31			

FEBRUARY

Su	M	Tu	W	Th	F	Sa
				1	2	3
4	5	6	7	8	9	10
11	12	13	14	15	16	17
18	19	20	21	22	23	24
25	26	27	28	29		

MARCH

Su	M	Tu	W	Th	F	Sa
					1	2
3	4	5	6	7	8	9
10	11	12	13	14	15	16
17	18	19	20	21	22	23
24	25	26	27	28	29	30
31						

APRIL

Su	M	Tu	W	Th	F	Sa
	1	2	3	4	5	6
7	8	9	10	11	12	13
14	15	16	17	18	19	20
21	22	23	24	25	26	27
28	29	30				

MAY

Su	M	Tu	W	Th	F	Sa
			1	2	3	4
5	6	7	8	9	10	11
12	13	14	15	16	17	18
19	20	21	22	23	24	25
26	27	28	29	30	31	

JUNE

Su	M	Tu	W	Th	F	Sa
						1
2	3	4	5	6	7	8
9	10	11	12	13	14	15
16	17	18	19	20	21	22
23	24	25	26	27	28	29
30						

JULY

Su	M	Tu	W	Th	F	Sa
	1	2	3	4	5	6
7	8	9	10	11	12	13
14	15	16	17	18	19	20
21	22	23	24	25	26	27
28	29	30	31			

AUGUST

Su	M	Tu	W	Th	F	Sa
				1	2	3
4	5	6	7	8	9	10
11	12	13	14	15	16	17
18	19	20	21	22	23	24
25	26	27	28	29	30	31

SEPTEMBER

Su	M	Tu	W	Th	F	Sa
1	2	3	4	5	6	7
8	9	10	11	12	13	14
15	16	17	18	19	20	21
22	23	24	25	26	27	28
29	30					

OCTOBER

Su	M	Tu	W	Th	F	Sa
		1	2	3	4	5
6	7	8	9	10	11	12
13	14	15	16	17	18	19
20	21	22	23	24	25	26
27	28	29	30	31		

NOVEMBER

Su	M	Tu	W	Th	F	Sa
					1	2
3	4	5	6	7	8	9
10	11	12	13	14	15	16
17	18	19	20	21	22	23
24	25	26	27	28	29	30

DECEMBER

Su	M	Tu	W	Th	F	Sa
1	2	3	4	5	6	7
8	9	10	11	12	13	14
15	16	17	18	19	20	21
22	23	24	25	26	27	28
29	30	31				

10

JANUARY

Su	M	Tu	W	Th	F	Sa
		1	2	3	4	5
6	7	8	9	10	11	12
13	14	15	16	17	18	19
20	21	22	23	24	25	26
27	28	29	30	31		

FEBRUARY

Su	M	Tu	W	Th	F	Sa
					1	2
3	4	5	6	7	8	9
10	11	12	13	14	15	16
17	18	19	20	21	22	23
24	25	26	27	28	29	

MARCH

Su	M	Tu	W	Th	F	Sa
						1
2	3	4	5	6	7	8
9	10	11	12	13	14	15
16	17	18	19	20	21	22
23	24	25	26	27	28	29
30	31					

APRIL

Su	M	Tu	W	Th	F	Sa
		1	2	3	4	5
6	7	8	9	10	11	12
13	14	15	16	17	18	19
20	21	22	23	24	25	26
27	28	29	30			

MAY

Su	M	Tu	W	Th	F	Sa
				1	2	3
4	5	6	7	8	9	10
11	12	13	14	15	16	17
18	19	20	21	22	23	24
25	26	27	28	29	30	31

JUNE

Su	M	Tu	W	Th	F	Sa
1	2	3	4	5	6	7
8	9	10	11	12	13	14
15	16	17	18	19	20	21
22	23	24	25	26	27	28
29	30					

JULY

Su	M	Tu	W	Th	F	Sa
		1	2	3	4	5
6	7	8	9	10	11	12
13	14	15	16	17	18	19
20	21	22	23	24	25	26
27	28	29	30	31		

AUGUST

Su	M	Tu	W	Th	F	Sa
					1	2
3	4	5	6	7	8	9
10	11	12	13	14	15	16
17	18	19	20	21	22	23
24	25	26	27	28	29	30
31						

SEPTEMBER

Su	M	Tu	W	Th	F	Sa
	1	2	3	4	5	6
7	8	9	10	11	12	13
14	15	16	17	18	19	20
21	22	23	24	25	26	27
28	29	30				

OCTOBER

Su	M	Tu	W	Th	F	Sa
			1	2	3	4
5	6	7	8	9	10	11
12	13	14	15	16	17	18
19	20	21	22	23	24	25
26	27	28	29	30	31	

NOVEMBER

Su	M	Tu	W	Th	F	Sa
						1
2	3	4	5	6	7	8
9	10	11	12	13	14	15
16	17	18	19	20	21	22
23	24	25	26	27	28	29
30						

DECEMBER

Su	M	Tu	W	Th	F	Sa
	1	2	3	4	5	6
7	8	9	10	11	12	13
14	15	16	17	18	19	20
21	22	23	24	25	26	27
28	29	30	31			

11   PERPETUAL CALENDAR (cont.)

JANUARY

Su	M	Tu	W	Th	F	Sa
			1	2	3	4
5	6	7	8	9	10	11
12	13	14	15	16	17	18
19	20	21	22	23	24	25
26	27	28	29	30	31	

FEBRUARY

Su	M	Tu	W	Th	F	Sa
						1
2	3	4	5	6	7	8
9	10	11	12	13	14	15
16	17	18	19	20	21	22
23	24	25	26	27	28	29

MARCH

Su	M	Tu	W	Th	F	Sa
1	2	3	4	5	6	7
8	9	10	11	12	13	14
15	16	17	18	19	20	21
22	23	24	25	26	27	28
29	30	31				

APRIL

Su	M	Tu	W	Th	F	Sa
			1	2	3	4
5	6	7	8	9	10	11
12	13	14	15	16	17	18
19	20	21	22	23	24	25
26	27	28	29	30		

MAY

Su	M	Tu	W	Th	F	Sa
					1	2
3	4	5	6	7	8	9
10	11	12	13	14	15	16
17	18	19	20	21	22	23
24	25	26	27	28	29	30
31						

JUNE

Su	M	Tu	W	Th	F	Sa
	1	2	3	4	5	6
7	8	9	10	11	12	13
14	15	16	17	18	19	20
21	22	23	24	25	26	27
28	29	30				

JULY

Su	M	Tu	W	Th	F	Sa
			1	2	3	4
5	6	7	8	9	10	11
12	13	14	15	16	17	18
19	20	21	22	23	24	25
26	27	28	29	30	31	

AUGUST

Su	M	Tu	W	Th	F	Sa
						1
2	3	4	5	6	7	8
9	10	11	12	13	14	15
16	17	18	19	20	21	22
23	24	25	26	27	28	29
30	31					

SEPTEMBER

Su	M	Tu	W	Th	F	Sa
		1	2	3	4	5
6	7	8	9	10	11	12
13	14	15	16	17	18	19
20	21	22	23	24	25	26
27	28	29	30			

OCTOBER

Su	M	Tu	W	Th	F	Sa
				1	2	3
4	5	6	7	8	9	10
11	12	13	14	15	16	17
18	19	20	21	22	23	24
25	26	27	28	29	30	31

NOVEMBER

Su	M	Tu	W	Th	F	Sa
1	2	3	4	5	6	7
8	9	10	11	12	13	14
15	16	17	18	19	20	21
22	23	24	25	26	27	28
29	30					

DECEMBER

Su	M	Tu	W	Th	F	Sa
		1	2	3	4	5
6	7	8	9	10	11	12
13	14	15	16	17	18	19
20	21	22	23	24	25	26
27	28	29	30	31		

12

JANUARY

Su	M	Tu	W	Th	F	Sa
				1	2	3
4	5	6	7	8	9	10
11	12	13	14	15	16	17
18	19	20	21	22	23	24
25	26	27	28	29	30	31

FEBRUARY

Su	M	Tu	W	Th	F	Sa
1	2	3	4	5	6	7
8	9	10	11	12	13	14
15	16	17	18	19	20	21
22	23	24	25	26	27	28
29						

MARCH

Su	M	Tu	W	Th	F	Sa
	1	2	3	4	5	6
7	8	9	10	11	12	13
14	15	16	17	18	19	20
21	22	23	24	25	26	27
28	29	30	31			

APRIL

Su	M	Tu	W	Th	F	Sa
				1	2	3
4	5	6	7	8	9	10
11	12	13	14	15	16	17
18	19	20	21	22	23	24
25	26	27	28	29	30	

MAY

Su	M	Tu	W	Th	F	Sa
						1
2	3	4	5	6	7	8
9	10	11	12	13	14	15
16	17	18	19	20	21	22
23	24	25	26	27	28	29
30	31					

JUNE

Su	M	Tu	W	Th	F	Sa
		1	2	3	4	5
6	7	8	9	10	11	12
13	14	15	16	17	18	19
20	21	22	23	24	25	26
27	28	29	30			

JULY

Su	M	Tu	W	Th	F	Sa
				1	2	3
4	5	6	7	8	9	10
11	12	13	14	15	16	17
18	19	20	21	22	23	24
25	26	27	28	29	30	31

AUGUST

Su	M	Tu	W	Th	F	Sa
1	2	3	4	5	6	7
8	9	10	11	12	13	14
15	16	17	18	19	20	21
22	23	24	25	26	27	28
29	30	31				

SEPTEMBER

Su	M	Tu	W	Th	F	Sa
			1	2	3	4
5	6	7	8	9	10	11
12	13	14	15	16	17	18
19	20	21	22	23	24	25
26	27	28	29	30		

OCTOBER

Su	M	Tu	W	Th	F	Sa
					1	2
3	4	5	6	7	8	9
10	11	12	13	14	15	16
17	18	19	20	21	22	23
24	25	26	27	28	29	30
31						

NOVEMBER

Su	M	Tu	W	Th	F	Sa
	1	2	3	4	5	6
7	8	9	10	11	12	13
14	15	16	17	18	19	20
21	22	23	24	25	26	27
28	29	30				

DECEMBER

Su	M	Tu	W	Th	F	Sa
			1	2	3	4
5	6	7	8	9	10	11
12	13	14	15	16	17	18
19	20	21	22	23	24	25
26	27	28	29	30	31	

13   **PERPETUAL CALENDAR (cont.)**

JANUARY

Su	M	Tu	W	Th	F	Sa
					1	2
3	4	5	6	7	8	9
10	11	12	13	14	15	16
17	18	19	20	21	22	23
24	25	26	27	28	29	30
31						

FEBRUARY

Su	M	Tu	W	Th	F	Sa
	1	2	3	4	5	6
7	8	9	10	11	12	13
14	15	16	17	18	19	20
21	22	23	24	25	26	27
28	29					

MARCH

Su	M	Tu	W	Th	F	Sa
		1	2	3	4	5
6	7	8	9	10	11	12
13	14	15	16	17	18	19
20	21	22	23	24	25	26
27	28	29	30	31		

APRIL

Su	M	Tu	W	Th	F	Sa
					1	2
3	4	5	6	7	8	9
10	11	12	13	14	15	16
17	18	19	20	21	22	23
24	25	26	27	28	29	30

MAY

Su	M	Tu	W	Th	F	Sa
1	2	3	4	5	6	7
8	9	10	11	12	13	14
15	16	17	18	19	20	21
22	23	24	25	26	27	28
29	30	31				

JUNE

Su	M	Tu	W	Th	F	Sa
			1	2	3	4
5	6	7	8	9	10	11
12	13	14	15	16	17	18
19	20	21	22	23	24	25
26	27	28	29	30		

JULY

Su	M	Tu	W	Th	F	Sa
					1	2
3	4	5	6	7	8	9
10	11	12	13	14	15	16
17	18	19	20	21	22	23
24	25	26	27	28	29	30
31						

AUGUST

Su	M	Tu	W	Th	F	Sa
	1	2	3	4	5	6
7	8	9	10	11	12	13
14	15	16	17	18	19	20
21	22	23	24	25	26	27
28	29	30	31			

SEPTEMBER

Su	M	Tu	W	Th	F	Sa
				1	2	3
4	5	6	7	8	9	10
11	12	13	14	15	16	17
18	19	20	21	22	23	24
25	26	27	28	29	30	

OCTOBER

Su	M	Tu	W	Th	F	Sa
						1
2	3	4	5	6	7	8
9	10	11	12	13	14	15
16	17	18	19	20	21	22
23	24	25	26	27	28	29
30	31					

NOVEMBER

Su	M	Tu	W	Th	F	Sa
		1	2	3	4	5
6	7	8	9	10	11	12
13	14	15	16	17	18	19
20	21	22	23	24	25	26
27	28	29	30			

DECEMBER

Su	M	Tu	W	Th	F	Sa
				1	2	3
4	5	6	7	8	9	10
11	12	13	14	15	16	17
18	19	20	21	22	23	24
25	26	27	28	29	30	31

14

JANUARY

Su	M	Tu	W	Th	F	Sa
						1
2	3	4	5	6	7	8
9	10	11	12	13	14	15
16	17	18	19	20	21	22
23	24	25	26	27	28	29
30	31					

FEBRUARY

Su	M	Tu	W	Th	F	Sa
		1	2	3	4	5
6	7	8	9	10	11	12
13	14	15	16	17	18	19
20	21	22	23	24	25	26
27	28	29				

MARCH

Su	M	Tu	W	Th	F	Sa
			1	2	3	4
5	6	7	8	9	10	11
12	13	14	15	16	17	18
19	20	21	22	23	24	25
26	27	28	29	30	31	

APRIL

Su	M	Tu	W	Th	F	Sa
						1
2	3	4	5	6	7	8
9	10	11	12	13	14	15
16	17	18	19	20	21	22
23	24	25	26	27	28	29
30						

MAY

Su	M	Tu	W	Th	F	Sa
	1	2	3	4	5	6
7	8	9	10	11	12	13
14	15	16	17	18	19	20
21	22	23	24	25	26	27
28	29	30	31			

JUNE

Su	M	Tu	W	Th	F	Sa
			1	2	3
4	5	6	7	8	9	10
11	12	13	14	15	16	17
18	19	20	21	22	23	24
25	26	27	28	29	30	

JULY

Su	M	Tu	W	Th	F	Sa
						1
2	3	4	5	6	7	8
9	10	11	12	13	14	15
16	17	18	19	20	21	22
23	24	25	26	27	28	29
30	31					

AUGUST

Su	M	Tu	W	Th	F	Sa
		1	2	3	4	5
6	7	8	9	10	11	12
13	14	15	16	17	18	19
20	21	22	23	24	25	26
27	28	29	30	31		

SEPTEMBER

Su	M	Tu	W	Th	F	Sa
					1	2
3	4	5	6	7	8	9
10	11	12	13	14	15	16
17	18	19	20	21	22	23
24	25	26	27	28	29	30

OCTOBER

Su	M	Tu	W	Th	F	Sa
1	2	3	4	5	6	7
8	9	10	11	12	13	14
15	16	17	18	19	20	21
22	23	24	25	26	27	28
29	30	31				

NOVEMBER

Su	M	Tu	W	Th	F	Sa
		1	2	3	4
5	6	7	8	9	10	11
12	13	14	15	16	17	18
19	20	21	22	23	24	25
26	27	28	29	30		

DECEMBER

Su	M	Tu	W	Th	F	Sa
					1	2
3	4	5	6	7	8	9
10	11	12	13	14	15	16
17	18	19	20	21	22	23
24	25	26	27	28	29	30
31						

Time Zones (USA)

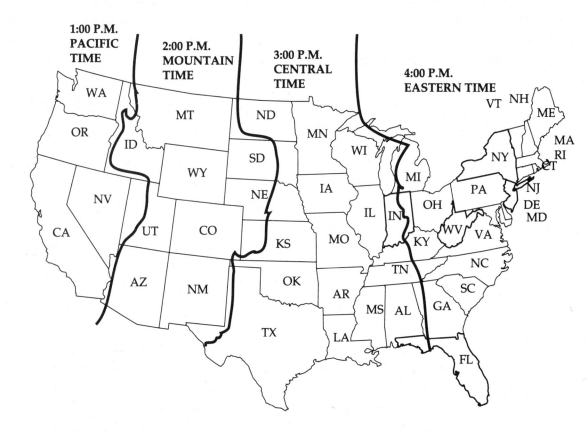

Alaska falls into four time zones: Pacific, Yukon (one hour behind Pacific), Alaska/Hawaii (two hours behind Pacific), Yukon (three hours behind Pacific). Hawaii is two hours behind Pacific time.

Weather Symbols

Conditions			
Clear	Partly cloudy	Overcast	Hazy
Showers (rain)	Hail	Thunderstorm	Tornado
Hurricane	Tropical storm	Drizzle	Sand or duststorm
Lightning	Snow	Drifting snow	Sleet

Light fog	Heavy fog	Smoke-reduced visibility	

Wind Speeds				
Calm	About 1 m.p.h. (1 knot)	About 6 m.p.h. (5 knots)	About 12 m.p.h. (10 knots)	About 58 m.p.h. (50 knots)

Fronts			
Warm	Cold	Occluded	Stationary

INDEX

Credit cards
  affinity group, 386
  bank, 387–88
  in booking hotel room, 464
  insurance hotline registration, 413
  lost or stolen, 771–72
  safeguarding, 389
  scams involving, 369
  telephone, 772
  and travel abroad, 482–85
Credit counselors, 391
Credit life insurance, 412–13
Credit rating, maintaining, 773
Credit report, 389–90
Credit Union National Association, 379
Crime. *See also* Fraud
  abducted children, 105–10
  battered women, 115–17
  burglarproofing, 96
  carjacking, 101–3
  car theft, 100–101
  child abuse, 111–15
  credit card, 389
  domestic violence as, 111–20
  elder abuse, 117–18
  and gun safety, 103–4
  and hotel safety, 465–66
  neighborhood watch, 104
  rape, 118–20
  safety at ATM machine, 92
  and self-defense, 93–95
  stalking as, 92–93
  street, 91–92
  tips on security, 96–100
  witnessing, 95–96
Crime Prevention Council, 104
Crime victims
  civil legal remedies for, 124–25
  organizations for, 125
  rights of, 123–24
Crossed eyes, 25
Crossword puzzles, 549–50
Crowns, 28
Cruise Line International Association (CLIA), 472
Cruisers, 537
Cruises, 472–73
Cryptorchidism, 322
Crystal, buying, 210
Crystal healing, 82
Cucumbers, 611
Cumin, 626
Curly endive (chicory), 620

Currants, 614
Current Checks, 381
Custom Direct Check Printers, 381
Customs and manners in foreign countries, 490–91
Cut-and-loop carpet, 205
Cut-end carpet, 205
Cuts, home remedy for, 16
Cystic fibrosis, 51
Cystic Fibrosis Foundation, 51

D

Daisy wheel printer, 222
Damage claims in moving, 178
Dancer, tips to make you a better, 578
Dandruff, 674
Dark sweet chocolate, 630
Dash, 718
Database, 222
Data file, 222
Day care
  adult, 299
  centers for, 255
  family, 255
  in-home care, 254
  questions on, 255–57
Daylighting, 211
Deadly nightshade, 569
Dealer invoice price, 427–28
Debit cards, lost or stolen, 771–72
Debts
  and declaring bankruptcy, 390, 392–93
  handling out of control, 391–92
  warning signs of problems with, 391
Decimal equivalents of common fractions, 832
Decongestants, 48, 49
  interaction with food, 46
Deductions
  nonqualifying, as audit trigger, 416
  unusually high itemized, as trigger for tax audit, 415
Default insurance, 463
Defenders of Wildlife, 160
Deforestation, 155
Defrosting products in a microwave, 623
Degradable, 162

Delay claims in moving, 178
Dill, 626
DELTA Society, 132, 133
Denial of crime victim, 121–22
Dental health
  and AIDS, 29
  bad breath in, 679–80
  brushing in, 27
  flossing, 27
  glossary in, 28–29
  other tips, 27–28
Dentistry, cosmetic, 706–7
Dependents, fake, as audit trigger, 416
Depression. *See also* Suicide
  clinical, 66–67
  risk and information on, 53
Dermabrasion, 705
Dermatology, 75
  specialty board for, 77
Desktop computer, 222
Deterrents, 99
Dewey Decimal System, 830
Diabetes
  in dogs, 322
  as risk factor for heart disease, 57
  risk and information on, 53
  risk for, 53, 61–62
  and travel abroad, 488
Dialog box, 222
Dialysis at Sea Cruises, 475
Diamond, determining value of, 690–91
Diet. *See also* Eating; Foods Nutrition
  healthy, 587–89
  as risk factor for heart disease, 57
Diet aids, fraudulent, 6
Diet guide, 5–6
Diet patches, 6
Differences-World Cities, 482
Digestive disorders, 51
Dinner etiquette, 650–54
  place settings, 651, 652, 653
  seating arrangements, 650
  serving food, 651
  table manners, 651, 653–54
Dinnerware, buying, 209–10
Diplomatic Corps., 729
Direct Marketing Association, 372
  Telephone Preference Service, 372
Director, 223